9th
EDITION

COST ACCOUNTING

PLANNING AND CONTROL

Milton F. Usry, PhD, CPA
Mary Ball Washington
Professor of Accountancy
College of Business
University of West Florida

Lawrence H. Hammer, DBA, CPA
Associate Professor of Accounting
College of Business Administration
Oklahoma State University

Adolph Matz, PhD
Late Professor Emeritus of Accounting
The Wharton School
University of Pennsylvania

Published by

A88   **SOUTH-WESTERN PUBLISHING CO.**

CINCINNATI   WEST CHICAGO, IL   CARROLLTON, TX   LIVERMORE, CA

PREFACE

The ninth edition of COST ACCOUNTING: PLANNING AND CONTROL maintains its focus on the twin management functions of planning and control in the context of modern concepts and techniques. The connecting link between these functions is the cost accounting information system, rightly termed a tool of management. Although the information and underlying data required for the planning and control functions are often quite different, the cost accounting information system is expected to provide the answers and respond to the needs of both functions. This dual responsibility of the cost accounting information system strongly influenced the authors in structuring the presentation followed in this textbook.

▼ HIGHLIGHTS OF CHANGES IN THE NINTH EDITION

The textbook has undergone a significant reorganization and rewrite throughout to enhance clearness and thoroughness of the coverage. The most noticeable changes from the eighth edition are as follows:

1. The first process costing chapter (Chapter 4) discusses both lost unit calculations and the addition of materials, with a clearer cost of production report presentation of the effect on unit costs.
2. The elements of cost—materials, labor, and factory overhead—are grouped in Part 3 and are presented in their cost of goods sold statement order.
3. The materials chapters (Chapters 7 and 8) include statistical methods for computing safety stock covering both conditions of random demand variability as well as deviations from forecast demand; modern inventory and production management tools, such as materials requirements planning and just-in-time inventory systems; and flexible manufacturing systems, including robotics.
4. The discussion of productivity in the first labor chapter (Chapter 9) is expanded.
5. Cost behavior analysis is the focal point of Chapter 11, which is positioned as a foundation to the text's coverage of the use of cost data for planning and control.
6. Chapter 13 includes a comprehensive illustration of service department cost allocation methods.
7. Flexible budgeting is restructured to stress the control phase of budgeting and is placed at the end of the second budgeting chapter (Chapter 16).
8. An additional method of factory overhead variance analysis in standard costing is presented, along with a discussion of a detailed analysis for each type of factory overhead expense. Also, the discussion of responsibilities for standard cost variances has been expanded.
9. In Part 5, Break-Even and Cost-Volume-Profit Analysis (Chapter 20) and Differential Cost Analysis (Chapter 21) are logically positioned, immediately following Chapter 19—Direct Costing and the Contribution Margin.
10. Chapter 20 contains an expanded discussion of break-even and cost-volume-profit analysis under conditions of multiple products and shifts in the sales mix.
11. The linear programming chapter (Chapter 22) visually demonstrates the step-by-step development of simplex tableaus and has broadened the discussion of sensitivity analysis to include the objective function coefficients.
12. The capital expenditures coverage has been expanded into two chapters (Chapters 23 and 24) to include a comprehensive discussion of risk and uncertainty conditions.
13. The Marketing Cost and Profitability Analysis chapter (Chapter 25) now integrates gross profit analysis.

▼ ORGANIZATION OF THE BOOK

Parts One and Two of the ninth edition fuse planning and control into a harmonious whole by first presenting fundamental cost accounting concepts and objectives, followed by a comprehensive illustration depicting the flow of costs in a manufacturing enterprise, including its interface with the balance sheet and income statement. Cost data accumulation procedures using job order and process costing are then developed as a fundamental means of providing reliable cost data.

Part Three deals with the cost elements of materials and labor from both the planning and control phases, followed by consideration of cost behavior analysis which provides the foundation for cost planning and control. The part concludes with an in-depth treatment of factory overhead and responsibility accounting.

Part Four elaborates on the heart of the planning function—budgeting—including the flexible budget. This part also treats standard costing, which is basic to effective cost control.

Part Five, the final section, covers the entire spectrum of analysis of costs and profits, including direct costing; break-even and cost-volume-profit analysis; differential cost analysis; linear programming; the planning, evaluating, and control of capital expenditures; marketing cost and profitability analysis, including gross profit analysis; profit performance measurements; transfer pricing; and product pricing.

Like many other disciplines, cost accounting has been influenced by the development of quantitative techniques and behavioral science concepts. These tools and their applications are presented in a clear and concise manner throughout the textbook as they relate to particular topics. Also, the appropriate consideration of income tax effects is integrated throughout this edition, as is the relevance of inflation's impact on the management process. The concepts and techniques developed in this textbook are intended to have broad applicability to all phases of business and nonprofit organizations, both large and small.

▼ ORGANIZATION FOR INSTRUCTION

The presentation of the fundamental theoretical and practical aspects of cost accounting provides wide flexibility for classroom usage. In addition to its applicability to the traditional two-semester course sequence, the textbook may be used in a variety of one-semester courses. For these alternative courses, a suggested outline, by chapter numbers, follows:

Course	Textbook Chapters
Cost Accounting (two-semester course)	Chapters 1-14 (first semester)
	Chapters 15-26 (second semester)
Cost Accounting (one-semester course)	Chapters 1-14 and 19
Cost Control (one-semester course)	Chapters 1-3, 7-14, 17-18
Budgetary Control (one-semester course)	Chapters 1-3, 11, 15-19, 25
Cost Analysis (one-semester course)	Chapters 11, 15-26

▼ END-OF-CHAPTER MATERIALS

Most of the end-of-chapter materials are new or revised and include discussion questions, exercises, problems, and cases. For each topic, these materials afford coverage of relevant concepts and techniques at progressive levels in the learning process, thereby providing a significant student-learning benefit. The end-of-chapter materials include numerous items from the examinations administered by the American Institute of Certified Public Accountants (designated AICPA adapted), the Institute of Certified Management Accountants of the National Association of Accountants (ICMA adapted), the Institute of Internal Auditors (CIA adapted), the Canadian Institute of Chartered Accountants (CICA adapted), and the Certified General Accountants' Association of Canada (CGAAC adapted). The authors are indebted to these organizations for permission to use their materials.

▼ SUPPLEMENTARY MATERIALS

The materials accompanying the text include a solutions manual, an instructor's manual, transparencies of solutions and illustrations, an examinations booklet, and software. For the student, a study guide, four practice cases, and check figures are available.

For the Instructor

Solutions Manual. This manual contains detailed solutions to the end-of-chapter materials, including the discussion questions, exercises, problems, and cases.

Instructor's Manual, prepared by William K. Carter of the McIntire School of Commerce, University of Virginia. This manual contains a Summary section, which gives an abbreviated restatement of the contents of each chapter; and a Discussion section, which gives additional material for use in responding to students' questions and in clarifying some of the more difficult points in a chapter. In addition, a schedule of concepts covered by the exercises and problems, and a schedule of estimated time requirements for solving problems are included.

Transparencies. Transparencies of solutions to all exercises, problems, and cases are available. Also included with the transparencies are illustrations from the textbook.

Examinations Booklet, prepared by Edward J. VanDerbeck of Xavier University, Cincinnati. A test bank of multiple choice questions and examination problems, with solutions, is available to adopters. These materials may be readily reproduced by those instructors who wish to construct their own tests. A microcomputer version (MicroSWAT II) of the test bank is also available.

Template Diskette. This data disk is used with Lotus[®]1-2-3[®1] for solving selected end-of-chapter exercises and problems. The diskette is copyable and may be ordered, upon adoption, from South-Western Publishing Co.

Tools Diskette. This diskette, which is designed for use with the IBM PC[2], contains eight basic procedures that solve the following types of problems: inventory planning models, cost behavior analysis, factory overhead service department allocation, standard cost variance analysis, gross profit analysis, probability analysis, linear programming routines, and capital expenditure analysis.

For the Student

Study Guide, prepared by Edward J. VanDerbeck. This study guide contains a brief summary of each chapter, as well as questions and exercises with answers, thus providing students with immediate feedback on their comprehension of material.

Practice Cases, prepared by Lawrence H. Hammer and William K. Carter. Four cases—a job order cost case, a process cost case, a standard cost analysis case, and a budgeting case—are available. Each case, new with this edition, acquaints students with basic procedural and analytical characteristics without involving time-consuming details. Also, each case is available in a microcomputer version for use with Lotus 1-2-3.

Check Figures. Instructors may order check figures for distribution to students. These check figures may be used by students in checking their solutions to end-of-chapter problems.

▼ ACKNOWLEDGEMENTS

The authors wish to express appreciation to the many users of the previous editions who offered helpful suggestions. Thanks are given to the students and teachers of Oklahoma State University, the University of West Florida, and the University of Virginia who class-tested new materials and made suggestions for improvements.

The central person in this textbook's success from its origin through the eighth edition was the late Adolph Matz, Professor Emeritus of Accounting, The Wharton School, University of Pennsylvania. In this ninth edition, his legacy is carried forward and is coupled with the evolutionary modernization needed in a dynamic subject area. For Adolph's significant contribution to accounting education and to his wife, Trean Benfer Matz, we wish to express our special appreciation.

Milton F. Usry
Lawrence H. Hammer

[1]Lotus 1-2-3 are trademarks of the Lotus Development Corporation. Any reference to Lotus or 1-2-3 refers to this footnote.
[2]IBM is a registered trademark of International Business Machines Corporation. Any reference to the IBM Personal Computer refers to this footnote.

ABOUT THE
AUTHORS

Milton F. Usry is the Mary Ball Washington Professor of Accountancy at the University of West Florida, Pensacola, after previously serving on the Oklahoma State University faculty (1961-1986). He earned his BBA from Baylor University, MBA from the University of Houston, PhD from the University of Texas at Austin, and is a CPA. He has written numerous articles, especially in the areas of cost accounting and accounting education. Dr. Usry served as Associate Editor of two American Accounting Association books: *Accounting Education: Problems and Prospects* and *Researching the Accounting Curriculum: Strategies for Change.*

Professor Usry received the Oklahoma State University College of Business Administration Outstanding Teacher Award on three occasions. He has served in numerous professional responsibilities on behalf of the American Accounting Association, the American Institute of CPAs, and the National Association of Accountants.

In the area of professional certification, Dr. Usry has been a member of the AICPA Board of Examiners and the Institute of Certified Management Accountants Board of Regents. In the field of government service, he has just completed serving on the National Board of the Fund for the Improvement of Postsecondary Education of the U.S. Department of Education.

Lawrence H. Hammer teaches primarily in the areas of managerial accounting and income taxation at Oklahoma State University. He earned a BS from Sam Houston State University, MBA from North Texas State University, and DBA from Indiana University at Bloomington. He is a CPA in Texas and Oklahoma.

Dr. Hammer is widely published in the tax literature, and he has served on the editorial review boards of *The Accounting Review* and *The Journal of Accounting Education.* He is a member of the American Accounting Association Management Accounting Section, the American Taxation Association, the American Institute of CPAs, and the National Association of Accountants.

The late **Adolph Matz** was one of the original authors of this textbook, whose first edition was published in 1952. At the time of his death, he was Professor Emeritus of the Wharton School of the University of Pennsylvania. He was educated at the University of Pennsylvania, which granted him BA, MA, and PhD degrees. A Jusserand Travelling Fellowship made it possible to study two years at the University of Heidelberg, Germany. Visiting professorships included the Free University, Berlin, as well as Waseda University in Tokyo. Practical experience included banking in his native Germany, work as a consultant in electronic data processing for Lybrand, Ross Bros. and Montgomery, two years with the Budd Manufacturing Company as budget and cost supervisor, as well as work in the European automobile industry. In 1952, he was appointed cost specialist with the Foreign Operations Administration in Paris as part of the Marshall Plan, working in individual companies and lecturing to management groups in France, Italy, Germany, Austria, and the Netherlands. Other consulting work, combined with training courses, took him to Chile, Costa Rica, Panama, Guatemala, and Nicaragua.

Through much of the effort of Dr. Matz, COST ACCOUNTING has been translated into fourteen languages. In addition, Professor Matz published approximately 40 articles and reviews in American, Australian, Canadian, English, Belgian, Japanese, and German journals and periodicals, as well as a chapter for several editions of the *Mechanical Engineering Handbook.*

Dr. Matz's professional memberships included the American Accounting Association, the National Association of Accountants, and der Verband der Hochschullehrer fuer Betriebswirtschaft.

CONTENTS
IN BRIEF

CONTENTS

PART 5   ANALYSIS OF COSTS AND PROFITS

PART
1

Costs: Concepts and Objectives

CHAPTER 1

The Management Concept and the Function of the Controller

The management of a business enterprise is composed of individuals who belong to one of three groups: (1) the operating management group, consisting of supervisors; (2) the middle management group, represented by department heads, division managers, and branch managers; and (3) the executive management group, consisting of the president, the executive vice-presidents, and the executives in charge of the various functions of marketing, purchasing, engineering, manufacturing, finance, and accounting. Executive management is principally concerned with long-range decisions, middle management with decisions of medium-range impact, and operating managers with short-range decisions.

One of management's chief concerns is the effective use of company capital. This capital is invested in productive facilities, such as factory buildings, tools, and equipment, as well as in circulating capital, or current assets. The use of this capital is determined by management's short- and long-range plans for the future.

▼ THE MANAGEMENT CONCEPT

The management concept may be described by such phrases as "making decisions, giving orders, establishing policies, providing work and rewards, and hiring people to carry out policies." Management sets objectives that may be achieved by integrating its knowledge and skills with the ability and experience of the employees. To be successful, management must effectively perform the basic functions of planning, organizing, and control. Planning and organizing are primarily functions of executive management, while control is principally the duty of operating management. All three functions require appropriate participation of the various levels of the management team.

For theoretical purposes, planning and control are divided. Similarly, time frames are divided into discrete operating periods. However, one must keep in mind that these divisions are artificially designed for the convenience of analysis and for operations management and do not reflect the dynamic manner in which an entity evolves and changes. In the reality of management, planning and control are inseparable, interwoven processes; and time frames, such as short- and long-range periods, are not clearly distinguishable. Plans are made for the immediate future and for the long term, controlled action takes place, feedback from operations is obtained, plans are adjusted, and the continuum repeats itself.[1]

Planning

Planning refers to the construction of a detailed operating program for all phases of operations. Planning is the process of sensing external opportunities and threats, determining desirable objectives, and employing resources to accomplish these objectives. Planning includes such areas of investigation as the nature of the company's business, its major policies, and the timing of major steps and other factors related to short-range and to long-range plans. Effective planning is based on analyses of collected facts. Such analyses require reflective thinking, imagination, and foresight in order to make rational decisions.

The establishment of an effective plan also requires the participation of the engineering, manufacturing, marketing, research, finance, and accounting functions. No single group should plan and act independently from other groups. Failure to recognize this fundamental principle may cause unnecessary planning difficulties and may result in financial disaster for the organization.

Closely allied with proper planning is the determination of company objectives. An objective is a target or an end result. In stating the objectives of a business enterprise, many people point to the need for realizing a profit. Although profits are the indispensable element in a successful business, profit is a limited concept in today's economic society. Profits cannot remain the sole objective of a business enterprise. The companies best able to maximize profits are those which produce products or render services in a definite manner, in a volume, at a time, at a cost, and at a price that will, in the long run, assure a profit and also win the cooperation of employees, gain the goodwill of customers, and meet social responsibilities. Business logic and changing public expectations suggest that plans should be formulated within a framework of four major parameters—economic, technological, social, and political.

Organizing

Organizing is essentially the establishment of the framework within which required activities are to be performed. The terms "organize" and "organization" refer to the systematization of various interdependent parts into one

---

[1]*Management Accounting Guidelines, No. 3*, "Framework for Internal Control (exposure draft)" (Hamilton, Ontario: The Society of Management Accountants of Canada, 1984).

unit. Organizing requires (1) bringing the many functional units of an enterprise into a well-conceived structure and (2) assigning authority and responsibility to certain individuals. These organizational efforts include the task of motivating people to work together for the good of the company. Because of the attitudes and ambitions of the many persons involved, the desired organizational structure is developed through instruction and patience.

Creation of an organization involves the establishment of functional divisions, departments, sections, or branches. These units are created for the purpose of dividing tasks, which leads to specialization of labor. A manufacturing enterprise usually consists of at least three large fundamental activities: manufacturing, marketing, and administration. Within these three units, numerous departments are formed according to the nature and the amount of work, the degree of specialization, the number of employees, and the location of the work.

After organizational units have been created, management must assign the work to be done within each unit. The appropriate distribution of work among employees is vital to the attainment of company objectives. Of greater importance to a company's success are the relationships between superiors and subordinates and among managers within the management team.

Control

Control is management's systematic effort to achieve objectives by comparing performance to plans. Activities should be continuously supervised if management expects to stay within previously defined boundaries. Actual results of each activity classification are compared with plans, and if significant differences are noted, remedial actions may be taken. The following diagram illustrates the control process:

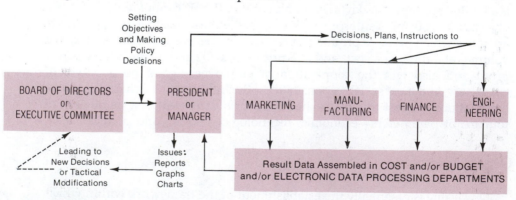

Authority, Responsibility, and Accountability

In a small company, planning and control activities are usually performed by one person, without elaborate analysis. This person will probably be the owner or general manager, who has an intimate knowledge of employees, materials, financing, and customers. In a large company with numerous divisions and a variety of products or services, planning and control of the activities of individual units is complex. For this reason, large firms assign the planning and control functions to more than one person, so that reports and any corrective actions are closer to the activity.

Authority is the power to command others to perform or not perform activities. Authority is the key to the managerial job and the basis for responsibility. It is the force that binds the organization together.

Authority originates with executive management, which delegates it to the various managerial levels. Such delegation is essential to the existence of an organizational structure. Through delegation, the chief executive's area of operations is extended. However, the chief executive retains overall authority for assigned functions, since delegation does not mean release from responsibility.

Responsibility or obligation, is closely related to authority. It originates particularly in the superior-subordinate relationship because the superior has the authority to require specific work from other people. As these people accept the obligation to perform the work, they create their own responsibility. The superior, however, is ultimately responsible for the subordinates' performance or nonperformance.

In addition to the aspect of achieving results, another facet of responsibility is *accountability*—reporting results to higher authority. Reporting is important because it makes possible the measurement—in terms of quantity, quality, time, and cost—of the extent to which objectives have been reached.

Accountability is basically an individual rather than a group problem. This principle of single accountability is well established in profit and nonprofit organizations. If the organizational structure permits pooling of judgment, responsibility is diffused and accountability is nullified. Without single accountability, control reports would not only be meaningless, but corrective actions would be delayed or not forthcoming at all.

The Organization Chart

The organization chart sets forth each principal management position and helps to define authority, responsibility, and accountability. An organization chart is essential to the development of a cost system and cost reports which indicate the responsibilities of individuals for implementing management plans. The coordinated development of a company's organization with the cost and budgetary system will lead to an approach to accounting and reporting called *responsibility accounting*.

Generally, an organization chart is based on the line-staff concept. The basic assumption of this concept is that all positions or functional divisions may be categorized into two groups: the line, which makes decisions and performs the true management functions; the staff, which gives advice or performs any technical functions. A line-staff organization chart is illustrated as follows:

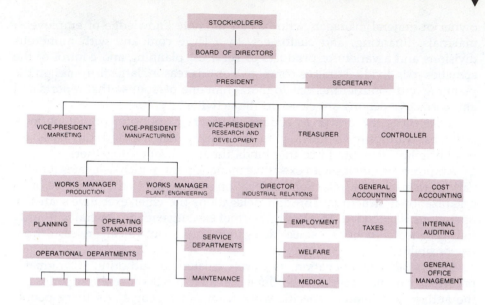

Organization Chart Based on Line-Staff Concept

Another type of organization chart is based on the functional-teamwork concept of management, which is structured to emphasize the most important functions of an enterprise: resources, processes, and human interrelations. The *resources function* involves the acquisition, disposal, and prudent management of a wide variety of resources—tangible and intangible, human and physical. The *processes function* deals with activities such as product design, research and development, purchasing, manufacturing, advertising, marketing, and billing. The *human interrelations function* directs the company's efforts in relation to the behavior of people inside and outside the company. An organization chart based on the functional-teamwork concept is illustrated as follows:

Organization Chart Based on Functional-Teamwork Concept

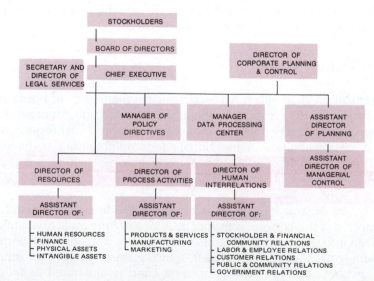

▼ THE CONTROLLER'S PARTICIPATION IN PLANNING AND CONTROL

The controller is the executive manager responsible for a company's accounting function. The controller coordinates management's participation in the planning and control phases of attaining objectives, in determining the effectiveness of policies, and in creating organizational structures and procedures. The controller is also responsible for observing the methods of planning and control throughout the enterprise and for proposing improvements in the planning and control system.

Effective cost control depends upon the proper communication of accounting information to management. Through the issuance of performance reports, the controller advises the various levels of management in regard to activities requiring corrective action. These reports emphasize deviations from a predetermined plan, following the principle of *management by exception*.

Through the conventional accounting system models, the controller provides management with information which it uses in planning a company's future and controlling its daily activities. These models—the balance sheet, the income statement, and the statement of cash flows—are based on historical dollars. Management also has access to much information which is outside these models, yet obtainable from the information system.

External users, including stockholders, future investors, and government agencies, must also receive information by which management's effectiveness may be judged. This information is usually communicated to external users via the company's annual report, which includes the basic financial statements of the company. These statements often lack explanatory detail, since it is impossible to include all the data which the large variety of external users would find useful.

▼ THE COST DEPARTMENT

The cost department, under the direction of the controller, is responsible for keeping records of a company's manufacturing and nonmanufacturing activities. This department must also analyze all costs of manufacturing, marketing, and administration. It must issue significant control reports and other decision-making data to those managers who assist in controlling and improving costs and operations. The analysis of costs and the preparation of reports are greatly facilitated through the proper division of functions within the cost department. These functions must be coordinated with other accounting functions, such as general accounting, which are closely tied to cost accounting.

In addition to the cost and other accounting departments, a company may have one or more of the following departments: manufacturing, personnel, treasury, marketing, public relations, and legal. The functions of the cost department are also coordinated with some of the functions of these departments.

The *manufacturing departments*, under the direction of engineers and factory superintendents, design and control production. In research and design, cost estimates for each type of material, labor, and machine process are used in deciding whether to accept or reject a design. Likewise, the scheduling, producing, and inspecting of jobs and products by the manufacturing departments are measured for efficiency in terms of the costs incurred.

The *personnel department* interviews and selects employees for various job classifications. It maintains personnel records, which include the wage rates and the methods of remuneration for each employee. This information forms the basis for the computation of payroll costs.

The *treasury department* is responsible for the financial administration of a company. In scheduling cash requirements and expectations, it relies upon budgets and related reports from the cost department.

The *marketing department* needs a good product at a competitive price in order to attract customers. While prices should not be set merely by adding a predetermined percentage to cost, costs cannot be ignored. Marketing managers use pertinent cost data to determine which products are most profitable and to determine sales policies.

The *public relations department* has the primary function of maintaining good relations between the company and its public, especially its customers and stockholders. Points of friction are most likely to be prices, wages, profits, and dividends. The cost department may be asked to provide basic information for public releases concerning policies in these areas.

The *legal department* uses cost information as an aid in maintaining company affairs according to law. Some of these legal areas include the Equal Pay Act, terms of industry-wide union contracts, the Robinson-Patman Act, social security taxes, unemployment compensation, the Employee Retirement Security Act of 1974, and income tax.

▼ THE ROLE OF COST ACCOUNTING

Cost accounting furnishes management with the necessary accounting tools for planning and control of activities. Specifically, the collection, presentation, and analysis of cost data should help management accomplish the following tasks:

1. Creating and executing plans and budgets for operating under expected competitive and economic conditions.
2. Establishing costing methods and procedures that permit control and, if possible, reductions or improvements of costs.
3. Creating inventory values for costing and pricing purposes and, at times, controlling physical quantities.
4. Determining company costs and profit for an annual accounting period or a shorter period.
5. Choosing from among two or more alternatives which might increase revenues or decrease costs.

Budgeting

The *budget* is the written expression of management's plan for the future. All levels of management should be involved in creating the budget program and welding it into a homogeneous unit. A workable, realistic budget will not only help promote coordination of people, clarification of policies, and crystallization of plans, but it will also create greater internal harmony and unanimity of purpose among managers and workers.

In recent years, considerable attention has been given to the behavioral implications of providing managers with the data required for planning and control of activities. Cost accounting and budgeting play an important role in influencing individual and group behavior at all stages of the management process, including: (1) setting goals; (2) informing individuals about what they must do to contribute to the accomplishment of these goals; (3) motivating desirable performance; (4) evaluating performance; and (5) suggesting when corrective action should be taken. In short, accountants cannot ignore the behavioral sciences (psychology, social-psychology, and sociology) because the decision-making function of accounting is essentially a behavioral function.

An individual manager's attitude toward the budget will depend greatly upon the existing good relationship within the management group. Guided by the company plan, with an opportunity for increased compensation, greater satisfaction, and eventually promotion, the middle and lower management group might achieve remarkable results. On the other hand, a discordant management group, unwilling to accept the budget's underlying figures, might show such poor performance that the administration would be compelled to defer implementation of the planning and control concept.

The following elements have been suggested as a means for motivating personnel to aim for the goals set forth in the budget:[2]

1. A compensation system that builds and maintains a clearly understood relationship between results and rewards.
2. A system for performance appraisal that employees understand with regard to their individual effectiveness and key results, their tasks and their responsibilities, their degree and span of influence in decision making, as well as the time allowed to judge their results.
3. A system of communication that allows employees to query their superiors with trust and honest communication.
4. A system of promotion that generates and sustains employee faith in its validity and judgment.
5. A system of employee support through coaching, counseling, and career planning.
6. A system that not only considers company objectives, but also employees' skills and capacities.

---

[2]Paul E. Sussman, "Motivating Financial Personnel," *The Journal of Accountancy*, Vol. 141, No. 2, p. 80.

7. A system that will not settle for mediocrity, but which reaches for realistic and attainable standards, stressing improvement and providing an environment in which the concept of excellence can grow.

Empirical research in this field aids in providing a useful understanding of the interrelationships of budgeting and human behavior. Numerous research projects have been undertaken and more of such research is needed. To illustrate the insights that can be offered by such studies, the results of one research project indicated that budgetary participation and budget goal clarity had positive and significant effects on managers' job-related and budget-related attitudes as well as on their budgetary performance, while excessively high goals that were difficult to attain resulted in adverse effects on attitudes and performance. The study also found that budgetary evaluation and feedback had only weak or insignificant effects on managers' attitudes and performance.[3] Such conclusions, however, must be viewed as tentative until additional research produces similar results.

Controlling Costs

The responsibility for cost control should be assigned to specific individuals, who are also responsible for budgeting the costs under their control. The responsibilities should be limited to controllable costs, and the performance of the individuals should be measured by comparing actual costs with budgeted costs. The responsibility for sales revenues and profits should also be assigned to certain managers.

To aid the process of controlling, the cost accountant may use *standard costs*. These predetermined costs for direct materials, direct labor, and factory overhead are established by using information accumulated from past experience and from scientific research. When standards are used, they form the foundation for the budget and for reports which identify variances between actual and standard costs.

Pricing

Management's pricing policy should assure not only the recovery of all costs but also the securing of a profit, even under adverse conditions. Although supply and demand are usually determining factors in pricing, the establishment of a profitable sales price depends upon consideration of costs.

Determining Profits

One of the primary objectives of cost accounting is the consistent allocation of manufacturing costs to units of products in the ending inventory and to

---

[3]Izzettin Kenis, ''Effects of Budgetary Goal Characteristics on Managerial Attitudes and Performance,'' *The Accounting Review*, Vol. LIV, No. 4, pp. 707-721.

units sold during a period. At the end of a fiscal period, the matching of costs with revenues determines profits for the period. These costs and profits may be reported for segments of the firm or for the entire firm, depending upon management's needs and generally accepted accounting principles.

The matching process requires an identification of short-run and long-run costs and variable and fixed (capacity) costs. Variable manufacturing costs are assigned first to the units manufactured and then matched with the units sold; variable nonmanufacturing costs typically are matched with the units sold. Fixed costs are arbitrarily allocated to units by one of the following alternatives:

1. Matching total fixed costs assigned to a period with revenues of that period (direct costing).
2. Matching manufacturing fixed costs to units of product and matching all other fixed costs with revenues of the period (absorption costing, the generally accepted method).

These alternatives give the same results in the long run, but yield a different profit for individual short periods.

Choosing Among Alternatives

Cost accounting is the source of information concerning the different revenues and different costs which might result from alternative courses of action. Based on this information, management must make both short-range and long-range decisions that involve such matters as entering new markets, developing new products, discontinuing product lines, and buying or leasing equipment.

Inflation's Impact

In the various activities of furnishing relevant information to management, the impact of inflation must be considered. Thus, in the development and use of budgets, in using cost control data, in pricing decisions, in evaluating profit, and in choosing among alternatives, the effect of any change in the purchasing power of the dollar becomes important for the intelligent use of information. Also, the use of physical measures of performance (e.g., pounds of product produced per machine hour of usage) avoids the confusion of the impact of inflation on historical cost financial data.

▼ CERTIFICATION AND ETHICS

The subject matter of this textbook, which is broadly described as cost accounting, encompasses the concepts outlined above and discussed in detail in the chapters that follow. Those engaged in the activities of cost accounting may be referred to as "management accountants" or "internal accountants." They may also be referred to by their professional certification, *Certified*

Management Accountant (CMA), which was established by the National Association of Accountants (NAA) in 1972 as a formal means of recognizing professional competence and educational achievement in this field.

Requirements for the CMA certificate include passing a five-part examination and completing two years of professional experience in management accounting within seven years of having passed the examination. The five parts of the examination are:

1. Economics and business finance.
2. Organization and behavior, including ethical considerations.
3. Public reporting standards, auditing, and taxes.
4. Internal reporting and analysis.
5. Decision analysis, including modeling and information systems.

In 1983, the NAA issued a code of ethics for management (internal or cost) accountants, whether CMAs or not. While individuals practicing as independent certified public accountants have been subject to a code of conduct for many decades, these standards are the first ever issued for management accountants. Such standards should contribute to the public's faith in the integrity of the business community.

The *Standards of Ethical Conduct for Management Accountants* present fifteen responsibilities of the management accountant, grouped under four main headings: competence, confidentiality, integrity, and objectivity. The standards also outline procedures for management accountants to follow if they have knowledge of, or think they are being asked to do, something unethical. The procedures call for going to each superior level of management, in turn, and to the board of directors, if necessary, until the matter is resolved. If no internal resolution is achieved, the standards specify that the accountant should resign. Communication of internal problems to authorities or individuals outside the organization is not considered appropriate unless required by law.

▼ THE INFLUENCE OF PRIVATE AND GOVERNMENTAL ORGANIZATIONS

In the private sector, major research and pronouncements by professional organizations contribute to the development, improvement, and revision of both financial and cost accounting theory and practice. These organizations include the Financial Accounting Standards Board (FASB), the Governmental Accounting Standards Board (GASB), the American Institute of Certified Public Accountants (AICPA), the National Association of Accountants (NAA), the American Accounting Association (AAA), and the Financial Executives Institute (FEI). In addition, accounting is influenced by public accounting firms, nonprofit organizations, individuals, and private companies.

The rapid growth of international business activities has led several international organizations to become involved in setting standards of accounting and reporting. These organizations include the International

Accounting Standards Committee (IASC) and the Organization for Economic Cooperation and Development (OECD).

In the public sector, federal, state, and local governments prescribe regulations that may often be embodied in the accounting system. At the federal level, the Securities and Exchange Commission (SEC), the Internal Revenue Service (IRS), and the pronouncements of the Cost Accounting Standards Board (CASB) have a significant influence on financial and cost reporting.

Securities and Exchange Commission

The federal government, through the actions of the SEC and other regulatory agencies, is showing an increasing interest in the external reports of private companies. In *Regulation S-X*, requirements are set forth for financial statements filed with the SEC.

Congress and the Internal Revenue Code

Federal income tax liability is determined in accordance with the Internal Revenue Code[4] as enacted and amended by Congress. The Treasury Department, acting under authority granted by Congress, issues regulations[5] which interpret the tax statutes enacted by Congress. Although the Internal Revenue Service (IRS) is actually the Treasury Department's enforcement branch, charged with the responsibility of collecting the tax, it issues rulings and procedures as guidance to taxpayers.[6] The influence of the income tax statutes, regulations, rulings, and procedures on financial statements and cost accounting procedures cannot be ignored. Any meaningful analysis for planning and decision making must carefully consider federal as well as state and local tax consequences.

Cost Accounting Standards Board

On August 15, 1970, Congress established the Cost Accounting Standards Board. The purposes of the board, as outlined in an amendment to Section 719 of the Defense Production Act of 1950, were stated as follows:

> The Board shall from time to time promulgate cost-accounting standards designed to achieve uniformity and consistency in the cost-accounting principles followed by defense contractors and subcontractors under Federal contracts. Such promulgated standards shall be used by all relevant Federal agencies and by defense contractors and subcontractors in estimating, accumulating, and reporting costs in connection with the pricing, administration, and settlement of all negotiated prime contract and subcontract

---

[4]*Title 26 of the United States Code.*
[5]*Title 26 of the Code of Federal Regulations.*
[6]Revenue Rulings and Revenue Procedures are published weekly in the *Internal Revenue Bulletin* and semiannually in the *Cumulative Bulletin.*

national defense procurements with the United States in excess of $100,000, other than contracts or subcontracts where the price negotiated is based on (1) established catalog or market prices of commercial items sold in substantial quantities to the general public, or (2) prices set by law or regulation. In promulgating such standards . . . the Board shall take into account the probable costs of implementation . . . compared to the probable benefits. . . . Such regulations shall require defense contractors and subcontractors as a condition of contracting to disclose in writing their cost-accounting principles, including methods of distinguishing direct costs from indirect costs and the basis used for allocating indirect costs, and to agree to a contract price adjustment, with interest, for any increased costs paid to the defense contractor by the United States because of the defense contractor's failure to comply with duly promulgated cost-accounting standards or to follow consistently his disclosed cost-accounting practices in pricing contract proposals and in accumulating and reporting contract performance cost data.

On September 30, 1980, the CASB was dissolved because Congress believed that the board's purpose of establishing basic cost accounting standards had been accomplished. Since the board's standards, rules, and regulations have been incorporated into all major federal procurement regulations, they are currently in effect. In addition, various governmental agencies are continuing certain aspects of the board's work.

Significant Standards Issued. During its existence, the CASB issued a series of Cost Accounting Standards (CASs), which govern the determination and allocation of specific costs. These standards are defined as formal statements that (1) enunciate a principle or principles to be followed, (2) establish practices to be applied, or (3) specify criteria to be employed in selecting from alternative principles and practices in estimating, accumulating, and reporting costs of contracts subject to the rules of the board. To achieve increased uniformity and consistency in accounting for costs of negotiated contracts, the standards provide criteria for the allocation of the cost of resources used to cost objectives. *Cost* in this discussion is the monetary value of the resources used. As defined by the board, a *cost objective* is "a function, organizational subdivision, contract, or other work unit for which cost data are desired and for which provision is made to accumulate and measure the cost of processes, products, jobs, capitalized projects, etc." CASs deal with all aspects of cost allocability, including:

1. The definition and measurement of costs which may be allocated to cost objectives.
2. The determination of the cost accounting period to which such costs are assignable.
3. The determination of the methods by which costs are to be allocated to cost objectives.

The board's pronouncements adhere to the concept of full costing whenever appropriate. Full allocation of all costs of a period, including general administrative expenses and all other indirect costs, is considered to be the basis for determining the cost of negotiated defense contracts.

Although specific CASs are discussed as appropriate in subsequent chapters, it should be noted here that three of the standards—CASs 409, 414, and 417—have the potential for impact far beyond the government contracting area. CAS 409 requires contractors to depreciate their assets for contract costing purposes over lives that are based on documented historical usefulness, irrespective of the lives used for either financial or income tax purposes. CASs 414 and 417 recognize as a contract cost the imputed cost of capital committed to facilities, thereby overturning the government's long-standing practice of disallowing interest and other financing-type costs.

Contractor's Coverage. The CASB standards are to be followed by defense contractors and subcontractors in estimating, accumulating, and reporting costs for negotiated contracts in excess of $100,000. Since all nondefense agencies have also implemented the CASB's standards, rules, and regulations, most negotiated contracts and subcontracts are subject to these standards. The standards have also been adopted by some state and local governments.

On January 1, 1975, smaller contractors and business units with insignificant amounts of government business were removed from the CASB's coverage. Coverage now extends only to business units (segments or profit centers) of a contractor that has received a covered prime or subcontract in excess of $500,000. Once a business unit receives such a contract, it must comply with applicable standards for all subsequently awarded prime or subcontracts in excess of $100,000 unless otherwise exempt. The coverage ceases only when all covered contracts in excess of $100,000 are completed by a contractor and becomes operative again for contracts in excess of $100,000 upon acceptance of an award exceeding $500,000. A firm qualifying as a small business under the regulations of the Small Business Administration is exempt from the CASB's requirements.

In 1978, the Board issued a rule exempting contracts and subcontracts awarded to foreign concerns and governments from most CASB standards. The exemptions are intended to remove impediments to efficient and successful contracting with foreign groups.

Statement of Disclosure. As a condition of contracting, contractors can be required to disclose in writing their cost accounting practices. For this purpose, the board provided for a detailed disclosure statement. The instructions pertaining thereto indicate that a contractor must state the practices of each profit center, division, or similar organizational unit. A *profit center* is defined as "the smallest organizationally independent segment of a company which has been charged by management with profit and loss responsibility."

Although a detailed presentation of the disclosure statement is beyond the scope of this text, it should be noted that the statement requires information regarding the three major elements of direct costs (direct materials, direct labor, and other direct costs); the methods used to charge out materials (fifo, lifo, standard costs, or others); the accumulation of variances; the method of charging direct labor (individual/actual rates, average rates, standard cost rates, or others) and a description of the types of variances; the method used to cost interorganizational transfers; and the allocation bases used for charging indirect costs to government contracts or similar cost objectives.

DISCUSSION QUESTIONS

1. Define the concepts of planning and control and discuss how they relate to each other and contribute to progress toward achieving objectives.

2. What is the meaning of assignment of responsibility?

3. Explain the relationship between assignment of responsibility and control.

4. Is responsibility accounting identical with the concept of accountability? Explain.

5. In what manner does the controller exercise control over the activities of other members of management?

6. Discuss the functions of the cost department.

7. Numerous nonaccounting departments require cost data and must also feed basic data to the cost department. Discuss.

8. Why must the controller be aware of the latest developments in the field of communications?

9. Why is the budget an essential tool in cost planning?

10. Will the *Standards of Ethical Conduct for Management Accountants* prevent management fraud?

11. How are CASB standards defined and what degree of authority do they have?

CHAPTER 2

Cost Concepts and the Cost Accounting Information System

Cost accounting is usually considered only as it applies to manufacturing operations. In today's economy, however, every type and size of organization should benefit from the use of cost accounting concepts and techniques. For example, cost accounting principles may be applied by financial institutions, transportation companies (airlines, railroads, bus companies), churches, schools, colleges, universities, and governmental units, as well as the nonmanufacturing activities of manufacturing firms. Although these numerous applications of cost accounting are not discussed in depth in this text, they are mentioned in appropriate places.

▼ THE COST CONCEPT

Cost concepts and terms have developed according to the needs of accountants, economists, and engineers. Accountants have defined cost as "an exchange price, a forgoing, a sacrifice made to secure benefit. In financial accounting, the forgoing or sacrifice at date of acquisition is represented by a current or future diminution in cash or other assets."[1]

Frequently the term "cost" is used synonymously with the term "expense." However, an expense may be defined as a measured outflow of goods or services, which is matched with revenue to determine income, or:

> . . . the decrease in net assets as a result of the use of economic services in the creation of revenues or of the imposition of taxes by governmental units. Expense is measured by the amount of the decrease in assets or the increase in liabilities related to the production and delivery of goods and the rendering of services . . . expense in its broadest sense includes all expired costs which are deductible from revenues.[2]

---

[1]Robert T. Sprouse and Maurice Moonitz, *Accounting Research Study No. 3*, "A Tentative Set of Broad Accounting Principles for Business Enterprises," (New York: American Institute of Certified Public Accountants, 1962), p. 25.
[2]*Ibid.*, p. 49.

When the term ''cost'' is used specifically, it should be modified by such descriptions as direct, prime, conversion, indirect, fixed, variable, controllable, product, period, joint, estimated, standard, sunk, or out-of-pocket. Each modification implies a certain attribute which is important in measuring cost, and which may be recorded and accumulated for assigning costs to inventories, preparing financial statements, and planning and controlling costs. The accountant who is involved in planning, analyzing, and decision making must also work with future, replacement, imputed, differential, or opportunity costs, none of which is recorded.

A *cost object* is defined as a product, job order, contract, project, organization department (or other subdivision), or other unit for which an arrangement is made to accumulate and measure cost. Such accumulations in cost accounting systems are multidimensional because of the multiple needs in cost finding, planning, and control. For example, it is necessary to assign costs to each product unit, but it is also necessary to plan and control costs for which individual managers are assigned responsibility, i.e., on a departmental basis. The design of accounting systems and their implementation must address these multiple cost object requirements.

▼ THE COST ACCOUNTING INFORMATION SYSTEM

To manage an enterprise, systematic and comparative cost information as well as analytical cost and profit data are needed. This information helps management set the company's profit goals, establish departmental targets which direct middle and operating management toward the achievement of the final goal, evaluate the effectiveness of plans, pinpoint successes or failures in terms of specific responsibilities, and analyze and decide on adjustments and improvements to keep the entire organization moving forward, in balance, toward established objectives. An integrated and coordinated information system should provide only that information which is needed by each responsible manager. To accomplish these objectives, the system must be designed to provide information promptly. Furthermore, the information must be communicated effectively. Cost control needs and profit opportunities may be delayed or missed because of poor communication.

The accumulation of accounting data requires many forms, methods, and systems due to the varying types and sizes of businesses. A successful information system should be tailored to give the blend of sophistication and simplicity that is most efficient and economical for a specific organization. Designing a cost accounting information system requires a thorough understanding of the organizational structure of the company and the type of cost information required by all levels of management. This interface between the system, management, and employees has significant behavioral implications. The system may enhance or thwart the achievement of desired results, depending on the extent to which sound behavioral judgment is applied in developing, administering, and improving the system and in educating employees to observe cost control procedures.

The cost accounting information system must be closely associated with the division of authority, so that individual managers can be held accountable for the costs incurred in their departments. The system should be designed to promote the concept of management by exception; i.e., it should provide information that enables management to take prompt remedial action. The system should also reflect the manufacturing and administrative procedures of the particular company for which it is designed. Although the accounting records will not provide all the necessary information for effective management, the accountant who designs the system must know how employees are paid, how inventories are controlled, how equipment is costed, machine capacities, and other operating information.

The information system should provide the proper focus for management's attention. Certain significant aspects of performance may be difficult to measure, while more easily measured but less significant factors may cause the firm to pursue or overemphasize activities that are not in its long-run best interest. Managers should be informed as to the appropriate, intended uses as well as the limitations of information. At the same time, the information system's utility should be extended if possible.

Requirements for record keeping and reporting may be imposed on an organization by external forces, such as the Internal Revenue Code, the Federal Insurance Contributions Act, the Securities and Exchange Commission, Cost Accounting Standards, other governmental regulatory agencies and taxing authorities, as well as creditors and labor unions. These legal and contractual requirements must be met by a system that is designed in a cost-conscious manner. Any sophistication in a system, beyond the basic requirements, must be justified solely on the basis of its value to management.

The Chart of Accounts

Every profit and nonprofit organization, irrespective of its size and complexity, must maintain some type of general ledger accounting system. For such a system to function effectively, data must be collected, identified, and coded for recording in journals and posting to ledger accounts. The prerequisite for efficiently accomplishing these tasks is a well-designed *chart of accounts* for classifying costs and expenses.

In constructing a chart of accounts, the following basic considerations should be observed:

1. Accounts should be arranged and designated to give maximum information with a minimum of supplementary analysis.
2. Account titles should reflect the purpose rather than the nature of expenditures.
3. Manufacturing, marketing, and administrative cost accounts should receive particular attention because these accounts are used to highlight variations in operating efficiency. They should be identifiable with the manager responsible for the costs involved.

A typical chart of accounts is divided into (1) balance sheet accounts for assets, liabilities, and capital, and (2) income statement accounts for sales, cost of goods sold, factory overhead, marketing expenses, administrative expenses, and other expenses and income. The use of numbers to represent these accounts is the simplest form of symbolizing, which is essential to the processing of information, especially when electronic data processing equipment is being used. A condensed chart of accounts is illustrated as follows:

BALANCE SHEET ACCOUNTS (100-299)

Current Assets (100-129)	Current Liabilities (200-219)
Property, Plant, and Equipment (130-159)	Long-Term Liabilities (220-229)
Intangible Assets (170-179)	Capital (250-299)

INCOME STATEMENT ACCOUNTS (300-899)

Sales (300-349)	Administrative Expenses (600-699)
Cost of Goods Sold (350-399)	Other Expenses (700-749)
Factory Overhead (400-499)	Other Income (800-849)
Marketing Expenses (500-599)	Income Taxes (890-899)

Electronic Data Processing

Successful management of a business is essentially a continuous process of decision making. The decision making becomes even more complex when multiple plants are located throughout the nation and in foreign countries; when product lines carry an array of sizes, colors, and options; when various reports are necessary for taxing authorities, regulatory agencies, employees, and stockholders; and when policies and objectives must be communicated from executive management to several operating levels. The information system aids the decision-making process by collecting, classifying, analyzing, and reporting business data. These activities are called *data processing,* and the procedures, forms, and equipment used in the process are called the *data processing system.* Any accounting system, even a cash register in a supermarket, is a data processing system that should be designed to provide pertinent and timely information to management.

The speed and flexibility of computers have led many businesses to convert the processing of data to electronic systems, which replace ledgers with magnetic tape or magnetic disks as media for the recording and storing of account data. These systems can handle routine information easily, verify its accuracy, automatically write checks and remittance statements, classify and post data files, prepare general and subsidiary records and analytical reports, and compute ratios and other statistics for analytical purposes.

An electronic data processing system may be used to recognize and report any circumstances which deviate from a norm or standard. The concept of management by exception is thereby applied efficiently. The system also greatly expands the ability of management to use mathematical models or simulations to plan operations. For example, with a computer, it is possible to simulate a complete operating budget and manipulate product mix, price, cost factors, and the marketing program. By studying alternative combinations of the variables, the uncertainty in making decisions is reduced.

When an electronic data processing system is used, accounting procedures must be carefully programmed for the system. The programming process includes analyzing the procedure, preparing extensive flowcharts that reduce the procedure to a logical design for the system, and writing the detailed code of instructions for the system to follow. As a result of the extensive analysis required in programming, an inherent advantage of an electronic data processing system is that possibly vague accounting procedures become more concise and efficient.

The use of electronic data processing systems enables controllers and their staffs to become the nerve centers of large corporations. With such systems, controllers can assemble data concerning human resources, money, materials, and machines, which may form the basis for proposing alternatives in planning crucial operations. The data are based on (1) the company's historical costs and revenues, (2) management's evaluation of the present and future, and (3) economic forecasts originating outside the company.

Sensitivity to Changing Methods

It is vital that cost accounting systems and procedures be in harmony with the manufacturing methods in current usage. For example, highly automated, robotics-oriented manufacturing processes may employ little if any direct labor, thus minimizing the focus of planning and controlling direct labor cost and requiring alternate bases for allocating factory overhead costs to production. Also, contemporary manufacturing methods are often based on a philosophy that seeks to reduce dramatically the investments in raw materials as well as in work in process inventories. Systems design, redesign, and implementation must be responsive to changing methods and account for them in a manner that is consistent with and representative of current operations.

▼ CLASSIFICATIONS OF COSTS

Cost classifications are needed for the development of cost data that will aid management in achieving its objectives. These classifications are based on the relationship of costs to:

1. The product
2. Volume of production
3. Manufacturing departments
4. An accounting period

Costs in Relation to a Product

The process of classifying costs and expenses may begin by relating costs to the operations of a business. In a manufacturing concern, total operating cost consists of (1) manufacturing cost and (2) commercial expenses. The chart on the next page illustrates this division of total operating cost and identifies some of the elements included in each division.

Manufacturing Costs. Manufacturing cost, often called production cost or factory cost, is the sum of the three cost elements: direct materials, direct labor, and factory overhead. Direct materials and direct labor may be combined into another classification called *prime cost*. Direct labor and factory overhead may be combined into a classification called *conversion cost,* which represents the cost of converting direct materials into finished products.

Direct materials are all materials that form an integral part of the finished product and that can be included directly in calculating the cost of the product. Examples of direct materials are the lumber to make furniture and the crude oil to make gasoline. The ease with which the materials items may be traced to the final product is a major consideration in classifying items as direct materials. For example, tacks to build furniture undoubtedly form part of the finished product, but to cost the furniture expeditiously, such items may be classified as indirect materials.

Direct labor is labor expended to convert direct materials into the finished product. It consists of employees' wages which can feasibly be assigned to a specific product.

Factory overhead—also called manufacturing overhead, manufacturing expenses, or factory burden—may be defined as the cost of indirect materials, indirect labor, and all other manufacturing costs that cannot be charged directly to specific products. Simply stated, factory overhead includes all manufacturing costs except direct materials and direct labor.

Indirect materials are those materials needed for the completion of a product, but the consumption of which is so minimal or so complex that treating them as direct materials is futile. Factory supplies, a form of indirect materials, consist of such items as lubricating oils, grease, cleaning rags, and brushes needed to maintain the working area and machinery in a usable and safe condition.

Indirect labor may be defined as expended labor which does not directly affect the construction or the composition of the finished product. Indirect labor includes the wages of supervisors, shop clerks, general helpers, and employees engaged in maintenance work that is not directly related to production.

Commercial Expenses. Commercial expenses fall into two large classifications: (1) marketing (distribution or selling) expenses and (2) administrative (general and administrative) expenses. *Marketing expenses* begin at the point where the factory costs end, i.e., when manufacturing has been completed and the product is in salable condition. These expenses include the expenses of selling and delivery. *Administrative expenses* include expenses incurred in directing and controlling the organization. Some of these expenses, such as a vice-president's salary, are often allocated to and included in manufacturing costs and marketing expenses.

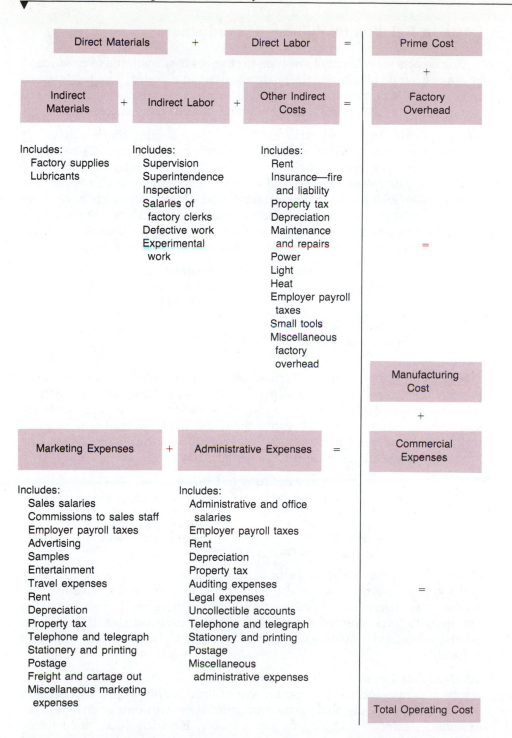

| Direct Materials | + | Direct Labor | = | Prime Cost |

+

| Indirect Materials | + | Indirect Labor | + | Other Indirect Costs | = | Factory Overhead |

Includes:
Factory supplies
Lubricants

Includes:
Supervision
Superintendence
Inspection
Salaries of
  factory clerks
Defective work
Experimental
  work

Includes:
Rent
Insurance—fire
  and liability
Property tax
Depreciation
Maintenance
  and repairs
Power
Light
Heat
Employer payroll
  taxes
Small tools
Miscellaneous
  factory
  overhead

=

Manufacturing
Cost

+

| Marketing Expenses | + | Administrative Expenses | = | Commercial Expenses |

Includes:
Sales salaries
Commissions to sales staff
Employer payroll taxes
Advertising
Samples
Entertainment
Travel expenses
Rent
Depreciation
Property tax
Telephone and telegraph
Stationery and printing
Postage
Freight and cartage out
Miscellaneous marketing
  expenses

Includes:
Administrative and office
  salaries
Employer payroll taxes
Rent
Depreciation
Property tax
Auditing expenses
Legal expenses
Uncollectible accounts
Telephone and telegraph
Stationery and printing
Postage
Miscellaneous
  administrative expenses

=

Total Operating Cost

Classification of Costs in Relation to a Manufactured Product

Costs in Relation to Volume of Production

Some costs vary directly in relation to changes in the volume of production or output, while others remain relatively fixed in amount. The tendency of costs to vary with output must be considered by management if it desires to plan a company's strategy intelligently and control costs successfully.

Variable Costs. In general, *variable costs* have the following characteristics: (1) variability of total amount in direct proportion to volume, (2) relatively constant cost per unit as volume changes within a relevant range, (3) assignable, with reasonable ease and accuracy, to operating departments, and (4) controllable by a specific department head. The costs which have these characteristics generally include direct materials and direct labor. Some factory overhead and nonmanufacturing costs are also variable. The following list identifies overhead costs which are usually classified as variable:

VARIABLE FACTORY OVERHEAD

Supplies	Receiving costs
Fuel	Hauling within plant
Power	Royalties
Small tools	Communication costs
Spoilage, salvage, and reclamation expenses	Overtime premium

Fixed Costs. The characteristics of *fixed costs* are: (1) fixed total amount within a relevant output range, (2) decrease in per unit cost as volume increases within a relevant range, (3) assignable to departments on the basis of arbitrary managerial decisions or cost allocation methods, and (4) control responsibility resting with executive management rather than operating supervisors. The following overhead costs are usually classified as fixed:

FIXED FACTORY OVERHEAD

Salaries of production executives	Wages of security guards and janitors
Depreciation	
Property tax	Maintenance and repairs of buildings and grounds
Patent amortization	
Insurance—property and liability	Rent

Fixed costs may be thought of as the costs of *being* in business, while variable costs are the costs of *doing* business. In some cases, management actions may determine whether a cost is classified as fixed or variable. For example, if a truck is rented at a rate per mile, the cost is variable. If the truck is purchased and subsequently depreciated by the straight-line method, the cost is fixed.

Semivariable Costs. Some costs contain fixed and variable elements. These *semivariable costs* include an amount that is fixed within a relevant range of output and an amount that varies proportionately with output changes. For example, electricity cost may be semivariable. Electricity used for lighting tends to be a fixed cost, since lights will be needed when the plant is operating, regardless of the level of output. Conversely, electricity used as power to operate equipment will vary, depending upon the usage of the equipment. Other examples of semivariable overhead costs are as follows:

SEMIVARIABLE FACTORY OVERHEAD

Supervision	Maintenance and repairs of machinery
Inspection	and plant equipment
Payroll department services	Compensation insurance
Personnel department services	Health and accident insurance
Factory office services	Payroll taxes
Materials and inventory services	Industrial relations expenses
Cost department services	Heat, light, and power

For analytical purposes, all manufacturing and nonmanufacturing costs should be classified as either fixed or variable. Therefore, semivariable costs must be divided into their fixed and variable components. Methods of accomplishing this division are discussed in Chapter 11.

Costs in Relation to Manufacturing Departments

For administrative purposes, a business may be divided into departments, segments, or functions. The division of a factory into departments, cost centers, or cost pools also serves as the basis for classifying and accumulating product costs and assigning responsibility for cost control. As a product passes through a department or cost center, it is charged with direct materials, direct labor, and a share of factory overhead.

To achieve the greatest degree of control, department managers should participate in the development of budgets for their respective departments or cost centers. Such budgets should clearly identify those costs about which the manager can make decisions and for which the manager accepts responsibility. At the end of a reporting period, the efficiency of a department and the manager's success in controlling costs may be measured by comparing actual costs with the budget.

Producing and Service Departments. The departments of a factory generally fall into two categories: (1) producing departments and (2) service departments. In a *producing department*, manual and machine operations, such as forming and assembling, are performed directly upon the product or its parts. The costs incurred by such departments are charged to the product. If two or more different types of machines perform operations on a product within the same department, the accuracy of product costs may be increased by dividing the department into cost centers.

In a *service department*, service is rendered for the benefit of other departments. In some instances, these services benefit other service departments as well as the producing departments. Although a service department does not directly engage in production, its costs are part of the total factory overhead and must be included in the cost of the product. Service departments which are common to many industrial concerns include maintenance, payroll, cost accounting, data processing, and food services.

Direct and Indirect Departmental Charges. Cost Accounting Standard No. 418, "Allocation of Direct and Indirect Costs," issued in 1980 by the Cost Accounting Standards Board, requires that costs be consistently classified as direct or indirect. In connection with materials and labor, the term "direct" refers to costs which are chargeable directly to the product. Factory overhead is considered "indirect" with regard to the product. The terms "direct" and "indirect" may be used, however, in connection with charging overhead costs to manufacturing departments and in charging expenses to the departments of nonmanufacturing organizations. If an expense is readily identifiable with (i.e., traceable to) the department in which it originates, it is referred to as a *direct* departmental expense. The salary of the departmental supervisor is an example of a direct expense. If an expense is shared by several departments that benefit from its incurrence, it is referred to as an *indirect* or *nontraceable* cost. Building rent and building depreciation are examples of indirect expenses which are allocated to departments.

Service department expenses are also indirect expenses for other departments. When all service department expenses have been allocated, each producing department's overhead will consist of its own direct and indirect departmental expense and the apportioned charges from service departments.

Common Costs and Joint Costs. Both common costs and joint costs are types of indirect costs. *Common costs* are costs of facilities or services employed by two or more operations. Common costs are particularly prevalent in organizations with many departments or segments. The degree of segmentation increases the tendency of costs to be common costs. For example, the salary of the marketing vice-president is not a common cost if the segment is the entire marketing function. If the segment encompasses only the southwestern marketing region, however, the vice-president's salary is a common cost to that region.

Joint costs occur when the production of one product may be possible only if one or more other products are manufactured at the same time. The meat-packing, oil and gas, and liquor industries are excellent examples of production that involves joint costs. In such industries, joint costs can be allocated to joint products only by arbitrary procedures. Therefore, data resulting from joint cost allocation must be analyzed carefully.

Costs in Relation to an Accounting Period

Costs may be classified as capital expenditures or as revenue expenditures. A *capital expenditure* is intended to benefit future periods and is recorded as an asset. A *revenue expenditure* benefits the current period and is recorded as an expense. Ultimately, an asset will flow into the expense stream as it is consumed or when it loses its usefulness.

The distinction between capital and revenue expenditures is essential to the proper matching of costs and revenue and to the accurate measurement of periodic income. However, a precise distinction between the two classifications is not always feasible. In many cases, the initial classification depends upon management's attitude toward such expenditures and the nature of the company's operations. The amount of the expenditure and the number of detailed records required are also factors that influence the distinction between these two classifications.

▼ THE FLOW OF COSTS IN A MANUFACTURING ENTERPRISE

Cost accounting neither adds new steps to the familiar accounting cycle nor discards the principles and procedures studied in financial accounting. Cost accounting consists of a system which is concerned with precise recording and measurement of cost elements as they originate and flow through the productive processes. This flow is illustrated in the following diagram:

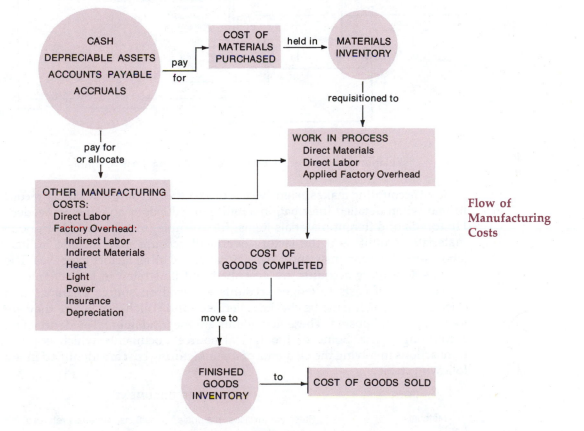

Flow of Manufacturing Costs

The manufacturing process and the physical arrangement of the factory are the basis for determining cost accumulation procedures. Generally, the accounts which describe manufacturing operations are: Materials, Payroll, Factory Overhead Control, Work in Process, Finished Goods, and Cost of Goods Sold. These accounts are used to recognize and measure the flow of costs in each fiscal period—from the acquisition of materials, through factory operations, to the cost of products sold. Cost accounts are expansions of general accounts and are related to general accounts, as shown in the following diagram:

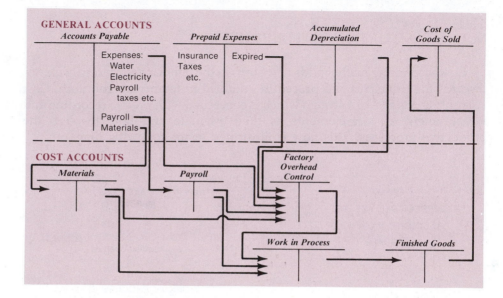

Relationship Between General Accounts and Cost Accounts

Cost accounting makes extensive use of a control account-subsidiary record format when detailed information about general ledger accounts is needed. Hundreds of different materials items, for example, may be included in one materials account, and the factory overhead account may include indirect labor, supplies, rent, insurance, taxes, repairs, and other factory expenses. The various subsidiary accounts are described and illustrated in later chapters.

The flow of costs to ledger accounts is based on source or transaction documents, which must be checked, verified, and vouchered before they are journalized and posted. These documents are the fundamental evidence of an accounting event. Some of the typical source documents which support transactions involving the elements of manufacturing cost are identified in the following table:

COST	SOURCE DOCUMENT
Materials	Purchase invoices, materials requisitions, materials returned slips, etc.
Labor	Time tickets or time sheets, clock cards, job tickets, etc.
Factory overhead	Vouchers prepared to set up depreciation or prepaid expenses, vendors' invoices, utility bills, time sheets, etc.

The flow of accounting information from source document to ledger accounts may be facilitated by using the journal voucher control system.

Whether manual or computerized, this system involves the use of journal vouchers on which information from the source documents is summarized and identified according to the chart of accounts. The journal voucher is the basis for the preparation of journal entries which record the transactions for a given period and the posting of these transactions to the ledger accounts. The journal voucher should indicate the voucher number, the date, the accounts with their numbers or codes, the amounts to be debited or credited, and approval. Columns may be added to accommodate the subsidiary ledger details, or these details may be posted directly from the source documents.

To illustrate the flow of costs in a manufacturing enterprise, assume that New Hope Manufacturing Company begins a new fiscal year with the financial position as shown in the following balance sheet:

New Hope Manufacturing Company
Balance Sheet
January 1, 19--

Assets

Current assets:			
Cash		$ 183,000	
Marketable securities		76,000	
Accounts receivable		313,100	
Inventories:			
Finished goods	$ 68,700		
Work in process	234,300		
Materials	135,300	438,300	
Prepaid expenses		15,800	
Total current assets			$1,026,200
Property, plant, and equipment:			
Land		$ 41,500	
Buildings	$ 580,600		
Machinery and equipment	1,643,000		
	$2,223,600		
Less accumulated depreciation	1,010,700	1,212,900	
Total property, plant, and equipment			1,254,400
Total assets			$2,280,600

Liabilities

Current liabilities:			
Accounts payable		$ 553,000	
Estimated income tax payable		35,700	
Due on long-term debt		20,000	
Total current liabilities			$ 608,700
Long-term debt			204,400
Total liabilities			$ 813,100

Stockholders' Equity

Common stock		$ 528,000	
Retained earnings		939,500	
Total stockholders' equity			1,467,500
Total liabilities and stockholders' equity			$2,280,600

During the month of January, New Hope completed the transactions which are summarized, recorded, and posted to the ledger accounts as follows. The revenue and expense accounts are not closed at the end of January, because such formal closing, in practice, is usually done only at year end.

Transactions	Journal Entries

(a) Materials purchased and received on account................................... $100,000

Materials... 100,000
   Accounts Payable.............................   100,000

This is a summary entry. The materials account is an inventory control account; subsidiary records will indicate the details of the materials received.

(b) Materials requisitioned during the month:

   For production... $ 80,000
   For indirect factory use............................ 12,000

Work in Process.................................... 80,000
Factory Overhead Control.................... 12,000
   Materials...   92,000

The indirect factory materials are kept in the inventory control account as well as in subsidiary records to control their purchase and usage.

(c) Total gross payroll.. $160,000
Payroll was paid to employees for the month, after deducting 7.5% FICA tax and 11.5% federal income tax withheld*........... 129,600

*Here and in later chapters, the various tax rates are used for illustration only. Current rates and wage bases to which the taxes apply may be found in published government regulations.

Payroll... 160,000
   Employees Income Tax Payable.....   18,400
   FICA Tax Payable............................   12,000
   Accrued Payroll...............................   129,600

Accrued Payroll.................................... 129,600
   Cash...   129,600

The accrued payroll account is used to establish a record until the payroll department has prepared the paychecks to be distributed to the employees.

(d) The distribution of the payroll was:
   Direct labor.. 65%
   Indirect factory labor...................................... 15
   Marketing salaries.. 13
   Administrative salaries................................... 7

Work in Process.................................... 104,000
Factory Overhead Control.................... 24,000
Marketing Expenses Control............... 20,800
Administrative Expenses Control......... 11,200
   Payroll..   160,000

(e) An additional 10% is recorded for the employer's payroll taxes:
   FICA tax.. 7.5%
   Federal unemployment insurance tax......... .8
   State unemployment insurance tax............. 1.7

Payroll taxes are distributed in the same proportion as the distribution of payroll. Payroll taxes related to factory activities (direct and indirect labor) are charged to the factory overhead control account.

Factory Overhead Control.................... 12,800
Marketing Expenses Control............... 2,080
Administrative Expenses Control......... 1,120
   FICA Tax Payable............................   12,000
   Federal Unemployment Tax Payable   1,280
   State Unemployment Tax Payable..   2,720

The company is required to pay the same amount of FICA tax as the employees. In addition, the company must pay federal and state unemployment taxes, from which the employee is exempt. The state unemployment tax rate is lower if the employer stabilizes employment; otherwise, it may be as high as 5.4%.

(f) Factory overhead consisting of:
   Depreciation.. $8,500
   Prepaid insurance.. 1,200

Factory Overhead Control.................... 9,700
   Accumulated Depreciation...............   8,500
   Prepaid Expenses............................   1,200

(g) General factory overhead costs (not itemized)... $26,340
70% of these expenses were paid in cash; the balance was credited to Accounts Payable.

Factory Overhead Control.................... 26,340
   Cash...   18,438
   Accounts Payable.............................   7,902

(h) Amount received from customers in
payment of their accounts............................ $205,000

Cash..	205,000	
Accounts Receivable........................		205,000

(i) The following liabilities were paid:
    Accounts payable....................................... $227,000
    Estimated income tax.............................. 35,700

Accounts Payable................................	227,000	
Estimated Income Tax Payable..........	35,700	
Cash..		262,700

(j) Factory overhead accumulated in the factory overhead control account was transferred to the work in process account.

Work in Process....................................	84,840	
Factory Overhead Control................		84,840

(k) Work completed and transferred to
finished goods... $320,000

Finished Goods....................................	320,000	
Work in Process..............................		320,000

(l) Sales... $384,000

40% was paid in cash; the balance was charged to Accounts Receivable. The cost of goods sold was 75% of sales.

Cash..	153,600	
Accounts Receivable............................	230,400	
Sales..		384,000
Cost of Goods Sold.............................	288,000	
Finished Goods................................		288,000

(m) Provision for income tax............................... $ 26,000

Provision for Income Tax.....................	26,000	
Estimated Income Tax Payable.......		26,000

Cash

1/1	183,000	(c)	129,600
(h)	205,000	(g)	18,438
(l)	153,600	(i)	262,700
	541,600		410,738
	130,862		

Marketable Securities

1/1	76,000	

Accounts Receivable

1/1	313,100	(h)	205,000
(l)	230,400		
	543,500		
	338,500		

Finished Goods

1/1	68,700	(l)	288,000
(k)	320,000		
	388,700		
	100,700		

Work in Process

1/1	234,300	(k)	320,000
(b)	80,000		
(d)	104,000		
(j)	84,840		
	503,140		
	183,140		

Materials

1/1	135,300	(b)	92,000
(a)	100,000		
	235,300		
143,300			

Prepaid Expenses

1/1	15,800	(f)	1,200
14,600			

Land

1/1	41,500	

Buildings

1/1	580,600	

Machinery and Equipment

1/1	1,643,000	

Accumulated Depreciation

		1/1	1,010,700
		(f)	8,500
			1,019,200

Accounts Payable

(i)	227,000	1/1	553,000
		(a)	100,000
		(g)	7,902
			660,902
		433,902	

Accrued Payroll				Employees Income Tax Payable		
(c)	129,600	(c)	129,600		(c)	18,400

Estimated Income Tax Payable				FICA Tax Payable		
(i)	35,700	1/1	35,700		(c)	12,000
		(m)	26,000		(e)	12,000
			61,700			24,000
		26,000				

Federal Unemployment Tax Payable				Factory Overhead Control		
		(e)	1,280	(b)	12,000	(j)	84,840

(Factory Overhead Control continued)

State Unemployment Tax Payable		
	(e)	2,720

Factory Overhead Control		
(b)	12,000	(j)	84,840
(d)	24,000	
(e)	12,800	
(f)	9,700	
(g)	26,340	
	84,840	

Due on Long-Term Debt		
	1/1	20,000

Payroll			
(c)	160,000	(d)	160,000

Long-Term Debt		
	1/1	204,400

Marketing Expenses Control		
(d)	20,800	
(e)	2,080	
	22,880	

Common Stock		
	1/1	528,000

Administrative Expenses Control		
(d)	11,200	
(e)	1,120	
	12,320	

Retained Earnings		
	1/1	939,500

Sales		
	(l)	384,000

Provision for Income Tax		
(m)	26,000	

Cost of Goods Sold	
(l)	288,000

▼ REPORTING THE RESULTS OF OPERATIONS

The results of operations of a manufacturing enterprise are reported in the conventional financial statements. These statements summarize the flow of costs and revenues, and show the financial position at the end of a period of operations.

Income Statement

The following statement shows the revenues and expenses of New Hope Manufacturing Company for the month of January:

```
                        New Hope Manufacturing Company
                                Income Statement
                        For Month Ended January 31, 19--
Sales.................................................................              $384,000
Less cost of goods sold (Schedule 1)......................              288,000
Gross profit...........................................................            $ 96,000
Less commercial expenses:
   Marketing expense............................................  $22,880
   Administrative expense.......................................   12,320            35,200
Income from operations..........................................                   $ 60,800
Less provision for income tax..................................                     26,000
Net income............................................................            $ 34,800
```

In the income statement, the cost of goods sold is shown in one figure. Although this procedure is followed in published reports, additional information is necessary for internal uses. Therefore, a supporting schedule of the cost of goods sold is usually produced, illustrated as follows for New Hope:

```
                        New Hope Manufacturing Company
                                   Schedule 1
                           Cost of Goods Sold Statement
                        For Month Ended January 31, 19--

①  Direct materials:
       Materials inventory, January 1, 19--........................  $135,300
       Purchases...................................................   100,000
       Materials available for use................................  $235,300
       Less: Indirect materials used.............. $ 12,000
             Materials inventory, January 31.....  143,300           155,300
       Direct materials consumed................................              $ 80,000
②  Direct labor.....................................................            104,000
③  Factory overhead:
       Indirect materials..........................................  $ 12,000
       Indirect labor..............................................    24,000
       Payroll taxes...............................................    12,800
       Depreciation................................................     8,500
       Insurance...................................................     1,200
       General factory overhead...................................    26,340     84,840
    Total manufacturing cost......................................             $268,840
④  Add work in process inventory, January 1.....................               234,300
                                                                               $503,140
    Less work in process inventory, January 31.................                183,140
    Cost of goods manufactured....................................            $320,000
⑤  Add finished goods inventory, January 1.....................                 68,700
    Cost of goods available for sale..............................            $388,700
    Less finished goods inventory, January 31.................                100,700
    Cost of goods sold.............................................            $288,000
```

① The direct materials section is comprised of the beginning materials inventory, purchases, and the ending inventory of materials, with an adjustment for the indirect materials that were added to factory overhead. This section identifies the cost of materials that became part of the finished product.

② The direct labor section indicates the cost of labor which can be identified directly with the products manufactured.

③ Factory overhead includes all costs that are indirectly involved in manufacturing the product. (Note: The next chapter and the factory overhead chapters will introduce and demonstrate the use of a predetermined factory overhead rate.)

④ The total manufacturing costs incurred during the period are adjusted for the work in process inventories at the beginning and end of the period.

⑤ The cost of goods manufactured during the period is adjusted for the finished goods inventory at the beginning and end of the period.

Balance Sheet

The balance sheet complements the income statement. Neither statement alone offers a sufficiently clear picture of the status and progress of a company. The following balance sheet shows the financial position of New Hope Manufacturing Company at the end of January:

New Hope Manufacturing Company
Balance Sheet
January 31, 19--

Assets

Current assets:			
Cash..		$ 130,862	
Marketable securities..		76,000	
Accounts receivable...		338,500	
Inventories:			
Finished goods..	$ 100,700		
Work in process......................................	183,140		
Materials..	143,300	427,140	
Prepaid expenses...		14,600	
Total current assets..................................			$ 987,102
Property, plant, and equipment:			
Land..		$ 41,500	
Buildings...	$ 580,600		
Machinery and equipment.................................	1,643,000		
	$2,223,600		
Less accumulated depreciation.........................	1,019,200	1,204,400	
Total property, plant, and equipment.........			1,245,900
Total assets...			$2,233,002

Liabilities

Current liabilities:			
Accounts payable...		$ 433,902	
Estimated income tax payable..........................		26,000	
Other current liabilities.....................................		46,400	
Due on long-term debt......................................		20,000	
Total current liabilities..............................			$ 526,302
Long-term debt...			204,400
Total liabilities...			$ 730,702

Stockholders' Equity

Common stock...		$ 528,000	
Retained earnings:			
Balance, January 1..................................	$939,500		
January net income.................................	34,800	974,300	
Total stockholders' equity.................................			1,502,300
Total liabilities and stockholders' equity............			$2,233,002

DISCUSSION QUESTIONS

1. (a) Explain the meanings of the terms "cost" and "expense" as used for financial reporting in conformity with generally accepted accounting principles. The explanation should indicate distinguishing characteristics of the terms, their similarities and interrelationships.
   (b) Classify each of the following items as a cost, expense, or other category, with an explanation of how the classification of each item may change: (1) cost of goods sold; (2) uncollectible accounts expense; (3) depreciation expense for plant machinery; (4) organization costs; (5) spoiled goods.

2. What are cost objects and why are they important?

3. Define a cost system.

4. Enumerate the requirements of a good information system.

5. What is the purpose of a chart of accounts?

6. What are the advantages of an electronic data processing system?

7. Enumerate the various classifications of costs.

8. Describe indirect materials and give an appropriate example.

9. Describe indirect labor and give an appropriate example.

10. (a) What is a service department? Name a few.
    (b) What are some characteristics of a service department in connection with the establishment of a product cost?

11. Expenditures may be divided into two general categories: capital expenditures and revenue expenditures.
    (a) Distinguish between these two categories of expenditures and their treatment in the accounts.
    (b) Discuss the impact on both present and future balance sheets and income statements of improperly distinguishing between capital and revenue expenditures.
    (c) What criteria do firms generally use in establishing a policy for classifying expenditures under these two general categories?

12. Enumerate the five parts of the cost of goods sold section of the income statement.

13. Discuss the complementary relationship between the balance sheet and the income statement.

14. A corporation's annual financial statements and reports were criticized because it was claimed that the income statement does not by any means give a clear picture of annual earning power, and the balance sheet does not disclose the true value of the plant assets. Considering the criticism made, offer an explanation of the nature and purpose of the income statement and of the balance sheet, together with comments on their limitations.

EXERCISES

1. **Manufacturing costs.** The estimated unit costs for a company operating at a production and sales level of 12,000 units are as follows:

Cost Item	Estimated Unit Cost
Direct materials.....................................	$32
Direct labor...	20
Variable factory overhead.....................	15
Fixed factory overhead..........................	6
Variable marketing.................................	3
Fixed marketing.....................................	4

Required:

(1) Identify the estimated conversion cost per unit.
(2) Identify the estimated prime cost per unit.
(3) Determine the estimated total variable cost per unit.
(4) Compute the total cost that would be incurred during a month with a production level of 12,000 units and a sales level of 8,000 units. *(ICMA adapted)*

2. Fixed and variable costs. In 19A, the Mercaldo Company had sales of $19,950,000, with $11,571,000 variable and $7,623,000 fixed costs. 19B sales are expected to decrease 15% and the cost relationship is expected to remain constant (the fixed costs will not change).

Required: Determine Mercaldo Company's expected operating income or loss for 19B.

3. Manufacturing costs; cost of goods manufactured; cost of goods sold. The December 31, 19B trial balance of Crockett Company showed:

Sales.........................	$14,500,500	Sales returns and	
Purchases (net)............	2,400,000	allowances......................	$ 25,200
Transportation in..........	32,000	Factory overhead..............	1,885,600
Direct labor..................	3,204,000	Advertising expense..........	155,000
Sales salaries...............	200,000	Delivery expense..............	65,000

Inventories:	December 31, 19B	December 31, 19A
Finished goods........................	$567,400	$620,000
Work in process.....................	136,800	129,800
Materials................................	196,000	176,000

Required: Determine (1) the total manufacturing cost, (2) the cost of goods manufactured, and (3) the cost of goods sold. *(CGAAC adapted)*

4. Journal entries for the cost accounting cycle. The following transactions pertain to manufacturing operations:

(a) Materials were issued as follows: direct, $24,500; indirect, $4,500.
(b) A payroll of $44,000 was recorded. Income tax withheld, $7,000; FICA tax rate, 7.5%.
(c) The payroll consisted of $30,000 direct labor, $6,000 indirect factory labor, and $8,000 sales salaries. State unemployment insurance is 5.4%, and federal is .8%. The employer's FICA tax rate was 7.5%.
(d) Miscellaneous factory expenses incurred will require a cash expenditure of $7,500. (Do not journalize the cash payment.)
(e) Factory overhead of $22,932 was charged to production.
(f) Cost of production completed during the period totaled $60,000.
(g) Materials purchased totaled $50,000.
(h) Goods costing $20,000 were shipped to customers at a sales price of $26,000.

Required: Prepare journal entries for the above transactions.

5. Journal entries for the cost accounting cycle. MultiElectro Incorporated completed the following transactions during February:

(a) Direct materials of $120,000 were purchased on terms of n/30.

(b) Total gross payroll was $90,000, with employee payroll deductions recorded at these rates: 7.5% of gross earnings for FICA tax; 17.5% of gross earnings for income tax. The payroll consisted of $45,000 direct labor, $9,000 indirect factory labor, $15,000 sales salaries, and $21,000 administrative salaries.

(c) Indirect factory materials and supplies amounting to $26,250 were purchased; terms n/30.

(d) Employer payroll tax expense includes: state unemployment, 3.1%; federal unemployment, .8%; FICA tax, 7.5%.

(e) Analysis of the materials requisitioned reveals:

Production orders..	$60,000
Indirect factory materials and supplies........................	15,000
Shipping supplies..	4,500

(f) Defective shipping supplies of $900 were returned to the vender.

(g) Accounts payable totaling $142,500, including the accrued payroll, were paid.

(h) Depreciation of $1,000 was recorded on the factory machinery.

(i) Sundry factory expenses of $6,900 were recorded as liabilities.

(j) Actual factory overhead of $38,056 was applied to production.

(k) Goods completed with a total cost of $126,000 were transferred to finished goods.

(l) Sales were $150,000 and cost $96,000 to produce.

Required: Prepare journal entries to record the transactions.

6. Journal entries for the cost accounting cycle. Selected transactions of the Romer Company for February are as follows:

(a) Materials requisitioned: $18,500 for production and $2,800 for indirect use.

(b) Work completed and transferred to finished goods amounted to $51,800.

(c) Materials purchased and received, $32,000.

(d) The payroll, after deducting 7.5% FICA tax, 17.5% federal income tax, and 5% state income tax, was $35,000. The wages due the employees were paid.

(e) Of the total payroll, 55% was direct labor, 18% indirect factory labor, 17% marketing salaries, and 10% administrative salaries.

(f) An additional 13.7% is entered for employer's payroll taxes, representing 7.5% FICA tax, .8% federal unemployment tax, and 5.4% state unemployment tax. Payroll taxes related to factory production are charged to the factory overhead control account.

(g) Other factory overhead consisted of $9,450 depreciation on the factory building and equipment, $600 expired insurance, and $1,250 other unpaid bills.

(h) Factory overhead of $28,100.50 was charged to production.

(i) Sales on account totaled $92,120, with a markup of 40% on the cost of goods sold.

(j) Cash collections from accounts receivable totaled $76,000.

Required: Prepare journal entries for these transactions.

7. Cost of goods manufactured statement. Thornton Company manufactures special machines made to customer specifications. The following information was available at the beginning of October:

Materials inventory.................................	$16,200
Work in process inventory.....................	3,600

During October, direct materials costing $20,000 were purchased, direct labor cost totaled $16,500, and factory overhead was $8,580.

October 31 inventories were:

Materials inventory	$17,000
Work in process inventory	7,120

Required: Prepare a cost of goods manufactured statement for October, 19A.

(AICPA adapted)

8. Cost of goods sold statement. The following data are provided by the controller of Pensacola Corporation:

Cash		$ 240,000
Accounts receivable		348,000
Inventories:		

	January 1	December 31
Finished goods	$54,200	$66,000
Work in process	29,800	38,800
Materials	88,000	64,000

Materials purchased	366,000
Sales discounts	8,000
Factory overhead (excluding depreciation)	468,400
Marketing and administrative expenses (excluding depreciation)	344,200
Depreciation (90% manufacturing, 10% marketing and administrative expenses)	116,000
Sales	1,844,000
Direct labor	523,600
Freight on materials purchased	6,600
Rental income	64,000
Interest on bonds payable	16,000

Required: Prepare a cost of goods sold statement.   (CGAAC adapted)

PROBLEMS

2-1. Cost of goods manufactured; prime and conversion costs. Mat Company's purchases of materials during March totaled $110,000, and the cost of goods sold for March was $345,000. Factory overhead was 50% of direct labor cost. Other information pertaining to Mat Company's inventories and production for March is as follows:

Inventories:	Beginning	Ending
Finished goods	$102,000	$105,000
Work in process	40,000	36,000
Materials	20,000	26,000

Required:

(1) Prepare a schedule of cost of goods manufactured for March.
(2) Compute the prime cost charged to work in process during March.
(3) Compute the conversion cost charged to work in process during March.

(AICPA adapted)

2-2. Income statement relationships. The following information is available for three companies at the end of their fiscal years:

Company A: Finished goods, January 1 *beg* .... $ 600,000
Cost of goods manufactured 3,800,000
Sales 4,000,000
Gross profit on sales 20% *800,000*
Finished goods inventory, December 31 .... ?

Company B: Freight in .... $ 20,000
Purchases returns and allowances 80,000
Marketing expense 200,000
Finished goods, December 31 *end* 190,000
Cost of goods sold 1,300,000
Cost of goods available for sale .... ?

Company C: Gross profit .... $ 96,000
Cost of goods manufactured *beg* 340,000
Finished goods, January 1 *beg* 45,000
Finished goods, December 31 *end* 52,000
Work in process, January 1 *beg* 28,000
Work in process, December 31 38,000
Sales .... ?

Required: Determine the amounts indicated by the question marks for each company.   (AICPA adapted)

2-3. Cost accounting cycle entries in T accounts. Dekker Company charges the total actual factory overhead to Work in Process. Following are selected account balances for September:

	September 1	September 30
Finished Goods	$34,000	$ 30,000
Work in Process	7,000	?
Materials and Supplies	20,000	15,000
Accrued Payroll (ignore payroll taxes)	13,000	9,000
Accounts Receivable	54,000	22,000
Accounts Payable	18,000	6,000
Sales		500,000

Additional information:

(a) All sales are on account.
(b) The accounts payable account is used for the purchase of materials and supplies only.
(c) Dekker's markup is 30% of sales.
(d) Work in process at the end of September had $2,000 of materials, $6,000 of direct labor, and $3,000 of factory overhead charged to it.
(e) Actual factory overhead costs for September were:

Supplies	$20,000
Indirect labor	55,000
Depreciation	10,000
Insurance	2,000
Miscellaneous	13,000

(f) Materials and supplies purchased on account, $65,000.

Required: Using T accounts, determine:

(1) Materials issued to production.
(2) Direct labor.
(3) Total factory overhead.
(4) Cost of goods manufactured.
(5) Cost of goods sold.
(6) Payment of accounts payable.
(7) Collection of accounts receivable.
(8) Payment of payroll.   *(CGAAC adapted)*

2-4. Journal entries for the cost accounting cycle. Waterlux Company incurred $50,000 direct labor cost in 19A and had the following selected account balances at the beginning and end of 19A:

	January 1	December 31
Finished Goods.............................	28,000	45,000
Work in Process............................	12,000	14,000
Materials..	17,000	24,000
Cost of Goods Sold......................	—	140,000
Factory Overhead Control.............	—	25,000

Required: Reconstruct the journal entries that recorded the above information in 19A.   *(CGAAC adapted)*

2-5. The cost accounting cycle. Montana Company's January 1 account balances are:

Dr.		Cr.	
Cash..	$20,000	Accounts Payable.............................	$15,500
Accounts Receivable......................	25,000	Accrued Payroll................................	2,250
Finished Goods...............................	9,500	Accumulated Depreciation................	10,000
Work in Process.............................	4,500	Common Stock..................................	60,000
Materials..	10,000	Retained Earnings.............................	21,250
Machinery..	40,000		

During January, the following transactions were completed:

(a) Materials purchased on account, $92,000.
(b) Miscellaneous factory overhead incurred on account, $18,500.
(c) Labor, accumulated and distributed using a payroll account, was consumed as follows: for direct production, $60,500; indirect labor, $12,500; sales salaries, $8,000; administrative salaries, $5,000. 9.5% of the wages is withheld for income tax. The state and federal unemployment tax rates are 2.7% and .8%, respectively; the employer and employee FICA tax rate is 7.5% each. The total accrued payroll was paid.
(d) Materials were consumed as follows: direct materials, $82,500; indirect materials, $8,300.
(e) Factory overhead charged to production was $47,330.
(f) Work finished and placed in stock cost $188,000.
(g) All but $12,000 of the finished goods were sold, terms 2/10, n/60. The markup was 30% above production cost. The sale and the receivable are recorded in the gross amount.
(h) Of the total accounts receivable, 80% was collected, less 2% discount. (Round to the nearest dollar.)

(i) A liability was recorded for various marketing and administrative expenses totaling $30,000. Of this amount, 60% was marketing and 40% was administrative.

(j) The check register showed payments of $104,000 for liabilities other than payrolls.

Required:

(1) Prepare T accounts with January 1 balances.
(2) Prepare journal entries and post January transactions into the ledger accounts. Open new accounts as needed.
(3) Prepare a trial balance as of January 31.

2-6. Cost of goods sold statement; income statement. The following data are available for Mandmeyer Company for the year ended November 30, 19B:

Sales..	$56,000
Finished goods inventory:	
November 30, 19B..............................	5,100
December 1, 19A...............................	3,500
Work in process inventory:	
November 30, 19B..............................	7,500
December 1, 19A...............................	4,000
Materials inventory:	
November 30, 19B..............................	4,250
December 1, 19A...............................	4,000
Materials purchased...............................	18,000
Direct labor..	7,500

Factory overhead charged to production, $5,000.
Marketing expenses, 5% of sales.
Administrative expenses, 2% of sales.
Other expenses, 1% of sales.

Required:

(1) Prepare a cost of goods sold statement.
(2) Prepare an income statement.   *(CGAAC adapted)*

PART
2

Cost Accumulation
Procedures

CHAPTER 3
Job Order Costing

The previous chapter presented an overall view of the flow of costs and expenses, generally known as the manufacturing cost accounting cycle for cost determination. This chapter discusses refinements in accounting for the flow of costs by distinguishing actual and standard cost systems and job order and process cost accumulation. Job order costing, which is used to determine costs and profit for specific jobs or orders, is then described and illustrated in detail.

▼ COST SYSTEMS AND COST ACCUMULATION PROCEDURES

Costs which are allocated to units of production may be actual costs or standard costs. In an *actual* or *historical* cost system, costs are collected as they occur, but the presentation of results is delayed until manufacturing operations have been performed or services rendered. In a *standard* cost system, products, operations, and processes are costed using standards for both quantities and dollar amounts. These standards are predetermined in advance of production. Actual costs are also recorded, and variances or differences between actual costs and standard costs are collected in separate accounts. The presentation in this and subsequent chapters is in the context of actual cost systems, with the details of standard cost systems deferred to Chapters 17 and 18.

The actual cost system and the standard cost system may be used with either job order or process cost accumulation procedures. In *job order costing*, costs are accumulated by job or specific order. This method presupposes the possibility of physically identifying the jobs produced and of charging each job with its own cost. Job order costing is applicable to job order work in factories, workshops, and repair shops, as well as to work by builders, construction engineers, and printers.

Many modern manufacturing processes are becoming highly automated. Increasingly, labor-intensive production processes such as assembly lines are being automated through the use of robotics. In such systems, manufacturing changes can be made more efficiently than in labor-intensive systems because the learning period required by humans is eliminated. In a robotics production process, the first unit of product is produced as efficiently as the last unit. As a consequence, robotics systems enhance the likelihood of manufacturing heterogeneous products and using job order costing to accumulate the manufacturing costs.

A variation of the job order cost method is that of costing orders by lots. A lot is the quantity of product which can conveniently and economically be produced and costed. In the shoe manufacturing industry, for example, a contract is typically divided into lots which consist of 100 to 250 pairs of one size and style of shoe. The costs are then accumulated for each lot.

When a job produces a specific quantity for inventory, job order costing permits the computation of a unit cost for inventory costing purposes. When jobs are performed on the basis of customer specifications, job order costing permits the computation of a profit or loss on each order. Since costs are revealed as an order goes through production, these costs may be compared with estimates which were made when an order was taken. Job order costing thereby provides opportunities for controlling costs.

Process costing, which is discussed in Chapters 4, 5, and 6, accumulates costs by production process or by department. This method is used when units are not separately distinguishable from one another during one or more manufacturing processes. Because of the nature of the output, a unit cost must be computed for each process. The following conditions may also exist:

1. The product of one process becomes the material of the next process.
2. Different products, or even by-products, are produced by the same process.

The process cost method is applicable to industries such as flour mills, breweries, chemical plants, and textile factories.

Many companies use both the job order and the process cost methods. For example, a company manufacturing a railway car built according to the customer's specifications uses job order costing to collect the cost per railway car. However, the multiple small metal stampings required are manufactured in a department which uses fast and repetitive stamping machines. The cost of these stampings is accumulated by the process cost method.

Although the textbook discussion of job order and process costing emphasizes manufacturing activity, the job order and process costing methods can also be used by service organizations. For example, an automobile repair shop uses job order costing to accumulate the costs associated with work performed on each automobile. Process costing may be used by an airline to accumulate costs per passenger mile, or by a hospital to accumulate costs per patient day.

When the job order or process cost methods are used, costs must be accumulated for control purposes according to the unit in which the product cost is to be stated. For example, coal is measured by the ton, chemicals by the gallon, and lumber by board feet. Products such as machines, automobiles, and shoes are measured either by the individual unit or by a multiple thereof, such as a dozen or a gross. The unit selected must conform to the type of product and the manufacturing processes, and it should not be too large or too small. If the unit is too large, the averaging of costs may cause significant cost trends to pass unnoticed. If the unit is too small, unnecessarily detailed and expensive clerical work may be required.

▼ JOB ORDER COSTING

In job order costing, the cost of each order produced for a given customer or the cost of each lot to be placed in stock is recorded on a *job order cost sheet*, sometimes called simply a *cost sheet*. The cost sheets are subsidiary records which are controlled by the work in process account. Although several jobs or orders may be going through a factory at the same time, each cost sheet is designed to collect the cost of materials, labor, and factory overhead charged to a specific job. Each cost sheet is assigned a job number, which is placed on each materials requisition and labor time ticket used in connection with a job. These forms for materials and labor are totaled daily or weekly by job number, for summary journal entries, and the details are entered on the cost sheets. The factory overhead entered on the cost sheets is preferably computed on the basis of an estimate rather than actual costs incurred. As discussed later in the chapter, the amount computed is referred to as *applied factory overhead*.

Cost sheets differ in form, content, and arrangement in each business. An example is shown on page 48. The upper section of each cost sheet provides space for the job number, the name of the customer, a description of the items to be produced, the quantity, the date started, and the date completed. The lower section summarizes the production costs, the marketing and administrative expenses, and the profit for the job when it is completed on the basis of customer specifications. The job cost sheet may also provide space for estimated costs and a comparison of actual costs to the estimated amounts. In the cost sheet for a departmentalized operation, the materials, labor, and factory overhead applied are shown for each department or cost center.

In the remainder of the chapter, job order cost accumulation procedures are described and illustrated for Rayburn Company. The flow of costs for Rayburn Company is summarized in the following diagram:

Accounting for Materials

In manufacturing enterprises, materials and supplies are usually recorded in one control account, Materials, although supplies may be recorded in a separate supplies or indirect materials account. Cost accounting procedures that affect the materials account involve (1) the purchase of materials and (2) the issuance of materials for factory use. These procedures are discussed in greater detail in Chapters 7 and 8.

Recording the Purchase and Receipt of Materials. Cost accounting techniques for the purchase of materials are similar to those studied in general accounting. As materials are received, the account debited is Materials or Materials Inventory, rather than Purchases, as shown in the following entry:

```
Materials...........................................................................................    25,000
      Accounts Payable..........................................................................              25,000
```

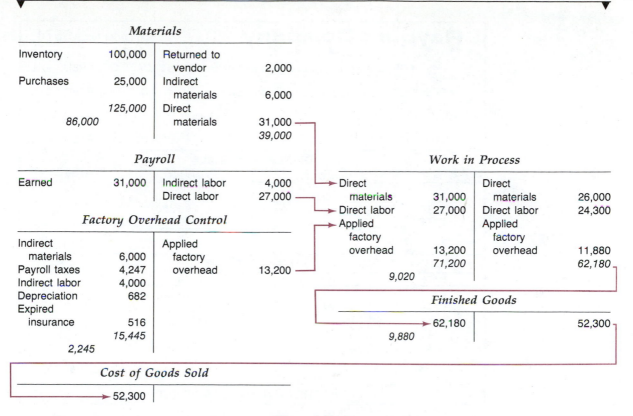

Flow of Costs

The quantity received, unit cost, and amount of each purchase is also entered on a materials ledger card which is maintained for each materials item. Materials ledger cards function as a subsidiary ledger and provide a perpetual inventory record of each item.

Recording the Issuance of Materials. When a job is started, the necessary materials are issued to the factory on the basis of materials requisitions, which are prepared by production scheduling clerks or other employees. The requisition bears the job order number and specifies the type and quantity of materials required. A copy of the requisition is sent to the storekeeper, who assembles the materials called for on the requisition. The quantity, unit cost, and the total cost of each item is entered on the requisition and posted to the materials ledger cards.

The flow of direct materials from storeroom to factory is recorded as a transfer of materials from the materials account to the work in process account. Materials requisitions are summarized and recorded as follows:

Work in Process	31,000	
Materials		31,000

A copy of each requisition is also sent to the cost department. In this department, the requisitions are totaled, sorted by job numbers, and entered in

Rayburn Company
Job Order No. 5574
1101 Maple Street, Cincinnati, OH 45227

FOR: Lawrenceville Construction Co.   DATE ORDERED: 1/10

PRODUCT: #14 Maple Drain Boards   DATE STARTED: 1/14

SPECIFICATION: 12'x 20"x 1" Clear Finishes   DATE WANTED: 1/22

QUANTITY: 10   DATE COMPLETED: 1/18

DIRECT MATERIALS

DATE	REQ. NO.	AMOUNT	TOTAL
1/14	516	$1,420.00	
1/17	531	780.00	
1/18	544	310.00	
			$2,510.00

DIRECT LABOR

DATE	HOURS	COST	
1/14	40	$ 320.00	
1/15	32	256.00	
1/16	36	288.00	
1/17	40	320.00	
1/18	48	384.00	
	196		$1,568.00

FACTORY OVERHEAD APPLIED

DATE	RATE OF APPLICATION	COST	
1/18	$6 per direct labor hour	$1,176.00	$1,176.00

Direct Materials..... $2,510.00		Selling Price................... $7,860.00
Direct Labor........ 1,568.00		Factory Cost $5,254.00
Factory Overhead		Marketing Expense 776.00
Applied 1,176.00		Admin. Expense .. 420.00
		Cost to Make
Total Factory Cost.. $5,254.00		and Sell 6,450.00
		Profit $1,410.00

the materials section of the cost sheet for the jobs indicated. The quantity and cost of materials used in each job are thereby accumulated.

When materials originally requisitioned for a job are not used, a returned materials report is prepared and the materials are returned to the storeroom. The return requires a journal entry in which Materials is debited and Work in Process is credited. Entries on the materials ledger card and the job order cost sheet are also required.

Materials requisitions are also used to secure indirect materials or supplies from the storeroom. Supplies that will not be used by the factory may be charged to marketing or administrative expense accounts. Supplies to be used by the factory are charged to the factory overhead control account when the supplies are issued, as shown in the following entry:

	Subsidiary Record	Dr.	Cr.
Factory Overhead Control......................		6,000	
Indirect Materials...........................	6,000		
Materials...			6,000

For control purposes, the requisitions for factory supplies must also be recorded in a subsidiary ledger for overhead, which may be a *factory overhead analysis sheet*.

The accounting entries required when materials are purchased and used are illustrated in the two-stage diagram on the next page. In Stage 1, an invoice for materials purchased in the amount of $500 is recorded. A materials ledger card is required for each kind of material. In Stage 2, a materials requisition calls for $400 of materials for use on one order. Another requisition for $50 of indirect materials is also recorded.

Accounting for Labor

The accounting procedures for labor, discussed in detail in Chapters 9 and 10, may be divided into two distinct phases:

1. Collection of payroll data, computation of earnings, calculation of payroll taxes, and payment of wages.
2. Distribution and allocation of labor costs to jobs, departments, and other cost classifications.

In most factories, time clocks register workers' hours on individual clock cards which the workers punch as they enter and leave the plant. These clock cards are used by the timekeeper for maintaining a record of the days or hours worked by each employee. The clock cards are also the basis for computing the gross earnings of employees who are paid hourly wages.

To compute the direct and indirect labor cost, the time spent on each job during a day must be recorded on labor time tickets for each worker. The time tickets for the various jobs are sorted, priced, and summarized, and the time ticket hours should be reconciled with the clock card hours.

At regular intervals, usually daily or weekly, the labor time and labor cost for each job are entered on the job order cost sheets. For each payroll period—weekly, every two weeks, or monthly—the summary of employees' earnings and the liability for payment is journalized and posted to the general ledger.

Entries to record and distribute the payroll costs for Rayburn Company are shown in the two-stage diagram on page 51. Rayburn Company incurred $13,800 of labor costs on the 15th of the month and $17,200 of labor costs on the 31st. Of the $31,000 total labor cost incurred during the month, $27,000 was direct labor and $4,000 was indirect labor. Deducted from gross earnings is 15% for employees income tax and 7.5% for FICA tax. The gross earnings might also be subject to deductions for pension payments, personal insurance policies, savings bonds, union dues, and United Fund contributions. The company incurs additional payroll costs for FICA tax (7.5%), federal unemployment tax

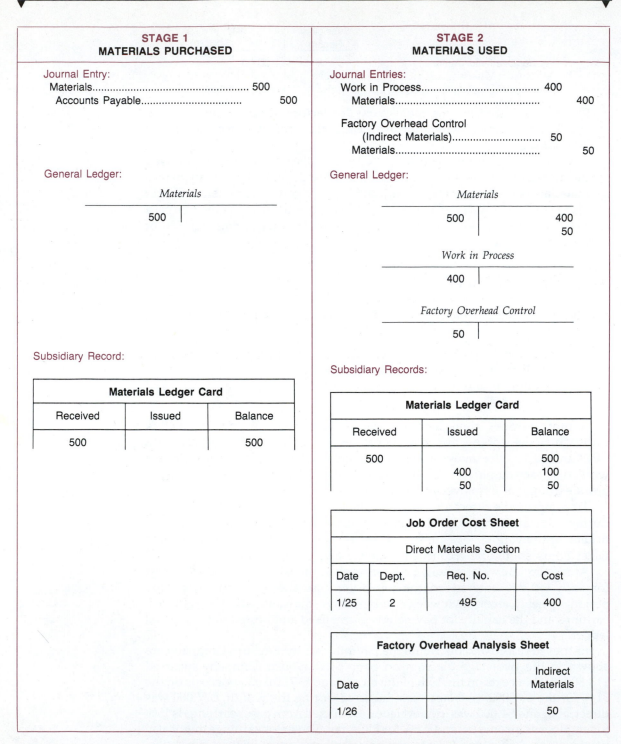

STAGE 1	STAGE 2
MATERIALS PURCHASED	**MATERIALS USED**

STAGE 1 — MATERIALS PURCHASED

Journal Entry:

Materials.. 500
    Accounts Payable..................................   500

General Ledger:

Materials

500	

Subsidiary Record:

Materials Ledger Card		
Received	Issued	Balance
500		500

STAGE 2 — MATERIALS USED

Journal Entries:

Work in Process... 400
    Materials...   400

Factory Overhead Control
    (Indirect Materials)...............................   50
    Materials...   50

General Ledger:

Materials

500	400
	50

Work in Process

400	

Factory Overhead Control

50	

Subsidiary Records:

Materials Ledger Card		
Received	Issued	Balance
500		500
	400	100
	50	50

Job Order Cost Sheet			
Direct Materials Section			
Date	Dept.	Req. No.	Cost
1/25	2	495	400

Factory Overhead Analysis Sheet			
Date			Indirect Materials
1/26			50

Entries Required for Materials Purchased and Used

(.8%), and state unemployment tax (5.4%). These rates, which apply to maximum wage bases, are used here for illustration only. Current rates and bases may be found in published government regulations.

The payroll account is a clearing account in which labor costs are accumulated, pending their distribution to the proper cost accounts. This

STAGE 1 PAYROLL COMPUTED AND PAID	STAGE 2 PAYROLL COSTS DISTRIBUTED

STAGE 1 — PAYROLL COMPUTED AND PAID

Journal Entries:

15th

Payroll.................................	13,800	
Employees Income Tax Payable.........................		2,070
FICA Tax Payable....................		1,035
Accrued Payroll......................		10,695
Accrued Payroll.........................	10,695	
Cash.......................................		10,695

31st

Payroll.................................	17,200	
Employees Income Tax Payable............................		2,580
FICA Tax Payable....................		1,290
Accrued Payroll......................		13,330
Accrued Payroll.........................	13,330	
Cash.......................................		13,330
Factory Overhead Control (Payroll Taxes)......................	4,247	
FICA Tax Payable..................		2,325
State Unemployment Tax Payable................................		1,674
Federal Unemployment Tax Payable...........................		248

General Ledger:

Factory Overhead Control

4,247	

Subsidiary Records:
Employees' earnings records
Employees' tax records
and other deduction records

STAGE 2 — PAYROLL COSTS DISTRIBUTED

Journal Entry:

31st

Work in Process...........................	27,000	
Factory Overhead Control (Indirect Labor)........................	4,000	
Payroll.......................................		31,000

General Ledger:

Work in Process

27,000	

Factory Overhead Control

4,247	
4,000	

Subsidiary Records:

Job Order Cost Sheets[1]		
Direct Labor Section		
Date	Hours	Amount
1/31	5,000	$27,000

Factory Overhead Analysis Sheet[2]			
Date	Payroll Taxes	Indirect Labor	Indirect Materials
1/31	4,247	4,000	

[1]There is a separate cost sheet for every job. Entries in the direct labor section of all jobs worked on during the period are made daily and total $27,000, as shown by the work in process account.
[2]There is an analysis sheet for each department or cost center.

Entries Required in Recording Labor Cost

distribution is usually recorded on a daily or weekly basis, so that labor costs remain current on the job order cost sheets and are available to operating management. The payroll account and employer payroll taxes account may also include amounts applicable to marketing and administrative personnel. Such costs would be charged to marketing and administrative expense accounts.

Accounting for Factory Overhead

If a planing mill contracts to make fifty cabinet assemblies for an apartment complex, the materials used and the labor expended can be charged to the cabinets on the basis of requisitions and time tickets. The amount of factory overhead which should be charged to the cabinets is more difficult to determine. Some of the overhead costs, such as rent or depreciation of the factory building, insurance, property taxes, and the plant manager's salary, are fixed regardless of the amount of production. Other expenses, such as power and lubricating oil, vary with the quantity of goods manufactured. To overcome these difficulties, the actual overhead may be charged to jobs by using a rate based on direct labor hours, direct labor cost, machine hours, or some other factor which exhibits a relationship to factory overhead. As automation increases and the use of direct labor decreases, the rate used will more likely be based on machine hours or machine hours weighted for varying degrees of overhead usage.

Many of the overhead costs may not be known until the end of a fiscal period, long after a job has been completed. Therefore, actual overhead cannot be charged to jobs on a timely basis. To enhance cost control in such cases, it is common to use a *predetermined overhead rate*, which is based on an estimate of factory overhead. For example, assume that an accountant for Rayburn Company determines that a relationship exists between direct labor hours and factory overhead. The accountant estimates that direct labor hours will total 75,000 and factory overhead will total $165,000 for the year. These estimates lead to the assumption that for each hour of direct labor, factory overhead of $2.20 ($165,000 ÷ 75,000 hours) is incurred. The amount of factory overhead for any job, called *applied factory overhead*, is determined by multiplying the direct labor hours during a period by the factory overhead rate.

The applied factory overhead entered on the job order cost sheet for each job is the basis for the following entry:

Work in Process..	13,200	
Applied Factory Overhead (6,000 direct labor hours × $2.20).....		13,200

At the end of the accounting period, the applied factory overhead account is closed to the factory overhead control account by the following entry:

Applied Factory Overhead...	13,200	
Factory Overhead Control...		13,200

this reduces the FOH control acct by the amt. applied to WIP

An applied factory overhead account is used because it keeps applied overhead and actual overhead costs in separate accounts. Some companies do not use the applied factory overhead account, but credit Factory Overhead Control when Work in Process is debited. This procedure eliminates the need to transfer applied overhead to Factory Overhead Control.

Some actual overhead costs, such as indirect materials, indirect labor, and payroll taxes, are charged to Factory Overhead Control as they are incurred. Other overhead costs, such as depreciation and expired insurance, are charged to Factory Overhead Control when adjusting entries are recorded. For example, factory depreciation and expired insurance are recorded at the end of the accounting period by the following entries:

	Subsidiary Record	Dr.	Cr.
Factory Overhead Control...		682	
Depreciation...	682		
Accumulated Depreciation—Machinery........................			682
Factory Overhead Control...		516	
Insurance Expense...	516		
Prepaid Insurance...			516

These entries are posted to the factory overhead control account shown in the diagram on the next page. This account shows on the debit side the $6,000 of indirect materials, the $4,247 of payroll taxes on factory labor, the $4,000 of indirect labor, the $682 of depreciation, and the $516 of expired insurance. The $13,200 on the credit side is the applied factory overhead.

The $2,245 debit balance in the factory overhead control account indicates that actual expenses exceeded the overhead applied to the job orders. Stated differently, overhead was underapplied by $2,245. The cost control significance and disposition of such a balance, either overapplied or underapplied, are discussed in Chapter 12. Typically, a relatively small balance is charged to the cost of goods sold. An in-depth discussion of accounting for factory overhead, including departmentalization and responsibility accounting, is included in Chapters 12, 13, and 14.

Accounting for Jobs Completed and Products Sold

During a month's operations, the amounts charged to the work in process account represent the total cost of materials placed in process, labor used, and factory overhead applied. As jobs are completed, cost sheets are moved from the in-process category to a finished work file. When a job for replenishing stock for sale is completed, the quantity and cost are recorded on finished goods ledger cards, which are subsidiary records for the finished goods account. In the journal, the following entry is recorded, assuming a total cost of $62,180:

Finished Goods...	62,180	
Work in Process...		62,180

STAGE 1 ACTUAL FACTORY OVERHEAD INCURRED	STAGE 2 ESTIMATED FACTORY OVERHEAD APPLIED

General Ledger:

Factory Overhead Control

	6,000	13,200
	4,247	
	4,000	
	682	
	516	
2,245	15,445	

Materials

	Indirect materials	6,000

Payroll

	Indirect labor	4,000

Payroll Taxes Payable

	Taxes on factory payroll	4,247

Accumulated Depreciation—Machinery

	682

Prepaid Insurance

	516

Subsidiary Record:

Factory Overhead Analysis Sheet

Date	Depr.	Payroll Taxes	Insurance	Indirect Labor	Indirect Materials
1/31	682	4,247	516	4,000	6,000

General Ledger:

Work in Process

13,200	

Applied Factory Overhead

13,200	13,200

Subsidiary Record:

Job Order Cost Sheets				
Factory Overhead Section				
Job 1	Job 2	Job 3	Job 4	Job 5
$2,420	$2,640	$2,200	$3,300	$2,640

NOTE: The application of overhead to the five jobs is merely for the purpose of illustrating a typical factory overhead section as it appears on job cost sheets.

Flow of Factory Overhead Through Accounting Records

When finished goods are delivered or shipped to customers, sales invoices are prepared, and the sales and the cost of goods sold are recorded as follows, assuming total sales of $70,000 and total cost of goods sold of $52,300:

Accounts Receivable	70,000	
Sales		70,000
Cost of Goods Sold	52,300	
Finished Goods		52,300

If the job in this illustration had been produced for a specific customer, the sale would be recorded as above, at the same time that the completed job's cost would be debited directly to Cost of Goods Sold, as follows:

Cost of Goods Sold	62,180	
Work in Process		62,180

Work in Process would be credited for the total cost of the job.

When the purpose of a job is to replenish the stock of a component used in subsequent manufacturing processes, the completed job may be charged to Materials.

DISCUSSION QUESTIONS

1. The statement has often been made that an actual product cost does not exist in the sense of absolute authenticity and verifiability. Why?

2. What is the primary objective in job order costing?

3. What is the rationale supporting the use of process costing instead of job order costing for product costing purposes?

    (AICPA adapted)

4. Describe the uses of a job order cost sheet.

5. What is the function of the work in process account in job order costing?

6. How is control over prime costs achieved in job order costing?

7. Distinguish between actual and applied factory overhead.

EXERCISES

1. Manufacturing costs. A schedule of cost of goods manufactured shows:

Materials used	$300,000
Direct labor	800,000
Overhead costs	640,000
Work in process, ending inventory	140,000

Required:

(1) Calculate the rate of factory overhead to direct labor cost.
(2) Determine the cost of direct materials included in the work in process ending inventory, assuming that the direct labor cost included in the inventory of work in process is $50,000.

2. Manufacturing costs. The payroll records of the E. W. Grant Company show payments for labor of $400,000, of which $80,000 is indirect labor. Materials requisitions show $300,000 for materials used, of which $280,000 represents direct materials. Other manufacturing expenses total $124,000. Finished goods on hand at the end of the period are stated at cost, $176,000, of which $40,000 is direct materials cost. Factory overhead is allocated on the basis of direct labor cost.

Required: Determine the amount of direct labor and the amount of factory overhead in Finished Goods.

3. Manufacturing costs. Selected data concerning last year's operations of Televans Company are as follows (000s omitted):

	Inventories	
	Beginning	Ending
Finished goods......................	$90	$110
Work in process....................	80	30
Materials................................	75	85

Other data:

Materials used..	$326
Total manufacturing costs charged to jobs during the year (includes materials, direct labor, and factory overhead applied at a rate of 60% of direct labor cost).........................	686
Cost of goods available for sale...	826
Marketing and administrative expenses..	25

Required: Compute the following:

(1) Cost of materials purchased.
(2) Direct labor cost charged to production.
(3) Cost of goods manufactured.
(4) Cost of goods sold.   (ICMA adapted)

4. Manufacturing costs. Krieger Company is to submit a bid on the production of 11,250 ceramic plates. It is estimated that the cost of materials will be $13,000, and the cost of direct labor will be $15,000. Factory overhead is applied at $2.70 per direct labor hour in the Molding Department and at 35% of the direct labor cost in the Decorating Department. It is estimated that 1,000 direct labor hours at a cost of $9,000 will be required in Molding. The company wishes a markup of 45% of its total production cost.

Required: Determine the following:

(1) Estimated cost to produce.
(2) Estimated prime cost.
(3) Estimated conversion cost.
(4) Bid price.

5. Income statement. Hansford Inc. submits the following data for September:
Direct labor cost, $30,000.
Cost of goods sold, $111,000, before adjusting for over- or underapplied overhead. Factory overhead is applied at the rate of 150% of direct labor cost. Over- or underapplied factory overhead is closed to the cost of goods sold account.
Inventory accounts showed these beginning and ending balances:

	September 1	September 30
Finished goods......................	$15,000	$17,500
Work in process....................	9,600	13,000
Materials................................	7,000	7,400

Other data:

Factory overhead (actual)...	$ 48,200
Marketing expense..	14,100
General and administrative expenses....................	22,900
Sales for the month...	182,000

Required: Prepare an income statement with a schedule showing the cost of goods manufactured and sold.

6. Job order cost sheet. Wadsworth Machine Works collects its cost data by the job order cost accumulation procedure. For Job 909, the following data are available:

Direct Materials			Direct Labor	
9/14 Issued.....................	$600	Week of Sept. 20.....................	90 hrs. @ $6.20/hr.
9/20 Issued.....................	331	Week of Sept. 26.....................	70 hrs. @ $7.30/hr.
9/22 Issued.....................	200		

Factory overhead is applied at the rate of $5 per direct labor hour.

Required:

(1) Enter the appropriate information on a job order cost sheet.
(2) Determine the sales price of the job, assuming that it was contracted with a markup of 40% of cost.

7. Job order costing. The following job order cost detail pertains to the three jobs that were in process at Dandy Machine Company during January:

	Job 36	Job 37	Job 38
Cost charged in prior period...	$36,000	$18,000	—
Costs added in January:			
Direct materials...	44,000	34,000	32,000
Direct labor...	40,000	48,000	42,000
Factory overhead (60% of direct labor).....................	24,000	28,800	25,200

Required: Prepare the appropriate journal entry (including subsidiary ledger detail for job orders) to record each of the following transactions:

(1) Direct materials were issued from the materials storeroom to work in process.
(2) The payroll was distributed to work in process.
(3) Factory overhead was applied to production for the period.
(4) Jobs 36 and 37 were completed and transferred to the finished goods storeroom.

8. Job order costing. The following job order cost sheets were prepared for three jobs that were in production during January:

	Job 97	Job 98	Job 99
Materials...	$ 60,000	$30,000	$40,000
Labor...	120,000	70,000	80,000
Applied factory overhead.....................	60,000	35,000	40,000
Gross profit margin.............................	60,000		

On January 1, Job 97 was 40% complete as to materials, labor, and factory overhead and was completed and sold on account during the month. Job 98 was started and completed during January but was not sold, and Job 99 was started but not completed during the month.

Required: Prepare the journal entries for January to record job costs in Work in Process and Finished Goods and to record the sale. Show subsidiary record detail for job orders.

9. Journal entries for the cost accounting cycle; predetermined overhead rate. The following account balances were selected from the general ledger accounts of Thornton Manufacturing Company.

	December 1	December 31
Finished Goods	$ 40,000	$ 55,000
Work in Process	35,000	15,000
Materials	5,000	10,000
Factory Overhead Control	375,000	492,000
Applied Factory Overhead (applied at a rate of 75% of direct labor cost)	400,000	520,000
Cost of Goods Sold	600,000	975,000

Thornton's accounting year is the calendar year.

Required:

(1) Prepare journal entries for the transactions that were entered in the above accounts for December.
(2) Close over- or underapplied factory overhead to Cost of Goods Sold.

PROBLEMS

3-1. Manufacturing costs. Last month, Hulse Company put into process $60,000 of materials. The Grinding Department used 8,000 labor hours at $5.60 per hour, and the Machining Department used 4,600 hours at a cost of $6 per hour. Factory overhead is applied at a rate of $6 per labor hour in the Grinding Department and $8 per labor hour in the Machining Department. Inventory accounts had the following beginning and ending balances:

	Beginning	Ending
Finished goods	$22,000	$17,000
Work in process	15,000	17,600
Materials	20,000	18,000

Required: Without preparing a formal income statement, compute the following:

(1) Total cost of work put into process.
(2) Cost of goods manufactured.
(3) Cost of goods sold.
(4) Conversion cost.
(5) Cost of materials purchased.

3-2. Manufacturing costs. The following account balances and other information for Saskatoon Company pertain to November operations:

	Account Balances	
	November 1	November 30
Finished Goods..	$70,000	$60,000
Work in Process..	50,000	?
Direct Materials...	10,000	25,000
Accounts Payable...	?	15,000
Accrued Payroll...	10,000	20,000
Accumulated Depreciation—		
Factory Equipment................................	80,000	90,000

Other information:

(a) Direct materials purchased on account during November, $50,000.

(b) Saskatoon Company applies factory overhead at a predetermined rate of $3 per direct labor hour.

(c) During November, direct labor employees worked 25,000 hours at a rate of $4 per hour.

(d) Jobs 385, 386, and 387 were still in process at the end of November. A total of $5,000 of direct materials has been charged to these three jobs. To date, 5,000 direct labor hours have been worked on these jobs.

(e) The accrued payroll account is used for factory employees only. Assuming no payroll deductions, payment to factory employees during the month totaled $140,000.

(f) Factory overhead was underapplied by $5,000.

(g) Payments on account totaled $55,000.

Required: Compute the following:

(1) Direct materials charged to production.
(2) Factory overhead applied during the month.
(3) Ending inventory of work in process.
(4) Cost of goods manufactured.
(5) Cost of goods sold, before disposition of underapplied factory overhead.
(6) Indirect labor.
(7) Miscellaneous factory overhead.
(8) Accounts payable, November 1.   (CGAAC adapted)

3-3. Income statement; cost of goods sold statement; factory overhead analysis. On October 1, the accountant of Columbus Company prepared a trial balance from which the following accounts were extracted:

Finished Goods (2,800 units)...	$ 9,800	
Work in Process (1,200 units)...	4,070	
Materials and Supplies...	40,700	
Buildings..	48,000	
Accumulated Depreciation—Buildings...............................		$ 6,000
Machinery and Equipment...	96,000	
Accumulated Depreciation—Machinery and Equipment.....................		37,500
Office Equipment..	3,200	
Accumulated Depreciation—Office Equipment.....................................		1,000
Accrued Payroll..		650

The following transactions and other data have been made available for October:

Purchased materials and supplies	$ 24,800
Paid factory overhead	20,100
Paid marketing expenses	25,050
Paid administrative expenses	19,700
Requisitions for:	
Direct materials	29,800
Indirect materials	3,950
Depreciation:	
Building, 5% (75% to manufacturing, 15% to marketing, and 10% to administrative expenses)	
Machinery and equipment, 10%	
Office equipment, 15% (40% to marketing and 60% to administrative expenses)	
Sales (20,700 units)	144,900
Sales returns and allowances	1,300
Cash payments for:	
Accounts payable	75,000
Payroll	21,800
Distribution of payroll earned:	
Direct labor	18,600
Indirect labor	4,400
Cash collected from customers	116,900
Applied factory overhead	27,450
Units transferred to finished goods, 20,400	
Cost of goods sold is calculated on the fifo basis.	
Work in process inventory on October 31	4,440

Required:

(1) Prepare in detail the cost of goods sold section of the income statement for October, assuming that over- or underapplied factory overhead is deferred until the end of the calendar year.

(2) Prepare the income statement for October.

(3) Calculate the amount of over- or underapplied factory overhead for October.

3-4. Balance sheet; income statement. On December 31, 19A, Morrisville Canning Company, with outstanding common stock of $30,000, had the following assets and liabilities:

Cash	$ 5,000
Accounts receivable	10,000
Finished goods	6,000
Work in process	2,000
Materials	4,000
Prepaid expenses	500
Property, plant, and equipment (net)	30,000
Current liabilities	17,500

During 19B, the retained earnings account increased 50% as a result of the year's business. No dividends were paid during the year. Balances of accounts receivable, prepaid expenses, current liabilities, and common stock were the same on December 31, 19B, as they had been on December 31, 19A. Inventories were reduced by exactly 50%, except for the finished goods inventory, which was reduced by 33⅓%. Plant assets (net) were reduced by depreciation of $4,000, charged ¾ to factory overhead and ¼ to administrative expense. Sales of $60,000 were made on account, costing $38,000. Direct labor cost was $9,000. Factory overhead was applied at a rate of 100% of direct labor cost, leaving $2,000 underapplied that was closed into the cost of goods sold account. Total marketing and administrative expenses amounted to 10% and 15%, respectively, of the gross sales.

Required:

    (1) Prepare a balance sheet as of December 31, 19B.
    (2) Prepare an income statement for the year 19B, with details of the cost of goods
        manufactured and sold.   *(AICPA adapted)*

3-5. Job order costing. The books of Booth Manufacturing Company showed the following balances on May 1:

Finished Goods	$10,000
Work in Process	16,400
Materials	8,000

The work in process account is supported by the following detail:

Job 2001	$10,000
Job 2002	6,400
Total	$16,400

The following information pertains to May operations:

  (a) Materials purchased and received, $6,000, terms n/30.
  (b) Materials issued: Job 2001, $2,500; Job 2002, $1,400.
  (c) Job 2003 was started with requisitions for materials of $1,800.
  (d) Indirect materials and supplies issued, $1,700.
  (e) Materials were returned to the storeroom as follows: Job 2001, $400; indirect
       materials and supplies, $100.
  (f) Materials returned to vendors, $600.
  (g) Gross payroll for the month was $10,000. FICA taxes were 7.5% and federal income
       taxes withheld were 10.5%.
  (h) The payroll amount due each employee was paid.
  (i) The payroll was distributed as follows: direct labor, 60%; indirect labor, 20%; sales
       salaries, 12%; administrative salaries, 8%. Of the direct labor, 50% pertained to Job
       2001; 30%, Job 2002; and 20%, Job 2003.
  (j) Employer's payroll taxes for the month were 7.5% for FICA taxes, 3.4% for state
       unemployment tax, and .8% for federal unemployment tax.
  (k) Factory overhead, other than any previously mentioned, amounted to $1,504. These
       expenses were paid during the month.
  (l) Factory overhead charged to production was 100% of the direct labor cost for May.
  (m) Job 2001 was completed and shipped directly to the customer at a contract price of
       $22,500.
  (n) Goods costing $8,000 were sold on account during the month at a sales price of
       $10,000.
  (o) Cash collections on accounts receivable were $26,000.
  (p) Over- or underapplied factory overhead was closed to the cost of goods sold account.

Required:

(1) Prepare journal entries for the above transactions. Indicate subsidiary ledger detail for Work in Process. No other subsidiary ledger detail is necessary.

(2) Post and reconcile the work in process subsidiary ledger accounts and the general ledger control account.

3-6. Job order costing. Topper Inc. had the following inventories on March 1:

Finished goods.........................	$15,000
Work in process.....................	19,070
Materials................................	14,000

The work in process account controls three jobs:

	Job 621	Job 622	Job 623
Materials...	$2,800	$3,400	$1,800
Labor...	2,100	2,700	1,350
Applied factory overhead....................	1,680	2,160	1,080
Total...	$6,580	$8,260	$4,230

The following information pertains to March operations:

(a) Materials purchased and received, $22,000; terms, n/30.

(b) Materials requisitioned for production, $21,000. Of this amount, $2,400 was for indirect materials; the difference was distributed: $5,300 to Job 621; $7,400 to Job 622; and $5,900 to Job 623.

(c) Materials returned to the storeroom from the factory, $600, of which $200 was for indirect materials, the balance from Job 622.

(d) Materials returned to vendors, $800.

(e) Payroll, after deducting 7.5% for FICA tax and 11.5% for employees income tax, was $30,780. The payroll amount due the employees was paid during March.

(f) Of the payroll, direct labor represented 55%; indirect labor, 20%; sales salaries, 15%; and administrative salaries, 10%. The direct labor cost was distributed: $6,420 to Job 621; $8,160 to Job 622; and $6,320 to Job 623.

(g) An additional 13.7% was entered for employer payroll taxes, representing the employer's 7.5% FICA tax, 5.4% state unemployment insurance tax, and .8% federal unemployment insurance tax. Employer payroll taxes related to direct labor are charged to the factory overhead control account.

(h) Factory overhead, other than any previously mentioned, amounted to $5,500. Included in this figure were $2,000 for depreciation of factory building and equipment and $250 for expired insurance on the factory. The remaining overhead, $3,250, was unpaid at the end of March.

(i) Factory overhead applied to production: 80% of the direct labor cost to be charged to the three jobs based on the labor cost for March.

(j) Jobs 621 and 622 were completed and transferred to the finished goods warehouse.

(k) Both Jobs 621 and 622 were shipped and billed at a gross profit of 40% of the cost of goods sold.

(l) Cash collections from accounts receivable during March were $69,450.

Required:

(1) Prepare job order cost sheets to post beginning inventory data.

(2) Journalize the March transactions with current postings to general ledger inventory accounts and to job order cost sheets.

(3) Prepare a schedule of inventories on March 31.

3-7. Ledger accounts covering cost accounting cycle and job order cost accumulation.
The books of Galveston Products Company show the following account balances as of March 1:

Finished Goods...	$ 78,830
Work in Process..	292,621
Materials...	65,000
Over- or Underapplied Factory Overhead.....................	12,300 (Cr.)

The work in process account is supported by the following job order cost sheets:

Job	Item	Direct Materials	Direct Labor	Factory Overhead	Total
204	80,000 Balloons	$ 15,230	$ 21,430	$ 13,800	$ 50,460
205	5,000 Life Rafts	40,450	55,240	22,370	118,060
206	10,000 Life Belts	60,875	43,860	19,366	124,101
		$116,555	$120,530	$ 55,536	$292,621

During March, the following transactions occurred:

(a) Purchase of materials, $42,300.

(b) Purchase of special materials, $5,800, for new Job 207, which calls for 4,000 life jackets.

(c) Payroll data for March:

Job	Amount	Hours
204	$26,844	3,355.5
205	22,750	3,250.0
206	28,920	3,615.0
207	20,370	2,910.0

Indirect labor cost, $9,480; factory superintendence, $3,000. Payroll deductions: FICA tax, 7.5%; employees income tax, 11.5%.

(d) Employer's payroll taxes: FICA, 7.5%; state unemployment, 5.4%; federal unemployment, .8%. These taxes are charged to Factory Overhead Control.

(e) Materials issued:

Job 204......................	$ 9,480
Job 205......................	11,320
Job 206......................	10,490
Job 207......................	16,640 (excluding $5,800 of special materials, which are also issued at this time)

(f) Other factory overhead incurred or accrued (credit Various Credits):

Insurance on factory............................	$ 830	Coal expense.................................	$1,810
Tax on real estate................................	845	Power...	3,390
Depreciation—machinery.....................	780	Repairs and mainte-	
Depreciation—factory building...	840	nance... Indirect supplies............................	2,240 1,910
Light..	560		

(g) Factory overhead is applied at the rate of $2.30 per direct labor hour. An applied factory overhead account is used.

(h) Job 204 was shipped and billed at a contract price of $117,500.

Required:

(1) Construct ledger accounts, inserting beginning balances and entering transactions for March. (Factory overhead is to be posted to the control account only.)
(2) In itemized form, compute the total cost of each job at the end of March.
(3) Determine the amount remaining in the over- or underapplied factory overhead account.

3-8. Job order costing. Targon Inc. manufactures lawn equipment. Job order costing is used because the products are manufactured on a batch rather than a continuous basis. The balances in selected general ledger accounts for the eleven-month period ended August 31 are as follows:

Finished Goods......................................	$ 2,785,000
Work in Process...................................	1,200,000
Materials..	32,000
Factory Overhead Control.....................	2,260,000
Cost of Goods Sold..............................	14,200,000

The work in process inventory consists of two jobs:

Job	Units	Item	Accumulated Cost
3005-5	48,000	Estate sprinklers	$ 700,000
3006-4	40,000	Economy sprinklers	500,000
			$1,200,000

The finished goods inventory consists of five items:

Item	Quantity and Unit Cost	Accumulated Cost
Estate sprinklers	5,000 units @ $22 each	$ 110,000
Deluxe sprinklers	115,000 units @ $17 each	1,955,000
Brass nozzles	10,000 gross @ $14 per gross	140,000
Rainmaker nozzles	5,000 gross @ $16 per gross	80,000
Connectors	100,000 gross @ $ 5 per gross	500,000
		$2,785,000

Factory overhead is applied using a predetermined rate of $6 per direct labor hour. A total of 367,000 direct labor hours have been worked through August 31.

The September transactions are summarized as follows:

(a) All direct materials, purchased parts, and supplies are charged to materials inventory. The September purchases were as follows:

Direct materials......................	$410,000
Purchased parts....................	285,000
Supplies................................	13,000

(b) The direct materials, purchased parts, and supplies were requisitioned from materials inventory, as shown in the following table:

Job:	Direct Materials	Purchased Parts	Supplies	Total Requisitions
3005-5	$100,000	$110,000	$ —	$210,000
3006-4	6,000	—	—	6,000
4001-3 (30,000 gross rainmaker nozzles)	181,000	—	—	181,000
4002-1 (10,000 deluxe sprinklers)	92,000	—	—	92,000
4003-5 (50,000 ring sprinklers)	—	163,000	—	163,000
Supplies	—	—	20,000	20,000
	$379,000	$273,000	$20,000	$672,000

(c) The payroll summary for September is as follows:

Job:	Hours	Cost
3005-5	6,000	$ 62,000
3006-4	2,500	26,000
4001-3	18,000	182,000
4002-1	500	5,000
4003-5	5,000	52,000
Indirect labor	8,000	60,000
Supervision	—	24,000
Sales and administration	—	120,000
		$531,000

(d) Other factory costs incurred during September were as follows:

Depreciation	$42,500
Employer payroll taxes	20,000
Utilities	15,000
Insurance	1,000
Property taxes	3,500
Miscellaneous	5,000
	$87,000

(e) Jobs completed during September and the actual output were as follows:

Job No.	Quantity	Items
3005-5	48,000 units	Estate sprinklers
3006-4	39,000 units	Economy sprinklers
4001-3	29,500 gross	Rainmaker nozzles
4003-5	49,000 units	Ring sprinklers

(f) The following finished products were shipped to customers during September:

Item	Quantity
Estate sprinklers	16,000 units
Deluxe sprinklers	32,000 units
Economy sprinklers	20,000 units
Ring sprinklers	22,000 units
Brass nozzles	5,000 gross
Rainmaker nozzles	10,000 gross
Connectors	26,000 gross

Required:

(1) Calculate the over- or underapplied factory overhead for the year ended September 30.
(2) Compute the dollar balance in the work in process account as of September 30.
(3) Calculate the dollar balance in the finished goods inventory of estate sprinklers as of September 30, using a fifo basis, i.e., assuming that the oldest units are sold first.

(ICMA adapted)

3-9. Job order cost cycle; general and subsidiary ledgers; cost of goods sold statement.

On January 1, the general ledger of Mid-State Company contained the following accounts and balances:

Cash............................	$47,000	Machinery...	$ 45,300
Accounts Receivable.....	50,000	Accumulated Depreciation — Machinery.....	10,000
Finished Goods.............	32,500	Accounts Payable...	59,375
Work in Process............	7,500	Common Stock...	100,000
Materials.......................	22,000	Retained Earnings..	34,925

Details of the three inventories are:

Finished goods inventory:	Item X—1,000 units @ $12.50..	$12,500
	Item Y—2,000 units @ 10.00..	20,000
	Total...	$32,500

Work in process inventory:	Job 101	Job 102
Direct materials:		
500 units of A @ $5...	$2,500	
200 units of B @ 3...		$ 600
Direct labor:		
500 hours @ $4..	2,000	
200 hours @ 5..		1,000
Factory overhead applied at the rate of $2 per hour..................	1,000	400
Total...	$5,500	$2,000

Materials inventory:	Material A—2,000 units @ $5.....................................	$10,000
	Material B—4,000 units @ 3.....................................	12,000
	Total..	$22,000

During January, the following transactions were completed:

(a) Purchases on account: Material A, 10,000 units @ $5.20; Material B, 12,000 units @ $3.75; indirect materials, $17,520.
(b) Payroll totaling $110,000 was accrued, and the amount payable to employees was paid. Payroll deductions consisted of $14,950 for employees income tax and 7.5% for FICA tax.
(c) Payroll was distributed as follows: Job 101, 2,500 direct labor hours @ $8; Job 102, 4,000 direct labor hours @ $10; Job 103, 3,000 direct labor hours @ $6; indirect labor, $12,000; marketing and administrative salaries, $20,000. Employer's payroll taxes were: FICA, 7.5%; state unemployment, 4.9%; federal unemployment, .8%.
(d) Materials were issued on a fifo basis as follows: Material A, 10,000 units (charged to Job 101); Material B, 12,000 units (charged to Job 102); Material A, 1,000 units, and

Material B, 2,500 units (charged to Job 103). (*Note: Transactions are to be taken in consecutive order.*) Indirect materials amounting to $7,520 were issued.

(e) Factory overhead was applied to Jobs 101, 102, and 103, based on a rate of $4.50 per direct labor hour.

(f) Jobs 101 and 102 were completed and sold on account for $120,000 and $135,000, respectively. (*Use a finished goods subsidiary account, titled "Completed Jobs."*)

(g) After allowing a 5% cash discount, a net amount of $247,000 was collected on accounts receivable.

(h) Marketing and administrative expenses (other than salaries) paid during the month amounted to $15,000. Miscellaneous factory overhead of $10,800 was paid. Depreciation on machinery was $2,000.

(i) Payments on account, other than payrolls paid, amounted to $85,000.

(j) The over- or underapplied factory overhead is to be closed to the cost of goods sold account.

Required:

(1) Open general and subsidiary ledger accounts and record January 1 balances.

(2) Journalize the January transactions, including subsidiary ledger detail.

(3) Post January transactions to the general ledger and the subsidiary ledgers for materials, work in process, finished goods, and factory overhead incurred.

(4) Prepare a trial balance of the general ledger as of January 31, reconciling control accounts with subsidiary ledgers.

(5) Prepare a cost of goods sold statement for January.

CHAPTER 4

Process Costing: Cost of Production Report

Cost accumulation procedures used by manufacturing concerns are classified as either (1) job order costing or (2) process costing. In this chapter, the basic aspects of process costing are discussed. These aspects include the cost of production reports for producing departments, the calculation of departmental unit costs, the computation of cost transferred to other departments or to the finished goods storeroom, the costing of work in process, the effect of lost units on unit costs, and the effect of adding materials in departments other than the first. Chapter 5 discusses beginning work in process inventories and Chapter 6 deals with the problem of assigning costs to by-products and joint products.

▼ PROCESS COST ACCUMULATION PROCEDURES

The objective of either job order or process costing is to match costs of a period with units produced in the same period. The type of manufacturing operations performed determines the cost procedures that must be used. For example, a company manufacturing custom machinery will use job order cost procedures, whereas a chemical company will use process cost procedures. In the case of the machinery manufacturer, a job order cost sheet accumulates materials, labor, and factory overhead costs for each order. In contrast, the chemical company cannot identify materials, labor, and factory overhead with each order, which is part of a batch or a continuous process. The individual order identity is lost, and the cost of a completed unit must be computed by dividing the total cost incurred during a period by total units completed.

Process costing is used when products are manufactured under conditions of continuous processing or under mass production methods. These conditions exist in industries that produce such commodities as plastics, petroleum, textiles, steel, flour, and sugar. Process costing is used by firms that manufacture bolts and small electrical parts, and by assembly-type industries (automobiles, airplanes, and household appliances). Some utilities (gas, water, and heat) cost their products by using process costing methods.

The characteristics of process costing are:

1. Costs are charged to departmental work in process accounts.
2. A cost of production report is used to collect, summarize, and compute total and unit costs. Unit costs are determined by dividing the total cost charged to a department by the total production of the department for a specific period.
3. Production in process at the end of a period is restated in terms of equivalent units.
4. Costs of completed units of a department are transferred to the next processing department in order to arrive eventually at the total cost of the finished products during a period, and costs are assigned to units still in process.

Costing by Departments

In manufacturing firms, production may take place in several departments. Each department performs a specific operation or process leading to the completion of the product. In a process costing situation, for example, the first department performs the starting phase of work on the product and transfers the units to a second department. The second department completes its work and transfers the units to a third department which completes them and sends them to the finished goods storeroom. The costs of materials, labor, and factory overhead are charged to work in process accounts which are maintained for each department. When the units are transferred from one producing department to another, the accumulated costs are transferred to the subsequent department.

In process costing, departmental total and unit costs are summarized in a cost of production report, which is described and illustrated in this chapter. The cost of a completed unit is used in determining the cost of units transferred out and still in process. This breakdown of departmental costs not only accommodates the primary purposes of inventory costing and income determination but also provides summary cost control data.

Product Flow

A product can move through a factory in a variety of ways. Three product flow formats associated with process costing—sequential, parallel, and selective—are illustrated here to indicate that the same basic costing procedures can be applied to all types of product flow situations.

Sequential Product Flow. In a sequential flow, each product is processed in the same series of steps. In a company with three departments, such a flow may be illustrated as follows:

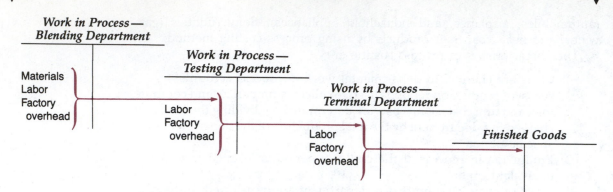

The processing of materials begins in the Blending Department, and labor and factory overhead costs are added. When the work is finished in this department, it moves to the Testing Department. Any succeeding processes may add more materials or simply work on the partially completed input from the preceding process, adding only labor and factory overhead, as in this example. After the product has been processed by the Terminal Department, it is complete and becomes a part of Finished Goods.

Parallel Product Flow. In a parallel product flow, certain portions of the work are done simultaneously and then brought together in a final process or processes for completion and transfer to Finished Goods. The following accounts illustrate a parallel flow for a production process in which materials are added in subsequent departments:

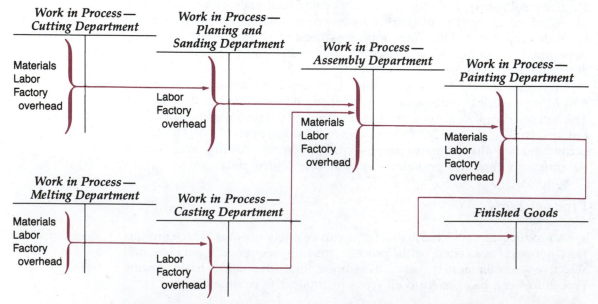

Selective Product Flow. In a selective flow, the product moves to different departments within the plant, depending upon the desired final product. The following accounts illustrate a selective flow in a meat processing plant. After the initial butchering process is completed, some of the product goes directly to the Packaging Department and then to Finished Goods; some goes to the Smoking Department and then to the Packaging Department and Finished Goods; some to the Grinding Department, then to the Packaging Department and finally to Finished Goods.

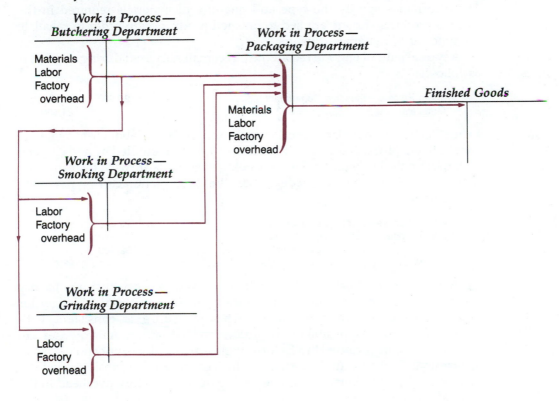

Procedures for Materials, Labor, and Factory Overhead Costs

The details involved in process cost procedures are usually fewer than those in job order costing, where accumulation of costs for many orders may become unwieldy. The job order procedures for accumulating materials, labor, and factory overhead costs generally apply, however, to process costing. Costs are charged to departments or processes by appropriate journal entries.

Materials Costs. In job order costing, materials requisitions are the basis for charging direct materials to specific jobs. If requisitions are used in process costing, the details are considerably reduced because materials are charged to departments rather than to jobs and the number of departments using materials is usually less than the number of jobs which a firm handles at a given time. Frequently materials are issued only to the process-originating department; subsequent departments add labor and factory overhead.

Materials requisition forms may be useful for materials control purposes. If the requisitions are not priced individually, the cost of materials used may be determined at the end of the production period through inventory difference procedures; i.e., adding purchases to beginning inventory and deducting ending inventory. Consumption reports which state the cost or quantity of materials put into process by various departments may also be used. The costs or quantities charged to departments may be based on formulas or prorations. These formulas specify the type and quantity of materials required in the various products and are applied to finished production in order to calculate the amount of materials consumed.

A typical journal entry to record the direct materials used during a period is as follows:

Work in Process—Blending Department	24,500	
Materials		24,500

Labor Costs. The detailed clerical work of accumulating labor costs by jobs is eliminated in process costing because labor costs are identified by and charged to departments. Daily time tickets or weekly clock cards are used instead of job time tickets. A summary entry distributes the direct manufacturing payroll to departments, as follows:

Work in Process—Blending Department	29,140	
Work in Process—Testing Department	37,310	
Work in Process—Terminal Department	32,400	
Payroll		98,850

Factory Overhead Costs. In both job order and process costing, factory overhead should be accumulated in a factory overhead subsidiary ledger for producing and service departments. This procedure is consistent with requirements for responsibility accounting and reporting. As expenses are incurred, they are recorded in a factory overhead control account and posted to departmental expense analysis sheets, which constitute the subsidiary ledger. The following entry illustrates the recording of actual factory overhead in the general ledger:

Factory Overhead Control	81,500	
Accounts Payable		24,500
Accumulated Depreciation—Machinery		42,500
Prepaid Insurance		8,000
Materials (for indirect materials and supplies)		4,500
Payroll (for indirect labor)		2,000

At the end of each period, either actual overhead or overhead using actual or predetermined rates is charged to the producing departments. When rates are used to apply overhead in process costing, the rates are multiplied by the respective actual activity base (e.g., direct labor hours) for each producing department. The following entry illustrates this procedure for Clonex Corporation, using predetermined rates:

Work in Process—Blending Department	28,200	
Work in Process—Testing Department	32,800	
Work in Process—Terminal Department	19,800	
Applied Factory Overhead		80,800

The $700 difference between the actual factory overhead of $81,500 and the applied amount of $80,800 represents underapplied factory overhead. The significance and disposition of such a balance, either overapplied or underapplied, is discussed in detail in Chapter 12.

▼ THE COST OF PRODUCTION REPORT

In process costing, all costs chargeable to a department are summarized in a departmental cost of production report. This report is a device for presenting the amount of costs accumulated and disposed of during a month. It is also the source of information for preparing summary journal entries which record activity in the cost accounts.

A cost of production report for a department shows (1) total and unit costs transferred from a preceding department; (2) materials, labor, and factory overhead added by the department; (3) unit costs added by the department; (4) total and unit costs accumulated at the end of operations in the department; (5) the cost of the beginning and ending work in process inventories, which are in various stages of completion; and (6) cost transferred to a succeeding department or to the finished goods storeroom. The cost section of the report is usually divided into two parts: one showing total costs for which the department is accountable, the other showing the disposition of these costs. The cost of production report or a supporting schedule should indicate the cost elements for each department because these detailed data are needed for cost control and for determining the cost of the ending work in process inventories.

The cost of production report also includes a quantity schedule which shows the total number of units for which a department is accountable and the disposition of these units. Information in this schedule, adjusted for equivalent production, is used to determine the unit costs added by a department, the costing of the ending work in process inventory, and the cost to be transferred out of the department.

To illustrate the details involved in the preparation of cost of production reports, the cost procedures of Clonex Corporation are discussed on the following pages. This company manufactures one product in three producing departments: Blending, Testing, and Terminal. The Clonex reports are condensed to show the total materials, labor, and factory overhead charged to departments. Unit costs are computed for each cost element rather than for each item.

Blending Department

The cost of production report of the Blending Department, the originating department of Clonex Corporation, is on page 74. The quantity schedule of this report shows that the Blending Department put 50,000 units in process. Of these 50,000 units for which the department was responsible, 45,000 units were transferred to the next department (Testing), 4,000 units are still in process, and 1,000 units were lost in processing.

Clonex Corporation
Blending Department
Cost of Production Report
For January, 19—

Quantity Schedule

Units started in process.. 50,000

Units transferred to next department.. 45,000
Units still in process (all materials—½ labor and factory overhead).. 4,000
Units lost in process.. 1,000   50,000

Cost Charged to the Department	Total Cost	Unit Cost
Cost added by department:		
Materials..	$24,500	$ .50
Labor..	29,140	.62
Factory overhead..	28,200	.60
Total cost to be accounted for....................................	**$81,840**	**$1.72**

Cost Accounted for as Follows

Transferred to next department (45,000 × $1.72)............................. $77,400
Work in process—ending inventory:
Materials (4,000 × $.50)... $ 2,000
Labor (4,000 × ½ × $.62)... 1,240
Factory overhead (4,000 × ½ × $.60)... 1,200   4,440
Total cost accounted for.. **$81,840**

Additional Computations:

Equivalent production: Materials = 45,000 + 4,000 = 49,000 units

$$\text{Labor and factory overhead} = 45{,}000 + \frac{4{,}000}{2} = 47{,}000 \text{ units}$$

$$\text{Unit costs: Materials} = \frac{\$24{,}500}{49{,}000} = \$.50 \text{ per unit}$$

$$\text{Labor} = \frac{\$29{,}140}{47{,}000} = \$.62 \text{ per unit}$$

$$\text{Factory overhead} = \frac{\$28{,}200}{47{,}000} = \$.60 \text{ per unit}$$

The units reported by the Blending Department are assumed to be measured in gallons. Generally, each department should report units in terms of the finished product. If materials issued to a department are stated in pounds, for example, and the finished product is reported in gallons, units in the quantity schedule should be stated in gallons by using a product conversion table.

Equivalent Production. To assign costs equitably to the ending work in process inventory and to transferred units, the stage of completion of the in-process inventory must be analyzed by a supervisor or by the use of formulas. Units still in process must be restated in terms of completed units and added to units actually completed in order to arrive at the equivalent production figure for the period. Units in process at the beginning of the period must also be restated and included in equivalent production. The discussion of this procedure is deferred to Chapter 5.

The equivalent production figure represents the number of units for which materials, labor, and overhead issued or used during a period were sufficient to complete those units. To compute unit costs by elements, the equivalent production figure is divided into the materials, labor, and overhead costs.

If the cost elements are at different stages of completion with respect to units in process, then separate equivalent production figures must be computed for each element. In many manufacturing processes, all materials are issued at the start of production. Unless stated otherwise, the illustrations in this discussion assume such a procedure. The 4,000 units still in process in the Clonex factory have all the materials needed for their completion, but only 50 percent of the labor and factory overhead needed to complete the units has been used. In terms of equivalent production, labor and factory overhead in process are sufficient to complete 2,000 units.

Unit Costs. Department cost of production reports indicate the cost of units as they leave each department. These individual departmental unit costs are accumulated into a completed unit cost for the period. The report for the Blending Department shows a materials cost of $24,500, labor cost of $29,140, and factory overhead of $28,200. The materials cost of $24,500 is sufficient to complete 49,000 units (the 45,000 units transferred out of the department as well as the work in process for which enough materials are in process to complete 4,000 units). The unit materials cost is $.50 ($24,500 ÷ 49,000). To determine the number of units actually and potentially completed with the labor and overhead costs, the 2,000 equivalent units in process are added to the 45,000 units completed and transferred. When this production figure of 47,000 units is divided into the labor cost of $29,140 for the month, a unit cost of $.62 ($29,140 ÷ 47,000) for labor is computed. The unit cost for factory overhead is $.60 ($28,200 ÷ 47,000).

The departmental unit cost, or the cost added by the department, is $1.72, which is the sum of the materials, labor, and overhead unit costs. This departmental unit cost figure cannot be determined by dividing total departmental costs of $81,840 by a single equivalent production figure. No such figure exists, since units in process are at different stages of completion as to materials, labor, and factory overhead.

Proper unit costs are required in order to identify the cost of units transferred out, the cost of an abnormal loss of units (as will be discussed later in this chapter), and the cost of units in work in process inventory. In some manufacturing operations, the costs assigned to work in process inventory as well as finished goods inventory may be relatively small. In any situation, however, unit costs provide vital information for cost control and for decision making.

Disposition of Departmental Costs. In the departmental cost report, the section titled "Cost Charged to the Department" shows a total departmental cost of $81,840. The section titled "Cost Accounted for as Follows" shows the disposition of this cost. The 45,000 units transferred to the next department have a cost of $77,400 (45,000 units multiplied by the departmental completed unit cost of $1.72). The balance of the cost to be accounted for, $4,440 ($81,840 − $77,400), is the cost of the work in process.

The work in process inventory must be broken down into its component parts. The $2,000 cost of materials in process is obtained by multiplying 4,000 total units in process by the materials unit cost of $.50. The costs of labor and factory overhead in process are similarly calculated by multiplying equivalent units by unit cost. Since the amount of labor and overhead in process is sufficient to complete only 50 percent of the units in process, the cost of labor in process is $1,240 (2,000 × $.62) and the cost of factory overhead in process is $1,200 (2,000 × $.60).

Lost Units. Continuous operating and processing lead to the possibility of waste, seepage, shrinkage, defects, and other factors which cause loss or spoilage of production units, referred to as lost units for purposes of this discussion. Lost units, units reported as complete, and units still in process must be reconciled with the quantities put in process. One method of making such reconciliations is to establish the expected process yield; i.e., the finished production that should have resulted from processing the various materials. This yield is computed as follows:

$$\text{Percent Yield} = \frac{\text{Weight of finished product}}{\text{Weight of materials charged in}} \times 100$$

Various yields are established as normal. Yields below normal are measures of inefficiencies and are sometimes used to compute lost units. The yield figure is useful in controlling materials consumption and ties in closely with a firm's quality control procedures as the cost vs. benefit of improvement is considered.

When units are lost during processing in the first department, the total cost must be spread over a reduced number of units. Therefore, the effect of losing units is an increase in the unit cost of the remaining good units. If 1,000 units had not been lost in the Blending Department, the equivalent production figure would have been 50,000 units for materials and 48,000 units for labor and factory overhead. The unit cost for materials would have been $.49 instead of $.50; labor, $.607 instead of $.62; and factory overhead, $.588 instead of $.60.

Testing Department

The Blending Department transferred 45,000 units to the Testing Department, where labor and factory overhead were added before the units were transferred to the Terminal Department. Costs incurred by the Testing Department resulted in additional departmental as well as cumulative unit costs.

The cost of production report of the Testing Department, shown on page 77, differs from that of the Blending Department in several respects. Several additional calculations are made, for which space has been provided on the report. The additional information includes (1) costs received from the preceding department, (2) an adjustment of the preceding department's unit cost because of lost units, and (3) costs received from the preceding department to be included in the cost of the ending work in process inventory.

The quantity schedule for the Testing Department shows that the 45,000 units received from the Blending Department were accounted for as follows: 40,000 units were sent to the Terminal Department, 3,000 units are still in process, and 2,000 units were lost. An analysis of the work in process indicates that units in process are only one-third complete as to labor and factory overhead. Therefore, equivalent production of the Testing Department is 41,000 units [40,000 + (⅓ × 3,000)], the labor unit cost is $.91 ($37,310 ÷ 41,000), and the factory overhead unit cost is $.80 ($32,800 ÷ 41,000). No materials were added by the department, so the departmental unit cost is the sum of the labor unit cost of $.91 and the factory overhead unit cost of $.80, or $1.71.

Clonex Corporation
Testing Department
Cost of Production Report
For January, 19—

Quantity Schedule

Units received from preceding department..		45,000
Units transferred to next department..	40,000	
Units still in process (⅓ labor and factory overhead)....................	3,000	
Units lost in process..	2,000	45,000

2000 units were lost during process in this dept.

	Total Cost	Unit Cost
Cost Charged to the Department		
Cost from preceding department:		
Transferred in during the month (45,000 units)...........................	$ 77,400	$1.72
Adjusted cost from preceding department		
[$77,400 ÷ (45,000 units − 2,000 lost units)]........................		$1.80
Cost added by department:		
Labor...	$ 37,310	$ .91
Factory overhead..	32,800	.80
Total cost added..	$ 70,110	$1.71
Total cost to be accounted for...	**$147,510**	**$3.51**

1.80
1.71
3.51

Cost Accounted for as Follows

Transferred to next department (40,000 × $3.51).......................		$140,400
Work in process—ending inventory:	*units still in process*	
(Adjusted) cost from preceding department (3,000 × $1.80).......	$ 5,400	
Labor (3,000 × ⅓ × $.91)...	910	
Factory overhead (3,000 × ⅓ × $.80).....................................	800	7,110
Total cost accounted for..		**$147,510**

Additional Computations:

Equivalent production: Labor and factory overhead = $40,000 + \dfrac{3,000}{3} = 41,000$ units

Unit costs: Labor = $\dfrac{\$37,310}{41,000} = \$.91$ per unit

Factory overhead = $\dfrac{\$32,800}{41,000} = \$.80$ per unit

The cost of production report for the Testing Department indicates that this department is also responsible for the cost of units received from the Blending Department. This cost is included in the section titled "Cost Charged to the Department." The cost transferred in was $77,400, which was previously shown in the cost report of the Blending Department as cost transferred out of that department. This cost was charged to the Testing Department by the following entry:

Work in Process—Testing Department...	77,400	
Work in Process—Blending Department...		77,400

Since the work in process account of the Testing Department is also charged with $70,110 of departmental labor and factory overhead, a total cost of $147,510 must be accounted for by the department.

Units Lost in Departments Subsequent to the First. The Blending Department's unit cost was $1.72 when 45,000 units were transferred to the Testing Department. However, because 2,000 of these 45,000 units were lost during processing in the Testing Department, the $1.72 unit cost figure must be adjusted. The total cost of the units transferred remains at $77,400, but 43,000 units must now absorb this total cost, causing an increase of $.08 in the cost per unit, from $1.72 to an adjusted cost of $1.80 [$77,400 ÷ (45,000 units − 2,000 lost units)].

The $1.80 "Adjusted cost from preceding department" and the $1.71 departmental unit cost are totaled to obtain the $3.51 cumulative unit cost for work done up to the end of operations in the Testing Department. The departmental unit cost of $1.71 does not have to be adjusted for units lost, since the cost of any Testing work on lost units has automatically been absorbed in the departmental unit costs by using the equivalent production figure of 41,000 instead of 43,000 units.

Disposition of Testing Department Costs. The cost of production report on page 77 shows a total cost of $147,510 to be accounted for by the Testing Department. The department completed and transferred 40,000 units to the Terminal Department at a cost of $140,400 (40,000 × $3.51). The remaining cost is assigned to the work in process inventory and is broken down by the various costs in process. When the cost of the ending work in process inventory of any department subsequent to the first is computed, costs received from preceding departments must be included.

(Even when there are no lost units)

The 3,000 units still in process but completed by the Blending Department at a unit cost of $1.72 were later adjusted by $.08 (to $1.80) because of the loss of some of the units transferred. Therefore, the Blending Department's cost of the 3,000 units still in process is $5,400 (3,000 × $1.80). The separate cost elements in this $5,400 figure are not identified, since such information is not pertinent to the Testing Department's operations. However, the amount is listed separately in the cost of production report because it is part of the Testing Department's ending work in process inventory.

Materials (if any), labor, and factory overhead added by a department are costed separately to arrive at the total work in process. Since the Testing Department added no materials to the units received, the ending inventory shows no materials in process. However, labor and factory overhead costs were incurred. The work in process analysis indicates that labor and factory overhead used on the units in process were sufficient to complete 1,000 units. The cost of labor in process is $910 (1,000 × $.91) and factory overhead in process is $800 (1,000 × $.80). The total cost of the 3,000 units in process is $7,110 ($5,400 + $910 + $800). This cost and the $140,400 transferred to the Terminal Department account for the $147,510 total cost charged to the Testing Department.

Terminal Department

The cost of production report of the Terminal Department of Clonex Corporation is illustrated below. Total and unit cost figures were derived by

Clonex Corporation
Terminal Department
Cost of Production Report
For January, 19—

Quantity Schedule

Units received from preceding department.....................................		40,000
Units transferred to finished goods storeroom...............................	35,000	
Units still in process (¼ labor and factory overhead)....................	4,000	
Units lost in process..	1,000	40,000

	Total Cost	Unit Cost
Cost Charged to the Department		
Cost from preceding department:		
Transferred in during the month (40,000 units).........................	$140,400	$3.51
Adjusted cost from preceding department		
[$140,400 ÷ (40,000 units − 1,000 lost units)].......................		$3.60
Cost added by department:		
Labor..	$ 32,400	$ .90
Factory overhead...	19,800	.55
Total cost added...	$ 52,200	$1.45
Total cost to be accounted for...	**$192,600**	$5.05

Cost Accounted for as Follows		
Transferred to finished goods storeroom (35,000 × $5.05)...........		$176,750
Work in process—ending inventory:		
Adjusted cost from preceding department (4,000 × $3.60).......	$ 14,400	
Labor (4,000 × ¼ × $.90)...	900	
Factory overhead (4,000 × ¼ × $.55)...................................	550	15,850
Total cost accounted for..		**$192,600**

Additional Computations:

Equivalent production: Labor and factory overhead = $35,000 + \dfrac{4,000}{4} = 36,000$ units

Unit costs: Labor = $\dfrac{\$32,400}{36,000} = \$.90$ per unit

Factory overhead = $\dfrac{\$19,800}{36,000} = \$.55$ per unit

using procedures discussed for the cost of production report of the Testing Department (page 77). Costs charged to the Terminal Department come from the payroll distribution and the department's expense analysis sheet. These costs include costs transferred from the Testing Department when the following journal entry was recorded:

> Work in Process—Terminal Department...................................... 140,400
>   Work in Process—Testing Department.................................... 140,400

Since the Terminal Department is the final processing department, the work completed is transferred to the finished goods storeroom. This transfer is recorded as follows:

> Finished Goods.. 176,750
>   Work in Process—Terminal Department................................... 176,750

Combined Cost of Production Report

The three cost of production reports for Clonex Corporation have been discussed and computed separately. These reports would most likely be consolidated in a single report summarizing manufacturing operations of the firm for a specified period. Such a report, illustrated on page 81, emphasizes the interrelationship of the various departmental reports.

▼ OTHER FACTORS IN ACCOUNTING FOR LOST UNITS

In the Testing Department as well as in the Blending and Terminal Departments of Clonex Corporation, it was assumed that the loss of units applied to all good units and was within normal tolerance limits. Thus, the loss of units resulted in an increase in the unit cost of the remaining good units, i.e., the units completed and the units still in process. Other lost unit situations require the application of the procedures that are discussed in the following paragraphs.

Timing of Lost Units

Situations may arise in which the cost of lost units does not pertain to the ending work in process inventory, because the identification of lost units occurs at a point beyond the stage of completion of the units still in process. Thus, any measured loss pertains only to units completed. No part of the loss is charged to units still in process.

To illustrate, assume that the 2,000 units lost by the Testing Department of Clonex Corporation were the result of spoilage which was discovered by the Quality Control Department at its final inspection. The cost of these units would be charged only to the 40,000 finished units, as illustrated in the cost of production report for the Testing Department on page 82.

Clonex Corporation
Cost of Production Report
All Producing Departments
For January, 19—

Quantity Schedule	Blending		Testing		Terminal	
Units started in process......................	50,000					
Units received from preceding department..			45,000		40,000	
Units transferred to next department.......................................	45,000		40,000			
Units transferred to finished goods storeroom...					35,000	
Units still in process.............................	4,000		3,000		4,000	
Units lost in process.............................	1,000	50,000	2,000	45,000	1,000	40,000

Cost Charged to the Department	Total Cost	Unit Cost	Total Cost	Unit Cost	Total Cost	Unit Cost
Cost from preceding department:						
Transferred in during the month......			$ 77,400	$1.72	$140,400	$3.51
Adjusted cost from preceding department (lost units).................				$1.80		$3.60
Cost added by department:						
Materials...	$24,500	$ .50				
Labor...	29,140	.62	$ 37,310	$ .91	$ 32,400	$ .90
Factory overhead............................	28,200	.60	32,800	.80	19,800	.55
Total cost added.............................	$81,840	$1.72	$ 70,110	$1.71	$ 52,200	$1.45
Total cost to be accounted for.	**$81,840**	**$1.72**	**$147,510**	**$3.51**	**$192,600**	**$5.05**

Cost Accounted for as Follows						
Transferred to next department..........	$77,400		$140,400			
Transferred to finished goods storeroom..					$176,750	
Work in process—ending inventory:						
Adjusted cost from preceding department.....................................			$ 5,400		$ 14,400	
Materials..	$ 2,000					
Labor...	1,240		910		900	
Factory overhead.............................	1,200	4,440	800	7,110	550	15,850
Total cost accounted for.............		**$81,840**		**$147,510**		**$192,600**

Since the lost units were discovered after completion in the Testing Department, unit costs are based on equivalent production for good units plus lost units. Therefore, no adjustment of the preceding department unit cost is required, and none of the cost of the spoiled units is included in the cost assigned to the ending work in process inventory. Only the cost transferred to the next department includes the full cost of the spoiled units.

The differences between the two cost of production reports for the Testing Department (pages 77 and 82) as to amounts for costs of units transferred and work in process inventory are as follows. A comparison of the differences indicates that the increases and decreases are offsetting.

Cost of units transferred:		Work in process inventory:	
On page 77	$140,400	On page 77	$7,110
On page 82	140,720	On page 82	6,790
Increase	$ 320	Decrease	$ 320

In this illustration, the 2,000 lost units identified at the end of the process were assumed to be complete as to all costs. However, lost units may not be entirely complete when the loss actually occurs, even though the loss is not

Clonex Corporation
Testing Department
Cost of Production Report
For January, 19—

Quantity Schedule

Units received from preceding department		45,000
Units transferred to next department	40,000	
Units still in process (⅓ labor and factory overhead)	3,000	
Units lost in process (at end of process)	2,000	45,000

Cost Charged to the Department	Total Cost	Unit Cost
Cost from preceding department:		
Transferred in during the month (45,000 units)	$ 77,400	$1.72
Cost added by department:		
Labor	$ 37,310	$ .87
Factory overhead	32,800	.76
Total cost added	$ 70,110	$1.63
Total cost to be accounted for	**$147,510**	**$3.35**

Cost Accounted for as Follows

Transferred to next department [40,000 units × ($3.35 + $.1675) or (40,000 × $3.35) × (2,000 lost units × $3.35)]		$140,720*
Work in process—ending inventory:		
From preceding department (3,000 × $1.72)	$ 5,160	
Labor (3,000 × ⅓ × $.87)	870	
Factory overhead (3,000 × ⅓ × $.76)	760	6,790
Total cost accounted for		**$147,510**

Additional Computations:

Equivalent production: Labor and factory overhead = $40,000 + \frac{3,000}{3} + 2,000$ lost units

= 43,000 units

Unit costs: Labor = $\frac{\$37,310}{43,000}$ = $.87 per unit

Factory overhead = $\frac{\$32,800}{43,000}$ = $.76 per unit

Lost unit cost = $3.35 × 2,000 units = $6,700; $6,700 ÷ 40,000 units = $.1675 per unit to be added to $3.35 to make the transfer cost $3.5175.

*40,000 units × $3.5175 = $140,700. To avoid a decimal discrepancy, the cost transferred is computed: $147,510 − $6,790 = $140,720.

[handwritten margin note] No adjusted cost from preceding dept. when units are lost at end of process but there is still a preceding dept. cost.

identified until the end of the process. In other instances, the loss may be discovered when production checks are made prior to the end of the process, but, again, the loss cannot be associated with units still in process. In both of these cases, the lost units should be adjusted for their equivalent stage of completion. For instance, 2,000 units lost at the 90 percent stage of conversion in the Testing Department would appear as 1,800 equivalent units with regard to labor and factory overhead costs and would be added to the good units in determining equivalent production for use in computing unit costs.

Normal vs. Abnormal Loss of Units

Units are lost through evaporation, shrinkage, substandard yields, spoiled work, poor workmanship, or inefficient equipment. In many instances, the nature of operations makes certain losses normal or unavoidable. When such losses are determined to be within normal tolerance limits for human and machine errors, the cost of the lost units does not appear as a separate item of cost but is spread over the remaining good units.

A different situation is created by abnormal or avoidable losses that are not expected to arise under normal, efficient operating conditions. Again, the procedure involves computing unit costs based on equivalent production for good units plus lost units. Therefore, no adjustment of the preceding department unit cost is required. The lost units are multiplied by the resulting unit costs to determine the cost applicable to the abnormal loss. This cost is charged to Factory Overhead or to a current-period expense account which is reported as a separate item in the income statement. Such a procedure assumes that a predetermined overhead rate is used. Charging abnormal spoilage cost to a current-period expense account would be mandatory if a predetermined factory overhead rate is not used. Otherwise, the actual factory overhead rate would include this cost, thereby assigning it to the cost of units produced.

If the cost of the abnormal loss is charged to Factory Overhead, as shown in the following entry, it will be reported as an additional unfavorable factory overhead variance, since abnormal spoilage is not included in the overhead rate.

	Subsidiary Record	Dr.	Cr.
Factory Overhead Control..		6,700	
Abnormal Lost Units..	6,700		
Work in Process—Testing Department.................			6,700

The cost of production report would show the abnormal spoilage or loss as follows:

Transferred to next department (40,000 units × $3.35).......................................	$134,020*
Transferred to factory overhead—cost of abnormal loss	
(2,000 lost units × $3.35)..	6,700

*40,000 units × $3.35 = $134,000. To avoid decimal discrepancy, the cost transferred is computed: $147,510 − $6,790 ending inventory − $6,700 = $134,020.

When the lost units are only partially complete, their stage of completion should be considered, and the costing of the abnormal loss should be weighted accordingly.

If one part of a loss is normal and another part abnormal, each portion should be treated in accordance with the above illustrations and discussion. The critical factor in distinguishing between the normal and abnormal portions of a loss is the degree of controllability. Normal or unavoidable loss is produced under efficient operating conditions and is uncontrollable. Abnormal or avoidable loss is considered unnecessary, because the conditions resulting in the loss are controllable. For this reason, within the limits set by the refinement of the production process, the difference is a short-run condition. In the long run, management would attempt to adjust and control all factors of production and eliminate all abnormal conditions.

Although any value assigned to spoiled units may be credited to a sales account, it preferably should be credited (1) to the work in process account if the spoilage is normal, or (2) to either Factory Overhead or the appropriate current period expense account if the spoilage is abnormal. If the market for these spoiled units is reasonably stable and reliable, and if the value is relatively high, the entry should occur at the time the physical units can be measured; otherwise, the entry should await the time of sale.

▼ ADDITION OF MATERIALS

The addition of materials in departments subsequent to the first has two possible effects on units and costs in process:

1. The additional materials increase the unit cost, since these materials become a part of the product manufactured, but do not increase the number of final units. For example, in a finishing plant of a textile company, the material added is often a bleach; in a wire company, a plating mixture; in an automobile assembly plant, additional parts. These materials are needed to give the product certain specified qualities, characteristics, or completeness; or
2. The added materials increase the number of units and also cause a change in unit cost. For example, in processing a chemical, water is often added to a mixture. As a result, the number of units increases and costs are spread over a greater number of units.

Increase in Unit Cost

In the simplest case, added materials, such as parts of an automobile, do not increase the number of units but increase the total cost and unit costs. A materials unit cost must be computed for the department, and a materials cost must be included in the work in process inventory.

The cost of production report of the Terminal Department of Clonex Corporation (page 79) is used to illustrate the different effects of the addition of materials on total and unit costs of a department. Assume that additional materials costing $17,020 are placed in process and charged to the Terminal Department. Assume further that these materials are sufficient to complete 2,000 of the 4,000 units in ending inventory; that is, units in process at the end of the period are 50 percent complete as to materials cost. The effect of the additional materials cost is shown in the following cost report:

Clonex Corporation
Terminal Department
Cost of Production Report
For January, 19—

Quantity Schedule

Units received from preceding department............................		40,000
Units transferred to finished goods storeroom............................	35,000	
Units still in process (½ materials; ¼ labor and factory overhead)............................	4,000	
Units lost in process............................	1,000	40,000

Cost Charged to the Department	Total Cost	Unit Cost
Cost from preceding department:		
Transferred in during the month (40,000 units)............................	$140,400	$3.51
Adjusted cost from preceding department [$140,400 ÷ (40,000 units − 1,000 lost units)]............................		$3.60
Cost added by department:		
Materials............................	$ 17,020	$ .46
Labor............................	32,400	.90
Factory overhead............................	19,800	.55
Total cost added............................	$ 69,220	$1.91
Total cost to be accounted for............................	**$209,620**	**$5.51**

Cost Accounted for as Follows

Transferred to finished goods storeroom (35,000 × $5.51)...........		$192,850
Work in process—ending inventory:		
Adjusted cost from preceding department (4,000 × $3.60).......	$ 14,400	
Materials (4,000 × ½ × $.46)............................	920	
Labor (4,000 × ¼ × $.90)............................	900	
Factory overhead (4,000 × ¼ × $.55)............................	550	16,770
Total cost accounted for............................		**$209,620**

Additional Computations:

$$\text{Equivalent production: Materials} = 35,000 + \frac{4,000}{2} = 37,000 \text{ units}$$

$$\text{Labor and factory overhead} = 35,000 + \frac{4,000}{4} = 36,000 \text{ units}$$

$$\text{Unit costs: Materials} = \frac{\$17,020}{37,000} = \$.46 \text{ per unit}$$

$$\text{Labor} = \frac{\$32,400}{36,000} = \$.90 \text{ per unit}$$

$$\text{Factory overhead} = \frac{\$19,800}{36,000} = \$.55 \text{ per unit}$$

The only differences in the two cost reports (pages 79 and 85) are the $17,020 materials cost charged to the department and the $.46 materials unit cost ($17,020 ÷ 37,000). The additional materials cost is also reflected in the total cost to be accounted for, in the cost of units transferred to finished goods, and in the ending work in process inventory.

Increase in Units and Change in Unit Cost

When additional materials result in additional units, different computations are necessary. The greater number of units causes a decrease in unit cost, which necessitates an adjustment of the preceding department's unit cost, since the increased number of units will absorb the same total cost transferred from the preceding department.

To illustrate this situation, assume Terminal Department costs for labor and factory overhead of $32,400 and $19,800, respectively, an additional materials cost of $17,020, and an increase of 8,000 units as the result of added materials. The effect of these assumptions on the Terminal Department's cost of production report is shown on page 87.

The additional 8,000 units are entered in the department's quantity schedule as "Additional units put into process." The quantity schedule reports that 44,000 units were completed and transferred to the finished goods storeroom and that 4,000 units are still in process, 50 percent complete as to materials and 25 percent complete as to labor and factory overhead. Therefore, equivalent production is 46,000 units for materials and 45,000 units for labor and factory overhead. Dividing departmental materials, labor, and factory overhead costs for the period by these production figures results in a unit cost of $.37 ($17,020 ÷ 46,000) for materials, $.72 ($32,400 ÷ 45,000) for labor, and $.44 ($19,800 ÷ 45,000) for factory overhead.

These computations do not differ from those already discussed. Peculiar to this situation of additional materials is the adjustment of the preceding department's unit cost. Total cost charged to the Terminal Department as cost transferred in from the preceding department must now be allocated over a greater number of units, thereby reducing the unit cost of work done in the preceding department.

In the illustration on page 85, the $140,400 cost transferred to the Terminal Department was absorbed by 40,000 units, resulting in a unit cost of $3.51. Because of the increase in units, the $140,400 cost must now be spread over 48,000 units, resulting in a unit cost of $2.925 for the preceding department. This adjusted cost is inserted in the production report on page 87 as "Adjusted cost from preceding department" and is added to departmental unit costs to arrive at the unit cost accumulated to the end of operations in the Terminal Department.

When additional materials increase the number of units being processed, it is still possible to have lost units. However, if both an increase and a loss occur, a separate calculation for the lost units is not necessarily required, and net units added can be used. In the illustration above, 8,000 additional units resulted

Clonex Corporation
Terminal Department
Cost of Production Report
For January, 19—

Quantity Schedule

Units received from preceding department.....................................	40,000	
Additional units put into process..	8,000	48,000
Units transferred to finished goods storeroom..............................	44,000	
Units still in process (½ materials; ¼ labor and factory over-head)...	4,000	48,000

Cost Charged to the Department	Total Cost	Unit Cost
Cost from preceding department:		
Transferred in during the month (40,000 units)..........................	$140,400	$3.510
Adjusted cost from preceding department [$140,400 ÷ (40,000 units + 8,000 additional units)]............		$2.925
Cost added by department:		
Materials...	$ 17,020	$ .370
Labor..	32,400	.720
Factory overhead..	19,800	.440
Total cost added...	$ 69,220	$1.530
Total cost to be accounted for...	**$209,620**	**$4.455**

Cost Accounted for as Follows

Transferred to finished goods storeroom (44,000 × $4.455).........		$196,020
Work in process—ending inventory:		
Adjusted cost from preceding department (4,000 × $2.925).....	$ 11,700	
Materials (4,000 × ½ × $.370)...	740	
Labor (4,000 × ¼ × $.720)..	720	
Factory overhead (4,000 × ¼ × $.440)......................................	440	13,600
Total cost accounted for..		**$209,620**

Additional Computations:

Equivalent production: Materials $= 44,000 + \dfrac{4,000}{2} = 46,000$ units

Labor and factory overhead $= 44,000 + \dfrac{4,000}{4} = 45,000$ units

Unit costs: Materials $= \dfrac{\$17,020}{46,000} = \$.370$ per unit

Labor $= \dfrac{\$32,400}{45,000} = \$.720$ per unit

Factory overhead $= \dfrac{\$19,800}{45,000} = \$.440$ per unit

from added materials. It is quite possible, though, that the materials added should have yielded 10,000 additional units. If 2,000 units were lost in processing, the effect is similar to that of units lost in the first department; that is, the cost is absorbed within the department as an increase in unit costs. However, if desired, it is also possible to report separately the effect of the loss, which can be determined as follows: (1) compute the unit cost of work done in preceding departments and in the Terminal Department as if no loss had occurred; (2) compute the loss by multiplying the unit cost obtained in the preceding computation by the 2,000 lost units.

DISCUSSION QUESTIONS

1. What is the primary objective in process costing?

2. Job order and process costing procedures are used by different types of industries. Discuss the procedure appropriate for each type.

3. For the following products, indicate whether job order or process cost procedures would be required:

   (a) Gasoline   (e) Dacron yarn
   (b) Sewing machines   (f) Cigarettes
   (c) Chocolate syrup   (g) Space capsules
   (d) Textbooks   (h) Men's and women's suits

4. What are the distinguishing characteristics of process cost procedures?

5. Discuss three product flow formats.

6. Compare the cost accumulation and summarizing procedures of job order costing and process costing.

7. Can predetermined overhead rates be used in process costing?

8. What is the purpose of a cost of production report?

9. What are the various sections of a cost of production report?

10. Separate cost of production reports are prepared for each producing department. Why is this method used in preference to one report for the entire firm?

11. Are month-to-month fluctuations in average unit costs computed in a cost of production report meaningful data in attempting to control costs?

12. What is equivalent production? Explain in terms of its effect on computed unit costs.

13. What is the justification for spreading the cost of lost units over the remaining good units? Should the cost of these units ever be charged to overhead? Will the answer be different if units are lost (a) in the originating department, (b) at the beginning of a department's operations, (c) during operations, or (d) at the end of operations?

14. What are the possible effects on units and costs in process when materials are added in subsequent departments?

EXERCISES

1. **Equivalent production.** During April, 20,000 units were transferred in from Department A at a cost of $39,000. Materials cost of $6,500 and conversion cost of $9,000 were added in Department B. On April 30, Department B had 5,000 units of work in process 60% complete as to conversion cost. Materials are added in the beginning of the process in Department B.

Required:

(1) Compute equivalent production for materials and conversion cost.
(2) Calculate the cost per equivalent unit for conversion cost. *(AICPA adapted)*

2. Costing of units transferred; lost units. Rude Inc. instituted a new process in October, during which it started 10,000 units in Department A. Of the units started, 1,000 units, a normal number, were lost during the process; 7,000 were transferred to Department B; and 2,000 remained in work in process inventory at the end of the month, 100% complete as to materials and 50% complete as to conversion cost. Materials and conversion costs of $27,000 and $40,000, respectively, were charged to the department in October.

Required: Compute the total cost transferred to Department B.   *(AICPA adapted)*

3. Cost of production report; no lost units. A company's Department 2 costs for June were:

Cost from Department 1.............................	$16,320
Cost added in Department 2:	
Materials..	43,415
Labor...	56,100
Factory overhead......................................	58,575

The quantity schedule shows 12,000 units were received during the month from Department 1; 7,000 units were transferred to finished goods; and 5,000 units in process at the end of June were 50% complete as to materials cost and 25% complete as to conversion cost.

Required: Prepare a cost of production report.

4. Cost of production report; normal spoilage. Wade Company uses process costing. All materials are added at the beginning of the process. The product is inspected when it is 80% converted, and spoilage is identified only at that point. Normal spoilage is expected to be 5% of good output.

During March, 10,500 units were put into process. Current costs were $52,500 for materials, $39,770 for labor, and $31,525 for factory overhead. The 3,000 units still in process at the end of March were estimated to be 90% complete. A total of 7,000 units were transferred to finished goods.

Required: Prepare a cost of production report for March.

5. Cost of production report; normal loss. For December, the Production Control Department of Lauren Chemical Inc. reported the following production data for Department 2:

Transferred in from Department 1...	55 000 liters
Transferred out to Department 3..	39 500 liters
In process at end of December (with ⅓ labor and factory overhead)....................	10 500 liters

All materials were put into process in Department 1. The Cost Department collected these figures for Department 2:

Unit cost for units transferred in from Department 1......................	$1.80
Labor cost in Department 2..	$27,520
Applied factory overhead...	$15,480

Required: Prepare a cost of production report for Department 2 for December.

6. Cost of production report; normal spoilage. Alabama Milling Company produces one product, processed in three departments. During May, 110,000 units were completed in Department 1 at a total cost of $176,000 and were transferred to the next department.

From this quantity, Department 2 completed and transferred out 85,000 units. The May 31 work in process inventory of Department 2 is 22,000 units, ¼ completed as to labor and factory overhead. Department 2's labor and factory overhead costs for May were $26,245 and $12,670, respectively, and the department's spoilage was normal and occurred during processing.

Required: Prepare a cost of production report for Department 2. Compute the adjusted cost from preceding department to five decimal places.

7. Cost of production report; spoilage at end of process, all normal. Norman Company produces toy plastic boats which require processing in three departments. During May, 160,000 units were completed in Department 1 at a total cost of $280,000 and were transferred to the next department. Of these units, Department 2 completed and transferred out 123,000 units. All materials are put into process in Department 1. The May 31 work in process inventory of Department 2 was 34,500 units, ½ completed as to labor and factory overhead. Spoilage in Department 2, a normal amount, occurs at the end of processing. Department 2's labor cost for May was $45,680, and applied factory overhead was $22,840.

Required: Prepare a cost of production report for Department 2.

8. Cost of production report; units lost at end, all normal. Rogers Milling Company manufactures a product requiring processing in three departments, with all materials put into process in the first department. During May, 110,000 units were completed in Department 1 at a total cost of $176,000 and were transferred to the next department. From this lot, Department 2 completed and transferred out 85,000 units, incurring labor cost of $26,180 and factory overhead cost of $13,090. The May 31 work in process inventory of Department 2 is 22,000 units, ¼ completed as to labor and factory overhead. Department 2's spoilage occurs at the end of processing and is normal.

Required: Prepare a cost of production report for Department 2, rounding unit costs to the nearest cent.

9. Cost of production report; abnormal loss. During February, the Assembly Department received 60,000 units from the Cutting Department at a unit cost of $3.54. Costs added in the Assembly Department were: materials, $41,650; labor, $101,700; and factory overhead, $56,500. There was no beginning inventory. Of the 60,000 units received, 50,000 were transferred out; 9,000 units were in process at the end of the month (all materials, ⅔ converted); 1,000 lost units were ½ complete as to materials and conversion costs. The entire loss is considered abnormal and is to be charged to factory overhead.

Required: Prepare a cost of production report.

10. Cost of production report; addition of materials. Oloroso Inc. produces a cologne, Mi Sudor, which requires processing in three departments. In the third department, materials are added, doubling the number of units. The following data pertain to the operations of Department 3 for March:

Units received from Department 2..	20,000
Units transferred to finished goods storeroom..	32,000
The balance of the units are still in process—100% complete as to materials, 50% complete as to labor and overhead.	
Cost transferred from Department 2..	$30,000

Cost added by the department:

Materials...	$8,800	
Labor...	9,000	
Factory overhead..	7,200	$25,000

There was no beginning work in process inventory.

Required: Prepare a cost of production report for Department 3 for March.

11. Cost of production report; addition of materials. Crescent Corporation produces hand cream, which requires processing in three departments. Materials are added at the beginning of the process in Department 2. The following data pertain to the operations of Department 2 for February:

Units received from Department 1...	20,000
Units added in Department 2...	10,000
Units transferred to Department 3...	24,000
Units in ending inventory (50% complete as to conversion cost)...	6,000
Cost transferred in from Department 1...................................	$60,000
Materials cost added in Department 2...................................	$30,000
Conversion cost added in Department 2..............................	$54,000

Required: Prepare a cost of production report for Department 2 for February.

PROBLEMS

4-1. Equivalent production. Trenton Manufacturing Company uses a process cost system to account for the cost of its only product, known as Nino. Production begins in the Fabrication Department, where units of raw material are molded into various connecting parts. After fabrication is complete, the units are transferred to the Assembly Department. There is no material added in the Assembly Department. After assembly is complete, the units are transferred to the Packaging Department, where the units are packaged for shipment. At the completion of this process, the units are complete and are transferred to the Shipping Department.

At year end, December 31, the following inventory of Nino is on hand:

(a) No unused raw material or packaging material.
(b) Fabrication Department: 6,000 units, 25% complete as to raw material and 40% complete as to direct labor.
(c) Assembly Department: 10,000 units, 75% complete as to direct labor.
(d) Packaging Department: 3,000 units, 60% complete as to packaging material and 75% complete as to direct labor.
(e) Shipping Department: 8,000 units.

Required: As of December 31, compute:

(1) The number of equivalent units of raw material in all inventories.
(2) The number of equivalent units of Fabrication Department direct labor in all inventories.
(3) The number of equivalent units of Packaging Department material and direct labor in the Packaging Department inventory.   *(AICPA adapted)*

4-2. Quantity and equivalent production schedules; lost units. Fleming Laboratories Inc. produces an antibiotic product in its three producing departments. The following quantitative and cost data have been made available:

	Department		
	Blending	Testing	Terminal
Production data:			
Started into production......................................	8 000 kg	5 400 kg	3 200 kg
Transferred to next department........................	5 400	3 200	
Transferred to finished goods storeroom.........			2 100
In process (100% materials, ⅓ labor and overhead).................................	2 400	1 800	
In process (100% materials, ⅔ labor and overhead).................................			900
Cost charged to departments:			
Materials...	$20,670	$ 7,980	$14,400
Labor...	11,160	5,016	11,520
Factory overhead..	5,580	2,280	5,040
Total..	$37,410	$15,276	$30,960

Lost units are normal and apply to all production.

Required:

(1) Prepare a quantity schedule for each of the three departments.
(2) Prepare an equivalent production schedule for each of the three departments.
(3) Compute the unit cost of factory overhead in the Blending Department.
(4) Compute the adjusted cost from preceding department in the Testing Department if the unit cost transferred in from the Blending Department is $5.35.

4-3. Cost of production report; spoilage at end of process, both normal and abnormal. Process costing is used in Department 1 of The Dallas Company. Materials are added at the beginning of the process. An inspection occurs at the end of the process. Normal spoilage is expected to be 5% of the good units that pass inspection, while abnormal spoilage is charged to a current period expense account.

Department 1 records for April show:

Units started in process..	10,000
Units transferred to Department 2...	8,000
Units still in process (100% materials; 25% conversion cost)..........	1,200
Materials cost..	$50,000
Conversion cost...	$45,500

Required: Prepare a cost of production report for Department 1 for April.

4-4. Cost of production report; normal and abnormal spoilage. Menninger Inc. uses process costing in its two producing departments. In Department 2, inspection takes place at the 96% stage of completion, after which materials are added to good units. A spoilage rate of 3% of good output is considered normal.

Department 2 records for April show:

Received from Department 1..	30,000 units
Cost...	$135,000
Materials...	$ 12,500

Conversion cost...	$139,340
Transferred to finished goods...	25,000 units
Ending work in process inventory (50% complete).....................	4,200 units

Required: Prepare a cost of production report for Department 2.

4-5. Cost of production report; normal and abnormal spoilage. Yares Company uses process costing in its two producing departments. The following information pertains to Department 2 for November.

Normal spoilage is 5% of good output; inspection and identification of spoilage take place at the 90% stage of completion; materials are added after inspection.

Department 2 received 14,000 units from Department 1 at a cost of $140,000. Department 2 costs were $12,000 for materials and $89,250 for conversion costs.

A total of 8,000 units were completed and transferred to finished goods. At the end of the month, 5,000 units were still in process, estimated to be 60% complete as to conversion costs.

Required: Prepare a cost of production report for Department 2.

4-6. Cost of production report; normal and abnormal spoilage. Neltner Company uses process costing in accounting for its production department, which uses two materials. Material A is added at the beginning of the process. Inspection is at the 90% stage. Material B is then added to the good units. Normal spoilage units amount to 5% of good output. Company records contain the following information for January:

Started during the period..	10,000 units
Material A..	$13,370
Material B..	$ 4,500
Direct labor cost...	$37,580
Factory overhead..	$46,975
Transferred to finished goods..	7,000 units
Ending inventory (95% complete, and includes all Material B).....................	2,000 units

Required: Prepare a cost of production report.

4-7. Cost of production report; normal and abnormal spoilage. Farniente Company uses process costing. In Department B, conversion costs are incurred uniformly throughout the process. Materials are added following inspection, which occurs at the 90% stage of completion. Normal spoilage is discovered during the inspection and is expected to be 5% of good output.

The following information relates to Department B for January:

	Units	Dollars
Received from Department A..	12,000	$84,000
Transferred to finished goods...	9,000	
Ending inventory (95% conversion cost; all materials)....................	2,000	
Cost incurred:		
Materials..		18,000
Labor and factory overhead...		45,200

Required: Prepare a cost of production report for Department B. Compute unit costs to the nearest cent.

4-8. Cost of production report; addition of materials. Ferry Inc. manufactures a product in two departments. Materials are added in each department, increasing the

number of units manufactured. A summary of the cost information for the company's first month of operations (January) is as follows:

	Dept. 1	Dept. 2
Materials..................................	$ 90,000	$ 67,500
Labor..	39,000	41,400
Factory overhead.....................	7,800	20,700
Total....................................	$136,800	$129,600

The production supervisor reports that 300,000 units were put into production in Department 1. Of this quantity, 75,000, a normal number, were lost in production, and 180,000 were completed and transferred to Department 2. The units in process at the end of the month were complete as to materials, but only one-third complete as to labor and factory overhead.

In Department 2, 45,000 units of materials were purchased outside and added to the units received from Department 1; 195,000 units were completed and transferred to finished goods inventory. The units in process at the end of the month were complete as to materials, but only 40% complete as to labor and factory overhead.

Required: Prepare a cost of production report for January for both departments. (Carry unit cost computations to three decimal places.)

CHAPTER 5
Process Costing: Average and Fifo Costing

The previous process costing chapter discussed the fundamentals of the cost of production report, lost unit calculations, and the effect of adding materials in departments other than the first. The discussion of process costing is now continued to include the effect of beginning work in process inventories.

▼ BEGINNING WORK IN PROCESS INVENTORIES

The cost of production reports illustrated in Chapter 4 list ending work in process inventories. These inventories become beginning inventories of the next period. Two of the possible methods of accounting for these beginning inventory costs are:

1. *Average costing.* Beginning inventory costs are added to the costs of the new period.
2. *First-in, first-out (fifo) costing.* Beginning inventory costs are kept separate from the new costs necessary to complete the work in process inventory.

Average Costing

The average costing method of accounting for beginning work in process inventory costs involves merging these costs with the costs of the new period. To accomplish this relatively simple task, representative average unit costs must be determined.

The February cost reports of the three departments reviewed in Chapter 4 are used to illustrate the treatment of beginning work in process inventory and to show the relationship of costs from one period to the next. Ending inventories in January departmental cost reports become beginning work in process inventories for February and are summarized as follows:

	Blending	Testing	Terminal
Units..	4,000	3,000	4,000
Cost from preceding department......................	—	$5,400	$14,400
Materials in process..	$2,000	—	—
Labor in process...	1,240	910	900
Factory overhead in process...........................	1,200	800	550

Blending Department. The February 1 work in process inventory of the Blending Department shows a $2,000 materials cost, a $1,240 labor cost, a $1,200 factory overhead cost, and 4,000 units in process. During February, additional charges to the department are: materials, $19,840; labor, $24,180; and factory overhead, $22,580. The additional materials put into process are for the production of 40,000 units. Therefore, units to be accounted for total 44,000 (4,000 + 40,000). Of the total units put into process, 39,000 are completed, with 38,000 units transferred to the Testing Department and 1,000 units awaiting transfer. At month end, 3,000 units are in process, 100 percent complete as to materials but only 66⅔ percent complete as to labor and overhead. During the month, 2,000 units were lost. In the Blending Department as well as in the subsequent departments in this illustration, it is assumed that the loss applies to all good units and that the loss is within normal tolerance limits. Therefore, the effect of losing units is an increase in the unit cost of the remaining good units.[1] The above facts are illustrated in the cost of production report on page 97.

The unit cost of work done in the Blending Department is $1.72, consisting of $.52 for materials, $.62 for labor, and $.58 for factory overhead. The $.52 unit cost for materials is computed by adding the materials cost in the beginning work in process inventory to the materials cost for the month ($2,000 + $19,840) and dividing the $21,840 total by the equivalent production figure of 42,000 units. These units include the 38,000 units completed and transferred, the 1,000 units completed but still on hand, and the 3,000 units in process, which are complete as to materials. The cost of materials already in process is added to the materials cost for the month before dividing by the equivalent production figure. This method results in an average unit cost for work done in the current and preceding periods.

The same procedure is followed in computing unit costs for labor and factory overhead. The $.62 unit cost for labor is the result of dividing equivalent production of 41,000 units [39,000 + (⅔ × 3,000)] into the sum of the beginning inventory labor cost of $1,240 and the departmental labor cost of $24,180 for the month. The factory overhead unit cost is $.58 [($1,200 + $22,580) ÷ 41,000].

Of the total cost charged to the department, $65,360 is transferred to the Testing Department when the following entry is recorded:

Work in Process—Testing Department	65,360	
Work in Process—Blending Department		65,360

The cost remaining in the Testing Department, $5,680, is assigned to the ending work in process inventory. The work in process inventory consists of $1,720 (1,000 units × $1.72) for units completed and on hand and of the following costs assigned to units still in process: $1,560 (3,000 units × $.52) for materials; $1,240 (2,000 units × $.62) for labor; and $1,160 (2,000 units × $.58)

(3000 × ⅔)   (3000 × ⅔)

---

[1]Reference should be made to Chapter 4 (pages 80-84) for discussion and illustration of other factors in accounting for lost units.

for factory overhead. The 1,000 units completed but on hand are listed as work in process in the Blending Department because this department is still responsible for these units.

Clonex Corporation
Blending Department
Cost of Production Report—Average Costing
For February, 19—

Quantity Schedule

Units in process at beginning (all materials; ½ labor and factory overhead)	4,000	
Units started in process	40,000	44,000
Units transferred to next department	38,000	
Units completed and on hand	1,000	
Units still in process (all materials; ⅔ labor and factory overhead)	3,000	
Units lost in process	2,000	44,000

	Total Cost	Unit Cost
Cost Charged to the Department		
Cost added by department:		
Work in process—beginning inventory:		
Materials	$ 2,000	
Labor	1,240	
Factory overhead	1,200	
Cost added during period:		
Materials	19,840	$ .52
Labor	24,180	.62
Factory overhead	22,580	.58
Total cost to be accounted for	**$71,040**	**$1.72**

Cost Accounted for as Follows

Transferred to next department (38,000 × $1.72)		$65,360
Work in process—ending inventory:		
Completed and on hand (1,000 × $1.72)	$ 1,720	
Materials (3,000 × $.52)	1,560	
Labor (3,000 × ⅔ × $.62)	1,240	
Factory overhead (3,000 × ⅔ × $.58)	1,160	5,680
Total cost accounted for		**$71,040**

Additional Computations:

Equivalent production: Materials = 38,000 + 1,000 + 3,000 = 42,000 units
Labor and factory overhead = 38,000 + 1,000 + (⅔ × 3,000)
= 41,000 units

Unit costs: Materials = $2,000 + $19,840 = $21,840; $\frac{$21,840}{42,000}$ = $.52 per unit

Labor = $1,240 + $24,180 = $25,420; $\frac{$25,420}{41,000}$ = $.62 per unit

Factory overhead = $1,200 + $22,580 = $23,780; $\frac{$23,780}{41,000}$ = $.58 per unit

Testing Department. Accounting for the beginning work in process inventory cost in a department other than the first requires additional analysis. When the prior period's ending work in process inventory was computed, part of the cost of this inventory came from costs added by the preceding department. Because costs assigned to the beginning work in process inventory are added to costs incurred during the period and the total is divided by equivalent production, the beginning work in process inventory of departments other than the first must be split into the following two parts:

1. Cost transferred from preceding departments.
2. Cost added by the department itself.

The portion of the beginning work in process inventory cost from preceding departments is entered in the section of the cost report entitled "Cost from preceding department." It is added to the cost of transfers received from the preceding department during the current period. An average unit cost for work done in preceding departments is then computed. The other portion of the beginning inventory cost, which was added by the Testing Department, is entered as a departmental cost to be added to other departmental costs incurred during the current period. Average unit costs are then computed.

The cost of production report of the Testing Department presented on page 99 illustrates these procedures. The analysis of the beginning work in process inventory of this department (page 95) lists 3,000 units in process with a cost of $5,400 from the preceding department, a labor cost of $910, and $800 for factory overhead. The following costs pertain to February: cost from the preceding department, $65,360; labor, $34,050; factory overhead, $30,018. Units completed and transferred to the Terminal Department totaled 36,000; 4,000 units are in process, 50 percent complete as to labor and factory overhead; 1,000 units were lost in process.

The $5,400 portion of the beginning work in process inventory, which is cost from the preceding department, is entered in the current month's cost report as work in process—beginning inventory. It is added to the $65,360 of cost transferred from the Blending Department to the Testing Department during the month. The average unit cost for work done in the preceding department is $1.726, computed by dividing total cost received from the Blending Department, $70,760 ($5,400 + $65,360), by 41,000 units. These units consist of 3,000 units in the beginning work in process inventory and 38,000 units received during the month. The unit cost is a weighted average, since it considers all units and costs received from the preceding department. It is not the average of the two unit costs, $1.80 and $1.72. A simple average would not be accurate, since there are more units with a unit cost of $1.72 (38,000 units) than with a unit cost of $1.80 (3,000 units).

The $1.726 average unit cost for work done in the Blending Department pertains to the 41,000 units transferred to the Testing Department. However, because 1,000 of these 41,000 units were lost during processing in the Testing Department, the $1.726 unit cost figure must be adjusted. The "Adjusted cost from preceding department" is computed on the assumption that units lost

Clonex Corporation
Testing Department
Cost of Production Report—Average Costing
For February, 19—

Quantity Schedule

Units in process at beginning (⅓ labor and factory overhead)......	3,000	
Units received from preceding department.................................	38,000	41,000
Units transferred to next department.................................	36,000	
Units still in process (½ labor and factory overhead).................	4,000	
Units lost in process..	1,000	41,000

Cost Charged to the Department	Total Cost	Unit Cost
Cost from preceding department:		
Work in process—beginning inventory (3,000 units)................	$ 5,400	$1.800
Transferred in during this period (38,000 units)	65,360	$1.720
Total (41,000 units)............	$ 70,760	$1.726
Adjusted cost from preceding department		
[$70,760 ÷ (41,000 units − 1,000 lost units)]......................		$1.769
Cost added by department:		
Work in process—beginning inventory:		
Labor..	$ 910	
Factory overhead..	800	
Cost added during period:		
Labor..	34,050	$ .920
Factory overhead..	30,018	.811
Total cost added...	$ 65,778	$1.731
Total cost to be accounted for...........................	**$136,538**	**$3.500**

Cost Accounted for as Follows

Transferred to next department (36,000 × $3.500)......................		$126,000
Work in process—ending inventory:		
Adjusted cost from preceding department (4,000 × $1.769).....	$ 7,076	
Labor (4,000 × ½ × $.920).............................	1,840	
Factory overhead (4,000 × ½ × $.811)......................	1,622	10,538
Total cost accounted for...................................		**$136,538**

Additional Computations:

$$\text{Unit cost from preceding department} = \frac{\$70,760}{41,000} = \$1.726 \text{ per unit}$$

$$\text{Equivalent production: Labor and factory overhead} = 36,000 + \frac{4,000}{2} = 38,000 \text{ units}$$

$$\text{Unit costs: Labor} = \$910 + \$34,050 = \$34,960; \frac{\$34,960}{38,000} = \$.920 \text{ per unit}$$

$$\text{Factory overhead} = \$800 + \$30,018 = \$30,818; \frac{\$30,818}{38,000} = \$.811 \text{ per unit}$$

cannot be identified as coming from either units in process at the beginning or from units received during the period, but proportionately from both sources. The total cost of the units transferred remains at $70,760, but 40,000 units must now absorb this total cost, causing an increase of $.043 in the cost per unit, from $1.726 to an adjusted cost of $1.769 [$70,760 ÷ (41,000 units − 1,000 lost units)].

Departmental unit costs for labor and factory overhead are computed as explained in discussing the cost report of the Blending Department. The $910 of labor in process at the beginning is added to labor put in process during the month, $34,050. The total of these two labor costs, $34,960, is divided by an equivalent production figure of 38,000 units [36,000 + (4,000 × ½)] to arrive at a unit cost of $.920. The factory overhead unit cost of $.811 is the result of dividing total factory overhead, $30,818 ($800 + $30,018), by equivalent production of 38,000 units. The departmental unit cost is the sum of these two unit costs, $.920 + $.811, or $1.731. The departmental unit cost of $1.731 does not have to be adjusted for units lost, since the cost of any testing work on lost units has automatically been absorbed in the departmental unit cost by excluding lost units from the equivalent production figure. Lost units are excluded on the assumption that the loss applies to good units and that the loss is within normal tolerance limits. The $1.769 "Adjusted cost from preceding department" and the $1.731 departmental unit cost are totaled to give a cumulative unit cost figure of $3.50.

The total cost to be accounted for is $136,538. Of this total, $126,000 is the cost of the 36,000 units completed and transferred. The balance is cost assigned to the ending work in process inventory. The following entry transfers the cost of the 36,000 units to the next department:

Work in Process—Terminal Department.................................... 126,000
    Work in Process—Testing Department....................................   126,000

Terminal Department. To complete this discussion of operations for February, the cost of production report of the Terminal Department is shown on page 101. The following entry transfers the cost of the 36,000 finished units to finished goods:

Finished Goods.. 182,160
    Work in Process—Terminal Department..................................   182,160

Combined Cost of Production Report—Average Costing. Although the cost reports of each department are presented separately, operations for the month would also be combined in a single cost report as illustrated on page 102.

First-In, First-Out (Fifo) Costing

The first-in, first-out method may be used to account for beginning work in process inventory costs in process costing. Under this method, the beginning work in process inventory costs are separated from costs incurred in the current period and are not averaged with the additional new costs. This procedure gives one unit cost for units completed from the beginning work in process inventory and another for units started and finished in the same

Clonex Corporation
Terminal Department
Cost of Production Report—Average Costing
For February, 19—

Quantity Schedule

Units in process at beginning (¼ labor and factory overhead)...... 4,000
Units received from preceding department....................................... 36,000   40,000

Units transferred to finished goods storeroom.............................. 36,000
Units still in process (⅓ labor and factory overhead)................... 3,000
Units lost in process.. 1,000   40,000

	Total Cost	Unit Cost
Cost Charged to the Department		
Cost from preceding department:		
Work in process—beginning inventory (4,000 units).................	$ 14,400	$ 3.60
Transferred in during this period (36,000 units).................	126,000	$ 3.50
Total (40,000 units).................	$140,400	$ 3.51
Adjusted cost from preceding department		
[$140,400 ÷ (40,000 units − 1,000 lost units)]......................		$ 3.60
Cost added by department:		
Work in process—beginning inventory:		
Labor..	$ 900	
Factory overhead..	550	
Cost added during period:		
Labor..	33,140	$ .92
Factory overhead..	19,430	.54
Total cost added...	$ 54,020	$ 1.46
Total cost to be accounted for...	**$194,420**	**$ 5.06**

Cost Accounted for as Follows

Transferred to finished goods storeroom (36,000 × $5.06)...........		$182,160
Work in process—ending inventory:		
Adjusted cost from preceding department (3,000 × $3.60).......	$ 10,800	
Labor (3,000 × ⅓ × $.92)...	920	
Factory overhead (3,000 × ⅓ × $.54).....................................	540	12,260
Total cost accounted for...		**$194,420**

Additional Computations:

Unit cost from preceding department = $\frac{\$140,400}{40,000}$ = $3.51 per unit

Equivalent production: Labor and factory overhead = 36,000 + $\frac{3,000}{3}$ = 37,000 units

Unit costs: Labor = $900 + $33,140 = $34,040; $\frac{\$34,040}{37,000}$ = $.92 per unit

Factory overhead = $550 + $19,430 = $19,980; $\frac{\$19,980}{37,000}$ = $.54 per unit

equiv 36,000 + (3,000 × ⅓)
= 37,000 units
33,140 + 900 = 34,040
34,040 ÷ 37,000 = .92

period. The cost of completing units in process at the beginning of the period is computed first, followed by the computation of the cost of units started and finished within the period.

Clonex Corporation
All Producing Departments
Cost of Production Report—Average Costing
For February, 19—

	Blending		Testing		Terminal	
Quantity Schedule						
Units in process at beginning.........................	4,000		3,000		4,000	
Units started in process.................................	40,000	44,000				
Units received from preceding department.................................			38,000	41,000	36,000	40,000
Units transferred to next department.............	38,000		36,000			
Units transferred to finished goods storeroom...					36,000	
Units completed and on hand........................	1,000					
Units still in process......................................	3,000		4,000		3,000	
Units lost in process......................................	2,000	44,000	1,000	41,000	1,000	40,000
	Total Cost	Unit Cost	Total Cost	Unit Cost	Total Cost	Unit Cost
Cost Charged to the Department						
Cost from preceding department:						
Work in process—beginning inventory..			$ 5,400	$ 1.800	$ 14,400	$3.60
Transferred in during this period................			65,360	$ 1.720	126,000	$3.50
Total...			$ 70,760	$ 1.726	$140,400	$3.51
Adjusted cost from preceding department..				$ 1.769		$3.60
Cost added by department:						
Work in process—beginning inventory:						
Materials..	$ 2,000					
Labor...	1,240		$ 910		$ 900	
Factory overhead.................................	1,200		800		550	
Cost added during period:						
Materials..	19,840	$ .52				
Labor...	24,180	.62	34,050	$ .920	33,140	$ .92
Factory overhead.................................	22,580	.58	30,018	.811	19,430	.54
Total cost added...................................	$71,040	$ 1.72	$ 65,778	$ 1.731	$ 54,020	$1.46
Total cost to be accounted for........	**$71,040**	**$ 1.72**	**$136,538**	**$ 3.500**	**$194,420**	**$5.06**
Cost Accounted for as Follows						
Transferred to next department....................		$65,360		$126,000		
Transferred to finished goods storeroom...						$182,160
Work in process—ending inventory:						
Completed and on hand............................	$ 1,720					
Adjusted cost from preceding department..			$ 7,076		$ 10,800	
Materials..	1,560					
Labor...	1,240		1,840		920	
Factory overhead.......................................	1,160	5,680	1,622	10,538	540	12,260
Total cost accounted for.....................		**$71,040**		**$136,538**		**$194,420**

To illustrate the fifo method, the February cost of production reports for Clonex Corporation are presented on the following pages, using the same data and assumptions as were used in the average costing illustration. A comparison of these reports with those illustrated for the average costing method indicates that the two methods do not result in significantly different unit costs, since manufacturing operations in process cost type industries are more or less uniform from period to period.

Blending Department. The February cost of production report of the Blending Department, using the fifo method, is shown on pages 104 and 105. When the report is compared to the average costing report on page 97, the following differences are apparent:

1. Under fifo costing, the beginning work in process inventory cost of $4,440 is kept separate and is not broken down into its component parts.
2. Under fifo costing, the degree of completion of the beginning work in process inventory must be stated in order to compute completed unit costs.

Under fifo costing, the cost of completing the 4,000 units in process at the beginning of February must be computed first. No additional materials were needed; but since these units were only 50 percent complete as to labor and factory overhead, more labor and overhead cost must be added.

To determine costs expended in completing the units in the beginning inventory and to arrive at the cost of units started and finished within the current period, unit costs are computed for materials, labor, and factory overhead added during the period. Materials added during February, costing $19,840, were sufficient to complete an equivalent production of 38,000 units. Of these 38,000 units, 34,000 were started and completed during the period, 3,000 units are in process at month end, with all the necessary materials, and 1,000 units were complete but still on hand. Therefore, the unit cost for materials is $.522 ($19,840 ÷ 38,000).

The labor cost for February is $24,180, and the overhead cost is $22,580. The labor and overhead unit costs are computed after determining the number of units that could have been completed from these total costs. The labor cost and the overhead cost were sufficient to complete (1) 50 percent or 2,000 of the 4,000 units in the beginning inventory; (2) 34,000 units started and completed this period; (3) 1,000 units still on hand; and (4) ⅔ or 2,000 of the 3,000 units still in process. Therefore, the equivalent production for labor and overhead is 39,000 units. The unit cost for labor is $.620 ($24,180 ÷ 39,000), and the unit cost for factory overhead is $.579 ($22,580 ÷ 39,000).

In average costing, the cost of the units transferred to the next department was computed by multiplying the number of units transferred by the final unit cost. Under fifo costing, units in process at the beginning must be completed first and will usually have a completed unit cost that is different from the unit cost for work started and finished during the period. Two separate computations determine the total cost transferred to the next department.

dept. ! (handwritten)

Clonex Corporation
Blending Department
Cost of Production Report—Fifo Costing
For February, 19—

Quantity Schedule

Units in process at beginning (all materials; ½ labor and factory overhead)..	4,000	
Units started in process..	40,000	44,000
Units transferred to next department..	38,000	
Units completed and on hand..	1,000	
Units still in process (all materials; ⅔ labor and factory overhead)..	3,000	
Units lost in process..	2,000	44,000

not broken down ? (handwritten)

Cost Charged to the Department

	Total Cost	Unit Cost
Work in process—beginning inventory..	$ 4,440	
Cost added by department:		
Materials.. 38000	$19,840	$ .522
Labor.. 39000	24,180	.620
Factory overhead................................... 29000	22,580	.579
Total cost added..	$66,600	$ 1.721
Total cost to be accounted for..	**$71,040**	

Cost Accounted for as Follows

Transferred to next department—			
From beginning inventory:			
Inventory cost..	$4,440		
Labor added (4,000 × ½ × $.620)............................	1,240		
Factory overhead added (4,000 × ½ × $.579)...........	1,158	$ 6,838	
From current production:			
Units started and finished (34,000 × $1.721)............................		58,517*	$65,355
Work in process—ending inventory:			
Completed and on hand (1,000 × $1.721)................................		$ 1,721	
Materials (3,000 × $.522)..		1,566	
Labor (3,000 × ⅔ × $.620)...		1,240	
Factory overhead (3,000 × ⅔ × $.579).....................................		1,158	5,685
Total cost accounted for...			**$71,040**

Additional Computations:

Equivalent production:	Materials	Labor and Factory Overhead
Transferred out...	38,000	38,000
Less beginning inventory (all units).............................	4,000	4,000
Started and finished this period...................................	34,000	34,000
Add beginning inventory (work this period)..................	-0-	2,000
Add ending inventory:		
Completed and on hand...	1,000	1,000
Still in process (work this period)...............................	3,000	2,000
	38,000 units	39,000 units

4,000×½ (handwritten) *3000×⅔* (handwritten)

*34,000 units × $1.721 per unit = $58,514. To avoid a decimal discrepancy, the cost transferred from current production is computed as follows: $71,040 − ($6,838 + $5,685) = $58,517.

$$\text{Unit costs: Materials} = \frac{\$19,840}{38,000} = \$.522 \text{ per unit}$$

$$\text{Labor} = \frac{\$24,180}{39,000} = \$.620 \text{ per unit}$$

$$\text{Factory overhead} = \frac{\$22,580}{39,000} = \$.579 \text{ per unit}$$

No additional materials were needed to complete the beginning work in process inventory. The cost of labor and factory overhead used during the period in completing the beginning inventory units is added to the $4,440 already included as a cost of these units. Labor and overhead were added at unit costs of $.620 for labor and $.579 for factory overhead to complete the equivalent of 2,000 of the 4,000 units in process. The labor cost added was $1,240 (2,000 × $.620), and factory overhead was $1,158 (2,000 × $.579). The total cost of the 4,000 units completed and transferred was $6,838 ($4,440 + $1,240 + $1,158). The other 34,000 units were transferred at a unit cost of $1.721, or at a total of $58,517. The remaining $5,685 cost to be accounted for is in work in process at the end of the period and is computed as shown on the cost of production report on page 104.

The following entry transfers the total cost of the 38,000 units sent to the next department:

Work in Process—Testing Department...	65,355	
Work in Process—Blending Department................................		65,355

Testing Department. The cost report of the Testing Department is illustrated on page 106. Although the cost transferred out of the Blending Department was the result of two separate computations, the total cost transferred into the Testing Department is shown as only one amount in its cost report. The unit cost of $1.72 is obtained by dividing the 38,000 total units received into the total cost received of $65,355 ($6,838 + $58,517). This procedure seems to cancel out the apparent advantages of the fifo method and has been criticized by some writers.

The balance of the Testing Department report is consistent with the fifo method of costing. The beginning work in process inventory, valued at $7,110, is shown in total and is not broken down into its component parts. Labor and factory overhead costs needed to complete the units in the beginning inventory are added to this figure to determine the completed cost of these units which are transferred to the next department. The $.920 unit cost for labor and the $.811 unit cost for factory overhead are computed by dividing the equivalent production figure of 37,000 units for labor and factory overhead into the labor cost of $34,050 and factory overhead of $30,018, respectively. The equivalent production figure of 37,000 units consists of (1) 2,000 units of beginning inventory completed; (2) 33,000 units started and finished this period; and (3) 2,000 of the 4,000 units in the ending work in process inventory. The labor cost added to the beginning work in process inventory was $1,840 (2,000 × $.920), and factory overhead added was $1,622 (2,000 × $.811). These two amounts are added to the beginning inventory cost of $7,110 to give a total cost of

Clonex Corporation
Testing Department
Cost of Production Report—Fifo Costing
For February, 19—

Quantity Schedule

Units in process at beginning (⅓ labor and factory overhead)......	3,000	
Units received from preceding department....................................	38,000	41,000
Units transferred to next department...................................	36,000	
Units still in process (½ labor and factory overhead)..................	4,000	
Units lost in process..	1,000	41,000

Cost Charged to the Department	Total Cost	Unit Cost
Work in process—beginning inventory...	$ 7,110	
Cost from preceding department:		
Transferred in during the month (38,000 units)...........................	$ 65,355	$ 1.720
Adjusted cost from preceding department		
[$65,355 ÷ (38,000 units − 1,000 lost units)].....................		$ 1.766
Cost added by department:		
Labor...	$ 34,050	$ .920
Factory overhead...	30,018	.811
Total cost added..	$ 64,068	$ 1.731
Total cost to be accounted for..	**$136,533**	**$ 3.497**

Cost Accounted for as Follows

Transferred to next department—			
From beginning inventory:			
Inventory cost...		$7,110	
Labor added (3,000 × ⅔ × $.920).......................		1,840	
Factory overhead added (3,000 × ⅔ × $.811).......		1,622	$ 10,572
From current production:			
Units started and finished (33,000 × $3.497)........................		115,435*	$126,007
Work in process—ending inventory:			
Adjusted cost from preceding department (4,000 × $1.766).....		$ 7,064	
Labor (4,000 × ½ × $.920)...		1,840	
Factory overhead (4,000 × ½ × $.811)...............................		1,622	10,526
Total cost accounted for..			**$136,533**

Additional Computations:

Equivalent production:	Labor and Factory Overhead
Transferred out..	36,000
Less beginning inventory (all units)................................	3,000
Started and finished this period....................................	33,000
Add beginning inventory (work this period)...................	2,000
Add ending inventory (work this period).........................	2,000
	37,000 units

Unit costs: Labor = $\dfrac{\$34,050}{37,000}$ = $.920 per unit

Factory overhead = $\dfrac{\$30,018}{37,000}$ = $.811 per unit

*33,000 units × $3.497 per unit = $115,401. To avoid a decimal discrepancy, the cost transferred from current production is computed as follows: $136,533 − ($10,572 + $10,526) = $115,435.

$10,572. This is the completed cost of the 3,000 units in the beginning inventory transferred to the Terminal Department.

Because 1,000 units were lost during February, computation of the cost accumulated to the end of operations in the Testing Department requires an adjustment for lost units. This adjustment is determined by dividing the previous department's total cost of $65,355 by the good units (37,000) of the period, resulting in an adjusted unit cost of $1.766. In fifo costing, the lost units must be identified as all units from the beginning inventory, all new units started during the period (assumed in this illustration), or a portion in each of these two categories. The identification is needed to determine which unit cost(s) should be adjusted. Such a determination in fifo costing is also required in cases involving the addition of materials in departments subsequent to the first, when an increase in units and a resulting change in unit cost occur.

In this illustration, the loss is assumed to apply to good units started this period, whether transferred out or in ending inventory, and the loss is assumed to be normal. If the normal loss does not pertain to the ending inventory or if the loss is abnormal, it is necessary in fifo costing to identify the extent to which the loss is from units started during the period or from beginning inventory. This determination is required in order to calculate equivalent production and the resulting unit costs properly.

For the various lost units conditions or when the addition of materials increases the number of units, the unit costs include not only the cost from the preceding department but the unit costs for materials, labor, and factory overhead that originate in the respective producing departments. This illustration, for all three departments, is consistent with the assumption used in the Testing Department in adjusting the preceding department unit cost. That is, for all unit costs, the lost units are assumed to come entirely from those units started in process during the current period, adjusted for the effect of beginning and ending work in process inventories on the computed equivalent production for the current period.

The Testing Department completed and transferred 36,000 units, of which 3,000 units came from those in process at the beginning of the period. The cost of the 3,000 units is $10,572. The remaining 33,000 units came from units started and finished during the month. These units are transferred at a cumulative unit cost of $3.497 and a total cost of $115,435. The following entry transfers the cost of the 36,000 units to the next department:

Work in Process—Terminal Department......................	126,007	
Work in Process—Testing Department....................		126,007

The remaining $10,526 cost to be accounted for is the ending work in process inventory, which is computed in the conventional manner.

Terminal Department. To complete the illustration of fifo costing, the cost of production report of the Terminal Department is presented on page 108. Based on this report, the entry to transfer the cost of the 36,000 finished units is:

Finished Goods...	182,166	
Work in Process—Terminal Department...................................		182,166

Clonex Corporation
Terminal Department
Cost of Production Report—Fifo Costing
For February, 19—

Quantity Schedule

Units in process at beginning (¼ labor and factory overhead)......	4,000	
Units received from preceding department....................................	36,000	40,000
Units transferred to finished goods storeroom............................	36,000	
Units still in process (⅓ labor and factory overhead)...................	3,000	
Units lost in process..	1,000	40,000

	Total Cost	Unit Cost
### Cost Charged to the Department		
Work in process—beginning inventory...	$ 15,850	
Cost from preceding department:		
Transferred in during the month (36,000 units)...........................	$126,007	$ 3.500
Adjusted cost from preceding department [$126,007 ÷ (36,000 units − 1,000 lost units)]......................		$ 3.600
Cost added by department:		
Labor...	$ 33,140	$ .921
Factory overhead...	19,430	.540
Total cost added...	$ 52,570	$ 1.461
Total cost to be accounted for...	**$194,427**	**$ 5.061**

Cost Accounted for as Follows

Transferred to finished goods storeroom—			
From beginning inventory:			
Inventory cost..	$15,850		
Labor added (4,000 × ¾ × $.921).........................	2,763		
Factory overhead added (4,000 × ¾ × $.540).....	1,620	$ 20,233	
From current production:			
Units started and finished (32,000 × $5.061).........................		161,933*	$182,166
Work in process—ending inventory:			
Adjusted cost from preceding department (3,000 × $3.60).......		$ 10,800	
Labor (3,000 × ⅓ × $.921)..		921	
Factory overhead (3,000 × ⅓ × $.540).....................................		540	12,261
Total cost accounted for..			**$194,427**

Additional Computations:

	Labor and Factory Overhead
Equivalent production:	
Transferred out...	36,000
Less beginning inventory (all units)...	4,000
Started and finished this period..	32,000
Add beginning inventory (work this period)...................................	3,000
Add ending inventory (work this period).......................................	1,000
	36,000 units

Unit costs: Labor = $\frac{\$33,140}{36,000}$ = $.921 per unit

Factory overhead = $\frac{\$19,430}{36,000}$ = $.540 per unit

*32,000 × $5.061 per unit = $161,952. To avoid a decimal discrepancy, the cost transferred from current production is computed as follows: $194,427 − ($20,233 + $12,261) = $161,933.

Combined Cost of Production Report—Fifo Costing. The illustration below is a combined cost of production report for February, using fifo costing. This report should be compared with the report (page 102) in which average costing is used.

Clonex Corporation
All Producing Departments
Cost of Production Report—Fifo Costing
For February, 19—

	Blending		Testing		Terminal	
Quantity Schedule						
Units in process at beginning........................	4,000		3,000		4,000	
Units started in process.................................	40,000	44,000				
Units received from preceding department...............................			38,000	41,000	36,000	40,000
Units transferred to next department.............	38,000		36,000			
Units transferred to finished goods storeroom..					36,000	
Units completed and on hand........................	1,000					
Units still in process.......................................	3,000		4,000		3,000	
Units lost in process.......................................	2,000	44,000	1,000	41,000	1,000	40,000

	Total Cost	Unit Cost	Total Cost	Unit Cost	Total Cost	Unit Cost
Cost Charged to the Department						
Work in process—beginning inventory..........	$ 4,440		$ 7,110		$ 15,850	
Cost from preceding department:						
Transferred in during the month...............			$ 65,355	$ 1.720	$126,007	$ 3.500
Adjusted cost from preceding department...				$ 1.766		$ 3.600
Cost added by department:						
Materials..	$19,840	$ .522				
Labor..	24,180	.620	$ 34,050	$ .920	$ 33,140	$ .921
Factory overhead......................................	22,580	.579	30,018	.811	19,430	.540
Total cost added.......................................	$66,600	$ 1.721	$ 64,068	$ 1.731	$ 52,570	$ 1.461
Total cost to be accounted for...........	**$71,040**	**$ 1.721**	**$136,533**	**$ 3.497**	**$194,427**	**$ 5.061**
Cost Accounted for as Follows						
Transferred to next department—						
From beginning inventory:						
Inventory cost...	$ 4,440		$ 7,110		$ 15,850	
Labor added..	1,240		1,840		2,763	
Factory overhead added.........................	1,158	$ 6,838	1,622	$ 10,572	1,620	$ 20,233
From current production:						
Units started and finished......................		58,517		115,435		161,933
		$65,355		$126,007		$182,166
Work in process—ending inventory:						
Completed and on hand............................	$ 1,721					
Adjusted cost from preceding department...			$ 7,064		$ 10,800	
Materials..	1,566					
Labor..	1,240		1,840		921	
Factory overhead......................................	1,158	5,685	1,622	10,526	540	12,261
Total cost accounted for......................		**$71,040**		**$136,533**		**$194,427**

Average Costing vs. Fifo Costing

Both average costing and fifo costing have certain advantages. It would be arbitrary to state that one method is either simpler or more accurate than the other. The selection of either method depends entirely upon management's opinion regarding the most appropriate and practical cost determination procedures. Each firm should select the method which offers reliable figures for managerial guidance.

The basic difference between the two methods concerns the treatment of beginning work in process inventory. The averaging method adds beginning work in process inventory cost to the cost from the preceding department and to materials, labor, and factory overhead costs incurred during the period. Unit costs are determined by dividing these costs by equivalent production figures. Units and costs are transferred to the next department as one cumulative figure.

The fifo method retains the beginning work in process inventory cost as a separate figure. Costs necessary to complete the beginning inventory units are added to this total cost. The sum of these two cost totals is transferred to the next department. Units started and finished during the period have their own unit cost, which is usually different from the completed unit cost of units in process at the beginning of the period. The fifo method thus separately identifies for management the current period unit cost originating in a department. Unfortunately, these costs are averaged out in the next department, resulting in a loss of much of the value associated with the use of the fifo method.

If the fifo method is used, units lost or added during a period must be identified as to whether they came from units in process at the beginning or from units started or received during the period. Also, in computing equivalent production figures in fifo costing, the degree of completion of both the beginning and ending work in process inventories must be considered.

The principal disadvantage of fifo costing is that if several unit cost figures are used at the same time, extensive detail is required within the cost of production report, which can lead to complex procedures and even inaccuracy. Whether the extra detail yields more representative unit costs than the average costing method is debatable, especially in a firm where production is continuous and more or less uniform and appreciable fluctuations in unit costs are not expected to develop. Under such conditions, the average costing method leads to more satisfactory cost computations.

▼ DIFFICULTIES ENCOUNTERED IN PROCESS COST ACCOUNTING PROCEDURES

The following difficulties in using process costing may be encountered in actual practice:

1. The determination of production quantities and their stages of completion presents problems. Every computation is influenced by these figures. Since the data generally come to the cost department

from operating personnel often working under circumstances that make a precise count difficult, a certain amount of doubtful counts and unreliable estimates are bound to exist. Yet, the data submitted form the basis for the determination of inventory costs.

2. Materials cost computations frequently require careful analysis. In the illustrations, materials cost is generally part of the first department's cost. In certain industries, materials costs are not even entered on production reports. When materials prices are influenced by fluctuating market quotations, the materials cost may be recorded in a separate report designed to facilitate management decisions in relation to the materials market.

3. When units are lost by shrinkage, spoilage, or evaporation, the time when the loss occurs influences the final cost calculation. Different assumptions concerning the units to which the loss pertains would result in different departmental unit costs which, in turn, affect inventory costs, the cost of units transferred, and the completed unit cost. Another consideration involves the treatment of cost attributable to avoidable loss as an expense of the current period. An increase in units resulting from materials added in departments subsequent to the first requires special consideration as well.

4. Industries using process cost procedures are generally of the multiple product type. Joint processing cost must be allocated to the products resulting from the processes. Weighted unit averages or other bases are used to prorate the joint cost to the several products. If units manufactured are used as a basis for cost allocation, considerable difficulties may arise in determining reasonable unit costs.

Management must decide whether economy and low operational cost are compatible with increased information, based on additional cost computations and procedures. Some companies use both job order and process costing procedures for various purposes in different departments. The basis for using either method should be reliable production and performance data for product costing which, when combined with output, budget, or standard cost data, will provide the foundation for effective cost control and analysis.

DISCUSSION QUESTIONS

1. Distinguish between the fifo and average methods of process costing.

2. Why are units completed and on hand in a processing department included in the department's work in process?

3. How are equivalent production figures computed when fifo costing is used?

4. The Wiring Department is the second stage of Flem Company's production cycle. On May 1, the beginning work in process contained 25,000 units which were 60% complete as to conversion costs. During May, 100,000 units were transferred in from the first stage of Flem's production cycle. On May 31, the ending work in process contained 20,000 units which were 80% complete as to conversion costs. Materials costs are added at the end of the process. Using the average method, compute the equivalent units of production. (AICPA adapted)

5. Ace Company computed the flow of physical units for Department A for April, as follows:

Units completed:
From work in process on
   April 1.. 10,000
From April production................................. 30,000
                                        40,000

Materials are added at the beginning of the process. Units of work in process at April 30 were 8,000. The work in process at April 1 was 80% complete as to conversion costs and the work in process at April 30 was 60% complete as to conversion costs. What are the equivalent units of production for April, using the fifo method?   *(AICPA adapted)*

6. What are some of the disadvantages of the fifo costing method?

7. Enumerate several of the basic difficulties frequently encountered in process costing.

8. Express an opinion as to the usefulness of data, derived from process costing, for the control of costs.

EXERCISES

1. Computation of equivalent production. TSA Company operates two producing departments, whose quantity reports appear as follows:

	Department 1	Department 2
Beginning inventory...	200	80
Department 1—all materials; 25% conversion cost		
Department 2—60% conversion cost		
Started in process..	2,260	2,160
	2,460	2,240
Transferred out...	2,160	2,000
Ending inventory....ᴼᶠ ᵂᴵᴾ..	300	240
Department 1—all materials; 60% conversion cost		
Department 2—80% conversion cost		
	2,460	2,240

Required: Compute equivalent production figures for each department, using (1) average costing and (2) fifo costing.

2. Computation of equivalent production. The following data originate from three different situations:

(a) Beginning inventory, 6,600 units, 1/3 complete as to materials, labor, and factory overhead; started in process, 10,200 units; in process at end of period, 4,800 units, 1/2 complete as to materials and 1/4 complete as to labor and factory overhead; transferred 12,000 units to next department.

(b) Started in process, 9,200 units; completed and on hand, 700 units; in process at end of period, 1,000 units, complete as to materials and 4/10 complete as to labor and factory overhead; transferred 7,500 units to next department.

(c) Beginning inventory, 2,000 units, 1/2 complete as to materials, 1/5 complete as to labor and factory overhead; transferred out, 20,000 units; units lost at beginning of production, 500, a normal quantity; in process at end of period, 2,500 units, complete as to materials, 1/2 complete as to labor and factory overhead.

Required: Compute the equivalent production figures in each situation, using (1) average costing and (2) fifo costing.

3. Computation of equivalent production. The following data originate from three different situations:

(a) Started in process, 18,000 units; in process at end of period, 6,000 units, complete as to materials, ½ complete as to conversion cost; transferred 12,000 units to finished goods.

(b) Beginning inventory, 11,000 units, ¼ complete as to materials, ⅛ complete as to conversion cost; transferred out, 12,000 units; units lost at end of production, 1,500; in process at end of period, 6,200 units, ⅛ complete as to materials, ¼ complete as to conversion cost.

(c) Beginning inventory, 4,500 units, complete as to materials, ¼ complete as to conversion cost; started in process, 12,500 units; in process at end of period, 2,100 units, complete as to materials, ⅓ complete as to conversion cost, and 1,700 units, ½ complete as to materials, ¼ complete as to conversion cost; units lost when units ¼ converted, 1,100, a normal amount.

Required: Compute the equivalent production figures in each situation, using (1) average costing and (2) fifo costing.

4. Computation of equivalent production—fifo costing; addition of materials. Elibach Inc. produces a chemical compound in two departments, A and B, using the following procedure: The chemical compound requires one pound of Chemical X and one pound of Chemical Y. One pound of Chemical X is processed in Department A and transferred to Department B, where one pound of Chemical Y is added when the process is 50% complete. When the processing is complete in Department B, the finished chemical compound is transferred to finished goods. The process is a continuous 24-hour-a-day operation. Normal spoilage occurs in Department A, where 5% of Chemical X is lost in the first few minutes of processing. Department A's conversion cost is incurred uniformly throughout the process and is allocated to good pounds produced, since spoilage is normal. Department B's conversion cost is allocated equally to each equivalent pound of output. No spoilage occurs in Department B.

Data available for October are:

	Department A	Department B
Work in process, October 1	8,000 pounds	10,000 pounds
Stage of completion of beginning inventory (one batch per department)	3/4	3/10·
Started or transferred in	50,000 pounds	?
Transferred out	46,500 good pounds	?
Work in process, October 31	?	12,000 pounds
Stage of completion of ending inventory (one batch per department)	1/3	1/5
Total equivalent pounds of material added in Department B		44,500 pounds

Required:

(1) Prepare a quantity schedule for each department.
(2) Prepare an equivalent production schedule for each department, using the fifo method.   *(AICPA adapted)*

5. Average costing. Information concerning Department B of Pace Company is as follows:

Units in beginning inventory	5,000
Units transferred in	35,000
	40,000
Units completed	37,000
Units in ending inventory	3,000

	Costs			
	Trans-ferred In	Materials	Conversion	Total Cost
Beginning inventory	$ 2,900	—	$ 3,400	$ 6,300
Units transferred in	17,500	$25,500	15,000	58,000
	$20,400	$25,500	$18,400	$64,300

Conversion costs were 20% complete as to the beginning inventory and 40% complete as to the ending inventory. All materials are added at the end of the process. Pace uses average costing.

Required:

(1) Compute the cost per equivalent unit for conversion costs, rounded to the nearest penny.
(2) Determine the portion of the total cost of ending inventory attributable to transferred-in cost.   *(AICPA adapted)*

6. Inventory costing; average vs. fifo costing. The Cutting Department is the first stage of Monk Company's production cycle. Conversion cost for this department was 80% complete as to the beginning work in process and 50% complete as to the ending work in process. Information as to conversion cost in the Cutting Department for January is as follows:

	Units	Conversion Cost
Work in process at January 1	25,000	$ 22,000
Units started and costs incurred during January	135,000	143,000
Units completed and transferred to next department during January	100,000	

Required: Compute the conversion cost of the Cutting Department's January 31 work in process inventory, using (1) the average method and (2) the fifo method. (Carry unit cost computations to three decimal places.)   *(AICPA adapted)*

7. Cost of production report; average costing. Escott Corporation is a manufacturer that uses average costing to account for costs of production. Escott manufactures a product that is produced in three separate departments: Molding, Assembling, and Finishing. The following information was obtained by the Assembling Department for June:

Work in process, June 1—2,000 units, composed of:

	Amount	Degree of Completion
Transferred in from the Molding Department	$32,000	100%
Cost added by the Assembling Department:		
Direct materials	20,000	100
Direct labor	7,200	60
Factory overhead	5,500	50

The following activity occurred during June:
- (a) 10,000 units were transferred in from the Molding Department at a cost of $160,000.
- (b) $150,000 of costs were added by the Assembling Department: direct materials, $96,000; direct labor, $36,000; and factory overhead, $18,000.
- (c) 8,000 units were completed and transferred to the Finishing Department.

At June 30, 4,000 units were still in work in process, with the following degrees of completion: direct materials, 90%; direct labor, 70%; and factory overhead, 35%.

Required: Prepare the June cost of production report for the Assembling Department.   (AICPA adapted)

8. Cost of production report; average costing. A product called Aggregate is manufactured in one department of Creek Corporation. Materials are added at the beginning of the process. Shrinkage of 10% to 14%, all occurring at the beginning of the process, is considered normal. Labor and factory overhead are added continuously throughout the process.

The following information relates to November production:

Work in process, November 1 (4,000 pounds, 75% complete):
Materials...	$ 22,800
Labor...	24,650
Factory overhead...	21,860

November costs:

Materials (fifo costing):
Inventory, November 1, 2,000 pounds.......................................	10,000
Purchase, November 3, 10,000 pounds.....................................	51,000
Purchase, November 18, 10,000 pounds....................................	51,500
Released to production during November, 16,000 pounds	
Labor...	103,350
Factory overhead...	93,340

Transferred out, 15,000 pounds
Work in process, November 30, 3,000 pounds, 33⅓%
complete (average costing)

Required: Prepare a cost of production report for November.   (ICMA adapted)

9. Cost of production report; average costing. Carmel Corporation uses the average process costing method. All spoilage that occurred in Department 2 during August was normal and applicable to all production.

August cost data for Department 2 were as follows:

	Beginning Inventory	August Cost Incurred
Cost transferred from Department 1.....................	$12,000	$89,200
Conversion cost...	6,000	60,400

The Department 2 beginning inventory (⅔ converted) was 1,200 units, and 8,000 units were transferred from Department 1. The ending inventory was 1,000 units (½ converted), and 7,800 units were transferred to Department 3.

Required: Prepare the August cost of production report for Department 2.

10. Manufacturing costs; fifo costing. Ferguson Motors is engaged in the production of a standard type of electric motor. Manufacturing costs for April totaled $66,000. At the beginning of April, inventories appeared as follows:

Motors in production, estimated 80% complete (2,500 units).....................	$32,000
Motors on hand and in finished goods (1,200 units).................................	19,200

During the month, 5,500 completed units were placed in finished stock. At the end of April, inventories were:

Motors in production, estimated 50% complete...........................	1,000 units
Motors on hand, completed and in finished goods....................	1,400

The company uses fifo costing for production and goods sold. In costing finished goods, the unit cost for units completed from beginning work in process inventory is kept separate from the unit cost of motors started and completed during the month.

Required:

(1) Compute the cost assigned to the ending work in process inventory.
(2) Compute the cost assigned to the ending finished goods inventory.
(3) Compute the cost of goods sold.   *(CGAAC adapted)*

11. Cost of production report; fifo costing. Dentex Plastics Corporation produces nonbreakable containers for cosmetics, using three departments: Mixing, Molding, and Finishing. On July 1, the work in process inventory in the Molding Department was 1,000 units, 50% complete as to materials and conversion costs, while the July 31 work in process inventory consisted of 2,800 units, 75% complete as to materials and conversion costs. During July, the Finishing Department received 20,000 units from the Molding Department. In the Molding Department, 800 units (a normal quantity) that came from the Mixing Department in July were lost during processing. Fifo costing is used.

Relevant cost data are as follows:

Work in process, July 1.................................	$ 6,000
July costs:	
Cost from Mixing Department....................	97,632
Materials..	16,200
Labor..	26,568
Factory overhead..	19,872

Required: Using the fifo costing method, prepare the cost of production report for the Molding Department for July. Round unit costs to the nearest cent.

12. Cost of production report; fifo costing. Cannery Row Company uses the fifo process costing method. All spoilage that occurred in Department 2 during June was normal and applicable to units received during June from the preceding department.

June cost data for Department 2 were as follows:

	Beginning Inventory	Cost Added
Cost transferred from Department 1.....................	$13,200	$91,200
Conversion cost..	6,000	60,000

The Department 2 beginning inventory (⅔ converted) was 1,200 units, and 8,000 units were transferred from Department 1. The ending inventory was 1,000 units (½ converted), and 7,800 units were transferred to Department 3.

Required: Prepare the June cost of production report for Department 2.

PROBLEMS

5-1. Cost of production report; fifo vs. average costing. Santa Rosa Corporation has two producing departments, Fabricating and Finishing. In the Fabricating Department, Polyplast is prepared from Miracle Mix and Bypro. In the Finishing Department, each unit of Polyplast is converted into six Tetraplexes and three Uniplexes. Service departments provide services to both producing departments.

The Fabricating and Finishing Departments use process cost procedures. Actual production costs, including factory overhead, are allocated monthly.

Service department expenses are allocated to producing departments as follows:

Expenses	Fabricating	Finishing
Building maintenance..................................	$30,000	$15,000
Timekeeping and personnel......................	16,500	11,000
Others..	19,500	19,500

Materials inventory and work in process are costed on a fifo basis. The Fabricating Department's records for December show:

Quantities (units of Polyplast):	
In process, December 1...	3,000
Started in process...	25,000
Total units to be accounted for..	28,000
Transferred to Finishing Department...	19,000
In process, December 31..	6,000
Normal losses throughout the process...	3,000
Total units accounted for..	28,000
Cost of work in process, December 1:	
Materials..	$ 13,000
Labor...	17,500
Factory overhead..	21,500
	$ 52,000
Direct labor cost...	$154,000
Departmental factory overhead (excluding service department	
allocation)...	$132,000

Polyplast work in process at the beginning and end of the month was partially completed as follows:

	Materials	Labor and Factory Overhead
December 1........................	66⅔%	50%
December 31......................	100%	75%

Materials inventory records for December indicate:

	Miracle Mix		Bypro	
	Quantity	Amount	Quantity	Amount
Balance, December 1....................................	62,000	$62,000	265,000	$18,550
Purchases:				
December 12...	39,500	49,375		
December 20...	28,500	34,200		
Fabricating Department usage....................	83,200		50,000	

Required:

(1) Compute the equivalent number of units of Polyplast for materials and conversion costs for the fifo method. (For the fifo method, assume that the loss came from units started in process during December.)

(2) For the fifo method:

(a) Determine the total Fabricating Department cost to be accounted for.

(b) Compute the unit costs for materials, labor, and factory overhead for the Fabricating Department.

(c) Compute the cost of units transferred to the Finishing Department, and the cost of the ending work in process inventory in the Fabricating Department.

(3) Complete requirements (1) and (2) above, assuming that work in process inventory is costed using the average method. (Round unit costs to the nearest cent.)
                                                            (AICPA adapted)

5-2. Cost of production report; fifo vs. average costing. Deterra Inc. uses three departments to produce a detergent. The Finishing Department is the third and last step before the product is transferred to storage.

All materials needed to give the detergent its final composition are added at the beginning of the process in the Finishing Department. Any lost units occur only at this point and are considered to be normal.

The company uses fifo costing. The following data for the Finishing Department for October have been made available:

Production data:

In process, October 1 (labor and factory overhead, ¾ complete)......................	10,000 gals.
Transferred in from preceding department...	40,000
Finished and transferred to storage..	35,000
In process, October 31 (labor and factory overhead, ½ complete)....................	10,000

Additional data:

Work in process inventory, October 1:	
Cost from preceding department.......................................	$ 38,000
Cost from this department:	
Materials...	21,500
Labor...	39,000
Factory overhead..	42,000
Total work in process inventory, October 1....................	$140,500
Transferred in during October...	$140,000
Cost added in this department:	
Materials...	$ 70,000
Labor...	162,500
Factory overhead..	130,000
Total cost added...	$362,500
Total cost to be accounted for...	$643,000

Required:

(1) Prepare a cost of production report for the Finishing Department for October, using fifo costing.

(2) Prepare a cost of production report for the Finishing Department for October, using average costing. (Carry unit cost computations to three decimal places, and round up the digit "5" in the fourth decimal place.)　　*(AICPA adapted)*

5-3. Inventory costing; average method. In attempting to verify the costing of the December 31, 19A inventory of work in process and finished goods recorded on Shelton Corporation's books, the auditor finds:

Finished goods, 200,000 units... $1,009,800
Work in process, 300,000 units, 50% complete as to labor and
    factory overhead... 660,960

    The company uses average costing. Materials are added to production at the beginning of the manufacturing process, and factory overhead is applied at the rate of 60% of direct labor cost. Shelton's inventory cost records disclosed zero finished goods on January 1, 19A, and the following additional information for 19A:

| | | Costs | |
	Units	Materials	Labor
Work in process, January 1 (80% complete as to labor and factory overhead)............................	200,000	$ 200,000	$ 315,000
Units started in production..	1,000,000		
Materials cost..		$1,300,000	
Labor cost...			$1,995,000
Units completed..	900,000		

Required:

    (1) Compute the equivalent units of production.
    (2) Compute the unit production costs of materials, labor, and factory overhead.
    (3) Cost the ending finished goods and work in process inventories and compare to book balances.
    (4) Prepare the necessary journal entry to correctly state the finished goods and work in process ending inventories. *(AICPA adapted)*

5-4. Cost of production report; average costing. Callaway Company produces sleeping pills in two departments: Mixing, and Compounding and Packaging. The company uses average costing. For February, in the Mixing Department, the ending inventory is complete as to materials and ½ complete as to labor and factory overhead, and lost units occur at the end of the department's processing. In the Compounding and Packaging Department, the ending inventory is ⅔ complete as to labor and factory overhead.

	Mixing Department	Compounding and Packaging Department
Production data:		
Beginning inventory...	1,000 units	500 units
Started in process..	15,000	—
Received from prior department......................	—	12,500
Transferred out..	12,500	11,500
Ending inventory..	3,000	1,500
Lost units (all normal)......................................	500	—
Cost summary:		
Beginning inventory:		
Cost from prior department..........................	—	$ 650
Materials..	$ 980	—
Labor..	230	175
Factory overhead...	400	100
Cost for February:		
Materials..	15,020	—
Labor..	5,570	6,700
Factory overhead...	8,300	4,275

Required: Prepare a cost of production report for both departments for February.

5-5. Average costing method; normal and abnormal spoilage. Larrman Company manufactures various lines of bicycles. Because of the high volume of each type of product, the company employs a process cost system, using the average method to determine unit costs. Bicycle parts are manufactured in the Molding Department. The parts are consolidated into a single bike unit in the Molding Department and transferred to the Assembly Department, where they are partially assembled. After assembly, the bicycle is sent to the Packing Department.

Cost per unit data for the 20-inch dirt bike have been completed through the Molding Department. Annual cost and production figures for the Assembly Department are presented in the following schedules:

Cost data:

	Transferred In from Molding Department	Assembly Materials	Assembly Conversion Cost	Total Cost of Dirt Bike Through Assembly
Prior period costs..................	$ 82,200	$ 6,660	$ 11,930	$ 100,790
Current period costs.............	1,237,800	96,840	236,590	1,571,230
Total cost...........................	$1,320,000	$103,500	$248,520	$1,672,020

(handwritten: 2nd dept. assembly Dept) *(handwritten: labor & FOH)*

Production data:

	Bicycles	Percent Complete		
		Transferred In	Assembly Materials	Assembly Conversion
Beginning inventory.........................	3,000	100%	100%	80%
Transferred in from Molding during year.....................	45,000	100	—	—
Transferred out to Packing during year.....................	40,000	100	100	100
Ending inventory..............................	4,000	100	50	20

(handwritten: Inspection at 70% includes all materials)

Defective (spoiled) bicycles are identified at an inspection point when the assembly conversion process is 70% complete. All assembly materials have been added at this stage of the process. The normal rejection percentage for defective bicycles is 5% of those reaching the inspection point, and the cost of these units is absorbed by the good units. Any defective bicycles in excess of the 5% allowance are considered abnormal, and their cost is charged to a current period expense account. All defective bikes are removed from the production process and scrapped.

Required:

(1) Compute the number of defective bikes considered to be (a) normal and (b) abnormal.
(2) Compute equivalent units of production for transferred in, assembly materials, and assembly conversion costs.
(3) Compute unit costs for equivalent production.
(4) Compute the amount of total production cost associated with (a) units transferred out to Packing, (b) abnormal spoilage charged to a current period expense account, and (c) Assembly Department work in process ending inventory.
(5) Describe how the applicable dollar amounts would be presented in the financial statements for (a) units transferred out to Packing, (b) abnormal spoilage, and (c) Assembly work in process ending inventory. *(ICMA adapted)*

5-6. Cost of production report; average costing; spoilage at end of process, both normal and abnormal. Wing Company manufactures a product which passes through two departments. The company uses average process costing.

In Department 1, two materials are used. The process begins with Material A. Conversion costs are applied evenly throughout the process. At the end of the process, units are inspected before the addition of Material B. Normal spoilage is considered to be 2% of good output.

There were 5,000 units in process at the beginning of the period, 40% complete. During the period, 25,000 units were started in process, with 27,000 units transferred to Department 2, and 2,000 units remaining in process at the end of the period, 70% complete.

Cost information is as follows:

	Beginning Inventory	Current Period
Material A..................................	$14,400	$ 75,600
Material B..................................	—	13,500
Conversion costs....................	7,600	110,000
	$22,000	$199,100

Required: Prepare a cost of production report for Department 1. *(CGAAC adapted)*

5-7. Cost of production report; average costing; addition of materials. Pain-Away Company manufactures liquid aspirin and accounts for production using average process costing. In Department 2, five gallons of liquid, weighing 8 pounds per gallon, are added to each pound of powder transferred from Department 1. Each Department 2 unit weighs one pound. The following information is available for August:

	Units	Dollars
Beginning inventory (all materials;		
⅓ labor and factory overhead)........................	30,000	
Cost from preceding department.....................		$ 57,000
Materials..		29,100
Labor..		5,300
Factory overhead..		41,000
Ending inventory (all materials;		
½ labor and factory overhead)........................	20,000	
Cost added during August:		
Cost from preceding department.....................	10,000 lbs. of powder	823,000
Materials..	400,000	410,900
Labor..		209,700
Factory overhead..		1,679,000

Required: Prepare a cost of production report for Department 2 for August.

5-8. Cost of production report; fifo costing; addition of materials. Adept Company manufactures a product known as Prep. The manufacturing process covers two departments, Grading and Saturating, in which fifo costing is used.

The manufacturing process begins in the Grading Department, where raw materials are started in process. The output is transferred to the Saturating Department for the final phase of production, where water is added at the beginning of the production process, resulting in a 50% gain in weight of the materials in production.

The following information is available for November:

	November 1		November 30
	Quantity (pounds)	Amount	Quantity (pounds)
Work in process inventories:			
Grading Department...............................	—	—	—
Saturating Department..............................	1,600	$17,600	2,000

	Materials	Labor and Factory Overhead
November costs of production:		
Grading Department................................	$259,200	$86,400
Saturating Department............................	—	86,000

The work in process inventory in the Saturating Department is estimated to be 50% complete as to conversion costs at both the beginning and end of November. The material used in the Grading Department during November weighed 28,800 pounds.

Required: Prepare a cost of production report for each department for November.

(AICPA adapted)

5-9. Cost of production report; average and fifo costing. Lullaby Company manufactures baby sleepwear in three processes: Cutting, Sewing, and Packaging. Average costing is used in the Cutting and Sewing Departments, while fifo costing is used in Packaging. The closing inventory in Cutting is complete as to materials and 1/2 complete as to labor and factory overhead; in Sewing, it is 2/3 complete as to labor and factory overhead; and in Packaging, the closing inventory is 1/6 complete, while the beginning inventory is 1/2 complete as to materials, labor, and factory overhead. Lost units are within normal limits and occur at the end of processing in Cutting and at the beginning of processing in Packaging. The following production and cost data for December are available:

	Cutting Department	Sewing Department	Packaging Department
Production data (quantity schedule):			
Units in process at beginning...............................	1,000	500	500
Units started in process..	15,000		
Units received from preceding department...........		12,500	11,500
	16,000	13,000	12,000
Units transferred to next department.....................	12,500	11,500	
Units transferred to finished goods........................			10,400
Lost units..	500		1,000
Units still in process...	3,000	1,500	600
	16,000	13,000	12,000
Cost data:			
Work in process—beginning inventory:			
Cost from preceding department........................		$ 650	$ 1,500
Materials..	$980		30
Labor...	230	175	65
Factory overhead...	400	100	50
Cost added during period:			
Materials..	15,020		615
Labor...	5,570	6,700	1,435
Factory overhead...	8,300	4,275	1,230

Required: Prepare a cost of production report, excluding the quantity schedule. (Carry unit costs to five decimal places.)

5-10. Cost of production report; average and fifo costing. Relaxo Company manufactures tranquilizers. Production is divided into three processes: Mixing, Compounding, and Packaging. Average costing is used in the first two departments, and fifo costing is used in the Packaging Department.

The following data are available for September:

Quantity schedule:

	Mixing	Compounding	Packaging
Units in process at beginning...	4,000	2,000	2,000
Units started in process..	60,000	—	—
Units received from preceding department...	—	50,000	46,000
	64,000	52,000	48,000
Units transferred to next department.............................	50,000	46,000	
Units transferred to finished goods.................................			41,600
Units lost during process*..	2,000		4,000**
Units still in process...	12,000	6,000	2,400
	64,000	52,000	48,000

*Losses are within normal tolerance limits and pertain to ending inventories as well as to units transferred out.
**Loss is assumed to be entirely from units transferred in this period.

	Mixing	Compounding	Packaging
Stage of completion of units in process at beginning of period:			
Materials..100%	1/1	—	1/2
Labor and factory overhead.......................................	5/6	2/3	1/2
Stage of completion of units in process at end of period:			
Materials..100%	1/1	—	1/6
Labor and factory overhead.......................................	1/2	2/3	1/6
Cost data:			
Work in process—beginning inventory:			
Cost from preceding department...........................	—	$ 2,260	$3,000
Materials...	$ 1,960	—	60
Labor..	770	350	130
Factory overhead...	1,060	200	100
Cost added during period:			
Materials...	29,040	—	1,230
Labor..	10,430	13,400	2,870
Factory overhead...	15,740	8,550	2,460

Required:

(1) Compute the equivalent units of production for each department.
(2) Prepare a combined cost of production report for September. (Carry unit cost computations to five decimal places.)

CHAPTER 6
Costing By-Products and Joint Products

Many industrial concerns are confronted with the difficult and often rather complicated problem of assigning costs to their by-products and/or joint products. Chemical companies, petroleum refineries, flour mills, coal mines, lumber mills, dairies, canners, meat packers, and many others produce in their manufacturing or conversion processes a multitude of products to which some costs must be assigned. Assignment of costs to these various products is required for inventory costing for income determination and financial statement purposes. Another aspect of by-product and joint product costing is that it furnishes management with data that may be useful in planning maximum profit potentials and evaluating actual profit performance. However, management should recognize the limited usefulness of arbitrary allocations in the analysis of individual products. The last section of this chapter elaborates on this limitation.

▼ BY-PRODUCTS AND JOINT PRODUCTS DEFINED

The term *by-product* is generally used to denote one or more products of relatively small total value that are produced simultaneously with a product of greater total value. The product with the greater value, commonly called the "main product," is usually produced in greater quantities than the by-products. Ordinarily, the manufacturer has only limited control over the quantity of the by-product that comes into existence. However, the introduction of more advanced engineering methods, such as in the petroleum industry, has permitted greater control over the quantity of residual products. For example, one company, which formerly paid a trucker to haul away and dump certain waste materials, discovered that the waste was valuable as fertilizer, and this by-product is now an additional source of income for the entire industry.

Joint products are produced simultaneously by a common process or series of processes, with each product possessing a more than nominal value in the form in which it is produced. The definition emphasizes the point that the manufacturing process creates products in a definite quantitative relationship.

An increase in one product's output will bring about an increase in the quantity of the other products, or vice versa, but not necessarily in the same proportion. To the point of split-off or to the point where these several products emerge as individual units, the cost of the products forms a homogeneous whole.

Nature of By-Products and Joint Products

The accounting treatment of by-products necessitates a reasonably complete knowledge of the technological factors underlying their manufacture, since the origins of by-products may vary. By-products arising from the cleansing of the main product, such as gas and tar from coke manufacture, generally have a residual value. In some cases, the by-product is leftover scrap or waste, such as sawdust in lumber mills. In other cases, the by-product may not be the result of any manufacturing process but may arise from preparing raw materials before they are used in the manufacture of the main product. The separation of cotton seed from cotton, cores and seeds from apples, and shells from cocoa beans are examples of this type of by-product.

By-products can be classified into two groups according to their marketable condition at the split-off point: (1) those sold in their original form without need of further processing and (2) those which require further processing in order to be salable.

The classic example of joint products is found in the meat-packing industry, where various cuts of meat and numerous by-products are processed from one original carcass with one lump-sum cost. Another example of joint product manufacturing is the production of gasoline, where the derivation of gasoline inevitably results in the production of such items as naphtha, kerosene, and distillate fuel oils. Other examples of joint product manufacturing are the simultaneous production of various grades of glue and the processing of soybeans into oil and meal. Joint product costing is also found in industries that must grade raw material before it is processed. Tobacco manufacturers (except in cases where graded tobacco is purchased) and virtually all fruit and vegetable canners face the problem of grading. In fact, such manufacturers have a dual problem of joint cost allocation: (1) materials cost is applicable to all grades; (2) subsequent manufacturing costs are incurred simultaneously for all the different grades.

Joint Costs

A *joint cost* may be defined as that cost which arises from the common processing or manufacturing of products produced from the same process. Whenever two or more different joint or by-products are created from a single cost factor, a joint cost results. A joint cost is incurred prior to the point at which separately identifiable products emerge from the same process.

The chief characteristic of a joint cost is the fact that the cost of several different products is incurred in an indivisible sum for all products, rather than in individual amounts for each product. The total production cost of multiple products involves both joint cost and separate, individual product costs. These separable product costs are identifiable with the individual product and, generally, need no allocation. However, a joint production cost requires allocation or assignment to the individual products.

Difficulties in Costing By-Products and Joint Products

By-products and joint products are difficult to cost because a true joint cost is indivisible. For example, an ore might contain both lead and zinc. In the raw state, these minerals are joint products, and until they are separated by reduction of the ore, the cost of finding, mining, and processing is a joint cost; neither lead nor zinc can be produced without the other prior to the split-off stage. The cost accumulated to the split-off stage must be borne by the difference between the sales price and the cost to complete and sell each mineral after the split-off point.

Because of the indivisibility of a joint cost, cost allocation and apportionment procedures used for establishing the unit cost of a product are far from perfect and are, indeed, quite arbitrary. The costing of joint products and by-products highlights the problem of assigning costs to products whose origin, use of equipment, share of raw materials, share of labor costs, and share of other facilities cannot truly be determined. Whatever methods of allocation are employed, the total profit or loss figure is not affected—provided there are no beginning or ending inventories—by allocating costs to the joint products or by-products, since these costs are recombined in the final income statement. However, a joint cost is ordinarily allocated to the products on some acceptable basis to determine product costs needed for inventory carrying costs. For this reason, there is an effect on periodic income, because different amounts may be allocated to inventories of the numerous joint products or by-products under various allocation methods.

The allocation of costs to joint products may be required for such special purposes as justifying sales prices before governmental regulatory bodies. However, the validity of splitting a joint cost to determine fair, regulated prices for products has been questioned by both accountants and economists.

▼ METHODS OF COSTING BY-PRODUCTS

The accepted methods for costing by-products fall into two categories:

1. A joint production cost is not allocated to the by-product. Any revenue resulting from sales of the by-product is credited either to income or to cost of the main product. In some cases, costs subsequent to split-off may be offset against the by-product revenue. For inventory costing, an independent value may be assigned to the by-product. The methods most commonly used in industry are:

★ For inventory costing an independent value is assigned to the by-product

Method 1. Revenue from sales of the by-product is listed on the income statement as:
   a. Other income.
   b. Additional sales revenue.
   c. A deduction from the cost of goods sold of the main product.
   d. A deduction from the total production (manufacturing) cost of the main product. — *a sales value is deducted*

Joint production cost is not assigned to by-product

Method 2. Revenue from sales of the by-product less the costs of placing the by-product on the market (marketing and administrative expenses) and less any additional processing cost of the by-product is shown on the income statement in a manner similar to that indicated in Method 1.

Method 3. The replacement cost method.

2. Some portion of the joint production cost is allocated to the by-product. Inventory costs are based on this allocated cost plus any subsequent processing cost. In this category, the following method is used:

Method 4. The market value (reversal cost) method.

Method 1: Recognition of Gross Revenue

Method 1 is a typical noncost procedure in which the final inventory cost of the main product is overstated to the extent that some of the cost belongs to the by-product. However, this shortcoming is somewhat removed in Method 1 (d), although a sales value rather than a cost is deducted from the production cost of the main product.

By-Product Revenue as Other Income. To illustrate this procedure, the following income statement is presented:

Sales (main product, 10,000 units @ $2)...............................		$20,000
Cost of goods sold:		
Beginning inventory (1,000 units @ $1.50)............................	$ 1,500	
Total production cost (11,000 units @ $1.50)........................	16,500	
Cost of goods available for sale...	$18,000	
Ending inventory (2,000 units @ $1.50)................................	3,000	15,000
Gross profit..		$ 5,000
Marketing and administrative expenses...................................		2,000
Operating income..		$ 3,000
Other income: Revenue from sales of by-product....................		1,500
Income before income tax...		$ 4,500

By-Product Revenue as Additional Sales Revenue. In this case, the income statement above would show the $1,500 revenue from sales of the by-product as an addition to sales of the main product. As a result, total sales revenue would be $21,500, and gross profit and operating income would increase accordingly. All other figures would remain the same.

By-Product Revenue as a Deduction from the Cost of Goods Sold. In this case, the $1,500 revenue from the by-product would be deducted from the

$15,000 cost of goods sold figure, thereby reducing the cost and increasing the gross profit and operating income. The income before income tax remains at $4,500.

By-Product Revenue Deducted from Production Cost. In this case, the $1,500 revenue from by-product sales is deducted from the $16,500 total production cost, giving a net production cost of $15,000. This revised cost results in a new average unit cost of $1.3625 for the main product. The final inventory will consequently be $2,725 instead of $3,000. Similarly, the beginning inventory of $1.35 per unit results from crediting revenue from by-product sales in the prior period to the main product's production costs incurred in that period. The income statement would appear as follows:

Sales (main product, 10,000 units @ $2)			$20,000
Cost of goods sold:			
Beginning inventory (1,000 units @ $1.35)		$ 1,350	
Total production cost (11,000 units @ $1.50)	$16,500		
Revenue from sales of by-product	1,500		
Net production cost		15,000	
Cost of goods available for sale (12,000 units			
@ $1.3625 average cost)		$16,350	
Ending inventory (2,000 units @ $1.3625)		2,725	13,625
Gross profit			$ 6,375
Marketing and administrative expenses			2,000
Operating income			$ 4,375

The preceding methods require no complicated journal entries. The revenue received from by-product sales is debited to Cash (or Accounts Receivable). In the first three cases, Income from Sales of By-Product is credited; in the fourth case, the production cost of the main product is credited.

Method 2: Recognition of Net Revenue

Method 2 recognizes the need for assigning some cost to the by-product. It does not attempt, however, to allocate any main product cost to the by-product. Any expenses involved in further processing or marketing the by-product are recorded in separate accounts. All figures are shown on the income statement, following one of the procedures described in Method 1.

Journal entries in Method 2 would involve charges to by-product revenue for the additional work required and perhaps for factory overhead. The marketing and administrative expenses might also be allocated to the by-product on some equitable predetermined basis. Some firms carry an account called By-Product, to which all additional expenses are debited and all income is credited. The balance of this account would be presented in the income statement, following one of the procedures outlined in Method 1. However, accumulated manufacturing costs applicable to by-product inventory should be reported on the balance sheet.

Method 3: Replacement Cost Method

The replacement cost method ordinarily is applied by firms whose by-products are used within the plant, thereby avoiding the necessity of purchasing certain materials and supplies from outside suppliers. The production cost of the main product is credited for such materials, and the offsetting debit is to the department that uses the by-product. The cost assigned to the by-product is the purchase or replacement cost existing in the market. In the steel industry, for example, many by-products are sold in the open market. Other products, such as blast furnace gas and coke oven gas, are mixed and used for heating in open-hearth furnaces. The waste heat from open hearths is used again in the generation of steam needed by the various producing departments. The resourceful use of these by-products and their accounting treatment are indicated by the following procedure used by a steel company:

1. Coke oven by-products are credited to the cost of coke at the average sales price per unit for the month.
2. Coke oven and blast furnace gas are credited respectively to the cost of coke and the cost of pig iron at a computed value based on the cost of fuel oil yielding equivalent heat units.
3. Tar and pitch used as fuel are credited respectively to the cost of coke at a computed value based on the cost of fuel oil yielding equivalent heat units.
4. Scrap steel remelted is credited to the cost of finished steel at market cost of equivalent grades purchased.
5. Waste heat from furnaces used to generate steam is credited to the steel ingot cost at a computed value based on the cost of coal yielding equivalent heat units.[1]

The costing of by-products that are used within a plant is actually a form of intracompany transfer pricing, which is discussed in Chapter 26. In this chapter, alternatives to the use of a replacement cost or market price are discussed. For example, a price based on the cost to produce the by-product, a negotiated price, or an arbitrary price might be used. Whatever the price used, the credit is made to the production cost of the main product from which the by-product comes and the offsetting debit is made to the department that uses the by-product.

Method 4: Market Value Method

by product revenue deducted from production cost

The market value (reversal cost) method is basically similar to the last technique illustrated in Method 1. However, it reduces the manufacturing cost of the main product, not by the actual revenue received, but by an estimate of the by-product's value at the time of recovery. This estimate must be made

[1]Howard C. Greer, "Accounting for By-Products and Joint Products," *NA(C)A Bulletin*, Vol. XVII, No. 24, Section 1, p. 1413.

prior to split-off from the main product. Dollar recognition depends on the stability of the market as to price and salability of the by-product; however, control over quantities is important as well. The by-product account is charged with this estimated amount and the production (manufacturing) cost of the main product is credited. Any additional costs of materials, labor, or factory overhead incurred after the by-product is separated from the main product are charged to the by-product. Marketing and administrative expenses might also be allocated to the by-product on some equitable basis. The proceeds from sales of the by-product are credited to the by-product account. The balance in this account can be presented on the income statement in one of the ways outlined for Method 1, except that the manufacturing cost applicable to by-product inventory should be reported in the balance sheet.

The market value (reversal cost) method of ascertaining main product and by-product costs may be illustrated as follows:

Item	Main Product	By-Product
Materials..	$ 50,000	
Labor..	70,000	
Factory overhead...	40,000	
Total production cost (40,000 units)...........................	$160,000	
Market value (5,000 units @ $1.80)...........................		$9,000
Estimated gross profit consisting of:		
Assumed operating profit		
(20% of sales price)...		$1,800
Marketing and administrative expenses		
(5% of sales price)...		450 2,250
		$6,750
Estimated production costs after split-off:		
Materials...		$1,000
Labor..		1,200
Factory overhead...		300 2,500
Estimated value of by-product at split-off		
to be credited to main product.............................	4,250	$4,250
Net cost of main product...	$155,750	
Add back *actual* production cost after		
split-off...		2,300
Total...		$6,550
Total number of units...	40,000	5,000
Unit cost..	$ 3.894	$ 1.31

[handwritten margin note: estimate of by products value at time of recovery]

This illustration indicates that an estimated value of the by-product at the split-off point results when estimated gross profit and production cost after split-off are subtracted from the by-product's ultimate market value. Alternatively, if the by-product has a market value at the split-off point, the by-product account is charged with this market value, less its estimated gross profit, and the main product's production cost would be credited. It is also possible to use the total market values of the main product and the by-product at the split-off point as a basis for assigning a share of the prior-to-split-off cost to the by-product, applying the offsetting credit to the production cost of the main product. In any event, subsequent-to-split-off cost related to the by-product would be charged to the by-product.

Method 4 is based on the theory that the cost of a by-product is related to its sales value. It is a step toward the recognition of a by-product cost prior to its split-off from the main product. It is also the nearest approach to methods employed in joint product costing.

▼ METHODS OF ALLOCATING JOINT PRODUCTION COST TO JOINT PRODUCTS

Joint production cost, incurred up to the split-off point, can be allocated to joint products by using one of the following methods:

1. The market or sales value method, based on the relative market values of the individual products.
2. The quantitative or physical unit method, based on some physical measurement unit such as weight, linear measure, or volume.
3. The average unit cost method.
4. The weighted average method, based on a predetermined standard or index of production.

Market or Sales Value Method

Proponents of the market or sales value method often argue that the market value of any product is to some extent a manifestation of the cost incurred in its production. The contention is that if one product sells for more than another, it is because more cost was expended to produce it. In other words, were it not for such a cost, a sales value would not exist. Yet, by definition, the effort required to produce each of the joint products cannot be determined. If it could be determined, the allocation could be made on the basis of the relative amount of effort expended on each of the joint products. Furthermore, according to economic theory, prices in a competitive market economy are determined on the basis of the relative scarcity of goods demanded by consumers, not on the basis of the relative cost of producing those goods.

Probably the best argument for using the market value method of allocating joint costs is that it is neutral, i.e., it does not affect the relative profitability of the joint products. Thus, decisions which must be based on an analysis of the relative profitability of the various joint products are not distorted by arbitrary cost allocations.

Joint Products Salable at Split-Off. The market value method prorates the joint cost on the basis of the relative market values of the items produced. The method is based on a weighted market value, using the total market or sales value of each product (quantity produced multiplied by the unit sales price). To illustrate, assume that joint products A, B, C, and D are produced at a total joint production cost of $120,000. Quantities produced are: A, 20,000 units; B, 15,000 units; C, 10,000 units; and D, 15,000 units. Product A sells for $.25; B, for $3, C, for $3.50; and D, for $5. These prices are market or sales values for the products at the split-off point; i.e., it is assumed that they can be sold at that point.

Management may have decided, however, that it is more profitable to process certain products further before they are sold. Nevertheless, this condition does not destroy the usefulness of the sales value at the split-off point for the allocation of the joint production cost. The proration of this joint cost is made in the following manner:

Product	Units Produced	Market Value per Unit	Total Market Value	Ratio of Product Value to Total Market Value	Apportionment of Joint Production Cost
A	20,000	$ .25	$ 5,000	3.125%	$ 3,750
B	15,000	3.00	45,000	28.125	33,750
C	10,000	3.50	35,000	21.875	26,250
D	15,000	5.00	75,000	46.875	56,250
Total..			$160,000	100.000%	$120,000

The same results can be obtained if the total joint production cost ($120,000) is divided by the total market value of the four products ($160,000). The resulting 75 percent is the percentage of joint cost in each individual market value. By multiplying each market value by this percentage, the joint cost will be apportioned as shown in the preceding table.

Under the market value method, each joint product yields the same unit gross profit percentage, assuming that the units are sold without further processing. This can be illustrated as follows, assuming no beginning inventories:

	Total	A	B	C	D
Sales—units...................................	52,000	18,000	12,000	8,000	14,000
Ending inventories........................	8,000	2,000	3,000	2,000	1,000
Sales—dollars...............................	$138,500	$ 4,500	$36,000	$28,000	$70,000
Production cost............................	$120,000	$ 3,750	$33,750	$26,250	$56,250
Less ending inventory.................	16,125	375*	6,750	5,250	3,750
Cost of goods sold.......................	$103,875	$ 3,375	$27,000	$21,000	$52,500
Gross profit..................................	$ 34,625	$ 1,125	$ 9,000	$ 7,000	$17,500
Gross profit percentage...............	25%	25%	25%	25%	25%

*$3,750 production cost ÷ 20,000 units produced = $.1875; $.1875 × 2,000 units in ending inventory = $375.

Joint Products Not Salable at Split-Off. Products not salable in their stage of completion at the split-off point and therefore without any market value require additional processing to place them in marketable condition. In such cases, the basis for allocation of the joint production cost is a hypothetical market value at the split-off point. To illustrate the procedure, the following assumptions are added to the preceding example:

Product	Ultimate Market Value per Unit	Processing Cost After Split-Off
A	$ .50	$ 2,000
B	5.00	10,000
C	4.50	10,000
D	8.00	28,000

To arrive at the basis for the apportionment, it is necessary to use a working-back procedure, whereby the after-split-off processing cost is subtracted from the ultimate sales value to find a hypothetical market value. After-split-off marketing and administrative expenses traceable to specific products and an allowance for profit should also be considered if their amounts are proportionately different among the joint products, because the joint cost apportionment would be affected. The following table indicates the steps to be taken:

Product	Ultimate Market Value per Unit	Units Produced	Ultimate Market Value	Processing Cost After Split-Off	Hypothetical Market Value*	Apportionment of Joint Production Cost**	Total Production Cost	Total Production Cost Percentage***
A	$ .50	20,000	$ 10,000	$ 2,000	$ 8,000	$ 4,800	$ 6,800	68.0
B	5.00	15,000	75,000	10,000	65,000	39,000	49,000	65.3
C	4.50	10,000	45,000	10,000	35,000	21,000	31,000	68.8
D	8.00	15,000	120,000	28,000	92,000	55,200	83,200	69.3
Total..			$250,000	$50,000	$200,000	$120,000	$170,000	68.0

*At the split-off point
**Percentage to allocate joint production cost (using the joint cost total determined on page 132):

$$\frac{\text{Total joint production cost}}{\text{Total hypothetical market value}} = \frac{\$120,000}{\$200,000} = .60 = 60\%;$$

60% × hypothetical market value = apportionment of joint production cost
***The production cost percentage is calculated by dividing total production cost by the ultimate market value; e.g.,

$$\frac{\$49,000}{\$75,000} = .653 = 65.3\% \text{ for Product B, and } \frac{\$170,000}{\$250,000} = .68 = 68\% \text{ for all products combined.}$$

If in a given situation, certain of the joint products are salable at the split-off point while others are not, the market values at the split-off point would be used for the former group. For the latter group, hypothetical market values would be required.

The following gross profit statement uses the same number of units sold as was used in the preceding illustration, but the sales prices have been increased as a result of additional processing.

	Total	A	B	C	D
Sales—units...	52,000	18,000	12,000	8,000	14,000
Ending inventories..............................	8,000	2,000	3,000	2,000	1,000
Sales—dollars......................................	$217,000	$ 9,000	$60,000	$36,000	$112,000
Cost of goods sold:					
Joint production cost......................	$120,000	$ 4,800	$39,000	$21,000	$ 55,200
Further processing cost.................	50,000	2,000	10,000	10,000	28,000
Total...	$170,000	$ 6,800	$49,000	$31,000	$ 83,200
Less ending inventory........................	22,227	680*	9,800	6,200	5,547
Cost of goods sold.............................	$147,773	$ 6,120	$39,200	$24,800	$ 77,653
Gross profit..	$ 69,227	$ 2,880	$20,800	$11,200	$ 34,347
Gross profit percentage......................	32%	32%	35%	31%	31%

*$6,800 production cost ÷ 20,000 units produced = $.34; $.34 × 2,000 units in ending inventory = $680.

Since the statement has often been made that every joint product should be equally profitable, the sales value technique may be modified by using the overall gross profit percentage to determine the gross profit for each product. In the following table, the gross profit (32 percent) is deducted from the sales value to find the total cost, which is reduced by each product's further processing cost to find the joint cost allocation for each product.

	Total	A	B	C	D
Ultimate sales value......................	$250,000	$10,000	$75,000	$45,000	$120,000
Less 32% gross profit..................	80,000	3,200	24,000	14,400	38,400
Total cost.......................................	$170,000	$ 6,800	$51,000	$30,600	$ 81,600
Further processing cost................	50,000	2,000	10,000	10,000	28,000
Joint cost......................................	$120,000	$ 4,800	$41,000	$20,600	$ 53,600

If sales value, gross profit percentage, or further processing costs are estimated, the balance labeled "Joint cost" would serve as the basis for allocating the actual joint cost to the four products.

Quantitative Unit Method

The quantitative unit method attempts to distribute the total joint cost on the basis of some unit of measurement, such as pounds, gallons, tons, or board feet. However, if the joint products are not measurable by the basic measurement unit, the joint units must be converted to a denominator common to all units produced. For instance, in the manufacture of coke, products such as coke, coal tar, benzol, sulfate of ammonia, and gas are measured in different units. The yield of these recovered units is measured on the basis of quantity of product extracted per ton of coal.

The following table illustrates the use of weight as a quantitative unit method of joint cost allocation:

Product	Yield in Pounds of Recovered Product per Ton of Coal	Distribution of Waste to Recovered Products	Revised Weight of Recovered Products	Materials Cost of Each Product per Ton of Coal
Coke....................................	1,320.0 lbs.	69.474 lbs.*	1,389.474 lbs.	$27.790**
Coal tar...............................	120.0	6.316	126.316	2.526
Benzol.................................	21.9	1.153	23.053	.461
Sulfate of ammonia............	26.0	1.368	27.368	.547
Gas.......................................	412.1	21.689	433.789	8.676
Waste (water)....................	100.0			
Total..............................	2,000.0 lbs.	100.000 lbs.	2,000.000 lbs.	$40.000

*[1,320 ÷ (2,000 − 100)] = 69.474
**(1,389.474 ÷ 2,000) × $40 = $27.790

Average Unit Cost Method

The average unit cost method attempts to apportion the total joint production cost to the various products on the basis of an average unit cost obtained by dividing the total number of units produced into the total joint production cost. Companies using this method argue that all products turned out by the same process should receive a proportionate share of the total joint production cost based on the number of units produced. As long as all units produced are measured in terms of the same unit and do not differ greatly, this method can be used without too much misgiving. When the units produced are not measured in like terms or the units differ markedly, the method should not be applied.

Using figures in the market value example, the average unit cost method can be illustrated as follows:

$$\frac{\text{Total joint production cost}}{\text{Total number of units produced}} = \frac{\$120,000}{60,000} = \$2 \text{ per unit}$$

average unit cost method

Product	Units Produced	Apportionment of Joint Production Cost
A	20,000	$ 40,000
B	15,000	30,000
C	10,000	20,000
D	15,000	30,000
	60,000	$120,000

Weighted Average Method

In many industries, the previously described methods do not give a satisfactory answer to the joint cost apportionment problem. For this reason, weight factors are often assigned to each unit, based upon size of the unit, difficulty of manufacture, time consumed in making the unit, difference in type of labor employed, amount of materials used, etc. Finished production of every kind is multiplied by weight factors to apportion the total joint cost to individual units.

Using figures from the previous example, weight factors assigned to the four products might be as follows:

Product A— 3   points
Product B—12   points
Product C—13.5 points
Product D—15   points

The joint production cost allocation would result in the following values:

Product	Units Produced	× Points	=	Weighted Units	×	Cost Per Unit*	=	Apportionment of Joint Production Cost
A	20,000	3		60,000		$.20		$ 12,000
B	15,000	12		180,000		.20		36,000
C	10,000	13.5		135,000		.20		27,000
D	15,000	15		225,000		.20		45,000
				600,000				$120,000

$$* \frac{\text{Total joint production cost}}{\text{Total number of weighted units}} = \frac{\$120,000}{600,000} = \$.20 \text{ per unit}$$

▼ FEDERAL INCOME TAX LAWS AND THE COSTING OF JOINT PRODUCTS AND BY-PRODUCTS

Federal income tax laws concerning the costing of joint products and by-products are not numerous. Legislators recognize the impossibility of establishing a specific code of law for every conceivable situation involving this type of cost problem. Consequently, the written pronouncement of the law does not precisely establish the boundaries of acceptable procedures. A digest of legal viewpoint is given in the Federal Income Tax Regulations, which state the following:

> *Inventories of miners and manufacturers. A taxpayer engaged in mining or manufacturing who by a single process or uniform series of processes derives a product of two or more kinds, sizes, or grades, the unit cost of which is substantially alike, and who in conformity to a recognized trade practice allocates an amount of cost to each kind, size, or grade of product, which in the aggregate will absorb the total cost of production, may, with the consent of the Commissioner [of the Internal Revenue Service], use such allocated cost as a basis for pricing inventories, provided such allocation bears a reasonable relation to the respective selling values of the different kinds, sizes, or grades of product.*[2]

The quotation does not fully and unequivocally authorize the utilization of the market value theory of costing joint products and by-products. The words "in conformity to a recognized trade practice" and "with the consent of the Commissioner" clearly imply that the multiplicity of conceivable situations is far too great to be covered by definite rules that allow or prohibit a particular costing procedure. Thus, when the size of the business warrants the trouble and expense and before any joint product and by-product inventories are assigned costs for income tax purposes, the Commissioner must study the proposed costing program and inform the producer whether it will be allowed. It is a genuine problem for the Commissioner to decide whether a cost policy conforms closely enough to the accepted standards of the industry, or whether the alleged cost of a joint product or a by-product is reasonably related to the market values. So much depends upon the judgment of the Commissioner that a person might justifiably claim that in joint product and by-product costing disputes, the Commissioner is virtually the enactor of the law. Of course, decisions may be appealed, but the higher tribunals find themselves beset by the same vague, general statute. Thus, they too must rely almost entirely upon their own independent discretion and practically make the law.

Clearly, tax laws have not solved the problem of costing joint products and by-products for the accountant and the manufacturer. Tax officials find themselves in exactly the same predicament as any coke producer, petroleum refiner, or chemical manufacturer, even though their immediate objective may be limited to collecting a proper tax. The necessity of defining and interpreting accepted practices in a given industry proves, at least partially, that if the present income tax law on joint product and by-product costing—with its implication that the market value method is desirable—is unfair or manifestly

---

[2]*Regulations*, Section 1.471-7.

inaccurate and illogical, it can and will be changed if industry and the accounting profession can offer better reasons for the use of other procedures.

▼ JOINT COST ANALYSIS FOR MANAGERIAL DECISIONS AND PROFITABILITY ANALYSIS

Joint cost allocation methods indicate only too forcefully that the amount of the cost to be apportioned to the numerous products emerging at the point of split-off is difficult to establish for any purpose. Furthermore, the acceptance of an allocation method for the assignment of the joint production cost does not solve the problem. The thought has been advanced that no attempt should be made to determine the cost of individual products up to the split-off point; rather, it seems important to calculate the profit margin in terms of total combined units. Of course, costs incurred after the split-off point will provide management with information needed for decisions relating to the desirability of further processing to maximize profits.

Production of joint products is greatly influenced by both the technological characteristics of the processes and by the markets available for the products. This establishment of a product mix which is in harmony with customer demands appears profitable but is often physically impossible. It is interesting to note that cost accounting in the meat-packing industry serves primarily as a guide to buying, since aggregate sales realization values of the various products that will be obtained from cutting operations are considered in determining the price that a packer is willing to pay for livestock. Sales realization values are also considered when deciding to sell hams or other cuts in a particular stage or to process them further.

A joint cost is often incurred for products that are either interchangeable or not associated with each other at all. Increasing the output of one will in most joint cost situations unavoidably increase to some extent the output of the other. These situations fall into the category of the cost-volume-profit relationship and differential cost analysis (Chapters 20 and 21). Evaluation of many alternative combinations of output can lead to time-consuming computations. Often such evaluations are carried out on a computer using sophisticated simulation techniques. Developments in operations research procedures have provided techniques helpful in solving such problems (Chapter 22 on linear programming).

For profit planning, and perhaps as the only reliable measure of profitability, management should consider a product's contribution margin after separable or individual costs are deducted from sales. This contribution margin allows management to predict the amount that a segment or product line will add to or subtract from company profits. This margin is not the product's net profit figure. It only indicates relative profitability in comparison with other products. "Net profit determined by allocating to segments an 'equitable' share of all costs, both separable and joint, associated with the group of segments is not a reliable guide to profit planning decisions because these data cannot be used for predicting the outcome of decisions in terms of the change in aggregate net profit."[3] For these reasons, attempts to allocate joint marketing cost to products and customers by time studies of salespersons' activities, as well as attempts to allocate the joint production cost, often yield results which are unreliable for appraising segment profitability.

DISCUSSION QUESTIONS

1. Distinguish between joint products and by-products.

2. How may the revenue from the sale of by-products be shown on the income statement?

3. Does the showing of revenue from by-products on the income statement influence the unit cost of the main product?

4. By what method can production cost be relieved of the value of a by-product that can be further utilized in production processes? Explain.

5. By-products which require no additional processing after the point of separation are often accounted for by assigning to them a cost of zero at the point of separation and crediting the cost of production of the main product as sales are made.
   (a) Justify the above method of treating by-products.
   (b) Discuss the possible shortcomings of the treatment.   *(AICPA adapted)*

6. Are by-products ever charged with any cost? Explain.

7. Describe methods for allocating the total joint production cost to joint products.

8. Discuss the advantages and disadvantages of the market value and average unit cost methods of joint cost allocation.

9. When is it necessary to allocate joint costs to joint products?

10. Does the Internal Revenue Service prescribe any definite joint product or by-product cost allocation methods for tax purposes? Explain.

11. Oregon Logging Company obtains its cost information by dividing total cost by the number of board feet of lumber produced. The president states that money is lost on every foot of low grade lumber sold but is made up on the high grades. Appraise the statement.

12. In making a decision about the further processing of joint products, what costs are relevant?

EXERCISES

1. By-product costing and entries. Okalala Soap Company produces a product known as Okay. In the manufacturing of Okay, a by-product results which can be sold as is for $.36 per pound or processed further and sold for $1.30 per pound. The additional processing for each pound of by-product requires $.125 for materials, $.075 for labor, and $.05 for factory overhead.

   For May, production costs of the main product and by-product up to the point of separation were: materials, $250,000; labor, $200,000; and factory overhead, $170,000. These costs were charged to the main product. During the month, 315,000 pounds of Okay and 80,000 pounds of by-product were produced.

---

[3]Walter B. McFarland, *Concepts for Management Accounting* (New York: National Association of Accountants, 1966), p. 49.

Required: Prepare journal entries for the by-product when it is:

(1) Stored without assigning it any cost and later sold on account at $.36 per pound, with no additional costs incurred.
(2) Stored and costed at $.36 per pound, reducing the main product cost by the amount allocated to the by-product.
(3) Further processed and stored, with no cost prior to separation allocated to it.
(4) Further processed and stored, with the market value method being used to allocate the cost prior to separation, the cost of the main product being reduced by the cost allocated to the by-product, and the main product selling at $2 per pound.

2. By-product costing and entries. Lares Confectioners Inc. makes a candy bar called Rey, which sells for $.50 per pound. The manufacturing process also yields a by-product known as Nagu. Without further processing, Nagu sells for $.10 per pound; with further processing, Nagu sells for $.30 per pound. During April, total joint manufacturing costs up to the point of separation consisted of the following charges to work in process:

Raw materials...........................	$75,000
Direct labor...............................	60,000
Factory overhead......................	15,000

Production for the month aggregated 394,000 pounds of Rey and 30,000 pounds of Nagu. To complete Nagu during April and to obtain a sales price of $.30 per pound, further processing of Nagu would entail the following additional costs:

Raw materials...........................	$2,000
Direct labor...............................	1,500
Factory overhead......................	500

Required: Prepare the April journal entries for Nagu, if Nagu is:

(1) Transferred as a by-product at sales value to the warehouse without further processing, with a corresponding reduction of Rey's manufacturing cost.
(2) Further processed as a by-product and transferred to the warehouse, with prior-to-separation cost being assigned to Nagu at the market value at the split-off point, and a corresponding reduction of Rey's manufacturing cost, thus assuming no gross profit attributable to Nagu at the split-off point.
(3) Further processed as a by-product and transferred to finished goods, with cost prior to separation being allocated between Rey and Nagu based on relative sales value at the split-off point. The joint cost assigned to Nagu correspondingly reduces Rey's manufacturing cost. *(AICPA adapted)*

3. By-product costing—market value (reversal cost) method. Jackman Company manufactures one main product and two by-products, A and B. For April, the following data are available:

	Main Product	By-Product A	By-Product B	Total
Sales..	$75,000	$6,000	$3,500	$84,500
Manufacturing cost after separation...	$11,500	$1,100	$ 900	$13,500
Marketing and administrative expenses...	6,000	750	550	7,300
Manufacturing cost before separation...				37,500

Profit allowed for A and B is 15% and 12%, respectively.

Required:

(1) Calculate manufacturing cost before separation for by-products A and B, using the market value (reversal cost) method.
(2) Prepare an income statement, detailing sales and costs for each product.

4. By-product costing. In the manufacture of its main product, the Hominy Company produces a by-product. Joint production costs incurred to the point of separation totaled $150,000. After separation, costs totaling $100,000 were incurred to complete the main product, and $2,000 was incurred to complete the by-product. The main product had a final market value of $350,000, and the by-product had a final market value of $10,000. There is no ending inventory.

Required:

(1) Assume that the net revenue method is used to account for the by-product as other income and that the by-product's marketing and administrative expenses are zero. How much other income should be reported on the income statement?
(2) Assume that management wants to allocate $1,000 of marketing and administrative expenses to the by-product and still have a profit of 15% of the sales price. Using the market value (reversal cost) method, how much of the joint cost should be allocated to the by-product?

5. Joint product cost allocation—market value method. Helen Corporation manufactures products W, X, Y, and Z from a joint process. Additional information follows:

Product	Units Produced	Market Value at Split-Off	If Processed Further Additional Cost	Market Value
W........................	6,000	$ 80,000	$ 7,500	$ 90,000
X........................	5,000	60,000	6,000	70,000
Y........................	4,000	40,000	4,000	50,000
Z........................	3,000	20,000	2,500	30,000
Total........................	18,000	$200,000	$20,000	$240,000

Required: Assuming that the market value method is used, allocate a share of the total joint production cost of $160,000 to each product. *(AICPA adapted)*

6. Joint product cost allocation—market value method; by-product cost allocation—market value (reversal cost) method. Whatley Company manufactures joint products X and Y as well as by-product Z. Cumulative joint cost data for the period show $204,000, representing 20,000 completed units processed through the Refining Department at an average cost of $10.20. Costs are assigned to X and Y by the market value method, which considers further processing costs in subsequent operations. To determine the cost allocation to Z, the market value (reversal cost) method is used. Additional data:

	Z	X	Y
Quantity processed...	2,000 units	8,000 units	10,000 units
Sales price per unit..	$6	$20	$25
Further processing cost per unit.....................	2	5	7
Marketing and administrative			
expenses per unit..	1	—	—
Operating profit per unit..................................	1	—	—

Required: Compute the joint cost allocated to Z, then the amount to X and Y.

7. Joint product cost allocation—market value method. Arlington Company manufactures three different products from a single raw material. A summary of production costs shows:

	Product			
	S	K	Y	Total
Output in kilograms...........................	80 000	200 000	160 000	440 000
Sales price per kilogram....................	$.75	$1.00	$1.50	—

	Separable Costs			Total Cost
	S	K	Y	
Production costs:				
Materials...	—	—	—	$ 90,000
Direct labor...	$ 3,000	$20,000	$30,000	80,000
Variable factory overhead...................	2,000	10,000	16,000	45,000
Fixed factory overhead........................	15,000	34,000	30,000	115,000

All separable costs have been assigned to products but the joint cost has not been allocated. All of the year's output was sold.

Required: Compute the gross profit for each product, allocating the joint cost by the market value method. *(CGAAC adapted)*

8. Joint product cost allocation—market value method. Cagle Company spent $158,400 on raw materials, then processed this material at a cost of $171,600, resulting in three products: 6,000 units of B, 4,000 units of R, and 3,000 units of Y.

To make these products salable, an additional $50,000 is spent on B, $30,000 on R, and $40,000 on Y. Unit sales prices are: B, $40; R, $50; and Y, $60.

Required:

(1) Compute a unit cost for each product for inventory costing, using the market value method for joint cost allocation.
(2) The company has an opportunity to sell all of its B output at the split-off point for $34 per unit. Advise management as to whether B output should be sold at the split-off point or after further processing. *(CGAAC adapted)*

9. Joint product cost allocation—average unit cost and market value methods. Miller Company manufactures three products, A, B, and C, from a joint process. The joint costs for January totaled $100,000. Additional January information follows:

Product	Quantity	Processing Cost After Split-Off	Ultimate Market Value
A	3,000	$20,000	$ 60,000
B	4,000	30,000	110,000
C	3,000	50,000	90,000

Required:

(1) Compute the total production cost for each product, using the average unit cost method.
(2) Compute the total production cost for each product, using the market value method.

10. Joint product cost allocation—market value and weighted average methods. Buildon Company produces three joint products: Buildon, Buildeze, and Buildrite. Total joint production cost for November was $21,600.

The units produced and unit sales prices at the split-off point were:

Product	Units	Unit Sales Price
Buildon......................	6,000	$2.20
Buildeze....................	8,000	1.25
Buildrite.....................	10,000	1.28

In determining costs by the weighted average method, each unit is weighted as follows:

Product	Per Unit Weighting
Buildon.......................	3
Buildeze.....................	2
Buildrite.....................	2

Required: Allocate the joint production cost, using (1) the market value method, and (2) the weighted average method.

11. Joint product cost allocation. Perry Company produces four joint products, which have a manufacturing cost of $224,000 at the split-off point. Data pertaining to these products follow:

Product	Sales Value at Split-Off per Unit	Units Produced	Weight Factors
Kon...........................	$12.00	20,000	3.0
Lon...........................	3.50	32,000	5.5
Mon..........................	6.00	36,000	5.0
Non..........................	5.50	24,000	6.0

Required: Allocate the joint cost, using:

(1) Market or sales value method.
(2) Average unit cost method.
(3) Weighted average method.

12. Joint product cost allocation—weighted average method. A department's production schedule shows 10,000 units of X and 8,000 units of Y. Both articles are made from the same raw materials, but units of X and Y require estimated quantities of materials in the ratio of 3:2, respectively. Both articles pass through the same conversion process, but X and Y require estimated production times per unit in the ratio of 5:4, respectively.

Required: Compute the unit materials and conversion costs for each product if the total costs are: materials, $92,000; conversion cost, $123,000.

PROBLEMS

6-1. Joint product cost allocation—market value method. Charlottetown Company produces three products jointly. During May, joint costs totaled $200,000, and the following individual product information was available:

	C	L	T
Production...	15,000	10,000	20,000
Sales units..	13,000	9,000	16,000
Sales price..	$ 20.00	$ 15.00	$ 9.50
Separable processing cost....................	$75,000	$25,000	$40,000

Required:

(1) Compute the May gross profit for each product and in total, using the market value allocation method.

(2) A customer has offered to buy all of Product T output at the split-off point for $7 per unit. Advise the Charlottetown management.

6-2. Joint product cost allocation—market value method. Vallarta Company manufactures three products—D, F, and L. The first part of the manufacturing process is joint and the current period joint costs total $100,000. Other current information is as follows:

Product	Processing Cost After Split-Off	Number of Units Produced	Number of Units Sold	Unit Sales Price
D	$ 60,000	5,000	4,000	$20
F	40,000	2,000	1,500	30
L	140,000	7,000	6,300	40

Required:

(1) Compute the dollars that should be assigned to finished goods inventory for financial statement presentation, allocating joint cost by the market value method.

(2) Vallarta now discovers that it would be possible to sell products D and F at the split-off point for $10 and $8, respectively. Should the company sell these products at the split-off point or process them further?   *(CGAAC adapted)*

6-3. Cost allocation—joint products and by-product. Mobile Corporation produces three products, Alpha, Beta, and Gamma. Alpha and Gamma are joint products, while Beta is a by-product of Alpha. No joint cost is to be allocated to the by-product. The production processes for a given year are as follows:

(a) In Department 1, 110,000 pounds of material Rho are processed at a total cost of $120,000. After processing, 60% of the units are transferred to Department 2 and 40% of the units (now Gamma) are transferred to Department 3.

(b) In Department 2, the material is further processed at a total additional cost of $38,000. Seventy percent of the units (now Alpha) are transferred to Department 4 and 30% emerge as Beta, the by-product, to be sold at $1.20 per pound. The marketing expense related to Beta is $8,100.

(c) In Department 4, Alpha is processed at a total additional cost of $23,660. After processing, Alpha is ready for sale at $5 per pound.

(d) In Department 3, Gamma is processed at a total additional cost of $165,000. In this department, a normal loss of units of Gamma occurs, which equals 10% of the good output of Gamma. The remaining good output is sold for $12 per pound.

Required:

(1) Prepare a schedule showing the allocation of the $120,000 joint cost between Alpha and Gamma, using the market value at split-off point and treating the net realizable value of Beta as an addition to the sales value of Alpha.

(2) Prepare a statement of gross profit for Alpha, independent of the answer to requirement (1), assuming that:
   (a) $102,000 of total joint cost was appropriately allocated to Alpha.
   (b) 48,000 pounds of Alpha and 20,000 pounds of Beta were available for sale.
   (c) During the year, sales of Alpha were 80% of the pounds available for sale. There was no beginning inventory.

(d) The net realizable value of Beta available for sale is to be deducted from the cost of producing Alpha. The ending inventory of Alpha is to be based on the net cost of production.

(e) All other costs, sales prices, and marketing expenses are those presented in the facts of the original problem.   *(AICPA adapted)*

6-4. Cost allocation—joint products and by-product. Matson Chemical Company manufactures several products in its three departments:

(a) In Department 1, the raw materials amanic acid and bonyl hydroxide are used to produce Amanyl, Bonanyl, and Am-Salt. Amanyl is sold to others, who use it as a raw material in the manufacture of stimulants. Bonanyl is not salable without further processing. Although Am-Salt is a commercial product for which there is a ready market, the company does not sell this product, preferring to submit it to further processing.

(b) In Department 2, Bonanyl is processed into the marketable product, Bonanyl-X. The relationship between Bonanyl used and Bonanyl-X produced has remained constant for several months.

(c) In Department 3, Am-Salt and the raw material colb are used to produce Colbanyl, a liquid propellant. As an inevitable part of this process, Demanyl is also produced. Demanyl was discarded as scrap until discovery of its usefulness as a catalyst in the manufacture of glue. For two years, Matson has been able to sell all of its Demanyl production.

In its financial statements, the company states inventory at the lower of cost (on the first-in, first-out basis) or market. Unit costs of the items most recently produced must therefore be computed. The cost allocated to Demanyl is computed so that after allowing $.04 per pound for packaging and selling costs, no profit or loss will be recognized on sales of this product.

The following data on October production and inventories are available:

Raw materials	Pounds Used	Total Cost
Amanic acid............................	6,300	$5,670
Bonyl hydroxide.....................	9,100	6,370
Colb.......................................	5,600	2,240

Conversion costs (labor and factory overhead)	Total Cost
Department 1...	$33,600
Department 2...	3,306
Department 3...	22,400

	Pounds Produced	Inventories in Pounds September 30	Inventories in Pounds October 31	Sales Price per Pound
Amanyl..........................	3,600	—	—	$ 6.65
Bonanyl........................	2,800	210	110	—
Am-Salt........................	7,600	400	600	6.30
Bonanyl-X....................	2,755	—	—	4.20
Colbanyl.......................	1,400	—	—	43.00
Demanyl.......................	9,800	—	—	.54

Required: Prepare schedules for the following items for October, with supporting computations prepared in good form and answers rounded to the nearest cent:

(1) Cost per pound of Amanyl, Bonanyl, and Am-Salt produced, using the market or sales value method.

(2) Cost per pound of Amanyl, Bonanyl, and Am-Salt produced, using the average unit cost method.

(3) Cost per pound of Colbanyl produced, assuming that the cost per pound of Am-Salt produced was $3.45 in September and $3.55 in October.

(AICPA adapted)

6-5. Joint product and by-product cost allocation—market value method. Dot Corporation grows, processes, cans, and sells three main pineapple products—sliced pineapple, crushed pineapple, and pineapple juice. The outside skin is cut off in the Cutting Department and processed as animal feed. The skin is treated as a by-product. Dot's production process is as follows:

(a) Pineapples first are processed in the Cutting Department. The pineapples are washed and the outside skin is cut away. Then the pineapples are cored and trimmed for slicing. The three main products (sliced, crushed, and juice) and the by-product (animal feed) are recognizable after processing in the Cutting Department. Each product is then transferred to a separate department for final processing.

(b) The trimmed pineapples are forwarded to the Slicing Department where they are sliced and canned. Any juice generated during the slicing operation is packed in the cans with the slices.

(c) The pieces of pineapple trimmed from the fruit are diced and canned in the Crushing Department. Again, the juice generated during this operation is packed in the can with the crushed pineapple.

(d) The core and the surplus pineapple generated from the Cutting Department are pulverized into a liquid in the Juicing Department. As the juices are heated, there is an evaporation loss equal to 8% of the weight of the good output produced in this department.

(e) The outside skin is chopped into animal feed in the Feed Department.

Dot Corporation uses the market value method to assign the cost of the joint process to its main products. The by-product is inventoried at its market value reduced by after-split-off processing cost, i.e., using the net revenue method.

A total of 270,000 pounds were entered into the Cutting Department during May. The schedule presented below shows the cost incurred in each department, the proportion by weight transferred to the four final processing departments, and the sales price of each end product:

Department	Cost Incurred	Proportion by Weight Transferred to Departments	Sales Price per Pound of End Product
Cutting	$60,000	—	—
Slicing	4,700	35%	$.60
Crushing	10,580	28	.55
Juicing	3,250	27	.30
Animal feed	700	10	.10
Total	$79,230	100%	

Required:

(1) (a) Compute the pounds of pineapple that result as output for pineapple slices, crushed pineapple, pineapple juice, and animal feed.

(b) Compute the hypothetical market value at the split-off point for the three main products.

(c) Compute the amount of the Cutting Department cost apportioned to the by-product and to each of the three main products in accordance with company policy.

(d) Compute the gross profit (revenue less total production cost) for each of the three main products.

(2) Comment on the significance to management of the gross profit information for main products.   *(ICMA adapted)*

6-6. Cost of production report—fifo process costing method; joint products and by-product. The following data were gathered from the records of Rodomontade Company for February:

	Process		
	1	2	3
Unit data:			
Beginning work in process inventory			
(⅓ complete in Processes 2 and 3)	—	3,000	3,000
Started or received	32,000	10,000	20,000
	32,000	13,000	23,000
Transferred to Process 2	10,000	—	—
Transferred to Process 3	20,000	—	—
Transferred to finished goods storeroom	—	9,000	20,000
Transferred out as by-product	2,000	—	—
Normal loss (all from units transferred in during February)	—	—	1,000
Ending work in process inventory (¼ complete in			
Process 2 and ½ complete in Process 3)	—	4,000	2,000
	32,000	13,000	23,000
Partial summary of costs:			
Beginning work in process inventory	—	$ 8,000	$14,500
Cost added by department:			
Materials	$58,000	—	—
Labor and factory overhead	30,000	18,000	60,000
	$88,000		
Less market value of by-product	4,000		
	$84,000		

Materials are issued in Process 1. At the end of processing in Process 1, the by-product appears and the balance of production is transferred to Process 2 for additional processing of one main product and to Process 3 for additional processing of the other main product.

The joint cost of Process 1, less the market value of the by-product, is apportioned to the main products using the market value method at the split-off point. Sales prices for the finished products of Processes 2 and 3 are $10 and $15, respectively. The by-product sells for $2. The company uses the fifo costing method.

Required: Prepare a departmental cost of production report for February. (Carry unit cost computations to four decimal places and round off the adjusted cost from preceding department unit cost to the nearest cent.)

6-7. Cost of production report—fifo process costing method; joint products and by-product. Colloid Chemical Company produces two principal products known as XO and MO. Incidental to this process is the production of a by-product known as Bypo. The company has three producing departments, which it identifies as Departments 101, 201, and 301. Raw materials A and B are started in process in Department 101. Upon completion of processing in that department, one fifth of the material is by-product and is transferred directly to stock. One third of the remaining output of Department 101 goes to Department 201, where it is made into XO, and the other two thirds goes to Department 301, where it becomes MO. The processing of XO in Department 201 results in a 50% gain in weight of materials transferred into the department due to the addition of water at the start of the processing. There is no gain or loss of weight in the other processes.

The company considers the income from Bypo, after allowing $.05 per pound for estimated selling and delivery costs, to be a reduction of the costs of the two principal products. The company assigns Department 101 costs to the two principal products in proportion to their net sales value at the point of separation, computed by deducting costs to be incurred in subsequent processes from the sales value of the products.

The following information concerns operations during April:

Inventories	March 31		April 30
	Quantity (Pounds)	Cost	Quantity (Pounds)
Department 101.............................	—	—	—
Department 201.............................	800	$17,160	1,000
Department 301.............................	200	2,340	360
Finished stock—XO.........................	300	7,260	80
Finished stock—MO........................	1,200	18,550	700
Finished stock—Bypo.....................	—	—	—

Inventories in process are estimated to be one-half complete in Departments 201 and 301, both at the beginning and at the end of the month. The company uses the fifo method for inventory costing.

Costs	Materials Used	Labor and Factory Overhead
Department 101.....................	$134,090	$87,418
Department 201.....................	—	31,950
Department 301.....................	—	61,880

The materials used in Department 101 weighed 18,000 pounds.

Sales Prices

XO —$29.50 per pound
MO — 17.50 per pound
Bypo— .50 per pound

Prices as of April 30 are unchanged from those in effect during the month.

Required: Prepare a departmental cost of production report for April. (Carry unit cost computations to three decimal places and round off cost amounts to the nearest dollar.)
(AICPA adapted)

CASE

Joint cost analysis for managerial decisions. Talor Chemical Company is a highly diversified chemical processing company. The company manufactures swimming pool chemicals, chemicals for metal processing companies, specialized chemical compounds for other companies, and a full line of pesticides and insecticides.

Currently, the Noorwood plant is producing two derivatives, RNA-1 and RNA-2, from the chemical compound VDB developed by Talor's research labs. Each week 1,200,000 pounds of VDB is processed at a cost of $246,000 into 800,000 pounds of RNA-1 and 400,000 pounds of RNA-2. The proportion of these two outputs from this joint process is fixed and cannot be altered. RNA-1 has no market value until it is converted into a product with the trade name Fastkil. The cost to process RNA-1 into Fastkil is $240,000. Fastkil wholesales at $50 per 100 pounds.

RNA-2 is sold as is for $80 per hundred pounds. However, Talor has discovered that RNA-2 can be converted into two new products through further processing. The further processing would require the addition of 400,000 pounds of compound LST to the 400,000 pounds of RNA-2. This additional joint process would yield 400,000 pounds each of DMZ-3 and Pestrol—the two new products. The additional raw materials and related processing costs would be $120,000. DMZ-3 and Pestrol would each be sold for $57.50 per 100 pounds. Talor management has decided not to process RNA-2 further, based on the analysis presented below. Talor uses the average unit cost method to allocate costs arising from joint processing.

The following analysis of the two options has been prepared:

	Sell as RNA-2	Process Further DMZ-3	Pestrol	Total
Production in pounds	400,000	400,000	400,000	
Revenue	$320,000	$230,000	$230,000	$460,000
Costs:				
VDB cost*	$ 82,000	$ 61,500	$ 61,500	$123,000
Additional raw materials (LST) and processing of RNA-2		60,000	60,000	120,000
Total cost	$ 82,000	$121,500	$121,500	$243,000
Weekly gross profit	$238,000	$108,500	$108,500	$217,000

*If RNA-2 is sold as is, the allocation basis is 1,200,000 pounds; if RNA-2 is processed further, the allocation basis is 1,600,000 pounds for VDB cost.

A new staff accountant who was to review the analysis commented that it should be revised, stating: "Product costing of products such as these should be done on a sales value basis not an average unit cost basis."

Required:

(1) Discuss whether the use of the sales value method would provide data more relevant for the decision to market DMZ-3 and Pestrol.

(2) Critique Talor's analysis and make any revisions that are necessary. The critique and analysis should indicate:
   (a) Whether Talor Chemical Company made the correct decision.
   (b) The gross savings (loss) per week of Talor's decision not to process RNA-2 further, if different from the company-prepared analysis.

(ICMA adapted)

PART

3

Planning and Control
of the Elements of Cost

CHAPTER 7

Materials: Controlling and Costing

Effective materials management is essential in order to (1) provide the best service to customers, (2) produce at maximum efficiency, and (3) manage inventories at predetermined levels to stabilize investments in inventories. Successful materials management requires the development of a highly integrated and coordinated system involving sales forecasting, purchasing, receiving, storage, production, shipping, and actual sales. Both the theory of costing materials and other inventories and the practical mechanics of cost calculations and record keeping must be considered.

Costing materials presents some important, often complex, and sometimes highly controversial questions concerning the costing of materials used in production and the cost of inventory remaining to be consumed in a future period. In financial accounting, the subject is usually presented as a problem of inventory valuation; in cost accounting, the primary problem is the determination of the cost of various materials consumed in production and a proper charge to the cost of goods sold. The discussion of materials management in this chapter deals with:

1. Procedures for materials procurement and use.
2. Materials costing methods.
3. Inventory valuation at cost or market, whichever is lower.
4. Inventory pricing and interim financial reporting.
5. Costing procedures for scrap, spoiled goods, and defective work.

▼ PROCEDURES FOR MATERIALS PROCUREMENT AND USE

Although production processes and materials requirements vary according to the size and type of industry, the cycle of procurement and use of materials usually involves the following steps:

1. *Engineering, planning,* and *routing* determine the design of the product, the materials specifications, and the requirements at each stage of operations. Engineering and planning not only determine the

150

maximum and minimum quantities to run and the bill of materials for given products and quantities, but also cooperate in developing standards where applicable.

2. The *production budget* provides the master plan from which details concerning materials requirements are eventually developed.

3. The *purchase requisition* informs the purchasing agent concerning the quantity and type of materials needed.

4. The *purchase order* contracts for appropriate quantities to be delivered at specified dates to assure uninterrupted operations.

5. The *receiving report* certifies quantities received and may report results of inspection and testing for quality.

6. The *materials requisition* notifies the storeroom or warehouse to deliver specified types and quantities of materials to a given department at a specified time or is the authorization for the storeroom to issue materials to departments.

7. The *materials ledger cards* record the receipt and the issuance of each class of materials and provide a perpetual inventory record.

Procedures for materials procurement and use involve forms and records necessary for general ledger financial accounting as well as those necessary for costing a job, process, or department, and for maintaining perpetual inventories and other statistical summaries. Some of these forms and records are identified in the flowchart on page 152, which shows procedures for purchasing, receiving, recording, and paying for materials, i.e., the procurement phase.

Purchases of Productive Materials

The actual purchase of all materials is usually made by the purchasing department headed by a general purchasing agent. In some small and medium-size companies, however, department heads or supervisors have authority to purchase materials as the need arises. In any case, systematic procedures should be in writing in order to fix responsibility and to provide full information regarding the ultimate use of materials ordered and received.

The purchasing department should (1) receive purchase requisitions for materials, supplies, and equipment; (2) keep informed concerning sources of supply, prices, and shipping and delivery schedules; (3) prepare and place purchase orders; and (4) arrange for adequate and systematic reports between the purchasing, the receiving, and the accounting departments. An additional function of the purchasing department in some enterprises is to verify and approve for payment all invoices received in response to purchase orders placed by the department. This procedure has the advantage of centralizing the verification and approval of invoices in the department that originates the purchases and that has complete information concerning items and quantities ordered, prices, terms, shipping instructions, and other conditions and details of the purchases. However, invoice verification and approval by the purchasing department may violate sound procedures and principles of

Flowchart for Purchasing, Receiving, Recording, and Paying for Materials

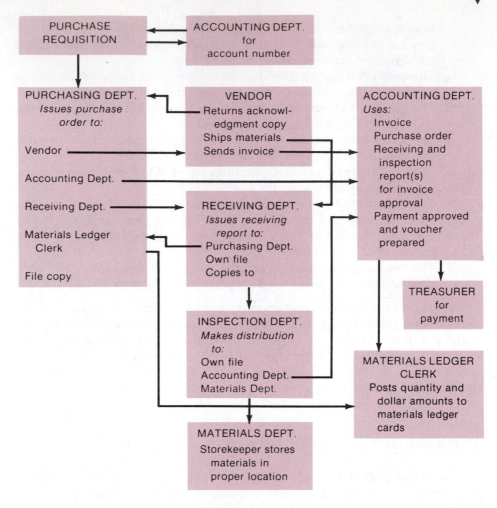

internal control, particularly if the same individual prepares an order and later approves the invoice. Consequently, invoice audit and approval in many instances have been made a function of the accounting department, which receives a copy of the purchase order. The purchase order carries all necessary information regarding price, discount agreement, and delivery stipulations, as well as the number of the account to which the order is to be charged. Furthermore, the centralization of invoice approval in the accounting department helps avoid delaying payments beyond the discount period.

Purchases of Supplies, Services, and Repairs

The procedure followed in purchasing productive materials should apply to all departments and divisions of a business. Purchase requisitions, purchase orders, and receiving reports are appropriate for accounting department supplies and equipment, the company cafeteria, the first aid unit, and the treasurer's office, as well as all other departments. If, for example, the accounting department needs new forms printed, a requisition should be sent to the purchasing department in the usual manner, and a purchase order should be prepared and sent to the printer.

In the case of magazine subscriptions, trade and professional association memberships for company officials, and similar services, the official or department head may send in a requisition in the usual manner. A requisition, an order, and an invoice for all goods and services purchased are a necessity in properly controlling purchases.

Repair contracts on an annual basis for typewriters, electronic data processing equipment, and some types of factory equipment may be requisitioned and ordered in the usual manner. In other cases, a department head or other employee may telephone for service and shortly thereafter may have a machine repaired and back in operation. In such cases, the purchasing agent issues a so-called blanket purchase order that amounts to approval of all repair and service costs of a specific type without knowing the actual amount charged. When the repair bill is received, the invoice clerk checks the amount of the bill with the head of the department where the repairs took place and then approves the invoice for payment.

Purchasing Forms

The principal forms required in purchasing are the purchase requisition and the purchase order.

Purchase Requisition. The *purchase requisition* originates with (1) a stores or warehouse clerk, who observes that the quantity on hand is at a set ordering minimum, (2) a materials ledger clerk, who may be responsible for notifying the purchasing agent when to buy, (3) a works manager, who foresees the need for special materials or unusual quantities, (4) a research, engineering, or other department employee or supervisor, who needs materials or supplies of a special nature, or (5) a computer that has been programmed to produce replenishment advice for the purchasing department. One copy remains with the originator, and the original is sent to the purchasing department for execution of the request. For standard materials, the requisition may indicate only the stock number of an item, and the purchasing agent uses judgment and established policy concerning where to buy and the quantity to order. For other purchase requests, it may be necessary to give meticulous descriptions, blueprints, catalog numbers, weights, standards, brand names, exact quantities to order, and suggested prices.

Purchase Order. The *purchase order*, signed by the purchasing agent or other official, is a written authorization to a vendor to supply specified quantities of described goods at agreed terms and at a designated time and place. As a convenience, the vendor's order forms may be used. In typical practice, however, the order forms are prepared by the purchasing company, and the form is adapted to the particular needs of the purchaser. As a matter of record and for accounting control, a purchase order should be issued for every purchase of materials, supplies, or equipment. When a purchase commitment is made by mail, telephone, or a sales representative, the purchase order serves as confirmation to the vendor and places the required documents in the hands of those concerned in the purchasing company.

The purchase order gives the vendor a complete description of the goods and services desired, the terms, the prices, and the shipping instructions. When necessary, the description may refer to attached blueprints and specification pages. The original and an acknowledgment copy are sent to the vendor. Other copies are distributed as shown in the flowchart on page 152. The vendor is asked to sign and return the acknowledgment copy to the purchaser, indicating that the order was received and will be delivered according to the specifications enumerated in the purchase order.

Receiving

The functions of the receiving department are to (1) unload and unpack incoming materials; (2) check quantities received against the shipper's packing list; (3) identify goods received with descriptions on the purchase order; (4) prepare a receiving report; (5) notify the purchasing department of discrepancies discovered; (6) arrange for inspection when necessary; (7) notify the traffic department and the purchasing department of any damage in transit; and (8) route accepted materials to the appropriate factory location.

The *receiving report* shows the purchase order number, the account number to be charged, the name of the vendor, details relating to transportation, and the quantity and type of goods received. The form also provides a space for the inspection department to note either the complete approval of the shipment or the quantity rejected and the reason for the rejection. If inspection does not take place immediately after receipt of the materials, the receiving report is distributed as follows: (1) the receiving department keeps one copy and sends another copy to the purchasing department as notice of the arrival of the materials; (2) all other copies go to the inspection department, and are distributed when inspection is completed. After inspection, one copy of the receiving report, with the inspection result noted thereon, is sent to the accounting department, where it is matched with the purchase order and the vendor's invoice and then paid. Other copies go to various departments such as materials and production planning. One copy accompanies the materials, so that the storekeeper knows the quantity and the kind of materials received.

Invoice Approval and Data Processing

By the time materials reach the receiving department, the company usually will have received the invoice from the vendor. This invoice and a copy of the purchase order are filed in the accounting department. When the receiving report with its inspection report arrives, the receiving report and the invoice are compared to see that materials received meet purchase order specifications as to items, quantities, prices, price extensions, discount and credit terms, shipping instructions, and other possible conditions. If the invoice is found to be correct or has been adjusted because of rejects as noted by the inspection department, the invoice clerk approves it, attaches it to the purchase order and the receiving report, and sends these papers to another clerk for the preparation of the voucher.

Invoice approval is an important step in materials control procedure, since it verifies that the goods have been received as ordered and that payment can be made. The verification procedure is handled by responsible invoice clerks, thus assuring systematic examination and handling of the paper work necessary for adequate control of materials purchases.

The preparation of a voucher is based on an approved invoice. The voucher data are entered first in the purchases journal and are posted to the subsidiary records. They are then entered in the cash payments journal according to the due date for payment. The original voucher and two copies are sent to the treasurer for issuance of the check. The treasurer mails the check with the original voucher to the vendor, files one copy of the voucher, and returns another copy to the accounting department for the vendor's file. Purchase transactions entered in the purchases journal affect the control accounts and the subsidiary records as shown in the chart below.

TRANSACTION	GENERAL LEDGER CONTROL		SUBSIDIARY RECORDS
	Debit	Credit	
Materials purchased for stock	Materials	Accounts Payable	Entry in the Received section of the materials ledger card
Materials purchased for a particular job or department	Work in Process	Accounts Payable	Entry in the Direct Materials section of the production report or job order cost sheet
Materials and supplies purchased for factory overhead purposes	Materials	Accounts Payable	Entry in the Received section of the materials ledger card
Supplies purchased for marketing and administrative offices	Materials Marketing Expenses Control Administrative Expenses Control	Accounts Payable	Entry in the Received section of the materials ledger card or in the proper columns of the marketing or administrative expense analysis sheets
Purchases of services or repairs	Factory Overhead Marketing Expenses Control Administrative Expenses Control	Accounts Payable	Entry in the proper account columns of the expense analysis sheets
Purchases of equipment	Equipment	Accounts Payable	Entry on the equipment ledger card

Correcting Invoices

When the purchase order, receiving report, and invoice are compared, various adjustments may be needed as a result of the following circumstances:

1. Some of the materials ordered are not received and are not entered on the invoice. In this case, no adjustment is necessary, and the invoice may be approved for immediate payment. On the purchase order, the invoice clerk will make a notation of the quantity received in place of the quantity ordered. If the vendor is out of stock or otherwise unable to deliver specified merchandise, an immediate ordering from other sources may be necessary.

2. Items ordered are not received but are entered on the invoice. In this situation, the shortage is noted on the invoice and is deducted from the total before payment is approved. A letter to the vendor explaining the shortage is usually in order.

3. The seller ships a quantity larger than called for on the purchase order. The purchaser may keep the entire shipment and add the excess to the invoice, if not already invoiced; or the excess may be returned or held, pending instructions from the seller. Some companies issue a supplementary purchase order that authorizes the invoice clerk to pay the overshipment.

4. Materials of a wrong size or quality, defective parts, and damaged items are received. If the items are returned, a correction on the invoice should be made before payment is approved. It may be advantageous to keep damaged or defective shipments if the seller makes adequate price concessions, or the items may be held subject to the seller's instructions.

5. It may be expedient for a purchaser to pay transportation charges, even though delivered prices are quoted and purchases are not made on this basis. The amount paid by the purchaser is deducted on the invoice, and the paid freight bill is attached to the invoice as evidence of payment.

Electronic Data Processing for Materials Purchases

The preceding description of invoice approval and payment was for a manual operation performed by an accounts payable clerk or an invoice clerk. In an electronic data processing (EDP) system, the computer—to a great extent—replaces the clerk. Upon receipt of the invoice (the source document), the accounts payable clerk enters the account distribution on the invoice. The data are then directly inputted from the invoice to the computer data bank via a terminal device. The data are edited, audited, and merged with the purchase order and the receiving order data, both of which have been stored in the computer data bank. The common matching criterion on all documents is the purchase order number. Quantities, dollar values, due dates, terms, and unit prices are matched. When in agreement, the cost data are entered in the accounts payable computer file with a date for later payment, or a printout of a check is transmitted for payment. Listings in journal form can be produced as needed.

The above procedure deals with the accounts payable phase of a purchase transaction. Of equal importance is the need for posting the data in quantities and dollar values to the materials inventory file in the EDP system. The information enters the EDP system from either the invoice or the invoice approval form, which would have to include all computer-necessary data. The internal computer program updates the materials inventory file. The withdrawal of materials could also be computerized, so that manual postings to the materials inventory file, as well as other manual operations, would be eliminated.

Cost of Acquiring Materials

A guiding principle in accounting for the cost of materials is that all costs incurred in entering a unit of materials into factory production should be included. Acquisition costs, such as the vendor's invoice price and transportation charges, are visible costs of the purchased goods. Less obvious costs of materials entering factory operations are costs of purchasing, receiving, unpacking, inspecting, insuring, storing, and general and cost accounting.

Controversial concepts and certain practical limitations result in variations in implementing the principles of costing materials, even with respect to easily identified acquisition costs. Calculating a number of cost additions and adjustments to each invoice involves clerical expenses which may be greater than benefits derived from the increased accuracy. Therefore, materials are commonly carried at the invoice price paid the vendor, although all acquisition costs and price adjustments affect the materials cost. As a result, acquisition costs are generally charged to factory overhead when it is not practical to follow a more accurate costing procedure.

Purchases Discounts. The handling of discounts on purchases is a problem in accounting for materials costs. Trade discounts and quantity discounts normally are not on the accounting records but are treated as price reductions. Cash discounts should be handled as price adjustments but at times are accounted for as other income, although income is not produced by buying. A lower purchase cost may well widen the margin between sales price and cost, but it takes the sale to produce income. When the vendor quotes terms such as 2/10, n/30 on a $100 invoice, is the sales price $100 or $98? The purchaser has two dates to make payment: on the tenth day, which allows time to receive, unpack, inspect, verify, voucher, and pay for the goods; or twenty days later. For the additional twenty days, an additional charge or penalty of 2 percent is assessed. If regarded as interest, the extra charge is 36 percent per year [(360 days ÷ 20 days) × 2%]. On these terms the seller is pricing on essentially a cash basis, and the purchaser has no reasonable choice except to buy on the cash basis.

Although the nature of a purchases discount is readily understood, for practical reasons the gross materials unit cost of the invoice may be recorded in the materials account and the cash discount recorded as a credit account item. Otherwise it would be necessary to compute the discount on each item, with unit costs having four or more decimal places.

Freight In. Freight or other transportation charges on incoming shipments are obviously costs of materials, but differences occur in the allocation of these charges. A vendor's invoice for $600 may show 25 items, weighing 1,700 pounds, shipped in five crates, with the attached freight bill showing a payment of $48. The delivered cost is $648. But how much of the freight belongs to each of the invoice items, and what unit price should go on the materials ledger card? When the purchased units are not numerous and are large in size and unit cost, computation of actual amounts of freight may be feasible; otherwise, some logical, systematic, and expedient procedure is necessary.

If freight charges are debited to Materials, the total amount should be added proportionately to each materials card affected. This might be done by assuming that each dollar of materials cost carries an equal portion of the freight. For example, freight of $48 on materials costing $600 would add $.08 ($48 ÷ $600) to each dollar on the invoice. The relative weight of each item on the invoice might be determined and used as a basis for calculating the applicable freight. If an invoice item is estimated to weigh 300 pounds, then $8.47 [(300 ÷ 1,700) × $48] would be added for freight. This procedure is also likely to result in unit costs having four or more decimal places on the materials ledger cards.

To simplify procedures, all freight costs on incoming materials and supplies may be charged to Freight In. As materials are issued for production, an applied rate for freight in might be added to the unit price on the ledger cards. The same amount is included in the debit to Work in Process or Factory Overhead (Indirect Materials), and Freight In is credited. Any balance in Freight In at the end of a period is closed to Cost of Goods Sold or prorated to Cost of Goods Sold and inventories.

Another method of accounting for incoming freight costs on materials is to estimate the total for an accounting period and include this amount in computing the factory overhead rate. Freight In would then become one of the accounts controlled by Factory Overhead. For materials or supplies used in marketing and administrative departments, freight, transportation, or delivery costs should be charged to the appropriate nonmanufacturing account.

Applied Acquisition Costs. If it is decided that the materials cost should include other acquisition costs as well, an applied rate might be added to each invoice and to each item, instead of charging these costs directly to factory overhead. A single rate for these costs could be used, but a more accurate method would be to use separate rates for each class of costs, as follows:

$$\frac{\text{Estimated purchasing department cost for budget period}}{\text{Estimated number of purchases or estimated amount of purchases}} = \begin{array}{l}\text{Rate per purchase or} \\ \text{rate per dollar purchased}\end{array}$$

$$\frac{\text{Estimated receiving department cost for budget period}}{\text{Estimated number of items to be received during period}} = \text{Rate per Item}$$

$$\frac{\text{Estimated materials department cost for budget period}}{\text{Estimated number of items, feet of space, dollar value, etc.}} = \begin{array}{l}\text{Rate per item, cubic} \\ \text{foot, dollar value, etc.}\end{array}$$

$$\frac{\text{Estimated applicable accounting department cost for budget period}}{\text{Estimated number of transactions}} = \begin{array}{l}\text{Rate per} \\ \text{transaction}\end{array}$$

This procedure results in the following accounting treatment:

Materials..	xxx	
Applied Purchasing Department Expenses.....................		xxx
Applied Receiving Department Expenses......................		xxx
Applied Materials Department Expenses......................		xxx
Applied Accounting Department Expenses....................		xxx

Actual expenses incurred by each of the departments for which applied rates are used will be debited to the applied accounts. Differences between the expenses incurred by the departments during the period and the expenses applied to the materials cost would represent over- or underapplied expenses and would be closed to Cost of Goods Sold or prorated to Cost of Goods Sold and inventories.

Inventory Costing for Income Tax Purposes. The Tax Reform Act of 1986 requires new inventory costing procedures.[1] The "uniform capitalization rules" require inclusion in inventory of certain costs that previously either were or could be charged to expense for tax reporting purposes. Costs such as depreciation for tax purposes in excess of the amount for financial reporting, rework labor, scrap and spoilage, materials procurement, warehousing and handling expenses, factory administrative expenses, and office salaries related to production services now must be inventoried for tax purposes. Generally, these costs are properly capitalizable for financial reporting purposes as well, with the exception of excess depreciation and conditions wherein rework labor, scrap, and spoilage are more properly expensed.

Storage and Use of Materials

Materials, together with a copy of the receiving report, are forwarded to the storeroom from the receiving or inspection department. The storekeeper and assistants are responsible for safeguarding the materials, which means that materials and supplies are placed in proper bins or other storage spaces, that they are kept safely until required in production, and that all materials taken from the storeroom are properly requisitioned. It is good policy to restrict

---

[1]*Internal Revenue Code of 1986*, Section 263A.

admittance to the storeroom to employees of that department only and to have these employees work behind locked doors, issuing materials through cage windows.

Since the cost of storing and handling materials may be substantial, careful design and arrangement of storerooms can result in significant cost savings. Materials can be stored according to (1) the materials account number; (2) the frequency of use of the item; (3) the factory area where the item is used; or (4) the nature, size, and shape of the item. In practice, no single base is likely to be suitable, but the size and shape of materials usually dictate the basic storeroom arrangement. Variations can then be introduced, such as placing the most frequently used items nearest the point of issue and locating materials used primarily in one factory area nearest that area.

Bin cards or *stock cards* are effective ready references that may be attached to storage bins, shelves, racks, or other containers. Bin cards usually show quantities of each type of material received, issued, and on hand. They are not a part of the accounting records as such, but they show the quantities on hand in the storeroom at all times and should agree with the quantities on the materials ledger cards in the accounting department.

Issuing and Costing Materials

To control the quantity and cost of materials, supplies, and services requires a systematic and efficient system of purchasing, recording, and storing. Equally necessary is a systematic and efficient procedure for issuing materials and supplies.

Materials Requisition. The *materials requisition* is a written order to the storekeeper to deliver materials or supplies to the place designated or to give the materials to the person presenting a properly executed requisition. It is drawn by someone who has the authority to requisition materials for use in the department. The authorized employee may be a production control clerk, a department head, a supervisor, a group leader, an expediter, or a materials release analyst.

The materials requisition is the basic form used to withdraw materials from the storeroom. Its preparation results in entries in the Issued section of the materials ledger cards and in postings to the job order cost sheets, production reports, or the various expense analysis sheets for individual departments. All withdrawals result in debits to Work in Process or to control accounts for factory overhead, marketing expenses, or administrative expenses, and in credits to Materials. A materials requisition is illustrated at the top of the next page.

Materials Requisitioned Journal. With the posting to the materials ledger cards, the job order cost sheets, the production reports, and the expense analysis sheets completed, it is still necessary to post the materials withdrawals to the proper ledger control accounts. This task is greatly facilitated by the use

MATERIALS REQUISITION   NO. **534871**

Deliver To Finishing Department

Requested By *Albert Baker*

Charge To Job. No. 952   Date October 23, 19--

                                                 Approved By _____

MATERIALS ACCOUNT NUMBER	QUANTITY RECEIVED	DESCRIPTION	QUANTITY ISSUED	UNIT COST	TOTAL COST
125	M	Carbon	M	$12.40	$12.40
130	M	Carbon	M	10.60	10.60
85	2M	Carbon	2M	4.50	9.00

FILLED BY	PRICED BY	ENTERED BY	RECEIVED BY	DATE RECEIVED
Hal	*WB*	*L.E.R.*	*Harry Long*	*Oct. 24*

MATERIALS LEDGER CLERK	→	COST DEPARTMENT	MATERIALS DEPARTMENT	FILE COPY

of a *materials requisitioned journal*. This journal, illustrated as follows, is a form of materials summary. At the end of the month, the totals of the various columns are posted directly to the ledger accounts, except for the Sundries column, from which items are posted individually.

MATERIALS REQUISITIONED JOURNAL

Date		Credit Materials	Description	Req. No.	Job or Acct. No.	Work in Process	Factory Overhead Control	Marketing Expenses Control	Administrative Expenses Control	Acct. No.	Post. Ref.	Amount
19-- Oct.	1	600 00	Direct materials	4101	5317	600 00						
	1	225 00	Indirect materials	4102	411		225 00					
	3	1,800 75	Direct materials	4103	5318	1,800 75						
	3	195 50	For installation	4104						135	✓	195 50
	4	75 00	Supplies	4105	630				75 00			
	4	112 80	Supplies	4106	530			112 80				
		41,160 90				36,400 00	2,280 00	1,525 40	760 00			195 50

Electronic Data Processing for Materials Requisitions. With the use of electronic data processing, materials requisition transactions would be inputted from the materials requisition form to the computer data bank. The computer program would produce a materials summary, similar to the materials requisitioned journal, as well as postings to the appropriate subsidiary ledger and ledger control accounts.

Bill of Materials. The *bill of materials,* a kind of master requisition, is a printed or duplicated form that lists all materials and parts necessary for a typical job or production run. Time is saved and efficiency is promoted through the use of a bill of materials. When a job or production run is started, all the materials listed on the bill of materials are sent to the factory or are issued on a prearranged time schedule. The bill of materials is a rather cumbersome medium for posting purposes, however, electronic data processing improves the procedure. A computer program will provide the printouts of the bill of materials and process the information internally to update the accounting records.

Just-in-Time Inventory Procedures. Manufacturing processes are increasingly being based on the receipt of raw materials from suppliers "just-in-time" for their use on the plant floor. When a firm's raw materials can be handled in this immediate use mode, the traditional storeroom receipt, storage, and issuance procedures are abbreviated. Storage, except for brief periods directly on the plant floor, is eliminated. Receipt and issuing documentation can be combined. As a result, there is a savings in paperwork and, more importantly, a savings in inventory investment, storage, and handling costs.

Materials Ledger Card—Perpetual Inventory

As purchased materials go through the systematic verification of quantities, prices, physical condition, and other checks, the crux of the accounting procedure is to establish a perpetual inventory—maintaining for each type of materials a record showing quantities and prices of materials received, issued, and on hand. In a perpetual inventory system, an entry is made each time the inventory is increased or reduced.

Materials ledger cards or stock ledger sheets constitute a subsidiary materials ledger controlled by the materials or inventory accounts in the general ledger. Materials ledger cards commonly show the account number, description or type of material, location, unit measurement, and maximum and minimum quantities to carry. These cards are the *materials ledger,* with new cards prepared and old ones discarded as changes occur in the types of materials carried in stock. The ledger card arrangement is basically the familiar debit, credit, and balance columns under the description of Received, Issued, and Balance, and is illustrated at the top of the next page.

The approved invoice with supporting documents, such as the purchase order and receiving report, goes to the materials ledger clerk. These documents enable the clerk to make the necessary entries in the Received section of the materials ledger card. Each receipt increases the balance on hand, and the new balance is extended upon entry of the receipt.

Unsatisfactory goods or defective units should be detected by the inspection department before being stored or even paid for. The receiving report should show materials actually accepted, and the ledger entries are

MATERIALS LEDGER CARD

Piece or Part No. _____ Reorder Point _____

Description _____ Reorder Quantity _____

Maximum Quantity _____

	Received				Issued				Balance		
Date	Rec. No.	Qty.	Amount	Date	Req. No.	Qty.	Amount	Quantity	Unit Cost	Amount

made after all adjustments. However, goods accepted in the storeroom may be found unsatisfactory after part of a shipment has been used in the factory, and the balance may then be returned to the vendor. Since these units were entered in the Received and Balance sections of the materials ledger card when they were placed in the storeroom, an adjustment must be made. The recommended procedure is to enter the quantity and the cost of the returned shipment in brackets in the Received section and to reduce the balance accordingly.

When the storekeeper issues materials, a copy of the requisition is sent to the materials ledger clerk, who then makes an entry in the Issued section of the materials ledger card, showing the date; requisition number; job, lot, or department number; quantity; and cost of the issued materials. The new balance is computed and entered in the Balance column. As already explained, these manual operations can be performed in an EDP system based on the computer program designed for materials transactions.

Physical Inventory. The alternative to a perpetual inventory system is the periodic inventory system, whereby purchases are added to the beginning inventory, the ending (remaining) inventory is counted and costed, and the difference is considered the cost of materials issued. Regardless of whether a periodic or a perpetual inventory system is used, periodic physical counts are necessary to discover and eliminate discrepancies between the actual count and the balances on materials ledger cards. These discrepancies may be due to errors in transferring invoice data to the cards, mistakes in costing requisitions, unrecorded invoices or requisitions, or spoilage, breakage, and theft. In some enterprises, plant operations are suspended periodically during a seasonal low period or at the end of the fiscal year while a physical inventory is taken. In others, an inventory crew or members of the internal audit department make a count of one or more stock classes every day throughout the year, presumably on a well-planned schedule, so that every materials item will be inventoried at least once during the year.

Adjusting Materials Ledger Cards and Accounts to Conform to Inventory Count. When the inventory count differs from the balance on the materials ledger card, the ledger card is adjusted to conform to the actual count. If the ledger card balance shows more materials units than the inventory card, an entry is made in the Issued section, and the Balance section is reduced to equal the verified count. In case the materials ledger card balance is less than the physical count, the quantity difference may be entered in the Received section or may be entered in brackets in the Issued section, with the Balance section being increased to agree with the actual count.

In addition to the corrections on the materials ledger cards, the materials account must be adjusted for the increase or decrease. For example, if the inventory count is less than that shown on the materials ledger card, the following entry should be recorded:

	Subsidiary Record	Dr.	Cr.
Factory Overhead Control.....................................		xxxx	
Inventory Adjustment to Physical Count...	xxxx		
Materials...			xxxx

▼ MATERIALS COSTING METHODS

The ultimate objective in cost accounting is to produce accurate and meaningful figures for the cost of goods sold. These figures can be used for purposes of control and analysis and are eventually matched against revenue produced in order to determine operating income.

After the unit cost and total cost of incoming materials are entered in the Received section of a materials ledger card, the next step is to cost these materials as they move either from storeroom to factory as direct or indirect materials or from storeroom to marketing and administrative expense accounts as supplies. The more common methods of costing materials issued and inventories are:

1. First-in, first-out (fifo).
2. Average cost.
3. Last-in, first-out (lifo).
4. Other methods—such as market price at date of issue or last purchase price, and standard cost.

These methods relate to assumptions as to the flow of costs. The physical flow of units may coincide with the method of cost flow, though such a condition is not a necessary requirement. Although this discussion deals with materials inventory, the same costing methods are also applicable to work in process and finished goods inventories.

Previous discussion as well as the following illustrations assume a perpetual inventory system. Such a procedure is especially useful in enhancing materials control and is needed to accurately identify the various general and subsidiary ledger accounts to which materials issued should be charged. Cost flow assumptions other than fifo, however, may result in unit costs that differ, depending on whether the perpetual or periodic inventory system is used.

First-In, First-Out (Fifo) Method of Costing

The first-in, first-out (fifo) method of costing is used to introduce the subject of materials costing. This illustration is based on the following transactions:

Feb. 1. Beginning balance: 800 units @ $6 per unit.
   4. Received 200 units @ $7 per unit.
   10. Received 200 units @ $8 per unit.
   11. Issued 800 units.
   12. Received 400 units @ $8 per unit.
   20. Issued 500 units.
   25. Returned 100 excess units from the factory to the storeroom—to be recorded at the latest issued price (or at the actual issued price if physically identifiable).
   28. Received 600 units @ $9 per unit.

Calculations for these transactions would be as follows:

FIFO COSTING METHOD ILLUSTRATED

Feb. 1. Beginning balance	800 units	@ $6 =	$4,800	
4. Received	200	@ $7 =	1,400	
10. Received	200	@ $8 =	1,600	$7,800
11. Issued	800	@ $6 =		4,800
Balance	{200	@ $7 =	1,400	
	200	@ $8 =	1,600	3,000
12. Received	400	@ $8 =	3,200	6,200
20. Issued	{200	@ $7 =	1,400	
	300	@ $8 =	2,400	3,800
Balance	300	@ $8 =	$2,400	
25. Returned to storeroom	100	@ $8 =	800	
28. Received	600	@ $9 =	5,400	8,600
Balance	{400	@ $8 =	3,200	
	600	@ $9 =	5,400	$8,600

The fifo method of costing issued materials follows the principle that materials used should carry the actual experienced cost of the specific units used. The method assumes that materials are issued from the oldest supply in stock and that the cost of those units when placed in stock is the cost of those same units when issued. However, fifo costing may be used even though physical withdrawal is in a different order. Advantages claimed for the fifo costing method are:

1. Materials used are drawn from the cost records in a logical and systematic manner.
2. Movement of materials in a continuous, orderly, single-file manner represents a condition necessary to and consistent with efficient materials control, particularly for materials subject to deterioration, decay, and quality or style changes.

The fifo method is recommended whenever (1) the size and cost of materials units are large, (2) materials are easily identified as belonging to a particular purchased lot, and (3) not more than two or three different receipts of the materials are on a materials card at one time. Fifo costing is definitely awkward if frequent purchases are made at different prices and if units from several purchases are on hand at the same time. Additional costing difficulties arise when returns to vendors or to the storeroom occur.

Average Costing Method

Issuing materials at an average cost assumes that each batch taken from the storeroom is composed of uniform quantities from each shipment in stock at the date of issue. Often it is not feasible to mark or label each materials item with an invoice price in order to identify the used unit with its acquisition cost. It may be reasoned that units are issued more or less at random as far as the specific units and the specific costs are concerned and that an average cost of all units in stock at the time of issue is a satisfactory measure of materials cost. However, average costing may be used even though the physical withdrawal is in an identifiable order. If materials tend to be made up of numerous small items low in unit cost and especially if prices are subject to frequent change, average costing is advantageous because:

1. It is a realistic costing method useful to management in analyzing operating results and appraising future production.
2. It minimizes the effect of unusually high or low materials prices, thereby making possible more stable cost estimates for future work.
3. It is a practical and less expensive perpetual inventory system.

The average costing method divides the total cost of all materials of a particular class by the number of units on hand to find the average price. The cost of new invoices is added to the total in the Balance column; the units are added to the existing quantity; and the new total cost is divided by the new quantity to arrive at the new average cost. Materials are issued at the established average cost until a new purchase is recorded. Although a new average cost may be computed when materials are returned to vendors and when excess issues are returned to the storeroom, for practical purposes it seems sufficient to reduce or increase the total quantity and cost, allowing the unit price to remain unchanged. When a new purchase is made and a new average is computed, the discrepancy created by the returns will be absorbed.

Using the data of the fifo illustration (page 165), the transactions can be summarized as shown at the top of the next page.

To insure quick costing and early reporting of completed jobs or products, some companies at the close of each month establish an average cost for each kind of material on hand and use this cost for all issues during the following month. When perpetual inventory costing procedures are not used, a variation of this method is to wait until the end of a costing period to compute the cost of materials consumed. The cost used is obtained by adding both quantities and dollars of purchases to beginning inventory figures, thus deriving an average cost.

AVERAGE COSTING METHOD ILLUSTRATED

				Average Cost
Feb. 1. Beginning balance............................	800 units @ $6	= $4,800		
4. Received..	200	@ $7	= 1,400	
Balance..	1,000		6,200	$6.20
10. Received..	200	@ $8	= 1,600	
Balance..	1,200		7,800	6.50
11. Issued..	800	@ $6.50 =	5,200	
Balance..	400		2,600	6.50
12. Received..	400	@ $8	= 3,200	
Balance..	800		5,800	7.25
20. Issued..	500	@ $7.25 =	3,625	
Balance..	300		2,175	7.25
25. Returned to storeroom......................	100		725	
Balance..	400		2,900	7.25
28. Received..	600	@ $9	= 5,400	
Balance..	1,000		$8,300	8.30

Last-In, First-Out (Lifo) Method of Costing

The last-in, first-out (lifo) method of costing materials issued is based on the premise that materials units issued should carry the cost of the most recent purchase, although the physical flow may actually be different. The method assumes that the most recent cost (the approximate cost to replace the consumed units) is most significant in matching cost with revenue in the income determination process.

Under lifo procedures, the objective is to charge the cost of current purchases to work in process or other operating expenses and to leave the oldest costs in the inventory. Several alternatives can be used to apply the lifo method. Each procedure results in different costs for materials issued and the ending inventory, and consequently in a different profit. It is mandatory, therefore, to follow the chosen procedure consistently.

The fifo data on page 165 are used to illustrate lifo costing, as shown at the top of the next page.

In this illustration, a new inventory balance is computed after each issue of materials, with the ending inventory consisting of 1,000 units costed at $7,800. If, however, a periodic rather than a perpetual inventory procedure is used, whereby the issues are determined at the end of the period by ignoring day-to-day issues and subtracting total ending inventory from the total of the beginning balance plus the receipts, the ending inventory would consist of:

800 units @ $6, on hand in the beginning inventory......................	$4,800
200 units @ $7, from the oldest purchase, Feb. 4........................	1,400
1,000 units, lifo inventory at the end of February.............................	$6,200

LIFO COSTING METHOD ILLUSTRATED

Feb. 1. Beginning balance............................	800 units	@ $6 =	$4,800	
4. Received..	200	@ $7 =	1,400	
10. Received..	200	@ $8 =	1,600	$7,800
	⎧ 200	@ $8 =	1,600	
11. Issued..	⎨ 200	@ $7 =	1,400	
	⎩ 400	@ $6 =	2,400	5,400
Balance.................................	400	@ $6 =	2,400	
12. Received..	400	@ $8 =	3,200	5,600
	⎰ 400	@ $8 =	3,200	
20. Issued...	⎱ 100	@ $6 =	600	3,800
Balance.................................	300	@ $6 =	1,800	
25. Returned to storeroom......................	100	@ $6 =	600	
28. Received..	600	@ $9 =	5,400	7,800
	⎰ 400	@ $6 =	2,400	
Balance.................................	⎱ 600	@ $9 =	5,400	$7,800

Both procedures are often referred to as the *item-layer identification method* of applying lifo and are acceptable variations of the lifo method, even though the cost of materials used and the ending inventory figures differ.

Regardless of the cost flow assumption, the latter procedure is particularly appropriate in process costing where individual materials requisitions are seldom used and the materials move into process in bulk lots, as in flour mills, spinning mills, oil refineries, and sugar refineries. The procedure also functions smoothly for a company that charges materials to work in process from month-end consumption sheets which provide the cost department with quantities used.

Lifo Advantages and Disadvantages. The advantages of the lifo costing method are:

1. Materials consumed are priced in a systematic and realistic manner. It is argued that current acquisition costs are incurred for the purpose of meeting current production and sales requirements; therefore, the most recent costs should be charged against current production and sales.
2. Unrealized inventory gains and losses are minimized, and reported periodic operating profits are stabilized in industries subject to sharp materials price fluctuations.
3. Inflationary prices of recent purchases are charged to operations in periods of rising prices, thus reducing profits, resulting in a tax saving, and therewith providing a cash advantage through deferral of income tax payments. The tax deferral creates additional working capital as long as the economy continues to experience an annual inflation rate increase.

The disadvantages of the lifo costing method are:

1. In a period of declining volume and/or disinflation, the lifo method will result in increasing profits, thus increasing taxes and therewith causing

a cash disadvantage. This same phenomenon may occur in high-technology companies because the effect of rapid technological improvements means that the first costs may be higher than the last costs; hence, the fifo method may actually result in a lower taxable income (and cash savings) than lifo.[2]

2. The election of lifo for income tax purposes is binding for all subsequent years unless a change is authorized or required by the Internal Revenue Service (IRS).[3]

3. Lifo is a "cost only" method, with no write-down to the lower of cost or market allowed for income tax purposes. Furthermore, the IRS requires that when lifo is adopted, an adjustment must be made to restore any previous write-downs from actual cost. Should the market fall below lifo cost in subsequent years, the business would be at a tax disadvantage. When prices drop, the only option may be to charge off the older (higher) costs by liquidating the inventory. However, liquidation for income tax purposes must take place at year end. According to IRS regulations, liquidation during the fiscal year is not acceptable if the inventory returns to its original level at the end of the year.[4]

4. Lifo must be used in financial statements if it is elected for income tax purposes. However, for financial reporting purposes, the lower of lifo cost or market can be used without violating IRS lifo conformity rules.[5]

5. Record keeping requirements under lifo, as well as fifo, are substantially greater than those under alternative costing and pricing methods.

6. Under lifo, the balance sheet reflects the earliest inventory costs incurred. Consequently, in periods of rising prices, the company's inventory, current and total assets, and stockholders' equity are understated.

7. End-of-period variations in the level of inventory purchases can permit income manipulation, using lifo procedures, that would not occur with the use of fifo.

Since the use of lifo reduces profits during periods of rising prices, managers whose rewards are based on immediate profits may not be inclined to use lifo. Therefore, if lifo is in the best interests of the firm, it may be necessary to modify the management reward system.

Dollar-Value Lifo. The item-layer identification method and the previous illustrations of the characteristics of lifo costing are generally not practicable for a company that has a wide variety of inventory items. The item-layer identification method is also particularly unsuitable for a company whose range or mix of inventory frequently changes. Use of this method under such

[2]Eugene H. Flegm, *Accounting: How to Meet the Challenges of Relevance and Regulation* (New York: John Wiley & Sons, Inc., 1984), p. 191.
[3]*Internal Revenue Code of 1986*, Section 472(e).
[4]*Regulations*, Section 1.472-2(b), (c), and (d).
[5]*Regulations*, Section 1.472-2(e) (1) and (7).

conditions virtually ensures frequent liquidation of lifo layers and a corresponding loss of the benefits from using lifo. As a result, companies in using lifo may employ some version of the *dollar-value lifo method* for financial reporting and for income tax purposes.[6] This method reduces the cost of administering lifo and reduces the likelihood of liquidating lifo layers. Also, the income tax savings during periods of rising prices is greater if dollar-value lifo is used, rather than the item-layer identification method. Thus, units issued to jobs or products are costed according to the company's established cost flow assumptions, whatever they may be, for internal costing purposes, and inventories are adjusted to dollar-value lifo figures for financial reporting and for income tax purposes.

The distinguishing feature of the dollar-value method is that similar inventory items are grouped into a pool and layers are determined, based upon the pool's total dollar changes. Under this method, year-end inventory costed at current prices is first adjusted to its base period cost, using the current period price index. The inventory change is then determined by comparing the ending inventory measured in base period dollars with the beginning inventory measured in base period dollars. Increases are adjusted back to current cost, using the current year price index, and are then added to the prior year's reported inventory. Decreases are adjusted by using the price index in effect when the depleted inventory layer was added to inventory and are then subtracted from the prior year's reported inventory.[7]

Other Materials Costing Methods

Although fifo, average cost, and lifo are commonly used methods of costing materials units into work in process, various other methods exist.

Market Price at Date of Issue or Last Purchase Price. Materials precisely standardized and traded on commodity exchanges, such as cotton, wheat, copper, or crude oil, are sometimes costed into production at the quoted price at date of issue. In effect, this procedure substitutes replacement cost for experienced or consumed cost and has the virtue of charging materials into production at a current and significant cost. This method of materials costing and that of using the last purchase price are often used for small, low-priced items.

Standard Cost. This method charges issued materials at a predetermined or estimated cost reflecting a normal or an expected future cost. Receipts and issues of materials are recorded in quantities only on the materials ledger cards or in the computer data bank, thereby simplifying the record keeping and reducing clerical or data processing costs.

---

[6]*Regulations*, Section 1.472-8.

[7]For a detailed discussion of dollar-value lifo, retail-dollar-value lifo, and other simplifying procedures, see Jay M. Smith, Jr. and K. Fred Skousen, *Intermediate Accounting*, 9th ed. (Cincinnati: South-Western Publishing Co., 1987), Chapter 9.

For materials purchases, the difference between actual and standard cost is recorded in a purchase price variance account. The variance account enables management to observe the extent to which actual materials costs differ from planned objectives or predetermined estimates. Materials are charged into production at the standard price, thereby eliminating the erratic costing inherent in the actual cost methods. Standard quantities for normal production runs at standard prices enable management to detect trouble areas and take corrective action immediately. Materials pricing under standard costs is discussed in Chapters 17 and 18.

Analysis and Comparison of Costing Methods

The several methods of costing materials represent industry's intense effort to measure costs. Undoubtedly, there is no one best method applicable to all situations. Methods may vary even within the same company, since the same method need not be used for the entire inventory of a business. Whatever method of costing is chosen, it should be followed consistently from period to period.

The various costing methods represent different views of the cost concept. The best method to use is the one that most clearly reflects periodic income when consumed cost is subtracted from current revenue. Perhaps no costing method will reflect consumed materials cost with complete accuracy at all times in all situations. The most appropriate method will, as nearly as possible, (1) relate current cost to current sales; (2) reflect the procurement, manufacturing, and sales policies of a particular company; and (3) carry forward to the new fiscal period a previously incurred residual cost which will be consumed in subsequent periods.

Adequate comparison of the various methods of costing is difficult and involved. However, certain generalizations can be made relative to the use of fifo, average cost, and lifo. In periods of rising prices, fifo costing will result in materials being charged out at lowest costs; lifo will result in materials being charged out at highest costs; and averaging costing will result in a figure between the two. In a period of falling prices, the reverse situation will develop, with fifo showing the highest cost of materials consumed, lifo showing the lowest cost of materials used, and average cost showing a result between the other two methods.

For internal costing purposes, the average method dominates because of the advantages already described for it and because of the awkwardness of both the fifo and lifo methods. For external purposes, i.e., for financial reporting and for income tax purposes, the lifo method is more likely to be used, largely because of the income tax advantage associated with patterns of rising prices. Lifo for external costing purposes will usually be dollar-value lifo. To restate inventory from the cost assigned for internal costing purposes to the amounts computed for external purposes, an end-of-the-period inventory adjustment is required, with the offset debited or credited to Cost of Goods Sold. The adjustment is then reversed at the beginning of the next accounting period.

CASB Costing of Materials

In accounting for government contracts to which CASB regulations apply, materials may be charged directly to a contract if the contract is specifically identified at the time of purchase or manufacture. Materials drawn from company-owned inventory can be priced using fifo, lifo, average, or the standard costing method. However, the method(s) selected must be used consistently for similar categories of materials. Furthermore, the contractor must prepare in writing the procedure for accumulating and allocating the cost of materials.[8]

Transfer of Materials Cost to Finished Production

The ultimate, intended destination of direct materials is finished products delivered to customers. The cost of materials used on each job or in each department is transferred from the materials requisition to the job order cost sheet or to the cost of production report. When the job or process is completed, the effect of materials used, as well as labor distributed and factory overhead applied, is expressed in the following entry:

Finished Goods.......................... xxxx
    Work in Process..................... xxxx

In production devoted to filling specific orders, cost sheets should provide sufficient information relative to the cost of goods sold. If a considerable portion of production is to be used for stock, a finished goods ledger is advantageous in maintaining adequate and proper control over the inventory. The finished goods ledger, controlled by the finished goods account in the general ledger, is similar in form and use to materials ledger cards.

Some production may consist of components manufactured for use in subsequent manufacturing operations. If the units move directly into these operations, the transfer is simply from one departmental work in process account to the next. However, if the components must be held in inventory, their cost should be debited to Materials and credited to Work in Process.

▼ INVENTORY VALUATION AT COST OR MARKET, WHICHEVER IS LOWER

American accounting principles follow the practice of pricing year-end inventories (materials as well as work in process and finished goods) at *cost or market, whichever is lower*. This departure from any experienced cost basis is generally defended on the grounds of conservatism. A more logical

---

[8]*Standards, Rules and Regulations, Part 411*, "Accounting for Acquisition Costs of Materials" (Washington, D.C.: Cost Accounting Standards Board, 1975), p. 226.

justification for cost or market inventory valuation is that a full stock is necessary to expedite production and sales. If physical deterioration, obsolescence, and price declines occur, or if stock when finally utilized cannot be expected to realize its stated cost plus a normal profit margin, the reduction in inventory value is an additional cost of the goods produced and sold during the period when the decline in value occurred.

Cost or Market Rules

Generally accepted accounting principles state that cost may properly be determined by any of the common methods already discussed in this chapter, but that cost must be abandoned in valuing inventory when the usefulness of goods is no longer as great as cost. This principle of *cost or residual useful cost, whichever is lower,* is described as follows:

> Where there is evidence that the utility of goods, in their disposal in the ordinary course of business, will be less than cost, whether due to physical deterioration, obsolescence, changes in price levels, or other causes, the difference should be recognized as a loss of the current period. This is generally accomplished by stating such goods at a lower level commonly designated as market.
>
> As used in the phrase lower of cost or market, the term "market" means current replacement cost (by purchase or by reproduction, as the case may be) except that:
>
> 1. Market should not exceed the net realizable value (i.e., estimated selling price in the ordinary course of business less reasonably predictable costs of completion and disposal); and
> 2. Market should not be less than net realizable value reduced by an allowance for an approximately normal profit margin.[9]

In analyzing the cost or market approach to inventory valuation, it is clear that the rules do not indicate that a replacement cost should be used for inventory value merely because it is lower than the acquisition cost figure. The real test is the usefulness of the inventory (whether it will sell at its cost). The rules in regard to inventory valuation may be interpreted as follows:

1. In principle, inventories are to be priced at cost.
2. Where cost cannot be recovered upon sale in the ordinary course of business, a lower figure is to be used.
3. This lower figure is normally market replacement cost, except that the amount should not exceed the expected sales price less a deduction for costs yet to be incurred in making the sale. On the other hand, this lower market figure should not be less than the expected amount to be realized in the sale of the goods, reduced by a normal profit margin.

To illustrate, assume that a certain commodity sells for $1; the marketing expense is 20 cents; the normal profit is 25 cents. The lower of cost or market as limited by the foregoing concepts is developed in each case as follows:[10]

---

[9] *Accounting Research and Terminology Bulletins—Final Edition* (New York: American Institute of Certified Public Accountants, 1961), pp. 30-31.

[10] Adapted from Jay M. Smith, Jr. and K. Fred Skousen, *Intermediate Accounting,* 9th ed. (Cincinnati: South-Western Publishing Co., 1987), Chapter 10.

			Market			
Case	Cost	Replace-ment Cost	Floor (Estimated Sales Price Less Costs of Completion and Disposal and Normal Profit)	Ceiling (Estimated Sales Price Less Costs of Completion and Disposal)	Market (Limited by Floor and Ceiling Values)	Lower of Cost or Market
A	$.65	$ .70	$.55	$.80	$.70	$.65
B	.65	.60	.55	.80	.60	.60
C	.65	.50	.55	.80	.55	.55
D	.50	.45	.55	.80	.55	.50
E	.75	.85	.55	.80	.80	.75
F	.90	1.00	.55	.80	.80	.80

A: Market is not limited by floor or ceiling; cost is less than market.
B: Market is not limited by floor or ceiling; market is less than cost.
C: Market is limited to floor; market is less than cost.
D: Market is limited to floor; cost is less than market.
E: Market is limited to ceiling; cost is less than market.
F: Market is limited to ceiling; market is less than cost.

The lower of cost or market procedure may be applied to each inventory item, to major inventory groupings, or to the inventory as a whole. Application of this procedure to the individual inventory items will result in the lowest inventory value. However, application to inventory groups or to the inventory as a whole may provide a sufficiently conservative valuation with less effort. The application method selected by a company must be followed consistently from period to period. The mix within a group or within the total inventory should not change erratically from period to period, so that inventory value is not distorted by the mix changes.

Adjustments for Cost or Market, Whichever Is Lower

The problem of year-end inventory valuation is primarily a question of the materials cost consumed in products manufactured and sold to customers and the cost assignable to goods in inventory ready to move into production and available for sales the next fiscal period. This question is important, because the materials ledger cards would have to be adjusted for any change in unit prices if there is a departure from cost. However, the detailed task of changing hundreds and even thousands of cards may not be possible or at least may be cumbersome and time-consuming, since the lower of cost or market procedure may be applied to inventory groups or to the inventory as a whole, and since the new unit price generally is not available to the materials ledger clerk until some time after the year-end inventory is priced. Instead of adjusting the ledger cards, companies may create an inventory valuation account, as illustrated by the following journal entry:

	Subsidiary Record	Dr.	Cr.
Cost of Goods Sold (or Factory Overhead Control)..		5,000	
Inventory Adjustment—Lower of Cost or Market..	5,000		
Materials—Allowance for Inventory Decline to Market...			5,000

If the debit is to Factory Overhead Control, the effect is to increase the amount of the unfavorable factory overhead variance.

Use of the valuation account retains the cost of the inventory and at the same time reduces the materials inventory for statement purposes to the desired cost or market, whichever is lower valuation, without disturbing the materials ledger cards. The preceding entry should result in the following balance sheet presentation:

Materials, at cost..	$100,000	
Less allowance for inventory decline to market........................	5,000	
Materials, at cost or market, whichever is lower......................		$95,000

The net charge to Cost of Goods Sold may be shown in the cost of goods sold statement or deducted from the ending inventory at cost, thus increasing the cost of materials used. In the subsequent fiscal period, Materials—Allowance for Inventory Decline to Market is closed out to Cost of Goods Sold (or Factory Overhead Control) to the extent necessary to bring the materials consumed that are still carried at a higher cost to the desirable lower cost level.

Whenever the lower of cost or market procedure is applied to each inventory item and the adjustment of materials ledger cards to a lower market figure is not burdensome and the data are available early in the next year, the adjustment should be accomplished by dating the entry with the last day of the fiscal period just ended and entering in the Balance section the units on hand at the unit price determined for inventory purposes. In such a case, the credit portion of the adjusting entry would be to the materials account.

▼ INVENTORY PRICING AND INTERIM FINANCIAL REPORTING

Companies should generally use the same inventory pricing methods and make provisions for write-downs to market at interim dates on the same basis as used at annual dates when preparing published financial statements. However, the following exceptions are appropriate at interim reporting dates:

1. Some companies use estimated gross profit rates to determine the cost of goods sold during interim periods or use other methods different from those used at annual inventory dates. These companies should disclose the method used at the interim date and any significant

adjustments that result from reconciliations with the annual physical inventory.

2. Companies that use the lifo method may encounter a liquidation of base period inventories at an interim date that is expected to be replaced by the end of the annual period. In such cases the inventory at the interim reporting date should not give effect to the lifo liquidation, and cost of sales for the interim reporting period should include the expected cost of replacement of the liquidated lifo base.

3. Inventory losses from market declines should not be deferred beyond the interim period in which the decline occurs. Recoveries of such losses on the same inventory in later interim periods of the same fiscal year through market price recoveries should be recognized as gains in the later interim period. Such gains should not exceed previously recognized losses. Some market declines at interim dates, however, can reasonably be expected to be restored in the fiscal year. Such *temporary* market declines need not be recognized at the interim date, since no loss is expected to be incurred in the fiscal year.[11]

The second exception indicates that if the liquidation of base period inventories is considered temporary and is expected to be replaced prior to year end, the company should charge Cost of Goods Sold at current prices. The difference between the carrying value of the inventory and its current replacement cost is a current liability for replacement of temporarily depleted lifo base inventory. When the liquidated inventory is replaced, inventory is debited for the original lifo value, and the liability is removed from the books.

▼ COSTING PROCEDURES FOR SCRAP, SPOILED GOODS, AND DEFECTIVE WORK

Generally, manufacturing operations cannot escape the occurrence of certain losses or output reduction due to scrap, spoilage, or defective work. Management and the entire personnel of an organization should cooperate to reduce such losses to a minimum. Indeed, an important aspect of current Japanese manufacturing success results from a philosophy that losses such as those attributable to defects can be eliminated. Advocates of this zero defect approach claim that measures to reduce these losses are cost effective because total long-term manufacturing costs decrease as the percentage of defects decreases.[12] As long as losses do occur, however, they must be accounted for and, with the aid of effective reporting, better controlled.

---

[11]*Opinions of the Accounting Principles Board, No. 28,* "Interim Financial Reporting" (New York: American Institute of Certified Public Accountants, 1973), par. 14.

[12]Robert S. Kaplan, "Measuring Manufacturing Performance: A New Challenge for Managerial Accounting Research," *The Accounting Review,* Vol. LVIII, No. 4, p. 690.

Scrap and Waste

In many manufacturing processes, waste and scrap result from (1) the processing of materials, (2) defective and broken parts, (3) obsolete stock, (4) revisions or abandonment of experimental projects, and (5) worn-out or obsolete machinery. This scrap should be collected and placed in storage for sale to scrap dealers. At the time of sale, the following entry may be made:

```
Cash (or Accounts Receivable)......................  xxxx
     Scrap Sales (or Other Income)...................          xxxx
```

The full amount realized from the sale of scrap and waste can be included in income of the period in either of two ways:

1. The amount accumulated in Scrap Sales may be closed directly to Income Summary and shown on the income statement under Scrap Sales or Other Income.
2. The amount accumulated may be credited to Cost of Goods Sold, thereby reducing the total costs charged against sales revenue for the period, which results in the same increase in income as when the amount is reported as Scrap Sales or Other Revenue.

Alternatively, the amount received for the sale of scrap may be credited to Factory Overhead Control. If the amount can be predicted (even if not exactly), it should be included in the predetermined factory overhead rate, which will reduce the total factory overhead charged to goods manufactured during the period. Even if the amount is not subject to prediction (because it is not expected to occur), it may nevertheless be credited to Factory Overhead Control with the expectation that it will reduce the amount of underapplied factory overhead or increase the amount of overapplied factory overhead for the period. In either case, the entry would be:

```
Cash (or Accounts Receivable)......................  xxxx
     Factory Overhead Control...........................          xxxx
```

When scrap is collected from a job or department, the amount realized from the sale of scrap is often treated as a reduction in the materials cost charged to the individual job or product. In this case, the entry to record the sale would be:

```
Cash (or Accounts Receivable)......................  xxxx
     Work in Process.........................................          xxxx
```

When the quantity and value of scrap material is relatively high, it should be stored in a designated place under the supervision of a storekeeper. One of the following procedures may then be used:

1. The materials ledger clerk may open a materials ledger card, filling in the quantity only. The dollar value would not be needed. When the scrap is sold, the entries and treatment of the income item might be handled as discussed previously.

2. The quantity as well as the dollar value of the scrap delivered to the storekeeper may be recorded. The value would be based on scrap prices quoted on the market at the time of entry. The entry would be:

Scrap Materials.. xxxx
    Scrap Sales (or Other Income or Factory Overhead
      Control or Work in Process)... xxxx

When the scrap is sold, the entry would be:

Cash (or Accounts Receivable)... xxxx
    Scrap Materials.. xxxx

Any difference between the price at the time the inventory is recorded and the price realized at the time of sale would be a plus or minus adjustment in the scrap sales account, the work in process account, or the factory overhead control account, consistent with the account credited in the first entry.

To reduce accounting for scrap to a minimum, often no entry is made until the scrap is actually sold. At that time, Cash or Accounts Receivable is debited, while Scrap Sales or Other Income is credited. This method is expedient and is justified when a more accurate accounting becomes expensive and burdensome, the scrap value is relatively small, or the price is uncertain.

Proceeds from the sale of scrap are in reality a reduction in production cost. As long as the amounts are relatively small, the accounting treatment is not a major consideration. What is important is an effective scrap control system based on periodic reporting to responsible supervisory personnel. Timely scrap reports for each producing department call attention to unexpected items and unusual amounts and should induce prompt corrective action.

Spoiled Goods

Cost accounting should provide product costs and cost control information. In the case of spoilage, the first requirement is to know the nature and cause of the spoiled units. The second requirement, the accounting problem, is to record the cost of spoiled units and to accumulate spoilage costs and report them to responsible personnel for corrective action.

Attaining the degree of materials and machine precision and the perfection of labor performance necessary to eliminate spoiled units entirely may, in many cases, involve incurring costs in excess of the costs of a normal or tolerable level of spoilage. The related cost vs. benefit must be considered in setting such tolerances. As a result, the occurrence of spoilage in manufacturing processes often does occur. The following discussion and illustrations of accounting for spoiled goods pertain to job order costing. The appropriate procedures for process costing were covered in Chapter 4.

Two methods of accounting for the cost of spoilage are appropriate, depending upon the circumstances. First, if spoilage is normal but does not occur at a fairly uniform rate with each job or if spoilage is abnormal and attributable to an event that is not expected to recur (for example, a setup error, an accident attributable to carelessness or inexperience, or an employee's failure to follow instructions), the cost of the spoiled units in excess of their net realizable value should be charged to Factory Overhead Control. If some or all of these costs are subject to estimation (as would likely be the case with normal spoilage, since it would be expected to recur each period), an estimated amount should be included in the predetermined factory overhead rate, based on previous experience, thereby spreading the expected cost of such spoilage over all of the jobs and products produced during the period. To the extent that such costs were not expected and thus were not included in the predetermined factory overhead rate, an unfavorable variance would be created in factory overhead for the period (i.e., the amount of underapplied factory overhead would be increased or the amount of overapplied factory overhead would be decreased).

Second, if spoilage is normal and occurs at a fairly uniform rate with each job or if spoilage is directly attributable to requirements imposed by the customer (for example, changes after the job was begun or requiring unusually close production tolerances), the cost of the spoiled units in excess of the net realizable value should be charged to the job and excluded from the overhead rate. If normal spoilage occurs fairly uniformly from job to job, the periodic amount could be estimated, based on previous experience, and included in the predetermined factory overhead rate (as should be done when spoilage does not occur uniformly from job to job). If spoilage is included in the predetermined rate, each job would be charged with a share of the cost when factory overhead is applied to the job via the predetermined rate. To avoid double charging in such a case, the unrecoverable cost of such spoilage must be determined and charged to Factory Overhead Control. Whether the cost of uniformly occurring normal spoilage is charged to the job on which it occurs or is included in the predetermined factory overhead rate, the amount charged to each good unit produced during the period will be approximately the same. However, charging such costs to the job is more economical because the cost of spoiled units need not be separately determined, removed from the job in which spoilage occurs, and then tracked over time, as would be required if spoilage were included in the predetermined factory overhead rate. If the customer is responsible for the spoilage, the job should be charged, so that the costs can be passed on to the customer during the billing process.

Spoiled Materials Charged to Total Production. Nevada Products Company has a monthly capacity to manufacture 125,000 three-inch coil springs for use in mechanical brakes. Production is scheduled in response to orders received. Spoilage is caused by a variety of unpredictable factors and averages $.05 per spring. During November, 100,000 springs were produced, with a materials cost of $.40 per unit, a labor cost of $.50 per unit, and factory overhead charged to production at a rate of 150% of the direct labor cost. This rate is based on an estimate that includes $.05 per spring for spoilage. The entry to record work put into production during the month is:

Work in Process...	165,000	
Materials...		40,000
Payroll..		50,000
Applied Factory Overhead......................		75,000

On the last working day of the month, the entire day's production of 4,000 units is spoiled due to improper heat treatment; however, these units can be sold for $.50 each in the secondhand market. To record this normal loss on spoiled goods and the possible resale value, the entry that charges all production during the period with a proportionate share of the spoilage is:

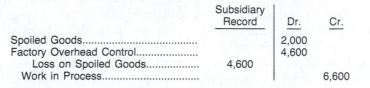

	Subsidiary Record	Dr.	Cr.
Spoiled Goods......................................		2,000	
Factory Overhead Control.....................		4,600	
Loss on Spoiled Goods.................	4,600		
Work in Process...............................			6,600

The materials, labor, and factory overhead in the spoiled units, reduced by the recovery or sales value of these units ($1,600 materials + $2,000 labor + $3,000 factory overhead − $2,000 cost recovery = $4,600 spoilage loss) is transferred from Work in Process to Factory Overhead Control. Each of the 96,000 good units produced during the month has a charged-in cost of $.05 for spoilage (96,000 × $.05 = $4,800); the actual spoilage during the period is $4,600.

The good units produced during the week or on the order where spoilage did occur carry a cost of $.40 for materials, $.50 for labor, and $.75 for overhead because spoilage is charged to all production—not to the lot or order which happens to be in process at the time of spoilage. In other words, the $165,000 monthly production cost less the $6,600 credit resulting from spoiled units leaves $158,400 to be divided by the 96,000 good units manufactured during the month at a cost of $1.65 per good unit. The entry transferring the good units to Finished Goods is:

Finished Goods...........................	158,400	
Work in Process.....................		158,400

During the month, the amounts charged to Factory Overhead Control represent the depreciation, insurance, taxes, indirect materials, and indirect labor actually experienced, along with the $4,600 spoilage cost. All production during the month is charged with overhead of $.75 per unit. Overhead analysis reveals a $200 favorable variance ($4,600 actual minus $4,800 applied) attributable to the spoilage units. Any difference between the price when the inventory was recorded and the price realized at the time of sale would be a positive or negative adjustment to Factory Overhead Control (Loss on Spoiled Goods).

Spoiled Materials Charged to a Particular Job. Nevada Products Company has a contract to manufacture 10,000 heavy-duty coil springs for Tri-State Supply Company. This order requires a steel wire that is harder and slightly heavier than stock normally used, but the production process, as well as labor time and overhead factors, is identical, with the standard product. Materials cost for each of these springs is $.60. This special order requires exacting specifications, and normal spoilage is to be charged to the order. The $.05 per unit spoilage factor is now eliminated from the overhead rate, and 140% of direct labor cost, or $.70 per unit, is the rate used on this job. The order is put into production the first day of December, and sampling during the first hour of production indicates that eleven units of production are required to secure ten good springs. The entry to record costs placed into production for 11,000 units is:

Work in Process..	19,800	
Materials...		6,600
Payroll..		5,500
Applied Factory Overhead......................		7,700

One thousand units, a normal number, did not meet specifications and are spoiled but can be sold as seconds for $.45 per unit. The entry to record the spoilage is:

Spoiled Goods..	450	
Work in Process......................................		450

The entry transferring the completed order to Finished Goods would be:

Finished Goods..	19,350	
Work in Process......................................		19,350

The net result of this treatment is to charge the spoilage loss of $1,350 ($1,800 − $450 cost recovery) to the 10,000 good units that are delivered at the original contract price. The unit cost of completed springs is $1.935 ($19,350 ÷ 10,000 units).

Any difference between the price when the inventory was recorded and the price realized at the time of sale should be an adjustment to Work in Process, Finished Goods, or Cost of Goods Sold, depending on the completion status of the particular job order. As an expedient, the difference might be closed to Factory Overhead Control.

In the situation just described, in which spoilage is charged to the particular job, the overhead rate is adjusted downward from 150% to 140%. This adjustment, which eliminates the normal spoilage unit cost factor, is the theoretically correct procedure. For expediency, however, a firm may elect not to make an adjustment in the overhead rate if such a charge to a specific job is an unusual occurrence.

Defective Work

In the manufacturing process, imperfections may arise because of faults in materials, labor, or machines. The cost of such occurrences, both before and after delivery to customers, must be compared to the related cost of their prevention. If the unit can be reprocessed in one or more stages and made into a standard salable product, it is often profitable to rework the defective unit. Although spoiled work cannot usually be made into a first-class finished unit without uneconomical expenditures, defective work can be corrected to meet specified standards by adding materials, labor, and factory overhead.

Two methods of accounting for the added cost to upgrade defective work are appropriate, depending upon the circumstances:

1. If defective work is experienced in regular manufacturing but does not occur at a fairly uniform rate from job to job or if the defective work is the result of an unusual event that is not expected to recur (for example, an employee error), the additional cost to correct the defective units should be charged to Factory Overhead Control. If the defects are normal, they can be included in the predetermined factory overhead rate, based on previous experience. When the cost is included in the predetermined factory overhead rate, all units produced during the period are charged with a portion of the rework cost as overhead is applied to production. If the cost is not included in the predetermined factory overhead rate, the cost of rework will create an unfavorable factory overhead variance.

   To illustrate, assume that a company has an order for 500 units of a product that has direct production costs of $5 for materials and $3 for labor, with factory overhead charged to production at 200% of labor cost, including a 5% allowance for reworking defective units. Fifty units are found to be defective and are to be reworked at a total cost of $30 for materials, $60 for labor, and overhead at 200% of direct labor cost. The entries are:

	Subsidiary Record	Dr.	Cr.
Work in Process.....................................		7,000	
Materials..			2,500
Payroll..			1,500
Applied Factory Overhead...................			3,000
Factory Overhead Control......................		210	
Defective Work................................	210		
Materials..			30
Payroll..			60
Applied Factory Overhead...................			120
Finished Goods.......................................		7,000	
Work in Process................................			7,000

The unit cost of the completed units is $14 ($7,000 ÷ 500 units).

2. If defective work is expected to occur at a fairly uniform rate from job to job or is directly attributable to requirements imposed by the customer, the additional cost to correct the defective units should be charged to the job. For example, suppose that the company in the preceding example received a special order for 500 units, with the agreement stating that any defective work is chargeable to the contract. During production, 50 units are improperly assembled. The total cost to correct these defective units is $30 for materials, $60 for labor, and 195% of the direct labor cost for factory overhead. Observe that the factory overhead rate has been reduced by the 5% allowance for reworking defective units, because the rework cost is to be charged directly to the job instead of to factory overhead. The entries in this case are:

Work in Process......................................	6,925	
Materials...		2,500
Payroll...		1,500
Applied Factory Overhead....................		2,925
Work in Process......................................	207	
Materials...		30
Payroll...		60
Applied Factory Overhead....................		117
Finished Goods.......................................	7,132	
Work in Process...................................		7,132

The unit cost is $14.264 ($7,132 ÷ 500 units) instead of $14. In this second case, in which the particular job is charged for defective work, the overhead rate is adjusted downward from 200% to 195%. This adjustment, which eliminates the allowance for reworking defective units from the overhead rate, is the theoretically correct procedure. For expediency, however, a firm may decide not to make an adjustment in the overhead rate if such charge to a specific job is an unusual occurrence.

▼ SUMMARY OF MATERIALS MANAGEMENT

Materials managers are constantly confronted with the following problems and requirements:

1. Inventories account for a large portion of the working capital requirements of many businesses. This fact makes materials and/or inventory management a major problem requiring constant attention by all three management levels.
2. At present, the problem of materials management has become even more acute due to market conditions and inflation.
3. Effective materials management and materials control is found in an organization in which individuals have been vested with responsibility for, and authority over, the various details of procuring, maintaining, and disposing of inventory. Such a person or persons must have the ability to obtain, coordinate, and evaluate the necessary facts and to take action when and where needed.

DISCUSSION QUESTIONS

1. List the forms most frequently used in the procurement and use of materials.

2. Should formal purchase requisitions and purchase orders be prepared for the purchase of incidental supplies, services, and repairs? Explain.

3. How is an invoice approved for payment?

4. If a firm purchases raw materials from its supplier on a 2/10, n/60 cash discount basis, what is the equivalent annual interest rate (using a 360-day year) of forgoing the cash discount?

5. Diane Company, a retailer and wholesaler of national brand name household lighting

Planning and Control of the Elements of Cost—Part 3

fixtures, purchases its inventories from various suppliers.

(a) What criteria should be used to determine which of Diane's costs are inventoriable?

(b) Are Diane's administrative costs inventoriable? Explain. *(AICPA adapted)*

6. A company's own power plant uses coal as the principal fuel. Coal is delivered by rail and stored in an open field close to the powerhouse, from which it is fed into furnaces by conveyor belts. What method should be used to determine coal consumption during a time period and the coal on hand at the end of the period?

7. Describe the fundamental cost flow assumptions of the average cost, fifo, and lifo inventory costing methods.

8. Discuss the reasons for using lifo in an inflationary economy.

9. Proponents of lifo and fifo procedures ascribe certain merits to each. Identify the inventory procedure, lifo or fifo, to which the following features are attributed:

(a) Matches actual physical flow of goods.
(b) Matches old costs with new prices.
(c) Costs inventory at approximate replacement cost.
(d) Matches new costs with new prices.
(e) Emphasizes the balance sheet.
(f) Emphasizes the income statement.
(g) Opens door for profit manipulation.
(h) Understates the current ratio in a period of inflation.
(i) Overstates inventory turnover in a period of inflation.
(j) Gives higher profits in a period of inflation.

(k) Matches current cost with current revenue.
(l) Reflects more accurately the profit available to owners.
(m) Gives lower profits in a period of deflation.
(n) Results in a procession of costs in the same order as incurred.
(CGAAC adapted)

10. Does the method of inventory costing have its principal effect on the balance sheet or on the income statement?

11. What are the theoretical arguments for inventory valuation at cost or market, whichever is lower?

12. In applying inventory valuation at cost or market, whichever is lower, the replacement cost of the inventories is below the net realizable value less a normal profit margin, which, in turn, is below the original cost. What amount should be used to value the inventories? Why?
(AICPA adapted)

13. Several methods of accounting for scrap materials are discussed in this chapter. Which method could be regarded as most accurate?

14. In the control of materials cost, why is the knowledge that there is excessive waste likely to be of greater value than the income derived from the sale of scrap?

15. In some situations, labor and materials costs incurred on defective work are treated as factory overhead. In other cases the cost of perfecting defective work is charged directly to the job. Explain the appropriate use of each accounting treatment.

EXERCISES

1. Freight-in allocation. An invoice for Pepto, Lenco, and Bilco is received from Wellright Company. Invoice totals are: Pepto, $1,125; Lenco, $1,350; Bilco, $1,575. The freight charges on this shipment of 1,800 pounds total $162. Weights for the respective materials are 450, 600, and 750 pounds.

Required:

(1) Allocate freight to materials, based on cost.
(2) Allocate freight to materials, based on shipping weight.

2. Materials costing methods. Lacy Company made the following materials purchases and issues during January:

Inventory: January 1 — 500 units @ $1.20   Issues: January 15 — 560
Receipts: January 6 — 200   @ 1.25   27 — 400
                   10 — 400   @ 1.30
                   25 — 500   @ 1.40

Required: Compute the cost of materials consumed and the cost assigned to the inventory at the end of the month, using a perpetual inventory system and:

(1) Average costing, rounding unit costs to the nearest cent.
(2) Fifo costing.
(3) Lifo costing.

3. Materials costing methods. Rosalita Company's record of transactions for October was as follows:

October 1 Beginning inventory.......................   700 units @ $5.00

Received

October	4..	300	@	5.20
	8..	300	@	5.20
	13..	1,000	@	5.10
	21..	400	@	5.50
	29..	300	@	5.60
		2,300		

Issued

October	3..	400
	9..	500
	11..	300
	23..	600
	27..	800
		2,600

Required: Compute the cost of materials used and the cost assigned to the inventory at the end of the month, using a perpetual inventory system and:

(1) Fifo costing.
(2) Lifo costing.
(3) Average costing, rounding unit costs to the nearest cent. *(CGAAC adapted)*

4. Materials costing methods. The following information is to be used in costing inventory on October 31:

October 1. Beginning balance: 800 units @ $6
         5. Purchased 200 units @ $7
         9. Purchased 200 units @ $8
        16. Issued 400 units
        24. Purchased 300 units @ $9
        27. Issued 500 units

Required: Compute the cost of materials used and the cost assigned to the October 31 inventory by each of these perpetual inventory costing methods:

(1) First-in, first-out.
(2) Last-in, first-out.
(3) Average, using a materials ledger card and rounding unit costs to the nearest cent.
(4) Market price at date of issue.

5. Average costing method—perpetual and periodic inventory costing. The following information was available from Milner Company's January inventory records:

	Units	Unit Cost	Total Cost
Balance at January 1......................	2,000	$ 9.775	$19,550
Received			
January 6...	1,500	10.300	15,450
January 26.......................................	3,400	10.750	36,550
Issued			
January 7...	1,800		
January 31.......................................	3,200		
Balance at January 31.....................	1,900		

Required: Compute the cost of materials used and the cost assigned to the January 31 inventory, using (a) perpetual inventory records and the average costing method, and (b) the periodic inventory costing system at average cost. For (b), round the unit cost to the nearest cent and add the rounding difference to the cost of materials used.

(AICPA adapted)

6. Materials costing methods. Barnes Company, a wholesaler, made the following purchases of Material X during 19A:

January 7...........................	8,000 units	@	$12.00	$ 96,000
March 30............................	8,800	@	12.40	109,120
May 10...............................	12,000	@	12.00	144,000
July 5.................................	16,000	@	12.60	201,600
September 2.......................	6,400	@	12.80	81,920
December 14......................	7,200	@	12.68	91,296
	58,400			$723,936

The December 31, 19A inventory was 15,200 units, and on January 1, 19A, 4,000 units at $11.92 each were on hand. The sales price during the year was stable at $16.

Required:

(1) Prepare a schedule of December 31, 19A inventory, assuming a periodic inventory system and lifo as the costing method.
(2) Prepare a statement showing Material X's sales, cost of goods sold, and gross profit for 19A, assuming the fifo costing method.   *(CGAAC adapted)*

7. Inventory costing method related to income computation. Ajax Company uses lifo in costing inventory. During its first three years of operations, the year-end inventory, computed by different methods for comparative purposes, was as follows:

	Ending Inventory		
	19A	19B	19C
Lifo..	$360,000	$400,000	$320,000
Fifo...	300,000	320,000	280,000
Average cost.....................	340,000	420,000	300,000

Operating income computed using the lifo method was: 19A, $80,000; 19B, $140,000; 19C, $60,000.

Required: Determine operating income, using the (a) fifo method and (b) average cost method.   *(CGAAC adapted)*

8. Fifo, lifo, and cash flow. Due to rising prices for materials, the problem of using the most appropriate inventory costing method has become acute. With the wide variety of methods available to account for inventories, it is important to select one that will be the most beneficial for a company. To illustrate, assume that two companies are almost identical, except that one uses fifo and the other lifo costing. Both companies have a beginning inventory of 200 units @ $2 per unit. The ending inventory is 240 units. The price paid for all purchases during the fiscal period was $2.40, and sales totaled 180 items at a sales price of $3.60. The income tax rate is 50% for both companies.

Required:

(1) Compute the amount of total materials available for sale.
(2) Prepare income statements showing aftertax earnings for both companies.
(3) Compute the cost assigned to the ending inventory, based on the fifo and lifo costing methods.
(4) Determine the cash position at the end of the fiscal year, assuming that all transactions, materials purchases, sales, and income tax were paid in cash.
(5) Write a brief evaluation of the results.

9. Inventory valuation at cost or market, whichever is lower. The following information has been gathered for four inventory items:

Item	Original Cost	Replacement Cost	Sales Price	Estimated Cost to Complete and Sell	Normal Profit Margin
Delta	$ .67	$ .62	$ .72	$ .04	$ .08
Sigma	2.20	2.12	2.22	.12	.08
Beta	.19	.20	.24	.03	.01
Nu	.93	.87	.97	.05	.04

Required: Determine the unit value that would be assigned to each item for inventory valuation purposes, using the lower of cost or market rules.

10. Materials costing methods and cost or market, whichever is lower. The following lots of a particular material were available for use during the year:

Beginning inventory.....................	20 units	@ $80
First purchase............................	20	@ 82
Second purchase........................	30	@ 85
Third purchase...........................	30	@ 87
Ending inventory.........................	25	

The company uses a periodic inventory system.

Required:

(1) Compute the cost assigned to ending inventory, assuming fifo as the costing method.
(2) Compute the cost assigned to ending inventory, assuming fifo as the costing method, if the current replacement cost is $86 per unit and if this replacement cost is between the ceiling and the floor of the rules for cost or market, whichever is lower.
(3) Compute the cost assigned to ending inventory, assuming the average costing method.
(4) Compute the cost assigned to ending inventory, assuming lifo as the costing method.   *(CGAAC adapted)*

11. Inventory valuation at cost or market, whichever is lower. EAH Corporation uses the lower of cost or market rules to value inventory. Data regarding items in work in process inventory are as follows:

	Inventory Item		
	Markers	Pens	Highlighters
Cost..	$12,000	$ 9,440	$15,000
Sales price..	18,000	18,000	18,000
Estimated cost to			
complete...	2,400	2,400	3,400
Replacement cost...............................	10,400	8,400	15,900
Normal profit margin as			
a percentage of sales			
price...	25%	25%	10%

Required:

(1) Identify the value for cost to be used in the lower of cost or market comparison for markers.
(2) Compute the market value to be used in the lower of cost or market comparison for pens.
(3) Determine the inventory valuation for highlighters, using the lower of cost or market method.   *(ICMA adapted)*

12. Journal entries to correct materials accounts. The following transactions were completed by Patterson Company:

(a) The inventory of materials on the average costing basis was $4,200 and represented a book quantity of 8,000 units. An actual count showed 7,780 units.
(b) Materials of $150 issued to Job 182 should have been charged to the Repair Department.
(c) Excess materials returned from the factory amounted to $382 for Job 257.
(d) Materials returned to vendor amounted to $165. Freight out on this shipment, to be borne by Patterson Company, was $14, paid in cash.
(e) Finished goods returned by customers: cost, $1,500; sales price, $2,100.
(f) Materials requisitions totaled $4,814.50, of which $214.50 represented supplies used.
(g) Materials purchased and placed in stockroom, $6,150, of which $500 represented supplies. Freight in paid, applicable to direct materials, was $70.
(h) Supplies returned to the storeroom, $150.
(i) Scrap materials sent to the storeroom, valued at sales price (debit Scrap Materials):

From direct materials.....................	$190
From supplies................................	10

(j) Spoiled work received in storeroom: original cost, $60; sales value, $20. Loss is charged to total production.

(k) Scrap was sold for $250 cash; the book value of the scrap was $200 [see (i)].

Required: Prepare the general ledger entries or adjustments, if any, for each of the above transactions. Carry all computations to three decimal places. Indicate the appropriate subsidiary ledger account for debits or credits to Factory Overhead Control.

13. Accounting for spoiled materials. Fashioncraft Company had a production run of 6,000 pairs of slacks during the last week of June. Upon completion of the run, accumulated cost figures resulted in the following journal entry:

Work in Process..	60,900	
Materials...		24,000
Payroll..		18,000
Appied Factory Overhead (105% of direct labor)......................		18,900

Inspection revealed that 500 pairs were spoiled and did not meet quality standards, but can be sold as seconds at a price of $5 a pair.

Required:

(1) Prepare the journal entry to record the spoilage, if the number of spoiled units is normal for such a production run.

(2) Prepare the journal entry to record the spoilage, if the spoilage is due to exacting specifications and is chargeable to a particular customer order, in which case the applied factory overhead for this production run would have been at 100% of direct labor.

14. Accounting for spoiled work. Alba Company had a production run of 4,000 pairs of jeans during the last week of June, with the following unit costs:

Direct materials..	$ 5.00
Direct labor..	4.00
Factory overhead (includes a $.50 allowance for spoiled work)...	3.50
	$12.50

Final inspection revealed that 300 pairs, a normal number, did not meet quality standards, but can be sold as seconds at a price of $7 a pair.

Required: Prepare journal entries for all of the described transactions if:

(1) The loss is charged to all production.

(2) The loss is due to exacting specifications and is charged to the production run.

15. Journal entries to correct defective work. Florida Fabricators manufacture golf carts and other recreational equipment. One order from Wisconsin Wholesale Company for 1,000 carts showed the following costs per unit: direct materials, $40; direct labor, $20; and factory overhead applied at 140% of direct labor cost if defective work is charged to a specific job and 150% if it is not.

Final inspection revealed that wheels were assembled with improper bearings. The wheels were disassembled and the proper bearings inserted. The cost of correcting each defective cart consists of $2 added cost for bearings, $4 for labor, and factory overhead at the predetermined rate.

Required: Prepare journal entries to record correction of the defective units and transfer of the work in process to finished goods if:

(1) The Wisconsin Wholesale Company order is to be charged with the cost of defective units.

(2) The cost of correcting the defective work is not charged to the Wisconsin Wholesale Company order.

PROBLEMS

7-1. Applied acquisition costs. Shelton Industries, Inc. records incoming materials at invoice price less cash discounts plus applied receiving and handling cost. For product Zingo, the following data are available:

	Budgeted for the Month	Actual Cost for the Month
Freight in and cartage in............................	$ 2,500	$ 2,580
Purchasing Department cost......................	4,800	4,500
Receiving Department cost........................	3,900	4,200
Storage and handling................................	4,200	3,800
Testing, spoilage, and rejects...................	2,600	3,120
Total..	$18,000	$18,200

The purchasing budget shows estimated net purchases of $144,000 for the month. Actual invoices net of discounts total $148,500 for the month.

Required:

(1) Determine the applied acquisition costing rate for the month.

(2) Determine the amount of applied cost added to materials purchased during the month.

(3) Indicate the possible disposition to be made of the variance.

7-2. Materials costing methods. A corporation that uses a perpetual inventory system had the following transactions during June:

June 1. Beginning balance: 200 units @ $3.00 per unit.
       2. Purchased 500 units @ $3.20 per unit.
       7. Issued 400 units.
     11. Purchased 300 units @ $3.30 per unit.
     14. Issued 400 units.
     17. Purchased 400 units @ $3.20 per unit.
     21. Issued 200 units.
     24. Purchased 300 units @ $3.40 per unit.
     26. Purchased 400 units @ $3.50 per unit.
     29. Issued 600 units.

Sales were 1,600 units @ $7 per unit. Marketing and administrative expenses totaled $2,100.

Required:

   (1) Prepare comparative income statements based on the transactions for June, using the lifo and fifo methods and a 40% income tax rate.

   (2) For each costing method, determine the cash position at the end of June, assuming that all transactions, purchases, sales, and nonmanufacturing expenses were paid in cash.

7-3. Materials costing methods. During 19A, the records of Redford Trading Company show the following information about Item A:

Balance on January 1, 200 units @ $10 per unit.

	Purchased Units	Purchase Price per Unit	Sales Units
January 12........................	100	$11	
February 1........................			200
April 16..............................	200	12	
May 1.................................			100
July 15...............................	100	14	
November 10.....................			100
December 5.......................	200	17	
	600		400

The Item A selling price throughout 19A was $21.

Required:

   (1) Determine the cost of the ending inventory under the fifo method when a periodic inventory system is followed.

   (2) Determine the cost of the ending inventory under the lifo method when perpetual inventory records are maintained.

   (3) Prepare the required journal entry or entries to record the sale on account and the cost of the goods sold on February 1, assuming that perpetual inventory records are maintained and the lifo method is used. *(CGAAC adapted)*

7-4. Inventory costing and valuation. Grant Company uses perpetual inventory costing for inventory Item 407, which it purchases for resale. The company began its operations on January 1 and is in the process of preparing its first financial statements.

Upon examining the inventory ledger and other accounting records, the following information was gathered pertaining to the first four months of operations:

Purchases			Sales	
	Units	Cost per Unit		Units
January 2.......................	2,000	$5	January 15........................	500
February 2.....................	1,200	6	January 31........................	700
March 2..........................	1,500	8	February 15.....................	600
April 2............................	1,900	7	February 28.....................	900
			March 15..........................	600
			March 31..........................	800
			April 15............................	700
			April 30............................	700

On April 30, the following additional information was obtained:

(a) Current replacement cost, $6.50 per unit.
(b) Net realizable value, $8 per unit.
(c) Net realizable value reduced by a normal profit margin, $5 per unit.

Management has not decided which of the following three inventory costing methods should be selected to evaluate the cost of goods sold:

(a) Average method.
(b) First-in, first-out method.
(c) Last-in, first-out method.

Required:

(1) Prepare the perpetual inventory ledger for Item 407, using each of the above methods. (Carry all computations to three decimal places.)
(2) Prepare a comparative statement showing the effect of each method on gross profit. The sales price is $10 per unit.
(3) Prepare the necessary adjusting journal entry under each of the three inventory costing methods, assuming that the company decides to show its April 30 inventory at the lower of cost or market. *(CGAAC adapted)*

7-5. Lifo vs. fifo costing methods using periodic procedures. Great Northern Company accounts for Product X using lifo periodic procedures. Data relative to this product for the year ended December 31, 19A, are:

Inventory, January 1, 19A...4,000 units @ $8

	Purchases	Sales
First quarter..........................	8,000 units @ $10	5,000 units @ $16
Second quarter.....................	20,000 @ 12	16,000 @ 18
Third quarter........................	16,000 @ 15	18,000 @ 20
Fourth quarter......................	8,000 @ 16	12,000 @ 22

Required:

(1) Compute the gross profit on sales of Product X for 19A.
(2) Repeat requirement (1), assuming that 4,000 rather than 8,000 units were purchased in the fourth quarter.
(3) Repeat requirement (1), assuming that 12,000 rather than 8,000 units were purchased in the fourth quarter.
(4) Solve requirements (1), (2), and (3) on the assumption that Great Northern uses the fifo rather than the lifo inventory costing method. *(CGAAC adapted)*

7-6. Fifo and cost or market, whichever is lower. Kenny Company, a food wholesaler, supplies independent grocery stores in the immediate region. The company has a fifo inventory system for all of its food products. Kenny records all purchases net of purchases discounts and takes all purchases discounts. The following transactions and other related information regarding two items (instant coffee and sugar) are given for October, the last month of Kenny's fiscal year.

	Instant Coffee	Sugar
Standard unit of packaging:	Case containing 24 one-pound jars	Baler containing 12 five-pound bags
Inventory, October 1:	1,200 cases @ $53.22 per case	600 balers @ $6.50 per baler

Purchases (before purchases discounts):

Instant Coffee	Sugar
October 10—1,600 cases @ $56.40 per case plus freight of $480.	October 5—640 balers @ $5.76 per baler, plus freight of $320.
October 20—1,600 cases @ $57 per case plus freight of $480.	October 16—640 balers @ $5.40 per baler, plus freight of $320.
	October 24—640 balers @ $5.04 per baler, plus freight of $320.

	Instant Coffee	Sugar
Purchase terms:	2/10, net/30, FOB shipping point	Net 30 days, FOB shipping point
October sales:	3,400 cases @ $76 per case	2,200 balers @ $7.80 per baler
Sales terms:	1/10, net/30, FOB shipping point	1/10, net/30, FOB shipping point
Returns and allowances:	A customer returned 50 cases which had been shipped by error. The customer's account was credited for $3,800.	As the October 16 purchase was unloaded, 20 balers were discovered to be damaged. A representative of the trucking firm confirmed the damage and the balers were discarded. Credit of $108 for the merchandise and $10 for the freight was received by Kenny.

	Instant Coffee	Sugar
October 31: Most recent quoted price (before deducting purchases discounts, excluding freight)	$56.65 per case	$5.30 per baler
Net realizable value	$60.80 per case	$5.20 per baler
Net realizable value less a normal markup	$53.20 per case	$4.55 per baler

Required:

(1) Compute the number of units in inventory and the related unit cost for instant coffee and sugar as of October 31.

(2) Compute the total dollar amount of the October 31 instant coffee and sugar inventory, applying the lower of cost or market rules on an individual product basis.

(3) State whether or not the company could apply the lower of cost or market rule to groups of products or to the inventory as a whole, rather than on an individual product basis. *(ICMA adapted)*

7-7. Journal entries for spoiled work. Fannin Company had a production run of 8,000 pairs of slacks during the last week of June, at the following costs per pair:

Materials..	$5
Labor...	4
Factory overhead (includes $.70 allowance for spoiled work)...	3

Final inspection revealed 600 pairs as not meeting quality standards, salable as seconds at $4 a pair.

Required: Prepare the journal entries to record all related costs if:

(1) The loss is to be charged to the production run.
(2) The loss is to be charged to all production of the fiscal period.

7-8. Journal entries to correct defective work. Lindale Fabricators manufactures jacks and other lifting equipment. One order from Athens Supply House for 1,000 jacks showed the following costs per unit: materials, $4; labor, $1.75; factory overhead applied at 160% of direct labor cost (150% in cases in which any defective unit costs are to be charged to a specific order).

Final inspection revealed that 75 of the units were improperly riveted. To correct each defective unit requires $.20 for materials, $.30 for labor, and factory overhead at the appropriate rate.

Required: Prepare entries to record all costs related to the order when the:

(1) Order is charged with the cost of defective work.
(2) Cost of correcting defective work is not charged to a specific order.

CASES

A. Purchasing procedures. Long, CPA, has been engaged to examine and report on the financial statements of Maylou Corporation.

During the review phase of the study of Maylou's system of internal accounting control over purchases, Long was given the following document flowchart for purchases:

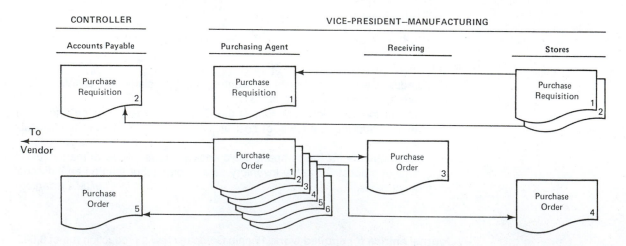

Required: Specify the procedures, relating to purchase requisitions and purchase orders, that Long would expect to find if Maylou's system of internal accounting control over purchases were effective. For example, purchase orders should be prepared only after giving proper consideration to the time to order and quantity to order. Do not comment on the effectiveness of the flow of documents as presented in the flowchart or on separation of duties.   (AICPA adapted)

B. Procedures for materials procurement and use. Creek Company produces a variety of chemical products for use by plastics manufacturers. The plant operates on two shifts, five days per week, with maintenance work performed on the third shift and on Saturdays as required.

An audit conducted by the staff of the new corporate Internal Audit Department has recently been completed, and the comments on inventory control were not favorable. Audit comments were particularly directed to the control of raw materials and maintenance materials and supplies.

Raw Materials. Raw materials are received at the back of the plant, signed for by one of the employees of the Batching Department and stored near the location of the initial batching process. During the day, receiving tallies are given to the supervisor, who forwards the tallies to the Inventory Control Department at the end of the day. The Inventory Control Department calculates raw materials usage, using weekly reports of actual production and standard formulas. Physical inventories are taken quarterly. Purchase requisitions are prepared by the Inventory Control Department and rush orders are frequent. In spite of the need for rush orders, the production superin-tendent regularly gets memos from the controller, stating that there must be excess inventory because the raw materials inventory dollar value is too high.

Maintenance Materials and Supplies. Maintenance materials and supplies are received and stored in a storeroom to which a clerk is assigned for each operating shift. A requisition is to be filled out for items taken from the storeroom, but this practice is not always followed. Because of the need to obtain parts quickly, the storeroom is not locked when the clerk is out. The storeroom is also open during the third shift and on Saturdays, so that maintenance crews can get needed materials and supplies. Purchase requisitions are prepared by the storeroom clerk and rush orders are frequent. A physical inventory is taken on a cycle-count basis.

Required: Identify weaknesses and recommended improvements in the procedures used for (1) the raw materials and (2) the maintenance materials and supplies inventories.

(ICMA adapted)

CHAPTER 8

Materials: Quantitative Models for Planning and Control

The planning and control of inventory from product design to final delivery are of considerable strategic significance to management. Inventories serve as a cushion between the production and consumption of goods and exist in various forms: materials awaiting processing; partially completed products or components; and finished goods at the factory, in transit, at warehouse distribution points, and in retail outlets. At each of these stages, a sound economic justification for the inventory should exist, since each additional unit carried in inventory generates some additional costs.

Any inventory planning and control method should have but one goal that might be expressed in two ways: (1) to minimize total cost or (2) to maximize profit within specified time and resource allocations. For example, the size of inventory at production sites should reflect the profitability inherent in large production runs, in the economic ordering, handling, and shipping of lots, and in the need for flexibility to meet uncertain future demand.

▼ PLANNING MATERIALS REQUIREMENTS

Materials planning begins with the design of a product. Whether it is a regular product or a special contract, a series of planning stages is necessary to get materials into production. In the preliminary stages, the engineering department studies the proposal, design, blueprints, and other available specifications and prepares a product requirement statement. The tooling department studies the work details necessary to manufacture the product in a particular plant. The manufacturing control department examines production in terms of existing and contemplated production schedules. The materials planning and cost estimating departments study the cumulative information and submit a cost estimate for the production proposal. The long-range or economic planning section suggests a product price based on considerations of present product lines, economic conditions and expectations, company

196

policies, and expansion plans. Executive management must finally decide whether to proceed with, reject, or modify the proposal.

To plan manufacturing requirements, every stock item or class of items must be analyzed periodically to:

1. Forecast demand for the next month, quarter, or year.
2. Determine acquisition lead time.
3. Plan usage during the lead time.
4. Establish quantity on hand.
5. Place units on order.
6. Determine reserve or safety stock requirements.

These six steps are illustrated below in determining the quantity to order in September for a November delivery. In this illustration, the *lead time*, the time between the order and delivery, is two months. The desired inventory cushion, or *safety stock*, is approximately a two weeks' supply.

Planned or forecast usage from review date:		Units
September production		2,500
October production		2,000
November production		2,500
Desired inventory, November 30		1,000
Total to be provided		8,000
Quantity on hand, September 1	1,600	
On order for September delivery	2,000	
On order for October delivery	2,000	5,600
Quantity to order for November delivery		2,400

Future requirements for each purchased or produced item play a central role in materials control. If usage requirements are not accurately planned, even the most elaborate control system will result in the wrong level of inventory during and at the end of a future period.

Materials planning deals with two fundamental factors—the quantity and the time to purchase. Determination of how much and when to buy involves two conflicting kinds of cost—the cost of carrying inventory and the cost of inadequate carrying. The nature of these conflicting costs is indicated in the following comparison:

Cost of Carrying Inventory	Estimate	Cost of Inadequate Carrying
Interest on investment in working capital	10.00%	Extra purchasing, handling, and transportation costs
Property tax and insurance	1.25	Higher prices due to small order quantities
Warehousing or storage	1.80	Frequent stockouts resulting in disruptions of production schedules, overtime, and extra setup time
Handling	4.25	Additional clerical costs due to keeping customer back-order records
Deterioration and shrinkage of stocks	2.60	Inflation-oriented increases in prices when inventory purchases are deferred
Obsolescence of stocks	5.20	Lost sales and loss of customer goodwill
Total	25.10%	

Inventory Carrying and Ordering Costs for Economic Order Quantity Calculations

The *economic order quantity (EOQ)* is the amount of inventory to be ordered at one time for purposes of minimizing annual inventory cost. If a company buys in large quantities, the cost of carrying the inventory is high because of the sizable investment. If purchases are made in small quantities, frequent orders with correspondingly high ordering costs will result. Therefore, the quantity to order at a given time must be determined by balancing two factors: (1) the cost of possessing (carrying) materials and (2) the cost of acquiring (ordering) materials.

The cost factors of carrying an inventory, listed previously, are expressed as percentages of the average inventory investment and can be estimated and measured. These cost factors should include only those costs that vary with the level of inventory. For example, in the case of warehousing or storage, only those costs that will vary with changes in the number of units ordered should be included. The cost of labor and equipment used in the storeroom is normally a fixed cost and should not be considered a part of the carrying charge. Similarly, the insurance cost is included only when the company has a monthly reporting type of policy with premiums charged on the fluctuating inventory value. A standard insurance policy for one year or more should be considered a fixed cost that is irrelevant to the decision.

It is difficult to determine the costs of not carrying enough inventory; yet they must be considered in deciding upon order quantities and order points. Such costs include ordering costs, although the fixed cost of placing an order is not relevant. Only the variable or out-of-pocket cost of procuring an order should be included. Ordering costs include preparing the requisition and the purchase order, handling the incoming shipment and preparing a receiving report, communicating in case of quantity/quality errors or delays in receipts of materials, and accounting for the shipment and the payment. Other costs of not carrying enough inventory relate to such questions as savings in freight and quantity discounts as well as to the question of when to order, including an appropriate allowance for safety stock.

Depending upon many factors, it may cost from $10 to $50 or more to process an order and from 10 to 35 percent of the average inventory investment to hold materials. Techniques for analyzing cost behavior, described and illustrated in Chapter 11, should facilitate the determination of realistic carrying and ordering cost estimates, provided due consideration is given to current costs, including the impact of inflation. Mathematical and statistical techniques permit improved planning and control in an endeavor to maximize profits and minimize costs.

Tabular Determination of the Economic Order Quantity

A tabular arrangement of data relative to a materials item allows the determination of an approximate economic order quantity, and thereby the number of orders that need to be placed annually. To illustrate, assume the following data:

Estimated requirements for next year..	2,400 units	
Cost of the item per unit..	$ .75	
Ordering cost (per order)...	$20.00	
Inventory carrying cost (% of average inventory investment)....................	20%	

Based on these data, various possible order sizes can be evaluated:

QUANTITATIVE DATA

Order size in units...	300	400	800	1,200	2,400
Number of orders..	8	6	3	2	1
Average inventory (order size ÷ 2)....................	150	200	400	600	1,200

COST DATA

Average inventory investment............................	$112.50	$150	$300	$450	$900
Total carrying cost (20% of average inventory)...	$ 22.50	$ 30	$ 60	$ 90	$ 180
Total ordering cost..	160.00	120	60	40	20
Cost to order and carry.......................................	$182.50	$150	$120	$130	$ 200

Of the order sizes calculated, 800 is the most economical; thus, an order should be placed every four months. However, the most economical order size may not have been calculated; there may be some unit quantity between 400 and 800 or between 800 and 1,200 with a cost to order and carry that is lower than $120.

Graphic Determination of the Economic Order Quantity

The following graph shows the lowest point of the total-cost-to-order-and-carry curve, about $120, and the most economic order quantity of about 800 units. The ideal order size is the point where the sum of the ordering and carrying costs is at a minimum, i.e., where the total cost curve is at its lowest. This point generally occurs where the annual carrying charges equal the ordering charges, i.e., where these two cost lines intersect.

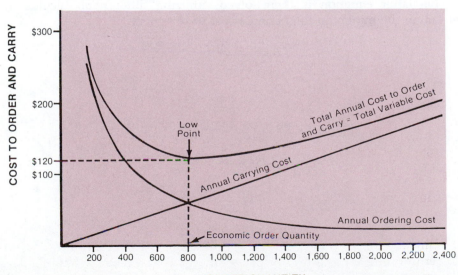

Graphic Determination of the Economic Order Quantity

The Economic Order Quantity Formula

To determine the economic order quantity by a tabular or graphic method is lengthy and may not provide the most accurate answer. Companies using order-point calculations based upon economic order quantities usually prefer to use a formula. With information as to quantity required, unit price, inventory carrying cost percentage, and cost per order, differential calculus makes it possible to compute economic order quantity by formula. One formula variation follows:

$$\text{Economic order quantity} = \sqrt{\frac{2 \times \text{Annual required units} \times \text{Cost per order}}{\text{Cost per unit of material} \times \text{Carrying cost percentage}}}$$

$$\text{OR} \quad \text{EOQ} = \sqrt{\frac{2 \times \text{RU} \times \text{CO}}{\text{CU} \times \text{CC}}}$$

Given the terms EOQ, RU, CO, CU, and CC as specified, the formula is based on the following relationships:

$$\frac{\text{RU}}{\text{EOQ}} = \text{Number of orders placed annually}$$

$$\frac{\text{RU} \times \text{CO}}{\text{EOQ}} = \text{Annual ordering cost}$$

$$\frac{\text{EOQ}}{2} = \text{Average number of units in inventory at any point in time}$$

$$\frac{\text{CU} \times \text{CC} \times \text{EOQ}}{2} = \text{Annual carrying cost}$$

$$\frac{\text{RU} \times \text{CO}}{\text{EOQ}} + \frac{\text{CU} \times \text{CC} \times \text{EOQ}}{2} = \text{Total annual cost of ordering and carrying inventory, designated as AC}$$

This latter equation is then solved, utilizing differential calculus to determine the minimum total annual cost of inventory:

$$\text{AC} = \frac{\text{RU} \times \text{CO}}{\text{EOQ}} + \frac{\text{CU} \times \text{CC} \times \text{EOQ}}{2}$$

$$\text{AC} = \text{RU} \times \text{CO} \times \text{EOQ}^{-1} + \frac{\text{CU} \times \text{CC} \times \text{EOQ}}{2}$$

$$\frac{d\text{AC}}{d\text{EOQ}} = -\text{RU} \times \text{CO} \times \text{EOQ}^{-2} + \frac{\text{CU} \times \text{CC}}{2}$$

$$\frac{d\text{AC}}{d\text{EOQ}} = \frac{-\text{RU} \times \text{CO}}{\text{EOQ}^2} + \frac{\text{CU} \times \text{CC}}{2}$$

$$\text{Let } \frac{d\text{AC}}{d\text{EOQ}} = 0; \quad \frac{-\text{RU} \times \text{CO}}{\text{EOQ}^2} + \frac{\text{CU} \times \text{CC}}{2} = 0$$

$$\frac{\text{CU} \times \text{CC}}{2} = \frac{\text{RU} \times \text{CO}}{\text{EOQ}^2}$$

$$EOQ^2 \times CU \times CC = 2 \times RU \times CO$$

$$EOQ^2 = \frac{2 \times RU \times CO}{CU \times CC}$$

$$EOQ = \sqrt{\frac{2 \times RU \times CO}{CU \times CC}}$$

The formula for the economic order quantity, or least-cost order quantity in units, is the square root of a fraction whose numerator is twice the product of the annual unit demand and the cost per order and whose denominator is the product of the unit price and the annual carrying rate. The formula assumes a constant rate of materials usage. Using the formula, the EOQ for the data on page 199 is:

$$EOQ = \sqrt{\frac{2 \times 2,400 \times \$20}{\$.75 \times 20\%}} = \sqrt{\frac{\$96,000}{\$.15}} = \sqrt{640,000} = 800 \text{ units}$$

It is also possible to express EOQ in dollars rather than in units. The following formula is employed:

$$EOQ = \sqrt{\frac{2 \times RU \times CU \times CO}{CC}}$$

Using the data from the previous illustration, the EOQ in dollars is computed as follows:

$$EOQ = \sqrt{\frac{2 \times 2,400 \times \$.75 \times \$20}{20\%}} = \sqrt{\frac{\$72,000}{.20}} = \sqrt{\$360,000} = \$600 \text{ total cost}$$

The EOQ can be converted to units by dividing the EOQ total cost by the cost per unit ($600 ÷ $.75 = 800 units).

The following example is given to indicate the results when new cost data enter the formula, since any shift in cost data will affect the answer. Again, only those cost components that vary directly with order or production quantities should be used, i.e., the variable costs.

RU = 2,400 units of materials used per year (200 units per month)
CO = $10 ordering cost per order
CU = $1.50 cost per unit of materials
CC = 20% carrying cost as a percent of average inventory investment

$$EOQ = \sqrt{\frac{2 \times 2,400 \times \$10}{\$1.50 \times 20\%}} = \sqrt{\frac{\$48,000}{\$.30}} = \sqrt{160,000} = 400 \text{ units}$$

The economic order quantity for the stock item is 400 units, or six orders per year. Other order quantities resulting in more or less than six orders per year are not so economical, as proven by the following table, which is based on $3,600 (2,400 units × $1.50 cost per unit) annual usage of materials:

Orders per Year	Units per Order	Value per Order	Ordering Cost	Carrying Cost	Total Cost
1	2,400	$3,600	$10	$360	$370
2	1,200	1,800	20	180	200
3	800	1,200	30	120	150
4	600	900	40	90	130
5	480	720	50	72	122
6	400	600	60	60	120
7	343	515	70	52	122
8	300	450	80	45	125

In the EOQ formula as illustrated, the carrying cost per unit (the denominator in the formula) is the product of the acquisition cost per unit of material and the carrying cost expressed as a percentage of the average inventory investment (CU × CC). An alternative is to estimate the carrying cost per unit directly by itemizing each component of carrying cost as a cost per unit of holding items in inventory, rather than as a percentage of average inventory investment. Thus, the denominator in the EOQ formula becomes the carrying cost per unit expressed directly, instead of as CU × CC.

Quantity Price Discounts. By purchasing in quantities larger than the minimum, quantity price discounts and/or freight savings may be realized, resulting in a lower cost per unit and altering the economic order quantity. Buying in larger quantities also alters the frequency of orders, and thus changes the total ordering cost. At the same time, it involves a larger investment in inventories.

To illustrate, assume that annual usage of an inventory item is 3,600 units, costing $1 each, with no quantity discount available. The carrying cost is 20 percent of the average inventory investment, and the cost to place an order is $10. The EOQ is:

$$\sqrt{\frac{2 \times 3,600 \times \$10}{\$1 \times 20\%}} = \sqrt{\frac{\$72,000}{\$.20}} = \sqrt{360,000} = 600 \text{ units}$$

Now assume the availability of the following quantity discounts:

Order Size	Quantity Discount
3,600 units	8%
1,800	6
1,200	5
900	5
720	4½
600	4
450	4

The following table considers the effect of quantity price discounts, using a cost-comparison approach. Observe that the order quantity that minimizes total cost (900 units per order) differs from the EOQ computed when no quantity discount is available (600 units per order).

			Number of orders per year				
	1	2	3	4	5	6	8
List price per unit....................	$1	$1	$1	$1	$1	$1	$1
Quantity discount.....................	8%	6%	5%	5%	4½%	4%	4%
Discount price per unit.............	$.92	$.94	$.95	$.95	$.955	$.96	$.96
Size of order in units...............	3,600	1,800	1,200	900	720	600	450
Average inventory in units.......	1,800	900	600	450	360	300	225
Cost of average inventory.......	$1,656.00	$ 846.00	$ 570.00	$ 427.50	$ 343.80	$ 288.00	$ 216.00
Annual cost of materials......(a)	$3,312.00	$3,384.00	$3,420.00	$3,420.00	$3,438.00	$3,456.00	$3,456.00
Carrying cost							
(20% of average)............. (b)	331.20	169.20	114.00	85.50	68.76	57.60	43.20
Cost to order........................(c)	10.00	20.00	30.00	40.00	50.00	60.00	80.00
Total cost per year							
(a) + (b) + (c).....................	$3,653.20	$3,573.20	$3,564.00	$3,545.50	$3,556.76	$3,573.60	$3,579.20

With quantity discounts, the cost of materials is not constant but is affected by the quantity discount. Therefore, the objective becomes the identification of an order quantity that minimizes not only the sum of the ordering and carrying costs [(b) + (c) in the table], but the sum of these costs *plus* the cost of the materials, i.e., (a) + (b) + (c). Since variable carrying cost in this example is assumed to fluctuate directly with and is expressed as a percentage of the average inventory investment, carrying cost is also affected by the quantity discount, because the cost per unit contained in the average inventory investment is reduced.

The EOQ Formula and Production Runs. The EOQ formula is equally appropriate in computing the optimum size of a production run, in which case CO represents an estimate of the setup cost and CU is the variable manufacturing cost per unit. To illustrate, assume that stock item A88 is manufactured rather than purchased; the setup cost (CO), such as the cost of labor to rearrange and adjust machines, is $62; variable manufacturing cost (CU) is $2 per unit; annual required units total 6,000; and the carrying cost is 20 percent. The optimum size of a production run is computed as follows:

$$\sqrt{\frac{2 \times 6{,}000 \text{ units} \times \$62 \text{ setup cost}}{\$2 \text{ variable manufacturing cost per unit} \times 20\%}} = \sqrt{\frac{\$744{,}000}{\$.40}} = \sqrt{1{,}860{,}000} = 1{,}364 \text{ units}$$

This model assumes that the setup cost is constant for various production run quantities. In fact, the setup cost to put in place a larger production run may be greater than for a smaller quantity. This possibility should be considered if it is relevant and if it would shift the optimum quantity to a lower figure.

The reduction of setup costs permits reduced production runs and an associated lower investment in inventories. Reductions can come from improving equipment design, equipment and assembly line configurations, and worker training and attitude, and from computerized automation. For example, a computer-controlled robot machine tool does not care whether it makes one part 12 times or 12 different items, each just once. This factor alters the need to extend production runs of standard products, so that it is only necessary to produce enough variety of products to keep the factory going day after day and week after week.[1] The savings from reduced investments in inventories is thus enhanced.

Determining the Time to Order

The EOQ formula answers the quantity problem of inventory planning. However, the question of when to order is equally important. This question is controlled by three factors: (1) time needed for delivery, (2) rate of inventory usage, and (3) safety stock. Unlike the economic order quantity, the order point has no generally applicable and acceptable formula. Determining the order point would be relatively simple if *lead time*—the interval between placing an order and having materials on the factory floor ready for production—and the usage pattern for a given item were definitely predictable. For most stock items, there is a variation in either or both of these factors, which almost always causes one of three results: (1) if lead time or usage is below expectation during an order period, the new materials will arrive before the existing stock is consumed, thereby adding to the cost of carrying inventory; (2) if lead time or usage is greater than expected, a *stockout* will occur, with the resultant incurrence of costs associated with not carrying enough inventory; (3) if average or normal lead time and usage are used to determine an order point, a stockout could be expected on every other order.

Forecasting materials usage requires the expenditure of time and money. In materials management, forecasts are an expense as well as an aid to balancing the cost to acquire and the cost to carry inventory. Since perfect forecasts are rarely possible, an inventory cushion or safety stock is often the least costly device for protecting against a stockout. The basic problem is to determine the safety stock quantity. If the safety stock is greater than neded, the carrying cost will be too high; if too small, frequent stockouts will occur and inconveniences, disruptions, and additional costs will result. The optimum safety stock is that quantity which results in minimal total annual cost of stockouts and safety stock carrying cost. This carrying cost is determined in the same manner as in calculating the economic order quantity. The annual cost of stockouts depends upon the frequency of occurrence and the actual cost of each stockout.

To illustrate, assume that a company uses an item for which it places 10 orders per year, the cost of a stockout is $30, and the carrying cost is $.50 per unit. The following probabilities of a stockout have been estimated for various levels of safety stock:

Probability	Safety Stock Level
40%	0 units
20	50
10	100
5	200

[1]Steven S. Ross, "The Shape of Things to Come," *Pan Am Clipper*, Vol. 23, No. 10, p. 54.

The total carrying cost and stockout cost at each level of safety stock is determined as follows:

Safety Stock Level	Expected Annual Stockouts (Probability × Number of Orders)	Total Stockout Cost	Total Carrying Cost	Total Stockout and Carrying Cost
0 units	4.0	$120	-0-	$120
50	2.0	60	$ 25	85
100	1.0	30	50	80
200	.5	15	100	115

In this illustration, the optimum level of safety stock is 100 units, since the total stockout and safety stock carrying cost is minimized at this level. Such an analysis of important stock items leads to smooth operations and effective materials management.

Order Point Formula

Order points are based on usage during the time necessary to requisition, order, and receive materials, plus an allowance for protection against stockout. The *order point* is reached when inventory on hand and quantities due in are equal to the lead time usage quantity plus the safety stock quantity. In equation form, the order point may be expressed as:

$$I + QD = LTQ + SSQ, \text{ where:}$$

I = Inventory balance on hand
QD = Quantities due in from orders previously placed, materials transfers, and returns to stock
LTQ = Lead time quantity equals normal lead time in months, weeks, or days multiplied by normal month's, week's, or day's use
SSQ = Safety stock quantity

The following situations are illustrated, both of which are solved mathematically and graphically:

1. Usage and lead time are known with certainty; therefore, no safety stock is provided.
2. A safety stock is injected into the calculation.

Order Point Illustrated—No Safety Stock. Assume the weekly use of 175 units of a stock item, and that a lead time of four weeks establishes an order point at 700 units (175 units × 4 weeks). Assuming that the unit cost is $.50, the carrying cost is 20%, the order cost is $24, and annual usage is 9,100 units (175 units × 52 weeks), then the EOQ is computed as follows:

$$EOQ = \sqrt{\frac{2 \times 9{,}100 \times \$24}{\$.50 \times 20\%}} = \sqrt{\frac{\$436{,}800}{\$.10}} = \sqrt{4{,}368{,}000} = 2{,}090 \text{ units}$$

Each order provides a 12 weeks' supply (2,090 ÷ 175). Figure 1 shows the control pattern of this item if usage and lead time are definitely known. It is apparent that (1) if lead time is more than four weeks, a stockout will result; and (2) if usage exceeds 700 units in any four-week period following an order point, a stockout is inevitable. Since perfect prediction of usage and lead time is usually unrealistic, a safety stock allowance is needed.

Figure 1—Rate of Usage and Lead Time known with Certainty

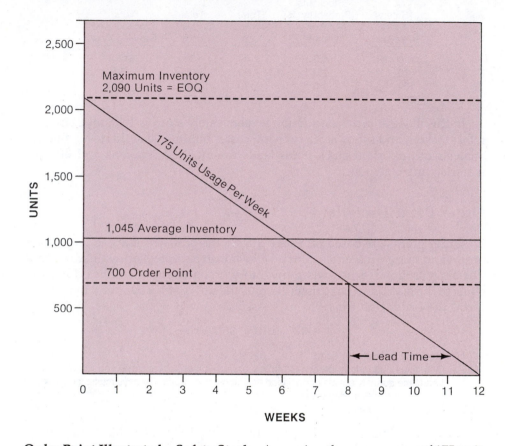

Order Point Illustrated—Safety Stock. Assuming the same usage of 175 units per week, shown in Figure 1, with a lead time of normally four weeks but possibly as long as nine weeks, the order point would be 1,575 units: 700 units usage during normal lead time (175 units × 4 weeks) plus 875 units of safety stock (175 units × 5 weeks). Assuming a beginning inventory of 2,800 units and no orders outstanding, the usage, order schedule, and inventory levels would be:

2,800 units in beginning inventory
<u>1,225</u> usage to order point (1,225 ÷ 175 weekly usage = 7 weeks)
1,575 order point
<u> 700</u> usage during normal lead time (700 ÷ 175 weekly usage = 4 weeks)
  875 maximum inventory or safety stock at date of delivery, assuming normal lead time and usage
<u>2,090</u> EOQ units received
<u>2,965</u> maximum inventory, assuming normal lead time and usage

The average inventory, assuming normal lead time and usage, is 1,920 units [(2,090 EOQ ÷ 2) + 875 units of safety stock]. Figure 2 depicts materials planning under the above assumptions and shows that a stockout would not occur unless lead time exceeds nine weeks, assuming normal usage.

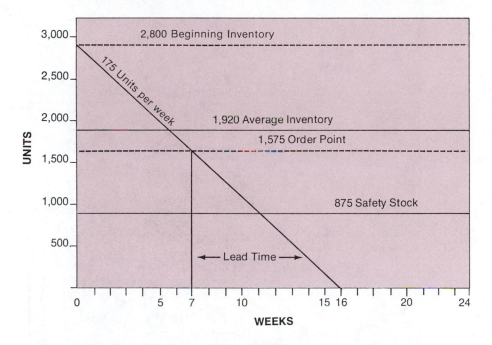

Figure 2—Rate of Usage Known with Certainty and Lead Time Known but Variable

In most businesses, a constant normal usage is not likely to occur because usage depends upon production schedules, and production depends upon sales. For instance, if the usage rate is as high as 210 units per week, with lead time normally four weeks or possibly as long as nine weeks, the safety stock would be 1,190 units and the order point 1,890 units, calculated as follows:

Normal usage for normal lead time of four weeks
  (175 units × 4 weeks).. 700 units
Safety stock:
  Normal usage for five weeks' delay (175 units × 5 weeks)..................... 875
  Usage variation [(210 − 175) × 9 weeks].................................... 315   1,190
  Order point.. 1,890 units

Assuming a beginning inventory of 2,800 units, with no orders outstanding, the usage, order schedule, and inventory levels would be:

2,800 units in beginning inventory
  910 usage to order point (910 ÷ 210 maximum weekly usage = 4.3 weeks)
1,890 order point
  700 normal usage for normal lead time (700 ÷ 175 normal weekly usage = 4 weeks)
1,190 maximum inventory or safety stock at date of delivery, assuming normal lead time and usage
2,090 EOQ units received
3,280 maximum inventory, assuming normal lead time and usage

The average inventory, assuming normal lead time and usage, is 2,235 units [(2,090 EOQ ÷ 2) + 1,190 units of safety stock]. Figure 3 shows materials planning under the assumptions that the rate of usage and lead time are known but variable.

Figure 3—Rate of Usage and Lead Time Known but Variable

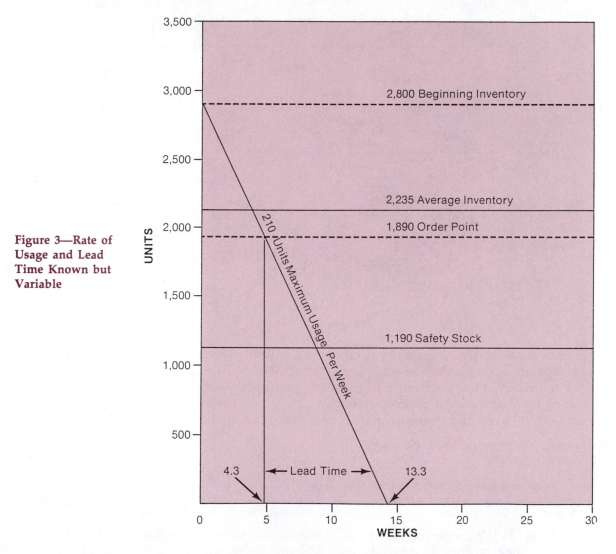

Safety Stock Calculations by Statistical Methods

The preceding situations tend to provide a safety stock for the extreme boundaries of usage and lead time variability. In other situations, the amount of safety stock is often calculated by traditional rules of thumb, such as a two-weeks' supply. These approaches have given way to statistical techniques which provide ways of determining the probability of incurring a stockout at different levels of safety stock, based on historical data. Such methods furnish management with a sound basis for determining the level of safety stock to carry. As the situation increases in complexity, computers may be used for handling calculations.

In the following paragraphs, two statistical techniques are discussed: (1) variability in demand and (2) deviations from forecast demand. The technique selected for use depends on which one most represents the conditions of a specific situation.

Variability in Demand. In this case, periodic demand is assumed to follow a random normal distribution, and the distribution of periodic demand expected in the lead time period is assumed to be the same as in the sample period. The safety stock formulation is:

$$SSQ = D\,\sigma\,\sqrt{L}, \text{ where:}$$

SSQ = Safety stock quantity
D = Desired confidence level
σ = Standard deviation of periodic historical demand
L = Lead time in months, weeks, or days

The standard deviation of periodic historical demand is defined as:

$$\sigma = \sqrt{\frac{\Sigma(x_i - \bar{x})^2}{n - 1}}, \text{ where}$$

n = The number of periods in the sample
x_i = Actual demand in period i
$\bar{x}$ = Average demand over the sample period, i.e., $\frac{\Sigma x_i}{n}$

Using the following historical data for Material J-2, the standard deviation of historical demand is computed as follows:

	x_i Actual Demand	$(x_i - \bar{x})$ Deviations from Mean	$(x_i - \bar{x})^2$ Deviations Squared
January	250	− 6.25	39.0625
February	225	− 31.25	976.5625
March	275	18.75	351.5625
April	240	− 16.25	264.0625
May	280	23.75	564.0625
June	260	3.75	14.0625
July	240	− 16.25	264.0625
August	280	23.75	564.0625
Total	2,050	-0-	3,037.5000

$$\bar{x} = \frac{\Sigma x_i}{n} = \frac{2,050}{8} = 256.25$$

$$\sigma = \sqrt{\frac{\Sigma(x_i - x)^2}{n - 1}} = \sqrt{\frac{3,037.5}{8 - 1}} = 20.83$$

Although demand is usually assumed to follow a standard normal distribution, for small samples, as in this illustration, the student's t distribution is a more appropriate assumption. A table of selected t values follows, based on the assumption that only one tail of the distribution is of interest, i.e., that managers are concerned about the occurrence rather than the nonoccurrence of a stockout:

Degrees of Freedom (df)[2]	Desired Confidence Level			
	95%	97.5%	99%	99.5%
1	6.314	12.706	31.821	63.657
2	2.920	4.303	6.965	9.925
3	2.353	3.182	4.541	5.841
4	2.132	2.776	3.747	4.604
5	2.015	2.571	3.365	4.032
6	1.943	2.447	3.143	3.707
7	1.895	2.365	2.998	3.499
8	1.860	2.306	2.896	3.355
9	1.833	2.262	2.821	3.250
10	1.812	2.228	2.764	3.169
11	1.796	2.201	2.718	3.106
12	1.782	2.179	2.681	3.055
13	1.771	2.160	2.650	3.012
14	1.761	2.145	2.624	2.977
15	1.753	2.131	2.602	2.947
20	1.725	2.086	2.528	2.845
25	1.708	2.060	2.485	2.787
30	1.697	2.042	2.457	2.750
40	1.684	2.021	2.423	2.704
60	1.671	2.000	2.390	2.660
120	1.658	1.980	2.358	2.617
∞	1.645	1.960	2.326	2.576

Given a sample size of 8, the $8 - 1 = 7$ degrees of freedom row in the table indicates that for a 97.5 percent confidence level, 2.365 should be multiplied by the standard deviation. The 97.5 percent figure includes all of the area under the curve plotted for the assumed probability distribution, except for the 2.5 percent right tail of the curve, which represents the probability of a stockout. Thus, the safety stock required to avoid a stockout approximately 97.5 percent of the time in the example above, with a lead time of one month, would be computed as follows:

$$SSQ = D \sigma \sqrt{L} = (2.365)(20.83)(\sqrt{1}) = 49.26 \text{ or about 50 units}$$

The order point would be:

$$LTQ + SSQ = (256.25)(1 \text{ month}) + (49.26) = 305.51 \text{ or about 306 units}$$

As shown in the table, the student's t distribution approaches the standard normal distribution as the sample size increases. Therefore, for large samples, the appropriate z value for the standard normal distribution may be used. The t values presented in the table above for df = ∞ are equal to the z values for the standard normal distribution at the probability levels indicated at the head of each column. For sample sizes of 30 or more, two standard deviations would approximate the appropriate factor at the 97.5 percent confidence level.

---

[2]Degrees of freedom (df) refers to the number of values that are free to vary after certain restrictions have been placed on the data. It is expressed as df = n − p, where n is the number of observations and p is the number of unknown parameters. Here, the unknown parameter is the mean of the demand distribution for this statistical procedure. For the next method to be discussed, the unknown parameter is the mean of the forecast error distribution.

Deviations from Forecast Demand. In this application, the safety stock formulation is based on the variability in forecast errors, i.e., the differences between forecast demand and actual demand. The technique assumes that variations between forecast demand and actual demand during the future lead time periods can be modeled by the variations experienced during the sample period. The eight months of actual consumption of Material J-2, previously illustrated, together with the forecast monthly usage, provide the following data for the statistical approach:

	x'_i Forecast Demand	x_i Actual Demand	$(x'_i - x_i)$ Deviations from Forecast	$(x'_i - x_i)^2$ Deviations Squared
January......................	260	250	10	100
February.....................	218	225	− 7	49
March.........................	260	275	−15	225
April............................	230	240	−10	100
May.............................	275	280	− 5	25
June............................	270	260	10	100
July.............................	245	240	5	25
August........................	270	280	−10	100
Totals.........................	2,028	2,050	−22	724

The standard deviation of the periodic forecast demand is defined as:

$$\sigma = \sqrt{\dfrac{\Sigma(x'_i - x_i)^2 - \dfrac{[\Sigma(x'_i - x_i)]^2}{n}}{n - 1}} \text{ , where}$$

n = The number of periods in the sample

x'_i = Forecast demand in period i

x_i = Actual demand in period i

The standard deviation for this illustration is computed as follows:

$$\sigma = \sqrt{\dfrac{724 - \dfrac{(-22)^2}{8}}{8 - 1}} = \sqrt{\dfrac{663.5}{7}} = 9.74$$

Since the forecasting model underestimated demand for the sample period, the level of safety stock must be increased by the average forecasting bias, multiplied by the number of periods expected during the lead time. Here, the safety stock required to avoid a stockout approximately 97.5 percent of the time (a confidence level of 97.5 percent) with a lead time of one month, would be:

$$SSQ = (D\sigma\sqrt{L}) - \left[\dfrac{\Sigma(x'_i - x_i)}{n}(L)\right]$$

$$= [(2.365)(9.74)(\sqrt{1})] - \left[\left(\dfrac{-22}{8}\right)(1)\right] = 23.035 + 2.75$$

$$= 25.785 \text{ or about 26 units}$$

The order point for September, assuming a forecast demand of 260 and a lead time of one month, would be:

$$\text{LTQ} + \text{SSQ} = 260 + 25.785 = 285.785 \text{ or about } 286 \text{ units}$$

Note that lead time periods must be measured in the same units, such as months, weeks, or days, as those used in computing the standard deviation.

An additional safety stock allowance may be needed if lead time varies, again giving consideration to the degree of protection desired by management. When the inventory stock reaches the order point level, it should trigger an order for the most economical order quantity.

Forecasting Usage

The number of units needed during the lead time and the lead time itself are the two variables which influence the when-to-order decision. It is usually possible to estimate fairly accurately the time required to receive materials. It is seldom possible to forecast exactly the materials needed even for a short future period; and when thousands of items are involved, the task becomes prodigious even with the aid of a computer. Some forecasting techniques are briefly mentioned in order to indicate the scope and complexity of the task:

1. Factor listing or barometric methods.
2. Statistical methods.
3. Forecasting surveys.

Factor listing involves enumerating the favorable and unfavorable conditions likely to influence sales of the various divisions or products of a company and relies upon the forecaster's judgment to evaluate the degree of the influence factor. *Barometric methods* result in systematized factor listing.

Statistical methods describe historical patterns in time series. The methods may be simple or complex, but the purpose is to reveal patterns that have occurred in the past and project them into the future. The usual procedure results in plotting time series data (such as total sales, sales of specific lines or products, inventory units or dollars, labor hours, or machine hours) on a graph, thus revealing a trend or a seasonal or cyclical pattern. A moving average may be used to smooth a series and remove irregular fluctuations, but the intent is to describe mathematically the growth or decline over a period of time. Regression analysis usually employs the least-squares method (see Chapter 11) to determine economic relationships between a dependent variable and one or more independent variables, such as sales territory, family incomes, advertising expenditures, and price of the product.

Forecasting surveys are used to avoid complete dependence on historical data. They are commonly made in order to determine consumer buying intentions, opinions, or feelings about the business outlook, and capital investment plans.

General Observations

The primary key to good inventory planning is sufficient knowledge of the fundamental techniques to develop enough self-confidence to permit their practical adaptation to the specific needs of the company. Basically, economic order quantity and computed order points assume:

1. Relatively uniform average demand.
2. Uniform rate of inventory usage.
3. Normal distribution of demand forecast errors.
4. Constant purchase price per unit, regardless of order size.
5. Available funds when the order point is reached.
6. Statistical independence of demand for all inventory items.

Aside from the technical and mathematical steps, it is important to remember that the following fundamentals largely determine the success of inventory planning procedures.

1. The order point is a significant factor affecting inventory planning, since it establishes the inventory level. It determines the investment in inventories and the ability to provide satisfactory customer service. The order point depends primarily on the accuracy of the sales or usage forecast.
2. Of equal importance is the establishment of unit costs, carrying and ordering costs, and the investment factor. These elements, along with estimated requirements, are involved in determining the economic order quantity.
3. The inventory model should be sensitive and adaptive to seasonal usage variations and other nonstatic data influencing order point quantity computations.

Computer Simulation for Materials Requirements Planning

Materials requirements planning (MRP) is a computer simulation for managing materials requirements, using each product's bill of materials as well as inventory status and the process of manufacture. A master schedule of items to be produced and due dates are entered into the computer, which then accesses the bill of materials, materials delivery lead times, and on-hand and on-order inventory balances.

The computer then determines component parts requirements and projects the time-phased production demands on various work centers. These demands, when compared with work-center capacities representing machines and personnel, determine the feasibility of meeting the master schedule of products to be produced. If work-center overloads cannot be resolved, the master schedule must be revised.

Only when the master schedule is determined to be feasible is it released, along with purchase order and work-center operation schedules. By using such simulations, the feasibility of schedules can be tested prior to their release.[3]

▼ MATERIALS CONTROL

Materials control is accomplished through functional organization, assignment of responsibility, and documentary evidence obtained at various stages of operations. These stages begin with the approval of sales and production budgets and with the completion of products which are ready for sale and shipment to warehouse stocks or to customers.

Two levels of inventory control exist: unit control and dollar control. Purchasing and production managers are primarily interested in unit control; they think, order, and requisition in terms of units instead of dollars. Executive management is primarily interested in the financial control of inventories. These executives think in terms of an adequate return on capital employed; i.e., dollars invested in inventory must be utilized efficiently and effectively. Inventory control is operating successfully when inventory increases or decreases follow a predetermined and predictable pattern, related in amount and time to sales requirements and production schedules.

The control of materials must meet two opposing needs: (1) maintenance of an inventory of sufficient size and diversity for efficient operations and (2) maintenance of a financially favorable inventory. A basic objective of materials control is the ability to place an order at the appropriate time with the best source to acquire the proper quantity at the right price and quality. Effective inventory control should:

1. Provide a supply of required materials and parts for efficient and uninterrupted operations.
2. Provide ample stocks in periods of short supply (seasonal, cyclical, or strike), and anticipate price changes.
3. Store materials with a minimum of handling time and cost and protect them from loss by fire, theft, elements, and damage through handling.
4. Keep inactive, surplus, and obsolete items to a minimum by systematic reporting of product changes which affect materials and parts.
5. Assure adequate inventory for prompt delivery to customers.
6. Maintain the amount of capital invested in inventories at a level consistent with operating requirements and management's plans.

Control Principles

Inventory control systems and techniques should be based on the following principles:

---

[3]Dale G. Sauers, "Analyzing Inventory Systems," *Management Accounting*, Vol. LXVII, No. 11, p. 31.

1. Inventory is created by purchasing (a) materials and parts and (b) additional labor and overhead to process the materials into finished goods.
2. Inventory is reduced through sales and spoilage.
3. Accurate sales and production schedule forecasts are essential for efficient purchasing, handling, and materials investment.
4. Management policies, which attempt to balance size and diversity of inventory for efficient operations and cost of maintaining that inventory, are the greatest factor in determining inventory investment.
5. Ordering materials is a response to forecasts; scheduling production controls inventory.
6. Inventory records alone do not achieve inventory control.
7. Control is comparative and relative, not absolute. It is exercised by people with varying experiences and judgment. Rules and procedures guide these individuals in making evaluations and decisions. For example, by establishing closer controls, experts in the field of materials control commonly expect to reduce inventory by 15 percent or more without significantly affecting customer service or production scheduling.

Organizing for Materials Control

Materials control is commonly centralized in one department called the materials management or materials control department. Size of the company, number of purchased items in a finished product, time required to manufacture a product, and physical size, weight, and unit value of items are factors that influence the organization and personnel required for effective materials control. A materials management organization may include some or all of the following sections:

Planning and Scheduling	Finished Goods
Purchasing	Warehousing
Receiving	Packing
Inspection	Traffic
Stores	Shipping
Materials Handling	Statistical Analysis

Materials Control Methods

Materials control methods differ primarily in the care and cost expended. Critical items and high-value items require greater attention than do low-value items. For example, for low-cost items, large safety stocks and large orders of three to six months' supply are appropriate, since carrying costs are usually low and the risk of obsolescence is often negligible. Control methods include the order cycling and the min-max method.

The *order cycling* or *cycle review method* examines periodically (e.g., each 30, 60, or 90 days) the status of quantities on hand of each item or class. Different companies use different time periods between reviews and may use different cycles for different types of materials. High-value items and items that would tie up normal operations if out of stock usually require a short review cycle. On low-cost and noncritical items, a longer review cycle is common, since these materials would be ordered in large quantities and a stockout would not be as costly. At each review period in the order cycling system, orders are placed to bring quantities up to some determined and desired level. This quantity is often expressed as a number of days' or weeks' supply and can be adjusted to projected sales for seasonal items.

The *min-max method* is based on the premise that the quantities of most stock items are subject to definable limits. A maximum quantity for each item is established. A minimum level provides the margin of safety necessary to prevent stockouts during a reorder cycle. The minimum level sets the order point, and the quantity to order will usually bring inventory to the maximum level.

Min-max procedures may be based on physical observation or they may be keyed to the accounting system. Physical observation that an order point has been reached is illustrated by the two-bin procedure, which separates each stock item into two bins, piles, or bundles. The first bin contains enough stock to satisfy usage that occurs between receipt of an order and the placing of the next order; the second bin contains the normal amount used from order date to delivery date plus the safety stock. When the first bin is empty and the second bin is tapped, a requisition for a new supply is prepared. The second bin or reserve quantity is determined originally by estimating usage requirements and adding a safety stock adequate to cover the time required for replenishing the materials. For example, if monthly usage of an item is ten dozen, a one-month safety stock is desired, and if 30 days are required to place an order and receive delivery, the second bin should contain 20 dozen units. A purchase order must be written when the reserve stock is tapped; otherwise, a stockout is likely to occur. The two-bin or "last bag" system requires little paper work, since reordering takes place when the "last bag" is opened.

The min-max method may be implemented through the accounting system by triggering an order when a materials ledger record shows that the balance on hand has dropped to the order point. The system is especially advantageous in companies using electronic data processing equipment. The materials control department reviews materials items, forecasts usage and lead time, establishes safety stock requirements, and determines economic order quantities. Thereafter, subject to quarterly or semiannual review, receipts and issues are electronically recorded on the materials record. When the quantity on hand drops to the established order point, the information is automatically routed to order clerks who activate orders for the quantity specified. Companies with computers may go even further in their use of the automatic order system. The computer reviews and updates order points, recalculates economic order quantities, and even writes purchase orders.

Just-in-Time Materials Control. The savings that can result from a minimum inventory investment and associated carrying costs has led to increasing attention to a *just-in-time (JIT) inventory system*. Such a procedure calls for heightened coordination with suppliers so that materials arrive immediately prior to their use. Japanese industry is credited with pioneering this procedure that is now being used by some U.S. manufacturers. For example, General Motors has implemented this approach with a fully automated JIT parts inventory system.

In JIT, authorization for a part to be made at a work station is generated by a requirement for the part at the next work station in the production line. As parts are used in final assembly, the need for production of their replacements is authorized. The process is repeated at all preceding work stations, thus "pulling" parts through the production system as they are needed and eventually pulling raw materials and purchased parts from suppliers.

JIT pertains to raw materials inventory as well as to work in process inventory between interacting work centers. The objective is that both raw materials and work in process inventories are held to absolute minimums.[4] JIT places a new emphasis on the desirability of minimum inventory levels and on improving integrated manufacturing processes rather than focusing on individual materials or operations. It is intended to complement the appropriate use of other materials planning and control tools, such as EOQ and safety stock calculations. For JIT to operate properly, machine setup time must be kept short. Furthermore, production flow through the various work stations must be uniform, which is usually characteristic of repetitive manufacturing.

A successful just-in-time system requires a change in manufacturing processes to accommodate this new inventory philosophy. What is involved is process management, not merely inventory management. The fundamental objective of JIT is to produce and deliver what is needed, when it is needed, at all stages of the production process—just in time to be fabricated, subassembled, assembled, and shipped to the customer. Although in practice there are no such plants, JIT is an ideal and therefore a worthy goal. The benefits are low inventory, high manufacturing cycle rates, high output per employee, minimum floor space requirements, minimum indirect labor, and perfect in-process control. An associated requirement of a successful JIT operation is the pursuit of perfect quality in order to reduce, to an absolute minimum, delays caused by defective product units.[5]

Selective Control—The ABC Plan. Segregation of materials for *selective control*, called the *ABC plan*, is an analytical approach based upon statistical averages. The ABC plan measures the cost significance of each materials item. "A," or high-value, items would be under the tightest control and the responsibility of the most experienced personnel. "C" items would be under simple physical controls, such as the two-bin system with safety stocks. The plan provides an impressive saving in materials cost.

The ABC plan concentrates on important items and is also known as *control by importance and exception (CIE)*. Because it is impractical to give equal attention to all items in inventory, stock items are classified and ranked in descending order on the basis of the annual dollar value of each item, thus providing a

[4]*Ibid.*, pp. 31-32.
[5]Larry Utzig, "Reconciling the Two Views of Quality," *Journal of Cost Management*, Vol. 1, No. 1, p. 68.

proportional value analysis. In most situations, an arbitrary number of items can be selected on a percentage basis to approximate, for example:

10% of the items to equal 70% of the dollar cost of materials used
30% of the items to equal 25% of the dollar cost of materials used
60% of the items to equal 5% of the dollar cost of materials used

The following table suggests the handling of high-, middle-, and low-value items to achieve effective control:

	High-Value Items (A)	Middle-Value Items (B)	Low-Value Items (C)
Quality of personnel....................................	Best available	Average	Low
Records needed...	Complete	Simple	Not essential
Order point and quantity used....................	As guides, frequent review	Infrequent review	Strictly used
Number of orders per year.........................	Generally high	Two to six	One or two
Replacement time..	As short as possible	Normal	Can be long
Amount of safety stock...............................	Low	Moderate	High
Inventory turnover.......................................	High	Moderate	Low

The procedure for segregating materials for selective control consists of six steps:

1. Determining future use in units over the review forecast period—month, quarter, or year.
2. Determining the price per unit for each item.
3. Multiplying the projected price per unit by the projected unit requirement to determine the total cost of that item during the period.
4. Arranging the items in terms of total cost, listing first the item with the highest total cost.
5. Computing for each item its percentage of the total for (a) units—number of units of each item divided by total units of all items, and (b) total cost—total cost of each item divided by total cost of all materials.
6. Plotting the percentages on a graph.

The following table and graph demonstrate ABC inventory classification:

Item	Units	% of Total	Unit Cost	Total Cost	% of Total
1	800	8⎤ 12%	$20.00	$16,000	32.0⎤ 56%—A
2	400	4⎦	30.00	12,000	24.0⎦
3	1,600	16⎤	4.50	7,200	14.4⎤
4	1,400	14⎬ 42%	5.00	7,000	14.0⎬ 38%—B
5	1,200	12⎦	4.00	4,800	9.6⎦
6	2,000	20⎤	1.00	2,000	4.0⎤
7	1,600	16⎬ 46%	.50	800	1.6⎬ 6%—C
8	1,000	10⎦	.20	200	.4⎦
Total	10,000	100		$50,000	100.0

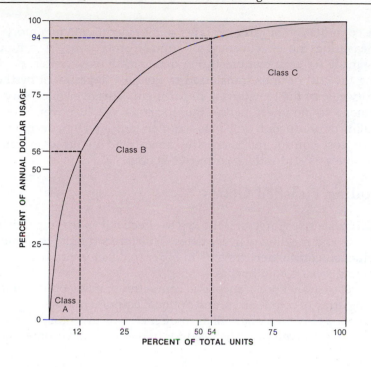

Distribution of Inventory Usage Values (Cumulative Percentages)

Controlling Materials in Process

The materials cost control responsibility is not ended when materials are requisitioned for production. Until goods are finished, packed, sold, and shipped, inventory control problems and cost savings potentials exist. This is particularly true of in-process inventories, which are intimately related to production processes and schedules but often are not controlled. Generally, the objective is to maintain inventory levels based on maximum production or the lowest unit cost.

Work in process inventory investment is largely determined by the time necessary for goods to pass through the production process. The time involved includes:

1. Setup time—preparing to run a job on a machine.
2. Running time—actually performing the work.
3. Queue time—the amount of time that the job spends waiting to be worked on.
4. Move time—transporting the goods to the next processing location.
5. Wait time—time spent waiting to be moved.

In most job shops, queue time accounts for 70 to 90 percent of the total time. Therefore, a large portion of the dollars invested in in-process inventory is tied up in nonproductive, idle goods. Although cutting queue time can result in significant reductions in inventory investment, some minimum level of queues is required in order to keep operations from running out of work.[6]

[6]Jay Severance and Ronald R. Bottin, "Work-in-Process Inventory Control Through Data Base Concepts," *Management Accounting*, Vol. LX, No. 7, pp. 37-38.

The computation of turnover rates aids in identifying inventory problems and measuring the effectiveness of control procedures. A computation is usually made for each manufacturing department, cost center, or process by dividing the cost of units transferred to the next department by the average inventory cost of the transferring department. Turnover rates vary from one department to another; hence the focus is on turnover rate changes. Scheduling or production problems are often indicated by a declining turnover rate. For cost control purposes, the downtrend in turnover rates should suggest analysis and induce corrective action.

Controlling Finished Goods

An accurate sales forecast is the key to effectively managing finished goods inventories and meeting delivery dates. This forecast must be communicated to production control departments in order to develop production schedules for meeting sales commitments.

To meet customer preferences and competition, many product lines feature a growing array of colors, sizes, and optional equipment. This results in added finished goods inventory as well as more materials inventory items and more work in process inventory. The need for tighter control becomes increasingly important.

Control of Obsolete and Surplus Inventory

Almost every organization is faced with the problem of surplus and obsolete inventory at one time or other. Whatever the many possible reasons for such conditions, some action is required in order to reduce or eliminate these items from inventory and free the related capital. To accomplish a reduction, management should first make certain that the buildup will not continue due to present ordering policies, and should then take steps to dispose of stock. Accurate perpetual inventory records showing acquisition and issue quantities and dates, as well as periodic review of the records, are necessary to identify obsolete and surplus items. Obsolete inventory usually results from changing a design or dropping a product. Prompt sale of the inventory for the first reasonable offer is often the best policy.

Reporting on Inventory Control

Management requires timely information concerning inventory control efforts. This information should be reported in a concise, easily understood form. Quantitative as well as graphic comparisons of actual and budgeted inventory, such as those illustrated on the next page, provide an indication of the efficiency of use of the total inventory and the major categories of raw materials, work in process, and finished goods.[7]

[7]Anker V. Andersen, *Graphing Financial Information—How Accountants Can Use Graphs to Communicate* (New York: National Association of Accountants, 1983), p. 39. Copyright 1983 by the National Association of Accountants. All rights reserved. Reprinted by permission.

INVENTORY TRENDS

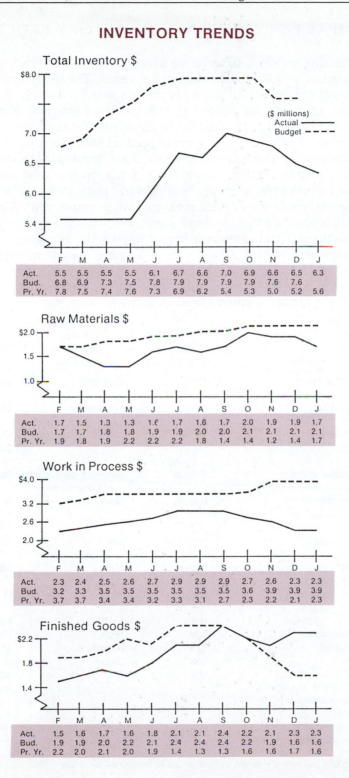

Total Inventory $

($ millions)
Actual ———
Budget - - - -

	F	M	A	M	J	J	A	S	O	N	D	J
Act.	5.5	5.5	5.5	5.5	6.1	6.7	6.6	7.0	6.9	6.6	6.5	6.3
Bud.	6.8	6.9	7.3	7.5	7.8	7.9	7.9	7.9	7.9	7.6	7.6	
Pr. Yr.	7.8	7.5	7.4	7.6	7.3	6.9	6.2	5.4	5.3	5.0	5.2	5.6

Raw Materials $

	F	M	A	M	J	J	A	S	O	N	D	J
Act.	1.7	1.5	1.3	1.3	1.6	1.7	1.6	1.7	2.0	1.9	1.9	1.7
Bud.	1.7	1.7	1.8	1.8	1.9	1.9	2.0	2.0	2.1	2.1	2.1	2.1
Pr. Yr.	1.9	1.8	1.9	2.2	2.2	2.2	1.8	1.4	1.4	1.2	1.4	1.7

Work in Process $

	F	M	A	M	J	J	A	S	O	N	D	J
Act.	2.3	2.4	2.5	2.6	2.7	2.9	2.9	2.9	2.7	2.6	2.3	2.3
Bud.	3.2	3.3	3.5	3.5	3.5	3.5	3.5	3.5	3.6	3.9	3.9	3.9
Pr. Yr.	3.7	3.7	3.4	3.4	3.2	3.3	3.1	2.7	2.3	2.2	2.1	2.3

Finished Goods $

	F	M	A	M	J	J	A	S	O	N	D	J
Act.	1.5	1.6	1.7	1.6	1.8	2.1	2.1	2.4	2.2	2.1	2.3	2.3
Bud.	1.9	1.9	2.0	2.2	2.1	2.4	2.4	2.4	2.2	1.9	1.6	1.6
Pr. Yr.	2.2	2.0	2.1	2.0	1.9	1.4	1.3	1.3	1.6	1.6	1.7	1.6

▼ THE IMPACT OF MODERNIZED FACTORY PROCESSES

In increasing numbers, factories are moving from manufacturing processes involving manual and/or fixed automated systems. The shift is toward *flexible manufacturing systems,* which consist of an integrated collection of automated production processes, automated materials movement, and computerized system controls to utilize the facilities in the efficient manufacture of a highly flexible variety of products. The extent of product variety is constrained by the need for the products to share certain broad characteristics that allow grouping within a particular family of products while maintaining considerable flexibility. For example, at the General Electric plant in Erie, Pennsylvania, diesel engines of substantially different sizes can be manufactured on the same automated production line, without significant retooling and setups.

Flexible manufacturing systems impact upon and alter many of the factors that management should consider in evaluating a system, especially the planning and control of raw materials and work in process inventories. The effect of each system—manual, fixed automation, and flexible manufacturing—on these factors is summarized as follows:

Factor	Manual Systems	Fixed Automation Systems	Flexible Manufacturing Systems
Numbers of kinds of products	Many	Only one	Several
Viable production volumes	Low	High range	Middle
Product quality	Varies	Tightly constrained	Consistent
Setup times	High (learning curve)	Very high	Short
Learning curve effect	Substantial	Depends on degree of automation	None
Lead times (per unit) to supply customer demands	Usually high	Moderate	Moderate/low
Direct labor cost (per unit)	High	Low	Very low
Direct labor cost (in total)	High	High	Very low
Inventories: Materials*	High	High	High
Work in process*	High	High	Low
Machine utilization	Low	High	High
Space required	Extensive	Extensive	Moderate
Capital cost	Low	High	High
Sensitivity to effects of breakdowns of single machine or group of machines	Low	High	Low
Responsiveness to changes in demand	High	Low	High

*Incorporation of a just-in-time inventory system will cause inventories to be low.

A comparison of these factors make the flexible manufacturing system attractive. However, there is a need to consider the substantial capital cost and the scarcity of expert knowledge in the field. Nevertheless, the rate of growth of such modernized factory processes is expected to accelerate.[8]

DISCUSSION QUESTIONS

1. In designing an inventory control system, what are three key questions which must be answered?

2. How can a firm benefit from economic order quantity and order point techniques?

3. What is the purpose of the economic order quantity model?

4. Explain each of the following terms: (a) order point, (b) lead time, and (c) safety stock.

5. What types of costs should be considered in deriving the economic order quantity?

6. To manage inventory levels effectively, both cost savings and risk reduction must be achieved. Which risks or uncertainties does an inventory manager strive to reduce. *(CIA adapted)*

7. How is the economic order quantity model affected by an increase in the uncertainty of usage of the inventory item?

8. What are the consequences of maintaining inadequate inventory levels? What are the difficulties of measuring precisely the costs associated with understocking?

9. Define materials requirements planning (MRP).

10. Is general management concerned primarily with unit control or financial control of inventory?

11. The control of materials must meet two opposing needs. What are they?

12. Discuss the purpose of a just-in-time inventory system.

13. In what situation are selective control and automatic control of materials effective?

14. What is the key to controlling finished goods inventory in a manufacturing company?

15. What characterizes flexible manufacturing systems?

EXERCISES

1. Quantity to order. Gladewater Company's production schedule calls for 5,000 units of Material B for January operations, 4,950 for February, and 5,550 for March. On January 1, the Material B inventory is 5,600 units, with 4,100 on order for January delivery and 5,100 for February delivery. The desired inventory level to begin second-quarter production is 75% of the January 1 inventory.

Required: Compute the number of Material B units to order for March delivery.

[8]David M. Dilts and Grant W. Russell, "Accounting for the Factory of the Future," *Management Accounting*, Vol. LXVI, No. 9, pp. 34-40. Copyright March, 1985, by the National Association of Accountants. All rights reserved. Reprinted by permission.

2. Usage forecast and inventory balances. On January 1, a materials analyst is asked to determine the number of units of Material Z to order for March delivery. The production schedule calls for 4,800 units of this material for January operations, 5,000 units for February, and 5,600 units for March. On January 1, the Material Z inventory is 6,000 units, 3,800 units are on order for January delivery, and 4,600 units are on order for February delivery. The desired inventory level to begin second-quarter production is 80% of the January 1 inventory.

Required:

(1) Compute the quantity to order for March delivery.
(2) If the planned usage occurs and outstanding orders are received on expected delivery dates, compute the number of units on hand (a) on March 1 and (b) on March 31.

3. Computations and applications of the EOQ formula. (Round off all answers to the nearest whole number.)

(a) Shilders Inc. has an annual usage of 100 units of Item M, with a purchase price of $55 per unit. The following data are applicable to Item M:

    Ordering cost....................................... $5 per order
    Carrying cost percentage....................   15%

    Required: Compute the economic order quantity.

(b) Ambler Company has developed the following information for one of its inventory items: units required per year, 30,000; cost of placing an order, $100; unit carrying cost per year, $600.

    Required: Compute the economic order quantity.

(c) Tyler Equipment Company estimates a need for 2,250 Ajets next year at a cost of $3 per unit. The estimated carrying cost is 20%, and the cost to place an order is $12.

    Required: Compute the economic order quantity.

(d) Bailey Inc. requires 6,750 containers next year at a list price of $12 per container. The estimated carrying cost is 25% of average inventory, and the cost to place an order is $20.

    Required: Compute the economic order quantity.

(e) Shubert Company estimates that it will need 12,500 cartons next year at a cost of $8 per carton. The estimated carrying cost is 25% of average inventory investment, and the cost to place an order is $20.

    Required: Compute (1) the economic order quantity and (2) the frequency in days that orders should be placed, based on a 365-day year.

(f) Cleveland Sporting Goods Inc. buys baseballs at $20 per dozen from its wholesaler. Brown will sell 48,000 dozen balls evenly throughout the year. The firm incurs interest expense of 10% on its average inventory investment. In addition, rent, insurance, and property tax for each dozen baseballs in the average inventory is $.40. The cost involved in handling each purchase order is $10.

    Required: Compute (1) the economic order quantity and (2) the total annual inventory expense to sell 48,000 dozen baseballs, if orders of 800 dozen each are placed evenly throughout the year.

(g) A customer has been ordering 5,000 specially designed metal columns at the rate of 1,000 per order during the past year. The variable production cost is $8 per unit: $6 for materials and labor, and $2 for factory overhead. It costs $1,000 to set up for one run of 1,000 columns, and the inventory carrying cost is 20%. Since this customer may buy at least 5,000 columns per year, the company would like to avoid making five different production runs.

Required: Compute the most economical production run.

(h) King Company manufactures 10,000 blades annually for its electric lawn mower division. Blades are used evenly throughout the year. The setup cost each time a production run is made is $80, and the cost to carry a blade in inventory is $.40. Management's objective is to produce the blades at the lowest possible cost.

Required: Compute the most economical number of annual production runs, if each run is scheduled for the same number of blades.

(i) Fairmont Company estimates that it will need 12,000 units of Material W next year at a cost of $9 per unit. The estimated carrying cost is 20%, and the cost to place an order is calculated to be $16.

Required: Compute (1) the economic order quantity, (2) the frequency of order placement, and (3) the economic order quantity if forecast usage is changed to 8,000 and the carrying cost percentage is 22%.

(j) An item costs $10, has a yearly usage volume of 500 units, an ordering cost of $6, and a carrying cost of 25%.

Required:

(1) Compute the economic order quantity and the total ordering and carrying cost per year.
(2) Determine the effect on the total ordering and carrying cost if the order quantity is 10% above the EOQ. Comment on the magnitude of the effect.

(k) Bahner Inc. manufactures a line of walnut office products. Management estimates the annual demand for the double walnut letter tray at 6,000 units. The tray sells for $80. The costs relating to the letter tray are (a) the manufacturing cost per tray, $50; (b) the cost to initiate a production run, $300; and (c) the annual cost of carrying the tray in inventory, 20%. In prior years, the production of the tray has been scheduled in two equal production runs.

Required: Find the expected annual cost savings the company could experience if it employed the economic order quantity model to determine the number of production runs which should be initiated during the year.

4. Economic order quantity and quantity discount. A particular material is purchased for $3 per unit. Monthly usage is 1,500 units, the ordering costs are $50 per order, and the annual carrying cost is 40%.

Required:

(1) Compute the economic order quantity.
(2) Determine the proper order size if the material can be purchased at a 5% discount in lots of 2,000 units.

5. Ordering and carrying costs, economic order quantity, and quantity discount. Pattersen Company buys 500 boxes of Item X-100 every 2 months. Order costs are $380 per order; carrying costs are $1 per unit and vary directly with inventory investment. Currently the company purchases the item for $5 each.

Required:

(1) Determine total ordering and carrying costs under current policy.
(2) Determine the economic order quantity and the related ordering and carrying costs.
(3) What is the order-size decision Pattersen should make, if the supplier offers a 5% discount for order sizes of 3,000 units?   (CGAAC adapted)

6. Safety stock and order point. Eagle Company's usage of Material A is 7,200 units during 240 working days per year. Normal lead time and maximum lead time are 20 working days and 45 working days, respectively.

Required: Assuming Material A will be required evenly throughout the year, what is the safety stock and order point?   (AICPA adapted)

7. Economic order quantity, order point, and safety stock. Yost Company has obtained the following costs and other data pertaining to one of its materials:

Working days per year...	250
Normal use per day..	500 units
Maximum use per day...	600 units
Minimum use per day..	100 units
Lead time..	5 days
Variable cost of placing one order.............................	$36
Variable carrying cost per unit per year....................	$4

Required: Compute the following:

(1) Economic order quantity.
(2) Safety stock (maximum).
(3) Order point.
(4) Normal maximum inventory.
(5) Absolute maximum inventory.
(6) Average inventory, assuming normal lead time and usage.

(CGAAC adapted)

8. Safety stock. Jackson & Sons Inc. would like to determine the safety stock to maintain for a product, so that the lowest combination of stockout cost and carrying cost would result. Each stockout will cost $75; the carrying cost for each safety stock unit will be $1; the product will be ordered five times a year. The following probabilities of running out of stock during an order period are associated with various safety stock levels:

Safety Stock Level	Probability of Stockout
10 units	40%
20	20
40	10
80	5

Required: Determine the combined stockout and safety stock carrying cost associated with each level and the recommended level of safety stock.   (AICPA adapted)

9. Safety stock calculation by a statistical method—deviations from forecast demand. Because of erratic customer demand, Atlanta Company has been experiencing stockouts on one of its important inventory items, even though deliveries arrive on a dependable schedule—one month from the date of an order. Records provide the usage forecast and the actual consumption on this item for the past nine months. The sum of the deviations squared is 2,888 and the sum of forecast minus units consumed is zero. A 97.5% protection against stockout is desired.

Required:

(1) Compute the safety stock, using the student's t table on page 210.
(2) Determine the order point if average usage is 262 units per month.
(3) Calculate the safety stock for 97.5% protection if four months are required from order to delivery.

10. ABC plan of control. Fremont Industries Inc. is considering a system of selective control of materials, using the following data:

Materials Stock No.	Quarterly Usage in Units	Unit Cost	Total Cost
24	2,000	$20.00	$ 40,000
25	20,400	.25	5,100
26	5,600	10.50	58,800
27	1,000	30.00	30,000
28	18,600	1.00	18,600
29	7,560	2.50	18,900
30	8,880	3.25	28,860
31	4,920	2.00	9,840
32	6,840	2.00	13,680
33	30,000	.50	15,000
34	9,980	1.50	14,970
35	8,220	2.50	20,550
Total	124,000		$274,300

Required:

(1) Prepare an arrangement of the data for presentation to management, assuming that the ABC plan of selective control is indicated. (Round off all percentages to two decimal places.)
(2) Construct a graph to depict the situation.

PROBLEMS

8-1. Economic order quantity—tabular, graphic, and formula determination. Karson Company uses 5,000 units of EL-304 each year. The relevant ordering cost is $250 per order and the carrying cost is $4 per unit per year.

Required:

(1) For order quantities of 5,000, 2,500, 1,250, 800, 500, 250, and 100 units of EL-304, calculate the annual ordering cost, the annual carrying cost, and the sum of the two types of costs.
(2) Graphically illustrate the annual ordering cost function, the annual carrying cost function, and the annual total cost function for EL-304.
(3) In the graph, indicate the EOQ and its approximate value.
(4) Mathematically determine the EOQ. *(CGAAC adapted)*

8-2. EOQ; order point; graphic illustration of materials management. The new financial vice-president of Morton Products Corporation is directing an intensive analysis of working capital management. The objective is to attain more efficient resource allocation and higher earnings from each dollar of assets.

Materials cost of one important manufactured product is $12 per unit; sales average 100 units per month; and the lead time is one month. Calculations show that the variable cost of placing an order and handling the incoming shipment is $50, and the cost of holding units in stock is 25% of the average inventory.

Required:

(1) Compute the economic order quantity.
(2) Determine the order point.
(3) Construct a graphic presentation of materials management.

8-3. Economic order quantity and quantity discount. Yoeman Company, a regional supermarket chain, orders 480,000 cans of frozen orange juice per year from a California distributor. A 24-can case of frozen juice delivered to Yoeman's central warehouse costs $4.80, including freight charges. The company borrows funds at a 10% interest rate to finance its inventories.

Yoeman Company's purchasing agent has calculated that it costs $15 to place an order for frozen juice and that the annual variable storage expense (electricity, insurance, handling) is $.08 for each can of juice.

Required:

(1) Compute the number of cases of frozen juice that Yoeman Company should request in each order.
(2) Determine the order-size decision that Yoeman should make, if the California distributor offers a 10% discount off the delivery price for minimum orders of 72,000 cans.   *(CGAAC adapted)*

8-4. Economic order quantity and quantity discount. EDP Associates is a small data processing company. Waring Paper Products, a regional distributor of paper products, has proposed a quantity discount on one type of computer paper purchased by EDP Associates. EDP currently pays $12 per carton for this paper and uses 15,000 cartons annually. Waring has offered a 5% cash discount on all quantity orders in excess of 1,000 cartons, provided an order is for 5,000 cartons, i.e., for each order of 5,000 cartons, EDP would pay the full price of $12 per carton on the first 1,000 cartons and a discounted price of $11.40 for each additional carton.

It has been determined that the cost to place an order is $64.80, and that the estimated carrying cost is 20% of the average inventory investment.

Required:

(1) Compute the optimum number of cartons of paper EDP Associates should be ordering currently without consideration of the quantity discount.
(2) Determine the cost effect of orders of 5,000 units instead of ordering the number computed in requirement (1).   *(ICMA adapted)*

8-5. Ordering and carrying costs, economic order quantity, and quantity discount. Kimes Company buys 15,000 units of Material X4 annually in lots of 1,000. Order costs are $20 per order; carrying costs are 25% of average inventory investment. Currently the company purchases the item for $5 each.

Required:

    (1) Determine the ordering and carrying costs under current policy.

    (2) Determine the economic order quantity using the tabular method. Include a range from 250 to 1,500 units in 250-unit increments.

    (3) Determine the economic order quantity using the formula method and compute the related ordering and carrying costs.

    (4) What is the order-size decision Kimes should make, if the supplier offers a 5% discount for order sizes of 3,000 units?

(Based on an article in Management Accounting*)*

8-6. Optimum production run size. A manufacturer expects to produce 100,000 Widgets during the year ending June 30, to supply a demand which is uniform throughout the year. The setup cost for each production run of Widgets is $144 and the variable cost of producing each Widget is $5. The cost of carrying one Widget in inventory is $.20 per year. After a batch of Widgets is produced and placed in inventory, it is sold at a uniform rate, and inventory is exhausted when the next batch of Widgets is completed.

    Management would like to have an equation to describe the above situation and determine the optimum quantity of Widgets in each production run in order to minimize total production and inventory carrying costs.

    Let: AC = Total annual cost of producing and carrying Widgets in inventory.

        X = Number of Widgets to be produced in each production run.

Required: Using the above notation, show (1) the derivation, $\partial AC/\partial X$, of the equation which determines the optimum quantity of Widgets produced during each production run in the fiscal year, and (2) the quantity of Widgets (to the nearest whole number) that should be produced in each production run in the fiscal year in order to minimize total cost.

(AICPA adapted)

8-7. EOQ formula and safety stock. Lauren Company sells a number of products to many restaurants in the area. One product is a special meat cutter with a disposable blade. Blades are sold in a package of 12 at $20 per package. It has been determined that the demand for the replacement blades is at a constant rate of 2,000 packages per month. The packages cost the company $10 each from the manufacturer and require a three-day lead time from date of order to date of delivery. The ordering cost is $1.20 per order, and the carrying cost is 10% per annum. The company uses the economic order quantity formula.

Required:

    (1) Compute the economic order quantity.

    (2) Compute the number of orders needed per year.

    (3) Compute the cost of ordering and of carrying blades for the year.

    (4) Determine the date on which the next order should be placed, assuming that there is no reserve (safety stock) and that the present inventory level is 200 packages. (360 days = 1 year.)

    (5) Discuss the difficulties that most firms would have in attempting to apply the EOQ formula to their inventory problems.

(ICMA adapted)

8-8. Determining the EOQ and time to order. Newton Products Company has developed the following costs and other data pertaining to one of its raw materials:

Normal use per day	400 units
Maximum use per day	600 units
Minimum use per day	100 units
Working days per year	250
Lead time	8 days
Cost of placing one order	$20.00
Cost per unit of material	$ 2.50
Carrying cost percentage	10%

Required: Compute the following:

(1) Economic order quantity.
(2) Safety stock.
(3) Reorder point.
(4) Normal maximum inventory.
(5) Absolute maximum inventory.
(6) Average normal inventory.

(CGAAC adapted)

8-9. Safety stock. For Product D, ordered 5 times per year, stockout cost per occurrence is $80 and safety stock carrying cost is $2 per unit. Available options are:

Units of Safety Stock	Probability of Running Out of Safety Stock
10	50%
20	40
30	30
40	20
50	10
55	5

Required: Compute the safety stock resulting in the lowest cost.   *(AICPA adapted)*

8-10. Safety stock calculation by a statistical method—variability in demand. Historical data indicating actual demand for Material A88 are as follows:

January	640 units	July	540 units
February	630	August	550
March	625	September	600
April	615	October	620
May	595	November	615
June	600	December	630

Lead time is one month. Management has determined that 97.5% protection against a stockout is adequate.

Required:

(1) Prepare a schedule showing the safety stock required, using the variability in demand statistical method and the student's t table on page 210. (Round off all amounts to two decimal places.)
(2) Compute the safety stock required if the normal lead time is two months.

8-11. Safety stock calculation by a statistical method—deviations from forecast demand. The forecast and actual usage data for Material A88 for a 12-month period are as follows:

	Forecast Demand	Actual Demand		Forecast Demand	Actual Demand
January............	600 units	640 units	July......................	600 units	540 units
February..........	610	630	August.................	575	550
March..............	620	625	September..........	575	600
April..................	620	615	October..............	590	620
May..................	610	595	November...........	600	615
June.................	600	600	December...........	610	630

Lead time can be depended upon to be one month. Management has determined that a 97.5% protection against a stockout is adequate.

Required:

    (1) Prepare a schedule showing the safety stock required, using the deviations from forecast demand statistical method and the student's t table on page 210. (Round off all amounts to two decimal places.)

    (2) Compute the safety stock required if the normal lead time is two months.

8-12. Economic order quantity; order point; safety stock using probabilities.
Sanborn Company is a regional distributor of automobile window glass, including windshields for subcompact cars. The expected daily demand for these windshields is 36, and the unit purchase price is $50.

Other costs associated with ordering and maintaining an inventory of the subcompact car windshields are as follows:

    (a) Cost incurred in the Purchase Order Department for placing and processing orders during the last three years is:

Year	Orders Placed and Processed	Cost
19A	20	$12,300
19B	55	12,475
19C	100	12,700

    Management expects this cost to increase 16% over the amounts and rates experienced the last three years.

    (b) The windshield manufacturer charges Sanborn a $75 shipping fee per order.

    (c) A clerk in the Receiving Department receives, inspects, and secures the windshields as they arrive from the manufacturer. This activity requires 8 hours per order received and the clerk is assigned to other duties when not performing this work. The clerk is paid at the rate of $9 per hour, and related variable overhead costs in this department are applied at the rate of $2.50 per hour.

    (d) Storage space for the windshields is rented as needed in a public warehouse at an estimated cost of $2,500 per year plus $5.35 per windshield.

    (e) Breakage cost is estimated to be 6% of each windshield's purchase price.

    (f) Property tax and fire insurance on the inventory are $1.15 per windshield.

    (g) The interest rate on the inventory investment is 21% of the purchase price.

Six working days are required from the time the order is placed with the manufacturer until it is received. Sanborn uses a 300-day work year when making economic order quantity computations.

Required:

    (1) Calculate the following:
        (a) Cost to place an order.

(b) Carrying cost per unit.

(c) Economic order quantity.

(d) The minimum annual relevant cost at the EOQ point.

(e) The order point in units, with no allowance for safety stock.

(2) Without prejudice to the requirement (1) answer, assume that the EOQ is 400 units, the carrying cost is $28 per unit, and the stockout cost is $12 per unit. Sanborn wants to determine the best safety stock in order to minimize its relevant costs. Using the following schedule of stockout probabilities during the reorder period, determine the proper amount of safety stock.

Safety Stock Level in Units	Stockout in Units	Probability
0	60	12%
	120	5
	180	2
60	60	5
	120	2
120	60	2
180	0	0

(ICMA adapted)

CASES

A. Estimating ordering and carrying costs. Evanston Inc., a large wholesale distributor, deals exclusively in baby shoes. Due to substantial ordering and storing costs, management decided to use the EOQ model to help determine the optimum quantities to order from the different manufacturers.

As a starting point, management has decided to develop values for the ordering cost and carrying cost by using data from the most recent fiscal year. The company had placed 4,000 purchase orders during the year, the largest of which was 400 orders in June and the smallest, 250 in December. Selected cost data for these two months and for the year were:

	Cost for High Activity Month (June—400 Orders)	Cost for Low Activity Month (December—250 Orders)	Annual Cost
Purchasing Department:			
Purchasing manager	$ 1,750	$ 1,750	$ 21,000
Buyers	2,500	1,900	28,500
Clerks	2,000	1,100	20,600
Supplies	275	150	2,500
Accounts Payable Department:			
Clerks	2,000	1,500	21,500
Supplies	125	75	1,100
Data processing	2,600	2,300	30,000
Warehouse:			
Supervisor	1,250	1,250	15,000
Receiving clerks	2,300	1,800	23,300
Receiving supplies	50	25	500
Shipping clerks	3,800	3,500	44,000
Shipping supplies	1,350	1,200	15,200
Freight out	1,600	1,300	16,800
Total	$21,600	$17,850	$240,000

The Purchasing Department is responsible for placing all orders. The costs listed for the Accounts Payable Department relate only to the processing of purchase orders for payment. The Warehouse costs reflect two operations, receiving and shipping. The receiving clerks inspect all incoming shipments and place the orders in storage. The shipping clerks are responsible for processing all sales orders to retailers.

The company leases space in a public warehouse where the rental fee is priced according to the square feet occupied during a month. The annual charges during the year totaled $34,500. Annual insurance and property tax on the shoes stored in the warehouse were $5,700 and $7,300, respectively. The company pays 8% a year for a small amount of short-term, seasonal bank debt. Long-term capital investments are expected to produce a rate of return of 12% after income tax; the effective income tax rate is 40%.

The inventory balances tend to fluctuate during the year, depending upon the demand for baby shoes. Selected data on inventory balances for the year are:

Inventory, January 1	$160,000
Inventory, December 31	120,000
Highest inventory balance (June)	220,000
Lowest inventory balance (December)	120,000
Average monthly inventory	190,000

The boxes in which the baby shoes are stored are all approximately the same size and occupy about the same amount of storage space in the warehouse.

Required:

(1) Estimate values appropriate for (a) the cost of placing an order (CO), and (b) the annual carrying cost per dollar of average investment in inventory (CC).
(2) Explain whether the costs should be developed solely from the historical data used in the EOQ model.   (ICMA adapted)

B. Setup cost. Pointer Furniture Company manufactures and sells office desks. For efficiency and quality control reasons, the desks are manufactured in batches. For example, 10 high-quality desks might be manufactured during the first two weeks in October and 50 units of a lower-quality desk during the last two weeks. Because each model has its own unique manufacturing requirement, the change from one model to another requires the factory's equipment to be adjusted. Pointer management wishes to determine the most economical production run for each of the items in its product lines by adapting the economic order quantity inventory model.

One of the cost parameters that must be determined before the model can be employed is the setup cost incurred when there is a change to a different furniture model. As an example, the Accounting Department has been asked to determine the setup cost for Model JE 40 in its junior executive line.

The Equipment Maintenance Department is responsible for all of the changeover adjustments on production lines, in addition to the preventive and regular maintenance of all the production equipment. The equipment maintenance employees are paid $9 per hour and employee benefits average 20% of wage costs. The other departmental costs, which include such items as supervision, depreciation, and insurance, total $50,000 per year. Two people from the Equipment Maintenance Department are required to make the production change for Model JE 40. Each person spends an estimated 5 hours in setting up the equipment as follows:

Machinery changes	3 hours
Testing	1 hour
Machinery readjustments	1 hour
Total	5 hours

The production line on which Model JE 40 is manufactured is operated by five workers. During the changeover, these workers assist the maintenance workers when needed and operate the line during the test run. However, they are idle for approximately 40% of the time required for the changeover and cannot be assigned to other jobs. The production workers are paid a basic wage of $7.50 per hour. Two factory overhead bases are used to apply the indirect costs because some of the costs vary in proportion to direct labor hours, while others vary with machine hours. The factory overhead rates applicable for the current year are as follows:

	Based on Direct Labor Hours	Based on Machine Hours
Variable....................	$2.75	$ 5.00
Fixed..........................	2.25	15.00
	$5.00	$20.00

These department overhead rates are based on an expected activity of 10,000 direct labor hours and 1,500 machine hours for the current year. This department is not scheduled to operate at full capacity because production capability currently exceeds sales potential.

The estimated cost of the direct materials used in the test run totals $200. Salvage materials from the test run should total $50.

Required:

(1) Estimate Pointer's setup cost for desk Model JE 40, for use in the economic production run model.
(2) Identify cost items to include in estimating Pointer's inventory carrying cost.

(ICMA adapted)

C. Cost of carrying inventory. Lacy Products is a regional firm that operates with a typical manufacturing plant involving raw materials, work in process, and finished goods inventories. Raw materials are purchased and stored until their introduction into the manufacturing process. Upon completion, the finished products are stored in the company's warehouse, awaiting final sale.

A recent study indicated that Lacy's annual cost of carrying inventory is more than 25% of the average inventory investment. Management believes that inventory carrying costs might be an excellent area to implement cost reductions and proposes (1) not requesting raw materials from suppliers until near the time needed in the manufacturing process and (2) transferring the finished goods to customers immediately following completion.

Required: Identify and discuss the circumstances necessary to make such a proposal feasible with respect to (1) raw materials inventory and (2) finished goods inventory.

(ICMA adapted)

CHAPTER 9

Labor: Controlling and Accounting for Costs

Labor cost represents the human contribution to production and is an important cost factor requiring constant measurement, control, and analysis. Labor cost consists of basic pay and fringe benefits. The basic pay for work performed is called the *base rate* or *job rate*. A base rate should be established for each operation in a plant or office and grouped by class of operation. An equitable wage rate or salary structure requires an analysis, description, and evaluation of each job within the plant or office. The value of all jobs must relate to wages and salaries paid for similar work in the community and in the industry or business as a whole. Maintaining competitive wage rates and salaries facilitates the acquisition and retention of quality personnel.

Fringe benefits also form a substantial element of labor cost. Fringe costs, such as the employer's share of FICA tax, unemployment taxes, holiday pay, vacation pay, overtime premium pay, insurance benefits and pension costs, must be added to the base rate in order to arrive at the full labor cost. While these fringe costs are generally included in overhead, they should not be overlooked in management's planning and control responsibilities, in decision-making analyses, or in labor-management wage negotiations. Workers' demands for a 50¢ per hour increase in pay may result in far greater expenditures by the company when related fringe costs are considered.

Wages and fringe benefits are only one element in employer-employee relations, however. Adequate records, easily understood and readily available, are also an important factor in harmonious relations between management, employees, labor unions, government agencies, and the general public.

▼ PRODUCTIVITY AND LABOR COSTS

All wage payments are directly or indirectly based on and limited by the productivity and skill of the worker. Therefore, proper planning, motivation, control, and accounting for this human cost factor is one of the most important problems in the management of an enterprise. A cooperative and enthusiastic labor force, loyal to the company and its policies, can contribute greatly toward efficient, low-cost operations.

Labor productivity may be defined as the measurement of production performance using the expenditure of human effort as a yardstick. It is the amount of goods and services a worker produces. In a broader sense, productivity could be described as the efficiency with which resources are converted into commodities and/or services. Greater productivity can be achieved by more efficient production processes, improved or modern equipment, or any other factor that improves the utilization of resources. Changes in the utilization of a labor force often require changes in methods of compensating labor, followed by changes in accounting for labor costs.

Planning Productivity

Improving productivity requires careful planning that transforms productivity improvement from an indirect residual of other planning efforts into a free standing, tracked effort in its own right. The plan should assign direct responsibilities for productivity improvement action as well as specifying interrelationships with other existing plans (e.g., the operating budget, capital investment, research and technology, and human resource development). Questions typically answered by the plan include:

1. How does the organization define productivity and quality of work life?
2. What priority should be attached to productivity improvement? Who is responsible?
3. How will executive management's commitment be communicated?
4. How much uniformity of application is desired?
5. How much employee involvement in planning and implementation is appropriate?
6. How will progress be measured?[1]

Measuring Productivity

Once plans have been formulated, productivity should be measured, analyzed, understood, and reported. The objective of productivity measurement is to provide management with a concise and accurate index for the comparison of actual results with a standard of performance. Productivity measurement should recognize the individual contribution of factors such as employees (including management), plant and equipment used in production, products and services utilized in production, capital invested, and government services utilized (as indicated by taxes). However, the most generally utilized measurement has been physical output per labor hour, which takes into account only one element of input—labor. Thus, productivity measurement ratios are, at their best, crude statistical devices that often ignore such essential factors as capital and land. This point is supported by a 1984 study, which

---

[1]Carl G. Thor, ''Planning Your Productivity Efforts,'' *Management Accounting*, Vol. LXIV, No. 12, pp. 28-29.

concluded: "Despite a decade of intense concern for productivity improvement in U.S. industry and some notable advances in techniques, measurement is still in its infancy."[2]

Setting a standard of labor performance is not easy, since it is often accompanied by serious disputes between management and unions. The pace at which the observed person is working is noted and referred to as a *rating* or *performance rating*. The rating factor is applied to the selected task to obtain a *normal time*, i.e., the time it should take a person working at a normal pace to do the job. Allowances are added for personal time, rest periods, and possible delays. The final result is the *standard time* for the job, expressed in minutes per piece or in units to be produced per hour.

The *productivity-efficiency ratio* measures the output of an individual, relative to the performance standard. This ratio can also be used to measure the relative operating achievement of a machine, an operation, a department, or an entire organization. To illustrate, if 4,000 hours is standard for a department and if 4,400 hours are used, then there is an unfavorable ratio of 90.9 percent (4,000 ÷ 4,400).

Economic Impact of Productivity

When productivity increases, business profits and the real earnings of workers should also increase. Furthermore, increased productivity enables society to get more and better output from the basic resources of the economy. In recent years, productivity has generally been increasing, resulting in more available goods and services. However, the normal productivity gain has fallen below the average gain of earlier years. This slowdown has given rise to increased costs. When increases in output do not keep pace with rising costs, unit costs—and, therefore, selling prices—increase. *inflation*

If prices are to be kept from rising, then wage increases should not exceed an amount that reflects the unit cost reduction resulting from increased productivity. In recent years, employment costs—wages, salaries, and fringe benefits—have risen more than output or production per labor hour, leading to inflationary higher prices to meet higher unit costs.

In 1980, the Congressional Joint Economic Committee issued a report, *Productivity and Inflation*, in which the role of productivity in reducing the nation's rate of inflation was assessed. The report stated that each increase of 1 percent in productivity growth would reduce inflation by at least 2.1 percent two years after the change and 2.8 percent four years later. The report further states that productivity growth should be considered in designing any wage and price standards, and that wage settlements which would otherwise be inflationary might not be, if accompanied by large productivity gains.[3]

---

[2]Jerome Kraus, *How U.S. Firms Measure Productivity* (New York: National Association of Accountants, 1984), p. 55.

[3]For an extended discussion of productivity, see Harold E. Arnett and Neill R. Schmeichel, *Increasing Productivity in the United States—A Political, Social, and Economic Policy Approach* (Montvale, New Jersey: National Association of Accountants, 1984).

Increasing Productivity by Better Management of Human Resources

Better management of human resources offers the prospect of increasing productivity as well as boosting product quality by enabling workers to participate more directly in the management of their work and the overall goals of their company. A long-term rather than short-term perspective is required, involving extensive training and a long-term view of results. Four fundamental assumptions characterize better human resource management:

1. People who do the work are best qualified to improve it.
2. Decision making should be pushed down to the lowest level possible.
3. Worker participation increases both job satisfaction and commitment to company objectives.
4. There is a vast pool of ideas in the work force waiting to be tapped.

Quality Costs

Productivity impacts significantly on product quality and a category of costs that might be labeled "quality of conformance costs." *Quality of conformance refers to the degree to which a product meets its specifications, i.e., its fitness for use.* These costs can be classified into four types:

1. Prevention costs are the costs associated with designing, implementing, and maintaining the quality system. They include engineering quality control systems, quality planning by various departments, quality training programs, and working with suppliers to improve the quality of incoming materials.
2. Appraisal costs are the costs incurred to ensure that materials and products meet quality standards. They include inspection of raw materials, work in process, and the finished product, as well as laboratory tests, quality audits, and field testing.
3. Internal failure costs are the costs associated with materials and products that fail to meet quality standards and result in manufacturing losses before a product reaches the customer. Included here are the cost of scrap, repair, and rework of defective products identified before shipment to customers, as well as downtime or work stoppages caused by defects.
4. External failure costs are those incurred because inferior quality products are shipped to customers. They include the costs of handling complaints, warranty replacement, repairs of returned products, and the difficult to measure but nevertheless real cost of damaged company reputation among existing as well as prospective customers.[4]

These categories of quality costs are interrelated. As more is invested in appraisal and prevention costs, failure costs decrease, with the objective of

---

[4]Harold P. Roth and Wayne J. Morse, "Let's Help Measure and Report Quality Costs," *Management Accounting,* Vol. LXV, No. 2, pp. 50-53.

lowering total quality costs. Moreover, effective preventive actions reduce failure costs as well as appraisal costs, although the payoff may require some time. Although the total elimination of failure costs may be neither feasible nor cost effective, management should be made aware of the trade-offs associated with these various quality costs and take appropriate action. Therefore, the accounting information system should track these costs by the accounting records to the extent that they are measurable, or by good estimates to the extent that they are not measurable.[5]

Quality of conformance costs occur in many different departments within the organization. Their order of magnitude may be substantial. Not only labor cost, but materials and factory overhead costs, marketing and administrative costs, and the opportunity cost of lost future sales all impact on the total. These costs pertain not just to manufacturing industries, but to service industries as well. Banking institutions are a prime example in the service category.

One recent estimate is that quality costs, while amounting to 10 to 20 percent of sales dollars for many U.S. companies, with proper control should be reduced to about 2.5 percent, which approximates the experience in the Japanese automobile industry. There is, indeed, tremendous room for improvement, and the accounting system should contribute toward this end. Some of these costs can be measured rather precisely, while others will probably have to be estimated. The more precise measurement is useful as long as the cost of obtaining the added precision is not excessive.

As is the case for cost control in general, the earlier in the production process that poor quality can be identified, the greater the potential quality cost savings. For example, if a faulty resistor costing two cents and used in manufacturing a computer is found before it is used, the cost is only the two cents. However, if it is not caught until it is soldered into a computer component, a substantially greater cost results. Even more severe is the cost of not catching the faulty part before shipment to a customer and having to recall and repair a computer that has been delivered.

In summary, productivity and its related costs demand careful planning and measurement if the associated economic impact is to be controlled effectively. Better management of human resources and careful balancing of quality of conformance costs are essential requirements leading to increased productivity.

▼ INCENTIVE WAGE PLANS

In the modern industrial enterprise with mass production and many employees, a worker's wage is based on negotiated labor contracts, productivity studies, job evaluations, profit sharing, incentive wage plans, and guaranteed annual wages. Because all wages are paid for work performed, an element of incentive is present in all wage plans. In contrast with pay by the

---

[5]James B. Simpson and David L. Muthler, "Quality Costs: Facilitating the Quality Initiative," *Journal of Cost Management*, Vol. 1, No. 1, pp. 25-34.

hour, week, or month, an incentive wage plan should reward workers in direct proportion to their increased output. A fair day's work standard should be established so that the worker can meet and even exceed it with a reasonable effort, thereby receiving full benefit from the incentive wage plan.

The installation and operation of incentive wage plans require not only the combined efforts of the personnel department, labor unions, factory engineers, and accountants, but also the cooperation and willingness of each worker. To be successful, an incentive wage plan must: (1) be applicable to situations in which a worker can increase output, (2) provide for proportionately more pay for output above standard, (3) set fair standards so that extra effort will result in bonus pay, and (4) result in immediate reward every payday. Along with these essentials, the plan needs to be reasonably simple and understandable to workers as well as to managers.

Purpose of an Incentive Wage Plan

The primary purpose of an incentive wage plan is to induce a worker to produce more, to earn a higher wage, and at the same time to reduce unit costs. The plan seeks to insure greater output, to increase control over labor cost by insuring more uniform unit costs, and to change the basis for reward from hours served to work accomplished. Naturally, producing more in the same period of time should result in higher pay for the worker. Because of the greater number of units produced, it should also result in a lower cost per unit for factory overhead and labor cost combined.

To illustrate, assume that a factory operation takes place in a building that is rented for $2,400 per month ($80 per day or $10 per hour) and that depreciation, insurance, and property tax amount to $64 per day or $8 per hour. Assume further that 10 workers on an 8-hour day are paid $6 per hour and that each worker produces 40 units of product per day (an individual production rate of 5 units per hour). The workers and the management agree that a rate of $6.60 per hour will be paid if a worker produces 48 units per day, thereby increasing the hourly output from 5 to 6 units.

The following table shows the cost per hour and cost per unit for the two systems, and indicates how a wage incentive can reduce unit costs and at the same time provide the worker with a higher income.

Cost Factor	Original System, $6 Per Hour (10 workers)			New System, $6.60 Per Hour (10 workers)		
	Amount per Hour	Units per Hour	Unit Cost	Amount per Hour	Units per Hour	Unit Cost
Labor	$60	50	$1.20	$66	60	$1.1000
Rent	10	50	.20	10	60	.1667
Depreciation, insurance, and property tax	8	50	.16	8	60	.1333
Total	$78	50	$1.56	$84	60	$1.4000

Effect of an Incentive Wage Plan on Unit Costs

Although the hourly labor cost of the work crew increases from $60 to $66, the cost of a complete unit of product is reduced from $1.56 to $1.40. The unit cost decrease is caused by two factors: (1) unit output per worker is increased 20 percent, with a 10 percent increase in wages, and (2) the same amount of factory overhead is spread over 60 instead of 50 units of production an hour. For greater precision, such an analysis should also include labor-related costs, such as employer's payroll taxes, as well as any other relevant factory overhead that would influence the unit cost. In this example, both labor and factory overhead unit costs were reduced. But even if the incentive wage causes the labor cost per unit to increase, the reduction of factory overhead cost per unit may be sufficient to result in a net reduction in unit cost, thus supporting the desirability of the incentive wage plan.

The lowering of conversion or manufacturing cost resulting from an incentive wage plan, illustrated here on a cost per unit basis, should also be analyzed in terms of differential (marginal or incremental) cost (Chapter 21). The marginal revenue associated with the additional output and the marginal cost of an incentive wage plan should influence management's decision to install a plan.

Types of Incentive Wage Plans

In actual practice, time wages and output wages are not clear-cut and distinct. Incentive plans typically involve wage rates based upon various combinations of output and time. Many wage incentive systems retain the names of the industrial engineers and efficiency experts who originated the plans—the Taylor differential piece-rate plan, the Halsey premium plan, the Bedaux point system, the Gantt task and bonus plan, and the Emerson efficiency bonus plan. Most of these plans are no longer used, but many adaptations are still in use. To demonstrate the operation of incentive wage plans, the straight piecework plan, the 100 percent bonus plan, and the group bonus plan are discussed as representative examples.

Straight Piecework Plan. The *straight piecework plan*, one of the simplest incentive wage plans, pays wages above the base rate for production above the standard. The production standard is computed in minutes per piece and is then translated into money per piece. If time studies determine that 2.5 minutes is to be the standard time required for producing one unit, the standard rate is 24 pieces per hour. If a worker's base pay rate is $7.44 per hour, the piece rate is $.31. Workers are generally guaranteed a base pay rate, even if they fail to earn that amount in terms of output. If a worker's production exceeds 24 pieces per hour, the $.31 per unit still applies. In the table at the top of the next page, the labor cost per unit of output declines until the standard is reached and then remains constant at any level of output above standard.

While piece rates reflect an obvious cause-effect relationship between output and pay, the incentive is effective only when workers can control their rates of output. Piece rates would not be effective when output is machine-paced. Also, modification of production standards and labor rates

Units per Hour	Guaranteed Hourly Rate	Piece Rate	Earned per Hour	Labor Cost per Unit	Over-head per Hour	Over-head per Unit	Conversion Cost per Unit
20	$7.44	$ 0	$7.44	$.372	$4.80	$.240	$.612
22	7.44	0	7.44	.338	4.80	.218	.556
standard 24	7.44	.31	7.44	.310	4.80	.200	.510
26	7.44	.31	8.06	.310	4.80	.185	.495
28	7.44	.31	8.68	.310	4.80	.171	.481
30	7.44	.31	9.30	.310	4.80	.160	.470
32	7.44	.31	9.92	.310	4.80	.150	.460

Straight Piecework Plan

becomes necessary when increases in output are the result of the installation of new and better machines.

100 Percent Bonus Plan. The *100 percent bonus plan* is a variation of the straight piecework plan. It differs in that standards are stated not in terms of money, but in time per unit of output. Instead of a price per piece, a standard time is allowed to complete a job or unit, and the worker is paid for the standard time at the hourly rate if the job or unit is completed in standard time or less. Thus, if a worker produces 100 units in an 8-hour shift and the standard time is 80 units per shift (or 10 units per hour), the worker would be paid the hourly rate for 10 hours. In other variations of the 100 percent bonus plan, savings are shared with the supervisor and/or the company.

Each payroll period, an efficiency ratio must be figured for every worker before earnings can be computed. Production standards in units of output per hour are set by industrial engineers. Hours of work and units produced are reported to the payroll department, where the reported hours worked are multiplied by the hourly production standard to determine the standard units. The worker's production is then divided by the standard quantity, resulting in the efficiency ratio. The efficiency ratio multiplied by the worker's base rate results in the hourly earnings for the period. The following table illustrates how earnings are computed, assuming that standard production is 15 units per hour.

Worker	Hours Worked	Out-put Units	Stan-dard Units	Effi-ciency Ratio	Base Rate	Base × Effi-ciency Ratio	Total Earned	Labor Cost per Unit	Over-head per Hour	Over-head per Unit	Conver-sion Cost per Unit
Abrams	40	540	600	.90	$7.50	—*	$300.00	$.5556	$5.40	$.4000	$.9556
Gordon	40	660	600	1.10	7.50	$ 8.250	330.00	.5000	5.40	.3273	.8273
Hanson	40	800	600	1.33	7.50	9.975	399.00	.4988	5.40	.2700	.7688
Jonson	38	650	570	1.14	7.60	8.664	329.23	.5065	5.40	.3157	.8222
Stowell	40	750	600	1.25	8.00	10.000	400.00	.5333	5.40	.2880	.8213
Wiebold	40	810	600	1.35	7.72	10.422	416.88	.5147	5.40	.2667	.7814

*When the efficiency ratio is less than 1.00, no bonus is earned.

100 Percent Bonus Plan

The 100 percent bonus plan has gained in popularity because of the frequency of wage increases. The standards, stated in terms of time and output quantity, need no adjustment when wage rates change. Since the system emphasizes time rather than money, the plan lends itself to the development of controls and efficiency standards.

Group Bonus Plan. Industry uses a great variety of incentive wage plans, some of which depend upon a superior productive performance of a whole department or an entire factory. Factory operations often require employees to work in groups or crews using large machines. Although the work of each employee is essential to the machine operation, it is frequently impossible to separate the work of one member of a crew. A worker on an assembly line cannot increase output without the cooperation of the entire group. Group bonus plans have proven successful in such situations.

Group bonus plans, like those designed for individual incentive, are intended to encourage production at rates above a minimum standard. Each worker in the group receives an hourly rate for production up to the standard output. Units produced in excess of the standard are regarded as time saved by the group, and each worker is in effect paid a bonus for time saved as well as being paid for time worked. Usually, the bonus earned by the group is divided among the group members in accordance with their respective base rates.

Group plans reduce the amount of clerical work necessary to compute labor cost and payrolls and the amount of supervision necessary to operate the incentive system. Group plans may also contribute to better cooperation among workers, and good workers are likely to bring pressure upon poor workers who might jeopardize the group bonus. Group plans quite often lead to the reduction of accidents, spoilage, waste, and absenteeism. For example, a bonus may be paid to a crew or department which has not had an accident for a specified period of time, or which has a reject rate in units of output below a specified ratio.

The following table illustrates the operation of a 100 percent group bonus plan. A crew of 10 workers uses costly equipment, and each is paid $10 an hour for a regular 8-hour shift. Standard production is 50 units per hour, or 400 units per shift; overhead is $320 per 8-hour shift, or $40 per hour.

Units Produced	Standard Hours for Units Produced	Actual Hours	Regular Group Wage	Bonus (Hrs. Saved @ $10)	Total Group Earnings	Labor Cost per Unit	Over-head Cost per Unit	Conversion Cost per Unit
350	70	80	$800	$ 0	$ 800	$2.286	$.914	$3.200
400	80	80	800	0	800	2.000	.800	2.800
425	85	80	800	50	850	2.000	.753	2.753
450	90	80	800	100	900	2.000	.711	2.711
475	95	80	800	150	950	2.000	.674	2.674
500	100	80	800	200	1,000	2.000	.640	2.640

100 Percent Group Bonus Plan

▼ TIME STANDARDS VIA LEARNING CURVE THEORY

Incentive wage plans assume that monetary bonuses will motivate workers to achieve higher productivity rates. In turn, the greater the output, the lower the conversion cost per unit. Yet, the previous discussion also stresses the fact that motivation is not always based on financial rewards. Furthermore, an incentive wage plan based on fixed time standards—no matter how scientifically engineered—often does not appear to motivate workers.[6] Even with such drawbacks, many current incentive wage plans still use fixed time standards for rewarding individual performance through bonus payments; however, the deficiencies existing in such wage incentive standards have been remedied by means of the learning curve theory.

The *learning curve theory* stipulates that every time the cumulative quantity of units produced is doubled, the cumulative average time per unit is reduced by a given percentage. If it is assumed that this reduction is 20 percent, it means that the second unit requires 80 percent of the cumulative average time per unit required for the first unit; the fourth unit, 80 percent of the second; the eighth unit, 80 percent of the fourth; and so on. Based on this theory, the following table of values for an 80 percent learning curve can be computed, assuming that 10 direct labor hours are required to produce the first unit:[7]

Units	×	Cumulative Average Required Labor Hours per Unit	=	Estimated Total Hours Needed To Perform the Task
1		10.0 hours		10.0 hours
2		8.0 (10.0 × 80%)		16.0
4		6.4 (8.0 × 80%)		25.6
8		5.1 (6.4 × 80%)		40.8
16		4.1 (5.1 × 80%)		65.6
32		3.3 (4.1 × 80%)		105.6
64		2.6 (3.3 × 80%)		166.4

The results indicate that the rate is constant at each doubling of the accumulated number of times the task is performed. The figures in the third column are the cumulative average hours times the number of units. To estimate the total time needed to perform the task the first 32 times, the calculation is 32 × 3.3, or 105.6 hours.

The 80 percent learning curve is used here for illustrative purposes. The 80 percent rate is frequent among industries, and typically the percentage is no lower than 60 nor higher than 85. The actual percentage will depend on the particular situation. Generally, for more complicated tasks in terms of labor skill, there is more room for learning to occur and, therefore, a greater likelihood of a lower labor input percentage as production increases. For a lower learning curve percentage, i.e., for more rapid learning rates, more of the increase in efficiency occurs earlier as cumulative units are produced.

At the extremes, the actual percentage could range from 100 percent (if no learning occurs) to 50 percent. At the latter extreme, if the average accumulated

---

[6]A fixed time standard is best explained by referring to the 100 percent bonus plan (page 242), in which the standard is fixed at 80 units per day (or 10 units per hour).

[7]James A. Broadston, "Learning Curve Wage Incentives," *Management Accounting*, Vol. XLIX, No. 12, pp. 15-23.

time for the first unit is 100 minutes, then the time for the second unit must equal zero (i.e., 100 minutes × 50% = 50 minutes − accumulated average time per task unit at the 2 task units level, or a total of 100 minutes for the 2 units). Thus, the 50 percent rate is an upper limit of learning—one that can never be reached. If the production period is long or the labor operations are routine, a point in production is reached when any improvement through repetition would become imperceptible, and the learning curve would level out to a steady-state condition.[8] It must be observed that in highly automated modern manufacturing processes, especially those that are computer-controlled and perhaps involving robots, there is no learning curve. The machine is as efficient producing one item as it is producing one thousand items.

After the learning curve percentage has been empirically determined for a specific operation, time requirements for successive increments in output can be estimated as long as conditions remain the same. Conditions which may cause deviations from times predicted by an established learning curve include changes in product design, changes in proportions of manufactured and purchased components, and changes in equipment.[9] Of course, conditions may also change because of improvements in engineering design and in manufacturing techniques.

When production is discontinuous, with comparatively long lapses of time and changes in personnel, relearning will be required. Furthermore, there may be a certain element of influence on learning curve behavior that is associated with individual worker variants over time, such as temporary productivity variations caused by health or emotional problems, or the Friday afternoon downturn of production as the weekend approaches. Worker group productivity attitudes may also have their impact.

By means of the learning curve, the time standard used for determining a worker's earnings has now changed to a variable time instead of the fixed time standard. The variable time standard meets the need of an incentive wage system more equitably.

> *The improvement phenomenon, as well as its mathematical model, the learning curve, provides an insight into human capabilities that bears directly upon the ability of workers to do work and the time required for them to learn new skills. An actual learning curve may show small irregularities; yet it will eventually follow an underlying natural characteristic of group or individual human activity.*[10]

As soon as workers have passed the learning stage and begin to produce the expected number of units (i.e., reach the standard proficiency), they will begin to draw bonus pay for doing the operation in less than standard time. They may even slow down a little and yet perform the operation in standard time or better, drawing the bonus pay but working less hard for it.

Government procurement agencies have used the learning curve as a tool for cost evaluation in negotiating prices for contracts. When a bid on a contract

---

[8]For further discussion of learning curves, see Richard B. Chase and Nicholas J. Aquilano, *Production and Operations Management* (Homewood, Illinois: Richard D. Irwin, Inc., 1981), pp. 602-610.
[9]Walter B. McFarland, *Manpower Cost and Performance Measurement* (New York: National Association of Accountants, 1977), p. 43.
[10]Broadston, *op. cit.*, p. 15.

is entered, the unit labor cost is usually estimated. The learning curve permits the determination of lot costs for various stages of production. As production progresses, the cumulative average unit labor cost should decrease.

By comparing the budgeted cost with the experienced labor cost in the initial stages of production, the trend of the labor cost can be determined. If, for example, an average labor cost of $20 per unit is to be achieved, the following output and cost table with 80, 85, and 90 percent learning curves can be predetermined.[11]

Cumulative Quantity	Learning Curve		
	80%	85%	90%
25	$61.02	$45.06	$33.86
50	48.82	38.30	30.47
100	39.06	32.56	27.43
200	31.25	27.68	24.69
400	25.00	23.53	22.22
800	20.00	20.00	20.00

doesn't say how many hours per unit ?

The learning curve allows projection of the cumulative average unit cost at any stage of production. It also predicts labor hours with accuracy and reliability, establishes work load, and allows production control to take advantage of reducing time per unit by increasing lot sizes, thereby maintaining a level work force. It also provides a basis for standard cost variance calculations (Chapter 17), allows judgment of a manager's performance relative to the department's target, and provides a basis for cost control through analysis of undesirable shifts of the curve.

▼ ORGANIZATION FOR LABOR COST ACCOUNTING AND CONTROL

Labor costing procedures involve:

1. The employment history of each worker—date hired, wage rate, initial assignment, promotions, tardiness, sickness, and vacations.
2. Adequate information for compliance with union contracts, social security laws, wage and hour legislation, income tax withholdings, and other federal, state, and local government requirements.
3. The establishment of labor time and cost standards for comparative purposes.
4. Productivity in relation to type of wage payment, creating the best system of compensation for each kind of work.
5. Each employee's time worked, wage rate, and total earnings for each payroll period.
6. The computation of deductions from gross wages for each employee.
7. The output or accomplishment of each employee.

---

[11]William H. Boren, "Some Applications of the Learning Curve to Government Contracts," *NAA Bulletin*, Vol. XLVI, No. 2, pp. 21-22.

8. The amount of direct labor cost and hours to be charged to each job, lot, process, or department, and the amount of indirect labor cost. The direct labor cost or hours information may be used as a basis for factory overhead application.
9. Total labor cost in each department for each payroll period.
10. The compilation of cumulative earnings and deductions detail for each employee.

The accounting principles, procedures, and objectives in labor costing are relatively simple, although considerable difficulty in their application may be experienced with large numbers of workers or when workers shift from one type of work to another under various factory conditions. Basically, two sets of underlying detailed records are kept, one for financial accounting and the other for cost accounting. The procedures for labor accounting are outlined as follows. The journal entries associated with these procedures, as well as those pertaining to labor-related costs, are discussed and illustrated in Chapter 10.

FINANCIAL ACCOUNTING	COST ACCOUNTING
A record is kept of the total time worked and the total amount earned by each worker.	A record is kept of the time worked on each job, process, or department by each worker and the cost thereof.
The daily or weekly amount earned by each worker is entered on the payroll record.	The direct labor hours and cost are entered on the respective job cost sheets or production reports; the indirect labor cost is entered in the proper column of the departmental expense analysis sheets.
Each payroll period, the total amount of wages paid to workers results in the following entry:	The weekly or month-end entry for labor distribution is:

Payroll.....................................	xxx	Work in Process..................................		xxx
Employees Income Tax Payable...........	xxx	Factory Overhead Control..................		xxx
FICA Tax Payable.................................	xxx	Indirect Labor................................	xxx	
Accounts Payable or Cash....................	xxx	Payroll..		xxx

Labor cost control begins with an adequate production planning schedule supported by labor-hour requirements and accompanying labor costs, determined well in advance of production runs. In most manufacturing plants, it is usually possible to establish a reasonably accurate ratio of direct labor hours and number of employees to dollar sales by product lines, and by relating this ratio to the sales forecast, to predict future labor requirements. The relationship between sales volume and personnel needs is perhaps more direct and predictable in wholesale, retail, financial, and service enterprises. The entire labor cost control process begins with the design of the product and continues until the product is sold. The departments that should cooperate in this process include the personnel, production planning, timekeeping, payroll, and cost departments.

Personnel Department

The chief function of a personnel department is to provide an efficient labor force. In a general way, this department is responsible for seeing that an entire organization follows good personnel policies. However, very little of the real personnel work is done by employees of the personnel department. Personnel relations are personal relations—between department heads and their subordinates, between supervisors and workers, and among all employees.

Personnel functions, dealing with the human resources of the organization, involve recruiting and employment procedures, training programs, job descriptions, job evaluations, and time and motion studies. Hiring of employees may be for replacement or for expansion. Replacement hiring starts with a labor requisition sent to the personnel department by a department head or supervisor. Expansion hiring requires authorization by executive management, in which case the authority to hire results from approval of the labor requirements of a production schedule rather than from separate requisitions to fill individual jobs. The personnel department, in conjunction with the department heads concerned, plans the expansion requirements and agrees upon promotions and transfers to be made, the number and kinds of workers to be hired, and the dates at which new employees will report for work.

Employment practices must comply not only with regulations set forth at the federal level (i.e., the Equal Employment Opportunity Commission and the Department of Labor) but also with regulations of human rights commissions in several of the states.

Production Planning Department

A production planning department is responsible for the scheduling of work, the release of job orders to the producing departments, and the dispatching of work in the factory. The release of orders is generally accompanied by materials requisitions and labor time tickets that indicate the operations to be performed on the product. A specific and understandable listing of detailed labor and machine operations is important if work is to be performed within the time allowed and with the materials provided. Delays caused by lack of materials, machine breakdowns, or need for additional instructions give rise to complaints by the workers and lead to additional labor costs. Production schedules prepared several weeks in advance, utilizing labor time standards for each producing department, lead to cost control through the use of departmental labor budgets similar to the one at the top of the next page.

Timekeeping Department

Securing an accurate record of the time purchased from each employee is the first step in labor costing. To do so, it is necessary to provide a:

1. Clock card (or time card) as unquestionable evidence of the employee's presence in the plant from the time of entry to departure.
2. Time ticket (or job ticket) to secure information as to the type of work performed.

LABOR BUDGET

Department __Cooler Assembly__   For __October, 19--__

Prepared __September 10, 19--__

Model No.	Units Scheduled	Budgeted Assembly Hours per Unit			Total Budgeted Direct Labor Hours
		Motor	Fan	Freon	
625	2,000	1.5	.25	.5	4,500
748	1,000	1.5	.30	.6	2,400
500	3,000	1.5	.20	.4	6,300
600	1,500	1.3	.40	.5	3,300
	7,500				16,500

Variable and Fixed Costs	Total Cost	Cost per Unit	No. of Employees*
Variable costs:			
Direct labor -- 16,500 hrs. @ $6	$ 99,000	$13.200	94
Indirect labor -- 1,000 hrs. @ $4.80 ..	4,800	.640	6
Total variable labor budget	$103,800	$13.840	
Fixed costs:			
Supervision -- 700 hrs. @ $7	$ 4,900	$ .653	4
Clerical & Packing -- 350 hrs. @ $4.60	1,610	.215	2
Total fixed labor budget	$ 6,510	$ .868	
Total for October	$110,310	$14.708	106

*No. of hrs. ÷ 176 (22 days x 8 hrs.)

Both forms, which are illustrated at the top of the next page, are supervised, controlled, and collected by the timekeeping department. Since the earnings of the employee depend mainly upon these two forms and the timekeeper processes them in the first step toward final payment, the timekeeping department forms a most valuable link in harmonious labor-management relationships. In fact, to many workers, the timekeeper *is* management. Frequently the timekeeper's performance is the basis for a worker's first opinion of the company.

Clock Card. A *clock card* provides space for the name and number of the employee and usually covers an entire payroll period. When completed, the clock card shows the time a worker started and stopped work each day or shift of the payroll period, with overtime and other premium hours clearly indicated.

The *time clock* (or *time recorder*) is a mechanical instrument for recording employee time in and out of the office and the factory. Under a typical procedure, each employee is assigned a clock number that identifies the department and the employee. The clock number is used for identification on the payroll and in charging labor time to departments and production orders.

Time Ticket. In accounting for materials, the receiving report and the invoice are evidence that the goods have been received and payment is in order. In

Clock Card

DEPT.	NUMBER
03 —	01064

NAME — Ed Gordon

REG. HRS.	HOURS 39¾	RATE 6.60	AMOUNT 262.35
O.T. HRS.			
GROSS EARNINGS 262.35	TOTAL HOURS 39¾	DAYS WORKED 5	

03 — 01064 — 268-28-5042 — 3/17/--

DEPT. CLOCK NO. SOCIAL SECURITY NUMBER WEEK ENDING

⅀17:05	℞17:07 ⅀17:04 ℥17:03 ℉17:06
⅀13:00	℞12:59 ⅀12:50 ℥12:58 ℉12:55
⅀12:03	℞12:00 ⅀12:01 ℥12:02 ℉12:05
	℥ 8:18
⅀ 7:59	℞ 7:50 ⅀ 7:51 ℉ 8:00

MON.	TUE.	WED.	THURS.	FRI.	SAT.	SUN.
8	8	8	7¾	8		

TOTAL HOURS SHOWN IS CORRECT

Ed Gordon
AUTHORIZED SIGNATURE

Time Ticket

DATE 5/27/—		TIME TICKET
EMPLOYEE'S NAME *Warren Mayes*		SHIFT A
TIME STARTED 8:00	TIME STOPPED 12:00	CHARGE ACCOUNT NUMBER 361
HRS. WORKED 4	EARNINGS 23.40	DESCRIPTION OF WORK *Finishing*
OVERTIME HRS. —	OVERTIME EARN. —	PIECE NO. OR JOB NO. 748 / CLOCK NO. 01065
RATE 5.85	TOTAL EARNINGS 23.40	PIECES COMPLETED 14 / OPERATION NO. 27
		SUPERVISOR'S APPROVAL EDV

accounting for labor, the clock card is evidence that time has been purchased and is comparable to the receiving report. The *time ticket* shows the specific use that has been made of the time purchased and is comparable to the materials requisition. When an individual time ticket is used, a new ticket must be made out for each job worked on during the day. Since this procedure may lead to many tickets per employee, some plants use a *daily time report* on which the worker lists jobs.

The best procedure for filling in time tickets depends upon many factors peculiar to shop operations. In some factories, the workers prepare their own time tickets, approved by the supervisor, or the supervisor prepares them. Remote computer terminals enable employees to report time distributions by direct entry to the computer. These entries are later confirmed by the supervisors, based on reports received from the computer center. In other factories, timekeepers, dispatch clerks, and supervisors have desks near the work stations. Employees report to the timekeeper when changing jobs, get a new assignment from the dispatch clerk, secure instructions at the supervisor's desk, get the required tools at the tool crib, and thus shift from one job to another.

Each day, usually after the morning shift has clocked in, the timekeeper collects all the time tickets or the daily time reports of the previous day, together with the clock cards. Before the daily time tickets are sent to the payroll department, the total time reported on each time ticket is compared with the total hours of each employee's clock card. If there is any difference, an adjustment is made. If the clock card shows more hours than the time tickets, the difference is reported as idle time. If the time tickets show more hours than the clock card, the error is corrected in consultation with the supervisor and the worker.

The degree of accuracy in reporting time varies from plant to plant, but in most situations a report to the exact minute is neither necessary nor practical. Many companies find it advantageous to use a decimal system, which is fast and which measures the hour in ten periods of six minutes each rather than the regular clock interval of five-minute periods and twelve periods per hour. On a decimal system, a job started at 9:23 a.m. and finished at 11:38 a.m. would be reported as 9.3 and 11.6, with an elapsed time of 2.3 hours.

Time tickets form the basis for calculating bonuses under a wage incentive plan. When wages are based on hours worked, the time tickets provide a means of auditing the clock cards and a source of data concerning efficient utilization of labor.

Payroll Department

Payroll data are processed in two steps: (1) computing and preparing the payroll and (2) distributing the payroll to jobs, processes, and departments. These steps may be performed by a payroll department, depending on the size and complexity of a company. Some companies require only a small payroll department staffed by one or two payroll clerks who perform the work manually; others require an elaborate payroll department with many employees and computerized procedures. In any case, the payroll department is responsible for the important task of recording the job classification, department, and wage rate for each employee. It records hours worked and wages earned, makes payroll deductions, determines the net amount due each employee, maintains a permanent earnings record for each employee, prepares the paychecks or provides the cashier's or treasurer's office with the necessary records to make the payments, and may prepare the payroll distribution.

Payroll Computation and Preparation. The company's payroll is prepared from the clock cards. The final computed payroll may be recorded in a payroll journal or payroll record. The record must show total wages, deductions, and the net payroll. A record of individual employee earnings and deductions must also be maintained.

In most instances, employees are paid by check. Payroll checks may be drawn against the regular checking account or a special payroll deposit. The special payroll bank account is especially advantageous with large numbers of workers. When a payroll fund is deposited in the bank, the payroll department certifies the amount required for a particular payment date, a voucher is drawn for the specified amount, and a check is drawn against the regular deposit account and is deposited in the payroll fund. By utilizing this procedure, only one check, drawn on the general bank account, appears in the cash payments journal each payroll period. For each employee, the paymaster prepares a check drawn against the special payroll account. When computerized methods are used for payroll accounting, the payroll journal, the checks, the check register, and the employees' earnings records are commonly prepared in one simultaneous operation.

Payroll Distribution. The individual time ticket or daily time report shows the use made of the time purchased from each factory employee. The tickets for each employee must agree with the employee's total earnings for the week. Time tickets are sorted by jobs, departments, and types of indirect labor to permit the distribution of the total payroll to Work in Process and to the departmental expense analysis sheets controlled by Factory Overhead Control. Distribution of the payroll is speeded up when automated methods are used. If the payroll department does not prepare the distribution summary, the time tickets are sent to the cost department, which must perform this task. Labor costs distributed to jobs, processes, or departments must agree with the total amount recorded in the payroll account. The distribution summary may also show the labor hours when they are the basis for the application of factory overhead.

Cost Department

On the basis of the labor distribution summary or the time tickets, the cost department records the direct labor cost on the appropriate job cost sheets or production reports, and the indirect cost on the departmental expense analysis sheets. In some factories, cost accounting activities are decentralized, and cost work becomes largely a matter of organization and direction in carrying out a system for recording payroll information and labor costs. In such a situation, cost clerks may be stationed in producing departments to assist in accumulating and classifying labor costs, using the time tickets to compute production costs and services by job orders, units of output, departmental operations, and product types. In other factories, the cost department may be highly centralized and may not direct and control any timekeeping or payroll preparation.

Summary

The organization chart on page 253 summarizes the departmental inter-relationships required for effective labor cost control and accounting.

The preceding labor costing procedures have emphasized manufacturing labor. Labor costing of nonmanufacturing labor, such as marketing and administrative employees, also requires the same detailed cost accumulation and distribution procedures.

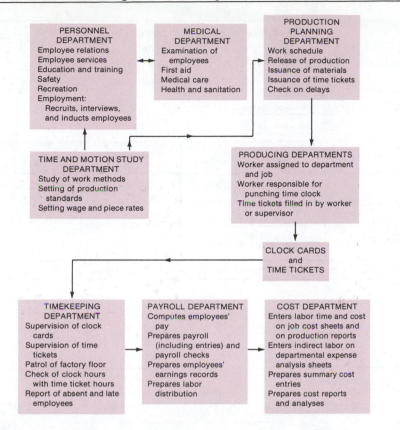

Organization Chart for Labor Cost Control and Accounting

▼ LABOR PERFORMANCE REPORTS

Production schedules, performance standards, and labor budgets represent plans and expectations, but effective control of labor efficiency and costs depends upon meaningful and timely performance reports sent to department heads and supervisors who are directly responsible for departmental production. Labor performance reports are designed to compare budgets and standards with actual results attained, thereby pointing to variances from planned performance. The departmental direct labor cost report, the plant-wide labor cost report issued weekly or monthly, the daily performance report for labor, and daily idle time reports are the media used to provide supervisors and plant managers with information needed for effective cost control.

In the following report, the expected direct labor cost for the week is computed from the October labor budget for the Cooler Assembly Department, shown on page 249. For example, in motor assembling, the Cooler Assembly Department produced 600 units of Model No. 625 requiring 1.5 hours of budgeted labor per unit, 800 units of Model No. 500 with 1.5 hours of budgeted labor per unit, and 500 units of Model No. 600 with 1.3 hours of budgeted labor per unit, for a total of 2,750 budgeted labor hours at $6 per hour, or $16,500.

DEPARTMENTAL DIRECT LABOR COST REPORT

Department: Cooler Assembly
Supervisor: H. Stevenson
Week Ending: October 12, 19--

Production:
No. 625--600 units
No. 500--800 units
No. 600--500 units

Operation	Actual Cost	Budgeted Cost	Variance*	Reasons
Motor.........	$16,925.00	$16,500.00	$425 over 2.6%	Reboring hangers
Fan...........	3,000.00	3,060.00	60 under 2.0%	Good group
Freon.........	5,675.00	5,220.00	455 over 8.7%	Overtime and reweld
Total...	$25,600.00	$24,780.00	$820 over	

*Expressed as a percentage of budgeted cost, e.g., $425 ÷ $16,500 = 2.6%

LABOR COST REPORT

Plant: Midville
Week Ending: October 12, 19--

Department	Labor Class	Actual Labor Cost			Estimated Labor Cost		
		This Week	Last Week	Year to Date	This Week	Last Week	Year to Date
Cutting	Direct....	$28,500	$28,200	$1,174,380	$28,200	$28,000	$1,172,500
	Indirect..	2,200	2,250	81,640	2,240	2,200	81,800
	Total..	$30,700	$30,450	$1,256,020	$30,440	$30,200	$1,254,300
Forming	Direct....	$13,600	$13,400	$ 430,525	$13,750	$13,450	$ 431,000
	Indirect..	1,600	1,600	65,600	1,600	1,620	65,700
	Total..	$15,200	$15,000	$ 496,125	$15,350	$15,070	$ 496,700
Cooler Assembly	Direct....	$25,600	$26,100	$1,152,250	$24,780	$24,000	$1,150,000
	Indirect..	2,825	2,800	117,880	2,750	2,750	117,000
	Total..	$28,425	$28,900	$1,270,130	$27,530	$26,750	$1,267,000

Timely reporting is required for effective cost control. While weekly reports, as illustrated above, are informative and serve a useful purpose, daily reports may be required as well. The following daily performance report and the daily idle time report[12] combine three types of daily labor reports: (1) employee performance, (2) departmental performance, and (3) idle time. Physical factors such as hours are coupled with percentages to improve the effectiveness of these reports.

[12]William L. Ferrara, "An Integrated Approach to Control of Production Costs," *NAA Bulletin*, Vol. LXI, No. 9, p. 65. Copyright March, 1960, by the National Association of Accountants. All rights reserved. Reprinted by permission.

DAILY PERFORMANCE REPORT FOR LABOR

Daily Performance Report by Employees				Daily Performance Report by Departments			
Employee No.	Actual Producing Hours	Standard Hours of Output	Percent Performance	Department	Actual Producing Hours	Standard Hours of Output	Percent Performance
105	8	10	125.0	1	110	90	81.8
110	6	7	116.7	2	280	300	107.1
112	5	4	80.0	3	150	145	96.7

handwritten: 10÷8 ... *handwritten: 90÷110 = .81 81 × 100 = 81.81*

DAILY IDLE TIME REPORT

Depart-ment	Total Direct Labor Hours	Productive Direct Labor Hours		Idle Time Due To							
				Maintenance		No Materials		Other		Total	
		Amount	%	Amount	%	Amount	%	Amount	%	Amount	%
1	3,200	2,900	90.6	200	6.2	50	1.6	50	1.6	300	9.4
2	1,300	1,200	92.3	25	1.9	25	1.9	50	3.9	100	7.7
3	600	550	91.7	20	3.3	30	5.0			50	8.3
4	200	180	90.0	10	5.0			10	5.0	20	10.0
Total	5,300	4,830	91.1	255	4.8	105	2.0	110	2.1	470	8.9

handwritten: 2900÷3200

▼ THE COMPUTER'S CONTRIBUTION TO LABOR COST ACCOUNTING AND CONTROL

Payroll procedures were among the first to be programmed for computers because most businesses had well-defined payroll accounting procedures. Computerized labor accounting begins the day an employee is hired and the data for the employee's name, number, job classification, shift, department, direct/indirect pay rate, deductions, etc., are entered in the employee's master file. From that moment on, the employee's activities and those of every other employee are inputted for payroll data, labor distribution, and a permanent employment data bank. Computerized payroll procedures are depicted in the flowchart on the next page.

Computerized procedures can be used to produce the types of reports that have been illustrated, including use of a computer program to calculate and report each worker's daily earnings and efficiency. Because such a report is too voluminous and impractical for a plant manager or supervisor to use, one procedure is to program for significant unfavorable shifts in performance from one day to the next. This type of report provides for management by exception, whereby the supervisor can work to correct problems of a very few workers

Flowchart of Computerized Payroll Procedures

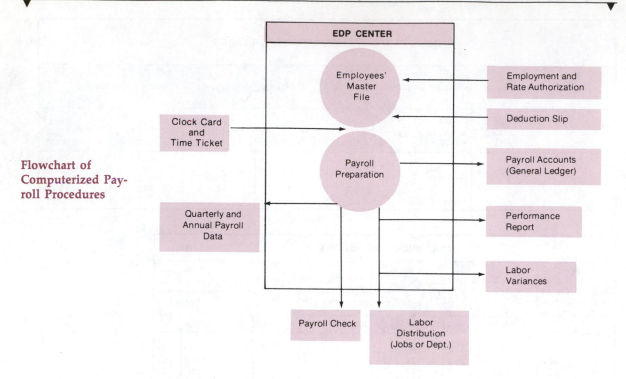

and prevent chronic difficulties. With a work force of five hundred employees, a daily report from the computer, identifying significant adverse changes, might appear as follows. This report is focused on adverse changes in performance from the workers' historical pattern. For example, Perez is a highly efficient performer, but the 81% efficiency rate seems too low for this worker, and management has an opportunity to take early corrective action if needed.

	Employee Performance Report (Significant Adverse Change)					May 19, 19--					
Employee	% Efficiency Last Month			% Efficiency Yesterday	Previous Five Days % Efficiency					Number of Times Reported This Month
	Low	High	Average							
Bowan, T.	72%	84%	78%	64%	76	79	83	81	78	1
Duram, A.	75	91	83	69	71	73	85	90	90	2
Gordon, E.	70	78	74	31	76	71	75	78	74	1
Hoesl, A.	62	88	75	56	80	84	76	65	87	3
Perez, G.	86	98	92	81	85	93	97	94	92	1

With daily efficiency performances in computer storage, management can be provided with monthly or quarterly reports on chronically inefficient workers. The following illustration indicates the information needed to increase effectiveness in labor utilization and labor cost control. Even with no knowledge of the situation, a reading of the illustration suggests that Asbury, Clarke, and probably Varney are not likely to be satisfactory workers in this department if 75% of the standard rate is considered minimal. Dettmer and Mayes seem to be improving, while Shaw appears capable of attaining the desired productivity level.

	Employee Performance Report (Chronically Low Performance)				November 30, 19--						
Employee	% Efficiency Last 12 Months			% Efficiency This Month	Previous Five Months % Efficiency					Number of Times Reported This Year
	Low	High	Average		Oct.	Sep.	Aug.	Jul.	Jun.	
Asbury, M.	33%	43%	38%	40%	42	49	43	51	46	6
Clarke, G.	42	58	50	52	56	45	51	45	51	7
Dettmer, C.	58	74	66	71	70	68	66	58	63	3
Mayes, W.	60	66	63	66	64	60	56	54	50	2
Shaw, T.	70	84	77	68	70	75	68	75	80	5
Varney, M.	45	73	59	64	60	65	68	66	64	4

Effective control is best achieved by careful use of comparisons between actual performance and predetermined standards of performance. Daily or weekly comparisons may be in aggregate (i.e., by department or division), or they may be made for each employee. Departmental labor cost reports can be combined to form a plant summary of operating performance, which is most useful to the plant superintendent and other production officials.

DISCUSSION QUESTIONS

1. Is it generally true that all wage payments are ultimately limited by and are usually based, directly or indirectly, on the productivity of the worker? Explain.

2. Define productivity.

3. Why is productivity important to the firm, to workers, and to society?

4. What are the four major types of quality of conformance costs and why are these costs important?

5. How can labor efficiency be determined or measured?

6. What is the purpose of an incentive wage plan?

7. In most incentive wage plans, does production above standard reduce the labor cost per unit of output? Discuss.

8. Wage incentive plans are successful in plants operating near full capacity.
   (a) Discuss the desirability of using these plans during periods of curtailed production.
   (b) Is it advisable to install an incentive wage plan in a plant operating at 60% of capacity? Discuss.

9. Describe the straight piecework plan, the 100 percent bonus plan, and the group bonus plan.

10. State the basic concept underlying the relationship involved in the learning curve theory.

11. Name some situations for the application of the learning curve theory.

12. Accounting for labor has a two-fold aspect: financial accounting and cost accounting. Differentiate between the two.

13. In what way are the creation and maintenance of an efficient labor force a cooperative effort?

14. What is the purpose of determining the labor hours (a) worked by each employee; (b) worked on each job, or in each department?

15. What purpose is served by the (a) clock card; (b) time ticket?

16. If employees' clock cards show more time than their time tickets, how is the difference reconciled?

EXERCISES

1. 100 percent bonus plan. J. Martin, employed by the Beach City Canning Company, submitted the following labor data for the first week in June:

	Units	Hours
Monday............................	270	8
Tuesday..........................	230	8
Wednesday.....................	300	8
Thursday.........................	240	8
Friday..............................	260	8

Required: Prepare a schedule showing Martin's weekly earnings, the effective hourly rate, and the labor cost per unit, assuming a 100 percent bonus plan with a base wage of $9 per hour and a standard production rate of 30 units per hour. (Round off the bonus percentage to two decimal places.)

2. 100 percent group bonus plan. Dove Plains Inc. produces printed circuits for the electronics industry. The firm has recently initiated a 100 percent group bonus plan with standard production set at 50 units per hour.

The company employs 10 workers on an 8-hour shift at $8 per hour. Depreciation on plant equipment is $10 per hour, and other overhead is applied at $7 per hour.

Production for the first week under the 100 percent group bonus plan was:

	Units
Monday............................	3,800
Tuesday..........................	4,500
Wednesday.....................	4,600
Thursday.........................	4,500
Friday..............................	4,400

Management is interested in appraising the results of the new incentive wage plan.

Required: Prepare a schedule showing employee earnings, unit labor cost, unit overhead cost, and conversion cost per unit. (Round off unit costs to three decimal places.)

3. Incentive wage plans. Standard production for an employee in the Assembly Department is 20 units per hour in an 8-hour day. The hourly wage rate is $8.

Required: Compute the employee's earnings under each of the following conditions (carrying all computations to three decimal places):

(1) If an incentive plan is used, with the worker receiving 80% of the time saved each day, and records indicate:

	Units	Hours
Monday...........................	160	8
Tuesday...........................	170	8
Wednesday.....................	175	8

(2) If the 100 percent bonus plan is used and 840 units are produced in a 40-hour week.

(3) If an incentive plan is used, providing an hourly rate increase of 5% for all hours worked each day that quota production is achieved, and records indicate:

	Units	Hours
Monday...........................	160	8
Tuesday...........................	168	8
Wednesday.....................	175	8

4. Incentive wage plan evaluation. McDaniel Company, a relatively small supplier of computer-oriented parts, is currently engaged in producing a new component for the computer sensory unit. The company has been producing 150 units per week, and factory overhead (all fixed) was estimated to be $1,200 per week. The following is a schedule of the pay rates of three workers assigned to the new component:

Employee	Hourly Rate
Clancy, D......................	$6.00
Luken, T........................	8.00
Schott, J........................	7.00

Customers have been calling in for additional units, but management does not want to work more than 40 hours per week. To motivate its workers to produce more, the company decided to institute an incentive wage plan. Under the plan, each worker would be paid a base rate per hour, as shown in the following schedule, and a premium of $1 per unit for all units when the total number exceeds 150.

Employee	Base Rate
Clancy, D......................	$3.50
Luken, T........................	5.50
Schott, J........................	4.50

The first week the plan was put into operation, production increased to 165 units. The shop superintendent studied the results and considered the plan too costly. Production had increased 10%, but the labor cost had increased by approximately 23.2%. The superintendent requested permission to redesign the plan in order to make the labor cost increase proportionate to the productivity increase.

Required:

(1) Calculate the dollar amount of the 23.2% labor cost increase.
(2) Give an opinion, supported by figures, as to whether the shop superintendent was correct in assuming that the incentive wage plan was too costly, and discuss other factors to be considered.

5. Learning curve and production cost. A company's new process will be carried out in one department. The production process has an expected learning curve of 80%. The cost subject to the learning effect for the first batch produced by the process was $30,000.

Required: Compute the cumulative average cost per batch subject to the learning effect after the 16th batch has been produced, using the learning curve function.

6. Learning curve and construction time. A construction company has just completed a bridge over the Escambia River. This is the first bridge the company has built and it required 100 weeks to complete. Now, having a bridge construction crew with some experience, the company would like to continue building bridges. Because of the investment in heavy machinery needed continuously by this crew, the company believes it would have to bring the average construction time to less than one year (52 weeks) per bridge in order to earn a sufficient return on investment. The average construction time will follow an 80% learning curve.

Required: Compute the number of additional bridges the crew must build to bring the average construction time (over all bridges constructed) below one year per bridge.

(ICMA adapted)

7. Learning curve. Romer Company uses labor standards in manufacturing its products. Based upon past experience, the company considers the effect of an 80% learning curve when developing standards for direct labor costs.

The company is planning the production of an automatic electrical timing device requiring the assembly of purchased components. Production is planned in lots of five units each. A steady-state production phase with no further increases in labor productivity is expected after the eighth lot. The first production lot of 5 units required 90 hours of direct labor time at a standard rate of $9 per hour.

Required:

(1) Compute the standard amount the company should establish for the total direct labor cost required for the production of the first 8 lots.
(2) Discuss the factors that should be considered in establishing the direct labor standards for each unit of output produced beyond the first 8 lots.

(ICMA adapted)

8. Labor performance report. Saxon Inc. prepares monthly production budgets for its three departments. Budgeted and actual amounts for April for one of its products are as follows:

Department	Budgeted Hours	Actual Labor Cost	Units Produced
Mixing..............................	1,100	$ 9,798	740
Processing......................	3,320	28,275	615
Packaging......................	580	3,816	800

The following standards have been adopted for this product:

Department	Standard Hours per Unit	Standard Labor Cost per Hour
Mixing..............................	1.5	$9.15
Processing......................	5.0	9.75
Packaging......................	0.5	9.00

Required: Prepare a labor cost report for April, comparing actual and standard labor cost.

PROBLEMS

9-1. Incentive wage plans. For the first week in March, the record of A. Stewart shows:

	Hours Worked	Units Produced
Monday............................	8	180
Tuesday..........................	8	200
Wednesday.....................	8	220
Thursday.........................	8	224
Friday.............................	8	192

Stewart's guaranteed hourly wage rate is $6 and standard production is 24 units per hour. Factory overhead per labor hour is $3.

Required:

(1) If Stewart receives 90% of the labor value of time saved during a day, prepare a schedule to show Stewart's pay, using the following headings:

Day	Premium Wage
Units Produced	Total Pay
Daily Wage	Labor Cost per Unit (to nearest 1/100¢)
Units Above Standard	Overhead per Unit (to nearest 1/100¢)
Hours Saved	Conversion Cost per Unit (to nearest 1/100¢)

(2) If the 100 percent bonus plan is used (for each week's total production), prepare a schedule to show Stewart's pay, using the following headings:

Hours Worked	Base × Efficiency Ratio
Units Produced	Week's Earnings
Standard Production	Labor Cost per Unit (to nearest 1/100¢)
Efficiency Ratio (nearest %)	Conversion Cost per Unit (to nearest 1/100¢)
Base Wage	

(3) If the daily quota is standard production of 192 units and the hourly rate increases 5% for total wages for each day of quota production and above, prepare a schedule to show Stewart's pay, using the following headings:

Day	Amount Earned
Units Produced	Labor Cost per Unit (to nearest 1/100¢)
Hourly Wage	Conversion Cost per Unit (to nearest 1/100¢)

9-2. Incentive wage plans. The company's union steward complained to the Payroll Department that several union members' wages had been miscalculated in the previous week. The schedule at the top of the next page indicates the wages and conditions of the earnings of the workers involved.

The company's union contract contains the following description of the systems for computing wages in various departments of the company. The minimum wage for a worker is the base rate, which is also paid for any downtime when the worker's machine is under repair or there is no work. Workers are paid 150% of base rates for overtime production in a standard workweek of 40 hours.

(a) Straight piecework. The worker is paid at the rate of $.66 per piece produced.
(b) Percentage bonus plan. Standard quantities of production per hour are established by the Engineering Department. The worker's average hourly production, determined from the total hours worked and the worker's production, is divided by

Worker	Incentive Wage Plan	Total Hours	Down-time Hours	Units Pro-duced	Stan-dard Units	Base Rate	Gross Wages per Books
Dodd	Straight piecework	40	5	400	—	$6.00	$284.00
Hare	Straight piecework	46	—	455*	—	6.00	277.20
Lowe	Straight piecework	44	4	420**	—	6.00	302.20
Ober	Percentage bonus plan	40	—	250	200	6.00	280.00
Rupp	Percentage bonus plan	40	—	180	200	5.00	171.00
Suggs	Emerson efficiency system	40	—	240	300	5.60	233.20
Ward	Emerson efficiency system	40	2	590	600***	5.60	280.00

*Includes 45 pieces produced during the 6 overtime hours.
**Includes 50 pieces produced during the 4 overtime hours. The overtime, brought about by the downtime, was necessary to meet a production deadline.
***Standard units for 40 hours production.

the standard quantity of production to determine an efficiency ratio. The efficiency ratio is then applied to the base rate to determine the worker's hourly earnings for the period.

(c) Emerson efficiency system. A minimum wage is paid for total hours worked. A bonus, calculated from the following table of rates, is paid when the worker's production exceeds 66⅔% of standard output or efficiency. The bonus rate is applied only to wages earned during productive hours.

Efficiency	Bonus
Up to 66⅔%	0
66⅔ — 79%	10%
80 — 99%	20
100 — 125%	45

Required: Prepare a schedule comparing each individual's gross wages per books with the gross wages calculated.   (AICPA adapted)

9-3. Group bonus plans. Employees of Evans and Troup Enterprises work in groups of five, plus a group leader. Standard production for a group is 400 units for a 40-hour week. The workers are paid $6 an hour until production reaches 400 units; then a bonus of $1.20 per unit is paid for production over 400 units, with $1 being divided equally among the five workers and the remainder passing to the group leader (who is also paid a weekly salary of $300). Factory overhead is $7 per direct labor hour and includes the group leader's earnings.

The production record of a group for one week shows:

	Hours Worked	Units Produced
Monday	40	72
Tuesday	40	81
Wednesday	40	95
Thursday	40	102
Friday	40	102

Required:

(1) Compute the week's earnings of the group (excluding the leader), the labor cost per unit, the overhead cost per unit, and the conversion cost per unit, based upon the above data and bonus plan. (Round off unit costs to four decimal places.)

(2) Prepare a schedule showing daily earnings of the group (excluding the leader), unit labor cost, unit overhead cost, and the conversion cost per unit, assuming that the company uses the group bonus plan, as described on page 243.

9-4. Quarterly bonus allotment. Whitlock Inc., manufacturers of standard pipe fittings for water and sewage lines, pay a bonus to their employees, based upon the production recorded each calendar quarter. Normal production is set at 240,000 units per quarter. A bonus of $.50 per unit is paid for any units in excess of the normal output for each quarter. Distribution of the bonus is made on the following point basis:

Employees Participating	Points Allowed For Each Employee
1 Works manager.............................	250
2 Production engineers.....................	200
5 Shop supervisors...........................	200
1 Storekeeper....................................	100
5 Factory office clerks.......................	10
150 Factory workers..............................	20

The employees' earnings are not penalized for any month in which the actual output falls below the monthly average of the normal quarterly production. In such a case, the deficiency is deducted from any excess in subsequent months before any bonus is earned by and paid to the employees.

At the end of March, cumulative actual production amounted to 270,000 units.

Required:

(1) Calculate the amount of bonus payable to each group of employees. (Carry all calculations to three decimal places.)

(2) Prepare journal entries at the end of each month to record the bonus liability on the basis of the following production figures: January, 75,000 units; February, 94,000 units; March, 101,000 units. Assume that all of the bonus is charged to Factory Overhead Control.

9-5. Learning curve in contract price negotiation. Catonic Inc. recently developed a new product that includes a rather complex printed circuit board as a component (Catonic's part number PCB-31). Although Catonic has the ability to manufacture the PCB-31 internally, the circuit board is purchased from an independent supplier because the company's printed circuit line has been operating at capacity for some time.

The first contract for 50 units of the PCB-31 was awarded to Rex Engineering Company in September, 19A, on the basis of a competitive bid. Rex was significantly lower than other bidders. Additional orders for 50 units each were placed with Rex, as shown in the following purchase history schedule:

Date Ordered	Quantity	Unit Price	Total Price
September 15, 19A	50	$374	$18,700
November 15, 19A	50	374	18,700
January 1, 19B	50	374	18,700
February 1, 19B	50	374	18,700

Mark Polmik, a buyer for Catonic, has determined that the next order for PCB-31 should be for 600 units. He has contacted Kathy Wentz, a Rex salesperson. Polmik indicated that the next PCB-31 order would be for 600 units and that he believed that Catonic should receive a lower unit price because of the increased quantity. A few days later, Wentz provided a proposal of $355 per unit for the 600-unit contract.

Polmik has scheduled a meeting with Wentz for next week for the purpose of negotiating the 600-unit contract. He has asked Catonic's Cost Accounting Department for assistance in evaluating the $355 unit price for the PCB-31 circuit board.

The price bid on the original contract for 50 units was estimated to be a full cost-based price, since at that time Catonic was not sure if there would be future contracts for the PCB-31 board. The cost of materials included in the PCB-31 is estimated to be $180 per unit. The Cost Accounting Department is fairly sure that Rex applies overhead at 100% of direct labor and employee benefit cost. Because Rex Engineering recently received a good deal of coverage by the local media when a strike was narrowly averted, the labor and fringe benefit costs at Rex are known to be approximately $20 per hour. The printed circuit line at Rex is similar to the one at Catonic, and Rex's overhead is believed to be approximately 50% variable and 50% fixed. Similar work at Catonic evidences a 90% learning curve effect. However, it is assumed that the learning curve effect on fixed overhead per unit is negligible.

Using the foregoing data, the price of a 50-unit order is estimated to be comprised of the following cost components:

Materials..	$	180
Labor and employee benefits (4 labor hours × $20).....................		80
Overhead (100% of labor and employee benefits).........................		80
Full cost of PCB-31 component..	$	340
Profit contribution (10% of full cost)...		34
Unit price...	$	374
Units purchased..		50
Total contract price...		$18,700

Required:

(1) Prepare a schedule that may be used by Mark Polmik during his meeting with Kathy Wentz next week. This schedule should incorporate the learning curve effect that Rex would have experienced on the first 200 units already produced, which should be of use to Polmik in negotiating a contract with Rex Engineering. (Past production was, and future production will be, in lots of 50 units each.)

(2) What are the implications of an 80% learning curve as opposed to a 90% learning curve?

(3) Identify factors that would tend to reduce the degree of learning that takes place in an industrial operation.   *(ICMA adapted)*

9-6. Planning labor costs. Elliston Inc., a relatively new company in the environmental control industry, is experiencing tremendous growth in product demand. To meet customers' increasing demands, management is considering the addition of a nighttime production shift beginning October 1.

Production takes place in three departments: Assembly, Molding, and Finishing. Standard time in the Molding Department is 10 minutes per unit produced, while the Finishing Department averages 12½ items per hour. Employees in these two departments are paid $8 per hour. Two people are needed in the Assembly Department, each with a monthly salary of $1,500, to serve the extra shift. Five cleanup employees are needed, and one supervisor for each 19 workers (including cleanup employees) is required in the Molding and Finishing Departments. Supervisors are paid $1,900 per month, and each member of the cleanup crew is paid $5.50 per hour.

Under normal conditions, the company schedules 20 workdays per month, with a standard monthly production of 120,000 units.

Required: Prepare a monthly labor budget for the extra shift, showing the time required in each department, the labor cost for each department and service, the unit labor cost, and the number of employees required. (Round off unit costs to four decimal places.)

CASES

A. Setting productivity standards. Anvil, Inc. intends to expand its Punch Press Department with the purchase of three new presses from Presco, Inc. Mechanical studies indicate that for Anvil's intended use, the output rate for one press should be 1,000 pieces per hour. The company has similar presses now in operation that average 600 pieces per hour. This average is derived from these individual outputs:

Worker	Daily Output (In Pieces)
Allen, W.	750
Miller, G.	750
Salermo, J.	600
Velasquez, E.	500
Underwood, P.	550
Keppinger, J.	450
Total	3,600
Average daily output	600

Anvil's management also plans to institute a standard cost accounting system in the very near future. The company's engineers are supporting a standard based upon 1,000 pieces per hour; the Accounting Department, a standard based upon 750 pieces per hour; and the Punch Press Department supervisor, a standard based upon 600 pieces per hour.

Required:
  (1) Specify arguments which each proponent could use.
  (2) Discuss the alternative which best reconciles the needs of cost control and the motivation of improved performance, with an explanation for the choice made. *(ICMA adapted)*

B. Incentive wage plan. Morac Industries is a rapidly growing ten-year-old company specializing in plumbing supplies. The company employs 100 persons. There are 25 salaried employees in office and management positions. The remaining 75 employees perform various production line functions and are paid on an hourly basis. Sales for 19A are forecasted at $3 million.

Management has been so preoccupied with its goals of growth and financial stability that employee relations have been virtually ignored. Many hourly employees do not believe their wage adjustments have kept pace either with industry standards or inflation. Additionally, these same employees do not believe they have been adequately rewarded for their contributions to the company's increase in productivity and performance.

Warren McMan, president of Morac, believes wage incentive programs can be developed to deal with current discontent. Mr. McMan, along with the company controller and manufacturing vice-president, developed a new wage incentive plan they hope will meet the hourly employees' concerns. It would apply to workers once they have completed the company's six-month training program. Currently, unskilled workers are hired at $5 per hour and immediately are put through the training program, at the end of which the workers are assigned to a specific job and awarded wage increases of about $2 per hour. Under the proposed plan, subsequent merit wage increases would be approved by fellow employees and would work as follows:

(a) Employees who believe they deserve merit wage increases would file a wage increase request form. This form would indicate the current wage rate, the amount of the requested pay increase, and the justification for the increase.

(b) Each employee's request would be posted for one week, giving the employee's peers ample time to study the request and observe performance. During this week, records of the employee's history, productivity, and job responsibilities would be available to the other employees.

(c) Fellow employees would vote on each individual's merit wage request by secret ballot. If the majority vote is favorable, the request for a merit wage increase would be approved.

Required: Discuss the advantages and disadvantages to Morac Industries of the new plan for approving merit wage increases. Specifically address the following issues:

(1) Employee motivation.
(2) Employee productivity.
(3) Goal congruence between employee and company.
(4) Administration of the plan.

(ICMA adapted)

C. Learning curve. Kelly Company plans to manufacture a product called Electrocal, which requires a substantial amount of direct labor on each unit. Based on the company's experience with other products that required similar amounts of direct labor, management believes that there is a learning factor in the production process used to manufacture this product.

Each unit of Electrocal requires 50 square feet of raw materials at a cost of $30 per square foot for a total materials cost of $1,500. The standard direct labor rate is $25 per direct labor hour. Variable factory overhead is assigned to products at a rate of $40 per direct labor hour. The company adds a markup of 30% on variable manufacturing cost in determining an initial bid price for all products.

Data on the production of the first two lots (16 units) of Electrocal are as follows:

(a) The first lot of eight units required a total of 3,200 direct labor hours.

(b) The second lot of eight units required a total of 2,240 direct labor hours.

Based on prior production experience, Kelly anticipates that there will be no significant improvement in production time after the first 32 units. Therefore, a standard for direct labor hours will be established, based on the average hours per unit for units 17-32.

Required:

(1) What is the basic premise of the learning curve?

(2) Based on the data presented for the first 16 units, what learning rate appears to be applicable to the direct labor required to produce Electrocal?

(3) Calculate the standard for direct labor hours which Kelly Company should establish for each unit of Electrocal.

(4) After the first 32 units were manufactured, Kelly was asked to submit a bid on an additional 96 units. What price should Kelly bid on this order of 96 units?

(5) Knowledge of the learning curve phenomenon can be a valuable management tool. Explain how management can apply the learning curve in the planning and controlling of business operations.

(ICMA adapted)

D. Payroll procedures. A team of internal auditors was assigned to review the Galena Plant's Payroll Department, including the procedures used for payroll processing. Their findings are as follows:

(a) The payroll clerk receives the clock cards from the various department supervisors at the end of each pay period, checks the employee's hourly rate against information provided by the Personnel Department, and records the regular and overtime hours for each employee.

(b) The payroll clerk sends the clock cards to the plant's Data Processing Department for compilation and processing.

(c) The Data Processing Department returns the clock cards with the printed checks and payroll journal to the payroll clerk upon completion of the processing.

(d) The payroll clerk verifies the hourly rate and hours worked for each employee by comparing the detail in the payroll journal to the clock cards.

(e) If errors are found, the payroll clerk voids the computer-generated check, prepares another check for the correct amount, and adjusts the payroll journal accordingly.

(f) The payroll clerk obtains the plant signature plate from the Accounting Department and signs the payroll checks.

(g) An employee of the Personnel Department picks up the checks and holds them until they are delivered to department supervisors for distribution to employees.

Required: Discuss the shortcomings in Payroll Department procedures and suggest corrective action.   (ICMA adapted)

E. Production planning and control reports. Wilguess Inc., a supplier of bulk metals and alloys, recently negotiated a contract to supply 3,000 sections of aluminum air-conditioning ductwork for an office building under construction. The order required fabricating, cutting, and assembly. Based on experience, the supervisor prepared the following daily budget:

Department	Sections Scheduled	Hours Budgeted
Fabricating	100	50
Cutting	100	30
Assembly	100	25

Realizing the need for up-to-the-minute production information, the supervisor obtained the following results for the first two days:

	Department	Sections Produced	Hours Required
First day:	Fabricating	112	48
	Cutting	81	30
	Assembly	77	22
Second day:	Fabricating	120	49
	Cutting	96	30
	Assembly	96	23

Required:

(1) Discuss the action to be taken by the supervisor, based on the first day's report.

(2) Discuss the action needed according to the results on the second day's report.

CHAPTER 10

Labor: Accounting for Labor-Related Costs

According to a U.S. Chamber of Commerce study, American workers have enjoyed a spectacular growth in nonwage benefits because (1) new benefits have been introduced (e.g., insurance for vision, dentistry, and legal needs), (2) benefit costs have increased, (3) the duration of benefits has increased, and (4) more employees are covered by benefits.[1] Some of the data collected by the U.S. Chamber of Commerce, for the three decades ending in 1979, are summarized in the following table:

EMPLOYEE BENEFITS 1951-1979

Cost Measure	1951	1979
Percent of payroll cost...............................	18.7%	36.6%
Amount per hour...	$.32	$2.68
Yearly amount per employee.....................	$644	$5,560
Total benefits paid in U.S...........................	$26 (billion)	$390 (billion)

Recent data indicate that these benefits have tended to stabilize and in some companies have declined. Nevertheless, employee benefits are substantial. In addition to the basic earnings computed on hours worked or units produced, nonwage benefits are cost elements that enter into labor cost. The following possible labor-related costs that would not be included in the basic wages are expressed as a percentage of straight-time earnings.

FICA tax for employees' old-age, survivors, and disability insurance and the hospital insurance program..	7.5%
Federal unemployment insurance tax (FUTA)...	.8
State unemployment insurance tax (representing a typical rate, with most companies paying less than the 5.4% maximum)..	4.0
State workmen's compensation insurance (rates vary with the hazards—a fraction of 1% to 3% and over)...	1.0
Vacation pay and paid holidays (two weeks of vacation and 7 to 10 holidays in relation to 52 weeks of 40 hours)...	8.0
Contributions to pension fund (probable average)...	7.0
Recreation, health services, life insurance, medical care.....................................	5.5
Contributions to supplemental unemployment pay funds....................................	2.0
Time off for voting, jury duty, grievance meetings..	1.3
Services related to parking lots, income tax, legal advice, meal money, uniforms.........	1.5
Total..	38.6%

[1]*Employee Benefits—Historical Data: 1951-1979* (Washington, D.C.: U.S. Chamber of Commerce, 1981).

Some of the percentages, such as those for FICA, FUTA, and state unemployment insurance tax, apply to a base that may be less than total annual wages, which tends to lower the average annual percentage.

In addition to the elements listed, labor cost usually includes overtime earnings; premium pay for work on holidays, Saturdays, and Sundays when overtime is not involved; shift bonuses or differentials; bonuses for attendance, length of service, no accidents, and year end; apprenticeship or trainee costs; and dismissal or severance pay. This chapter discusses the accounting procedures for many of these fringe benefits.

▼ OVERTIME EARNINGS

The Fair Labor Standards Act of 1938, commonly referred to as the Federal Wage and Hour Law, established a minimum wage per hour with time and a half for hours worked in excess of 40 in one week. Subsequently the act has been amended, broadening the coverage and raising the minimum wage. Some types of organizations and workers are exempt from the provisions of the act and its amendments, or have lower minimums.

A number of payroll practices are mandatory to comply with the Federal Wage and Hour Law. For each employee, records must show:

1. Hours worked each working day and the total hours worked during each workweek.
2. Basis on which wages are paid.
3. Total daily or weekly earnings at straight time.
4. Total extra pay for overtime worked each week.
5. Total wages paid during each pay period, the date of payment, and the work period covered by the payment.

Overtime earnings consist of two elements: (1) the regular pay due for the employee's work and (2) the overtime premium pay, which is an additional amount for work done beyond the 40-hour workweek or a regular 8-hour workday (as specified in some labor union contracts). For most workers, an employer must pay as a minimum the regular rate plus one half the rate for overtime employment. For example, if an employee is paid $8 per hour for a regular workweek of 40 hours, but works 45 hours, the gross earnings are:

Regular workweek	40 hours @ $8 =	$320
Overtime	5 hours @ 8 =	40
Overtime premium	5 hours @ 4 =	20
Gross earnings		$380

Charging overtime premium pay to a specific job or product or to factory overhead depends primarily upon the reason for the overtime work. The contract price of a particular job, taken as a rush order with the foreknowledge that overtime will be necessary, may include the premium wage factor, which should be charged to the specific job. When orders cannot be completed in the regular working hours, the overtime premium pay should be included in the predetermined factory overhead rate as factory overhead, because it cannot properly be allocated to work that happens to be in process during overtime hours.

▼ BONUS PAYMENTS

Bonus payments may be a fixed amount per employee or job classification, a percentage of profits, a fraction of one month's wages, or some other calculated amount. The amount of bonus for each employee may be a fixed and long-established tradition of a company, or the amount may vary from year to year. Bonus payments are a production cost, a marketing expense, or an administrative expense. If a direct-labor employee's average weekly earnings are $250 and the company intends to pay two weeks' pay as a bonus at the end of the year, then earnings actually amount to $260 per week, but the additional $10 per week is paid in a lump sum of $500 ($10 × 50 weeks, assuming two weeks of vacation time) at the end of the year. To spread the bonus cost over production throughout the year via the predetermined factory overhead rate, the weekly entry would be:

	Subsidiary Record	Dr.	Cr.
Work in Process..................................		250	
Factory Overhead Control.....................		10	
Bonus Pay.......................................	10		
Payroll...			250
Liability for Bonus.............................			10

When the bonus is paid, the liability account is debited and Cash and the withholding accounts are credited.

In theory, this and other direct-labor-related costs are additional labor costs that should be charged to Work in Process. In practice, such a procedure usually is impractical, and these costs are generally included in the predetermined factory overhead rate.

▼ VACATION PAY

Vacation pay presents cost problems similar to those of bonus payments. When an employee is entitled to a paid vacation of 2 weeks, the vacation pay is accrued over the 50 weeks of productive labor. For example, assume that a direct labor employee has a base wage of $300 per week and is entitled to a paid vacation of 2 weeks. The cost of labor is $300, plus $12 per week. In 50 weeks at $12 per week, the deferred payment of $600 will equal the expected vacation pay. The entry to record the weekly labor cost, including the provision for vacation pay, would be:

$$\frac{600}{50} = 12$$

	Subsidiary Record	Dr.	Cr.
Work in Process...................................		300	
Factory Overhead Control....................		12	
Vacation Pay.....................................	12		
Payroll...			300
Liability for Vacation Pay...................			12

When a vacation is taken, the liability account is debited and Cash and the withholding accounts are credited. Similarly, accrual should be made for employer liability pertaining to sick leave, holidays, military training, or other personal activities for which employees receive compensation. If it becomes necessary to use temporary replacements to perform the duties of personnel who are absent, this additional expense should be charged to the department for which the replacement is made.

FASB Statement No. 43, "Accounting for Compensated Absences," requires an employer to accrue a liability for employees' rights to receive compensation for future absences when all of the following conditions are met: (1) the rights are attributable to employees' services already rendered, (2) the rights vest or accumulate, (3) payment is probable, and (4) the amount can be reasonably estimated. While the statement requires accrual of vacation benefits, it generally does not require a liability to be accrued for future sick pay benefits (unless the rights vest), holidays, and similar compensated absences until employees are actually absent.[2] In accounting for government contracts, CASB regulations require the accrual of employer obligations for labor-related costs for personal absences.[3]

▼ GUARANTEED ANNUAL WAGE PLANS

While a guaranteed annual wage plan for all industrial workers is far from realization, a step in that direction has been taken in labor contracts that provide for the company to pay employees who are laid off. For example, assume that an unemployed worker is guaranteed 60 to 65 percent of normal take-home pay, beginning the second week of layoff and continuing for as long as 26 weeks. The company pay is a supplement to the state unemployment insurance. To provide funds from which payments can be made during unemployment periods, a specified amount, such as $.15 an hour for each worker, is paid into a fund by the company.

In principle, if it is assumed that layoffs will eventually occur, it is clear that the employee while working is earning $.15 an hour that is not included in the paycheck at the end of the payroll period. This amount is held in reserve by the company in order to make payments during unemployment periods. For a

[2]*Statement of Financial Accounting Standards*, No. 43, "Accounting for Compensated Absences" (Stamford: Financial Accounting Standards Board, 1980).
[3]*Standards, Rules and Regulations*, Part 408, "Accounting for Costs of Compensated Personal Absence" (Washington, D.C.: Cost Accounting Standards Board, 1974).

direct-labor employee whose base pay rate is $8 an hour, the cost effect of unemployment pay for a 40-hour week is illustrated by the following entry:

	Subsidiary Record	Dr.	Cr.
Work in Process..		320	
Factory Overhead Control................................		6	
Unemployment Pay.....................................	6		
Payroll..			320
Liability for Unemployment Pay....................			6

▼ APPRENTICESHIP AND TRAINING PROGRAMS

In many plants, new workers receive some preliminary training before they become economically productive. Of the wages paid, the portion in excess of the average or standard paid for the productive output, plus the cost of instruction, is an indirect labor cost to be charged to the total annual output through inclusion in the factory overhead rates. When unusual training programs are needed as a result of the opening of a new plant or the activating of a second or third shift, a case can be made for treating the training cost as development or starting load cost and deferring a portion of the cost over a period of time.

▼ HUMAN RESOURCE ACCOUNTING

In annual reports, management often speaks in glowing terms of its employees as the company's most valuable asset. Yet management makes little effort to assess the value of this asset, and the company's accounting system does little to provide any assistance. For example, many firms invest heavily in personnel training programs without evaluating the expected payoff or the return on such investments. A firm is apt to send its managers to a variety of executive development programs whose value is essentially taken on faith and which are discontinued when profits cannot afford them.

Human resource accounting is the process of developing financial assessments of people or groups of people within organizations and society and of monitoring these assessments over time. It deals with the value of investments in human beings and with the related economic results. Managers are being asked to give more serious consideration to human resource investment decisions and to the human resource impact of all their decisions. Thus, the personnel function within an organization may serve more efficiently its role of acquisition, development, and utilization of human resource potential.

A human resource accounting system, separate from and supplemental to the formal accounting system, attempts to identify incurred human resource costs that are to be separated from the firm's other costs. The techniques and procedures used should distinguish between the asset and expense components of human resource costs. The resulting human resource assets would then be classified into functional categories, such as recruiting, hiring, training, development, and familiarization. Such information would purportedly enable management to make decisions based on a realistic cost/benefit analysis and cost amortization and would provide investors with an improved basis to assess the value of an enterprise.

The quantification of human resources appears to be the first stumbling block in the creation of human resource accounting. All companies have methods of measuring sales, profits, investments in plant and equipment, and investments in inventories. Similarly, incurred human resource costs, such as training programs, can be measured, although determining the time period for amortization may be difficult. But beyond the possibility of capitalizing certain incurred human resource costs, how does a company set a quantitative value for such attributes as loyalty, skills, morale, decision-making ability, and intelligence? Since it seems difficult to quantify these human factors, it seems equally difficult to assign asset status to human resources except when measured incurred costs can be identified. The justification for measuring an asset value is based on the economic concept that an asset is capable of providing future benefits to the firm. It is argued that, since the employee group is important to the future success of the company, it has value that should be considered as an asset on the human resource balance sheet. Asset determination for human resources is particularly meaningful for professional sports franchises, where a superstar is essentially the asset that creates gate receipts. As with any other asset, the professional athlete can be sold or traded, which increases the litigation involving player contracts.

In spite of the difficulties, a number of proposals have attempted to utilize human resource accounting. Some proposals focus on incurred costs only, while others encompass estimated values. These proposals are:

1. *Capitalizing salaries*—whereby a firm assumes that what the employees are doing will be of some future benefit to the firm and that appropriate rates of capitalization can be determined.

2. *Capitalizing the cost of acquiring an employee*—a plan that would require collecting the costs of acquiring, hiring, and training. (A precedent for this method exists in professional sports.)

3. *Capitalizing startup costs*—involves not only capitalizing startup costs but goes one step further by considering the synergistic components of cost and time required for members of a firm to establish effective cooperative working relationships.

4. *Behavioral variables approach*—involves periodic measurements of the key causal and intervening variables for the corporation as a whole. Statistical variation in leadership styles and technical proficiency levels (causal variables) and the resulting changes in subordinate attitudes, motivations, and behavior (intervening variables) can establish relationships between such variables. These changes would produce changes in the end-result variables such as productivity, innovation, and human resource developments. Trends in earnings could then be predicted. These forecasts are discounted to find the present value of the human resources.

5. *Opportunity costs*—suggest that investment center managers are encouraged to bid for any scarce employee they desire. The winning manager includes the bid in the investment base. The division's benefit is the increased profit produced by the new employee.

6. *Economic value approach*—compares differences in present and future earnings of similar firms in the same industry. Ostensibly, the differences are due to human organization. Future earnings are forecast and discounted to find their present value. A portion thereof is allocated to human resources based on their contribution.

7. *Present value method*—involves determining wage payments over perhaps a five-year period, and then discounting these payments at the rate of return of owned assets in the economy for the most recent year. This calculation yields the present value of the future five-years' wage payments based on this year's return.

8. *Stochastic rewards valuation model*—involves a stochastic process defined as a natural system that changes in time in accordance with the law of probability. To measure an individual's value to an organization requires:

    (a) An estimate of the time interval during which an individual is expected to render services to the organization, and

    (b) A measure of the services expected to be derived from the individual during this interval.

    The resource's expected value is then multiplied by a discount factor to arrive at the present value of expected future services.[4]

Human resource data may be part of a large-scale human resource accounting system or merely part of a specific project application. Although the human resource accounting movement might gain an aura of respectability from inclusion as supplemental data in external reports, these data seem more useful for managerial decisions, i.e., an internal reporting focus.

At present, the value of human resource accounting systems for specific purposes must be determined by designing models and methods which can be empirically tested. Further research is required to demonstrate both the feasibility and the effects of human resource accounting on management's attitude, behavior, and decisions.[5]

▼ PENSION PLANS

A *pension plan* is an arrangement whereby a company provides retirement benefit payments for all employees in recognition of their work contribution to the company. A pension plan is probably the most important as well as the

---

[4]Roger Jauch and Michael Skigen, "Human Resources Accounting: A Critical Evaluation," *Management Accounting,* Vol. LV, No. 11, pp. 33-36.

[5]For an example of empirical research, see Lawrence A. Tomassini, "Assessing the Impact of Human Resource Accounting: An Experimental Study of Managerial Decision Preferences," *The Accounting Review,* Vol. LII, No. 4, pp. 904-913. In this study, human resources accounting cost data caused different preferences to be expressed between the experimental and control group subjects.

most complicated factor associated with labor and labor costs. It influences personnel relations, company financing, income determination, income tax considerations, and general economic conditions. It must also comply with governmental regulations.

Pension Cost Estimate

The ultimate cost of a company pension plan depends upon several related factors:

1. The number of employees reaching retirement age each year.
2. The average benefit to be paid to each retired employee.
3. The average period over which benefits will be paid.
4. Income from pension fund investments.
5. Income tax allowances.
6. Expense of administration.
7. Treatment of benefits to employees who leave the company before reaching the pension age.

Pension Cost Allocation

In the case of bonuses and paid vacations, part of the total earnings of an employee is withheld or accrued for a period of months and then paid in a lump sum. In the case of pension payments, the wage is earned and the labor cost is incurred many years before the payment is made. As a matter of principle, if an employee is paid a base wage for a 40-hour week and if the employer's pension cost will amount to $1.50 an hour, the pension cost incurred is $60 per week and is chargeable to factory overhead, marketing expense, or administrative expense. An employer may also elect to accrue post-retirement benefits, such as health care coverage, during the years of employment, rather than expensing them on a pay-as-you-go basis.[6]

Employee Retirement Income Security Act of 1974

The Employee Retirement Income Security Act of 1974 (more commonly known as ERISA or the Pension Reform Act of 1974) was enacted in order to make certain that promised pensions are actually paid at retirement. This act sets minimum government standards for vesting, participation, funding, management, and a variety of other matters. The act also covers a wide range of employee welfare plans for health, accident, and death benefits. In addition, it covers pension or retirement plans and establishes both labor standards (administered by the Secretary of Labor) and tax standards (administered by

---

[6]For an extensive study of accounting for pension plans and post-retirement benefits, refer to: *AICPA Research Study No. 8* (1965) by E. L. Hicks; *APB Opinion No. 8* (1966); *FASB Interpretation No. 3* (1974); *CAS No. 412* (1975) and *CAS No. 413* (1977); and *FASB Statement No. 35* (1980), *Statement No. 36* (1980), and *FASB Technical Bulletin 1987-1*.

the Secretary of the Treasury). The labor and tax standards taken together form a common body of legislation pertaining to practically all employee benefit plans not specifically exempted from the act.

Virtually every private pension, profit-sharing, thrift, or savings plan had to be amended in order to comply with the act. All plans must contend with increased record keeping, compliance, and reporting. Many plans have experienced increased costs and/or funding obligations.

The Pension Reform Act of 1974, including its amendments, is a comprehensive piece of legislation. The presentation here enumerates only a few matters relevant to labor-related costs. Among the more important requirements affecting employers and employees are:

1. New employees cannot be denied participation for more than one year unless an employee is under twenty-five years of age or benefits are fully vested at the end of a three-year waiting period. The law prohibits a plan from excluding an employee because of advanced age if employment began at least five years prior to normal retirement age.

2. An employer's minimum annual contribution generally must include the normal cost for the year plus amortization of initial past service liabilities, liabilities resulting from plan amendments, and experienced gains and losses. Amortization payments must be calculated on a level payment basis. The amortization period for initial past service costs is forty years for existing plans and thirty years for new plans. The periods for liabilities resulting from plan amendments and experienced gains and losses are thirty years and fifteen years, respectively.

3. In case the assets of a terminated or insolvent plan are not sufficient to pay the insured benefits, the Pension Benefit Guaranty Corporation (PBGC) guarantees certain specified vested benefits for each participant or beneficiary. To finance this insurance program, the PBGC collects a premium from all covered plans.

4. Descriptions of the plan and annual financial, actuarial, and other information must be provided to participants and beneficiaries, the Secretaries of Labor and the Treasury, and the PBGC.

Vesting. A participant of a pension plan is assured of receiving future benefits under a plan when rights to the benefits become vested. *Vesting* means that benefits will not be forfeited even in the event of dismissal or discontinuance of company operations. Employees who resign will still be entitled upon reaching retirement age to receive the benefits in which their rights were vested. The act sets minimum vesting standards that must be met by all plans subject to the participation standards.

Funding. The act establishes minimum funding standards for certain defined benefit plans. The effect of these standards is to impose time limitations for accumulating sufficient assets to pay retirement benefits to participants. Generally, employers must currently contribute the normal cost of the plan for the plan year plus a level funding, including interest, of past service costs and certain other costs. The law does not permit the use of the so-called pay-as-you-go method, whereby employers would make periodic pension payments directly to retired employees.

Present Value (PV). Basic to all funding methods is the concept of present value (PV), sometimes referred to as capitalized value. The *present value* principle permits the value at any given point of time to be expressed as the equivalent value at a different point in time under a set of future conditions. The principle is particularly useful in dealing with financial transactions involving a time series, such as periodic contributions and retirement annuities. It permits the computation of an entire series of financial transactions over a period of time to be expressed as a single value at any point in time.

The Role of the Actuary. Computations relating to pension plan costs, contributions, and benefits are made by an *actuary*, an expert in pension, life insurance, and related matters involving life contingencies. An actuary employs mathematical, statistical, financial, and other techniques to compute costs or benefits, to equate costs with benefits, and to evaluate and project actuarial experience under a plan. Membership in the American Academy of Actuaries, or one of the other recognized actuarial organizations, identifies a person as a member of the actuarial profession.

Administrative Problems. The Pension Reform Act of 1974 mandated sweeping changes in the structure and administration of all types of qualified employee benefit plans. In addition, the act created a staggering number of complicated requirements in such areas as disclosure, reporting, investments, and insurance. For example, an employer must report to four government agencies: the Department of Labor, the Pension Benefit Guaranty Corporation, the Internal Revenue Service, and the Secretary of Labor. A summary description report must also be prepared and sent to all participants and beneficiaries.

CASB Pension Cost Standards

In 1975, the Cost Accounting Standards Board promulgated CAS No. 412, "Cost Accounting Standards for Composition and Measurement of Pension Cost," establishing the components of pension cost, the bases for measuring such cost, and the criteria for assigning pension cost to cost accounting periods. This standard is to be used in accounting for government contracts to which CASB regulations apply. This standard is compatible with the requirements of the Pension Reform Act of 1974, although certain of its provisions are more restrictive than the Pension Reform Act. Furthermore, the CASB standard, while attempting to stay within the general constraints of APB Opinion No. 8, "Accounting for the Cost of Pension Plans," specifies certain features of the opinion which are considered not appropriate for government contract costing purposes. In 1977, CAS No. 413, "Adjustment and Allocation of Pension Cost," declared that actuarial gains and losses should be calculated and gave criteria for assigning pension expense to accounting periods and to segments, as well as for valuing pension fund assets.

▼ ADDITIONAL LEGISLATION AFFECTING LABOR-RELATED COSTS

Costing labor and keeping payroll records were relatively simple prior to the first social security act. This legislation made it necessary for many employers to initiate or redesign payroll procedures in order to account accurately for payroll deductions. Later, other state and federal legislation imposed additional requirements affecting the accounting for wages and salaries. For example, the Federal Insurance Contributions Act, federal and state unemployment tax laws, and workmen's compensation laws require periodic reports.[7] As a result of the multiplicity of forms and regulations, competent personnel are needed in a company's payroll department.

Federal Insurance Contributions Act (FICA)

This legislation is administered and operated entirely by the federal government. Originally enacted in August of 1935 and operative January 1, 1936, the act provided that employers in a covered industry must withhold 1 percent of the wages paid to each employee up to $3,000 of earnings in any one year, which amounted to a maximum of $30 of FICA tax. The employer was required to contribute an equal amount. Employees in several types of work, such as agricultural workers, domestic services, federal, state, and municipal employees, nonprofit organizations, self-employed persons, and a variety of others, were specifically excluded in the 1935 act.

The Federal Insurance Contributions Act has been amended many times since 1935, the amendments tending to bring more employees under the act and to increase the benefits, the tax rate, and the wage base upon which the tax is levied.[8] Under the 1965 FICA amendments, the Hospital Insurance Program (Medicare) was enacted.[9]

Records Necessitated by the FICA. The Federal Insurance Contributions Act requires that employers who are subject to its provisions keep records of:

1. The name, address, and social security account number of each employee.
2. The total amount and the date of each remuneration payment and the period of service covered by such payment.

employers contribute equal amt. as employees

---

[7]These pages summarize the major provisions. U.S. Treasury Department Internal Revenue Service Circular E, entitled "Employer's Tax Guide," is an excellent source for a more comprehensive coverage of these regulations. A free copy of the current edition can be obtained by writing to the nearest District Director, Internal Revenue Service.

[8]The Tax Reform Act of 1984 amended the _Internal Revenue Code_, Section 3121(a), to require the inclusion of fringe benefits (not specifically excluded by statute) in wages subject to FICA tax.

[9]A rate of 7.5 percent for FICA tax, used in the illustrations and in the end-of-chapter material, is not the current rate. The actual rate changes from time to time. The wage base to which the tax applies, assumed in the textbook to be annual wages up to $42,000 per employee, is also subject to change.

3. The amount of such remuneration payment that constitutes taxable wages.
4. The amount of tax withheld or collected.

Although the legislation does not order, suggest, or recommend forms or details for securing the required information, the employer must keep records that will enable a government agency to ascertain whether the taxes for which the employer is liable are correctly computed and paid. These records must be kept for at least four years after the date the tax becomes due or the date the tax is paid, whichever is later. Employees are not required to keep records, but the act recommends that each employee keep accurate and permanent records showing the name and address of each employer, dates for beginning and termination of employment, wages earned, and tax withheld during employment.

Collection and Payment of the FICA Tax. Employers are required to pay a tax on wages paid, equal to the amount paid by the employees. The employer is further required to collect the FICA tax from employees by deducting the current percent from the wages paid each payday up to the current annual limit or base to which the tax applies. Federal income tax withheld and employee and employer FICA taxes must be deposited with either an authorized commercial bank depository or a Federal Reserve Bank on a periodic basis, depending on the amount of taxes to be remitted, and a quarterly report must be filed.

Federal Unemployment Tax Act (FUTA)

Unemployment compensation insurance is another phase of social security legislation affecting labor costs and payroll records. Unlike FICA, which is strictly a federal program, FUTA provides for cooperation between state and federal governments in the establishment and administration of unemployment insurance. When the initial legislation was enacted by the federal government in August, 1935, provisions of FUTA forced various states to pass adequate unemployment laws.

Under the provisions of the Federal Unemployment Tax Act, an employer in covered employment pays an unemployment insurance tax of 6.2 percent. The annual earnings base is $7,000 of each employee's wages paid, with .8 percent payable to the federal government and 5.4 percent to the state. States generally provide an experience rating plan under which an employer who stabilizes employment may pay less than 5.4 percent to the state agency, with zero as a possible payment. State legislation may provide for a higher rate or a larger annual earnings base in computing the state portion of the tax. While the federal act requires no employee contribution, some states also levy an unemployment insurance tax on the employee.[10]

---

[10]The earnings base and rates are subject to change. To be current, consult published government regulations. Also, the percentage payable to the federal government may be greater than .8 percent in certain states because those states failed to repay prior year advances that came from the federal government to the state unemployment compensation funds.

The payroll and personnel departments should work together in striving to earn an experience rating that minimizes the firm's state unemployment tax. An awareness of the effect of claims on the rate may provide stronger incentives for a more stable work force, a desirable condition for the employees as well.

Records Necessitated by the FUTA. Every employer subject to unemployment taxes must keep records of:

1. The total amount of remuneration paid to each employee during the calendar year.
2. The total amount of such remuneration that constitutes taxable wages.
3. The amount of contributions paid into each state unemployment compensation fund, showing separately (a) payments made and not deducted from the remuneration of employees and (b) payments made and deducted from the remuneration of employees.
4. All information required to be shown on the prescribed tax return.

As with the FICA tax, the Federal Unemployment Tax Act does not prescribe or recommend forms or procedures for securing the required information. Each employer is expected to use accounting procedures and to maintain records that will enable the Internal Revenue Service to determine whether the tax is correctly computed and paid.

Payment of the FUTA Tax. The federal portion of the unemployment tax is payable quarterly. However, if the employer's tax liability (plus any accumulated tax liability for previous quarters) is $100 or less for the fiscal year, only one payment is required by January 31 of the following year. The related tax return is due annually on January 31.

State Unemployment Reports and Payments. The various state unemployment compensation laws require reports from employers to determine their liability to make contributions, the amount of taxes to be paid, and the amount of benefit to which each employee is entitled if unemployment occurs. While the reports and report forms vary from state to state, the more important requirements are:

1. *Status Report.* The status report determines whether an employer is required to make contributions to the state unemployment insurance fund.
2. *Contribution and Wage Report.* All employers covered by the state unemployment compensation laws are required to file a quarterly contribution and wage report. This report provides a summary of wages paid during the quarter, a computation of the tax, names of employees, and wages paid to each during the quarter.
3. *Separation Report.* When it becomes necessary to lay off workers, printed materials prepared by the state employment commission are provided, informing employees how to secure new employment and how to make an application for unemployment benefits. An employee who quits without good cause or before working a certain number of

weeks, is discharged for ample reason, or has been unemployed for a short period may be ineligible for unemployment payments. In these cases, an employer files a separation notice with the state employment commission. Since any unemployment benefits paid to a former employee may increase the employer's state rate, the separation notice is filed in order to prevent the charge-back that the state employment commission would otherwise make. Charge statements from the state should be checked by the employer to verify their accuracy.

Workmen's Compensation Insurance

Workmen's compensation insurance laws provide insurance benefits for workers or their survivors for losses caused by accidents and occupational diseases suffered in the course of employment. In most states, these laws have been in effect for many years. While the benefits, premium costs, and various other details vary from state to state, the total insurance cost is borne by the employer. The employer may have the option of insuring with an approved insurance company or through a state insurance fund. In some cases, if the size and the financial resources are sufficient, the enterprise may carry its own risk.

Withholding of Federal Income Tax, State Income Tax, and City Wage Tax

The employer is required to withhold federal income tax—and state income and city wage taxes if applicable—from salary and wage payments to employees and to furnish information to the Internal Revenue Service and to state and city taxing authorities, showing the amount of compensation paid each employee and the amount of income taxes withheld.[11] The collection of income taxes from employees and the remittance of these taxes affect payroll accounting. Before new employees begin work, they are required to fill out a withholding exemption certificate (W-4 form).

Income taxes are withheld from each wage payment in accordance with the amount of the employee's earnings and the exemptions claimed on the W-4 form. Employers are required to furnish a written statement or receipt to each employee from whom taxes have been withheld, showing the total wages earned and the amount of taxes withheld (income taxes and FICA) during a calendar year. This withholding statement (W-2 form) must be delivered to the employee on or before January 31 of the following year. If employment is terminated before December 31, the W-2 form, if requested by the employee, must be furnished within 30 days (1) from the date requested or (2) from the last payment of wages, whichever is later. If it is not requested by the employee, the normal January 31 deadline applies.

---

[11]The Tax Reform Act of 1984 amended the *Internal Revenue Code*, Section 61(a)(1), to require the inclusion of employee fringe benefits in the definition of gross income, i.e., income subject to taxation. Consequently, employers must include employee fringe benefits that are not specifically excluded by statute in income subject to withholding.

As mentioned previously, each employer must periodically deposit federal income tax withheld and FICA taxes. Also, a reconciliation of the quarterly reports with duplicate copies of the W-2 forms furnished employees must be filed annually. Therefore, payroll records must show the names of persons employed during the year, the periods of employment, the amounts and dates of payment, and the taxes withheld each payroll date.

The state may also levy an income tax that must be withheld from employees' wages. The tax withheld must be remitted to the taxing authorities along with the required reports. Information must also be supplied to the employee.

A city or municipality may levy a wage earnings tax on an employee working within its boundaries even though the employee is not a resident. Here, too, not only must reports and payments be made to the local taxing authority, but information must also be supplied to the employee.

▼ LABOR-RELATED DEDUCTIONS

In addition to compulsory payroll deductions, a variety of other deductions may be withheld from take-home pay, with the consent of the employee.

Insurance

Many companies provide various benefits for their employees, such as health, accident, hospital, and life insurance. It is common for the company and the employees to share the cost, with the employees' share being deducted from wages each payroll period or at regular intervals. If the company has paid insurance premiums in advance, including the employees' share, an asset account, such as Prepaid Health and Accident Insurance, will be debited at the time that the payments are made. The employer's share will subsequently be credited to the asset account and debited to expenses, and the asset account will be credited for the employees' share of the premiums when the payroll deductions are made. In this payroll deduction, as in all similar cases, a subsidiary ledger showing the contributions of each employee is necessary, and one or more general ledger accounts are maintained.

Union Dues

Many enterprises employing union labor agree to a union shop and to a deduction of initiation fees and regular membership dues from the wages of each employee. To account for these deductions, a column is provided in the payroll journal, and a general ledger account entitled Union Dues Payable shows the liability for amounts withheld from the employees. At regular intervals, the company prepares a report and remits the dues collected to the union treasurer.

U.S. Savings Bonds

To cooperate with the federal government, an employer and an employee frequently agree to some systematic plan of withholding from wages a fixed amount for the purpose of purchasing U.S. Savings Bonds. A deduction column is provided in the payroll journal, and a general ledger account entitled U.S. Savings Bonds Payable is set up to show the liability for wages withheld for this purpose. When the accumulated amount withheld from a given employee is sufficient to purchase a bond, an entry is made debiting U.S. Savings Bonds Payable and crediting Cash. Similar procedures may be used for other employee savings and investment plans.

Payroll Advances

For a variety of reasons, payroll advances may be made to officers, sales representatives, and factory workers. The advances may be in the form of cash, materials, or finished goods. To provide control, an advance authorization form should be executed by a responsible official and should be sent to the payroll department. The asset account debited for all advances represents a receivable to the company and may be entitled Salary and Wage Advances.

When the advances take the form of merchandise, Materials or Finished Goods is credited. If the merchandise is charged to the employee at a figure above cost, Sales may be credited. When the price is above cost but substantially less than the regular sales price, an account entitled Sales to Employees might be maintained. At the regular payroll date, the employee's earnings are entered in the payroll journal as usual, and the advance is deducted from wages to be paid. The amount of the advance being deducted is credited to Salary and Wage Advances.

▼ RECORDING LABOR COSTS

The basic principle of labor costing is simple and straightforward. A record of the labor time "purchased" is made through use of the clock card; a record of the performance received is made through the use of time tickets or the daily time report. The accounting entries required are:

1. To record wage payments due employees and the liability for all amounts withheld from wages.
2. To charge the total labor cost to appropriate jobs, processes, and departments.

Weekly, semimonthly, monthly, or as often as a payroll is met, the total amount earned by workers is debited to Payroll, with credits to Accrued Payroll and to the withholding accounts. The cost of labor purchased is summarized and recorded as debits to Work in Process, Factory Overhead Control, Marketing Expenses Control, and Administrative Expenses Control and as a credit to Payroll. Employer payroll taxes and other labor-related costs are recorded, and at appropriate times, payments are made to discharge payroll-related liabilities.

The accounting for labor costs and payroll liabilities is illustrated in general journal form on pages 285 and 286, based upon these assumptions:

1. The payroll period is for January, 19B.
2. The payroll is paid on January 9, 19B, and on January 23, 19B, covering wages earned through the preceding Saturday. Note that the wages of the last week of December, 19A, would be paid on January 9 and that the payment of January 23 would cover work done through January 19. Refer to the following calendar.

JANUARY, 19B

Sun	Mon	Tue	Wed	Thu	Fri	Sat
		1	2	3	4	5
6	7	8	9	10	11	12
13	14	15	16	17	18	19
20	21	22	23	24	25	26
27	28	29	30	31		

3. Payroll figures for wages earned during January are:

Direct factory labor...	$38,500
Indirect factory labor..	18,000
Sales salaries..	20,000
Office and administrative salaries.....................	12,000
Total payroll..	$88,500

4. Wages paid during January, 19B: $50,000 on January 9, and $40,000 on January 23. Of the federal income tax withheld, $6,000 is on the payroll of January 9 and $5,500 on that of January 23.
5. Wages earned and unpaid on December 31, 19A, total $26,000. On January 31, the amount is $24,500.
6. The cost of the employer's payroll taxes is recorded when the month-end labor cost distribution entry is made, with separate liability accounts for federal and state agencies. Employees' FICA taxes are recorded when they are withheld at the payroll date, in compliance with the regulations.

Added assumptions:

FICA tax, 7.5%.
Workmen's compensation, 1% of payroll.
Unemployment insurance: .8% federal, 5.4% state.

Pension cost estimated to be $4,000 per month, divided as follows:
   direct labor, $1,540; indirect labor, $900; sales salaries, $1,000; office
   and administrative salaries, $560.
Payroll advances, $2,200 deducted on January 9 payroll.
Union dues collected, $1,000 each payroll period.
Savings bonds deductions, $1,200 on January 9 and $900 on January 23.
Health and accident insurance, 2% of payroll, shared equally—
   employees' share as wages paid, employer's share as wages earned.
Cost for supplemental unemployment benefits, 2% of factory labor earned.

	Subsidiary Record	Dr.	Cr.
Reversing entry for wages payable as of December 31:			
Jan. 2 Accrued Payroll..		26,000.00	
Payroll..			26,000.00
9 Payroll..		50,000.00	
Accrued Payroll...			35,350.00
Employees Income Tax Payable....................................			6,000.00
FICA Tax Payable..			3,750.00
Salary and Wage Advances...			2,200.00
Union Dues Payable..			1,000.00
U.S. Savings Bonds Payable...			1,200.00
Prepaid Health and Accident Insurance........................			500.00
9 Accrued Payroll...		35,350.00	
Cash..			35,350.00
23 Payroll..		40,000.00	
Accrued Payroll...			29,200.00
Employees Income Tax Payable....................................			5,500.00
FICA Tax Payable..			3,000.00
Union Dues Payable..			1,000.00
U.S. Savings Bonds Payable...			900.00
Prepaid Health and Accident Insurance........................			400.00
23 Accrued Payroll...		29,200.00	
Cash..			29,200.00
31 Payroll..		24,500.00	
Accrued Payroll...			24,500.00
31 Work in Process..		38,500.00	
Factory Overhead Control..		8,354.50	
FICA Tax..	2,887.50		
Unemployment Insurance Taxes...............................	2,387.00		
Workmen's Compensation..	385.00		
Pension Expense...	1,540.00		
Health and Accident Insurance................................	385.00		
Estimated Unemployment Expense..........................	770.00		
Payroll..			38,500.00
FICA Tax Payable...			2887.50
Federal Unemployment Tax Payable..........................			308.00
State Unemployment Tax Payable.............................			2,079.00
Prepaid Workmen's Compensation...........................			385.00
Liability for Pensions..			1,540.00
Prepaid Health and Accident Insurance....................			385.00
Liability for Unemployment Pay..................................			770.00

	Subsidiary Record	Dr.	Cr.
Jan. 31 Factory Overhead Control....................................		22,086.00	
Indirect Labor..	18,000.00		
FICA Tax...	1,350.00		
Unemployment Insurance Taxes...............................	1,116.00		
Workmen's Compensation....................................	180.00		
Pension Expense...	900.00		
Health and Accident Insurance.................................	180.00		
Estimated Unemployment Expense......................	360.00		
Payroll..			18,000.00
FICA Tax Payable...			1,350.00
Federal Unemployment Tax Payable......................			144.00
State Unemployment Tax Payable.........................			972.00
Prepaid Workmen's Compensation.............................			180.00
Liability for Pensions.....................................			900.00
Prepaid Health and Accident Insurance........................			180.00
Liability for Unemployment Pay....................................			360.00
31 Marketing Expenses Control...............................		24,140.00	
Sales Salaries...	20,000.00		
FICA Tax...	1,500.00		
Unemployment Insurance Taxes...............................	1,240.00		
Workmen's Compensation....................................	200.00		
Pension Expense...	1,000.00		
Health and Accident Insurance.................................	200.00		
Payroll..			20,000.00
FICA Tax Payable...			1,500.00
Federal Unemployment Tax Payable......................			160.00
State Unemployment Tax Payable.........................			1,080.00
Prepaid Workmen's Compensation.............................			200.00
Liability for Pensions.....................................			1,000.00
Prepaid Health and Accident Insurance........................			200.00
31 Administrative Expenses Control...............................		14,444.00	
Office and Administrative Salaries...........................	12,000.00		
FICA Tax...	900.00		
Unemployment Insurance Taxes...............................	744.00		
Workmen's Compensation....................................	120.00		
Pension Expense...	560.00		
Health and Accident Insurance.................................	120.00		
Payroll..			12,000.00
FICA Tax Payable...			900.00
Federal Unemployment Tax Payable......................			96.00
State Unemployment Tax Payable.........................			648.00
Prepaid Workmen's Compensation.............................			120.00
Liability for Pensions.....................................			560.00
Prepaid Health and Accident Insurance........................			120.00

This illustration records the employer's payroll taxes as a liability when the wages are earned, which follows the accrual concept of accounting. As a practical matter, many employers do not accrue payroll taxes at the end of each fiscal period because the legal liability does not occur until the next period when the wages are paid. This latter practice may be considered acceptable if it is consistently applied or if the amounts are not material. It is, however, required for income tax purposes.

DISCUSSION QUESTIONS

1. The hourly wage of an employee is $9, but the labor cost of the employee is considerably more than $9 an hour. Explain.

2. Discuss the accounting treatment of fringe benefits to factory employees.

3. Give two costing methods of accounting for the premium costs of overtime direct labor. State circumstances under which each method would be appropriate.
   (AICPA adapted)

4. For many years, a company has paid all employees one week's wages as a year-end bonus. It is also company policy to give 2-week paid vacations. What accounting procedures should be followed with respect to the bonus and vacation pay?

5. The productive efficiency of a company depends upon superior group leaders. The company management suggests that group leaders and selected workers organize a class in personnel administration and group leadership. The class is set up at a nearby university, with one of the regular professors in charge. The employees attend the class at night on their own time, but the company pays the tuition charges. How should the company account for this cost?

6. (a) Define human resource accounting.
   (b) What are the objectives of the concept?
   (c) State the theoretical proposals that have been made in favor of human resource accounting.
   (d) What are some of the more serious drawbacks of this concept?

7. The total cost of contributions that must be paid ultimately to provide pensions for the present participants in a plan cannot be determined precisely in advance; however, reasonably accurate estimates can be made by the use of actuarial techniques. List the factors entering into the determination of the ultimate cost of a funded pension plan.
   (AICPA adapted)

8. The term "pension plan" has been referred to as a formal arrangement for employee retirement benefits, whether established unilaterally or through negotiation, by which specific or implied commitments have been made and used as the basis for estimating costs. Explain the preferable procedure for computing and accruing the costs under a pension plan.
   (AICPA adapted)

9. What is meant by the experience-rating provisions of the unemployment compensation laws of various states?

EXERCISES

1. Overtime earnings. An employee in the Assembly Department is paid $7 an hour for a regular week of 40 hours. During the week ended April 30, the employee worked 56 hours and earned time and a half for overtime hours.

Required:

(1) Prepare the journal entry to record the labor cost if the overtime premium is charged to production worked on during the overtime hours.

(2) Prepare the journal entry to record the labor cost if the overtime premium is not charged to production worked on during the overtime hours.

2. Bonus and vacation pay liability. A production worker earns $1,150 per month and the company pays the worker a year-end bonus equal to one month's wages. The worker is also entitled to a half-month paid vacation per year. Company policy dictates that bonus and vacation benefits be treated as indirect costs and accrued during the 11½ months the employee is at work.

Required: Prepare the journal entry to record and distribute (simultaneously) the labor cost of the production worker for a month. Assume that there are no deductions from gross wages.

3. **Bonus and vacation pay liability.** Four factory workers and a supervisor comprise a team in the Machining Department. The supervisor earns $10 per hour and the combined hourly direct wages of the four workers is $32. Each employee is entitled to a two-week paid vacation and a bonus equal to four weeks' wages each year. Vacation pay and bonuses are treated as an indirect cost and are accrued over the 50-week work year. A provision in the union contract does not allow these employees to work in excess of 40 hours per week.

Required: Prepare the journal entry to record the bonus and vacation pay liability applicable to one week's production.

4. **Pension cost allocation.** Midatlantic Corporation has just installed a pension plan for its 100 employees. Normal operations are 50 weeks per year at 40 hours each week. After working 25 years, the workers are to receive a pension of $4,800 a year for an average of 10 years. For July, the number of labor hours was 18,000. Pension cost is recorded monthly on the basis of labor hours.

Required: Ignoring administrative cost and earnings from invested funds, compute the following:

(1) Pension cost per labor hour.
(2) Pension cost for July.

5. **Fringe benefits.** A production worker earns $1,656 a month, and the company pays one month's salary as a bonus at the end of the year. The worker is also entitled to a half-month paid vacation, and the company pays $1,840 a year into a pension fund for the worker. Bonus, vacation pay, and pension costs are charged to production during the 11½ months the employee is at work. The federal and state unemployment insurance tax rates are .8% and 3.6%, respectively. The employer's share of FICA tax is 7.5%. All labor-related fringe benefits for production workers are treated as factory overhead.

Required: Prepare the journal entries to record the March payroll distribution and the cost of fringe benefits.

6. **Employer's labor-related expenses.** Digby Company has employees engaged in manufacturing, marketing, and administrative functions. The February payroll was:

Direct labor........................	$25,000
Indirect labor......................	10,000
Marketing...........................	8,000
Administrative....................	7,000
	$50,000

The company incurs the following labor-related expenses as a percentage of the payroll:

Pension plan	7.8%
FICA tax	7.5
Federal unemployment insurance	.8
State unemployment insurance	4.6
Workmen's compensation	4.0
Medical insurance	1.0

Required: Present the journal entry to record the employer's labor-related expenses.

(CGAAC adapted)

7. Payroll entries. For the second week in February, Wisconsin Products Company's records show direct labor, $18,000; indirect factory labor, $3,000; sales salaries, $4,200; and administrative office salaries, $1,500. The FICA tax rate is 7.5%; state and federal unemployment compensation insurance taxes are 3.2% and .7%, respectively; state and federal income taxes withheld are $500 and $2,500, respectively; and the city wage tax is 1% on employee gross earnings and is paid by the employee. The company treats employer payroll taxes on factory personnel as an indirect cost.

Required:

(1) Prepare the entry to record the payroll liability.
(2) Prepare the entry to distribute the payroll cost.
(3) Prepare the entry to record the employer's payroll taxes.

8. Payroll entries. For the first payroll in November, the records of Nans Company show direct labor, $20,000; indirect labor, $4,000; sales salaries, $5,000; and office salaries, $3,600. FICA tax is applicable to 75% of the payroll in each department, while unemployment insurance tax applies to only 25%. Federal income tax to be withheld totals $3,000, and employees pay a city income tax of 1% on gross earnings.

Required: Prepare the journal entries to record the payroll liability, distribute the payroll, and record the employer's payroll taxes, treated as an indirect cost. The state unemployment tax rate is 3%, the FUTA tax rate is .8%, and the FICA tax rate is 7.5%.

PROBLEMS

10-1. Entries for payroll and payroll taxes. For the December 1-15 payroll, which totaled $28,000, employees' FICA deductions amounted to only $1,230, since some of the employees had already earned the maximum applicable during the year. For the same period, income tax withheld totaled $2,872.

The company should apportion employer FICA taxes as follows: 60% to factory overhead, 30% to marketing expense, and 10% to general office expense. The state unemployment insurance tax rate is 4%, the FUTA tax rate is .8%, and only $5,000 of the payroll (all factory employees) is subject to this tax, since all other employees had earned more than $7,000 by December 1. The company closed for the year on December 15 and had no more payroll expenses.

Required: Prepare the entry to record the payroll for the period December 1-15, the entry to pay the payroll of December 1-15, and the entry to record the employer's payroll taxes for the period December 1-15.

10-2. Payroll, tax deductions, and payroll distribution. The following information, taken from the daily time tickets of a producing department, summarizes time and piecework for the week ended April 30:

Employee	Clock No.	Job No.	Hours Worked	Production Pieces	Hourly Rate	Piece Rate
Belcastro, V......................	90	641	40	960	—	$.30
Cherpack, C.....................	91	—	46	—	$7.00	—
Meadows, A.....................	92	638	40	—	5.80	—
Smeltzer, S......................	93	—	40	—	7.20	—

The company operates on a 40-hour week and pays time and a half for overtime. Additional information:

(a) A FICA tax deduction of 7.5% should be made for each employee.
(b) An advance of $20 was made to Belcastro on April 26.
(c) A 2% deduction is to be made from each employee's wage for the company's employee health and hospital benefit plan.
(d) Cherpack works in the storeroom issuing materials; Smeltzer is the supervisor; the others work directly on special orders as noted.
(e) Use 10% in computing income tax withheld. The state unemployment tax rate is 4%, and the federal unemployment tax rate is .8%.

Required:

(1) Compute each employee's gross pay, deductions, and net pay.
(2) Prepare journal entries to (a) set up the accrued payroll and other liabilities, (b) pay the payroll, and (c) distribute the payroll and record the employer's payroll taxes. Include subsidiary record detail.

10-3. Payroll taxes, vacation pay, and payroll. The normal workweek at Starks Publishing Inc. is Monday through Friday, with payday being the following Tuesday. On April 1, after the reversing entry was posted, the payroll account showed a $2,230 credit balance, representing labor purchased during the last two days of March. (See the following calendar.)

APRIL

Sun	Mon	Tue	Wed	Thu	Fri	Sat
			1	2	3	4
5	6	7	8	9	10	11
12	13	14	15	16	17	18
19	20	21	22	23	24	25
26	27	28	29	30		

Deductions of 7.5% for FICA tax and 9.5% for income tax are withheld from each payroll check.

The labor summary for April shows $16,400 of direct labor and $5,600 of indirect labor. Vacation pay is charged to current production at a rate of 8% of total payroll. Payrolls were:

April 7......................	$5,890
14......................	4,920
21......................	5,900
28......................	4,880

Required:

- (1) Prepare entries to record each payroll.
- ⚡(2) Prepare the entry on April 30 to distribute the payroll and to record the employer's payroll taxes for wages earned during April, treating the employer's payroll taxes and vacation pay as factory overhead. The state unemployment tax rate is 4%, and the federal unemployment tax rate is .8%. Include subsidiary record detail.
- (3) Prepare T-accounts for Payroll and Accrued Payroll and the entry to record accrued wages at the end of April.

10-4. Payroll entries. Cleanaire Inc. manufactures air pollution control devices. There are four producing departments, supported by two factory service departments, Toolroom and Storeroom. For manufacturing employees, overtime premium wages are treated as factory overhead, as are payroll taxes borne by the employer. The Finished Goods Stockroom and Shipping departments are located in the manufacturing plant facilities but are a part of marketing expenses. The separate sales and administrative offices' payroll expenses are charged to marketing expenses and administrative expenses, respectively.

For the week ended February 14, the following payroll summary was prepared:

Department	Labor Hours	Payroll (Earned Hours)	Overtime Premium	Federal Income Tax Withheld (10%)	FICA Tax (7.5%)	Net Pay
Casting..........................	240	$ 1,620	$108	$ 172.80	$129.60	$1,425.60
Forging..........................	410	2,542	160	270.20	202.65	2,229.15
Machining.....................	560	3,976	120	409.60	307.20	3,379.20
Assembly......................	160	960	—	96.00	72.00	792.00
Toolroom......................	84	428	16	44.40	33.30	366.30
Storeroom....................	82	410	8	41.80	31.35	344.85
Finished Goods						
Stockroom................	40	180	—	18.00	13.50	148.50
Shipping.......................	40	192	—	19.20	14.40	158.40
Total plant payroll.....	1,616	$10,308	$412	$1,072.00	$804.00	$8,844.00
Sales Office.................	—	$ 2,200	—	$ 220.00	$165.00	$1,815.00
Administrative Office....	—	1,550	$150	170.00	127.50	1,402.50

Required: Prepare journal entries, including subsidiary record detail, to record:

- (1) Preparation of the payroll.
- (2) Payment of the payroll.
- (3) Distribution of the payroll.
- (4) Recording of the employer's payroll taxes. (The state unemployment tax rate is 3.2%, and the federal unemployment tax rate is .8%.)

10-5. Payroll cycle. The payroll department of Banderillo Company Inc. prepares its monthly and biweekly payroll using the following payroll data:

- (a) The payroll period deals with August and September; the last payment was made on August 25. Refer to the calendars on page 292.
- (b) The company pays its factory, marketing, and office and administrative personnel on a biweekly basis. The workweek is Monday through Friday; paychecks are distributed on the Friday following the close of the two weeks. Executives, superintendents, and department heads are paid on a monthly basis on the first

			AUGUST							SEPTEMBER			
Sun	Mon	Tue	Wed	Thu	Fri	Sat	Sun	Mon	Tue	Wed	Thu	Fri	Sat
		1	2	3	4	5						1	2
6	7	8	9	10	11	12	3	4	5	6	7	8	9
13	14	15	16	17	18	19	10	11	12	13	14	15	16
20	21	22	23	24	25	26	17	18	19	20	21	22	23
27	28	29	30	31			24	25	26	27	28	29	30

Friday following the last day of the month. The 4th of September is Labor Day; all employees will be paid, but the direct labor cost is charged to factory overhead.

(c) The payroll is based on these data:

Monthly salaries:

2 executives: $3,000 each per month
3 superintendents: $2,500 each per month
2 department heads: $2,000 each per month

Hourly workers:

Direct factory labor: 200 employees; 40 hours per week; average pay, $6 per hour
Indirect factory labor: 30 employees; 40 hours per week; average pay, $4 per hour

Weekly rates:

Marketing personnel: 12 employees; average pay, $350 per week
Office and administrative personnel: 9 employees; average pay, $305 per week

(d) Additional information:

Federal income tax withheld: 15% on monthly salaries; 10% on all others

FICA tax: 7.5% (maximum $42,000 earnings per year)

Federal unemployment tax: .8% up to $7,000 per employee

State unemployment tax: 5.4% up to $7,000 per employee

The FICA tax is recorded as a liability when it is withheld at the payroll date, in compliance with regulations. The employer's payroll taxes are recorded when the cost distribution entry is made; separate liability accounts are kept for federal and state agencies; month-end payroll accrual entries are made only at the end of the calendar year.

Workmen's compensation insurance: 1% of total payroll

Pension cost: 5% for monthly salaries, with equal contributions by these employees deducted from their paychecks; 3% for all other employees, with no contributions by them

Union dues: $.50 deducted each payday from each hourly worker

Health insurance: 1% of earnings, shared equally between employees and employer

Required: Prepare journal entries, including subsidiary record detail, to record:

(1) The monthly salaries to be paid in September, with all applicable deductions and employer-borne labor-related costs. Distribution is to be made as follows: 2 executives to administration; 3 superintendents to factory; 1 department head to marketing; 1 department head to administration (office).

(2) Factory, marketing, and office employees' earnings to be paid in September on a biweekly basis, with all applicable deductions and employer-borne labor-related costs. Distribution is to be made on the basis of the four categories.

(3) The earnings of one direct factory laborer for the first of the two-week payroll periods, in order to illustrate the procedure required for an individual employee.

CASES

A. Cost principles and cost determination. As a subcontractor under a prime contract with a governmental agency, a company operating a machine shop undertook to produce certain parts on a cost-plus-fixed-fee basis. The hours of operation were about evenly divided between the above contract and the regular business of the company.

Each day, the work required for the regular company business was completed first. The remainder of the day, with whatever overtime was necessary, was devoted to production under the contract. During the contract period, overtime hours represented a substantial portion of the total hours worked. Under an agreement with the employees, time and a half was paid for all hours over eight worked each day.

Job sheets recorded the actual costs of materials and direct labor, including any overtime premium paid. Factory overhead was applied on the basis of the labor cost so recorded, and the job sheets were adjusted each month to eliminate any balance in the overhead variance account.

Required: State objections to the cost accounting principles applied, reasons for any incorrectness of the client's statements, and the procedure for making a revised cost determination. *(AICPA adapted)*

B. Human resource accounting. The Consumer Products Division of Liberty Manufacturing Company experienced reduced sales in the first quarter of 19B and has forecasted that the decline in sales will continue through the remainder of the year.

Liberty's executive management believes in a decentralized organization, and division managers have considerable managerial latitude, receiving bonuses of a specified percentage of division profits, in addition to their annual salaries. At the end of the first quarter of 19B, J. Spassen, the Consumer Products Division manager, felt that drastic action was needed to reduce costs and improve the division's performance. Consequently, 20 highly-trained, skilled employees were dismissed as one cost-reduction step. Five of these employees are expected to be available for reemployment when business is projected to return to normal in 19C.

Executive management, upon reviewing the steps taken by Spassen, was concerned about the consequences of dismissing the 20 skilled employees. The company officials had recently attended a seminar on human resource accounting and wondered if Spassen would have taken that particular action if a cost-based human resource accounting system had been in operation.

Required:

(1) Explain what is accounted for in a cost-based human resource accounting system.
(2) Explain how information generated by such a system might apply to the decision to dismiss the 20 skilled employees. *(ICMA adapted)*

CHAPTER 11
Cost Behavior Analysis

Some costs vary in total directly with changes in production activity, while others remain relatively unaffected. Because of the dynamic nature of business, companies are often faced with the need to make changes in the level and mix of their business activities. In order for management to plan a company's activities intelligently and control its costs effectively, the relationship of cost incurrence to changes in activity must be thoroughly understood. This chapter classifies costs, with respect to activity, as fixed, variable, or semivariable, and it illustrates techniques used to segregate the fixed and variable components of semivariable costs. Although the discussion centers on production costs and activities, the concepts and techniques are equally applicable to marketing and administrative activities.

▼ CLASSIFYING COST

Success in planning and controlling cost depends upon careful study and analysis of the relationship of cost to changes in business activity and requires classifying each type of expenditure as a fixed, variable, or semivariable cost.

Fixed Cost

A *fixed cost* remains the same in total as activity increases or decreases. However, a cost will remain fixed only within a limited range of activity. This range of activity is referred to as the *relevant range*. Total fixed cost will change outside the relevant range of activity. The changes in fixed cost at different levels of activity and the relevant range are depicted in the graph on page 295.

In the long run, all costs are variable. If all business activity decreases to zero and there is no prospect for an increase, a firm will liquidate, thereby avoiding all costs. If activity is expected to increase beyond the capacity of current facilities, fixed costs must be increased to handle the expected excess volume. For example, fixed factory overhead includes items such as supervision, depreciation, rent, property insurance, and property taxes. If management expects demand for the company's products to increase beyond the capacity of the present production facilities, it must acquire additional plant

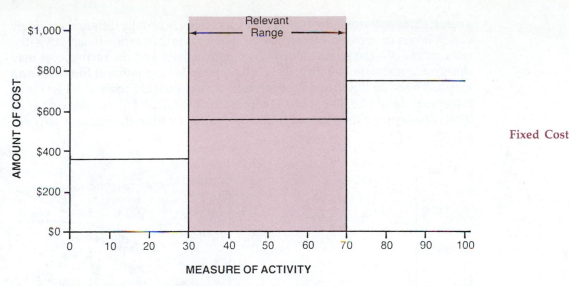

Fixed Cost

and equipment, personnel, and possibly supervisors in order to produce the level of output necessary to meet demand. As a consequence of this action, the company would experience an incremental change in fixed factory overhead.

Some expenditures acquire the fixed characteristic through the dictates of management policy. For example, the level of advertising expenditure and the amount of charitable contribution (or the cost of other community service projects) are determined by management and are not directly related to sales or production activity. Such expenses are sometimes referred to as *programmed fixed expenses*. Expenditures that require a series of payments over a long-term period of time are often called *committed fixed expenses*. Examples include interest on long-term debt and rentals on long-term lease agreements.

Variable Cost

A *variable cost* increases in total proportionately with an increase in activity and decreases proportionately with a decrease in activity. Variable costs include the cost of direct materials, direct labor, some supplies, some indirect labor, perishable tools, rework, and normal spoilage. Variable costs can usually be directly identified with the activity that gives rise to the incurrence of cost.

In practice, the relationship between a business activity and the related variable cost usually is treated as if it were linear; that is, total variable cost is assumed to increase by a constant amount for each unit increase in activity. However, the actual relationship is rarely perfectly linear over the entire range of possible activity. Productive efficiency usually declines when the work load is lighter than normal and, at the opposite extreme, when labor and machinery are pushed to the limit of capacity. When the volume of activity increases to a certain level, management may add newer, more efficient production machinery or replace existing machinery with more productive machinery. As a result of these factors, the cost per unit of activity is usually different at widely varied levels of activity. Nevertheless, within a limited range of activity—the relevant range—the relationship between an activity and the related cost may closely approximate linearity. This relationship is illustrated in the following graph. The solid line (Line B) represents actual variable costs at all levels of activity, and the dash line (Line A) represents the calculated variable cost at all levels of activity as determined from observations within the relevant range of activity.

Calculated Variable Cost

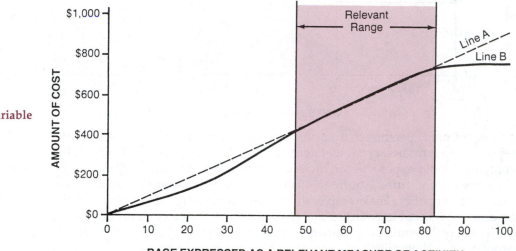

In cases such as the one illustrated in the graph, a constant variable cost rate is a sufficient approximation of the relationship between the variable cost and the related activity within the relevant range. However, to plan and control variable costs effectively, the underlying conditions that give rise to the incurrence of cost should be reviewed frequently to determine whether or not the variable cost per unit of activity has changed. When conditions change or the level of activity is outside the relevant range, a new variable cost rate should be computed.

Semivariable Cost

A *semivariable cost* displays both fixed and variable characteristics. Examples include the cost of electricity, water, gas, fuel oil, coal, some supplies, maintenance, some indirect labor, employee group-term life insurance, pension cost, payroll taxes, and travel and entertainment.

Three reasons for the semivariable characteristic of some expenses are:

1. A minimum of organization may be needed, or a minimum quantity of supplies or services may need to be consumed, in order to maintain readiness to operate. Beyond this minimum level of cost, which is essentially fixed, additional cost varies with volume.

2. Accounting classifications, based upon the object of expenditure or function, commonly group fixed and variable items together. For example, the cost of steam used for

heating, which is dependent upon the weather, and the cost of steam used for manufacturing, which is dependent upon the volume of production, may be charged to the same account.

3. Production factors are divisible into infinitely small units. When such costs are charted against their volume, their movements appear as a series of steps rather than as a continuous straight line. This situation is quite noticeable in moving from a one-shift to a two-shift or from a two-shift to a three-shift operation. Such moves result in definite steps in the cost line because a complete set of workers must be added at one point.[1]

A semivariable cost is illustrated in the following graph. The solid line in the graph represents actual costs at all levels of activity. In this illustration, the actual cost line (Line C) is nonlinear. This situation could occur because of the use of different production techniques or equipment and/or because of different degrees of capacity utilization at different levels of activity. The dash lines are linear and represent the calculated fixed and variable components of the semivariable cost (Line A and Line B, respectively) at all levels of activity, as determined from observations within the relevant range. Where Line B and Line C coincide, the linear assumption closely approximates the actual relationship. This area of coincidence is the relevant range. The calculated fixed expense and the variable expense rate are inaccurate and should be recalculated for activity outside of the relevant range.

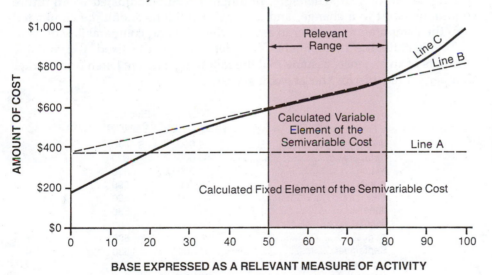

Calculated Fixed and Variable Elements of Semivariable Cost

DETERMINING THE FIXED AND VARIABLE ELEMENTS OF A SEMIVARIABLE COST

The determination of the fixed and variable elements of a semivariable cost is necessary in order to plan, analyze, control, measure, or evaluate costs at

[1]*NA(C)A Bulletin*, Vol. 30, No. 20, pp. 1224-1225.

different levels of activity. As discussed in later chapters, the fixed and variable components of semivariable costs must be segregated for the purposes of:

1. Predetermined factory overhead rate computation and variance analysis.
2. Flexible budget preparation and variance analysis.
3. Direct costing and contribution margin analysis.
4. Break-even and cost-volume-profit analysis.
5. Differential and comparative cost analysis.
6. Short-run profit maximization and cost minimization analysis.
7. Capital budgeting analysis.
8. Marketing profitability analysis by territories, products, and customers.

The following methods are used in determining the fixed and variable elements of a semivariable expense: (1) high and low points method, (2) statistical scattergraph method, and (3) method of least squares. These methods are also used to determine the rate of variability of expenses that are entirely variable. Since these methods deal primarily with past costs, the values determined thereby might not fit the situation expected to exist in the coming month or year. Therefore, findings should be adjusted when future conditions point to a change, and unusual conditions should be eliminated from the computation in order to assure reliability and comparability of data.

To illustrate the three methods of determining the fixed and variable elements of an expense, assume that the following data are taken from Barker Company's records for the preceding year:

Month	Direct Labor Hours	Electricity Expense
January..	34,000	$ 640
February......................................	30,000	620
March..	34,000	620
April..	39,000	590
May...	42,000	500
June..	32,000	530
July...	26,000	500
August...	26,000	500
September....................................	31,000	530
October..	35,000	550
November.....................................	43,000	580
December.....................................	48,000	680
Total......................................	420,000	$6,840
Monthly average......................	35,000	$ 570

High and Low Points Method

In the high and low points method, the fixed and variable elements of a semivariable cost are computed from two data points. The data points (periods) selected from the historical data being analyzed are the high and low periods as to activity level. These periods are usually, but not necessarily, also the highest and lowest figures for the expense being analyzed. If the periods having the highest or lowest activity levels are not the same as those having the highest or lowest expense being analyzed, the activity level should govern in making the selection. The high and low periods are selected because they represent conditions for the two activity levels which are the farthest apart. However, care must be taken not to select data points distorted by abnormal conditions.

Using the data for Barker Company, the fixed and variable elements are determined as follows:

	Activity Level	Expense
High...............................	48,000 hours	$680
Low................................	26,000 hours	500
Difference......................	22,000 hours	$180

Variable rate: $180 ÷ 22,000 hours = $.00818 per direct labor hour   = variable rate

	High	Low
Total expense..	$680	$500
Variable expense (rounded)....................	− 393	− 213 ← 26,000 × .00818
Fixed expense..	= $287	= $287

The high and low activity levels differ by 22,000 direct labor hours, with a cost variation of $180. The assumption is that the difference in the costs at the two levels of activity occurred because of the activity being measured and is therefore pure variable cost. The variable rate is determined by dividing the difference in expense ($180) by the difference in activity (22,000 direct labor hours). In this example, the variable rate is determined to be $.00818 per direct labor hour. The total variable expense at either the high or low level of activity can be determined by multiplying the variable rate times the activity level. This results in a total variable cost at the high level of $393 ($.00818 × 48,000 hours) and at the low level, $213 ($.00818 × 26,000 hours). The difference between the total expense and the total variable expense is the fixed expense, which in this example is determined to be $287. The fixed expense is the same, whether computed from the high or low data.[2] With variable and fixed elements established, the expense totals for various levels of activity can be calculated.

The high and low points method is simple, but it has the disadvantage of using only two data points to determine cost behavior, and it is based on

---

[2]The high and low points method is equivalent to solving two simultaneous equations, based on the assumption that both points fall on the locus of the true variable cost line. Using the above figures, equations could be set up and solved as follows:

$$F + 48,000V = \$\ 680$$
$$-F - 26,000V = \ -500$$
$$22,000V = \$\ 180$$
$$V = \frac{\$180}{22,000} = \$.00818 \text{ per direct labor hour}$$

the assumption that the other data points lie on a straight line between the high and low points. Because it uses only two data points, it may result in estimates of fixed and variable components of semivariable costs that are biased. Consequently, total cost estimates are often more inaccurate than estimates derived by other methods that consider a larger number of data points.

Statistical Scattergraph Method

The statistical scattergraph method can be used for analyzing semivariable expenses. In this method, various costs (the dependent variable) are plotted on a vertical line—the *y-axis*—and measurement figures (the independent variable, e.g., direct labor dollars, direct labor hours, units of output, or percentage of capacity) are plotted along a horizontal line—the *x-axis*.

The data from the electricity expense illustration on page 298 are plotted on the following graph. Each point on the graph represents the electricity expense for a particular month. For instance, the point labeled "Nov." represents the electricity expense for November, when 43,000 direct labor hours were worked. The x-axis shows the direct labor hours, and the y-axis shows the electricity expense. Line B is plotted by visual inspection. This line represents the trend shown by the majority of data points. Generally, there should be as many data points above as below the line. Another line (Line A) is drawn parallel to the base line from the point of intersection on the y-axis, which is read from the scattergraph as approximately $440. This line represents the fixed element of the electricity expense for all activity levels within the relevant range.

Statistical Scattergraph Representing the Fixed and Variable Elements for Electricity Expense

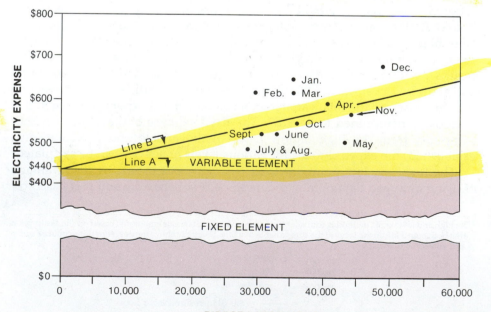

The triangle formed by Lines A and B shows the increase in electricity expense as direct labor hours increase. This increase, based on direct labor hours, is computed as follows:

Average monthly	−	Fixed	=	Average monthly variable
expense		element		element of expense
$570	−	$440	=	$130

$$\frac{\text{Average monthly variable element of expense}}{\text{Average monthly direct labor hours}} = \frac{\text{Variable cost per}}{\text{direct labor hour}}$$

$$\frac{\$130}{35,000 \text{ hours}} = \$.0037 \text{ per direct labor hour}$$

Thus, the electricity expense consists of $440 fixed expense per month and of a variable factor of $.0037 per direct labor hour.

In the statistical scattergraph on page 300, Line B is drawn as a straight line, even though the points do not follow a perfect linear pattern. In most analyses, a straight line is adequate, because it is a reasonable approximation of cost behavior within the relevant range.

The statistical scattergraph method is an improvement over the high and low points method because it utilizes all available data rather than only two data points. Nevertheless, the results are still likely to be biased because the cost line drawn through the data plot is based on visual interpretation.

Method of Least Squares

The *method of least squares* (sometimes called *simple regression analysis*) determines mathematically a line of best fit or a linear regression line through a set of plotted points, so that the sum of the squared deviations of each actual plotted point from the point directly above or below it on the regression line is at a minimum.[3]

---

[3]The formula for a straight line is $y = a + bx$; consequently, the regression equation is:

$$y_i = a + bx_i + e_i$$

where y_i = dependent variable (expense) at period i
x_i = independent variable (activity) at period i
a = intercept (estimate of fixed expense)
b = slope (estimate of variable expense per unit of activity)
e_i = prediction error, i.e., the difference between y_i (an actual observation) and $a + bx_i$ (an estimate of y_i)

Since the regression line exactly splits the plotted sample y_is, so that the sum of the values of the e_is above the line will exactly equal the sum of the values of the e_is below the line, the e_is will equal zero if they are totaled. To have a value to work with, the e_is are squared before being summed. This sum of the squared error terms, SSE, is expressed as follows:

$$SSE = \Sigma (y_i - a - bx_i)^2 = \Sigma y_i^2 - 2b\Sigma x_i y_i + 2ab\Sigma x_i + b^2\Sigma x_i^2 + na^2 - 2a\Sigma y_i$$

where y, a, b, and x are as previously defined and n is the sample size. For ease of presentation, the subscripts for x and y have been omitted in the remainder of the footnote. To find the minimum value of SSE, first partial derivatives are taken with respect to the two unknowns, i.e., a and b, and set equal to zero as follows:

$$\frac{\partial SSE}{\partial a} = 2b\Sigma x + 2na - 2\Sigma y = 0$$

$$\frac{\partial SSE}{\partial b} = -2\Sigma xy + 2a\Sigma x + 2b\Sigma x^2 = 0$$

Rearranging terms and dividing through by 2 yields the so-called normal equations: *(See next page.)*

To illustrate this method, the data from page 298 are used in completing the following table:

Month	(1) x_i Direct Labor Hours	(2) $(x_i - \bar{x})$ Difference from Average of 35,000 Hours	(3) y_i Electricity Expense	(4) $(y_i - \bar{y})$ Difference from Average of $570 Electricity Expense	(5) $(x_i - \bar{x})^2$ (2) Squared	(6) $(x_i - \bar{x})(y_i - \bar{y})$ (2) × (4)	(7) $(y_i - \bar{y})^2$ (4) Squared
January	34,000	−1,000	$ 640	$ 70	1,000,000	$− 70,000	$ 4,900
February	30,000	−5,000	620	50	25,000,000	− 250,000	2,500
March	34,000	−1,000	620	50	1,000,000	− 50,000	2,500
April	39,000	4,000	590	20	16,000,000	80,000	400
May	42,000	7,000	500	−70	49,000,000	− 490,000	4,900
June	32,000	−3,000	530	−40	9,000,000	120,000	1,600
July	26,000	−9,000	500	−70	81,000,000	630,000	4,900
August	26,000	−9,000	500	−70	81,000,000	630,000	4,900
September	31,000	−4,000	530	−40	16,000,000	160,000	1,600
October	35,000	0	550	−20	0	0	400
November	43,000	8,000	580	10	64,000,000	80,000	100
December	48,000	13,000	680	110	169,000,000	1,430,000	12,100
Total	420,000	0*	$6,840	0*	512,000,000	$2,270,000	$40,800

*The sum of these columns is always zero, except for rounding differences.

To prepare this table, the following steps are required:

1. First, determine the average direct labor hours, $\bar{x}$, and the average electricity expense, $\bar{y}$. The total direct labor hours are 420,000. When this amount is divided by the sample size, 12, the average of 35,000 hours per month results. The total electricity expense is $6,840, or an average of $570 per month ($6,840 ÷ 12).
2. Compute the differences between actual monthly figures for direct labor hours, x_i, and electricity expense, y_i, and their respective monthly

---

[3]Concluded:

$$\Sigma y = na + b\Sigma x$$
$$\Sigma xy = a\Sigma x + b\Sigma x^2$$

The normal equations each contain two unknowns. However, since the two equations are not linear transformations of one another, they can be solved. One way would be to multiply both sides of the first equation by $\Sigma x/n$ and then to subtract the first equation from the second in order to eliminate one of the unknowns (a in this case):

$$\Sigma xy = a\Sigma x + b \Sigma x^2$$
$$-\frac{\Sigma x\Sigma y}{n} = -a\Sigma x - \frac{b\Sigma x\Sigma x}{n}$$
$$\Sigma xy - \frac{\Sigma x\Sigma y}{n} = b\Sigma x^2 - \frac{b\Sigma x\Sigma x}{n} \quad \text{or} \quad n\Sigma xy - \Sigma x\Sigma y = nb\Sigma x^2 - b\Sigma x\Sigma x$$

Solving for b yields:

$$b = \frac{n\Sigma xy - \Sigma x\Sigma y}{n\Sigma x^2 - \Sigma x\Sigma x} = \frac{\Sigma xy - \dfrac{\Sigma x\Sigma y}{n}}{\Sigma x^2 - \dfrac{\Sigma x\Sigma x}{n}} = \frac{\Sigma(x - \bar{x})(y - \bar{y})}{\Sigma(x - \bar{x})^2}$$

where $\bar{x} = \Sigma x/n$
and $\bar{y} = \Sigma y/n$

Since $y = a + bx$, then the remaining unknown, a, is computed as follows:

$$a = \bar{y} - b\bar{x}$$

averages, $\bar{x}$ and $\bar{y}$ computed in Step 1. These differences are entered in Columns 2 and 4.

3. Next, two multiplications must be made. First, square each of the differences entered in Column 2, $(x_i - \bar{x})$, and enter in Column 5, $(x_i - \bar{x})^2$. Second, multiply each of the differences in Column 2, $(x_i - \bar{x})$, by the corresponding differences in Column 4, $(y_i - \bar{y})$, and enter the products in Column 6, $(x_i - \bar{x})(y_i - \bar{y})$. [The differences entered in Column 4, $(y_i - \bar{y})$, are also squared and entered in Column 7, $(y_i - \bar{y})^2$. This column will be used on page 304 in computing the coefficient of determination.]

The variable rate for electricity expense, b, is computed as follows:

$$b = \frac{\Sigma(x_i - \bar{x})(y_i - \bar{y})}{\Sigma(x_i - \bar{x})^2} = \frac{\text{Column 6 total}}{\text{Column 5 total}} = \frac{\$2,270,000}{512,000,000} = \$.0044 \text{ per direct labor hour}$$

formula for variable rate

The fixed expense, a, can be computed, using the formula for a straight line as follows:

$$\bar{y} = a + b\bar{x}$$

$$\$570 = a + (\$.0044)(35,000)$$

$$\$570 = a + \$154$$

$$a = \$416 \text{ fixed element of electricity expense per month}$$

formula for fixed expense

The answer above differs somewhat from the figure determined by the scattergraph method because fitting a line visually through the data points is not as accurate as fitting a line mathematically. The mathematical preciseness of the method of least squares injects a high degree of objectivity into the analysis. However, it is still useful to plot the data in order to verify visually the existence of a linear relationship between the dependent variable and the independent variable. Plotting the data makes it easier to spot abnormal data (sometimes referred to as outliers) which can distort the least squares estimate of the fixed and variable components of the semivariable cost being analyzed. If abnormal data are found, they should be removed from the sample data set before using the least squares formulas. In this illustration, the sample size was small in order to simplify the computations. In practice, the sample size should be sufficiently large to represent normal operating conditions.

Correlation Analysis. The application of the statistical scattergraph method accomplishes visual verification of a reasonable degree of correlation. *Correlation* is a measure of the covariation between two variables—the independent variable (x, or direct labor hours in the illustration) and the dependent variable (y, or electricity expense in the illustration). After the computation of the fixed cost and the variable rate for semivariable expenses or the variable rate for entirely variable expenses, the correlation between the independent variable and the dependent variable should be assessed. If all plotted points fall on the regression line, perfect correlation exists.

Mathematical measurements may be used to quantify correlation. In statistical theory, the *coefficient of correlation*, denoted r, is a measure of the extent to which two variables are related linearly. When r = 0, there is no correlation; and when r = ±1, the correlation is perfect. As r approaches +1, the correlation is positive, which means that the dependent variable, y, increases as the independent variable, x, increases, and the regression line slopes upward to the right. As r approaches −1, the correlation is negative or inverse, which means that the dependent variable, y, decreases as the independent variable, x, increases, and the regression line slopes downward to the right.

The *coefficient of determination, r^2,* is found by squaring the coefficient of correlation. The coefficient of determination is considered easier to interpret than the coefficient of correlation, r, because it represents the percentage of variance in the dependent variable explained by the independent variable. The larger the coefficient of determination, the closer it comes to the coefficient of correlation until both coefficients equal 1. The word "explained" means that the variations in the dependent variable are related to, but not necessarily caused by, the variations in the independent variable. Although the coefficient of correlation and the coefficient of determination are mathematical measures of covariation, they do not establish a cause-and-effect relationship between the dependent variable and the independent variable. Such a relationship must be theoretically developed or physically observed.

The formula for calculating the coefficient of correlation is:

$$r = \frac{\Sigma(x_i - \bar{x})(y_i - \bar{y})}{\sqrt{\Sigma(x_i - \bar{x})^2 \Sigma(y_i - \bar{y})^2}}$$

where $x_i - \bar{x}$ is the difference between each observation of the independent variable (direct labor hours in the Barker Company illustration) and its average; and $y_i - \bar{y}$ is the difference between each observation of the dependent variable (electricity expense) and its average. The coefficient of correlation, r, and the coefficient of determination, r^2, for the data on page 302 are calculated as follows:

$$r = \frac{\Sigma(x_i - \bar{x})(y_i - \bar{y})}{\sqrt{\Sigma(x_i - \bar{x})^2 \Sigma(y_i - \bar{y})^2}} = \frac{\text{Column 6 total}}{\sqrt{(\text{Column 5 total})(\text{Column 7 total})}}$$

$$= \frac{2{,}270{,}000}{\sqrt{(512{,}000{,}000)(40{,}800)}} = \frac{2{,}270{,}000}{\sqrt{20{,}889{,}600{,}000{,}000}}$$

$$= \frac{2{,}270{,}000}{4{,}570{,}514.2} = +.49666$$

$$r^2 = .24667$$

The coefficient of determination of less than .25 means that less than 25 percent of the change in electricity expense is related to the change in direct labor hours. The conclusion is that the cost is related not only to direct labor hours but to other factors as well, such as the time of day for production or the season of the year. Furthermore, some other independent variable, such as machine hours, may afford a better correlation.

To illustrate a case in which a high degree of correlation exists, the cost of electricity from the previous example is slightly altered, with direct labor hours remaining on the same level. The following solution indicates an almost perfect

r^2 = coefficient of determination

correlation between the two variables, which means that this relationship could be accepted as the basis for calculating electricity expense for planning and control.

Month	(1) x_i Direct Labor Hours	(2) $(x_i - \bar{x})$ Difference from Average of 35,000 Hours	(3) y_i Electricity Expense	(4) $(y_i - \bar{y})$ Difference from Average of $655 Electricity Expense	(5) $(x_i - \bar{x})^2$ (2) Squared	(6) $(x_i - \bar{x})(y_i - \bar{y})$ (2) × (4)	(7) $(y_i - \bar{y})^2$ (4) Squared
January	34,000	−1,000	$ 660	$ 5	1,000,000	$ −5,000	$ 25
February	30,000	−5,000	590	− 65	25,000,000	325,000	4,225
March	34,000	−1,000	660	5	1,000,000	−5,000	25
April	39,000	4,000	680	25	16,000,000	100,000	625
May	42,000	7,000	740	85	49,000,000	595,000	7,225
June	32,000	−3,000	610	− 45	9,000,000	135,000	2,025
July	26,000	−9,000	580	− 75	81,000,000	675,000	5,625
August	26,000	−9,000	550	− 105	81,000,000	945,000	11,025
September	31,000	−4,000	630	− 25	16,000,000	100,000	625
October	35,000	0	640	− 15	0	0	225
November	43,000	8,000	750	95	64,000,000	760,000	9,025
December	48,000	13,000	770	115	169,000,000	1,495,000	13,225
Total	420,000	0	$7,860	0	512,000,000	$5,120,000	$53,900

$$r = \frac{\Sigma(x_i - \bar{x})(y_i - \bar{y})}{\sqrt{\Sigma(x_i - \bar{x})^2 \Sigma(y_i - \bar{y})^2}} = \frac{\text{Column 6 total}}{\sqrt{(\text{Column 5 total})(\text{Column 7 total})}}$$

$$= \frac{5,120,000}{\sqrt{(512,000,000)(53,900)}} = \frac{5,120,000}{\sqrt{27,596,800,000,000}}$$

$$= \frac{5,120,000}{5,253,265.7} = +.97463$$

$$r^2 = .94991$$

Standard Error of the Estimate. The regression equation, which in the Barker Company illustration is $y_i' = \$416 + \$.0044x_i$, can be used to predict expense at a given level of activity. However, since the regression equation is determined from a limited sample and since variables which are not included in the regression equation may have some influence on the expense being predicted, the calculated expense will usually be different from the actual expense at the same level of activity. The visual scatter around the regression line portrayed in the graph on page 300 illustrates that the actual electricity expense will likely vary from what might be estimated using the calculated fixed expense and the variable expense rate. Because some variation can be expected, management should determine an acceptable range of tolerance for use in exercising control over expenses. Expenses within the limits of variation can be accepted. Expenses beyond the limits should be investigated, and any necessary corrective action should be taken.

The *standard error of the estimate* is defined as the standard deviation about the regression line. A small value for the standard error of the estimate indicates a good fit. For an r^2 equal to one, the standard error would equal zero. Management can use this concept to develop a confidence interval which, in turn, can be used to decide whether a given level of expense indicates a need for management action. To illustrate, the following table can be prepared from the data on page 298.

Month	(1) x_i Direct Labor Hours	(2) y_i Actual Electricity Expense	(3) $(y_i' = a + bx_i)$ Predicted Electricity Expense*	(4) $(y_i - y_i')$ Prediction Error [(2) − (3)]	(5) $(y_i - y_i')^2$ Prediction Error Squared [(4) Squared]
January	34,000	$ 640	$ 566	$ 74	$ 5,476
February	30,000	620	548	72	5,184
March	34,000	620	566	54	2,916
April	39,000	590	588	2	4
May	42,000	500	601	− 101	10,201
June	32,000	530	557	− 27	729
July	26,000	500	530	− 30	900
August	26,000	500	530	− 30	900
September	31,000	530	552	− 22	484
October	35,000	550	570	− 20	400
November	43,000	580	605	− 25	625
December	48,000	680	627	53	2,809
Total	420,000	$6,840	$6,840	0**	$30,628

*Calculated regression line, y_i', values, (direct labor hours × $.0044) + $416, are rounded to the nearest dollar.
**The sum of this column is always zero, except for rounding differences.

The standard error of the estimate is then calculated as follows:

$$s' = \sqrt{\frac{\Sigma(y_i - y_i')^2}{n - 2}} = \sqrt{\frac{\text{Column 5 total}}{12 - 2}} = \sqrt{\frac{\$30,628}{10}} = \sqrt{\$3,062.80} = \$55.34$$

The prediction errors are usually assumed to follow a standard normal distribution. However, for small samples, the Student's t distribution is a more appropriate assumption. A table of selected t values (based on the assumption that two tails of the distribution are of concern, i.e., that managers are concerned about both favorable and unfavorable variances) is given at the top of page 307.

The acceptable range of actual expense around the predicted expense would be computed for a sample of size n by multiplying the standard error of the estimate by the t value for n − 2 degrees of freedom[4] at the desired confidence level, t_p, and by a correction factor for small samples as follows:

$$y_i' \pm t_p s' \sqrt{1 + \frac{1}{n} + \frac{(x_i - \bar{x})^2}{\Sigma(x_i - \bar{x})^2}}$$

where all variables above are as previously defined.

To illustrate the computation and use of the confidence interval, assume that the actual level of activity for a period is 40,000 direct labor hours. The electricity expense computed for the budget from the regression equation determined in the previous example is $592 [$416 + $.0044 (40,000)]. Assume

---

[4]Degrees of freedom (df) refers to the number of values which are free to vary after certain restrictions have been placed on the data. In general, if a regression equation involves p unknown parameters, then df = n − p. In linear bivariate regression, there are two unknown parameters, a and b; thus, df = n − 2.

Degrees of Freedom	Desired Confidence Level			
	90%	95%	99%	99.8%
1	6.314	12.706	63.657	318.310
2	2.920	4.303	9.925	22.326
3	2.353	3.182	5.841	10.213
4	2.132	2.776	4.604	7.173
5	2.015	2.571	4.032	5.893
6	1.943	2.447	3.707	5.208
7	1.895	2.365	3.499	4.785
8	1.860	2.306	3.355	4.501
9	1.833	2.262	3.250	4.297
10	1.812	2.228	3.169	4.144
11	1.796	2.201	3.106	4.025
12	1.782	2.179	3.055	3.930
13	1.771	2.160	3.012	3.852
14	1.761	2.145	2.977	3.787
15	1.753	2.131	2.947	3.733
20	1.725	2.086	2.845	3.552
25	1.708	2.060	2.787	3.450
30	1.697	2.042	2.750	3.385
40	1.684	2.021	2.704	3.307
60	1.671	2.000	2.660	3.232
120	1.658	1.980	2.617	3.160
∞	1.645	1.960	2.576	3.090

t values

t value for n−2 degrees freedom
12−2=10
10 @ 95% = 2.228

further that management wants to be 95 percent confident that the actual electricity expense is within acceptable tolerance limits. Based on the table factor of 2.228 for t at the 95 percent confidence level, with df = 12 − 2, and on the standard error of the estimate computed above (s′ = $55.34), the confidence interval would be:

$$y_i' \pm t_{95\%} s' \sqrt{1 + \frac{1}{n} + \frac{(x_i - \bar{x})^2}{\Sigma(x_i - \bar{x})^2}}$$

actual level of activity in direct labor hours

See bottom P. 306

$$\$592.00 \pm (2.228)(\$55.34) \sqrt{1 + \frac{1}{12} + \frac{(40,000 - 35,000)^2}{512,000,000}}$$

See P. 302 & P. 305 $(x - \bar{x})^2$

$$\$592.00 \pm (2.228)(\$55.34)(1.064)$$

$$\$592.00 \pm \$131.19$$

from standard error of estimate

Management can expect the actual electricity expense to be between $460.81 ($592.00 − $131.19) and $723.19 ($592.00 + $131.19) about 95 percent of the time. Electricity expense outside of these limits will occur because of random chance only 5 percent of the time. If the actual electricity expense is less than $460.81 or greater than $723.19, management should investigate the cause and take any necessary corrective action.

For large samples, the Student's t distribution approaches the standard normal distribution and the correction factor for small samples (the square root term) approaches one. For large samples, therefore, the computation of the acceptable range of actual expense around the predicted expense may be simplified by omitting the correction factor and using the appropriate z value for the standard normal distribution.[5] If the sample size used in computing the regression equation and the standard error of the estimate in the illustration were large, the 95 percent confidence interval for electricity expense at 40,000 direct labor hours would be:

$$\$592.00 \pm (1.960)(\$55.34)$$
$$\$592.00 \pm \$108.47$$

After the fixed and variable components of cost have been computed using the method of least squares, it is useful to plot the regression line against the sample data, so that the pattern of deviations of the actual observations from the corresponding estimates on the regression line can be inspected. Normally, the distribution of observations around the regression line should be uniform for all values of the independent variable (referred to as *homoscedastic*) and randomly distributed around the regression line as depicted in Figure 1. However, if the variance differs at different points on the regression line (referred to as *heteroscedastic*) as depicted in Figure 2 or the observations around the regression line appear to be correlated with one another (referred to as *serial correlation* or *autocorrelation*) as depicted in Figure 3, the standard error of the estimate and the confidence intervals based on the standard error are unreliable measures.[6]

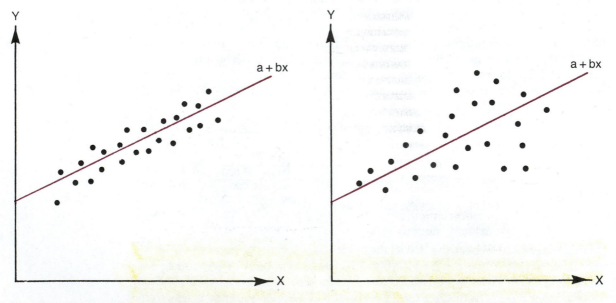

Figure 1—Homoscedasticity—Random Error Term   **Figure 2—Heteroscedasticity**

---

[5]The t values presented in the table on page 307 for df = ∞ are equal to the z values for the standard normal distribution at the probability levels indicated at the head of each column.

[6]For a comprehensive discussion, see Chapter 19, "Multiple Regression and Correlation," Michael J. Brennan and Thomas M. Carroll, *Preface to Quantitative Economics & Econometrics* (Cincinnati: South-Western Publishing Co., 1987).

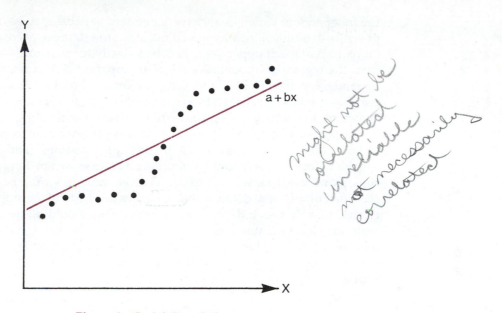

Figure 3—Serial Correlation

Method of Least Squares for Multiple Independent Variables. Typically, cost behavior is shown as dependent on a single measure of volume or on some other independent variable. In the discussion above, for example, the behavior of the dependent variable, electricity expense, was described by the independent variable, direct labor hours. However, a cost may vary because of more than one factor.

Multiple regression analysis is a further application and expansion of the method of least squares, permitting consideration of more than one independent variable. In multiple regression analysis, the simple least squares equation for a straight line, $y_i = a + bx_i + e_i$, is expanded to include more than one independent variable. For example, in the equation $y_i = a + bx_i + cz_i + e_i$, c is the degree of variability for an additional independent variable z. Although the cost relationship can no longer be shown on a two-dimensional graph and the arithmetical computations become more complex, the widespread availability of computer programs makes the use of multiple regression analysis feasible.

The least-squares concept is fundamentally the same when there are two or more independent variables as when there is only one. The assumption of normality still applies. In the case of multiple regression, however, it is the joint probability distribution of the variables that is assumed to be normally distributed (sometimes referred to as multivariate normal). One additional assumption is that the independent variables are not correlated with one another. When the independent variables are correlated with one another, they are said to be collinear, a condition referred to as *multicollinearity*. When the degree of multicollinearity is high, the relationship between one or more of the independent variables and the dependent variable may be obscured.[7] The presence of multicollinearity would not affect the estimate of cost unless one or more important independent variables—activity measures—were omitted from the regression model because of an apparent lack of relationship to the dependent variable—cost. Omitting important variables from the multiple regression model is referred to as *specification error* and is more of a problem in analyzing the sources of cost incurrence than in estimating cost.

If the cost behavior of a group of expenses in one or more expense accounts is being described, an alternate to multiple variables (and hence to the considerations necessitated by multiple variables when applying the least squares method) may be possible. That is, expenses may be grouped and classified in sufficient detail so that expenses in a particular group are all largely related to only one independent variable. This would allow the use of the method of least squares as earlier illustrated, i.e., simple regression analysis. If this approach is not feasible, i.e., if more than one independent variable is still required to describe the cost behavior, then multiple regression analysis should be employed.[8]

DISCUSSION QUESTIONS

1. Explain the difference between fixed, variable, and semivariable costs.

2. What is meant by the term "relevant range?"

3. Why should semivariable costs be segregated into their fixed and variable components?

4. What methods are available for separating the fixed and variable components of semivariable costs?

5. What are the advantages and disadvantages of each of the three different methods of separating fixed and variable components of semivariable costs?

6. Explain the meaning of the $200 and the $4 in the regression equation,

$y_i = \$200 + \$4x_i$, where y_i denotes the total monthly cost of indirect supplies and x_i is machine hours per month.

(ICMA adapted)

7. Define and explain the difference between the coefficient of correlation and the coefficient of determination.

8. With respect to the method of least squares, what is meant by the term "heteroscedasticity," and what problem is likely to occur if it is present?

9. Define and explain the significance of the term "serial correlation."

10. What is meant by the term "multicollinearity" as it is applied in multiple regression analysis?

obscures the cause can't be sure which is the cause

---

[7] *Ibid.*
[8] *Ibid.*

EXERCISES

1. High and low points method. Edd Company wishes to segregate the fixed and variable portions of maintenance expense, believed to be a semivariable expense, as measured against machine hours. The following information has been provided for the first six months of the current year:

Month	Machine Hours	Maintenance Expense
January........................	2,500	$1,250
February.....................	2,200	1,150
March..........................	2,100	1,100
April...........................	2,600	1,300
May............................	2,300	1,180
June...........................	2,400	1,200

Required: Using the high and low points method, compute the variable expense rate and the fixed expense for maintenance expense.

2. Statistical scattergraph. Peepers Company production management is interested in determining the fixed and variable components of supplies expense, a semivariable expense, as measured against direct labor hours. Data for the first ten months of the current year follow:

Month	Direct Labor Hours	Supplies Expense
January........................	450	$600
February.....................	475	700
March..........................	500	750
April...........................	550	650
May............................	725	900
June...........................	750	800
July............................	675	825
August........................	525	725
September..................	600	775
October.......................	625	850

Required: Graph the data provided and determine the fixed and variable components of supplies expense.

3. Method of least squares. Biff Company management is interested in predicting travel and entertainment expense based on the number of expected sales calls on customers. Over the past 50 weeks, the company's sales department reported that its sales force made 6,250 calls on customers, an average of 125 calls per week. Travel and entertainment expenses over the same period totaled $500,000, an average of $10,000 per week. The travel and entertainment expense deviations from its average multiplied by the sales call deviations from its average [$\Sigma(x_i - \bar{x})(y_i - \bar{y})$] is 87,000, and the sales call deviations from its average squared and summed [$\Sigma(x_i - \bar{x})^2$] is 1,450.

Required: Using the method of least squares, estimate the total cost of travel and entertainment for a week in which the company's sales personnel make 200 sales calls.

4. Method of least squares. The management of Raton Inc. would like to separate the fixed and variable components of electricity expense as measured against machine hours in one of its plants. Data collected over the most recent twelve months follow:

Month	Electricity Expense	Machine Hours
January......................	$1,100	4,500
February....................	1,110	4,700
March........................	1,050	4,000
April..........................	1,200	5,000
May...........................	1,060	4,100
June..........................	1,120	4,600
July...........................	1,170	4,900
August.......................	1,020	3,700
September.................	1,130	4,700
October.....................	1,040	3,900
November..................	1,000	3,400
December..................	1,080	4,100

Required: Using the method of least squares, compute the fixed cost and the variable cost rate for electricity expense. Round the estimate of variable cost to a tenth of a cent and the estimate of fixed cost to even cents.

5. **Correlation analysis.** The controller of Berry Electronics Company would like to know how closely the incurrence of factory overhead in the company's semiconductor manufacturing department correlates with machine hours. Total factory overhead over the past 12 months is $108,000, and 5,760 machine hours were logged in for the same period. The machine hour differences from its average and summed $[\Sigma(x_i - \bar{x})^2]$ are 850, and the factory overhead cost differences from its average and summed $[\Sigma(y_i - \bar{y})^2]$ is $3,400. The machine hour differences from average multiplied by the factory overhead cost differences from average and summed $[\Sigma(x_i - \bar{x})(y_i - \bar{y})]$ is 1,564.

Required: Compute the coefficient of correlation, r, and the coefficient of determination, r^2, for factory overhead and machine hours in the semiconductor manufacturing department.

6. **Correlation analysis.** The following data were collected for the most recent twelve-month period by the marketing department of Chaffey Company.

Month	Shipping Expense	Sales Revenue
January......................	$360	$26,000
February....................	400	30,000
March........................	400	29,000
April..........................	380	28,000
May...........................	370	28,000
June..........................	350	25,000
July...........................	390	30,000
August.......................	410	33,000
September.................	450	35,000
October.....................	420	32,000
November..................	430	34,000
December..................	440	30,000

Required: Compute the coefficient of correlation, r, and the coefficient of determination, r^2, for shipping expense and sales revenue.

7. **Cost behavior and correlation analysis.** Total maintenance expense for the past ten months is $48,000. Some of the maintenance activity appears related to the operation of machinery, and the accountant desires to determine whether machine hours should be used as a basis upon which to estimate maintenance expense at various levels of

capacity. Machine hours for the same period totaled 80,000 hours. The machine hour differences from average multiplied by the maintenance expense differences from its average and summed $[\Sigma(x_i - \bar{x})(y_i - \bar{y})]$ is 1,800. The machine hour differences from average squared and summed $[\Sigma(x_i - \bar{x})^2]$ is 4,000, and the maintenance expense differences from average squared and summed $[\Sigma(y_i - \bar{y})^2]$ is 1,000.

Required:

(1) Compute the coefficient of correlation, r, and the coefficient of determination, r^2, for maintenance expense and machine hours.
(2) Compute the variable maintenance expense per machine hour, using the method of least squares.
(3) Compute the fixed maintenance expense, using the method of least squares.

8. Choosing appropriate activity measure and separating fixed and variable costs. Total electricity expense for the past 20 months is $42,000. An activity measure upon which to base estimates of electricity expense is needed. The two activity measures being considered are direct labor hours and machine hours. Direct labor hours for the period totaled 180,000, and machine hours totaled 120,000. The direct labor hour differences from average multiplied by the electricity expense differences from its average and summed $[\Sigma(x_i - \bar{x})(y_i - \bar{y})]$ is 5,700. The direct labor hour differences from average squared and summed $[\Sigma(x_i - \bar{x})^2]$ is 28,500. The electricity expense differences from average squared and summed $[\Sigma(y_i - \bar{y})^2]$ is 1,264. The machine hour differences from average multiplied by the electricity expense differences from its average and summed $[\Sigma(x_i - \bar{x})(y_i - \bar{y})]$ is 7,000. The machine hour differences from average squared and summed $[\Sigma(x_i - \bar{x})^2]$ is 50,000.

Required:

(1) Compute the coefficient of correlation, r, and the coefficient of determination, r^2, for direct labor hours and electricity expense.
(2) Compute the coefficient of correlation, r, and the coefficient of determination, r^2, for machine hours and electricity expense.
(3) Which activity measure should be used for the estimation of fixed and variable electricity expense? Explain.
(4) Compute the variable electricity expense rate and the fixed expense, using the method of least squares.

9. Standard error of the estimate. The controller of Frinzy Company used the method of least squares to compute the fixed and variable components of utility expense from the following data:

Month	Utility Expense	Labor Hours
January........................	$356	2,600
February.....................	381	3,000
March...........................	397	3,100
April.............................	403	3,300
May..............................	433	3,500
June.............................	426	3,200
July..............................	387	2,800
August.........................	455	3,600
September...................	399	2,900
October........................	434	3,300
November....................	414	3,200
December....................	375	2,700

Required: Assuming that the least squares estimate of fixed cost is $142 and the variable rate is $0.085, compute the standard error of the estimate to three decimal places for the data presented above.

10. Standard error of the estimate and confidence interval estimation. production supervisor of Tylow Inc. would like to know the range of maintenance expense that should be expected about 90 percent of the time at the 1,500 machine hour level of activity. The least squares estimate of maintenance expense at that level of activity is $500. The least squares parameter estimates, i.e., the estimates of fixed cost and the variable cost rate, were derived from a sample of data for a recent 15-month period. The machine hour average for the sample period is 1,300, and the machine hour deviations from its average squared and summed $[\Sigma(x_i - \bar{x})^2]$ is 150,000. The prediction error squared $[\Sigma(y_i - y_i')^2]$ over the same sample period is $49,972.

Required: Compute the standard error of the estimate and the 90 percent confidence interval estimate for maintenance expense at the 1,500 machine hour level of activity.

PROBLEMS

11-1. Correlation analysis. The Cost Department of Quick Supply Company attempts to establish a budget to assist in the control of marketing expenses. An examination of individual expenses shows:

Item	Fixed Portion	Variable Portion
Sales staff:		
Salaries.............................	$1,200	none
Retainers..........................	2,000	none
Commissions.....................	none	4% on sales values
Advertising............................	5,000	none
Travel expense....................	?	?

Statistical analysis is needed to split the travel expense satisfactorily into its fixed and variable portions. Before beginning such an analysis, it is thought that the variable portion of the travel expense might vary in accordance either with the number of calls made on customers each month or the value of orders received each month. Records reveal the following details over the past twelve months:

Month	Calls Made	Orders Received	Travel Expense
January.......................	410	$53,000	$3,000
February.....................	420	65,000	3,200
March.........................	380	48,000	2,800
April...........................	460	73,000	3,400
May............................	430	62,000	3,100
June...........................	450	67,000	3,200
July............................	390	60,000	2,900
August........................	470	76,000	3,300
September..................	480	82,000	3,500
October.......................	490	62,000	3,400
November...................	440	64,000	3,200
December....................	460	80,000	3,400

Required:

(1) Compute the coefficient of correlation, r, and coefficient of determination, r^2, between (a) the travel expense and the number of calls made and (b) the travel expense and orders received. (Round off to four decimal places.)
(2) Compare the answers obtained in (1a) and (1b).

11-2. Choosing appropriate activity measure; cost behavior analysis. The controller of Stone Products Corporation has asked for help in the selection of the appropriate activity measure to be used in estimating variable supplies expense for the company's budget. The following information about past expenses and two potential activity measures has been supplied:

Month	Supplies Expense	Direct Labor Hours	Machine Hours
January......................	$ 1,500	3,900	2,100
February....................	1,400	4,200	2,000
March.........................	1,600	4,200	2,100
April...........................	1,550	3,950	2,000
May............................	1,450	3,800	1,950
June...........................	1,450	3,900	2,000
July............................	1,500	4,200	2,050
August.......................	1,550	4,300	2,100
September.................	1,650	4,250	2,400
October......................	1,550	4,300	2,300
Total...........................	$15,200	41,000	21,000

Required:

(1) Compute the coefficient of correlation, r, and the coefficient of determination, r^2, between supplies expense and each of the two activity measures.
(2) Which of the two activity measures above should be used as a basis upon which to estimate the allowable supplies expense?
(3) Using the activity measure selected in requirement (2) above, determine the fixed expense and the variable expense rate by the method of least squares.

11-3. Cost behavior analysis; correlation analysis; standard error of the estimate. A company making tubing from aluminum billets uses a process in which the billets are heated by induction to a very high temperature before being put through an extruding machine that shapes the tubing from the billets. The inducer, a very large coil into which the billet is placed, must sustain a great flow of current to heat the billets to the desired temperature. Regardless of the number of billets to be processed, the coil is kept on during the entire operating day because of the time involved in starting it up. The Cost Department wants to charge the variable electricity cost to each billet and the fixed electricity cost to factory overhead. The following data have been assembled:

Month	Number of Billets	Cost of Electricity	Month	Number of Billets	Cost of Electricity
January................	2,000	$400	July............................	1,400	$340
February...............	1,800	380	August......................	1,900	390
March....................	1,900	390	September...............	1,800	380
April......................	2,200	420	October....................	2,400	440
May.......................	2,100	410	November................	2,300	430
June......................	2,000	400	December................	2,200	420

Required:

(1) Provide a fixed-variable expense analysis using the method of least squares.
(2) Prepare a graph indicating the results calculated.
(3) Compute the coefficient of correlation, r, and the coefficient of determination, r^2.
(4) Compute the standard error of the estimate and the 95% confidence interval for electricity expense at the 2,200 billets level of activity.

11-4. Cost behavior analysis; correlation analysis; standard error of the estimate.
The following data have been collected by the controller of Wilson Corporation over the past ten months:

Month	Maintenance Expense	Machine Hours
January..................................	$ 2,200	25,000
February................................	2,150	23,500
March....................................	2,000	20,000
April.....................................	2,150	24,000
May......................................	2,050	21,000
June.....................................	2,200	26,000
July......................................	2,150	24,500
August..................................	2,250	25,500
September.............................	2,300	27,000
October.................................	2,150	24,500
Total..................................	$21,600	241,000

Required:

(1) Using the high and low points method, determine the average amount of fixed maintenance expense per month and the variable maintenance rate per machine hour.
(2) Determine the fixed expense and the variable expense rate, using the method of least squares.
(3) Compute the coefficient of correlation, r, and the coefficient of determination, r^2, between the machine hours and the maintenance expense.
(4) Determine the 95% confidence interval for maintenance expense at the 25,000 machine hour level of activity.

11-5. Cost behavior analysis; correlation analysis; standard error of the estimate.
The management of the Roberts Hotel is interested in an analysis of the fixed and variable costs in the electricity used relative to hotel occupancy. The following data have been gathered from records for the year:

Month	Guest Days	Electricity Cost
January.......................	1,000	$ 400
February.....................	1,500	500
March..........................	2,500	500
April............................	3,000	700
May.............................	2,500	600
June............................	4,500	800
July.............................	6,500	1,000
August........................	6,000	900
September...................	5,500	900
October.......................	3,000	700
November....................	2,500	600
December....................	3,500	800
Year total..............	42,000	$8,400

Required:

(1) Determine the fixed and variable elements of the electricity cost, using (a) the method of least squares, (b) the high and low points method, and (c) a scattergraph with trend line fitted by inspection. (Round off the variable rate to four decimal places.)

(2) What other elements, besides occupancy, might affect the amount of electricity used in any one month?

(3) Compute the coefficient of correlation, r, and the coefficient of determination, r^2, for guest days and electricity expense.

(4) Compute the standard error of the estimate.

(5) Compute the 90% confidence interval for electricity expense at the 2,000 guest days capacity.

11-6. Cost behavior analysis; correlation analysis; standard error of the estimate. Randal Company manufactures a wide range of electrical products at several different plant locations. Due to fluctuations, its Franklin plant has been experiencing difficulties in estimating the level of monthly overhead.

Management needs more accurate estimates to plan its operational and financial needs. A trade association publication indicates that for companies like Randal, overhead tends to vary with direct labor hours. Based on this information, one member of the accounting staff proposes that the overhead cost behavior pattern be determined in order to calculate the overhead cost in relation to budgeted direct labor hours. Another member of the accounting staff suggests that a good starting place for determining the cost behavior pattern of the overhead cost would be an analysis of historical data to provide a basis for estimating future overhead costs.

Direct labor hours and the respective factory overhead costs for the past three years are as follows:

	19A		19B		19C	
Month	Direct Labor Hours	Factory Overhead Costs	Direct Labor Hours	Factory Overhead Costs	Direct Labor Hours	Factory Overhead Costs
January.........................	2,000	$8,500	2,100	$8,700	2,000	$8,600
February.....................	2,400	9,900	2,300	9,300	2,300	9,300
March...........................	2,200	8,950	2,200	9,300	2,300	9,400
April.............................	2,300	9,000	2,200	8,700	2,200	8,700
May..............................	2,000	8,150	2,000	8,000	2,000	8,100
June.............................	1,900	7,550	1,800	7,650	1,800	7,600
July..............................	1,400	7,050	1,200	6,750	1,300	7,000
August.........................	1,000	6,450	1,300	7,100	1,200	6,900
September...................	1,200	6,900	1,500	7,350	1,300	7,100
October.......................	1,700	7,500	1,700	7,250	1,800	7,500
November....................	1,600	7,150	1,500	7,100	1,500	7,000
December....................	1,900	7,800	1,800	7,500	1,900	7,600

Required:

(1) Compute the amount of fixed factory overhead and the variable cost rate, using the method of least squares. (Round fixed factory overhead to the nearest dollar and the variable cost rate to the nearest cent.)

(2) Compute the coefficient of correlation, r, and the coefficient of determination, r^2, for factory overhead costs and direct labor hours. (Round to four decimal places.)

(3) Compute the standard error of the estimate. (Round to the nearest dollar.)

(4) Compute the 95% confidence interval for factory overhead costs at the 2,200 direct labor hour level of activity. (Assume that the sample size is sufficiently large

that the standard normal probability distribution can be assumed and that the correction factor for small samples can be omitted. Round to the nearest dollar.)

CASES

A. Cost behavior analysis using method of least squares. Alma Company's plant management wishes to develop a budget formula to use in estimating factory overhead which can be expected to be incurred at various activity levels. The formula is to be developed using the method of least squares. Sufficient evidence is available to conclude that factory overhead varies with direct labor hours, and monthly data for the last three years were provided from plant records.

The three-year period contained various occurrences not uncommon to many businesses. During the first year, production was severely curtailed for two months because of wildcat strikes. In the second year, production was reduced in one month because of material shortages and materially increased (overtime scheduled) during two months to meet the units required for a one-time sales order. At the end of the second year, employee benefits were raised significantly as the result of a labor agreement. Production during the third year was not affected by any special circumstances.

Various members of Alma's staff raised some issues regarding the historical data collected for the cost behavior analysis.

(a) Some believed that the use of data from all 36 months would provide a more accurate portrayal of cost behavior. While they recognized that any of the monthly data could include efficiencies and inefficiencies, they believed these efficiencies and inefficiencies would tend to balance out over a longer period of time.

(b) Others suggested that only those months which were considered normal should be used, so that the analysis would not be distorted.

(c) Still others felt that only the most recent 12 months should be used, because they were the most relevant.

(d) Some questioned whether historical data should be used at all to form the basis for a budget formula.

The Accounting Department ran two methods of least squares analyses of the data—one using the data from all 36 months and the other using only the data from the last 12 months. The following information was derived:

	Data from All 36 Months	Data from Most Recent 12 Months
Coefficients:		
Fixed cost	$123,810	$109,020
Variable rate	$ 1.6003	$ 4.1977
Coefficient of correlation	.4710	.6891
Standard error of the estimate	$ 13,003	$ 7,473

Required:

(1) From the analysis that used data from all 36 months, determine:
  (a) The least squares budget formula to use in estimating monthly factory overhead.
  (b) The factory overhead estimate when 25,000 direct labor hours are worked.

(2) Select the analysis results (36 months vs. 12 months) to be preferred as a basis for cost behavior estimation.

(3) Comment on the four specific issues raised by members of Alma's staff.

(ICMA adapted)

B. Regression and correlation analysis—utility and implementation. Ned McCarty, controller of Arkansas Distribution Company, is responsible for development and administration of the company's internal information system as well as the coordination of the company's budget preparation.

At a meeting with Donna Tuma, the vice-president, McCarty proposed that the company employ regression analysis (the least squares method) and correlation analysis as a standard part of its internal information system relating to sales and expenses. He felt that such analyses, including projections, would be significant decision-making aids.

Tuma admitted that she had forgotten the exact mechanics of regression and correlation analysis. However, she did comment that:

(a) Regression and correlation calculations for weekly or monthly amounts would involve enormous numbers of calculations because the company's budget and control system uses weekly amounts for sales and some expenses and monthly amounts for other expenses.

(b) A great deal of caution must be exercised when relying on predictions calculated by regression analysis techniques.

McCarty agreed that a large number of calculations would be required, but felt that this problem might be overcome by computerizing the analysis. The computerized analysis would have to suit the company's budget and control system and cover all significant sales and expense accounts, of which there are about 100.

The company's microcomputer is not large and operates only with a flexible diskette data storage device. No standard computer programs are available for this kind of analysis. Therefore, a program must be specially written, its accompanying data gathered, and the processing problems solved.

To pursue his idea, McCarty decided to obtain sample data regarding sales and related selling expenses for the past five years. Using regression analysis, he predicted sales of $30,500,000 for the coming year and calculated a coefficient of correlation of .4 between sales and the selling expenses.

Required:

(1) What are the advantages and limitations of using regression and correlation analysis according to McCarty?

(2) Identify those matters that should be considered before the regression analysis is made, based on the sample data collected.

(3) Provide an outline of the programming and operating problems that might be encountered if the analysis is computerized using the available computer.

(CICA adapted)

C. Cost behavior analysis; correlation analysis; standard error of the estimate. A company's cost department has compiled weekly records of production volume (in units), electric power used, and direct labor hours employed. The range of output for which the following statistics were computed is from 500 to 2,000 units per week:

Electric power:
$y = 1,000 + .4x$, where y is electric power
and x is units of production
Standard error of the estimate: 100
Coefficient of correlation: .45

Direct labor:
$y = 100 + 1.2x$, where y is direct labor
hours and x is units of production
Standard error of the estimate: 300
Coefficient of correlation: .70

Required:

(1) Compute the best estimate of the additional number of required direct labor hours, if production for the next period should be 500 units greater than production in this period.

(2) Comment on the reliability of the above equations for estimating electric power and direct labor requirements, together with the necessary assumptions if the estimating equations are to be used to predict future requirements. An interpretation of the coefficient of correlation and the standard error of the estimate should be included.

(CGAAC adapted)

D. Cost behavior analysis; alternative models. Motorco Corporation plans to acquire several retail automotive parts stores as part of its expansion program. Motorco carries out extensive review of possible acquisitions prior to making any decision to approach a specific company. Projections of future financial performance are one of the aspects of such a review. One form of projection relies heavily on using past performance (normally ten prior years) to estimate future performance.

Currently, Motorco is conducting a preacquisition review of Alpha Auto Parts, a regional chain of retail automotive parts stores. Among the financial data to be projected for Alpha are the future rental cost for its stores. The following schedule presents the rent and revenues (in millions of dollars) for the past ten years:

Year	Revenues	Annual Rent Expense
19A	$22	$1.00
19B	24	1.15
19C	36	1.40
19D	27	1.10
19E	43	1.55
19F	33	1.25
19G	45	1.65
19H	48	1.60
19I	61	1.80
19J	60	1.95

The following three alternative methods of estimating future rental expense are being considered:

Alternative A: A linear regression using time as the independent variable was performed. The resultant formula is as follows:

$$\text{Rental expense} = .93 + .0936y$$
$$r = .895$$
$$\text{Standard error of the estimate} = .150$$

where y is equal to (actual year − 19A), e.g., 19J = 10.

Alternative B: The annual rental expense was related to annual revenues through linear regression. The formula for predicting rental expense in this case is as follows:

$$\text{Rental expense} = .5597 + .02219y$$
$$r = .978$$
$$\text{Standard error of the estimate} = .070$$

where y is equal to (Revenues/1,000,000), e.g., y for 19J is 60.

Alternative C: The third alternative is to calculate rental expense as a percentage of revenues using the arithmetical average for the ten-year period of 19A-19J inclusive. The

formula for predicting rental expense in this case is as follows:

$$\text{Rental expense} =$$
$$(\Sigma E \div \Sigma R)y =$$
$$(14.45 \div 399)y = .0362y$$

where ΣE is equal to the sum of the rental expenses for the ten-year period, ΣR is equal to the sum of the revenues for the ten-year period, and y is equal to revenue in the prediction year; e.g., y for 19J is 60.

Required:

(1) Discuss the advantages and disadvantages of each of the three alternative methods for estimating the rental expense for Alpha Auto Parts.
(2) Identify one method from Alternatives A, B, or C that Motorco should use to estimate rental expense and explain why that alternative was selected.
(3) Explain whether a statistical technique is an appropriate method in this situation for estimating rental expense.

(ICMA adapted)

E. Multiple regression analysis. Multiple regression is a procedure used to measure the relationship of one variable with two or more other variables. Regression provides a rational statement rather than a causal statement with regard to the relationship. The basic formula for a multiple regression equation is:

$$y_i' = a + bx_i + cz_i + e_i$$

For a regression equation to provide meaningful information, it should comply with the basic criteria of goodness of fit and specification analysis. Specification analysis is determined by examining the data and the relationships of the variables for (1) linearity within a relevant range, (2) constant variance of error terms (homoscedasticity), (3) independence of observations (serial correlation), (4) normality, and (5) multicollinearity.

Required:

(1) Explain what is meant by "regression provides a rational statement rather than a causal statement."

(2) Explain the meaning of each of the symbols which appear in the basic formula of the multiple regression equation above.

(3) Identify the statistical factors which are used to test a regression equation for goodness of fit and, for each item identified, indicate whether a high or low value describes a "good" fit.

(4) Explain what each of the following terms means with respect to regression analysis:
(a) Linearity within a relevant range
(b) Constant variance (homoscedasticity)
(c) Serial correlation
(d) Normality
(e) Multicollinearity   *(ICMA adapted)*

CHAPTER 12

Factory Overhead: Planned, Actual, and Applied; Variance Analysis

The use of a predetermined factory overhead rate for the purpose of charging a fair share of factory overhead to products was introduced briefly in earlier chapters. This chapter (1) discusses the methods, procedures, and bases available for applying factory overhead; (2) describes methods and procedures for classifying and accumulating actual factory overhead; (3) shows computations for over- or underapplied factory overhead; and (4) analyzes the total net variance, showing the spending and idle capacity variances. Chapter 13 discusses (1) the departmentalization of factory overhead, (2) the creation and use of separate departmental overhead rates, and (3) departmentalization in nonmanufacturing businesses and nonprofit organizations. Chapter 14 discusses (1) the relationship of product costing to responsibility accounting, (2) monthly overhead variance analysis for use in responsibility accounting and reporting for producing and service departments, and (3) responsibility reporting fundamentals and systems.

▼ THE NATURE OF FACTORY OVERHEAD

Factory overhead is generally defined as indirect materials, indirect labor, and all other factory expenses that cannot conveniently be identified with nor charged directly to specific jobs or products or final cost objectives, such as government contracts. Other terms used for factory overhead are *factory burden, manufacturing expense, manufacturing overhead, factory expense,* and *indirect manufacturing cost.*

Factory overhead possesses two characteristics that require consideration if products are to be charged with a fair share of this expense. These characteristics deal with the particular relationship of factory overhead to (1) the product itself and (2) the volume of production. Unlike direct materials and direct labor, factory overhead is an invisible part of the finished product. There is no materials requisition or labor time ticket to indicate the amount of overhead, such as factory supplies or indirect labor, that enters into a job or product. Yet factory overhead is as much a part of a product's manufacturing cost as direct materials and direct labor. Since automation has increased in modern manufacturing processes, factory overhead as a percentage of total product cost has increased, while the portion of direct labor has declined.

The second characteristic deals with the change in cost that many items of overhead undergo with a change in production volume; i.e., overhead may be fixed, variable, or semivariable. As discussed in Chapter 11, fixed overhead remains relatively constant regardless of changes in production volume, while the fixed overhead per unit of output varies inversely with production volume. Variable overhead varies proportionately with production output. Semivariable overhead varies but not in proportion to units produced. As production volume changes, the combined effect of these different overhead patterns can cause unit manufacturing cost to fluctuate considerably, unless some method is provided to stabilize overhead charged to the units produced. The following chart illustrates the relationship of overhead and volume:

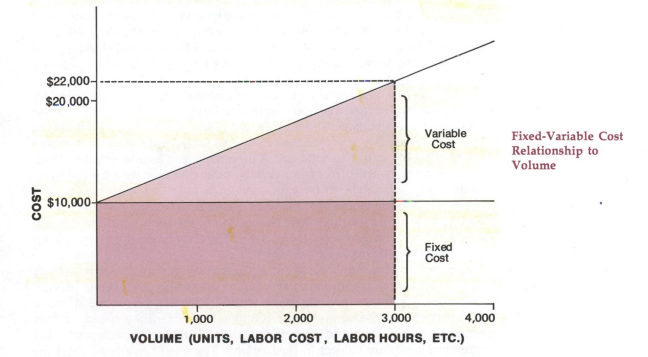

Fixed-Variable Cost Relationship to Volume

▼ THE USE OF A PREDETERMINED FACTORY OVERHEAD RATE

The various overhead expenses must be charged to all work done during any period. The problem is how to make such a charge. It is possible to allocate actual overhead to all work completed during the month, using a base such as actual direct labor dollars, direct labor hours, or machine hours. As long as the volume of work completed each month is the same, and costs are within control limits, this method would result in a consistent charge to production each period. As variations occur, work completed during different months would receive a greater or smaller charge—an inequitable situation. For example, costing problems would result if actual costs incurred for repairs and maintenance are charged directly to a job or product when repairs are made. Ordinarily, repairs are necessary because of wear and tear over a much longer period than one month and are made to permit continuous operations in any month. Moreover, since overhead cost needs to be assigned promptly to production and inefficiencies need to be identified, it is argued that factory overhead should be charged to work done on an estimated basis. However, the use of estimates can cause certain difficulties because underlying data are the result of opinions and judgments. Consequently, estimates must be the outcome of careful studies.

Because of the impossibility of tracing all items of factory overhead to specific jobs or specific products, an arbitrary overhead allocation must be made. A predetermined factory overhead rate permits an equitable and logical allocation. For both job order and process cost accumulation procedures, it provides the only feasible method of computing product overhead costs promptly enough to serve management needs, identify inefficiencies, and smooth out uncontrollable and somewhat illogical month-to-month fluctuations in unit costs.

In job order costing, actual costs of direct materials and direct labor used on a job are determined from materials requisitions and time cards and are entered on job order cost sheets. Overhead costs are predetermined from cost data to arrive at the total amount of overhead estimated for the activity level to be used in computing the rate. This total cost is then related to estimated direct labor hours, machine hours, direct labor dollars, or some other base for the same activity level, ultimately to be expressed in a rate. For example, factory overhead applicable to a job would be calculated by multiplying actual direct labor hours incurred on the job by the predetermined rate, and the amount would be entered on the job order cost sheet. The cost of a job is thereby known at the time the job is completed.

In process costing, unit costs are computed by dividing total weekly or monthly costs of each process by the output of that process. While process costing could produce product costs without the use of overhead rates, predetermined overhead rates are recommended, since they speed up unit product cost calculations and offer other distinct advantages when overhead or production levels are subject to fluctuations. The use of overhead rates for process costing is similar to that for job order costing.

▼ FACTORS TO BE CONSIDERED IN THE SELECTION OF OVERHEAD RATES

The types of overhead rates used differ not only from company to company but also from one department, cost center, or cost pool to another within the same company. The type, significance, and use of factory overhead items must be considered when deciding upon applicable rates. At least five main factors influence the selection of overhead rates. The first three of these factors, which are identified as follows, are discussed in this chapter. The last two factors are discussed in Chapters 13 and 14.

I. Base To Be Used
   a. Physical output
   b. Direct materials cost
   c. Direct labor cost
   d. Direct labor hours
   e. Machine hours

II. Activity Level Selection
   a. Theoretical capacity
   b. Practical capacity
   c. Expected actual capacity
   d. Normal capacity
      1. Purposes of establishing normal capacity
      2. Factors involved in determining normal capacity

   e. Effect of capacity on overhead rates
   f. Idle capacity vs. excess capacity

III. Including or Excluding of Fixed Overhead
   a. Absorption costing
   b. Direct costing

IV. Use of a Single Rate or Several Rates
   a. Plant-wide or blanket rate
   b. Departmental rates

V. Use of Separate Rates for Service Activities

Base To Be Used

Selection of the most appropriate base for applying overhead is of utmost importance if a cost system is to provide reasonably proper costs and if management is to receive meaningful and valuable data. Therefore, the primary objective in selecting a base is to ensure the application of factory overhead in a reasonable proportion to the beneficial or causal relationship to jobs, products, or work performed. Since factory overhead rates are also used for estimating purposes, the overhead distribution base quantity needed can be translated easily and efficiently into a factory overhead cost to arrive at total estimated production cost.

Ordinarily, the base selected should be closely related (correlated) to functions represented by the overhead cost being applied. If, for example, factory overhead is predominantly labor-oriented, such as supervision and indirect labor, the proper base is probably direct labor cost or direct labor hours. If overhead items are predominantly investment-oriented, related to the ownership and operation of machinery, then a machine hour base is probably most appropriate. If overhead is mainly materials-oriented, such as costs associated with the purchasing and handling of materials, then the materials cost might be considered as the base. Correlation analysis tools discussed in Chapter 11 are especially useful in selecting the base to be used.

A secondary objective in selecting a base is to minimize clerical cost and effort relative to the benefits attained. When two or more bases provide approximately the same applied overhead cost to specific units of production, the simplest base should be used. Although the cost of administering the various methods differs from one company to another, the direct labor cost base and the direct materials cost base seem to cause the least clerical effort and cost. The labor and machine hour bases generally require additional clerical work and expense.

Physical Output. The physical output or units of production base, the simplest and most direct method of applying factory overhead, is computed as follows:

$$\frac{\text{Estimated factory overhead}}{\text{Estimated units of production}} = \text{Factory overhead per unit}$$

If the estimated expense is $300,000 and the company intends to produce 250,000 units during the next period, each completed unit would be charged with $1.20 ($300,000 ÷ 250,000 units) as its share of factory overhead. An order with 1,000 completed units would be charged with $1,200 (1,000 units × $1.20) of factory overhead.

The physical output base is satisfactory when a company manufactures only one product; otherwise, the method is either unsatisfactory or subject to arbitrary allocation procedures. However, if the several products manufactured are alike or closely related, their difference being merely one of weight or volume, application of factory overhead can be made on a weight, volume, or point base. The weight base applies overhead according to the weight of each unit of product as follows:

	Product		
	A	B	C
Estimated number of units manufactured.............	20,000	15,000	20,000
Unit weight of product..	5 lbs.	2 lbs.	1 lb.
Estimated total weight produced.........................	100,000 lbs.	30,000 lbs.	20,000 lbs.
Estimated factory overhead per pound ($300,000 ÷ 150,000).....................................	$2	$2	$2
Estimated factory overhead for each product...	$200,000	$60,000	$40,000
Estimated factory overhead per unit....................	$10	$4	$2

If the weight or volume base does not seem to yield a just apportionment of overhead, the method can be improved by assigning a certain number of points to each unit to compensate for differences. For example, a company manufacturing Products L, S, M, and F computes an overhead rate per product as follows:

Product	Estimated Quantity	Points Assigned	Estimated Total Points	Estimated Factory Overhead per Point	Estimated Factory Overhead for Each Product	Estimated Factory Overhead Cost per Unit
L	2,000	5	10,000	$3	$ 30,000	$15
S	5,000	10	50,000	3	150,000	30
M	3,000	8	24,000	3	72,000	24
F	4,000	4	16,000	3	48,000	12
			100,000		$300,000	

If products are different in any respect, such as time to produce or method of production not considered in the allocation base, a uniform charge based on physical output may result in inappropriate costing. Other methods must be adopted in such instances.

Direct Materials Cost Base. In some companies, a study of past costs will reveal a correlation between direct materials cost and factory overhead. The study might show that factory overhead has remained approximately the same percentage of direct materials cost. Therefore, a rate based on materials cost might be applicable. In such instances, the charge is computed by dividing total estimated factory overhead by total direct materials cost expected to be used in the manufacturing processes:

$$\frac{\text{Estimated factory overhead}}{\text{Estimated materials cost}} \times 100 = \frac{\text{Percentage of overhead}}{\text{per direct materials cost}}$$

If the estimated overhead is $300,000 and the estimated materials cost is $250,000, each job or product completed would be charged with an additional 120 percent [($300,000 ÷ $250,000) × 100] of its materials cost as its share of factory overhead. For example, if the materials cost of an order is $5,000, the order would receive an additional charge of $6,000 ($5,000 × 120%) for factory overhead.

The materials-related cost base has only limited use, because in most cases no logical relationship exists between the direct materials cost of a product and factory overhead used in its production. One product might be made from high-priced materials, another from less expensive materials; yet, both products might require the same manufacturing process, or even the same materials-oriented overhead costs, and thus use approximately the same amount of factory overhead. If the materials cost base is used to charge overhead, the product using expensive materials will, in this case, be charged with more than its share. To overcome this unfairness, two overhead rates might be calculated: one (based on materials cost, weight, volume, or some other measure of use) for items that are materials-oriented, such as purchasing, receiving, inspecting, handling, and storage costs; the other for the remaining overhead costs.

Direct Labor Cost Base. The direct labor cost base method of applying overhead to jobs or products entails dividing estimated factory overhead by estimated direct labor cost to compute a percentage:

$$\frac{\text{Estimated factory overhead}}{\text{Estimated direct labor cost}} \times 100 = \text{Percentage of direct labor cost}$$

If estimated factory overhead is $300,000 and total direct labor cost for the next period is estimated at $1,200,000, the overhead rate would be 25 percent [($300,000 ÷ $1,200,000) × 100]. A job or product with a direct labor cost of $12,000 would be charged with $3,000 ($12,000 × 25%) for factory overhead.

Factory overhead items that are used over a period of time must be taken into consideration. The direct labor cost base does so, since the labor cost is computed by multiplying the number of work-hours by an hourly wage rate. The more hours worked, the higher the labor cost, the greater the use of time-related items, and the greater the charge for factory overhead.

The direct labor cost base is relatively easy to use, since information needed to apply overhead is readily available. Its use is particularly favored when (1) a direct relationship between direct labor cost and factory overhead exists and (2) the rates of pay per hour for similar work are comparable. The weekly payroll provides the direct labor cost without any additional record keeping. As long as economy in securing underlying information remains a main prerequisite, the direct labor cost base can be accepted as the best and quickest of the available methods of applying factory overhead.

On the other hand, this method can be objected to for two reasons:

1. Factory overhead must be looked upon as adding to the value of a job or product. The added value often comes about through depreciation charges of high-cost machinery, which might not bear any relationship to direct labor payroll.

2. Total direct labor cost represents the sum of wages paid to high- and low-wage production workers. By applying overhead on the basis of direct labor cost, a job or product is charged with more overhead when a high-wage operator performs work. Such a method can lead to incorrect distribution of factory overhead, particularly when numerous operators, with different hourly rates in the same department, perform similar operations on different jobs or products.

Direct Labor Hour Base. The direct labor hour base is designed to overcome the second disadvantage of using the direct labor cost base. The overhead rate based on direct labor hours is computed as follows:

$$\frac{\text{Estimated factory overhead}}{\text{Estimated direct labor hours}} = \text{Rate per direct labor hour}$$

If estimated factory overhead is $300,000 and total direct labor hours are estimated to be 200,000, an overhead rate based on direct labor hours would be $1.50 per hour of direct labor ($300,000 ÷ 200,000 hours). A job or product that required 400 direct labor hours would be charged with $600 (400 hours × $1.50) for factory overhead.

The use of this method requires accumulation of direct labor hours by job or product. Timekeeping forms and records must be organized to provide the additional data. The use of the direct labor hour base requires, first, a direct relationship between direct labor hours and factory overhead and, second, different rates of pay per hour for similar work, caused, for example, by seniority rather than increased output. As long as labor operations are the chief factor in production processes, the direct labor hour method is acceptable as an equitable base for applying overhead. However, if shop or factory departments use machines extensively, the direct labor hour method might lead to unreasonable costing.

Management goals in manufacturing in recent years have focused on decreasing the amount of direct labor as a component of total cost. The shift has been away from direct labor toward increasing levels of automation. As a result, the use of direct labor cost or direct labor hours for purposes of factory overhead application has become less appropriate, often giving way to the use of machine hours as the preferred base.

Machine Hour Base. When machines are used extensively, machine hours may be the most appropriate base. This method is based on time required to perform identical operations by a machine or group of machines. Machine hours expected to be used are estimated, and a machine hour rate is determined as follows:

$$\frac{\text{Estimated factory overhead}}{\text{Estimated machine hours}} = \text{Rate per machine hour}$$

If factory overhead is estimated to be $300,000 and 50,000 machine hours are estimated, the rate is $6 per machine hour ($300,000 ÷ 50,000 machine hours). Work that required 120 machine hours would be charged with $720 (120 hours × $6) for factory overhead.

If a machine or group of machines differ with respect to the overhead costs related to them, then a weighting procedure such as that discussed for the physical output base is required. An alternative is to use a separate rate for each machine or machine group, which requires segmentation of cost estimation, accumulation, and application, following the procedures discussed in the next chapter. A third alternative is to use process time as the base. *Process time* is the total time that the manufacturing process requires to produce a unit of product.

The machine hour method requires additional clerical work. A reporting system must be designed to assure correct accumulation of all required data for proper overhead accounting. Generally, shop personnel, supervisors, or timekeepers collect machine hour data needed to charge overhead to jobs, products, or work performed. The machine hour method is considered the most reasonable method of applying overhead if the overhead cost is comprised predominantly of facility-related costs, such as depreciation, maintenance, and utilities. Indeed, with modern manufacturing technology, direct labor becomes an increasingly smaller portion of manufacturing costs, and facility costs become a proportionately greater portion. As a result, more and more situations require the use of a non-direct labor base, such as machine hours or weighted machine hours.

Activity Level Selection

In calculating an overhead rate, a great deal depends on the activity level selected. The greater the assumed activity, the lower the fixed portion of the overhead rate, because fixed overhead will be spread over a greater number of direct labor dollars, hours, etc. The variable portion of the rate will tend to remain constant at various activity levels.

The following terms are used to describe different activity levels: theoretical capacity, practical capacity, expected actual capacity, and normal capacity. These descriptions are discussed in the following paragraphs. Current federal income tax regulations permit the use of practical, expected actual, or normal capacity in assigning factory overhead costs to inventories.[1]

---

[1] *Regulations*, Section 1.471-11.

Theoretical Capacity. The *theoretical capacity* of a department is its capacity to produce at full speed without interruptions. It is achieved if the plant or department produces at 100 percent of its rated capacity.

Practical Capacity. It is highly improbable that any company can operate at theoretical capacity. Allowances must be made for unavoidable interruptions, such as time lost for repairs, inefficiencies, breakdowns, setups, failures, unsatisfactory materials, delays in delivery of materials or supplies, labor shortages and absences, Sundays, holidays, vacations, inventory taking, and pattern and model changes. The number of work shifts must also be considered. These allowances reduce theoretical capacity to the *practical capacity* level. This reduction is caused by internal influences and does not consider the chief external influence—lack of customers' orders. Reduction from theoretical to practical capacity typically ranges from 15 percent to 25 percent, which results in a practical capacity level of 75 percent to 85 percent of theoretical capacity.

Expected Actual Capacity. The short-range or short-term planning and control approach, the *expected actual capacity* concept, advocates a rate in which overhead and production are based on the expected actual output for the next production period. This method usually results in the use of a different predetermined rate for each period, depending on increases or decreases in estimated factory overhead and production figures. The use of expected actual capacity is feasible with firms whose products are of a seasonal nature and whose market and style changes allow price adjustments according to competitive conditions and customer demands. However, the use of a predetermined rate based on expected actual production is more often due to the difficulty of judging current performance on a long-range or normal capacity level.

Normal Capacity. The long-range or long-term planning and control approach, the *normal capacity* concept, advocates an overhead rate in which expenses and production are based on average utilization of the physical plant over a time period long enough to level out the highs and lows that occur in every business venture. The normal capacity rate is based on the concept that the overhead rate should not be changed because existing plant facilities are used to a greater or lesser degree in different periods; therefore, a more useful unit cost results. A job or product should not cost more to produce in any one accounting period just because production was lower and fixed charges were spread over a fewer number of units. The rate will be changed, however, when prices of certain expense items change or when fixed costs increase or decrease.

As a result of the use of normal production figures for estimating factory overhead and the selected bases, applied overhead will usually differ from actual overhead incurred. The possibility of such a difference or variance must be recognized, but should not serve to discourage the use of an overhead rate nor encourage the change of this rate. In fact, when this variance, generally called over- or underapplied factory overhead, is further analyzed, it reveals useful management information (pages 336-340).

Purposes of Establishing Normal Capacity. Although there may be some differences between a normal long-run volume and the sales volume expected in the next period, normal capacity is useful in establishing sales prices and controlling costs. It is fundamental to the entire budget system, and it can be used for the following purposes and aims:

1. Preparing departmental flexible budgets and computing predetermined factory overhead rates.
2. Compiling the standard cost of each product.
3. Scheduling production.
4. Assigning cost to inventories.
5. Determining the break-even point.
6. Measuring the effects of changing volumes of production.

Although other capacity assumptions are sometimes used due to existing circumstances, normal capacity fulfills both long- and short-term purposes. The long-term utilization of the normal capacity level relates the marketing phase and therewith the pricing policy of the business to the production phase over a long period of time, leveling out fluctuations that are of short duration and of comparatively minor significance. The short-term utilization relates to management's analysis of changes or fluctuations that occur during an operating year. This short-term utilization measures temporary idleness and aids in an analysis of its causes.

Factors Involved in Determining Normal Capacity. In determining the normal capacity of a plant, both its physical capacity and average sales expectancy must be considered. Neither plant capacity nor sales potential alone is sufficient. As previously mentioned, sales expectancy should be determined for a period long enough to level out cyclical variations, rather than on the sales expectancy for a short period of time. It should also be noted that unused machinery and machinery bought for future use must be excluded from the considerations which lead to the determination of the normal capacity level.

Calculation of the normal capacity of a plant requires many different judgment factors. Normal capacity should be determined first for the business as a whole and then broken down by plants and departments. Determination of a departmental capacity figure might indicate that for a certain department the planned program is an overload, while in another it will result in excess capacity. The capacities of several departments will seldom be in such perfect balance as to produce an unhampered flow of production. For the department with the overload, often termed the "bottleneck" department, actions such as the following might have to be taken:

1. Working overtime.
2. Introducing an additional shift.
3. Temporarily transferring operations to another department where spare capacity is available.
4. Subcontracting the excess load.
5. Purchasing additional equipment.

On the other hand, the excess facilities of other departments might have to be reduced. Alternatively, the sales department might be asked to search for additional orders to utilize the spare capacity in these departments.

Effect of Capacity on Overhead Rates. The effect of the various capacity levels on predetermined factory overhead rates is illustrated in the following table. In this illustration, if the 75 percent capacity level (normal capacity) is the selected level, the overhead rate is $2.40 per direct labor hour. At higher capacity levels, the rate is lower, because the fixed overhead is spread over more hours.

EFFECT OF VARIOUS CAPACITY LEVELS ON PREDETERMINED FACTORY OVERHEAD RATES

Item	Expected Actual Capacity	Normal Capacity	Expected Actual Capacity	Practical Capacity	Theoretical Capacity
Percentage of theoretical capacity......................	70%	75%	80%	85%	100%
Direct labor hours..	7,000 hrs.	7,500 hrs.	8,000 hrs.	8,500 hrs.	10,000 hrs.
Budgeted factory overhead:					
Fixed..	$12,000	$12,000	$12,000	$12,000	$12,000
Variable...	5,600	6,000	6,400	6,800	8,000
Total..	$17,600	$18,000	$18,400	$18,800	$20,000
Fixed factory overhead rate per direct labor hour............................	$1.71	$1.60	$1.50	$1.41	$1.20
Variable factory overhead rate per direct labor hour............................	.80	.80	.80	.80	.80
Total factory overhead rate per direct labor hour............................	$2.51	$2.40	$2.30	$2.21	$2.00

Idle Capacity vs. Excess Capacity. A distinction must be made between idle capacity and excess capacity. *Idle capacity* results from the idleness of production workers and facilities due to a temporary lack of sales. When sales demand increases, the idle production workers and facilities are restored to full use. When idle capacity is budgeted for the period, its cost is usually included in the factory overhead application rate and thus becomes a part of the product cost. When idle capacity is not budgeted, a factory overhead idle capacity variance results which is related to idle facilities. Costs associated with idle production workers are included in the spending variance. An overhead idle capacity variance should be (1) treated as a period cost or (2) allocated to inventories and cost of goods sold. If it is not material, it is typically charged to expense of the period.

Excess capacity, conversely, results either from greater productive capacity than the company could ever hope to use, or from an imbalance in equipment or machinery. This imbalance involves the excess capacity of one machine in contrast with the output of other machines with which it must be synchronized. Any expense arising from excess capacity should be excluded from the factory overhead rate and from the product cost. The expense should be treated as a deduction in the income statement. In many instances, it may be wise to dispose of excess plant and equipment.

Including or Excluding of Fixed Overhead Items

Ordinarily, cost accounting procedures apply all factory costs to the output of a period. Under these procedures, called *absorption costing, conventional costing,* or *full costing,* both fixed and variable expenses are included in overhead rates. Another method of costing, termed *direct costing,* is sometimes used, but only for internal management purposes. Under this method of costing, only variable overhead is included in overhead rates. The fixed expense does not become a product cost but is treated as a period cost, meaning that it is charged off in total each period as are marketing and administrative expenses. It is not included in either work in process or finished goods inventories. Direct costing is discussed in detail in Chapter 19.

Absorption costing and direct costing are the results of two entirely different cost concepts with respect to product cost, period cost, gross profit, and operating income. Although the two methods result in different inventory costs and different period profits, each of the various bases discussed for applying overhead may be used with absorption costing or direct costing.

▼ THE CALCULATION OF A FACTORY OVERHEAD RATE

The first step in calculating the overhead rate is to determine the activity level to be used for the base selected and then estimate or budget each individual expense at the estimated activity level in order to arrive at the total estimated factory overhead. To illustrate, assume that DeWitt Products estimates a normal capacity level of 200,000 direct labor hours. The total factory overhead is estimated to be $300,000. This overhead is classified into fixed or variable categories, as shown in the statement on page 334.

The classification of expenses according to changes in volume attempts to establish a variability pattern for each expense item. This classification must, in turn, consider certain specific assumptions regarding plant facilities, prices (including inflation estimates), managerial policy, and the state of technology. Once the classification has been decided upon, the expense may remain in this category for a limited period of time. Should underlying conditions change, the original classification must be reviewed and expenses reclassified as necessary.

Variable expenses change with production volume and are considered a function of volume; that is, the amount of variable expense per unit is constant. Fixed expenses, on the other hand, are just the opposite. The total amount is fixed, but the expense per unit is different for each production level. Increased production causes a decrease in fixed expense per unit. Knowledge of the effect of fixed and variable expenses on the product unit cost is highly important in any study of factory overhead. A knowledge of the behavior of all costs is fundamental to the planning and analytical processes for decision-making purposes as well as for cost control.

DeWitt Products
Estimated Factory Overhead for 19—

Expense	Fixed	Variable	Total
Supervisors..	$ 70,000		$ 70,000
Indirect labor...	9,000	$ 66,000	75,000
Overtime premium..		9,000	9,000
Factory supplies..	4,000	19,000	23,000
Repairs and maintenance....................................	3,000	9,000	12,000
Electric power..	2,000	18,000	20,000
Fuel..	1,000	5,000	6,000
Water..	500	500	1,000
FICA tax...	3,000	15,000	18,000
Unemployment taxes..	1,500	3,500	5,000
Workmen's compensation.....................................	500	2,500	3,000
Hospitalization insurance.....................................	500	1,500	2,000
Pensions..	2,000	13,000	15,000
Vacations and holidays...	2,000	10,000	12,000
Group insurance..	1,000	3,000	4,000
Depreciation—building...	5,000		5,000
Depreciation—equipment.....................................	13,000		13,000
Property tax..	4,000		4,000
Insurance (fire)...	3,000		3,000
Total estimated factory overhead....................	$125,000	$175,000	$300,000

An examination of fixed and variable expenses indicates the difficulty of segregating all expenses as either fixed or variable. Some expenses are partly fixed and partly variable; some are fixed to a certain production level and then increase as production increases. Also, costs may change in step-like fashion at various production levels. Such expenses are classified as semivariable. Because expenses are to be classified as either fixed or variable, the fixed portion of any semivariable expense and the degree of change in the variable part must be determined.

Chapter 11 (pages 298-303) presented the methods available to aid in finding the constant portion and the degree of variability in the variable portion for determining cost behavior patterns. These procedures determine the relationship between increases in production and increases in total and individual expenses. For example, when production is expected to increase 10 percent, it is possible to determine the corresponding increase in total expense as well as the increase in individual expenses such as supplies, power, or indirect labor.

After the activity level for the selected base and the factory overhead have been estimated, the overhead rates can be computed. Assuming that the direct labor hour base is used and direct labor hours for the coming year are estimated to be 200,000 (normal capacity level) for DeWitt Products, the factory overhead rate at this selected activity level would be:

$$\text{Factory overhead rate} = \frac{\text{Estimated factory overhead}}{\text{Estimated direct labor hours}} = \frac{\$300,000}{200,000} = \frac{\$1.50 \text{ per}}{\text{direct labor hour}}$$

This rate should be used to charge overhead to jobs, products, or work performed. Amounts applied are first entered in subsidiary ledgers such as job order cost sheets and cost of production reports. Direct labor hours, direct labor cost, or other similar data already recorded determine the amount of overhead chargeable to each job or product.

The factory overhead rate can be further broken down into its fixed and variable components as follows:

$$\frac{\$125,000 \text{ Estimated fixed factory overhead}}{200,000 \text{ Estimated direct labor hours}} = \$ .625 \text{ fixed portion of the factory overhead rate}$$

$$\frac{\$175,000 \text{ Estimated variable factory overhead}}{200,000 \text{ Estimated direct labor hours}} = .875 \text{ variable portion of the factory overhead rate}$$

$$\text{Total factory overhead rate} = \underline{\$1.500} \text{ per direct labor hour}$$

▼ ACTUAL FACTORY OVERHEAD

Deciding upon the base and activity level to be utilized, estimating the factory overhead, and calculating the overhead rate take place prior to the incurrence or recording of the actual expenses. Factory overhead is applied as soon as the necessary data, such as direct labor hours, have been made available. Each day, however, actual overhead transactions are journalized and posted to general and subsidiary ledgers, independent of the application of factory overhead based on the predetermined overhead rate.

A basic objective for accumulating factory overhead is the gathering of information for purposes of control. Control, in turn, requires (1) reporting costs to the individual department heads responsible for them and (2) making comparisons with amounts budgeted for the level of operations achieved. The mechanics for collecting overhead items are based on the chart of accounts, which indicates the accounts to which various factory overhead items are to be charged.

The principal source documents used for recording overhead in the journals are (1) purchase vouchers, (2) materials requisitions, (3) labor time tickets, and (4) general journal vouchers. These documents provide a record of the overhead information which must be analyzed and accumulated in proper accounts. To obtain accurate and useful information, each transaction must be properly classified at its inception. Those responsible for this identification must be thoroughly familiar with names and code numbers of cost accounts as well as with the purpose and function of each account.

Factory overhead includes numerous items which can be classified in many different ways. Every firm, because of its own manufacturing peculiarities, will devise its own particular accounts and methods of classifying them. However, regardless of these possible variations, expenses are summarized in a factory overhead control account kept in the general ledger. Details of this general ledger account are kept in a subsidiary overhead ledger. This subsidiary ledger also can take many forms, and it may be difficult to recognize it as such, particularly when electronic data processing equipment is used. A subsidiary ledger will group various expense items together under significant selective titles as to kinds of expenses and may also detail the expenses chargeable to individual producing and service departments (discussed in Chapter 13), thereby permitting stricter control over factory overhead.

The accumulation of factory overhead in accounting records presents several distinct problems. Due to the many varied potential requests and uses of factory overhead data for managerial decision-making purposes, it is almost impossible to set up an all-purpose system for accumulating factory overhead.

▼ APPLIED FACTORY OVERHEAD—OVER- OR UNDERAPPLIED AND VARIANCE ANALYSIS

At the end of the month or year, applied factory overhead and actual factory overhead are analyzed. The comparison between actual and applied figures leads to computation of the spending variance and the idle capacity variance. The following paragraphs present the mechanics of applying factory overhead, determining the over- or underapplied overhead, and analyzing the overhead variances.

The Mechanics of Applying Factory Overhead

The job order cost sheets or the departmental cost of production reports receive postings as soon as direct materials or direct labor data become available. Factory overhead is applied to the work done after the direct materials and the direct labor costs have been recorded. If direct labor hours or machine hours are the basis for overhead charges, these data must also be available to the cost department.

To continue the illustration for DeWitt Products, assume that actual direct labor hours worked totaled 189,000, and actual factory overhead totaled $292,000. The overhead applied during the period is $283,500 (189,000 hours × $1.50 per hour). The journal entry for summarizing factory overhead applied is:

Work in Process...	283,500	
Applied Factory Overhead.....................		283,500

Charges made to subsidiary records (the job order cost sheets or departmental cost of production reports) list in detail applied factory overhead charged to jobs or process costing departments. The debit to the work in process control account brings total applied overhead into the general ledger.

The applied factory overhead account would subsequently be closed to the factory overhead control account by the following entry:

Applied Factory Overhead.........................	283,500	
Factory Overhead Control.....................		283,500

It is common practice to use an applied factory overhead account because it keeps applied costs and actual costs in separate accounts. However, some companies post the credit directly to Factory Overhead Control.

After the actual and applied overhead have been recorded, the factory overhead control account for DeWitt Products appears as follows:

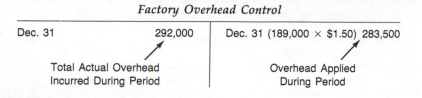

Factory Overhead Control

Dec. 31	292,000	Dec. 31 (189,000 × $1.50) 283,500

Total Actual Overhead Incurred During Period   Overhead Applied During Period

Over- or Underapplied Factory Overhead

Debits to the factory overhead control account are for actual expenses incurred during the period, while credits are for applied expenses. There may also be credit adjustments (e.g., the return of supplies to the storeroom) which reduce the total actual factory overhead. Since the debits and credits are seldom equal, there is usually a debit or credit balance in the account. A debit balance indicates that overhead has been underapplied; a credit balance means that overhead has been overapplied. These over- or underapplied balances must be analyzed carefully, because they are the source of much information needed by management for controlling and judging the efficiency of operations and the use of available capacity during a particular period.

For DeWitt Products, applied factory overhead for the period is $8,500 less than the actual factory overhead incurred. Therefore, factory overhead for the period was $8,500 underapplied. This difference must be analyzed to determine the reason or reasons for the underapplied overhead.

Variance Analysis

Two separate variances are computed in analyzing over- or underapplied overhead:

1. Spending variance—a variance due to budget or expense factors.
2. Idle capacity variance—a variance due to volume or activity factors.

The analysis can be made in the following manner, using the factory overhead data given on pages 333-335:

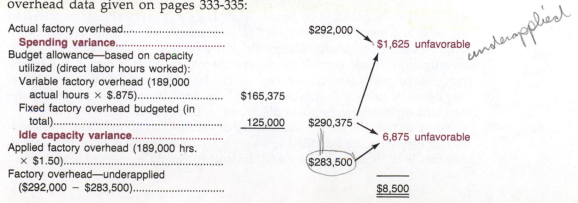

Actual factory overhead...............................		$292,000	
Spending variance......................................			$1,625 unfavorable
Budget allowance—based on capacity utilized (direct labor hours worked):			
Variable factory overhead (189,000 actual hours × $.875)...........................	$165,375		
Fixed factory overhead budgeted (in total)...	125,000	$290,375	
Idle capacity variance................................			6,875 unfavorable
Applied factory overhead (189,000 hrs. × $1.50)..		$283,500	
Factory overhead—underapplied ($292,000 − $283,500).............................			$8,500

underapplied

Spending Variance. The $1,625 spending variance is the difference between the actual factory overhead incurred and the budget allowance estimated for the capacity utilized, i.e., for the actual activity of 189,000 direct labor hours worked. The spending variance can also be computed as follows:

Actual factory overhead incurred during the period...	$292,000
Less budgeted fixed overhead...	125,000
Actual variable overhead incurred during the period......................................	$167,000
Variable overhead applied during the period (189,000 hours × $.875)........	165,375
Spending variance—unfavorable...	$ 1,625

If actual overhead had been less than budgeted, the spending variance would have been favorable. Any difference between actual and budgeted fixed overhead would be included as part of the spending variance or separately identified as an additional variance.

A breakdown of the $1,625 spending variance, as well as a comparison of each actual expense with its budgeted figure, is useful. Details of the actual expenses are recorded in the factory overhead subsidiary ledger. The comparison of actual with budgeted overhead for capacity worked (189,000 direct labor hours) is illustrated for DeWitt Products on page 339.

The budgeted figures utilize the concept of the flexible budget discussed in Chapter 16. Basically, the budget figures represents the budget for the level of activity attained. For example, from the estimates for indirect labor on page 334, fixed overhead is $9,000; the variable part of the overhead cost is $.33 per hour ($66,000 estimated variable indirect labor ÷ 200,000 estimated direct labor hours). The budgeted indirect labor for the activity level attained is $9,000 fixed overhead plus $62,370 (189,000 direct labor hours × $.33) variable overhead.

Some of the actual expenses exceed while others are less than the budgeted figures. Each difference must be analyzed, the reason for the difference must be determined, and discussion must be initiated with the individual responsible for its incurrence. Corrective action should be taken where called for; likewise, effective and efficient performance should be recognized and rewarded. Observe that even underexpenditures may be undesirable. For example, the $1,305 underspent repairs and maintenance amount may suggest insufficient attention to preventive maintenance.

In deciding which expenses to investigate, tolerance limits should be established. The question becomes, "How large a variance should be tolerated before it is considered excessive?" If an expense falls within the tolerance range, it can be considered acceptable. If the variance is outside the range, an investigation should occur if the cost of the investigation is reasonable. Thus, the notion of management by exception can be employed. The tolerance limits may be set by rules of thumb or preferably by applying procedures such as the standard error of the estimate discussed in Chapter 11.

Some of the spending variance may be attributable to inflation. Although budget estimates are intended to incorporate inflationary effects, the level of inflation is difficult to predict and difficult to isolate as part of a variance.

DeWitt Products
Comparison of Actual and Factory Overhead Budget Allowance for 19—
(Capacity Utilized: 189,000 Direct Labor Hours = 94.5% of Normal)

	Budget Allowance	Actual	Spending Variance
Variable overhead:			
Indirect labor	$ 62,370	$ 63,550	$1,180
Overtime premium	8,505	8,700	195
Factory supplies	17,955	18,720	765
Repairs and maintenance	8,505	7,200	(1,305)
Electric power	17,010	17,650	640
Fuel	4,725	4,300	(425)
Water	472	500	28
FICA tax	14,175	14,450	275
Unemployment taxes	3,308	3,425	117
Workmen's compensation	2,362	2,400	38
Hospitalization insurance	1,418	1,435	17
Pensions	12,285	12,550	265
Vacations and holidays	9,450	9,300	(150)
Group insurance	2,835	2,820	(15)
Total	$165,375	$167,000	$1,625
Fixed overhead:			
Supervisors	$ 70,000	$ 70,000	—
Indirect labor	9,000	9,000	—
Factory supplies	4,000	4,000	—
Repairs and maintenance	3,000	3,000	—
Electric power	2,000	2,000	—
Fuel	1,000	1,000	—
Water	500	500	—
FICA tax	3,000	3,000	—
Unemployment taxes	1,500	1,500	—
Workmen's compensation	500	500	—
Hospitalization insurance	500	500	—
Pensions	2,000	2,000	—
Vacations and holidays	2,000	2,000	—
Group insurance	1,000	1,000	—
Depreciation—building	5,000	5,000	—
Depreciation—equipment	13,000	13,000	—
Property tax	4,000	4,000	—
Insurance (fire)	3,000	3,000	—
Total	$125,000	$125,000	—
Total	$290,375	$292,000	$1,625 unfav.

Idle Capacity Variance. For DeWitt Products, the rate used for applying factory overhead was $1.50 per direct labor hour, which was based on 200,000 normal capacity hours. However, direct labor hours worked during the period totaled only 189,000 hours; capacity not used was 11,000 direct labor hours. The capacity attained was 94.5 percent (189,000 ÷ 200,000) of normal.

The $1.50 overhead rate was considered the proper costing price for each direct labor hour used. The fact that operations were at a level below normal should not increase the factory overhead cost of each unit. The cost of idle capacity should be recorded separately and considered a part of total manufacturing cost. The $6,875 idle capacity variance arises because 11,000 available hours were not used. It is computed as follows:

Budget allowance (based on capacity utilized)	$290,375
Applied factory overhead	283,500
Idle capacity variance—unfavorable	$ 6,875

The idle capacity variance can also be computed by multiplying the 11,000 idle hours by the $.625 fixed expense rate or by multiplying the total budgeted fixed expense of $125,000 by 5.5 percent (100% − 94.5%).

Responsibility for the idle capacity variance rests with executive management, since this variance indicates the under- or overutilization of plant and equipment. The cause of a capacity variance, whether favorable or unfavorable, should always be determined and possible reasons for the variance discovered. One cause may be a lack of proper balance between production facilities and sales. On the other hand, it might be due to a favorable sales price that recovers fixed overhead at an unusually low volume level.

Disposition of Over- or Underapplied Factory Overhead. Because of its importance, the analysis of the over- or underapplied factory overhead is presented in detail. Disposition of this figure is generally quite simple. Although total over- or underapplied overhead is analyzed, showing spending and idle capacity variances, it need not be journalized and posted in two parts. At the end of the fiscal period, overhead variances may be (1) treated as a period cost or (2) allocated between inventories and the cost of goods sold.

For financial reporting purposes, the procedure often used for disposing of over- or underapplied overhead, provided the amount involved is insignificant, is to close it directly to Income Summary or to Cost of Goods Sold, thereby treating the over- or underapplied overhead as a period cost. The entries are:

Income Summary	8,500	
Factory Overhead Control		8,500

or

Cost of Goods Sold	8,500	
Factory Overhead Control		8,500

In the second case, the $8,500 is subsequently closed to the income summary account as a part of the total cost of goods sold account balance.

The over- or underapplied figure is closed to the cost of goods sold account if the variances are considered a manufacturing function responsibility; if not, the balance is closed to Income Summary. If it is closed to the income summary account, it will appear in the income statement as follows:

DeWitt Products
Income Statement
For Year Ended December 31, 19—

Sales...		$1,600,000
Less: Cost of goods sold at normal......................	$1,193,500	
Underapplied factory overhead....................	8,500	1,202,000
Gross profit..		$ 398,000
Less: Marketing expense...	$ 150,000	
Administrative expense................................	100,000	250,000
Operating income...		$ 148,000

If the over- or underapplied overhead is closed to the cost of goods sold account, it will appear in the cost of goods sold statement. This statement and the income statement would appear as follows:

DeWitt Products
Cost of Goods Sold Statement
For Year Ended December 31, 19—

Direct materials used..	$ 400,000
Direct labor used..	500,000
Applied factory overhead..	283,500
Total manufacturing cost..	$1,183,500
Less increase in work in process inventory....................	20,000
Cost of goods manufactured at normal............................	$1,163,500
Plus decrease in finished goods inventory......................	30,000
Cost of goods sold at normal..	$1,193,500
Plus underapplied factory overhead................................	8,500
Cost of goods sold at actual...	$1,202,000

[handwritten annotations:] 32,500 beg invent WIP / 32,200 applied to WIP / 300 add the decrease in WIP
18,000 / −68,000 / 50,000 less an increase

DeWitt Products
Income Statement
For Year Ended December 31, 19—

Sales...		$1,600,000
Less cost of goods sold at actual......................		1,202,000
Gross profit..		$ 398,000
Less: Marketing expense...	$150,000	
Administrative expense................................	100,000	250,000
Operating income...		$ 148,000

Over- or underapplied overhead may be allocated between inventories and the cost of goods sold. This procedure has the effect of restating applied overhead at amounts approximating actual overhead, and it is appropriate for financial reporting purposes if the variances are significant.

Internal Revenue Service regulations require that inventories include an allocated portion of significant annual overhead variances. When the amount involved is not significant in relation to total actual factory overhead, an allocation is not required, unless such allocation is made for financial reporting purposes. Also, the taxpayer must treat both over- and underapplied overhead consistently. The regulations, however, do permit expensing of the idle capacity variance.[2]

Regardless of the disposition made of the over- or underapplied figure, the computation, analysis, and reporting of both the spending and idle capacity variances are significant and important. In the disposition of over- or underapplied factory overhead for financial reporting purposes, companies should generally follow the same procedures at interim dates as are followed at year end. Variances that occur at an interim date and that are expected to be absorbed prior to year end should be deferred rather than disposed of immediately. Further discussion of the disposition of variances is reserved for the standard cost chapters (17 and 18).

▼ CHANGING OVERHEAD RATES

Overhead rates are usually reviewed annually. This procedure helps level out costing through the year and ties overhead control in with budget control. If rates are changed during a fiscal or budget period, meaningful comparisons will be difficult. Changes in production methods, prices (because of inflation or for other reasons), efficiencies, and sales expectancy make review and, possibly, revision of overhead rates necessary at least annually. Revisions should be based on a complete review of all factors involved. The extent to which a company revises its overhead rates depends on the frequency of changes, on factors which affect overhead rates, and on management's need and desire for current costs and realistic overhead variance information.

An overhead rate may be incorrect because of misjudgments regarding estimated overhead or anticipated activity. A large over- or underapplied overhead figure does not necessarily mean that the overhead rate was wrong. As mentioned, use of a normal overhead rate is purposely designed to show spending variances as well as the extent to which normal capacity is or is not used. Likewise, when an overhead rate based on expected actual conditions is used, seasonal variations may result in a large amount of over- or underabsorbed overhead, which will tend to even itself out during a full year. The best way to detect an incorrect overhead rate is to analyze the factors used in its predetermination. Since a rate is an estimate, small errors should be expected, and the rate need not be changed for such errors.

▼ SUMMARY OF FACTORY OVERHEAD

This chapter's discussion of estimating, accounting for, and analyzing factory overhead is summarized diagrammatically on page 343.

---

[2]*Regulations*, Section 1.471-11(d)(3).

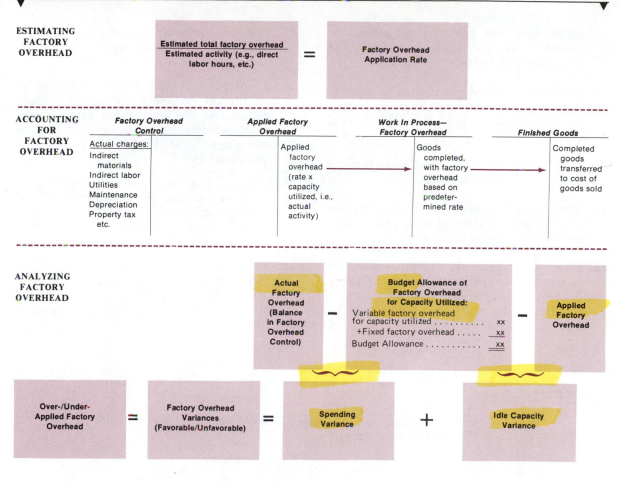

DISCUSSION QUESTIONS

1. List some of the main expenses that are considered to be factory overhead.

2. Why will factory overhead vary from month to month?

3. When and why must predetermined factory overhead rates be used? Indicate the impracticalities and inaccuracies of charging actual overhead to jobs and products.

4. Name five bases used for applying overhead. What factors must be considered in selecting a particular base?

5. Why is the selection of a proper predetermined rate so essential to reasonable costing? Explain.

6. Discuss the objectives and criteria that should be used in deciding whether to use direct labor hours or machine hours as the overhead rate base.   *(AICPA adapted)*

7. Differentiate between (a) theoretical capacity, (b) practical capacity, (c) expected actual capacity, and (d) normal capacity.

8. How does the selection of normal or maximum capacity affect operating profit in setting the factory overhead rate?

9. (a) What situations give rise to idle capacity costs? (b) How and why should such costs be accounted for? (c) What is excess capacity cost?

10. What are the steps involved in accounting for actual factory overhead?

11. The factory overhead control account has a credit balance at the end of the period. Was overhead over- or underapplied?

12. Over- or underapplied overhead can be analyzed into two parts called variances. Name these variances, state the reason(s) for their titles, and show their computations.

13. What are the purposes of a factory overhead variance analysis report, such as the one shown on page 339?

14. A company applies factory overhead to production on the basis of direct labor dollars. At the end of the year, factory overhead has been overapplied to the extent of $60,000. What factors could cause this situation?

15. Describe two methods for disposing of over- or underapplied factory overhead and explain how the decision to use one of these methods rather than the other would affect net income.

16. If large underabsorbed (underapplied) factory overhead variances occur month after month, the factory overhead rate should be revised to make unit costs more accurate. Comment.

EXERCISES

1. Factory overhead application. On November 30, the work in process account of Watkins Company showed:

Work In Process

Materials	23,800	Finished	
Direct		goods	48,600
labor	20,160		
Factory			
overhead	15,840		

Materials charged to the work still in process amounted to $4,560. Factory overhead is a fixed percentage of direct labor cost.

Required: Compute the individual amounts of factory overhead and direct labor charged to work still in process. (Round off all amounts to four decimal places.)

2. Calculation of estimated labor hours. Venice Company employs 150 people, who work 8 hours a day, 5 days a week. Normal capacity for the firm is based on the assumption that the equivalent of 47 weeks of work can be expected from an employee.

Required: Calculate the following:

(1) The number of direct labor hours to be used in setting up the firm's factory overhead rate based on normal capacity.
(2) The number of direct labor hours if management and workers agree on a 10-hour, 4-day workweek.

3. Various factory overhead rates. Colbey Corporation estimates factory overhead of $276,000 for the next fiscal year. It is estimated that 47,500 units will be produced at a materials cost of $400,000. Conversion will require 28,750 direct labor hours at a cost of $9.60 per hour, with 23,000 machine hours.

Required: Compute the factory overhead rate that may be used in applying factory overhead to production on each of the following bases:

(1) Units of production   (4) Direct labor cost
(2) Materials cost   (5) Machine hours
(3) Direct labor hours

4. Normal and expected actual capacity. Normal capacity for Baltimore Products Company is 50,000 direct labor hours. The actual capacity attained for the fiscal year ended June 30, 19A, was 43,000 hours. It is estimated that 40,000 hours will be worked in the next fiscal period. Fixed factory overhead is $200,000, and variable factory overhead is $6.69 per direct labor hour.

Required:

(1) Assuming normal capacity, compute (a) the factory overhead rate, (b) the fixed part of the factory overhead rate, and (c) the 19A idle capacity variance.
(2) Assuming expected actual capacity, compute (a) the factory overhead rate and (b) the fixed part of the factory overhead rate.

5. Factory overhead—applied, over- or underapplied. Carlo Company budgeted factory overhead at $255,000 for the period for Department A, based on a budgeted volume of 100,000 machine hours. At the end of the period, the actual factory overhead was $270,000, and actual machine hours were 105,000.

Required: Calculate the applied and over- or underapplied factory overhead for the period.

6. Entries for factory overhead. Lancaster Co. assembles and sells electric mixers. All parts are purchased, and the cost of the parts per mixer totals $40. Labor is paid on the basis of $32 per mixer assembled. Since the company handles only this one product, the unit cost base for applying factory overhead is used. Estimated factory overhead for the coming period, based on a production of 30,000 mixers, is as follows:

Indirect materials.....................	$220,000
Indirect labor...........................	240,000
Light and power.......................	30,000
Depreciation............................	25,000
Miscellaneous..........................	55,000

During the period, 29,000 mixers were assembled and actual factory overhead was $559,600. These units were completed but not yet transferred to the finished goods storeroom.

Required:

(1) Prepare the journal entries to record the above information.
(2) Determine the amount of over- or underapplied factory overhead.

7. Factory overhead variance analysis. Normal annual capacity for Remington Company is 60,000 units, with production being constant throughout the year. The October budget shows fixed factory overhead of $2,500 and a variable factory overhead rate of $2.50 per unit. During October, actual output was 4,800 units, with a total factory overhead of $15,500.

Required: Compute the spending and idle capacity variances.

8. Applied factory overhead and variance analysis. Normal annual capacity for Maddax Company is 36,000 labor hours, with fixed factory overhead budgeted as $16,920 and an estimated variable factory overhead rate of $2.10 per labor hour. During October, actual production required 2,700 labor hours, with a total overhead of $7,959.

Required: Compute (1) the applied factory overhead and (2) the spending and idle capacity variances.

9. Variance analysis. Mitchell Company made the following data available from its accounting records and reports:

(a) $\dfrac{\$600,000 \text{ estimated factory overhead}}{200,000 \text{ estimated machine hours}} = \$3$ predetermined factory overhead rate

(b) Further analysis indicates that one third of the rate is variable-cost oriented.

(c) During the year, the company worked 210,000 machine hours, and actual factory overhead expenditures were $631,000.

Required: Compute the spending and idle capacity variances.

10. Factory overhead application and analysis. Normal operating capacity of Warren Inc. is 150,000 machine hours per month, the level used to compute the predetermined factory overhead application rate. At this level of activity, fixed factory overhead is estimated to be $300,000, and variable factory overhead is estimated to be $150,000. During March, actual production required 140,000 machine hours, and actual factory overhead totaled $435,000.

Required:

(1) Determine the fixed portion of the factory overhead application rate.
(2) Determine the variable portion of the factory overhead application rate.
(3) Is factory overhead for March over- or underapplied and by how much?
(4) How much is the spending variance, and is it favorable or unfavorable?
(5) How much is the idle capacity variance, and is it favorable or unfavorable?

11. Variance analysis procedure. Kornbrant Company was totally destroyed by fire during June. However, certain fragments of its cost records with the following data were recovered: idle capacity variance, $1,266 favorable; spending variance, $879 unfavorable; and applied factory overhead, $16,234.

Required: Determine (1) the budget allowance, based on capacity utilized, and (2) the actual factory overhead.

PROBLEMS

12-1. Determining variable and fixed factory overhead cost behavior. Noblenz Company had the following production, sales, and costs in March and October, 19A, which are considered to be typical months:

	March	October
Production in units...	10,000	15,000
Sales in units..	12,000	16,000
Costs:		
Depreciation on factory building and equipment...	$16,000	$ 16,000
Heat, light, and power (factory)............................	6,000	8,000
Supplies used (factory)...	7,000	10,500
Direct materials used...	50,000	75,000
Taxes on factory building.......................................	2,000	2,000
Bad debt expense..	1,000	1,500
Indirect labor (factory)..	60,000	70,000
Advertising expense..	6,000	8,000
Maintenance (factory)..	12,000	18,000
Direct labor...	70,000	105,000

Required:

(1) Compute the variable overhead per unit for each factory overhead expense.
(2) Compute the fixed overhead for each factory overhead expense.

(CGAAC adapted)

12-2. Factory overhead accumulation and application. Bullock Company uses job order cost accumulation procedures. Manufacturing-related costs for November were:

Work in process, November 1 (Job 50)......................	$54,000
Materials and supplies requisitioned for:	
Job 50..	$45,000
Job 51..	37,500
Job 52..	25,500
Supplies..	2,000
Factory direct labor hours:	
Job 50..	3,500
Job 51..	3,000
Job 52..	2,000
Labor costs:	
Direct labor wages..	$102,000
Indirect labor wages...	15,000
Supervisory salaries...	6,000
Building occupancy costs...	3,500
Factory equipment costs...	6,000
Other factory costs...	5,000

Jobs 50 and 51 were completed during November. The predetermined factory overhead rate is $4.50 per direct labor hour.

Required:

(1) Compute the total cost of Job 50.
(2) Determine the factory overhead costs applied to Job 52 during November.
(3) Compute the total factory overhead costs applied during November.
(4) Determine the actual November factory overhead incurred.
(5) How should Bullock dispose of any over- or underapplied factory overhead, assuming that the amount is not significant in relation to total factory overhead? *(ICMA adapted)*

12-3. Variance analysis. Following are eight sets of partial factory overhead data, with favorable variances shown in parentheses:

Actual Factory Overhead	Applied Factory Overhead	Budget Allowance (Based on Capacity Utilized)	Spending Variance	Idle Capacity Variance
(a) $30,000	$29,000	$32,000	$?	$?
(b) ?	15,000	?	1,000	7,000
(c) 24,000	24,000	?	(6,000)	?
(d) ?	?	18,000	1,000	2,000
(e) 18,000	20,000	?	3,000	?
(f) 27,000	?	?	(6,000)	(2,000)
(g) 16,000	16,000	?	-0-	?

Required: Compute the missing figures.

12-4. Factory overhead costing; job order cost accumulation. The following manufacturing cost data are available for Department 203:

Work in process—beginning of period:

Job No.	Materials	Labor	Factory Overhead	Total
1376	$17,500	$22,000	$33,000	$72,500

Costs for 19—:

Incurred by Jobs	Materials	Labor	Other	Total
1376..	$ 1,000	$ 7,000	—	$ 8,000
1377..	26,000	53,000	—	79,000
1378..	12,000	9,000	—	21,000
1379..	4,000	1,000	—	5,000

Not Incurred by Jobs				
Indirect materials and supplies..............................	15,000	—	—	15,000
Indirect labor..................................	—	53,000	—	53,000
Employee benefits.........................	—	—	$23,000	23,000
Depreciation..................................	—	—	12,000	12,000
Supervision....................................	—	20,000	—	20,000
Total..	$58,000	$143,000	$35,000	$236,000

Factory overhead rate for 19—:
Budgeted overhead:

Variable—Indirect materials and supplies...	$ 16,000
Indirect labor...	56,000
Employee benefits...	24,000
Fixed—Depreciation...	12,000
Supervision...	20,000
Total..	$128,000
Budgeted direct labor cost...	$ 80,000
Overhead rate per direct labor dollar ($128,000 ÷ $80,000)............	160%

Required:

(1) Compute the actual factory overhead.
(2) Determine the over- or underapplied factory overhead.

(3) Calculate the spending variance.

(4) Calculate the amount included in cost of goods sold for Job 1376, which was the only job completed and sold in 19—.

(5) Determine the cost assigned to the work in process account at the end of 19—, unadjusted for any over- or underapplied factory overhead.

(6) Assume that factory overhead was $14,000 underapplied. Compute the underapplied factory overhead charged to the ending work in process inventory if it was distributed between this account and cost of goods sold.

(ICMA adapted)

12-5. Variance analysis. Prince Goods Company set normal capacity at 60,000 machine hours. The expected operating level for the period just ended was 45,000 hours. At this expected actual capacity, variable expenses were estimated to be $29,250 and fixed expenses, $18,000. Actual results show that 47,000 machine hours were used and that actual factory overhead totaled $49,400 during the period.

Required:

(1) Compute the predetermined factory overhead rate based on normal capacity.

(2) Compute the predetermined factory overhead rate based on expected actual capacity.

(3) Compute the amount of factory overhead charged to production if the company used the normal capacity rate.

(4) Compute the amount of factory overhead charged to production if the company used the expected actual capacity rate.

(5) Would there be a favorable idle capacity variance if the normal capacity rate were used? Illustrate by variance computation.

(6) Would there be a favorable idle capacity variance if the expected actual capacity rate were used? Illustrate by variance computation.

(7) Determine the difference in the amount of the spending variance, depending on whether normal or expected actual capacity was used. Illustrate by variance computation.

12-6. Variance analysis. In June, the factory overhead idle capacity variance for Sterner Company was $800 favorable and the spending variance was zero. In July, the factory overhead idle capacity variance was zero, but the spending variance was $500 unfavorable. June actual factory overhead was $9,000 for an output of 700 tons, while July factory overhead was $7,500 for a 500-ton output. In August, output was 400 tons, actual factory overhead was $5,900, and the budget allowance was $6,000.

Required: Complete the variance analysis for each of the three months.

12-7. Variance analysis. The June idle capacity variance was zero, and the spending variance was $600, unfavorable. The July idle capacity variance was $800, unfavorable, and the spending variance was zero. June overhead was $7,000 for an output of 800 tons, while July overhead was $5,600, and output was 600 tons. In August, output was 900 tons and actual factory overhead was $7,100.

Required: Prepare a columnar analysis, indicating actual, budget allowance, applied, total variance, spending variance, and idle capacity variance for each month.

12-8. Inventory costing; overhead analysis; statement of cost of goods sold. The Cost Department of Ingot Company received the following monthly data, pertaining solely to manufacturing activities, from the general ledger clerk:

Work in process inventory, January 1	$ 32,500
Materials inventory, January 1	21,000
Direct labor	256,000
Materials purchased	108,000
Materials returned to suppliers	5,050
Supervision	18,500
Indirect labor	29,050
Heat, light, and power	22,800
Depreciation—factory buildings	7,500
Property tax	4,000
Insurance on factory buildings	3,000
Transportation in (factory overhead)	6,500
Repairs and maintenance—factory equipment	8,250
Depreciation—factory equipment	7,500
Miscellaneous factory overhead	9,900
Finished goods inventory, January 1	18,000
Applied factory overhead	115,200

Additional data:

(a) Physical inventory taken January 31 shows $9,000 of materials on hand.

(b) The January 31 work in process and finished goods inventories show the following direct materials and direct labor contents:

	Direct Materials	Direct Labor
Work in process	$ 9,000	$16,000 (2,000 hrs.)
Finished goods	10,000	40,000 (5,000 hrs.)

ending inventories

(c) Factory overhead is applied to these two ending inventories on the basis of a factory overhead rate of $3.60 per direct labor hour.

Required:

(1) Determine the cost assigned to the ending work in process and finished goods inventories, including factory overhead.

(2) Prepare a schedule of the total actual factory overhead for the month.

(3) Prepare an analysis of the over- or underapplied factory overhead, assuming that the predetermined factory overhead rate was based on the following data:

Variable factory overhead	$70,875
Fixed factory overhead	$42,525
Direct labor hours	31,500

estimate
estimate
actual   estimate of normal capacity
budget × 3.60 = 113,400

(4) Prepare a detailed cost of goods sold statement, assuming that over- or underapplied overhead is closed to the cost of goods sold account.

CASES

A. Cost behavior analysis; utility of cost behavior information. Tastee-Treat Food Company assigns factory overhead by a predetermined rate on the basis of direct labor hours.

Factory overhead costs for two recent years, adjusted for changes using current prices and wage rates, are as follows:

	Year 1	Year 2
Direct labor hours worked......	2,760,000	2,160,000

Factory overhead costs:

	Year 1	Year 2
Indirect labor....................	$11,040,000	$ 8,640,000
Employee benefits..............	4,140,000	3,240,000
Supplies...........................	2,760,000	2,160,000
Power..............................	2,208,000	1,728,000
Heat and light...................	552,000	552,000
Supervision......................	2,865,000	2,625,000
Depreciation.....................	7,930,000	7,930,000
Property taxes and insurance..........................	3,005,000	3,005,000
Total factory overhead cost.................	$34,500,000	$29,880,000

Required:

(1) The company expects to operate at a 2,300,000 direct labor hour level of activity next year. Using the data from the two recent years, calculate the estimated total factory overhead for next year.

(2) Explain how the company can use the computed cost behavior information for:

(a) Evaluation of product pricing decisions.

(b) Cost control evaluation.

(c) Development of budgets.

(ICMA adapted)

B. **Factory overhead rate bases.** Herbert Manufacturing Company, a manufacturer of custom designed restaurant and kitchen furniture, uses job order costing. Actual factory overhead costs incurred during the month are applied to the products on the basis of actual direct labor hours required to produce the products and consist primarily of supervision, employee benefits, maintenance costs, property tax, and depreciation.

Herbert recently won a contract to manufacture the furniture for a new fast food chain which is expanding rapidly in the area. In general, this furniture is durable but of a lower quality than the company normally manufactures. To produce this new line, Herbert must produce more molded plastic parts for the furniture than for its current line. Through innovative industrial engineering, an efficient manufacturing process for this new furniture has been developed, requiring only a minimum capital investment. Management is optimistic about the profit improvement the new product line will bring.

At the end of October, the start-up month for the new line, and again in November, the controller prepared a separate income statement for the new product line. On a consolidated basis, the gross profit percentage was normal; however, the profitability for the new line was less than expected. Management is concerned that knowledgeable stockholders will criticize the decision to add this lower-quality product line at a time when profitability appeared to be increasing with their standard product line. Gross profit results for the first nine months, for October, and for November are as follows:

Herbert Manufacturing Company
Statement of Gross Profit
(000s omitted)

	First Nine Months			October			November		
	Fast Food Furniture	Custom Furniture	Consolidated	Fast Food Furniture	Custom Furniture	Consolidated	Fast Food Furniture	Custom Furniture	Consolidated
Sales........................	—	$8,100	$8,100	$400	$900	$1,300	$800	$800	$1,600
Direct materials.........	—	$2,025	$2,025	$200	$225	$ 425	$400	$200	$ 600
Direct labor:									
Forming................	—	758	758	17	82	99	31	72	103
Finishing...............	—	1,314	1,314	40	142	182	70	125	195
Assembly..............	—	558	558	33	60	93	58	53	111
Factory overhead.......	—	1,779	1,779	60	180	240	98	147	245
Cost of goods sold.....	—	$6,434	$6,434	$350	$689	$1,039	$657	$597	$1,254
Gross profit...........	—	$1,666	$1,666	$ 50	$211	$ 261	$143	$203	$ 346
Gross profit percentage.............	—	20.6%	20.6%	12.5%	23.4%	20.1%	17.9%	25.4%	21.6%

The controller contends that the factory overhead allocation based solely on direct labor hours is inappropriate and that only supervision and employee benefits should use this base, with the balance of factory overhead allocated based on machine hours. In the controller's judgment, the increase in custom design furniture profitability is partially a result of overhead misallocation.

The actual direct labor hours and machine hours for the past two months are as follows:

	Fast Food Furniture	Custom Furniture
Machine hours:		
October:		
Forming......................	660	10,700
Finishing....................	660	7,780
Assembly...................	—	—
	1,320	18,480
Direct labor hours:		
October:		
Forming......................	1,900	9,300
Finishing....................	3,350	12,000
Assembly...................	4,750	8,700
	10,000	30,000
Machine hours:		
November:		
Forming......................	1,280	9,640
Finishing....................	1,280	7,400
Assembly...................	—	—
	2,560	17,040
Direct labor hours:		
November:		
Forming......................	3,400	8,250
Finishing....................	5,800	10,400
Assembly...................	8,300	7,600
	17,500	26,250

The actual factory overhead costs for the past two months were:

	October	November
Supervision......................	$ 13,000	$ 13,000
Employee benefits.............	95,000	109,500
Maintenance.....................	50,000	48,000
Depreciation.....................	42,000	42,000
Property tax....................	8,000	8,000
All other.........................	32,000	24,500
Total...........................	$240,000	$245,000

Required:

(1) Reallocate actual factory overhead for October and November, following the controller's preference. (Round allocated costs to the nearest $100.)

(2) Present support or criticism of the controller's contention, based on requirement (1) results, and include revised statements of gross profit for October and for November.

(3) The controller has also recommended that consideration be given to using predetermined factory overhead rates calculated on an annual basis rather than allocating actual cost over actual volume each month. The controller stated that this is particularly applicable now that the company has two distinct product lines. Discuss the advantages of predetermined factory overhead rates.   *(ICMA adapted)*

CHAPTER 13

Factory Overhead: Departmentalization

The preceding chapter discussed the establishment and use of one factory-wide predetermined overhead rate, the accumulation of actual factory overhead, and the analysis of over- or underapplied factory overhead. These phases are now expanded through the use of predetermined departmental factory overhead rates, which improves the charging of overhead to jobs and products and leads to cost control via responsibility accounting.

The computation of predetermined overhead rates requires a series of departmental allocation processes with respect to estimated expenses. These allocations are necessary for computing overhead rates prior to the beginning of the fiscal period. Actual overhead accumulated during the month or year should remain with the individual department until the end of the accounting period.

▼ THE CONCEPT OF DEPARTMENTALIZATION

Methods for the control of materials and labor costs are discussed in other chapters. However, because each product manufactured requires a certain minimum amount of materials and labor, there is a limit to the amount of cost reduction for materials and labor which can be realized through the use of such methods. The control potential and control methods are different for factory overhead.

Departmentalization of factory overhead means dividing the plant into segments, called departments, cost centers, or cost pools, to which expenses are charged. For accounting purposes, dividing a plant into separate departments provides improved costing of jobs and products and responsible control of overhead costs, which is necessary if unit and total costs are to stay within predetermined or budgeted ranges.

Improved costing of jobs and products is possible because departmentalization uses different departmental overhead rates for applying factory overhead. A job or product going through a department is charged with factory overhead for work done in that department, using the department's predetermined overhead rate. Depending on the type and number of departments through which they pass, jobs or products are charged with varying amounts of factory overhead, rather than with a single plant-wide overhead rate.

Responsible control of overhead costs is possible because departmentalization makes the incurrence of expenses the responsibility of a supervisor or manager. Expenses which originate directly and completely in a department are identified with the individual responsible for the supervision of the department.

The entire process of departmentalizing factory overhead is an extension of methods previously discussed. Estimating or budgeting expenses and selecting a proper base for applying them is still necessary; but, in addition, departmentalizing overhead requires separate estimates or budgets for each department. Actual expenses of a period must still be recorded in a factory overhead control account and a factory overhead subsidiary ledger for each department, according to the nature of the expense. This procedure permits comparison of actual departmental expenses with departmentally applied factory overhead. Over- or underapplied factory overhead is computed departmentally and analyzed separately to determine departmental spending and idle capacity variances.

▼ PRODUCING AND SERVICE DEPARTMENTS

Departments are classified as either producing or service departments. A *producing department* engages in the actual manufacture of the product by changing the shape, form, or nature of the material worked upon, or by assembling the parts into a finished article. A *service department* renders a service that contributes in an indirect manner to the manufacture of the product but which does not itself change the shape, form, or nature of the material that is converted into the finished product. The following table lists examples of producing and service departments:

PRODUCING		SERVICE	
Cutting	Mill Room	Utilities	Shipping
Planing	Plating	Materials Handling	Medical
Assembly	Knitting	Inspection	Production Control
Upholstery	Mixing	Storage	Personnel
Finishing	Refining	Plant Security	Maintenance
Machining		Purchasing	Cafeteria
		Receiving	General Factory Cost Pool

Selection of Producing Departments

A manufacturing company is usually organized along departmental lines for production purposes. Manufacturing processes dictate the type of organization needed to handle the different operations efficiently, to obtain the best production flow, and to establish responsibility for physical control of production.

The cost information system is designed to fit the departmentalization required for production purposes. The system accumulates manufacturing costs according to such departmentalization, whether operations are of the job type or the continuous process type. Factors to be considered in deciding the kinds of departments required for establishing accurate departmental overhead rates with which to control costs are:

1. Similarity of operations, processes, and machinery in each department.
2. Location of operations, processes, and machinery.
3. Responsibilities for production and costs.
4. Relationship of operations to flow of product.
5. Number of departments or cost centers.

The establishment of producing departments for the purpose of costing and controlling expenses is a problem for the management of every company. Although no hard and fast rules can be given, the most common approach divides the factory along lines of functional activities, with each activity or group of activities constituting a department. Division of the factory into separate, interrelated, and independently governed units is important for the proper control of factory overhead and the reasonable costing of jobs and products.

The number of producing departments used depends on the emphasis the cost system puts on cost control and the development of overhead rates. If the emphasis is on cost control, separate departments might be established for the plant manager and for each superintendent or supervisor. When the development of departmental overhead rates emphasizes costing, fewer departments might be used. Sometimes the number of departments needed for cost control is larger than that needed for overhead rates. In such cases, the cost control system can be adapted to proper overhead rates by combining departments, thus reducing the number of rates used without sacrificing control of costs.

In certain instances, particularly when different types of machines are used, departments are further subdivided for cost control and overhead rate purposes. This results in a refinement in applying and controlling overhead with respect to the jobs or products passing through a department.

Selection of Service Departments

The selection and designation of service departments has considerable bearing on effective costing and control. Services available for the benefit of producing departments and other service departments can be organized in several ways by (1) establishing a separate service department for each function, (2) combining several functions into one department, or (3) placing service costs in a department called "general factory cost pool." The specific service is not identified if service costs applicable to producing and service functions are accumulated in a general factory cost pool.

Determination of the kinds and numbers of service departments should consider the number of employees needed for each service function, the cost of providing the service, the importance of the service, and the assignment of supervisory responsibility. Establishing a separate department for every service function is rarely done, even in large companies. When relatively few employees are involved and activities are closely related, service functions are generally combined for the sake of economy and expediency. Decisions with respect to combining service functions are governed by the individual circumstances existing in each company. Since factory overhead rates for job and product costing are generally calculated for producing departments only, service department expenses are transferred ultimately to producing departments for rate setting and variance analysis.

CAS 418, "Allocation of Direct and Indirect Costs," states that a department should be homogeneous and specifies that this criterion is met ". . . if each significant activity whose costs are included therein has the same or a similar beneficial or causal relationship . . . as the other activities whose costs are included in the [department]."

▼ DIRECT DEPARTMENTAL EXPENSES IN PRODUCING AND SERVICE DEPARTMENTS

The majority of direct departmental overhead costs can be categorized as follows:

1. Supervision, indirect labor, and overtime.
2. Labor fringe benefits.
3. Indirect materials and factory supplies.
4. Repairs and maintenance.
5. Equipment depreciation.

These expense categories are generally readily identified with the originating department, whether producing or service. In the discussion that follows, detailed attention is given to each of the categories.

Supervision, Indirect Labor, and Overtime

These factory labor categories, in contrast to direct labor, do not alter the shape or content of a product; they are auxiliary to its manufacture. It is important to realize that the labor control and accounting procedures discussed in Chapters 9 and 10 are relevant to supervision, indirect labor, and overtime, as well as to their related labor fringe benefits.

Any factory labor not classified as direct labor is automatically classified as factory overhead. Since overhead is allocated to all products, a lax or incorrect classification would cause direct labor that applies to only one product to be allocated as indirect labor in the form of overhead to other products, thereby understating the one product cost and overstating the others. Thus, decisions on whether or not to classify costs as direct labor can have an important effect on overhead rates, especially since direct labor cost is often used as the base for determining the rates. In such a case, a decision to classify certain labor as indirect reduces the denominator and increases the numerator of the ratio (factory overhead ÷ direct labor cost) used to compute overhead rates. The following illustration points out the possible effect of incorrect identification of $1,000 of direct labor as indirect labor:

	Correctly Identified as Direct Labor	Incorrectly Identified as Indirect Labor
Direct labor	$6,000	$5,000
Factory overhead:		
Indirect labor	$5,000	$6,000
Other overhead	1,000	1,000
Total factory overhead	$6,000	$7,000

$$\text{Factory overhead rates} = \frac{\text{Factory overhead}}{\text{Direct labor cost}} \qquad \frac{\$6,000}{\$6,000} = 100\% \qquad \frac{\$7,000}{\$5,000} = 140\%$$

The premium portion of overtime paid should generally be charged as overhead to the departments in which the overtime occurred. This method should be followed for all labor except for special cases, which are discussed in the labor chapters. However, the straight-time portion of overtime paid to direct labor employees should be charged to direct labor.

Labor Fringe Benefits

Labor fringe benefits include such costs as vacation and holiday pay, FICA tax, state and federal unemployment taxes, workmen's compensation insurance, pension costs, hospitalization benefits, and group insurance. In theory, these labor fringe benefits are additional labor costs and should—when they pertain to direct labor employees—be added to the direct labor cost. In practice, such a procedure is usually impractical; therefore, these costs that pertain to direct as well as to other factory workers are generally included in factory overhead and become part of the factory overhead rate.

Indirect Materials and Factory Supplies

The materials control and costing procedures and quantitative models discussed in Chapters 7 and 8 are equally appropriate in dealing with indirect materials and factory supplies. However, incorrectly distinguishing between direct and indirect materials (the latter being part of overhead) has the same adverse effects on product costing as failure to make proper distinction between direct and indirect labor. However, distinguishing between direct and indirect materials is usually not as difficult. In a manufacturing operation, direct materials are those which are changed in form through processing and become an integral part of the end product. Indirect materials, often referred to as factory supplies, are auxiliary to the processing operations and do not become an essential part of the end product. Although insignificant amounts of direct materials may be distinguishable, they may be charged to overhead as an expediency.

Repairs and Maintenance

With respect to repairs and maintenance costs, it is essential to establish control over the total cost incurred by the repairs and maintenance department and to devise effective means for charging maintenance costs to departments receiving the service. Repairs and maintenance costs are generally traceable to benefiting departments and are thus classified here as direct departmental expenses, even though they first may originate in a maintenance department.

As a rule, the work of repair and maintenance crews is supervised by a maintenance superintendent. If possible and practical, all actual maintenance costs should be charged to a maintenance department, so that the total cost is controlled by the maintenance superintendent and kept within a maintenance budget. However, since maintenance is a service function, its costs must ultimately be distributed to departments that receive the service.

Most maintenance work performed for departments is generally of a recurring nature, and charges are incurred evenly throughout the year. However, certain types of maintenance work, such as breakdowns and overhauls, occur at irregular intervals and often involve large expenditures. In such cases, companies using departmental budgets may spread major repair costs over the year by making monthly charges to operations, based on a predetermined rate. These rates are commonly derived from previous years' experiences. Monthly provisions are charged to Maintenance Expense and credited to an allowance account. Actual repair costs are charged to the allowance account. In this manner, large maintenance costs are charged to operations in direct proportion to the operating rate and presumably approximate the actual deterioration of the equipment.

Equipment Depreciation

Depreciation is usually a cost not controllable by departmental supervisors. However, their use of equipment influences maintenance and depreciation costs. This is true with respect to all types of depreciable assets—machinery and equipment, buildings, vehicles, and furniture and fixtures. For effective costing and controlling, depreciation is usually identified with the departments using the assets, and the cost is charged directly to departments. The recommended method is to compute depreciation by departments, based on the cost of equipment as recorded on detailed plant asset records. When no records are available or equipment is used by more than one department, depreciation is frequently accumulated in the general factory cost pool.

For assets acquired in earlier years, depreciation of historical costs results in failure to consider both price-level changes and/or current values, especially as they relate to inflationary trends. The result is a mingling of these older costs with other costs acquired with more current dollars. Inflation accounting, while not incorporated in the historical-cost accounting records, should be considered by management in using accounting data for planning and decision making. Discussion of inflation adjustment procedures is left to financial accounting textbooks.

▼ INDIRECT DEPARTMENTAL EXPENSES IN PRODUCING AND SERVICE DEPARTMENTS

Expenses such as power, light, rent, and depreciation of factory buildings, when shared by all departments, are not charged directly to a department. These expenses do not originate with any specific department. They are incurred for all to use and must, therefore, be prorated to any or all departments using them.

Selecting appropriate bases for the distribution of indirect departmental expenses is difficult and arbitrary. At best, allocations will be intuitively reasonable. To charge every department with its share of an expense, a base using some factor common to all departments must be found. For example, square footage may be used for prorating such expenses as rent. In plants with departments occupying parts of the factory with ceilings of unequal height, cubic measurement rather than square footage might be used. Areas occupied by stairways, elevators, escalators, corridors, and aisles must also be considered. Some of the indirect departmental expenses that require prorating, together with the bases most commonly used, are:

Indirect Departmental Expenses	Distribution Bases
Factory rent	Square footage
Property tax	Square footage
Depreciation—buildings	Square footage
Insurance (fire)	Square footage
Building repairs	Square footage
Heat	Square footage
Superintendence	Number of employees
Telephone and telegraph	Number of employees or number of telephones
Workmen's compensation insurance	Department payroll
Light	Kilowatt-hours
Freight in	Materials used
Power	Horsepower-hours

At times a service that could be obtained separately by each of several departments can be obtained centrally at a lower aggregate cost. In such cases, the cost if each department obtained the service separately, i.e., the "stand-alone" cost, may be the most equitable base for allocation of the centralized cost.[1] For example, assume that individual departments can obtain necessary rental space separately as follows:

Department	Cost of Rental Space Obtained Separately
A	$ 500,000
B	500,000
C	250,000
D	50,000
	$1,300,000

[1]Richard B. Troxel, "Corporate Cost Allocation Can Be Peaceful . . . Is Sharing the Key?" *Management Focus*, Vol. 28, No. 1, pp. 3-5.

Assume further that the rental space can be provided under a consolidated rental agreement for a total cost of $1,030,000. Proration of the aggregate cost on a "stand-alone" base would yield the following result:

$$A = \frac{500,000}{1,300,000} = 396,154$$

Department	Aggregate Cost	Allocation Base	Allocated Aggregate Cost
A	$1,030,000 ×	$500,000/$1,300,000 =	$ 396,154
B	1,030,000 ×	500,000/1,300,000 =	396,154
C	1,030,000 ×	250,000/1,300,000 =	198,077
D	1,030,000 ×	50,000/1,300,000 =	39,615
			$1,030,000

The Cost Accounting Standards Board Disclosure Statement requires that covered federal government contractors identify and describe allocation bases for all factory overhead, service center, and general and administrative cost pools used by the contractor. CAS 418 sets forth guidance for accumulating as well as for allocating indirect costs. The allocation is to be based on one of the following, listed in order of preference: (1) a resource consumption measure, (2) an output measure, or (3) a surrogate that is representative of resources consumed.[2] While specified for costing government contracts, this hierarchy affords guidance for more general cost accounting system uses.

▼ ESTABLISHING DEPARTMENTAL OVERHEAD RATES

For convenience, factory overhead is usually applied on the basis of direct labor cost or hours when only one factory overhead rate is used for the entire plant. However, the use of departmental rates requires a distinct consideration of each producing department's overhead, which often results in the use of different bases for applying overhead for different departments. For example, it is possible to use a direct labor hour rate for one department and a machine hour rate for another. A further refinement might possibly lead to different bases and rates for cost centers within the same producing department.

Since all factory overhead, whether from producing departments or from service departments, is ultimately allocated to producing departments, the establishment of departmental factory overhead rates proceeds in the following manner:

1. Estimate or budget total direct factory overhead of producing departments and total direct expenses of service departments at the selected activity levels; determine, if possible, the fixed and variable nature of each expense category.
2. Prepare a factory survey for the purpose of distributing indirect factory overhead and service department costs.
3. Estimate or budget total indirect factory overhead, such as electric power, fuel, water, building depreciation, property tax, and fire

---

[2]*Standards, Rules and Regulations, Part 418*, "Allocation of Direct and Indirect Costs" (Washington, D.C.: Cost Accounting Standards Board, 1980).

insurance at the selected activity levels; allocate these costs, based on selected methods.

4. Distribute service department costs to benefiting departments.
5. Calculate departmental factory overhead rates.

These procedures are illustrated with the total estimated factory overhead for DeWitt Products (page 334), which has now been departmentalized. The figures have been modified for ease in calculating departmental rates, but the fixed-variable cost classification has been retained. The illustration uses four producing departments: Cutting, Planing, Assembly, and Upholstery; and four service departments: Materials Handling, Inspection, Utilities, and General Factory.

Materials handling involves the operation of equipment such as cranes, trucks, forklifts, and loaders. Since many departments are served by this function, a preferred method of organization establishes a separate service department for materials handling activities. All handling costs are charged to this department, with a supervisor responsible for their control. Costs charged to such a service department are the same as those charged to any department and include wages and labor fringe costs of the department's employees; supplies, such as batteries and gasoline; and repairs and maintenance of the equipment. In addition to centralizing responsibility for materials handling operations, departmentalization has the advantage of collecting all materials handling costs in one place.

For cost control, inspection costs are treated in the same manner as other service department costs. However, in certain instances, a special work order may require additional inspection or testing. This type of inspection cost is chargeable to the order and must be so identified. To accumulate these specific charges, separate cost centers may be established for the purpose of charging time and materials for special inspections.

Power and fuel are consumed for two major purposes: for operating manufacturing facilities such as machines, electric welders, and cranes, and for what might be termed "working condition" purposes, such as lighting, cooling, and heating. Although a single billing is common for electric power or natural gas, a direct departmental allocation is often possible. To make such an allocation possible, separate meters to measure power or fuel consumed by specific types of equipment may be installed. In other instances, separate power sources (fuel, natural gas, coal, or electricity) may be used for different facilities or equipment, thus permitting the determination of an individual utility cost by department.

For purposes of departmental and product costing, two methods of accounting for costs of utilities are recommended:

1. Charge all power and fuel costs to a separate utilities department; then allocate to the benefiting departments.
2. Charge specific departments with power or fuel cost if separate meters are provided, and charge the remaining power and fuel costs to a separate utilities department or to a general factory account; this remainder is then allocated to the benefiting departments.

Allocation of utilities costs to specific departments is based on special studies that determine such information as each department's horsepower of machines and the number of machines.

Certain expenses other than those discussed above come under the category "general factory," because they represent a variety of miscellaneous factory services. Therefore, a separate general factory cost pool is established to accumulate and control such expenses. Such an organizational unit is usually the direct responsibility of the plant superintendent. Salaries of management personnel directly concerned with production are charged to this cost pool if they cannot be charged to specific departments except by arbitrary allocations. Janitor labor and supplies may be charged to general factory unless charged to maintenance or to "building occupancy." Unless separate service departments for plant security and yard operation are established, these costs are also charged to general factory.

Estimating Direct Departmental Expenses

Estimating or budgeting the direct expenses of producing and service departments (Exhibit 1, page 363) is a joint undertaking of department heads, supervisors, and members of the budget or cost department of the company. Labor fringe costs are calculated by the office personnel, since the individual supervisor has little influence or knowledge with respect to the underlying rates and figures. Costs of indirect labor and indirect materials are of greater interest to the supervisor. Repairs and maintenance costs are often disputed items unless a definite maintenance program has been established, and, while not illustrated here, they first may be charged to the maintenance department and then assigned to the benefiting department. Departmental depreciation charges are based on management's decision regarding depreciation methods and rates. In the illustration, depreciation of equipment is charged directly to the departments on the basis of asset values and rates set by the controller. The plant manager, working with budget personnel, estimates and supervises the general factory costs.

Factory Survey

Before indirect departmental and service department expenses can be prorated to benefiting and ultimately to producing departments, certain underlying data must be obtained. A survey of factory facilities and records usually produces the information needed, such as rated horsepower of equipment in each department, estimated kilowatt-hour consumption, number of employees in each department, estimated payroll costs, square footage, estimated materials consumption, and asset values. Functions performed by each service department must be studied carefully to determine

DeWitt Products
Estimated Departmental Factory Overhead
For the Year 19—

Cost Account	F or V	Total	Producing Departments				Service Departments			
			Cutting	Planing	Assembly	Upholstery	Materials Handling	Inspection	Utilities	General Factory
Direct departmental expenses:										
Supervisors	F	$ 70,000	$ 9,000	$ 8,000	$ 8,000	$ 8,000	$10,000	$ 6,000	$ 9,000	$12,000
Indirect labor	F	9,000	1,000	2,000	1,000	1,500	1,000	500	1,000	1,000
Labor fringe costs	V	66,000	9,000	3,000	5,000	5,500	11,000	8,500	10,000	14,000
	F	10,000	1,500	1,000	1,000	1,000	2,000	1,000	1,500	1,000
	V	47,000	10,500	11,800	9,400	8,200	1,800	1,400	1,900	2,000
Indirect materials	F	4,000	500	500	800	1,200	300	200	200	300
	V	19,000	2,500	2,500	3,200	4,800	1,700	800	1,800	1,700
Repairs and maintenance	F	3,000	600	500	700	600			300	300
	V	9,000	1,400	1,500	1,300	1,800	500	200	1,700	600
Depreciation—equipment	F	13,000	1,500	3,500	1,000	3,000				4,000
Total direct departmental expense		$250,000	$37,500	$34,300	$31,400	$35,600	$28,300	$18,600	$27,400	$36,900
Indirect departmental expenses:										
Electric power	V	$ 2,000							$ 2,000	
Fuel	V	20,000							20,000	
		1,000							1,000	
Water	V	10,000							10,000	
		1,000							1,000	
		4,000							4,000	
Depreciation—buildings	F	5,000	$ 1,250	$ 1,000	$ 1,500	$ 1,250				
Property tax	F	4,000	1,000	800	1,200	1,000				
Insurance (fire)	F	3,000	750	600	900	750				
Total indirect departmental expense		$ 50,000	$ 3,000	$ 2,400	$ 3,600	$ 3,000			$38,000	
Total departmental factory overhead		$300,000	$40,500	$36,700	$35,000	$38,600	$28,300	$18,600	$65,400	$36,900
Total fixed factory overhead		$125,000	$17,100	$17,900	$16,100	$18,300	$13,300	$ 7,700	$16,000	$18,600
Total variable factory overhead		$175,000	$23,400	$18,800	$18,900	$20,300	$15,000	$10,900	$49,400	$18,300

Exhibit 1

the most reasonable basis for distributing their expenses. The factory survey for DeWitt Products appears as follows:

DEWITT PRODUCTS
SCHEDULE A—FACTORY SURVEY PREPARED AT THE BEGINNING OF THE YEAR

Producing Department	Number of Employees	%	Kilo-watt Hours	%	Horse-power Hours	%	Floor Area (Sq. Ft.)	%	Cost of Materials Requisi-tioned	%
Cutting	30	20	12 800	20	200,000	40	5,250	25	$180,000	45
Planing	25	17	6 400	10	120,000	24	4,200	20	40,000	10
Assembly	45	30	19 200	30	80,000	16	6,300	30	40,000	10
Upholstery	50	33	25 600	40	100,000	20	5,250	25	140,000	35
Total	150	100	64 000	100	500,000	100	21,000	100	$400,000	100

Estimating and Allocating Indirect Expenses

Indirect departmental expenses, such as heat, electric power, fuel, water, and building depreciation, must be estimated and then allocated to either producing and service departments or perhaps only to producing departments. The method depends upon management's decision. In Exhibit 1, indirect departmental expenses are prorated in two ways: (1) electric power, fuel, and water are charged to Utilities, from which a distribution is made to producing departments only; (2) depreciation of building, property tax, and fire insurance are prorated only to producing departments on the basis of floor area as shown in the Factory Survey (Schedule A); e.g., 25 percent of $5,000, or $1,250, is charged to the Cutting Department for building depreciation. However, as an alternative, these costs could be allocated to service departments as well as to producing departments. This procedure would more completely measure the total cost for individual service departments as well as provide information needed for cost planning and control.

Distributing Service Department Costs

The number and types of service departments in a company depend on its operations and the degree of expense control desired. As shown in Exhibit 1, each service department of DeWitt Products is charged with its direct expenses. These costs and any indirect departmental expenses charged to the service departments should be distributed equitably to either producing departments and service departments or just to producing departments, again depending on management's decision. The distribution might be based on number of employees, kilowatt-hour consumption, horsepower-hour consumption, floor space, asset value, or cost of materials to be requisitioned. The expenses of service departments are ultimately transferred to producing departments to establish predetermined factory overhead rates and to analyze variances. The commonly used procedures for allocating service department overhead to benefiting departments are the direct method, the step method, and the algebraic method.

Direct Method. In some companies, service department expenses are transferred only to producing departments. This procedure minimizes clerical work. It can be justified for product costing if there is no material difference in the final costs of a producing department when the expenses of a service department are not prorated to other service departments. However, this procedure fails to measure the total cost for individual service departments when such information is needed for cost planning and control.

The direct procedure for the distribution of estimated service department costs for DeWitt Products is illustrated in Exhibit 2, page 366. Since the illustration shows no transfer of service department costs to other service departments, the order of distribution does not matter. The distribution begins with Materials Handling. The overhead of this department is distributed on the basis of the estimated cost of materials requisitioned per Schedule A. For example, 45 percent of $28,300, or $12,735, is transferred to the Cutting Department. The Inspection cost is transferred to the Assembly and Upholstery producing departments on a 50-50 basis, because these two departments are the only ones receiving this type of service and they receive it in equal amounts.

The Utilities cost is transferred in a three-fold manner: 20 percent of the cost based on kilowatt-hours; 50 percent, on horsepower-hours; and 30 percent, on floor area. The amount of $13,080 represents 20 percent of $65,400, the total cost of the Utilities Department. According to Schedule A, 20 percent of $13,080, or $2,616, is distributed to the Cutting Department. The same method is followed for the other costs and departments. General Factory is distributed on the basis of number of employees. For example, 20 percent of $36,900, or $7,380, is distributed to the Cutting Department.

The distribution of the service department costs in this illustration is based on percentages in the Factory Survey, page 364. Alternatively, such costs could be allocated by calculating a rate per square foot, per kilowatt-hour, or per employee. For example, the amount of General Factory cost allocated to the Cutting Department may be determined as follows:

$$\frac{\$36,900 \text{ General Factory cost}}{150 \text{ employees}} = \$246 \text{ per employee}$$

$$\$246 \times 30 \text{ employees in the Cutting Department} = \$7,380$$

DeWitt Products

Distribution of Estimated Service Department Costs

and

Calculation of Departmental Factory Overhead Rates

For the Year 19—

Cost Account	Total	Producing Departments				Service Departments			
		Cutting	Planing	Assembly	Upholstery	Materials Handling	Inspection	Utilities	General Factory
Total departmental factory overhead before distribution of service depts.	$300,000	$40,500	$36,700	$35,000	$38,600	$28,300	$18,600	$65,400	$36,900
Distribution of service department costs:									
Materials handling (Base: estimated cost of materials requisitioned)		$12,735	$ 2,830	$ 2,830	$ 9,905	(28,300)			
Inspection (Base: equally to assembly and upholstery departments)				9,300	9,300		(18,600)		
Utilities: (Bases: 20% on kwh		2,616	1,308	3,924	5,232			(13,080)	
50% on hph		13,080	7,848	5,232	6,540			(32,700)	
30% on floor area)		4,905	3,924	5,886	4,905			(19,620)	
General factory (Base: no. of employees)		7,380	6,273	11,070	12,177				(36,900)
Total service department cost distributed		$40,716	$22,183	$ 38,242	$48,059				
Total departmental factory overhead after distribution of service departments	$300,000	$81,216	$58,883	$ 73,242	$86,659				
Bases: Direct labor hours		40,608			48,140				
Machine hours			18,400						
Direct labor cost				$122,000					
Rates		$2.00 per direct labor hour	$3.20 per machine hour	60% of direct labor cost	$1.80 per direct labor hour				

Exhibit 2

An additional and more compact illustration of the direct method, and other methods to be discussed, is based on the following data for Nickleby Company:

Department	Factory Overhead Before Distribution of Service Departments	Services Provided Dept. Y	Services Provided Dept. Z
Producing—A....................................	$ 60,000	40%	20%
Producing—B....................................	80,000	40	50
Service—Y.......................................	36,300	—	30
Service—Z.......................................	20,000	20	—
Total factory overhead.....................	$196,300	100%	100%

Recall that the service provided to other service departments is ignored by the direct procedure because this method allocates service department overhead only to producing departments. Thus, the order of distribution does not matter. For Nickleby Company, the distribution is as follows:

Distribution of Service Department Overhead Using the Direct Method

	Total	Producing Departments A	Producing Departments B	Service Departments Y	Service Departments Z
Factory overhead before distribution of service departments..............................	$196,300	$60,000	$ 80,000	$36,300	$20,000
Distribution of:					
Department Y............................		18,150	18,150	(36,300)*	
Department Z............................		5,714	14,286		(20,000)**
Total factory overhead................	$196,300	$83,864	$112,436		

*40/80 to A, 40/80 to B
**20/70 to A, 50/70 to B

Step Method. An alternate procedure is to transfer by steps, that is, in a prescribed order by departments, the expenses of service departments, primarily on the basis of producing and other service departments' use of the respective services. To use this procedure, a decision must be made with respect to the service department which should be closed first, second, etc., because no further distributions are made to a service department, once its costs have been distributed. Thus, a more complete recognition of interrelated benefits among service departments occurs than is the case using the direct method in which no such interrelationships are recognized. However, this procedure is still only a partial consideration of the service departments' mutual benefits, since after distribution of a service department's costs, no further distributions are made to it.

Usually, expenses are transferred in the order of the amount of service rendered and received, with the expenses of the department serving the greatest number of other departments and receiving service from the smallest number of other departments transferred first, and so on. When service rendered and received by departments cannot be determined reasonably, however, the expenses of the service department which has the largest total expense may be distributed first, then by descending expense size for other departments. With this latter approach, it is assumed that the department with the largest amount of expense provided the greatest amount of service.

The Nickleby Company data can be used to demonstrate the step method, with Department Y distributed first, as follows:

Distribution of Service Department Overhead Using the Step Method

	Total	Producing Departments		Service Departments	
		A	B	Y	Z
Factory overhead before distribution of service departments...............................	$196,300	$60,000	$ 80,000	$36,300	$20,000
Distribution of:					
Department Y............................		14,520	14,520	(36,300)*	7,260
Department Z............................		7,789	19,471		(27,260)**
Total factory overhead.................	$196,300	$82,309	$113,991		

*40/100 to A, 40/100 to B, 20/100 to Z
**20/70 to A, 50/70 to B

Y is closed 1st

Algebraic Method. Incompleteness in proration arises using the step method because one department would be closed out before the other and therefore before receiving any expense proration from the other. While the resulting difference in the final costs of a producing department may or may not be materially different, the direct method and to a lesser extent the step method fail to measure the total cost for individual service departments. This total cost information may be quite useful for cost planning and control.

The algebraic method, sometimes referred to as the simultaneous method, offers a means of accomplishing a complete consideration of interrelationships among the various service departments. The Nickleby Company data from page 367 are again used to illustrate the procedure. Here the expenses of the service departments are allocated simultaneously, using the following algebraic technique.[3]

Let:	$Y = \$36,000 + .30Z$
	$Z = \$20,000 + .20Y$
Substituting:	$Y = \$36,300 + .30 (\$20,000 + .20Y)$
Solving:	$Y = \$36,300 + \$6,000 + .06Y$
	$.94Y = \$42,300$
	$Y = \$45,000$
Substituting:	$Z = \$20,000 + .20 (\$45,000) = \$20,000 + \$9,000 = \$29,000$

[3]Matrix algebra can also be used, and it is especially efficient when there is a large number of service departments and the allocation is done by computer. See Thomas H. Williams and Charles H. Griffin, "Matrix Theory and Cost Allocation," *The Accounting Review,* Vol. XXXIX, No. 3, pp. 671-678, and John L. Livingstone, "Matrix Algebra and Cost Allocation," *The Accounting Review,* Vol. XLIII, No. 3, pp. 503-508.

The distribution is then accomplished as follows:

Distribution of Service Department Overhead Using the Algebraic Method

		Producing Departments		Service Departments	
	Total	A	B	Y	Z
Factory overhead before distribution of service departments................................	$196,300	$60,000	$ 80,000	$36,300	$20,000
Distribution of:					
Department Y.............................		18,000	18,000	(45,000)*	9,000
Department Z.............................		5,800	14,500	8,700	(29,000)**
Total factory overhead.................	$196,300	$83,800	$112,500		

*40/100 to A, 40/100 to B, 20/100 to Z
**20/100 to A, 50/100 to B, 30/100 to Y

Calculating Departmental Overhead Rates

After service department expenses have been distributed, producing department overhead rates can be calculated in terms of direct labor hours, direct labor cost, machine hours, or some other appropriate base. In Exhibit 2, three different bases are used: direct labor hours, machine hours, and direct labor cost.

This discussion has described procedures by which all factory overhead costs, for both producing and service departments, are assigned to work in process by ultimate accumulation of factory overhead in producing departments and then by use of overhead rates for producing departments only. However, it is possible to assign certain service department costs directly from the service department to work in process. For example, materials handling costs might be accumulated in a materials handling department and a materials-cost-oriented rate used for assigning these costs directly to work in process, with any difference between actual and applied costs analyzed into spending and idle capacity variances.

▼ USE OF DEPARTMENTAL FACTORY OVERHEAD RATES

During the fiscal year, as information becomes available at the end of each week or month, factory overhead is applied to a job or product by inserting the applied overhead figure in the overhead section of a job sheet or production report. Amounts applied must be summarized periodically for entry in the general journal. The summary entry applicable to DeWitt Products is illustrated as follows:

Work in Process..285,000

    Applied Factory Overhead—Cutting Department (42,010 actual
       direct labor hours × $2)... 84,020

    Applied Factory Overhead—Planing Department (17,000 actual
       machine hours × $3.20).. 54,400

    Applied Factory Overhead—Assembly Department ($111,700 ac-
       tual direct labor cost × 60%)... 67,020

    Applied Factory Overhead—Upholstery Department (44,200 ac-
       tual direct labor hours × $1.80).. 79,560

A separate work in process account may be used for each producing department, instead of the single work in process account illustrated here. In such a case, the debit would be to each of these departmental work in process accounts in the same amount as for the corresponding applied departmental factory overhead figure.

▼ ACTUAL FACTORY OVERHEAD—DEPARTMENTALIZED

Actual factory overhead is summarized in the factory overhead control account in the general ledger. Details are entered in the factory overhead subsidiary ledger. Departmentalization of actual factory overhead also involves the detailed adaptation of previously outlined procedures for handling actual factory overhead.

Departmentalization of factory overhead requires that each expense be charged to a department as well as to a specific expense account. Such charges are collected on departmental expense analysis sheets, which serve as the subsidiary ledger. A portion of the form used for both producing and service departments is reproduced as follows:

DEPARTMENTAL EXPENSE ANALYSIS SHEET

Department No.   1 — Cutting   For   March, 19--

Explanation	Date	411	412	413	421	433	451	453	Summary

In this form, each column represents a certain class of factory overhead that will be charged to the department. For example, the column coded 411 represents supervisors, and 412 represents indirect labor. Entries to departmental expense analysis sheets are facilitated by combining department numbers and expense codes. A code such as 1412 indicates that Department No. 1 (Cutting) is charged with indirect labor (Code 412). Similar combinations are used for other departments. The chart of accounts establishes the codes. The subsidiary ledger must also include a sheet for each indirect factory expense not originally charged to a department, so that the total of the subsidiary overhead ledger will equal the total in the factory overhead control account.

▼ STEPS AND PROCEDURES AT END OF FISCAL PERIOD

At the end of the fiscal period, actual costs of producing and service departments, as well as those of a general indirect nature, are again assembled in the same manner as for estimated factory overhead at the beginning of the year. When all overhead has been assembled in the producing departments, it is then possible to compare actual with applied overhead and to determine the over- or underapplied factory overhead. The procedures are summarized as follows:

1. Prepare a summary of the actual direct departmental factory overhead of producing departments, direct expenses of service departments, and indirect factory overhead. (See Exhibit 3 on page 372.)
2. Prepare a second factory survey based on the actual data experienced during the year. (See Schedule B below).
3. Allocate actual indirect factory overhead based on the results of the factory survey at the end of the year. (See Exhibit 3 and Schedule B.)
4. Distribute actual service department costs to benefiting departments on the basis of the end-of-the-year factory survey. (See Exhibit 4 on page 373 and Schedule B.)
5. Compare actual total and departmental factory overhead with the total and departmental factory overhead applied to jobs and products during the year, and determine the total and departmental over- or underapplied factory overhead. (See Exhibit 4.)

DEWITT PRODUCTS
SCHEDULE B—FACTORY SURVEY—DECEMBER 31, 19—

Producing Department	Number of Employees	%	Kilo-watt Hours	%	Horse-power Hours	%	Floor Area (Sq. Ft.)	%	Cost of Materials Requisi-tioned	%
Cutting	35	24	16 978	26	210,000	42	5,250	25	$193,500	45
Planing	25	17	5 224	8	110,000	22	4,200	20	43,000	10
Assembly	40	28	16 325	25	90,000	18	6,300	30	47,300	11
Upholstery	45	31	26 773	41	90,000	18	5,250	25	146,200	34
Total	145	100	65 300	100	500,000	100	21,000	100	$430,000	100

Over- or Underapplied Factory Overhead

With the year-end overhead distribution sheet completed, total actual departmental factory overhead can now be transferred to the individual

DeWitt Products
Actual Departmental Factory Overhead
For the Year 19—

Cost Account	F or V	Total	Producing Departments				Service Departments			
			Cutting	Planing	Assembly	Upholstery	Materials Handling	Inspection	Utilities	General Factory
Direct departmental expenses:										
Supervisors	F	$ 70,000	$ 9,000	$ 8,000	$ 8,000	$ 8,000	$10,000	$ 6,000	$ 9,000	$12,000
Indirect labor	F	9,000	1,000	2,000	1,000	1,500	1,000	500	1,000	1,000
Labor fringe costs	V	63,000	9,800	2,800	4,200	6,000	10,000	7,300	9,000	13,900
	F	10,000	1,500	1,000	1,000	1,000	2,000	1,000	1,500	1,000
Indirect materials	V	45,000	10,000	11,400	9,700	8,000	1,700	1,300	1,600	1,300
	F	4,000	500	500	800	1,200	300	200	200	300
Repairs and maintenance	V	23,000	4,300	3,600	2,900	5,400	1,800	1,200	2,100	1,700
	F	3,000	600	500	700	600	600	300	300	300
	V	12,000	1,700	1,800	2,000	2,100			2,500	1,000
Depreciation—equipment	F	13,000	1,500	3,500	1,000	3,000				4,000
Total direct departmental expense		$252,000	$39,900	$35,100	$31,300	$36,800	$27,400	$17,800	$27,200	$36,500
Indirect departmental expenses:										
Electric power	F	$ 2,000							$ 2,000	
	V	14,000							14,000	
Fuel	F	1,000							1,000	
	V	7,000							7,000	
Water	F	1,000							1,000	
	V	3,000							3,000	
Depreciation—buildings	F	5,000	1,250	1,000	1,500	1,250				
Property tax	F	4,000	1,000	800	1,200	1,000				
Insurance (fire)	F	3,000	750	600	900	750				
Total indirect departmental expense		$ 40,000	$ 3,000	$ 2,400	$ 3,600	$ 3,000			$28,000	
Total actual departmental factory overhead before distribution of service departments		$292,000	$42,900	$37,500	$34,900	$39,800	$27,400	$17,800	$55,200	$36,500

Exhibit 3

DeWitt Products
Distribution of Actual Service Department Costs
and
Computation of Departmental Over- or Underapplied Factory Overhead
For the Year 19—

Cost Account	Total	Producing Departments				Service Departments			
		Cutting	Planing	Assembly	Upholstery	Materials Handling	Inspection	Utilities	General Factory
Total actual departmental factory overhead before distribution of service depts.	$292,000	$42,900	$37,500	$ 34,900	$39,800	$27,400	$17,800	$55,200	$36,500
Distribution of service department costs:									
Materials handling (Base: actual cost of materials requisitioned)		$12,330	$ 2,740	$ 3,014	$ 9,316	(27,400)			
Inspection (Base: equally to assembly and upholstery departments)				8,900	8,900		(17,800)		
Utilities: (Bases: 20% on kwh / 50% on hph / 30% on floor area)		2,870 / 11,592 / 4,140	883 / 6,072 / 3,312	2,760 / 4,968 / 4,968	4,527 / 4,968 / 4,140			(11,040) / (27,600) / (16,560)	
General factory (Base: no. of employees)		8,760	6,205	10,220	11,315				(36,500)
Total service department cost distributed		$39,692	$19,212	$ 34,830	$43,166				
Total actual departmental factory overhead after distribution of service departments	$292,000	$82,592	$56,712	$ 69,730	$82,966				
Total applied factory overhead	285,000	84,020	54,400	67,020	79,560				
(Over-) or underapplied factory overhead	$ 7,000	$(1,428)	$ 2,312	$ 2,710	$ 3,406				

Exhibit 4

departmental factory overhead control accounts. Using the figures provided by the overhead distribution sheet (Exhibit 4), the following entry can be made:

Factory Overhead—Cutting Department............................	82,592	
Factory Overhead—Planing Department...........................	56,712	
Factory Overhead—Assembly Department........................	69,730	
Factory Overhead—Upholstery Department.....................	82,966	
Factory Overhead Control...		292,000

A comparison of actual and applied overhead of each producing department as well as of the total overhead of the company results in the following (over-) underapplied factory overhead:

Total	Cutting	Planing	Assembly	Upholstery
$7,000	$(1,428)	$2,312	$2,710	$3,406

Spending and Idle Capacity Variance Analysis

In the previous chapter, page 337, the $8,500 underapplied factory overhead was analyzed and a $1,625 unfavorable spending variance and a $6,875 unfavorable idle capacity variance were determined. The $1.50 overhead rate used there and based on 200,000 direct labor hours and the variance results are not applicable for the departmentalized illustration. New rates with different bases and variance results have been created. However, it is possible to analyze each departmental over- or underapplied figure and determine a departmental spending and idle capacity variance. What is particularly needed is the amount of overhead budgeted for the level of operation attained (capacity utilized), which, in turn, requires a knowledge of the fixed and variable overhead in each producing department. To develop the budget allowance, the estimates shown in the summaries of the departmental factory overhead (Exhibit 1) and the distribution of service department costs (Exhibit 2) are examined. Exhibit 1 indicates the fixed and variable departmental costs at the bottom line of the estimates. The service department costs distributed to the producing departments, as shown in Exhibit 2, are considered variable costs for the producing departments. The fixed-variable classification does not apply after the distribution.

The following spending and idle capacity variance analysis is prepared for executive management on the basis of the actual annual data after the books have been closed. However, the middle- and operating-management levels require current cost control information at least once a month. With ever greater emphasis placed upon the control of costs by responsible supervisory personnel, control information must be communicated to all levels of management in a manner that permits the charging and discharging of responsibility of cost incurrence. This is discussed in Chapter 14.

CALCULATION OF ESTIMATED FIXED AND VARIABLE OVERHEAD RATES
Producing Departments

	Cutting	Planing	Assembly	Upholstery
Fixed departmental overhead*.....................	$17,100	$17,900	$ 16,100	$18,300
Variable departmental overhead*................	$23,400	$18,800	$ 18,900	$20,300
Variable service department costs**...........	40,716	22,183	$ 38,242	48,059
Total variable overhead...............................	$64,116	$40,983	$ 57,142	$68,359
Bases:**				
Direct labor hours....................................	40,608			48,140
Machine hours.......................................		18,400		
Direct labor cost...................................			$122,000	
Fixed overhead rate..................................	$ .42	$ .97	13%	$ .38
Variable overhead rate...............................	1.58	2.23	47	1.42
Total overhead rate:				
Per direct labor hour...............................	$ 2.00			
Per machine hour....................................		$ 3.20		
Of direct labor cost................................			60%	
Per direct labor hour...............................				$ 1.80

*From Exhibit 1, p. 363.
**From Exhibit 2, p. 366.

CALCULATION OF BUDGET ALLOWANCES*
Producing Departments

	Cutting	Planing	Assembly	Upholstery
Variable overhead:				
42,010 direct labor hours × $1.58..........	$66,376			
17,000 machine hours × $2.23..............		$37,910		
$111,700 direct labor cost × 47%..........			$52,499	
44,200 direct labor hours × $1.42..........				$62,764
Fixed overhead..	17,100	17,900	16,100	18,300
Total budget allowance...............................	$83,476	$55,810	$ 68,599	$81,064

*Based on capacity utilized, i.e., actual activity.

SPENDING AND IDLE CAPACITY VARIANCE ANALYSIS

Producing Department	(1) Actual Overhead*	(2) Budget Allowance**	(3) Applied Overhead***	Total Variance (1) − (3)	Spending Variance (1) − (2)	Idle Capacity Variance (2) − (3)
Cutting...........................	$ 82,592	$ 83,476	$ 84,020	$(1,428)	$ (884)	$ (544)
Planing...........................	56,712	55,810	54,400	2,312	902	1,410
Assembly.......................	69,730	68,599	67,020	2,710	1,131	1,579
Upholstery.....................	82,966	81,064	79,560	3,406	1,902	1,504
Total..............................	$292,000	$288,949	$285,000	$7,000	$3,051	$3,949

  *From Exhibit 4, p. 373.
  **From calculations above.
***From journal entry, p. 370.

▼ OVERHEAD DEPARTMENTALIZATION IN NONMANUFACTURING BUSINESSES AND NONPROFIT ORGANIZATIONS

The responsible control of departmental expenses is equally essential in nonmanufacturing activities. The following large complex entities should be divided into administrative and supervisory departments, sections, or service units for cost planning and control:

Nonmanufacturing segments of manufacturing concerns (e.g., marketing departments—see Chapter 25)
Retail or department stores
Financial institutions (banks, savings and loan associations, and brokerage houses)
Insurance companies
Educational institutions (school systems, colleges, and universities)
Service organizations (hotels, motels, hospitals, and nursing homes)
Federal, state, and local governments (and their agencies)

Retail or department stores have practiced departmentalization for many years by grouping their organizations under the following typical headings: administration, occupancy, sales promotion and advertising, purchasing, selling, and delivery. These groups incur costs similar to those in manufacturing businesses. The group "Occupancy" is almost identical with General Factory, and includes such expenses as building repairs, rent and property taxes, insurance on buildings and fixtures, light, heat, power, and depreciation on buildings and fixtures. Again, similar to factory procedures, group costs are prorated to revenue-producing sales departments via a charging or billing rate.

Financial institutions (banks, savings and loan associations, and brokerage houses) should departmentalize their organizations in order to control expenses and establish a profitability rating of individual activities. The size of the institution and the types of services offered determine the number of departments. The accumulation of departmental costs again follows factory procedure: (1) direct expenses, such as salaries, supplies, and depreciation of equipment, are charged directly; (2) general expenses, such as light, heat, and air conditioning, are prorated to the departments on appropriate bases. As income and expenses are ascertained, it is possible to create a work cost unit that permits the charging of accounts for services rendered and the analysis of an account's profitability.

The work of insurance companies is facilitated by dividing the office into departments. Some departments have several hundred clerks, and the work is highly organized. Insurance companies were one of the first businesses to install computers to reduce the clerical costs connected with the insurance business and to calculate new insurance rates and coverage on a more expanded basis for greater profitability. This quite detailed departmentalization might include actuarial, premium collection, group insurance, policyholders' service, registrar, medical, and legal information. While some costs are unique to the individual group, most are identical with expenses experienced in any office.

Educational institutions (such as public and private school systems, colleges, and universities) and service organizations (such as hotels, motels, hospitals, and nursing homes) find it increasingly necessary to budget their expenses on a departmental basis in order to control expenses and be able to charge an adequate cost recovering fee for their services. The services of social security via Medicare make a knowledge of costs mandatory in hospitals and nursing homes. Departmentalization will assist management in creating a costing or charging rate for short- or long-term care, for special services, for nurses' instruction, and for professional services (surgical, medical, X-rays, laboratory examinations, and filling of prescriptions).

The federal government employs a great number of people in a vast number of departments and agencies. A similar situation exists in state and local governments. This discussion uses the municipality as an example, since its varied services are better known to the public. Some common services or departments are street cleaning, street repairing and paving, public works projects, police and fire departments, city hospitals, sewage disposal plants, and trash and garbage collection. These services should be budgeted and their costs controlled on a responsibility accounting basis. Since the costs incurred are generally not revenue- but service-benefit-oriented, an attempt should be made to measure the operating efficiency of an activity based on some unit of measurement such as per capita (police), per mile (street paving and cleaning), and per ton (trash and garbage collection). Increasing costs require additional revenue, which means additional taxes. Taxpayers, however, expect efficient service in return for their tax money.

The state and federal governments must be made equally aware of the need for responsible cost control methods, so that services may be rendered at the lowest cost with greatest efficiency. With their many departments and agencies and huge sums budgeted for all of these units, governments must ensure that these activities are being administered by cost-conscious and service-minded people. The departmentalization process helps to assure the achievement of such a goal in any governmental unit.

DISCUSSION QUESTIONS

1. State reasons for the preference of departmental overhead rates over a single plant-wide rate.

2. The statement has been made that the entire process of departmentalizing factory overhead is an extension of methods used when a single overhead rate is used. Explain.

3. A company uses departmental factory overhead rates based on direct labor hours. Would the sum of departmental over- or underapplied overhead be any different if a plant-wide or blanket rate were used? Would the costs of goods sold and inventory be different?

4. What is a producing department? A service department? Give illustrations of each.

5. What are some of the factors that must be considered in deciding the kinds and number of departments required to control costs and to establish accurate departmental overhead rates?

6. For effective control of overhead, a supervisor, superintendent, manager, or department head can be held accountable for more than one cost center; but responsibility for a single cost center should not be divided between two or more individuals. Discuss.

7. State reasons for using a general factory cost pool for certain types of overhead instead of allocating it directly to producing and service departments.

8. Justify classifying overtime premiums for factory employees as factory overhead. List some of the difficulties in estimating this item in the creation of predetermined overhead rates.

9. Most companies keep plant asset records to identify equipment and its original cost by location or department. However, charges for depreciation, property tax, and fire insurance are often accumulated in general factory accounts and charged to departments on the basis of equipment values. Is this the best method for controlling such costs? If not, suggest possible improvements.

10. What are the important factors involved in selecting the rate to be used for applying the factory overhead of a producing department?

11. What are the several steps followed in establishing departmental factory overhead rates?

12. What questions must be resolved in allocating service department costs to benefiting departments, and how can cost information aid in service department cost control?

13. What methods can be used for allocating service department costs to producing departments? Which is recommended?

14. Procedures followed in computing departmental factory overhead rates determine the accounting for actual factory overhead. Explain.

15. Describe how departmental over- or underapplied overhead is determined, and explain the computations of departmental spending and idle capacity variances.

16. Overhead control in a nonmanufacturing business can be achieved through departmentalization. Explain.

17. Federal, state, and local governments should practice cost control via responsibility accounting. Discuss.

EXERCISES

1. Entries with overhead subsidiary ledger. The general ledger of Niehart Company contains a factory overhead control account supported by a subsidiary ledger showing details by departments. The plant has one service department and three producing departments. The following table shows details with respect to these departments:

	Machining Dept.	Painting Dept.	Assembly Dept.	General Factory Cost Pool
Building space (sq. ft.)	10,000	4,000	4,000	2,000
Cost of machinery	$300,000	$100,000	$60,000	$20,000
Horsepower rating	1,000	-0-	100	150
Workmen's compensation insurance rate (per $100)	$1.50	$1.50	$1.00	$1.00

During January, certain assets expired and some liabilities accrued as follows:

(a) Depreciation on buildings, $1,500.
(b) Depreciation on machinery, $9,600.
(c) Property tax for the year ending December 31 is estimated to be $12,000 (60% on buildings and 40% on machinery).
(d) Workmen's compensation insurance for January is based on the following earnings of factory employees: Machining Department, $30,000; Painting Department, $12,000; Assembly Department, $16,000; and General Factory Cost Pool, $6,000.
(e) The power meter reading at January 31 shows 12 500 kilowatt-hours consumed. The rate is $.06 per kilowatt-hour.
(f) The heat and light bill for January is $900.
(g) Supplies requisitions show $1,800 used in the Machining Department, $2,300 in the Assembly Department, and $410 in the General Factory Cost Pool.

Required: Prepare journal entries, with details entered in the departmental factory overhead subsidiary ledger columns.

2. Rate calculation—plant-wide vs. departmental direct method. West Florida Company uses the direct method in allocating service department costs to producing departments. Costs of Department S1 are allocated on the basis of number of employees, while costs of Department S2 are allocated on the basis of machine hours. The allocation bases used in calculating predetermined overhead rates are machine hours in Department P1 and direct labor hours in Department P2.

	Producing Departments		Service Departments	
	P1	P2	S1	S2
Budgeted factory overhead....................	$410,000	$304,000	$100,000	$50,000
Number of employees...........................	90	210	20	28
Machine hours.......................................	64,000	16,000		
Direct labor hours.................................	35,000	100,000		

The following data pertain to Job 437:

	Department P1	Department P2
Materials cost............................	$90	$40
Direct labor hours.....................	1	2
Machine hours...........................	3	1

Required:

(1) Calculate predetermined factory overhead rates for the producing departments and compute the resulting overhead cost of Job 437.
(2) Calculate a plant-wide predetermined factory overhead rate based on direct labor hours and compute the resulting overhead cost of Job 437.

(CGAAC adapted)

3. Rate calculation—plant-wide vs. departmental step method. LA Company allocates some service department expenses to other service departments. However, after a department's expenses have been allocated, no expenses are assigned back to it. Buildings and Grounds is allocated first, using square feet as a base. The number of employees is used as a base for allocating Factory Administration.

	Machining	Assembly	Buildings and Grounds	Factory Administration
Budgeted factory overhead.....................	$360,000	$420,000	$40,000	$25,000
Square feet...	9,000	10,000	1,500	1,000
Number of employees............................	440	460	50	30
Direct labor hours...................................	452,000	567,250		
Machine hours..	195,600	23,000		

Required:

(1) Compute a plant-wide factory overhead rate, using direct labor hours as a base. Round answer to the nearest cent.
(2) Compute the factory overhead rate for Machining, using machine hours as a base, and for Assembly, using direct labor hours as a base. Round answers to the nearest cent.   *(CGAAC adapted)*

4. Departmental distribution of estimated overhead—direct method; rate calculation. Gulf Breeze Company's factory is divided into four departments—two producing departments, Cutting and Finishing, serviced by the Buildings and Grounds and the Factory Administration departments. Service department costs are allocated to producing departments only—Buildings and Grounds based on square feet, and Factory Administration based on direct labor hours. In calculating predetermined overhead rates, machine hours are used as the base in Cutting, and direct labor hours as the base in Finishing.

	Cutting	Finishing	Buildings and Grounds	Factory Administration
Budgeted factory overhead.....................	$200,000	$300,000	$40,000	$60,000
Direct labor hours...................................	100,000	50,000		
Machine hours..	212,000			
Square feet...	50,000	30,000	1,000	2,000

The following data pertain to Job 2375:

Cutting:	Direct materials......................................	$35
	Direct labor, 3 hrs. @ $6......................	18
	Machine hours, 7	
Finishing:	Direct materials......................................	$10
	Direct labor, 5 hrs. @ $8......................	40

Required:

(1) Calculate predetermined factory overhead rates for the producing departments.
(2) Determine the total cost of Job 2375.   *(CGAAC adapted)*

5. Departmental distribution of estimated overhead—direct method; rate calculation. Naughton Company's factory contains two producing departments—Cutting and Assembly, and two service departments—Maintenance and Administration. Maintenance Department cost is allocated based on square feet, and Administration Department cost is allocated based on number of employees. Service department costs are allocated to producing departments only. Producing department overhead rates are computed based on direct labor hours.

The estimated annual data are as follows:

	Cutting	Assembly	Maintenance	Administration
Number of employees....................	150	100	40	30
Square feet......................................	21,000	9,000	4,000	3,000
Direct labor hours............................	300,000	200,000		
Overhead budget............................	$520,000	$400,000	$200,000	$150,000

Required: Prepare a factory overhead distribution and compute overhead rates.

(CGAAC adapted)

6. Departmental distribution of estimated overhead—step method; rate calculation. Morgan Company has two production and two service departments. Budgeted monthly costs and other operating data are as follows:

	Process A	Process B	General Plant	Maintenance
Direct labor hours......................................	30,000	38,500		
Machine hours..	60,000	30,000		
Maintenance hours....................................	1,800	1,200		
Direct labor cost.......................................	$162,000	$218,500		
Indirect labor cost:				
Variable..	5,000	10,000	—	$6,000
Fixed...	3,000	4,000	$13,900	1,500
Indirect material:				
Variable..	2,500	7,000	—	800
Fixed...	—	—	1,500	400
Miscellaneous factory overhead:				
Fixed...	4,000	4,000	1,000	1,500

It is assumed that the other three departments benefit from general plant services in relation to their budgeted labor costs, including both direct and indirect, variable and fixed.

Required:

    (1) Allocate service department costs, first General Plant, then Maintenance. It is Morgan Company's policy that after a department's expenses have been allocated, no expenses are assigned back to it. The producing departments benefit from maintenance service in relation to budgeted maintenance hours.

    (2) Develop factory overhead rates for the producing departments, using machine hours as the base for Process A and direct labor hours as the base for Process B.

(CGAAC adapted)

7. Departmental distribution of actual overhead—step method. Beaumont Municipal Hospital uses the step method for allocating nonrevenue-generating departments to revenue departments. For this method, the nonrevenue department serving the greatest number of other revenue and nonrevenue departments and receiving services from the smallest number is to be allocated first. Once the cost of a nonrevenue department has been allocated, no costs from any other department may be allocated to it, even though services may have been provided.

Beaumont Municipal Hospital has received approval to use the following order of allocation: Depreciation, Maintenance and Utilities, Laundry. June's costs are:

June Costs

Department	Original Departmental Cost
Operating Room...............................	$100,000
Radiology...	65,000
Laboratory.......................................	45,000
Patient Rooms.................................	250,000
Depreciation....................................	100,000
Maintenance and Utilities.................	50,000
Laundry..	20,000
	$630,000

Revenue / *NonRevenue*

Cost allocation data (expressed as percentages) have been determined as follows:

Department	Depreciation*	Maintenance and Utilities**	Laundry***
Operating Room...................................	7%	10.7%	21.2%
Radiology...	5	9.3	3.0
Laboratory...	10	6.7	—
Patient Rooms.....................................	50	60.0	75.8
Depreciation..	—	—	—
Maintenance and Utilities....................	25	—	—
Laundry..	3	13.3	—
	100%	100.0%	100.0%

*Buildings on the basis of square footage; equipment on the basis of dollar value.
**On the basis of square footage.
***On the basis of pounds used in each department.

Required: Allocate the June costs to final revenue departments.

(Based on an article in Management Accounting)

8. Departmental distribution of actual overhead—step method; variance analysis.

Yares Company has two producing departments, A and B, and four service departments, C, D, E, and F. Expenses are distributed from Department F first, D second, C third, and E fourth. The company assigns some service department expenses to other service departments; however, after a department's expenses have been allocated, no expenses are assigned back to it.

Department F distributes one-half of its expenses to A and the remainder, on the basis of the number of employees, to Departments D and E. Department D distributes its expenses on the basis of the investment in equipment. C's expenses are assigned to B, and E's expenses are distributed on the basis of floor space.

The following information for March is available:

Department	Actual Expenses	Square Feet	Employees	Investment in Equipment (000s omitted)
A.................................	$100,000	1,500	20	$12,500
B.................................	80,000	2,500	10	6,000
C.................................	120,000	3,000	10	10,000
D.................................	56,000	1,500	15	5,000
E.................................	15,000	1,000	10	4,000
F.................................	30,000	1,200	5	2,000
Total...........................	$401,000	10,700	70	$39,500

Required:

(1) Distribute service department expenses, based on the data given.
(2) Department A's predetermined overhead rate is based on machine hours. The total rate is $4, 25% of which is fixed. Fixed factory overhead budgeted is $40,000. The actual machine hours for March were 38,500. Compute the spending and idle capacity variances for Department A.

9. Departmental distribution of actual overhead—algebraic method; variance analysis. Sherlock Company has decided to distribute the costs of service departments by the algebraic method. The producing departments are P1 and P2, the service departments are S1 and S2, and the monthly data are:

	Actual Factory Overhead Costs Before Distribution	Services Provided By S1	S2
P1.....................	$94,000	40%	50%
P2.....................	85,000	50	30
S1.....................	20,000	—	20
S2.....................	17,600	10	—

Required:

(1) Compute the total factory overhead of producing department P1 after distribution of service department costs.
(2) P1's predetermined overhead rate is based on direct labor hours. The total rate is $3, 40% of which is fixed. Fixed factory overhead budgeted is $46,000. The actual direct labor hours for the month were 34,000. Compute the spending and idle capacity variances for department P1.

10. Departmental distribution of estimated overhead—algebraic method. The estimated departmental factory overhead for Producing Departments S and T and the estimated expenses of Service Departments E, F, and G (before any service department allocations) are:

Producing Department		Service Department	
S....................	$60,000	E.....................	$20,000
T	90,000	F.....................	20,000
		G	10,000

The interdependence of the departments is as follows:

Department	Services Provided E	F	G
Producing—S.....................	—	30%	40%
Producing—T.....................	50%	40	30
Service—E.........................	—	20	—
Service—F.........................	20	—	—
Service—G.........................	30	10	—
Marketing...........................	—	—	20
General Office....................	—	—	10
	100%	100%	100%

Required:

(1) Compute the final amount of estimated overhead of each service department after reciprocal transfer costs have been calculated algebraically.

(2) Compute the total factory overhead of each producing department and the amount of Department G cost assigned to the Marketing Department and to General Office.

PROBLEMS

13-1. Journal entries; revision of overhead rates. Baumert Furniture Company manufactures laboratory benches in three producing departments: Cutting, Assembling, and Finishing. All overhead costs are charged directly to producing departments without the use of auxiliary or service departments.

For the first six months of the calendar year, management had approved the following predetermined factory overhead rates:

Cutting.............................. $1.50 per machine hour
Assembling...................... 1.90 per direct labor hour
Finishing......................... 100% of direct labor cost

Factory overhead costs for the first six months were:

Cutting............................. $16,950
Assembling...................... 12,143
Finishing......................... 8,405

For the same period, the following data were also accumulated:

Cutting............................. 12,900 machine hours
Assembling...................... 8,100 direct labor hours
Finishing......................... $9,100 direct labor

As of June 30, the company revised its annual budget in the light of experience to that date and projections for the remainder of the year. Data on factory overhead from the new budget follow:

	Cutting	Assembling	Finishing
Total budgeted factory overhead....................	$26,975	$20,160	$14,805
Application basis (estimated).........................	20,750 machine hours	12,600 direct labor hours	$16,450 direct labor

Required: Prepare journal entries to record:

(1) Incurred and applied overhead for the first six months.

(2) Adjustment of the applied overhead based on the new rates, retroactive to January 1. Analysis of the job cost sheets shows the total overhead adjustment should be distributed 10% to work in process, 30% to finished goods, and 60% to cost of goods sold.

13-2. Departmental distribution of actual overhead—direct and step methods. Bash Inc. has two producing departments and three service departments. A summary of costs and other data for each department prior to allocation of service department costs for the year ended June 30, 19—, shows:

	Producing Departments		Service Departments		
	Fabrication	Assembly	General Factory Cost Pool	Mainte-nance	Cafeteria
Direct labor cost................................	$2,100,000	$4,100,000	$180,000	$164,200	$174,000
Direct materials cost...........................	3,130,000	950,000	—	67,700	91,000
Factory overhead cost.........................	1,650,000	1,850,000	70,000	56,100	62,000
Direct labor hours...............................	562,500	437,500	31,000	27,000	42,000
Number of employees.........................	280	200	12	8	20
Square footage occupied.....................	88,000	72,000	1,750	2,000	4,800

The costs of General Factory Cost Pool, Maintenance, and Cafeteria are allocated on the basis of direct labor hours, square footage occupied, and number of employees, respectively. There are no factory overhead variances.

Required:

(1) Compute the amount of Maintenance cost allocated to Fabrication, assuming that the company elects to distribute service department costs directly to the producing departments without inter-service-department cost allocation.

(2) Compute the amount of General Factory Cost Pool cost allocated to Assembly, assuming the same policy of allocating service departments to producing departments only.

(3) Assuming that the company elects to distribute service department costs to other service departments (starting with the service department with the greatest total cost) as well as to the producing departments and that once a service department's cost has been allocated, no subsequent service department cost is recirculated back to it, compute (a) the amount of Cafeteria cost allocated to Maintenance and (b) the amount of Maintenance cost allocated to Cafeteria.

(AICPA adapted)

13-3. Departmental distribution of estimated overhead—step method; rate calculation.

The president of Mellow Products Company has been critical of the product costing methods whereby factory overhead is charged to products by a plant-wide overhead rate. The chief accountant suggested a departmentalization of the factory for the purpose of calculating departmental factory overhead rates. The following estimated direct departmental overhead data on an annual basis were accumulated:

Overhead Items	Producing Departments			Service Departments		
	Dept. 10	Dept. 12	Dept. 14	Store-room	Repairs and Maintenance	General Factory Cost Pool
Supervision.....................................	$20,500	$16,000	$14,000	$ 7,200	$ 8,000	$24,000
Indirect labor....................................	5,400	6,000	8,000	6,133	7,200	18,000
Indirect supplies...............................	4,850	5,600	5,430	1,400	3,651	1,070
Labor fringe benefits.........................	6,872	9,349	10,145	640	760	2,100
Equipment depreciation......................	6,000	8,000	10,000	560	1,740	1,100
Property tax, depreciation of buildings, etc..						20,000
Total..	$43,622	$44,949	$47,575	$15,933	$21,351	$66,270

The annual light and power bill is estimated at $9,300 and is allocated on the basis of electricity usage.

The order and bases of distribution of service department expenses (using the step method) are as follows:

(a) General Factory Cost Pool—area occupied
(b) Storeroom—estimated requisitions
(c) Repairs and Maintenance—estimated repairs and maintenance hours

The following departmental information is provided:

	Dept. 10	Dept. 12	Dept. 14	Store-room	Repairs and Maintenance	General Factory Cost Pool
Percentage of usage of electricity..........	20%	25%	30%	3%	12%	10%
Area occupied (sq. ft.)............................	21,000	25,200	29,400	3,360	5,040	—
Estimated number of requisitions...........	124,200	81,000	40,500	—	24,300	—
Estimated number of repairs and maintenance hours..............................	4,800	4,200	6,000	—	—	—
Estimated direct labor hours..................	80,000	90,000	80,000	—	—	—

Required: Prepare a factory overhead distribution sheet, with calculation of overhead rates for the producing departments based on direct labor hours.

13-4. Departmental distribution of actual overhead—algebraic method; variance analysis.
The controller of Mitchell Corporation instructs the cost supervisor to use an algebraic procedure for allocating service department costs to producing departments. The corporation's three producing departments are served by three service departments, each of which consumes part of the services of the other two. After primary but before reciprocal distribution, the account balances of the service departments and the interdependence of the departments were tabulated as follows:

Department	Departmental Overhead Before Distribution of Service Departments	Services Provided		
		Powerhouse	Personnel	General Factory
Mixing..	$200,000	25%	35%	25%
Refining......................................	90,000	25	30	20
Finishing....................................	105,000	20	20	20
Powerhouse...............................	16,000	—	10	20
Personnel..................................	29,500	10	—	15
General Factory........................	42,000	20	5	—
	$482,500	100%	100%	100%

Required:

(1) Compute the final amount of overhead of each service department after reciprocal transfer costs have been calculated algebraically.
(2) Compute the total factory overhead of each producing department.
(3) The Mixing Department's predetermined overhead rate is based on machine hours. The total rate is $6, 40% of which is fixed. Fixed factory overhead budgeted is $96,000. The actual machine hours for the period were 37,000. Compute the spending and idle capacity variances for the Mixing Department.

13-5. Departmental distribution of estimated overhead—direct vs. algebraic method; rate calculation.
Barrylou Corporation is developing departmental overhead rates based upon direct labor hours for its two production departments—Molding and

Assembly. The Molding Department employs 20 people, and the Assembly Department employs 80 people. Each person in these two departments works 2,000 hours per year. The production-related overhead costs for the Molding Department are budgeted at $200,000, and the Assembly Department costs are budgeted at $320,000. Two service departments—Repair and Power—support the two production departments and have budgeted costs of $48,000 and $250,000, respectively. The production departments' overhead rates cannot be determined until the service departments' costs are properly allocated. The following schedule reflects the use of the Repair Department's and Power Department's output by the various departments.

| | Services Provided | |
Department	Repair Hours	KWH
Molding.........................	1,000	840 000
Assembly......................	8,000	120 000
Repair.........................	—	240 000
Power.........................	1,000	—
	10,000	1 200 000

Required:

(1) Calculate the overhead rates per direct labor hour for the two producing departments, allocating service department costs to producing departments only. (Round rates to the nearest cent.)
(2) Calculate the overhead rates per direct labor hour for the two producing departments, using the algebraic method to distribute service department costs. (Round rates to the nearest cent.)
(3) Explain the difference between the methods and indicate arguments to support the algebraic method.   *(ICMA adapted)*

13-6. Departmental distribution of actual overhead—direct, step, and algebraic methods. Petit Company operates with two producing departments, P1 and P2, and two service departments, S1 and S2. Actual factory overhead before distribution of service department costs, together with the usage of services from the service departments, follows:

Department	Actual Factory Overhead Before Distribution of Service Department Costs	Services Provided S1	S2
P1	$20,000	40%	20%
P2	23,800	50	40
S1	7,200	—	40
S2	9,000	10	—
	$60,000	100%	100%

Required:

(1) Determine the total factory overhead (including service department costs) for each producing department, allocating service department costs to producing departments only.
(2) Determine the total factory overhead (including service department costs) for each producing department, allocating service department costs stepwise, beginning with Department S2. After a department's expenses have been allocated, no expenses are assigned back to it.   *(Continued)*

(3) Determine the total factory overhead (including service department costs) for each producing department, using the algebraic method.

13-7. Cost center rates and variance analysis. The Cost Department of Montpelier Company applies factory overhead to jobs and products on the basis of predetermined cost center overhead rates. In each of the two producing departments, two cost centers have been set up. For the coming year, the following estimates and other data have been made available:

	Estimated Annual Factory Overhead			Estimated Annual Hours
Department 10	Fixed	Variable	Total	
Cost Center 10-1.....................	$14,040	$23,400	$37,440	15,600
Cost Center 10-2.....................	26,910	43,290	70,200	23,400
Department 10				
Cost Center 20-1.....................	$ 8,320	$21,580	$29,900	26,000
Cost Center 20-2.....................	6,240	19,760	26,000	20,800

Required:

(1) Compute the annual normal cost center overhead rates, based on the estimated machine hours in Department 10 and the estimated direct labor hours in Department 20.

(2) Apply factory overhead to the four cost centers on the basis of these actual machine or labor hours used or worked during February:

Cost Centers	10-1	10-2	20-1	20-2
Machine hours......................	1,220	2,000		
Labor hours..........................			2,250	1,650

(3) Compute the spending and the idle capacity variances for the two producing departments. Actual factory overhead in Department 10 amounted to $9,430 and in Department 20 to $4,005.

(4) Analyze the total idle capacity variance of Department 10, determining the idle capacity variances of the two cost centers. Use 1/12 of the total annual estimated hours as normal monthly hours.

13-8. Transfer entries and variance analysis. The distribution of a company's actual factory overhead for the past year is given as follows. Budgeted factory overhead for the four producing departments (including apportioned service department expenses) is also given for two levels of activity.

Actual Factory Overhead

	A	B	C	D	X	Y	Z	Total
Actual expenses....................	$11,000	$16,000	$4,000	$8,000	$3,000	$5,000	$6,000	$53,000
Z's expenses........................	1,500	750	1,250	500	1,000	1,000	(6,000)	
Y's expenses........................	1,800	1,200	1,800	600	600	(6,000)		
X's expenses........................	2,000	1,000	1,200	400	(4,600)			
Total.....................................	$16,300	$18,950	$8,250	$9,500				$53,000

	Budgeted Factory Overhead 20,000 Hours (Normal)	16,000 Hours
Department A.....................	$17,800	$15,000
Department B.....................	20,200	17,800
Department C...................	10,600	9,400
Department D...................	10,600	9,400
Total..............................	$59,200	$51,600

The company uses a predetermined rate for each producing department, based on labor hours at the normal capacity level. Actual hours worked last year were 17,000 for Department A and 18,000 for B.

Required:

(1) Prepare entries to record:
  (a) The transfer of the actual factory overhead to producing departments, assuming that the actual factory overhead was accumulated in a single factory overhead control account.
  (b) The applied factory overhead for Department A and for B.
(2) Compute the spending and idle capacity variances for Department A and for B.

CASES

A. Types of factory overhead rates. Vukovich Inc. engages the services of a CPA firm for the installation of a job order cost system. Preliminary investigation of manufacturing operations discloses these facts:

(a) The company makes a line of light fixtures and lamps. The materials cost of any particular item ranges from 15% to 60% of total factory cost, depending on the kind of metal and fabric used.
(b) The business is subject to wide cyclical fluctuations, since the sales volume follows new housing construction.
(c) About 60% of the manufacturing is normally finished during the first quarter of the year.
(d) For the whole plant, the direct labor wage rates range from $6.50 to $12 an hour. However, within each of the eight individual departments, the spread between the high and low wage rate is less than 5%.
(e) Each product requires the use of all eight of the manufacturing departments, but not proportionately.

(f) Within the individual manufacturing departments, factory overhead ranges from 30% to 80% of conversion cost.

Required: Prepare a letter to the president of Vukovich Inc., explaining whether its cost system should use the following procedures, and including the reasons supporting each of these recommendations:

(1) A predetermined overhead rate or an actual overhead rate—departmental or plant-wide.
(2) A method of factory overhead distribution based on direct labor hours, direct labor cost, or prime cost.

(AICPA adapted)

B. Assigning costs to activity centers in a data processing department. Fitzgerald Associates recently reorganized its computer and data processing activities. In the past, small computer units were located in accounting departments at the firm's plants and subsidiaries. These units have been replaced with a single Electronic Data Processing Department at corporate headquarters. The new department has been in operation for two years, regularly producing reliable and timely data for the past twelve months.

Because the department has focused its activities on converting applications to the new system and producing reports for the plant and subsidiary managements, little attention has been devoted to data processing costs. Now that the department's activities are operating relatively smoothly, company management has requested that the department manager recommend a cost accumulation system to facilitate cost control and the development of suitable service charging rates.

For the past two years, the data processing costs have been recorded in one account. The costs have then been allocated to user departments on the basis of computer time used. Following are the costs and charging rate for the current year:

(a) Salaries and benefits	$ 622,600
(b) Supplies	40,000
(c) Equipment maintenance contract	15,000
(d) Insurance	25,000
(e) Heat and air conditioning	36,000
(f) Electricity	50,000
(g) Equipment and furniture depreciation	285,400
(h) Building improvement depreciation	10,000
(i) Building occupancy and security	39,300
(j) Corporate administrative charge	52,700
Total cost	$1,176,000
Computer hours for user processing*	2,750
Hourly rate ($1,176,000 ÷ 2,750)	$428

*Use of available computer hours:	
Testing and debugging programs	250
Setup of jobs	500
Processing jobs	2,750
Downtime for maintenance	750
Idle time	742
Total	4,992

The department manager recommends that the data processing costs be accumulated by five activity centers within the department: Systems Analysis, Programming, Data Preparation, Computer Operations (processing), and Administration. The Administration activity cost should be allocated to the other four activity centers before a separate rate for charging users is developed for each of the first four activities.

The manager noted that the subsidiary accounts within the department contained the following charges:

(a) Salaries and benefits—the salary and benefit costs of all employees in the department.

(b) Supplies—diskette cost, paper cost for printers, and a small amount for miscellaneous other costs.

(c) Equipment maintenance contracts— charges for maintenance contracts covering all equipment.

(d) Insurance—cost of insurance covering the equipment and the furniture.

(e) Heat and air conditioning—a charge from the corporate Heating and Air Conditioning Department estimated to be the differential costs which meet the special needs of the Electronic Data Processing Department.

(f) Electricity—the charge for electricity, based upon a separate meter within the department.

(g) Equipment and furniture depreciation— the depreciation charges for all owned equipment and furniture within the department.

(h) Building improvement depreciation— the depreciation charges for the building changes which were required to provide proper environmental control and electrical service for the computer equipment.

(i) Building occupancy and security—the department's share of the depreciation, maintenance, heat, and security costs of the building; these costs are allocated to the department on the basis of square feet occupied.

(j) Corporate administrative charge—the department's share of the corporate administrative cost which is allocated to the department on the basis of number of employees in the department.

Required:

(1) State whether each of the ten cost items (lettered a through j) should be allocated to the five activity centers. For each cost item which should be distributed, specify the basis upon which the distribution

should be made. Justify your answer in each case, including an indication as to whether the cost would be included in a rate designed to include only variable costs as opposed to a full cost rate.

(2) Calculate the total number of hours that should be employed to determine the charging rate for Computer Operations, using the analysis of computer utilization shown as a footnote to the department cost schedule, and assuming that the Computer Operations activity cost will be charged to the user departments on the basis of computer hours. Explain.

(ICMA adapted)

C. Overhead analysis and causes for variances. Beachmont Company uses predetermined departmental overhead rates. The rate for the Fabricating Department is $4 per direct labor hour. Direct labor employees are paid $10.50 per hour. A total of 15,000 direct labor hours were worked in the department during the year. Total overhead charged to the department for supervisors' salaries, indirect labor, labor fringe benefit costs, indirect materials, and service department costs was $65,000.

Required:

(1) Determine the over- or underapplied factory overhead.

(2) Determine the effect on the amount of over- or underapplied factory overhead in each of the following situations. Discuss each item separately as though the other factors had not occurred.

(a) Direct laborers worked one hundred overtime hours for which time-and-a-half was paid. Overtime premium, the amount in excess of the regular rate, is charged as overhead to the department in which the overtime is worked.

(b) A $.35 per hour wage increase was granted November 1. Direct labor hours worked in November and December totaled 2,500.

(c) The company cafeteria incurred a $1,500 loss, which was distributed to producing departments on the basis of number of employees. Nine of the 120 employees work in the Fabricating Department. No loss was anticipated when predetermined overhead rates were computed.

CHAPTER 14

Factory Overhead: Responsibility Accounting and Reporting

Factory overhead creates two distinct problems:

1. Allocation to products for the purpose of inventory costing and profit determination, and
2. Control of factory overhead with the aid of responsibility accounting.

The well-designed information system should yield product costs for inventory costing and profit determination. It should also provide a control mechanism encompassing *responsibility accounting* and make meaningful cost data available for setting policies and making decisions. The predetermined or budgeted revenue and expense items form the foundation for comparison with actual results, leading to variance analysis and the management by exception principle.

The establishment of such a system allows and maintains the most efficient and profitable balance between manufacturing and marketing. On the one hand, management needs to decide the kinds and costs of its products; on the other hand, it must decide the prices of its products. The greatest profit results from the proper balance of these considerations. For these reasons, product costs must be fairly accurate, include all relevant costs, and recognize cost differentials between products.

▼ RESPONSIBILITY ACCOUNTING AND CONTROL OF FACTORY OVERHEAD

Webster's dictionary defines being *responsible* as "liable to be called upon to answer." Kohler's *A Dictionary for Accountants* defines *responsibility* as "the obligation prudently to exercise assigned or imputed authority attaching to the assigned or imputed role of an individual or group participating in organizational activities or decisions." The N.A.(C.)A. Research Series, No. 22, says: "A responsibility may be defined as an organizational unit having a single head accountable for activities of the unit."

Responsibility Accounting—Basic Concepts

The following concepts are prerequisites to the initiation and maintenance of a responsibility accounting system:

1. Responsibility accounting is based on a classification of managerial responsibilities (departments) at every level in the organization for the purpose of establishing a budget for each. The individual in charge of each responsibility classification should be responsible and accountable for the expenses of his or her activity. This concept introduces the need for the classification of costs into controllable and not controllable by a department head. Generally, costs charged directly to a department, with the exception of fixed costs, are controllable by the department's manager.

2. The starting point for a responsibility accounting information system rests with the organization chart in which the spheres of jurisdiction have been determined. Authority leads to the responsibility for certain costs and expenses which, with the knowledge and cooperation of the supervisor, department head, or manager, are presented in the budget.

3. Each individual's budget should clearly identify the costs controllable by that person. The chart of accounts should be adapted to permit recording of controllable or accountable expenses within the jurisdictional framework.

Factors Influencing Responsible Cost Control

The fundamental tenet of responsibility accounting limits the individual's control effort to controllable costs. Yet, studies have shown that in departmental situations, several factors may influence the extent of controllability and the effectiveness of the departmental control efforts. These factors are summarized in the following performance model.[1]

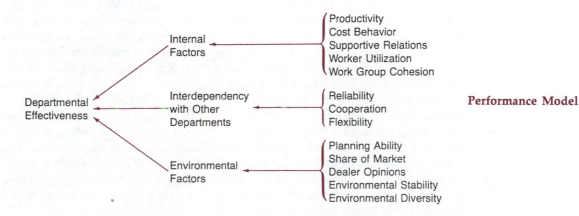

Internal Factors
- Productivity
- Cost Behavior
- Supportive Relations
- Worker Utilization
- Work Group Cohesion

Departmental Effectiveness

Interdependency with Other Departments
- Reliability
- Cooperation
- Flexibility

Environmental Factors
- Planning Ability
- Share of Market
- Dealer Opinions
- Environmental Stability
- Environmental Diversity

Performance Model

[1]David C. Hayes, "The Contingency Theory of Managerial Accounting," *The Accounting Review*, Vol. LII, No. 1, pp. 22-39.

Human Behavior in Responsibility Accounting

A program to develop management accounting controls must be considered a prime responsibility of executive management, with the accounting department providing technical assistance. To assure the follow-through of the program and its ultimate success, management must provide a complete clarification of the objectives and responsibilities of all levels of the organization. This prerequisite requires an understanding by middle and operating management of executive management's goals. The acceptance of responsibility for certain costs and expenses does not always follow the issuance of directives and orders. Supervisory personnel, particularly at the foreman level, need guidance and training to achieve the control and/or profit results expected from them. Control responsibility does not happen naturally, but requires a certain fundamental attitude or frame of mind for the task.

One of the most beneficial influences is executive management's own exemplary adherence to the cost-and-profit responsibility it created. Of equal importance is the motivation for corrective action by the responsible individual. The issuance of reports based on the organization's responsibility concept is not sufficient. The successful achievement of effective management control depends upon the lines of communication between the accounting department, the responsible supervisors, and their superiors. Responsibility accounting requires teamwork in the truest sense of the word.

Responsibility for Overhead Costs

As the preceding factory overhead chapters indicate, many overhead items are directly chargeable to a given department and become the direct responsibility of the departmental supervisor. Other overhead items must be allocated or distributed in order to calculate a departmental factory overhead rate that will charge all costs to a job, a product, or the work performed. This allocation procedure, however, is not necessary or useful for cost control, i.e., for responsibility accounting. For responsibility accounting purposes, any allocated charges should be limited to those expenses for which control and responsibility have been assumed by the originating department. However, the assignment of responsibility depends a great deal upon the methods of cost accumulation and allocation used by a firm.

In some firms, the cost system provides for a normal volume distribution of service hours, use hours, and/or maintenance hours to producing or other service departments. The distribution can be looked upon as a purchase by the recipient department and a sale by the providing service department. The distribution to the recipient department is based on what is termed a *billing rate,* a *sold-hour rate,* a *charging rate,* or a *transfer rate.* The method is based on the idea that these departments purchase the services in the same manner as direct materials and direct labor.

The determination of the billing rate follows the procedures discussed in the previous factory overhead chapters.

1. Estimate or budget the costs of any service department according to their nature (supervision, supplies, electricity, etc.)
2. Classify costs as fixed or variable. This classification often leads to the realization that many costs of service departments are fixed over fairly wide ranges of service volume.
3. Determine a rate by dividing total estimated departmental cost by the number of hours the service is expected to be needed.
4. Compare actual service department costs with estimated or budgeted costs.

The establishment of the use hours is as important for billing rates as it is for factory overhead rates. The hours can be based either on past experience in a representative period or on future activity or volume as expressed in the budget. A refinement of the rate is the apportionment of fixed costs to cost centers on the basis of service capacity, i.e., readiness or ability to provide services, as defined for each benefiting department. The variable cost is then assigned on the basis of actual usage.[2]

The comparison of actual and budgeted costs is made (1) in the service department to which the expenses are originally charged, by comparing actual costs with charged-out or sold-out amounts; and (2) in the benefiting (recipient) departments in which the charges for service departments' services are linked with the budget allowances. This step is the control phase of the service department's charging-out procedure. The supervisor of the service department is responsible for the actual cost versus the cost for services charged out to benefiting departments. The benefiting department supervisor is responsible for the number of service department hours purchased, and the resulting cost charged to his or her department. Variances for service and producing departments are calculable.

Billing Rates for Electronic Data Processing Services. Electronic data processing (EDP) services offer an excellent illustration of the need for careful attention to the use of appropriate billing rates. EDP services usually start as a support group, with costs classified as general overhead. These costs may be allocated to broad functional classifications, such as manufacturing (factory overhead), marketing, and administrative expenses. As data processing matures and becomes an integral part of the organization's operations, more precise cost accounting mechanisms are considered. The EDP center might apportion costs to users on the basis of a percentage of general utilization; e.g., assigning 10 percent of the costs to one department, 15 percent to another, and so forth. This approach has limitations, because it fails to contribute to efficient use of the EDP facility and does not aid the recipient in making selective judgments about the application requested. Users need to understand the cost and value of the services which they require.

The electronic data processing department should develop a price (charge) for the services which users can include in their departmental budgets. The price of a given system is usually a fixed amount plus a variable amount per

---

[2]An example of more sophisticated allocation procedures is found in Daniel L. Jensen's "A Class of Mutually Satisfactory Allocations," *The Accounting Review*, Vol. LII, No. 4, pp. 842-856.

transaction, the volume of which would affect the total processing time. The difference between actual price and actual cost provides one measure of the data processing department's efficiency.[3]

The general, one-rate allocation to functional classifications may be superseded by the partitioning of the computer into cost centers, with major expenses classified as direct expenses to a cost center. To illustrate, a budget for a data processing department which has been partitioned into eight cost centers is shown on page 397.[4]

The "percent utilization expected" is important to a data processing department. Experience indicates that available hours are often utilized at only a 70 to 80 percent rate. The difference between utilized and available hours represents nonproductive activity which, for a systems analyst or a programmer, consists of vacation, holiday, illness, training, staff meetings, administrative tasks, professional societies, initial examination of requests, and other miscellaneous tasks. Time recording procedures established in all cost centers would allow the data processing administration to:

1. Keep a close watch over the productive utilization percentage and take action if and when it gets out of line.
2. Calculate the cost of each project or system, based on actual time incurred multiplied by the budgeted hourly rates.
3. Compare the actual productive hours to budgeted productive hours, and be aware of variances on a weekly or monthly basis.
4. Note the variance between total actual monthly data processing cost and the summation of project and system costs.
5. For subsequent years, estimate more accurately the expected productive hours by cost centers.

The use of a "budgeted hourly rate" provides the following benefits:

1. Aids in controlling or reducing data processing costs.
2. Permits accurate and realistic costing of all work performed by project, system, user department, and/or line of business served.
3. Provides realistic rates to be used in estimating the cost of requested or proposed projects.
4. Permits a comparison of actual costs of processing a system to those costs which were estimated prior to implementation.
5. Aids in the evaluation of operating efficiency of a data processing installation.
6. Provides one measure of profitability for each data processing cost center and for the entire department in those cases where services are charged to a user or customer.

Maintenance Costs. Maintenance expense, like any other factory cost, is charged ultimately to producing departments in order to be included in the

---

[3]Adapted from "The Fair Measure," *Data Processor*, Vol. 18, No. 2, pp. 10-13.
[4]Adapted from "Costing in the Data Processing Department" by John E. Finney, *Management Accounting*, Vol. LVI, No. 4, pp. 29-35. Copyright October, 1974, by the National Association of Accountants. All rights reserved. Reprinted by permission.

DATA PROCESSING BUDGET BY COST CENTER

Item	Annual Budget	Systems	Programming	Computer Background	Computer Foreground 1	Computer Foreground 2	Off-Line Devices	Data Entry	Data Control
Data processing administration	$ 48,000	$ 7,400	$ 5,200	$ 4,700	$ 8,900	$ 5,600	$ 500	$ 13,000	$ 2,700
Group managers and secretaries	82,000	20,000	15,000	5,000	10,000	10,000	2,000	10,000	10,000
Other salaries and fringe benefits	528,300	114,000	84,000	10,000	23,000	15,000	4,000	230,000	48,300
Training costs	11,000	3,500	3,500	300	900	500	200	1,600	500
Supplies	34,600	2,300	1,700	1,000	8,000	12,600	2,000	6,000	1,000
Travel expenses	7,700	4,000	2,000	500	700	500			
Consulting fees	9,000	6,000	3,000						
Rent, insurance, and utilities	78,000	13,500	13,500	8,000	11,000	9,000	2,000	17,000	4,000
Equipment rental and depreciation	356,000			80,000	150,000	77,000	1,000	47,000	1,000
Equipment maintenance	30,700			8,000	12,000	10,000	500		200
Depreciation on furniture and fixtures	6,100	1,700	1,700	200	400	400	300	400	1,000
Employment agency fees	7,000	4,000	3,000						
Dues and subscriptions	1,600	1,000	600						
Total budgeted cost	$1,200,000	$177,400	$133,200	$117,700	$224,900	$140,600	$ 12,500	$325,000	$ 68,700
Available or purchased hours		14,560	14,560	7,488	7,488	7,488	1,040	60,320	12,480
Percent utilization expected		70	80	35	60	20	85	86	80
Expected productive hours		10,192	11,648	2,621	4,493	1,498	884	51,875	9,984
Budgeted hourly rate		$ 17.41	$ 11.44	$ 44.91	$ 50.06	$ 93.86	$ 14.14	$ 6.27	$ 6.88

calculation of overhead rates. The basic problem is assigning cost responsibility for this expense. Maintenance supervisors often believe that their department really incurs no cost at all, since any cost incurrence is for the benefit and at the request of other departments. Factory supervisors, on the other hand, may argue that they have no influence on either personnel or machinery costs of the maintenance department. The control is in reality twofold: the factory supervisors control the amount of maintenance work, while maintenance engineers or supervisors control the quantity of people and materials required to serve the various departments. Since maintenance work is done at the request of production supervisors, the problem arises as to whether control should be exercised at the source level or the recipient level.

At the source level, maintenance labor is organized and supervised. Control at this point requires predetermination of labor-hour requirements in each of the producing and service departments for each maintenance function. At the recipient level, the cost system establishes budget allowances for this indirect cost. Budget allowances based on planned levels of production permit the determination of the labor-hour budgets and advance scheduling of the work force of each shop service or maintenance unit. Preplanning is the heart of the control, providing an opportunity for corrective action before the hours are worked. Maintenance department supervisors are apprised of the maintenance allowance or budgeted service for individual recipient cost centers, but the distribution or scheduling of the work is left largely to their discretion.[5]

One major problem, however, is how much maintenance or repair work is needed in a department. Up to a point, the costs of preventive maintenance services generally will be more than offset by reductions in cost due to fewer equipment failures. Beyond this point, costs of providing additional preventive maintenance services will outweigh the benefits gained and total cost will increase. A basic problem of maintenance, therefore, is the determination of the balance—in terms of both effectiveness and cost—between prevention of equipment failure and correction of equipment failure.[6]

The solution may be determined by the executive management group. When a factory is laid out and the machinery installed, a maintenance program should be planned. The size of the maintenance department, the type or class of workers (carpenters, plumbers, electricians, pipefitters, masons, millwrights, machinists, etc.), and the kind of equipment and tools are greatly influenced by early decisions. On the other hand, experience indicates that such maintenance objectives are lacking in many companies due to management's own lack of interest as well as alleged difficulties in planning, measuring, and controlling the maintenance function. Although many organizations engage the services of outside firms for part or all of their

---

[5]For additional discussion and illustration of responsibility accounting for maintenance, see James H. Bullock, *Maintenance Planning and Control* (New York: National Association of Accountants, 1979), pp. 29-33.

[6]*Ibid.*, p. 14.

maintenance, the need for careful planning and control of maintenance cost is not negated.

When management and the supervisors of the producing, service, and maintenance engineering departments agree on a preventive maintenance program, their objective is to keep equipment in such condition that breakdowns and the need for emergency repairs are within control. Preventive maintenance facilitates the scheduling of maintenance work and helps to obtain better utilization of the maintenance work force and the productive equipment.

A preventive maintenance program can work automatically so that inspection, minor repairs, adjustments, and lubrication are completed as a matter of course. The method further provides for a check on the effectiveness of the maintenance work by the supervisor of the serviced or buying unit. The maintenance supervisor, in turn, is responsible for the inspection and the upkeep of the facilities.

Responsibility for Other Costs

The discussion has intentionally focused on factory overhead items, since their assignment and control occupies the attention of many executives, department heads, and supervisors. However, other cost elements as well as functions in administration and marketing also require supervision and control by responsible managers.

Basically, the best approach to assigning responsibility for any cost element is to identify those individuals who are in the most favored position to keep the costs under control. The assignment of responsibility for overhead expenses to supervisors and department heads provides a certain degree of control. Admittedly, however, certain expenses (e.g., maintenance expenses) are often troublesome. In the direct materials and direct labor areas, many individuals may be assigned the responsibility for costs incurred, and this responsibility often becomes obscure and nearly impossible to identify. Of course, it seems advisable to insist upon the assignment on the basis of relative control rather than absolute control.

In the direct materials area, the variances or deviations from a predetermined norm or standard will result in (1) materials price variances, (2) materials quantity, or mix and yield variances, and/or (3) excessive defective work, rejects, or scrap costs. In the direct labor area, the variances or deviations from a predetermined norm or standard will result in (1) pay rate variations, (2) efficiency variations, (3) and/or overtime costs.

Other factors also may be subject to change for which a manager may be held responsible. In later chapters, the deviations from budgeted gross or net profit figures require explanation. The changes in sales prices, sales volume, and sales mix are the responsibility of the marketing department. Yet the gross profit and net profit figures contain elements of cost as well, so that a further investigation is warranted.

Cost Control Characteristics

An effective cost control system has two major characteristics:

1. A sound technical design with goals set at a challenging but attainable performance level and with a reporting system that distinguishes controllable costs within each managerial responsibility from costs controllable elsewhere in the organization.
2. A managerial style sensitive to the behavior of people in a particular organizational setting. This requires a proper blend of:
   (a) Involvement by managers in setting goals for their own activities.
   (b) Leadership provided by executive management.
   (c) Open communication channels through which individual managers feel their views receive serious consideration.
   (d) Review procedures which disclose and discourage suboptimization and individual gains at the expense of the whole organization.

Cost control techniques are effective only with sufficient managerial appreciation of the behavioral aspects of control systems.[7]

Variance Analysis for Responsibility Accounting

Today with the emphasis on responsible control of financial results via the return-on-capital-employed concept, assets, liabilities, net worth, revenue, and costs form a vast area in which the entire management spectrum, from the top executive to the supervisor, holds some share of responsibility. Like blocks within a pyramid (page 407), the responsibility travels from the lowest to the highest level of supervision. All supervisors are responsible for costs incurred by their subordinates.

To exercise this control, the cost and/or budget department should issue monthly reports that compare actual results with predetermined amounts or budget allowances. An analysis prepared at the end of the annual fiscal period, as shown in Chapter 13, is not very helpful for immediate control actions. Reports on a monthly or more frequent basis are advisable to allow short-range comparisons of those costs for which operating management is responsible.

In general, variable expenses are controllable at the departmental level, while fixed expenses are not. In some circumstances, however, certain variable expenses may be controlled at a higher level in the organization; e.g., employee fringe benefits may be determined by negotiations between executive management and the labor union or by government regulations. Such costs should be analyzed and separately identified to relieve a department manager of this responsibility. Conversely, a department manager may have some control over certain fixed costs—those that involve a long-term

---

[7]Walter B. McFarland, *Manpower Cost and Performance Measurement* (New York: National Association of Accountants, 1977), p. 101.

commitment (sometimes called *committed fixed expenses*), such as equipment depreciation or lease expense, and those that can be readily changed in the short run (sometimes called *programmed fixed expenses*), such as the number of supervisors in the department. These costs should be individually identified as controllable by the manager of the department. Whether fixed or variable, some costs may be indirect or common with respect to two or more departments and thus may require arbitrary allocation. Accordingly, their controllability by a single department manager is restricted.

Attention must be called to the fact that in the long run, all costs are controllable. Variable costs are generally controllable over short time periods. Some fixed costs, such as supervisory labor or equipment rental, can also be altered on short notice. Other fixed costs, such as depreciation of plant assets or a long-term lease agreement, involve a fixed commitment over a long period of time. Finally, some costs possess a dual short- and long-run controllability characteristic. For example, a five-year contract as to the price of a raw material, representing a long-term commitment, is not immediately controllable and the contract may be negotiable only at a higher management level. However, waste and spoilage of the same material is immediately controllable by the department. Generally, department managers should be well enough informed to explain cost variances, even though the control or certain aspects of the control do not fall within their scope of authority and responsibility.

To illustrate monthly variance analysis on a departmental basis, the DeWitt Products data used in Chapter 13 are modified to accommodate a monthly comparison, and for conciseness of the illustration only one service department, Utilities, is used. The four departmental factory overhead rates computed in Chapter 13 are maintained as follows:

Cutting Department..........................	$2.00 per direct labor hour
Planing Department..........................	$3.20 per machine hour
Assembly Department.......................	60% of direct labor cost
Upholstery Department......................	$1.80 per direct labor hour

At the end of January, the following actual data for DeWitt Products are assembled:

Department	Actual Hours (Labor or Machine) or Labor Cost	Actual Consumption for the Month kwh	hph	Actual Departmental Overhead Before Billing Out Utilities
Cutting...........................	3,046 direct labor hours	1 180	19,000	$3,575
Planing...........................	1,620 machine hours	700	10,800	3,125
Assembly.......................	$11,400 direct labor cost	1 700	7,000	2,900
Upholstery......................	4,100 direct labor hours	1 980	8,000	3,570
Utilities...........................				5,860
		5 560	44,800	

Based on the actual production and cost data, the cost department would apply the following amounts of factory overhead to products passing through the four departments:

Cutting Department, 3,046 direct labor hours × $2.00............................	$6,092
Planing Department, 1,620 machine hours × $3.20...............................	5,184
Assembly Department, $11,400 direct labor cost × 60%.......................	6,840
Upholstery Department, 4,100 direct labor hours × $1.80.....................	7,380

To determine and analyze the amount of over- or underapplied factory overhead, service department costs must be added to the actual direct and indirect departmental overhead to put actual and applied figures on a comparable basis. These procedures were presented in Chapter 13.

Spending Variance. In responsibility accounting, the emphasis rests upon the comparison of actual departmental expenses with budgeted or estimated costs before service department costs are allocated, because it is at these departmental points of origin that costs are best controlled. Furthermore, many accountants believe that only the variable portion of these point-of-origin costs should be compared and not the total overhead, since these variable costs tend to be the most readily controllable at the department level. Naturally, the procedures for different organizations vary.

In this example, both procedures are illustrated for the four producing departments and one service department. The first computation shows total actual departmental overhead, both fixed and variable, compared with budgeted or predetermined departmental overhead. The second computation shows only variable actual departmental overhead compared with its budgeted or predetermined amount. In both situations, the analysis is made for producing and service departments prior to any service department cost allocation.

PROCEDURE 1

	Departments				
	Cutting	Planing	Assembly	Upholstery	Utilities
Actual departmental overhead.......	$3,575	$3,125	$2,900	$3,570	$5,860
Budget allowances:					
Variable overhead:					
3,046 hours × $.5762*	$1,755				
1,620 hours × $1.0217*		$1,655			
$11,400 × 15.5%*			$1,767		
4,100 hours × $.4217*				$1,729	
5 560 kwh × $.1544*					$ 858
44,800 hph × $.0494*					2,213
1,750 sq. ft.** × $.7057*					1,235
Fixed overhead (1/12 annual fixed cost; e.g.,					
$17,100*** ÷ 12 = $1,425)...	1,425	1,492	1,342	1,525	1,333
Budget allowances..............	$3,180	$3,147	$3,109	$3,254	$5,639
Spending variances.............	$ 395	$ (22)	$ (209)	316	$ 221
	unfav.	fav.	fav.	unfav.	unfav.

*Variable cost rate, as calculated on the next page.
**1,750 sq. ft. is 1/12 of 21,000 sq. ft. (to convert to a one-month period), as shown on page 364.
***Estimated fixed cost for the Cutting Department, page 363.

PROCEDURE 2

	Departments				
	Cutting	Planing	Assembly	Upholstery	Utilities
Actual variable departmental overhead (e.g., $3,575– $1,425 fixed cost)......................	$2,150	$1,633	$1,558	$2,045	$4,527
Budgeted variable overhead..........	1,755	1,655	1,767	1,729	4,306
Spending variances....................	$ 395	$ (22)	$ (209)	$ 316	$ 221
	unfav.	fav.	fav.	unfav.	unfav.

The variable cost rates for the producing departments are calculated by dividing the variable departmental overhead, before service department distribution, by the predetermined or estimated direct labor hours, direct labor cost, or machine hours, using data from pages 363 and 366.

	Estimated Variable Departmental Overhead	÷	Direct Labor Hours	Estimated Direct Labor Cost	Machine Hours	=	Variable Departmental Cost Rates
Cutting............................	$23,400		40,608				$ .5762
Planing...........................	$18,800				18,400		$1.0217
Assembly........................	$18,900			$122,000			15.5%
Upholstery......................	$20,300		48,140				$ .4217

In the producing departments, actual hours or actual costs for the month are multiplied by the variable cost rate to arrive at the budgeted or estimated variable cost.

The variable rates for Utilities (using data from pages 363 and 366) are calculated as follows:

Total departmental expense......................	$65,400
Less fixed expense.................................	16,000
Total variable expense.............................	$49,400

$49,400 × 20% = $9,880 ÷ 64 000 kwh = $.1544 variable rate per kwh
$49,400 × 50% = $24,700 ÷ 500,000 hph = $.0494 variable rate per hph
$49,400 × 30% = $14,820 ÷ 21,000 sq. ft. = $.7057 variable rate per sq. ft.

The estimated allowance for Utilities is based on the actual monthly consumption figures multiplied by the corresponding variable rates.

Idle Capacity Variance. Responsibility accounting stresses the control of variable expenses and the calculation of the departmental spending variance. It is possible, however, to continue the analysis and calculate an idle capacity variance based entirely on departmental costs without any allocation of service department costs or charges. To illustrate, the data from page 363 are used in determining the idle capacity variance for the Cutting Department, as shown in the following table.

(1)	(2)	(3)	(4) Total Variance	(5) Spending Variance	(6) Idle Capacity Variance
Actual Overhead	Budget Allowance	Applied Overhead	(1) − (3)	(1) − (2)	(2) − (3)
$3,575	$3,180	$3,038*	$537 unfav.	$395 unfav.	$142** unfav.

*3,046 actual hours × $.9973 = $3,038
**3,384 (40,608 hours ÷ 12 months) predetermined hours − 3,046 actual hours = 338 idle hours × $.4211 = $142

The Cutting Department's total estimated overhead cost is $40,500, with $17,100 fixed and $23,400 variable. The variable overhead rate is $.5762 and the fixed rate is $.4211 ($17,100 ÷ 40,608 estimated hours), providing a total of $.9973. In the Cutting Department, a factory overhead rate of $2 per direct labor hour is used for product costing purposes. The difference of $1.0027 ($2.00 − $.9973) is accounted for by service department costs assigned to this department.

A similar analysis can be made as follows for the service department, Utilities:

(1)	(2)	(3)	(4) Total Variance	(5) Spending Variance	(6) Idle Capacity Variance
Actual Overhead	Budget Allowance	Utilities Cost Charged Out	(1) − (3)	(1) − (2)	(2) − (3)
$5,860	$5,639	$5,701*	$159 unfav.	$221 unfav.	$(62) fav.

*The amount of cost charged out is based on the total predetermined utilities cost of $65,400 (from page 363), which was to be distributed 20% or $13,080 based on kwh, 50% or $32,700 on hph, and 30% or $19,620 on floor area, resulting in these charging rates: $.2044 ($13,080 ÷ 64 000 kwh); $.0654 ($32,700 ÷ 500,000 hph); and $.9343 ($19,620 ÷ 21,000 sq. ft.). The $5,701 is the result of:

$$
\begin{array}{rl}
5\ 560 \text{ actual kwh} \times \$.2044 = & \$1,136 \\
44,800 \text{ actual hph} \times \$.0654 = & 2,930 \\
1,750 \text{ sq. ft. converted to a one-month period (1/12 of 21,000 sq. ft.)} \times \$.9343 = & \underline{1,635} \\
& \underline{\$5,701}
\end{array}
$$

Responsibility for Service Department Variances. While the responsibility for the cost incurred is, generally speaking, easily identifiable in the producing departments, a service department's cost variances need a great deal of additional investigation. With a service department such as Utilities, the analysis is not so easy because:

1. Utilities can be charged accurately to consuming departments only when departmental or cost center meters are used.
2. Even with meters, the quantity used might differ from the quantity produced, due to line losses. The pinpointing of the responsibility for these losses is often impossible.
3. Since any utility can often be either purchased from outside or manufactured inside, it could be possible that the interchangeable use of one source with another will give rise to variances for which the cause is also difficult to detect.

Similar difficulties regarding the pinpointing of responsibility for the cost incurrence and the resulting variance are experienced with any service department. The maintenance department has already been cited as an example. In many instances, service department costs are largely fixed, at least over a relevant range of activity or volume. For this reason, responsibility is difficult to establish. The idle capacity variance is particularly troublesome when calculated on a monthly basis. The spending variance is somewhat more meaningful, since actual and budgeted costs can be compared with their increases and decreases.

As a rule, the manager of the service department is responsible for the variance between the actual cost and the cost based on the number of hours or service units charged out or sold. The manager of the producing or services received department, together with the service department supervisor, is responsible for the number of hours or service units consumed in the department. This statement indicates that a kind of dual responsibility exists between the charges to the services received departments and the credits to the services rendered departments. The consuming department's cost must be compared with the allowed or budgeted service cost to determine the cost increase or decrease in that department, while the service department must examine its cost on the basis of the quantity consumed or sold.

▼ RESPONSIBILITY REPORTING

Responsibility accounting is a program encompassing all operating management for which the accounting, cost, or budget divisions provide technical assistance in the form of daily, weekly, or monthly control reports. Responsibility reporting includes the reporting phase of responsibility accounting. In fact, the terms, "responsibility accounting" and "responsibility reporting" are generally considered synonymous.

Reporting to the various levels of management can be divided into responsibility-performance reporting and information reporting. A clear distinction between the two is important; each serves different goals or objectives. *Responsibility-performance reports* are accountability reports with two purposes:

1. To inform managers and superiors of their performance in responsible areas.
2. To motivate managers and superiors to generate the direct action necessary to improve performance.

Information reports are issued for the purpose of providing managers with information relevant to their areas of interest, although not necessarily associated directly with their specific responsibility for performance. Information reports serve a broader and different set of goals than performance reports. In the short view, responsibility-performance reports are more important than information reports because of the immediate and pressing needs to keep the business on course. However, from the long view, information reports bearing on the progress and growth of the business are also important.

Fundamentals of Reports

Reports should be based on the following fundamental qualities and characteristics:

1. Reports should fit the organization chart; that is, they should be addressed primarily to the individuals responsible for controlling the items covered by the reports. Managers must be educated to use the results of the reporting system.
2. Reports should be consistent in form and content each time they are issued. Changes should be made only for good reasons and with clear explanations to users.
3. Reports should be prompt and timely. Prompt issuance of a report requires that cost records be organized so that information is available when it is needed.
4. Reports should be issued with regularity. Promptness and regularity are closely tied in with the mechanical aids used to assemble and issue reports.
5. Reports should be easy to understand. Often they contain accounting terminology that managers with little or no accounting training find difficult to understand, and vital information may be incorrectly communicated. Therefore, accounting terms should be explained or modified to fit the user. Management should have some knowledge of the kind of items chargeable to an account as well as the methods used to compute overhead rates, allocate costs, and analyze variances.
6. Reports should convey sufficient but not excessive detail. The amount and nature of the detail depend largely on the management level receiving the report. Reports to management should neither be flooded with immaterial facts nor so condensed that management lacks vital information essential to carrying out its responsibilities.
7. Reports should give comparative figures (a comparison of actual with budgeted figures, or of predetermined standards with actual results) and should isolate variances.
8. Reports should be analytical. Analysis of underlying papers, such as time tickets, scrap tickets, work orders, and materials requisitions, provides reasons for poor performance which might have been due to power failure, machine breakdown, an inefficient operator, poor quality of materials, or other similar factors.
9. Reports for operating management should be stated in physical units as well as in dollars, since dollar information may be irrelevant to a supervisor not trained in the language of the accountant. Also, dollars may be more difficult to compare over time because of the impact of inflation.
10. Reports may tend to highlight supposed departmental efficiencies and inefficiencies. Care should be exercised to see that such reports do not encourage departmental activities aimed at "making a good showing" regardless of the effect on the entire organization.

To be of value, information must be used; to be used, it must be effectively communicated. Both the form and the method of the reporting techniques are critical, whether written or oral.

The written report should include tabular presentation as well as the use of charts and graphs.[8] Narrative comments are useful for conveying qualitative information and for analyzing and interpreting quantitative data. Oral presentations are especially effective in offering opportunities to convey information, raise questions, and voice opinions.

Responsibility-Reporting Systems Illustrated

The first step in a responsibility-reporting system is the establishment of lines of responsibility and responsibility areas. Each block in a company's organization chart represents a segment (cost center, division, department, etc.) that is reported upon and that receives reports on the functions responsible to it. Any report prepared according to this concept easily fits into one of the blocks illustrated in the following organization chart for a manufacturing concern:

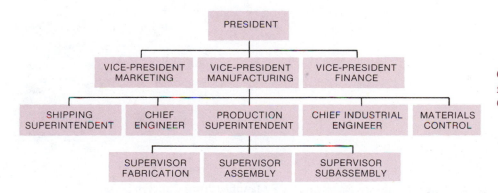

Organization Chart for a Manufacturing Concern

The following reports illustrate the factory overhead reporting structure for each level of responsibility and the relationship of each report to the next higher echelon of responsibility.[9] Starting with Report D (bottom of the pyramid), the Subassembly Department supervisor is provided with the factory overhead expenses for this area. The supervisors for the Fabrication and Assembly Departments also receive similar reports. The supervisors of these three departments are responsible to the production superintendent. Report C summarizes the overhead expenses for the production superintendent and the three departments for which the production superintendent is accountable. Report B provides the vice-president of manufacturing with

---

[8]For discussion and illustrations of these communication aids, see Anker V. Andersen, *Graphing Financial Information—How Accountants Can Use Graphs to Communicate* (New York: National Association of Accountants, 1983).

[9]James D. Wilson, "Human Relations and More Effective Reporting," *NAA Bulletin*, Vol. XLII, No. 9, pp. 13-24. Copyright May, 1961, by the National Association of Accountants. All rights reserved. Reprinted by permission.

performance figures for this office and for the five responsibility areas within this division. Finally, the president receives a summary, Report A, indicating overhead expenses not only for the president's own area but also for the three divisions (Marketing, Manufacturing, Finance) reporting to that office.

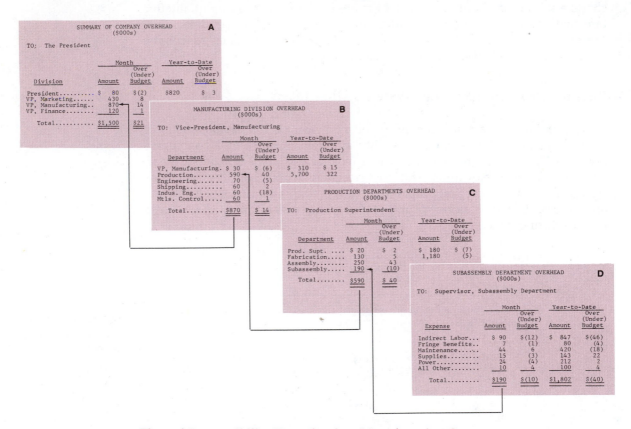

Flow of Responsibility Reporting in a Manufacturing Concern

The illustration on page 409 depicts responsibility reporting in a bank, utilizing a reporting system that accurately identifies and reports expenses along the bank's organizational lines.[10] This permits effective expense control through the proper assignment of responsibility and control at each management level, with expenses at each management level identified by area of responsibility as well as by natural classification.

Reviewing the Reporting Structure

To provide all levels of management with all the facts when needed, the reporting system should be geared to the requirements of all managerial personnel. Each report should be so arranged that exceptions are highlighted

[10]Edward T. Kennedy, "Computer-Based Bank Financial Information Systems," *The Arthur Andersen Chronicle* (Chicago: Arthur Andersen & Co.), Vol. 29, No. 2, p. 28.

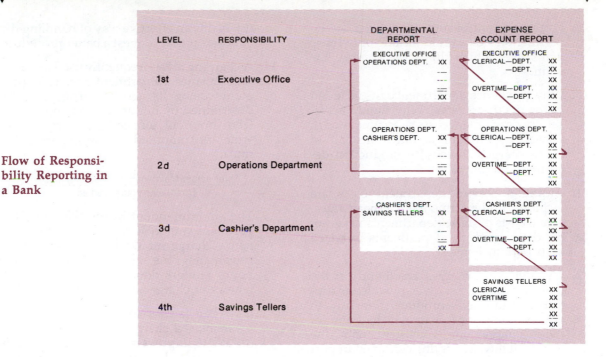

Flow of Responsibility Reporting in a Bank

and brought to the attention of the responsible manager without too much searching and extensive reading. The number of reports issued and sent to a manager also needs constant examination. Too many times a reporting system is cluttered with old, detailed, and voluminous reports, without consideration of the cost of their preparation or their justification. No reporting system is ever perfect. It requires continuous checking and examination in the light of changing times and the vicissitudes of business itself.

DISCUSSION QUESTIONS

1. Explain responsibility accounting and the classification of revenues and expenses under this concept.

2. Responsibility accounting does not involve a drastic change in accounting theory or principles. Discuss.

3. Explain what is meant by controllable costs and how the idea of controllability is related to responsibility accounting.

4. What is the significance of controllable as compared to uncontrollable costs?

5. Enumerate general requirements that are absolutely necessary for a successful responsibility accounting system.

6. Enumerate the benefits that should result from responsibility accounting.

7. Why is some knowledge of human behavior important to responsibility accounting?

8. The departmentalization of factory overhead is essential for maximum control of overhead. Explain in terms of responsibility reporting.

9. Overhead control reports received by department heads should include only those items over which they have control. Explain.

10. Why are service department costs included in the overhead rates? Why should actual service department costs be accumulated in service department accounts instead of being charged directly to production department accounts?

11. Although service department costs are included in departmental overhead rates, actual costs of these departments need not be distributed to departments serviced each period. Explain.

12. The following charges are found on the monthly report of a division which manufactures and sells products primarily to outside companies. State which, if any, of these charges are consistent with the responsibility accounting concept. Support each answer with a brief explanation.

(a) A charge for general corporation administration at 10% of division sales.
(b) A charge for the use of the corporate computer facility. The charge is determined by taking the actual annual Computer Department cost and allocating an amount to each user on the ratio of its use to total corporation use.
(c) A charge for goods purchased from another division. (The charge is based upon the competitive market price for the goods.)   (ICMA adapted)

13. The electric bill of the Emmons Company increased from $5,000 to $7,500 between January and February. As a bill is received, its cost is allocated to various departments on the basis of actual usage.
(a) What factors may have caused the increase?

(b) Is this an effective way of handling this cost? If not, suggest a better procedure.

14. A charging rate is frequently used to charge Maintenance Department cost to departments using its services. The charge is determined by multiplying the number of labor hours of service by a charging rate which is computed by the following formula:

$$\frac{\text{Total actual Maintenance Department cost}}{\text{Total labor hours worked}}$$

The superintendent of the Stamping Department was upset by a $15,000 maintenance charge for work that involved approximately the same number of labor hours as work done in a previous month when the charge was $12,000.

(a) What factors may have caused the increased charge?
(b) What improvements can be made in the distribution of this company's Maintenance Department cost?

15. Discuss the information which a well-designed cost report should give to the management from the point of view of production and of control. Is there any other information with which the cost figures should be amplified? In what terms should such information be given?

16. On what fundamentals should the method of presenting cost data to management be based?

17. Why is usefulness of the figures so important in accounting?

18. A frequent complaint made by management is that cost reports arrive too late to be of any value to the executives. What are the main contributing causes of this condition, and how can it be remedied?

EXERCISES

1. **Billing rates; variance analysis.** Baars Company uses predetermined departmental overhead rates to apply factory overhead. In computing these rates, every attempt is

made to transfer service department costs to producing departments on the most equitable bases. Budgeted cost and other data for Baar's two service departments, Maintenance and General Factory, are as follows:

	Maintenance	General Factory
Monthly fixed cost..................................	$7,500	$30,000
Variable cost..	$8.50 per maintenance labor hour	$20 per employee (producing departments only)
Normal level of activity.........................	15,000 maintenance hours per month	1,000 producing department employees
Actual November results:		
Total cost...	$132,000	$51,000
Actual level of activity.......................	14,000 maintenance hours	980 producing department employees

Required:

(1) Compute the charging or billing rates to be used to transfer estimated maintenance and general factory costs to other departments, together with a description of the method used.

(2) Compute the spending and idle capacity variances for the service departments.

2. Sold-hour rates; variance analysis. A company's two service departments provide the following data:

Service Center	Monthly Budget	Service-Hours Available	Actual Monthly Expense
Carpenter Shop.....................	$20,000	2,000	$19,800
Electricians.............................	30,000	2,500	28,900

The two service departments serve three producing departments that show the following budgeted and actual cost and service-hours data:

Department No.	Estimated Services Required		Actual Services Used	
	Carpenter Shop	Electricians	Carpenter Shop	Electricians
1.....................	600 hrs.	900 hrs.	400 hrs.	1,000 hrs.
2...................	750 hrs.	1,000 hrs.	800 hrs.	850 hrs.
3...................	650 hrs.	600 hrs.	450 hrs.	550 hrs.

Required:

(1) Compute the sold-hour rates for the two service departments.

(2) Compute the amounts charged to the producing departments for services rendered.

(3) Compute the spending variances for the two service departments, assuming that 70% of the budgeted expense is fixed in the Carpenter Shop and 80% for Electricians.

3. Billing rates; variance analysis. The management of Paley Company wishes to secure greater control over service departments and decides to create a billing rate for the Maintenance and Payroll Departments. For September, the following predetermined and actual operating and cost data have been made available:

Maintenance Department

Predetermined data (beginning of the month):
Normal level of maintenance hours per month... 3,200
Average hourly rate for maintenance worker... $8.70
Other maintenance costs:

	Fixed Cost per Month	Variable Cost per Maintenance Labor Hour
Supervision.......................................	$9,800	$.50
Tools and supplies.........................	2,300	.75
Other miscellaneous items..............	700	.05

Actual data (end of the month):
Maintenance hours worked.. 3,355
Maintenance workers' earnings.. $29,610
Other costs (supervision, etc.).. $17,590

Payroll Department

Predetermined data (beginning of the month):
Average number of employees in factory and office... 1,200
Budgeted cost for department... $12,000 plus $2 for each employee in factory and office

Actual data (end of the month):
Number of employees in factory and office... 1,165
Total cost in the Payroll Department.. $13,875

Required:

  (1) Compute the billing rate for the two departments.
  (2) Compute the variances for the two departments for September.

4. Readiness-to-serve and billing rates. During November, the actual expense of operating a power plant was $12,800, of which $6,000 was considered a fixed cost. The schedule of horsepower-hours for the producing and service departments is as follows:

	Producing Departments		Service Departments	
	A	B	X	Y
Needed at capacity production.....................	10,000	20,000	12,000	8,000
Used during November...............................	8,000	13,000	7,000	6,000

Required:

  (1) Compute the dollar amounts of the power plant expense to be allocated to each producing and service department. The fixed cost is assigned on the basis of the power plant's readiness to serve.
  (2) State reasons for allocating one service department's cost to other service departments as well as to producing departments.

5. Readiness-to-serve and billing rates; variance analysis. Mowen Company operates its own power-generating plant. Power cost is distributed to the producing departments by charging the fixed cost according to the standby capacity provided and the variable cost on the basis of a predetermined rate multiplied by actual consumption. The rated standby capacity of the three departments, Cutting, Grinding, and Polishing, is 35 000, 26 250, and 8 750 kwh, respectively, per month.

The following information relates to the producing departments and the power plant for April, May, and June:

	Consumption in Kilowatt-Hours			Power Plant Costs	
	Cutting	Grinding	Polishing	Fixed	Variable
April......................	22 500	20 000	6 000	$7,000	$5,450
May......................	27 500	17 500	5 000	7,000	5,350
June....................	23 750	21 000	5 500	7,000	5,750

The predetermined variable power cost is $.11 per kwh.

Required:

(1) Separately identify the fixed and variable power cost charged to each department for each of the three months.
(2) Compute the over- or underdistributed variable cost of the power plant for each of the three months.

6. Overhead analysis; report to supervisor. The cost and operating data on April factory overhead for Department 10 are as follows:

	Budgeted Factory Overhead	Actual Factory Overhead
Variable departmental overhead:		
Supplies...	$ 2,000	$ 1,800
Repairs and maintenance............................	800	600
Indirect labor..	4,000	3,800
Power and light..	1,200	1,150
Heat..	400	350
Subtotal...	$ 8,400	$ 7,700
Fixed departmental overhead:		
Building expense..	$ 800	$ 840
Depreciation—machinery.............................	2,400	2,400
Property tax and insurance.........................	400	420
Subtotal...	$ 3,600	$ 3,660
Total..	$12,000	$11,360
Operating data:		
Normal capacity hours.................................	8,000	
Factory overhead rate per hour..................	$1.50	
Actual hours...		6,400

Required:

(1) Prepare a variance analysis of the factory overhead for Department 10.
(2) Prepare a departmental report for the supervisor of Department 10, with explanations regarding the format used.

PROBLEMS

14-1. Variance analysis of producing and service departments overhead. Wright Products Inc. decided to push for a greater amount of cost consciousness and cost responsibility among its departmental supervisors. The allocation of service department costs to the producing departments, using predetermined rates, has been in use for some time. Now the management asks the Cost Department, with the cooperation of the departmental supervisors, not only to prepare departmental budgets but also to give the supervisors monthly reports for cost control information.

The company operates with three producing departments, A, B, and C, and two service departments, Repairs and Maintenance, and Utilities. For the year 19—, the Cost Department prepared the following departmental factory overhead budgets and determined the factory overhead rates based on direct labor hours:

	Producing Departments			Service Departments	
	A	B	C	Repairs and Maintenance	Utilities
Total budgeted expense..............................	$52,000	$52,450	$41,900	$56,000	$49,000
Allocation of service departments:					
Utilities (based on kilowatt-hours)...........	14,000	15,750	12,250	7,000	(49,000)
Repairs and maintenance					
(based on direct labor hours)..............	18,000	27,900	17,100	(63,000)	
Total..	$84,000	$96,100	$71,250		
Bases:					
Kilowatt-hours...	40 000	45 000	35 000	20 000	
Direct labor hours....................................	20,000	31,000	19,000		
Service department allocation rates...........				$.90 per direct labor hour	$.35 per kilowatt-hour
Departmental overhead rates.....................	$4.20 per direct labor hour	$3.10 per direct labor hour	$3.75 per direct labor hour		

Actual cost and operating data before allocation of service department costs at the end of the budget period are:

	Producing Departments			Service Departments	
	A	B	C	Repairs and Maintenance	Utilities
Total actual expense............	$56,020	$52,850	$42,580	$56,320	$50,040
Operating data:					
Direct labor hours..............	20,480	29,850	20,100		
Kilowatt-hours...................	39 300	46 200	35 800	18 950	

Required:

(1) Compute the amount of factory overhead applied for each of the three producing departments.
(2) Compute the amount of over- or underapplied factory overhead for each of the three producing departments, charging them with service department costs on the basis of actual kilowatt-hours or labor hours multiplied by the billing rate.
(3) Compute the total variance for each of the two service departments.

14-2. Billing rates; estimated factory overhead and variance analysis. Perdido Tool Co. has two producing departments, Planers and Radial Drills, and two service departments, Maintenance and Utilities. The following data were collected:

	Producing Departments		Service Departments	
	Planers	Radial Drills	Maintenance	Utilities
Estimated data for 19—:				
Fixed overhead.............................	$18,000	$15,000	$ 6,000	$ 4,800
Variable overhead.........................	15,000	9,000	4,500	3,600
Total...	$33,000	$24,000	$10,500	$ 8,400
Direct labor hours.........................	12,000	7,500		
Maintenance hours........................	2,500	1,000	3,500	
Kilowatt-hours................................	45 000	25 000		70 000
Actual data for January 19—:				
Fixed overhead.............................	$ 1,500	$ 1,250	$ 500	$ 400
Variable overhead.........................	1,620	1,050	670	310
Total...	$ 3,120	$ 2,300	$ 1,170	$ 710
Direct labor hours.........................	1,020	680		
Maintenance hours........................	320	80	400	
Kilowatt-hours................................	4 000	2 000		6 000

Required:

(1) Compute the billing (or charging) rate for each of the two service departments.
(2) Calculate the total predetermined factory overhead for each of the two producing departments and their departmental factory overhead rates based on direct labor hours. Service department expenses are to be distributed on the basis of the billing rates calculated in (1). (Carry all computations to three decimal places.)
(3) Prepare an analysis of the over- or underapplied factory overhead of each of the two producing departments for January, including the spending and idle capacity variances. Service department expenses are to be charged on the basis of actual hours (maintenance or kilowatt) multiplied by the billing rate. This method treats these expenses as being wholly variable.
(4) Prepare a calculation and analysis of the over- or underapplied factory overhead in each of the two service departments, including the spending and idle capacity variances. (Round off all amounts to four decimal places.)
(5) Prepare a reconciliation of the total variances.

14-3. Budget allowance; variance analysis based on responsibility reporting. The controller of Ushco Corporation prepared the following forecast income statement for the year:

		Amount	Unit
Sales (60,000 units)...		$600,000	$10.00
Cost of goods sold (Schedule I).......................................		384,000	6.40
Gross profit..		$216,000	$ 3.60
Operating expenses:			
Marketing expense..	$80,000		
Administrative expense....................................	70,000	150,000	2.50
Income before income tax..		$ 66,000	$ 1.10
Schedule I—Estimated cost of goods sold:			
Direct materials..		$102,000	$ 1.70
Direct labor...		162,000	2.70
Factory overhead..		120,000	2.00
Total...		$384,000	$ 6.40

The product's manufacturing processes require two producing departments that make use of the services of Department 76, Maintenance, and Department 95, Janitorial. To charge the products moving through the two departments, the cost accountant has prepared an overhead distribution sheet and calculated predetermined factory overhead rates as follows:

| | Producing Departments | | Service Departments | |
	Dept. 10	Dept. 12	Dept. 76 Maintenance	Dept. 95 Janitorial
Production units..................................	60,000	60,000		
Direct labor hours..............................	15,000	12,000		
Direct labor cost................................	$90,000	$72,000		
Factory overhead:				
Variable overhead...........................	$27,000	$22,800	$ 5,100	$2,700
Fixed overhead................................	17,520	34,230	8,400	7,200
			$13,500	$9,900
Share of Department 76..................	7,500	6,000	(13,500)	
Share of Department 95..................	1,980	2,970		(4,950)
Total factory overhead........................	$54,000	$66,000		
To marketing and administrative expenses..				(4,950)
Factory overhead rate (based on direct labor hours)...........................	$3.60	$5.50		

Actual hours and costs at the end of the month:

	Dept. 10	Dept. 12	Dept. 76	Dept. 95
Hours worked......................................	1,340	1,030		
Actual factory overhead:				
Variable overhead...........................	$2,700	$2,240	$650	$440
Fixed overhead................................	1,500	3,000	700	600

The Department 76 cost was allocated to the two producing departments on the basis of the direct labor hours. The Department 95 cost was prorated 50% to the factory and 50% to the general offices. The two producing departments shared the 50% factory allocation on a 40:60 basis, respectively.

For January, the Planning Department scheduled 5,000 units. At the end of the month, sales and production showed the following results:

Sales..	4,900 units
Production—completed in both departments....................	5,200 units

Required:

(1) Compute the budget allowance for each of the two producing departments for January, based on (a) scheduled production hours and (b) actual production hours.

(2) Compute the spending and idle capacity variances for each of the two producing departments, based on actual production hours.

(3) Compute the spending variance for each of the two service departments. (Round off all amounts to three decimal places.)

14-4. Overhead rates; variance analysis in producing and service departments.
Roderick Products Co. prepared the following budgeted and actual data:

				Actual Data March, 19—	
	Budgeted Data, 19—				
	Direct Labor	Factory Overhead		Direct Labor	Factory Overhead
Department	Hours	Fixed	Variable	Hours	Cost
Machining..................................	22,000	$12,840	$14,400	2,130	$3,586*
Assembly....................................	28,000	14,100	18,300	2,310	3,341*
Tools and Supplies...................	-0-	3,600	5,600	-0-	920
Materials Handling.....................	-0-	5,700	6,000	-0-	1,090

*Includes service departments

The fixed cost of the service departments is apportioned to the producing departments on a 60:40 basis and the variable cost at a predetermined rate on the basis of direct labor hours. Budgeted direct labor hours are based on normal capacity utilization. Factory overhead is applied on the basis of direct labor hours.

Required:

(1) Compute the departmental factory overhead rates for the producing departments. (Round off all amounts to three decimal places.)

(2) Compute the spending and idle capacity variances of producing and service departments for March. (Round off calculations to three decimal places.)

14-5. Setting sewage treatment usage charge rates. The city of Alpine, Texas, estimates its sewage treatment costs for next year as follows:

Fixed

Debt service cost associated with excess capacity...	$350,000
Costs attributable to infiltration and inflow (basically rain water and subsurface ground water):	
Debt service...	150,000
Operating and maintenance...	140,000
Administration and office overhead..	250,000
Remaining debt service...	110,000

Variable

Sewage volume and strength processing costs..	$1,000,000

Its user census profile is estimated to be:

User Class	Number of Users	Volume/Strength Units
Wet industry...	3	80,000
Commercial and dry industry......................	150	50,000
Residential..	8,675	120,000
Total..	8,828	250,000

Required:

(1) Compute the user charging rate, based on volume/strength units.

(2) Compute the fixed and variable user charging rates, assuming that:

(a) Excess capacity cost and infiltration and inflow debt service cost are excluded from rates and recovered through property tax, and

(b) All other fixed costs are charged to industry/commercial users and residential users at a per user ratio of 25:1, which is based on the user's relative size of lateral pipe.

(3) Calculate allocations to user classes, based on (1) and (2), and identify the more equitable method, giving reasons.

CASES

A. Cost responsibility and the attitude of managers. Declining profits compelled the management of the Wilmington Corporation to approach employees to work for production economy and increased productivity. Production managers were promised a monetary incentive based on cost reductions.

The production managers responded with (1) an increased rate of production; (2) a higher rejection rate for quantities of raw materials and parts received from the storeroom; (3) a postponement of repairs and maintenance work; and (4) a reliance on quick emergency repairs to avoid breakdowns.

The repair and maintenance policy is causing serious conflicts. The maintenance supervisor argues that the postponement of certain repairs in the short run and the use of emergency repair techniques could result in increased costs later and, in some instances, could reduce the life of machines as well as machine safety.

Even more serious is the growing bitterness caused by pressures placed on the maintenance managers by individual production managers to obtain service. Also, in several instances, some production departments whose production has been halted due to machine breakdown have had to wait while another production department, with an aggressive manager, has received repair service on machines not needed in the current production run. Furthermore, the demand for immediate service sometimes results in substandard repair work.

The production departments are charged with the actual cost of the repairs. A record of the repair work conducted in individual production departments is prepared by the maintenance managers. This record, when complet-

ed in the Accounting Department, shows the repair hours, the hourly rate of the maintenance worker, the maintenance overhead charge, and the cost of any parts. The record serves as the basis for the charges to production departments. Production managers have complained about the charging system, claiming that charges depend upon which maintenance worker does the work (hourly rate and efficiency), when the work is done (the production department is charged for the overtime premium), and how careful the worker is in recording the time on the job.

Required:

(1) Identify and briefly explain the motivational factors which may cause friction between the production and maintenance managers.
(2) Develop a plan which revises the system employed to charge production departments for repair costs, so that the production departments' complaints are eliminated or reduced.

(ICMA adapted)

B. Maintenance cost control. Mobile Company is a medium-size manufacturer in a capital-intensive industry. The corporation's profitability is low at the moment and, as a result, investment funds are limited and hiring is restricted. These consequences of the corporation's problems have placed a strain on the plant's repair and maintenance program. The result has been a reduction in work efficiency and cost control effectiveness in the repair and maintenance area.

The controller proposes the installation of a maintenance work order system to overcome these problems. This system would require a work order to be prepared for each repair request and for each regular maintenance activity. The maintenance superintendent would record the estimated time to complete a job and would send one copy of the work order to the department in which the work was to be done. The work order would also serve as a job cost sheet. The actual cost of the parts and supplies used on the job as well as the actual labor costs incurred in completing the job would be recorded directly on the work order. A copy of the completed work order with the actual costs would be the basis of the charge to the department in which the repair or maintenance activity occurred.

The maintenance superintendent opposes the program on the grounds that the added paperwork will be costly and nonproductive. He states that the departmental clerk who now schedules repair and maintenance activities is doing a good job without all the extra forms the new system would require. The real problem, in the superintendent's opinion, is that the Maintenance Department is understaffed.

Required:

(1) Discuss how the maintenance work order system would aid cost control.
(2) Explain how the maintenance work order system might aid the maintenance superintendent in obtaining authorization to employ more mechanics. *(ICMA adapted)*

C. **Readiness-to-serve and billing rates.** The Independent Underwriters Insurance Co. (IUI) established a Systems Department two years ago to implement and operate its own data processing systems. IUI believed that its own department would be more cost effective than the service bureau it had been using.

IUI's three-departments—Claims, Records, and Finance—have different requirements with respect to hardware and other capacity-related resources and operating resources. The system was designed to recognize these differ-

ing needs. In addition, the system was designed to meet IUI's long-term capacity needs. The excess capacity designed into the system would be sold to outside users until needed by IUI. The estimated resource requirements used to design and implement the system are shown in the following schedule:

	Hardware and Other Capacity-Related Resources	Operating Resources
Records	30%	60%
Claims	50	20
Finance	15	15
Expansion (outside use)	5	5
Total	100%	100%

IUI currently sells the equivalent of its expansion capacity to a few outside clients.

At the time the system became operational, management decided to redistribute total expenses of the Systems Department to the user departments, based on actual computer time used. The actual costs for the first quarter of the current fiscal year were distributed to the user departments as follows:

Department	Percentage Utilization	Amount
Records	60%	$330,000
Claims	20	110,000
Finance	15	82,500
Outside	5	27,500
Total	100%	$550,000

The three user departments have complained about the cost distribution method since the Systems Department was established. The Records Department's monthly costs have been as much as three times the costs experienced with the service bureau. The Finance Department is concerned about the costs distributed to the outside user category because these allocated costs form the basis for the fees billed to the outside clients.

James Dale, IUI's controller, decided to review the distribution method by which the Systems Department's costs have been allocated for the past two years. The additional information he gathered for his review is reported in the following three tables:

Table 1

Systems Department Costs and Activity Levels

| | Annual Budget | | First Quarter | | | |
| | | | Budget | | Actual | |
	Hours	Dollars	Hours	Dollars	Hours	Dollars
Hardware and other capacity-related costs....................	—	$ 600,000	—	$150,000	—	$155,000
Software development...	18,750	562,500	4,725	141,750	4,250	130,000
Operations:						
Computer related..	3,750	750,000	945	189,000	920	187,000
Input/output related..	30,000	300,000	7,560	75,600	7,900	78,000
		$2,212,500		$556,350		$550,000

Table 2

Historical Utilization by Users

| | Hardware and Other Capacity Needs | Software Development | | Operations | | | |
| | | | | Computer | | Input/Output | |
		Range	Average	Range	Average	Range	Average
Records......................	30%	0-30%	12%	55-65%	60%	10-30%	20%
Claims.........................	50	15-60	35	10-25	20	60-80	70
Finance.......................	15	25-75	45	10-25	15	3-10	6
Outside......................	5	0-25	8	3-8	5	3-10	4
	100%		100%		100%		100%

Table 3

Utilization of Systems Department's Services
in Hours—First Quarter

| | Software Development | Operations | |
		Computer Related	Input/ Output
Records...........	425	552	1,580
Claims..............	1,700	184	5,530
Finance............	1,700	138	395
Outside............	425	46	395
Total.............	4,250	920	7,900

Dale has concluded that the method of cost distribution should be changed to show more directly the actual benefits received by the departments. He believes that the hardware and capacity-related costs should be allocated to the user departments in proportion to the planned, long-term needs. Any difference between actual and budgeted hardware costs would not be allocated to the departments but remain with the Systems Department.

The remaining costs for software development and operations would be charged to the user departments, based on actual hours used multiplied by a predetermined hourly rate based on annual budget data. The hourly rates that would be used for the current fiscal year are as follows:

Function	Hourly Rate
Software development....................	$ 30
Operations:	
Computer related........................	$200
Input/output related....................	$ 10

Dale plans to use first quarter activity and cost data to illustrate his recommendations. The recommendations will be presented to the Systems Department and the user departments for their comments and reactions. He then expects to present his recommendations to management for approval.

Required:

(1) Calculate the amount of data processing costs that would be included in the Claims Department's first quarter budget according to the method James Dale has recommended.

(2) Prepare a schedule to show how the actual first quarter costs of the Systems Department would be charged to the users if Dale's recommended method was adopted.

(3) Explain whether Dale's recommended system for charging costs to the user departments will:

   (a) Improve cost control in the Systems Department.

   (b) Improve planning and cost control in the user departments.

   (c) Be a more equitable basis for charging costs to user departments.

(ICMA adapted)

D. Improving reports. Denny Daniels is production manager of the Alumalloy Division of WRT Inc. Alumalloy has limited contact with outside customers and has no sales staff. Most of its customers are other divisions of WRT. All sales and purchases with outside customers are handled by other corporate divisions. Therefore, Alumalloy is treated as a cost center for reporting and evaluation purposes rather than as a revenue or profit center.

Daniels perceives the Accounting Department as a historical number-generating process that provides little useful information for conducting his job. Consequently, the entire accounting process is perceived as a negative motivational device that does not reflect how hard or how effectively he works as a production manager. Daniels tried to discuss these perceptions and concerns with Jana Scott, the controller for the Alumalloy Division. Daniels told Scott, "I think the cost report is misleading. I know I've had better production over a number of operating periods, but the cost report still says I have excessive costs. Look, I'm not an accountant, I'm a production manager. I know how to get a good quality product out. Over a number of years, I've even cut the raw materials used to do it. But the cost report doesn't show any of this. Basically, it's always negative, no matter what I do. There's no way you can win with accounting or the people at corporate headquarters who use those reports."

Scott gave Daniels little consolation. Scott stated that the accounting system and the cost reports generated by headquarters are almost impossible for an individual to change. "Although these accounting reports are pretty much the basis for evaluating the efficiency of your division and the means corporate headquarters uses to determine whether you have done the job they want, you shouldn't worry too much. You haven't been fired yet! Besides, these cost reports have been used by WRT for the last 25 years."

Daniels perceived from talking to the production manager of the Zinc Division that most of what Scott said was probably true. However, some minor cost reporting changes for Zinc had been agreed to. He also knew from the trade grapevine that the turnover of production managers was considered high at WRT, even though relatively few were fired. Most seemed to end up quitting, usually in disgust, because of beliefs that they were not being evaluated fairly. Typical comments of production managers who have left WRT are:

   (a) "Corporate headquarters doesn't really listen to us. All they consider are those misleading cost reports. They don't want them changed and they don't want any supplemental information."

   (b) "The accountants may be quick with numbers but they don't know anything about production. As it was, I either had to ignore the cost reports entirely or pretend they were important even though they didn't tell how good a job I had done. No matter what they say about not firing people, negative reports mean negative evaluations. I'm better off working for another company."

A recent copy of the cost report prepared by corporate headquarters for the Alumalloy Division is as follows. Daniels does not like this report because he believes it fails to reflect the division's operations properly, thereby resulting in an unfair evaluation of performance.

Alumalloy Division
Cost Report for April, 19A
($000s omitted)

	Master Budget	Actual Cost	Excess Cost
Aluminum	$ 400	$ 437	$ 37
Labor	560	540	(20)
Overhead	100	134	34
Total	$1,060	$1,111	$ 51

Required:

(1) What are Daniel's perceptions of (a) Scott, the controller; (b) corporate headquarters; (c) the cost report; and (d) himself as a production manager.

(2) Discuss how Daniel's perceptions affect his behavior and probable performance as a production manager and employee of WRT.

(3) Identify and explain changes that could be made in the cost reports that would make the information more meaningful and less threatening to the production managers. *(ICMA adapted)*

E. Reviewing the reporting structure.
McCumber Company employs a computer-based data processing system for maintaining all company records. The present system was developed in stages over the past five years and has been fully operational for the last 24 months.

When the system was being designed, all department heads were asked to specify the types of information and reports they would need for planning and controlling operations. The Systems Department attempted to meet the specifications of each department head. Company management specified that certain other reports be prepared for department heads. During the five years of systems development and operations, there have been changes in the department head positions due to attrition and promotions. New department heads have often requested additional reports according to their specifications; the Systems

Department has complied with all of these requests. Consequently, the data processing system has generated a large quantity of reports each reporting period. Occasionally, a report has been discontinued upon request by a department head, but only if it was not a standard report required by executive management.

Company management became concerned about the quality of information being produced by the system, and the Internal Audit Department was asked to evaluate the effectiveness of these reports. The audit staff noted the following reactions to this information overload:

(a) Many department heads would not act on certain reports during periods of peak activity. The department head would let these reports accumulate with the hope of catching up during a subsequent lull.

(b) Some department heads had so many reports that they did not act at all upon the information or made incorrect decisions because of misuse of the information.

(c) Frequently, action required by the nature of the report data was not taken until the department head was reminded by someone who needed the decision. These department heads did not appear to have developed a priority system for acting on the information produced by the data processing system.

(d) Department heads often would develop the information they needed from alternative, independent sources, rather than utilize the reports generated by the data processing system. This was often easier than trying to search among the reports for the needed data.

Required:

(1) Explain whether each of the observed reactions is a functional or dysfunctional behavioral response.

(2) Recommend procedures that the company could employ to eliminate any dysfunctional behavior and to prevent its recurrence. *(ICMA adapted)*

PART

4

Budgeting and Standard Costing

CHAPTER 15

Budgeting: Profits, Sales, Costs, and Expenses

Management formulates intelligent plans for achieving an organization's objectives. Effective control of operations then depends upon cost accounting, which provides management with detailed statements of the actual cost of materials, labor, factory overhead, marketing expenses, and administrative expenses. Comparisons and analyses of these actual costs with estimates and standards prepared in advance of production and sales enable management to identify the reasons for any differences and to take appropriate corrective action.

▼ PROFIT PLANNING

The terms "profit planning" and "budgeting" can be viewed as synonymous. *Profit planning* is a well thought-out operational plan with its financial implications expressed in the form of long- and short-range income statements, balance sheets, and cash and working capital projections. A budget is simply a plan expressed in financial and other quantitative terms. Profit planning is directed to the ultimate objectives of the organization and serves as a guide to maintaining a definite course of activity.

Budgets should be distinguished from forecasts. A profit plan or budget represents the expected profit level or target which management strives to achieve, whereas a forecast is a level of revenue or cost that the organization predicts will occur. The notion of a weather forecast illustrates the distinction: one forecasts the weather; one does not budget the weather.

Sound and intelligent planning of profits is a difficult task, because technology changes rapidly, and economic, social, and political factors exert strong influences on business. To accomplish this task, managers must be motivated to strive for attainment of their personal objectives in congruence with the organization's objectives.

424

Setting Profit Objectives

Fundamentally, three different procedures can be followed in setting profit objectives:

1. The *a priori* method, in which the profit objectives take precedence over the planning process. At the outset, management specifies a given rate of return, which it seeks to realize in the long run by means of planning toward that end.
2. The *a posteriori* method, in which the determination of profit objectives is subordinated to the planning, and the objectives emerge as the product of the planning itself.
3. The *pragmatic* method, in which management uses a profit standard that has been tested empirically and sanctioned by experience. By using a target rate of profit derived from experience, expectations, or comparisons, management establishes a relative profit standard which is considered satisfactory for the company.[1]

In setting profit objectives, management needs to consider the following factors:

1. Profit or loss resulting from a given volume of sales.
2. Sales volume required to recover all consumed costs, to produce a profit adequate to pay dividends on preferred and common stock, and to retain sufficient earnings in the business for future needs.
3. Break-even point.
4. Sales volume that the present operating capacity can produce.
5. Operating capacity necessary to attain the profit objectives.
6. Return on capital employed.

Public expectations with regard to social responsibilities compel companies to also consider the social consequences of profit objectives. Increasingly, important actions must be evaluated in a context that includes social as well as economic impacts. Potential social impacts specifically pertain to ". . . environmental pollution, the consumption of nonrenewable resources, and other ecological factors; the rights of individuals and groups; the maintenance of public service; public safety; health and education; and many other social concerns.[2]

Long-Range Profit Planning

Business has become increasingly aware of a need to develop long-range profit plans. *Long-range planning* has been defined as "the continuous process of making present decisions systematically and, with the best possible

---

[1]*Research Report No. 42*, "Long-Range Profit Planning" (New York: National Association of Accountants, 1964), pp. 60-65.
[2]Robert K. Elliott, "Social Accounting and Corporate Decision-Making," *Management Controls*, Vol. XXI, No. 1, p. 2.

knowledge of their futurity, organizing systematically the efforts needed to carry out these decisions, and measuring the results of these decisions against the expectations through organized, systematic feedback."[3] Long-range plans are not stated in precise terms, nor are they expected to be completely coordinated future plans. They deal rather with specific areas such as sales, capital expenditures, extensive research and development activities, and financial requirements.

In long-range profit planning, management attempts to find the most probable course of events. Of greatest importance, however, is the ability to be flexible and adaptable to changing conditions. Long-range planning does not eliminate risk, for risk taking is the essence of economic activity. An end result of successful long-range profit planning is a capacity to take a greater risk, which is a fundamental way to improve entrepreneurial performance.

Market trends and economic factors, inflation, growth of population, personal consumption expenditures, and indexes of industrial production form the background for long-range planning. Quantitative and dollar sales estimates for a three- to five-year forecast may be developed from this information. A prospective income statement can then be prepared, showing anticipated sales, fixed and variable costs (factory, marketing, and administrative), contribution margin, and operating income by years. A balance sheet by years should indicate anticipated cash balances, inventory levels, accounts receivable balances, and liabilities. This financial long-range plan might also be supported by a cash flow statement.

The rate of return on capital (total assets) employed is an important statistic in long-range profit planning and in setting profit objectives. To measure the effectiveness with which management is likely to use the assets, rates of return are computed for each individual year covered in the long-range plan. These figures show whether planned increases in total net income will keep pace with increases in assets at the corporate as well as divisional or operating levels. Though return on capital employed is the basic measure of profit performance (discussed in detail in Chapter 26), companies typically use several other measures, such as the ratio of net income to sales, the ratio of sales to shareholders' capital, and earnings per common share.[4]

Short-Range Plans or Budgets

Management's long-range plans can only be achieved through successful long-run profit performance, which requires growth and a reasonably high and stable level of profit. Long-range plans with their future expectancy of profits and growth must, however, be incorporated into a shorter-range budget for both planning and control of the contemplated course of action. Although one year is the usual planning period, the short-range budget may cover periods of three, six, or twelve months, depending upon the nature of the business. For efficient planning, the annual budget should be expanded

[3]Peter F. Drucker, "Long-Range Planning," *Management Science*, Vol. 5, No. 3, p. 240.
[4]*Research Report No. 42, loc. cit.*

into an eighteen-month budget, allowing for a three-month period at the end of the old year, twelve months for the regular budget period, and an additional three months into the third year. These overlapping months are needed in order to allow transition from year to year and to make adjustments based on prior months' experience. The budget period should:

1. Be divided into months.
2. Be long enough to complete production of the various products.
3. Cover at least one entire seasonal cycle for a business of a seasonal nature.
4. Be long enough to allow for the financing of production well in advance of actual needs.
5. Coincide with the financial accounting period to compare actual results with budget estimates.

Some organizations use a continuous budget, by which a month or quarter in the future is added as the month or quarter just ended is dropped, and the budget for the entire period is revised and updated as needed. This procedure forces management to think continuously about its short-range plans.

Advantages of Profit Planning

Profit planning, or budgeting, has the advantages of:

1. Providing a disciplined approach to the solution of problems.
2. Obliging management to make an early study of its problems and instilling into an organization the habit of careful study before making decisions.
3. Developing throughout the organization an atmosphere of profit-mindedness, and encouraging an attitude of cost-consciousness and maximum resource utilization.
4. Enlisting the aid and coordinating the operating plans of the diverse segments of the entire management organization so that the final decisions and contingency plans represent the total organization in the form of an integrated, comprehensive plan.
5. Affording the opportunity of appraising systematically every facet of the organization as well as examining and restating periodically its basic policies and guiding principles.
6. Coordinating and correlating all efforts, since no management activity reveals weaknesses in organization as quickly as the orderly procedure necessary for systematic budgeting.
7. Aiding in directing capital and effort into the most profitable channels.
8. Encouraging a high standard of performance by stimulating competition, providing a sense of purpose, and serving as an incentive to perform more effectively.
9. Providing yardsticks or standards for measuring performance and gauging the managerial judgment and ability of the individual executive.

Limitations of Profit Planning

While the advantages of profit planning are unquestionably impressive and far-reaching, certain limitations and pitfalls need to be mentioned:

1. Forecasting is not an exact science; a certain amount of judgment is present in any estimate. Since a budget must be based on forecasts of future events, a revision or modification of the budget should be made when variations from the estimates warrant a change of plans.

2. The budget could focus a manager's attention on goals (e.g., high production, high credit sales, etc.) which are not necessarily in harmony with the organization's overall objectives. Thus, care must be used to properly channel the managers' efforts.

3. A profit planning program needs the cooperation and participation of all members of management. The basis for success is executive management's sustained adherence to and enthusiasm for the profit plan. Too often a profit plan has failed because executive management has paid only lip service to its execution. Also, involvement at all levels is needed to avoid the feeling at lower management levels that the budget is being imposed on them without their participation.

4. A budgetary system is inadequate whenever it motivates an individual to take an action that is not in the best interest of the organization. Regardless of how sophisticated budgetary systems become, their effectiveness ultimately depends upon how they influence human behavior and attitudes.[5]

5. Profit planning does not eliminate or take over the role of administration. Executives should not feel restricted by the budget. Rather, the profit plan is designed to provide detailed information that allows the executives to operate with strength and vision toward achievement of the organization's objectives.

6. Installation takes time. Management often becomes impatient and loses interest because it expects too much too soon. The budget must first be sold to the responsible people; and they, in turn, must then be guided, trained, and educated in the fundamental steps, methods, and purposes of a budgetary system.

▼ PRINCIPLES OF BUDGETING

A company's organization chart and its chart of accounts form the basic framework on which to build a coordinated and efficient system of managerial planning and budgetary control. The organization chart defines the functional responsibilities of executives and thereby justifies their budgets. Although

---

[5]Paul J. Carruth and Thurrell O. McClendon, "How Supervisors React to 'Meeting the Budget' Pressure," *Management Accounting*, Vol. LXVI, No. 5, p. 54.

final responsibility for the budget rests with executive management, all managers are responsible for the preparation and execution of their departmental budgets. If a budgetary control system is to be successful, these managers must fully cooperate and must understand their role in making the budget system successful. The budget must be the joint effort of many people—a working document that forms the basis for action.

The Budget Committee

The budgeting process is usually directed by a budget committee, which is composed of the sales manager, the production manager, the chief engineer, the treasurer, and the controller. The principal functions of the budget committee are to:

1. Decide on general policies.
2. Request, receive, and review individual budget estimates.
3. Suggest revisions in individual budget estimates.
4. Approve budgets and later revisions.
5. Receive and analyze budget reports.
6. Recommend actions designed to improve efficiency where necessary.

In performing these functions, the budget committee becomes a management committee. It is a powerful force in coordinating the various activities of the business and in controlling operations.

Budget Development and Implementation

The procedure used in developing a budget may be as important as its content and should include these fundamental principles:

1. Provide adequate guidance so that all management levels are working on the same assumptions, targeted objectives, and agenda. All managers should understand the limitations and constraints of their participation and the bounds of their decision making. Participants should be told, prior to the time the budget is established, how their activities will fit into the entire organization and what constraints will be placed upon them and their activities by upper-level administrative decisions.
2. Encourage participation in the budgeting process at each level within the organization. Structure the activity of developing the budget to involve the people who will be responsible for implementing the budget and who will be rewarded according to its accomplishments.
3. Structure the climate of budget preparation to eliminate anxiety and defensiveness. Individuals should have the freedom and authority to influence and accept their own performance levels, and should assume the responsibility for accomplishment. Budget preparation should be oriented to the problems and opportunities of the participants.

4. Structure the preparation of the budget so that there is a reasonably high probability of successful attainment of objectives. When challenging but attainable objectives are achieved, feelings of success, confidence, and satisfaction are produced and aspiration levels are raised. If objectives are not accomplished, the reasons for this failure should be clear. A careful distinction should be made between controllable factors for which individuals should be responsible and for uncontrollable factors for which they are not.

5. Evaluate numerous sets of assumptions in developing the budget. This iterative process is facilitated by the use of computers and also probabilities, both of which are discussed in Chapter 16.

If the proper procedure for developing a budget has been followed, implementation difficulties are minimized. Proper budget implementation requires adherence to the following principles:

1. Establish rewards and reward contingencies that will lead to achieving the organizational objectives. Too often, the budgeting process does not provide sufficient rewards to induce employees to accomplish organizational objectives.

2. The organization should focus on rewarding achievement rather than punishing failure. Feelings of success or failure largely determine attitudes toward the budget and the level of performance to which employees will aspire.

3. Provide rapid feedback on the performance of each work team or individual. This principle necessitates the use of reports and reporting procedures that are understandable to workers and supervisors at the department level, so that they can analyze their results and initiate corrective action.[6]

▼ THE COMPLETE PERIODIC BUDGET

A complete set of budgets generally consists of:

1. A sales budget.
2. Estimates of inventory and production requirements.
3. Budgets of materials, labor, and factory overhead, combined into a cost of goods manufactured and sold schedule.
4. Budgets for marketing and administrative expenses.
5. Estimates of other income and expense items and income tax.
6. A budgeted income statement.
7. A budget of capital expenditures and of research and development expenditures.

---

[6]J. Owen Cherrington and David J. Cherrington, "Budget Games for Fun and Frustration," *Management Accounting*, Vol. LVII, No. 7, p. 32.

8. A cash receipts and disbursements budget.
9. A budgeted balance sheet showing the estimated financial position of the company at the end of the budget period.

Items 1 through 6 form the basis for preparing the budgeted income statement. They are discussed and illustrated in the remainder of this chapter, while items 7 through 9 are covered in the first portion of Chapter 16.

The following data are used to illustrate the budget components that comprise the income statement. As each budget component is discussed, the relevant data are used to illustrate the preparation of the related budget schedule. Subsequent schedules are cross-referenced to show the linkage between the various budget parts, building to the budgeted income statement. Assume that Franklin Company manufactures three products, A, B, and C, which are marketed in two territories, the Midwest and the Southwest. The production departments are designated Cutting, Assembling, and Finishing. The management and the department heads have made the following estimates for the coming year ending December 31:

1. Sales:

Product	Midwest	Southwest	Sales Price
A............................	4,000 units	3,000 units	$200 per unit
B............................	6,000	5,000	150
C............................	9,000	6,000	100

2. Inventories:
    Materials:

Material	Beginning Inventory Units	Ending Inventory Units	Unit Cost
X............................	30,000	40,000	$ 1.00
Y............................	10,000	12,000	14.00
Z............................	2,000	2,500	2.50

Work in process: None at the beginning or end of the period. Finished goods (fifo):

Product	Beginning Inventory Units	Unit Cost	Ending Inventory Units
A............................	200	$125.70	250
B............................	400	82.50	200
C............................	500	64.00	400

3. Materials requirements and unit cost:

	Material		
	X	Y	Z
Product A..................................	12	5	2
Product B..................................	8	3	1
Product C..................................	6	2	1
Materials unit cost.....................	$1.00	$14.00	$2.50

4. Labor time requirements and rate per hour:

	Cutting	Assembling	Finishing
Product A..........................	.500 hour	2.500 hours	.800 hour
Product B..........................	.375	2.000	.500
Product C..........................	.375	1.750	.500
Rate per hour.....................	$8.00	$10.00	$9.00

5. Unit overhead rates:

Product	Cutting	Assembling	Finishing	Total
A..............................	$3.00	$7.50	$4.80	$15.30
B..............................	2.25	6.00	3.00	11.25
C..............................	2.25	5.25	3.00	10.50

6. Marketing expenses: $450,000.
   Administrative expenses: $270,000.
   Other income: $70,000.
   Other expenses: $105,000.
   Income tax rate: 40%.

To achieve a concise yet comprehensive illustration, only annual data are shown. As previously noted, however, monthly budget details are often desirable and necessary. Also, customer group classifications for sales are omitted, and factory overhead, marketing and administrative expenses, and other income and expense items are not shown in detail.

Sales Budget

One of the most important elements in a budgetary control system is a realistic sales estimate that is based on analyses of past sales and the present market. Yet, the sales variable is often the budget component that is the most difficult to predict with reasonable precision. The demand for an entity's products or services normally depends on forces and factors largely beyond the scope of management's control. In most instances, this uncertainty makes expected sales the focal point of the planning process.[7]

The task of preparing the sales budget is usually approached from two different angles: (1) judging and evaluating external influences and (2) considering internal influences. These two influences are brought together in a workable sales budget. External influences include the general trend of industrial activity, actions of competitors, governmental policies, cyclical phases of the nation's economy, price-level expectations, purchasing power of the population, population shift, and changes in buying habits and modes of living. Internal influences are sales trends, factory capacities, new products, plant expansion, seasonal products, sales estimates, and establishment of quotas for salespeople and sales territories. The profit desired by the company is a highly significant consideration.

[7]Eugene A. Imhoff, Jr., *Sales Forecasting Systems* (Montvale, N.J.: National Association of Accountants, 1986), pp. 5-6.

The following annual sales budget for Franklin Company, detailed by product and by territory, is prepared from the data on page 431.

Schedule 1

Franklin Company
Sales Budget
For the Year Ending December 31, 19—

| | Territories | | |
	Midwest	Southwest	Total
Product A			
Units.........................	4,000	3,000	7,000
Unit price..................	$200	$200	$200
Total.......................	$ 800,000	$ 600,000	$1,400,000
Product B			
Units.........................	6,000	5,000	11,000
Unit price..................	$150	$150	$150
Total.......................	$ 900,000	$ 750,000	$1,650,000
Product C			
Units.........................	9,000	6,000	15,000
Unit price..................	$100	$100	$100
Total.......................	$ 900,000	$ 600,000	$1,500,000
Total sales..................	$2,600,000	$1,950,000	$4,550,000

Estimating Sales. The preparation of sales estimates is usually the responsibility of the marketing manager, assisted by individual salespeople and market research personnel. Because of the many dissimilarities in the marketing of products, actual methods used to estimate sales vary widely. One method used by many companies is the preparation of sales estimates by individual salespeople. All salespeople supply their district managers with estimates of probable sales in their territories. These estimates are consolidated and adjusted by the district marketing manager. They are then forwarded to the general marketing manager, who makes further adjustments. These adjustments include allowances for expected economic conditions and competitive conditions of which salespeople are unaware, as well as allowances for expected canceled orders and sales returns that salespeople would likely disregard because their estimates are based on the orders they expect to procure. During the budget preparation process, it is not unusual for sales estimates to be revised a number of times. The ultimate sales estimates tend to be improved when forecasts from several sources, such as a group of managers, are averaged.

In estimating sales as well as expenditures, the tendency to over- or underestimate plans must be recognized. Individuals tend to be overly pessimistic or optimistic in setting goals and in making plans. Therefore, the budgeting system should be designed to monitor this tendency in order to keep goals and plans within reasonable bounds.

In most large organizations, the estimating procedure usually starts with known factors; namely, (1) the company's sales of past years broken down by product groups and profit margins, (2) industry or trade sales volume and perhaps profits, and (3) unusual factors influencing sales in the past. The company's past sales figures often require a restudy or reclassification due to changes in products, profit margins, competition, sales areas, distribution methods, or changes within the industry. Industry or trade sales and profits are secured from trade associations, trade publications, and various business magazines. For some industries, the U.S. Department of Commerce publishes information that is useful as background data. Unusual factors influencing past sales are inventory conditions, public economic sentiment, competition, and customer relations.

Charting a company's volume in units of various products for a three- to five-year period and comparing it with the industry's volume will disclose the company's sales trend and will pinpoint factors that affected past sales. However, a recent study indicated that, for most companies, the use of historical sales data is generally limited to the most recent two years. Thus, the amount of time-series data used is reduced. The study also finds that managers tend to use current and prospective information in preference to historical trends, even though there is research evidence that time-series models are often good predictors of future sales.[8]

Although the feeling frequently exists that the sales budget is a crystal-ball area, a sound basis for estimating future sales often can be established by using time-series models and by applying probability analysis techniques to the consideration of general business conditions, the industry's prospects, the company's potential share of the total industry market, and the plans of competitive companies.

Seasonal Variations. When the annual sales estimate has been approved, it must be placed on an operating period basis, which is usually a month. The monthly sales budget should show seasonal sales patterns for each product manufactured. These patterns are evident from the company's experience and from records of a product's trend during past years. Any fluctuations in a trend should be considered, as well as the causes of fluctuations, such as customs or habits based on local or national traits, climate, holidays, or even the influences of companies in the firm's own industry.

The seasonal or operating sales budget is of great help in judging the records of individual salespeople. Averaging sales over a budget period is not sufficient to assure success of a sales program. Too many times, low sales in one month have been excused with the optimistic statement that sales in the following month will make up the difference. When this does not happen, the sales budget and the entire budget plan suffer.

Sales Budget on a Territory and Customer Basis. A sales budget should not only be placed on a monthly basis for each product, but should also be classified by territories or districts and by types of customers. The customer

---

[8]*Ibid.*, pp. 20, 36.

classification should show sales to jobbers, wholesalers, retailers, institutions, governmental agencies, schools and colleges, foreign businesses, etc. Such a breakdown indicates the contribution of each territory and customer class to total sales and profits. An analysis of this type often reveals that certain territories or classes of customers are not given sufficient attention by sales managers and sales representatives. A detailed sales budget can be a strong means for analyzing possible new trade outlets. It also assists in identifying reasons for a drop in sales, in investigating such a decrease, and in taking remedial steps.

Estimating Production and Inventory Requirements. Prior to the final acceptance of a sales budget, the factory's capacity to produce the estimated quantities must be determined. The production level should maintain inventories that are sufficient to fulfill periodic sales requirements.

If factory capacity is available, production should be planned at a level that will keep workers and equipment operating all year. Serious fluctuations in employment are expensive and do not promote good labor relations. If the sales budget indicates that factory employment in certain months would fall below a desirable level, it would be necessary to attempt to increase sales volume or increase inventories. At the same time, the investment in inventories should be held to a level consistent with sound financial policy. If estimated sales are higher than available capacity, the purchase or rental of new machinery and factory space must be considered as a means of increasing plant capacity.

Sales Estimate Follow-Up. Follow-up review should occur at intervals influenced by the frequency of change in the company, its industry, and general economic conditions. The review should determine (1) the accuracy of past estimates, (2) the location of the major estimation errors, (3) the best method by which to update estimates, and (4) the steps needed for improvement of the making and monitoring of future estimates.

Past errors indicate the reliance that can be placed on sales estimates and provide insight into the company and the personal bias built into the estimate. When estimates are monitored, comparison with actual results should extend beyond financial results to include consideration of the underlying factors and key assumptions. Such comparisons might require the monitoring of unit sales volumes, prices, production rates, backlogs of sales orders, changes in capacity, and economic indicators.

Production Budget

The production budget deals with the scheduling of operations, the determination of volume, and the establishment of maximum and minimum quantities of finished goods inventories. It provides the basis for preparing the budgets of materials, labor, and factory overhead.

A production budget is stated in physical units. As shown in the following illustration, this budget is frequently the budgeted sales quantity adjusted for any inventory changes.

Schedule 2

Franklin Company
Production Budget
For the Year Ending December 31, 19—

	Products		
	A	B	C
Units required to meet sales budget (Schedule 1).....................	7,000	11,000	15,000
Add desired ending inventory..	250	200	400
Total units required...	7,250	11,200	15,400
Less beginning inventory..	200	400	500
Planned production for the year...	7,050	10,800	14,900

If there is work in process inventory, the equivalent number of such units in the ending inventory would be added to, and units in the beginning inventory would be subtracted from, the above calculations in order to determine the units to be produced.

The production budget, like other budgets, may be detailed by months or quarters as well as annually. For comparison with actual production, the detailed budget should be broken down by work stations. The nature of this division will be determined by plant layout, type of production, and other factors.

For a company that does not manufacture standard products but produces only on orders, a detailed production budget may not be possible. In special-order work, the primary problem is to be prepared for production when orders are received. Work must be routed and scheduled through the factory, so that delays are prevented and production facilities are fully utilized.

No division of a manufacturing business has made so much progress in scientific management as the production department. Constant effort is directed toward devising new ways and shortcuts that will lead to more efficient production and cost savings which will be reflected in earnings.

Manufacturing Budgets

With the forecast sales translated into physical units in the production budget, the estimated manufacturing costs essential to the sales and production program can be computed. Detailed budgets are prepared for direct materials and direct labor in order to identify these costs with products and responsible managers. Factory overhead is budgeted in detail by responsibility centers or departments. This budget information becomes part of the master budget to be used as a standard or target against which the performance of the individual department is judged and evaluated.

Direct Materials Budget. The budgeting of direct materials specifies the quantity and cost of materials required to produce the predetermined units of finished goods. It (1) leads to the determination of quantities of materials that must be on hand, (2) permits the purchasing department to set up a purchasing schedule that assures delivery of materials when needed, and (3) establishes a means by which the treasurer can include in the cash budget the necessary funds for periodic purchases as well as for all other cash payments. Although the materials budget usually deals only with direct materials, these budgeting procedures are also applicable to supplies and indirect materials that are included in the factory overhead budget and the commercial expenses budget.

The schedules for Franklin Company below and on page 438 consist of (1) the direct materials budget expressed in units required for production (Schedule 3), (2) the purchases budget, specifying inventory levels and units as well as the cost of purchases (Schedule 4), and (3) the calculation of the cost of materials required for production (Schedule 5).

The production planning department determines the quantity and type of materials required for the various products manufactured by a company. Most companies have standard parts lists and bills of materials which detail all materials requirements. These requirements are given to the purchasing department, which sets up a buying schedule. This schedule is based on the objective of providing sufficient materials, without overstocking, and entails an increasing trend by manufacturers to minimize inventory by utilizing a just-in-time inventory stocking policy. In preparing a buying schedule, the purchasing department must consider changes in possible delivery promises by the supplier and changes in the rate of materials consumption because of unforeseen circumstances.

Franklin Company
Direct Materials Budget in Units
For the Year Ending December 31, 19—

	Units To Be Manufactured	Materials X	Materials Y	Materials Z
Product A				
Units to be manufactured (Schedule 2).......	7,050			
Materials rate..		12	5	2
Units of materials required...........................		84,600	35,250	14,100
Product B				
Units to be manufactured (Schedule 2).......	10,800			
Materials rate..		8	3	1
Units of materials required...........................		86,400	32,400	10,800
Product C				
Units to be manufactured (Schedule 2).......	14,900			
Materials rate..		6	2	1
Units of materials required...........................		89,400	29,800	14,900
Total units of materials required....................		260,400	97,450	39,800

Schedule 3

Schedule 4

Franklin Company
Purchases Budget
For the Year Ending December 31, 19—

| | Materials | | | |
	X	Y	Z	Total
Units required for production (Schedule 3)..	260,400	97,450	39,800	
Add desired ending inventory...............	40,000	12,000	2,500	
	300,400	109,450	42,300	
Less beginning inventory......................	30,000	10,000	2,000	
Units to be purchased..........................	270,400	99,450	40,300	
Unit cost..	$1.00	$14.00	$2.50	
Total cost of purchases........................	$270,400	$1,392,300	$100,750	$1,763,450

Schedule 5

Franklin Company
Cost of Materials Required for Production
For the Year Ending December 31, 19—

| | Materials | | | |
	X	Y	Z	Total
Product A				
Units of materials required for production (Schedule 3)..................	84,600	35,250	14,100	
Unit cost..	$1.00	$14.00	$2.50	
Total...	$ 84,600	$ 493,500	$35,250	$ 613,350
Product B				
Units of materials required for production (Schedule 3)..................	86,400	32,400	10,800	
Unit cost..	$1.00	$14.00	$2.50	
Total...	$ 86,400	$ 453,600	$27,000	567,000
Product C				
Units of materials required for production (Schedule 3)..................	89,400	29,800	14,900	
Unit cost..	$1.00	$14.00	$2.50	
Total...	$ 89,400	$ 417,200	$37,250	543,850
Total cost of materials required for production........................	$260,400	$1,364,300	$99,500	$1,724,200

Direct Labor Budget. The annual budget is the principal tool for the overall planning for human resources. When the budget is completed and approved, it should include a human resources plan that is coordinated with planned sales and production activities as well as the profit goal.

The direct labor budget, based on specifications drawn up by product engineers, guides the personnel department in determining the number and type of workers needed. If the labor force has been with the firm for several years and if the production schedule does not call for additional workers, the task of the personnel department is rather easy. If an increase or decrease in the labor force is required, the personnel department must make plans in advance to assure the availability of workers. Frequently, the personnel department must provide a training program which provides workers to the production department at the proper time. When workers are to be laid off, the personnel department must prepare a list of those affected, giving due recognition to skill and seniority rights. In many companies, this schedule is prepared in collaboration with union representatives in order to protect employees from any injustice or hardship.

For each type of labor, the hours or the number of workers must be translated into dollar values. Established labor rates as agreed upon in union contracts are generally used. If conditions indicate that labor rates might change, the new rates should be used, so that the financial budget reflects the most recent figures available. The following direct labor budget for Franklin Company is prepared from the data on page 432:

<table>
<tr><td colspan="5" align="center">Franklin Company
Direct Labor Budget
For the Year Ending December 31, 19—</td></tr>
<tr><td></td><td>Cutting</td><td>Assembling</td><td>Finishing</td><td>Total</td></tr>
<tr><td>Product A</td><td></td><td></td><td></td><td></td></tr>
<tr><td>Hours per unit.............................</td><td>.500</td><td>2.500</td><td>.800</td><td></td></tr>
<tr><td>Units to be manufactured
(Schedule 2)............................</td><td>7,050</td><td>7,050</td><td>7,050</td><td></td></tr>
<tr><td>Hours of labor required........................</td><td>3,525</td><td>17,625</td><td>5,640</td><td></td></tr>
<tr><td>Labor cost per hour............................</td><td>$8</td><td>$10</td><td>$9</td><td></td></tr>
<tr><td>Total labor cost............................</td><td>$ 28,200</td><td>$176,250</td><td>$ 50,760</td><td>$255,210</td></tr>
<tr><td>Product B</td><td></td><td></td><td></td><td></td></tr>
<tr><td>Hours per unit.............................</td><td>.375</td><td>2.000</td><td>.500</td><td></td></tr>
<tr><td>Units to be manufactured
(Schedule 2)............................</td><td>10,800</td><td>10,800</td><td>10,800</td><td></td></tr>
<tr><td>Hours of labor required........................</td><td>4,050</td><td>21,600</td><td>5,400</td><td></td></tr>
<tr><td>Labor cost per hour............................</td><td>$8</td><td>$10</td><td>$9</td><td></td></tr>
<tr><td>Total labor cost............................</td><td>$ 32,400</td><td>$216,000</td><td>$ 48,600</td><td>297,000</td></tr>
<tr><td>Product C</td><td></td><td></td><td></td><td></td></tr>
<tr><td>Hours per unit.............................</td><td>.375</td><td>1.750</td><td>.500</td><td></td></tr>
<tr><td>Units to be manufactured
(Schedule 2)............................</td><td>14,900</td><td>14,900</td><td>14,900</td><td></td></tr>
<tr><td>Hours of labor required........................</td><td>5,587.5</td><td>26,075</td><td>7,450</td><td></td></tr>
<tr><td>Labor cost per hour............................</td><td>$8</td><td>$10</td><td>$9</td><td></td></tr>
<tr><td>Total labor cost............................</td><td>$ 44,700</td><td>$260,750</td><td>$ 67,050</td><td>372,500</td></tr>
<tr><td>Total direct labor.........................</td><td>$105,300</td><td>$653,000</td><td>$166,410</td><td>$924,710</td></tr>
</table>

Schedule 6

Indirect labor is included in the factory overhead budget and consists of such employees as helpers in producing departments, maintenance workers, crane operators, materials clerks, and receiving clerks. Labor requirements for marketing and administrative activities must be budgeted as part of the commercial expenses budget.

Factory Overhead Budget. The detailed factory overhead budget is prepared on the basis of the chart of accounts, which properly classifies expense accounts and details the various cost centers for planning and control and assignment of factory overhead to product cost. As discussed and illustrated in Chapter 13, expenses are grouped according to:

1. Natural expense classification, such as indirect materials and supplies, indirect labor, freight, light, and power.

2. Departmental or functional classification according to the producing or service department or cost center in which the expense originated.
3. Behavior, i.e., variable and fixed, using the cost behavior analysis tools described in Chapter 11.

The natural expense (primary account) classification alone is not useful for budget purposes, since expenses are usually incurred by various departments. By classifying expenses according to individual departments, the value and importance of budgetary control for expenses becomes significant.

Preparation of any expense budget should be guided by the principle that every expense is chargeable to a department, and that an executive, department head, or supervisor should be held accountable and responsible for expenses incurred. Those expenses for which the department supervisor is directly responsible should be identified in the supervisor's budget. Allocated expenses for which the supervisor has little or no responsibility should also be identified.

If department supervisors accept the budget, they are more likely to cooperate in its execution. Therefore, supervisors should be asked to prepare their own estimates of departmental expenses, based on the department's projected activity for the budget period. These estimates and any revisions should be reviewed and coordinated with other budgets before they are incorporated into the overall budget.

The detailed expense estimates lead to calculation of departmental factory overhead rates (as illustrated in Chapter 13), which are then used to estimate factory overhead for units to be manufactured. For Franklin Company, these costs are shown in the following budget:

Schedule 7

Franklin Company
Factory Overhead Budget
For the Year Ending December 31, 19—

	Cutting	Assembling	Finishing	Total
Product A				
Units to be manufactured (Schedule 2)	7,050	7,050	7,050	
Estimated departmental factory overhead per unit	$3.00	$7.50	$4.80	
Total cost	$21,150	$ 52,875	$ 33,840	$107,865
Product B				
Units to be manufactured (Schedule 2)	10,800	10,800	10,800	
Estimated departmental factory overhead per unit	$2.25	$6.00	$3.00	
Total cost	$24,300	$ 64,800	$ 32,400	121,500
Product C				
Units to be manufactured (Schedule 2)	14,900	14,900	14,900	
Estimated departmental factory overhead per unit	$2.25	$5.25	$3.00	
Total cost	$33,525	$ 78,225	$ 44,700	156,450
Total factory overhead	$78,975	$195,900	$110,940	$385,815

Beginning and Ending Inventories. Not only must inventory quantities be determined for materials, work in process, and finished goods, but the inventories must be costed in order to make available the necessary information leading to preparation of a budgeted cost of goods manufactured and sold statement and ultimately to an income statement and a balance sheet. For Franklin Company, beginning and ending inventory quantities and costs are summarized in the following schedule. Observe that the ending inventory unit costs for finished goods are the summation of estimates for direct materials, direct labor, and factory overhead.

Franklin Company
Beginning and Ending Inventories
For the Year Ending December 31, 19—

	Beginning Inventory			Ending Inventory		
	Units	Cost	Total	Units	Cost	Total
Materials:						
X..............................	30,000	$ 1.00	$ 30,000	40,000	$ 1.00	$ 40,000
Y..............................	10,000	14.00	140,000	12,000	14.00	168,000
Z..............................	2,000	2.50	5,000	2,500	2.50	6,250
Total.....................			$175,000			$214,250
Work in process: None						
Finished goods:						
Product A.................	200	$125.70	$ 25,140	250	$138.50*	$ 34,625
Product B.................	400	82.50	33,000	200	91.25	18,250
Product C.................	500	64.00	32,000	400	72.00	28,800
Total.....................			$ 90,140			$ 81,675
Total inventories..........			$265,140			$295,925

*Ending inventory unit costs for finished goods:

	Product A	Product B	Product C
Materials:			
X: 12 × $ 1.00...................................	$ 12.00		
8 × 1.00...................................		$ 8.00	
6 × 1.00...................................			$ 6.00
Y: 5 × $14.00...................................	70.00		
3 × 14.00...................................		42.00	
2 × 14.00...................................			28.00
Z: 2 × $ 2.50...................................	5.00		
1 × 2.50...................................		2.50	
1 × 2.50...................................			2.50
Direct labor:			
Cutting: .500 × $ 8.....................	4.00		
.375 × 8.....................		3.00	
.375 × 8.....................			3.00
Assembling: 2.500 × $10.....................	25.00		
2.000 × 10.....................		20.00	
1.750 × 10.....................			17.50
Finishing: .800 × $ 9.....................	7.20		
.500 × 9.....................		4.50	
.500 × 9.....................			4.50
Factory overhead.....................................	15.30	11.25	10.50
Total unit costs..	$138.50	$91.25	$72.00

Schedule 8

Budgeted Cost of Goods Manufactured and Sold Statement. This statement requires no new estimates. Figures taken from various manufacturing schedules are arranged in the form of a cost of goods manufactured and sold statement, illustrated as follows. Source schedules are referenced to indicate the linkage with the budget components previously discussed and illustrated.

Schedule 9

Franklin Company
Budgeted Cost of Goods Manufactured and Sold Statement
For the Year Ending December 31, 19—

Materials:		
Beginning inventory (Schedule 8)	$ 175,000	
Add purchases (Schedule 4)	1,763,450	
Total goods available for use	$1,938,450	
Less ending inventory (Schedule 8)	214,250	
Cost of materials used (Schedule 5)		$1,724,200
Direct labor (Schedule 6)		924,710
Factory overhead (Schedule 7)		385,815
Total manufacturing cost		$3,034,725
Add beginning inventory of finished goods (Schedule 8)		90,140
Cost of goods available for sale		$3,124,865
Less ending inventory of finished goods (Schedule 8)		81,675
Cost of goods sold		$3,043,190

Budgeting Commercial Expenses

The company's chart of accounts is also the basis for budgetary control of commercial expenses, which include both marketing (selling or distribution) and administrative expenses. These expenses may be classified by primary accounts and by functions.

Budgeting and analyzing commercial expenses by primary accounts is the simplest method of classification. This method stresses the nature or the type of expenditure, such as salaries, commissions, repairs, light and heat, rent, telephone and telegraph, postage, advertising, travel expenses, sales promotion, entertainment, delivery expense, freight out, insurance, donations, depreciation, taxes, and interest. As expenses are incurred, they are recorded in primary expense accounts, posted to ledger accounts, and then taken directly to the income statement. No further allocation is made. At the end of an accounting period, actual expenses are compared with either budgeted expenses or expenses of the previous month or year.

To control commercial expenses effectively, it is necessary to group them by functional activities or operating units. Classification by function emphasizes departmental activities, such as selling, advertising, warehousing, billing, credit and collection, transportation, accounting, purchasing, engineering, and financing. Such a classification is consistent with the concept of responsibility accounting and may be compared to collecting factory overhead by departments or cost centers. A departmental classification adds to rather than replaces the process of classifying expenses by primary accounts, because primary account classifications are maintained within each department.

When a departmental classification system is used, it is important that each expense be charged to a department, and that the classification conforms to the company's organization chart at the corporate level as well as each marketing territory level. However, it is impossible to suggest exact classifications, since organizational structures vary so much in business organizations. Departments known by the same name may perform widely differing functions.

Commercial expenses grouped by department may be subclassified as direct and indirect expenses. Direct expenses, such as salaries and supplies, are charged directly to a department. Indirect expenses are general or service department expenses that are prorated to benefiting departments. Expenses such as rent, insurance, and utilities, when shared by several departments, constitute this type of expense. Also, expenses should be estimated and identified as to their variable and fixed components, again utilizing the cost behavior analysis tools described in Chapter 11. Such identification will help highlight control responsibility.

To identify an outlay of cash or the incurrence of a liability with a function requires considerably more work than is required by the primary account method. However, the chart of accounts will normally provide the initial breakdown of expenses. Usually the allocation of expenses to departments and the identification of the primary account classification within each department can be made when the voucher is prepared. This procedure requires coding the expenditure when it is requisitioned for purchase. Any increase in expenses caused by the use of this functional method is more than offset by the advantages of improved cost control. Furthermore, to the extent that the identifications are practical and meaningful, commercial expenses may be assigned to individual products or product groups and to individual marketing territories.

Commercial expenses are not detailed in the Franklin Company illustration, but rather are shown only in summary form in the budgeted income statement. Budget detail for primary accounts as well as for functional activities, products, and territories is shown in Chapter 25, using marketing expenses as the basis for illustration.

Marketing Expenses Budget. A company's marketing activities can be divided into two broad categories:

1. Obtaining the order—involves the functions of selling and advertising.
2. Filling the order—involves the functions of warehousing, packing and shipping, credit and collection, and general accounting (for marketing).

The supervisors of functions connected with marketing activities should prepare budget estimates of these costs. Some estimates are based on individual judgment, while others are based on the costs experienced in previous years, modified by expected sales volume. Expenses such as depreciation and insurance depend upon the policy established by management.

Administrative Expenses Budget. Administrative expenses include some costs which are peculiar to the administrative function, such as directors' fees, franchise taxes, capital stock taxes, and professional services of accountants, lawyers, and engineers. Other expenses, such as purchasing, engineering, personnel, and research, are shared by the production and marketing as well as the administrative functions.

As a result of the problem of classifying certain expenses, the budgeting and control of administrative expenses is often quite difficult. The difficulty is increased because the persons responsible for the control of certain of these expenses may not be identifiable. However, an attempt should be made to place every item of expense under the jurisdiction and control of an executive, such as the chief executive, treasurer, controller, general accounting supervisor, or office manager. This person should be responsible for estimating the administrative expenses of a specific section or division, and should have authority to control the incurrence of the division's expenses. For example, the office manager should supervise filing clerks, mail clerks, librarians, stenographers, secretaries, and receptionists. This arrangement permits better control and more intense utilization of personnel in clerical jobs, where overlapping and overexpansion are common.

▼ BUDGETED INCOME STATEMENT

A budgeted income statement contains summaries of the sales, manufacturing, and expense budgets. It projects net income, the goal toward which all efforts are directed, and it offers management the opportunity to judge the accuracy of the budget work and to investigate causes for variances. The budgeted income statement for Franklin Company is as follows:

Schedule 10

Franklin Company Budgeted Income Statement For the Year Ending December 31, 19—		
	Amount	% of Sales
Sales (Schedule 1)..	$4,550,000	100.0%
Cost of goods sold (Schedule 9)......................	3,043,190	66.9
Gross profit..	$1,506,810	33.1%
Commercial expenses:		
Marketing expenses......... $450,000 (9.9%)		
Administrative expenses... 270,000 (5.9%)	720,000	15.8%
Income from operations....................................	$ 786,810	17.3%
Other (income) expense....................................	35,000	.8%
Income before income tax................................	$ 751,810	16.5%
Less provision for income tax..........................	300,724	6.6
Net income...	$ 451,086	9.9%

The sales budget gives expected sales revenue, from which the budgeted cost of goods sold is deducted to give the estimated gross profit. Budgeted marketing and administrative expenses are subtracted from estimated gross profit to arrive at income from operations, which is then adjusted for other income and expense to determine income before income tax. Finally, the provision for income tax is deducted to determine net income. The inclusion of percentages of sales may aid in determining whether various income statement components are in line with expectations.

The budgeted income statement and related supporting budgets may be shown by months or quarters. They may also be segmented by individual products or product groups and by individual marketing territories.

DISCUSSION QUESTIONS

1. Profit planning includes a complete financial and operational plan for all phases and facets of the business. Discuss.

2. Distinguish between a budget and a forecast.

3. Discuss the three different procedures that a company's management might follow to set profit objectives.

4. Differentiate between long-range profit planning and short-range budgeting.

5. What is a budget and how is it related to the control function?

6. The development of a budgetary control program requires specific systems and procedures needed in carrying out management's functions of planning, organizing, and control. Enumerate these steps.

7. Explain whether the periodic budget represents a formal or informal communication channel within a company.
(ICMA adapted)

8. "Budgets are meaningless in my business because I simply cannot estimate my sales for next year. Only if you can tell me which of my bids will be accepted can I prepare a meaningful budget," protested the president of a small custom manufacturer of die-cast parts for the automobile industry. Discuss, with respect to the above statement, the role of budgets and explain to the president how budgeting could help in bidding.
(CGAAC adapted)

9. The human factors in budget preparation are more important than its technical intricacies. Explain.

10. Commercial expenses are generally identified as marketing and administrative expenses. How should these expenses be grouped for budgetary purposes?

11. The budgeted income statement may be viewed as the apex of budgeting. Explain this statement.

EXERCISES

1. **Sales budget.** Whatley Brothers is a wholesaler for three chemical compounds, Barb, Shir, and Bett, for which the following information relates to the year 19A:

Product	Sales (In Pounds)	Average Sales Price per Pound	Gross Profit per Pound
Barb	10,000	$30	$9
Shir	7,500	18	2
Bett	7,500	23	2

Barb has greatly increased in popularity, and demand is expected to double in 19B. Shir will probably experience a 40% increase in demand, while demand for Bett is expected to remain constant. In line with the overall economy, sales prices will increase by 4%, except for Barb, whose market value will increase to $37. Unit costs of goods sold are expected to increase by the following multiples: Barb, 1/3; Shir, 1/8; Bett, 1/10.

Required: Prepare a schedule presenting budgeted sales revenue and gross profit, by product, for 19B.

2. Sales and production estimates. Swisher Company produces and sells commercial printing presses. Accounting records from the past four years reveal the following:

Press Model Number	Sales in Units			
	Year 1	Year 2	Year 3	Year 4
222	100	110	120	130
333	100	120	160	240
444	100	95	85	70

The trends over the past four years are expected to extend to Year 5.
Inventory estimates for Year 5 are:

Press Model Number	Beginning Inventory	Ending Inventory
222	2	4
333	5	5
444	4	5

Required: Prepare sales and production estimates for Year 5, in units and by product.

3. Production budget. Schwankenfelder Company's sales forecast for the next quarter, ending June 30, indicates the following:

Product	Expected Sales
Ceno..........................	21,000 units
Nepo..........................	37,500
Teno..........................	54,300

Inventories at the beginning and desired quantities at the end of the quarter are as follows:

Product	March 31	June 30
Ceno........................	5,800 units	6,200 units
Nepo........................	11,000	10,500
Teno........................	14,500	12,200

Required: Prepare a production budget for the second quarter.

4. Production budget. Magic Enterprises produces three perfumes. The sales department prepared the following tentative sales budget for the first quarter of the coming year:

Perfume	Units
Moon Glow.....................	250,000
Enchanting.....................	175,000
Day Dream....................	300,000

The following inventory levels have been established:

| | Work in Process | | | | Finished Goods | |
| | Beginning | | Ending | | Beginning | Ending |
Perfume	Units	% Processed	Units	% Processed	Units	Units
Moon Glow...............	4,000	50%	7,000	60%	16,000	15,000
Enchanting...............	6,000	30	5,000	40	12,000	10,000
Day Dream...............	8,000	80	8,000	75	25,000	20,000

Required: Prepare a production budget, by product.

5. Production budget and raw materials purchases requirements. Manford Industries produces television antennas and has estimated sales for the next six-month period as follows:

Model Number	Units
1001.................................	200
1002.................................	150
1003.................................	425
2001.................................	175
2002.................................	325
2003.................................	215

Raw materials requirements for each model are:

| | Raw Materials in Pounds | |
Model Number	X	Y
1001.................................	5	2
1002.................................	7	2
1003.................................	10	3
2001.................................	4	1.5
2002.................................	6	2
2003.................................	8	2.5

Estimated inventories are:

	Beginning Inventory	Ending Inventory
Raw Materials:		
X...	5,000 lbs.	7,000 lbs.
Y...	2,000	1,500
Finished Goods:		
1001.................................	50 units	40 units
1002.................................	25	25
1003.................................	75	60
2001.................................	15	20
2002.................................	35	35
2003.................................	20	20

Required:

    (1) Prepare a production budget, by product.
    (2) Compute the raw materials purchases requirements, by raw material.

6. Production budget, purchase requirements, and manufacturing costs. Provence Company prepared the following figures as a basis for its annual budget:

Product	Expected Sales	Estimated per Unit Sales Price	Required Materials per Unit A	B
Tribolite........................	80,000 units	$1.50	1 kg	2 kg
Polycal..........................	40,000	2.00	2	—
Powder X.....................	100,000	.80	—	1

Estimated inventories at the beginning and desired quantities at the end of the year are:

Material	Beginning	Ending	Purchase Price per Kilogram
A.................................	10 000 kg	12 000 kg	$.20
B.................................	12 000	15 000	.10

Product	Beginning	Ending	Direct Labor Hours per 1,000 Units
Tribolite........................	5,000 units	6,000 units	50.0
Polycal..........................	4,000	2,000	125.0
Powder X.....................	10,000	8,000	12.5

The direct labor cost is budgeted at $8 per hour and variable factory overhead at $6 per hour of direct labor. Fixed factory overhead, estimated to be $40,000, is a common cost and is not allocated to specific products in developing the manufacturing budget for internal management use.

Required:

(1) Prepare a production budget.
(2) Prepare a purchases budget for each material.
(3) Prepare a budget of manufacturing costs, by product and in total.

7. Budgeted cost of goods sold statement. Sandersen Inc, with $20,000,000 of par stock outstanding, plans to budget earnings of 6%, before income tax, on this stock.

The Marketing Department budgets sales at $12,000,000. The budget director approves the sales budget and expenses as follows:

Marketing.............................	15% of sales
Administrative	5%
Financial.............................	1%

Labor is expected to be 50% of the total manufacturing cost; materials issued for the budgeted production will cost $2,500,000; therefore, any savings in manufacturing cost will have to be in factory overhead.

Inventories are to be as follows:

	Beginning of Year	End of Year
Finished goods........................	$800,000	$1,000,000
Work in Process.....................	100,000	300,000
Materials.................................	500,000	400,000

Required: Prepare the budgeted cost of goods manufactured and sold statement, showing the budgeted purchases of materials and the adjustments for inventories of materials, work in process, and finished goods.

8. Budgeted income statement. Starnes Company has just received a franchise to distribute air conditioners. The company began business on January 1 with the following assets:

Cash	$ 45,000
Inventory	94,000
Warehouse, office, and delivery facilities and equipment	800,000

All facilities and equipment have a useful life of 20 years and no residual value. First quarter sales are expected to be $360,000 and should be doubled in the second quarter. Third quarter sales are expected to be $1,080,000. Two percent of sales are considered to be uncollectible. The gross profit margin should be 30%. Variable marketing expenses (except uncollectible accounts) are budgeted at 10% of sales and fixed marketing expenses at $48,000 per quarter, exclusive of depreciation. Variable administrative expenses are expected to be 3% of sales and fixed administrative expenses should total $34,200 per quarter, exclusive of depreciation.

Required: Prepare a budgeted income statement for the second quarter.

(CGAAC adapted)

9. Budgeted income statement. Calcor Company has been a wholesale distributor of automobile parts for domestic automakers for 20 years. Calcor has suffered through the recent slump in the domestic auto industry, and its performance has not rebounded to the levels of the industry as a whole.

Calcor's income statement for the year ended November 30, 19A, is as follows:

Calcor Company
Income Statement
For the Year Ended November 30, 19A
(000s omitted)

Net sales	$8,400
Expenses:	
Cost of goods sold	$6,300
Marketing expenses	780
Administrative expenses	900
Interest expense	140
Total expense	$8,120
Income before income tax	$ 280
Income tax	112
Net income	$ 168

Calcor's management team is considering the following actions for fiscal 19B, which they expect will improve profitability and result in a 5% increase in unit sales:

(a) Increase sales prices 10%.

(b) Increase advertising by $420,000 and hold all other marketing and administrative expenses at fiscal 19A levels.

(c) Improve customer service by increasing average current assets (inventory and accounts receivable) by a total of $300,000, and hold all other assets at fiscal 19A levels.

(d) Finance the additional assets at an annual interest rate of 10% and hold all other interest expense at fiscal 19A levels.

(e) Improve the quality of products carried; this will increase the unit cost of goods sold by 4%.

Calcor's 19B effective income tax rate is expected to be 40%—the same as in fiscal 19A.

Required: Prepare a budgeted income statement for Calcor Company for the year ending November 30, 19B, assuming that Calcor's planned actions would be carried out and that the 5% increase in unit sales would be realized.   (ICMA adapted)

PROBLEMS

15-1. **Sales and manufacturing budgets.** Scarborough Corporation manufactures and sells two products, Thingone and Thingtwo. In July, 19A, Scarborough's Budget Department gathered the following data in order to project sales and budget requirements for 19B:

19B projected sales:

Product	Units	Price
Thingone	60,000	$ 70
Thingtwo	40,000	100

19B inventories (in units):

Product	Expected—January 1, 19B	Desired—December 31, 19B
Thingone	20,000	25,000
Thingtwo	8,000	9,000

To produce one unit of Thingone and Thingtwo, the following raw materials are used:

Raw Material	Amount Used per Unit Thingone	Thingtwo
A	4 lbs.	5 lbs.
B	2 lbs.	3 lbs.
C	—	1 unit

Projected data for 19B with respect to raw materials are as follows:

Raw Material	Anticipated Purchase Price	Expected Inventories January 1, 19B	Desired Inventories December 31, 19B
A	$8	32,000 lbs.	36,000 lbs.
B	5	29,000 lbs.	32,000 lbs.
C	3	6,000 units	7,000 units

Projected direct labor requirements and rates for 19B are as follows:

Product	Hours per Unit	Rate per Hour
Thingone	2	$8
Thingtwo	3	9

Factory overhead is applied at the rate of $2 per direct labor hour.

Required: Based on the above projections and budget requirements for 19B for Thingone and Thingtwo, prepare the following 19B budgets:

(1) Sales budget.
(2) Production budget.
(3) Raw materials purchases budget.
(4) Direct labor budget.
(5) Budgeted finished goods inventory at December 31, 19B.   *(AICPA adapted)*

15-2. Production and direct labor budget. Roletter Company makes and sells artistic frames for pictures of weddings, graduations, christenings, and other special events. Lynn Anderson, controller, is responsible for preparing Roletter's budget and has accumulated the following information for 19B:

	19B				
	January	February	March	April	May
Estimated unit sales........................	10,000	12,000	8,000	9,000	9,000
Sales price per unit.........................	$50.00	$47.50	$47.50	$47.50	$47.50
Direct labor hours per unit..............	2.0	2.0	1.5	1.5	1.5
Wage per direct labor hour.............	$ 8.00	$ 8.00	$ 8.00	$ 9.00	$ 9.00

Labor-related costs include pension contributions of $.25 per hour, workers' compensation insurance of $.10 per hour, employee medical insurance of $.40 per hour, and social security and unemployment taxes of 10% of wages. The cost of employee benefits paid by Roletter on its employees is treated as a direct labor cost.

Roletter has a labor contract that calls for a wage increase to $9 per hour on April 1, 19B. New labor saving machinery has been installed and will be fully operational by March 1, 19B.

Roletter expects to have 16,000 frames on hand at December 31, 19A, and has a policy of carrying an end-of-month inventory of 100% of the following month's sales plus 50% of the second following month's sales.

Required:

(1) Prepare a production budget and a direct labor budget for Roletter Company by month and for the first quarter of 19B. Both budgets may be combined in one schedule. The direct labor budget should include direct labor hours and show the detail for each direct labor cost category.
(2) For each item used in Roletter's production budget and its direct labor budget, identify the other component(s) of the periodic budget that would also use these data.   *(ICMA adapted)*

15-3. Production and manufacturing budgets. The following data are provided for Hanska Corporation:
Sales:
Sales through June 30, 19A, the first six months of the current year, are 24,000 units. Expected sales for the full year are 60,000 units. Actual sales in units for May and June and estimated unit sales for the next four months are as follows:

May...............................	4,000 units
June...............................	4,000
July	5,000
August............................	6,000
September.....................	7,000
October.........................	7,000

Direct materials:

At each month end, Hanska desires to have sufficient materials on hand to produce the next month's estimated sales. Data regarding materials are as follows:

Direct Material	Units of Material Required	Cost per Unit	Inventory Units, June 30, 19A
101	6	$2.40	35,000
211	4	3.60	30,000
242	2	1.20	14,000

Direct labor:

Process	Hours per Unit	Hourly Labor Rate
Forming.........................	.80	$8.00
Assembly.....................	2.00	5.50
Finishing.....................	.25	6.00

Factory overhead:

The company produced 27,000 units during the six-month period through June 30, 19A, and expects to produce 60,000 units during the year. The actual variable factory overhead costs incurred during this six-month period are as follows. The controller believes that these costs will be incurred at the same rate during the remainder of 19A.

Supplies..	$ 59,400
Electricity..	27,000
Indirect labor...	54,000
Other...	21,600
Total variable factory overhead....................	$162,000

The fixed factory overhead costs incurred during the first six months of 19A amounted to $93,000. Fixed overhead costs are budgeted for the full year as follows:

Supervision..	$ 60,000
Property tax..	7,200
Depreciation...	86,400
Other...	32,400
Total fixed factory overhead.........................	$186,000

Finished goods inventory:

The desired monthly ending finished goods inventory in units is 80% of the next month's estimated sales. There are 5,600 finished units in the June 30, 19A inventory.

Required:

(1) Prepare the production budget for the third quarter ending September 30, 19A.
(2) Prepare the direct materials purchases budget for the third quarter.
(3) Prepare the direct labor budget for the third quarter.
(4) Prepare the factory overhead budget for the six months ending December 31, 19A, presenting two figures, i.e., for total variable and fixed overhead.

(ICMA adapted)

15-4. Sales budget; purchases and materials requirements. The management of Bannister Food Products decided to install a budgetary control system under the supervision of a budget director and a committee. Among its products, the company manufactures a patented breakfast food that is sold in packages of two sizes—1 lb. and 2 lb. The cereal is made from two types of grain, called R(rye) and S(soy) for this purpose. There are two operations: (a) processing and blending and (b) packaging. The grains are purchased by the bushel measure, a bushel of R containing 70 lbs. and a bushel of S containing 80 lbs. Three bushels of grain mixed in the proportion of 2R:1S produce 198 lbs. of finished product. The entire loss occurs in the first department.

To prepare estimated sales figures for the first six months of the coming year, the budget committee first asked the salespeople to prepare sales estimates in units. The following data were submitted:

	Territories				
	I	II	III	Other	6-Month Total
1-lb. package.....................	10,000	15,000	12,000	613,000	650,000
2-lb. package.....................	12,000	18,000	12,000	783,000	825,000
Total.................................	22,000	33,000	24,000	1,396,000	1,475,000

The figures submitted are analyzed by the budget committee in the light of general business conditions. The company uses the Federal Reserve Board Index together with its own trade index to prepare a trend percentage that exists in the business. The trend percentage indicates that a .90 general index figure should be applied to the estimates in order to arrive at the final sales figures. The finished goods inventory is to be kept at zero if possible. The work in process inventory is to be kept near the present level, which is about 160,000 lbs. of blended material.

Factory facilities permit processing sales requirements as stated in the sales budget. The production manager decided to accept the monthly sales figures for the production budget.

Purchases of grains in bushels have been arranged as follows:

	Type R		Type S	
	Quantity	Price	Quantity	Price
January..	5,000 bu.	$1.30	2,000 bu.	$1.20
February..	2,000	1.40	1,000	1.20
March...	-0-	-0-	3,000	1.25
April..	8,000	1.50	3,000	1.00
May...	3,000	1.50	-0-	-0-
June..	4,000	1.60	4,000	1.00
Beginning inventory, January 1.....................	10,000	1.20	3,000	1.00

Materials are charged into production on the fifo basis.

Required:

(1) Prepare a revised sales budget in units for the six-month period, based on the index.
(2) Prepare a sales budget in dollars, assuming that the 1-lb. package sells for $.25 and the 2-lb. package for $.50.
(3) Prepare a schedule of materials purchases.
(4) Prepare a computation of materials requirements for production. (Round off to the nearest whole amount.)
(5) Prepare a schedule of the materials account (fifo basis), in units and dollars, indicating beginning inventory, purchases, usage, and ending inventory for the six-month period taken as a whole.

15-5. Budgeted income statement. The president of a hardware manufacturing company has asked the controller to prepare an income forecast for the next year, by quarters, with sales reported for each of the two major segments—commercial and government.

The Marketing Department provided the following sales estimates:

	1st Quarter	2d Quarter	3d Quarter	4th Quarter
Commercial sales......................	$250,000	$266,000	$275,000	$300,000
Government sales.....................	100,000	120,000	110,000	115,000

The controller's office assembled these figures:

    (a) Cost of goods sold: 46% of total sales.
    (b) Advertising expenditures: $6,000 each quarter.
    (c) Selling expenses: 10% of total sales.
    (d) Administrative expenses: 16.8% of gross profit.
    (e) General office expenses: 12% of gross profit.
    (f) Other income: $8,000 per quarter.
    (g) Corporate income tax rate: 40%.

Required:

    (1) Prepare a budgeted income statement, by quarters and in total. All figures should be shown in thousands of dollars and rounded to the nearest thousand, adding four quarters across to obtain total figures.
    (2) Prepare an analysis of the effect of a 5% increase in commercial sales revenue, using the same income statement format as for (1).

15-6. Preliminary profit plan. Yorio Food Manufacturing Company is a medium-size publicly held corporation, producing a variety of consumer food and specialty products. Current-year data were prepared as follows for the salad dressing product line, using five months of actual expenses and a seven-month projection:

Projected Income Statement
For the Year Ending December 31, 19A
(5 months actual; 7 months projected)
(000s omitted)

Volume in gallons...	5,000
Gross sales..	$30,000
Freight, allowances, and discounts.....................	3,000
Net sales..	$27,000
Less manufacturing costs:	
Variable...	$13,500
Fixed..	2,100
Depreciation..	700
Total manufacturing cost.................................	$16,300
Gross profit..	$10,700
Less expenses:	
Marketing...	$ 4,000
Brokerage...	1,650
General and administrative...............................	2,100
Research and development..............................	500
Total expenses..	$ 8,250
Income before income tax....................................	$ 2,450

The current-year projection was accepted as being accurate, but it was agreed that the projected income was not at a satisfactory level. The president wants, at a minimum, a 15% increase in gross sales dollars and not less than 10% before-tax profit on gross sales for 19B. The president also intends to reduce general and administrative expenses $200,000 to help achieve the profit goal.

Both the vice-president—marketing and the vice-president—production felt that the president's objectives would be difficult to achieve; however, they offered the following suggestions to reach the objectives:

(a) Sales volume—Yorio's current share of the salad dressing market is 15% and the total salad dressing market is expected to increase by 5% for 19B. Yorio's current market share can be maintained by a marketing expenditure of $4,200,000. The two vice-presidents estimated that the market share could be increased by additional expenditures for advertising and sales promotion. For an additional expenditure of $525,000, the market share can be raised by one percentage point until the market share reaches 17%. To achieve further market penetration, an additional $875,000 must be spent for each percentage point until the market share reaches 20%. Any advertising and promotion expenditures beyond this level are not likely to increase the market share to more than 20%.

(b) Sales price—The sales price, which will remain at $6 per gallon, is very closely related to the cost of the ingredients, which is not expected to change in 19B from that experienced in 19A.

(c) Variable manufacturing cost—Variable manufacturing cost is projected at 50% of the net sales dollar (gross sales less freight, allowances, and discounts).

(d) Fixed manufacturing cost—An increase of $100,000 is projected for 19B.

(e) Depreciation—A projected increase in equipment will increase depreciation by $25,000 over the 19A projection.

(f) Freight, allowances, and discounts—The current rate of 10% of gross sales dollars is expected to continue in 19B.

(g) Brokerage expense—A rate of 5% of gross sales dollars is projected for 19B.

(h) General and administrative expense—A $200,000 decrease in general and administrative expense from the 19A forecast is projected, an amount consistent with the president's commitment.

(i) Research and development expense—A 5% increase from the absolute dollars in the 19A forecast will be necessary to meet divisional research targets.

Required: Prepare a profit plan (budgeted income statements) for 15% through 20% market shares, at 1% increments, indicating the market share percentage most in harmony with the president's objectives.   (ICMA adapted)

15-7. Budgeted income statement and related schedules. A1 Sound Systems manufactures speakers for component stereo systems. Three models are produced: Model 150, Model 100, and Model 50. The speakers are marketed in two regions, the South and Southwest. The production departments are designated Cutting, Assembling, and Finishing. Lumber, speakers, and a finishing compound are the materials used in producing the speakers.

The following estimates have been made for the coming year:

(a) Sales forecast:

Model	South	Southwest	Sales Price
150........................	3,000 units	4,000 units	$175 per unit
100........................	5,000	7,000	120
50........................	7,000	8,000	90

(b) Inventories:
   Materials:

	Beginning Inventory	Ending Inventory	
	Units	Units	Unit Cost
Lumber (board feet).....................	40,000	30,000	$ .75
Speakers..	10,000	8,000	15.00
Finish (pints).................................	1,500	2,000	2.00

Work in process: None at the beginning or end of the period.

Finished goods (fifo):

Model	Beginning Inventory		Ending Inventory	
	Units	Unit Cost	Units	Unit Cost
150....................	200	$98.00	200	$105.50
100....................	300	62.00	400	66.75
50....................	400	47.00	300	50.25

(c) Materials requirements:

Model	Lumber (Board Feet)	Speakers	Finish (Pints)
150....................	12	5	2
100....................	8	3	1
50....................	6	2	1

(d) Estimated materials cost:
   Lumber, $.75 per board foot
   Speakers, $15 per speaker
   Finish, $2 per pint

(e) Estimated labor cost:

	Cutting	Assembling	Finishing
Rate per hour.....................	$6.00	$5.00	$4.00

Estimated labor time requirements:

Model	Cutting	Assembling	Finishing
150....................	.375 hour	2.0 hours	.375 hour
100....................	.375	1.5	.250
50....................	.375	1.5	.250

(f) Factory overhead budgets show the following unit overhead rates:

Model	Cutting	Assembling	Finishing
150....................	$1.00	$2.00	$.75
100....................	1.00	1.50	.50
50....................	1.00	1.50	.50

(g) Marketing expenses: $500,000.
   Administrative expenses: $300,000.
   Income tax rate: 50%.

Required: Prepare annual budget schedules utilizing the budget estimates provided. The schedules should be designed to provide essential data in an easily understood form. Titles and schedule numbers to be used are as follows. Cross-references should be made using schedule numbers.

Schedule	Title
(1)	Sales budget—by models and by sales regions
(2)	Production budget—by models and by units
(3)	Direct materials budget in units—by materials and by models
(4)	Purchases budget—by materials and by cost
(5)	Cost of materials required for production—by materials and by models
(6)	Direct labor budget—by models and by departments
(7)	Factory overhead budget (applied overhead)—by models and by departments
(8)	Beginning and ending inventories—by materials and by models
(9)	Budgeted cost of goods manufactured and sold statement
(10)	Budgeted income statement—with each item shown as a percentage of sales (round off percentages to the nearest tenth of a percent)

CASES

A. Need for profit planning. George Mai invented a special valve for application in the paper manufacturing industry. At the time of its development, he could not find any company willing to manufacture the valve. As a result, he formed Maiton Company to manufacture and sell the valve.

Maiton Company grew quite slowly. George Mai found it difficult to persuade paper companies to try this new valve designed and manufactured by an unknown company. However, the company has prospered and now has a number of smaller paper companies as regular customers. In fact, there is increasing interest by a number of large paper companies because of the very good results experienced by the smaller paper companies.

The size of the potential new customers and their probable needs over the next several years will dramatically increase the sales of the valve. George Mai was an engineer for a large company prior to his invention. His business experience is limited to the activities of Maiton Company.

Required:

(1) Explain why it is important for George Mai to introduce business planning and budgeting activities into his company at this time.

(2) Identify major problems that likely would be disclosed as Maiton Company attempts to prepare a five-year plan. Explain why the problems identified were selected.   (ICMA adapted)

B. Long-range planning; periodic sales budget. Marval Products manufactures and wholesales several lines of luggage. Each luggage line consists of various pieces and sizes. One line is a complete set of luggage designed to be used by both men and women, but some lines are designed specifically for men or women. Some lines also have matching attaché cases. Luggage lines are discontinued and introduced as tastes change or as product improvements are developed.

Marval Products also manufactures luggage for large retail companies according to each company's specifications. This luggage is marketed under the retail companies' own private labels rather than the Marval label.

Marval has been manufacturing several lines of luggage under its own label and private lines for retail companies for the last ten years.

Required:

(1) Identify the factors Marval Products needs to consider in its periodic review of long-range planning.

(2) Identify the factors Marval Products needs to consider when developing its sales component of the annual budget. *(ICMA adapted)*

C. Budget preparation.

RV Industries manufactures and sells recreation vehicles. The company has eight divisions strategically located near major markets. Each division has a sales force and two to four manufacturing plants. These divisions operate as autonomous profit centers responsible for purchasing, operations, and sales.

Dale Collins, the corporate controller, described the divisional performance measurement system as follows: "We allow the divisions to control the entire operation from the purchase of raw materials to the sale of the product. We, at corporate headquarters, only get involved in strategic decisions, such as developing new product lines. Each division is responsible for meeting its market needs by providing the right products at a low cost on a timely basis. Frankly, the divisions need to focus on cost control, delivery, and services to customers in order to become more profitable.

"While we give the divisions considerable autonomy, we watch their monthly income statements very closely. Each month's actual performance is compared with the budget in considerable detail. If the actual sales or contribution margin is more than 4 or 5% below the budget, we jump on the division people immediately. I might add that we don't have much trouble getting their attention. All of the management people at the plant and division level can add appreciably to their annual salaries with bonuses if their actual profit is considerably greater than budget."

The budgeting process begins in August when division sales managers, after consulting with their sales personnel, estimate sales for the next calendar year. These estimates are sent to plant managers who use the sales forecasts to prepare production estimates. At the plants, production statistics, including raw material quantities, labor hours, production schedules, and output quantities, are developed by operating personnel. Using the statistics prepared by the operating personnel, the plant accounting staff determines costs and prepares the plant's budgeted variable cost of goods sold and other plant expenses for each month of the coming calendar year.

In October, each division's accounting staff combines plant budgets with sales estimates and adds additional division expenses. "After the divisional management is satisfied with the budget," said Collins, "I visit each division to go over their budget and make sure it is in line with corporate strategy and projections. I really emphasize the sales forecasts because of the volatility in the demand for our product. For many years, we lost sales to our competitors because we didn't project high enough production and sales, and we couldn't meet the market demand. More recently, we were caught with large excess inventory when the bottom dropped out of the market for recreational vehicles.

"I generally visit all eight divisions during the first two weeks in November. After that, the division budgets are combined and reconciled by my staff, and they are ready for approval by the board of directors in early December. The board seldom questions the budget.

"One complaint we've had from plant and division management is that they are penalized for circumstances beyond their control. For example, they failed to predict the recent sales decline. As a result, they didn't make their budget and, of course, they received no bonuses. However, I point out that they are well rewarded when they exceed their budget. Furthermore, they provide most of the information for the budget, so it's their own fault if the budget is too optimistic."

Required: Discuss the following:

(1) Biases which corporate management should expect in the communication of budget estimates prepared by its division and plant personnel.
(2) Sources of information which corporate management can use to monitor the budget estimates prepared by its divisions and plants.

(3) Services which corporate management could offer the divisions to aid them in their budget development, without appearing to interfere with division budget decisions.

(4) Factors which corporate management should consider in deciding whether or not it should become more involved in the budget process. *(ICMA adapted)*

D. Evaluation of budget procedures. Schaffer Company, a large multidivision firm with several plants in each division, uses a comprehensive budgeting system for planning operations and measuring performance. The annual budgeting process begins in August, five months prior to the beginning of the fiscal year. At this time, the division managers submit proposed budgets for sales, production and inventory levels, and expenses. Capital expenditure requests also are formalized at this time. The expense budgets include direct labor and all factory overhead items, separated into fixed and variable components. Direct materials are budgeted separately in developing the production and inventory schedules.

The expense budgets for each division are developed from each plant's results, as measured by the percent variation from an adjusted budget in the first six months of the current year, and a target expense reduction percentage established by the corporation.

To determine plant percentages, the plant budget for the just completed half-year period is revised to recognize changes in operating procedures and costs outside the control of plant management (e.g., labor wage rate changes and product style changes). The difference between this revised budget and the actual expenses is the controllable variance, expressed as a percentage of the actual expenses. If unfavorable, this percentage is added to the corporate target expense reduction percentage. A favorable plant variance percentage is subtracted from the corporate target. If a plant had a 2% unfavorable controllable variance and the corporate target reduction was 4%, the plant's budget for next year should reflect costs approximately 6% below this year's actual costs.

Next year's final budgets for the corporation, its divisions, and plants are adopted after corporate analysis of the proposed budgets and a careful review with each division manager of the changes made by corporate management.

Division profit budgets include allocated corporate costs, and plant profit budgets include allocated division and corporate costs.

Required: Evaluate the budget procedures of Schaffer Company with respect to its effectiveness for planning and controlling operations. *(ICMA adapted)*

E. Budget evaluation. Executive management receives the following budget information for 19B from a subsidiary, the Papion Men's Clothing Company:

The Papion Men's Clothing Company expects the operating results for 19B to be better than for 19A, because several actions have been taken which will improve sales and solve operating problems. Sales should increase substantially due to the introduction of a new line of women's sportswear to be distributed through company-owned stores. Progress was also made last year in attracting other retailers to handle Papion's lines. Additional sales increases can be expected this year if negotiations to induce a major chain to distribute Papion lines are successful. The budget on the next page includes the sales expected to be made through this large chain retailer.

Operating costs should be lower this year. A new production facility should be completed in February to replace an older plant. This older plant has caused production shortages due to frequent equipment breakdowns. Also, labor problems which existed at the Midwest Plant have been resolved, thus correcting the lower output and higher costs of that plant.

Required:

(1) Evaluate the report's usefulness to executive management in exercising control over the subsidiary.

(2) Identify the report changes needed to improve its effectiveness in communicating Papion's 19B plans.

(ICMA adapted)

Original Budget for 19A
Forecast of Actual Operations for 19A
Proposed Budget for 19B
(000s omitted)

Prediction

	19A Budget *target*	19A Forecast of Actual Operations	19B Budget *target*
Sales...	$10,000	$8,500	$12,000
Cost of goods sold:			
Materials......................................	$ 1,050	$ 975	$ 1,260
Labor...	1,400	1,400	1,680
Factory overhead..........................	1,750	1,600	1,800
Marketing expenses:			
Sales force...................................	500	425	600
Advertising and promotion..............	600	500	950
Company stores.............................	1,000	950	1,100
General administration....................	750	755	825
Total expenses..............................	$ 7,050	$6,605	$ 8,215
Income before income tax...............	$ 2,950	$1,895	$ 3,785

Prepared and submitted: October, 19A.

F. Budgetary control. Two divisional managers of the same company were overheard in conversation:

Manager X: "You know, comparison of my division's performance against the budget shows my group falling further and further behind each month. I'm really depressed. Conditions in our markets have changed so much since the budget was established that there is no way I can achieve those figures. In fact, our divisional performance is worse and worse by comparison with the budget for the balance of the year."

Manager A: "Yes, I know what you mean and sympathize with you. I had that problem last year. But this year I'm in the opposite situation. Our actual performance vis-a-vis the budget just gets better and better. It's nothing we're doing—conditions in our markets have changed for the good since the budget was established. We are, in a sense, just along for the ride, but it sure makes me look good at the head office."

Required: Discuss the role of the budgeting process in achieving objectives and what (if anything) is wrong with the process in this company.   (CGAAC adapted)

CHAPTER 16

Budgeting: Capital Expenditures, Research and Development Expenditures, and Cash; PERT/Cost; The Flexible Budget

Budgeting is usually an iterative process. Budgets are prepared, reviewed, and revised until executive management is satisfied that the result represents the best plans that can be devised under existing circumstances. Furthermore, management may develop contingency plans for dealing with various eventualities. As the planning period unfolds, budget revisions may be required, and such revisions will be facilitated if management has anticipated alterations called for by changing circumstances and conditions.

This chapter discusses specific budgets, such as capital expenditures and research and development budgets, which play a significant part in the long- and short-range plans of any management. Closely related thereto is the cash budget, which reveals excesses or shortages of funds. The budgeted income statement (Chapter 15) and balance sheet serve as a master budget and final check on the ultimate results expected from the combined sales-cost-profit plan. Computerized budgeting, prospective financial information for external users, budgeting for nonmanufacturing businesses and nonprofit organizations, zero-base budgeting, PERT and PERT/cost, probabilistic budgets, and the flexible budget conclude the presentation.

▼ CAPITAL EXPENDITURES BUDGET

Capital expenditures are long-term commitments of resources to realize future benefits. Budgeting capital expenditures is one of the most important areas of managerial decision. Facility improvements and plant expansion programs must be geared to a limited supply of funds from internal operations and external sources. The magnitude of funds involved in each expenditure and the length of time required to recover the investment call for penetrating analysis and capable judgment. Decisions regarding current manufacturing

461

operations can always be changed, but because the benefits of a capital expenditure will be reaped over a fairly extended length of time, managerial errors could be quite costly.

Evaluating Capital Expenditures

To minimize the number of capital expenditure errors, many firms have established definite procedures for evaluating the merits of a project before funds are released. True control of capital expenditures is exercised in advance by requiring that each request be based on evaluation analyses, described and illustrated in Chapters 23 and 24. Managerial control requires facts regarding engineering estimates, expected sales volumes, production costs, and marketing costs. Management usually has a firm conviction as to what is consistent with the long-range objectives of the business. It is fundamentally interested in making certain that the project will contribute to the earnings position of the company.

Short- and Long-Range Capital Expenditures

Capital expenditure programs involve both short- and long-range projects. Short-range projects must be examined in the light of their economic worth as compared with other projects seeking final approval. The process of budgeting provides the only opportunity to examine these projects side by side and to evaluate their contribution to future periods. For short-range capital expenditures, the current budget should include a detailed capital expenditures budget as well as a determination of the impact on budgeted depreciation expense, cash, fixed asset, and liability accounts.

Long-range projects which will not be implemented in the current budget period need only be stated in general terms, since the exchange and addition of capital assets are only significant in the current budget period. In the main, long-range capital expenditure plans are a management responsibility and are translated into budget commitments only as the opportune time for their implementation approaches. Timing is most important to the achievement of the most profitable results in planning and budgeting capital expenditures.

▼ RESEARCH AND DEVELOPMENT BUDGET

Research and development (R & D) activities have been defined as follows:

1. *Research* is planned search or critical investigation aimed at discovery of new knowledge with the hope that such knowledge will be useful in developing a new product or service (hereinafter "product") or a new process or technique (hereinafter "process") or in bringing about a significant improvement to an existing product or process.
2. *Development* is the translation of research findings or other knowledge into a plan or design for a new product or process or for a significant

improvement to an existing product or process whether intended for sale or use. It includes the conceptual formulation, design, and testing of product alternatives, construction of prototypes, and operation of pilot plants. It does not include routine or periodic alterations to existing products, production lines, manufacturing processes, and other ongoing operations even though those alterations may represent improvements, and it does not include market research or market testing activities.[1]

The managements of many firms are acutely aware of the increased necessity for and rapid growth of research and development activities and of the need to consider their costs from both the long- and short-range points of view. From the long-range viewpoint, management must assure itself that a program is in line with future market trends and demands and that the future cost of a program is not at odds with forecast economic and financial conditions. From the short-range viewpoint, management must be assured that experimental efforts are being expended on programs which promise a satisfactory rate of return on the dollars invested.

R & D projects compete with other projects for available financial resources. The value of the research and development program must be shown as clearly as possible, so that management can compare it with similar programs and other investment opportunities. Therefore, the motivation and intent of experimental activities must be carefully identified.

R & D efforts may require significant resources and may involve considerable risk. The cost of the resources may be estimated by using a "rule of sevens." That is, if an incremental technology to be sold through existing channels costs $1 million for R & D, it will likely cost $7 million for design and $7 million more to produce the first commercial unit. To these costs must be added working capital requirements and consideration of lead time. Studies have shown that generally if the time to complete the research is one year, the time to produce the first unit is another three years, with still another two years before significant profit occurs.[2]

As to risk, on average the probabilities are .6, .6, and .7, respectively, of successfully completing the phases of (1) determining that the product is technologically sound, (2) deciding that the product can be commercially successful, and (3) actually achieving commercial success. Thus, one in four projects can be expected to succeed (.6 × .6 × .7 = .25). Therefore, while many businesses require R & D efforts, they should be planned with a realistic understanding of the associated resource commitment and risk.[3]

The research and development budget involves identifying program components and estimating their costs. Other planning devices are used at times, but the budget is considered best for (1) balancing the research and development program, (2) coordinating the program with the company's other

---

[1] *Statement of Financial Accounting Standards*, No. 2, "Accounting for Research and Development Costs" (Stamford: Financial Accounting Standards Board, 1974), par. 8.
[2] Francis W. Wolek, "The Business of Technology, Part I: A Board Guide to Progress and Profits," *Directors & Boards*, Vol. 9, No. 4, p. 33.
[3] *Ibid.*

projects, and (3) checking certain phases of nonfinancial planning. The budget forces management to think in advance about planned expenditures, both in total amounts and in sphere of effort. It helps achieve coordination, because it presents an overall picture of proposed R & D activities which can be reviewed and criticized by other operating managers. Exchange of opinions and information at planning meetings is management's best control over the program.

Another important purpose of research and development budgeting is to coordinate these plans with the immediate and long-term financial plans of the company. The budget also forces the R & D director and staff to think in advance about major aspects of the program: personnel requirements, individual or group work loads, equipment requirements, special materials, and necessary facilities. These phases of the research and development program are often overlooked or duplicated.

Forms of a Research and Development Budget

Management expects the R & D staff to present ideas along with a complete and detailed budget which can be evaluated as part of the entire planning program. The controller's staff may assist in the preparation of budgets with clearly defined goals and properly evaluated cost data.

Submission of data takes many forms. Information regarding segmentation and allocation of time and effort to various phases of the program is of particular interest to executive management as well as to divisional managers. The following example of a research and development budget has been proposed.[4]

RESEARCH AND DEVELOPMENT BUDGET
PROGRAM PLANNED FOR 19—

(Percentages of Total Effort by Area of Inquiry and by Phase)

Phase	Cost Reduction			Improved Products			New Products			Total
	A*	B	C	A	B	C	A	B	C	
Basic research	4%	3%	3%	2%	4%	4%	1%	1%	3%	25%
Applied research	5	12	3	4	1		2		3	30
Development	7	6	2	5			10		15	45
Total by product lines	16%	21%	8%	11%	5%	4%	13%	1%	21%	100%
Total by area of inquiry		45%			20%			35%		

*A, B, and C refer to product lines.

---

[4]J. B. Quinn, "Study of the Usefulness of Research and Development Budgets," *NAA Bulletin*, Vol. XL, No. 1, pp. 79-90. Copyright July, 1958, by the National Association of Accountants. All rights reserved. Reprinted by permission.

The overall R & D program should be supported by a specific budget request which indicates the jobs or steps within each project, the necessary labor hours, the service department time required, and required direct departmental funds. Each active project should be reviewed monthly, comparing projected plans with results attained.

The Franklin Company illustration from the preceding chapter did not include budgeted research and development expenditures. Such a budget could be detailed in dollars, using a format similar to the budget shown above. The dollar amount would be included in the budgeted income statement, consistent with the accounting procedures described in the following paragraph.

Accounting for Research and Development Costs

Research and development costs generally should be expensed in the period incurred because of the uncertainty of the extent or length of future benefit to the company. An exception to the expensing requirement applies to costs of R & D expenditures that are (1) conducted for others, (2) unique to extractive industries, or (3) incurred by a government-regulated enterprise, such as a public utility, which often defers research and development costs because of the rate-regulated aspects of its business. Equipment and purchased intangibles having alternative future uses should be recorded as assets and expensed through depreciation or amortization. R & D costs, when expensed, should be reported as one item in the operating expense section of the income statement.[5]

For government contract costing, the Cost Accounting Standards Board promulgated a standard dealing with accounting for independent research and development costs and bid and proposal costs. It provides criteria for (1) accumulation of such costs, (2) their allocation among contractor divisions, and (3) allocation of these costs to contracts.[6]

▼ CASH BUDGET

A *cash budget* involves detailed estimates of anticipated cash receipts and disbursements for the budget period or some other specific period. It has generally been recognized as an extremely useful and essential management tool. Planning and controlling cash is basic to good management.

Effective cash management entails having the right amounts of cash in the right places at the right times. It involves the management of flows of cash by looking at an organization's liquid funds as an income-producing asset rather

---

[5]*Statement of Financial Accounting Standards, No. 2, op. cit.,* pars. 2, 3, and 11-14.
[6]For specifics, see *Standards, Rules and Regulations, Part 420,* "Accounting for Independent Research and Development Costs and Bid and Proposal Costs" (Washington, D.C.: Cost Accounting Standards Board, 1980).

than simply as currency for paying bills. Even if a company does not prepare extensive budgets for sales and production, it should set up a budget or estimate of cash receipts and disbursements as an aid to cash management.

Purpose and Nature of a Cash Budget

A cash budget:

1. Indicates cash requirements needed for current operating activities.
2. Aids in focusing on cash usage priorities currently unavoidable and required versus postponable or permanently avoidable.
3. Indicates the effect on the cash position of seasonal requirements, large inventories, unusual receipts, and slowness in collecting receivables.
4. Indicates the availability of cash for taking advantage of discounts.
5. Indicates the cash requirements for a plant or equipment expansion program.
6. Assists in planning the financial requirements of bond retirements, income tax installments, and payments to pension and retirement funds.
7. Shows the availability of excess funds for short-term or long-term investments.
8. Shows the need for additional funds from sources such as bank loans or sales of securities and the time factors involved. In this connection, it might also exert a cautionary influence on plans for plant expansion, leading to a modification of capital expenditure decisions.
9. Serves as a basis for evaluating the actual cash management performance of responsible individuals, using measurement criteria such as the target average daily balance as compared with the actual average daily balance in each cash account.

The cash budget for different time spans has different uses and origins. A long-range cash projection, which may cover periods ranging from three to five years, is useful in planning business growth, investments in projects, and introduction of new products. It focuses primarily on significant changes in the firm's cash position. A medium-range cash budget is related to the overall periodic, usually yearly, budgeting procedures for the business, detailed by quarters and months. Improved cash utilization within this time frame is obtained through control of accounts payable policies, control of inventory turnover, and a review of credit, billing, and collection procedures. The short-range cash budget details the daily availability of cash for current operations, usually 30 to 60 days, and indicates any need for short-term financing. This kind of projection generally is based on records of current transactions of the business.[7]

---

[7]Robert A. Leitch, John B. Barrack, and Sue H. McKinley, "Controlling Your Cash Resources," *Management Accounting*, Vol. LXII, No. 4, p. 59.

Preparation of a Periodic Cash Budget

Preparation of a periodic cash budget involves estimating cash receipts and disbursements by time periods. All anticipated cash receipts, such as cash sales, cash collections of accounts receivable, dividends, interest on notes and bonds, proceeds from sales of assets, royalties, bank loans, and stock sales, are carefully estimated. Likewise, cash requirements for materials purchases, supplies, payroll, repayment of loans, dividends, taxes, and purchases of plant or equipment must be determined.

The primary sources of cash receipts are cash sales and collections of accounts receivable. Estimates of collections of accounts receivable are based on the sales budget and on the company's collection experience. A study is made of a representative period to determine how customers pay their accounts, how many take the discount offered, and how many pay within 10 days, 30 days, and so forth. These experiences are set up in a schedule of anticipated collections from credit sales. Collections during a month will be the result of (1) this month's sales and (2) accounts receivable of prior months' sales. Seasonal variations should also be considered if they affect the collections pattern. To illustrate, assume that during each month, collections of credit sales show the following pattern:

From this month's sales..	10.8%
From prior months' accounts receivable:	
Last month's sales..	77.4
2 months old..	6.3
3 months old..	2.1
4 months old..	1.2
Cash discounts taken..	1.2
Doubtful accounts..	1.0
	100.0%

On the basis of these percentages, collections for January, as an illustrative month, are computed as follows:

Month	Assumed Estimate of Credit Sales	%	Collections
January...	$400,000	10.8	$ 43,200
December...	385,000	77.4	297,990
November...	420,000	6.3	26,460
October..	360,000	2.1	7,560
September..	340,000	1.2	4,080
Total collections for January........................			$379,290

Estimated cash disbursements are computed from the:

1. Purchases budget, which shows planned purchases of materials and supplies.
2. Direct labor budget, which indicates direct labor wages to be paid.
3. Various types of expense budgets, both factory overhead and commercial, which indicate expenses expected to be incurred. Noncash expenses such as depreciation are excluded.

4. Plant and equipment budget, which details cash needed for the purchase of new equipment or replacements.
5. Treasurer's budget, which indicates requirements for items such as dividends, interest and payments on loans and bonds, donations, and income tax.

For each item, the estimated timing of the cash disbursements is required. If indebtedness does not occur uniformly, variations in the pattern should be considered in estimating the timing of cash disbursements.

A cash budget includes no accrual items. For example, assume that direct labor payroll accrued at the beginning and the end of January is $14,800 and $13,300, respectively, and the budget shows that $90,000 will be earned by direct labor employees. The treasurer computes the monthly cash requirement for the direct labor payroll as follows:

Accrued payroll at beginning of January..............................	$ 14,800
Add payroll earned as per budget...	90,000
	$104,800
Deduct accrued payroll at end of January............................	13,300
Amount of cash to be paid out during January.....................	$ 91,500

A similar approach can be used to estimate the timing of other cash disbursements as well. Alternatively, a cash payment may be estimated in the following manner. Assume that direct materials purchases and other items such as factory overhead and commercial expenses occur fairly uniformly throughout each month and that approximately ten days (⅓ month) normally elapse between the recording of an indebtedness and its payment. Assume further that cash discounts are always taken and that they average 2 percent. Using data that would be obtained from the direct materials budget, the January cash disbursement for direct materials purchased is:

December purchases [($200,000 − 2% cash discount) × ⅓ paid in January]..	$ 65,333
January purchases [($130,000 − 2% cash discount) × ⅔ paid in January]..	84,933
January cash disbursement for direct materials purchased..	$150,266

After all the cash receipts and cash disbursements have been estimated for each month of the budget year, the year-end cash balance for inclusion in the budgeted balance sheet can be determined. This amount is the beginning of the budget year's cash balance, plus the estimated total annual cash receipts from all sources, less the estimated total annual disbursements necessary to satisfy all cash demands.

Development of Daily Cash Budget Detail

Daily cash receipts and disbursements schedules are necessary for prudent and efficient cash management. Such schedules bring the focus of the cash budget to the most relevant time frame.

Development of daily cash budget detail begins with identification of the timing of major cash flows for items such as taxes, dividends, lease payments, debt service, and wages. Most major cash flows are either easily forecast or if not forecastable, are offset by a single financial transaction, such as the use of short-term borrowing for an outflow or short-term investing for an inflow.

Numerous small receipts and payments may also occur. These minor flows are amenable to some combination of two basic approaches—distribution and scheduling. *Distribution* refers to using statistical estimation to spread a forecast of the total monthly minor flow components over the days of the month in order to reflect the known intramonth cash flow.[8] *Scheduling* refers to the construction of a forecast from information-system-based data, such as disbursement data from invoices, purchase authorizations, production schedules, and work plans.

Electronic Cash Management

The basic premise of cash management is that dollars in transit are not earning assets. They cannot be utilized until they are available as deposits. Similarly, cash lying idle in checking accounts contributes nothing to corporate profitability.

Organizations with multiple, geographically dispersed units, or firms with a widespread customer base making individual payments to dispersed collecting units can especially benefit from electronic cash management systems. The system involves cash concentration by means of nationwide electronic transfers which accelerate the collection of deposits from local banks into a central account on a same-day basis. By drawing checks on its centrally located account, the firm has the additional advantage of *float* for the time it takes the check to be cleared back to the central bank account.

For whatever number of bank accounts a firm may have, electronic balance reporting affords a valuable aid to efficient and effective cash management. This bank service provides accurate, up-to-date, and on-line daily information on amounts and locations of available cash. Depending on the level of service, the information furnished may be highly detailed, via a computer terminal, or abbreviated by means of a telephone-to-computer inquiry that results in each bank's computer "telling" the firm's balances. This information is especially useful in the short-term investment management of the day-to-day difference between the firm's book balance of cash and the bank's balance, that is, in the management of float.

Another and broader electronic cash management application is found in *electronic funds transfer systems* (EFTS). These systems are designed to reduce the number of paper documents and to increase the use of electronic data in carrying out banking cash transfer functions, thus reducing bank transaction costs and expediting cash transfers. These developing cash payment systems include unstaffed customer banking facilities, automated clearinghouses for

---

[8]For an illustration of this procedure, see Bernell K. Stone and Robert A. Wood, "Daily Cash Forecasting: A Simple Method for Implementing the Distribution Approach," *Financial Management*, Vol. 6, No. 3, pp. 40-50.

interbank cash transfers, point-of-sale facilities, pay-by-phone service, and corporate funds transfers.[9] For the manager, the potential for virtually instantaneous receipts and payments of cash requires consideration in the management of cash resources.

▼ BUDGETED BALANCE SHEET

A balance sheet for the beginning of the budget period is the starting point in preparing a budgeted balance sheet for the end of the budget period. The following budgeted balance sheet for Franklin Company incorporates all changes in assets, liabilities, and stockholders' equity in the budgets submitted by the various departments, functions, or segments.

Franklin Company
Budgeted Balance Sheet
At December 31, 19—

Assets

Cash...		$ 245,750
Accounts receivable..	$ 370,265	
Less allowance for doubtful accounts.....................	7,400	362,865
Inventories:		
Finished goods...		81,675
Materials..		214,250
Plant and equipment..	$1,604,740	
Less accumulated depreciation.............................	418,610	1,186,130
Other assets..		143,834
Total assets...		$2,234,504

Liabilities and Stockholders' Equity

Current liabilities...	$ 327,942
Long-term debt..	450,000
Common stock...	800,000
Retained earnings..	656,562
Total liabilities and stockholders' equity................	$2,234,504

The finished goods and materials inventory balances agree with those shown in the company's budgeted cost of goods manufactured and sold statement on page 442. While these inventory account changes are directly related to income statement transactions, other accounts may be affected in part by non-income statement transactions. For example, in the case of cash, proceeds from a bank loan or the payment of a cash dividend to stockholders are of the latter type of transaction.

Numerous advantages result from the preparation of a budgeted balance sheet. One advantage is that it discloses unfavorable ratios which management may wish to change for various reasons. Unfavorable ratios can lower credit ratings or cause a drop in the value of the corporation's securities. A second advantage is that it serves as a check on the accuracy of all other budgets. Still

---

[9]Howard C. Johnson and Edward C. Arnold, "The Emerging Revolution in Electronic Payments," *Price Waterhouse Review*, Vol. 22, No. 3, pp. 26-31.

another advantage is that a return-on-investment ratio can be computed by relating net income to capital employed. An inadequate return on investment would suggest a need for budget changes.

▼ COMPUTERIZED BUDGETING[10]

The time required to assemble the periodic budget and to achieve a consensus of the managers involved is so great that the budgeting process is often inhibited. Time constraints may be handled more effectively, however, by converting the elements of the conventional budgeting process into a functional planning tool through the use of computer modeling techniques. Tedious arithmetic can be eliminated by converting budgeting procedures into a computerized set of straightforward algebraic formulas. The resulting computerized model entails the following primary components:

1. A line-by-line outline which describes the format of the desired output of budget schedules and statements.
2. A structure of algebraic logic or procedures which demonstrates the computational processes in simple formulas.
3. Elements of data which, when passed through the computational process, will generate the desired output.

The development of a computerized budgeting process can result in substantial benefits. These benefits include:

1. Shortening the planning cycle time. By reducing computational effort, it is frequently possible to delay the start of budget preparation until more accurate inputs are available. Thus the quality of sales and cost estimates may be improved.
2. Reconsidering planning assumptions. Time savings make it feasible to reconsider planning assumptions early in the budgeting process. Cost and profit implications of various assumptions can be estimated before any commitment is made.
3. Continuous budgeting. Plans can be updated continuously throughout the budget period and, in some cases, planning horizons can be extended beyond the current budget period.
4. Operating analysis capability. If procedures and data are maintained in current form, the computerized model is available to produce instant answers to "what if" questions. More alternatives can be evaluated when such a model is used.
5. Discipline. Development of a model requires precise understanding and definition of the organization and its accounting system. Therefore, the discipline of developing the relationships inherent in a computerized budgeting model is of itself a valuable learning experience.

---

[10]This discussion adapted from Richard C. Murphy, "A Computerized Model Approach to Budgeting," *Management Accounting*, Vol. LVI, No. 12, pp. 34-36, 38.

▼ PROSPECTIVE FINANCIAL INFORMATION FOR EXTERNAL USERS

Recent years have seen increasing recognition of the importance of prospective financial information for external users, because investors and potential investors seek to enhance the process of predicting the future. What has happened in the past, as reported in the financial statements, may be viewed as an indicator of the future. Often, however, past results may not be indicative of future expectations and may need to be tempered accordingly.

The question of whether prospective information should be included in external financial statements is controversial. Opponents point out that the uncertainty of such information and the potential dangers of undue reliance upon it could result in added legal liability, a drop in credibility, or both. These concerns and potentially advantageous disclosures to competitors have been cited as causes of widespread opposition by management. On the positive side, however, it has been argued that the inclusion of prospective information in external financial statements "should be provided when it will enhance the reliability of user's predictions."[11]

In 1985, the AICPA issued a statement which establishes detailed procedures and reporting standards for engagements to examine, compile, or apply agreed-upon procedures to prospective financial information. Included are financial forecasts and financial projections. *Financial forecasts* are defined as an entity's expected financial position, results of operations, and changes in financial position, reflecting conditions expected to exist and the course of action expected to be taken. A financial forecast may be expressed in specific monetary amounts as a single point estimate of forecasted results or as a range.

Financial projections present an entity's financial statements based on one or more hypothetical assumptions. One or more hypothetical courses of action may be presented for evaluation, as in a response to a question such as "What would happen if . . . ?" The presentation reflects conditions expected to exist and the course of action expected to be taken, given the assumptions. A projection, like a forecast, may contain a range.

The AICPA statement includes minimum presentation guidelines. Generally, the prospective financial information should be in the format of the historical financial statements and should include a description of what management intends to present, a statement that the assumptions are based on information existing at the time the prospective information was prepared, a caveat that the prospective results may not be achieved, and a summary of significant assumptions.[12]

Securities and Exchange Commission regulations presently encourage but do not require inclusion of prospective financial data in external financial reports. Furthermore, a safe harbor rule gives SEC-regulated companies and their auditors protection from legal liability should public prospective

---

[11]Report of the Study Group on the Objectives of Financial Statements, *Objectives of Financial Statements* (New York: American Institute of Certified Public Accountants, 1973), p. 46.

[12]*Statement on Standards for Accountants' Services on Prospective Financial Information*, "Financial Forecasts and Projections" (New York: American Institute of Certified Public Accountants, 1985).

information fail to materialize. For the rule to apply, forecasts and projections must be made on a reasonable basis, in good faith, with assumptions disclosed. The Commission requires that materially incorrect predictions be corrected in subsequent financial reports. SEC guidelines are in harmony with AICPA requirements.

▼ PLANNING AND BUDGETING FOR NONMANUFACTURING BUSINESSES AND NONPROFIT ORGANIZATIONS

Many industrial concerns still pay only lip service to the suggested steps, methods, and procedures of budgeting. To an even greater extent, nonmanufacturing businesses—and especially nonprofit organizations—lack effective planning and control mechanisms. However, examples of effective budgeting do exist.

Nonmanufacturing Businesses

Under the guidance of the National Retail Merchants Association, department stores have followed merchandise budget procedures that have a long and quite successful history. A budget for a retail store is a necessity, since the profit per dollar of sales is generally low—usually from 1 to 3 percent. Planning, budgeting, and control administration is strongly oriented toward profit control on the total store as well as on a departmental basis. The merchandise budget shows predetermined sales and profits, generally on a six-month basis following the two merchandising seasons: spring-summer and fall-winter. The merchandise budget includes sales, purchases, expenses, capital expenditures, cash, and annual statements.

Although it is logical for a department store or a wholesaler to plan and budget its activities, banks, savings and loan associations, and insurance companies should also create a long-range profit plan coordinating long-term goals and objectives of the institution. In these businesses, forecasting would deal with deposit size and mix, number of insured and mix of policies, capital requirements, types of earning assets, physical facilities, personnel requirements, operational changes, and new, additional, or changed depositor or client services. The long-range goal should be translated into short-range budgets, starting at the lowest level of responsibility, building and combining the various organizational units into a whole.

Nonprofit Organizations

While business organizations are concerned with profits, the nonprofit sector is concerned with programs. Yet neither can succeed without sound budgeting. Management in a nonprofit organization, as in any entity, is a process that entails planning, resource allocation, execution, and evaluation. Budgeting is the common denominator that links these management activities.

Periodic budgets in any enterprise, nonprofit or business, are usually conceived at the bottom of the organizational hierarchy and then passed upward for refinement and approval. Department managers in nonprofit organizations develop their program needs in the context of policies, priorities, and assumptions expressed in long-range plans and in accordance with periodic budget guidelines established by senior management. A comprehensive budget format is required—presented by program to indicate the purpose of expenditures and with adequate detail to establish control. Each program should emphasize the relationship between the input of resources and the output of services to be performed, including the measures necessary to evaluate achievement of program objectives.[13]

Measuring the benefits or outputs of programs poses difficulties. A private enterprise measures its benefits in terms of increased revenue or decreased cost. In the nonprofit sector, however, social problems complicate the measurement of benefits. Consequently, such endeavors have often resulted in relatively meaningless monetary outcome data. Problems encountered in monetary output measurements suggest that monetary inputs (costs) might be more meaningfully related to nonmonetary outcomes for specific programs.[14]

Annual budgets for governments at all levels in the United States now exceed one trillion dollars—an enormous sum of money. Yet, in spite of the many decades in which governmental budgeting has been practiced, the general public is increasingly critical of services received for money spent. While the federal government might be under more obvious attack, state, county, and municipal governments are equally criticized not only for the lack of a satisfactory control system, but also for the ill-conceived procedure for planning the costs and revenues needed to govern. Therefore, a budget based on a managerial approach would go a long way toward responsibly meeting these criticisms.

An example of such an effort in government is found in the concept of a planning, programming, budgeting system, commonly referred to as PPBS. *PPBS* might be defined as an analytical tool to assist management (1) in the analysis of alternatives as the basis for rational decision making and (2) in allocating resources to accomplish stated goals and objectives over a designated time period. It had its origin in the Defense Department's attempt to quantify huge expenditures in terms of benefits derived from activities and programs of the public sector. This analysis technique is closely related to cost-benefit analysis, focusing upon the outputs or final results, rather than the inputs or the initial dollars expended. The outputs are directly relatable to the planned objectives through the use of performance budgets.

The idea that governmental programs should be undertaken in the light of final benefits has caused agencies in the field of health, education, and welfare services as well as other nonprofit organizations to apply PPBS to their activities and programs. However, PPBS has been criticized because its

---

[13]R. Schuyler Lesher, Jr., and Craig Becker, "Total Recall," *Management Focus*, Vol. 30, No. 5, pp. 13, 15.
[14]For additional discussion and illustration, see James E. Sorensen and Hugh D. Grove, "Cost-Outcome and Cost-Effectiveness Analysis: Emerging Nonprofit Performance Evaluation Techniques," *The Accounting Review*, Vol. LII, No. 3, pp. 658-675.

required specification of objectives cannot be transformed readily into operational outcome quantities or statistics. PPBS, if effective, needs a great deal of refinement and innovation, an understanding of its aims and methods, and active participation of executive and middle management.

In the same way that governmental units have become budget and cost conscious, nonprofit organizations, such as hospitals, churches, school districts, colleges, universities, fraternal orders, libraries, and labor unions, are adopting strong measures of budgetary control. In the past, efforts to control costs were generally exercised through pressure to reduce budget increases rather than through method improvements or program changes. Long-range planning was seldom practiced.

Basically, the objectives of nonprofit organizations are directed toward the economic, social, educational, or spiritual benefit of individuals or groups who have no vested interest in such organizations in the form of ownership or investment. The presidents, boards of directors, trustees, or administrative officers, like their counterparts in profit-seeking enterprises, are charged with the stewardship of economic resources, except that their job is primarily to use or spend these resources instead of trying to derive monetary gain. It is expressly for this nonprofit objective that these organizations should install adequate and effective methods and procedures in planning, budgeting, and cost control.[15]

▼ ZERO-BASE BUDGETING

Customarily, those in charge of an established budgetary program are required to justify only the increase sought above last year's appropriation. What they are already spending is usually accepted as necessary, with little or no examination. *Zero-base budgeting,* however, is a budget-planning procedure for the reevaluation of an organization's program and expenditures. It requires each manager to justify the entire budget request in detail and places the burden of proof on the manager to justify why authorization to spend any money at all should be granted. It starts with the assumption that zero will be spent on each activity—thus, the term "zero-base." What a manager is already spending is not accepted as a starting point.

Managers are asked to prepare for each activity or operation under their control a *decision package* that includes an analysis of cost, purpose, alternative courses of action, measures of performance, consequences of not performing the activity, and benefits. The zero-base budgeting approach asserts that in building the budget from zero, two types of alternatives should be considered by managers: (1) different ways of performing the same activity and (2) different levels of effort in performing the activity.

A decision package identifies an activity in a definitive manner for evaluation and comparison with other activities. Devising these decision

---

[15]Budgeting for nonprofit organizations other than governmental, health care, and higher education is discussed in considerable detail in *Financial Planning and Evaluation for the Nonprofit Organization,* by Anthony J. Gambino and Thomas J. Reardon (New York: National Association of Accountants, 1981).

packages, ranking them, and making funding decisions according to the rank order comprise the heart of the zero-base budgeting process.

Success in implementing zero-base budgeting requires:

1. Linkage of zero-base budgeting to the short- and long-range planning process.
2. Sustained support and commitment from executive management.
3. Innovation among the managers who make up the budget decision packages.
4. Sale of the procedure to the people who must perform the work necessary to keep the concept vigorous.

▼ PERT AND PERT/COST—SYSTEMS FOR PLANNING AND CONTROL

The accountant's involvement in management planning and control has led to the use of network analysis systems for planning, measuring progress to schedule, evaluating changes to schedule, forecasting future progress, and predicting and controlling costs. These systems are variously referred to as PERT (Program Evaluation and Review Technique) or CPM (Critical Path Method). The origin of PERT is military; it was introduced in connection with the Navy Polaris program. CPM's origin is industrial.

Many companies use these methods in planning, scheduling, and costing such diverse projects as constructing buildings, installing equipment, and research and development. There is also an opportunity for using PERT in business administration tasks, such as scheduling the closing of books, revising standard cost data, scheduling the time elements for the preparation of departmental budgets, cash flows, and preparing the annual profit plan, as well as for audit planning and control. In conjunction with PERT and critical path techniques, computer systems provide executive management with far better means for directing large-scale, complex projects. Management can measure cost, time, and technical performance on an integrated basis. Actual results can be compared with the network plan and revisions made as needed.

The PERT System

PERT is a probabilistic diagram of the interrelationships of a complex series of activities. Whether a military, industrial, or business administration task, time is the fundamental element of any of these activities. The major burden of PERT is the determination of the longest time duration for the completion of the entire project. This calculation is based on the length of time required for the longest sequence of activities.

All of the individual tasks to complete a given job or program must be visualized in a *network* of events and activities. An *event* represents a specified accomplishment at a particular instant in time, such as B or E in the following network. An *activity* represents the time and resources necessary to move from one event to another, e.g., B → E in the chart. Some of the activities may be in series; e.g., market research cannot be performed before the research design is planned. Other activities may be parallel; e.g., the engines for a ship can be built at the same time the hull is being constructed.

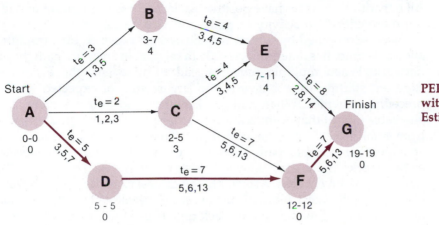

PERT Network with Time Estimates in Weeks

Time estimates for PERT are made for each activity on a three-way basis, i.e., optimistic (t_o), most likely (t_m), and pessimistic (t_p). In the network illustrated, the three time estimates, expressed in units of one week, are indicated under each activity line. From these estimates, an expected time (t_e) is calculated for each activity. The expected time represents the average time an activity would require if it were repeated a large number of times. The calculation is generally based on the assumption that the distribution of activity times closely approximates a Beta probability distribution. Such distributions may be symmetrical or skewed. The following formula is used to compute the mean of the Beta probability distribution, which is the expected time:

$$t_e = \frac{t_o + 4t_m + t_p}{6}$$

For example, the activity D-F has a value of $t_e = 7$, determined as follows:

$$\text{If: } t_o = 5$$
$$t_m = 6$$
$$t_p = 13$$
$$\text{Then: } t_e = \frac{5 + 4(6) + 13}{6} = \frac{42}{6} = 7$$

Below each event in the network are noted the earliest expected and latest allowable times, and below these two numbers, the slack time is shown. The *earliest expected time* is the earliest time that an activity can be expected to start, because of its relationship to pending activities. The *latest allowable time* is the latest time that an activity may begin and not delay completion of the project.

The Critical Path. The longest path through the network is known as the *critical path* and is denoted on the flowchart by the arrows connecting A-D-F-G.

Shortening of total time can be accomplished only by shortening the critical path. However, if the critical path A-D-F-G is shortened from nineteen weeks to fifteen weeks, A-C-F-G (assuming F-G remains unchanged) would then become the critical path because it would be the longest.

Slack Time. Activities along the critical path (A-D-F-G) have a slack of zero. All noncritical activities have positive slack. The less the amount of slack time, the more critical an activity or path, and vice versa.

Slack is computed by subtracting the earliest expected time from the latest allowable time. It is determinable only in relation to an entire path through the network. When multiple activities lead to an event, the event's earliest expected starting time is always the largest sum of expected times of the preceding activities. When multiple activities lead from an event, the latest allowable time at that event is always the smallest figure found by subtracting from total project time the sum of expected times of subsequent network activities. For example, path A-C-E-G at event C has an earliest expected time of two weeks and a latest allowable time of five weeks [19 − (7 + 7)], for a slack time of three weeks. At event E, the earliest expected time is seven weeks (3 + 4) and the latest allowable time is eleven weeks (19 − 8), for a slack time of four weeks. However, if any slack time is used up, that is, if a noncritical activity utilizes more than the expected time, the slack times for subsequent activities must be recomputed. Recomputation would also be necessary when less than the expected times are required.

Slack allows management some flexibility. If available slack time is not exceeded, noncritical activities can be delayed without delaying the project's completion date. Slack time information provides useful data for initial planning and continuous project monitoring when the project's status is compared with the plan.

The PERT/Cost System

PERT/cost is an integrated management information system designed to furnish management with timely information for planning and controlling schedules and costs of projects. The PERT/cost system is really an expansion of PERT. It assigns cost to time and activities, thereby providing total financial planning and control by functional responsibility.

The predetermination of cost is in harmony with the accountant's budgeting task and follows the organizational and procedural steps used in responsibility accounting. The PERT/cost estimates are activity- or project-oriented, and the addition of the cost component permits analyses involving time/cost tradeoffs. Each activity is defined at a level of detail necessary for individual job assignments and supervisory control. Control is on scheduled tasks, with time and cost as the common control factors. Cost accumulation methods must be devised to be compatible with PERT/cost control concepts.

In the following network, the activities noted by the dark circles, A, B, C, and D, represent completed events. The dollar figures in the white blocks represent estimated costs, e.g., $30,000 for activity F-G. Figures in the lightly shaded blocks to the right of the estimates are actual costs. Estimated times (t_e) and actual times (t_a) are shown below the activity lines.

PERT/Cost Network and Time (in Weeks) and Cost (in Thousands of Dollars)

Activities A-B, A-C, and A-D have been completed. A-B required one-half week more time than planned; however, it is not on the critical path and will not affect total project duration. If excess time were such that another path became long enough to be the critical path, then total time would be involved.

The actual activity cost of $10,000 for A-B compared to a budget of $12,000 indicates an underrun of $2,000. Activity A-C budget and actual figures coincide for time and cost. A-D had an overrun of $5,000 and a two-week slippage. The slippage requires immediate attention because A-D is on the critical path. Immediate investigation and corrective action seem needed for B-E and C-E. According to the present status report, both activities have consumed the budgeted time and cost and one or both are not yet completed.

While comparison of actual versus planned time and cost figures is essential, comparison alone is not enough to evaluate a project. Evaluation of performance is needed to complete the process. For example, a project is not necessarily in financial trouble when actual expenditures exceed budgeted. Progress may be correspondingly ahead of schedule. Nor is a project necessarily meeting performance standards when it is within the budget. To evaluate the true status, management needs to study performance, cost, and timing.

Computer Applications

Computer support provides distinct advantages to PERT and PERT/cost applications. PERT and PERT/cost procedures are mathematically oriented and are therefore ideally suited to the high-speed response of computers for deriving the critical path, slack times, and costs, and for storing and reporting results to management. Revisions to all schedule elements, whether during the initial estimating phase or during the active project phase, can be updated and the revised results promptly reported.

▼ PROBABILISTIC BUDGETS

The budget may be developed based on one set of assumptions as to the most likely performance in the forthcoming period. However, there is increasing evidence that several sets of assumptions are evaluated by management before the budget is finalized. One possibility is the PERT-like three-level estimates—optimistic, most likely, and pessimistic. This involves estimating each budget component assuming each of the three conditions. Probability trees can be used in which several variables can be considered in the analysis, e.g., number of units sold, sales price, and variable manufacturing and marketing costs.

To each discrete set of assumptions, a probability can be assigned, based on past experience and management's best judgment about the future, thus revealing to management not only a range of possible outcomes but also a probability associated with each. Further statistical techniques can then be applied, including an expected (weighted, composite) value, the range, and the standard deviation for the various budget elements, such as sales, manufacturing cost, and marketing cost. For example, the expected value for sales may be $960,000, with a range from a low of $780,000 to a high of $1,200,000 and a standard deviation of $114,600.

The computational capability of the computer facilitates the consideration of complex sets of assumptions and permits the use of simulation programs, making it possible to develop more objectively determined probabilities.[16]

▼ THE FLEXIBLE BUDGET FOR PLANNING AND CONTROL

Budgets are based on certain definite assumed conditions and results. The budgets discussed and illustrated in Chapter 15 and up to this point in the present chapter are known as fixed or expected budgets, while the budgets discussed in this section are known as flexible budgets. The term "fixed" is misleading, however, since a fixed budget is subject to revision. *Fixed* merely denotes that the budget is not adjusted to actual volume attained. It represents a prefixed point of sales and cost estimates with which actual results are compared. A *flexible budget*, however, is adjusted to actual volume.

Both fixed and flexible budgets provide management with information necessary to attain the major objectives of budgetary control, which include:

---

[16]An exhaustive treatment of these techniques is beyond the scope of this discussion. For expanded discussion and illustrations, see:

William L. Ferrara and Jack C. Hayya, "Toward Probabilistic Profit Budgets," *Management Accounting*, Vol. LII, No. 3, pp. 23-28.

Belverd E. Neddles, Jr., "Budgeting Techniques: Subjective to Probabilistic," *Management Accounting*, Vol. LIII, No. 6, pp. 39-45.

Edmund J. Hall and Richard J. Kolkmann, "A Vote for the Probabilistic Pro Forma Income Statement," *Management Accounting*, Vol. LVII, No. 7, pp. 45-48.

Davis L. S. Chang and Shu S. Liao, "Measuring and Disclosing Forecast Reliability," *The Journal of Accountancy*, Vol. 143, No. 5, pp. 76-87, (Monte Carlo simulation).

1. An organized procedure for planning.
2. A means for coordinating the activities of the various divisions of a business.
3. A basis for cost control.

Cost control is predicated on the idea that actual costs will be compared with budgeted costs, relating what did happen with what should have happened. When a company's activities can be estimated within close limits, the fixed budget is satisfactory. However, completely predictable situations exist in only a few cases. If actual volume differs from that planned, a comparison of actual results with a fixed budget may be misleading. For example, suppose that 1,000 units of product were planned at a budgeted cost of $10,000, but that 1,100 units are actually produced at a cost of $10,500. A simple comparison of budgeted costs with actual costs indicates an unfavorable variance of $500. However, further examination reveals that actual production exceeds that planned by 100 units. Since budgeted and actual costs contain both fixed and variable costs, it is not clear whether the variance is favorable or unfavorable. To make such a determination, actual costs must be compared with a budget based on the actual volume. A flexible budget provides an acceptable measure of what costs should be under any given set of conditions, i.e., a budget adjusted to actual volume.

Preparing a Flexible Budget

To prepare a flexible budget, a formula must be developed for each account within each department or cost center. Each formula indicates the fixed cost and/or the variable cost rate for the account. The variable portion of the formula is a rate of cost in relation to some measure of activity such as direct labor hours, machine hours, or units of production. The fixed amount and the variable rate remain constant within prescribed ranges of activity.

The application of these formulas to the level of activity actually experienced produces allowable budget expenditures for the volume of activity actually attained. These budget figures are compared with actual costs in order to compute the spending and idle capacity variances (see Chapter 12) and, thus, to measure the performance of each department or cost center.

Originally, the flexible budget was applied principally to the control of departmental factory overhead. Now, however, the idea is applied to the entire budget, so that marketing and administrative budgets as well as manufacturing budgets are prepared on a flexible budget basis. The flexible budget is also a useful planning tool because it provides cost behavior information that can be used to evaluate the effects of different volumes of activity on profits and on the cash position and to establish the approved periodic budget.

The following illustration is devoted to the preparation of a flexible budget for a producing department in a factory. It is not intended to convey the idea, however, that the factory overhead budget outranks the budgets for other functions of the business, because these other functions can also utilize the flexible budget concept. Any increase or decrease in business activity must be reflected throughout the enterprise. In some activities or departments, changes will be greater or smaller than in others. Certain departments have the ability to produce more without much additional cost. In others, costs increase or decrease in more or less direct proportion to production increases or decreases. The flexible budget attempts to deal with this problem.

When the fixed dollar amount and the variable rate of an expense have been determined, following the cost behavior analysis procedures covered in Chapter 11, budget allowances for any level within a relevant range of activity can be computed without difficulty. For example, a budget allowances schedule, based on normal capacity, for the Machining Department of a manufacturing company, is as follows:

BUDGET ALLOWANCES FOR MACHINING DEPARTMENT

Activity Base: Normal capacity, 4,000 direct labor hours per month = 80% of rated capacity

Expense	Fixed Expense	Variable Rate per Direct Labor Hour
Indirect labor	$ 600	$ .175
Clerical help	100	.050
Setup crew	800	.070
Rework operations	100	
Supervision	1,200	
Factory supplies	200	.055
Total controllable by department head	$ 3,000	$ .350
Insurance—fire, etc.	$ 80	
Taxes—state and local	50	
Depreciation	500	
Total noncontrollable	$ 630	
Maintenance	$ 600	$ .20
Building occupancy	780	.10
Gas, water, steam, and air	540	.30
General expenses	450	.05
Total service departments (apportioned)	$ 2,370	$ .65
Total	$ 6,000	$1.00

Summary:

Fixed expense	$ 6,000
Variable expense, 4,000 direct labor hours @ $1 per hour	4,000
Total cost at normal capacity	$10,000
Factory overhead rate of Machining Department at normal capacity ($10,000 ÷ 4,000 hours)	$2.50 per direct labor hour

The schedule of budget allowances is the basis for the following flexible budget. In this budget, the factory overhead rate declines steadily as production moves to the 90 percent operating level. As production approaches theoretical capacity, the overhead rate increases, because items such as rework operations and supervision increase faster than at lower levels and overtime premiums and night premiums are introduced. While such cost increases are revealed through the flexible budget, the situation indicates a possible departure from the use of the equation for a straight line, y = a + bx, or $6,000 fixed expense + $1.00(x) for all levels of activity. However, it should be emphasized that one definite level must be agreed upon and used for setting the predetermined factory overhead rate, for applying overhead cost to production, and for computing the spending and idle capacity variances, including a determination of the spending variance related to each expense category (discussed and illustrated in Chapter 12). These variances might warrant a rate change in the next period for the sake of more meaningful cost control and pricing procedures. In any case, the effective use of cost data for planning, control, and decision-making purposes requires reasonably accurate knowledge of cost behavior.

FLEXIBLE BUDGET FOR MACHINING DEPARTMENT

Operating level:				
Based on direct labor hours	3,500	4,000*	4,500	5,000
Percentage of rated capacity	70%	80%	90%	100%
Monthly allowances for expenses:				
Indirect labor	$1,212.50	$ 1,300.00	$ 1,387.50	$ 1,475.00
Clerical help	275.00	300.00	325.00	350.00
Setup crew	1,045.00	1,080.00	1,115.00	1,150.00
Rework operations	100.00	100.00	100.00	135.00
Supervision	1,200.00	1,200.00	1,200.00	1,400.00
Factory supplies	392.50	420.00	447.50	475.00
Overtime premium	—	—	—	500.00
Night premium	—	—	—	100.00
Total controllable by department head	$4,225.00	$ 4,400.00	$ 4,575.00	$ 5,585.00
Insurance—fire, etc.	$ 80.00	$ 80.00	$ 80.00	$ 80.00
Taxes—state and local	50.00	50.00	50.00	50.00
Depreciation	500.00	500.00	500.00	500.00
Total noncontrollable	$ 630.00	$ 630.00	$ 630.00	$ 630.00
Maintenance	$1,300.00	$ 1,400.00	$ 1,500.00	$ 1,600.00
Building occupancy	1,130.00	1,180.00	1,230.00	1,280.00
Gas, water, steam, and air	1,590.00	1,740.00	1,890.00	2,040.00
General expenses	625.00	650.00	675.00	700.00
Total service departments	$4,645.00	$ 4,970.00	$ 5,295.00	$ 5,620.00
Total factory overhead	$9,500.00	$10,000.00	$10,500.00	$11,835.00
Factory overhead rate per direct labor hour	$2.714	$2.500	$2.333	$2.367

*Normal capacity.

In the flexible budget for the Machining Department, the factory overhead rate based on direct labor hours means that all variable expenses are related to this activity base. In many instances, however, the activity base is not uniform for all overhead items. Certain departments within a firm may have different bases, and a single department may require different bases and rates for different groups of expenses. Within a department, only a low correlation or none at all may exist between some of the expenses and the activity base selected. It is therefore essential to study the correlation of volume in physical terms, such as units produced, labor hours worked, or machine hours used, with the dollar cost for each item or group of items (see Chapter 11). Such studies quite often indicate that a new base must be chosen for some or all of the expenses to arrive at the most acceptable separation of fixed and variable expenses. The use of statistical correlation analysis is suggested to discover the correct volume base to be used before attempting to separate the fixed and variable elements of the many expense items that are semivariable in nature and before describing the rate of variability of entirely variable expenses.

Flexible Budgeting Through Computers and Step Charts

The determination of the fixed and variable elements in each departmental expense is a time-consuming task, particularly when computations, calculations, and analyses are performed either manually or by a desk calculator. The application of computerized techniques can eliminate this tedious chore and at the same time provide the necessary tools for budgetary control and responsibility reporting throughout the year.

Predetermined rates are usually used. However, when increases or decreases in certain expenses are anticipated due to a change in the product or a change in processing, the projected overhead amounts are adjusted accordingly. Some expenses are budgeted on a step-chart basis which is in harmony with the relevant range idea mentioned previously.

The following step chart indicates the allowance for nonproduction personnel at various levels of production activity. Each bisected square is an

Step Chart for a Producing Department

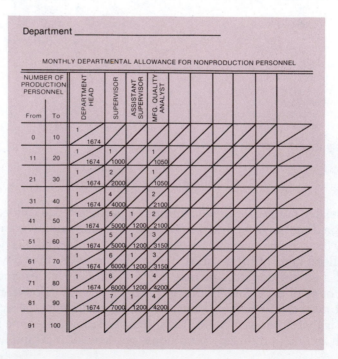

indication as to the number of nonproduction personnel (upper left-hand corner) and salary levels allowable (lower right-hand corner) at each step. The levels are based on the number of production workers.

In a step chart for a service department, the levels might be based on the total number of production hours in all producing departments. Such detailed data enhance the development of monthly departmental budgets by sub-expense classifications.

Flexible Budget for a Service Department

Flexible budgets for service departments permit (1) comparison of actual expenses with allowed expenses at the prevailing level of operations and (2) establishment of a fairer use rate or sold-hour rate by charging operating departments with fixed expenses regardless of activity and with a variable cost based on departmental activity. In the following flexible budget for the Maintenance Department of a company, the expenses of the department are estimated at a fixed amount of $4,200. At 80 percent capacity, the total expense is $27,000. Assuming that the company has two producing departments and two service departments to which a fixed cost of $1,200, $2,000, $600, and $400, respectively, is charged as the readiness-to-serve cost of the Maintenance Department, the remaining balance of $22,800 is divided by the total number of maintenance hours, 2,400, to arrive at a variable rate of $9.50 per hour.

FLEXIBLE BUDGET FOR MAINTENANCE DEPARTMENT				
Operating level:				
Maintenance hours............................	2,100	2,400	2,700	3,000
Percentage of plant capacity.......................	70%	80%	90%	100%
Monthly allowances for expenses:				
Artisans...	$12,600	$14,400	$16,200	$18,000
Supervision......................................	2,000	2,000	2,000	2,000
Factory supplies..............................	5,950	6,800	7,650	8,500
Tools..	1,400	1,600	1,800	2,000
Depreciation....................................	1,400	1,400	1,400	1,400
Building occupancy........................	800	800	800	800
Total expense............................	$24,150	$27,000	$29,850	$32,700
Fixed expense....................................	$ 4,200	$ 4,200	$ 4,200	$ 4,200
Variable expense...............................	19,950	22,800	25,650	28,500
Variable charging rate per maintenance hour...	$9.50	$9.50	$9.50	$9.50

Flexible Marketing and Administrative Budgets

In contrast to the factory overhead budget, which bases its expense levels in most cases on direct labor hours, machine hours, or direct labor dollars, the budget for commercial expenses is often based on net sales, as shown in the following illustration. This practice has been criticized, and other methods are suggested in Chapter 25.

FLEXIBLE MARKETING AND ADMINISTRATIVE BUDGET

Net sales		$600,000	$700,000	$800,000	$900,000	$1,000,000
Monthly allowances for marketing expenses:	Based on Sales					
Sales salaries	5%	$30,000	$35,000	$40,000	$45,000	$50,000
Advertising	1%	6,000	7,000	8,000	9,000	10,000
Sales expenses	2%	12,000	14,000	16,000	18,000	20,000
Misc. expenses	5%	3,000	3,500	4,000	4,500	5,000
Depreciation	Fixed	10,000	10,000	10,000	10,000	10,000
Total marketing		$61,000	$69,500	$78,000	$86,500	$95,000
Monthly allowances for administrative expenses:	Based on Sales					
Executives' salaries	Fixed	$20,000	$20,000	$20,000	$30,000	$50,000
General expenses	3%	18,000	21,000	24,000	27,000	30,000
Depreciation	Fixed	5,000	5,000	5,000	5,000	5,000
Insurance	Fixed	3,000	3,000	3,000	3,000	3,000
Taxes	Fixed	4,000	4,000	4,000	4,000	4,000
Total administrative		$50,000	$53,000	$56,000	$69,000	$92,000

DISCUSSION QUESTIONS

1. What is meant by a capital expenditure? How does it differ from a revenue expenditure?

2. Name some purposes of and some reasons for a research and development program.

3. Companies should establish budgetary procedures to provide control and accounting systems for research and development expenditures. What are such procedures specifically designed to achieve?

4. Managers consider a cash budget an extremely useful management tool. Why?

5. The budgeted balance sheet may indicate an unsatisfactory financial condition. Discuss.

6. What governing criterion has been suggested for determining whether to include prospective information in external financial statements?

7. Discuss the need for planning and budgeting in (a) nonmanufacturing businesses and (b) nonprofit organizations.

8. What is the objective of the control concept generally referred to as PPBS?

9. (a) Describe zero-base budgeting. (b) Explain how zero-base budgeting differs from traditional budgeting.

10. What strengths and weaknesses might be associated with zero-base budgeting?
(CICA adapted)

11. Discuss the role of PERT as it might apply to project development.

12. Discuss the conditions determining when PERT is appropriate.

13. Explain the computation of slack in the PERT network.

14. State the relationship between PERT and PERT/cost systems.

15. What does computer support offer to PERT and PERT/cost users?

16. Discuss how PERT/cost would be used in planning the audit of a state government's highway construction and maintenance operation.   (CIA adapted)

17. Contrast the probabilistic budget and the traditional budget in terms of information provided to management.

18. Name some relative advantages in the use of a flexible budget over a fixed budget.

19. What is the underlying principle of a flexible budget?

20. A company has been operating a budget system for a number of years. Production volume fluctuates widely, reaching its peak in the fall, but is quite low during the rest of the year. Manufacturing for stock during the dull period as a means of smoothing out the volume fluctuations is impractical because of frequent and sudden changes in specifications prescribed by the customers. Actual annual volume has been substantially below normal. The budget produces large unfavorable capacity variances since overhead rates are computed from normal volume and are inadequate to absorb the overhead which should be charged into production during the low-volume periods. This fixed type of budget based on an unrealistic normal production volume fails to serve its planning and control purpose. As a consultant, diagnose the situation and offer advice.

21. Can service departments' expenses be set up using flexible budget procedures? What makes the situation difficult? Suggest how the expenses can be allocated meaningfully to producing departments.

EXERCISES

1. Budgeted cash receipts. All sales of Salvey Company are made on account. A 3% discount is offered to customers who pay by the 10th of the next month, and 60% of the company's customers take advantage of the cash discount. Accounts are due at the end of the month after sale, and 25% of the customers pay by the due date but not within the discount period. A further 12% of the customers pay in the second month after sale, and 3% never pay. Budgeted sales are as follows:

January.......................	$35,000
February....................	40,000
March.........................	70,000
April...........................	25,000
May............................	20,000

Required: Compute the budgeted cash receipts for April from collections of accounts receivable.

2. Budgeted cash collections and accounts receivable. A company's actual sales on account were:

Month	Sales on Account
February....................	$160,000
March.........................	100,000
April...........................	180,000

Experience has shown that such sales are usually collected as follows:

Month of sale...	20%
Month after sale..	50
Second month after sale.............................	25
Never collected and written off in third month after sale...................	5
	100%

Required:

(1) Compute the budgeted cash collections in May, if May sales on account are budgeted at $150,000.
(2) Compute the balance of accounts receivable on the books at April 30.
(3) Compute the balance of accounts receivable on the books at May 31.
(4) What steps could the company take to reduce the balance in accounts receivable as of May 31st? Evaluate both the risks and advantages.

(CIA adapted)

3. Estimated cash disbursements. Thomas Corporation has estimated its activity for June, as follows:

(a) Sales...	$700,000
Gross profit (based on sales)..	30%
Increase in trade accounts receivable during month...................	$ 20,000
Change in accounts payable during month.................................	$ -0-
Increase in inventory during month..	$ 10,000

(b) Variable selling, general, and administrative expenses (S, G, & A) include a charge for uncollectible accounts of 1% of sales.
(c) Total S, G, & A is $71,000 monthly plus 15% of sales.
(d) Monthly depreciation expense of $40,000 is included in fixed S, G, & A.

Required: Determine the estimated June cash disbursements.

4. Cash budget for inventory purchases. Partee Company manufactures a product called Par. Each unit of Par requires 3 pieces of a material called Tee, whose standard price per piece is $5.

Budgeted inventory levels are as follows:

	Par	Tee
June 1.......................	5,000	20,000
July 1........................	3,000	14,000
August 1...................	3,000	11,000

Budgeted sales of Par are 50,000 for June and 30,000 for July.

The company intends to take advantage of a 2/10, n/30 discount. Assume one third of the purchases of any month due for discount are paid in the following month.

Required: Compute the cash required in July for purchases of Tee.

(CGAAC adapted)

5. Cash budget. Crockett Company is preparing a cash budget for July. The following estimates were made:

(a) Expected cash balance, July 1, $5,000.

(b) Income tax rate is 40%, based on accounting income for the month, payable in the following month.

(c) Crockett's customers pay for 50% of their purchases during the month of purchase and the balance during the following month. Bad debts are expected to be 2%.

(d) Merchandise is purchased on account for resale, with 25% of purchases paid for during the month of purchase and the balance paid during the following month.

(e) Marketing and administrative expenses are all paid in the current month.

(f) Dividends of $15,000 are expected to be declared and paid during July.

(g) Crockett's desire is to have a minimum month-end cash balance of $5,000.

(h) Other budgets include the following estimates:

	June	July
Sales (all on account)	$30,000	$40,000
Purchases	10,000	15,000
Depreciation expense	5,000	6,000
Cost of goods sold	12,000	16,000
Other marketing and administrative expenses	9,000	10,000

Required:

(1) Prepare a cash budget for July.

(2) What financial action needs to be taken as a result of this cash budget?

(CGAAC adapted)

6. PERT network. Crespi Construction Company will soon begin work on a building for Echelon Savings Bank. Work on the building was started by another construction firm that has gone out of business. Crespi has agreed to complete the project. Crespi's schedule of activities and related expected completion times for the Echelon Savings Bank project are presented in the following table:

Activity Code	Activity Description	Estimated Time (in weeks)
1-2	Obtain on-site work permit	1
2-5	Repair damage done by vandals	4
2-3	Inspect construction materials left on site	1
3-5	Order and receive additional construction materials	2
3-4	Apply for waiver to add new materials	1
4-5	Obtain waiver to add new materials	1
5-6	Perform electrical work	4
6-7	Complete interior partitions	2

Required:

(1) Prepare the PERT network.

(2) Identify the critical path and determine the expected time in weeks for the project.

(3) Explain the effect on the critical path and expected time for the project if Crespi were not required to apply for and obtain the waiver to add new materials.

(ICMA adapted)

7. PERT network. A company is faced with the following PERT network situation (time in days):

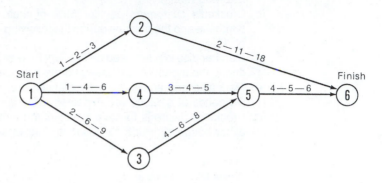

Required:

(1) Calculate t_e (expected time) for each activity, to two decimal places. For each activity, the estimates are t_o, t_m, and t_p, in that order.
(2) Calculate the total t_e for each path, and identify the critical path as well as total time for other paths. *(CGAAC adapted)*

8. PERT network. The following PERT network uses a weighted average of three times—optimistic, most likely, and pessimistic—to calculate expected time for a particular job's completion:

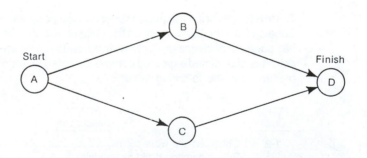

Activity	Time in Days			Crash Cost to Reduce One Day's Time
	t_o	t_m	t_p	
A-B	11	12	19	$300
B-D	22	24	32	200
A-C	12	14	28	100
C-D	22	23	30	200

Required:

(1) Compute the t_e (expected time) for each activity.
(2) Identify the critical path.
(3) Compute slack time at events B and C.
(4) If a $150 premium will be paid for each day of completion before the expected completion time, how many days should be reduced? *(CGAAC adapted)*

9. PERT network for auditing liabilities. All audits have a critical path, but auditors seldom recognize it as such without the aid of network analysis. In the auditing of liabilities, the following activities and expected times have been identified:

Activity Code	Activity Description	Expected Time (Hours)
6.10-6.11	Obtain schedule of liabilities....	2
6.11-6.12	Mail confirmations.........	12
6.12-6.16	Process confirmations......	39
6.16-6.17	Investigate debit balances.......	5
6.11-6.13	Vouch selected liabilities.....	64
6.13-6.14	Test accruals and amortization......	4
6.11-6.14	Test pension plan.......	4
6.14-6.15	Reconcile interest expense to debt.....	8
6.15-6.17	Verify debt restriction compliance.......	5
6.17-6.18	Review subsequent payments......	10

Required: Construct the PERT network, identifying the critical path and including slack times.

10. Critique of performance report. Jewell Company uses a fixed or forecast budget to measure its performance against the objectives set by the forecast and to help in controlling costs. At the end of a month, management received the following report, which compares actual performance with budgeted figures:

Items of Cost	Budget	Actual
Units produced.......	75,000	73,500
Direct materials........	$39,000	$37,020
Direct labor.......	6,000	5,950
Factory supplies........	1,500	1,550
Indirect labor......	726	710
Repairs and maintenance.......	2,250	2,300
Insurance and property tax.....	355	350
Rent.......	2,000	2,000
Depreciation.......	2,200	2,200
Total......	$54,031	$52,080

Required: What conclusions can be drawn from this report? Indicate weaknesses, if any, of this type of budget.

11. Flexible budget for performance evaluation. The University of Boyne offers an extensive continuing education program in many cities throughout the state. For the convenience of its faculty and administrative staff and to save costs, the university employs a supervisor to operate a motor pool. The motor pool operated with 20 vehicles until February, when an additional automobile was acquired. The motor pool furnishes gasoline, oil, and other supplies for its automobiles. A mechanic does routine maintenance and minor repairs. Major repairs are done at a nearby commercial garage.

Each year, the supervisor prepares an operating budget, which informs the university administration of the funds needed for operating the pool. Depreciation (straight-line) on the automobiles is recorded in the budget in order to determine the cost per mile.

The following schedule presents the annual budget approved by the university, with March's actual costs compared to one twelfth of the annual budget:

University Motor Pool
Budget Report for March

	Annual Budget	One-Month Budget	March Actual	(Over) Under
Gasoline..	$ 52,500	$ 4,375	$ 5,323	$(948)
Oil, minor repairs, parts, and supplies.............	3,600	300	380	(80)
Outside repairs..	2,700	225	50	175
Insurance...	6,000	500	525	(25)
Salaries and benefits..................................	30,000	2,500	2,500	—
Depreciation..	26,400	2,200	2,310	(110)
	$121,200	$10,100	$11,088	$(988)
Total miles..	600,000	50,000	63,000	
Cost per mile...	$ .2020	$ .2020	$ .1760	
Number of automobiles.................................	20	20	21	

The annual budget was constructed upon these assumptions:

(a) 20 automobiles in the pool.
(b) 30,000 miles per year per automobile.
(c) 16 miles per gallon per automobile.
(d) $1.40 per gallon of gasoline.
(e) $.006 per mile for oil, minor repairs, parts, and supplies.
(f) $135 per automobile for outside repairs.

The supervisor is unhappy with the monthly report comparing budget and actual costs for March, claiming it presents an unfair picture of performance. A previous employer used flexible budgeting to compare actual costs to budgeted amounts.

Required:

(1) Prepare a report showing budgeted amounts, actual costs, and monthly variations for March, using flexible budget techniques. (Round off computations to four decimal places.)
(2) Explain the basis of the budget figure for outside repairs.

(ICMA adapted)

12. Flexible budget. Basston Company produces electrical appliances. Its Assembly Department operates under a flexible budget, with monthly allowances established at 20% intervals. The following information shows fixed and total expenses at the 80% and 100% levels:

	Fixed	Total Cost 80%	Total Cost 100%
Direct materials.........................		$16,000	$20,000
Direct labor..............................		9,000	11,250
Supervision..............................	$ 500	500	500
Indirect materials......................	250	1,450	1,750
Property tax.............................	300	300	300
Maintenance.............................	600	1,400	1,600
Power.....................................	200	280	300
Insurance................................	175	175	175
Depreciation.............................	1,600	1,600	1,600

Required: Prepare a flexible budget at the 92% level.

13. Flexible budget. Operating at normal capacity, Birch Company employs 20 production workers in the Assembly Department, working 8 hours per day, 20 days per month at a wage rate of $9 per hour. Normal capacity is 3,800 units of production per month. Supplies average $.23 per direct labor hour, indirect labor cost is ⅛ of direct labor cost, and other charges are $.18 per direct labor hour. The flexible budget at the normal capacity activity level follows:

Direct materials..................................	$ 4,760
Direct labor..	28,800
Fixed factory overhead.....................	670
Supplies...	736
Indirect labor....................................	3,600
Other charges...................................	576
Total..	$39,142
Cost per unit.....................................	$ 10.30

Required: Prepare the flexible budget for one month at 60% and 75% capacity.

14. Flexible budget. Albanese Inc. employs 10 production workers, working 8 hours a day, 20 days per month, at a normal capacity of 2,400 units. The direct labor wage rate is $6.30 per hour; direct materials are budgeted at $2 per unit produced. Fixed factory overhead is $960; supplies average $.25 per direct labor hour; indirect labor is 1/6 of direct labor cost; and other charges are $.45 per direct labor hour.

Required: Prepare the flexible budget for one month at 60%, 80%, and 100% of normal capacity, showing itemized manufacturing costs, total manufacturing cost, and total manufacturing cost per unit.

PROBLEMS

16-1. Cash and purchases budget for a manufacturer. Huntsville Company seeks assistance in developing cash and other budget information for May, June, and July. On April 30, the company had cash of $5,500, accounts receivable of $437,000, inventories of $309,400, and accounts payable of $133,055. The budget is to be based on the following assumptions:

Sales:

(a) Each month's sales are billed on the last day of the month.
(b) Customers are allowed a 3% discount if payment is made within 10 days after the billing date. Receivables are recorded at the gross sales price.
(c) Sixty percent of the billings are collected within the discount period; 25% by the end of the month; 9% by the end of the second month; and 6% prove uncollectible.

Purchases:

(a) Fifty-four percent of all purchases of materials and a like percentage of marketing, general, and administrative expenses are paid in the month purchased, with the remainder paid in the following month.
(b) Each month's units of ending materials inventory are equal to 130% of next month's production requirement.

(c) The cost of each unit of inventory is $20.
(d) Wages and salaries earned each month by employees total $38,000.
(e) Marketing, general, and administrative expenses (of which $2,000 is depreciation) are equal to 15% of the current month's sales.

Actual and projected sales are as follows:

March	$354,000	June	$342,000
April	363,000	July	360,000
May	357,000	August	366,000

Actual and projected materials needed for production:

March	11,800 units	June	11,400 units
April	12,100	July	12,000
May	11,900	August	12,200

Accrued payroll at the end of each month is as follows:

March	$3,100	June	$3,400
April	2,900	July	3,000
May	3,300	August	2,800

Required: Compute the following:

(1) Budgeted cash disbursements during June.
(2) Budgeted cash collections during May.
(3) Budgeted units of inventory to be purchased during July.

(AICPA adapted)

16-2. Cash and purchases budgets. Russon Corporation is a retailer whose sales are all made on credit. Sales are billed twice monthly, on the 10th of the month for the last half of the prior month's sales and on the 20th of the month for the first half of the current month's sales. The terms of all sales are 2/10, net 30, from the billing date. Based upon past experience, the collection experience of accounts receivable is as follows:

Within the discount period	80%
On the 30th day	18
Uncollectible	2

Sales for May and forecast sales for the next four months are:

May (actual)	$500,000
June	600,000
July	700,000
August	700,000
September	400,000

Russon's average markup on its products is 20% of the sales price.

Russon purchases merchandise for resale to meet the current month's sales demand and to maintain a desired monthly ending inventory of 25% of the next month's sales. All purchases are on credit, with terms of net 30. Russon pays for one half of a month's purchases in the month of purchase and the other half in the month following the purchase.

All sales and purchases occur uniformly throughout the month.

Required: Compute the following:

(1) Russon's budgeted cash collections in July.
(2) Russon's budgeted cash collections in September from August sales.

(3) Desired August 31 inventory.

(4) Budgeted June purchases.   *(ICMA adapted)*

16-3. Cash budget. Mayne Manufacturing Co. has incurred substantial losses for several years and has become insolvent. On March 31, 19A, Mayne petitioned the court for protection from creditors and submitted the following balance sheet:

Mayne Manufacturing Co.
Balance Sheet
March 31, 19A

	Net Book Value	Liquidation Value
Assets		
Accounts receivable..	$100,000	$ 50,000
Inventories..	90,000	40,000
Plant and equipment.......................................	150,000	160,000
Total..	$340,000	$250,000
Liabilities and Stockholders' Equity		
Accounts payable—general creditors...............	$600,000	
Common stock outstanding..............................	60,000	
Deficit...	(320,000)	
	$340,000	

Mayne's management informed the court that the company has developed a new product, and that a prospective customer is willing to sign a contract for the purchase of 10,000 units of this product during the year ending March 31, 19B, 12,000 units during the year ending March 31, 19C, and 15,000 units during the year ending March 31, 19D, at a price of $90 per unit. This product can be manufactured using Mayne's present facilities. Monthly production with immediate delivery is expected to be uniform within each year. Receivables are expected to be collected during the calendar month following sales.

Unit production costs of the new product are expected to be as follows:

Direct materials.........................	$20
Direct labor................................	30
Variable overhead....................	10

Fixed costs (excluding depreciation) will amount to $130,000 per year.

Purchases of direct materials will be paid during the calendar month following purchase. Fixed costs, direct labor, and variable overhead will be paid as incurred. Inventory of direct materials will be equal to 60 days' usage. After the first month of operations, 30 days' usage of direct materials will be ordered each month.

The general creditors have agreed to reduce their total claims to 60% of their March 31, 19A balances, under the following conditions:

(a) Existing accounts receivable and inventories are to be liquidated immediately, with the proceeds turned over to the general creditors.

(b) The balance of reduced accounts payable is to be paid as cash is generated from future operations, but in no event later than March 31, 19C. No interest will be paid on these obligations.

Under this proposed plan, the general creditors would receive $110,000 more than the current liquidation value of Mayne's assets.

Required: Ignoring any need to borrow and repay short-term funds for working capital purposes, prepare a cash budget for the years ending March 31, 19B and 19C, showing the cash expected to be available to pay the claims of the general creditors, payments to general creditors, and the cash remaining after payment of claims. *(ICMA adapted)*

16-4. Cash budget. Reynard Furniture Company has the following forecast data available:

	September	October
Cash sales..	$ 40,000	$60,000
Sales on account..	77,500	95,000
Cash purchases...	20,000	20,000
Purchases on account.................................	100,000	80,000
Purchases discounts....................................	6,000	3,000
Accounts payable—beginning....................	10,000	12,000
Accounts payable—ending........................	12,000	9,000
Cash operating expenses...........................	46,500	10,000

Net sales on account are collected 50% in the month of sale, 40% in the month following, and 10% in the second following month. Such sales in July and August were $100,000 and $120,000, respectively. The estimated September 1 cash balance is $13,000.

Required: Prepare a cash budget for September and October.

16-5. Cash budget for nonprofit organization. Triple-F Health Club (Family, Fitness, and Fun) is a nonprofit family-oriented health club. The club's board of directors is developing plans to acquire more equipment and expand the club facilities. The board plans to purchase about $25,000 of new equipment each year and wants to begin a fund to purchase the adjoining property in four or five years. The adjoining property has a market value of about $300,000.

The club manager, Jane Crowe, is concerned that the board has unrealistic goals in light of its recent financial performance. She has sought the help of a club member with an accounting background to assist her in preparing for the board a report supporting her concerns.

The club member reviewed the club's records, including the following cash basis income statement. The review and discussions with Jane Crowe disclosed the additional information which follows the statement.

Triple-F Health Club
Statement of Income (Cash Basis)
For Years Ended October 31
(000s omitted)

	19B	19A
Cash revenues:		
Annual membership fees.............................	$355.0	$300.0
Lesson and class fees................................	234.0	180.0
Miscellaneous...	2.0	1.5
Total cash received..............................	$591.0	$481.5
Cash expenses:		
Manager's salary and benefits....................	$ 36.0	$ 36.0
Regular employees' wages and benefits.....................	190.0	190.0
Lesson and class employee wages and benefits.........	195.0	150.0
Towels and supplies....................................	16.0	15.5
Utilities (heat and light)..............................	22.0	15.0
Mortgage interest..	35.1	37.8
Miscellaneous...	2.0	1.5
Total cash expenses.............................	$496.1	$445.8
Cash income..	$ 94.9	$ 35.7

Additional information:

  (a) Other financial information as of October 31, 19B:
    (1) Cash in checking account, $7,000.
    (2) Petty cash, $300.
    (3) Outstanding mortgage balance, $360,000.
    (4) Accounts payable arising from invoices for supplies and utilities which are unpaid as of October 31, 19B, $2,500.
  (b) No unpaid bills are expected to exist on October 31, 19C.
  (c) The club purchased $25,000 worth of exercise equipment during the current year 19B. Cash of $10,000 was paid on delivery, and the balance was due on October 1 but was not paid as of October 31, 19B.
  (d) The club began operations six years ago in rental quarters. Two years later it purchased its current property (land and building) for $600,000, paying $120,000 down and agreeing to pay $30,000 plus 9% interest annually on November 1 until the balance was paid off.
  (e) Membership rose 3% during 19B. This is approximately the same annual rate the club has experienced since it opened.
  (f) Membership fees were increased by 15% in 19B. The board has tentative plans to increase the fees by 10% in 19C.
  (g) Lesson and class fees have not been increased for three years. The board policy is to encourage classes and lessons by keeping the fees low. The members have taken advantage of this policy and the number of classes and lessons have grown significantly each year. The club expects the percentage growth experienced in 19B to be repeated in 19C.
  (h) Miscellaneous revenues are expected to grow at the same percentage as experienced in 19B.
  (i) Operating expenses are expected to increase. Hourly wage rates and the manager's salary will need to be increased 15% because no increases were granted in 19B. Towels and supplies, utilities, and miscellaneous expenses are expected to increase 25%.

Required:

  (1) Construct a cash budget for 19C for Triple-F Health Club.
  (2) Identify and explain any operating problem(s) that this budget discloses for Triple-F Health Club.
  (3) Is Jane Crowe's concern that the board's goals are unrealistic justified? Explain.   (ICMA adapted)

16-6. Revenue projection for a school system. The Beaver County School Board bases its revenues budget for the fiscal year ending July 31, 19B, on projections of receipts for the fiscal year ending July 31, 19A. The actual revenues received as of April 30, 19A, are summarized by type and source as follows:

Type and Source	Sales Tax	State Grants	Federal Grants	Allocation Of Federal Revenue Sharing
City A	$ 300,000			$ 250,000
City B	450,000			300,000
All other cities	210,000			200,000
Unincorporated areas	150,000			
Federal government			$750,000	
State government	300,000	$200,000		1,000,000
Total	$1,410,000	$200,000	$750,000	$1,750,000

Projected receipts for the remainder of the fiscal year ending July 31, 19A, are (a) sales tax collections should continue at the same rate; (b) additional state grants are expected to total $50,000; (c) no more federal funds of any kind are forthcoming until after July 31, 19A.

Revenues for 19B are expected to change as follows: (a) sales tax collections are projected to increase by 10%; (b) state grants will remain the same; (c) federal grants will be cut by two thirds; (d) federal revenue-sharing allocations should increase by 10%.

Required:

(1) Prepare a schedule of actual and projected revenues (by type and source) for the fiscal year ending July 31, 19A.
(2) Prepare a schedule of projected revenues (by type and source) for the fiscal year ending July 31, 19B.

16-7. Prospective financial statements. CL Corporation appears to be experiencing a good year, with sales in the first quarter of 19B one third ahead of last year and the Sales Department predicting continuation of this rate throughout the year. The controller has been asked to prepare a new forecast for the year and to analyze the differences from 19A results. The forecast is to be based on actual results obtained in the first quarter plus the expected costs of programs to be carried out in the remainder of the year. Various department heads (production, sales, etc.) have provided the necessary information and the results are as follows:

CL Corporation
Prospective Trial Balance
For December 31, 19B
(000s omitted)

Cash	1,200	
Accounts Receivable	80,000	
Inventory (1/1/19A, 40,000 units)	48,000	
Plant and Equipment	130,000	
Accumulated Depreciation		41,000
Accounts Payable		45,000
Accrued Payables		23,250
Notes Payable (due within one year)		50,000
Common Stock		70,000
Retained Earnings		108,200
Sales		600,000
Other Income		9,000
Cost of Goods Sold	—	
Manufacturing Costs:		
Materials	213,000	
Direct Labor	218,000	
Variable Factory Overhead	130,000	
Depreciation	5,000	
Other Fixed Factory Overhead	7,750	
Marketing:		
Salaries	16,000	
Commissions	20,000	
Promotion and Advertising	45,000	
General and Administrative:		
Salaries	16,000	
Travel	2,500	
Office Costs	9,000	
Income Tax	—	
Dividends	5,000	
	946,450	946,450

Adjustments for the change in inventory and for income tax have not been made. The scheduled production for 19B is 450 million units, while the sales volume will reach 400 million units. Sales and production volume in 19A was 300 million units. A full-cost, first-in, first-out inventory system is used. The company is subject to a 40% income tax rate. The actual financial statements for 19A follow:

CL Corporation
Balance Sheet
As of December 31, 19A
(000s omitted)

Assets

Current assets:

Cash.........	$ 23,000	
Accounts receivable..........	50,000	
Inventory.........	48,000	$121,000
Plant and equipment........	$130,000	
Less accumulated depreciation........	36,000	94,000
Total assets.........		$215,000

Liabilities and Shareholders' Equity

Current liabilities:

Accounts payable........	$ 13,000	
Accrued payables........	12,800	
Notes payable........	11,000	$ 36,800

Shareholders' equity:

Common stock.........	$ 70,000	
Retained earnings.........	108,200	178,200
Total liabilities and shareholders' equity.........		$215,000

CL Corporation
Statement of Income and Retained Earnings
For Year Ended December 31, 19A
(000s omitted)

Revenue:

Sales.........	$450,000	
Other income.........	15,000	$465,000

Expenses:

Cost of goods manufactured and sold:

Materials.........	$132,000	
Direct labor.........	135,000	
Variable factory overhead.........	81,000	
Fixed factory overhead.........	12,000	
	$360,000	
Beginning inventory.........	48,000	
	$408,000	
Ending inventory.........	48,000	$360,000

Marketing:

Salaries.........	$13,500	
Commissions.........	15,000	
Promotion and advertising.........	31,500	60,000

General and administrative:

Salaries.........	$14,000	
Travel.........	2,000	
Office costs.........	8,000	24,000

Income tax.........	8,400	452,400
Net income.........		$ 12,600
Beginning retained earnings.........		100,600
		$113,200
Less dividends.........		5,000
Ending retained earnings.........		$108,200

Required:

(1) Prepare prospective financial statements (statement of income and retained earnings, and balance sheet) for 19B.
(2) Using the 19A information provided for comparison:
   (a) Evaluate the 19B prospective profit performance.
   (b) Specify areas of 19B operating performance to be investigated.
   (c) Recommend programs for improved management performance.

(ICMA adapted)

16-8. Budgeted balance sheet. Einhard Company has a comprehensive budgeting program that includes preparation of financial statements as the final step. Einhard's budgeted balance sheet as of June 30, 19A, is as follows:

Einhard Company
Budgeted Balance Sheet
June 30, 19A
(000s omitted)

Assets

Cash	$ 800
Accounts receivable	750
Direct materials inventory	506
Finished goods inventory	648
Total current assets	$ 2,704
Land	$ 1,500
Property, plant, and equipment	11,400
Less accumulated depreciation	$ (2,250)
Total long-term assets	$10,650
Total assets	$13,354

Liabilities and Equity

Vouchers payable	$ 1,230
Income tax payable	135
Notes payable (due 12/30/19A)	1,000
Total liabilities	$ 2,365
Common stock	$10,200
Retained earnings	789
Total equity	$10,989
Total liabilities and equity	$13,354

Various master budget data based upon plans for the fiscal year ending June 30, 19B, appear as follows:

Sales—2,100,000 units × $16 = $33,600,000
Production—2,110,000 units × $12 = $25,320,000
Raw materials purchases—4,320,000 lbs. × $2.75 = $11,880,000 (two pounds of raw materials are needed to make one unit of finished product)
Direct labor—2,110,000 units produced × $4 = $8,440,000 (one-half hour of direct labor is needed to make one unit of finished product)
Factory overhead:

Variable expenses	$2,954,000*
Depreciation	600,000
Other fixed expenses	1,721,000*
	$5,275,000

$5,275,000 ÷ 1,055,000 direct labor hours (DLH) at normal capacity = $5.00 factory overhead rate per DLH;   Marketing expenses—$2,525,000*;   Administrative expenses—$2,615,000*

*Requires cash expenditure, but not necessarily in current budget year.

All sales are made on account. Raw materials, direct labor, factory overhead, and marketing and administrative expenses are credited to Vouchers Payable. Federal income tax expense is charged to Income Tax Payable. The federal income tax rate is 40%.

Beginning inventory in quantity and dollars:

	Quantity	Cost per Unit	Total Cost
Direct materials.....................	184,000 pounds	$ 2.75 per lb.	$506,000
Finished goods......................	54,000 units	$12.00 per unit	$648,000

Cash receipts and disbursements (000s omitted):

Cash balance 7/1/19A (estimated)................................	$ 800	
Cash receipts:		
Collection of accounts receivable..............................	33,450	
Total cash available...		$34,250
Cash disbursements:		
Payment of vouchers payable:		
Direct material..	$11,900	
Direct labor..	8,400	
Factory overhead..	4,650	
Marketing and administrative expenses................	5,200	
Total vouchers payable...	$30,150	
Income tax..	1,100	
Purchase of equipment..	400	
Cash dividends...	820	
Total cash disbursements..		32,470
Excess cash..		$ 1,780
Financing:		
Repayment of note payable, 12/30/19A....................	$ 1,000	
Interest expense...	50	
Total financing cost...		1,050
Projected cash balance, 6/30/19B................................		$ 730

Required: Construct a budgeted balance sheet for Einhard Company as of June 30, 19B.   *(ICMA adapted)*

16-9. PERT/cost network. The following network has been prepared for a project:

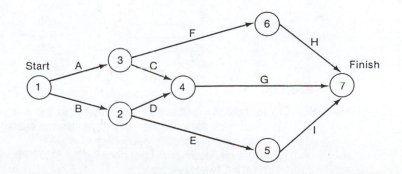

Expected time and cost estimates are:

Activity	Time	Cost
A	5 days	$ 4,000
B	5	4,000
C	10	15,000
D	7	3,500
E	5	10,000
F	7	14,000
G	5	5,000
H	10	20,000
I	10	30,000

Costs for each activity occur uniformly; e.g., activity A requires $800 each day.

Required:

    (1) Identify the critical path.
    (2) Prepare a daily activity and cost schedule.   *(CGAAC adapted)*

16-10. PERT/cost network for planning. Niswonger Construction Company is faced with the following PERT/cost network situation:

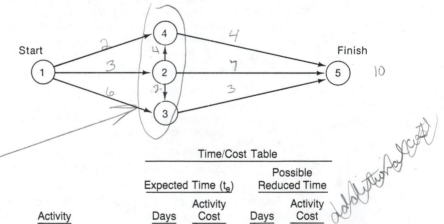

these are happening at same time (contemporaneous)

Time/Cost Table

Activity	Expected Time (t_e)		Possible Reduced Time	
	Days	Activity Cost	Days	Activity Cost
1-4......................	2	$ 800	1	$1,300
1-2......................	3	700	1	1,900
1-3......................	6	1,100	5	1,350
2-4......................	4	600	3	800
2-3......................	2	900	1	1,000
2-5......................	7	850	6	1,050
4-5......................	4	1,050	3	1,450
3-5......................	3	500	2	700
		$6,500		$9,550

Required:

    (1) Identify the critical path and determine the slack time.
    (2) Determine the cheapest way to reduce the critical path by one day and by two days and the cost in each case.
    (3) State management's best decision if a $1,000 bonus will be paid if the project is finished two days early.

16-11. PERT network and project planning. The following diagram and accompanying schedule have been prepared for a proposed retail store opening. The schedule describes the activities, the expected time (in weeks), the expected cost of each activity, and the possible reduced time (in weeks) and related incremental cost for those activities which can be accomplished in a shorter time period. It is estimated that the store should produce a contribution of about $2,000 per week to operating income.

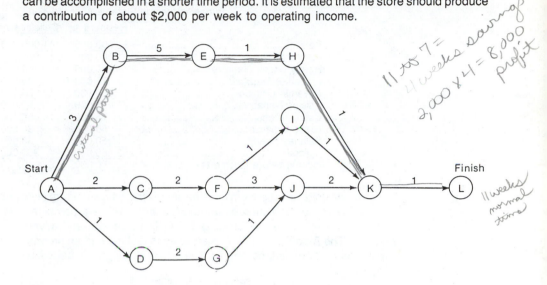

11 to 7 = 4 weeks savings
2,000 × 4 = 8,000 profit

critical path

Finish

11 weeks normal time

Activity	Description of Activity	Expected Time	Possible Reduced Time	Expected Cost	Incremental Cost To Achieve Reduced Time
A-B	Design exterior	3 weeks	1 week	$ 5,000	$4,500
A-C	Determine inventory needs	2	NC	500	0
A-D	Develop staffing plan	1	NC	500	0
B-E	Do exterior structural work	5	3	27,000	3,500
E-H	Paint exterior	1	NC	4,000	0
H-K	Install exterior signs	1	NC	15,000	0
C-F	Order inventory	2	NC	1,500	0
F-I	Develop special prices for opening	1	NC	2,000	0
I-K	Advertise opening and special prices	1	NC	8,000	0
F-J	Receive inventory	3	2	4,000	2,000
D-G	Acquire staff	2	1	3,000	1,000 *don't reduce time*
G-J	Train staff	1	NC	5,000	0
J-K	Stock shelves	2	1	3,500	1,500
K-L	Final preparations for grand opening	1	NC	6,000	0

NC denotes no change in time is possible.

8 weeks saved   *85,000*   *12,500 cost to save 8 weeks*   *11,500 cost*

Required:

(1) Determine the normal critical path, its length in weeks, and the normal cost to be incurred in opening the store.
(2) Compute the minimum time in which the store could be opened and the costs incurred to achieve the earlier opening.
(3) Explain whether the store should be opened following the normal schedule or the reduced program.   *(ICMA adapted)*

16-12. Flexible vs. fixed budget. Pearsons Inc. is a regional chain of restaurants, each with a carryout delicatessen department. Company management has prepared the following budget for a typical unit:

Typical Pearsons Restaurant—Deli
Budgeted Income Statement for the Year

	Restaurant	Delicatessen	Total
Sales..	$2,500,000	$1,000,000	$3,500,000
Purchases...	$1,000,000	$ 600,000	$1,600,000
Hourly wages (variable).....................	875,000	50,000	925,000
Franchise fee....................................	75,000	30,000	105,000
Advertising (fixed).............................	200,000	100,000	300,000
Utilities (variable)..............................	125,000	70,000	195,000
Depreciation.....................................	75,000	50,000	125,000
Lease expense..................................	50,000	30,000	80,000
Salaries (fixed).................................	50,000	30,000	80,000
Total..	$2,450,000	$ 960,000	$3,410,000
Income before income tax..................	$ 50,000	$ 40,000	$ 90,000

All units are approximately the same size, with a uniform style of building and facilities. The corporation charges a franchise fee, which is a percentage of sales, for use of the company name, the building and facilities design, and advertising advice.

The Akron, Ohio unit was selected to test the budget program. Its performance for the year just ended, compared to the typical budget, is as follows:

Pearsons Restaurant—Deli, Akron, Ohio
Income Statement for the Year Ended December 31, 19—

	Actual				Over (Under)
	Restaurant	Delicatessen	Total	Budget	Budget
Sales...................................	$2,000,000	$1,200,000	$3,200,000	$3,500,000	$(300,000)
Purchases.............................	$ 800,000	$ 780,000	$1,580,000	$1,600,000	$(20,000)
Hourly wages.........................	700,000	60,000	760,000	925,000	(165,000)
Franchise fee.........................	60,000	36,000	96,000	105,000	(9,000)
Advertising............................	200,000	100,000	300,000	300,000	—
Utilities.................................	100,000	76,000	176,000	195,000	(19,000)
Depreciation..........................	75,000	50,000	125,000	125,000	—
Lease expense.......................	50,000	30,000	80,000	80,000	—
Salaries.................................	50,000	30,000	80,000	80,000	—
Total...............................	$2,035,000	$1,162,000	$3,197,000	$3,410,000	$(213,000)
Income before income tax.......	$ (35,000)	$ 38,000	$ 3,000	$ 90,000	$ (87,000)

A review of the report and a discussion of its meaning by Pearsons' management led to the conclusion that a more meaningful comparison would result if a flexible budget analysis for each of the two lines were performed.

Required:

(1) Prepare an income statement for the Akron unit's deli line, comparing actual performance to a flexible budget.

(2) Discuss whether or not a complete report, comparing the performance of each of the two lines to its flexible budget, would make Akron's operating problems easier to identify.

(3) What are the advantages of comparing actual performance to a flexible budget as a part of the regular annual as well as monthly reporting system?

(ICMA adapted)

16-13. Flexible budget. The controller of Oakhill Corporation decided to prepare a flexible factory overhead budget ranging from 80% to 100% of capacity for the next year, with 50,000 hours as the 100% level. The data available are based on either past experiences, shop supervisors' figures, or management's decisions. For expenses of a semivariable nature, the fixed amount and the variable rate are determined via the high and low points method. The direct labor rate is $7.50 per hour. Additional data for factory overhead are:

Annual fixed expenses:
Depreciation..	$ 9,000
Insurance...	1,500
Maintenance cost (including payroll taxes and fringe benefits)............................	24,000
Property tax..	1,500
Supervisory staff (including payroll taxes and fringe benefits)............................	36,000

Variable expenses:
Shop supplies..	$.10 per direct labor hour
Indirect labor (excluding inspection)....................	$.45 per direct labor hour
Payroll taxes and fringe benefits.........................	18% of labor cost, direct and indirect

Semivariable expenses (from previous five years):

Year	Direct Labor Hours	Power and Light	Inspection (Including Payroll Taxes and Fringe Benefits)	Other Semi-Variable Expenses
19A	44,000	$1,500	$ 9,200	$8,000
19B	40,000	1,400	9,000	7,400
19C	45,000	1,600	9,200	8,200
19D	49,000	1,650	10,000	8,800
19E	50,000	1,700	10,200	8,900

Required: Prepare a flexible factory overhead budget ranging from 80% to 100% of capacity, with 10% intervals.

16-14. Flexible budget and overapplied fixed factory overhead. Salsbury Corporation uses a flexible budgeting system. The following flexible budget is provided for 80% and 100% of normal capacity.

	80% Capacity	100% Capacity
Units of production...	2,000	2,500
Direct labor..	$ 4,000	$ 5,000
Direct materials...	6,000	7,500
Total prime cost...	$10,000	$12,500
Factory overhead:		
Utilities...	$ 900	$ 1,000
Supplies...	800	1,000
Indirect labor..	1,000	1,250
Depreciation of plant and equipment................	3,000	3,000
Miscellaneous indirect factory expenses...........	1,000	1,200
Total factory overhead................................	$ 6,700	$ 7,450
Total budgeted manufacturing cost...............	$16,700	$19,950

Required:

(1) Prepare the allowable flexible budget on the assumption that 2,600 units are actually produced in the current period.

(2) If the factory overhead application rate were based on 100% of actual capacity and actual production costs were equal to the allowable budget for 2,600 units, what would be the amount of over- or underapplied factory overhead?

16-15. Flexible budget. Department A, one of 15 departments in the manufacturing plant, is involved in the production of all of the six products manufactured by Augustin Products Inc. Because Department A is highly mechanized, its output is measured in direct machine hours. Flexible budgets are utilized throughout the plant in planning and controlling costs, but this problem's focus is upon the application of flexible budgets in Department A only.

On March 15, 19A, the following flexible budget was approved for Department A to be used throughout the fiscal year 19A-B, beginning on July 1, 19A. This flexible budget was developed through the cooperative efforts of Department A's manager, the supervisor, and members of the Budget Department.

Flexible Budget for Department A
For Fiscal Year 19A-B

Controllable Cost	Fixed Amount per Month	Variable Rate per Direct Machine Hour
Employees' salaries......................	$ 9,000	
Indirect wages..............................	18,000	$.07
Indirect materials..........................		.09
Other costs...................................	6,000	.03
Total...	$33,000	$.19

On May 5, 19A, the annual sales plan and the production budget were completed. To continue preparation of the annual profit plan, which was detailed by month, the production budget was translated to planned activity for each of the 15 departments. The planned activity for Department A was:

	July	August	September	October-June	For Twelve Months Ending June 30, 19B
Planned output in direct machine hours............	22,000	25,000	29,000	249,000	325,000

On August 31, 19A, Department A's manager was informed that the planned September output had been revised to 34,000 direct machine hours. On September 30, 19A, Department A's accounting records showed the following actual data for September:

Actual output in direct machine hours.....................	33,000
Actual controllable costs incurred:	
Employees' salaries..	$ 9,300
Indirect wages..	20,500
Indirect materials..	2,850
Other costs..	7,510
Total...	$40,160

The following requirements relate primarily to the potential uses of the flexible budget for the period March through September, 19A.

Required:

(1) Explain how the range of the activity base to which the variable rates per direct machine hour are relevant should be determined.

(2) Illustrate the application of the high and low points method of determining the fixed and variable components of indirect wage costs for Department A. Assume that the high and low values for indirect wages are $19,400 at 20,000 direct machine hours and $20,100 at 30,000 direct machine hours.

(3) Explain and illustrate the use of the flexible budget in:

(a) Budgeting costs when the annual sales plan and production budget are completed (about May 5, 19A, or shortly thereafter).

(b) Budgeting a cost revision based upon a revised production budget (about August 31, 19A, or shortly thereafter).

(c) Preparing a cost performance report for September, 19A.

(AICPA adapted)

CASE

Flexible budget for performance evaluation.
Berwin Inc. is a manufacturer of small industrial tools with an annual sales volume of approximately $3.5 million. Sales growth has been steady during the year, and there is no evidence of cyclical demand. Production has increased gradually during the year and has been distributed evenly throughout each month. The company employs a sequential processing system. The four manufacturing departments—Casting, Machining, Finishing, and Packaging—are all located in the same building. Fixed factory overhead is assigned using a plant-wide rate.

Berwin has always been able to compete with other manufacturers of small industrial tools. However, its market has expanded only in response to product innovation. Thus, research and development is important and has helped Berwin to expand as well as maintain demand.

Carla Viller, controller, has designed and implemented a new budget system in response to concerns voiced by George Berwin, president. An annual budget that has been divided into 12 equal segments has been prepared to assist in the timely evaluation of monthly performance. Berwin was visibly upset upon receiving the performance report for May for the Machining Department, shown on page

508. Similar performance reports were prepared for the other three departments.

Berwin exclaimed, "How can they be efficient enough to produce nine extra units every working day and still miss the budget by $300 a day?" Gene Jordan, Machining Department supervisor, could not understand "all the red ink," when he knew the department had operated more efficiently in May than it had in several months. Jordan stated, "I was expecting a pat on the back and instead the boss tore me apart. What's more, I don't even know why!"

Required:

(1) Review the May performance report for the Machining Department of Berwin Inc. Based upon the information presented in the report:

(a) Discuss the strengths of the new budget system in general.

(b) Identify the weaknesses of the performance report and explain how the report should be revised to eliminate each weakness.

(2) Prepare a revised performance report for the Machining Department, using the data given for May.

(ICMA adapted)

Berwin Inc.
Machining Department Performance Report
For the Month Ended May 31, 19A

	Budget	Actual	(Over) Under Budget
Volume in units...	3,000	3,185	(185)
Variable manufacturing costs:			
Direct materials..	$24,000	$ 24,843	$ (843)
Direct labor..	27,750	29,302	(1,552)
Variable factory overhead................................	33,300	35,035	(1,735)
Total variable manufacturing cost.................	$85,050	$ 89,180	$(4,130)
Fixed factory overhead:			
Indirect labor...	$ 3,300	$ 3,334	$ (34)
Depreciation..	1,500	1,500	
Taxes..	300	300	
Insurance...	240	240	
Other...	930	1,027	(97)
Total fixed overhead cost.............................	$ 6,270	$ 6,401	$ (131)
Corporate costs:			
Research and development.............................	$ 2,400	$ 3,728	$(1,328)
Marketing and administrative...........................	3,600	4,075	(475)
Total corporate cost......................................	$ 6,000	$ 7,803	$(1,803)
Total cost..	$97,320	$103,384	$(6,064)

CHAPTER 17

StandardCosting: Setting Standards and Analyzing Variances

A *standard cost* is the predetermined cost of manufacturing a single unit or a specific quantity of product units during a specific period. It is the planned cost of a product under current and/or anticipated operating conditions. A standard cost has two components: a physical standard (i.e., a standard quantity of inputs per unit of output) and a price standard (i.e., a standard cost or rate per unit of input).

A standard is like a norm. Whatever is considered normal can generally be accepted as standard. For example, if a score of 72 is the standard for a golf course, a golfer's score is judged on the basis of this standard. In industry, the standards for making a desk, assembling a microcomputer, refining crude oil, or manufacturing automobiles are based on carefully determined quantitative and qualitative measurements and engineering methods. A standard should be thought of as a norm in terms of specific production inputs, such as units of materials, hours of labor, and percentage of plant capacity used.

To provide a foundation for understanding and effectively utilizing a standard cost system, this chapter begins by discussing the usefulness of standard costs and the setting of standards. This foundation is followed by a section which explains and illustrates the computation of the standard cost variances for materials, labor, and factory overhead. The chapter concludes with a discussion about the responsibility and control of these variances.

▼ USEFULNESS OF STANDARD COSTS

A standard cost system may be used in connection with either the process or job order cost accumulation method. Standard costing is most readily adaptable to manufacturing environments where production technology is relatively stable and the products manufactured are homogeneous within the cost accumulation unit, i.e., the department or the job. It is difficult to establish standards if the manufacturing technology changes rapidly or if each product manufactured is unique. Consequently, standard costing is typically found in firms that use process cost accumulation procedures (e.g., manufacturers of petroleum and chemical products, building supplies, steel, and soft drinks), and in firms that use job order cost accumulation procedures where homogeneous units are batch produced on each job (e.g., manufacturers of radios and televisions, furniture, paper products, and processed foods).

Standard cost systems aid in planning and controlling operations and in gaining insights into the probable impact of managerial decisions on costs and profits. Standard costs are used for:

1. Establishing budgets.
2. Controlling costs by motivating employees and measuring efficiencies.
3. Simplifying costing procedures and expediting cost reports.
4. Assigning costs to materials, work in process, and finished goods inventories.
5. Forming the basis for establishing contract bids and for setting sales prices.

Standards are quite useful in preparing budgets. With the use of standard costs, the preparation of budgets for any volume and mixture of products is more reliably and speedily accomplished. Reliability is enhanced because the standards are based on detailed analyses of the production processes. The time required to prepare the operating budget is reduced because production requirements are already documented for each product.

The effectiveness of controlling costs depends greatly upon a thorough understanding of both the processes that give rise to cost incurrence and the motivation of the personnel who control those processes. Standards provide performance goals for employees and a basis for evaluating actual operating results. Executives and supervisors become cost-conscious as they become aware of results. This cost-consciousness tends to reduce costs and encourage economies in all phases of the business.

The use of standard costs for accounting purposes simplifies costing procedures through the reduction of clerical labor and expense. A complete standard cost system is usually accompanied by standardization of productive operations. Standard production or manufacturing orders, which call for standard quantities of production and specific labor operations, can be prepared in advance of actual production. Materials requisitions, labor time tickets, and operation cards can be prepared in advance of production, and standard costs can be compiled. As orders for a part are placed into the shop, previously established standards are used to determine the quantities, production processes, and costs that will apply. As the production process becomes more standardized, the clerical effort becomes simpler. Reports can be systematized to present complete information regarding standards, actual costs, and variances.

Although some companies that use standard costs for planning and control do not record inventories at standard cost, the incorporation of standard costs into the regular accounting records leads to increased efficiency and accuracy in clerical work. A complete standard cost file by parts and operations simplifies assigning costs to materials, work in process, and finished goods inventories. Inventory costs are easily determined by multiplying the quantities of each product in inventory by the standard unit cost and adding the total cost for each product. The use of standard costs also tends to stabilize the influence of fluctuating input prices and capacity utilization on inventory costs. Incorporation of standard costs into the accounting records through journal entries is discussed and illustrated in Chapter 18.

The process of determining contract bids and establishing sales prices for products is greatly enhanced by utilization of a standard cost system. The computation of costs to be incurred on a contract is simplified and made more reliable by using standard costs for the products to be produced or, if a unique product is to be produced, by using standard costs for the production operations that will be required. Standards are useful in establishing sales prices for products by providing reliable, up-to-date cost information. When the market price of a product is not readily observable, as would be the case for new products or products that are in some way differentiated from those of competitors, product cost typically provides the starting point in establishing the sales price.

▼ SETTING STANDARDS

Calculation of a standard cost is based on physical standards—two types, basic and current, are often discussed in the literature. A *basic standard* is a yardstick against which both expected and actual performances are compared. It is similar to an index number against which all subsequent results are measured. *Current standards* are of three types:

1. The *expected actual standard* is a standard set for an expected level of operation and efficiency. It is a reasonably close estimate of actual results.
2. The *normal standard* is a standard set for a normal level of operation and efficiency, intended to represent challenging yet attainable results.
3. The *theoretical standard* is a standard set for an ideal or maximum level of operation and efficiency. Such standards constitute goals to be aimed for rather than performances that can be currently achieved.

Materials and labor costs are generally based on normal, current operating conditions, allowing for expected changes in prices and rates and tempered by the desired efficiency level. Factory overhead is based on normal operating conditions and volume at the desired efficiency level.

The success of a standard cost system depends on the reliability, accuracy, and acceptance of the standards. Extreme care should be taken to make sure that all factors are considered in the establishment of standards. In some cases, standards are set on the basis of an average of the actual results of previous periods. However, the most effective standards are set by industrial engineers on the basis of careful studies of product components and production operations, using appropriate sampling techniques and including participation by those individuals whose performance is to be measured by the standards.

Standards must be set, and the system implemented, in an atmosphere that gives full consideration to the behavioral characteristics of managers and workers. In the long run, workers and plant management will tend to react negatively if they feel threatened by imposed standards. If they participate in setting standards, they can more easily understand the basis upon which the standards are determined and more readily identify with the standard costing procedure. Under ideal conditions, employees will accept standards as personal production goals.

Standards which are too loose or too tight will generally have a negative impact on worker motivation. If standards are too loose, workers will tend to set their goals at this low level, thereby reducing productivity to a level below what is attainable. If the standard is too tight, workers will quickly realize the impossibility of attaining the standards, will become frustrated, and will soon begin to ignore the standard. A reasonable standard which can be attained under normal working conditions is likely to contribute to the workers' motivation to achieve the designated level of activity or production.

Mature products are better candidates for cost minimization and measures of productivity than are new products for which innovative behavior may be more appropriate. The new product is likely to begin in a somewhat fluid form, with process standardization evolving with maturity. Otherwise, ". . . managers introducing new products, but who are evaluated on the basis of cost minimization and productivity, may not be as responsive to customer needs, will freeze the design specifications of the products prematurely in an attempt to standardize production, and may not pay sufficient attention to producing consistently high-quality products."[1]

To be utilized effectively in the control and analysis of costs, standards must be established for a definite period of time. Standards are usually computed for a six- or twelve-month period, although a longer period is sometimes used. Standards should be changed only when underlying conditions change or when they no longer reflect the original concept. Changing physical standards more than once a year weakens their effectiveness and increases clerical details. Frequent changes in the physical standards create confusion and tend to give employees the impression that supervisors are not in control and do not know what level of efficiency can be achieved. Nevertheless, physical standards should be continuously monitored and frequently reviewed to determine their appropriateness. Events, rather than time, are the factors that determine when standards should be revised. These events may be classified as internal or external. Internal events such as technological advances, design revisions, method changes, labor rate adjustments, and changes in physical facilities are to some degree controllable by management. In contrast, external events such as price changes (including the impact of inflation), market trends, specific customer requirements, and changes in the competitive situation are generally not controllable by management. Consequently, price standards and product configuration standards may require frequent change as controlling external events occur.

---

[1] Robert S. Kaplan, "Measuring Manufacturing Performance: A New Challenge for Managerial Accounting Research," *The Accounting Review*, Vol. LVIII, No. 4, p. 695.

Once standards are set, standard cost cards should be prepared, on which the itemized cost of each materials part, labor operation, and overhead cost is shown. A master standard cost card, illustrated as follows, gives the standard unit cost of a product.

Date of Standard July 1, 19--   STANDARD COST CARD FOR PRODUCT Alpac

	ITEM CODE	QUAN-TITY	STANDARD UNIT PRICE	DEPARTMENT 1	2	3	4	5	TOTALS
DIRECT MATERIALS	2-234	4	$6.00/pc.		$24.00				
	3-671	24	3.00/doz.			$6.00			
	5-489	2	2.50/pc.					$ 5.00	
	5-361	8	6.50/pc.					52.00	
	TOTAL DIRECT MATERIALS COST								$ 87.00

	OPERA-TION NUMBER	STANDARD HOURS	STANDARD RATE PER HOUR	DEPARTMENT 1	2	3	4	5	
DIRECT LABOR	2-476	3	$9.00		$27.00				
	2-581	11½	9.40		108.10				
	3-218	4	9.30			$37.20			
	5-420	2½	9.20					$23.00	
	TOTAL DIRECT LABOR COST								195.30

	STANDARD HOURS	RATE PER DIRECT LABOR HOUR	DEPARTMENT 1	2	3	4	5	
FACTORY OVERHEAD	14½	$4.80		$69.60				
	4	2.00			$8.00			
	2½	3.50					$8.75	
	TOTAL FACTORY OVERHEAD.							86.35
	TOTAL MANUFACTURING COST PER UNIT							$368.65

Standard Cost Card

The master standard cost card is supported by individual cards that indicate how the standard cost was compiled and computed. Each subcost card represents a form of standard cost card.

▼ DETERMINING STANDARD PRODUCTION

The preceding discussion deals with the determination of the standards per unit of production. To determine the standard allowed for each cost component, the standard per unit must be multiplied by the quantity of equivalent units produced. This determination must consider the stage of completion of work in process inventories. Because the emphasis of control is on current period activity, it is essential to compute the production standard and identify the associated variances for the current period only. Thus, the equivalent units for each cost component would be computed as follows:

Units completed and transferred out.	xxxx
Less beginning inventory (all units).	xxx
Units started and completed this period.	xxxx
Add beginning inventory (work this period).	xxx
Add ending inventory (work this period).	xxx
Equivalent units of production this period.	xxxx

equivalent units of production

Generally, standards include an allowance for normal spoilage. In such a case, equivalent unit computations for standard costing are based on good units only. By this procedure, the cost of excess or abnormal spoilage becomes a part of the computed variances. However, if management wishes to segregate the cost of abnormal spoilage for separate identification and evaluation, equivalent production computations must include both good units and abnormal spoilage.

▼ DETERMINING STANDARD COST VARIANCES

For each item of direct material, for each labor operation, and for departmentalized factory overhead, actual costs are measured against standard costs, resulting in differences. These differences are analyzed and identified as specific types of standard cost variances. If the actual cost exceeds the standard cost, the variance is referred to as "unfavorable" because the excess has an unfavorable effect on income. Conversely, if the standard cost exceeds the actual cost, the variance is referred to as "favorable" because it has a favorable effect on income.

The analysis does not end with such labeling, however. A standard cost variance is a question, not an answer. To achieve cost control, managers must determine reasons for the occurrence of each material variance by investigating the circumstances that caused it. Effective management action can be taken only when the causes of cost variances are known. The responsibility and control of variances is more fully discussed later in this chapter.

Materials Standards and Variances

Two standards must be developed for direct materials costs:

1. A materials price standard
2. A materials quantity standard (sometimes referred to as a materials usage standard)

Price standards permit (1) checking the performance of the purchasing department and detecting the influence of various internal and external factors on materials cost and (2) measuring the effect of materials price increases or decreases on the company's profits. Determining the price or cost to be used as the standard cost is often difficult because materials prices are controlled more by external factors than by a company's management. Prices selected should reflect current market prices, and the standards should be revised at inventory dates or whenever there is a major change in the market price of any of the principal materials or parts. Typically, prices are determined at the beginning of the accounting period and used throughout the period. However, during periods of rapidly changing prices, it may be necessary to change the price standard frequently, especially if inventory is recorded in the accounting records at standard.

If the actual price paid is more or less than the standard price, a price variance occurs. Materials price variances may be recorded at the time the materials are purchased (referred to as a *materials purchase price variance*) or at the time the materials are issued to the factory (referred to as a *materials price usage variance*). To hold the purchasing department fully accountable for price variances at the date they occur, the variances should be recorded at the time of purchase. Otherwise, materials used in the current period may include price variances related to materials purchased in a prior period, or price variances applicable to current period purchases may be inventoried. In either case, the materials price usage variance would be difficult to interpret because of the compounding effects of inventory changes.

To illustrate the computation of a materials purchase price variance, assume that 5,000 units of Item 5-489 on the standard cost card for Alpac (page 513) are purchased at a unit price of $2.47. The materials purchase price variance is computed as follows:

	Quantity ×	Unit Cost	=	Amount	
Actual quantity purchased	5,000	$2.47 actual		$12,350	
Actual quantity purchased	5,000	2.50 standard		12,500	
Materials purchase price variance	5,000	$ (.03)		$ (150)	fav.

The $150 materials purchase price variance is favorable because the actual price is less than the standard price (i.e., the actual cost is $.03 per unit less than the standard permitted). As an alternative, the materials price usage variance could be computed. For example, if 3,550 units of Item 5-489 were issued and used by production, the materials price usage variance would be computed as follows:

	Quantity ×	Unit Cost	=	Amount	
Actual quantity used	3,550	$2.47 actual		$8,768.50	
Actual quantity used	3,550	2.50 standard		8,875.00	
Materials price usage variance	3,550	$ (.03)		$ (106.50)	fav.

The $150 favorable materials purchase price variance is $43.50 greater than the $106.50 favorable materials price usage variance. The reason for this difference is that 1,450 units of Item 5-489 which were purchased this period at a favorable variance of $.03 per unit (1,450 × $.03 = $43.50) were added to inventory and not used this period.

Quantity or usage standards are generally developed from materials specifications prepared by the departments of engineering (mechanical, electrical, or chemical) or product design. In a small or medium-size company, the superintendent or the departmental supervisors will provide basic specifications regarding type, quantity, and quality of materials needed and operations to be performed. Quantity standards should be set after the most economical size, shape, and quality of the product and the results expected from the use of various kinds and grades of materials have been analyzed. The standard quantity should be increased to include allowances for acceptable levels of waste, spoilage, shrinkage, seepage, evaporation, and leakage. The determination of the percentage of spoilage or waste should be based on figures that prevail after the experimental and development stages of the product have been completed.

The *materials quantity (or usage) variance* is computed by comparing the actual quantity of materials used with the standard quantity allowed, both priced at standard cost. The standard quantity allowed is determined by multiplying the quantity of materials that should be required to produce one unit of product (the standard quantity allowed per unit) by the actual number of units produced during the period. The units produced are the equivalent units of production for the materials cost being analyzed.

To illustrate the computation of the materials quantity (or usage) variance, assume that 1,750 equivalent units of Alpac are produced during the period, insofar as material Item 5-489 is concerned. Since the standard cost card calls for two units of Item 5-489 per unit of Alpac produced, the standard quantity allowed is 3,500 units (1,750 × 2). The materials quantity (or usage) variance for Item 5-489 is computed as follows:

	Quantity	×	Unit Cost	= Amount
Actual quantity used	3,550		$2.50 standard	$8,875
Standard quantity allowed	3,500		2.50 standard	8,750
Materials quantity variance	50		2.50 standard	$ 125 unfav.

The $125 materials quantity (or usage) variance is unfavorable because the actual quantity used exceeded the standard quantity allowed by 50 units.

Labor Standards and Variances

Two standards must also be developed for direct labor costs:

1. A rate (wage or cost) standard.
2. An efficiency (time or usage) standard.

In many plants, the standard is based on rates established in collective bargaining agreements that define hourly wages, piece rates, and bonus differentials. Without a union contract, rates are based on the earnings rate as determined by agreement between the employee and the personnel department. Since rates are generally based on definite agreements, labor rate variances are infrequent. If they occur, they are generally due to unusual short-term conditions existing in the factory.

To assure fairness in rates paid for each operation performed, job rating has become a recognized procedure in industry. When a rate is revised or a change is authorized temporarily, it must be reported promptly to the payroll department to avoid delays, incorrect pay, and faulty reporting. Any difference between the standard and actual rates results in a *labor rate (wage or cost) variance*.

To illustrate the computation of the labor rate variance for Operation 2-476 on the standard cost card for Alpac (page 513), assume that 1,880 hours are worked at a rate of $9.50 per hour to produce 530 equivalent units of Alpac. The labor rate variance is computed as follows:

	Hours ×	Rate	= Amount
Actual hours worked....................	1,880	$9.50 actual	$17,860
Actual hours worked....................	1,880	9.00 standard	16,920
Labor rate variance......................	1,880	$ .50	$ 940 unfav.

The labor rate variance of $940 is unfavorable because the actual rate exceeded the standard rate by $.50 per hour. The actual labor hours worked excludes nonproductive time, which is charged to factory overhead. Idle labor cost, to the extent that it is not included as a budgeted overhead item, will ulimately become part of the controllable variance in the two-variance method or the spending variance in the three- and four-variance methods, which are discussed later in the chapter.

Determination of labor efficiency standards is a specialized function. Therefore, they are best established by industrial engineers, using time and motion studies. Standards are set in accordance with scientific methods and accepted practices. They are based on actual performance of a worker or group of workers possessing average skill and using average effort while performing manual operations or working on machines operating under normal conditions. Time factors for acceptable levels of fatigue, personal needs, and delays beyond the control of the worker are studied and included in the standard. Such allowances are an integral part of the labor standard, but time required for setting up machines, waiting, or a breakdown is included in the factory overhead standard.

The establishment of time standards requires a detailed study of manufacturing operations. Standards based on operations should be understood by supervisors and used to enhance labor efficiency. However, time standards are of limited use "where operating times are strongly influenced by factors which cannot be standardized and controlled by management or where output from highly mechanized work is a function of machine time and speed rather than of labor hours worked."[2]

When a new product or process is started, the labor efficiency standard for costing and budget development should be based on the learning curve phenomenon (Chapter 9). The learning curve may well be, at least in part, an explanation of the labor efficiency variance associated with employees assigned to existing tasks that are new to them. Labor-related factory overhead costs and perhaps materials usage might also be affected.

The *labor efficiency variance* is computed at the end of any reporting period (day, week, or month) by comparing actual hours worked with standard hours allowed, both at the standard labor rate. The standard hours allowed is determined by multiplying the number of direct labor hours established or predetermined to produce one unit (the standard labor hours per unit) times the actual number of units produced during the period for which the variances

---

[2] Walter B. McFarland, *Manpower Cost and Performance Measurement* (New York: National Association of Accountants, 1977), p. 60.

are being computed. The units produced are the equivalent units of production for the labor cost being analyzed.

The labor efficiency variance for Operation 2-476 is computed as follows:

	Hours	×	Rate	=	Amount	
Actual hours worked	1,880		$9.00 standard		$16,920	
Standard hours allowed	1,590		9.00 standard		14,310	
Labor efficiency variance	290		9.00 standard		$ 2,610	unfav.

The standard hours allowed is the result of multiplying 530 units of Alpac by three standard hours per unit. The unfavorable labor efficiency variance of $2,610 is due to the use of 290 hours in excess of standard hours allowed. The actual labor hours worked excludes nonproductive time, which is charged to factory overhead. Idle labor cost to the extent it is not included as a budgeted overhead item will ultimately become part of the controllable variance in the two-variance method or the spending variance in the three- and four-variance methods.

Factory Overhead Standards and Variances

Procedures for establishing and using standard factory overhead rates are similar to the methods discussed in Chapters 12 and 13, dealing with the determination of predetermined factory overhead rates by department and their application to jobs and products. First, a factory overhead budget must be prepared for each department or cost center. This process involves estimating each item of factory overhead expense that is expected to be incurred within each department or cost center at some predetermined level of activity, typically normal capacity or expected actual capacity. Next, budgeted service department costs are allocated to producing departments on the basis of services that are expected to be provided. When all budgeted factory overhead costs have been allocated to producing departments, each producing department's standard factory overhead rate is determined by totaling the budgeted direct and indirect factory overhead in the department and dividing the total by the predetermined level of the allocation base used by the department, such as direct labor hours, direct labor dollars, machine hours, direct materials cost, or units of product.

The activity measure used as an allocation base may vary from department to department, depending upon the nature of the production process in each department. There are two important considerations in selecting the appropriate allocation base. First, in order to assign costs to products on a reasonably accurate basis, the activity measure chosen should be the one that reflects the primary source of cost incurrence within the department. For example, if the production process is labor intensive in one department and capital intensive in another, direct labor hours or direct labor cost should be used in the first department and machine hours in the latter. However, if only one product is produced within the department, the equivalent units of product is a reasonable allocation base, regardless of the nature of the production process. Second, the activity measure chosen must be one that is capable of being reasonably and accurately monitored on a per unit or per job basis within the existing data gathering system or with inexpensive modification to that system. If machine hours are selected, a data gathering system that can accurately record the number of machine hours incurred in the production of each unit or job must be in place. Because such data are not normally collected and because the installation and operation of a system that would accurately collect such data are costly, manufacturers have traditionally used readily available measures such as direct labor hours or direct labor cost to allocate factory overhead to production. However, with the increasing use of robotics in manufacturing, direct labor is becoming a less significant, and in some cases an insignificant, cost.[3] Consequently, many modern manufacturing companies are being forced to redesign their cost accounting systems and find new ways of allocating factory overhead.

The effect of choosing different levels of capacity on factory overhead cost per unit may be observed in the following illustration:

Production volume (units)	80,000	90,000	100,000	110,000
Factory overhead:				
Variable	$112,000	$126,000	$140,000	$154,000
Fixed	60,000	60,000	60,000	60,000
Total	$172,000	$186,000	$200,000	$214,000
Factory overhead per unit:				
Variable	$1.40	$1.400	$1.40	$1.400
Fixed	.75	.667	.60	.545
Total unit overhead cost	$2.15	$2.067	$2.00	$1.945

The illustration demonstrates the basic pattern of overhead behavior. Fixed expenses remain fixed within the relevant range of activity (assumed here to be between 80,000 and 110,000 units), as activity (volume of units produced) changes, but they vary per unit of activity. As the number of units produced increases, the amount of fixed factory overhead per unit decreases. In contrast, total variable expenses increase proportionately with each increase in activity and remain fixed per unit within the relevant range. Understanding this characteristic of overhead behavior is important in establishing a standard factory overhead rate because the level of activity chosen can have a material effect on the amount of factory overhead charged to production and, consequently, the amount of cost charged to products.

The data from the following flexible budget for Department 3, which is involved in producing Alpac (page 513), are used to illustrate the computation of the standard overhead rate and the overhead variances:

---

[3] Allen H. Seed, III, "Cost Accounting in the Age of Robotics," *Management Accounting*, Vol. LXVI, No. 4, pp. 39-43.

	Department 3 Monthly Flexible Budget			
Capacity......................................	80%	90%	100%	
Standard production..................	800	900	1,000	
Direct labor hours......................	3,200	3,600	4,000	
Variable factory overhead:				
Indirect labor..........................	$1,600.00	$1,800.00	$2,000.00	$ .50 per DLH
Indirect materials...................	960.00	1,080.00	1,200.00	.30
Supplies..................................	640.00	720.00	800.00	.20
Repairs....................................	480.00	540.00	600.00	.15
Power and light......................	160.00	180.00	200.00	.05
Total variable overhead.........	$3,840.00	$4,320.00	$4,800.00	$1.20 per DLH
Fixed factory overhead:				
Supervision.............................	$1,200.00	$1,200.00	$1,200.00	
Depreciation of machinery.....	700.00	700.00	700.00	
Insurance................................	250.00	250.00	250.00	
Property tax............................	250.00	250.00	250.00	
Power and light......................	400.00	400.00	400.00	
Maintenance............................	400.00	400.00	400.00	
Total fixed overhead..............	$3,200.00	$3,200.00	$3,200.00	
Total factory overhead..............	$7,040.00	$7,520.00	$8,000.00	$3,200 per month plus $1.20 per DLH

Assuming that the 100% column represents normal capacity, the standard factory overhead rate is computed as follows:

$$\frac{\text{Total factory overhead}}{\text{Direct labor hours}} = \frac{\$8,000}{4,000} = \$2 \text{ per standard direct labor hour}$$

At the 100% capacity level, the rate consists of:

$$\frac{\text{Total variable factory overhead}}{\text{Direct labor hours}} = \frac{\$4,800}{4,000} = \$1.20 \text{ variable factory overhead rate}$$

$$\frac{\text{Total fixed factory overhead}}{\text{Direct labor hours}} = \frac{\$3,200}{4,000} = .80 \text{ fixed factory overhead rate}$$

Total factory overhead rate at
  normal capacity................................... $2.00 per standard direct labor hour

The standard cost of factory overhead chargeable to each job or process is determined by multiplying the standard number of units of the allocation base allowed, direct labor hours in this illustration, by the predetermined standard factory overhead rate. The standard number of units of the allocation base allowed is determined by multiplying the standard number of units of the allocation base allowed per unit of product by the actual number of equivalent units of product produced during the period. At the end of each period, usually a month, the factory overhead actually incurred is compared with the standard cost of factory overhead chargeable to work in process for the period. The difference between these two amounts is referred to as the *overall (or net) factory overhead variance*. If the standard cost system is fully integrated into the regular accounting records, i.e., inventories are recorded in the accounts at standard, the overall factory overhead variance is equal to over- or underapplied factory overhead (see Chapter 18).

For illustration purposes, assume the data for Department 3 at the end of one month are as follows:

Actual overhead.. $7,384
Standard hours allowed for actual production (850 units × 4 standard
   labor hours per unit)... 3,400
Actual direct labor hours used... 3,475

The overall factory overhead variance is computed as follows:

Actual departmental factory overhead.. $7,384
Standard factory overhead chargeable to work in process (3,400
   standard hours × $2 standard overhead rate)............................... 6,800
Overall (or net) factory overhead variance... $ 584 unfav.

The overall factory overhead variance must be further analyzed to reveal the sources of the variance in order to provide a guide to management in determining its causes. Causes must be determined before effective remedial action can be taken. The overall variance can be broken down for analysis in many different ways; however, the most frequently used approaches are to compute two, three, or four factory overhead variances. Regardless of the method used, the sum of the variances computed must equal the overall factory overhead variance.

Two-Variance Method. The two-variance method is the most frequently used method in actual practice, perhaps because it is the easiest to compute. The two variances are (1) the controllable variance and (2) the volume variance.

The *controllable variance* is the difference between the actual factory overhead incurred and the budget allowance based on the standard number of units of the allocation base allowed for actual production. The budget allowance may be thought of as the amount of factory overhead that would have been budgeted at standard if the actual quantity produced had been known in advance, i.e., total budgeted variable overhead at standard for actual production plus total budgeted fixed factory overhead.

The controllable variance is the responsibility of department managers to the extent that they can exercise control over the costs to which the variances relate. It is composed of two elements: (1) the difference between actual variable factory overhead and standard variable factory overhead allowed and (2) the difference between actual fixed factory overhead and budgeted fixed factory overhead. Based on the data presented above for Department 3, the controllable variance is computed as follows:

Actual factory overhead.. $7,384
Budget allowance based on standard hours allowed:
  Variable overhead (3,400 standard hours × $1.20 variable
    overhead rate)... $4,080
  Fixed overhead budgeted....................................... 3,200 7,280
Controllable variance.. $ 104 unfav.

The *volume variance* is the difference between the budget allowance based on the standard number of units of the allocation base allowed for actual production and the standard factory overhead chargeable to work in process. It indicates the cost of capacity available but not utilized efficiently and, therefore, may be the responsibility of the department manager (to the extent caused by variances in production efficiencies) or of executive management (to the extent caused by unexpected changes in sales demand). The volume variance for Department 3 is computed as follows:

Budget allowance based on standard hours allowed..............................	$7,280
Standard factory overhead chargeable to work in process.....................	6,800
Volume variance...	$ 480 unfav.

When standard cost rather than actual cost is charged to production, the volume variance can be thought of as the amount of over- or underapplied budgeted fixed factory overhead. It is the difference between budgeted fixed factory overhead and the amount of fixed factory overhead chargeable to production, based on the standard number of units of the allocation base allowed for actual production. Consequently, the volume variance for Department 3 could be computed as follows:

Fixed factory overhead budgeted...	$3,200
Fixed factory overhead chargeable to production, based on the standard hours allowed for units produced (3,400 standard hours × $.80 fixed overhead rate)...	2,720
Volume variance...	$ 480 unfav.

Alternatively, it can also be computed as follows:

Normal (or budgeted) capacity in labor hours...............................	4,000
Standard hours allowed for actual production...............................	3,400
Capacity hours not utilized or not utilized efficiently....................	600
Fixed factory overhead rate..	× $.80
Volume variance...	$ 480 unfav.

The controllable variance plus the volume variance equals the overall factory overhead variance for Department 3, as follows:

Controllable variance...	$104 unfav.
Volume variance...	480 unfav.
Overall factory overhead variance.....................	$584 unfav.

Three-Variance Method. One of the problems with the two-variance method is that it conceals the over- or underutilization of the variable input used as the factory overhead allocation base, which is direct labor hours in the Department 3 illustration. The three-variance method attempts to remedy this problem. There are two commonly found alternative approaches for dividing the overall factory overhead variance into three variances. One method, referred to throughout this text as three-variance method A, requires the computation of (1) the spending variance, (2) the idle capacity variance, and (3) the efficiency variance. The other method, referred to throughout this text as three-variance method B, requires the computation of (1) the spending variance, (2) the variable efficiency variance, and (3) the volume variance. Each alternative provides a different view of the overall variance for management analysis.

Method A. The spending variance and the idle capacity variance computed in three-variance method A are the same variances discussed in Chapter 12. In this method, only the efficiency variance is unique to standard costing. The *spending variance* is the difference between the actual factory overhead incurred and the budget allowance based on the actual number of units of the allocation base used in actual production. It is composed of (1) the difference between the actual variable factory overhead incurred and the amount that would have been budgeted at the actual level of activity and (2) the difference between the actual fixed factory overhead and the budgeted fixed factory overhead. For Department 3, the spending variance would be computed as follows:

Actual factory overhead incurred...		$7,384
Budget allowance based on actual hours:		
Variable overhead (3,475 actual hours × $1.20 variable		
overhead rate)...	$4,170	
Fixed overhead budgeted........ *4,000 × .80*	3,200	7,370
Spending variance..		$ 14 unfav.

[handwritten: Spending Variance]

By basing the budget allowance on actual hours instead of on standard hours allowed, as shown above in the controllable variance, the manager of Department 3 receives a more favorable allowance, which reduces the variance from $104 to $14. This reduction, which is identified later in the chapter as the variable efficiency variance, is caused by the inefficient use of the variable production input used as the allocation base for factory overhead.

The *idle capacity variance* is the difference between the budget allowance based on the actual number of units of the allocation base used in actual production and the amount of factory overhead chargeable to production in the absence of a standard cost system (i.e., the actual number of units of the allocation base used multiplied by the factory overhead rate). It is a measure of the over- or underutilization of production capacity and is computed for Department 3 in the illustration as follows:

Budget allowance based on actual hours......................................	$7,370	
Actual hours (3,475) × factory overhead rate ($2)......................	6,950	
Idle capacity variance..	$ 420 unfav.	

[handwritten: Idle Capacity Variance]

Conceptually, the idle capacity variance is the difference between the budgeted fixed factory overhead and the fixed factory overhead that would be charged to production on the basis of the actual capacity employed. Consequently, it can be computed as follows:

Budgeted fixed factory overhead..	$3,200	
Actual hours (3,475) × fixed overhead rate ($.80)......................	2,780	
Idle capacity variance..	$ 420 unfav.	

Alternatively, it can also be computed as follows:

Normal (or budgeted) capacity in labor hours..............................	4,000	
Actual labor hours...	3,475	
Capacity hours not utilized..	525	
Fixed factory overhead rate...	×$.80	
Idle capacity variance..	$ 420 unfav.	

The *efficiency variance* is the difference between the actual number of units of the allocation base used and the standard number of units of the allocation base allowed for actual production, multiplied by the standard factory overhead rate. It is largely the responsibility of department management because it reflects the efficient or inefficient use of the variable production input used as the allocation base. When labor hours are used as the basis for applying factory overhead, this variance reflects the efficient or inefficient use of labor, and when machine hours are used as the allocation base, this variance reflects the efficiency of machine usage. This variance is affected by inexperienced labor, fatigue, poor employee morale, changes in operating procedures, new or worn-out machinery, and poor quality of materials.

The efficiency variance for Department 3 is computed as follows:

Actual hours (3,475) × standard overhead rate ($2)......................	$6,950
Standard factory overhead chargeable to production	
(3,400 standard hours × $2 overhead rate)...............................	6,800
Efficiency variance..	$ 150 unfav.

Alternatively, it can be computed as follows:

Actual hours worked..	3,475
Standard hours allowed for actual units produced.....................	3,400
Excess of actual hours over standard hours allowed.................	75
Standard factory overhead rate......................................	× $2.00
Efficiency variance..	$ 150 unfav.

The sum of the three variances computed under method A equals the overall factory overhead variance for Department 3, as follows:

Spending variance...	$ 14 unfav.
Idle capacity variance...	420 unfav.
Efficiency variance...	150 unfav.
Overall factory overhead variance....................	$584 unfav.

Method B. The spending variance computed in three-variance method B is the same as the spending variance computed in three-variance method A, and the volume variance is the same volume variance as computed in the two-variance method. The *variable efficiency variance* is the difference between the actual number of units of the allocation base used and the standard number of units of the allocation base allowed for actual production, multiplied by the variable factory overhead rate. It is the portion of the efficiency variance that measures the effect of the efficient or inefficient use of the input used as an allocation base on the cost of the variable factory overhead. The variable efficiency variance may be computed as follows:

Budget allowance based on actual hours worked..........................	$7,370
Budget allowance based on standard hours allowed.....................	7,280
Variable efficiency variance...	$ 90 unfav.

Alternatively, it can be computed as follows:

Actual hours worked..	3,475
Standard hours allowed for actual units produced.....................	3,400
Excess of actual hours over standard hours allowed.................	75
Variable factory overhead rate..	× $1.20
Variable efficiency variance..	$ 90 unfav.

The unfavorable spending variance of $14 plus the unfavorable variable efficiency variance of $90 equals the unfavorable controllable variance of $104 computed under the two-variance method illustrated for Department 3.

As is the case with method A, the sum of the three variances computed under method B equals the overall factory overhead variance for Department 3, as follows:

Spending variance...	$ 14 unfav.
Variable efficiency variance.................................	90 unfav.
Volume variance..	480 unfav.
Overall factory overhead variance......................	$584 unfav.

The primary difference in method A and method B is that since the volume variance is computed in method B, the effect of the efficient or inefficient use of the input used to allocate factory overhead is impounded in the measure of capacity utilization and not separately stated. Under method A, the idle capacity variance is computed along with the efficiency variance. The efficiency variance segregates the effects of production efficiency from the measure of capacity utilization. The effect of the efficient or inefficient use of the input used to allocate factory overhead on capacity utilization can be observed in the difference between the volume variance and the idle capacity variance, a measure identified in the next section as the fixed efficiency variance. If department management has no control over capacity utilization, the method B approach seems reasonable. On the other hand, if department management has some control over the level of capacity utilized, the method A approach seems more desirable because it charges management with the effect of productive efficiency on capacity utilization.

Four-Variance Method. The four-variance method is similar to the three-variance method A, except that the efficiency variance is divided into its fixed and variable components. The four variances are (1) the spending variance, (2) the variable efficiency variance, (3) the fixed efficiency variance, and (4) the idle capacity variance. The spending variance and the idle capacity variance are computed in the same manner as in the three-variance method A, and the variable efficiency variance is computed in the same manner as in the three-variance method B. All three of these variances were illustrated previously. The fourth variance, the *fixed efficiency variance*, is the difference between the amount of fixed factory overhead that would be charged to production if based on the actual number of units of the allocation base used and the amount that would be charged to production based on the standard number of units of the allocation base allowed for actual production. Based on the information provided for Department 3, the fixed efficiency variance would be computed as follows:

Actual hours (3,475) × fixed overhead rate ($.80)..	$2,780
Standard hours allowed (3,400) × fixed overhead rate ($.80).....................	2,720
Fixed efficiency variance..	$ 60 unfav.

Alternatively, it may be computed as follows:

Actual hours worked..	3,475
Standard hours allowed for actual units produced........................	3,400
Excess of actual hours over standard hours allowed.....................	75
Fixed factory overhead rate..	× $.80
Fixed efficiency variance..	$ 60 unfav.

When all four variances for Department 3 in the illustration are added together, the total is equal to the overall factory overhead variance, as follows:

Spending variance...	$ 14 unfav.
Variable efficiency variance...............................	90 unfav.
Fixed efficiency variance....................................	60 unfav.
Idle capacity variance..	420 unfav.
Overall factory overhead variance.....................	$584 unfav.

Reconciling from the four-variance method, the spending and variable efficiency variances combine to equal the controllable variance, and the fixed efficiency variance and the idle capacity variance combine to equal the volume variance. These relationships for the Department 3 illustration are demonstrated as follows:

Spending variance.....................................	$ 14 unfav.
Variable efficiency variance.....................	90 unfav.
Controllable variance...............................	$104 unfav.
Fixed efficiency variance..........................	$ 60 unfav.
Idle capacity variance..............................	420 unfav.
Volume variance.......................................	$480 unfav.

In addition, the variable efficiency and fixed efficiency variances combine to equal the efficiency variance of the three-variance method A. For the Department 3 illustration, this relationship is demonstrated as follows:

Variable efficiency variance......................	$ 90 unfav.
Fixed efficiency variance..........................	60 unfav.
Efficiency variance...................................	$150 unfav.

Other Methods. There are numerous other methods of breaking down the overall factory overhead variance for analysis. For example, any portion of the spending or controllable variance attributable to the difference between budgeted and actual fixed factory overhead may be isolated separately and labeled as the fixed spending variance. It is also possible to break down the spending variance into price and quantity variances for each item of factory overhead expense. The variance system chosen by management should be the one that it finds most useful in identifying the causes of the overall factory overhead variance. However, as a practical matter, management must weigh the costs of alternative data gathering and reporting systems with their expected benefits.

▼ MIX AND YIELD VARIANCES

Basically, the establishment of a standard product cost requires the determination of price and quantity standards. In many industries, particularly of the process type, materials mix and materials yield play significant parts in the final product cost, in cost reduction, and in profit improvement.

Materials specification standards are generally set up for various grades of materials and types of secondary materials. In most cases, specifications are based on laboratory or engineering tests. Comparative costs of various grades of materials are used to arrive at a satisfactory materials mix, and changes are often made when it seems possible to use less costly grades of materials or substitute materials. In addition, a substantial cost reduction might be achieved through the improvement of the yield of good product units in the factory. At times, trade-offs may occur; e.g., a cost saving resulting from use of a less costly grade of materials may result in a poorer yield, or vice versa. A variance analysis program identifying and evaluating the nature, magnitude, and causes of mix and yield variances is an aid to operating management.

Mix Variance

After the standard specification has been established, a variance representing the difference between the standard cost of formula materials and the standard cost of the materials actually used can be calculated. This variance is generally recognized as a *mix* (or *blend*) *variance*, which is the result of mixing basic materials in a ratio different from standard materials specifications. In a woolen mill, for instance, the standard proportions of the grades of wool for each yarn number are reflected in the standard blend cost. Any difference between the actual wool used and the standard blend results in a blend or mix variance.

Industries like textiles, rubber, and chemicals, whose products must possess certain chemical or physical qualities, find it quite feasible and economical to apply different combinations of basic materials and still achieve a perfect product. In cotton fabrics, it is common to mix cotton from many parts of the world with the hope that the new mix and its cost will contribute to improved profits. In many cases, the new mix is accompanied by either a favorable or unfavorable yield of the final product. Such a situation may make it difficult to judge correctly the origin of the variances. A favorable mix variance, for instance, may be offset by an unfavorable yield variance, or vice versa. Thus, any apparent advantage created by one may be canceled out by the other.

Yield Variance

Yield can be defined as the amount of prime product manufactured from a given amount of materials. The *yield variance* is the result of obtaining a yield different from the one expected on the basis of input.

In sugar refining, a normal loss of yield develops because, on the average, it takes approximately 102.5 pounds of sucrose in raw sugar form to produce 100 pounds of surose in refined sugars. Part of this sucrose emerges as black strap molasses, but a small percentage is completely lost.

In the canning industry, it is customary to estimate the expected yield of grades per ton of fruit purchased or delivered to the plant. The actual yield should be compared to the one expected and should be evaluated in terms of cost. If the actual yield deviates from predetermined percentages, cost and profit will differ.

Since the final product cost contains not only materials but also labor and factory overhead, a yield variance for labor and factory overhead should be determined when the product is finished. The actual quantities resulting from the processes are multiplied by the standard cost, which includes all three cost elements. A labor yield variance must be looked upon as the result of the quality and/or quantity of the materials handled, while the factory overhead yield variance is due to the greater or smaller number of hours worked. It should be noted that the overhead yield variance may have a significant effect on the amount of over- or underabsorbed factory overhead.

Illustration of Variances

To illustrate the calculation of mix and yield variances, assume that the Springmint Company, a manufacturer of chewing gum, uses a standard cost system. Standard product and cost specifications for 1,000 lbs. of chewing gum are as follows:

Material	Quantity	×	Unit Cost	=	Amount	
A............................	800		$.25 per lb.		$200	
B............................	200		.40		80	
C............................	200		.10		20	
Input..................	1,200 lbs.				$300;	$300 ÷ 1,200 lbs. = $.25 per lb.*
Output...............	1,000 lbs.				$300;	$300 ÷ 1,000 lbs. = $.30 per lb.*

*Weighted averages.

The production of 1,000 lbs. of chewing gum requires 1,200 lbs. of raw materials. Hence, the expected yield is 1,000 lbs. ÷ 1,200 lbs., or $\frac{5}{6}$ of input.

Materials records indicate:

Material	Beginning Inventory	Purchases in January	Ending Inventory
A	10,000 lbs.	162,000 lbs. @ $.24	15,000 lbs.
B	12,000	30,000 @ .42	4,000
C	15,000	32,000 @ .11	11,000

To convert 1,200 lbs. of raw materials into 1,000 lbs. of finished product requires 20 direct labor hours at $9 per hour, or $.18 per lb. of finished product. Actual direct labor hours and cost for January are 3,800 hours at $34,656.

Factory overhead is applied on a direct labor hour basis at a rate of $5 per hour ($3 fixed, $2 variable), or $.10 per lb. of finished product. Normal overhead is $20,000, with 4,000 direct labor hours. Actual overhead for the month is $22,000. Actual finished production for January is 200,000 lbs.

The standard cost per pound of finished chewing gum is:

Materials	$.30	per lb.
Labor	.18	
Factory overhead	.10	
	$.58	per lb.

Materials Variances. The materials variances for January consist of (1) price variances, (2) a mix variance, (3) a yield variance, and (4) quantity variances. The company computes the materials price variances as follows, using the procedure illustrated on page 515, and recognizes these variances when the materials are purchased.

Material	Actual Standard Quantity	Actual Cost	Standard Cost	Unit Cost Variation	Price Variance
A	162,000	$.24	$.25	$(.01)	$(1,620) fav.
B	30,000	.42	.40	.02	600 unfav.
C	32,000	.11	.10	.01	320 unfav.
Net materials purchase price variance					$ (700) fav.

The materials mix variance results from combining materials in a ratio different from the standard materials specifications. It is computed as follows:

Actual quantities at individual standard materials costs:

A	157,000 lbs. @ $.25	$39,250
B	38,000 @ .40	15,200
C	36,000 @ .10	3,600
	231,000 lbs.	$58,050

Actual quantity at weighted average of standard materials cost input (231,000 lbs. × $.25).......... 57,750*

Materials mix variance............. $ 300 unfav.

*This figure can also be determined by multiplying the standard (expected) output from actual input (192,500 lbs., or ⁵⁄₆ of 231,000 lbs.) by $.30 weighted average of standard materials cost output.

The influence of individual raw materials on the total materials mix variance can be computed in the following manner:

Material	Actual Quantity	Standard Formula	×	Total Actual Quantity	=	Actual Quantity Using Standard Formula	Quantity Variation	×	Standard Unit Cost	=	Materials Mix Variance	
A.....................	157,000 lbs.	$\frac{800}{1,200}$		231,000 lbs.		154,000 lbs.	3,000 lbs.		$.25		$750	unfav.
B.....................	38,000	$\frac{200}{1,200}$		231,000		38,500	(500)		.40		(200)	fav.
C.....................	36,000	$\frac{200}{1,200}$		231,000		38,500	(2,500)		.10		(250)	fav.
	231,000 lbs.					231,000 lbs.	-0-				$300	unfav.

The yield variance is computed as follows:

Actual input quantity at weighted average of standard materials cost.............. $57,750
Actual output quantity at weighted average of standard materials cost
(200,000 lbs. × $.30).. 60,000*
Materials yield variance... $(2,250)   fav.

*This figure can also be determined by multiplying the input needed to produce 200,000 lbs. (240,000 lbs.) by $.25.

The yield variance occurred because the actual production of 200,000 lbs. exceeded the expected output of 192,500 lbs. ($\frac{5}{6}$ of 231,000 lbs.) by 7,500 lbs. The yield difference multiplied by the standard weighted materials cost of $.30 per output pound equals the favorable yield variance of $2,250.

The materials quantity variance can be computed for each item as follows, using the procedure illustrated on page 516:

Material	Unit	×	Standard Unit Cost	=	Amount	Materials Quantity Variance
A: Actual quantity used...............................	157,000 lbs.		$.25		$39,250	
Standard quantity allowed.....................	160,000 lbs.*		.25		40,000	$ (750) fav.
B: Actual quantity used...............................	38,000 lbs.		$.40		$15,200	
Standard quantity allowed.....................	40,000 lbs.**		.40		16,000	(800) fav.
C: Actual quantity used...............................	36,000 lbs.		$.10		$ 3,600	
Standard quantity allowed.....................	40,000 lbs.***		.10		4,000	(400) fav.
Total materials quantity variance...						$(1,950) fav.

*An output of 200,000 lbs. should require an input of 240,000 lbs., with a standard yield of 1,000 lbs. ouput for each 1,200 lbs. input. Then the 240,000 lbs. × (800 lbs. ÷ 1,200 lbs.) Material A portion of the formula = 160,000 lbs.
**The 240,000 lbs. × (200 lbs. ÷ 1,200 lbs.) Material B portion of the formula = 40,000 lbs.
***The 240,000 lbs. × (200 lbs. ÷ 1,200 lbs.) Material C portion of the formula = 40,000 lbs.

The total materials quantity variance can also be determined by comparing actual quantities at standard prices, $58,050 ($39,250 + $15,200 + $3,600), to actual output quantity at the weighted average of standard materials cost, $60,000 (200,000 lbs. × $.30) for a total favorable variance of $1,950. The mix and yield variances separate the materials quantity variance into two parts:

Materials mix variance............................ $ 300   unfav.
Materials yield variance........................ (2,250)   fav.
Materials quantity variance.................... $(1,950)   fav.

Labor Variances. The expected output of 192,500 lbs. of chewing gum should require 3,850 standard labor hours (20 hours per thousand pounds of chewing gum produced). Similarly, the actual output of 200,000 lbs. of chewing gum should require 4,000 standard labor hours.

The labor variances are the (1) rate variance, (2) efficiency variance, and (3) yield variance. The computation of these variances for January is as follows:

Actual payroll..	$34,656
Actual hours (3,800) × standard labor rate ($9)...	34,200
Labor rate variance...	$ 456 unfav.

Actual hours × standard labor rate..	$34,200
Standard hours allowed for expected output (3,850) × standard labor rate ($9)...	34,650
Labor efficiency variance...	$ (450) fav.

Standard hours allowed for expected output × standard labor rate..	$34,650
Standard hours allowed for actual output (4,000) × standard labor rate ($9)...	36,000
Labor yield variance..	$(1,350) fav.

The labor rate variance is computed as shown on page 517. The traditional labor efficiency variance, as illustrated on page 518, is computed as follows:

	Hours	×	Standard Rate	=	Amount	
Actual hours worked..........................	3,800		$9		$34,200	
Standard hours allowed.....................	4,000		9		36,000	
Labor efficiency variance..................	(200)		9		$(1,800)	fav.

The labor yield variance identifies the portion of the labor efficiency variance attributable to obtaining an unfavorable or, as in this illustration, a favorable yield [(3,850 standard hours allowed for expected output − 4,000 standard hours allowed for actual output) × $9 standard labor rate = $1,350]. The favorable labor efficiency variance of $450 is the portion of the traditional labor efficiency variance that is attributable to factors other than yield. The sum of the two variances, $1,350 plus $450, equals the $1,800 traditional labor efficiency variance. When a standard mix of labor skills or classes is called for, mix and yield variances patterned after those computed for materials can be isolated.

Factory Overhead Variances. A yield variance can also be computed for factory overhead. When three-variance method A is used, the overhead variances consist of the (1) spending variance, (2) idle capacity variance, (3) efficiency variance, and (4) yield variance. These variances are computed as follows:

THREE-VARIANCE METHOD A ADAPTED TO COMPUTE A YIELD VARIANCE

Actual factory overhead..		$22,000
Budget allowance (based on actual hours):		
Variable overhead (3,800 hours × $2)..	$ 7,600	
Fixed overhead budgeted..	12,000	19,600
Spending variance..		$ 2,400 unfav.
Budget allowance (based on actual hours)..		$19,600
Actual hours (3,800) × standard overhead rate ($5)........................		19,000
Idle capacity variance...		$ 600 unfav.
Actual hours × standard overhead rate..		$19,000
Standard hours allowed for expected output (3,850) × standard overhead rate ($5)....		19,250
Overhead efficiency variance...		$ (250) fav.
Standard hours allowed for expected output × standard overhead rate........................		$19,250
Standard hours allowed for actual output (4,000) × standard overhead rate ($5).........		20,000
Overhead yield variance...		$ (750) fav.

The spending and idle capacity variances are computed in the same manner as discussed on page 523. The overhead efficiency variance and the overhead yield variance, when combined, equal the efficiency variance discussed earlier in this chapter. The overhead yield variance measures that portion of the total overhead variance resulting from a favorable yield [(3,850 hours − 4,000 hours) × $5 = $750].

When three-variance method B is used, the overhead variances are the (1) spending variance, (2) variable efficiency variance, (3) volume variance, and (4) yield variance. These variances are computed as follows:

THREE-VARIANCE METHOD B ADAPTED TO COMPUTE A YIELD VARIANCE

Actual factory overhead..		$22,000
Budget allowance (based on actual hours):		
Variable overhead (3,800 hours × $2)..	$ 7,600	
Fixed overhead budgeted..	12,000	19,600
Spending variance..		$ 2,400 unfav.
Budget allowance (based on actual hours)..		$19,600
Budget allowance (based on standard hours allowed for expected output):		
Variable overhead (3,850 standard hours × $2)........................	$ 7,700	
Fixed overhead budgeted..	12,000	19,700
Overhead variable efficiency variance..		$ (100) fav.
Budget allowance (based on standard hours allowed for expected output)..................		$19,700
Standard hours allowed for expected output (3,850) × standard overhead rate ($5)....		19,250
Overhead volume variance..		$ 450 unfav.
Standard hours allowed for expected output × standard overhead rate........................		$19,250
Standard hours allowed for actual output (4,000) × standard overhead rate ($5).........		20,000
Overhead yield variance...		$ (750) fav.

The spending variance is the same as that computed in three-variance method A. The difference between the overhead variable efficiency variance of method B and the overhead efficiency variance of method A is the $150 fixed part of the favorable overhead efficiency variance [(3,800 hours − 3,850 hours) × $3], which when added to the idle capacity variance yields the overhead volume variance.

When the two-variance method is used, the overhead variances are the (1) controllable variance, (2) volume variance, and (3) yield variance. These variances are computed as follows:

TWO-VARIANCE METHOD ADAPTED TO COMPUTE A YIELD VARIANCE		
Actual factory overhead..		$22,000
Budget allowance (based on standard hours allowed for expected output):		
Variable overhead (3,850 hours × $2)..	$ 7,700	
Fixed overhead budgeted..	12,000	19,700
Controllable variance..		$ 2,300 unfav.
Budget allowance (based on standard hours allowed for expected output).....................		$19,700
Standard hours allowed for expected output (3,850) × standard overhead rate ($5)..		19,250
Overhead volume variance..		$ 450 unfav.
Standard hours allowed for expected output × standard overhead rate........................		$19,250
Standard hours allowed for actual output (4,000) × standard overhead rate ($5)..		20,000
Overhead yield variance..		$ (750) fav.

The $2,300 unfavorable controllable variance equals the unfavorable spending variance, $2,400, combined with the $100 variable part of the favorable overhead efficiency variance [(3,800 hours − 3,850 hours) × $2]. The $450 unfavorable overhead volume variance equals the unfavorable idle capacity variance, $600, combined with the $150 fixed part of the favorable overhead efficiency variance [(3,800 hours − 3,850 hours) × $3].

The favorable overhead yield variance is the same as for the three-variance methods and can be viewed as consisting of $300 variable cost [(3,850 standard hours allowed for expected output − 4,000 standard hours allowed for actual output) × $2], and $450 fixed cost [(3,850 − 4,000) × $3].

▼ RESPONSIBILITY AND CONTROL OF VARIANCES

Management scrutinizes variances in an attempt to determine why they occur, what corrective action can be taken, and how efficient and effective performance should be rewarded. There is no substitute for competent supervision, but variance reporting can be a valuable aid to the supervisor in carrying out control responsibilities. However, managment should recognize that explanations for variations in costs have limited usefulness in improving the future control of costs because the explanations seldom suggest the corrective action that should be taken. If cost control is to be effective, the results of corrective action taken must be measured and reported.

The extent of variance investigation should be based on the estimated cost of making the investigation versus the value of the anticipated benefits. If the costs to be saved from investigating a variance and taking corrective action are expected to exceed the cost of making the investigation, management should investigate to determine the cause of the variance. Variances should be identified and reported to management as frequently as economically feasible. The closer the detection and reporting is to the point of occurrence, the more effective is the remedial action and the larger is the amount of cost that can be saved. It may also be desirable to report variances in physical units as well as in dollars of cost.

Causes of Variances

A variance is a signal. Large variances, whether favorable or unfavorable, should be investigated and critically analyzed. A variance may be caused by some random event that is not expected to recur, or it may be the result of some systematic problem that can be corrected. It is also possible that the standard is simply out-of-date. For example, the manufacturing process may change, thus changing physical standards, or unexpected price changes may cause monetary standards to be out-of-date. In some cases, variances in different departments may be related. Determination of such a relationship is particularly important where favorable variances in one area are more than offset by related unfavorable variances in another area. For example, a favorable materials price variance resulting from the purchase of inexpensive materials may be more than offset by unfavorable labor efficiency variances that result from increased labor time required to work with the poorer quality materials.

The purchasing department carries the primary responsibility for materials price variances. To be useful, variance reports should list the variance for each item of materials purchased during the period. Control of prices is obtained by getting several quotations, buying in economical lots, taking advantage of cash discounts, and selecting the most economical means of delivery. However, economic conditions and unexpected price changes by suppliers may be outside the limits of the department's control and may be caused by unexpected inflation, an excess or shortage of the quantity available in the market, or a fortunate buy. Thus, a materials price variance may be more a measure of forecasting ability than a failure to buy at predetermined prices. Internal factors, such as costly rush orders requiring materials shipments on short notice or in smaller than economical quantities, may have a negative impact on the materials price variance but would not be the fault of the purchasing department.

Materials quantity variances may result from many causes, which must be identified if the variances are to be controlled. Materials variance reports should be prepared on a departmental basis and should list the materials quantity variance for each item of materials used during the period. If the materials are of substandard quality, the fault may be with the person who prepared the purchase requisition informing the purchasing department about the quality of materials needed. If the materials purchased varied from the purchase requisition specification, the fault may lie with the purchasing department. Or perhaps the faulty materials went unnoticed during inspection when received. Other causes relate to the production activity and include inexperienced or inefficient labor, pilferage or theft, badly worn or new machinery, changes in production methods, faulty product planning, or lack of proper production supervision.

Labor rate variances tend to be fairly minor because labor rates are usually set by management for the period or by long-term union contract. Rate variances may occur, however, because of the use of a single average rate for a department, operation, or craft, while several different rates exist for the individual workers. In such cases, absenteeism or the assignment of workers to tasks that normally pay different rates can result in a rate variance. In this case, the planning or scheduling of work assignments would be the cause of the variance.

Labor efficiency variances may occur for a multitude of reasons. These reasons include a lack of materials or faulty materials, inexperienced workers and the related learning curve phenomenon (pages 244-246), badly worn or obsolete machinery, machinery breakdowns, new and unfamiliar machinery, changes in production methods, poor or incorrect production planning and scheduling, faulty blueprints or product design specifications, worker dissatisfaction, or work interruptions. From the point of view of department managers, the most useful labor efficiency report would be one that reports an efficiency variance for each worker. However, because of the high cost of such reports, labor efficiency variances are usually reported on a departmental or production operation basis.

Factory overhead variances relate to the variable and the fixed factory overhead. The variance computation methods discussed previously segregate controllable variances from capacity variances. The idle capacity variance and the volume variance are measures of capacity utilization. Capacity variances are generally attributed to executive management. The decision regarding the utilization of plant capacity and the setting of predetermined factory overhead rates rests with the planning group. Within the range of fixed costs, however, changes occur due to changes in depreciation rates, increases in insurance premiums and taxes, and increases in salaries of top-level managers. Such changes generally become a part of the controllable variance or the spending variance. The controllable variance can be broken down into the spending variance and the variable efficiency variance. The variable efficiency variance is caused by the efficient or inefficient use of the input used to allocate factory overhead, and the spending variance results from the efficient or inefficient use of the various items of factory overhead. Unless the portion of the spending variance attributable to each item of factory overhead expense is computed and reported to responsible management, large variances may go undetected. A report can also highlight a situation in which a large favorable variance for one item of expense is substantially offset by a large unfavorable variance for another item. An example of such a report for Department 3 is illustrated below, using three-variance method B. For this report, the budget allowance based on actual hours can be determined for each item by multiplying its standard overhead rate per labor hour (page 520) by the actual labor hours worked. The spending variance for each item is computed by subtracting the actual cost of each item from its budget allowance.

Department 3
Factory Overhead Variance Report
For Month Ending March 31, 19A

	(1) Budget Allowance Normal Capacity	(2) Budget Allowance Standard Hours	(3) Budget Allowance Actual Hours	(4) Actual Cost	(5) Variable Efficiency Variance (3) − (2)	(6) Spending Variance (4) − (3)
Direct labor hours..............................	4,000	3,400	3,475			
Capacity utilized................................	100%	85%	86.875%			
Variable factory overhead:						
Indirect labor....................................	$2,000.00	$1,700.00	$1,737.50	$1,960.00	$37.50	$222.50
Indirect materials.............................	1,200.00	1,020.00	1,042.50	1,044.00	22.50	1.50
Supplies...	800.00	680.00	695.00	652.50	15.00	(42.50)
Repairs..	600.00	510.00	521.25	335.00	11.25	(186.25)
Power and light...............................	200.00	170.00	173.75	183.60	3.75	9.85
Total variable overhead..................	$4,800.00	$4,080.00	$4,170.00	$4,175.10		
Fixed factory overhead:						
Supervision......................................	$1,200.00	$1,200.00	$1,200.00	$1,200.00	-0-	-0-
Depreciation of machinery..............	700.00	700.00	700.00	700.00	-0-	-0-
Insurance...	250.00	250.00	250.00	251.00	-0-	1.00
Property tax.....................................	250.00	250.00	250.00	257.90	-0-	7.90
Power and light...............................	400.00	400.00	400.00	400.00	-0-	-0-
Maintenance....................................	400.00	400.00	400.00	400.00	-0-	-0-
Total fixed overhead.......................	$3,200.00	$3,200.00	$3,200.00	$3,208.90		
Total factory overhead.......................	$8,000.00	$7,280.00	$7,370.00	$7,384.00	$90.00	$14.00
Standard overhead chargeable to work in process (3,400 std. hrs. × $2)...		6,800.00			unfav.	unfav.
Volume variance.................................		$ 480.00 unfav.				

Reconciliation of variances:
Actual factory overhead.. $7,384
Standard overhead chargeable to work in process................... 6,800
Overall factory overhead variance.. $ 584 unfav.

Spending variance.. $ 14 unfav.
Variable efficiency variance... 90 unfav.
Volume variance.. 480 unfav.
Overall factory overhead variance.. $ 584 unfav.

To further enhance the usefulness of the standard cost variance report, the spending variance could be broken down into price and quantity variances for each item of factory overhead expense. The computational procedures are similar to those used in computing price and quantity variances for direct materials and direct labor. To break the spending variance down into price and quantity variances, more data are needed. In the illustration for Department 3, the standard cost per unit, the actual cost per unit, and the actual quantity of each item of variable factory overhead used during March are as follows:

Item of Variable Overhead	Standard Cost per Unit	Actual Cost per Unit	Actual Quantity Used
Indirect labor............................	$10.00	$10.00	196 hours
Indirect materials......................	.60	.58	1,800 units
Supplies....................................	1.00	.90	725 units
Repairs......................................	15.00	16.75	20 hours
Power and light........................	.25	.27	680 kwh

The spending quantity variance for each item of factory overhead is determined first by computing the actual quantity of input at the standard unit cost for each item. That is, for each item of variable factory overhead, its standard cost per unit is multiplied by the actual quantity of the item used, and then the budget allowance based on actual hours for each item is subtracted. The spending price variance for each item can then be determined by subtracting the actual quantity of input used at the standard unit cost for each item from its actual cost. These variances are illustrated in the factory overhead variance report for Department 3 on page 538.

Tolerance Limits for Variance Control

The control of standard cost variances is the responsibility of a designated manager. All managers have many important time-consuming responsibilities other than variance investigation; therefore, their efforts should be concentrated on large variances first because they have the greatest impact on cost and profit. Some variance in cost measurements can be expected as a result of imperfect measurement techniques. Typically, the activity measure used to estimate a cost does not explain all of the variation in the cost. The question that should be asked is "How large a variance from standard should be tolerated before the variance should be investigated?" In other words, some tolerance limit or range should be established, so that if the cost variance falls within this range, it can be considered acceptable. If the variance is outside the range, an investigation should be made if the cost of doing so is reasonable. In this manner, the notion of management by exception can be employed effectively and efficiently.

Each variance should be highlighted in a manner indicating whether the variance is within the control limit. Such information enables the responsible manager or supervisor to accept deviations from the standard as a valuable tool for the control of costs and lessens the dangers of their being more averse to risk than upper-level managers prefer. A manager who is unduly concerned about the penalty for even small variances may perform in a manner that hampers rather than enhances efficient operations.

Past data on established operations, tempered by estimated changes in the future, may furnish reliable bases for estimating expected costs and calculating control limits that serve to indicate good as well as poor operation and that aid

Department 3
Factory Overhead Variance Report
For Month Ending March 31, 19A

	(1) Budget Allowance Normal Capacity	(2) Budget Allowance Standard Hours	(3) Budget Allowance Actual Hours	(4) Actual Quantity of Input at Standard Unit Cost	(5) Actual Cost	(6) Variable Efficiency Variance (3) − (2)	(7) Spending Variance (5) − (3)	(8) Spending Quantity Variance (4) − (3)	(9) Spending Price Variance (5) − (4)
Direct labor hours	4,000	3,400	3,475						
Capacity utilized	100%	85%	86.875%						
Variable factory overhead:									
Indirect labor	$2,000.00	$1,700.00	$1,737.50	$1,960.00	$1,960.00	$37.50	$222.50	$222.50	$ 0
Indirect materials	1,200.00	1,020.00	1,042.50	1,080.00	1,044.00	22.50	1.50	37.50	(36.00)
Supplies	800.00	680.00	695.00	725.00	652.50	15.00	(42.50)	30.00	(72.50)
Repairs	600.00	510.00	521.25	300.00	335.00	11.25	(186.25)	(221.25)	35.00
Power and light	200.00	170.00	173.75	170.00	183.60	3.75	9.85	(3.75)	13.60
Total variable overhead	$4,800.00	$4,080.00	$4,170.00	$4,235.00	$4,175.10	$90.00	$14.00	$65.00	$(51.00)
						unfav.	unfav.	unfav.	fav.
Fixed factory overhead:									
Supervision	$1,200.00	$1,200.00	$1,200.00	$1,200.00	$1,200.00	-0-	-0-	-0-	-0-
Depreciation of machinery	700.00	700.00	700.00	700.00	700.00	-0-	-0-	-0-	-0-
Insurance	250.00	250.00	250.00	250.00	251.00	-0-	1.00	-0-	1.00
Property tax	250.00	250.00	250.00	250.00	257.90	-0-	7.90	-0-	7.90
Power and light	400.00	400.00	400.00	400.00	400.00	-0-	-0-	-0-	-0-
Maintenance	400.00	400.00	400.00	400.00	400.00	-0-	-0-	-0-	-0-
Total fixed overhead	$3,200.00	$3,200.00	$3,200.00	$3,200.00	$3,208.90				
Total factory overhead	$8,000.00	$7,280.00	$7,370.00	$7,435.00	$7,384.00				
Standard overhead chargeable to work in process (3,400 std. hrs. × $2)		6,800.00							
Volume variance		$ 480.00 unfav.							

Reconciliation of variances:

Actual factory overhead.......................... $7384
Standard overhead chargeable to work in process.......................... 6800
Overall factory overhead variance.......................... $ 584 unfav.

Spending variance:
Spending quantity variance.......................... $ 65.00 unfav.
Spending price variance.......................... (51.00) fav.
.... $ 14 unfav.
Variable efficiency variance.......................... 90 unfav.
Volume variance.......................... 480 unfav.
Overall factory overhead variance.......................... $ 584 unfav.

in the decision to investigate a variance. The limits may be expressed as minimum dollar amounts or as percentage differences. Their determination may be based on subjective judgments, hunches, guesses, and biases, or on careful analysis and estimates, including the possible use of statistical procedures such as the standard error of the estimate (pages 305-308). In setting and applying tolerance limits, it is important to recognize that the relative magnitude of a variance is more significant than its absolute value. Furthermore, the cost vs. benefit of tighter controls must be considered as tolerance reduction alternatives are explored.

To illustrate the use of tolerance limits, assume that $10,000 appears in a factory overhead budget for maintenance expense. Based on past experience and future expectations, assume that the significant range should be ±$2,000. At the end of the month, the actual maintenance expense is $14,000, indicating a variance of $4,000 ($14,000 − $10,000). Such a result would call for further investigation into the causes of the variance. If the actual expense is only $10,900 and the variance is $900, the deviation is acceptable and requires no further investigation, at least at this time. If the unfavorable variance persists in subsequent report periods, however, the causes should be examined, because they may be significant in the long run.

In the preceding example, maintenance expense is classified as a fixed cost, since no deviation from the basic amount is expected as a result of a change in the level of activity. However, this cost is generally classified as a semivariable expense, i.e., a fixed amount plus a variable rate which depends, in this case, on direct labor hours as the source of activity or volume. Thus, a relationship between the variance and volume must be established for the maintenance expense.

To modify the previous example, assume a tolerance limit of $3,000 when activity is 10,000 direct labor hours. When direct labor hours increase or decrease, the tolerance limit is $3,000 ± $.05 per hour for any difference between the 10,000 direct labor hours and the standard hours allowed for actual production. Assuming that $10,000 is the budget allowance for 12,700 direct labor hours and the actual cost of $14,000 was incurred when standard direct labor hours allowed were 12,700, the tolerance limit would be $3,135 [$3,000 + ($.05 × 2,700)]. This amount would be used to evaluate the $4,000 variance.

DISCUSSION QUESTIONS

1. (a) Define standard costs.
   (b) Name some advantages of a standard cost system.

2. A team of management consultants and company executives concluded that a standard cost installation was a desirable vehicle for accomplishing the objectives of a progressive management. State some uses of standard costs that can be associated with the above decision.

3. The use of standard costs in pricing and budgeting is quite valuable, since decisions

in the fields of pricing and budgetary planning are made before the costs under consideration are incurred. Discuss.

4. Explain how standards relate to job order and process cost accumulation procedures.

5. Discuss the criteria to be used when selecting the operational activities for which standards are to be set.
   (ICMA adapted)

6. Discuss the behavioral issues to be considered when selecting the level of performance to be incorporated into a standard cost.
   (ICMA adapted)

7. Discuss the role that each of the following departments should play in establishing standard costs.
   (a) Accounting Department.

(b) The department whose performance is being measured.
(c) The Industrial Engineering Department.
   (ICMA adapted)

8. In a standard cost system, the computation of variances is a first step. What steps should follow?

9. Discuss the meaning of variance control and responsibility by various levels of management.

10. (a) Describe the features of tolerance limits.
    (b) Discuss potential benefits of tolerance limits to an organization.
    (c) Identify and discuss potential behavioral problems which can occur in using tolerance limits. *(ICMA adapted)*

EXERCISES

1. Materials variance analysis. The standard cost per unit of material V-31 is $13.50 per pound. During the month, 4,500 pounds of V-31 were purchased at a total cost of $60,975. In addition, 3,900 pounds of V-31 were used during the month; however, the standard quantity allowed for actual production is 3,800 pounds.

Required: Compute the materials purchase price variance, price usage variance, and quantity variance, indicating whether the variances are favorable or unfavorable.

2. Labor variance analysis. During the month, 1,200 units of Topo were produced. Actual direct labor required 650 direct labor hours at an actual total cost of $6,435. According to the standard cost card for Topo, one-half hour of labor should be required per unit of Topo produced, at a standard cost of $10 per labor hour.

Required: Compute the labor rate and efficiency variances, indicating whether the variances are favorable or unfavorable.

3. Materials and labor variance analysis. The following data pertain to the first week of operations during the month of June:

Materials:	Actual purchases..........	1,500 units at $3.80 per unit
	Actual usage.................	1,350 units
	Standard usage.............	1,020 units at $4.00 per unit
Direct labor:	Actual hours..................	310 hours at $12.10 per hour
	Standard hours.............	340 hours at $12.00 per hour

Required: Compute the following variances, indicating whether the variances are favorable or unfavorable:

(1) Materials purchase price variance, price usage variance, and quantity variance.
(2) Labor rate and efficiency variances.

4. Factory overhead variance analysis, two-variance method. The normal capacity of the Assembly Department is 12,000 machine hours per month. At normal capacity, the standard factory overhead rate is $12.50 per machine hour, based on $96,000 of budgeted fixed expenses per month and a variable expense rate of $4.50 per machine hour. During April, the department operated at 12,500 machine hours, with actual factory overhead of $166,000. The number of standard machine hours allowed for the production actually attained is 11,000.

Required: Compute the overall factory overhead variance and analyze it using the two-variance method. Indicate whether the variances are favorable or unfavorable.

5. Factory overhead variance analysis, three-variance method A. The normal capacity of Department 3 is 16,000 direct labor hours per month. At normal capacity, the standard factory overhead rate is $10.40 per direct labor hour, based on $64,000 of budgeted fixed expenses per month and a variable expense rate of $6.40 per direct labor hour. During November, the department operated at 15,000 direct labor hours, with actual factory overhead of $157,000. The number of standard direct labor hours allowed for the production actually attained is 15,300.

Required: Compute the overall factory overhead variance and analyze it using the three-variance method A. Indicate whether the variances are favorable or unfavorable.

6. Factory overhead variance analysis, three-variance method B. The normal capacity of the Die Cutting Department is 4,500 machine hours per month. At normal capacity, the standard factory overhead rate is $24.80 per machine hour, based on budgeted fixed factory overhead of $85,500 per month and a variable expense rate of $5.80 per machine hour. During July, the department operated at 4,600 machine hours, with actual factory overhead of $121,000. The number of standard machine hours allowed for the production actually attained is 4,200.

Required: Compute the overall factory overhead variance and analyze it using the three-variance method B. Indicate whether the variances are favorable or unfavorable.

7. Factory overhead variance analysis, four-variance method. Standard direct labor hours budgeted for February production were 2,000, with factory overhead at that level budgeted at $10,000, of which $3,000 is variable. Actual labor hours for the month were 1,900; however, the number of standard labor hours allowed for actual February production is 2,050. Actual factory overhead incurred during the month was $9,750.

Required: Compute the overall factory overhead variance and analyze it using the four-variance method. Indicate whether the variances are favorable or unfavorable.

8. Factory overhead variance analysis. Montana Machine Company has developed the following standard factory overhead costs for each SX unit assembled in Department 6, based on a monthly capacity of 80,000 direct labor hours:

Variable overhead....................	2 hours @ $6 per hour =	$12
Fixed overhead..........................	2 hours @ $3 per hour =	6
Department 6 factory overhead per unit of SX...................		$18

During the month of August, 38,000 units of SX were actually produced. Actual direct labor hours totaled 77,500, and actual factory overhead totaled $700,000.

Required: Determine the overall factory overhead variance and analyze it with each of the following variance analysis methods, indicating whether the variances computed are favorable or unfavorable.

(1) Two-variance method.
(2) Three-variance method A.
(3) Three-variance method B.
(4) Four-variance method.

9. Factory overhead variance analysis report. The Cost Department of Benjamin Products Company prepared the following flexible budget for Department 2 for June:

Production quantity based on standard....................	9,600	10,800	12,000
Direct labor hours at standard................................	4,800	5,400	6,000
Capacity utilization at standard...............................	80%	90%	100%
Variable overhead:			
Indirect labor...	$ 1,920	$ 2,160	$ 2,400
Manufacturing supplies..	1,680	1,890	2,100
Repairs..	640	720	800
Heat, power, and light..	80	90	100
Total variable overhead.......................................	$ 4,320	$ 4,860	$ 5,400
Fixed overhead:			
Superintendence...	$ 6,000	$ 6,000	$ 6,000
Indirect labor...	5,400	5,400	5,400
Manufacturing supplies..	1,020	1,020	1,020
Maintenance..	960	960	960
Heat, power, and light..	120	120	120
Machinery depreciation...	540	540	540
Insurance and taxes...	360	360	360
Total fixed overhead...	$14,400	$14,400	$14,400
Total budgeted factory overhead............................	$18,720	$19,260	$19,800

Factory overhead is charged to production at the rate of $3.30 per direct labor hour. The overhead rate was determined on the basis of 100% capacity utilization, considered to be normal. At the end of the month, cost records showed 10,200 units of product were manufactured, 5,040 direct labor hours were worked, and actual factory overhead was as follows:

Superintendence...	$ 6,200
Indirect labor..	7,500
Manufacturing supplies...................................	2,825
Repairs..	650
Maintenance..	960
Heat, power, and light.....................................	225
Machinery depreciation....................................	540
Insurance and taxes..	372
Total actual factory overhead....................	$19,272

Required: Prepare a departmental factory overhead variance report which includes (a) the spending variance and the variable efficiency variance for each item of factory overhead and (b) a single departmental volume variance. For each item of expense that contains both a fixed and a variable portion, assume that the actual fixed portion is equal to the budgeted fixed portion and that the balance of the actual expense is variable. Indicate whether the variances are favorable or unfavorable.

10. Price, mix, and yield variances. Malmuta Company uses a standard cost system. The standard cost card for one of its products shows the following materials standards:

Material	Pounds ×	Standard Cost per Pound	= Amount
A............................	20	$.70	$14
B............................	5	.40	2
C............................	25	.20	5
Total materials cost per unit................................			$21

The standard 50 lb. mix cost per lb. is $.42 ($21 ÷ 50 lbs.). The standard mix should produce 40 lbs. of finished product, and the standard cost of finished product per lb. is $.525 ($21 ÷ 40 lbs.).

Materials of 500,000 lbs. were used as follows:

Material A......................	230,000 lbs.	@ $.80
Material B.....................	50,000	@ $.35
Material C.....................	220,000	@ $.25

The output of the finished product was 390,000 lbs.

Required: Prepare a product analysis showing materials price, mix, and yield variances.

11. Price, mix, and yield variances. Chocolate manufacturing operations require close control of daily production and cost data. The computer printout for a batch of one ton of cocoa powder indicates the following materials standards:

Ingredients	Quantities (Pounds)	Unit Cost	Mix Cost
Cocoa beans......................	800	$.45	$ 360
Milk.....................................	3,700	.50	1,850
Sugar..................................	500	.25	125
Total batch.........................	5,000	$.467 (weighted average)	$2,335

On December 7, the company's Commodity Accounting and Analysis Section reported the following production and cost data for the December 6 operations:

Ingredients put in process:

Cocoa beans:	225,000 lbs. @ $.425...	$ 95,625
Milk:	1,400,000 lbs. @ $.533..	746,200
Sugar:	250,000 lbs. @ $.240..	60,000
	1,875,000 lbs.	$901,825

Transferred to cocoa powder inventory: 387 tons. There was no work in process inventory.

Required: Compute the materials price, mix, and yield variances.

12. Mix and yield variances for direct labor. When a standard mix of labor skills or classes is called for, mix and yield variances patterned after those computed for materials can be isolated, as demonstrated by Landeau Company, which has a process cost accumulation system utilizing standard costs.

The standard direct labor rates in effect for the current year and the standard hours allowed for the output for April are shown in the following schedule:

	Standard Direct Labor Rate per Hour	Standard Direct Labor Hours Allowed for Output
Labor Class III......................	$8.00	500
Labor Class II......................	7.00	500
Labor Class I.......................	5.00	500

The actual direct labor hours (DLH) worked and the actual direct labor rates per hour experienced for April were as follows:

	Actual Direct Labor Rate per Hour	Actual Direct Labor Hours
Labor Class III......................	$8.50	550
Labor Class II......................	7.50	650
Labor Class I.......................	5.40	375

Required:

(1) Compute the rate and efficiency variances for each labor class.
(2) Compute the direct labor mix and yield variances. (Compute the weighted average standard DLH rate to five decimal places and round computed variances to nearest dollar.)   *(ICMA adapted)*

PROBLEMS

17-1. Variance analysis: materials, labor, and factory overhead. Armando Corporation manufactures a product with the following standard costs:

Direct materials—20 yards @ $1.35 per yard..	$27
Direct labor—4 hours @ $9 per hour..	36
Factory overhead—4 direct labor hours @ $7.50 per hour; ratio of variable to fixed factory overhead is 2:1..	30
Total standard cost per unit of output..	$93

Standards are based on normal monthly capacity of 2,400 direct labor hours. The following information pertains to July, 19A:

Units produced in July..	500
Direct materials purchased—18,000 yards @ $1.38 per yard....................	$24,840
Direct materials used—9,500 yards	
Direct labor—2,100 hours @ $9.15 per hour...	19,215
Actual factory overhead..	16,650

Required:

(1) Compute the variable factory overhead rate per direct labor hour and the total fixed factory overhead based on normal monthly capacity.
(2) Compute two variances each for materials, labor, and factory overhead.
    (AICPA adapted)

17-2. Variance analysis: materials, labor, and factory overhead; process costing. Trutch Company manufactures a product which is accounted for using a standard process costing system with the following standards:

Materials—2 pieces @ $.48 each..	$ .96
Labor—½ hour @ $7.60 per hour..	3.80
Variable factory overhead—½ hour @ $1.40 per hour....................	.70
Fixed factory overhead—½ hour @ $.40 per hour............................	.20
	$5.66

The company's standards include an allowance for normal spoilage. Equivalent production computations for standard costing are made for good units only. By this procedure, excess spoilage becomes a contributing factor to the computed variances.

The following data are available for September:

Beginning inventory (all materials, 50% converted)—10,000 units.
Started in process—40,000 units.
Transferred to finished goods—42,000 units.
Ending inventory (all materials, 90% converted)—5,000 units.
Fixed factory overhead budgeted—$8,000.
Materials used (76,000 pieces)—$38,000.
Labor (22,500 hours)—$180,000.
Variable factory overhead incurred—$33,800.
Fixed factory overhead incurred—$8,200.

Required: Compute two variances for materials and labor, and compute three variances for factory overhead, using three-variance method A. Indicate whether the variances are favorable or unfavorable. *(CGAAC adapted)*

17-3. Variance analysis: materials, labor, and factory overhead. Alpha Company has developed the following standard unit cost for product Beta, the only product produced in Gamma Department:

Direct materials.........................	4 lbs. @ $3 =	$12
Direct labor.................................	2 hrs. @ 9 =	18
Variable overhead.....................	2 hrs. @ 2 =	4
Fixed overhead..........................	2 hrs. @ 5 =	10
Standard cost per unit of Beta produced..............		$44

The company recognizes the materials price variance at the point of purchase. Fixed factory overhead is budgeted at $120,000. Actual activity for January included:

50,000 lbs. of direct materials purchased for $149,000 total.
10,000 units of Beta were produced.
41,500 lbs. of direct materials were used in current production.
The direct labor payroll was $196,560 (21,000 hrs. @ $9.36).
Actual factory overhead costs totaled $158,000.

Required: Compute two variances for materials and labor, and reconcile the overall factory overhead variance using three-variance method B. Indicate whether the variances are favorable or unfavorable. *(CGAAC adapted)*

17-4. Variance analysis: materials, labor, and factory overhead. Terry Company manufactures a commercial solvent used for industrial maintenance. This solvent, which is sold by the drum, generally has a stable selling price. Terry produced and sold 60,000 drums in December.

The following information is available regarding Terry's operations for the month:

(a) Standard costs per drum of product manufactured were:

Materials:

10 gallons of raw material...	$20
1 empty drum...	1
Total materials...	$21

Direct labor: 1 hour..	$7
Factory overhead (fixed): per direct labor hour................	4
(normal capacity is 68,750 direct labor hours)	
Factory overhead (variable): per direct labor hour..............	6

(b) Costs incurred during December were:

Raw materials:
600,000 gallons were purchased at a cost of $1,150,000.
700,000 gallons were used.

Empty drums:
85,000 drums were purchased at a cost of $85,000.
60,000 drums were used.

Direct labor:
65,000 hours were worked at a cost of $470,000.

Factory overhead:

Depreciation of building and machinery (fixed)........................	$230,000
Supervision and indirect labor (semivariable)..........................	360,000
Other factory overhead (variable)...	76,500
Total factory overhead..	$666,500

Required: Compute two variances for each material and for labor and four variances for factory overhead. The materials price variance is determined at the time of purchase. Indicate whether the variances are favorable or unfavorable.   (AICPA adapted)

17-5. Equivalent production and standard costing variance analysis. Marshall Company uses a standard process costing system in accounting for costs in its one production department. Material A is added at the beginning of the process, and Material B is added when the units are 90% complete. Conversion costs are incurred uniformly throughout the process. Inspection takes place at the end of the process, and all spoilage is expected to be abnormal. The standard cost of abnormal spoilage is charged to a current period expense account. Normal capacity is 7,800 direct labor hours per month.

The standard cost per unit is as follows:

Material A: 4 gallons @ $1.20...	$ 4.80
Material B: 2 square feet @ $.70.......................................	1.40
Direct labor: 1 hour @ $11.50...	11.50
Variable factory overhead: 1 hour @ $1.80.....................	1.80
Fixed factory overhead: 1 hour @ $5.00..........................	5.00
Total..	$24.50

Additional data for January:

(a) Beginning work in process inventory—3,000 units (33⅓% converted).
(b) Started in process during the month—11,000 units.
(c) Finished during the month—8,000 units.
(d) Ending work in process inventory—5,000 units (40% converted).
(e) Actual costs incurred:

Material A used	50,000 gallons @ $1.00
Material B used	18,000 sq. ft. @ $.75
Direct labor	10,200 hours @ $12.00
Factory overhead	$60,100

Required:

(1) Compute the January equivalent production for Material A, Material B, and for conversion costs.
(2) Compute two variances each for Material A, Material B, direct labor, and factory overhead. Indicate whether the variances are favorable or unfavorable.

(CGAAC adapted)

17-6. Standard process costing; cost of production report at standard; variance analysis. Weissritter Company uses a standard process costing system in accounting for its one product, which is produced in one department. All materials are added at the beginning of the process. Inspection takes place at the end of the process. Any spoiled units revealed by inspection are considered abnormal and completed as to all cost elements, and the related standard cost is charged to a current period expense account.

Standard cost per unit:

Materials: 3 square meters @ $.60	$1.80
Direct labor: ¼ hour @ $10.00	2.50
Variable factory overhead: ¼ hour @ $2.00	.50
Fixed factory overhead: ¼ hour @ $2.80	.70
Total	$5.50

Normal capacity is 8,750 direct labor hours per month.
Actual data for November:

(a) Beginning work in process inventory—5,000 units (40% converted).
(b) Started in process during the month—30,000 units.
(c) Spoiled during November—1,000 units.
(d) Ending work in process inventory—2,000 units (80% converted).
(e) Actual costs incurred:

Materials purchased	100 000 square meters @ $.64, recorded at standard cost
Materials used	92 000 square meters
Direct labor	8,000 hours @ $10.60
Variable factory overhead	$17,000
Fixed factory overhead	$25,000

Required:

(1) Prepare a cost of production report, at standard, for November.
(2) Compute two variances each for materials and direct labor and three for factory overhead (method A). Indicate whether the variances are favorable or unfavorable.

(CGAAC adapted)

17-7. Equivalent production and standard costing variance analysis. Steeler Manufacturing Company manufactures product AB in a process which involves two departments, Department A and Department B. Units are transferred from Department A to Department B and from Department B to the Finished Goods Storeroom.

In Department B, units are inspected at the end of the process, and material is added only to those units that pass inspection. All spoilage is considered to be normal. The company uses a standard cost system; therefore, the cost of normal spoilage becomes a part of the computed standard cost variances. Steeler Manufacturing has set the following standards for Department B:

> Standard Cost for One Unit of Product AB:
>
> | | | |
> |---|---|---|
> | Materials.............................. | 1 pound @ $1.90 = | $ 1.90 |
> | Direct labor.......................... | 2 hours @ $8.00 = | 16.00 |
> | Variable overhead............... | 2 hours @ $ .75 = | 1.50 |
> | Fixed overhead................... | 2 hours @ $1.50 = | 3.00 |
> | | | $22.40 |

Normal capacity is 17,000 units of product AB (34,000 direct labor hours). The following information pertains to April:

> | | |
> |---|---|
> | Beginning inventory (50% complete), 2,000 units.............. | $ 28,800 |
> | Received from Department A, 18,000 units......................... | 190,100 |
> | Transferred to Finished Goods, 15,000 units | |
> | Ending inventory (75% complete), 4,000 units | |
> | Costs added in Department B this period: | |
> | Materials (14,800 lbs. @ $2.00 actual cost)..................... | 29,600 |
> | Direct labor (38,000 hours @ $7.80)............................... | 296,400 |
> | Variable factory overhead... | 28,000 |
> | Fixed factory overhead... | 56,500 |

Required:

(1) Compute the equivalent production for prior department costs, materials, and conversion costs for the month of April.

(2) Compute two variances each for materials and labor, and compute three variances for factory overhead using method B. Indicate whether variances are favorable or unfavorable.   *(CGAAC adapted)*

17-8. Equivalent production and standard costing variance analysis. The standard cost card for Torno Company's product is:

> | | |
> |---|---|
> | Materials: 7 liters @ $.50.. | $3.50 |
> | Labor: ½ hr. @ $6.00... | 3.00 |
> | Variable factory overhead: ½ hr. @ $2.00.................... | 1.00 ⎤ |
> | Fixed factory overhead: ½ hr. @ $4.00......................... | 2.00 ⎦ ½ @ $3.00 |
> | Standard product cost per unit.. | $9.50 |

Data for November:

(a) 1,000 units (40% converted) were in process at the beginning of the month.
  5,050 units were started during the month.
  5,000 units were transferred to finished goods.
  800 units (25% converted) were in process at the end of the month.

(b) Materials are all added at the beginning of the process. Conversion costs are incurred evenly throughout the process. Inspection takes place when the units are 80% converted. Under normal conditions, no spoilage should occur.

(c) 40 000 liters of materials were purchased for $19,200 and were charged to inventory at standard cost.

(d) 37 000 liters of materials were issued to production.

(e) Direct labor payroll was $15,600 for 2,400 hours. *= 6.50 per hour ÷ 2 = 3.25 per ½ hr.*

(f) Actual factory overhead costs were:

Indirect labor (variable).....................................		$ 4,000
Supervision...		4,000
Depreciation (based on time)........................		2,500
Supplies...		1,000
Heat, light, and power (variable)....................	$ 300	
(fixed)...........................	1,200	1,500
Property tax..		200
Insurance...		500
		$13,700

(g) Marketing and administrative expenses were:
Variable, $1 per unit sold
Fixed, $13,500.

(h) Normal output for a month is 4,000 units.

Required:

(1) Compute the November equivalent production for materials and for conversion costs. *(labor & FOH)*

(2) Determine the standard cost of:
  (a) Units transferred to finished goods.
  (b) Abnormal spoilage, to be charged directly to a current period expense account.
  (c) Ending inventory of work in process.

(3) Compute the (a) materials price and quantity variances, (b) labor rate and efficiency variances, and (c) factory overhead variances, using the four-variance method. Indicate whether the variances are favorable or unfavorable.

(CGAAC adapted)

17-9. Variance analysis: materials, labor, and factory overhead; job order costing.
Vogue Fashions Inc. manufactures ladies' blouses of one quality, produced in lots to fill each special order from its customers, comprised of department stores located in various cities. Vogue sews the particular stores' labels in the blouses. The standard costs for a dozen blouses are:

Direct materials....................................	24 yards @ $1.10	$26.40
Direct labor...	3 hours @ $4.90	14.70
Factory overhead.................................	3 hours @ $4.00	12.00
Standard cost per dozen.....................		$53.10

During June, Vogue worked on three orders, for which the month's job cost records disclose the following:

Lot No.	Units in Lot (dozens)	Material Used (yards)	Hours Worked
22.....................	1,000	24,100	2,980
23.....................	1,700	40,440	5,130
24.....................	1,200	28,825	2,890

The following information is also available:

(a) Vogue purchased 95,000 yards of material during June at a cost of $106,400. The materials price variance is recorded when goods are purchased. All inventories are carried at standard cost.

(b) Direct labor during June amounted to $55,000. According to payroll records, production employees were paid $5 per hour.

(c) Factory overhead during June amounted to $45,600.

(d) A total of $576,000 was budgeted for factory overhead for 19A, based on estimated production at the plant's normal capacity of 48,000 dozen blouses annually. Factory overhead at this level of production is 40% fixed and 60% variable. Factory overhead is applied on the basis of direct labor hours.

(e) There was no work in process at June 1. During June, Lots 22 and 23 were completed. All material was issued for Lot 24, which was 80% completed as to direct labor.

Required:

(1) Prepare a schedule showing the computation of standard cost of Lots 22, 23, and 24 for June.

(2) Prepare a schedule showing the computation of the materials price variance for June.

(3) Prepare a schedule showing, for each lot produced during June, computations of the following variances, indicating whether they are favorable or unfavorable.
   (a) Materials quantity variance.
   (b) Labor efficiency variance.
   (c) Labor rate variance.

(4) Prepare a schedule showing computations of the total controllable and volume factory overhead variances for June. Indicate whether the variances are favorable or unfavorable.   (AICPA adapted)

17-10. Factory overhead variance analysis report. The Cost Department of Coffman Manufacturing Company prepared the following flexible budget for Department X for the month of January:

Machine hours.......................................	4,000	4,500	5,000
Capacity utilized.....................................	80%	90%	100%
Variable factory overhead:			
Indirect labor......................................	$ 2,800	$ 3,150	$ 3,500
Supplies..	2,000	2,250	2,500
Machinery repairs.............................	800	900	1,000
Electric power....................................	4,000	4,500	5,000
Total variable overhead....................	$ 9,600	$10,800	$12,000
Fixed factory overhead:			
Supervision.......................................	$ 3,000	$ 3,000	$ 3,000
Supplies..	1,700	1,700	1,700
Machinery maintenance.....................	3,000	3,000	3,000
Depreciation of machinery................	6,500	6,500	6,500
Insurance...	1,800	1,800	1,800
Property tax.......................................	1,000	1,000	1,000
Gas heating.......................................	600	600	600
Electricity (lighting)............................	400	400	400
Total fixed overhead........................	$18,000	$18,000	$18,000
Total factory overhead.........................	$27,600	$28,800	$30,000

Factory overhead is allocated to production on the basis of machine hours. The factory overhead rate is computed on the basis of normal capacity, which is 5,000 machine hours. At the end of January, 4,650 machine hours were actually worked; however, based on the standard cost card, 4,800 machine hours were allowed for the actual quantity of production output. The following cost data have also been compiled by the cost department for January:

	Actual Quantity of Input at Standard Unit Costs	Actual Quantity of Input at Actual Unit Costs
Supervision..	$ 3,000	$ 3,100
Indirect labor...	3,300	3,400
Variable supplies....................................	2,600	2,200
Fixed supplies.......................................	1,700	1,650
Machinery repairs...................................	950	960
Machinery maintenance.........................	3,200	3,200
Depreciation of machinery.....................	6,500	6,500
Insurance...	1,800	1,900
Property tax...	1,000	1,100
Gas heating..	700	845
Variable electricity.................................	4,700	4,740
Fixed electricity......................................	400	405
Total factory overhead..........................	$29,850	$30,000

Required: Prepare a departmental factory overhead variance report which includes (a) a variable efficiency variance, a spending variance, a spending quantity variance, and a spending price variance for each item of factory overhead expense, and (b) a single departmental volume variance. Indicate whether the variances are favorable or unfavorable.

17-11. Materials, labor, and overhead variances; mix and yield variances. Century Cement Company uses a standard cost system. Cement is produced by mixing two major components, A (lime) and B (clay), with water and by adding a third component, C, quantitatively insignificant.

Materials standards and costs for the production of 100 tons of output are:

	Tons	Cost	Percent of Input Quantity	Amount	
Material A	55	$43	50%	$2,365	
Material B	44	35	40	1,540	
Material C	11	25	10	275	
Input	110		100%	$4,180	= $38.00 per ton
Output	100			$4,180	= $41.80 per ton

The monthly factory overhead budget for a normal capacity level of 16,500 direct labor hours is as follows:

	Fixed Overhead	Variable Overhead
Plant manager	$ 2,000	
Supervisors	1,800	
Indirect labor	2,220	$ 810
Indirect supplies	850	2,040
Power and light	300	2,200
Water	480	2,000
Repairs and maintenance	500	1,200
Insurance	450	
Depreciation—production facilities	3,775	
Total	$12,375	$8,250

To convert 110 tons of materials into 100 tons of finished cement requires 500 direct labor hours at $7.50 per hour or $37.50 per ton. Factory overhead is applied on a direct labor hour basis.

In producing 3,234 tons of finished cement in April, the following costs were incurred:

Direct labor	15,800 hrs. @ $7.95
Fixed factory overhead	$11,075
Variable factory overhead	$ 8,490

| | Materials Purchased | | Materials Requisitioned |
	Quantity	Cost per Ton	Quantity
Material A	2,000 tons	$44	1,870 tons
Material B	1,200	37	1,100
Material C	500	24	440

There were no inventories of materials or work in process at the beginning of April. The materials price variance is recognized at the time of purchase.

Required: Compute the following variances, indicating whether they are favorable or unfavorable:

(1) Materials price, mix, and yield variances.
(2) Direct labor rate, efficiency, and yield variances.
(3) Factory overhead spending, idle capacity, efficiency, and yield variances.

17-12. **Materials, labor, and overhead variances; mix and yield variances.** Bowman Crunchies Inc. manufactures breakfast cereal, using the following proportion of ingredients:

	Quantity	Unit Cost	Amount	
Wheat germ	25 lbs.	$2.00	$ 50	
Barley	100	1.00	100	
Oats	125	.80	100	
Input	250 lbs.		$250	= $1.00 per lb.
Output	200 lbs.		$250	= $1.25 per lb.

Materials records for October indicate:

	Beginning Inventory	Purchases	Unit Cost	Ending Inventory
Wheat germ	2,000 lbs.	8,000 lbs.	$2.05 per lb.	1,200 lbs.
Barley	5,000	35,000	1.10	5,300
Oats	4,000	45,000	.75	7,000

The materials price variance is recognized when the materials are purchased.

The conversion of 250 pounds of materials into 200 pounds of finished product requires 25 direct labor hours at $8 per hour. The actual direct labor for the month was 8,000 hours and cost $64,800.

Factory overhead is applied on a direct labor hour basis at a rate of $3 per hour ($1 fixed, $2 variable). Normal capacity overhead is $30,000 with 10,000 direct labor hours. Actual overhead for October was $28,000. Actual finished production for the month was 70,000 pounds.

Required: Compute the following variances, indicating whether they are favorable or unfavorable:

(1) Materials purchase price, mix, and yield variances and the materials quantity variance for each material.
(2) Labor rate, efficiency, and yield variances.
(3) Factory overhead (a) spending, idle capacity, efficiency, and yield variances, and (b) controllable, volume, and yield variances.

CASES

A. Motivation via standard costing. Kelly Company manufactures and sells pottery items. All manufacturing takes place in one plant, having four departments, with each department producing only one product. The four products are plaques, cups, vases, and plates. Sam Kelly, the president and founder, credits the company's success to well-designed, quality products and to an effective cost control system which was installed early in the firm's existence to improve cost control and to serve as a basis for planning.

With the participation of plant management, the company establishes standard costs for materials and labor. Each year, the plant manager, the department heads, and the time-study engineers are invited by executive management to recommend changes in the standards for the next year. Executive management reviews these recommendations and the records of actual performance for the current year before setting the new standards. As a general rule, tight standards representing very efficient performance are established, so that no inefficiency or slack will be included in cost goals. The plant manager and department heads are charged with cost control responsibility and the variances from standard costs are used to measure their performance in carrying out this charge.

No standards are set for factory overhead because management believes it is too difficult to predict and relate overhead to output. The actual factory overhead for the departments and the plant is accumulated in one "pool." The actual overhead is then allocated to the departments on the basis of departmental output.

The company's executives are convinced that more effective cost control can be obtained than is currently being realized from the standard cost system. A review of cost performance for recent years disclosed several factors that led them to this conclusion:

(a) Unfavorable variances were the norm rather than the exception, although the size of the variances was quite uniform.
(b) Employee motivation, especially among first-line supervisors, appeared to be low.

Required:

(1) Identify the probable effects on motivation of plant managers and department heads resulting from:
(a) The participative standard cost system.
(b) The use of tight standards.
(2) State the effect on the motivation of department heads to control overhead

costs when actual factory overhead costs are applied on the basis of actual units. *(ICMA adapted)*

B. Standard setting. John Stevens, plant manager of the Fairlee Plant of Lockstead Corporation called together the twenty-five employees of Department B and told them that production standards established several years previously were now too low in view of the recent installation of automated equipment. He gave the workers an opportunity to discuss the mitigating circumstances and to decide among themselves, as a group, what their standards should be. Stevens, on leaving the room, believed they would doubtlessly establish much higher standards than he himself would have dared propose.

After an hour of discussion, the group summoned Stevens and notified him that, contrary to his opinion, their group decision was that the standards were already too high, and since they had been given the authority to establish their own standards, they were making a reduction of 10%. These standards, Stevens knew, were far too low to provide a fair profit on the owner's investment. Yet it was clear that his refusal to accept the group decision would be disastrous.

Required:
(1) Identify the errors made by Stevens.
(2) Suggest a course of action to be taken by Stevens. *(CGAAC adapted)*

C. Standard setting. Associated Media Graphics (AMG) is a rapidly expanding company involved in the mass reproduction of instructional materials. Ruth Boston, owner and manager of AMG, has made a concentrated effort to provide a quality product at a fair price with delivery on the promised due date. Expanding sales have been attributed to this philosophy. Boston is finding it increasingly difficult to supervise personally the operations of AMG and is beginning to institute an organizational structure that would facilitate management control.

One change recently made was the designation of operating departments as cost centers, with control over departmental operations transferred from Boston to each departmental manager. However, quality control still reports directly to Boston, as do the finance and accounting functions. A materials manager was hired to purchase all raw materials and to oversee the inventory handling (receiving, storage, etc.) and recordkeeping functions. The materials manager also is responsible for maintaining an adequate inventory based upon planned production levels.

The loss of personal control over the operations of AMG caused Boston to look for a method of efficiently evaluating performance. Maryanne Cress, a new cost accountant, proposed the use of a standard cost system. Variances for materials, labor, and factory overhead could then be calculated and reported directly to Boston.

Required:
(1) Assume that Associated Media Graphics is going to implement a standard cost system and establish standards for materials, labor, and factory overhead. Identify and discuss for each of these cost components:
   (a) Who should be involved in setting the standards.
   (b) The factors that should be considered in establishing the standards.
(2) Describe the basis for assignment of responsibility under a standard cost system. *(ICMA adapted)*

D. Factory overhead variance analysis. Stringfellow Industries uses a standard cost system and budgets the following sales and costs for 19—:

Unit sales	20,000
Sales	$200,000
Total production cost at standard	130,000
Gross profit	70,000
Beginning inventories	None
Ending inventories	None

The 19— budgeted sales level was the normal capacity level used in calculating the factory overhead predetermined standard cost rate per direct labor hour.

At the end of 19—, Stringfellow Industries reported production and sales of 19,200 units. Total factory overhead incurred was exactly equal to budgeted factory overhead for the year and there was underapplied total factory overhead of $2,000 at December 31. Factory overhead is applied to the work in process inventory on the basis of standard direct labor hours allowed for units produced. Although there was a favorable labor efficiency variance, there was neither a labor rate variance nor materials variances for the year.

Required: Write an explanation of the underapplied factory overhead of $2,000, being as specific as the data permit and indicating the overhead variances affected. Stringfellow uses three-variance method A to analyze the total factory overhead. (AICPA adapted)

E. Price, mix, and yield variances and their use. LAR Chemical Company manufactures a wide variety of chemical compounds and liquids for industrial uses. The standard mix for producing a single batch of 500 gallons of one liquid is as follows:

Liquid Chemical	Quantity in Gallons	Cost per Gallon	Total Cost
Maxan	100	$2.00	$200
Salex	300	.75	225
Cralyn	225	1.00	225
	625		$650

There is a 20% loss in liquid volume during processing due to evaporation. The finished liquid is put into 10-gallon bottles for sale. Thus, the standard materials cost for a 10-gallon bottle is $13.

The actual quantities of raw materials and the respective cost of the materials placed in production during November were as follows:

Liquid Chemical	Quantity in Gallons	Total Cost	
Maxan	8,480	$17,384	2.05
Salex	25,200	17,640	.70
Cralyn	18,540	16,686	.90
	52,220	$51,710	

A total of 4,000 bottles (40,000 gallons) were produced during November.

Required:

(1) Compute the materials price, mix, and yield variances, including an analysis of the portion of the mix variance attributable to each material.

(2) Explain how LAR Chemical could use each of these variances to help control the cost to manufacture this liquid compound. (ICMA adapted)

F. Variance analysis; variance control responsibility. Cappels Corporation manufactures and sells a single product, using a standard cost system. The standard cost per unit of product is:

Materials: 1 pound of plastic @ $2	$ 2.00
Direct labor: 1.6 hours @ $4	6.40
Variable factory overhead cost per unit	3.00
Fixed factory overhead cost per unit	1.45
	$12.85

The factory overhead cost per unit was calculated from the following annual overhead cost budget for a 60,000-unit volume:

Variable factory overhead cost:	
Indirect labor (30,000 hours @ $4)	$120,000
Supplies (oil—60,000 gallons @ $.50)	30,000
Allocated variable service department cost	30,000
Total variable factory overhead cost	$180,000
Fixed factory overhead cost:	
Supervision	$ 27,000
Depreciation	45,000
Other fixed costs	15,000
Total fixed factory overhead cost	$ 87,000
Total budgeted annual factory overhead cost for 60,000 units	$267,000

The charges to the Manufacturing Department for November, when 5,000 units were produced, were:

Materials (5,300 pounds @ $2)	$10,600
Direct labor (8,200 hours @ $4.10)	33,620
Indirect labor (2,400 hours @ $4.10)	9,840
Supplies (oil—6,000 gallons @ $.55)	3,300
Allocated variable service department cost	3,200
Supervision	2,475
Depreciation	3,750
Other fixed costs	1,250
Total	$68,035

The Purchasing Department normally buys about the same quantity of plastic as is used in production during a month. In November, 5,200 pounds were purchased at a price of $2.10 per pound.

The company has divided its responsibilities so that the Purchasing Department is responsible for the price at which materials and supplies are purchased, while the Manufacturing Department is responsible for the quantities of materials used.

The Manufacturing Department manager performs the timekeeping function and, at various times, an analysis of factory overhead and direct labor variances has shown that the manager has deliberately misclassified labor hours (e.g., direct labor hours might be classified as indirect labor hours and vice versa), so that only one of the two labor variances is unfavorable. It is not economically feasible to hire a separate timekeeper.

Required:

(1) Calculate these variances from standard costs for the data given: (a) materials purchase price variance; (b) materials quantity variance; (c) direct labor rate variance; (d) direct labor efficiency variance; (e) factory overhead controllable variance, analyzed for each expense classification.

(2) Explain whether the division of responsibilities should solve the conflict between price and quantity variances.

(3) Prepare a report which details the factory overhead budget variance. The report, which will be given to the Manufacturing Department manager, should display only that part of the variance that is the manager's responsibility and should highlight information useful to that manager in evaluating departmental performance and in considering corrective action.

(4) Suggest a solution to the company's problem involving the classification of labor hours.   (ICMA adapted)

G. **In-depth analysis of labor variances.** Technowave Company manufactures a complete line of radios. Because a large number of models have plastic cases, the company has its own molding department for producing them. The month of April was devoted to the production of the plastic case for one of the portable radios—Model SX76.

The Molding Department has two operations—molding and trimming; there usually is no interaction of labor in these two operations. The standard labor cost for producing 10 plastic cases for Model SX76 is as follows:

Molding: ½ hour @ $6	$3
Trimming: ¼ hour @ $4	1
	$4

During April, 70,000 plastic cases were produced in the Molding Department; however, 10% of these cases had to be discarded because they were found to be defective at final inspection. The Purchasing Department had changed to a new plastic supplier to take advantage of a lower price for comparable plastic. The new plastic turned out to be of a lower quality, resulting in the rejection of the 7,000 cases.

Direct labor hours worked and direct labor costs charged to the Molding Department are as follows:

Molding: 3,800 hours @ $6.25	$23,750
Trimming: 1,600 hours @ $4.15	6,640
Total labor charges	$30,390

As a result of poor scheduling by the Production Scheduling Department, the supervisor of the Molding Department had to shift molders to the trimming operation for 200 hours during April. The company paid the molding workers their regular hourly rate, even though they were performing a lower-rated task. There was no significant loss of efficiency caused by the shift. In addition, as a result of unexpected machinery repairs required during the month, 75 hours and 35 hours of idle time occurred in the molding and trimming operations, respectively.

The monthly report which compares actual costs with standard cost of output for April shows the following labor variance for the Molding Department:

Actual labor cost for April	$30,390
Standard labor cost of output	
[63,000 × ($4 ÷ 10)]	25,200
Unfavorable labor variance	$ 5,190

This variance is significantly higher than normal.

Required:

(1) Prepare a detailed analysis of the unfavorable labor variance for the Molding Department, showing the variance resulting from (a) labor rates; (b) labor substitution; (c) material substitution; (d) operating efficiency; and (e) idle time.

(2) Evaluate the Molding Department supervisor's argument that the variances due to labor substitution and change in raw materials should not be charged to the department. *(ICMA adapted)*

CHAPTER 18

Standard Costing: Incorporating Standards Into the Accounting Records

Some companies prefer to use standard costs for planning, motivation, and evaluation purposes only. In such cases, standard costs do not enter into the company's journals and ledgers. However, the incorporation of standard costs into the regular accounting system permits the most efficient use of a standard cost system and leads to savings and increased accuracy in clerical work. In either case, variances can be analyzed for cost control, and standard costs can be used in developing budgets, bidding on contracts, and setting prices. The procedures for accumulating standard costs in the company's accounts and the disposition of standard cost variances are presented in this chapter. The illustrative data and the resulting variance computations used are the same as for Chapter 17.

▼ RECORDING STANDARD COST VARIANCES IN THE ACCOUNTS

Standard costs should be viewed as costs which pass through the data processing system into financial statements. However, variations exist in the methods of accumulating these costs. Some systems employ the partial plan; others, the single plan. Both plans center around the entries to the work in process account. Under either plan, the work in process account can be broken down by individual cost elements (materials, labor, and factory overhead) and/or by departments. The plans are summarized as follows:

Partial Plan

Work in Process	
Actual cost	Standard cost

Single Plan

Work in Process	
Standard cost	Standard cost

558

The Partial Plan

In the partial plan, the work in process account is debited for the actual cost of materials, labor, and factory overhead and is credited at standard cost when goods are completed and transferred to finished goods inventory. Any balance remaining in the work in process account consists of two elements: (1) the standard cost of work still in process and (2) the variances between actual and standard costs. To isolate these variances, additional analysis is needed.

The Single Plan

Since timely identification and reporting are major control features of standard cost accounting, prompt communication for very short time frames may be required. The single plan debits and credits the work in process account at standard costs only, and variances are recorded in separate variance accounts. These entries are periodic summaries of standard costs, actual costs, and resulting variances. They are discussed in detail in the following pages and are used in the exercises and problems of this chapter.

▼ STANDARD COST ACCOUNTING PROCEDURES FOR MATERIALS

The recording of materials purchased can be handled by three different methods:

1. *Record the price variance when materials are received and placed in stores.* The general ledger control account, Materials, is debited at standard cost and the materials ledger cards are kept in quantities only. A standard price is noted on the card when the standards are set. As purchases are made, no prices are recorded on these cards. This procedure results in clerical savings and speedier postings.
2. *Record the materials at actual cost when received, and determine the price variance when the materials are requisitioned for production.* The general ledger control account, Materials, is debited at actual cost and the materials ledger cards show quantities and dollar values as in a historical cost system.
3. *Use a combination of methods (1) and (2).* Calculate price variances when the materials are received, but defer charging them to production until the materials are actually placed in process. At that time, only the price variance applicable to the quantity used will appear as a current charge, the balance remaining as a part of the materials inventory. This method results in two types of materials price variances: (1) a materials purchase price variance originating when materials purchases are first recorded, and (2) a materials price usage variance when materials are used. The occurrence of the materials price usage variance is a reduction of the materials purchase price variance.

For control purposes, the price variance should be determined when the materials are received. If it is not computed and reported until the materials are requisitioned for production, then remedial action is difficult because the time of computation is so far removed from the time of purchase. Also, the problem of deciding which actual cost is applicable is again present.

These methods for recording materials purchased are illustrated below, using the following data for Item 5-489 (pages 515-516):

Standard unit price as per standard cost card........................	$2.50
Purchases...	5,000 pieces @ $2.47
Requisitioned..	3,550 pieces
Standard quantity allowed for actual production....................	3,500 pieces

Method 1

The journal entry when materials are purchased is:

Materials*..	12,500	
Accounts Payable**..		12,350
Materials Purchase Price Variance***.....................		150

*$2.50 standard price × 5,000 pieces purchased
**$2.47 actual price × 5,000 pieces purchased
***$.03 favorable price variance per piece × 5,000 pieces purchased

When materials issued to the factory are recorded, the entry is:

Work in Process*..	8,750	
Materials Quantity Variance**...................................	125	
Materials***...		8,875

*$2.50 standard price × 3,500 pieces (standard quantity allowed)
**$2.50 standard price × 50 piece unfavorable quantity variance
***$2.50 standard price × 3,550 pieces used

Method 2

When materials are purchased, no variance is computed and the entry is:

Materials*..	12,350	
Accounts Payable..		12,350

*$2.47 actual price × 5,000 pieces purchased

When materials issued to production are recorded, the entry is:

Work in Process*..	8,750.00	
Materials Quantity Variance**...................................	125.00	
Materials***...		8,768.50
Materials Price Usage Variance****.....................		106.50

*$2.50 standard price × 3,500 pieces (standard quantity allowed)
**$2.50 standard price × 50 piece unfavorable quantity variance
***$2.47 actual price × 3,550 pieces used
****$.03 favorable price variance per piece × 3,550 pieces used

For this computation, the cost used is $2.47 per piece. The assumption here is that there is no beginning materials inventory and that there are no other purchases during the period. In practice, the actual cost used would depend upon the type of inventory costing methods employed, such as perpetual or periodic, and the inventory cost flow assumptions, such as fifo, lifo, or average costing.

In this method, the materials price usage variance account appears on the books after the materials are issued, and then only for the quantity issued—not for the entire purchase. The price variance occurred because the actual cost of the materials issued was $.03 less than the standard price; the quantity variance, because 50 pieces were used in excess of the standard quantity allowed. Notice that the cost charged to Work in Process and the amount recorded as the quantity variance are the same for Method 1 and Method 2. Only the price variance and the charge to the materials inventory are different.

Method 3

The following entry, identical with the first entry in Method 1, would be made when the materials are purchased:

Materials*..	12,500	
Accounts Payable**...		12,350
Materials Purchase Price Variance***......................		150

*$2.50 standard price × 5,000 pieces purchased
**$2.47 actual price × 5,000 pieces purchased
***$.03 favorable price variance per piece × 5,000 pieces purchased

When the materials issued are recorded, two entries are made. The following entry, identical with the second entry in Method 1, recognizes the 50 pieces of material used in excess of the standard quantity allowed.

Work in Process*..	8,750	
Materials Quantity Variance**......................................	125	
Materials***...		8,875

*$2.50 standard price × 3,500 pieces (standard quantity allowed)
**$2.50 standard price × 50 piece unfavorable quantity variance
***$2.50 standard price × 3,550 pieces used

The next entry transfers $106.50 from the purchase price variance account to the price usage variance account.

Materials Purchase Price Variance.............................	106.50	
Materials Price Usage Variance*.............................		106.50

*$.03 favorable price variance per piece × 3,550 pieces used

In Method 3, any balance remaining in the materials purchase price variance account at the end of the accounting period is used to adjust the inventory to actual cost. This balance is shown in the balance sheet as follows:

Materials (at standard cost)...	$3,625.00
Less materials purchase price variance.....................	43.50
Materials (adjusted to actual cost).............................	$3,581.50

▼ STANDARD COST ACCOUNTING PROCEDURES FOR LABOR

The payroll is computed on the basis of clock cards, job tickets, and other labor time information furnished to the payroll department. In a standard cost system, these basic records supply the data for the computation of labor variances.

The necessary journal entries are illustrated with the following data for Operation 2-476 (pages 517-518):

Actual hours worked	1,880
Actual rate paid per hour	$9.50
Standard hours allowed for actual production	1,590
Standard rate per hour	$9.00

The following journal entry records the total actual direct labor payroll, assuming that there were no payroll deductions:

Payroll	17,860	
Accrued Payroll*		17,860

*$9.50 actual labor rate × 1,880 actual hours worked

To distribute the payroll and to set up the variance accounts, the journal entry is:

Work in Process*	14,310	
Labor Rate Variance**	940	
Labor Efficiency Variance***	2,610	
Payroll		17,860

*$9.00 standard labor rate × 1,590 standard hours allowed
**$.50 unfavorable labor rate × 1,880 actual hours worked
***$9.00 standard labor rate × 290 excess actual hours over standard

▼ STANDARD COST ACCOUNTING PROCEDURES FOR FACTORY OVERHEAD

The close relationship between standard costs and budgetary control methods is particularly important for the analysis of factory overhead. Actual factory overhead is measured not only against the applied overhead cost, but also against a budget based on actual and standard activity allowed for actual production.

The following data for Department 3 (pages 520-521) are used to illustrate the journal entries for the two-variance, three-variance, and four-variance methods.

Normal capacity (in direct labor hours)............................		4,000 hours
Total factory overhead at normal capacity:		
Fixed..	$3,200	
Variable...	4,800	$8,000
Factory overhead rate per direct labor hour:		
Fixed..	$ .80	
Variable...	1.20	$2.00
Actual factory overhead...		$7,384
Actual direct labor hours..		3,475 hours
Standard hours allowed for actual production....................		3,400 hours

In actual practice, numerous entries would be entered in the general journal during each month of the year to record the incurrence of actual factory overhead. A single entry is used as follows to illustrate the recording of actual factory overhead for the entire period:

Factory Overhead Control.........................	7,384	
Various Credits.....................................		7,384

Typically, an entry to record the factory overhead charged to Work in Process would be entered in the general journal at least once a month. Again, a single entry is used to illustrate the application of factory overhead to work in process:

Work in Process*......................................	6,800	
Applied Factory Overhead....................		6,800

*$2.00 factory overhead rate × 3,400 standard hours allowed

At the end of the period, when applied factory overhead is closed, the entry would be as follows:

Applied Factory Overhead....................	6,800	
Factory Overhead Control.................		6,800

The factory overhead control account now has a debit balance of $584, which will be closed into the appropriate factory overhead variance accounts. The computations for the two-variance, three-variance, and four-variance methods are illustrated and discussed in detail in Chapter 17. The journal entries to record each of the alternative methods are illustrated here.

Two-Variance Method

In the two-variance method, the balance in the factory overhead control account is divided between the controllable variance and the volume variance. The entry to close the factory overhead control account and to record the controllable and volume variances is as follows:

Factory Overhead Volume Variance*..................................	480	
Factory Overhead Controllable Variance**........................	104	
Factory Overhead Control***..		584

*$.80 fixed factory overhead rate $\times$ 600 hours [i.e., the difference between normal capacity (4,000 hours) and the standard hours allowed (3,400 hours)]
**The amount required to balance the entry (see page 521 for an illustration of the computation of the controllable variance)
***The amount of underapplied factory overhead [i.e., the difference between actual factory overhead ($7,384) and applied factory overhead ($6,800)]

Three-Variance Method A

In the three-variance method A, the amount of over- or underapplied factory overhead can be analyzed as spending, idle capacity, and efficiency variances. The entry to close the factory overhead control account and to record these three variances is as follows:

Factory Overhead Idle Capacity Variance*.........................	420	
Factory Overhead Efficiency Variance**............................	150	
Factory Overhead Spending Variance***...........................	14	
Factory Overhead Control****..		584

*$.80 fixed factory overhead rate $\times$ 525 hours [i.e., the difference between normal capacity (4,000 hours) and the actual hours required (3,475 hours)]
**$2.00 factory overhead rate $\times$ 75 hours [i.e., the difference between the actual hours required (3,475 hours) and the standard hours allowed (3,400 hours)]
***The amount required to balance the entry (see page 523 for an illustration of the computation of the spending variance)
****The amount of underapplied factory overhead [i.e., the difference between actual factory overhead ($7,384) and applied factory overhead ($6,800)]

Three-Variance Method B

In the three-variance method B, the amount of over- or underapplied factory overhead can be analyzed as spending, variable efficiency, and volume variances. The entry to close the factory overhead control account and to record these three variances is as follows:

Factory Overhead Volume Variance*..................................	480	
Factory Overhead Variable Efficiency Variance**....................	90	
Factory Overhead Spending Variance***...........................	14	
Factory Overhead Control****..		584

*$.80 fixed factory overhead rate $\times$ 600 hours [i.e., the difference between normal capacity (4,000 hours) and the standard hours allowed (3,400 hours)]
**$1.20 variable factory overhead rate $\times$ 75 hours [i.e., the difference between the actual hours required (3,475 hours) and the standard hours allowed (3,400 hours)]
***The amount required to balance the entry (see page 523 for an illustration of the computation of the spending variance)
****The amount of underapplied factory overhead [i.e., the difference between actual factory overhead ($7,384) and applied factory overhead ($6,800)]

Four-Variance Method

In the four-variance method, the amount of over- or underapplied factory overhead is divided into the spending, idle capacity, variable efficiency, and fixed efficiency variances. The entry to close the factory overhead control account and to record these four variances is as follows:

Factory Overhead Idle Capacity Variance*...............................	420	
Factory Overhead Variable Efficiency Variance**....................	90	
Factory Overhead Fixed Efficiency Variance***........................	60	
Factory Overhead Spending Variance****................................	14	
Factory Overhead Control*****...		584

*$.80 fixed factory overhead rate × 525 hours [i.e., the difference between normal capacity (4,000 hours) and the actual hours required (3,475 hours)]
**$1.20 variable factory overhead rate × 75 hours [i.e., the difference between the actual hours required (3,475 hours) and the standard hours allowed (3,400 hours)]
***$.80 fixed factory overhead rate × 75 hours [i.e., the difference between the actual hours required (3,475 hours) and the standard hours allowed (3,400 hours)]
****The amount required to balance the entry (see page 523 for an illustration of the computation of the spending variance)
*****The amount of underapplied factory overhead [i.e., the difference between actual factory overhead ($7,384) and applied factory overhead ($6,800)]

▼ STANDARD COST ACCOUNTING PROCEDURES FOR COMPLETED PRODUCTS

The completion of production requires the transfer of cost from the work in process account of one department to the work in process account of another department, or, in the case of the last department, to the finished goods inventory account. The cost transferred is the standard cost of the completed products.

To illustrate, assume that 500 units of Alpac were completed during the period and transferred to finished goods inventory. The standard cost card for Alpac (page 513) indicates that the total cost of manufacturing a unit is $368.65. The journal entry to record the transfer of the 500 finished units of Alpac follows:

| Finished Goods... | 184,325 | |
| Work in Process*.. | | 184,325 |

*$368.65 standard cost per unit × 500 completed units

The finished goods ledger card will show quantities only, because the standard cost of the units remains the same during a period unless substantial cost changes occur. The entry to record the sale of 460 units of Alpac during the year is:

| Cost of Goods Sold.. | 169,579 | |
| Finished Goods*... | | 169,579 |

*$368.65 standard cost per unit × 460 units sold

▼ JOURNAL ENTRIES FOR MIX AND YIELD VARIANCES

The following data for Springmint Company (page 528) are used to illustrate the journal entries for the mix and yield variances. Standard product and cost specifications for 1,000 lbs. of chewing gum are as follows:

Material	Quantity	×	Unit Cost	=	Amount
A	800 lbs.		$.25 per lb		$200
B	200		.40		80
C	200		.10		20
Input	1,200 lbs.				$300

Since 1,200 lbs. of materials are required to produce 1,000 lbs. of finished product, the standard cost of materials per lb. of chewing gum is $.30 ($300 standard cost for 1,200 lbs. of input ÷ 1,000 lbs. output). To convert 1,200 lbs. of raw materials into 1,000 lbs. of finished product requires 20 direct labor hours at $9 per hour, or $.18 per lb. of finished product. Factory overhead is applied on a direct labor hour basis at a rate of $5 per hour ($3 fixed and $2 variable), or $.10 per lb. of finished product. Factory overhead at the normal capacity of 4,000 hours is budgeted at $20,000. The standard cost per pound of finished chewing gum is:

Materials..................................	$.30 per lb.
Labor...	.18
Factory overhead.....................	.10
	$.58 per lb.

During the period, 200,000 lbs. of chewing gum were actually produced. The following actual costs were incurred during the month:

Materials	Quantity Purchased	Actual Price per Lb.	Quantity Issued
A	162,000 lbs.	$.24	157,000 lbs.
B	30,000	42	38,000
C	32,000	.11	36,000

Labor—$9.12 per hour for 3,800 actual hours

Factory overhead—$22,000

Materials. Since the materials price variance is recorded at the date of purchase, the entry to record the purchase of materials is:

Materials*..	55,700	
Accounts Payable**..		55,000
Materials Purchase Price Variance***....................		700

*Material	Quantity	× Standard Cost per Lb.	= Total Cost
A	162,000 lbs.	$.25 per lb.	$40,500
B	30,000	.40	12,000
C	32,000	.10	3,200
			$55,700

**Material	Quantity	× Actual Cost per Lb.	= Total Cost
A	162,000 lbs.	$.24 per lb.	$38,880
B	30,000	.42	12,600
C	32,000	.11	3,520
			$55,000

***The amount required to balance the entry (see page 529 for an illustration of the computation of the price variance)

The entry to record the materials charged to production and to isolate the materials mix and yield variances is:

Work in Process*..	60,000	
Materials Mix Variance**.............................	300	
Materials Yield Variance***......................		2,250
Materials****..		58,050

*$.30 standard cost per lb. of output × 200,000 lbs. output
**Actual quantity of input at actual mix and standard prices (computed below).................. $58,050
Actual quantity of input at standard mix and standard prices [231,000 lbs. of
input × ($300 ÷ 1,200 lbs. input)].. 57,750
Materials mix variance.. $ 300 unfav.

***Actual quantity of input at standard mix and standard prices (computed above)............. $57,750
Actual quantity of output at standard cost per lb. of output [200,000 lbs. of out-
put × ($300 ÷ 1,000 lbs. output)]... 60,000
Materials yield variance.. $ (2,250) fav.

****Material	Quantity Issued	× Standard Cost per Lb.	= Total Cost
A	157,000 lbs.	$.25 per lb.	$39,250
B	38,000	.40	15,200
C	36,000	.10	3,600
	231,000 lbs.		$58,050

Labor. The entry to record the liability for direct labor incurred during the period is:

Payroll*..	34,656	
Accrued Payroll...		34,656

*$9.12 actual labor rate per hour × 3,800 actual hours worked

To charge Work in Process with direct labor and to isolate the labor variances:

Work in Process*..	36,000	
Labor Rate Variance**.................................	456	
Labor Efficiency Variance***......................		450
Labor Yield Variance****...........................		1,350
Payroll...		34,656

*$.18 standard cost per lb. × 200,000 lbs. actual output
**$.12 unfavorable rate variance per hour × 3,800 actual hours
***$9 standard labor rate × 50 hours [i.e., the difference between 3,800 actual hours worked and 3,850 standard hours allowed for the expected output (20 hours × 231,000 lbs. of input ÷ 1,200 lbs. input per batch)]
****$9 standard labor rate × 150 hours [i.e., the difference between 3,850 standard hours allowed for the expected output (computed above) and 4,000 standard hours allowed for actual output (20 hours × 200,000 lbs. output ÷ 1,000 lbs. standard yield per batch)]

Factory Overhead (Two-Variance Method). The entry to record the cost of actual factory overhead for the period is:

Factory Overhead Control.........................	22,000	
Various Credits..		22,000

The entry to charge factory overhead to production is:

Work in Process*..	20,000	
Applied Factory Overhead.................................		20,000

*$.10 standard cost per lb. of output × 200,000 lbs. of output

To close applied factory overhead into factory overhead control:

Applied Factory Overhead...................................	20,000	
Factory Overhead Control.................................		20,000

When the two-variance method is used, the overhead variances are the (1) controllable variance, (2) volume variance, and (3) yield variance. The entry to close factory overhead control and record these variances is:

Factory Overhead Volume Variance*..............................	450	
Factory Overhead Controllable Variance**.....................	2,300	
Factory Overhead Yield Variance***...........................		750
Factory Overhead Control****.......................................		2,000

*$3 fixed factory overhead rate × 150 hours [i.e., the difference between the normal capacity of 4,000 labor hours and the standard hours allowed for the expected output (3,850 hours)]
**The amount required to balance the entry (see page 533 for an illustration of the computation of the factory overhead controllable variance)
***$5 factory overhead rate × 150 hours [i.e., the difference between the standard hours allowed for the expected output (3,850 hours) and the standard hours allowed for the actual output (4,000 hours)]
****$22,000 actual factory overhead − $20,000 applied factory overhead

The entry to close factory overhead control and to record the factory overhead variances for the other variance computation methods would be recorded in a manner similar to the two-variance method.

Assuming that there is no work in process ending inventory, the total cost of completed production would be as follows:

Materials..	$ 60,000
Direct labor...	36,000
Factory overhead...	20,000
Total cost charged to work in process at standard	$116,000

To record the transfer of the finished products to the finished goods warehouse, the following entry would be made:

Finished Goods..	116,000	
Work in Process.......................................		116,000

▼ DISPOSITION OF VARIANCES

Variances may be disposed of in either of the following ways: they may be (1) closed to Income Summary or (2) treated as adjustments to Cost of Goods Sold and to inventories.

Variances Closed to Income Summary

Stating the work in process and finished goods inventories and the cost of goods sold at standard costs allows comparison of sales revenue and standard cost by product class. At the end of the month or year, the procedure for handling cost variances is to consider them as profit or loss items. Unfavorable (or debit) manufacturing cost variances are deducted from the gross profit calculated at standard cost. Favorable (or credit) variances are added to the gross profit computed at standard cost. The treatment of manufacturing cost variances using this method is depicted in the following income statement, which should be supported by a variance analysis report:

Income Statement
For Year Ended December 31, 19—

Sales..			$52,000
Cost of goods sold (at standard)—Schedule 1........................			24,000
Gross profit (at standard)...			$28,000
Adjustments for standard cost variances:			
Unfavorable variances:			
Materials purchase price variance..	$ 1,200		
Labor efficiency variance..	600		
Factory overhead controllable variance...............................	720		
Factory overhead volume variance......................................	1,200		
Total unfavorable variances...		3,720	
Gross profit (adjusted)..		$24,280	
Less: Marketing expenses..	$12,000		
Administrative expenses..	6,000	18,000	
Operating income...		$ 6,280	

Schedule 1
Cost of Goods Sold
For Year Ended December 31, 19—

Materials purchased...	$20.000	
Less ending inventory..	4,000	
Materials used..		$16,000
Direct labor..		10,000
Factory overhead..		20,000
		$46,000
Less ending work in process inventory....................................		16,000
Cost of goods manufactured...		$30,000
Less ending finished goods inventory.....................................		6,000
Cost of goods sold..		$24,000

At the end of the period, variance accounts are closed to the income summary account, as follows:

Income Summary..	3,720	
Materials Purchase Price Variance............................		1,200
Labor Efficiency Variance...		600
Factory Overhead Controllable Variance.....................		720
Factory Overhead Volume Variance...........................		1,200

As an alternative, if variances are considered a manufacturing function responsibility, they are closed to the cost of goods sold account, rather than directly to the income summary account. The total amount in Cost of Goods Sold (the standard cost of units sold plus the variance) would then be closed to Income Summary. Variances closed to the cost of goods sold account will appear in the cost of goods sold statement. Variances closed to the income summary account will appear in the income statement.

Accountants who use these procedures believe that only the standard costs should be considered the true costs. Variances are treated not as increases or decreases in manufacturing costs but as deviations from contemplated costs, due to abnormal inactivity, extravagance, inefficiencies or efficiencies, or other changes of business conditions. This viewpoint leads to the closing of all variances to the income summary account, which is an acceptable procedure as long as standards are reasonably representative of what costs ought to be. However, some proponents of this procedure suggest that the unused portion of the materials purchase price variance should be linked with materials still on hand and shown on the balance sheet as part of the cost of the ending materials inventory.

If an adjustment is made for the materials purchase price variance, whereby a part of the variance is attached to the materials inventory, the following computation would be made in this example:

Balance in materials inventory: $4,000 or 20% of purchases made
Materials purchase price variance: $1,200
Variance transferred to the materials account: $240 (20% of $1,200)

The materials account would be increased and the amount closed to Income Summary would be decreased, thereby increasing the operating income from $6,280 to $6,520. The journal entry to close the variance accounts would be:

Income Summary..	3,480	
Materials..	240	
Materials Purchase Price Variance.............................		1,200
Labor Efficiency Variance..		600
Factory Overhead Controllable Variance......................		720
Factory Overhead Volume Variance............................		1,200

Variances Allocated to Cost of Goods Sold and Inventories

With respect to the cost of inventories, *Accounting Research Bulletin No. 43* implies that significant variances are to be allocated between cost of goods sold and inventories:

Standard costs are acceptable if adjusted at reasonable intervals to reflect current conditions so that at the balance-sheet date standard costs reasonably approximate costs computed under one of the recognized bases. In such cases descriptive language should be used which will express this relationship, as, for instance, "approximate costs determined on the first-in, first-out basis," or, if it is desired to mention standard costs, "at standard costs, approximating average costs."[1]

CASB regulations require that significant standard cost variances be included in inventories. Current Internal Revenue Service regulations also require the inclusion of a portion of significant variances in inventories. When the amount involved is not significant in relation to total actual factory overhead for the year, an allocation is not required by the IRS unless such allocation is made for financial reporting purposes. Also, the taxpayer must treat both favorable and unfavorable variances consistently. Regulations, however, do permit expensing of the idle capacity variance.[2]

To illustrate the allocation of variances, the percentage of cost elements in the inventories and cost of goods sold of the previous example are:

Account	Materials Amount	%	Labor Amount	%	Factory Overhead Amount	%
Work in Process	$ 6,000	37.5	$ 2,000	20	$ 8,000	40
Finished Goods	2,000	12.5	2,000	20	2,000	10
Cost of Goods Sold	8,000	50.0	6,000	60	10,000	50
Total	$16,000	100.0	$10,000	100	$20,000	100

The allocation of the variances shown on page 569 is summarized in the following table. The materials purchase price variance of $960 ($1,200 − $240 allocated to Materials) is multiplied by the respective percentage of materials in the inventories and cost of goods sold accounts (37.5%, 12.5%, and 50.0%). The labor and factory overhead variances are allocated in a similar manner.

Account	Total Amount	Work in Process	Finished Goods	Cost of Goods Sold
Materials Purchase Price Variance	$ 960	$ 360	$120	$ 480
Labor Efficiency Variance	600	120	120	360
Factory Overhead Controllable Variance	720	288	72	360
Factory Overhead Volume Variance	1,200	480	120	600
Total	$3,480	$1,248	$432	$1,800

(handwritten: 960 × 37.5%)

(handwritten: 360 + $120 = $480)

The proration of these variances to work in process, finished goods, and cost of goods sold results in the following income statement:

Income Statement For Year Ended December 31, 19—		
Sales		$52,000
Cost of goods sold (standard adjusted to actual)—Schedule 1		25,800
Gross profit (actual)		$26,200
Less: Marketing expenses	$12,000	
Administrative expenses	6,000	18,000
Operating income		$ 8,200

(handwritten: 24,000 + 1800)

[1]*Accounting Research Bulletin, No. 43*, "Inventory Pricing" (New York: American Institute of Certified Public Accountants, 1953), Chapter 4, par. 6.
[2]*Regulations*, Section 1.471-11(d)(3).

Schedule 1
Cost of Goods Sold
For Year Ended December 31, 19—

	Standard	Variance	Actual
Materials available..	$20,000		$21,200
Materials purchase price variance........................		$1,200	
Less materials inventory (ending)............................	4,000		– 4,240
Materials purchase price variance........................		240	
Materials used..	$16,000		$16,960
Materials purchase price variance........................		$ 960	
Direct labor..	10,000		+ 10,600
Efficiency variance..		600	
Factory overhead..	20,000		+ 21,920
Controllable variance..		720	
Volume variance..		1,200	
Total manufacturing cost....................................	$46,000	$3,480	$49,480
Less ending work in process inventory....................	16,000	1,248	– 17,248
Cost of goods manufactured................................	$30,000	$2,232	$32,232
Less ending finished goods inventory....................	6,000	432	– 6,432
Cost of goods sold..	$24,000	$1,800	$25,800

The $1,920 difference between the adjusted operating income of $8,200 and the operating income of $6,280 shown in the income statement on page 569 is summarized as follows:

Cost added to:		
	Materials...............................	$ 240
	Work in process.....................	1,248
	Finished goods.......................	432
	Total...................................	$1,920

Entries transfer the prorated amounts to the respective accounts in the general ledger only. Subsidiary inventory accounts and records are not adjusted. The various adjustment accounts could be shown on the balance sheet as valuation or contra accounts against standard inventory values, or combined with them to form one amount. At the beginning of the next period, the portion of these proration entries that affects inventory accounts is reversed in order to return beginning inventories to standard costs. At the end of that period, the amount reversed plus new variances are allocated in the same manner as before, based on ending inventory and cost of goods sold account balances.

In connection with closing variances, a problem arises in the allocation of variances to product or commodity groups. Preferably, standard cost variances are shown as deductions in total and are not allocated to major commodity groups to determine the profit and loss per commodity. Experience has shown that it is almost impossible to do otherwise. The basic idea of variance analysis is misconstrued when such prorations are attempted. The isolation of variances is for the purpose of controlling costs and determining what the variances are, where they occurred, and what caused them.

The Logic of Disposition of Variances

The treatment of variances depends upon the (1) type of variance (materials, labor, or factory overhead), (2) size of variance, (3) experience with standard costs, (4) cause of variance (e.g., incorrect standards), and (5) timing of variance (e.g., a variance caused by seasonal fluctuations). Therefore, determining the most acceptable treatment requires consideration of more than the argument that only actual costs should be shown in the financial statements. The determination of an actual cost may be impossible, and to argue that charging off variances in the period in which they arise might distort the operating income reveals a misunderstanding of standard costs.

One view of the disposition of variances has been expressed as follows:

1. Where the standards are current and attainable, companies would "state their inventories at standard cost and charge the variances against the income of the period in which the variances arise. They justify this practice on the grounds that variances represent inefficiencies, avoidable waste not recoverable in the selling price, and random fluctuations in actual cost."

2. Where standards are not current, "the general practice is to divide the variances between inventories and cost of goods sold or profit and loss thereby converting both inventories and cost of sales to approximate actual costs."[3]

Another view asserts that:

1. Any variances which are caused by inactivity, waste, or extravagance (outside acceptable tolerance limits) should be written off, since they represent losses. They should not be deferred by capitalizing them in the inventory accounts. This would include quantity variances on materials and labor as well as idle time (capacity) and efficiency variances on overhead. To assign a portion of such costs to inventory may cloud the product pricing decision. For example, "the inclusion of idle capacity costs in product costs has the effect of raising [inventory] costs when it is most difficult to raise prices [low volume periods] and lowering [inventory] costs when it is easiest to ask for higher prices [high volume periods]."[4]

2. An inventory reserve account should be established and charged with part of the price (spending and rate) variances (and quantity, capacity, and efficiency variances within acceptable tolerance limits) to an extent which would bring the materials, work in process, and finished goods inventories up to, but not in excess of, current market values. The rest of the price (spending and rate) variance amounts (as well as those variances described in (1) above) should be written off, since they

[3]*NAA Research Report, Nos. 11-15,* "How Standard Costs Are Being Used Currently" (New York: National Association of Accountants, 1948), pp. 65-66.
[4]Edwin Bartenstein, "Different Costs for Different Purposes," *Management Accounting,* Vol. LX, No. 2, p. 46.

represent excess costs. In this way, the inventory accounts themselves will be stated at standard cost while the inventories on the balance sheet will, as a whole, be shown at reasonable costs through the use of the inventory reserve account. In addition, losses caused by excessive costs and inefficiencies will be shown in the operating statement for the period in which they occur.[5]

Disposition of Variances for Interim Financial Reporting

The AICPA takes the following position concerning variance disposition for interim financial reporting in published financial statements:

Companies that use standard cost accounting systems for determining inventory and product costs should generally follow the same procedures in reporting purchase price, wage rate, usage or efficiency variances from standard cost at the end of an interim period as followed at the end of a fiscal year. Purchase price variances or volume or capacity cost variances that are planned and expected to be absorbed by the end of the annual period, should ordinarily be deferred at interim reporting dates. The effect of unplanned or unanticipated purchase price or volume variances, however, should be reported at the end of an interim period following the same procedures used at the end of a fiscal year.[6]

▼ REVISION OF STANDARD COSTS

As discussed in Chapter 17, standards should be changed only when underlying conditions change or when they no longer reflect the original concept. The idea that standards should be changed more than once a year weakens their effectiveness and increases operational details. Nevertheless, standard costs require continuous review and should be changed when conditions dictate.

When standard costs are changed, any adjustment to inventory should be made with care so that inventories are not written up or down arbitrarily. The National Association of Accountants made the following comments concerning adjustments to ending inventory for such changes:

1. *If the new standard costs reflect conditions which affected the actual cost of the goods in the ending inventory, most firms adjust inventory to the new standard cost and carry the contra side of the adjusting entry to cost of sales by way of the variance accounts. In effect, this procedure assumes that the standard costs used to cost goods in the inventory have been incorrect and that restatement of inventory cost is needed to bring inventories to a correct figure on the books. Since the use of incorrect standards has affected the variance accounts as well as the inventory, the adjustment is carried to the variance accounts.*
2. *If the standard costs represent conditions which are expected to prevail in the coming period but which have not affected costs in the past period, ending inventories are costed at the old standards. It appears to be common practice to adjust the detailed inventory records to new standard costs.*

---

[5]W. Wesley Miller, "Standard Costs and Their Relation to Cost Control," *NA(C)A Bulletin*, Vol. XXVII, No. 15, p. 692.

[6]*Opinions of the Accounting Principles Board, No. 28,* "Interim Financial Reporting" (New York: American Institute of Certified Public Accountants, 1973), par. 14.

In order to maintain the control relationship which the inventory accounts have over subsidiary records, the same adjustment is entered in the inventory control accounts; and the contra entry is carried to an inventory valuation account. Thus, the net effect is to state the inventory in the closing balance sheet at old standard costs. In the next period the inventory valuation account is closed to cost of sales when the goods to which the reserve relates move out of inventories. By use of this technique, the detailed records can be adjusted to new standards before the beginning of the year while at the same time the net charge to cost of sales in the new period is for old standard cost since the latter cost was correct at the time the goods were acquired.[7]

▼ BROAD APPLICABILITY OF STANDARD COSTING

The use of standard costing is not limited to manufacturing situations. This powerful working tool for planning and control can be used in other aspects of business organizations. For example, standards can be used for marketing activities, as discussed in Chapter 25, and for maintenance work.[8] The nonprofit organization sector (hospitals, governmental agencies, etc.) also affords many opportunities to utilize standard costing concepts and techniques. Though standard costs may not be formally recorded in the accounts, many relatively small organizations, such as automotive repair shops and construction contractors, can utilize the comparison of actual to standard quantities, times, and costs for bidding, pricing of jobs or projects, and the planning and control of routine operating activities.

DISCUSSION QUESTIONS

1. Some firms incorporate standard costs into their accounts; others maintain them only for statistical comparisons. Discuss these different uses of standard costs.

2. Compare the use of actual cost methods to standard costing systems for inventory costing.

3. Differences between actual costs and standard costs may be recorded in variance accounts. What considerations might determine the number of variance accounts?

4. Name several advantages of using standard costs for finished goods and goods sold.

5. The determination of periodic income depends greatly upon the cost assigned to materials, work in process, and finished goods inventories. What considerations determine the costing of inventories at standard or approximate actual costs by companies using standard costs?

6. Present arguments in support of each of the following three methods of treating standard cost variances for purposes of financial reporting:
   (a) As deferred charges or credits on the balance sheet.
   (b) As charges or credits on the income statement.
   (c) Allocated between inventories and cost of goods sold.   *(AICPA adapted)*

---

[7]*NAA Research Report,* Nos. 11-15, *op. cit.* p. 64.
[8]See James H. Bullock, *Maintenance Planning and Control* (New York: National Association of Accountants, 1979), Chapter 6, "Maintenance Standards and Performance Measurement," pp. 99-111.

EXERCISES

1. Journal entries for materials; variance analysis. Frisco Corporation uses a standard costing system. The standard for one of its products, Freako, is 2 units of raw material LEQ at a cost of $1 per unit. During April, 17,600 Freakos were manufactured. Inventory of raw material LEQ on April 1 was 8,000 units, costing $8,400; purchases were 32,000 units @ $1.04 per unit; and ending inventory was 6,000 units, costing $1.04 each.

Required: Prepare the journal entries for the purchase and issue of LEQ, using the three methods for recording materials purchased.

2. Journal entries for labor; variance analysis. The processing of one unit of Product X requires a standard of 1.75 hours at $9.08 per hour to perform Operation A88. During the month, 1,500 units were manufactured, requiring 2,590 hours at $9.28 per hour for this operation.

Required: Prepare the journal entries for labor operation A88, including variances.

3. Journal entries for factory overhead; two-variance analysis. Factory overhead is charged to production in Department A on the basis of the standard machine hours allowed for actual production. The following data relate to the results of operations for the month of May:

Normal capacity in machine hours..	15,000
Standard machine hours allowed for actual production.....................	12,000
Actual machine hours...	13,000

The factory overhead rate based on normal capacity machine hours follows:

Variable overhead...........................	$ 37,500 ÷ 15,000 hours =	$2.50
Fixed overhead.................................	67,500 ÷ 15,000 hours =	4.50
Total factory overhead.....................	$105,000 ÷ 15,000 hours =	$7.00

Actual factory overhead incurred during the month of May totaled $90,000.

Required: Prepare the journal entries necessary to record each of the following:

(1) The incurrence of actual factory overhead.
(2) The factory overhead actually charged to production.
(3) The closing of the applied factory overhead account.
(4) The closing of the factory overhead control account into the controllable variance and the volume variance accounts.

4. Journal entries for factory overhead: three-variance method A. Factory overhead is charged to production in the Assembly Department of Indiana Manufacturing Company on the basis of the standard direct labor hours allowed for actual production. The following data relate to the results of operations for the month of December:

Normal capacity in direct labor hours...	10,000
Standard labor hours allowed for actual production.....................	11,000
Actual direct labor hours worked...	10,500

The factory overhead rate based on normal capacity direct labor hours follows:

Variable overhead...........................	$ 30,000 ÷ 10,000 hours =	$3.00
Fixed overhead.................................	20,000 ÷ 10,000 hours =	2.00
Total factory overhead.....................	$ 50,000 ÷ 10,000 hours =	$5.00

Actual factory overhead incurred during December totaled $56,000.

Required: Prepare the journal entries necessary to record each of the following:

(1) The incurrence of actual factory overhead.
(2) The factory overhead actually charged to production.
(3) The closing of the applied factory overhead account.
(4) The closing of the factory overhead control account into three factory overhead variance accounts (method A).

5. **Journal entries for factory overhead; three-variance method B.** Factory overhead is charged to production in the Machining Department of Texas Tool Company on the basis of the standard machine hours allowed for actual production. The following data relate to the results of operations for November:

Normal capacity in machine hours	5,000
Standard machine hours allowed for actual production	4,800
Actual machine hours	5,200

The factory overhead rate based on normal capacity machine hours follows:

Variable overhead	$ 20,000	÷ 5,000 hours	=	$ 4.00
Fixed overhead	60,000	÷ 5,000 hours	=	12.00
Total factory overhead	$ 80,000	÷ 5,000 hours	=	$16.00

Actual factory overhead incurred during November totaled $78,000.

Required: Prepare the journal entries necessary to record each of the following:

(1) The incurrence of actual factory overhead.
(2) The factory overhead actually charged to production.
(3) The closing of the applied factory overhead account.
(4) The closing of the factory overhead control account into three factory overhead variances (method B).

6. **Journal entries for factory overhead; four-variance method.** Factory overhead is charged to production in the Finishing Department of Franklin Furniture Company on the basis of the standard direct labor hours allowed for actual production. The following data relate to the results of operations for February:

Normal capacity in direct labor hours	8,000
Standard labor hours allowed for actual production	7,000
Actual direct labor hours worked	7,600

The factory overhead rate based on normal capacity direct labor hours follows:

Variable overhead	$ 64,000	÷ 8,000 hours	=	$ 8.00
Fixed overhead	24,000	÷ 8,000 hours	=	3.00
Total factory overhead	$ 88,000	÷ 8,000 hours	=	$11.00

Actual factory overhead incurred during February totaled $86,000.

Required: Prepare the journal entries necessary to record each of the following:

(1) The incurrence of actual factory overhead.
(2) The factory overhead actually charged to production.

(3) The closing of the applied factory overhead account.
(4) The closing of the factory overhead control account into four factory overhead variance accounts.

7. Factory overhead variance analysis and journal entries. The theoretical capacity of Lawrence Products is 3,600 units or 9,000 direct labor hours. At the normal capacity level (80% of theoretical), the following factory overhead amounts have been budgeted:

Fixed.......................... $4,392
Variable.................... 5,904

Standards were set as follows:

Direct labor, 2.5 hours per unit
Factory overhead, $1.43 per direct labor hour

Actual data for May were:

Production, 2,870 units
Labor, 7,150 hours
Factory overhead, $10,236

Required:

(1) Compute the variances resulting when the two-, three-, and four-variance methods are used. For the three-variance method, use both method A and B.
(2) For each method, prepare the journal entries to record actual factory overhead, applied factory overhead, and variances.

8. Journal entries for materials mix and yield variances. Standard production and cost specifications for 1,000 pounds of product X are:

Material	Standard Mix	Standard Unit Cost
A	900 lbs.	$ .50 per lb.
B	450 lbs.	1.20 per lb.
C	150 lbs.	3.30 per lb.
	1,500 lbs.	

Materials price variances are recorded at the time the materials are purchased. During July, 10,100 pounds of product X were actually produced from the following material inputs:

A.......................... 8,900 lbs.
B.......................... 4,200 lbs.
C.......................... 1,800 lbs.
Total.................... 14,900 lbs.

Required: Prepare a journal entry to record the issue of materials to production at standard, along with the related mix and yield variances.

9. Disposition of variances. Nanron Company uses a standard process cost system for all its products. All inventories are carried at standard. Inventories and cost of goods sold are adjusted for financial statement purposes for all variances considered material in amount at the end of the fiscal year. All products are considered to flow through the manufacturing process to finished goods and ultimate sale in a first-in, first-out pattern.

The standard cost of one of Nanron's products is as follows:

Materials...	$2
Direct labor (.5DLH @ $8).............	4
Factory overhead..........................	3
Total standard cost....................	$9

There is no work in process inventory of this product due to the nature of the product and the manufacturing process.

The following schedule reports the manufacturing and sales activity measured at standard cost for the current fiscal year:

	Units	Dollars
Product manufactured...	95,000	$855,000
Beginning finished goods inventory......................	15,000	135,000
Goods available for sale.....................................	110,000	$990,000
Ending finished goods inventory..........................	19,000	171,000
Cost of goods sold...	91,000	$819,000

The balance of the finished goods inventory, $140,800, reported on the balance sheet at the beginning of the year included a $5,800 adjustment for variances from standard cost. The unfavorable standard cost variances for labor for the current fiscal year consisted of a wage rate variance of $32,000 and a labor efficiency variance of $20,000 (2,500 hours @ $8). There were no other variances from standard cost for this year.

Required: Assuming the unfavorable labor variances totaling $52,000 are considered material in amount by management and are to be allocated to finished goods inventory and to cost of goods sold, compute the amount that will be shown on the year-end balance sheet for finished goods inventory and the amount for cost of goods sold on the income statement prepared for the fiscal year. *(ICMA adapted)*

10. Disposition of variances. Atlas Bell Corporation uses standard costing in accounting for the manufacturing costs of its only product, Xerco. Variances are allocated to the cost of goods sold and ending inventories. The following information was extracted from the corporation's books for January:

	Debit	Credit
Materials purchase price variance.....................	$1,500	
Materials quantity variance.................................	660	
Labor rate variance...	250	
Labor efficiency variance...................................	290	
Controllable variance...		$300
Volume variance...	120	

The following inventories were on hand on January 31:

Finished goods.......................	900 units
Work in process....................	1,200 units
Raw materials........................	none

The work in process inventory was 100% complete as to materials and 50% complete as to direct labor and factory overhead. During January, 1,500 units were sold.

Required: Allocate the variances. Round distribution percentages to the nearest percent and allocations to the nearest dollar.

PROBLEMS

18-1. Journal entries; variance analysis. Irvine Company manufactures a product having the following standard costs:

Materials..	3 sq. ft. @ $2	$ 6.00
Labor..	½ hr. @ 8	4.00
Variable factory overhead...............................	½ hr. @ 3	1.50
Fixed factory overhead (normal capacity is 4,000 labor hours)...................	½ hr. @ 2	1.00
			$12.50

The following information pertains to actual activity for March:

(a) 9,000 units were produced.

(b) 30,000 sq. ft. of materials were purchased at $2.07. The materials price variance is recorded when the purchase is made.

(c) 28,000 sq. ft. of materials were used.

(d) Direct labor was $36,080 for 4,400 hours. The liability has been recorded, but the payroll account has not been distributed.

(e) Factory overhead was $22,600.

(f) 8,200 units were sold at $16.

(g) Marketing and administrative expenses were $20,000.

Required: Prepare the journal entries to record the above information, including two variances for each cost element.   *(CGAAC adapted)*

18-2. Journal entries; variance analysis. Alexandria Manufacturing Inc. produces custom-made, tie-dyed sweat shirts for distribution on college campuses. The following standards have been established.

Materials:		
Cotton cloth: 2 yards @ $1.........................	$2.00
Dyes: 1 pint @ $.50....................................	.50
Labor: ½ hour @ $6.......................................	3.00
Factory overhead: ½ hour @ $1.....................	.50
	$6.00

The yearly production budget is based upon normal plant operations of 20,000 hours, with fixed factory overhead of $6,000.
Inventories at January 1 were:

Cotton cloth (2,000 yards @ $1)...	$2,000
Dye (1,000 pints @ $.50)..	500
Work in process (1,000 units; ¼ finished as to conversion; all materials issued)...	3,375
Finished goods (500 @ $6)...	3,000

Production for January:

3,000 units completed
750 units ⅓ converted, all materials added

Transactions for January:

Cotton cloth purchased.............................	5,000 yds. @ $1.10
Dyes purchased..	2,500 pints @ $.49
Cotton cloth issued to factory.....................	5,600 yards
Dyes issued to factory.................................	2,700 pints
Direct labor payroll......................................	1,550 hours @ $5.90
Actual factory overhead.............................	$1,620
Sales on account...	3,100 sweat shirts @ $9

Required: Prepare the journal entries to record the January transactions, accounting for work in process at standard cost and recognizing variances in the proper accounts. Use the two-variance method in computing materials and labor, and three-variance method A in computing factory overhead variances; recognize the materials price variance at the time of purchase. Use separate inventory and variance accounts for each material. Close all variances into Cost of Goods Sold.

18-3. Journal entries; variance analysis. Manhattan Manufacturing Company uses a standard cost system in its accounting records. The standard costs for its one product are as follows:

Materials......................................	3 kilograms	@	$ 2.00 =	$ 6.00
Direct labor................................	2 hours	@	10.50 =	21.00
Variable overhead.....................	2 hours	@	3.00 =	6.00
Fixed overhead..........................	2 hours	@	1.00 =	2.00
				$35.00

Normal capacity is 2,000 direct labor hours per month. Materials, work in process, and finished goods are recorded in inventory at standard cost. The following information is taken from last month's records:

Production..	900 units
Materials purchased...................................	5 000 kilograms @ $ 1.95
Materials used in production.....................	2 800 kilograms
Direct labor payroll.....................................	1,740 hours @ $11.55
Actual overhead...	$8,600

Required: Prepare the journal entries to record the above information. Use the two-variance method to compute materials and labor variances and three-variance method B to compute overhead variances. *(CGAAC adapted)*

18-4. Journal entries; variance analysis. The following information pertains to production operations of Groff Company for April:

Inventories:
  Work in process: Beginning, 2,000 units, all materials, ½ converted; ending, 3,000
                     units, all materials, ⅓ converted; no spoilage.
  Finished goods: No beginning or ending inventory.

Standard and actual costs:
  Materials: Standard quantity, 5 square feet per unit; 50,000 square feet were
                     purchased @ $.52; the unfavorable materials purchase price

	variance was $1,000; 29,500 square feet of materials were requisitioned from the storeroom.
Labor:	Standard per unit, ½ hour at $9 per hour; actual labor rate was $9.05 per hour for 2,600 hours.
Factory overhead:	Normal capacity, 2,000 labor hours; fixed factory overhead standard, $2 per unit or $4 per labor hour; actual factory overhead was $5,500 variable and $8,200 fixed; efficiency variance, $700 unfavorable; spending variance, $400 unfavorable.

Five thousand units were sold for cash at $15 each.

Required: Prepare the journal entries to record the cost accounting cycle transactions, using standard costing. Variances will not be disposed of until June, the end of the fiscal year.

(CGAAC adapted)

18-5. Price, mix, and yield variances; journal entries. Medicope Company produces an antiseptic powder which is sold in bulk to institutions such as schools and hospitals. The product's mixture is tested at intervals during the production process. Materials are added as needed to give the mixture the desired drying and medicating properties. The standard mixture with standard prices for a 100-lb. batch is as follows:

10 lbs. of Hexachlorophene @ $.45
10 lbs. of Para-chlor-meta-xylenol @ $.30
30 lbs. of Bentonite @ $.08
20 lbs. of Kaolin @ $.10
50 lbs. of Talc @ $.05

During January, the following materials were purchased:

1,500 lbs. of Hexachlorophene @ $.47
1,100 lbs. of Para-chlor-meta-xylenol @ $.33
4,000 lbs. of Bentonite @ $.07
2,500 lbs. of Kaolin @ $.11
6,000 lbs. of Talc @ $.04

The materials price variance is recorded when materials are purchased. Production for the month consisted of 10,700 lbs. of finished product. There were no beginning or ending inventories of work in process. The following actual materials quantities were put into production:

1,050 lbs. of Hexachlorophene
1,125 lbs. of Para-chlor-meta-xylenol
3,080 lbs. of Bentonite
2,200 lbs. of Kaolin
5,300 lbs. of Talc

Required:

(1) Calculate materials variances (price, mix, and yield).
(2) Prepare the journal entries for (a) purchase, (b) usage, (c) completion of materials, and (d) disposition of variances, assuming all completed units were sold.

18-6. Income statement; variance analysis. Ensley Corporation manufactures Product G, which sells for $25 per unit. Material M is added before processing starts, and labor and overhead are added evenly during the manufacturing process. Production capacity is budgeted at 110,000 units of G annually. The standard costs per unit of G are:

Direct materials:		
M: 2 pounds @ $1.50..		$ 3.00
Direct labor: 1.5 hours at $8 per hour.....................		12.00
Factory overhead:		
Variable...	$1.50	
Fixed...	1.10	2.60
Total standard cost per unit......................................		$17.60

A process cost system is used. Inventories are costed at standard cost. All variances from standard costs are charged or credited to Cost of Goods Sold in the year incurred.

Inventory data for 19—:

	January 1	December 31
Material M...	50,000 pounds	60,000 pounds
Work in process:		
All materials, 2/5 processed......................	10,000 units	
All materials, 1/3 processed......................		15,000 units
Inventory, finished goods..............................	20,000 units	12,000 units

During 19—, 250,000 pounds of M were purchased at an average cost of $1.485 per pound; and 240,000 pounds were transferred to work in process inventory. Direct labor costs amounted to $1,313,760 at an average hourly labor rate of $8.16.

Actual factory overhead for 19—:

Variable.....................	$181,500
Fixed..........................	114,000

A total of 110,000 units of G were completed and transferred to finished goods inventory. Marketing and administrative expenses were $681,000.

Required: Prepare an income statement for 19—, including all manufacturing cost variances and using the two-variance method for factory overhead. *(AICPA adapted)*

18-7. Variance analysis: materials, labor, factory overhead; income statement. The following information concerns Boris Logan Company, which manufactures one product and uses a standard costing system:

Standard cost per unit:

Materials: 3 liters @ $2..	$ 6
Direct labor: 2 hours @ $8..	16
Variable factory overhead: 2 hours @ $3.....................	6
Fixed factory overhead: 2 hours @ $2..........................	4
	$32

Actual production—11,000 units
Materials purchased—50 000 liters @ $1.90; purchases are recorded at standard cost
Direct labor (23,000 hours)—$193,200

Depreciation of factory building and equipment—$10,000
Sales salaries—$12,000
Insurance: factory—$2,000; office—$200
Sales—9,000 units @ $45
Indirect labor (includes $25,000 fixed)—$60,000
Normal capacity—10,000 units or 20,000 direct labor hours
Heat and light—office—$800
Heat, light, and power—factory—$11,000 (includes $4,000 fixed)
Advertising—$8,000
Materials used—35 000 liters
Office supplies used—$500
Administrative salaries—$14,000
Depreciation of office building—$1,000
Indirect factory materials used (variable)—$20,000
Delivery expense—$4,000

Required:

(1) Prepare an analysis of the materials, direct labor, and factory overhead variances, using the three-variance method A for factory overhead.
(2) Prepare an income statement, supported by a schedule of variances and treating all variances as period costs.   *(CGAAC adapted)*

18-8. Journal entries; variance analysis; income statement. Halifax Company uses the following standard costs in accounting for its only product:

Materials: 3 liters × $4	$12.00
Direct labor: ½ hour × $7	3.50
Variable factory overhead: ½ hour × $6	3.00
Fixed factory overhead: ½ hour × $9	4.50
	$23.00

Fixed factory overhead budgeted was $49,500 per month.
Actual activity for November was:

(a) 40 000 liters of material were purchased for $159,200. The related price variance is recorded at the time of purchase.
(b) 10,000 units were produced.
(c) There was no work in process at the beginning or end of November.
(d) 31 000 liters of material were issued to production.
(e) The direct labor payroll to be distributed (credit the payroll account) is $35,616 for 4,800 hours.
(f) Actual factory overhead cost of $81,500 was incurred.
(g) 8,000 units were sold on account at $40 each.
(h) Marketing and administrative expenses of $60,000 were incurred.

Required:

(1) Prepare journal entries to record the November activity. (Ignore overhead variances.)
(2) Prepare a four-variance analysis of under- or overapplied factory overhead.
(3) Prepare an income statement, assuming that all variances are to be closed to Cost of Goods Sold.   *(CGAAC adapted)*

18-9. Allocating variances. Hamm Corporation commenced doing business on December 1. The corporation uses a standard cost system for the manufacturing costs of its only product, Hamex. The standard costs for a unit of Hamex are:

Materials: 10 kilograms @ .70..	$ 7
Direct labor: 1 hour @ $8...	8
Factory overhead (applied on the basis of $2 per direct labor hour)....................	2
Total..	$17

The following data were extracted from the corporation's books for December:

	Units	Debit	Credit
Budgeted production..	3,000		
Units sold...	1,500		
Sales..			$45,000
Sales discounts..		$ 500	
Materials price usage variance.................................		1,500	
Materials quantity variance......................................		660	
Direct labor rate variance..		250	
Factory overhead spending variance....................			300
Discounts lost...		120	

The company records purchases of materials net of discounts. The amounts shown for discounts lost and materials price usage variance are applicable to materials used in manufacturing operations during December.

Inventory data at December 31 indicate the following inventories were on hand:

Finished goods.......................	900 units
Work in process.....................	1,200 units
Materials................................	None

The work in process inventory was 100% complete as to materials and 50% as to direct labor and factory overhead. The corporation's policy is to allocate variances to the cost of goods sold and ending inventories, i.e., work in process and finished goods.

Required: Prepare schedules:

(1) Allocating the variances and discounts lost on purchases to the ending inventories and to cost of goods sold.
(2) Computing the cost of goods manufactured at standard cost and at actual cost for December. Amounts for materials, labor, and factory overhead should be shown separately.
(3) Computing the actual cost of materials, labor, and factory overhead included in the work in process inventory and in the finished goods inventory at December 31.   (AICPA adapted)

CASES

A. Disposition of Variances. Jonesboro Company manufactures office equipment. The company historically has utilized standard costing to aid management decisions. Variances from standard usually have been minor and always have been expensed in the audited financial statements. However, two problems have been encountered this year. First, variances from standard are large because of rapid increases in labor and materials costs and because of a slowdown in production during the last quarter. Second, a considerable portion of manufactured inventory remains unsold. The company wishes to expense the variances from standard.

Required: Discuss the acceptability of the proposal insofar as external reporting is concerned.   (CICA adapted)

B. Standard costs in inventory and variance disposition. Many advocates of standard costing take the position that these costs are a proper basis for inventory costing for external reporting purposes. Accounting Research Bulletin No. 43, however, reflects the widspread view that standard costs are not acceptable unless "adjusted at reasonable intervals to reflect current conditions so that at the balance-sheet date standard costs reasonably approximate costs computed under one of the recognized bases."

Required:
(1) Discuss the conceptual merits of using standard costs as the basis for inventory costing for external reporting purposes.
(2) Prepare general journal entries for three alternative dispositions of a $1,500 unfavorable variance, when all goods manufactured during the period are included in the ending finished goods inventory. Assume that a formal standard cost system is in operation, that $500 of the variance resulted from actual costs exceeding normal (attainable) standard cost, and that $1,000 of the variance resulted from the difference between the theoretical (ideal) standard and a normal standard.
(3) Discuss the conceptual merits of each of the three alternative methods of disposition requested in (2) above.
                                       (AICPA adapted)

PART

5

Analysis of Costs and Profits

CHAPTER 19
Direct Costing and the Contribution Margin

The factory overhead chapters (Chapters 12, 13, and 14) presented the use of the factory overhead rate for product costing. All budgeted factory overhead costs were combined into a composite, predetermined rate. To construct this rate, all factory overhead for the accounting period must be budgeted and the total divided by the expected volume of the activity measure used to allocate factory overhead to production. The objective of this process is to assign a portion of each item of factory overhead incurred during the period to each unit produced during the period. Since this process results in the assignment of a share of both fixed and variable factory overhead to production, it is referred to as *absorption*, *full*, or *conventional costing*.

Since the amount of factory overhead assigned to production is a function of the predetermined rate and the actual volume of production activity, actual factory overhead and the amount charged to production typically differ. This difference may be the result of differences in costs (i.e., actual factory overhead for the period is not the same as budgeted factory overhead adjusted to the actual level of activity) or differences in activity (i.e., the actual volume of production activity is not the same as the budgeted level of activity used in computing the predetermined rate) or both. When actual and budgeted activity differ, fixed factory overhead will be over- or underabsorbed. Whether this fixed cost variance is charged to period expense or ratably allocated between ending inventories and the cost of goods sold, fluctuations in the unit product cost occur.

If the predetermined factory overhead rate were based on an accurate measure of long-run or normal capacity, the fixed cost variance might be deferred on the theory that such variances would balance out in the long run. However, information accumulated in NAA research studies over a period of years indicates that the concept of long-range normal or standard unit cost for costing production, sales, and inventory is often not applied in practice. The reasons for this failure are:

1. *Long-range normal or standard volume cannot be reliably determined. First, this is a consequence of the fact that long-range volume for a growing company with indefinite future life cannot be defined in concrete terms capable of being implemented by*

measurement techniques. Second, long-range forecasts of future volume have, at best, a wide and unknown margin of error.

2. *The services of manufacturing facilities and organizations tend to expire with the passage of time whether or not utilized to produce salable goods. Consequently, the period costs of these services also expire with time. To carry such costs forward to future periods results in mismatching of costs with revenues because no benefits from such costs will be received in the future and nothing is contributed by the cost toward production of future revenues. Thus, the practice of charging unabsorbed period cost against revenues of the current period has been justified by reasoning that this charge measures cost of idle capacity and not cost of production. Similarly, apportionment of large overabsorbed balances reflects the opinion that unit product costs based on standard volume have been overstated.[1]*

The NAA study concludes that "the concept of long-run unit cost of production is unsatisfactory in measuring short period income. The fault in this case is that the wrong cost concept was chosen for the purpose—i.e., the long-run concept of cost was used to measure short-run operations."[2]

The normal capacity concept used for establishing overhead rates is long-range in nature; however, management wants monthly and even weekly earnings reports. It wants to know what was earned last month. It does not ask for a profit figure covering the firm's entire production and sales cycle. Although the usefulness of costing methods for managerial purposes has been aided immeasurably through the use of factory overhead rates and flexible budgets, management always asks for more direct and understandable answers. Direct costing seeks to satisfy these demands.

▼ DIRECT COSTING DEFINED

Direct costing, also referred to as *variable costing* or *marginal costing,* charges units of product with only those manufacturing costs that vary directly with volume. Prime costs (direct materials and direct labor) plus variable factory overhead are assigned to inventories (both work in process and finished goods) and to the cost of goods sold. Thus, only variable manufacturing costs are charged to the product, while all fixed manufacturing costs are expensed in the current period. Fixed manufacturing costs, such as depreciation, insurance, taxes, supervisory salaries, and the salaries of janitors, guards, maintenance, and office personnel, are excluded from the cost of the product. Because the incurrence of fixed costs appears to be more closely associated with the passage of time than with production activity, such costs are often referred to as *period costs* and are charged to period expense rather than to inventories. In contrast, variable costs are often referred to as *product costs* and are assigned to inventories because they are more closely associated with production activity than with the passage of time.

---

[1]*NAA Research Report*, No. 37, "Applications of Direct Costing" (New York: National Association of Accountants, 1961), pp. 72-73.

[2] *Ibid.*, p. 73.

▼ FACETS OF DIRECT COSTING

Direct costing focuses attention on the product and its costs. This interest moves in two directions: (1) to internal uses of the fixed-variable cost relationship and the contribution margin concept, and (2) to external uses involving the costing of inventories, income determination, and financial reporting. The internal uses deal with the application of direct costing in profit planning, product pricing, other phases of decision making, and in cost control. These facets of direct costing can be presented as follows:

Facets of Direct Costing

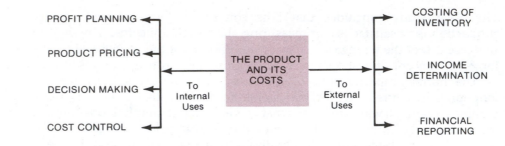

Contribution Margin Defined

The *contribution margin*, sometimes referred to as *marginal income*, is the difference between sales revenue and variable costs. It is computed by subtracting all variable costs, both manufacturing and nonmanufacturing, from sales revenue. In direct costing, contribution margin may be computed in total (for the entire firm or for each product line, sales territory, operating division, etc.) or on a per unit basis. However, income per unit is not computed. Total income is computed by subtracting total fixed costs from the total contribution margin, as shown in the following illustration. This illustration is based on the assumption that unit variable cost remains constant at $42 for all levels of activity, and that the fixed cost is fixed in total for all levels of activity.

	Per Unit	Total	Percentage of Sales
Sales (10,000 units)....................	$70	$700,000	100
Less variable cost........................	42	420,000	60
Contribution margin......................	$28	$280,000	40
Less fixed cost.............................		175,000	25
Operating income........................		$105,000	15

Internal Uses of Direct Costing

Executive managers, including marketing executives, production managers, and cost analysts, frequently praise the planning, control, and analytical potentialities of direct costing. Fixed costs calculated on a unit cost basis under absorption costing tend to vary for various volumes of production and sales.

Such variability in unit costs makes the use of absorption costing for many types of internal analysis difficult at best and misleading at worst. In contrast, variable unit costs and the contribution margin per unit tend to remain constant at all levels of activity. Consequently, managers often find direct costing more understandable and more useful than absorption costing for most types of internal analysis.

Many modern manufacturing plants are highly automated. In some cases, robotics technology has been used to replace direct labor, thereby significantly reducing variable manufacturing costs. In fully automated plants, variable costs may comprise no more than one or two percent of the total manufacturing cost. At first glance, one might assume that direct costing would be of little value to decision makers if variable costs comprise such a small component of the total cost of manufacturing. However, quite the opposite may be true. Since fixed costs comprise a larger share of total costs, the inclusion of fixed costs in the cost of the product will result in larger changes in product costs as production volume fluctuates between periods. Consequently, reliance on absorption costing figures can be even more misleading than in cases where fixed costs comprise a smaller share of the total cost of manufacturing.

Direct Costing as a Profit-Planning Tool. A *profit plan*, often called a *budget* or *plan of operations,* covers all phases of future operations to attain a stated profit goal. Although such a plan includes both long- and short-range operations, direct costing is quite useful in planning for short periods, in pricing special orders, or in making current operating decisions.

The variable cost and the contribution margin allow quick and fairly reliable profit approximations for making decisions in the short run. To be reliable in such situations, the change or shift of a small segment within the total volume must not require major changes in capacity, which would change fixed or period costs. Period costs that are specific or relevant to a single product, product line, or segment of the business should be isolated and attached to that unit in order to increase the usefulness of these costs for decision-making purposes.

With its separation of variable and fixed costs and its calculation of the contribution margin, direct costing facilitates analysis of the cost-volume-profit relationship. Direct costing aids in identifying the relevant analytical data for determining the break-even point, the rate of return on investment, the contribution margin by a segment of total sales, and the total profit from all operations based on a given volume. Direct costing also aids management in planning and evaluating the profit resulting from a change of volume, a change in the sales mix, make-or-buy situations, and the acquisition of new equipment. A knowledge of the variable or out-of-pocket costs, fixed costs, and contribution margin provides a basis for evaluating the profitability of products, customers, territories, and other segments of the entire business. These uses are discussed in later chapters.

Direct Costing as a Guide to Product Pricing. In a highly competitive market, prices are determined through the interaction of supply and demand. The best or optimum price is the one which will yield the maximum excess of total revenue over total cost. The volume at which the increase in total cost due to the addition of one more unit of volume is just equal to the increase in total revenue (i.e., the point at which marginal revenue is equal to marginal cost) is the profit-maximizing volume. The price at which this volume can be obtained is the optimum price. A higher price will lower the quantity demanded and decrease total profit. A lower price will increase the quantity demanded but decrease total profit. Although management can control supply, demand is a function of such factors as the tastes and preferences of consumers and their financial capacity, over which management has little control. Direct costing provides the marginal cost of the product necessary to determine the profit-maximizing volume.

In multiproduct pricing, management needs to know whether each product can be priced competitively and still contribute sufficiently to the company's total contribution margin for fixed cost recovery and profit. Direct costing provides the data necessary to compute the contribution margin from each product line for different unit sales prices and different levels of sales. Although such information is useful in short-term pricing decisions, a long-run pricing policy should ensure that all fixed costs are fully recovered.

Direct Costing for Managerial Decision Making. Installation of a direct costing system requires a study of cost trends and a segregation of fixed and variable costs. The classification of costs as either fixed or variable, with semivariable expenses properly subdivided into their fixed and variable components, provides a framework for the accumulation and analysis of costs. This also provides a basis for the study of contemplated changes in production levels or proposed actions concerning new markets, plant expansion or contraction, or special promotional activities. Of course, it is important to recognize that a study of cost behavior that identifies fixed and variable costs can be accomplished without the use of a formal direct costing system.

In NAA Research Report No. 37, findings on the usefulness of direct costing are summarized as follows:

> *Companies participating in this study generally feel that direct costing's major field of usefulness is in forecasting and reporting income for internal management purposes. The distinctive feature of direct costing which makes it useful for this purpose is the manner in which costs are matched with revenues.*
>
> *The marginal income [contribution margin] figure which results from the first step in matching costs and revenues in the direct costing income statement is reported to be a particularly useful figure to management because it can be readily projected to measure increments in net income which accompany increments in sales. The theory underlying this observed usefulness of the marginal income figure in decision making rests upon the fact that, within a limited volume range, period costs tend to remain constant in total when volume changes occur. Under such conditions, only the direct costs are relevant in costing increments in volume.*
>
> *The tendency of net income to fluctuate directly with sales volume was reported to be an important practical advantage possessed by the direct costing approach to income determination because it enables management to trace changes in sales to their consequence in net income. Another advantage attributed to the direct costing income statement was that management has a better understanding of the impact that period costs have on profits when such costs are brought together in a single group.[3]*

---

[3] *Ibid.*, pp. 84-85.

Direct Costing as a Control Tool. The direct costing procedure is designed to improve the usefulness of the income statement prepared for management. With absorption costing, inverse fluctuations of production costs and sales revenues can result from fixed manufacturing cost allocations between inventories and cost of goods sold. Such allocations do not occur in direct costing. By adopting direct costing, management and marketing management in particular believe that a more meaningful and understandable income statement can be furnished by the accountant. However, reports issued should serve not only the marketing department but all divisions of an enterprise. It seems appropriate, therefore, to prepare reports for all departments or responsibility centers based on standard costs, flexible budgets, and a division of all costs into their fixed and variable components.

The marketing manager should receive a statement placing sales and production costs in direct relationship to one another. Differences between intended sales and actual sales caused by changes in sales price, sales volume, or sales mix, which are the direct responsibility of the marketing manager, should be detailed for analysis as discussed in Chapter 25. Control of marketing costs is also vital to the total cost control framework.

Other managers can examine and interpret their reports with respect to the production cost variances originating in their respective areas of responsibility. The production manager is able to study the materials quantity variance, the labor efficiency variance, and the controllable overhead variance. Variable expenses actually incurred can be analyzed by comparing them with the budget allowance for work actually performed. The purchasing agent or manager can be held accountable for the purchase price variance, and the personnel manager for labor rate variances. General management, which originally authorized and approved plant capacity in the form of labor and machines, is primarily responsible for utilization of existing facilities. In direct costing, however, no variances result with respect to fixed expenses, because all fixed costs are charged currently against revenue instead of to the product.

Reports constructed on the direct costing basis and augmented by the additional information described become valuable control tools. A profit-responsible management group is continually reminded of the original profit objective for the period. Subsequent approved deviations from the objective are reappraised in light of the current performance. Accounting by organizational lines makes it possible to direct attention to the appropriate responsibility. Performance is no longer evaluated on the basis of last month or last year, since each period now has its own standard.

External Uses of Direct Costing

The proponents of direct costing believe that the separation of fixed and variable expenses, and the accounting for each according to some direct costing plan, simplifies both the understanding of the income statement and the assignment of costs to inventories.

To keep fixed overhead out of the reported product costs, variable and fixed expenses should be recorded in separate accounts. Therefore, the chart of accounts should be expanded so that each natural classification has two accounts, as needed—one for the variable and one for the fixed portion of the expense. Also, instead of one overhead control account, two should be used: Factory Overhead Control—Variable Expenses and Factory Overhead Control—Fixed Expenses. When a predetermined overhead rate is used to charge variable expenses to work in process, an applied overhead account labeled Applied Variable Factory Overhead is credited. Differences between actual and applied variable overhead constitute controllable or spending and variable efficiency variances when a standard cost system is used and a spending variance when standard costing is not used. Because fixed expenses are not charged to work in process, they are excluded from the predetermined overhead rate. The total fixed expense accumulated in the account, Factory Overhead Control—Fixed Expenses, is charged directly to Income Summary.

To illustrate the effects of direct costing on the income statement, assume that the normal capacity of a plant that produces only one kind of product is 20,000 units per quarter, or 80,000 units per year. Variable standard costs per unit are: direct materials, $30; direct labor, $22; and variable factory overhead, $8. Fixed factory overhead is $1,200,000 per year ($300,000 per quarter or $15 per unit under the absorption costing method at normal capacity). The units of production basis is used for applying factory overhead. Fixed marketing and administrative expenses are $200,000 per quarter, or $800,000 per year; and variable marketing expense is $5 per unit. The sales price per unit is $100.

Materials variances, labor variances, and the factory overhead controllable variance have a net unfavorable total of $15,000, $9,000, $14,000, and $17,000 for the first, second, third, and fourth quarters, respectively. These variances are not considered to be material and are closed to Cost of Goods Sold each quarter, whether absorption costing or direct costing is used, because they relate to variable costs which are included in the cost of the product under both methods. However, the factory overhead volume variance (i.e., the over- or underapplied fixed factory overhead) is computed and closed to Cost of Goods Sold only for the absorption costing method because fixed costs are not added to the cost of the product under direct costing.

In this illustration there is no work in process inventory. Standard costs are assigned to finished goods, and the standard costs for the previous year are the same as the standard costs for the current year. If work in process inventories were present, they would also be assigned standard costs. If standard costs were not used or if standard costs in the current period were different from standard costs in the prior period, an assumption about the flow of costs would be required to cost inventories. That is, the average, fifo, or lifo cost flow assumption would be used to cost inventories.

There are 4,000 units in finished goods inventory at the beginning of the first quarter. Actual production, planned production, sales, and finished goods inventories in units are:

	First Quarter	Second Quarter	Third Quarter	Fourth Quarter
Planned production in units.....................	20,000	20,000	20,000	20,000
Actual production in units........................	20,000	18,000	20,000	22,000
Actual sales in units.................................	20,000	20,000	18,000	18,000

From this information, income statements can be prepared. The following income statement (based on absorption costing) includes the fixed factory overhead in the unit cost of the product and also in the costs assigned to inventory:

	First Quarter	Second Quarter	Third Quarter	Fourth Quarter
Sales..	$2,000,000	$2,000,000	$1,800,000	$1,800,000
Standard cost of goods sold........	$1,500,000	$1,500,000	$1,350,000	$1,350,000
Materials, labor, and controllable variances................	15,000	9,000	14,000	17,000
Volume variance...........................	0	30,000	0	(30,000)
Adjusted cost of goods sold.........	$1,515,000	$1,539,000	$1,364,000	$1,337,000
Gross profit...................................	$ 485,000	$ 461,000	$ 436,000	$ 463,000
Marketing and administrative expenses...................................	300,000	300,000	290,000	290,000
Operating income..........................	$ 185,000	$ 161,000	$ 146,000	$ 173,000

The following income statement (based on direct costing) excludes the fixed factory overhead in the unit cost of products and also from the costs assigned to inventory:

	First Quarter	Second Quarter	Third Quarter	Fourth Quarter
Sales..	$2,000,000	$2,000,000	$1,800,000	$1,800,000
Standard variable cost of goods sold...	$1,200,000	$1,200,000	$1,080,000	$1,080,000
Materials, labor, and controllable variances..	15,000	9,000	14,000	17,000
Adjusted variable cost of goods sold...	$1,215,000	$1,209,000	$1,094,000	$1,097,000
Gross contribution margin....................	$ 785,000	$ 791,000	$ 706,000	$ 703,000
Variable marketing expenses...............	100,000	100,000	90,000	90,000
Contribution margin..............................	$ 685,000	$ 691,000	$ 616,000	$ 613,000
Fixed factory overhead.........................	$ 300,000	$ 300,000	$ 300,000	$ 300,000
Fixed marketing and administrative expenses...................	200,000	200,000	200,000	200,000
Total fixed expenses............................	$ 500,000	$ 500,000	$ 500,000	$ 500,000
Operating income.................................	$ 185,000	$ 191,000	$ 116,000	$ 113,000

Costs Assigned to Inventory. To determine the costs assigned to ending finished goods inventory, the number of units in ending inventory must first be computed:

	First Quarter	Second Quarter	Third Quarter	Fourth Quarter
Units in beginning inventory....................	4,000	4,000	2,000	4,000
Units produced during period...................	20,000	18,000	20,000	22,000
Units available for sale............................	24,000	22,000	22,000	26,000
Units sold..	20,000	20,000	18,000	18,000
Units in ending inventory.........................	4,000	2,000	4,000	8,000

Since standard costs are assigned to inventory and since the standard costs have not changed between periods, the cost assigned to the finished goods ending inventory under the absorption costing method and the direct costing method can be determined as follows:

	First Quarter	Second Quarter	Third Quarter	Fourth Quarter
Units in ending inventory......................	4,000	2,000	4,000	8,000
Standard full cost per unit....................	$ 75	$ 75	$ 75	$ 75
Cost of ending inventory under absorption costing..............................	$300,000	$150,000	$300,000	$600,000

	First Quarter	Second Quarter	Third Quarter	Fourth Quarter
Units in ending inventory......................	4,000	2,000	4,000	8,000
Standard variable cost per unit.............	$ 60	$ 60	$ 60	$ 60
Cost of ending inventory under direct costing......................................	$240,000	$120,000	$240,000	$480,000

only variable costs

	First Quarter	Second Quarter	Third Quarter	Fourth Quarter
Cost of ending inventory under absorption costing..............................	$300,000	$150,000	$300,000	$600,000
Cost of ending inventory under direct costing...	240,000	120,000	240,000	480,000
Difference...	$ 60,000	$ 30,000	$ 60,000	$120,000

These differences occur because fixed factory overhead is included in inventory in absorption costing but excluded in direct costing. In absorption costing, fixed factory overhead becomes a part of the predetermined factory overhead rate and, therefore, becomes a part of the product's cost. In direct costing, fixed factory overhead is charged to period expense and does not become a part of the product's cost.

Operating Profits. The inclusion or exclusion of fixed cost from inventories and the cost of goods sold causes the gross profit to vary considerably from the gross contribution margin. The gross contribution margin (sales less variable manufacturing cost) is greater than the gross profit in absorption costing. This difference has also resulted in some criticism of direct costing. Some opponents argue that a greater gross contribution margin might mislead marketing personnel about product profitability, thereby resulting in requests for lower product prices and demands for higher bonuses or benefits. In most cases, however, sales prices and bonuses are based not on gross profit but on operating income.

The income statements on page 595 also show differences in operating income. These differences are the result of charging fixed factory overhead to inventory under the absorption costing method but expensing it under direct costing. These differences are summarized and reconciled as follows:

	First Quarter	Second Quarter	Third Quarter	Fourth Quarter
Operating income under absorption costing..	$185,000	$ 161,000	$146,000	$173,000
Operating income under direct costing..........	185,000	191,000	116,000	113,000
Difference in operating income......................	0	$ (30,000)	$ 30,000	$ 60,000
Inventory change under absorption costing:				
Ending inventory...	$300,000	$ 150,000	$300,000	$600,000
Beginning inventory....................................	300,000	300,000	150,000	300,000
Increase (decrease)....................................	0	$(150,000)	$150,000	$300,000
Inventory change under direct costing:				
Ending inventory...	$240,000	$ 120,000	$240,000	$480,000
Beginning inventory....................................	240,000	240,000	120,000	240,000
Increase (decrease)....................................	0	$(120,000)	$120,000	$240,000
Difference in operating income......................	0	$ (30,000)	$ 30,000	$ 60,000

Since standard costing is used in this illustration, the differences in operating income determined under absorption costing and direct costing may be computed by multiplying the difference between the quantity produced and the quantity sold for each quarter by the fixed portion of the factory overhead rate used in absorption costing, as follows:

	First Quarter	Second Quarter	Third Quarter	Fourth Quarter
Units produced..	20,000	18,000	20,000	22,000
Units sold..	20,000	20,000	18,000	18,000
Unit change in inventories, increase (decrease)..	0	(2,000)	2,000	4,000
Fixed factory overhead rate under absorption costing..	$ 15	$ 15	$ 15	$ 15
Difference in operating income......................	$ 0	$(30,000)	$30,000	$60,000

The amount of fixed cost charged to inventory is affected not only by the quantities produced and sold but also by the inventory costing method employed—a fact that is frequently overlooked. In the illustrations presented above, the operating profit is larger in absorption costing than in direct costing when the quantity produced exceeds the quantity sold (third and fourth quarters). Conversely, the operating profit is smaller in absorption costing than in direct costing when the quantity produced is less than the quantity sold (second quarter). These relationships hold only for the standard costing method when the standard cost does not change between periods (as in the illustration) and for the lifo inventory method. Under the fifo and the average costing methods, the results may differ from those demonstrated, depending upon the magnitude and the direction of the changes in costs.[4]

The inventory change in this illustration is for finished goods only. If there were work in process inventories, they too would be included in the inventory change in order to reconcile the difference in operating income. Also, any

---

[4]Yuji Ijiri, Robert K. Jaedicke, and John L. Livingstone, ''The Effect of Inventory Costing Methods on Full and Direct Costing,'' *Journal of Accounting Research*, Vol. 3, No. 1, pp. 63-74.

volume variances (i.e., over- or underapplied fixed factory overhead) deferred on the balance sheet, rather than being currently expensed, would be a reconciling item in explaining the difference in operating income.

The operating income will be the same in each method when no inventories exist or, as demonstrated in the first quarter of the illustration, when no change in the total cost assigned to inventory occurs from the beginning to the end of the period. Although the illustrations of direct costing and absorption costing are prepared on a quarterly basis, they are equally representative of statements prepared on a monthly or an annual basis.

As previously explained, many managers favor direct costing because there is a direct correspondence between sales figures and cost figures. The variable cost of goods sold varies directly with sales volume, and the influence of production on profit is eliminated. The idea of "selling overhead to inventories" might sound plausible and appear pleasing at first; but when the prior period's inventories become this period's beginning inventories, the apparent advantages cancel out. The results of the third and fourth quarters with absorption costing offer good examples of the effects of large production with current period cost being deferred in inventories to be charged against income in a future period. The absorption costing income statement also demonstrates the effect of expensing the volume variance (i.e., the over- or underapplied fixed factory overhead resulting from fluctuations in production volume).

Financial Reporting. The use of direct costing for financial reporting is not accepted by the accounting profession as a generally accepted accounting principle. In addition, the Securities and Exchange Commission refuses to accept financial reports prepared on the basis of direct costing, and the Internal Revenue Service will not permit the computation of taxable income on the direct costing basis. The position of these groups is generally based on their opposition to excluding fixed costs from inventories.

The Position of the Accounting Profession. The basis for the accounting profession's position on direct costing is Accounting Research Bulletin No. 43. The "Inventory Pricing" chapter begins by stressing that "a major objective of accounting for inventories is the proper determination of income through the process of matching appropriate costs against revenues."

The bulletin continues by stating that "the primary basis of accounting for inventories is cost, which has been defined generally as the price paid or consideration given to acquire an asset. As applied to inventories, cost means in principle the sum of the applicable expenditures and charges directly or indirectly incurred in bringing an article to its existing condition and location." In discussing the second point, the bulletin states quite emphatically that "it should also be recognized that the exclusion of all overheads from inventory costs does not constitute an accepted accounting procedure." This last statement seems to apply to direct costing. Proponents of direct costing might argue, however, that while the exclusion of all overhead is not acceptable, by inference the exclusion of some is acceptable. This argument might sound true, but it does not seem to have any bearing on the accounting profession's acceptance of direct costing, since in an earlier discussion of cost, the bulletin states that "under some circumstances, items such as idle facility expense, excessive spoilage, double freight, and rehandling costs may be so abnormal as to require treatment as current period charges rather than as a portion of the inventory cost." This appears to be the type of overhead that the bulletin recognizes as excludable from inventories.

The Position of the IRS. The Internal Revenue Service position is directed by Section 1.471-3(c) of the Regulations, which defines inventory cost in the case of merchandise produced to be: "(1) the cost of raw materials and supplies entering into or consumed in connection with the product, (2) expenditures for direct labor, and (3) indirect production costs incident to and necessary for the production of the particular article, including in such indirect production costs an appropriate portion of management expenses. . . ." Furthermore, Section 1.471-11(a) of the Regulations specifically requires the use of the full absorption method of inventory costing. As a result of the Tax Reform Act of 1986, Section 263A of the Internal Revenue Code requires the capitalization of the indirect as well as the direct costs incurred in the manufacture of products held for sale to customers.

The Position of the SEC. The SEC's refusal to accept annual financial reports prepared on the basis of direct costing is generally the result of (1) its policy to favor consistency among reporting companies as far as possible and (2) its attitude that direct costing is not generally accepted accounting procedure. In filing reports with the SEC, a firm that uses direct costing must adjust its inventories and reported income to what they would have been had absorption costing been used.

Adjustment of Direct Costing Figures for External Reporting Purposes. Companies using direct costing internally make adjustments in preparing income tax returns and external financial reports. In actual practice, comparatively simple procedures are frequently used to determine the amount of periodic adjustment necessary to convert inventories recorded on the direct costing basis to the absorption costing basis required for external reporting purposes. According to NAA Research Report No. 37, one company reported that fixed factory overhead for the period is divided by actual production to create a costing rate which is applied to the units in the ending inventory. Another company expresses these fixed expenses as a rate per dollar of variable expenses at normal volume. The dollar amount of variable expenses in the ending inventory is then multiplied by the foregoing rate to arrive at the fixed factory overhead component.[5] In both cases, the excess of the fixed factory overhead incurred during the period over the amount charged to the ending inventory is closed to the cost of goods sold, and the adjustment to the ending inventory is reversed at the beginning of the next accounting period.

[5] *NAA Research Report, No. 37, op. cit.,* pp. 94-95.

DISCUSSION QUESTIONS

1. Differentiate between direct costs and direct costing.
2. Distinguish between product and period costs and relate this distinction to direct costing.
3. Describe the difference between direct costing and the current generally accepted method of costing inventory for external reporting.
4. What is the theoretical justification for excluding fixed manufacturing costs from inventories in direct costing?
5. What would be the rationale for using the direct costing method for internal reporting? *(AICPA adapted)*
6. In the process of determining a proper sales price, what kind of cost figures are likely to be most helpful?

7. Why must the chart of accounts be expanded when direct costing is used?
8. List the arguments for the use of direct costing.
9. List the arguments against the use of direct costing.
10. Assuming that the quantity of ending inventory is larger than the quantity of beginning inventory and that the lifo method is being used, would operating income using direct costing be different from operating income using absorption costing? If so, specify whether operating income would be larger or smaller, and explain the rationale for your answer. *(AICPA adapted)*

EXERCISES

1. Direct and absorption costing. During the past year, Morningstar Company produced 150,000 units (100% of normal capacity) of a product and sold 120,000 of these units. Production costs consisted of $300,000 direct materials, $375,000 direct labor, $150,000 variable factory overhead, and $187,500 fixed factory overhead.

Required:

(1) Using direct costing, compute (a) the per unit cost of production and (b) the year-end inventory cost.
(2) Using absorption costing, compute (a) the per unit cost of production and (b) the year-end inventory cost.

2. Absorption and direct costing. JV Company began its operations on January 1, 19A, and produces one product that sells for $7. Normal capacity is 100,000 units per year, with 100,000 units produced and 80,000 units sold in 19A.

Manufacturing costs and marketing and administrative expenses were as follows:

	Fixed Costs	Variable Costs
Materials..	—	$1.50 per unit produced
Direct labor..	—	1.00 per unit produced
Factory overhead..	$150,000	.50 per unit produced
Marketing and administrative expenses..................	80,000	.50 per unit sold

There were no variances from the standard variable costs. Any under- or overapplied overhead is written off directly at year end as an adjustment to the cost of goods sold.

Required:

(1) In presenting inventory on the December 31, 19A balance sheet, compute the unit cost under absorption costing.
(2) Determine the 19A operating income, using direct costing.

3. Operating income using direct costing. Jayhawk Company began its operations on January 1, 19A, and produces a single product that sells for $9 per unit. In 19A, 100,000 units were produced and 90,000 units were sold. There was no work in process inventory at December 31, 19A.

Manufacturing costs and marketing and administrative expenses for 19A were as follows:

	Fixed	Variable
Materials..	—	$1.75 per unit produced
Direct labor...	—	1.25 per unit produced
Factory overhead..	$100,000	.50 per unit produced
Marketing and administrative.....................	70,000	.60 per unit sold

Required: Prepare an operating income statement for 19A using direct costing.

(AICPA adapted)

4. Absorption costing vs. direct costing. Murphy Products began operations on January 3 of the current year. Standard costs were established in early January assuming a normal production volume of 160,000 units. However, Murphy Products produced only 140,000 units of product and sold only 100,000 units at a selling price of $180 per unit during the current year. Variable costs totaled $7,000,000, of which 60% were manufacturing and 40% were selling. Fixed costs totaled $11,200,000, of which 50% were manufacturing and 50% were selling. Murphy had no raw materials or work in process inventories at the end of the year. Actual input prices per unit of product and actual input quantities per unit of product were equal to standard.

Required:

(1) Determine Murphy Products' cost of goods sold at standard cost, using full absorption costing (excluding standard cost variances).
(2) How much cost would be assigned to Murphy Products' ending inventory using direct costing?
(3) Compute Murphy Products' factory overhead volume variance for the year.
(4) How much operating income would Murphy Products have using direct costing?

(ICMA adapted)

5. Absorption costing vs. direct costing. In April, Randall Corporation produced at its normal capacity level of 12,000 units. Variable costs per unit were: direct materials, $2; direct labor, $3; and factory overhead, $1. Fixed costs were: factory overhead, $24,000 and marketing and administrative expenses, $6,000. During the month, 10,000 units were sold at $10 each. There was no beginning inventory.

Required: Assuming absorption costing and direct costing, determine each of the following:

(1) Cost of goods sold.
(2) Gross profit/contribution margin.
(3) Operating profit.
(4) Finished goods inventory, April 30.

6. Inventory costs—absorption vs. direct costing. Bolson Company produces a product having the following standard cost per unit:

Direct materials......................................	$6
Direct labor...	8
Variable factory overhead....................	5
Fixed factory overhead.........................	2

Normal capacity is 80,000 units. During 19A, 75,000 units were produced and 60,000 were sold. There was no finished goods beginning inventory and no beginning or ending work in process inventory.

Actual 19A costs incurred were:

Direct materials......................................	$ 460,000
Direct labor...	625,000
Variable factory overhead....................	370,000
Fixed factory overhead.........................	148,500
Total...	$1,603,500

Required: Determine the cost assigned to finished goods ending inventory under each of the following methods:

(1) Direct costing, using standard cost, with variable cost variances prorated.
(2) Absorption costing, using actual cost.
(3) Absorption costing, using actual prime cost and applied factory overhead, based on normal capacity and assuming factory overhead variances are not prorated. *(CGAAC adapted)*

7. Comparison of direct costing to absorption costing. Hubert Corporation's November income statement, based on direct costing, is as follows:

Sales (100,000 units @ $24)..		$2,400,000
Variable cost of goods sold (100,000 units @ $12)....................		1,200,000
Contribution margin..		$1,200,000
Less fixed expenses:		
Factory overhead...	$600,000	
Marketing and administrative...	400,000	1,000,000
Operating income..		$ 200,000

Normal capacity for November is 150,000 units, with 145,000 units produced in November.

Required:

(1) Prepare the November income statement on an absorption costing basis, with applied factory overhead based on normal capacity and any over- or underapplied factory overhead closed to Cost of Goods Sold.
(2) Reconcile and explain the difference between the direct costing and the absorption costing operating income figures.
(3) Explain the features associated with direct costing income measurement that should be useful to management. *(ICMA adapted)*

8. Income statements—absorption costing vs. direct costing. The following data pertain to April:

Beginning inventory	-0-
Units sold	5,000
Units produced	8,000
Sales price per unit	$ 24
Direct manufacturing cost per unit	10
Fixed factory overhead—total	28,000
Fixed factory overhead—per unit	3.50
Commercial expense (all fixed)	10,000

Required:

(1) Prepare an income statement using absorption costing.
(2) Prepare an income statement using direct costing.
(3) Provide computations explaining the difference in operating income between the two methods.

PROBLEMS

19-1. Direct costing income statement. Moines Company has been using a standard absorption costing system. Standard variable manufacturing costs are $6 per unit. Standard fixed factory overhead is $1 per unit ($400,000 divided by 400,000 units of normal activity). The sales price is $10 per unit. Variable marketing and administrative costs are $2 per unit sold. Fixed marketing and administrative costs are $250,000. Beginning inventory in 19— was 70,000 units; ending inventory was 50,000 units. Variances from standard variable manufacturing costs in 19— totaled $30,000, unfavorable. All variances are written off directly at year end as an adjustment to the cost of goods sold. Sales in 19— were 370,000 units.

Required:

(1) It has been suggested that Moines switch to direct costing for internal reporting purposes. Prepare an income statement for 19— using direct costing.
(2) Determine 19— income using absorption costing. (An income statement is not required.)   *(CGAAC adapted)*

19-2. Direct costing income statement. Quebec Company wishes to use direct costing in accounting for its only product, with standard unit manufacturing costs as follows:

Materials	$ 5
Direct labor	4
Variable factory overhead	3
	$12

The fixed factory overhead budget is $160,000, and normal capacity is 80,000 units. During 19A, Quebec's first year of operations, 85,000 units were produced, of which 75,000 were sold at $25 each.
Actual costs were:

Materials used	$434,000
Direct labor	350,000
Variable factory overhead	250,000
Fixed factory overhead	162,000
Variable marketing and administrative expenses	75,000
Fixed marketing and administrative expenses	100,000

Required:

    (1) Prepare a direct costing income statement, assuming variances are written off in the current period.

    (2) Determine the difference in operating income if absorption costing were used. (An income statement is not required.)   *(CGAAC adapted)*

19-3. Direct costing income statement. Crawford Connections uses a standard cost system in accounting for its only product, Craw, which it sells for $22 per unit. The standard cost per unit is:

Direct materials..	$ 4
Direct labor...	6
Variable factory overhead..	2
Fixed factory overhead (based on normal capacity of 60,000 units)....................	3
	$15

All variances are closed to Cost of Goods Sold.

    On October 1, there were 10,000 units of Craw on hand. During October, 50,000 units were produced and 45,000 were sold. Costs incurred during October were:

Direct materials...	$198,000
Direct labor...	305,000
Variable factory overhead............................	103,000
Fixed factory overhead................................	186,000
Variable marketing and administrative..........	50,000
Fixed marketing and administrative..............	74,000

Required:

    (1) Explain whether Crawford uses direct or absorption costing.

    (2) Prepare an income statement for October, using direct costing.

    (3) Compute the operating income for October if absorption costing is used.

    (CGAAC adapted)

19-4. Absorption costing vs. direct costing. Goldschmidt Corporation developed the following standard unit costs at 100% of its normal production capacity, which is 50,000 units per year:

Direct materials......................................	$ 3
Direct labor..	3
Variable factory overhead.....................	2
Fixed factory overhead.........................	3
	$11

The selling price of each unit of product is $20. Variable commercial expenses are $1 per unit sold and fixed commercial expenses total $150,000 for the period. During the year, 49,000 units were produced and 52,000 units were sold. There are no work in process beginning or ending inventories, and finished goods inventory is maintained at standard cost, which has not changed from the preceding year. For the current year, there is a net favorable variable cost variance in the amount of $1,000.

Required:

    (1) Prepare an income statement on the absorption costing basis.

    (2) Prepare an income statement on the direct costing basis.

(3) Compute and reconcile the difference in operating income for the current year under absorption costing and direct costing.

19-5. Absorption costing vs. direct costing. Maxumm Corporation developed the following standard unit costs at 100% of its normal production capacity, which is 50,000 units per year:

Direct materials.....................................	$2
Direct labor...	3
Variable factory overhead....................	1
Fixed factory overhead.........................	2
	$8

The selling price of each unit of product is $15. Variable commercial expenses are $1 per unit sold and fixed commercial expenses total $100,000 for the period. During the year, 52,000 units were produced and 49,000 units were sold. There are no work in process beginning or ending inventories, and finished goods inventory is maintained at standard cost, which has not changed from the preceding year. For the current year, there is a net unfavorable variable cost variance in the amount of $1,000.

Required:

(1) Prepare an income statement on the absorption costing basis.
(2) Prepare an income statement on the direct costing basis.
(3) Compute and reconcile the difference in operating income for the current year under absorption costing and direct costing.

19-6. Direct costing statements; explanation of profit differences. In one of its divisions, Connects Inc. produces a connector sold primarily to commercial fertilizer distributors at $8 each. Normal production is 6,000 units per month, and at this level the variable manufacturing cost is $2.50 per unit and the fixed manufacturing cost is $9,000 per month. Gross profit statements for this product for the first three months of the year, using absorption costing, show:

	January		February		March	
Sales..................................		$36,000		$32,000		$48,000
Beginning inventory............	—0-		$ 6,000		$14,000	
Cost of goods manufactured..................	$24,000		24,000		24,000	
Cost of goods available for sale.............	$24,000		$30,000		$38,000	
Ending inventory.................	6,000		14,000		14,000	
Cost of goods sold.............		18,000		16,000		24,000
Gross profit........................		$18,000		$16,000		$24,000

Required:

(1) Prepare statements for each of the three months, using direct costing.
(2) Explain the statement differences for each month under absorption costing and direct costing.

19-7. Income statements—absorption costing vs. direct costing. On January 2, Commerce Reel Company began production of a new model. First quarter sales were 20,000 units and second quarter sales were 26,000 units at a unit price of $10. Unit production costs each quarter were: direct materials, $1; direct labor, $2; and variable factory overhead, $1.50. Fixed factory overhead was $62,400 each quarter and, for absorption costing, is assigned to inventory based on actual units produced.

Marketing and administrative expenses consisted of a $15,000 fixed portion each quarter and a variable portion which was 5% of sales. Units produced in the first quarter and the second quarter totaled 30,000 and 20,000, respectively. The fifo inventory costing method is used.

Required:

(1) Prepare comparative income statements for the first and second quarters under the absorption costing method.
(2) Prepare comparative income statements for the first and second quarters under the direct costing method.
(3) Compute and reconcile the differences in operating income under the two methods for each quarter.

19-8. Comparative income statements—absorption costing vs. direct costing. Lindell Corporation developed the following standard unit costs at normal production capacity, which is 100,000 units:

Direct materials.......................................	$ 5
Direct labor..	4
Variable factory overhead.....................	2
Fixed factory overhead..........................	9
	$20

The selling price for each unit of product is $35. Variable commercial expenses are $2 per unit. The selling price and the costs of the product have not changed since the company began operations two years ago. Data related to the operations of Lindell Corporation for the past two years follow:

	19A	19B
Units actually produced...	95,000	106,000
Units sold...	90,000	110,000
Fixed commercial expenses...	$500,000	$550,000
Unfavorable (favorable) variable standard cost variances..	$(85,000)	$40,000

Required:

(1) Prepare comparative income statements for 19A and 19B under the absorption costing method.
(2) Prepare comparative income statements for 19A and 19B under the direct costing method.
(3) Compute and reconcile the differences in income for the two years under the absorption costing and direct costing methods.

CASES

A. Sales and production volume effects—absorption costing vs. direct costing. Star Company, a wholly-owned subsidiary of Orbit Inc., produces and sells three main product lines. The company employs a standard cost accounting system for record-keeping purposes.

At the beginning of the year, the president of Star Company presented the budget to the parent company and accepted a commitment to contribute $15,800 to Orbit's consolidated profit in 19—. The president has been confident that the year's profit would exceed the budget target, since the monthly sales reports have shown that sales for the year will exceed the budget by 10%. The president is both disturbed and confused when the controller presents an adjusted forecast as of November 30, indicating that profit will be 11% under budget. The two forecasts are as follows:

	Forecasts as of	
	Jan. 1	Nov. 30
Sales..	$268,000	$294,800
Cost of goods sold at standard	212,000*	233,200
Gross profit at standard............	$ 56,000	$ 61,600
Less underapplied		
factory overhead.....................	—	6,000
Gross profit at actual.................	$ 56,000	$ 55,600
Marketing expense....................	$ 13,400	$ 14,740
Administrative expense.............	26,800	26,800
Total commercial expense........	$ 40,200	$ 41,540
Income from operations............	$ 15,800	$ 14,060

*Includes fixed factory overhead of $30,000.

There have been no sales price changes or product mix shifts since the January 1 forecast. The only cost variance on the income statement is the underapplied factory overhead. This arose because the company used only 16,000 standard machine hours (budgeted machine hours were 20,000) during the year as a result of a shortage of raw materials. Fortunately, Star Company's finished goods inventory was large enough to fill all sales orders received.

Required:

(1) Analyze and explain the forecast profit decline, in spite of increased sales and good cost control.

(2) Explain and illustrate an alternative internal cost reporting procedure which would avoid the confusing effect of the present procedure.

(ICMA adapted)

B. Sales and production volume effects—absorption costing vs. direct costing. RGB Corporation is a manufacturer of a synthetic element. A. B. Meek, president of the company, has been eager to get the operating results for the fiscal year just completed. Meek was surprised when the income statement revealed that operating income dropped to $645,000 from $900,000, although sales volume had increased by 100,000 units. This drop in operating income occurred even though Meek had implemented the following changes during the past 12 months to improve the profitability of the company.

(1) In response to a 10% increase in production costs, the sales price of the company's product was increased by 12%. This action took place on December 1, 19A.

(2) The managements of the selling and administrative departments were given strict instructions to spend no more in fiscal 19B than they did in fiscal 19A.

RGB's accounting department prepared and distributed to top management the following comparative income statements:

RGB Corporation
Statements of Operating Income
For the years ended November 30, 19A and 19B
(000s omitted)

	19A		19B	
Sales revenue..............		$9,000		$11,200
Cost of goods sold......	$7,200		$8,560	
Volume variance, (favorable) unfavorable..............	(600)	6,600	495	9,055
Gross profit.................		$2,400		$ 2,145
Selling and administrative expenses.................		1,500		1,500
Operating income........		$ 900		$ 645

The accounting staff also prepared related financial information that is presented in the following schedule to assist management in evaluating the company's performance. RGB uses the fifo inventory method for finished goods.

RGB Corporation
Selected Operating and Financial Data
For 19A and 19B

	19A	19B
Sales price per unit..................	$10.00	$11.20
Materials cost per unit.............	1.50	1.65
Direct labor cost per unit..........	2.50	2.75
Variable factory overhead per unit.......................................	1.00	1.10
Fixed factory overhead per unit..	3.00	3.30
Total fixed factory overhead.....	$3,000,000	$3,300,000
Total selling and administrative expenses........	1,500,000	1,500,000
Quantity of units budgeted (normal capacity)...................	1,000,000	1,000,000
Quantity of units actually produced..............................	1,200,000	850,000
Quantity of units sold...............	900,000	1,000,000
Quantity of units in beginning inventory...............................	0	300,000
Quantity of units in ending inventory...............................	300,000	150,000

more expensive inventory

Required:
(1) Explain to A. B. Meek why RGB Corporation's net income decreased in the current fiscal year, despite the sales price and sales volume increase.
(2) A member of RGB's accounting department has suggested that the company adopt direct costing for internal reporting purposes.
  (a) Prepare an operating income statement for the fiscal years ending November 19, 19A and 19B, for RGB Corporation using the direct costing method.
  (b) Present a numerical reconciliation of the difference in operating income between the absorption costing method currently in use and the direct costing method proposed.
(3) Identify and discuss some of the advantages and disadvantages of using the direct costing method for internal reporting purposes. (ICMA adapted)

CHAPTER 20

Break-Even and Cost-Volume-Profit Analysis

Break-even analysis, the construction of break-even charts, and the related cost-volume-profit analysis are analytical tools that provide management with important information about the relationships between costs, profits, product mix, and sales volume. *Break-even analysis* indicates the point at which the company neither makes a profit nor suffers a loss. *Cost-volume-profit analysis*, integrally related to break-even analysis, is concerned with determining the sales volume and mix of products necessary to achieve the desired level of profit with available resources. These analyses are based on the assumption that fixed and variable costs can be meaningfully measured, and they focus on the firm's short-run output decisions.

▼ THE NATURE OF BREAK-EVEN AND COST-VOLUME-PROFIT ANALYSIS

Break-even analysis is used to determine the level of sales and the mix of products which are required to just recover all costs incurred during the period. The *break-even point* is the point at which cost and revenue are equal. There is neither a profit nor a loss at the break-even point. The objective of cost-volume-profit analysis is to determine the level of sales and the mix of products which are required to achieve a targeted level of profit. Therefore, break-even analysis may be thought of as a special case of cost-volume-profit analysis, i.e., the determination of the level of sales and the mix of products necessary to achieve a zero level of profit.

Although management typically plans for a profit each period, the break-even point is of concern. If sales fall below the break-even point, losses will be incurred. Management must determine the break-even point in order to compute the *margin of safety*, which indicates how much sales may decrease from the targeted level before the company will incur losses. The margin of safety is a criterion used to evaluate the adequacy of planned sales.

Break-even and cost-volume-profit analysis may be based on historical data, past operations, or projected sales and costs. However, data for break-even and cost-volume-profit analysis cannot be taken directly from the absorption or full costing income statement, because the effect of activity on costs cannot be readily determined. Each item of expense must be analyzed to determine its fixed and variable components. In contrast to the absorption or full costing income statement, the direct or variable costing income statement segregates fixed costs from variable costs and, therefore, is quite useful in break-even and cost-volume-profit analysis. The flexible budget and standard cost cards are also good sources of data because fixed and variable costs are segregated in both data sources. Consequently, the data available in each source can be used directly and without alteration for break-even and cost-volume-profit analysis.

Break-even and cost-volume-profit analysis is based on the following accounting relationship:

Profit = Total Revenues − (Total Variable Costs + Total Fixed Costs)

which is equivalent to saying that:

Total Revenues = Total Fixed Costs + Total Variable Costs + Profit

Conventional break-even and cost-volume-profit analysis is based on the assumption that the total fixed cost and the variable cost per unit remain constant within the range of activity being analyzed. For notational convenience, the basic accounting relationship can be expressed in the form of a linear equation, as follows:

$$R = F + (V \times R) + \pi$$

where: R = Total sales revenue

F = Total fixed cost

V = Variable cost per dollar of sales revenue (i.e., total variable cost divided by total sales revenue)

π = Total profit

The objective of break-even and cost-volume-profit analysis is to determine the volume of sales and the mix of products required to achieve a targeted level of profit (zero profit in the case of break-even analysis). If only one product is produced, as assumed initially, the only unknown of concern is the volume of sales. The volume of sales can be measured in terms of sales revenue or in terms of units of product. To determine the required level of sales revenue, the equation above can be solved for R, as follows:

$$R = F + (V \times R) + \pi$$
$$R - (V \times R) = F + \pi$$
$$R(1 - V) = F + \pi$$
$$R = \frac{F + \pi}{1 - V} = \frac{\text{Total fixed cost} + \text{Profit}}{\text{Contribution margin per sales dollar}}$$

If profit were set equal to zero, the break-even point measured in sales revenue, R(BE), would be computed as follows:

$$R(BE) = \frac{F}{1 - V} = \frac{\text{Total fixed cost}}{\text{Contribution margin per sales dollar}}$$

The contribution margin per sales dollar, also referred to as the *contribution margin ratio* (C/M), is the portion of each sales dollar available to recover fixed costs and provide a profit. Below the break-even point, it is the portion of each sales dollar used to recover fixed cost. Above the break-even point, it is the portion of each sales dollar that provides an increase in profit. To illustrate the computation of the break-even point, assume that the following data are taken from the flexible budget of Northstar Company:

Total sales revenue at normal capacity......................	$6,000,000
Total fixed costs...	1,600,000
Total variable costs at normal capacity......................	3,600,000
Sales price per unit...	400
Variable costs per unit......................................	240

The break-even point would be computed as follows:

$$R(BE) = \frac{F}{1 - V}$$

$$= \frac{\$1,600,000}{1 - (\$3,600,000 \div \$6,000,000)} \text{ or } \frac{\$1,600,000}{1 - (\$240 \div \$400)}$$

$$= \frac{\$1,600,000}{.40}$$

$$= \$4,000,000$$

Once fixed costs have been recovered, the contribution margin from each additional dollar of sales revenue provides a profit. Consequently, if the sales revenue required to break even has already been computed, the sales revenue required to achieve a targeted level of profit can be determined by simply dividing the targeted profit by the contribution margin per sales dollar and adding the quotient to the sales revenue required to break even. For example, based on the data provided in the Northstar Company illustration, a targeted profit of $400,000 would require sales of $1,000,000 beyond the break-even point ($400,000 profit divided by $.40 contribution margin per dollar of sales). Therefore, total sales of $5,000,000 would be required to yield a profit of $400,000 ($4,000,000 of sales to break even plus $1,000,000 of sales beyond the break-even point). Alternatively, the required level of sales can be determined directly by adding the targeted level of profit to fixed costs and dividing the sum by the contribution margin per sales dollar, as indicated by the formula derived on page 610 and demonstrated as follows:

$$R = \frac{F + \pi}{1 - V}$$

$$= \frac{\$1,600,000 + \$400,000}{1 - (\$3,600,000 \div \$6,000,000)} \text{ or } \frac{\$1,600,000 + \$400,000}{1 - (\$240 \div \$400)}$$

$$= \frac{\$2,000,000}{.40}$$

$$= \$5,000,000$$

Since each unit sells for $400, the total quantity of product to be sold to break even would be 10,000 units ($4,000,000 break-even sales divided by $400 sales price per unit), and the total quantity to be sold to meet a targeted profit of $400,000 would be 12,500 units ($5,000,000 of sales divided by $400 sales price).

A units-of-product approach rather than the sales-revenue approach is sometimes taken in break-even and cost-volume-profit analyses. For some types of analyses, it is more expedient and convenient to work with units of product rather than sales revenue. Both approaches are conceptually the same. In the units-of-product approach, the basic equation is altered to include the quantity of product, the unit sales price, and the unit variable cost. Recall that the equation used in developing the sales-revenue approach to cost-volume-profit analysis on page 610 is:

$$R = F + (V \times R) + \pi$$

Since sales revenue, R, is equal to the unit sales price multiplied by the quantity of product sold, and total variable cost, $(V \times R)$, is equal to the variable cost per unit multiplied by the quantity of product sold, the equation above can be restated as follows:

$$P \times Q = F + (C \times Q) + \pi$$

where: P = Sales price per unit
Q = Quantity of product sold
F = Total fixed cost
C = Variable cost per unit
π = Total profit

The unknown in the modified equation is the quantity of product, Q. Solving for Q yields:

$$P \times Q = F + (C \times Q) + \pi$$
$$(P \times Q) - (C \times Q) = F + \pi$$
$$Q \times (P - C) = F + \pi$$
$$Q = \frac{F + \pi}{P - C}$$

If profit is set equal to zero, then the break-even point in units of product, Q(BE), would be:

$$Q(BE) = \frac{F}{P - C}$$

Based on the data provided in the Northstar Company illustration, the break-even point in units of product would be computed as follows:

$$Q(BE) = \frac{F}{P - C} = \frac{\$1,600,000}{\$400 - \$240} = \frac{\$1,600,000}{\$160} = 10,000 \text{ units}$$

A targeted profit of $400,000 would require sales of:

$$Q = \frac{F + \pi}{P - C}$$
$$= \frac{\$1,600,000 + \$400,000}{\$400 - \$240}$$
$$= \frac{\$2,000,000}{\$160}$$
$$= 12,500 \text{ units}$$

Constructing a Break-Even Chart

Break-even computations can be presented in a break-even chart, in which the cost line and the sales line intersect at the break-even point. The information needed to construct this chart is forecast sales and fixed and variable costs.

A conventional break-even chart for Northstar Company is illustrated as follows:

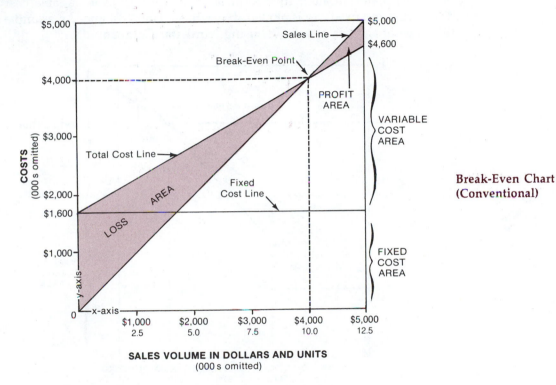

Break-Even Chart (Conventional)

The conventional break-even chart is constructed as follows:

1. A horizontal base line, the x-axis, is drawn and spaced into equal distances to represent the sales volume in dollars or in number of units, or as a percentage of some specified volume.
2. A vertical line, the y-axis, is drawn at the extreme left and right sides of the chart. The y-axis at the left is spaced into equal parts and represents sales and costs in dollars.
3. A fixed cost line is drawn parallel to the x-axis at the $1,600,000 point of the y-axis.
4. A total cost line is drawn from the $1,600,000 fixed cost point on the y-axis to the $4,600,000 cost point on the right side of the y-axis.
5. The sales line is drawn from the 0 point at the left (the intersection of the x-axis and y-axis) to the $5,000,000 point on the right y-axis.

6. The total cost line intersects the sales line at the break-even point, representing $4,000,000 sales or 10,000 units of sales.
7. The shaded area to the left of the break-even point is the loss area, while the shaded area to the right is the profit area.

In the conventional break-even chart, the fixed cost line is parallel to the x-axis and variable cost is plotted above the fixed cost. Such a chart emphasizes fixed cost at a definite amount for various levels of activity. Many analysts, however, prefer an alternative form of chart, in which the variable cost is drawn first and fixed cost is plotted above the variable cost line. An example of this type of chart is as follows, using Northstar Company data:

Break-Even Chart with Fixed Cost Plotted Above Variable Cost

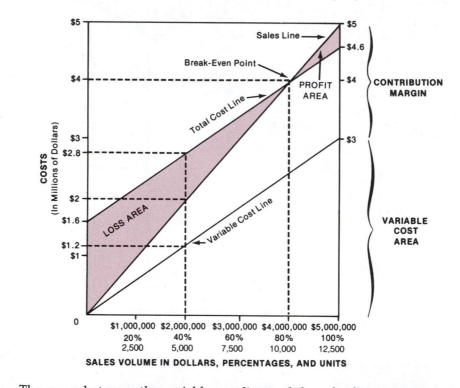

The space between the variable cost line and the sales line represents the contribution margin. Where the total cost line intersects the sales line, the break-even point has been reached. The space between the sales line and the total cost line beyond the break-even point represents the profit for the period at any volume. The space between the total cost line and the sales line to the left of the break-even point indicates the fixed costs not yet recovered by the contribution margin and is the loss for the period at any volume below the break-even point.

This alternative break-even chart indicates the recovery of fixed costs at various levels of percentage capacity and at dollar sales or unit sales. If sales, for example, drop to $2,000,000, variable costs would be $1,200,000 (60 percent of $2,000,000) while fixed costs remain at $1,600,000. The loss at this point would be $800,000 [$2,000,000 − ($1,200,000 + $1,600,000)]. The chart shows

$2,000,000 on the sales line to be $800,000 below the total cost line. In columnar form, the analysis can be illustrated as follows:

(1) Number of Units	(2) Sales	(3) Variable Cost	(4) Contribution Margin (2)-(3)	(5) Fixed Cost	(6) Profit (Loss) (4)-(5)
2,500	$1,000,000	$ 600,000	$ 400,000	$1,600,000	($1,200,000)
5,000	2,000,000	1,200,000	800,000	1,600,000	(800,000)
7,500	3,000,000	1,800,000	1,200,000	1,600,000	(400,000)
10,000	4,000,000	2,400,000	1,600,000	1,600,000	None
12,500	5,000,000	3,000,000	2,000,000	1,600,000	400,000

A break-even chart can be constructed in even greater detail by breaking down fixed and variable costs into subclassifications. Variable expenses, for example, may be classified as direct materials, direct labor, variable factory overhead, and variable marketing and administrative expenses. Fixed expenses may be divided in a similar manner, showing fixed factory overhead and fixed marketing and administrative expenses separately. Even the profit wedge might be subdivided to indicate application of the profit to income tax, interest and dividend payments, and retained earnings. Such a chart is illustrated as follows:

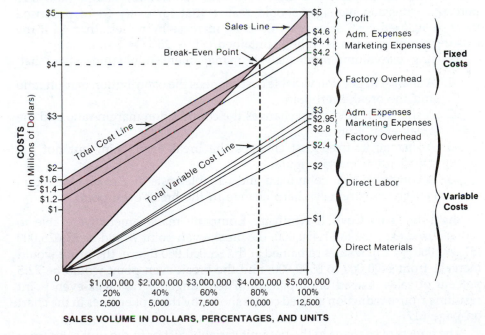

Break-Even Chart with Detailed Fixed and Variable Costs

Break-Even and Cost-Volume-Profit Analysis for Decision Making

The accounting data involved, the assumptions made, the manner in which the information is obtained, and the way the data are expressed are limitations that must be considered in connection with the results of cost-volume-profit analysis. The break-even chart is fundamentally a static analysis. In most cases, changes can only be shown by drawing a new chart or a series of charts. The notion of relevant range as stated in the discussion of classifying cost (pages 294-297) is applicable. That is, the amount of fixed and variable costs, as well as the slope of the sales line, is meaningful only in a defined range of activity and must be redefined for activity outside the relevant range. Furthermore, linear cost and sales behavior is assumed and has general acceptance within the relevant range of activity.[1]

Despite its limitations, cost-volume-profit analysis offers wide application for testing proposed actions, for considering alternatives, or for other decision-making purposes. For example, the technique permits determination of the effect on profit of a shift in fixed and/or variable expenses when old machinery is replaced by new equipment. Firms with multiple plants, products, and sales territories may prepare charts which show the effects of the shift in sales quantities, sales prices, and sales efforts. With such information, management is able to direct the firm's operations into the most profitable channels. For a company with numerous divisions, the analysis is particularly valuable in determining the influence on profits of an increase in divisional fixed cost. If, for example, a company's overall contribution margin ratio is 25 percent, a division manager should realize that for every $1 of proposed increase in fixed cost, sales revenue must increase by no less than $4 if the existing profit position is to be maintained ($1 ÷ 25% = $4).

In using cost-volume-profit analysis, management should understand that:

1. A change in per unit variable cost changes the contribution margin ratio and the break-even point.
2. A change in sales price changes the contribution margin ratio and the break-even point.
3. A change in fixed cost changes the break-even point but not the contribution margin figure.
4. A combined change in fixed and variable costs in the same direction causes an extremely sharp change in the break-even point.

Changes in Fixed Cost. If Northstar Company management were able to reduce fixed expense to $1,450,000, the break-even point would be $3,625,000 ($1,450,000 ÷ .40). If sales remained at the $5,000,000 figure, the profit would increase from $400,000 to $550,000, and the break-even point would be 72.5 percent of sales instead of 80 percent. The change in the break-even point resulting from a reduction in fixed cost is shown by the broken lines in the chart on page 617.

The effects of changes in the per unit variable cost or in the unit sales price could also be charted. Thus, a dynamic dimension could be added to the analysis.

---

[1] Calculus can be employed in dealing with curvilinear functions. See Travis P. Goggans, "Break-Even Analysis with Curvilinear Functions," *The Accounting Review*, Vol. XL, No. 4, pp. 867-871.

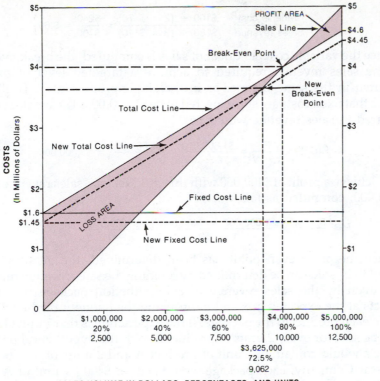

Break-Even Chart with a Reduction in Fixed Cost

SALES VOLUME IN DOLLARS, PERCENTAGES, AND UNITS

Multiple Products and Shifts in the Sales Mix. When firms produce more than one product, the variable costs per dollar of sales revenue may be different for different products. In such cases, the contribution margin ratio would be different for different sales mixes. As a consequence, the break-even point and the level of sales required to achieve targeted profit levels would be different for different mixes of products. The mathematical computations in the multiple-product case are essentially the same as those in the single-product case, except that the analyst must remember that the results are valid only for the sales mix used in the analysis. If the sales mix is expected to change, the results should be recomputed for the new mix.

To illustrate the computations in a multiple-product case, assume that Northstar Company expects the following product mix to be sold in the coming period:

Product	Unit Sales Price	Variable Cost per Unit	Expected Sales Mix
A	$180	$100	1
B	110	70	2

If the product mix is expected to remain constant at all levels of sales, the variable cost per dollar of sales revenue would be determined as follows:

$$V = \frac{\text{Variable cost}}{\text{Sales revenue}} = \frac{\$100 + (2 \times \$70)}{\$180 + (2 \times \$110)} = \frac{\$240}{\$400} = \$.60$$

Once the variable cost per dollar of sales is computed, the break-even point and the sales revenue required to achieve a targeted level of profit are computed in the same manner as in the single-product case. To illustrate, assume that fixed costs are still expected to be $1,600,000. The break-even point measured in sales revenue would be:

$$R(BE) = \frac{F}{1 - V} = \frac{\$1,600,000}{1 - .60} = \frac{\$1,600,000}{.40} = \$4,000,000$$

To achieve a profit of $400,000 with this product mix, sales revenue must be $5,000,000, computed as follows:

$$R = \frac{F + \pi}{1 - V} = \frac{\$1,600,000 + \$400,000}{1 - .60} = \frac{\$2,000,000}{.40} = \$5,000,000$$

Once the break-even point has been determined, the quantity of each product to be sold can be determined by dividing the sales revenue required to break even by the sales revenue of a hypothetical package of the firm's products at the expected mix and multiplying the quotient by the number of units of each product in the package. If the expectation is that 1 unit of product A will be sold for every 2 units of product B sold, the hypothetical package of products would contain one unit of product A and 2 units of product B. For Northstar Company, each package would sell for $400 [(1 unit of A × $180 each) + (2 units of B × $110 each)]. As a result, the quantity of each product to be sold to break even with this sales mix can be determined as follows:

$$Q(BE) = \frac{R(BE)}{\$400} = \frac{\$4,000,000}{\$400} = 10,000 \text{ hypothetical packages}$$

10,000 packages × 1 unit of A per package = 10,000 units of A
10,000 packages × 2 units of B per package = 20,000 units of B

The quantity of each product to be sold at this mix to achieve sales revenue of $5,000,000 and a profit of $400,000 would be determined as follows:

$$Q = \frac{R}{\$400} = \frac{\$5,000,000}{\$400} = 12,500 \text{ hypothetical packages}$$

12,500 packages × 1 unit of A per package = 12,500 units of A
12,500 packages × 2 units of B per package = 25,000 units of B

Alternatively, the quantity of hypothetical packages to be sold to break even or achieve a targeted level of profit can be computed directly using the units-of-product approach. In this case, the unit used in the formula presented on page 612 is the hypothetical package of the firm's products. For Northstar Company, the break-even point in hypothetical packages of product containing 1 unit of product A and 2 units of product B would be determined as follows:

Sales revenue per package = (1 unit of A × $180 each) + (2 units of B × $110 each) = $400
Variable cost per package = (1 unit of A × $100 each) + (2 units of B × $70 each) = $240

$$Q(BE) = \frac{F}{P - C} = \frac{\$1,600,000}{\$400 - \$240} = \frac{\$1,600,000}{\$160} = \frac{10,000}{\text{packages}}$$

The units of each product required to break even would then be computed by multiplying the number of hypothetical packages by the number of units of each product in the hypothetical package, as follows:

10,000 packages × 1 unit of A per package = 10,000 units of A
10,000 packages × 2 units of B per package = 20,000 units of B

The number of hypothetical packages required to achieve a targeted profit of $400,000 would be:

$$Q = \frac{F + \pi}{P - C} = \frac{\$1,600,000 + \$400,000}{\$400 - \$240} = \frac{\$2,000,000}{\$160} = 12,500 \text{ packages}$$

The number of units of each product would be:

12,500 packages × 1 unit of A per package = 12,500 units of A
12,500 packages × 2 units of B per package = 25,000 units of B

In this multiple-product case, the break-even point and the sales revenue required to achieve a targeted level of profit would be different for a different product mix because the variable cost and the contribution margin per dollar of sales would be different. For example, if the expected sales mix were 1 unit of product A for every 3 units of product B, the variable cost per dollar of sales would change from $.60 to $.607843, determined as follows:

$$V = \frac{\text{Variable cost}}{\text{Sales revenue}} = \frac{\$100 + (3 \times \$ 70)}{\$180 + (3 \times \$110)} = \frac{\$310}{\$510} = \$.607843$$

The increase in variable cost per dollar of sales revenue would result in a decline in contribution margin per dollar of sales revenue and an increase in the sales revenue required to break even. The sales revenue required to break even would increase from $4,000,000 to $4,080,000, determined as follows:

$$R(BE) = \frac{F}{1 - V} = \frac{\$1,600,000}{1 - .607843} = \frac{\$1,600,000}{.392157} = \$4,080,000$$

As a result of this change in sales mix, the quantity of each product that must be sold to break even also changes. The number of hypothetical packages required to break even would be determined as follows:

$$Q(BE) = \frac{R(BE)}{\$510} = \frac{\$4,080,000}{\$510} = 8,000 \text{ hypothetical packages}$$

or equivalently:

$$Q(BE) = \frac{F}{P - C} = \frac{\$1,600,000}{\$510 - \$310} = \frac{\$1,600,000}{\$200} = 8,000 \text{ hypothetical packages}$$

The number of units of each product that must be sold to break even with this mix would be:

8,000 packages × 1 unit of A per package = 8,000 units of A
8,000 packages × 3 units of B per package = 24,000 units of B

A change in the mix of products sold can have a material effect on not only the break-even point but also profitability. Based on a sales mix of 1 unit of product A to 2 units of product B, Northstar Company should have a $400,000 profit if it can generate sales revenue of $5,000,000. However, if the actual sales mix is 1 unit of product A to 3 units of product B, sales revenue of approximately $5,000,000 will result in only $360,800 of profit, determined as follows:

Sales: Product A (9,804 units @ $180)......................	$1,764,720	
Product B (29,412 units @ $110)....................	3,235,320	$5,000,040
Less variable cost of goods sold:		
Product A (9,804 units @ $100)......................	$ 980,400	
Product B (29,412 units @ $70)......................	2,058,840	3,039,240
Contribution margin..		$1,960,800
Less fixed costs..		1,600,000
Operating income..		$ 360,800

Because of uncertainty in the market place, this sort of situation is not uncommon. It illustrates the desirability of considering alternative sales mixes in break-even and cost-volume-profit analysis. One way to overcome this difficulty is to prepare a separate analysis for each product. However, if arbitrarily allocated common or joint costs are included in the analysis, the results are of limited value. Another approach is to evaluate the sensitivity of the results of the targeted, or most probable, sales mix by preparing a separate analysis for each of several possible alternative sales mixes and comparing the results. This approach makes it possible for management to identify an acceptable range of profit.

The Unit Profit Graph. A break-even chart is generally prepared on the basis of total revenue and expense. These dollar sales and expense figures can be translated into a profit-per-unit graph in order to show more vividly the influence of fixed cost on the product unit cost. Assume, for example, the following: normal capacity, 100 percent; total sales, $50,000 (500 units @ $100); variable cost, $30,000; fixed cost, $15,000; profit, $5,000. The break-even point is $37,500 ($15,000 ÷ .40) or 75 percent of normal capacity ($37,500 ÷ $50,000). The variable cost is $60 per unit, and the fixed cost is $30 per unit if 500 units are made and sold. As volume decreases, the fixed cost per unit increases. This relationship is illustrated in the graph on page 621.

The effect of varying volume on the fixed cost per unit can also be expressed as follows:

	Units					
	100	200	300	375	400	500
Variable unit cost.........................	$ 60	$ 60	$ 60	$ 60	$ 60.00	$ 60
Fixed unit cost..............................	150	75	50	40	37.50	30
Total unit cost..............................	$ 210	$135	$110	$100	$ 97.50	$ 90
Unit sales price............................	100	100	100	100	100.00	100
Profit (loss) per unit....................	$(110)	$ (35)	$ (10)	Break even	$ 2.50	$ 10

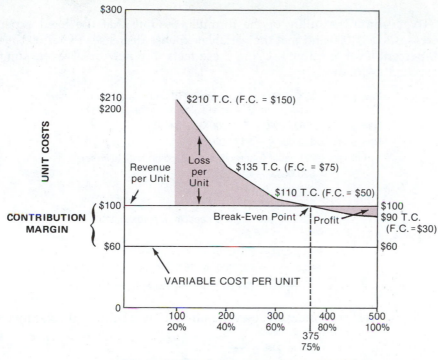

Unit Profit Graph Showing the Influence of Fixed and Variable Costs on Unit Cost

UNITS OF PRODUCT AND PERCENTAGE OF NORMAL CAPACITY

The analysis illustrated in the unit profit graph and in the tabular presentation, together with a break-even analysis, are important tools in determining which unit cost(s) should be used in setting sales prices. A break-even chart will help in understanding the effect on total profits when sales prices and fixed and variable costs are related to sales volume.

Unit Cost Formulas. The unit profit graph and the tabular presentation show a total unit cost that varies from a high of $210 per unit to a low of $90 per unit. To obtain a true comparison, unit costs must be computed at all levels of activity. When unit costs of various products are compared, the analyst must observe the production rates of each product, each of which may be at a different level.

Formulas can aid in determining the effect of changing costs or level of activity. For example, the following formula can be used to determine unit costs under conditions of fluctuating activity levels:

$$\text{Unit cost} = \frac{A + BX}{CX}$$

Where: A = total fixed cost
B = total variable cost at normal capacity
C = units of production at normal capacity
X = level of activity, expressed as a percentage of normal capacity

Using figures from the example introduced on page 620, the total cost of $45,000 ($15,000 + $30,000) divided by total units (500) gives a unit cost of $90 at the 100 percent level of activity.

To illustrate the utility of the formula, assume that the fixed expense increases to $17,000 and that the variable expense decreases to $27,000 at the 100-percent level of activity. Using these facts, the new break-even point is computed as follows:

$$\text{New profit} = (SX - BX) - A, \text{ where A, B, and X are as previously}$$
$$\text{defined and S = total sales at normal capacity}$$
$$\text{New profit} = (\$50,000X - \$27,000X) - \$17,000$$
$$\text{New profit} = \$23,000X - \$17,000$$

Let new profit equal 0 (the break-even point) and solve for X:

$$0 = \$23,000X - \$17,000$$
$$X = \frac{\$17,000}{\$23,000}$$
$$X = .739 \times 100, \text{ or } 74\% \text{ capacity (approximate)}$$

(or)

$$\text{Fixed cost} = \$17,000$$
$$\text{Variable cost} = \$27,000, \text{ or } \$54 \text{ per unit, or } 54\% \text{ of sales}$$
$$\frac{\$17,000}{1 - .54} = \frac{\$17,000}{.46} = \$37,000, \text{ or } 74\% \text{ capacity, or } 370 \text{ units}$$

The unit cost at the new break-even point can then be computed as follows:

$$\text{Unit cost} = \frac{A + BX}{CX}$$
$$= \frac{\$17,000 + \$27,000(.74)}{500(.74)}$$
$$= \frac{\$17,000 + \$19,980}{370}$$
$$= \$100 \text{ (approximate)}$$

Assuming the same changes in the fixed and variable expenses, the unit cost at 90 percent of capacity would be determined as follows:

$$\text{Unit cost} = \frac{\$17,000 + \$27,000(.90)}{500(.90)}$$
$$= \frac{\$17,000 + \$24,300}{450}$$
$$= \$92 \text{ (approximate)}$$

The above equations permit the development of unit costs, using data included in the budget. They further permit quick and easy computations in connection with problems raised by changing conditions. Budget data expressed in equation form permit quicker analysis of the effects of a variety of changes on unit costs.

Margin of Safety. Information developed from a break-even and cost-volume-profit analysis offers additional useful control data such as the *margin of safety*, which indicates how much sales may decrease from a selected sales figure before the company will break even, i.e., before the company will begin to suffer a loss. From the Northstar Company illustration on page 611, where sales are \$5,000,000, the margin of safety is \$1,000,000 (\$5,000,000 − \$4,000,000). The margin of safety expressed as a percentage of sales is called the *margin of safety ratio (M/S)* and is computed as follows:

$$\text{Margin of safety ratio (M/S)} = \frac{\text{Selected sales figure} - \text{Break-even sales}}{\text{Selected sales figure}}$$

$$= \frac{\$5,000,000 - \$4,000,000}{\$5,000,000}$$

$$= 20\%$$

Observe that the margin of safety and the margin of safety ratio would be negative if the break-even sales exceed the selected sales figure.

The margin of safety is directly related to profit. Using the same illustration from page 611, with a contribution margin ratio of 40 percent and a margin of safety ratio of 20 percent, then:

$$\text{Profit ratio} = \text{Contribution margin ratio} \times \text{Margin of safety ratio}$$
$$\text{PR} = \text{C/M} \times \text{M/S}$$
$$= 40\% \times 20\%$$
$$= 8\%$$

This computation indicates that of the margin of safety dollars, i.e., the sales above the break-even point, the contribution margin ratio portion is available for profit. Thus, 8 percent (40 percent of 20 percent) is the profit ratio, i.e., the percentage of the total selected sales figure that is profit.

$$\text{Proof: Profit} = \text{Margin of safety dollars} \times \text{Contribution margin ratio}$$
$$= \$1,000,000 \times 40\%$$
$$= \$400,000$$

and

$$\text{Profit} = \text{Selected sales figure} \times \text{Profit ratio}$$
$$= \$5,000,000 \times 8\%$$
$$= \$400,000$$

If the contribution margin ratio and the profit ratio are known, the margin of safety ratio is:

$$\text{M/S} = \frac{\text{PR}}{\text{C/M}} = \frac{8\%}{40\%} = 20\%$$

The Profit-Volume Analysis Graph

Break-even analysis and cost-volume-profit analysis also employ the *profit-volume (P/V) analysis graph,* which relates profit to volume. Using the figures from the illustration on page 611, a P/V analysis graph is illustrated on page 624.

The P/V analysis graph is constructed as follows:

1. The graph is divided into two parts by the sales line.
2. The total fixed cost is marked off below the sales line on the left-hand vertical line. The computed profit or loss figure is located by moving

horizontally to the point representing assumed sales dollars, then moving vertically to the point representing the computed profit or loss.
3. Fixed cost and profit points are joined by a diagonal line which crosses the sales line at the break-even point.

Profit-Volume Analysis Graph

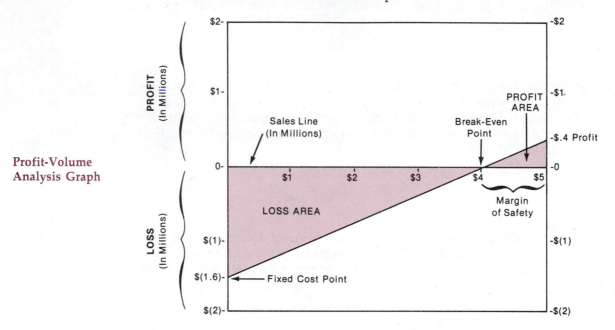

When management is considering various courses of action, a tabular report can present the possible results. For example, the effect of possible sales price increases and decreases for a product are shown in the following report:

| | Decrease | | Normal | Increase | |
	20%	10%	Volume	10%	20%
Units...	200,000	200,000	200,000	200,000	200,000
Sales...	$320,000	$360,000	$400,000	$440,000	$480,000
Variable cost.............................	200,000	200,000	200,000	200,000	200,000
Contribution margin..................	$120,000	$160,000	$200,000	$240,000	$280,000
Fixed cost..................................	160,000	160,000	160,000	160,000	160,000
Profit..	—	0	$ 40,000	$ 80,000	$120,000
Loss..	$ 40,000	0	—	—	—
Profit per unit...........................	—	—	$.20	$.40	$.60
Loss per unit.............................	$.20	—	—	—	—
% change in profit.....................	−200%	−100%	—	+100%	+200%
Return on investment of $200,000............................	− 20%	0%	20%	40%	60%
Break-even point.......................	$426,667	$360,000	$320,000	$293,333	$274,286

In this illustration, a 10 percent drop in price reduces the profit to the break-even point, and a 20 percent drop in price causes a $40,000 loss. However, the 10 percent and 20 percent price increases cause profit to increase

$40,000 and $80,000, respectively. These effects are indicated more effectively, however, in a P/V analysis graph, as follows:

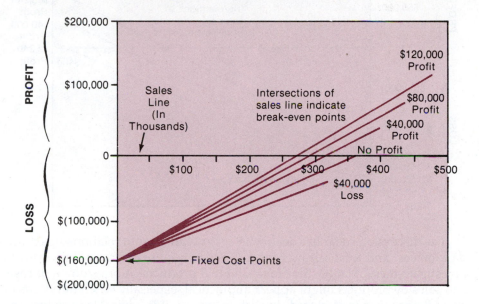

P/V Analysis Graph Illustrating the Effect of Possible Sales Price Changes on Profit

As another example of the use of a P/V analysis graph, assume that a company's management has the following plans regarding sales, costs, volume, and profit:

Plan 1		Plan 2	
Decrease in price.............................	10%	Increase in price................................	10%
Increase in volume..........................	12%	Decrease in volume..........................	12%
Variable cost increase....................	4%	Variable cost decrease....................	4%
Fixed cost increase..........................	5%	Fixed cost decrease..........................	5%

The effect of these plans is summarized as follows:

	Plan 1	Normal Volume	Plan 2
Units...	224,000	200,000	176,000
Sales...	$403,200	$400,000	$387,200
Variable cost................................	232,960	200,000	168,960
Contribution margin....................	$170,240	$200,000	$218,240
Fixed cost.....................................	168,000	160,000	152,000
Profit...	$ 2,240	$ 40,000	$ 66,240
Profit per unit..............................	$.01	$.20	$.3763
% change in profit.......................	− 94.4%	....	+ 65.6%
Return on investment of $200,000.............................	1.12%	20%	33.1%
Break-even point........................	$397,895	$320,000	$269,677

The following graph, based on the summary data, is a composite, highly informative P/V analysis graph:

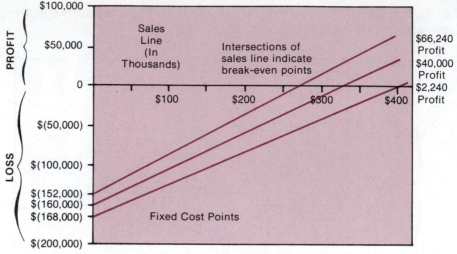

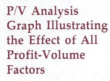

P/V Analysis
Graph Illustrating
the Effect of All
Profit-Volume
Factors

The discussion so far has dealt with cost-volume-profit relationships based on total cost and total sales revenue. It is much more desirable, however, to investigate these relationships for individual products. A breakdown of costs and sales by products might appear impractical, especially when hundreds of small items are manufactured. In such instances, it is advisable to reduce the large number of products to several major lines. To determine a better product cost for purposes of planning and control, many firms have departmentalized their sprawling factory output. With such departmentalization, the contribution that each product or product group makes to the total contribution margin can be gauged more satisfactorily.

Variable costs used in previous illustrations are a composite of the variable costs of the several manufacturing cost centers, the marketing departments, and administrative divisions. However, it is possible to determine the variable cost of each product line because:

1. Direct materials and direct labor costs can be based on standard costs.
2. Variable factory overhead can be based on normal production hours, labor cost, or machine hours established for the cost centers of the plant. The flexible budget for each cost center serves as an excellent basis for the determination of product factory overhead.
3. Variable marketing and administrative expenses can be charged directly to products or allocated on the basis of the sales value of each product or gross profit return or other bases discussed in Chapter 25. Of course, allocations of either nonmanufacturing or manufacturing costs are arbitrary, a limitation that should not be overlooked.

Once the sales value and the variable cost of each product have been determined, it will be apparent that each product has a different contribution margin and a C/M ratio. To illustrate cost-volume-profit analysis by products, the figures of the Normal Volume column of the summary on page 625 are divided between four products, resulting in the following data:

Product	Sales Value of Production	Variable Cost	% of Variable Cost to Sales	Contribution Margin	C/M Ratio
A	$120,000	$100,000	83%	$ 20,000	17%
B	140,000	60,000	43	80,000	57
C	90,000	30,000	33	60,000	67
D	50,000	10,000	20	40,000	80
Total	$400,000	$200,000	50	$200,000	50

$$\text{Less fixed cost}........\ 160,000$$
$$\text{Profit}......................\ \$\ 40,000$$

$$\text{Break-even point} = \frac{\$160,000}{.50} = \$320,000$$

The contribution margin and C/M ratio are shown for each product and in total. The C/M ratio varies from 17 percent for Product A to 80 percent for Product D. If the present sales mix can be altered or if sales can be expanded, products with higher C/M ratios afford greater relative contributions to profit per dollar of sales. But the product's C/M ratio, sales dollars, and contribution margin must be related to facility utilization. The product offering the higher C/M ratio is desirable only if the resulting contribution margin (C/M ratio × sales dollars) is greater than could be achieved by some alternative use of the same limited facilities. If unused or idle facilities are available, perhaps both alternatives can be pursued profitably.

The following P/V analysis graph indicates the profit path for each product, A, B, C, and D:

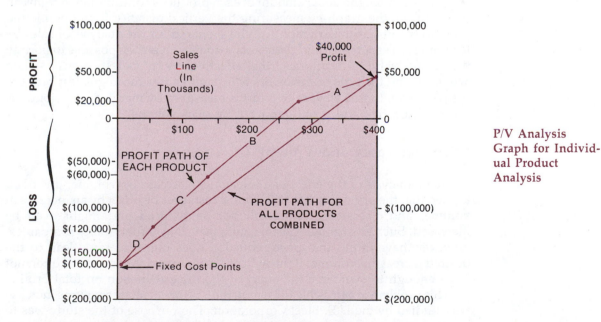

P/V Analysis Graph for Individual Product Analysis

This P/V analysis graph is constructed as follows:

1. The horizontal line 00 represents sales and is marked off from zero to $400,000.

2. The profit path for all products combined is then drawn, starting at the $(160,000) fixed cost point in the loss area and ending at the $40,000 profit point in the profit area. The break-even point is at the point of crossover from the loss to the profit area.

3. The profit path of each product is plotted next. It starts with the product with the highest C/M ratio, Product D. The line begins at the total fixed cost point and is drawn to the $(120,000) point in the loss area directly below the $50,000 sales volume point. The plotting indicates that $40,000 of the $160,000 fixed cost has been recovered.

4. The profit path of Product C starts at the point where D's path ended. The line for Product C ends opposite the loss figure of $(60,000) and below the sales volume figure of $140,000. The $(60,000) figure shows that $60,000 additional fixed cost was recovered. The $140,000 point on the sales line is the accumulated sales total of Products D and C ($50,000 + $90,000).

5. The profit path for Product B begins at the end of C's path and leads across the sales line into the profit area to the $20,000 profit point immediately above the sales volume figure of $280,000.

6. Product A with the lowest C/M ratio is charted last. It adds $20,000 to the profit, and its path ends at the $40,000 profit figure.

The plotting of the profit path of each product provides management with an interesting pictorial report—the steeper the slope, the higher the C/M ratio. If any product did not have a contribution margin, its path or slope would be downward. Also, the dollar amount of each product's contribution margin can be read from the graph by measuring the vertical distance from one plotted point to the next. Similar graphs can be prepared for the analysis of sales by territories, salespersons, and classes of customers. It is then possible to portray the profitability of territories, the effectiveness of salespersons' selling activities, and the type of customers whose purchases mean greatest profit to the company. In this way, sales effort is measured by marginal contributions toward fixed cost and profit—and not by sales volume.

Price Decreases and Volume Increases

In an analysis of the effect of a sales price decrease on volume, it is often argued that the price decrease will in most instances be offset by an increase in volume, and, therefore, profit will not be reduced and might even be increased. Such an argument seems quite plausible at first. Many companies, however, have found that price reduction does not necessarily lead to the desired increase in volume. If the increase in volume does occur, it is often not large enough to overcome the effect of the price reduction on total profit.

This problem of a possible price reduction being offset by a volume increase was studied by the U.S. Steel Corporation. The purpose of the study was to ascertain the increase in volume that would have to take place to offset various decreases in steel prices by the company's subsidiaries, taking into consideration the effect of increased volume on cost, and to estimate the financial gain or loss which would result from price reductions. The study concluded that, because of the low elasticity of demand for steel, the increase in volume resulting from a reduction in price would be less than the increase needed to offset the adverse effects of the lower price on profit. While offsetting volume increases may be more favorable in other types of businesses and industries, they are, in general, hardly enough to overcome reduced prices. In most cases, a price reduction must be accompanied not only by increased volume but also by a reduction in the cost of the product.

▼ THE FALLACY OF FULL COST ANALYSIS

When the profitability of a product is determined by distributing all fixed and variable costs to all products, it is likely that certain products will show a loss, depending on the methods used to allocate fixed cost. For example, the following illustration uses the figures for Products A, B, C, and D, from page 627, and shows the distribution of the fixed cost to each product on the basis of the variable cost ratios:

**FIXED COST DISTRIBUTION TO EACH PRODUCT
BASED ON VARIABLE COST RATIOS**

Product	Sales Value of Production	Total Cost*	Profit	Percentage of Profit to Sales
A	$120,000	$180,000	−$60,000	−50%
B	140,000	108,000	32,000	22.8
C	90,000	54,000	36,000	40
D	50,000	18,000	32,000	64
Total	$400,000	$360,000	$40,000	10

*Computation of total cost:

Product	Variable Cost	Variable Cost Ratio		Fixed Cost		Fixed Cost Distribution	Total Cost
A	$100,000	$\frac{\$100,000}{\$200,000}$	×	$160,000	=	$80,000	$180,000
B	60,000	$\frac{60,000}{200,000}$	×	160,000	=	48,000	108,000
C	30,000	$\frac{30,000}{200,000}$	×	160,000	=	24,000	54,000
D	10,000	$\frac{10,000}{200,000}$	×	160,000	=	8,000	18,000
Total	$200,000						

The analysis indicates that Product A is a loss item. Because it also contributes a lower contribution margin and C/M ratio than the other products, management might want to discontinue it. Product A, however, actually contributes $20,000 to the company's total profit picture.

Most methods used to distribute fixed costs to products confuse cost-volume-profit relations, for they do not recognize the change in costs and profits produced by a change in volume or product mix. This confusion is eliminated by following the contribution margin principle, which sets apart not only the fixed costs that must be allocated, but also those that are directly assignable to a specific product. Attention is then directed to the margin between sales and variable cost, rather than sales and total cost. Products make a favorable contribution as long as the sales revenue exceeds the related variable cost.

An alternative product should replace the existing one only if idle capacity is not available and only if the alternative product will yield a larger total dollar contribution toward recovering the fixed cost and profit for an equal amount of capacity constraint (e.g., machine hours). Since some fixed costs can be changed in the short run, the analysis must consider any change in fixed cost associated with dropping a product or moving from an existing product to an alternative product. It is assumed, of course, that the added product can be marketed without disturbing the market for other products of the company.

In the case of joint products, the variable as well as the fixed joint costs are best viewed in their relationship to the contribution made by the group of joint products rather than on the basis of an arbitrary allocation to each product (pages 137-138).

▼ USES OF BREAK-EVEN AND COST-VOLUME-PROFIT ANALYSIS SUMMARIZED

There are many specific uses of break-even and cost-volume-profit analysis which management can make. Among these, some of the more significant ones are summarized as follows:

1. Aiding budgetary control. Helps indicate what changes, if any, are needed to bring expenses into line with revenue.
2. Improving and balancing sales. Acts as a warning signal to alert management to potential trouble in the sales program. If sales relative to costs are not as high as they should be, this fact will show up. Then it may be time to reevaluate (a) sales techniques, (b) training of sales staff, and (c) lines carried in relation to customers.
3. Analyzing volume change impact. Provides answers to specific questions such as the following: (a) How much of the present sales volume can the company lose before profit disappears? (b) How much will profit increase with an increase in volume?
4. Analyzing sales price and cost change impact. Indicates the probable effects on profit of sales price changes in combination with other changes. For example: (a) What changes may be expected in profit with changes in price, assuming all other factors remain constant? (b) If prices are reduced, what is the most practical combination of volume and cost changes to expect and what is the net effect of the combination of changes on profit? (c) Similarly, if prices are increased, what combination of changes and what effect on profit may reasonably be expected?

5. Negotiating wages. Assists management by: (a) quickly reflecting the probable influence on profit of proposed wage changes (assuming no change in employee efficiency) and (b) providing aid in determining possible economies and efficiencies that might protect the profit position of the company.
6. Analyzing product mix. Enables critical examination of the product mix. Break-even and cost-volume-profit analysis for different sales mixes and for each product line is a valuable aid in determining which products should be pushed and which should possibly be eliminated.
7. Assessing further capitalization and expansion decisions. Provides a means of appraising in advance proposed capital expenditures which may change the cost structure of the business.
8. Analyzing margin of safety. Serves as a reminder of the margin of safety and of how changes may affect it.

DISCUSSION QUESTIONS

1. Define break-even point.
2. (a) Why must the conventional income statement be restated for computation of the break-even point? (b) What type of statement is constructed?
3. What is the contribution margin?
4. Give the formulas commonly used by firms with a single product to determine the break-even point (a) in dollars of sales revenue and (b) in units of product.
5. Identify the numbered components of the following break-even chart:

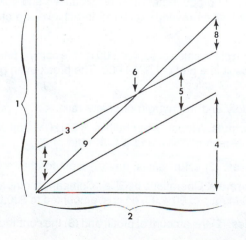

6. Discuss the significance of the concept of the relevant range to break-even analysis.
7. Discuss weaknesses inherent in the preparation and uses of break-even analysis.
8. How does the break-even point move when changes occur in (a) variable expense? (b) fixed expense?
9. The break-even chart and the unit profit graph intend to show the same information but seem to differ. How?
10. What is the margin of safety?
11. What is meant by the term "cost-volume-profit relationship?" Why is this relationship important in business management?
12. In accordance with classical economic theory, a reduction in prices should be accompanied by an increase in the volume of sales. Discuss the effect of such an action on revenue and profits.
13. Why is a cost-volume-profit analysis by products valuable to management?
14. Describe how the contribution of each product to the recovery of fixed expense and to the total profit of a company can be presented in graphic form.
15. What are some uses of break-even and cost-volume-profit analysis?

EXERCISES

1. Break-even analysis. Woliver Company plans to market a new product. Based on its market studies, Woliver estimates that it can sell 5,500 units during the first year. The sales price will be $2 per unit. Variable cost is estimated to be 40% of the sales price. Fixed cost is estimated to be $6,000.

Required: Compute the break-even point in dollars and in units.

2. Break-even analysis. The 19— sales of Jupiter Company were $7,640,000. Fixed expense was $2,451,000 and variable expense totaled $4,736,800.

Required: Compute (1) the contribution margin, (2) the contribution margin ratio, and (3) the break-even point in dollars.

3. Break-even analysis. The normal capacity of Mosier Company is 18,000 units and the per unit sales price is $2.50. Relevant costs are:

	Variable (Per Unit)	Fixed
Materials...	$.70	
Labor...	.60	
Factory overhead..	.175	$2,000
Marketing and administrative....................	.20	2,290

Required: Compute (1) the break-even sales in dollars, (2) the break-even sales in units, and (3) the sales dollars required to produce a profit of $8,250.

4. Break-even and cost-volume-profit analysis. Kenton Company produces only one product. Normal capacity is 20,000 units per year, and the unit sales price is $5. Relevant costs are:

	Unit Variable Cost	Total Fixed Cost
Materials...	$1.00	
Direct labor...	1.20	
Factory overhead................................	.50	$15,000
Marketing expenses............................	.30	5,000
Administrative expenses......................	3.00	6,000

Required: Compute (1) the break-even point in units of product, (2) the break-even point in dollars of sales, (3) the number of units of product that must be produced and sold to achieve a profit of $10,000, and (4) the sales revenue required to achieve a profit of $10,000.

5. Margin of safety. Marvel Corporation plans sales of $2,000,000 for the coming period, which top management expects will result in a profit of $200,000. The break-even point has been determined to be $1,500,000 of sales.

Required: Compute the margin of safety and the margin of safety ratio.

6. Break-even analysis and profit formula. A month's operations of Sureflite Company show fixed expense of $9,300, an M/S ratio of 25%, and a C/M ratio of 62%.

Required: Compute (1) break-even sales, (2) actual sales, and (3) profit for the month.

7. Break-even analysis and profit formula. Operations of Gilley Company for the year disclosed an M/S ratio of 20% and a C/M ratio of 60%. Fixed cost amounted to $30,000.

Required: Compute (1) break-even sales, (2) the amount of profit, and (3) the contribution margin.

8. Cost-volume-profit analysis. Semiconductor Company is planning to produce and sell 100,000 units of Chip A at $4 a unit and 200,000 units of Chip B at $3 a unit. Variable costs are 70% of sales for Chip A and 80% of sales for Chip B.

Required: If total planned operating profit is $140,000, what must the total fixed cost be? (AICPA adapted)

9. Unit cost formula. At 100% capacity, volume is 350 units, variable expense is $742, and fixed expense is $1,008.

Required: What is the unit cost at 90% capacity?

10. Break-even analysis. The income statement for one of Meek Company's products shows:

Sales (100 units at $100 a unit).....................		$10,000
Cost of goods sold:		
Direct labor...	$1,500	
Direct materials used................................	1,400	
Variable factory overhead..........................	1,000	
Fixed factory overhead.............................	990	
Total cost of goods sold.........................		4,890
Gross profit..		$ 5,110
Marketing expenses:		
Variable..	$1,000	
Fixed...	1,000	
Administrative expenses:		
Variable..	500	
Fixed...	1,000	
Total marketing and administrative expenses....................................		3,500
Operating income..		$ 1,610

Required: Compute (1) the break-even point in units, (2) the operating income if sales increase by 25%, and (3) the break-even point in dollars if fixed factory overhead increases by $690. (AICPA adapted)

11. Break-even analysis with multiple products. Redwood Company manufactures two products, tables and chairs. Tables sell for $60 each and chairs for $30 each. Twice as many chairs are sold each year as tables. Variable costs per unit are $35 and $20 for tables and chairs, respectively. Total fixed cost is $675,000.

Required: Compute the break-even point in sales dollars and in units of product.

12. Break-even and cost-volume-profit analysis. Puma Company manufactures two products, L and M. L sells for $20 and M for $15. Variable costs per unit are $12 and $10 for L and M, respectively. Total fixed cost is $372,000. Puma management has targeted profit for the coming period at $93,000. Two units of L are expected to sell for every three units of M sold during the period.

Required: Compute (1) the break-even point in units of product and in sales dollars and (2) the level of sales in units of product and dollars necessary to achieve Puma's profit goal.

13. Price decreases and volume increases—elasticity of demand. Basso Company forecasts next year's sales of Product X to be 50,000 units at a sales price of $10. Management is considering a price reduction to $9 with the expectation that sales and profit will increase. However, the elasticity of demand is questionable, ranging from an estimated low elasticity of only 2,000 additional units sold to a high elasticity of an increase of 30,000 units.

The variable unit manufacturing cost is estimated to be $5 and the variable nonmanufacturing cost is estimated to be 10% of sales revenue. At the high elasticity sales level, annual programmed fixed costs are expected to increase $5,000 and $1,000 for manufacturing and nonmanufacturing costs, respectively.

Required: Compute the change in the contribution to other fixed cost and to income before income tax if the sales price is reduced and the sales volume increases (a) 2,000 units; (b) 30,000 units.

14. Cost-volume-profit analysis. Citation Company expects to incur the following costs to produce and sell 70,000 units of its product:

Variable manufacturing costs..	$210,000
Fixed manufacturing costs..	80,000
Variable marketing expenses...	105,000
Fixed marketing and administrative expenses................	60,000

Required:

(1) What price would Citation have to charge for the product in order just to break even if all 70,000 units produced are sold?

(2) If Citation decides upon a price of $8 and has a profit objective of 10% of sales, what sales volume would be required?

(3) Citation plans to expand capacity next year to 100,000 units. The increased capacity will increase fixed manufacturing costs to $100,000. If the sales price of each unit of product remains at $8, how many units must Citation sell in order to produce a profit of 15% of sales.   *(CGAAC adapted)*

15. Break-even chart. Groff Company expects annual sales of 10,000 units of its product at $20 per unit. Variable costs are $10 per unit, and fixed costs are expected to total $70,000.

Required: Prepare a break-even chart for Groff Company.

PROBLEMS

20-1. Break-even analysis. Kimbrell Company has decided to introduce a new product. The new product can be manufactured by either a capital-intensive method or a labor-intensive method. The manufacturing method will not affect the quality of the product. The estimated unit manufacturing costs by the two methods follow:

	Capital Intensive	Labor Intensive
Materials..	$5.00	$5.60
Direct labor...	6.00	7.20
Variable factory overhead......................	3.00	4.80

Directly traceable incremental fixed factory overhead is expected to be $2,440,000 if the capital-intensive method is chosen and $1,320,000 if the labor-intensive method is chosen. Kimbrell's market research department has recommended an introductory unit sales price of $30. Regardless of the manufacturing method chosen, the incremental fixed marketing expenses are estimated to be $500,000 per year plus a variable marketing expense of $2 for each unit sold.

Required:

    (1) Calculate the estimated break-even point for the new product in annual units of sales, if Kimbrell Company uses the:
       (a) capital-intensive manufacturing method.
       (b) labor-intensive manufacturing method.
    (2) Determine the annual unit sales volume at which Kimbrell Company would be indifferent between the two manufacturing methods.   *(ICMA adapted)*

20-2. Break-even analysis. Wolverton Company manufactures and sells a single product, for which price and cost data are as follows:

Sales price per unit...	$ 25.00
Variable costs per unit:	
Raw materials..	$ 11.00
Direct labor..	5.00
Factory overhead..	2.50
Marketing and administrative....................	1.30
Total variable cost per unit....................	$ 19.80
Annual fixed costs:	
Factory overhead..	$192,000
Marketing and administrative....................	276,000
	$468,000
Income tax rate..	40%

Required:

    (1) Compute the break-even point in units.
    (2) Determine the units to sell in order to earn $156,000 after income tax.
    (3) Compute the break-even point in units if direct labor cost increases 8%.
    (4) If Wolverton's direct labor cost does increase 8%, determine the per unit sales price to maintain the same contribution margin ratio.   *(ICMA adapted)*

20-3. Break-even analysis; impact of new order. In 19A, Chesterton Inc. produced and sold 100,000 units of its product at a price of $2.75. The company can increase capacity to produce 125,000 units by increasing fixed cost $5,000 per year. The company receives an order for 15,000 unbranded units to be sold at $2.45 each. With the added volume plus other economies, the plant manager estimates that materials, labor, and variable factory overhead each can be reduced $.02 per unit for all the output. Nonmanufacturing expenses will be unaffected by the added 15,000-unit order. The president of the company wishes to see a projected gross profit statement for next year, assuming that the new order is accepted on January 2, 19B, that there are no other changes in sales volume, and that the economies can be affected.

    Data for 19A are as follows:

Sales..		$275,000
Cost of goods sold:		
Materials...	$80,000	
Labor..	62,000	
Variable factory overhead....................	45,000	
Fixed factory overhead........................	25,600	
Cost of goods sold..........................		212,600
Gross profit...		$ 62,400

Required:

    (1) Compute the break-even sales, contribution margin, and C/M ratio, based on 19A data and disregarding nonmanufacturing costs.

    (2) Prepare a projectd 19B statement of gross profit.

    (3) Compute the break-even sales, contribution margin, and C/M ratio, based on projected 19B data and disregarding nonmanufacturing costs. Round the C/M ratio to four decimal places.

20-4. Break-even and cost-volume-profit analysis. Castleton Company has analyzed the costs of producing and selling 5,000 units of its sole product to be as follows:

Direct materials	$60,000
Direct labor	40,000
Variable factory overhead	20,000
Fixed factory overhead	30,000
Variable marketing and administrative expenses	10,000
Fixed marketing and administrative expenses	15,000

Required:

    (1) Compute the number of units to break even at a per unit sales price of $38.50.

    (2) Determine the number of units that must be sold to produce an $18,000 profit, at a $40 per unit sales price.

    (3) Determine the price Castleton must charge at a 5,000-unit sales level, in order to produce a profit equal to 20% of sales.   *(CGAAC adapted)*

20-5. Cost behavior, break-even, and cost-volume-profit analysis. Fenton Office Equipment Company collected the following data for the second quarter of the year:

	Sales	Cost
April	$70,000	$56,000
May	77,000	59,990
June	85,000	64,550

Required: Compute the following amounts:

    (1) The fixed cost and the variable cost per sales dollar.

    (2) The contribution margin ratio.

    (3) The break-even point.

    (4) July profit if sales are $79,000.

    (5) August sales if the month's loss is $1,050.

20-6. Break-even analysis. Byrum Co. manufactures two products—Whistles and Bells. The following data are projected for the coming year:

	Whistles Units	Whistles Amount	Bells Units	Bells Amount	Total Amount
Sales	10,000	$10,000	8,000	$10,000	$20,000
Fixed cost		$ 2,000		$ 5,600	$ 7,600
Variable cost		6,000		3,000	9,000
Total cost		$ 8,000		$ 8,600	$16,600
Operating income		$ 2,000		$ 1,400	$ 3,400

Required: Compute the following:

    (1) The break-even sales in units for Whistles, assuming that the facilities are not jointly used.

(2) The break-even sales in dollars for Bells, assuming that the facilities are not jointly used.

(3) The composite unit contribution margin, assuming that consumers purchase composite units of four Whistles and three Bells.

(4) The break-even units for both products, assuming that consumers purchase composite units of four Whistles and three Bells.

(5) The composite contribution margin ratio, assuming that a composite unit is defined as one Whistle and one Bell. (Round to two decimal places.)

(6) The break-even point in dollars, assuming that Whistles and Bells become one-to-one complements and there is no change in the company's cost function. *(AICPA adapted)*

20-7. Break-even and cost-volume-profit analysis. Cabot Electronics produces and markets tape recorders and electronic calculators. Its 19A income statement follows:

Cabot Electronics
Income Statement
For Year Ended December 31, 19A

	Tape Recorders		Electronic Calculators		
	Total (000s omitted)	Per Unit	Total (000s omitted)	Per Unit	Total (000s omitted)
Sales..	$1,050	$15.00	$3,150	$22.50	$4,200.0
Production costs:					
Materials......................................	$ 280	$ 4.00	$ 630	$ 4.50	$ 910.0
Direct labor.................................	140	2.00	420	3.00	560.0
Variable factory overhead..............	140	2.00	280	2.00	420.0
Fixed factory overhead...................	70	1.00	210	1.50	280.0
Total production cost.................	$ 630	$ 9.00	$1,540	$11.00	$2,170.0
Gross profit.....................................	$ 420	$ 6.00	$1,610	$11.50	$2,030.0
Fixed marketing and administrative expenses...					1,040.0
Income before income tax..					$ 990.0
Income tax (55%)..					544.5
Net income...					$ 445.5

The tape recorder business has been fairly stable in recent years, and the company has no plans to change the tape recorder price. However, because of increasing competition and market saturation, management has decided to reduce its calculator price to $20, effective January 1, 19B, and to spend an additional $57,000 in 19B for advertising. As a result, Cabot estimates that 80% of its 19B revenue will be from electronic calculator sales. The sales units mix for tape recorders and calculators was 1:2 in 19A and is expected to be 1:3 in 19B at all volume levels. For 19B, materials costs are expected to drop 10% and 20% for the tape recorders and calculators, respectively; however, all direct labor costs are to increase 10%.

Required:

(1) Compute the number of tape recorders and electronic calculators to break even, using 19A data.

(2) Determine the sales dollars required to earn an aftertax profit of 9% on sales, using 19B estimates.

(3) Compute the number of tape recorders and electronic calculators to break even, using 19B estimates. *(ICMA adapted)*

20-8. Break-even and cost-volume-profit analysis; direct costing. The following data relate to a year's budgeted activity for Mariemont Corporation, which manufactures one product:

Beginning inventory	30,000 units
Production	120,000
Available for sale	150,000 units
Sales	110,000
Ending inventory	40,000 units
Sales price	$5.00 per unit
Variable manufacturing cost	1.00
Variable marketing cost	2.00
Fixed manufacturing cost (based on 100,000 units)	.25
Fixed marketing cost (based on 100,000 units)	.65

A special order is received for 10,000 units, in addition to budgeted sales, to be used in an unrelated market. The total fixed cost remains unchanged within the relevant range of 45,000 units to total capacity of 135,000 units.

Required: Compute the following:

(1) Projected annual break-even sales in units.
(2) Projected operating income for the year from budgeted sales (a) under direct costing; (b) under absorption costing, charging all variances to Cost of Goods Sold.
(3) Price per unit to be charged on the special order, given the original data, so that the operating income will increase by $5,000.
(4) Number of units to be sold to generate a profit equal to 10% of the contribution margin, assuming that the sales price increases by 20%; the variable manufacturing cost increases by 10%; the variable marketing cost remains the same; and the total fixed cost increases to $104,400. *(AICPA adapted)*

20-9. Break-even and cost-volume-profit analysis. Community Hospital is a general hospital, but it rents space and beds to separately owned entities rendering specialized services, such as pediatrics and psychiatrics. Community charges each separate entity for common services, such as patients' meals and laundry, and for administrative services, such as billings and collections. Space and bed rentals are fixed charges for the year, based on bed capacity rented to each entity.

Community charged the following costs to pediatrics for the preceding year:

	Patient Days (Variable Cost)	Bed Capacity (Fixed Cost)
Dietary	$ 600,000	—
Janitorial	—	$ 70,000
Laundry	300,000	—
Laboratory	450,000	—
Pharmacy	350,000	—
Repairs and maintenance	—	30,000
General and administrative	—	1,300,000
Rent	—	1,500,000
Billings and collections	300,000	—
Totals	$2,000,000	$2,900,000

During the preceding year, pediatrics charged each patient an average of $300 per day, had a capacity of 60 beds, and had revenue of $6,000,000 for 365 days.

In addition, pediatrics directly employed the following personnel:

	Annual Salaries
Supervising nurses.....................	$25,000
Nurses..	20,000
Aides...	9,000

Community has the following minimum departmental personnel requirements based on total annual patient days:

Annual Patient Days	Aides	Nurses	Supervising Nurses
Up to 21,900	20	10	4
21,901 to 26,000	26	13	4
26,001 to 29,200	30	15	4

These staffing levels represent full-time equivalents. Pediatrics always employs only the minimum number of required full-time equivalent personnel. Salaries of supervising nurses, nurses, and aides are therefore fixed within ranges of annual patient days.

Pediatrics operated at 100% capacity on 90 days during the preceding year. It is estimated that during these 90 days the demand exceeded 20 patients more than capacity. Community has an additional 20 beds available for rent for the current year. Such additional rental would increase pediatrics' fixed charges, based on bed capacity.

Required:

(1) Calculate the minimum number of patient days required for pediatrics to break even for the current year if the additional 20 beds are not rented. Patient demand is unknown, but assume that revenue per patient day, cost per patient day, cost per bed, and salary rates will remain the same for the current year as in the preceding year.

(2) Assume that patient demand, revenue per patient day, cost per patient day, cost per bed, and salary rates for the current year remain the same as in the preceding year. Prepare a schedule of increase in revenue and increase in costs for the current year in order to determine the net increase or decrease in earnings from the additional 20 beds if pediatrics rents this extra capacity from Community. *(AICPA adapted)*

20-10. Price decreases and volume increases. Regents Recording Company records and sells phonograph records to outlets across the nation. Competition has increased significantly in recent years, and Regents feels that a price reduction would boost sales volume and operating income.

The following data have been estimated for 19A:

Sales (937,500 units @ $5).....................	$4,687,500
Variable cost...	2,250,000
Fixed cost..	2,000,000

Management predicts that an 8% price cut would increase the estimated volume by 20% and that a 15% price cut would lead to a 40% volume increase. Total fixed cost and unit variable cost would not change if the volume increase does not exceed 50%.

Required: Calculate the expected operating income for 19A for each of the following situations: (1) no price cut, (2) an 8% price cut, and (3) a 15% price cut.

20-11. Price decreases and volume increases. The income statement of Lennholm Inc. for the year ended December 31, 19A, is as follows:

Sales (9,600,000 units)...		$160,000,000
Cost of goods sold:		
Direct materials...	$38,400,000	
Direct labor..	28,800,000	
Factory overhead...	48,000,000	115,200,000
Gross profit..		$ 44,800,000
Marketing and administrative expenses....................		28,800,000
Operating income..		$ 16,000,000

Production capacity of the installed machinery is 12,000,000 units. Company management is conscious of the high degree of underutilized capacity. It is uncertain, however, whether or not the market will absorb more units of product than at present. The task of assessing product demand was assigned to a marketing research consulting firm. The study made by the consultants predicted the following price-volume relationships:

Sales Price per Unit	Quantity Demanded
$16.00	10,000,000
15.50	12,000,000
14.50	14,000,000
14.25	18,000,000

An analysis of factory overhead reveals that in 19A, fixed factory overhead was $28,800,000 and fixed marketing and administrative expenses were $19,200,000. If new machinery is to be installed for increasing the production capacity to 18,000,000 units, an additional capital expenditure of $100,000,000 is required, resulting in a fixed factory overhead increase of $10,000,000 per year.

Required: Determine the recommended level of activity.

20-12. Use of limiting constraint. Moorehead Manufacturing Company produces two products, for which the following per unit data have been tabulated:

	XV-7	BD-4
Sales price...	$4.00	$3.00
Variable manufacturing cost.....................	2.00	1.50
Fixed manufacturing cost..........................	.75	.20
Variable marketing cost............................	1.00	1.00

Fixed manufacturing cost is applied at a rate of $1 per machine hour.

The sales manager has received a $160,000 increase in the budget allotment for advertising and wants to apply the money to the more profitable product. The products are not substitutes for one another.

Required:

(1) Calculate the minimum increase in sales units and dollars required to offset the advertising increase if the sales manager devotes the entire $160,000 to (a) XV-7, (b) BD-4.

(2) Moorehead has only 100,000 unused machine hours which can be made available to produce either XV-7 or BD-4, but not both. If all the unused machine hours are made available, compute the total estimated contribution margin increase for (a) XV-7, (b) BD-4.   *(ICMA adapted)*

CHAPTER 21
Differential Cost Analysis

Differential cost is the difference in the cost of alternative choices. Differential cost is often referred to as *marginal cost* by economists and as *incremental cost* by industrial engineers. It is essentially the *out-of-pocket cost,* i.e., the cost that requires an immediate or future cash outlay, that must be incurred if a project is undertaken or extended beyond its originally intended goal. Similarly, differential cost may be thought of as the cost that can be avoided if the project is not undertaken or extended. Differential cost does not include cost that must be incurred regardless of whether the project is undertaken. Consequently, *sunk costs* (such as the excess of the book value of an asset over its salvage value) and allocated fixed costs (such as building depreciation and supervisory salaries) are not differential costs. Since sunk costs cannot be recovered and allocated fixed costs must be incurred regardless of whether the project is undertaken or extended, they are not relevant to any decision concerning the desirability of undertaking or extending the project.

The purpose of this chapter is to discuss the application of differential cost analysis in short-term decision making. Differential cost studies are discussed and illustrated in the first section, and quantitative techniques that are useful in differential cost analysis are presented in the last section.

▼ DIFFERENTIAL COST STUDIES

Differential cost studies are undertaken to determine the marginal or incremental revenue, cost, and/or profit margin of alternative uses of fixed facilities or available capacity. In these studies, variable costs are relevant because they are typically costs that are avoidable if the projects being evaluated are not undertaken. In contrast, fixed costs are typically not avoidable costs and, therefore, not relevant to any decision about the relative cost or profitability of alternatives. If, however, fixed cost must be increased, for example, as a result of the purchase or rental of additional equipment or space, the additional fixed cost should be considered a differential cost. For purposes of determining the cost to be incurred in undertaking or extending a project, any out-of-pocket expenditure required to provide sufficient capacity is relevant to the decision.

Opportunity costs related to alternative uses of resources are also relevant to differential cost studies. An *opportunity cost* may be defined as the measurable value of the best forgone alternative, i.e., the measurable value of an opportunity bypassed by rejecting the best alternative use of resources. For example, money could either be spent in producing and selling a product or it could be invested in an interest-earning asset, such as a bond. If money were spent producing and selling a product, the interest that could have been earned from the alternative investment in the interest-earning asset would be an opportunity cost. Similarly, a machine could either be used in the manufacture of a product or it could be sold for salvage. The salvage value of the machine is an opportunity cost. Opportunity costs must be considered in evaluating alternatives in order to determine the most profitable use of resources.

Imputed costs may also be relevant to differential cost studies. *Imputed costs* are hypothetical costs representing the cost of a resource measured by its use value. Imputed costs do not ordinarily appear in conventional accounting records and do not necessarily entail dollar outlays. An imputed cost is similar to an opportunity cost, except that an imputed cost may be an arbitrary measure. A common example of an imputed cost is the inclusion of "interest" on ownership equity as a part of operating expenses.

Historical costs drawn from the accounting records generally do not give management the differential cost information needed to evaluate alternative courses of action. A flexible budget, however, with its revised current costs for each rise in the capacity level, can be useful in some differential cost analyses. The flexible budget shows the various expenses at different levels of production. It indicates that some expenses increase proportionately with an increase in capacity, while other expenses remain comparatively stationary through various levels of activity.

In the flexible budget on page 643, the $5.40 average unit cost at 60 percent of normal capacity is computed by dividing the total cost at that capacity by the number of units produced ($324,250 ÷ 60,000 units). The total differential cost is determined by subtracting the total estimated cost for one level of activity from that of another level (e.g., $423,400 − $324,250 = $99,150, the differential cost between the 80-percent and 60-percent levels). The differential unit cost is computed by:

1. Subtracting one level of output from the next higher level (80,000 units output at 80 percent minus 60,000 units output at 60 percent = 20,000 units).
2. Dividing the differential cost total between these two levels by the added number of units ($99,150 ÷ 20,000 units = $4.96).

Differential cost studies are typically short-term in orientation; i.e., they generally involve activities that do not extend beyond one year. If the alternatives being evaluated extend beyond one year, the capital budgeting evaluation techniques discussed in Chapters 23 and 24 should be used. Some

FLEXIBLE BUDGET FOR DIFFERENT RATES OF OUTPUT
(100,000 Units = 100% Normal Capacity)

Capacity	60%	80%	100%	120%
Variable costs				
Direct manufacturing costs:				
Direct materials	$102,000	$136,000	$170,000	$204,000
Direct labor	93,000	124,000	155,000	186,000
Total	$195,000	$260,000	$325,000	$390,000
Indirect manufacturing costs:				
Heat	$ 720	$ 960	$ 1,200	$ 1,440
Light and power	1,440	1,920	2,400	2,880
Repairs and maintenance	2,460	3,280	4,100	4,920
Supplies	1,260	1,680	2,100	2,520
Indirect labor	9,120	12,160	15,200	18,240
Total	$ 15,000	$ 20,000	$ 25,000	$ 30,000
Commercial expenses:				
Clerical help	$ 11,580	$ 15,440	$ 19,300	$ 23,160
Wages, general	6,960	9,280	11,600	13,920
Supplies	1,260	1,680	2,100	2,520
Total	$ 19,800	$ 26,400	$ 33,000	$ 39,600
Fixed costs (within ranges)				
Indirect manufacturing costs:				
Foremen	$ 15,250	$ 20,500	$ 20,500	$ 25,750
Superintendent	15,000	15,000	15,000	17,750
Setup crew	5,000	7,500	7,500	8,500
Depreciation and rent	8,000	9,400	9,400	9,400
Insurance	2,600	2,600	2,600	2,600
Total	$ 45,850	$ 55,000	$ 55,000	$ 64,000
Commercial expenses:				
Executives	$ 28,000	$ 35,000	$ 35,000	$ 40,000
Assistants	11,200	16,400	16,400	19,200
Property tax	3,400	3,400	3,400	3,400
Advertising	6,000	7,200	7,200	8,600
Total	$ 48,600	$ 62,000	$ 62,000	$ 71,200
Total cost	$324,250	$423,400	$500,000	$594,800
Units of output	60,000	80,000	100,000	120,000
Average unit cost	$5.40	$5.29	$5.00	$4.96
Differential cost total		$99,150	$76,600	$94,800
Differential cost per unit		$4.96	$3.83	$4.74

examples of short-term decisions that may require differential cost analysis include:

1. Accepting or refusing certain orders.
2. Reducing the price of a single, special order.
3. Making a price cut in a competitive market.
4. Evaluating make-or-buy alternatives.
5. Expanding, shutting down, or eliminating a facility.
6. Increasing, curtailing, or stopping production of certain products.
7. Determining whether to sell or process further.
8. Choosing among alternative routings in product manufacture.
9. Determining the maximum price that can be paid for raw materials.

Accepting Additional Orders

Differential cost is the cost that must be considered when a decision involves a change in output. The differential cost of added production is the difference between the cost of producing the present smaller output and that of the contemplated, larger output. If available capacity is not fully utilized, a differential cost analysis might indicate the possibility of selling additional output at a figure lower than the existing average unit cost. The new or additional business can be accepted as long as the variable cost is recovered, since any contribution to the recovery of fixed cost and profit is desirable.

To illustrate, assume that a plant has a maximum capacity of 100,000 units, but normal capacity production is set at 80,000 units, or 80 percent of maximum capacity. At this level, the predetermined overhead rate is computed so that fixed expenses are fully absorbed when operating at the 80,000-unit level. If fewer units are produced, unabsorbed fixed overhead results. If more units are produced, fixed overhead is overabsorbed. If this company makes only one unit, its cost would be:

Variable cost..........................	$	5 per unit
Total fixed cost.....................	100,000	for this unit
Total.................................	$100,005	

At normal capacity, the fixed cost per unit is reduced to $1.25 ($100,000 ÷ 80,000 units), and the total cost per unit is:

Variable cost................................	$5.00
Share of fixed cost.....................	1.25
Total..	$6.25

If additional capacity can be utilized to produce an additional 1,000 units, the unit cost of these units—the differential cost—would be only the $5 variable cost, unless the units require additional fixed expense outlays. An income statement comparing present operating results with the total results after additional units are produced and sold might appear as follows:

	Present Business	With Additional Business
Sales...	$720,000	$729,000
Variable cost................................	400,000	405,000
Contribution margin.....................	$320,000	$324,000
Fixed cost.....................................	100,000	100,000
Profit[1]..	$220,000	$224,000

The additional business requires variable cost only, since the capacity cost (i.e., the fixed cost) indicates that adequate unused capacity is available to handle the additional business. If the 1,000 units are sold at any price above the $5 variable cost, the sale will yield a positive contribution margin.

---

[1]The term "profit" in this discussion denotes operating income before income tax.

The illustration above can also be presented in the following manner to highlight the differential revenue of $9,000 and cost of $5,000:

	Present Business	Additional Business	Total
Sales...	$720,000	$9,000	$729,000
Variable cost..................................	400,000	5,000	405,000
Contribution margin.......................	$320,000	$4,000	$324,000
Fixed cost......................................	100,000	—0—	100,000
Profit..	$220,000	$4,000	$224,000

Reducing the Price of a Special Order

Differential cost analysis is an aid to management in deciding at what price the firm can afford to sell additional goods. To illustrate, assume that a company manufactures 450,000 units, using 90 percent of its normal capacity. The fixed factory overhead is $335,000, which is $.67 ($335,000 ÷ 500,000 units) for each unit manufactured when operations are at 100 percent of normal capacity. The variable factory overhead rate is $.50 per unit. The direct materials cost is $1.80, and the direct labor cost is $1.40 per unit. Each unit sells for $5. Marketing as well as general and administrative expenses are omitted to simplify the illustration. On the basis of these data, the accountant would prepare the following statement:

Sales (450,000 units @ $5)..		$2,250,000
Cost of goods sold:		
Direct materials (450,000 units @ $1.80).........................	$810,000	
Direct labor (450,000 units @ $1.40)...............................	630,000	
Variable factory overhead (450,000 units @ $.50).........................	225,000	
Fixed factory overhead (450,000 units @ $.67).............................	301,500	1,966,500
Income from operations..		$ 283,500
Unabsorbed fixed factory overhead [(500,000 units—450,000 units) @ $.67]..		33,500
Income from operations (adjusted).......................................		$ 250,000

The sales department reports that a customer has offered to pay $4.25 per unit for an additional 100,000 units. To make the additional units, an annual rental cost of $10,000 for new equipment would be incurred. The accountant computes the gain or loss on this order as follows:

Sales (100,000 units @ $4.25).......................................		$425,000
Cost of goods sold:		
Direct materials (100,000 units @ $1.80).........................	$180,000	
Direct labor (100,000 units @ $1.40)...............................	140,000	
Variable factory overhead (100,000 units @ $.50).....................	50,000	
Fixed factory overhead (100,000 units @ $.67).........................	67,000	437,000
Loss on this order...		$ 12,000

The accountant's computation would cause management to reject the offer. In this computation, all cost elements use the existing unit costs, and fixed overhead is allocated on the basis of the established rate ($.67 per unit). A second look, however, reveals the following effect of the new order on total fixed factory overhead:

Fixed factory overhead (at present)..		$335,000
Fixed factory overhead (because of additional business).....................		10,000
Total fixed factory overhead..		$345,000
Fixed factory overhead charged into production:		
For 450,000 units (old business)...	$301,500	
For 100,000 units (additional business)...	67,000	368,500
Overabsorbed fixed factory overhead...		$ 23,500

Instead of underabsorbed fixed factory overhead of $33,500, the additional business would result in overabsorbed factory overhead of $23,500 or a net composite gain of $57,000 ($67,000 − $10,000) in absorbed factory overhead. This $57,000 minus the computed $12,000 loss on the order results in a gain of $45,000, as shown in the following statement, which includes only the differential costs and revenue:

Sales (100,000 units @ $4.25)..		$425,000
Cost of goods sold:		
Direct materials (100,000 units @ $1.80)....................................	$180,000	
Direct labor (100,000 units @ $1.40)...	140,000	
Variable factory overhead (100,000 units @ $.50)....................	50,000	
Additional fixed cost to produce this order.................................	10,000	380,000
Gain on this order...		$ 45,000

The unit cost of the additional units can be computed as follows:

$$\frac{\text{Cost of goods sold}}{\text{Additional units}} = \frac{\$380,000}{100,000} = \$3.80 \text{ per additional unit}$$

Whenever a differential cost analysis leads management to accept an additional order at or above the differential cost, it is assumed that the order is not going to disturb the market of the other products being offered. The additional business may involve a product presently marketed by the firm, or a product that can be manufactured with existing facilities and personnel. If these products are placed in a competitive market, they might have to be marketed at established prices. Otherwise, competitors might retaliate by cutting prices to an unprofitable and therefore undesirable level, considering all relevant cost and market factors. The firm must also be careful not to violate the Robinson-Patman Act (discussed in Chapter 25) and other governmental pricing restrictions.

Make-Or-Buy Decisions

Another phase of alternative actions is the problem of whether to make or buy component parts or a finished product. The importance of the make-or-buy decision is evidenced by the fact that almost all manufacturing firms at some time during the course of their operations will have to make such a decision. The choice of whether to manufacture an item internally or purchase it on the outside can be applied to a wide variety of decisions that are often major determinants of profitability and that can be significant to the company's financial health.

The objective of a make-or-buy decision should be to best utilize the firm's productive and financial resources. The problem often arises in connection with the possible use of idle equipment, idle space, and even idle labor. In such situations, a manager is inclined to consider making certain units instead of buying them in order to utilize existing facilities and to maintain work-force stability. Commitments of new resources may also be involved.

Despite its importance, studies indicate that surprisingly few firms give adequate objective study to their make-or-buy problems.[2] Not only is this type of decision important to the firm, but it is also complicated by a host of factors, both financial (quantitative) and nonfinancial (qualitative) that must be considered. Faced with a make-or-buy decision, the manager should:

1. Consider the quantity, quality, and dependability of supply of the items as well as the technical know-how required, weighing such requirements for both the short-run and long-run period.
2. Compare the cost of making the items with the cost of buying them.
3. Compare the making of the items with possibly more profitable alternative uses that could be made of the firm's own facilities if the items are purchased.
4. Consider differences in the required capital investment and the timing of cash flows (Chapters 23 and 24).
5. Adopt a course of action related to the firm's overall policies. Customers' and suppliers' reactions often play a part in these decisions. Retaliation or ill will could result. Whether it is profitable to make or buy depends upon the circumstances surrounding the individual situation.

The accountant should present a statement that compares the company's cost of making the items with the vendor's price. The statement should present the differential costs of the item as well as a share of existing fixed expenses and a profit figure that places the total cost on a comparable basis. The budget should also be restated to indicate the effect on total costs and total profit when existing fixed costs are allocated to the additional items.

A cost study with only the differential costs and with no allocation of existing fixed overhead or of profit indicates possible cost savings in the short run. In practice, such studies seem to favor the making of the items in the majority of cases. However, if management were asked to sell the items at the differential price, it might be unwilling to do so, since, in the long run, the full cost must be covered and a reasonable profit achieved. Furthermore, if there is only a slight advantage in favor of making, the item will likely be purchased because more reliance will be put on a known cost to buy rather than an estimated cost to make.[3]

---

[2]Anthony J. Gambino, *The Make-or-Buy Decision* (New York: National Association of Accountants and Hamilton, Ontario: The Society of Management Accountants of Canada, 1980), pp. 9-10.

[3]*Ibid.*, p. 21.

A study by the National Association of Accountants makes the following observations about cost considerations:

To evaluate the alternatives properly, costs to make vs. costs to buy must be based on the same underlying assumptions. Thus, costs for each of the alternatives must be based on the identical product specifications, quantities, and quality standards.

Determination of the "cost to buy" cannot be limited to existing costs shown on supplier invoices. The competitive nature of supplier pricing requires that current optimum third-party prices based upon identical specifications and quantities be used for evaluation of this alternative. There are many examples of lower prices being obtained from suppliers for larger quantities, standardization of specifications, etc., as well as from the use of competitive bids and/or the threat of self-manufacture. All direct and indirect costs of functions and facilities which are properly allocable to the "buy" alternative, under the "full cost" concept, must be considered. Cost to buy must also include the "full cost" to bring the product to the same condition and location as if self-manufactured—including freight, handling, purchasing, incoming inspection, inventory carrying costs, etc.

Determination of the "cost to make" cannot be limited to those identified as manufacturing costs or used in the valuation of inventories. All direct and indirect costs of functions and facilities which are properly allocable to self-manufacture under the "full cost" concept must be considered.

It is concluded that in the case of short-run decisions, differential costs become more significant. However, . . . it is recommended that the long-term and full-cost consideration also be developed. The short-term judgments can then be properly evaluated against the alternative choices which will be required at a later date.

The long-term nature of most make-or-buy decisions requires that cost determinations not only consider present costs but also projections of future costs resulting from inflationary factors, technological changes, productivity, mechanization, etc. More specifically, the projection of the future cost to make and the cost to buy must give full consideration to what the costs "should be" under obtainable conditions and reflect all possible improvements—not just what may be achieved under existing operating conditions.[4]

Decisions to Shut Down Facilities

Differential cost analysis is also used when a business is confronted with the possibility of a shutdown of both manufacturing and marketing facilities. In the short run, a firm seems to be better off operating than not operating, as long as the products or services sold recover the variable cost and make a contribution toward the recovery of the fixed cost. A shutdown of facilities does not eliminate all costs. Depreciation, interest, property tax, and insurance continue during complete inactivity.

If operations are continued, certain expenses connected with the shutting down of the facilities would be saved. Furthermore, costs that would have to be incurred when a closed facility is reopened can be saved. Management might also consider the investment in the training of the active employees, which would be lost in the event of a shutdown. Morale of other employees, as well as community goodwill, may be adversely affected, and the recruiting and training of new workers would add to present costs. The loss of established markets is also a factor, since reentering a market requires a reeducation of the consumers of the company's products.

---

[4]*NAA Statement, No. 5*, "Criteria for Make-or-Buy Decisions" (New York: National Association of Accountants, June 21, 1973), pp. 5-8.

To orient management regarding the possible steps to be taken, the accountant might again resort to the flexible budget to determine the effects of continuing operations as long as differential costs or any amount above them can be secured. This does not mean, however, that the volume set in the budget should be considered final. In view of probable prices, the most advantageous operating level can be determined only by considering several different volume levels.

Decisions to Discontinue Products[5]

While an entire facility may not be closed or eliminated, management may decide to discontinue certain individual products because they are producing no profit or an inadequate profit. Decisions to discontinue products require careful analysis of relevant differential cost and revenue data through a structured and continuous product evaluation program. Several benefits can accrue from an effectively administered evaluation program that has as its objective the timely identification of products that should be eliminated or that can be made more profitable through appropriate corrective action. These benefits include:

1. Expanded sales.
2. Increased profits.
3. Reduced inventory levels.
4. Executive time freed for more profitable activities.
5. Important and scarce resources, such as facilities, materials, and labor, made available for more promising projects.
6. Greater management concern with why products get into difficulty or fail, thus enabling the institution of policies that will reduce the rate of product failure.

Care must be taken not only to consider the profitability of the product being analyzed but also to evaluate the extent to which sales of other products will be adversely affected when one product is removed. If the sales decrease of related products is severe enough, it might be desirable to retain the product being scrutinized.

Management needs data that will permit development of warning signals for products that may be in trouble. Such warning signals include:

1. Declining sales volume.
2. Product sales volume decreasing as a percentage of the firm's total sales.
3. Decreasing market share.
4. Malfunctioning of the product or introduction of a superior competitive product.
5. Past sales volume not up to projected amounts.

---

[5]This discussion is adapted from Stanley H. Kratchman, Richard T. Hise, and Thomas A. Ulrich, ''Management's Decision To Discontinue a Product,'' *The Journal of Accountancy*, Vol. 139, No. 6, pp. 50-54.

6. Expected future sales and market potential not favorable.
7. Return on investment below a minimum acceptable level.
8. Variable cost which approaches or exceeds revenue.
9. Various costs as a percentage of sales consistently increasing.
10. Increasingly greater percentage of executive time required.
11. Price which must be constantly lowered to maintain sales.
12. Promotional budgets which must be consistently increased to maintain sales.

Studies have shown that firms often do a poor job of identifying products that are in difficulty and should be eliminated. Probably the major deficiency is the lack of timely, relevant data. To determine what data are required for a successful product monitoring program and its effective implementation and operation, management must draw on the accountant's experience and expertise.

The conditions that bring about the need to evaluate products or facilities may be permanent or even long-term in nature. If profitable alternative asset usage is not foreseen, asset divestment may be needed.[6]

Additional Applications of Differential Cost Analysis

In the following pages, differential cost analysis is applied to the alternatives which confront the management of an oil refinery. The hypothetical cases, which illustrate the methods that may be employed in solving such problems, demonstrate additional examples of differential cost analysis and can be generalized for other industry settings.[7]

The oil refining industry is characterized by processes that require management to choose between alternatives at various points during the processes. The basic function of oil refining is the separation, extraction, and chemical conversion of the crude oil's component elements, employing skillful utilization of heat, pressure, and catalytic principles. The basic petroleum products are obtained through a physical change caused by the application of heat through a wide temperature range. Within a temperature differential of 300° (275°F to 575°F), the different liquid products, called fractions, ends, or cuts, pass off as vapors and are then condensed back into liquids. The initial application of heat drives off the lightest fractions—the naphthas and gasoline; the successively heavier fractions, such as kerosene and fuel oil, follow as the temperature rises. This process of vaporizing the crude oil and condensing the gaseous vapors to obtain the various cuts is commonly referred to as primary distillation.

---

[6]For an expanded development of this topic, see Douglas M. Lambert, *The Product Abandonment Decision* (Montvale, N.J.: National Association of Accountants, and Hamilton, Ontario: The Society of Management Accountants of Canada, 1985).

[7]Adapted from a study prepared by John L. Fox, later published in *NA(C)A Bulletin*, Vol. XXXI, No. 4, pp. 403-413, under the title, "Cost Analysis Budget to Evaluate Operating Alternatives for Oil Refiners."

Certain cuts (such as straight-run gasoline) are marketable with but little treating. Other products may undergo further processing in order to make them more salable. Thus, heavier fractions, such as kerosene and fuel oil, may be subjected to cracking, which will cause them to yield more valuable products such as gasoline. Cracking is a process during which, by the use of high temperatures and pressures and perhaps in the presence of a catalyst, a heavy fraction is subjected to destructive distillation and converted to a lighter hydrocarbon possessing different chemical characteristics, one of which is a lower boiling point. The heaviest of the fractions resulting from primary distillation is known as residuum or heavy bottoms. This residuum, after further processing, treating, and blending, forms lubricating oils and ancillary wax or asphalt products.

The management of a refinery must decide what to do with each distillate or fraction and at what stage of refining each should be sold; whether additional fractions should be bought from other refineries and what price should be paid for the additional units; or whether the company should enlarge the plant in order to handle a greater volume. They must also determine what alternate courses should be taken in order to break into the most profitable market at the moment.

The accountant can help management through the preparation of flexible budgets for the secondary operating departments in which further processing might take place. These departmental flexible budgets are called *cost analysis budgets*. They differ from the flexible budget used for control purposes in several respects: (1) all expenses are included in the analysis budget; (2) budgeted expenses of service departments are allocated to operating departments at corresponding capacity levels; and (3) their aim is to discover the departmental differential costs.

The amounts stated for each class of expense at each production level are computed on separate work sheets, in which various individual expenses are separated into their fixed and variable elements. This separation is necessary to arrive at the estimated expenses for each level of production.

Analysis budgets for various activities for the following departments, which represent secondary processing or finishing operations, are prepared:

Treating	Solvent Extraction
Filters and Burners	Wax Specialties
Cracking	Canning
Solvent Dewaxing	Barrel House

The analysis budget for cracking fuel oil in the Cracking Department is as shown at the top of page 652.

Sell or Process Further. A refiner has on hand 20,000 gallons of fuel oil and must decide whether to sell it as fuel oil or crack it into gasoline and residual fuel oil. The following current prices per gallon are available:

Fuel oil.....................	$1.40
Gasoline....................	1.68

ANALYSIS BUDGET

Department: Cracking

Period Budgeted: _____ to _____

Supervisor:_____

Normal Capacity (100%) 100,000 gallons through-put of fuel oil

	Shut-Down	60%	80%	100%	120%
Direct expenses....................................	$6,000	$14,000	$16,000	$17,000	$23,000
Allocated expenses (fixed and variable)	1,000	2,000	3,000	4,000	6,000
Total cost...	$7,000	$16,000	$19,000	$21,000	$29,000
Through-put:					
Total gallons....................................		60,000	80,000	100,000	120,000
Differential gallons............................		60,000	20,000	20,000	20,000
Differential cost...................................		$9,000	$3,000	$2,000	$8,000
Unit differential cost.............................		$ .150	$ .150	$ .100	$.4000
Unit average cost..................................		$ .267	$ .238	$ .210	$.2417

Cracking analysis budget:
  Present operations, 80% of normal capacity
  Differential cost (80% to 100%) = $.10 per input gallon
Cracking yields: 75% gasoline; 15% residual fuel oil; 10% loss

The refiner can then prepare the following differential income computation, utilizing the Cracking Department analysis budget:

Potential revenue—products from cracking:		
Gasoline (15,000 gallons @ $1.68)...	$25,200	
Fuel oil (3,000 gallons @ $1.40)...	4,200	
	$29,400	
Less differential cost (20,000 gallons @ $.10)................................	2,000	$27,400
Net potential revenue—fuel oil (20,000 gallons @ $1.40).....................		28,000
Loss from cracking of fuel oil...		$ 600*

*Not an accounting loss per se, but a loss of profit that would result from an improper choice of alternatives.

Thus, judging from a quantitative standpoint, it would be more profitable to sell the 20,000 gallons of fuel oil as such rather than to process them further.

Choice of Alternate Routings. A refiner is trying to decide whether to treat and sell the kerosene fraction or to crack it for its gasoline content. The current decision involves 10,000 gallons of raw kerosene. Pertinent available information follows (from an analysis budget for cracking kerosene):

Current prices per gallon:	
Kerosene...	$1.20
Gasoline..	1.68
Fuel oil..	1.40
Cracking yields:	
Gasoline..	85%
Residual fuel oil..	5
Loss..	10
Differential costs associated with potential gallons through-put of kerosene:	
Cracking..	$.12 per gallon
Treating...	.08

Using the above amounts, the refiner can prepare the following analysis:

Net potential revenue—products from cracking:
Gasoline (8,500 gallons @ $1.68)..	$14,280	
Fuel oil (500 gallons @ $1.40)..	700	
	$14,980	
Less differential cost (10,000 gallons @ $.12)................	1,200	$13,780

Net potential revenue—kerosene:
Total revenue (10,000 gallons @ $1.20)............................	$12,000	
Less differential cost (10,000 gallons @ $.08)................	800	11,200
Gain from cracking rather than treating.................................		$ 2,580

In this situation, the more profitable alternative is to crack the kerosene fraction.

Price To Pay for an Intermediate Stock. A refiner has been offered 10,000 gallons of cylinder stock. The usual bargaining process will determine the final price. The refiner is interested in knowing how high a price it can pay and still make a profit. The stock purchased would be processed into conventional bright stock and sold at that stage, since the blending unit for making finished motor oils is currently working at full capacity. Available information is as follows:

Cylinder stock is of such a quality and type that it will probably yield:
   90% bright stock
   5% petrolatum
   5% loss
Current prices: bright stock, $1 per gallon; petrolatum—no market

Differential costs associated with processing 10,000 gallons of cylinder stock through several units (from analysis budgets) are:

Solvent dewaxing......................	$.06 per gallon
Solvent extracting....................	.06
Filtering......................................	.03
Total..	$.15 per gallon

Using this information, the refiner's position can be analyzed and a bargaining margin can be determined:

Revenue—bright stock (9,000 gallons @ $1)......................	$9,000
Differential cost (10,000 gallons @ $.15)............................	1,500
Margin...	$7,500
Margin per gallon of cylinder stock......................................	$ .75

The refiner is now ready to bargain for the purchase of the cylinder stock, knowing that a purchase price of $.75 a gallon represents a critical maximum point—to pay more would produce a loss, to pay less would result in a gain. Management can then decide how much profit is required to justify the purchase. Here the concept of opportunity costs also enters into the final decision. If the available capacity could be more profitably used for another purpose, then perhaps the proposed purchase should not be consummated.

Proposed Construction of Additional Capacity. A refiner discovers that the market for finished neutrals is such that present capacity will not satsify the demand. The refiner feels certain that an addition to the solvent dewaxing and solvent extracting units would prove profitable. The additional wax distillate stock required would be purchased on the open market at the current rate. However, before going ahead with the construction, the chief accountant is consulted and presents the following information.

Unit differential cost:
    Capacity from 100% (normal) to 120% (increase of 10,000 gallons through-put)
        Solvent Dewaxing Department—$.10 per gallon through-put
        Solvent Extracting Department—$.10 per gallon through-put
Assumed yield from wax distillate:
    90% Viscous neutral
    1.5% Paraffin (8 pounds per gallon)
    8.5% Loss
Current market prices:
    Viscous neutrals—$1.50 per gallon
    Paraffin—$.24 per pound
    Wax distillate stock—$1.20 per gallon*

*Not a published market price but the price management believes it will have to pay to acquire the stock.

Using this information, the following analysis is prepared:

Differential revenue:
    9,000 gallons viscous neutrals @ $1.50... $13,500
    1,200 pounds paraffin @ $.24..   288
                                                                                                    $13,788
    Less cost of wax distillate stock (10,000 gallons @ $1.20).....................   12,000
Margin to apply against differential costs... $1,788
Differential costs:
    Solvent Dewaxing Department (10,000 gallons @ $.10)........................... $ 1,000
    Solvent Extracting Department (10,000 gallons @ $.10)..........................   1,000   2,000
Potential loss from differential production... $ 212

The accountant's analysis indicates that the proposed increase in the productive capacity would not be justified under the stated conditions. Furthermore, even a potential profit should yield a satisfactory return on the additional capital investment.

▼ QUANTITATIVE TECHNIQUES IN DIFFERENTIAL COST ANALYSIS

Differential cost studies are often involved in determining the most profitable short-run use of available capacity. Quantitative techniques, such as linear programming and probability analysis, are analytical tools that can be used in such studies to improve the quality of management decisions. Quantitative techniques aid management by giving structure to a decision problem, which helps the decision maker to include the relevant decision variables in the analysis and to weight properly the impact of each variable on the problem.

Linear Programming

A short-term resource allocation problem may become rather complex and involved when several products are involved and numerous constraints are imposed. One approach to solving the problem would be for the decision maker to model the production process and to make an educated guess about the appropriate level of inputs and outputs. Alternatively, after modeling the production process, the decision maker could input numerous different combinations of decision variables and select the combination that results in the best outcome from among those combinations evaluated. Microcomputer spreadsheets with cell linking and automatic recalculation features provide readily accessible tools for such a trial and error approach. However, the decision maker using such an approach may spend a great deal of time searching for the best combination of decision variables and still miss the optimum solution to the problem. In contrast to the trial and error approach, linear programming is a quantitative decision tool that will permit the decision maker to find the optimum solution to a short-term resource allocation problem without guessing. Chapter 22 is devoted entirely to this important mathematical technique.

Probability Analysis

In practice most decisions are based on a single best guess about the future value of each decision variable relevant to the decision problem. Although decision makers recognize that the future is uncertain, formal attempts to incorporate uncertainty into the decision are rarely made. Instead, the problem of uncertainty is usually handled by tempering the decision with business judgment and a "feel" for the uncertainty inherent in the relevant data. As a result, many biased and naive decisions are made.

Probability analysis is one approach to incorporating uncertainty specifically into the decision process. Probability analysis is an application of statistical decision theory that, under conditions of uncertainty, leads to more consistent and reliable decisions than single best guesses. Probabilities, based on available information, are utilized to reduce the amount of uncertainty present in the decision problem.

Technically, a probability is a number between 0 and 1 that represents the likelihood of the occurrence of a particular event. A probability may be thought of as the relative frequency of the occurrence of different recurring events. The probability is operational in the sense that historical events exhibit a frequency pattern, or conceptual in the sense that future events are expected to follow some frequency pattern. Alternatively, a probability may be thought of as the degree of belief about the outcome of a nonrecurring future event, such as the probability that the government will deregulate a particular industry before the end of the year. In either case, the probabilities are no more accurate than the data or subjective estimates upon which they are based. Nevertheless, the specific incorporation of probabilities into the decision process provides a systematic way to evaluate the effect of alternative outcomes on complex decision problems.

In some decision settings, a wealth of reasonably reliable historical data permits the assignment of fairly objective probabilities. As long as the underlying process that generates the decision variable does not change, historical data can be used to model the probability distribution. For example, the actual historical demand for a particular product may be a good predictor of the future demand as long as consumer tastes and preferences, the capacity of consumers to purchase the product, and the price and availability of competitive products do not change. If competitors introduce a new and better product, however, future demand for the old product is likely to decline, which in turn would mean that the frequency distribution of historic demand would not be a very reliable model of the probability distribution of future demand.

To illustrate the use of probabilities in decision making under uncertainty, assume that a company's contribution margin is $10 per unit sold. A study of a 40-month period reveals that sales demand is random; i.e., demand is irregular, with no discernible trend or pattern. Assuming that no change is expected in the underlying process that generates demand for the product (i.e., the action of competitors and the capacity and desire of consumers to purchase the product are not expected to change), experience is a reasonable basis for predicting the future. The relative frequency of the occurrence of each level of sales demand during the sample period can be used as a measure of the probability of the occurrence of each level of sales demand in the future [denoted as $P(x_i)$, where x_i is the ith event, i.e., level of sales demand]. The sum of the probabilities of all possible events must equal one, i.e., $\Sigma P(x_i) = 1$. Otherwise, some event other than those included in the distribution could occur.

Once the probability distribution for demand has been determined, the expected contribution margin from sales of the product [E(X), referred to as the expected value] is determined by adding the products of the contribution margin for each possible level of sales (x_i, referred to as the conditional value) multiplied by the relative probability of its occurrence, $P(x_i)$. That is, $E(X) = \Sigma[x_i \, P(x_i)]$, and the computation is illustrated as follows:

(1) Units of Sales per Month	(2) Historical Frequency in Months	(3) $P(x_i)$ Probability	(4) Contribution Margin per Unit	(5) x_i Conditional Value (1) × (4)	(6) E(X) Expected Value (3) × (5)
4,000	8	8/40 = .20	$10	$40,000	$ 8,000
5,000	10	10/40 = .25	10	50,000	12,500
6,000	12	12/40 = .30	10	60,000	18,000
7,000	6	6/40 = .15	10	70,000	10,500
8,000	4	4/40 = .10	10	80,000	8,000
	40	40/40 = 1.00			$57,000

The expected value in this illustration may be thought of as the average contribution margin that the company can expect in the future, based on past experience. The expected value is the mean of the probability distribution. If several alternative projects are being evaluated, the alternative with the largest expected value has the largest expected average contribution margin and, consequently, the largest expected total contribution margin in the long run. However, management may be concerned not only about profitability but also about risk.

The *variance* of a probability distribution [denoted σ^2 and defined as $\sigma^2 = \Sigma[P(x_i)\,(x_i - E(X))^2]$ and the *standard deviation* (which is the square root of the variance and is denoted σ) are measures of dispersion which are commonly used as measures of risk. Each provides a numerical measure of the scatter of the possible conditional values around the expected value. The greater the dispersion, the greater the likelihood, and consequently the greater the risk, that the actual value (contribution margin in the illustration) will differ materially from the expected value. Computation of the standard deviation is illustrated as follows:

(1) x_i Conditional Value	(2) $(x_i - E(X))$ Difference from Expected Value ($57,000)	(3) $(x_i - E(X))^2$ (2) Squared	(4) $P(x_i)$ Probability	(5) $P(x_i)\,(x_i - E(X))^2$ (3) × (4)
$40,000	$-17,000	$289,000,000	.20	$ 57,800,000
50,000	-7,000	49,000,000	.25	12,250,000
60,000	3,000	9,000,000	.30	2,700,000
70,000	13,000	169,000,000	.15	25,350,000
80,000	23,000	529,000,000	.10	52,900,000
Variance..				$151,000,000

$$\text{Variance } (\sigma^2) = \$151,000,000$$

$$\text{Standard deviation } (\sigma) = \sqrt{\$151,000,000} = \$12,288$$

If alternative expected values are being compared, such as the expected contribution margins for several different products, the relative riskiness of each alternative cannot be determined by simply comparing standard deviations. Because of the difference in the magnitudes of the expected values, an alternative with a large expected value would be expected to have a larger standard deviation than an alternative with a small expected value. The problem of comparing the relative riskiness of alternatives can be resolved by computing and comparing the *coefficient of variation*, a measure which relates the standard deviation of a probability distribution to its expected value, thereby compensating for differences in the relative size of values involved.

For the illustration above, the coefficient of variation is computed as follows:

$$\text{Coefficient of variation} = \frac{\text{Standard deviation } (\sigma)}{\text{Expected value (contribution margin) } E(X)} = \frac{\$12,288}{\$57,000} = .22$$

If another product were analyzed and an expected contribution margin of $100,000 and a standard deviation of $18,000 resulted, the relative risk as measured by the coefficient of variation would be less than for the product illustrated above [.18 ($18,000 ÷ $100,000) as compared to .22] even though the standard deviation is larger ($18,000 as compared to $12,288).

In this illustration, the number of possible outcomes is small and the probability distribution is discrete. However, when possible outcomes can take on any value within a defined range, a continuous probability distribution may provide a better description of the nature of the variable and be a better basis for prediction. As a practical matter, continuous probability distributions are usually assumed to have some familiar, well-behaved form such as a Poisson, binomial, or normal distribution, thereby making it possible to calculate the parameters of the distribution, such as the mean or expected value and the standard deviation.

Use of Probabilities in Strategy Analysis. Probabilities are especially useful in determining the best strategy under conditions of uncertainty. Where several courses of action are available, a payoff table can be constructed to aid in evaluating available alternatives.

For illustrative purposes, assume that the manager of a bakery must decide how many loaves of bread to bake each day. The normal sales price is $1 a loaf. However, the price of bread which is not sold on the day of delivery is reduced to $.30 a loaf. The variable cost of producing and distributing a loaf of bread is $.40. An additional cost of $.10 is incurred in distributing and selling each loaf which is sold at the reduced price. The unit contribution margin is computed as follows:

Regular sales price..................	$1.00	Reduced sales price........................		$.30
Less variable cost....................	.40	Less: Variable cost.........................	$.40	
Unit contribution margin		Additional distribution cost...	.10	.50
at regular sales price............	$ .60	Unit loss at reduced sales price......		$.20

Over the past 360 days, the company has experienced the following random sales demand (i.e., there are no cycles or trends in sales demand):

Unit Sales per Day	Number of Days	Probability
10,000	72	.20
11,000	108	.30
12,000	144	.40
13,000	36	.10
	360	1.00

Assuming that sales demand in the future is expected to be the same as in the past, a payoff table can be constructed. For each production level strategy, (1) the contribution margin (conditional value) for each unit sales possibility is computed and (2) the expected contribution margin (expected value) is determined, as follows:

Possible Actions (Quantities to be Produced)	Contribution Margin (Conditional Value) for Possible Sales Quantities				Contribution Margin (Expected Value of Each Strategy)
	10,000	11,000	12,000	13,000	
10,000	$6,000*	$6,000	$6,000	$6,000	$6,000
11,000	5,800**	6,600	6,600	6,600	6,440
12,000	5,600	6,400	7,200	7,200	6,640
13,000	5,400	6,200	7,000	7,800	6,520***
Probability	.20	.30	.40	.10	

Payoff Table

*10,000 units at the regular sales price × $.60 = $6,000
**(10,000 units at the regular sales price × $.60) − (1,000 units at the reduced price × $.20 negative contribution margin) = $5,800
***(.20 probability × $5,400) + (.30 probability × $6,200) + (.40 probability × $7,000) + (.10 probability × $7,800) = $6,520

In this situation, the best strategy in the long run would be to produce 12,000 loaves of bread each day, because such a strategy would result in the largest average expected profit.

As in the previous illustration, the standard deviation and the coefficient of variation can be computed for each strategy. For example, the computations for the 12,000-loaf daily production level follow:

(1) x_i Conditional Value	(2) $(x_i - E(X))$ Difference from Expected Value ($6,640)	(3) $(x_i - E(X))^2$ (2) Squared	(4) $P(x_i)$ Probability	(5) $P(x_i)(x_i - E(X))^2$ (3) × (4)
$5,600	$−1,040	$1,081,600	.20	$216,320
6,400	−240	57,600	.30	17,280
7,200	560	313,600	.40	125,440
7,200	560	313,600	.10	31,360
Variance...				$390,400

Standard deviation $(\sigma) = \sqrt{\$390,400} = \$625$

$$\frac{\text{Coefficient}}{\text{of variation}} = \frac{\text{Standard deviation }(\sigma)}{\text{Expected contribution margin } [E(X)]} = \frac{\$625}{\$6,640} = .09$$

Expected Value of Perfect Information. The opportunity may exist to acquire additional information that will be useful in selecting the best alternative. Information, however, like any good or service, is costly. For example, the baker in the illustration above might conduct a market survey which could improve the prediction of consumer demand. However, a market survey would cost money. Before making such a decision, the cost of the additional information should be weighed against the increase in the expected value that can be obtained by using the information. If the increase in the expected value to be derived from the use of the additional information is greater than the cost, the cost should be incurred. Otherwise, it should not.

In actual practice it is difficult to determine the value of information about a future event until the event has occurred. A market survey would probably result in a better estimate of demand but not a perfectly accurate prediction. On the other hand, it is possible to compute the maximum expected value of additional information by computing the expected value under conditions of certainty and comparing it with the expected value of the best strategy under uncertainty. The expected value under conditions of certainty is the expected value assuming that the probability distribution is an accurate representation of the relative frequency of future demand and that the decision maker knows exactly when each possible event will occur. The maximum increase in the expected value that could be obtained from additional information is the expected value of perfect information and, consequently, the maximum amount one would be willing to pay for additional information.

For the bakery illustration, the expected value of perfect information is the difference between (1) the average contribution margin if the manager knew the sales demand for bread each day with certainty (and consequently produced exactly the amount demanded) and (2) the average expected contribution margin using the best strategy under uncertainty. The expected value of perfect information is determined as follows:

(1) Unit Sales per Day	(2) Contribution Margin per Unit	(3) x_i Contribution Margin (Conditional Value)	(4) $P(x_i)$ Probability	(5) E(X) Contribution Margin (Expected Value)
10,000	$.60	$6,000	.20	$1,200
11,000	.60	6,600	.30	1,980
12,000	.60	7,200	.40	2,880
13,000	.60	7,800	.10	780

Expected value (contribution margin) with perfect certainty..	$6,840
Less the expected value (contribution margin) using the best strategy under uncertainty (production of 12,000 loaves per day)...	6,640
Expected value of perfect information (on a per-day basis).	$ 200

Management could afford to pay up to $200 per day for perfect information because with perfect information the contribution margin would be expected to increase an average of $200 a day. While perfect information is generally not available, this analysis determines the upper limit value of additional information.

Probability Revision. Probabilities should be revised as new information becomes available. One approach to probability revision is an application of Bayes' theorem. However, before presenting Bayes' theorem, the following additional notation is needed:

(1) Let $P(A)$, $P(B)$, and $P(C)$ be the symbols for the probabilities of the occurrence of events A, B, and C, respectively.

(2) Let $P(AB)$ be the symbol for the probability of the occurrence of both event A and event B, and let $P(BC)$ be the symbol for the probability of the occurrence of both event B and event C.

(3) Let $P(A|B)$ be the symbol for the probability of the occurrence of event A given the occurrence of event B, $P(B|A)$ be the symbol for the

probability of the occurrence of event B given the occurrence of event A, and P(B|C) be the probability of the occurrence of event B given the occurrence of event C.

P(AB) and P(BC) are referred to as joint probabilities. P(A|B), P(B|A), and P(B|C) are referred to as conditional probabilities; i.e., the events enclosed in parentheses are not independent, but instead, are related in some way. If P(A|B) < 1.0 and P(B|A) < 1.0, then A may occur without the occurrence of event B, and B may occur without the occurrence of event A, but there is some possibility that both events could occur because there is some logical link between the two events. For example, a company may introduce a new product before the end of the year (event A) without hiring any new employees, and the same company may hire new employees (event B) without introducing a new product, but it is also quite possible that the company may hire new employees in order to have sufficient capacity to be able to produce a new product. In this case, since event A and event B are not independent events, P(AB) = P(B|A)P(A) = P(A|B)P(B); or, in words, the joint probability of A and B (i.e., the occurrence of both events) is equal to the conditional probability of the occurrence of B, given the occurrence of A, multiplied by the probability of the occurrence of A, which is also equal to the conditional probability of the occurrence of A, given the occurrence of B, multiplied by the probability of the occurrence of B.

Now assume that event C is the event that will occur if event A does not occur, i.e., event C is that the company in the example above will not introduce a new product before the end of the year. In this case, event C and event A are mutually exclusive; i.e., the company either will or will not introduce a new product before the end of the year. However, both event C and event B may occur; i.e., the company may hire new employees but not introduce a new product. Since event A or event C must occur along with event B, then the probability of event B occurring would be:

$$P(B) = P(AB) + P(BC)$$

Recall from the discussion above that P(AB) = P(A|B)P(B). The conditional probability of the occurrence of event A, given the occurrence of event B, can be determined by dividing both sides of this equation by P(B), which yields:

$$P(A|B) = \frac{P(AB)}{P(B)}$$

Since P(AB) = P(A|B)P(B) = P(B|A)P(A), then P(B|A)P(A) can be substituted for P(AB) in the numerator on the right-hand side of the equation. Also, since P(B) = P(AB) + P(BC) = P(B|A)P(A) + P(B|C)P(C), then P(B|A)P(A) + P(B|C)P(C) can be substituted in the denominator for P(B). The following equation results:

$$P(A|B) = \frac{P(AB)}{P(B)} = \frac{P(B|A)P(A)}{P(B|A)P(A) + P(B|C)P(C)}$$

Similarly, since P(B|C)P(C) = P(C|B)P(B) = P(BC), the conditional probability of the occurrence of event C can be derived as follows:

$$P(C|B) = \frac{P(BC)}{P(B)} = \frac{P(B|C)P(C)}{P(B|A)P(A) + P(B|C)P(C)}$$

This formulation is Bayes' theorem expressed in its simplest form. Bayes' theorem can be used to revise the original probability estimates for events A and C when new information becomes available (in this case, the occurrence of event B). For this purpose, the term on the left-hand side of the equation (i.e., P(A|B) in the first equation or P(C|B) in the second equation) is the revised estimate of the probability of the occurrence of the event of concern (i.e., the probability that event A will occur in the first equation or that event C will occur in the second equation now that event B has occurred). This revised probability estimate is referred to as a *posterior probability*. P(A) and P(C) are the probability estimates of the occurrences of events A and C, respectively, before event B occurred. Since these estimates were made before the new information became available, they are referred to as *prior probabilities*. P(B|A) and P(B|C) are conditional probabilities that express the expected relationship of the new information to events A and C (i.e., the probability that event B would occur and be followed by event A or C). To revise the probabilities of the occurrence of events A and C using Bayes' theorem, each prior probability is multiplied by the conditional probability associated with the related event and, since the sum of the posterior probabilities must equal the sum of the prior probabilities (i.e., P(A) + P(C) = P(A|B) + P(C|B) = 1.0), the product is divided by the sum of the products of all of the prior probabilities multiplied by the conditional probabilities associated with the related event. In the simple two-event world depicted by the equations above, the numerator would be P(B|A)P(A) for the revision of the probability of the occurrence of event A and P(B|C)P(C) for the revision of the probability of the occurrence of event C. Since A and C are the only two events that can occur, the denominator in both cases would be the sum of these two products [i.e., P(B|A)P(A) + P(B|C)P(C)]. As a result, the sum of the revised probabilities (i.e., P(A|B) + P(C|B) = 1.0) is equal to the sum of the prior probabilities (i.e., P(A) + P(C) = 1.0).

To illustrate the use of Bayes' theorem in the revision of probabilities, assume that the top management of Kotts Company is planning to introduce a new version of their present product in order to expand its present market share. Market surveys indicate that there is a sizeable market for a less expensive version of the product and a smaller, but lucrative, market for a more expensive version. However, rumors are circulating that a competitor will introduce a new version of their product before the end of the year. The introduction of such a product by the competitor would have a material effect on the sales of Kotts Company's products. Based on familiarity with the competitor's previous actions, management assigns the following probabilities to each of the possible events:

	Event	Probability
A	No new product introduced..	.5
B	Less expensive product introduced....................................	.2
C	More expensive product introduced....................................	.2
D	Both a less expensive and a more expensive product introduced...	.1
		1.0

Given (a) expected market demand for the different products, (b) the expected share of each market given the alternative actions available to Kotts Company and the competitor, and (c) the unit contribution margin of each of Kotts Company's products, a payoff table is constructed as follows:

	Events (Actions of Competitor)				
	A	B	C	D	
Kotts Company Actions	No New Product	Less Expensive Product	More Expensive Product	Both Kinds of Products	Expected Value
No new product	$1,000,000	$ 700,000	$ 700,000	$500,000	$ 830,000
Less expensive product	1,300,000	800,000	1,100,000	800,000	1,110,000
More expensive product	1,400,000	1,200,000	800,000	800,000	1,180,000
Both kinds of products	1,500,000	900,000	800,000	700,000	1,160,000
Probability	.50	.20	.20	.10	

Before deciding on a course of action, management finds out that the competitor is hiring engineers (event E). Management believes that there is a .80 probability that the hiring of engineers means that the competitor is planning to manufacture and introduce a more expensive product. This means that there is a .20 probability that the competitor would hire more engineers, even if it had no intention of introducing a new product $[P(E|A) = .20]$, a .20 probability that it would hire more engineers if it were planning to introduce a new less expensive product $[P(E|B) = .20]$, a .80 probability that it would hire more engineers if it were planning to introduce a more expensive product $[P(E|C) = .80]$, and a .80 probability that it would hire more engineers if it were planning to introduce both less and more expensive products $[P(E|D) = .80]$. Based on these newly assessed conditional probabilities, the original probabilities can be revised as follows, using Bayes' theorem:

$$P(A|E) = \frac{P(E|A)P(A)}{P(E|A)P(A) + P(E|B)P(B) + P(E|C)P(C) + P(E|D)P(D)}$$

$$P(B|E) = \frac{P(E|B)P(B)}{P(E|A)P(A) + P(E|B)P(B) + P(E|C)P(C) + P(E|D)P(D)}$$

$$P(C|E) = \frac{P(E|C)P(C)}{P(E|A)P(A) + P(E|B)P(B) + P(E|C)P(C) + P(E|D)P(D)}$$

$$P(D|E) = \frac{P(E|D)P(D)}{P(E|A)P(A) + P(E|B)P(B) + P(E|C)P(C) + P(E|D)P(D)}$$

Events (Actions of Competitor)	(1) Prior Probability	(2) Conditional Probability of Hiring Engineers	(3) Prior Probability Times Conditional Probability (1) × (2)	(4) Posterior Probability (3) ÷ (3) total
A No new product	.50	.20	.10	5/19
B Less expensive product	.20	.20	.04	2/19
C More expensive product	.20	.80	.16	8/19
D Both kinds of products	.10	.80	.08	4/19
	1.00		.38	19/19

Notice that the original values in Column (3) correspond to the numerators in the equations that precede the table, and the Column (3) total corresponds to the denominator in each equation. If more information becomes available before the decision is made, the posterior probabilities would become prior probabilities, and the new conditional probabilities (i.e., the probabilities associated with the new information) would be used to compute new posterior probabilities. Also, notice that the conditional probabilities in column 2 were not totaled. Although each conditional probability must be less than one, the sum of the conditional probabilities need not equal one because they do not represent a collectively exhaustive set of possibilities.

The expected values of the alternative actions being considered by Kotts Company are computed as follows, using the payoff table and the revised probabilities:

Kotts Company Actions	Events (Actions of Competitor)				Expected Value
	A No New Product	B Less Expensive Product	C More Expensive Product	D Both Kinds of Products	
No new product	$1,000,000	$ 700,000	$ 700,000	$500,000	$ 736,842
Less expensive product	1,300,000	800,000	1,100,000	800,000	1,057,895
More expensive product	1,400,000	1,200,000	800,000	800,000	1,000,000
Both kinds of products	1,500,000	900,000	800,000	700,000	973,684
Probability	5/19	2/19	8/19	4/19	

The expected values of the alternatives changed when the probabilities were revised. In this case, the best course of action for Kotts Company also changed from the introduction of a more expensive product to the introduction of a less expensive product.

Decision Trees. Alternatives and their expected results may be portrayed graphically with a decision tree. A decision tree is a graphic representation of the decision points, the alternative actions available to the decision maker, the possible outcomes from each decision alternative along with the related probabilities, and the expected values of each event. A decision tree expedites the evaluation of alternatives by giving the decision maker a visual map of the expected result of each alternative. This kind of analysis is especially useful when sequential decisions are involved.

To illustrate the use of a decision tree in a sequential-decision problem, assume that Wildcat Oil Company is faced with the problem of deciding whether or not to drill a well on a newly acquired lease. Based on statistically available information, the probability of finding oil is .22, and the probability of finding no oil is .78. If oil is found, the company will have a $1,000,000 profit; however, if oil is not found, the company will lose $300,000.

Before deciding whether or not to drill, Wildcat could pay a seismographic service company $50,000 to conduct a seismic test of the proposed site. There is a .2 probability that the seismic test result would be favorable, and a .8 probability that it would not. If the results are favorable, the probability of finding oil would be .7 (with a .3 probability of finding no oil), and if the results are unfavorable, the probability of finding no oil would be .9 (with a .1 probability of finding oil).

In this situation, Wildcat is faced with making two sequential decisions; first, whether or not to purchase a seismic test, and second, whether or not to drill. Based on the data provided, a decision tree can be constructed as shown on page 666.

The decision points, i.e., the points at which the decision maker must choose some action, are denoted with squares. The chance points, i.e., the points at which some event related to the previous decision will occur, are denoted with circles. To determine the best choice of action, the expected values for the last alternatives in the sequence are first determined. Then, the expected values for the next preceding alternatives are determined, assuming that the best decision alternatives for the subsequent decisions are made. This process is sometimes referred to as "backward induction." The expected value of each action is written above the related chance point, and the expected value of the best choice of action is written above the related decision point.

Notice in Wildcat's decision tree that if a seismic test is not purchased, the expected values of drilling and not drilling are a $14,000 loss and $0 profit or loss, respectively. The best course of action, given that a seismic test is not conducted, is not to drill. On the other hand, if a seismic test is conducted, two possible results may occur. If the test result is favorable, the expected values of drilling and not drilling are a $560,000 profit and a $50,000 loss (the cost of the seismic test), respectively. If the test result is unfavorable, the expected values of drilling and not drilling are a $220,000 loss and a $50,000 loss, respectively. If the test result is favorable, the best course of action is to drill. If the test result is unfavorable, the best course of action is not to drill. If the best courses of action are taken, the expected value of conducting a seismic test is a $72,000 profit. Since the expected value of conducting a seismic test exceeds the expected value of no test, the seismic test should be purchased.

More complex decision trees can be constructed to incorporate additional events and additional sequential decisions. For example, if several different quantities of oil may be found, several different payoffs would be possible. In addition, further testing during the drilling process might decrease the uncertainty about the presence or absence of oil, thereby reducing the potential loss once drilling begins.

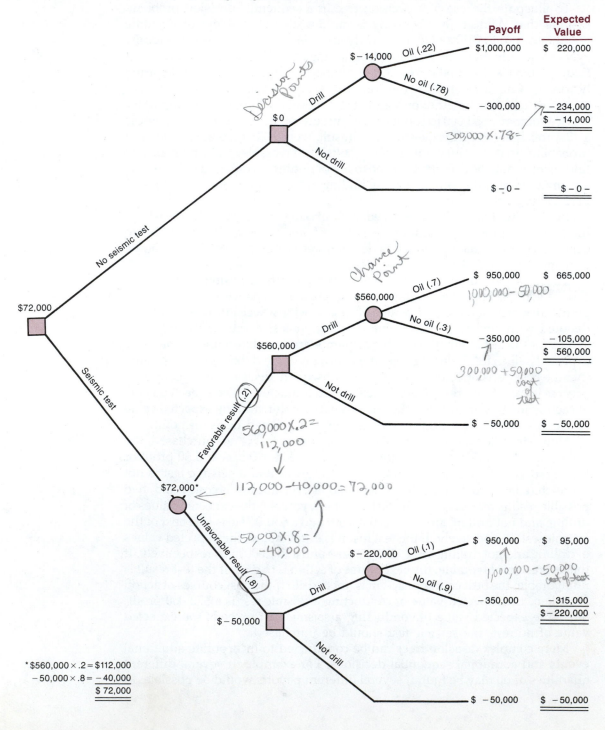

	Payoff	Expected Value
Oil (.22)	$1,000,000	$ 220,000
No oil (.78)	−300,000	−234,000
		$ −14,000

300,000 × .78 =

Decision Points

$−14,000

Drill

$0

Not drill

$ −0 − $ − 0 −

No seismic test

Chance Point

Oil (.7)	$ 950,000	$ 665,000

1,000,000 − 50,000

$560,000

Drill

No oil (.3)	−350,000	−105,000
		$ 560,000

300,000 + 50,000 cost of test

$560,000

Not drill

$ −50,000 $ −50,000

Favorable result (.2)

560,000 × .2 = 112,000

112,000 − 40,000 = 72,000

$72,000

$72,000*

−50,000 × .8 = −40,000

Unfavorable result (.8)

Oil (.1)	$ 950,000	$ 95,000

1,000,000 − 50,000 cost of test

$ −220,000

Drill

No oil (.9)	−350,000	−315,000
		$ −220,000

$ −50,000

Not drill

$ −50,000 $ −50,000

*$560,000 × .2 = $112,000
 −50,000 × .8 = −40,000
                $ 72,000

Seismic test

Monte Carlo Simulations. Many business problems contain variables over which decision makers have little or no control. Such variables may be treated as if they were generated by a stochastic process, i.e., a process that generates events that appear to the decision maker to occur at random. If the decision problem contains many stochastic variables, it becomes complex and difficult (and perhaps in some cases impossible) to evaluate with analytical techniques. In such cases, computer simulation may be a viable alternative. The primary requirement is that the decision problem be one that can be adequately modeled with one or more mathematical equations. Computer simulations that contain stochastic variables are often referred to as *Monte Carlo simulations*.

Monte Carlo simulation utilizes statistical sampling techniques in order to obtain a probabilistic approximation of the outcome of the business system being modeled. The probability distributions of the stochastic variables in the decision problem are simulated in the computer model, using a random number generator. The form of the stochastic processes simulated can be based on historical data or on estimates. The simulation is run numerous times in order to model the output of the business system. Based on the frequency distribution of the simulation results, the decision maker can determine the expected value (i.e., the mean of the simulated probability distribution) and a measure of risk (i.e., the variance and standard deviation) for the decision problem. Monte Carlo simulations are especially useful in planning and evaluating complex new business systems.

DISCUSSION QUESTIONS

1. Give a broad definition of the term "differential cost." What other terms are often used and by whom?

2. Distinguish between marginal cost and marginal costing (or direct costing).

3. Differential costs have also been called alternative costs. Why is the identification of alternative costs important in decision making?

4. Differential costs do not correspond to any possible accounting category. Explain.

5. How does the flexible budget assist in the preparation of differential cost analyses?

6. Why are historical costs usually irrelevant for decision making?

7. Why is variable cost so important in differential cost studies?

8. What are sunk costs?

9. Define opportunity costs.

10. Why should a manager try to assess the probabilities associated with possible outcomes before making a decision under conditions of uncertainty?

11. Define expected value.

12. In what way is the standard deviation of the expected value useful?

13. What is the coefficient of variation, and how is it used in evaluating alternatives?

14. Contrast joint probability and conditional probability.

15. What is a decision tree, and how is it used?

16. What is the purpose of Monte Carlo simulation?

EXERCISES

1. Differential cost. The Baytown Plant of Southwest Casting Company has a normal capacity of 75,000 units per month. At normal capacity, variable cost totals $10 per unit and the monthly fixed cost is $225,000.

Required:

(1) Compute the differential cost of the production between 80% and 90% of normal capacity.
(2) By increasing fixed cost $10,000 per month, the plant can produce 80,000 units. Compute:
   (a) The differential production cost of these 5,000 units.
   (b) The per unit total production cost.
   (c) The per unit differential production cost of these 5,000 units.

2. Analysis of proposed new business. Saugus Insecticide Company is currently producing and selling 30 000 kilograms of Sta Ded monthly. This volume is 70% of capacity for Sta Ded. A wholesaler outside the Saugus marketing area offers to buy 5 000 kilograms of this product per month on a two-year contract at $1.80 per kilogram, provided the present pinkish color can be changed to green. The product will be marketed under the wholesaler's brand name.

To change the color, a special mixing machine will need to be purchased at a cost of $3,000, but it will have no value at the end of the two-year contract period. Ingredients to change the color in the finished product will cost $.01 per kilogram.

Marketing expense will not be increased if the new business is accepted, but additional administrative expense of $150 per month is estimated. No additional cost for supervision or property tax is contemplated. Additional payroll taxes will be $210.

A monthly income statement for the current operations follows:

Sales...		$72,000
Cost to manufacture:		
Direct materials...	$18,000	
Direct labor...	15,000	
Factory overhead:		
Indirect labor..	6,000	
Supervisory labor..	4,000	
Power ($180 fixed)......................................	780	
Supplies..	600	
Maintenance and repair.............................	810	
Depreciation...	3,000	
Insurance...	210	
Property tax..	125	
Payroll taxes...	1,250	
Cost of goods produced and sold....................		49,775
Gross profit..		$22,225
Marketing expense.......................................	$11,000	
Administrative expense...................................	4,500	15,500
Income before income tax...............................		$ 6,725

Required: Prepare a differential cost analysis to show whether the company should accept the proposed new business.

3. Acceptance of a special order. Pacific Palmer Company has been producing and selling 10,000 units of its product per month, with the following total costs:

Direct materials..	$20,000
Direct labor..	35,000
Variable factory overhead...	15,000
Fixed factory overhead..	24,000
Variable marketing and administrative expenses.....................	10,000
Fixed marketing and administrative expenses..........................	13,000

The normal sales price is $15 and plant capacity is 18,000 units. The company has received an offer from a special customer who would like to buy exactly 5,000 units of Pacific Palmer's product for $9 per unit. Marketing and administrative expenses related to this special order would be $1,500.

Required:

(1) Present computations showing whether or not Pacific Palmer should accept this special order.
(2) Determine the effect on the answer to requirement (1) if the plant capacity were only 13,000 units.   *(CGAAC adapted)*

4. Minimum selling price for special order. Braxton Company sells product T5 at a price of $21 per unit. Braxton's cost per unit based on the full capacity of 200,000 units is as follows:

Direct materials..	$ 4
Direct labor...	5
Factory overhead (⅓ variable; ⅔ fixed).....................	6
	$15

A special order offering to buy 20,000 units was received from a foreign distributor. The only selling costs to be incurred on this order would be $2 per unit for shipping. Braxton has sufficient existing capacity to manufacture the additional units, and the foreign distributor does not compete with any of Braxton's regular customers.

Required: In negotiating a price for the special order, what should Braxton consider to be the minimum selling price per unit?   *(AICPA adapted)*

5. Make-or-buy decision. Huntington Products manufactures 10,000 units of Part M-1 annually for use in its production. The following costs are reported:

Direct materials.....................................	$ 20,000
Direct labor..	55,000
Variable factory overhead.....................	45,000
Fixed factory overhead..........................	70,000
	$190,000

Lufkin Company has offered to sell Huntington 10,000 units of Part M-1 annually for $18 per unit. If Huntington accepts the offer, some of the facilities presently used to manufacture Part M-1 could be rented to a third party at an annual rental of $15,000. Additionally, $4 per unit of the fixed factory overhead applied to Part M-1 would be totally eliminated.

Required: Should Huntington accept Lufkin's offer, and why?   *(AICPA adapted)*

6. Make-or-buy decision. Montrose Inc. manufactures Part 345 for use in one of its main products. Normal annual production for Part 345 is 100,000 units. The cost per 100-unit lot of the part follows:

Direct materials...................................	$260
Direct labor..	100
Factory overhead:	
Variable..	120
Fixed..	160
Total cost per 100 units....................	$640

Kalispell Inc. has offered to sell Montrose all 100,000 units it will need during the coming year for $600 per 100 units. If Montrose accepts the offer from Kalispell, the facilities used to manufacture Part 345 could be used in the production of Part 789. This change would save Montrose $90,000 in fixed cost related to the rental of capacity necessary to produce Part 789. In addition, a $50,000 cost item included in fixed factory overhead which is specifically related to Part 345 (rental of special equipment not usable in the manufacture of other products) would be eliminated.

Required: Determine whether or not Montrose Inc. should make Part 345 or buy it from Kalispell Inc. for $600 per unit. *(ICMA adapted)*

7. Sell or process further. Enid Company produces a variety of cleaning compounds and solutions for both industrial and household use. One of its products, a coarse cleaning powder called Grit 337, has a variable manufacturing cost of $1.60 and sells for $2 per pound.

A small portion of this product's annual production is retained for further processing in the Mixing Department, where it is combined with several other ingredients to form a paste which is marketed as a silver polish selling for $4 per jar. The further processing requires one-fourth pound of Grit 337 per jar; other ingredients, labor, and variable factory overhead associated with further processing cost $2.50 per jar, while unit variable marketing cost is $.30. If a decision were made to cease silver polish production, $5,600 of fixed Mixing Department costs could be avoided.

Required: Calculate the minimum number of jars of silver polish that must be sold to justify further processing Grit 337. *(ICMA adapted)*

8. Sell or process further. Martin Products, processor of peanuts, has on hand 50,000 lbs. of peanut hulls. The division producing fertilizer is currently operating at 80% of capacity, which is more than adequate to process the hulls into fertilizer. Current prices for hulls are $44 per ton; for fertilizer, $5 per 50-lb. bag.

The differential cost is $.05 per lb. of finished product. Processing yields 90% fertilizer and 10% loss from the hulls put into the system. Additional materials weighing 5,000 lbs. are to be added during processing.

Required: Prepare an analysis indicating whether Martin should sell or process further.

9. Product alternatives. S.W. Schwarz Company sells two products with the following characteristics:

	Product A	Product B
Quantity sold......................................	100,000 units	50,000 units
Standard cost per unit:		
Fixed..	$10	$20
Variable..	10	40
	$20	$60
Sales price per unit...........................	$30	$54

Required:

  (1) Compute the profit per unit and in total for each product, assuming that the firm operates at normal capacity and that the standard cost and the actual cost are the same.

  (2) Recommend whether the firm should continue its sales of both products, assuming that the fixed cost (in total) will remain the same.

  (3) Recommend a decision to either drop Product B or add Product C, assuming that facilities presently committed to B alternatively could be assigned to C, that the two products are mutually exclusive, and that C has the following characteristics:

Quantity sold......................................	25,000 units
Standard cost per unit:	
Fixed..	$40
Variable..	20
	$60
Sales price per unit...........................	$50

  (4) Compute the opportunity cost associated with Product B and with Product C.

10. New product analysis. Helene's, a high fashion women's dress manufacturer, is planning to market a new cocktail dress for the coming season. Helene's supplies retailers in the east and mid-Atlantic states.

Four yards of material are required to lay out the dress pattern. Some material remains after cutting and can be sold as remnants.

The leftover material could also be used to manufacture a matching cape and handbag. However, if the leftover material is to be used for the cape and handbag, more care will be required in the cutting, which will increase the cutting costs.

The company expects to sell 1,250 dresses if no matching cape and handbag are available. Helene's market research reveals that dress sales will be 20% higher if a matching cape and handbag are available. The market research indicates that the cape and/or handbag will not be sold individually but only as accessories with the dress. The various combinations of dresses, capes, and handbags which are expected to be sold by retailers are as follows:

	Percent of Total
Complete sets of dress, cape, and handbag.....................	70%
Dress and cape...	6
Dress and handbag..	15
Dress only...	9
Total..	100%

The material used in the dress costs $12.50 a yard, or $50 for each dress. The cost of cutting the dress if the cape and handbag are not manufactured is estimated at $20 a dress, and the resulting remnants can be sold for $5 for each dress cut out. If the cape and handbag are to be manufactured, the cutting costs will be increased by $9 per dress. There will be no salable remnants if the capes and handbags are manufactured in the quantities estimated.

The sales prices and the costs to complete the three items once they are cut are as follows:

	Sales Price per Unit	Unit Cost To Complete (Excludes Cost of Material and Cutting Operation)
Dress..........................	$200.00	$80.00
Cape..........................	27.50	19.50
Handbag....................	9.50	6.50

Required:

(1) Calculate Helene's differential contribution margin from manufacturing the capes and handbags in conjunction with the dresses.
(2) Identify any nonquantifiable factors which could influence Helene's management in this decision.   *(ICMA adapted)*

11. Choice of production method. Circutech Company is evaluating the use of AZ-17 Photo Resist for the manufacture of printed circuit boards. The major advantages in the utilization of this process versus the present silk-screen method are:

(a) Anticipated reduced manufacturing cycle and cost due to elimination of the need for silk circuit screens and shorter operator time to produce circuit boards.
(b) Improved ease of registration between front and back patterns.
(c) The ability to achieve finer line widths and closer spacing between circuit paths.

The proposed AZ-17 process is described as follows:
(a) Fabricate through the completion of the drilling and copper plating of inside holes.
(b) Pressure spray AZ-17 Photo Resist on one side, oven bake for 10 minutes, and repeat for other side.
(c) Use the photo negative and expose each side for seven minutes in a Nu-Arc Printer.
(d) Develop in AZ-17 Developer and proceed through normal operations for making printed circuit board.

Total direct labor time for the proposed AZ-17 process is 30 minutes.

The original silk-screen method uses a wire mesh stencil film, screening ink, and frames. The direct labor time to prepare the screen for each circuit board is 1½ hours. The direct labor time to screen patterns on the printed wire board is 20 minutes.

The hourly direct labor rate is $6.50. The monthly cost for materials and for equipment rental and operation needed for the proposed process is $4,000 greater than for the silk-screen method, excluding the direct labor.

The company manufactures 20,000 circuit boards annually.

Required: Compute the annual savings or added cost from changing from the silk-screen method to the new AZ-17 process. (Round off all computations to the nearest dollar.)

12. Expected value of probability distribution. Duguid Company is considering a proposal to introduce a new product, XPL. An outside marketing consultant prepared the following probability distribution describing the relative likelihood of monthly sales volume levels and related income (loss) for XPL:

Monthly Sales Volume	Probability	Income (Loss)
3,000	.05	$(35,000)
6,000	.15	5,000
9,000	.40	30,000
12,000	.30	50,000
15,000	.10	70,000

Required:

(1) Compute the expected contribution margin (expected value).
(2) Compute the standard deviation and the coefficient of variation.

(AICPA adapted)

13. Expected value and coefficient of variation. In planning its budget for the coming year, Princely Company prepared the following payoff probability distribution describing the relative likelihood of monthly sales volume levels and related contribution margins for product A:

Monthly Sales Volume	Contribution Margin	Probability
4,000	$ 80,000	.20
6,000	120,000	.25
8,000	160,000	.30
10,000	200,000	.15
12,000	240,000	.10

Required:

(1) What is the expected value of the monthly contribution margin for product A?
(2) Compute the coefficient of variation for product A. *(AICPA adapted)*

14. Revision of probabilities. Victoria Manufacturing Company plans to introduce a new product known as Quintex. Based on experience and contacts with customers, the vice-president of marketing believes that the demand for Quintex will be between 30,000 and 60,000 units. The following probabilities have been assigned to each possible level of demand:

Demand	Probability
30,000	.10
40,000	.10
50,000	.50
60,000	.30

Before beginning production, the president of the company asked the vice-president of marketing to have the market demand analyzed by an expert system computer program available from a local marketing service company. The program is a market demand analysis model built on the basis of decisions made by several successful experts in the field of market demand analysis. Although the model may overlook some factors unique to the market for Quintex, it captures many important variables and has generally been found to be useful in forecasting product demand. The vice-president complied with the president's request, and the results of the expert system analysis follow:

Demand	Probability
30,000	.20
40,000	.50
50,000	.20
60,000	.10

Required: Using Bayes' theorem, compute the posterior probabilities for the various levels of demand for Quintex, assuming that the demand probabilities generated by the expert's system provide new information (i.e., assume the expert system probabilities are conditional probabilities).

15. Decision tree. A land developer needs to decide which of two parcels of land to bid on for development. The developer assesses the chance of success on bids to be 60% for parcel A and 80% for parcel B. Development of either parcel would take two years, after which time parcel A is expected to generate a profit of $200,000, and parcel B is expected to generate a profit of $100,000. However, if the area where parcel B is located can be rezoned, this parcel could generate a $300,000 profit. Costs of $10,000 would be incurred in preparing and presenting the case for rezoning to the review board. The developer assesses the probability of a successful appeal for rezoning at 50%. An appeal for rezoning would not be undertaken unless parcel B were successfully acquired by bid.

Required: Construct the decision tree for the land developer's problem, and calculate the expected profits for each alternative. On which parcel should the developer place a bid? Should the developer apply for rezoning?   *(CGAAC adapted)*

PROBLEMS

21-1. Special order analysis. Auer Manufacturing Company received an order from Jaycor Company for a piece of special machinery, but just as the machine was completed, Jaycor Company defaulted on the order and forfeited the 10% deposit paid on the $72,500 sales price. Auer's manufacturing manager identified the costs already incurred in the production of the special machinery for Jaycor as follows:

Direct materials used...		$16,600
Direct labor incurred..		21,400
Factory overhead applied:		
Variable..	$10,700	
Fixed...	5,350	16,050
Fixed marketing and administrative expenses.....................		5,405
Total cost...		$59,455

KaTee Corporation would be interested in buying the special machinery if it is reworked to KaTee's specifications. Auer offered to sell the reworked special machinery to KaTee for a net price of $68,400. The additional identifiable costs to rework the machinery to the specifications of Katee are as follows:

Direct materials.....................	$ 6,200
Direct labor...........................	4,200
	$10,400

A second alternative available to Auer is to convert the special machinery to the standard model, which lists for $62,500. The additional identifiable costs to make the conversion are:

Direct materials.....................	$2,850
Direct labor...........................	3,300
	$6,150

A third alternative for Auer Manufacturing Company is to sell, as a special order, the machine as is (e.g., without modification) for a net price of $52,000.

The following additional information is available regarding Auer's operations:

(a) The sales commission rate on sales of standard models is 2%, while the sales commission rate on special orders is 3%. All sales commissions are calculated on net sales price (i.e., list price less cash discount, if any).

(b) Normal credit terms for sales of standard models are 2/10, n/30. Customers take the discounts, except in rare instances. Credit terms for special orders are negotiated with the customer.

(c) The application rates for factory overhead and the fixed marketing and administrative costs are as follows:

Factory overhead:
   Variable: 50% of direct labor cost
   Fixed: 25% of direct labor cost
Marketing and administrative:
   Fixed: 10% of the total of direct materials, direct labor, and factory overhead costs

Required:

(1) Compute the dollar contribution that each of the three alternatives will add to Auer's profit.

(2) If KaTee makes Auer a counteroffer, determine the lowest price Auer should accept from KaTee. *(ICMA adapted)*

21-2. Special order analysis. Framar Inc. manufactures automation machinery according to customer specifications. The company is relatively new and has grown each year. Framar operated at about 75% of practical capacity during its most recent fiscal year ended September 30, with operating results as follows:

Sales...		$25,000
Less sales commissions...............................		2,500
Net sales...		$22,500
Expenses:		
Direct materials.......................................		$ 6,000
Direct labor...		7,500
Factory overhead—variable:		
Supplies...	$ 625	
Indirect labor.......................................	1,500	
Power..	125	2,250
Factory overhead—fixed:		
Supervision..	$ 500	
Depreciation...	1,000	1,500
Corporation administration.......................		750
Total expense.....................................		$18,000
Income before income tax...........................		$ 4,500
Income tax (40%)....................................		1,800
Net income...		$ 2,700

Framar management has developed a pricing formula based on current operating costs, which are expected to prevail for the next year. This formula was used in developing the following bid for APA Inc.:

Direct materials cost..	$ 29,200
Direct labor cost..	56,000
Factory overhead calculated at 50% of direct labor............................	28,000
Corporate overhead calculated at 10% of direct labor........................	5,600
Total cost, excluding sales commission..	$118,800
Add 25% for profit and tax..	29,700
Suggested price (with profit) before sales commission........................	$148,500
Suggested total price (suggested price divided by .9 to adjust for 10% sales commission)...	$165,000

Required:

(1) Compute the impact on net income if APA accepts the bid.

(2) Determine the suggested decision if APA is willing to pay only $127,000.

(3) Calculate the lowest price Framar can quote without reducing current net income.

(4) Determine the effect on the most recent fiscal year's profit if all work were done at prices similar to APA's $127,000 counteroffer.   *(ICMA adapted)*

21-3. Comparative cost study to make or buy new product components. Meyers Surgical Products Company produces diverse lines of surgical instruments. It is considering a proposal, suggested by one of its sales managers, to produce dissection instrument sets for use by medical and premedical students. There is little competition in the market for the instrument sets, and the firm's present sales force could be used for effective distribution coverage. Moreover, the sales manager believes that the company could produce the instruments with the present facilities, except for the addition of certain minor auxiliary equipment.

Company management assigned two members of its Sales Department, two members from the Production Department, and an accounting staff representative to analyze the proposal. The team has assembled the following information:

(a) The proposed dissection instrument sets include:

(1)	Dissection knives.....................	3
(2)	Scissors....................................	2
(3)	Tweezers..................................	2
(4)	Scalpels....................................	2
(5)	Clamps......................................	4
(6)	Glass slides..............................	100
(7)	Cover slips................................	400
(8)	Case..	1

(b) The market price for such sets ranges from $55 to $65. An estimate of the total annual market demand ranges between 5,000 and 7,000 sets, and Meyers expects to sell 2,000 sets at $60.

(c) Set components can be purchased from suppliers at the following prices per unit:

(1)	Dissection knives.....................	$3.20
(2)	Scissors....................................	3.00
(3)	Tweezers..................................	2.97
(4)	Scalpels....................................	3.30
(5)	Clamps......................................	3.28
(6)	Glass slides..............................	.03
(7)	Cover slips................................	.01
(8)	Cases..	6.00

(d) Meyers has the option of manufacturing all of the components, except glass slides, cover slips, and the cases. The remaining components can be grouped into two categories for production and for product costing purposes:
(1) Group I—dissection knives and scalpels
(2) Group II—scissors, tweezers, and clamps
(e) Production costs were analyzed to be as follows:

	Group	
	I	II
Materials..	1 lb. of steel for 25 units @ $3.27 per lb.	1 lb. of steel for 20 units @ $3.60 per lb.
Labor..	2.5 hrs for 25 units @ $9.48 per hr.	2 hrs. for 20 units @ $12.16 per hr.
Variable factory overhead......................	150% of labor cost	150% of labor cost

(f) Set assembly and packing costs will average $3 per set.
(g) Additional fixed factory overhead directly related to the sets will be $7,040 and $6,000 annually for Groups I and II, respectively.
(h) The new product will have the following amounts of presently existing annual fixed overhead allocated to it:

(1) Group I manufacturing.. $4,000
(2) Group II manufacturing... 6,000
(3) All other dissection sets' production activity..................... 7,000

(i) All sales are FOB Meyers' plant.

Required: Advise management on the desirability of the proposal, including supporting computations. Compute unit costs to 1/10 of one cent.

·21-4. Minimum bid price. Chemco Inc. manufactures a combination fertilizer/weed-killer under the name Fertikil, the only product produced at the present time. Fertikil is sold nationwide, through normal marketing channels, to retail nurseries and garden stores.

National Nursery Company plans to sell a similar fertilizer/weed-killer compound through its regional nursery chain under its own private label. National Nursery has asked Chemco to submit a bid for a 25,000-pound order of the private brand compound. While the chemical composition of the National Nursery compound differs from Fertikil, the manufacturing process is similar.

The National Nursery compound would be produced in 1,000-pound lots. Each lot would require 60 direct labor hours and the following chemicals:

Chemicals	Quantity in Pounds
CW-3	400
JX-6	300
MZ-8	200
BE-7	100

The first three chemicals (CW-3, JX-6, and MZ-8) are all used in the production of Fertikil. BE-7 was used in a compound that Chemco has discontinued. This chemical was not sold or discarded because it does not deteriorate, and there have been adequate storage facilities. Chemco could sell BE-7 at the prevailing market price less $.10 per pound for selling and handling expenses.

Chemco also has on hand a chemical called CN-5, which was manufactured for use in another product that is no longer produced. CN-5, which cannot be used in Fertikil, can be substituted for CW-3 on a one-for-one basis without affecting the quality of the National Nursery compound. The quantity of CN-5 in inventory has a salvage value of $500.

Inventory and cost data for the chemicals which can be used to produce the National Nursery compound follow:

Chemical	Pounds in Inventory	Inventory Cost per Pound	Market Price per Pound
CW-3	22,000	$ .80	$ .90
JX-6	5,000	.55	.60
MZ-8	8,000	1.40	1.60
BE-7	4,000	.60	.65
CN-5	5,500	.75	salvage

The current direct labor rate is $7 per hour. The factory overhead rate is established at the beginning of the year and is applied consistently throughout the year, using direct labor hours (DLH) as the base. The predetermined overhead rate for the current year, based on a two-shift capacity of 400,000 total DLH with no overtime, follows:

Variable factory overhead................................ $2.25 per DLH
Fixed factory overhead.................................... 3.75 per DLH
Combined factory overhead rate.................... $6.00 per DLH

Chemco's production manager reports that the present equipment and facilities are adequate to manufacture the National Nursery compound. However, Chemco is within 800 hours of its two-shift capacity this month before it must schedule overtime. If need be, the National Nursery compound could be produced on regular time by shifting a portion of Fertikil production to overtime. Chemco's rate for overtime is one and one-half times the regular pay rate, or $10.50 per hour. There is no allowance for any overtime premium in the factory overhead rate.

Chemco's standard markup policy for new products is 25% on the full manufacturing cost.

Required:

(1) Calculate the lowest price Chemco should bid for the order and not reduce its net income. Assume that Chemco has decided to submit a bid for a 25,000-pound order of National Nursery compound. The order must be delivered by the end of the current month. It is presumed to be a one-time order (i.e., it will probably not be repeated).

(2) Without prejudice to your answer in requirement (1) above, calculate the price Chemco should quote National Nursery for each 25,000-pound lot of the compound, assuming that National Nursery plans to place regular orders for 25,000-pound lots of the new compound during the coming year. Chemco expects the demand for Fertikil to remain strong again in the coming year. Therefore, the recurring orders from National Nursery will put Chemco over its two-shift capacity. However, production can be scheduled so that 60% of each National Nursery order can be completed during regular hours, or Fertikil production could be shifted temporarily to overtime, so that the National Nursery orders could be produced on regular time. Chemco's production manager has estimated that the prices of all chemicals will stabilize at the current market rates

for the coming year, and that all other manufacturing costs are expected to be maintained at the same rates or amounts. *(ICMA adapted)*

21-5. Proposed construction of additional capacity. Westmore Company is considering expanding its production facilities with a building costing $260,000 and equipment costing $84,000. Building and equipment depreciable lives are 25 and 20 years, respectively, with straight-line depreciation and no salvage value. Of the additional depreciation cost, 5% is expected to be allocated to inventories.

The plant addition will increase volume by 50%; the product's sales price is expected to remain the same. The new union contract calls for a 5% increase in wage rates. Because of the increased plant capacity, quantity buying will yield an overall 6% decrease in materials cost, and one additional supervisor must be hired at a salary of $15,000.

The following data pertain to last year:

Sales, 50,000 units @ $10 per unit   Fixed factory overhead, $72,500

Direct materials, $2 per unit   Variable marketing expense, $12,000

Direct labor, $4 per unit   Fixed marketing expense, $7,000

Variable factory overhead, $1.30 per unit

With the volume increase, advertising, which is 10% of present fixed marketing expense, will be increased 25%.

Required: Prepare an analysis estimating the contribution margin and operating income for the present and the proposed plant capacities.

21-6. Evaluating production alternatives. Mowen Corporation has manufacturing plants in Boston and Chicago. Both plants produce the same product, Xoff, which sells for $20 per unit. Budgeted revenues and costs (000s omitted) for the coming year are as follows:

	Total	Boston	Chicago
Sales...	$6,200	$2,200	$4,000
Variable factory costs:			
Direct materials...	$1,550	$ 550	$1,000
Direct labor...	1,660	660	1,000
Variable factory overhead.............................	1,140	440	700
Fixed factory overhead.....................................	1,600	700	900
Fixed regional promotional costs....................	200	100	100
Allocated home office costs............................	310	110	200
Total costs..	$6,460	$2,560	$3,900
Operating income (loss).................................	$(260)	$(360)	$ 100

Home office costs are fixed and are allocated to manufacturing plants on the basis of relative sales levels. Fixed regional promotional costs are discretionary advertising costs needed to obtain budgeted sales levels. Because of the budgeted operating loss, Mowen is considering the possibility of ceasing operations at its Boston plant. If Mowen were to cease operations at its Boston plant, proceeds from the sale of plant assets would exceed their book value and exactly cover all termination costs. Fixed factory overhead costs of $50,000 would not be eliminated. Mowen is considering the following three alternative plans:

Plan A. Expand Boston's operations from the budgeted 110,000 units of Xoff to a budgeted 170,000 units. It is believed that this can be accomplished by increasing Boston's fixed regional promotional expenditures by $120,000.

Plan B. Close the Boston plant and expand Chicago's operations from the current budgeted 200,000 units of Xoff to 310,000 units in order to fill Boston's budgeted production of 110,000 units. The Boston region would continue to incur promotional costs in order to sell the 110,000 units. All sales and costs would be budgeted through the Chicago plant.

Plan C. Close the Boston plant and enter into a long-term contract with a competitor to serve the Boston region's customers. This competitor would pay Mowen a royalty of $2.50 per unit of Xoff sold. Mowen would continue to incur fixed regional promotional costs in order to maintain sales of 110,000 units in the Boston region.

Required:

(1) Without considering the effects of implementing Plans A, B, and C, compute the number of units of Xoff required by the Boston plant to cover its fixed factory overhead costs and fixed regional promotional costs.

(2) Prepare a schedule by plant and in total, computing Mowen's budgeted contribution margin and operating income resulting from the implementation of each of the three alternative plans.   (AICPA adapted)

21-7. Evaluation of alternatives for a charitable foundation. J. Watson recently was appointed executive director of a charitable foundation. The foundation raises money for its activities in a variety of ways, but the most important source of funds is an annual mail campaign. Although large amounts of money are raised each year from this campaign, the year-to-year growth in the amount derived from this solicitation has been lower than expected by the foundation's board. In addition, the board wants the mail campaign to project the image of a well-run and fiscally responsible organization in order to build a base for future contributions. Consequently, the major focus of Watson's first-year efforts will be devoted to the mail campaign.

The campaign takes place in the spring of each year. The foundation staff makes every effort to secure newspaper, radio, and television coverage of the foundation's activities for several weeks before the mailing. In prior years, the foundation has mailed brochures that described its charitable activities to a large number of people and requested contributions from them. The addresses for the mailing are generated from the foundation's own file of past contributors and from mailing lists purchased from brokers.

The foundation staff is considering three alternative brochures for use in the upcoming campaign. All three will be 8½″ × 11″ in size. The simplest and the one most likely to be available on a timely basis for bulk mailing is a sheet of white paper with a printed explanation of the foundation's program and a request for funds. A more expensive brochure on colored stock will contain pictures as well as printed copy. However, this brochure may not be ready in time to take advantage of bulk postal rates, but there is no doubt that it can be ready in time for mailing at first-class postal rates. The third alternative would be an elegant, multicolored brochure printed on glossy paper with photographs as well as printed copy. The printer assures the staff that it will be ready on time to meet the first-class mailing schedule, but asks for a delivery date one week later just in case there are production problems.

The foundation staff has assembled the following cost and gross revenue information for mailing the three alternative brochures to 2,000,000 potential contributors:

Type of Brochure	Design	Brochure Costs				Gross Revenue Potential (000s omitted)		
		Type-setting	Unit Paper Cost	Unit Printing Cost	Bulk Mail	First Class	Late First Class
Plain paper..................	$ 300	$ 100	$.005	$.003	$1,200	—	—
Colored paper.............	1,000	800	.008	.010	2,000	$2,200	—
Glossy paper..............	3,000	2,000	.018	.040	—	2,500	$2,200

The postal rates are $.04 per item for bulk mail and $.26 per item for presorted first-class mail. First-class mail is more likely to be delivered on a timely basis than bulk mail. The charge by outside companies who will be hired to handle the mailing is $.01 per unit for the plain and colored paper brochures and $.02 per unit for the glossy paper one.

Required:

(1) Calculate the net revenue potential for each brochure for each viable mailing alternative.
(2) The foundation must choose one of the three brochures for this year's campaign. The criteria established by the board—net revenue potential, image as a well-run organization, and image as a fiscally responsible organization—must be considered when making the choice. Evaluate the three alternative brochures in terms of the three criteria. (ICMA adapted)

21-8. Elimination of market. Justa Corporation produces and sells three products, A, B, and C. The three products are sold in a local market and in a regional market. At the end of the first quarter of the current year, the following income statement was prepared:

	Total	Local	Regional
Sales..	$1,300,000	$1,000,000	$300,000
Cost of goods sold...........................	1,010,000	775,000	235,000
Gross profit.......................................	$ 290,000	$ 225,000	$ 65,000
Marketing expense...........................	$ 105,000	$ 60,000	$ 45,000
Administrative expense....................	52,000	40,000	12,000
	$ 157,000	$ 100,000	$ 57,000
Operating income.............................	$ 133,000	$ 125,000	$ 8,000

Management has expressed special concern with the regional market because of the extremely poor return on sales. This market was entered a year ago because of excess capacity. It was originally believed that the return on sales would improve with time, but after a year, no noticeable improvement can be seen from the results as reported in the quarterly statement.

In attempting to decide whether to eliminate the regional market, the following information has been gathered:

	A	B	C
Sales..	$500,000	$400,000	$400,000
Variable manufacturing expense as a percentage of sales...	60%	70%	60%
Variable marketing expense as a percentage of sales...	3%	2%	2%

	Sales by Markets	
Product	Local	Regional
A	$400,000	$100,000
B	300,000	100,000
C	300,000	100,000

All fixed expense is based upon a prorated yearly amount. All administrative expense and fixed manufacturing expense are common to the three products and the two markets and are fixed for the period, regardless of whether a market is eliminated. Remaining marketing expense is fixed for the period and separable by market. All separable cost would be eliminated with the dropping of a market.

Required:

(1) Prepare the quarterly income statement, showing contribution margins by markets. Include a total column, combining the two markets.
(2) Assuming that there are no alternative uses for Justa Corporation's present capacity, should the regional market be dropped? Why or why not?
(3) Prepare the quarterly income statement, showing contribution margins by products.
(4) It is believed that a new product to replace Product C could be ready for sale next year if Justa Corporation decides to go ahead with continued research. The new product could be produced by simply converting equipment presently used in producing Product C. This conversion would increase fixed costs by $10,000 per quarter. Calculate the minimum contribution margin per quarter for the new product if Justa Corporation is to be no worse off financially than at present.

(ICMA adapted)

21-9. Sales probability and contribution margin analysis. Aplet Inc. purchased Avcont Company in 19A during Aplet's expansion period. The subsidiary has been quite profitable until recently. Beginning in 19I, the market share dropped, costs increased primarily due to increased prices of inputs, and the profits turned into losses.

Avcont management wants to take action to reverse the unsatisfactory results the company has been experiencing. One proposal under consideration is to increase the price of Avcont's product. Some members of management believe that the market might accept an 8% increase in prices at this time without affecting the expected 10% increase in unit sales volume because no price increases have taken place in this market since 19H. Several other companies are also considering price increases for 19L.

Other members of Aplet management question the feasibility of a price increase because Avcont is operating in an industry that is experiencing declining sales. In addition, the Marketing Department believes that a price increase will have an impact on the expected increase in unit sales volume during 19L. Its estimate of the possible outcomes on unit sales and the related probabilities for the 8% price increase are as follows:

Increase (Decrease) in 19L Unit Sales Volume	Probability
10%	.4
5	.3
0	.2
(5)	.1
	1.0

The income statements for 19I and 19J, along with an estimate of the 19K income made in October, 19K, are as follows:

AVCONT COMPANY
Income Statement for Years Ended December 31
(000s omitted)

	19I	19J	19K (Est.)
Industry unit sales	1,300	1,200	1,200
Avcont unit sales	120	110	110
Sales	$1,200	$1,100	$1,100
Less variable costs:			
Raw materials	$ 175	$ 170	$ 175
Labor	210	215	225
Factory overhead	100	99	100
Marketing	125	115	120
Administrative	50	50	60
	$ 660	$ 649	$ 680
Contribution margin	$ 540	$ 451	$ 420
Less fixed costs:			
Manufacturing*	$ 200	$ 210	$ 230
Marketing*	125	140	145
Administration*	135	145	145
	$ 460	$ 495	$ 520
Profit (loss)	$ 80	$ (44)	$ (100)

*Depreciation and amortization included in fixed costs:

Manufacturing	$ 60	$ 70	$ 70
Marketing	5	6	6
Administration	8	8	9
	$ 73	$ 84	$ 85

The subsidiary management is optimistic about the volume of sales for 19L. Recent sales promotion efforts seem to be beneficial, and Avcont expects to increase unit sales 10% during 19L, even though industry volume is expected to decline to 1,100,000 units. However, Avcont management also knows that its variable cost rates will increase 10% (as a percentage of sales dollars) in 19L over 19K levels.

Required:

(1) Determine Avcont's profits for 19L if the 8% price increase takes place and unit sales volume increases 10%.
(2) Will the 8% price increase and 10% volume increase reduce Avcont Company's need for funds from the corporate treasury during 19L? Explain.
(3) Compute Avcont's expected profits for 19L if the probabilistic sales data assembled by the Marketing Department are used.
(4) A member of the analysis team made the following observation to support the recommendation for a price increase: "Inflationary pressures make it reasonable for a company to forecast increased costs, increased product prices, and increased or at least constant volume because consumers can be expected to accept the product price increases." Comment on the validity of this statement for planning purposes. *(ICMA adapted)*

21-10. Make-or-buy decision using probability distribution. Unimat Company manufactures a thermostat designed for effective climatic control of large buildings. The thermostat requires a specialized thermocoupler, purchased from Cosmic Company at $15 each. For the past two years, an average of 10% of the purchased thermocouplers have not met quality requirements; however, the rejection rate is within the range agreed on in the purchase contract.

Unimat has most of the facilities and equipment needed to produce the components. Additional annual fixed cost of only $32,500 would be required. The Engineering Department has designed a manufacturing system that would hold the defective rate to 4 percent. At an annual demand level of 18,000 units, engineering estimates of the probabilities of various variable manufacturing unit costs, including allowance for defective units, are as follows:

Estimated Per Unit Variable Cost	Probability
$10	.1
12	.3
14	.4
16	.2

Required: Prepare a make-or-buy decision analysis, using probability distribution estimates.

(ICMA adapted)

21-11. Differential cost under uncertainty. The administrator for a large midwestern city continually seeks ways to reduce costs without cutting services. The administrator has asked all department heads to review their operations to determine if cost-saving procedures can be implemented.

The Department of Streets is responsible for the proper functioning of the city's computerized traffic control system, including the replacement of the 50,000-bulb units in the traffic lights. The department has kept detailed records regarding the failure rate of the bulb units over the past 18 months. The pattern of bulb failures that has been experienced is as follows:

Failure Occurs Within the Following Quarter of Replacement	Probability
First	.10
Second	.30
Third	.60

The Department of Streets has been replacing the bulb units as they have failed. Using this procedure, the estimated cost to replace the bulb units, exclusive of the cost of the bulb unit, is $5.40 per unit.

The manager of the Department of Streets is considering replacing all of the bulb units at once, such as at the beginning of every quarter, plus replacing bulbs as they fail. The manager estimates that the cost to replace all bulb units at once would be $1.40 per unit, exclusive of the cost of the bulb. The cost to replace each unit as it failed would still be $5.40 per unit.

Each bulb costs $1, regardless of the replacement procedure used.

Required:

(1) Calculate the average quarterly bulb and replacement cost to the Department of Streets if the present policy of replacing the bulb units as they fail is continued.

(2) Calculate the estimated average quarterly bulb and replacement cost if all bulb units are replaced on a regular basis at the beginning of:
(a) every quarter.
(b) every second quarter.
(c) every third quarter.
Show your calculations for all three alternatives.

(3) Why would there be such a large difference between the two estimated replacement costs per unit (replace as failure occurs, $5.40; replace all at once, $1.40)? Explain.   (ICMA adapted)

21-12. Probability analysis. The owner of Edward's Clothing Store must decide on the number of men's shirts to order for the coming season. One order must be placed for the entire season. The normal sales price is $12 per shirt; however, unsold shirts at season's end must be sold at half price. The following data are available:

Order Quantity	Unit Sales Price	Unit Cost	Unit Contribution Margin at Regular Price	Unit Loss at Half Price
100	$12.00	$10.00	$2.00	$4.00
200	12.00	9.50	2.50	3.50
300	12.00	9.00	3.00	3.00
400	12.00	8.50	3.50	2.50

Over the past 20 seasons, Edward's has experienced the following sales:

Quantity Sold	Frequency
100	4
200	6
300	8
400	2
	20

The historical sales have occurred at random; i.e., they have exhibited no cycles or trends, and the future is expected to be similar to the past.

Required:

(1) Prepare a payoff table representing the expected contribution margin of each of the four possible strategies of ordering 100, 200, 300, or 400 shirts, assuming that only the four quantities listed are ever sold.
(2) Select the best of the four strategies in (1), based on the expected contribution margin.
(3) Compute the expected value of perfect information in this problem.
(4) Compute the coefficient of variation for each alternative strategy.

21-13. Probability analysis. Jessica Company buys and resells a perishable product. A large purchase at the beginning of each month provides a lower per unit cost and assures that Jessica can purchase all the items it wishes. However, unsold units at the end of each month are worthless and must be discarded. If an inadequate quantity is purchased, additional units of acceptable quality are not available.

The units, which Jessica sells for $1.25 each, are purchased at a fixed fee of $50,000 per month plus $.50 each, if at least 100,000 units are ordered and they are ordered at the beginning of the month.

The needs of Jessica's customers limit the possible sales volumes to only four quantities per month—100,000, 120,000, 140,000, or 180,000 units. However, the total quantity needed for a given month cannot be determined prior to the date Jessica must make its purchases. The sales managers are willing to place a probability estimate on each of the four possible sales volumes each month. They noted that the probabilities for the four sales volumes change from month to month because of the seasonal nature of the customers' business. Their probability estimates for December, 19A sales units are 10% for 100,000, 30% for 120,000, 40% for 140,000, and 20% for 180,000.

Required:

(1) Prepare a table representing the expected value of each of the four possible strategies of ordering units, assuming that only the four quantities specified are ever sold and that the occurrences are random events, and identify the best strategy.

(2) Compute the amount Jessica would be willing to pay in order to ascertain with certainty its customers' December needs prior to placing its purchase order, rather than relying on the expected value decision model. (ICMA adapted)

21-14. Probability revision. L. J. Gant is a builder who has recently acquired a tract of unimproved real estate upon which new houses will be built. Gant feels that the local housing market is strong enough to absorb all of the houses built on the tract by the end of the year, provided that the size of houses built are those that meet the needs and preferences of the largest number of home buyers. Four different sizes of houses are being considered—1,600, 2,000, 2,400, and 2,800 square-foot houses. However, for economic and marketing reasons, only one size of house will be built on the tract. Based on past experience, George assigned the following subjective probabilities to the size of houses most in demand in the local market:

House Size	Probability
1,600	.20
2,000	.50
2,400	.20
2,800	.10

Before beginning construction, Gant read in the paper that an electronics firm announced it was considering locating a research laboratory in the community not far from Gant's planned housing site. If the firm locates a research facility in town, it will significantly increase demand for the 2,400 and 2,800 square-foot houses. Gant believes that there is a 75% probability that the electronics firm will locate its research facility in town and a 25% probability that it will not. The expected payoff for each alternative follows:

Actions House Size To Build	Events (House Size Most in Demand)			
	1,600	2,000	2,400	2,800
1,600 sq. ft.	$200,000	$180,000	$160,000	$140,000
2,000 sq. ft.	160,000	400,000	360,000	320,000
2,400 sq. ft.	120,000	320,000	600,000	540,000
2,800 sq. ft.	80,000	240,000	480,000	800,000

Required:

    (1) Compute the posterior probabilities for each of the alternatives related to the proposed housing project.

    (2) Compute the expected value of each alternative course of action, and make a recommendation to George about which course of action to take.

21-15. Decision tree. Strotz Brewery produces and sells nationally a popular premium beer and has enjoyed good profits for many years. In recent years, however, its sales volume has not grown with the general market. This lack of growth is due to the increasing popularity of light beer and the fact that Strotz has not entered this market.

Strotz is now developing its own light beer and is considering potential marketing strategies. Introducing the new light beer nationally would require a large commitment of resources for a full nationwide introduction because Strotz is a late entry into the light beer market. Strotz's advertising agency has helped assess the market risk and has convinced the Strotz management that there are only two reasonable alternative strategies to pursue.

Stragegy 1. Perform a test advertising and sales campaign in a limited number of states for a six-month period. Strotz would decide whether or not to introduce the light beer nationally and conduct a nationwide promotional campaign on the basis of the results of the test campaign.

Strategy 2. Conduct a nationwide promotion campaign and make the new light beer available in all fifty states immediately, without conducting any test campaign. The nationwide promotion and distribution campaign would be allowed to run for a full two years before a decision would be made to continue the light beer nationally.

Strotz management believes that, if Strategy 2 is selected, there is only a 50% chance of its being successful. The introduction of light beer nationally will be considered a success if $40 million of revenue is generated, while $30 million of variable costs are being incurred during the two-year period in which the nationwide promotion and distribution campaign is in effect. If the two-year nationwide campaign is unsuccessful, revenues are expected to be $16 million and variable costs will be $12 million. Total fixed costs for the two-year period will amount to $6 million, regardless of the result.

The advertising agency consultants believe that if Strategy 1 is selected, there is a 20% chance that the test will indicate that Strotz should conduct a nationwide promotion and distribution campaign when, in fact, a nationwide campaign would be unsuccessful. In addition, the consultants believe that there is a 20% chance that the test results will indicate Strotz should not conduct a nationwide promotion and distribution when, in fact, a nationwide campaign would be successful. The cost of the test campaign is estimated to be $500,000, and the probability of a successful test is 50%.

Required:

    (1) Prepare a decision tree representing Strotz's decision problem, including all decision alternatives and possible outcomes with related expected values.

    (2) Recommend the best strategy to Strotz management, based on the results indicated by the decision tree analysis.

    (3) Criticize the expected value decision criterion.   *(ICMA adapted)*

CASES

A. Relevant cost analysis data. Management is reviewing the Promotion Department's effectiveness to determine if the department's activities could be managed better and more economically by an outside promotion agency. As a part of this review, management has received the following summary of the Promotion Department's costs for the most recent year:

Promotion Department
Costs for the Year Ended November 30

Direct department costs....................................	$257,500
Charges from other departments....................	44,700
Allocated share of general administrative overhead..............................	22,250
Total..	$324,450

The direct department costs are those which can be traced directly to the activities of the Promotion Department, such as staff and clerical salaries, related employee benefits, and supplies. The charges from other departments represent the costs of services which are provided at the request of the Promotion Department. The company has developed a charging system for such interdepartmental uses of services. For instance, the "in-house" Printing Department charges the Promotion Department for the promotional literature printed. All such services provided to the Promotion Department by other departments are included in "Charges from other departments." General administrative overhead is comprised of such costs as executive management salaries and benefits, depreciation, insurance, and property taxes. These costs are allocated to all departments in proportion to the number of employees in each department.

Required: Discuss the usefulness of the Promotion Department cost figures as a basis for comparison with an outside agency bid to provide the same type of activities that are now provided by the Promotion Department.

(ICMA adapted)

B. Reducing the price of a special order. Ashley Company manufactures and sells a household product marketed through direct mail and advertisements in home improvement and gardening magazines. Although similar products are available in hardware and department stores, none is as effective as Ashley's model.

The company uses a standard cost system in its manufacturing accounting. The standards have not undergone a thorough review in the past 18 months. The general manager has seen no need for such a review because:

(a) The materials quality and unit costs were fixed by a three-year purchase commitment signed in July, 19A.
(b) A three-year labor contract was signed in July, 19A.
(c) There have been no significant variations from standard costs for the past three quarters.

The standard cost for the product, as established in July, 19A, is as follows:

Materials,	.75 lb. @ $1 per lb................	$ .75
Direct labor,	.3 hrs. @ $4 per hour..........	1.20
Factory overhead, .3 hrs. @ $7 per hour..........		2.10
Standard manufacturing cost per unit..............		$4.05

The standard for factory overhead cost was developed from the following budgeted costs, based upon an activity level of one million units (300,000 direct labor hours):

300,000 × $7 = 2,100,000

Variable factory overhead......................	$ 600,000
Fixed factory overhead..........................	1,500,000
Total factory overhead.........................	$2,100,000

$2.10 × 1,000,000 =

Action Hardware, a national chain, recently asked Ashley to manufacture a slightly modified version of the product which Action would distribute through its stores. Action has offered to buy a minimum quantity of 200,000 units each year over the next three years, beginning in 19C, and has offered to pay $4.10 for each unit, FOB shipping point.

The company has adequate capacity to meet the additional production requirements and anticipates no additional marketing or administrative expenses.

Required:

(1) Using the data given, present an analysis for the first year of the Action Hardware order.
(2) Identify additional financial data Ashley Company needs in order to prepare a more comprehensive analysis of the Action proposal for the (three-year) period.
(3) Specify the nonfinancial issues Ashley management should address in considering the Action proposal.

(ICMA adapted)

C. Make-or-buy decision. Until recently, when it discontinued five items, AME Company manufactured all electrical components that it sold. The items were dropped from the manufacturing process because the unit costs computed by the company's full (absorption) cost system did not provide a sufficient margin to cover shipping and selling costs. The five items are now purchased from other manufacturers at a price which allows AME to make a very small profit after shipping and selling costs. AME keeps these items in its product line in order to offer a complete line of electrical components.

The president thought that the switch from manufacture to purchase for the five items would improve profit performance. However, the reverse has occurred. All other factors affecting profits—sales volume, sales prices, and incurred marketing and manufacturing costs—were as expected, so the profit problem can be traced to this decision. Disappointed at recent profitability performance, the president has asked the Controller's Department to reevaluate the decision's financial effects.

The task was assigned to an assistant controller, who has reviewed the data used to reach the decision to purchase rather than manufacture and has concluded that the company should have continued to manufacture the item. In the assistant's opinion, the incorrect decision was made because full cost data rather than direct cost data were used.

Required: Explain the features of direct costing as compared to full costing that make it possible

for the assisant controller's conclusion to be correct. *(ICMA adapted)*

D. Analysis of differential business. Electrotech Manufacturing Inc. is presently operating at 50% of normal capacity, producing annually about 50,000 units of a patented electronic component. Electrotech recently received an offer from a company in Yokohama, Japan, to purchase 30,000 components at $6 per unit, FOB Electrotech's plant. Electrotech has not previously sold components in Japan. Budgeted production costs for 50,000 and 80,000 units of output follow:

Units	50,000	80,000
Costs:		
Direct materials	$ 75,000	$120,000
Direct labor	75,000	120,000
Factory overhead	200,000	260,000
Total cost	$350,000	$500,000
Cost per unit	$7.00	$6.25

The sales manager thinks the order should be accepted, even if it results in a loss of $1 per unit, since the sales may build up future markets. The production manager does not wish to have the order accepted, primarily because the order would show a loss of $.25 per unit when computed on the new average unit cost. The treasurer has made a quick computation indicating that accepting the order will actually increase gross profit.

Required:

(1) Determine causes of the drop in cost from $7 per unit to $6.25 per unit when budgeted production increases from 50,000 to 80,000 units.
(2) (a) Explain whether the production manager and/or the treasurer is correct.
   (b) Explain the conclusions of the production manager and the treasurer.
(3) Explain how each of the following may affect the decision to accept or reject the special order:
   (a) The likelihood of repeat special sales and/or all sales to be made at $6 per unit.

(b) Whether the sales are made to customers operating in two separate, isolated markets or whether the sales are made to customers competing in the same market.

(AICPA adapted)

E. New product proposal.

Calco Corporation, a producer and distributor of plastic products for industrial use, is considering a proposal to produce a plastic storage unit designed especially for the consumer market. The product is well suited for Calco's manufacturing process, with no costly machinery modifications or Assembly Department changes required. Adequate manufacturing capacity is available because of recent facility expansion and a leveling of sales growth in its industrial product line.

Management is considering two alternatives for marketing the product. The first is to add this responsibility to Calco's current Marketing Department. The other alternative is to acquire a small, new company named Jasco Inc. at a nominal cost. This company was started by some former employees of a firm which specialized in marketing plastic products for the consumer market when they lost their jobs because of a merger. Jasco has not yet started operations.

The Product Engineering Department has prepared the following unit manufacturing cost estimate for the new storage unit at both the 100,000- and the 120,000-unit levels of production:

Direct materials..	$14.00
Direct labor..	3.50
Factory overhead (25% variable)*.....................	10.00
Total...	$27.50

*Total fixed factory overhead will be $750,000 at the 100,000-unit level and $900,000 at the 120,000-unit level.

Calco's Marketing Department has used its experience in the sale of industrial products to develop a proposal for the distribution of the new consumer product. The Marketing Department would be reorganized so that several positions which were scheduled for elimination now would be assigned to the new product. The Marketing Department's forecast of the annual financial results for its proposals to market the storage units is as follows:

Sales (100,000 units @ $45).........		$4,500,000
Costs:		
Cost of units sold (100,000 units @ $27.50).....................................		$2,750,000
Marketing costs:		
Positions that were to be eliminated.......................................		600,000
Sales commission (5% of sales).................................		225,000
Advertising program................		400,000
Promotion program..................		200,000
Share of current Marketing Department's management costs.................................		100,000
Total cost......................................		$4,275,000
Income before income tax............		$ 225,000

The Jasco founders also prepared a forecast of the annual financial results, based upon their experience in marketing consumer products. The following forecast was based upon the assumption that Jasco would become part of Calco and be responsible for marketing the storage unit:

Sales (120,000 units @ $50).......................		$6,000,000
Costs:		
Cost of units sold (120,000 units @ $27.50).....................................		$3,300,000
Marketing costs:		
Personnel—sales..................................		660,000
Personnel—sales management............		200,000
Commission (10%)...............................		600,000
Advertising program.............................		800,000
Promotion program...............................		200,000
Office rental (the annual rental of a long-term lease already signed by Jasco)..		50,000
Total cost..		$5,810,000
Income before income tax,..........................		$ 190,000

Required:

(1) List factors Calco should consider before entering the consumer products market.

(2) Alter financial forecasts for use in deciding between the alternatives, if Calco decides to enter the consumer market.

(3) Compare the reliability of the two proposals.

(4) Identify the nonquantitative factors Calco should consider when choosing

between the alternatives. Indicate whether or not any one of these factors is sufficiently important to warrant selection of one alternative over the other, regardless of the estimated financial effect on profit.

(ICMA adapted)

F. Elimination of a product. Precision Gauge Corporation produces three gauges. These gauges, which measure density, permeability, and thickness, are known as D-gauges, P-gauges, and T-gauges, respectively. For many years, the company has been profitable and has operated at capacity. In the last two years, however, prices on all gauges were reduced and selling expenses increased to meet competition and to keep the plant operating at full capacity. The following third quarter results are representative of recent experiences:

Precision Gauge Corporation
Income Statement
For Third Quarter, 19A
(000s omitted)

	D-gauge	P-gauge	T-gauge	Total
Sales	$900	$1,600	$ 900	$3,400
Cost of goods sold	770	1,048	950	2,768
Gross profit	$130	$ 552	$ (50)	$ 632
Selling and administrative expenses	185	370	135	690
Income before income tax	$(55)	$ 182	$(185)	$(58)

Marvin Caplan, president of the company, is very concerned about the results of the pricing, selling, and production policies. After reviewing the third quarter results, he announced that he would ask his management staff to consider a course of action that includes the following three suggestions:

(a) Discontinue the T-gauge line immediately. T-gauges would not be returned to the line of products unless the problems with the gauge could be identified and resolved.

(b) Increase quarterly sales promotion by $100,000 on the P-gauge product line in order to increase sales volume 15%.

(c) Cut production on the D-gauge line by 50%, a quantity sufficient to meet the demand of customers who purchase P-gauges. In addition, the traceable advertising and promotion for this line would be cut to $20,000 each quarter.

Joan Garth, who is the controller, suggested that a more careful study of the financial relationships be made to determine the possible effect on the company's operating results as a consequence of the president's proposed course of action. The president agreed, and Tom Kirk, who is the assistant controller, was given the assignment to prepare an analysis. To prepare the analysis, he gathered the following information:

(a) All three gauges are manufactured with common equipment and facilities.

(b) The quarterly general selling and administrative expenses of $170,000 are allocated to the three gauge lines in proportion to their dollar sales volume.

(c) Special selling expenses (primarily advertising, promotion, and shipping) are incurred for each gauge as follows:

	Quarterly Advertising and Promotion	Shipping Expense
D-gauge	$100,000	$ 4 per unit
P-gauge	210,000	10 per unit
T-gauge	40,000	10 per unit

(d) The unit manufacturing costs for the three products are as follows:

	D-gauge	P-gauge	T-gauge
Direct materials	$17	$ 31	$ 50
Direct labor	20	40	60
Variable factory overhead	30	45	60
Fixed factory overhead	10	15	20
	$77	$131	$190

(e) The unit sales prices for the three products are $90, $200, and $180 for the D-gauge, P-gauge, and T-gauge, respectively.

(f) The company is manufacturing at capacity and is selling all the gauges it produces.

Required:

(1) Tom Kirk has suggested that the Precision Gauge Corporation product-line income statement presented for the third quarter of 19A is not suitable for analyzing proposals and making decisions such as the ones suggested by Marvin Caplan.

(a) Explain why the product-line income statement presented is not suitable for analysis and decision making.

(b) Describe an alternative income statement format that would be more suitable for analysis and decision making, and explain why it is better.

(2) Using the operating data presented for Precision Gauge Corporation and assuming that the president's proposed course of action had been implemented at the beginning of the third quarter of 19A, evaluate the president's proposed course of action by specifically responding to the following points:

(a) Are each of the three suggestions cost effective? The discussion should be supported by a differential cost analysis that shows the net impact on income before tax for each of the three suggestions.

(b) Was the president correct in eliminating the T-gauge line? Explain.

(c) Was the president correct in promoting the P-gauge line rather than the D-gauge line? Explain.

(d) Does the proposed course of action make effective use of Precision's capacity? Explain.

(3) Are there any nonquantitative factors that Precision Gauge Corporation should consider before it considers dropping the T-gauge line? Explain.

(ICMA adapted)

CHAPTER 22
Linear Programming for Planning and Decision Making

Quantitative tools and techniques are used by managers to make intelligent decisions and to control operations. At the heart of management's responsibility is the best or optimum use of limited resources that include money, personnel, materials, production equipment, facilities, and time. *Linear programming* is a mathematical tool that provides a way of determining the best use of available resources. It is a valuable aid to management because it provides a systematic and efficient procedure which can be used as a guide in decision making.

▼ LINEAR PROGRAMMING AND THE MAXIMIZATION OF CONTRIBUTION MARGIN

The contribution margin is a measure of business success and, consequently, it is often used as a measure of management performance. To maximize company profits, management must maximize the total contribution margin from the production and sale of products.

To illustrate the application of linear programming to the problem of maximizing the total contribution margin, assume that a machine shop manufactures two models of a product, standard and deluxe. Each unit of the standard model requires two hours of grinding and four hours of polishing. Each unit of the deluxe model requires five hours of grinding and two hours of polishing. The manufacturer has three grinders and two polishers; therefore, in a 40-hour work week there are 120 hours of grinding capacity and 80 hours of polishing capacity available. A unit of the standard model sells for $9, and a unit of the deluxe model sells for $12. The variable costs of producing and selling one unit total $6 and $8 for the standard model and the deluxe model, respectively. Consequently, the contribution margin from the production and sale of a standard unit and a deluxe unit is $3 and $4, respectively. Market demand for both products is strong enough to absorb all units that the company can produce and sell with its present capacity. To maximize the total contribution margin, management must decide on (1) the allocation of the available production capacity between the standard and deluxe models and (2) the resulting number of units of each model to produce.

The relevant information required to solve the problem is summarized as follows:

	Grinding Time	Polishing Time	Sales Price	Variable Cost	Contribution Margin
Standard model.............	2 hours	4 hours	$ 9	$6	$3
Deluxe model................	5	2	12	8	4
Plant capacity................	120	80			

This information is used in illustrating the two methods of solving linear programming problems—the graphic method and the simplex method.

Graphic Method

When a linear programming problem involves only two variables, a two-dimensional graph can be used to determine the optimal solution. In this example, let x be the symbol assigned to the number of units of the standard model and y be the number of units of the deluxe model. The maximum quantity of each model that can be produced, given the limited grinding and polishing capacity (referred to as constraints), is determined as follows:

Production Operation	Maximum Production Quantity	
	Standard Model (x)	Deluxe Model (y)
Grinding...	120 hrs. ÷ 2 = 60	120 hrs. ÷ 5 = 24
Polishing...	80 hrs. ÷ 4 = 20	80 hrs. ÷ 2 = 40

The smallest quantity in each of the two columns is the maximum quantity that can be produced with the limited capacity available. The company can produce no more than 20 units of the standard model, which would result in a contribution margin (CM) of $60 (20 units × $3 CM per unit), or 24 units of the deluxe model, which would result in a contribution margin of $96 (24 units × $4 CM per unit). However, producing a combination of standard and deluxe models would result in a different, perhaps better, solution.

To determine the production combinations possible, the constraints can be plotted on a graph. Once graphed, the production combinations can be evaluated to determine which alternative would result in the maximum contribution margin. Since the relationship between the usage of each available constraint and the quantity of each model produced in this example is linear, the polishing and grinding constraints may be drawn by connecting the points, plotted on each axis, representing the maximum number of units of each model that can be produced with each constraint. These points are:

When x = 0: $y \le 24$ for the grinding constraint
$y \le 40$ for the polishing constraint

When y = 0: $x \le 60$ for the grinding constraint
$x \le 20$ for the polishing constraint

A graph of the constraints for the illustrated problem appears as follows:

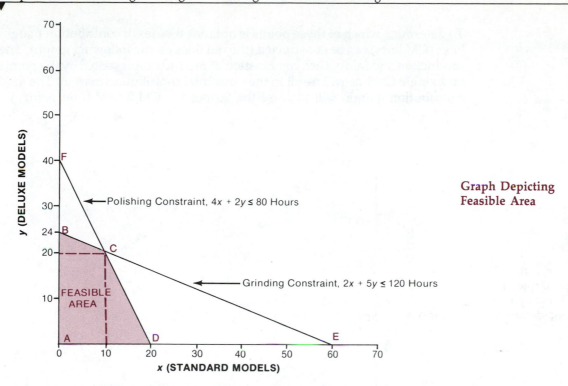

Graph Depicting Feasible Area

The solution space represents the area of feasible solutions and is bounded by the lines AB, BC, CD, and DA on the graph above. Any combination of standard and deluxe units that falls within the solution space can be physically produced. Any combination that falls outside the feasible area cannot be produced because there is not enough constraint available.

The best feasible solution is found at one of the corner points, labeled A, B, C, and D in the graph. To determine which corner point is best, each must be evaluated as follows:

$$
\begin{aligned}
A\ (x = 0, y = 0)\ &= (\$3)(0)\ + (\$4)(0)\ = \$\ \ 0\ \text{CM} \\
B\ (x = 0, y = 24)\ &= (\$3)(0)\ + (\$4)(24) = \$\ 96\ \text{CM} \\
C\ (x = 10, y = 20) &= (\$3)(10) + (\$4)(20) = \$110\ \text{CM} \\
D\ (x = 20, y = 0)\ &= (\$3)(20) + (\$4)(0)\ = \$\ 60\ \text{CM}
\end{aligned}
$$

In this case, the total contribution margin is maximized when 10 standard models and 20 deluxe models are produced and sold, i.e., the combination indicated at corner point C.

The fact that the optimal solution is found at one of the corner points can be demonstrated graphically. Notice in the graph above that the largest quantities for each product combination occur at the farthest distances from point A (i.e., the farthest away from 0 units of each product). Consequently, the production and sale of the product mix indicated at one of the points that lies on the line defining the outermost limit of the feasible area (i.e., the line defined by points B, C, and D, which will be called line BCD) would result in the maximum contribution margin possible, given the constraints imposed on the problem.

To determine which of those points is optimal, a series of contribution margin lines (CM lines) can be constructed (the red lines on the following graph). The production and sale of each combination of products represented by the points on a single CM line will result in the same total contribution margin. The total contribution margin will increase the farther the CM line is from point A.

Graph Depicting CM Lines and Optimal Solution

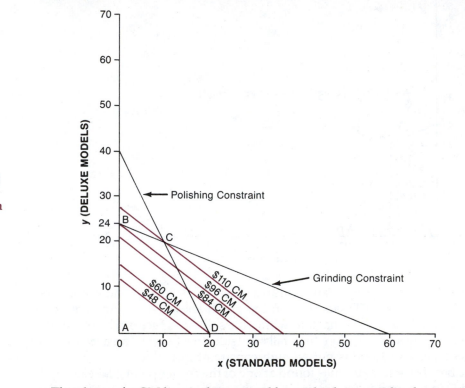

The slope of a CM line is determined by multiplying −1 by the quotient of the contribution margin available from the sale of one unit of the product designated by the horizontal axis, divided by the contribution margin available from the sale of one unit of the product designated by the vertical axis (e.g., −¾ for products x and y in the illustration). Since the total contribution margin in this example is $3x + $4y, a CM line can be constructed by drawing a line between a point plotted on the x axis (indicating the quantity of x's required to yield the contribution margin represented by the line, given that y is zero) and a point plotted on the y axis (indicating the quantity of y's required to yield the same contribution margin, given that x is zero). The following points are computed for the CM lines on the graph above:

CM	Quantity of x's Required When y = 0				Quantity of y's Required When x = 0			
$ 48	$ 48CM	÷	$3	= 16 units	$ 48CM	÷	$4	= 12 units
60	60CM	÷	3	= 20 units	60CM	÷	4	= 15 units
84	84CM	÷	3	= 28 units	84CM	÷	4	= 21 units
96	96CM	÷	3	= 32 units	96CM	÷	4	= 24 units
110	110CM	÷	3	= 36⅔ units	110CM	÷	4	= 27½ units

Notice in the graph above that the CM line is farthest from point A when it intersects point C.[1] Full utilization of all available resources will occur only at the point of common intersection of all of the constraint equations in the problem (point C in this example). However, utilization of all available resources does not necessarily result in an optimal solution. For example, if the contribution margin from the sale of a unit of x were $1 instead of $3, the optimal solution would be found at point B instead of point C (i.e., $1(0) + $4(24) = $96 contribution margin at point B would be greater than $1(10) + $4(20) = $90 contribution margin at point C). Therefore, to find the optimal solution, the contribution margin available from the production and sale of the combination of products indicated at each corner point must be computed and compared.

Simplex Method

Although linear programming problems with more than two constraints can be solved fairly easily using the graphic method, such an approach is not practical in solving problems with more than two variables in the objective function. A problem with three variables would require a three-dimensional graph, which, while not impossible, is certainly more difficult to handle than a two-dimensional graph. A problem with four or more variables would require a four- or more-dimensional graph, which would not be physically tractable. Fortunately, multivariable linear programming problems can be solved algebraically with an iterative procedure referred to as the *simplex method*. Based on matrix (or linear) algebra, the simplex method provides a systematic way of algebraically evaluating each corner point in the feasible area. The process begins at the origin (point A in the example) and systematically moves from one corner point to another until the optimal solution is found. Moves are selected which will provide the largest per unit improvement in the objective function. When the objective function can no longer be improved, the optimal solution has been found, and the iterative process stops.

The example described earlier in this chapter is used to illustrate the simplex method. However, before the simplex method can be applied, the problem must be expressed mathematically, as follows:

1. The objective function is the total contribution margin the manager can obtain from the production and sale of the two models of products. Let x and y represent the quantities of the standard model and the deluxe model to be produced and sold, respectively. Since a contribution margin of $3 is expected for each unit of the standard model and $4 for

---

[1] If the contribution margin changes for either product or for both products, the slope of the CM line would change. If the change in slope is sufficiently large, the optimal solution would shift to a different corner point. If the slope of the CM line were equal to the slope of line BC, all points on line BC would be equally profitable; however, notice that it would never be possible for a point on line BC between points B and C to be more profitable than points B and C.

each unit of the deluxe model, the total contribution margin available would be $3x + 4y$. Therefore, the objective function is:

$$\text{Maximize CM} = 3x + 4y$$

2. Next, the constraints for the problem must be expressed in mathematical form. In the illustration, there are two constraints available, grinding time and polishing time. There are 120 hours of grinding time available. It takes 2 hours of grinding to produce one unit of the standard model (denoted x) and 5 hours of grinding to produce one unit of the deluxe model (denoted y). Therefore, the grinding constraint can be expressed mathematically as follows:

$$2x + 5y \leq 120$$

Since there are 80 hours of polishing time available and it takes 4 hours to produce a unit of the standard model and 2 hours to produce a unit of the deluxe model, the polishing constraint can be expressed mathematically as follows:

$$4x + 2y \leq 80$$

Both constraints in this example are less-than-or-equal-to constraints, i.e., the amount of constraint that may be used must be less than or equal to the amount of constraint available. Maximization problems may also include equal-to constraints (i.e., all of the available constraint must be used) and/or greater-than-or-equal-to constraints (i.e., the amount of resource used must be greater than or equal to the amount specified on the right-hand side of the constraint inequality). These two types of constraints are illustrated in the linear programming minimization problem beginning on page 706.

3. Since the simplex method is an iterative algebraic procedure, the constraints must be converted to a system of equations. A less-than-or-equal-to inequality is converted to an equality by adding a slack variable to the left-hand side of the inequality. The *slack variable*, denoted s_1, may be thought of as the quantity of unused constraint, i.e., the quantity of constraint not used in the production of the two models in the illustration. The inequalities in the illustration rewritten as equalities are:

$$2x + 5y + s_1 = 120$$
$$4x + 2y + s_2 = 80$$

The unit contribution margin of the slack variables in this illustration is zero (but would be positive if the unused constraint had a salvage value), and the objective function equation becomes:

$$\text{Maximize CM} = 3x + 4y + 0s_1 + 0s_2$$

At this point, the simplex method can be applied, and the first tableau can be set up as follows:

	C_j	0	3	4	0	0	← Objective Row
V_i	Mix	Quantity (B_i)	x	y	s_1	s_2	← Variables Row
0	s_1	120	2	5	1	0	⎫
0	s_2	80	4	2	0	1	⎬ Problem Rows
	$Z_j - C_j$	0	−3	−4	0	0	← Index Row

Objective Column   Variables Column   Quantity Column

The simplex method records the relevant data in a matrix form known as the *simplex tableau*. The components of a simplex tableau follow:

1. The *objective row* consists of the coefficients of the objective function. These coefficients are denoted C_j.
2. The *variables row* is made up of the notation for the variables in the problem. It is simply a row which designates the names of each of the variables in the objective function, including slack variables (and artificial variables which are discussed on page 709).
3. The *problem rows* in the first tableau contain the coefficients of the variables in the constraints. Each row contains the coefficients of the variables in one constraint; consequently, as constraints are added to the problem, problem rows are added to the simplex tableau. Variables which are not included in a constraint are assigned a zero coefficient in the problem row of the initial tableau. In subsequent iterations of the tableau, new problem row values are computed, and the old values are replaced in the subsequent tableau. For notational convenience, the coefficients of the variables on the left-hand side of the constraint equations are denoted D_{ij}, where i denotes the row and j denotes the column in which the coefficient appears.
4. The *variables column* contains the names of the variables in the current solution and, therefore, it gives the mix of variables in the solution. Since the initial tableau begins with zero production, the variables column contains only slack variables (and artificial variables which are discussed on page 709). If no units are produced, all available constraints would be unused and, therefore, would be slack. In subsequent iterations of the tableau, different variables will enter the solution and their names will replace those in the current variables column.
5. The *objective column* contains the coefficients of the variables in the current solution. As variables enter and leave the solution in subsequent iterations, the coefficients in the objective column change. The value in the objective column is the coefficient for the variable in solution in the same row in the variables column.
6. The *quantity column* contains the values of the constraints in the initial tableau (i.e., the values on the right-hand side of the constraint

equations denoted B_i, where i is the row in which the value appears). As variables enter into the solution in subsequent iterations of the tableau, the values in the quantity column represent the quantities of the variables in the solution. For a variable representing a product, the value in the quantity column is the quantity of that product that can be produced in the current solution. For a slack variable, the value is the quantity of unused constraint available in the current solution (and for an artificial variable, the value is the excess constraint utilized over the minimum required).

7. The *index row* contains values computed by subtracting the C_j's (i.e., the coefficients of the variables in the objective function which are found on the objective row) from the Z_j's computed for each column. The Z_j's are computed by first multiplying the values in the quantity column (i.e., the B_j's) and each column of the problem rows (i.e., the D_{ij}'s) by the corresponding values in the objective column (i.e., the V_i's) and then adding the products for each column.

$$Z_j = \sum_{i=1}^{n} (V_i D_{ij}) \text{ where n is the number of constraints}$$

The index row for the first tableau is computed as follows:

Column	Z_j	$Z_j - C_j$
Quantity	$(120)(0) + (80)(0) = 0$	$0 - 0 = 0$
x	$(2)(0) + (4)(0) = 0$	$0 - 3 = -3$
y	$(5)(0) + (2)(0) = 0$	$0 - 4 = -4$
s_1	$(1)(0) + (0)(0) = 0$	$0 - 0 = 0$
s_2	$(0)(0) + (1)(0) = 0$	$0 - 0 = 0$

Since the slack variables are the only variables in the solution in the initial tableau, the contribution margin is zero. As variables with a positive contribution margin enter into the solution, the contribution margin increases. The optimal solution could be found by entering variables into the solution on a trial and error basis. However, a more efficient approach would be to enter the variable that will provide the largest improvement in the objective function first. Such an approach is taken in the simplex method. The optimal solution is found by manipulating the simplex tableau using the following step-by-step procedure:

1. Select the most negative value in the index row; i.e., select the $Z_j - C_j$ with the largest negative value (but do not select the value in the quantity column which could be negative if artificial variables are in the solution, as discussed on page 709). Call this column the pivot column. The largest negative $Z_j - C_j$ represents the largest per unit improvement in the objective function available by entering the variable at the top of the pivot column into the solution.

2. For each positive value in the pivot column (i.e., for each positive D_{ij} in the pivot column), divide the value in the quantity column by the value

in the pivot column (i.e., determine $B_i \div D_{ij}$ for each row in the pivot column), and select the smallest positive value. Call this number the pivot number and the corresponding row the pivot row. The smallest positive $B_i \div D_{ij}$ is the maximum quantity of the variable, entering into the solution, that can be produced because the B_i is the most limiting constraint. If any D_{ij} in the pivot column is zero or negative, the constraint for that problem row is not required in the production of the variable entering into the solution.

3. Create a new tableau and replace the variable in the solution in the old tableau with the variable entering the solution (i.e., the variable denoted at the top of the pivot column). Enter the name of the entering variable and its value in the row of the new tableau corresponding to the pivot row under the variables and objective columns, respectively.

4. Divide the values in the pivot row, the B_i and the D_{ij}'s, of the old tableau by the pivot number and enter the quotient in the corresponding cells of the new tableau. The value in the quantity column is the number of units of the new variable produced.

5. Multiply each element in the pivot row of the new tableau (i.e., the B_i and D_{ij}'s) by some D_{ij} in the pivot column of the old tableau (other than the pivot number) and subtract each product from the corresponding value in the row of the old tableau. Enter the difference for each subtraction in the corresponding row of the new tableau. Then, continue the process for each problem row in the old tableau until all problem rows in the new tableau are computed. This procedure will make each D_{ij} in the pivot column of the new tableau, other than the pivot number, equal to zero, and each B_i in the objective column will be adjusted to reflect the quantity of each product produced for the product variables in the solution and the unused quantity of constraint for the slack variables in the solution.

6. Compute the new $Z_j - C_j$ for each column, and enter the value in the index row of the new tableau. The value of the objective function is the value in the quantity column in the index row. Compare the value of the objective function in the new tableau with the value in the old tableau. An improvement should be observed.

7. Determine whether or not there are any negative $Z_j - C_j$ values in the index row. If there are any negative values, select the most negative $Z_j - C_j$ and continue the iterative process. If there are no negative values, the optimal solution has been found. Discontinue the iterative process because the objective function cannot be improved. The optimal solution requires producing the quantity of each variable in the solution in the final tableau, as indicated in the quantity column.

The solution procedure will be clearer by observing the computation of the tableaus for the example. First, notice that the most negative value in the index row of the first tableau, reported as follows, is -4. Therefore, the y column is the pivot column.

C_j			0	3	4	0	0
V_i	Mix	Quantity (B_i)	x	y	s_1	s_2
0	s_1	120	2	5	1	0
0	s_2	80	4	2	0	1
	$Z_j - C_j$		0	−3	−4	0	0

Next, divide each element in the quantity column by the corresponding value in the pivot column as follows:

B_i in Quantity Column	÷ D_{ij} in Pivot Column	= Quotient
120	5	24
80	2	40

Construct a new tableau and replace the variable from the row with the smallest positive $B_i \div D_{ij}$ with the variable entering the solution (i.e., the variable denoted in the variables row for the pivot column). Enter the name and value of the variable remaining in the solution and the value of the variable entering the solution in the objective column:

C_j			0	3	4	0	0
V_i	Mix	Quantity (B_i)	x	y	s_1	s_2
4	y					
0	s_2					
	$Z_j - C_j$					

Next, divide each element in the pivot row of the old tableau by the pivot number, and insert the quotients in the corresponding cells in the new tableau:

Column	Pivot Row Value in Old Tableau	÷ Pivot Number	= Pivot Row Value in New Tableau
Quantity	120	5	24
x	2	5	0.4
y	5	5	1
s_1	1	5	0.2
s_2	0	5	0

C_j			0	3	4	0	0
V_i	Mix	Quantity (B_i)	x	y	s_1	s_2
4	y	24	0.4	1	0.2	0
0	s_2					
	$Z_j - C_j$					

The next step is to multiply each value in the pivot row of the new tableau by the D_{ij} value in the pivot column, other than the pivot number, and then to subtract each product from the corresponding element in the old tableau:

(1) Column	(2) Values in Non-Pivot Row of Old Tableau	(3) Values in Pivot Row of New Tableau	(4) Value of D_{ij} in Pivot Column of Old Tableau	(5) Product (3) × (4)	(6) Remainder (2) − (5)
Quantity	80	24	2	48	32
x	4	0.4	2	0.8	3.2
y	2	1	2	2	0
s_1	0	0.2	2	0.4	−0.4
s_2	1	0	2	0	1

If there had been more than two constraints, this procedure would have been performed for each additional problem row; i.e., each element in the pivot row of the new tableau would be multiplied by the D_{ij} value in the pivot column of the additional problem row and then subtracted from the corresponding element in the additional problem row of the old tableau. Once computed, these values are entered into the corresponding problem row of the new tableau as follows:

C_j		0	3	4	0	0
V_i	Mix	Quantity (B_i)	x	y	s_1	s_2
4	y	24	0.4	1	0.2	0
0	s_2	32	3.2	0	−0.4	1
	$Z_j - C_j$					

The final step in completing the new tableau is to compute the values to be entered in the index row by first computing the Z_j's and then subtracting the corresponding C_j's from them as follows. The final tableau is completed by entering the new $Z_j - C_j$'s in the index row of the new tableau.

Column	Z_j		$Z_j - C_j$	
Quantity	(24)(4) +	(32)(0) = 96	96 − 0 = 96	
x	(0.4)(4) +	(3.2)(0) = 1.6	1.6 − 3 = −1.4	
y	(1)(4) +	(0)(0) = 4	4 − 4 = 0	
s_1	(0.2)(4) + (−0.4)(0) = 0.8		0.8 − 0 = 0.8	
s_2	(0)(4) +	(1)(0) = 0	0 − 0 = 0	

C_j		0	3	4	0	0
V_i	Mix	Quantity (B_i)	x	y	s_1	s_2
4	y	24	0.4	1	0.2	0
0	s_2	32	3.2	0	−0.4	1
	$Z_j - C_j$	96	−1.4	0	0.8	0

The solution for the second tableau is to produce 24 units of y (the deluxe model), which will result in a total contribution margin of $96. This solution is a considerable improvement over the zero contribution margin available from the solution in the first tableau. Also, notice that the simplex solution found after the first iteration is the same as corner point B in the graphic method on page 695. Each iteration of the simplex tableau will find a different corner point in the feasible area until no improvement in the objective function is possible. The solution in the second tableau also indicates that there are 32 units of the second constraint still available, i.e., 32 hours of polishing time still available. However, since one of the values in the index row is negative, the optimal solution has not been reached. If x is brought into the solution, the objective function will be increased by $1.40 for each unit manufactured. Therefore, a second iteration is required.

Since there is only one negative number in the index row of the second tableau, the new pivot column is readily identified as the x column. The ratio of the values in the quantity column divided by the corresponding values in the pivot column are determined as follows:

B_i in Quantity Column	÷ D_{ij} in Pivot Column	= Quotient
24	0.4	60
32	3.2	10

Since 10 is the smallest positive quotient, the s_2 row is identified as the pivot row, 3.2 becomes the new pivot number, and the s_2 variable is replaced in the solution with the x variable. The x variable is entered into the solution in the third tableau. The y variable remains in the solution and is entered into the new tableau:

C_j		0	3	4	0	0
V_i	Mix	Quantity (B_i)	x	y	s_1	s_2
4	y					
3	x					
	$Z_j - C_j$					

Next, each element in the new pivot row is divided by the new pivot number and entered into the new tableau:

Column	Pivot Row Value in Old Tableau	÷ Pivot Number	= Pivot Row Value in New Tableau
Quantity	32	3.2	10
x	3.2	3.2	1
y	0	3.2	0
s_1	−0.4	3.2	−0.125
s_2	1	3.2	0.3125

C_j		0	3	4	0	0
V_i	Mix	Quantity (B_i)	x	y	s_1	s_2
4	y					
3	x	10	1	0	−0.125	0.3125
	$Z_j - C_j$					

The next step is to multiply each value in the pivot row of the new tableau by the D_{ij} value in the pivot column, other than the pivot number, and then to subtract each product from the corresponding element in the old tableau:

(1)	(2)	(3)	(4)	(5)	(6)
	Values in Non-Pivot Row	Values in Pivot Row	Value of D_{ij} in Pivot Column		Remainder
Column	of Old Tableau	of New Tableau	of Old Tableau	Product (3) × (4)	(2) − (5)
Quantity	24	10	0.4	4	20
x	0.4	1	0.4	0.4	0
y	1	0	0.4	0	1
s_1	0.2	−0.125	0.4	−0.05	0.25
s_2	0	0.3125	0.4	0.125	−0.125

Once computed, these values are entered into the new tableau as follows:

C_j		0	3	4	0	0
V_i	Mix	Quantity (B_i)	x	y	s_1	s_2
4	y	20	0	1	0.25	−0.125
3	x	10	1	0	−0.125	0.3125
	$Z_j - C_j$					

The final step in completing the new tableau is to compute the values to be entered in the index row by first computing the Z_j's and then subtracting the corresponding C_j's from them as follows:

Column	Z_j			$Z_j - C_j$	
Quantity	(20)(4) +	(10)(3) =	110	110 − 0 =	110
x	(0)(4) +	(1)(3) =	3	3 − 3 =	0
y	(1)(4) +	(0)(3) =	4	4 − 4 =	0
s_1	(0.25)(4) +	(−0.125)(3) =	0.625	0.625 − 0 =	0.625
s_2	(−0.125)(4) +	(0.3125)(3) =	0.4375	0.4375 − 0 =	0.4375

The final tableau is completed by entering the new $Z_j - C_j$'s in the index row of the new tableau:

C_j		0	3	4	0	0
V_j	Mix	Quantity (B_j)	x	y	s_1	s_2
4	y	20	0	1	0.25	−0.125
3	x	10	1	0	−0.125	0.3125
	$Z_j − C_j$	110	0	0	0.625	0.4375

The solution for the second tableau is to produce 20 units of y (the deluxe model) and 10 units of x (the standard model), which will result in a total contribution margin of $110. This solution is an improvement over the $96 contribution margin available from the solution in the second tableau. Also, notice that the simplex solution found after the second iteration is the same as corner point C in the graphic method on page 695. Since none of the values in the index row are negative, the optimal solution has been reached. Therefore, no further iteration is required.

▼ LINEAR PROGRAMMING AND THE MINIMIZATION OF COST

The previous problem dealt with the maximization of the total contribution margin. Linear programming can also be used in problems whose objective is to minimize variable cost. To illustrate the cost minimization problem, assume that a pharmaceutical firm is planning to produce exactly 40 gallons of a mixture in which the basic ingredients, x and y, cost $8 per gallon and $15 per gallon, respectively. No more than 12 gallons of x can be used, and at least 10 gallons of y must be used. The firm wants to minimize cost.

The objective function can be written as:

$$\text{Minimize cost} = 8x + 15y$$

subject to the following constraints:

$$x + y = 40$$
$$x \leq 12$$
$$y \geq 10$$

The optimal solution in this case is obvious. Since x is cheaper than y, the maximum amount of x permitted by the constraint should be used first (12 gallons), and then the remaining required quantity (28 more gallons to meet the 40-gallon total requirement) should be filled with the more expensive y. However, in more complex problems, a solution may not be so obvious, especially if there are many ingredients, each having different constraints.

Graphic Method

The graphic method can be applied to minimization problems in the same manner as for maximization problems. As with maximization problems, the constraints define the solution space for minimization problems when they are graphed. The constraints for the illustration may be graphed as follows:

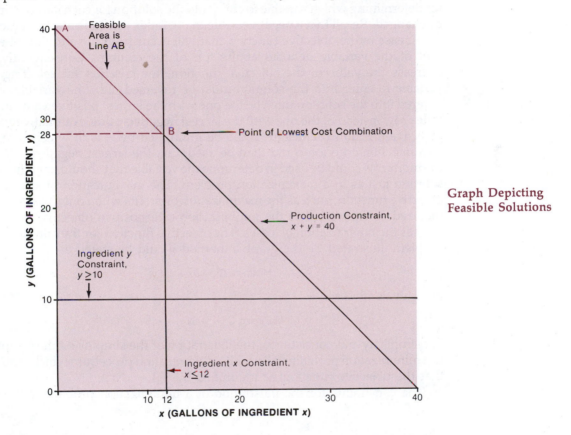

Graph Depicting
Feasible Solutions

The feasible area in this example is confined to the points on line AB. Any combination of x and y that lies on line AB will result in a total production quantity of exactly 40 gallons, of which more than 10 gallons will be y and no more than 12 gallons will be x. As in the case of the maximization problem, the optimal solution will be on one of the corner points of the feasible area, in this case point A or B. Consequently, the corner points must be evaluated to find the combination of inputs that minimizes the objective function, i.e., cost. The values at each of the two corner points are:

A (x = 0, y = 40) = $8(0) + $15(40) = $600 total cost
B (x = 12, y = 28) = $8(12) + $15(28) = $516 total cost

To minimize total cost, the company should use 12 gallons of x and 28 gallons of y, which will result in a total cost of $516.

Simplex Method

The procedure for solving a cost minimization problem using the simplex method is essentially the same as that used in solving a maximization problem. However, one alteration in the problem-solving procedure is required. Since the objective function is being minimized rather than maximized, the criterion for determining which variable to enter into the solution for each iteration must be changed. Recall that a negative value in the index row indicates the amount of increase in the objective function that will occur from the addition of each unit of the variable denoted at the top of the column. Consequently, to decrease the value of the objective function, the criterion for selecting the variable to enter into the solution must be reversed; i.e., the variable to be entered into the solution must be the one with the largest positive value in the index row instead of the one with the largest negative value. Alternatively, the objective function coefficients could be multiplied by -1, in which case the maximization criterion could then be used; i.e., the largest negative value in the index row could be used to determine the variable that should enter into the solution just as in a maximization problem. The maximization of a negative objective function, such as the maximization of profits when only losses can be incurred, is equivalent to the minimization of a positive objective function, such as the minimization of losses. The objective function for the minimization problem illustrated by the graphic method would be stated as:

$$\text{Minimize } C = 8x + 15y$$

or equivalently as:

$$\text{Maximize } C = -8x + -15y$$

For simplicity and consistency, the illustration of the simplex method applied to a minimization problem will use the maximization procedure which requires that the objective function be multiplied by -1.

The constraints for the illustration of a minimization problem are:

$$x + y = 40$$
$$x \quad\; \leq 12$$
$$y \geq 10$$

In the illustration of the maximization problem, the constraints were all of the less-than-or-equal-to kind. Recall that in order to use a less-than-or-equal-to constraint in an algebraic procedure, the inequality was converted to an equality by adding a slack variable to the left-hand side of the equation. In the set of constraints imposed on the minimization problem example, two additional kinds of constraints are introduced, an equal-to constraint and a greater-than-or-equal-to constraint. Since an equal-to constraint is already an equality, a slack variable need not be added. On the other hand, since a greater-than-or-equal-to constraint is an inequality, a negative slack variable must be added to the left-hand side of the equation to form an equality. In this case, the slack variable may be thought of as the excess amount of constraint used over the minimum amount required.

For computation purposes, an *artificial variable*, denoted a_i, must be added to equal-to and greater-than-or-equal-to constraints.[2] Since a_i is artificial, it must be given a very large cost to insure that the artificial variable will be driven out of the final solution. For hand computational purposes, the value m is used to denote that an artificial variable carries a very large cost (for a maximization problem, the artificial variable is a large negative contribution margin, i.e., $-m$). For computerized linear programming routines, a value of 10^{10} is often used as the cost of an artificial variable.

Adding the required slack and artificial variables, the constraint equations for the minimization problem are rewritten as follows:

$$x + y + a_1 \qquad\qquad = 40$$
$$x \qquad\qquad + s_1 = 12$$
$$y + a_2 - s_2 = 10$$

and the objective function equation becomes:

$$\text{Maximize } C = -8x - 15y - ma_1 - 0s_1 - ma_2 + 0s_2$$

For computational purposes, the artificial variables and the slack variable for less-than-or-equal-to constraints are always entered into the initial solution. Following the procedure presented in the discussion of the maximization problem, the first simplex tableau is set up as follows:

C_j		0	-8	-15	$-m$	0	$-m$	0
V_i	Mix	Quantity (B_i)	x	y	a_1	s_1	a_2	s_2
$-m$	a_1	40	1	1	1	0	0	0
0	s_1	12	1	0	0	1	0	0
$-m$	a_2	10	0	1	0	0	1	-1
$Z_j - C_j$		$-50m$	$-m+8$	$-2m+15$	0	0	0	m

---

[2] The set of constraints in a linear programming problem is essentially a set of linear equations. Consequently, the simplex method can make use of solution procedures common to matrix algebra. A single equation of the form $dx = b$, where x is the only unknown, can be solved by simple division, i.e., $x = b \div d$. However, for a system of equations expressed in matrix notation as $Dx = b$, where D is an $n \times n$ matrix, and x and b are $n \times 1$ vectors, solution by division is not possible. Matrices of identical dimensions may be added or subtracted, and matrices that are dimensionally compatible may be multiplied, but a matrix cannot be divided by another matrix. Nevertheless, multiplication by a reciprocal will result in the same solution as division. Therefore, if a matrix can be found which, when multiplied by D, would result in an identity matrix (i.e., a square matrix denoted as I which had ones on the diagonal and zeros elsewhere), a solution to the system of equations can be found. Such a matrix is referred to as an inverse, denoted D^{-1}. The solution to the vector of unknowns, x, of the system of equations, $Dx = b$, can be found by multiplying both sides of the equation by D^{-1}, i.e., $DD^{-1}x = D^{-1}b$ which yields $Ix = D^{-1}b$ or $x = D^{-1}b$. One method of computing an inverse, the Gaussian method, involves elementary row operations that transform the matrix to be inverted into an identity matrix and an identity matrix into an inverse. This method is essentially the method employed to solve the system of linear equations in the simplex method. As a result, a slack or artificial variable with a coefficient of one must be present in each constraint equation in order to construct the initial identity matrix.

The index row ($Z_j - C_j$ row) for the first tableau is computed as follows:

Column	Z_j					$Z_j - C_j$		
Quantity	$(40)(-m) +$	$(12)(0) +$	$(10)(-m) =$	$-50m$	$(-50m) -$	$(0) =$	$-50m$
x	$(1)(-m) +$	$(1)(0) +$	$(0)(-m) =$	$-m$	$(-m) -$	$(-8) =$	$-m+8$
y	$(1)(-m) +$	$(0)(0) +$	$(1)(-m) =$	$-2m$	$(-2m) -$	$(-15) =$	$-2m+15$
a_1	$(1)(-m) +$	$(0)(0) +$	$(0)(-m) =$	$-m$	$(-m) -$	$(-m) =$	0
s_1	$(0)(-m) +$	$(1)(0) +$	$(0)(-m) =$	0	$(0) -$	$(0) =$	0
a_2	$(0)(-m) +$	$(0)(0) +$	$(1)(-m) =$	$-m$	$(-m) -$	$(-m) =$	0
s_2	$(0)(-m) +$	$(0)(0) +$	$(-1)(-m) =$	m	$(m) -$	$(0) =$	m

The most negative value in the index row is under the y column. Therefore, y is the variable entering into the solution in the first iteration. Next, divide each element in the quantity column by the corresponding value in the pivot column as follows:

B_i in Quantity Column $\div$	D_{ij} in Pivot Column $=$	Quotient
40	1	40
12	0	Not defined
10	1	10

Since the smallest positive ratio is in the a_2 row, a_2 in the first tableau is replaced by y in the second tableau. The pivot row is divided by the pivot number as follows:

Column	Pivot Row Value in Old Tableau $\div$	Pivot Number $=$	Pivot Row Value in New Tableau
Quantity	10	1	10
x	0	1	0
y	1	1	1
a_1	0	1	0
s_1	0	1	0
a_2	1	1	1
s_2	-1	1	-1

Next, the non-pivot rows are computed for the second tableau as follows:

(1) Column	(2) Values in a_1 Row of Old Tableau	(3) Values in Pivot Row of New Tableau	(4) Value of D_{ij} in Pivot Column of Old Tableau	(5) Product (3) × (4)	(6) New a_1 Row (2) − (5)
Quantity	40	10	1	10	30
x	1	0	1	0	1
y	1	1	1	1	0
a_1	1	0	1	0	1
s_1	0	0	1	0	0
a_2	0	1	1	1	-1
s_2	0	-1	1	-1	1

(1)	(2) Values in s_1 Row of Old Tableau	(3) Values in Pivot Row of New Tableau	(4) Value of D_{ij} in Pivot Column of Old Tableau	(5) Product $(3) \times (4)$	(6) New s_1 Row $(2) - (5)$
Quantity	12	10	0	0	12
x	1	0	0	0	1
y	0	1	0	0	0
a_1	0	0	0	0	0
s_1	1	0	0	0	1
a_2	0	1	0	0	0
s_2	0	-1	0	0	0

The second tableau and the computation of the index row follow:

C_j		0	-8	-15	-m	0	-m	0
V_i	Mix	Quantity (B_i)	x	y	a_1	s_1	a_2	s_2
-m	a_1	30	1	0	1	0	-1	1
0	s_1	12	1	0	0	1	0	0
-15	y	10	0	1	0	0	1	-1
$Z_j - C_j$		-30m-150	-m+8	0	0	0	2m-15	-m+15

Column	Z_j	$Z_j - C_j$
Quantity	$(30)(-m) + (12)(0) + (10)(-15) = -30m-150$	$(-30m-150) - (0) = -30m-150$
x	$(1)(-m) + (1)(0) + (0)(-15) = -m$	$(-m) - (-8) = -m+8$
y	$(0)(-m) + (0)(0) + (1)(-15) = -15$	$(-15) - (-15) = 0$
a_1	$(1)(-m) + (0)(0) + (0)(-15) = -m$	$(-m) - (-m) = 0$
s_1	$(0)(-m) + (1)(0) + (0)(-15) = 0$	$(0) - (0) = 0$
a_2	$(-1)(-m) + (0)(0) + (1)(-15) = m-15$	$(m-15) - (-m) = 2m-15$
s_2	$(1)(-m) + (0)(0) + (-1)(-15) = -m+15$	$(-m+15) - (0) = -m+15$

Since there are negative values in the index row of the second tableau, the optimal solution has not been found. Notice, however, that an improvement has occurred in the objective function (total cost of 50m has been reduced to 30m + 150). The most negative $Z_j - C_j$ is under the x column; therefore, x will enter the solution in the third tableau. To determine which value x will replace, divide each element in the quantity column by the corresponding element in the pivot column as follows:

B_i in Quantity Column	÷ D_{ij} in Pivot Column	= Quotient
30	1	30
12	1	12
10	0	Not defined

Since the smallest positive ratio is in the s_1 row, s_1 in the second tableau is replaced by x in the third tableau. The pivot row is divided by the pivot number as follows:

Column	Pivot Row Value in Old Tableau	÷ Pivot Number =	Pivot Row Value in New Tableau
Quantity	12	1	12
x	1	1	1
y	0	1	0
a_1	0	1	0
s_1	1	1	1
a_2	0	1	0
s_2	0	1	0

Next, the non-pivot rows are computed for the third tableau as follows:

(1) Column	(2) Values in a_1 Row of Old Tableau	(3) Values in Pivot Row of New Tableau	(4) Value of D_{ij} in Pivot Column of Old Tableau	(5) Product (3) × (4)	(6) New a_1 Row (2) − (5)
Quantity	30	12	1	12	18
x	1	1	1	1	0
y	0	0	1	0	0
a_1	1	0	1	0	1
s_1	0	1	1	1	−1
a_2	−1	0	1	0	−1
s_2	1	0	1	0	1

(1) Column	(2) Values in y_1 Row of Old Tableau	(3) Values in Pivot Row of New Tableau	(4) Value of D_{ij} in Pivot Column of Old Tableau	(5) Product (3) × (4)	(6) New y Row (2) − (5)
Quantity	10	12	0	0	10
x	0	1	0	0	0
y	1	0	0	0	1
a_1	0	0	0	0	0
s_1	0	1	0	0	0
a_2	1	0	0	0	1
s_2	−1	0	0	0	−1

The third tableau and the computation of the index row follow:

C_j		0	−8	−15	−m	0	−m	0
V_i	Mix	Quantity (B_i)	x	y	a_1	s_1	a_2	s_2
−m	a_1	18	0	0	1	−1	−1	1
−8	x	12	1	0	0	1	0	0
−15	y	10	0	1	0	0	1	−1
$Z_j − C_j$		−18m−246	0	0	0	m−8	2m−15	−m+15

Column	Z_j			$Z_j - C_j$		
Quantity	$(18)(-m) + (12)(-8) + (10)(-15) =$	$-18m - 246$		$(-18m - 246) -$	$(0) =$	$-18m - 246$
x	$(0)(-m) + (1)(-8) + (0)(-15) =$	-8		$(-8) -$	$(-8) =$	0
y	$(0)(-m) + (0)(-8) + (1)(-15) =$	-15		$(-15) -$	$(-15) =$	0
a_1	$(1)(-m) + (0)(-8) + (0)(-15) =$	$-m$		$(-m) -$	$(-m) =$	0
s_1	$(-1)(-m) + (1)(-8) + (0)(-15) =$	$m - 8$		$(m - 8) -$	$(0) =$	$m - 8$
a_2	$(-1)(-m) + (0)(-8) + (1)(-15) =$	$m - 15$		$(m - 15) -$	$(-m) =$	$2m - 15$
s_2	$(1)(-m) + (0)(-8) + (-1)(-15) =$	$-m + 15$		$(-m + 15) -$	$(0) =$	$-m + 15$

Since there is a negative value in the index row of the third tableau, the optimal solution has not been found. Again an improvement has occurred in the objective function. Total cost has been reduced from $30m + 150$ to $18m + 246$. The only negative $Z_j - C_j$ is under the s_2 column; therefore, s_2 will enter the solution in the fourth tableau. To determine which value s_2 will replace, divide each element in the quantity column by the corresponding element in the pivot column as follows:

B_j in Quantity Column	÷	D_{ij} in Pivot Column	=	Quotient
18		1		18
12		0		Not defined
10		-1		Not relevant

Since the smallest positive ratio is in the a_1 row, a_1 in the second tableau is replaced by s_2 in the third tableau. The pivot row is divided by the pivot number as follows:

Column	Pivot Row Value in Old Tableau	÷ Pivot Number =	Pivot Row Value in New Tableau
Quantity	18	1	18
x	0	1	0
y	0	1	0
a_1	1	1	1
s_1	-1	1	-1
a_2	-1	1	-1
s_2	1	1	1

Next, the non-pivot rows are computed for the fourth tableau as follows:

(1) Column	(2) Values in x Row of Old Tableau	(3) Values in Pivot Row of New Tableau	(4) Value of D_{ij} in Pivot Column of Old Tableau	(5) Product (3) × (4)	(6) New x Row (2) − (5)
Quantity	12	18	0	0	12
x	1	0	0	0	1
y	0	0	0	0	0
a_1	0	1	0	0	0
s_1	1	-1	0	0	1
a_2	0	-1	0	0	0
s_2	0	1	0	0	0

Column	(2) Values in y Row of Old Tableau	(3) Values in Pivot Row of New Tableau	(4) Value of D_{ij} in Pivot Column of Old Tableau	(5) Product (3) × (4)	(6) New y Row (2) − (5)
Quantity	10	18	−1	−18	28
x	0	0	−1	0	0
y	1	0	−1	0	1
a_1	0	1	−1	−1	1
s_1	0	−1	−1	1	−1
a_2	1	−1	−1	1	0
s_2	−1	1	−1	−1	0

The fourth tableau and the computation of the index row follow:

C_j			0	−8	−15	−m	0	−m	0
V_i	Mix	Quantity (B_i)	x	y	a_1	s_1	a_2	s_2
0	s_2	18	0	0	1	−1	−1	1
−8	x	12	1	0	0	1	0	0
−15	y	28	0	1	1	−1	0	0
$Z_j - C_j$		−516	0	0	m−15	7	m	0

Column	Z_j				$Z_j - C_j$		
Quantity	(18)(0) +	(12)(−8) +	(28)(−15) = −516	(−516) −	(0) =	−516
x	(0)(0) +	(1)(−8) +	(0)(−15) = −8	(−8) −	(−8) =	0
y	(0)(0) +	(0)(−8) +	(1)(−15) = −15	(−15) −	(−15) =	0
a_1	(1)(0) +	(0)(−8) +	(1)(−15) = −15	(−15) −	(−m) =	m−15
s_1	(−1)(0) +	(1)(−8) +	(−1)(−15) = 7	(7) −	(0) =	7
a_2	(−1)(0) +	(0)(−8) +	(0)(−15) = 0	(0) −	(−m) =	m
s_2	(1)(0) +	(0)(−8) +	(0)(−15) = 0	(0) −	(0) =	0

Since there are no negative values in the index row, the optimal solution has been found. The company should use 12 gallons of x and 28 gallons of y, which will result in a total cost of $516.

▼ SENSITIVITY ANALYSIS

The optimal solution to a linear programming problem is determined on the basis of the mathematical relationships among the objective function and the constraints. Changes in the values of the coefficients of the objective function variables or in the amount of available constraint can result in changes in the optimal solution to the problem. Since future events typically are uncertain, it is often prudent to evaluate the sensitivity of the optimal solution to changes in the relevant variables. This evaluation process is referred to as *sensitivity analysis*.

Sensitivity Analysis of Objective Function Coefficients

If the contribution margin of one of the two products in the contribution margin maximization problem illustrated on pages 693 through 706 changes, the slope of the contribution margin (CM) line will change. (In a two-variable cost minimization problem, the slope of the cost line would change.) In most cases, a limited amount of change in the value of the objective function coefficients can occur without changing the optimal solution. The purpose of sensitivity analysis is to determine how much change can occur before the optimal solution is changed, i.e., before the optimal mix changes. Sensitivity analysis is a static analysis. It assumes that all variables remain unchanged, except the one being evaluated. The upper and lower limits determined for the objective function coefficient being analyzed are valid only if the constraints and the objective function coefficients of the other variables do not change.

The effect of changes in objective function coefficients can be evaluated graphically. Recall from page 696 that a CM line is a line describing all of the combinations that will result in the same total contribution margin. The slope is determined by multiplying a -1 by the quotient of the contribution margin available from the sale of one unit of the product designated by the horizontal axis, divided by the contribution margin available from the sale of one unit of the product designated by the vertical axis (which was $-\frac{3}{4}$ for the maximization problem illustrated). Notice that CM line 1 in the following graph has a slope of $-\frac{3}{4}$ and passes through corner point C. Since CM line 1 is the farthest possible distance from the origin (point A) that a line with a $-\frac{3}{4}$

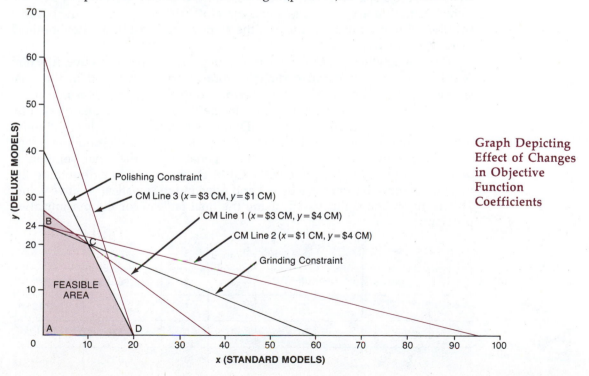

Graph Depicting Effect of Changes in Objective Function Coefficients

slope can be drawn and still remain in the feasible area, point C defines the mix of products that will maximize the total contribution margin subject to the production constraints imposed on the problem.

To observe the effect of a change in an objective function coefficient, assume that the contribution margin from the sale of a unit of the standard model (x) declines from $3 to $1, but the contribution margin from the sale of a deluxe model (y) remains unchanged. In such a case, the slope of the CM line would change from $-\frac{3}{4}$ to $-\frac{1}{4}$ (now 4 units of the standard model would have to be sold to generate as much profit as would be available from the sale of 1 unit of the deluxe model). Notice that the slope of the CM line has decreased, as illustrated by CM line 2 in the graph, and as a consequence, the CM line farthest from the origin now passes through point B. The optimal product mix has changed from point C (produce 20 units of y and 10 units of x) to point B (produce 24 units of y and no units of x). Now assume that the contribution margin from the sale of a unit of the standard model remains at $3, but that the contribution margin for a unit of the deluxe model (y) drops from $4 to $1. Now the slope of the CM line increases from $-\frac{3}{4}$ to $-\frac{3}{1}$, and the CM line farthest from the origin, illustrated by CM line 3 in the graph, now passes through point D. The optimal product mix has again changed, this time from point C (produce 20 units of y and 10 units of x) to point D (produce no units of y and 20 units of x).

Notice in the graph that CM line 1 could rotate somewhat around point C without changing the solution. The slope could decrease from $-\frac{3}{4}$ to $-\frac{24}{60}$ (which is the slope of the grinding constraint) or increase from $-\frac{3}{4}$ to $-\frac{40}{20}$ (which is the slope of the polishing constraint) without changing the optimal solution. But any further change in the slope would result in a new optimal production mix.

The maximum allowable increase or decrease in the objective function coefficients can be computed directly from information found in the final simplex tableau, i.e., the tableau for the optimal solution. The maximum allowable decrease for those variables in the final solution is determined by computing the quotient $(Z_j - C_j) \div D_{ij}$ for each variable that does not enter into the final solution and by selecting the smallest positive quotient. The maximum allowable increase for those variables in the final solution is determined by multiplying the $(Z_j - C_j) \div D_{ij}$ computed in determining the maximum allowable decrease by -1 and selecting the smallest positive value. This computation is illustrated, using the final tableau for the maximization problem:

C_j		0	3	4	0	0
V_j	Mix	Quantity (B_j)	x	y	s_1	s_2
4	y	20	0	1	0.25	-0.125
3	x	10	1	0	-0.125	0.3125
	$Z_j - C_j$	110	0	0	0.625	0.4375

Variable	$(Z_j - C_j) \div D_{ij}$ for s_1 Column	$(Z_j - C_j) \div D_{ij}$ for s_2 Column
x	$0.625 \div -0.125 = -5$	$0.4375 \div 0.3125 = 1.4$
y	$0.625 \div 0.25 = 2.5$	$0.4375 \div -0.125 = -3.5$

The maximum allowable decrease in the contribution margin of a unit of the standard model (x) is $1.40, and the maximum allowable increase is $5 (i.e., -5×-1). The maximum allowable decrease in the contribution margin of a unit of the deluxe model (y) is $2.50, and the maximum allowable increase is $3.50 (i.e., -3.5×-1). Notice that an increase of $5 in the contribution margin of an x, with y remaining constant, or a decrease of $2.50 in the contribution margin of a y, with x remaining constant, will result in a profit line with a slope of -2, which is equal to the slope of the polishing constraint in the graph. Similarly, a decrease of $1.40 in the contribution margin of an x, with y remaining constant, or an increase of $3.50 in the contribution margin of a y, with x remaining constant, will result in a profit line with a slope of $-.4$, which is equal to the slope of the grinding constraint in the graph. This result is consistent with the result predicted in the graph.

If the contribution margin of a unit of the standard model (x) increases exactly $5 (assuming all other variables remain constant), or the contribution margin of a unit of the deluxe model (y) decreases by exactly $2.50 (again assuming that all other variables remain constant), the firm would be indifferent between any of the product mixes indicated by line CD. Similarly, if the contribution margin of a unit of the standard model decreases by exactly $1.40, or the contribution margin of a unit of the deluxe model increases by exactly $3.50, the firm would be indifferent between any of the product mixes indicated by line BC. However, if the contribution margin of a unit of the standard model increases more than $5 or decreases more than $1.40, or if the sales price of a unit of the deluxe model increases by more than $3.50 or decreases by more than $2.50, the optimal product mix will change to a different corner point in the feasible area.

For variables that are not part of the optimal solution, the allowable decrease is infinity. Since the objective function coefficient of a variable that is not part of the optimal product mix is not large enough to keep it in the final solution, a decrease will not bring it back into the solution. As a result, the allowable decrease is infinity. On the other hand, an increase in the coefficient of a variable that is not in the final solution could bring it into the solution if the increase is large enough. The allowable increase for a variable that is not in the final solution is an amount equal to its $Z_j - C_j$ found in the index row of the final simplex tableau. If the C_j, which is the objective function coefficient, were to be increased to a point where it exceeded the Z_j for the variable column (in which case the $Z_j - C_j$ would be negative), the current solution would not be optimal. To make the solution optimal, the non-solution variable would have to be brought into the solution, resulting in a new solution and a new product mix. However, if the objective function coefficient were increased by an amount exactly equal to the $Z_j - C_j$ in the index row, the new $Z_j - C_j$ would be zero and the optimal solution would not change. Therefore, the maximum increase for a variable not in the final solution is an amount equal to the $Z_j - C_j$ in the index row of the final tableau.

In the case of a cost minimization problem, the procedures for determining the allowable increases and decreases in the objective function coefficients are essentially the same. However, the fact that an increase in unit cost will result in a decrease in contribution margin and that a decrease in unit cost will result in an increase in contribution margin should be considered. Consequently, the allowable increase in cost is determined in the same way as the allowable decrease in contribution margin [i.e., select the smallest positive $(Z_j - C_j) \div D_{ij}$ in the variable row], and the allowable decrease in cost is determined in the same way as the allowable increase in contribution margin [i.e., select the smallest negative $(Z_j - C_j) \div D_{ij}$ and multiply by -1]. Similarly, for a variable that does not enter into the final solution, the allowable increase in cost is the same as the allowable decrease in contribution margin (i.e., infinity), and the allowable decrease in cost is the same as the allowable increase in contribution margin (i.e., the non-solution variables $Z_j - C_j$ found in the index row).

Sensitivity Analysis for the Constraint Values

It may also be useful to consider the sensitivity of the optimal solution to the relaxation of a constraint. As was the case with a sensitivity analysis of the objective function coefficients, a sensitivity analysis of the constraint values is a static analysis. The objective function coefficients and the quantity of all other constraints are assumed not to change.

The purpose for evaluating the sensitivity of the optimal solution to changes in an available constraint is to determine the effect on the objective function (i.e., the increase or decrease in the total contribution margin or total cost) that will occur if there is an increase or decrease in an available constraint. The per unit change in the objective function that will occur by increasing or decreasing a constraint is called a *shadow price*. The shadow price for each constraint can be found in the index row of the final simplex tableau in the slack variable column for less-than-or-equal-to and greater-than-or-equal-to constraints and in the artificial variable column for equal-to constraints.

For the contribution margin maximization problem illustrated previously, there are two constraints and, therefore, two shadow prices. Shadow prices found in the index row of the final tableau are 0.625 in the s_1 column for the grinding constraint and 0.4375 in the s_2 column for the polishing constraint. These slack variables represent the trade-off in terms of product mix as the constraints are increased or decreased.[3] For example, one more hour of grinding time will increase the contribution margin by $0.625 (assuming that the cost of an additional hour of grinding time does not change). As one more grinding hour is made available, 0.25 units of y, the deluxe model, with a unit contribution margin of $4, will replace 0.125 units of x, the standard model,

---

[3]This discussion is adapted from Lanny G. Chasteen, "A Graphical Approach to Linear Programming Shadow Prices," *The Accounting Review*, Vol. XLVII, No. 4, pp. 819-823.

with a unit contribution margin of $3. The net increase in the total contribution margin is determined as follows:

$$\begin{array}{rl} 0.25 \times \$4 = & \$1\ 000 \\ 0.125 \times \$3 = & \underline{\$0.375} \\ \text{Net increase} & \underline{\$0.625} \end{array}$$

If additional grinding time could be obtained at no increase in unit variable cost, an increase of $0.625 in the contribution margin would result, and as much as $0.625 more than the present unit variable cost could be paid for an additional unit of grinding time (at which point a zero contribution margin per additional unit would occur). Thus, management may wish to consider paying an overtime premium if it does not exceed $0.625 per hour. A shadow price may also be interpreted as the opportunity cost of using the resource for some other purpose. The shadow price of $0.4375 has the same interpretation for each additional hour of polishing time that could be acquired.

The range of shadow prices for grinding and polishing hours can be computed from information available in the final simplex tableau. The allowable decrease is determined by dividing each value in the solution mix (i.e., each B_i in the final tableau) by the corresponding coefficients in the slack variable column (i.e., the D_{ij}'s in the shadow price column in the same row with the B_i) and selecting the smallest positive value. The allowable increase is determined by multiplying each quotient by -1 and selecting the smallest positive value. The computational procedure is illustrated as follows:

C_j		0	3	4	0	0
V_i	Mix	Quantity (B_i)	x	y	s_1	s_2
4	y	20	0	1	0.25	-0.125
3	x	10	1	0	-0.125	0.3125
$Z_j - C_j$		110	0	0	0.625	0.4375

Mix	B_i Quantity	D_{ij} in s_1 Column	D_{ij} in s_2 Column	$B_i \div D_{ij}$ for s_1	$B_i \div D_{ij}$ for s_2
y	20	0.25	-0.125	80	-160
x	10	-0.125	0.3125	-80	32

For the grinding constraint, the allowable decrease is 80 hours (the minimum positive value in the $B_i \div D_{ij}$ column for the s_1 slack variable) and the allowable increase is 80 hours (the minimum positive value in the $B_i \div D_{ij}$ column for the s_1 slack variable after all quotients are multiplied by -1, i.e., $-1 \times -80 = 80$). Therefore, the lower limit on the grinding constraint is 40 hours (120 hours $-$ 80 hours allowable decrease), and the upper limit is 200 hours (120 hours $+$ 80 hours allowable increase). For the polishing constraint, the allowable decrease is 32 hours (the minimum positive value in the $B_i \div D_{ij}$ column for the s_2 slack variable), and the allowable increase is 160 hours (the minimum positive value in the $B_i \div D_{ij}$ column for the s_2 slack variable after all quotients are multiplied by −1, i.e., −1 × −160 = 160). Therefore, the lower limit on the polishing constraint is 48 hours (80 hours − 32 hours allowable decrease), and the upper limit is 240 hours (80 hours + 160 hours allowable increase).

If only 40 hours of grinding time are available, maximum production is 20 units of x (40 hours ÷ 2 hours per unit) or 8 units of y (40 hours ÷ 5 hours per unit). If 200 hours are available, maximum production is 100 units of x (200 hours ÷ 2 hours per unit) or 40 units of y (200 hours ÷ 5 hours per unit). Similarly, if only 48 hours of polishing time is available, maximum production is 12 units of x (48 hours ÷ 4 hours per unit) or 24 units of y (48 hours ÷ 2 hours per unit). If 240 hours are available, maximum production is 60 units of x (240 hours ÷ 4 hours per unit) or 120 units of y (240 hours ÷ 2 hours per unit).

The effect of these limits can be observed in the following graph. Notice that if the grinding constraint is decreased below the lower limit, the polishing

Graph Depicting Allowable Increases and Decreases in Constraints

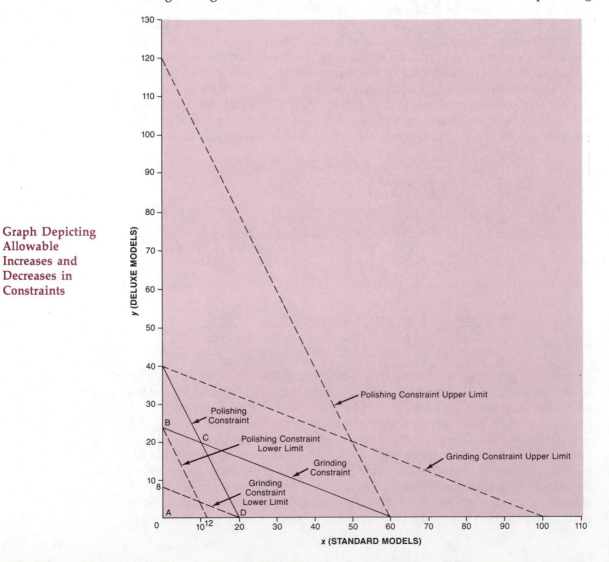

constraint will no longer be an effective production constraint, and if the grinding constraint is increased beyond the upper limit, it will no longer be an effective production constraint. Consequently, if either boundary is exceeded, the shadow price for grinding time will change. The same effect can be observed for the polishing constraint. If the polishing constraint is decreased below its lower limit or increased beyond its upper limit, the shadow price for the polishing constraint will change.

If the slack variable associated with a less-than-or-equal-to constraint enters into the final solution, the constraint is not binding because not all of the constraint available has been used; i.e., there is some slack available. However, if the amount of constraint available declines below the slack available, the optimal solution will change and, consequently, the shadow prices will change. Therefore, the allowable decrease in a non-binding less-than-or-equal-to constraint is the amount of unused constraint in the final simplex tableau, i.e., the amount of constraint in the quantity column for the slack variable in the final solution mix. Since the amount of constraint used is less than the amount available, any addition to the available constraint would have no influence on the optimal solution. As a result, the allowable increase in a non-binding less-than-or-equal-to constraint is infinity.

Since a greater-than-or-equal-to constraint constrains the objective function in a different way than a less-than-or-equal-to constraint (e.g., it sets a minimum quantity instead of a maximum), the allowable decrease and increase must be computed differently. The allowable *increase* for a binding greater-than-or-equal-to constraint is determined by dividing each value in the final solution mix (i.e., each B_i) by the corresponding coefficients in the slack variables column (i.e., the D_{ij}'s in the shadow price column in the same row with the B_i) and selecting the smallest positive value. The allowable *decrease* is determined by multiplying each quotient by -1 and selecting the smallest positive value. If the slack variable associated with a greater-than-or-equal-to constraint enters into the final solution, the allowable increase is the amount of excess constraint used over the minimum required (i.e., the value in the quantity column of the final simplex tableau for the greater-than-or-equal-to constraint associated with the slack variable in the solution). Any increase beyond the slack amount in the quantity column will make the constraint binding and alter the optimal solution. The allowable decrease is infinity because the quantity used is already greater than the minimum required. A decrease will not reduce the amount of constraint used and, therefore, will not impact on the solution.

▼ LINEAR PROGRAMMING TECHNIQUES—GENERAL OBSERVATIONS

The maximization and minimization problems illustrated in this chapter, together with those presented in the exercises and problems, are realistic examples of the types of problems faced by managers. Linear programming is a tool that can be effectively used by management to solve such problems. However, as the number of variables and the number of constraints increase, the computational difficulty increases. As a consequence, linear programming problems in actual practice are typically solved by using high-speed computers. The systematic, iterative procedures required in linear programming make it ideally suited and readily adaptable to computer solution. Although the computational difficulties are removed by using a computer, the decision maker must still formulate the problem in mathematical terms, select the proper data for entry into the program, and interpret the final solution. The accountant's role is to aid in this process.

DISCUSSION QUESTIONS

1. Explain what linear programming is.

2. What kind of unit costs are used in linear programming?

3. Examine the graph on page 695 and answer the following questions:
   a. The area bounded by the lines AB, BC, CD, and AD is called the solution space. Why?
   b. The triangles BCF and CDE are not part of the solution space. Why?
   c. Which point in the solution space designates the optimal solution? How can it be identified?

4. What is the simplex method?

5. What are the components of a simplex tableau? Explain.

6. What is a slack variable, and when is it used?

7. What is an artificial variable, and when is it used?

8. What effect will the change in an objective function coefficient have on the optimal solution?

9. What is a shadow price, and how may it be interpreted?

EXERCISES

1. Contribution margin maximization—problem formulation. Barnoski Company wants to maximize the profits on Products a, b, and c. The contribution margin for each product follows:

Product	Contribution Margin
a	$2
b	5
c	4

The production requirements and departmental capacities, by departments, are as follows:

Department	Production Requirement by Product (Hours)			Departmental Capacity (Total Hours)
	a	b	c	
Assembling......................	2	3	2	30,000
Painting............................	1	2	2	38,000
Finishing..........................	2	3	1	28,000

Required: Formulate the objective function and the constraints.

2. Contribution margin maximization—problem formulation. Styles Company manufactures two products, x and y. Each unit of x sells for $95, and each unit of y sells for $60. Variable manufacturing costs total $50 for a unit of x and $35 for a unit of y. It takes two hours of direct labor and one hour of machine time to produce a unit of x, and it takes one hour of direct labor and ¾ hour of machine time to produce a unit of y. No more than 500 hours of direct labor and 200 hours of machine time are available during a single month. The company wants to utilize fully all available machine time. Two units of material A are required to produce a unit of x, and three units of material A are required to produce a unit of y. In addition, two units of material B are required to produce a unit of x; however, material B is not required in the manufacture of y. There are 1,200 units of material A and 400 units of material B available.

Required: Assuming that Styles Company wants to maximize its profits, give the appropriate linear programming objective function and constraints for the production of x and y.

3. Cost minimization—problem formulation. A company seeks to minimize the total cost of Materials a and b. The per pound cost of a is $25 and of b, $10. The two materials are combined to form a product that must weigh 50 pounds. At least 20 pounds of a and no more than 40 pounds of b can be used.

Required: Formulate the objective function and the constraints.

4. Cost minimization—problem formulation. Harwell division of Berrett Company is a cost center. It manufactures component parts x and y for the company's Davidson division. Variable manufacturing costs of $40 are incurred in the manufacture of a unit of x and $60 in the manufacture of a unit of y. It is company policy to utilize fully all available direct labor each period. One-half hour of direct labor is required to manufacture a unit of x, and ¾ hour to manufacture a unit of y. Direct labor to be utilized during the period totals 200 hours. Two units of raw material are required to produce a unit of x, and three units are required to produce a unit of y. No more than 1,000 units of raw material are available for the period. To meet the production requirements of Davidson division, at least 150 units of x and y combined must be produced, at least 50 units of which must be units of y.

Required: Formulate the appropriate linear programming objective function and constraints for the Harwell division cost minimization problem.

5. Contribution margin maximization—graphic method. The following graph presents the constraints (all of the less-than-or-equal-to type) for a chair manufacturing company whose production problem can be solved by linear programming. The company earns a contribution margin of $5 for each office chair sold and $8 for each kitchen chair sold.

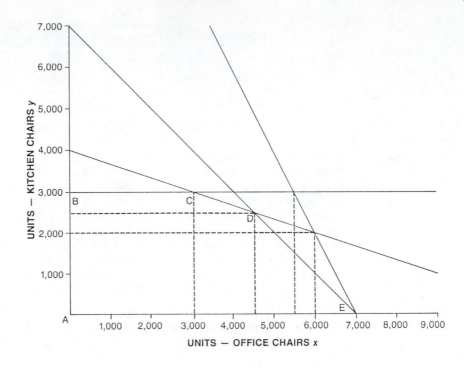

Required: What is the contribution margin maximizing production schedule?

(ICMA adapted)

6. Contribution margin maximization—graphic method. Chasteen Company manufactures two products, Alpha and Beta, that have contribution margins of $10 and $5 per unit, respectively. Each unit of Alpha requires 10 machine hours, while each unit of Beta requires 4 machine hours; 100 machine hours are available. Each unit of Beta requires two units of Material Z, of which 30 units are available.

Required: Determine the units of Alpha and Beta that must be manufactured to maximize the total contribution margin, using the graphic method.

7. Contribution margin maximization—graphic method. Green Nursery is considering the possibility of adding imported fruit trees and oriental yard shrubs to its line of nursery products. The fruit trees have a per unit contribution margin of $10; shrubs, $4. There are 12 square feet available for display. Each tree requires two square feet of space, while each shrub occupies three square feet. In addition, two hours each day are needed to prepare each tree for sale and one hour to prepare each shrub. Due to the many jobs to be performed in the nursery, only eight hours are available each day.

Required: Determine the number of imported fruit trees and oriental yard shrubs that should be stocked each day to maximize the contribution margin, using the graphic method.

8. Cost minimization—graphic method. Two additives are mixed with a plastic resin prior to extension into a final product. Over a period of time, empirical relationships were developed to meet quality specifications of the final product. Within the latitude of these relationships, the quantities are varied according to their current cost. Operating costs are not affected by the proportions of the two additives in the product.

The quality relationships per 100 kilograms of product are:

For tensile strength..................... $2a + b \geq 1.1$
For flexibility............................. $a + 3b \geq 1.5$

Additive a sells for $8 per kg, and b for $5 per kg.

Required: Determine the most economical (minimum cost) mixture, using the graphic method.

9. Cost minimization—graphic method. Certain animals at the Southport Zoo must receive an adequate amount of two vitamins in their daily food supply. The minimum daily requirement of Vitamin A is 30 units; of Vitamin B, 50 units.

One pound of foodstuff x can provide $3\frac{1}{3}\%$ of the minimum daily requirements of A and 4% of B. One pound of y will supply 10% of A and 2% of B requirements. The costs are: x, $.02 per pound; y, $.05 per pound.

Required: Determine the least possible cost to provide for the minimum requirements of the two vitamins, using the graphic method.

10. Sensitivity analysis. Voltz Metal Company produces three products, x, y, and z, with contribution margins of $10, $15, and $30, respectively. Production is constrained by the following three factors:

$x + 3y + 8z \leq 300$ hours of assembly time available
$x + y + 3z \leq 150$ hours of welding time available
$2x + y + z \leq 200$ hours of punch press time available

The production mix problem was formulated as the following linear programming problem and solved using the simplex method:

Maximize CM $= \$10x + \$15y + \$30z$
Subject To: $x + 3y + 8z + s_1 = 300$
$x + y + 3z + s_2 = 150$
$2x + y + z + s_3 = 200$

The final simplex tableau is as follows:

	C_j		0	10	15	30	0	0	0
V_i	Mix	Quantity (B_i)	x	y	z	s_1	s_2	s_3
0	s_2	10	0	0	1	$-.2$	1	$-.4$
10	x	60	1	0	-1	$-.2$	0	.6
15	y	80	0	1	3	.4	0	$-.2$
	$Z_j - C_j$	1,800	0	0	5	4	0	3

Required:

(1) Determine the maximum contribution margin available and the optimal production mix from the final simplex tableau.

(2) For each of the three products, determine the amount of increase and decrease in the contribution margin that could occur without changing the product mix indicated by the final simplex tableau.

(3) Identify the shadow prices for each of the three constraints and explain what they mean.

(4) Compute the allowable increase and decrease in each available constraint that could occur without changing the related shadow prices.

PROBLEMS

22-1. Contribution margin maximization—simplex method. Scraggs Company manufactures two products, x and y, with contribution margins of $5 and $3, respectively. One hour of machine time is required to produce one unit of each product. A maximum of 50 hours of machine time is available each period. It takes two hours of direct labor to produce one unit of x and one hour to produce a unit of y. No more than 60 direct labor hours are available each period.

Required: Using the simplex method, determine the product mix required to maximize the company's total contribution margin each period.

22-2. Contribution margin maximization—simplex method. Kevin Company manufactures two products, p and q, which have sales prices of $30 and $25, respectively. Variable manufacturing costs are $21 and $19 for p and q, respectively. The only two relevant production constraints are available cutting and assembly time. Production requirements and time available are:

Constraint	Quantity Required Product p	Product q	Maximum Available
Cutting time	3 hours	1 hour	120 hours
Assembly time	1 hour	1 hour	90 hours

Required: Using the simplex method, determine the product mix required to maximize the company's total contribution margin.

22-3. Cost minimization—simplex method. Dalton division of Calvin Manufacturing Company produces two products, f and g, which have variable costs of $30 and $50, respectively. These products are component parts for products produced by the Brandon division of Calvin Manufacturing Company. These parts are transferred at cost. To avoid laying off key personnel, Dalton must use at least 160 hours of direct labor each period. It takes one direct labor hour to manufacture a unit of f and 3 direct labor hours to manufacture a unit of g. To meet the minimum production requirements of Brandon division, Dalton must manufacture and transfer twice as many units of f as g, and the total combined quantity must be at least 100 units.

Required: Using the simplex method, determine the product mix required to minimize Dalton division's total cost.

22-4. Contribution margin maximization—graphic and simplex methods. Merz Inc. manufactures two kinds of leather belts—belt a (a high-quality belt) and belt b (of a lower quality). The respective contribution margins are $4 and $3 per belt. Production of belt a requires twice as much time as for belt b; and if all belts were of the belt b type, Merz Inc. could produce 1,000 per day. The leather supply is sufficient for only 800 belts per day (both belt a and belt b combined). Belt a requires a fancy buckle, and only 400 buckles per day are available for this belt.

Required: Determine the quantity of each type belt to be produced to maximize the contribution margin, using (1) the graphic method and (2) the simplex method.

22-5. Cost minimization—graphic and simplex methods. A company produces three products, a, b, and c, which use common materials, x and y. Material x costs $3 per ton and y $4 per ton. The amount of materials required per ton of product and the required weight per ton of product are:

	Product a	Product b	Product c
Material x...	4 lbs.	7 lbs.	1.5 lbs.
Material y...	8	2	5
Minimum weight required...................	32	14	15

Required: Determine the number of tons of each material needed to meet the requirements at minimum cost by (1) the graphic method and (2) the simplex method.

22-6. Contribution margin maximization—simplex method with sensitivity analysis. Sansei Inc. produces two types of promotional fans—oriental and domestic. The contribution margin on oriental fans is $5 per 100; on domestic fans, $4 per 100. Two hundred hours are available for the production of these fans. Two hours are required to produce 100 oriental fans, while one hour is required to produce 100 domestic fans. One pound of paper is required for each 100 fans, whether oriental or domestic. Sansei Inc. has 150 pounds of paper.

Required:

(1) Determine the product mix that provides the maximum contribution margin, using the simplex method.
(2) Determine the allowable increases and decreases in the objective function coefficients and the constraints.

22-7. Contribution margin maximization—simplex method with sensitivity analysis. Kipper Company manufactures two products, gaps and haps, which have unit contribution margins of $9 and $10, respectively. The only two restrictions on production of gaps and haps are available direct labor and machine time. Production requirements and available constraints are as follows:

	Quantity Required		Maximum
Constraint	Gaps	Haps	Available
Direct labor	2 hours	3 hours	300 hours
Machine time	1 hour	2 hours	180 hours

Required:

(1) Using the simplex method, determine the production mix required to maximize the company's total contribution margin.
(2) Compute the allowable increase and decrease in the unit contribution margin of gaps that could occur before the optimal production mix would change, assuming that the contribution margin of haps remains unchanged. Then compute the allowable increase and decrease in the contribution margin of haps that could occur, assuming that the contribution margin of gaps remains unchanged.

(Continued)

(3) Compute the allowable increase and decrease in each constraint that could occur before the shadow prices would change, assuming that all other contraints remain constant.

22-8. Cost minimization—simplex method with sensitivity analysis. Danford
Company wishes to minimize the costs of producing a product, with the following two constraints placed on its two primary components.

$$x + 4y \geq 150$$
$$x + y \geq 90$$

The variable cost of a unit of x is $5 and a unit of y is $8.

Required:

(1) Using the simplex method, determine the component mix that will minimize the cost of the product.
(2) Assuming that the cost of only one component changes at a time, compute the allowable increase and decrease in the unit cost of each component that could occur before the optimal mix of components would change.
(3) Assuming that only one constraint is varied at a time, compute the allowable increase and decrease in each constraint that could occur before the shadow prices would change.

22-9. Contribution margin maximization—graphic and simplex methods, with sensitivity analysis. Tarpo Corporation manufactures two products, Trinkets and
Gadgets. The information regarding these products is as follows:

| Product | Daily Capacities in Units | | Sales Price per Unit | Variable Cost per Unit |
	Cutting Department	Finishing Department		
Trinkets....................	400	240	$50	$30
Gadgets....................	200	320	70	40

The daily capacities of each department represent the maximum production for either Trinkets or Gadgets. However, any combination of Trinkets and Gadgets can be produced, as long as the maximum capacity of the department is not exceeded; i.e., two Trinkets can be produced in the Cutting Department for each Gadget not produced and three Trinkets can be produced in the Finishing Department for every four Gadgets not produced. Materials shortages prohibit the production of more than 180 Gadgets per day.

Required:

(1) Prepare a graph that expresses the production relationships stated in the information given.
(2) Identify and list the graphic locations (coordinates) of the:
    (a) Cutting Department's capacity.
    (b) Production limitations for Gadgets because of the materials shortages.
    (c) Area of feasible production combinations.
(3) Compute:
    (a) The contribution margin per unit for Trinkets and Gadgets.
    (b) The total contribution margin for each of the points of intersection of lines bounding the feasible production area.
    (c) The best production alternative.

(4) Determine the best production alternative, using the simplex method.
(5) Determine the allowable increases and decreases in the objective function coefficients and the constraints.   *(AICPA adapted)*

22-10. Cost minimization—graphic and simplex methods, with sensitivity analysis. Deane Pulp Paper Company uses softwood and hardwood pulp as basic materials for producing converter-grade paper. Hardwood is 80% pulp fiber and 20% pulp binder, while softwood is 50% pulp fiber and 50% pulp binder. The cost per pound for hardwood and softwood is $.50 and $.40, respectively.

The company's quality control expert specifies that in order for the product to meet quality standards, each batch must contain at least 12,000 pounds of pulp fiber and at least 6,000 pounds of pulp binder. Because of equipment limitations, the size of a batch cannot exceed 24,000 pounds.

The production department recently received a new standard from the Cost Department, allowing $8,200 per batch. The production manager feels that this amount is too low, because such costs have never been less than $8,400.

Required:

(1) Determine the hardwood and softwood mix necessary to minimize the cost per batch, using the (a) graphic method and (b) simplex method.
(2) Determine the allowable increases and decreases in the objective function coefficients and the constraints.

CASES

A. Contribution margin maximization—problem formulation. Leastan Company manufactures a line of carpeting which includes a commercial carpet and a residential carpet. Two grades of fiber—heavy duty and regular—are used in manufacturing both types of carpeting. The mix of the two grades differs in each type of carpeting, with the commercial grade using a greater amount of heavy duty fiber.

Leastan will introduce a new line of carpeting in two months to replace the current line. The present fiber in stock will not be used in the new line; therefore, management wants to exhaust the present stock during the last month of production.

Data regarding the current line of commercial and residential carpeting are:

	Commercial	Residential
Sales price per roll.........	$1,000	$800
Production specifications per roll of carpet:		
Heavy duty fiber.........	80 lbs.	40 lbs.
Regular fiber..............	20 lbs.	40 lbs.
Direct labor hours........	15 hrs.	15 hrs.
Standard cost per roll of carpet:		
Heavy duty fiber ($3/lb.).....................	$ 240	$120
Regular fiber ($2/lb.)...	40	80
Direct labor ($10/DLH)................	150	150
Variable factory overhead..................	90	90
Fixed factory overhead..................	180	180
Total standard cost per roll.....................	$ 700	$620

Leastan has 42,000 pounds of heavy duty fiber and 24,000 pounds of regular fiber in stock. All fiber not used in the manufacture of the present types of carpeting during the last month of production can be sold as scrap at $.25 a pound.

There is a maximum of 10,500 direct labor hours available during the month. The labor force can work on either type of carpeting.

Sufficient demand exists for the present line of carpeting so that all quantities produced can be sold.

Required:

(1) Compute the number of rolls of commercial carpet and residential carpet that Leastan must manufacture during the last month of production in order to exhaust completely the heavy duty and regular fiber still in stock.

(2) Explain whether or not the requirement (1) solution quantities can be manufactured during the last month of commercial and residential carpet production.

(3) Explain why linear programming would be useful in this application.

(4) Formulate the objective function and the constraints, so that this problem can be solved by linear programming.

(ICMA adapted)

B. Effect of changes on problem formulation.

Marlan Metal Products Company has just established a department for the production of two new products—metal trays and storage devices. This department is ready to begin operations with five metal forming machines and five metal cutting machines, which have been rented for $300 each per month from a local machine company. Both products require production time on both machines. Each of the machines is capable of 400 hours of production per month. No additional machines can be obtained.

| | Machine Hours per Unit | | Total Available |
	Trays	Storage Devices	Machine Hours per Month
Metal cutting machines.......	1	2	2,000
Metal forming machines.......	2	2	2,000

The controller's department has summarized expected costs and revenues as follows:

	Trays	Storage Devices
Selling price per unit....................	$18	$27
Variable cost per unit....................	14	20

Demand for the storage devices is unlimited, but Marlan believes that no more than 800 units of the trays can be sold per month.

The following linear programming formulation and accompanying graph represent the facts described above. Marlan must operate within the specified constraints as it seeks to maximize the contribution margin from this new operation. Marlan intends to operate at the optimal level, which it has determined to be the point labeled "OP" on the graph.

Linear programming formulation:

$$\text{Maximize CM} = \$4t + \$7s$$

Subject to:
$$t + 2s \leq 2,000$$
$$2t + 2s \leq 2,000$$
$$t \leq 800$$

Where: t = number of units of trays produced
s = number of units of storage devices produced
CM = contribution margin

Graphical presentation:

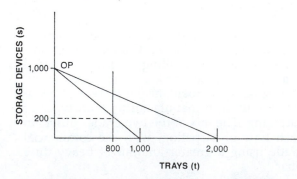

Required:

(1) Determine whether or not Marlan should be willing to incur additional advertising in order to increase tray demand per month to 1,000 units.

(2) Determine the effect on profit if one metal forming machine is returned to the rental agency, thus avoiding rent on the returned machine.

(3) What would the maximum contribution margin be if the storage device sales price is lowered to $23, assuming the problem as originally formulated?

(4) Assume that Marlan learns that a material needed for production of both products is in short supply. Enough material can be obtained to produce 1,200 trays, with each tray requiring ⅔ as much of this material as does each storage device. Formulate mathematically the constraint required to incorporate this additional information into the problem formulation. *(ICMA adapted)*

C. Interpreting the simplex solution.

Jansen Mills produces two grades of interior plywood from fir and pine lumber. The fir and pine lumber can be sold as saw lumber or used in the manufacture of plywood.

To produce the plywood, thin layers of wood are peeled from the logs in panels, and the panels are glued together to form plywood sheets and then dried. The peeler can peel enough panels from logs to produce 300,000 sheets of plywood in a month. The dryer has a capacity of 1,200,000 minutes for a month. The amount of lumber used and the drying time required for each sheet of plywood, by grade, are as follows:

	Grade A Plywood	Grade B Plywood
Fir (in board feet)...............	18	15
Pine (in board feet)...........	12	15
Drying time (in minutes)...	4	6

The only restriction on the production of fir and pine lumber is the capacity of the mill saws to cut the logs into boards. These saws have a capacity of 500,000 board feet per month, regardless of tree specie.

Jansen Mills has the following quantities of lumber available for June production:

Type of Lumber	Quantity Available in Board Feet
Fir	2,700,000
Pine	3,000,000

The contribution margins for each type of output are as follows:

Type of Output	Contribution Margin per Unit
Fir lumber	$ .20 per board foot
Pine lumber	.10 per board foot
Grade A plywood	2.25 per sheet
Grade B plywood	1.80 per sheet

The demand in June for plywood is expected to be a maximum of 80,000 sheets for grade A and a maximum of 100,000 sheets for grade B. There are no demand restrictions on pine and fir lumber.

Jansen Mills uses a linear programming model to determine the production quantities of each product. The correct formulation of the linear programing model and a summary of the solution is shown on page 732.

Required:

(1) How much fir, pine, grade A plywood, and grade B plywood should Jansen Mills produce, and what is the total contribution margin of the product mix?

(2) Will Jansen Mills use all of its resources to their capacities during June if it follows the solution derived from the linear programming model? Explain.

(3) In the list of variables that are not in the final solution, a value appears in the index row for two items regarding fir lumber: a value of .02 for fir lumber to be sold and a value of .12 for fir available as a constraint. Explain what these two items mean.

(4) Assuming that there is no change in price, should Jansen Mills attempt to acquire any more fir for use during June, and if so, how much should be acquired? Explain.

(5) Jansen Mills has been approached by one of its competitors asking it to sell some drying time. How much, if any, drying time should Jansen Mills sell to its competitor? Explain.

(6) Jansen Mills can acquire the use of additional mill saw capacity at the rate of $1,800 for an eight-hour day. The additional saw capacity can process 20,000 board feet of lumber in an eight-hour day. Should Jansen Mills

(Continued on page 733.)

Correct problem formulation:

f = board feet of fir lumber to be sold
p = board feet of pine lumber to be sold
a = number of sheets of grade A plywood to be sold
b = number of sheets of grade B plywood to be sold

Maximize CM = \$.20f + \$.10p + \$2.25a + \$1.80b

Subject to:

$$
\begin{array}{rrrrl}
f + &   & 18a + & 15b \le & 2{,}700{,}000 \text{ fir available} \\
    & p + & 12a + & 15b \le & 3{,}000{,}000 \text{ pine available} \\
    &   & a +   & b \le   & 300{,}000 \text{ peeler capacity} \\
    &   & 4a + & 6b \le & 1{,}200{,}000 \text{ dryer capacity} \\
f + & p   &   & \le   & 500{,}000 \text{ saw capacity} \\
    &   & a   & \le   & 80{,}000 \text{ grade A demand} \\
    &   &   & b \le   & 100{,}000 \text{ grade B demand}
\end{array}
$$

Summary of solution:

Variables in Final Solution	Quantity
Pine lumber to be sold......................................	500,000 board feet
Grade A plywood to be sold.............................	80,000 sheets
Grade B plywood to be sold.............................	84,000 sheets
Slack variables in solution:	
Pine available...	280,000 board feet
Peeler capacity..	136,000 sheets
Dryer capacity..	376,000 minutes
Demand for grade B plywood....................	16,000 sheets

Variables Not in Final Solution	Value in Index Row
Fir lumber to be sold...	.02
Constraints:	
Fir available..	.12
Saw capacity..	.10
Demand for grade A plywood....................	.09

Objective Function Variable	Initial Value	Allowable Decrease	Allowable Increase
Fir lumber...	$ .20	Infinity	$.02
Pine lumber..	.10	$.02	Infinity
Grade A plywood......................................	2.25	.09	Infinity
Grade B plywood......................................	1.80	.30	.075

	(000s omitted)		
Constraint	Initial Value	Allowable Decrease	Allowable Increase
Amount of fir available........................	2,700	1,260	240
Amount of pine available....................	3,000	280	Infinity
Peeler capacity....................................	300	136	Infinity
Dryer capacity......................................	1,200	376	Infinity
Saw capacity..	500	0	280
Grade A plywood demand...................	80	13	150
Grade B plywood demand...................	100	16	Infinity

acquire the use of extra saw capacity, and if so, how much time should it acquire? Explain.

(7) What is the range within which the contribution margin of the grade B plywood can fluctuate before the optimal solution changes? *(ICMA adapted)*

D. Product mix contribution margin. The illustration on page 693 assumes that the market for standard and deluxe models was stable and that the $3 and $4 per unit was maintainable for at least the near future. Increased demand for the deluxe model suggests the desirability of raising the price well above the level that produced the original $4 contribution margin.

Required: Determine the following:

(1) The product mix to be attained if deluxe models are priced to yield a $6 unit contribution margin.

(2) The product mix to be attained if deluxe models are priced to yield a $10 contribution margin.

(3) The contribution margin figure per deluxe model to make it possible to abandon production of standard units and operate at less than full capacity, maintaining maximum profits.

CHAPTER 23

Capital Expenditures: Planning, Evaluating, and Controlling

Capital expenditure planning, evaluating, and controlling, sometimes called *capital budgeting,* is the process of planning the continuing investment and reinvestment of an organization's resources and monitoring that investment. Capital expenditures involve long-term commitments of resources to realize future benefits. They reflect basic company objectives and have a significant, long-term effect on the economic well-being of the firm.

In the final analysis, a firm must earn a reasonable return on invested funds. Therefore, considerable attention has been devoted to techniques for evaluating capital expenditure proposals. Yet evaluation is only one essential requirement for the effective administration of a capital expenditure program. Equally important is the effective planning and control of such expenditures, because (1) the long-term commitment increases financial risk, (2) the magnitude of expenditures is substantial and the penalties for unwise decisions are usually severe, and (3) the decisions made in this area provide the structure that supports the operating activities of the firm.

▼ PLANNING FOR CAPITAL EXPENDITURES

Planning for capital expenditures consists of relating plans to objectives, structuring the framework, searching for proposals, budgeting the expenditures, and requesting authority for expenditures.

Relating Plans to Objectives

Individual projects must be consistent with objectives and must be capable of being blended into a firm's operations. To achieve this consistency, all levels of an organization need to be conscious of objectives and the different roles played by each level relative to these objectives. Ideally, executive management sets broad objectives; managers of functional activities formulate specific policies and programs for action which, when approved, are executed by operating levels of management. The lower the level at which a decision is authorized, the greater the need for guidelines extending to detailed procedures and standards; investment projects not conducive to such detail require handling at a higher level.

Structuring the Framework

An organization's established capital expenditure framework forms the basis for implementing the capital expenditure program. The framework is important because the very nature of performing tasks implies a sound frame of reference. Several factors influence the molding and revisions of a firm's framework: the company's organizational structure, its philosophy and applications of principles of organization, its size, the nature of its operations, and the characteristics of individual projects.

A company manual may be used to detail policies and procedures and to illustrate forms required for administering the capital expenditure program. Such manuals should be stripped down to helpful levels and should (1) encourage people to work on and submit ideas, (2) focus attention on useful analytical tasks, and (3) facilitate rapid project development and expeditious review.

Searching for Proposals

A capital investment program yields the best results only when the best available proposals are considered and all reasonable alternatives of each proposal have been brought into the analysis for evaluating and screening. Ideas should come from all segments of the enterprise. Everyone in the organization should participate in the search activity within the bounds of their technical knowledge and ability, their authority and responsibility, their awareness of operating problems, and existing management guidelines regarding desirable projects. Care must be taken to create and maintain an incentive to search out and bring good projects into the system. This incentive is strong when there is a genuine feeling that all proposals will be reviewed in a fair and objective manner.

Budgeting Capital Expenditures

The capital expenditures budget is typically prepared for a one-year period. It presents management's investment plans at the time the budget is prepared for the coming period.

Some projects never materialize; others are added through amendments to the budget during the budget year. Thus, the budget must be adaptable to changing needs. The capital expenditures budget is not an authorization to commit funds; it merely affords an opportunity to consolidate plans by looking at projects for the total organization, side by side. The capital expenditures budget should be reconciled with the other periodic budgeting activities of the firm, e.g., expense and cash budgets (as discussed in Chapters 15 and 16), and the annual capital budget should be reconciled with long-range capital investment and operating plans and objectives.

The capital expenditures budget passes through several management levels as it moves toward final approval at the executive management level. It follows that a clear explanation of the content of the approved budget should be transmitted to the various management levels to avoid misunderstandings.

Requesting Authority for Expenditures

The periodic budget is usually an approval of ideas and does not grant automatic approval to commit funds. Authority to commit funds for other than necessary preliminary administrative costs should come by means of an Authority for Expenditure (AFE). The AFE procedure is, in effect, a second look at budgeted projects, based on an up-to-date set of documents justifying and describing the expenditure. The AFE and supporting detail should be originated at the level at which the expenditure will occur, with staff assistance if needed.

Approval of the AFE should be delegated to the organizational level having the necessary competence to make the decision, as opposed to requesting executive management's approval for each AFE. The philosophy of companies varies as to the extent of decentralization of approval authority. The amount, type, and significance of the expenditure should be considered in determining the required level of approval. Required approvals also may be governed by whether certain designated evaluation criteria are met.

During the budget year, periodic reports should be prepared by categories, comparing approved AFE expenditures with the budget. The reports should be prepared for use by the organization levels originating the requests for expenditures as well as those granting approval. Higher echelons find summaries helpful, with out-of-line items reported in detail.

▼ EVALUATING CAPITAL EXPENDITURES

Evaluating capital expenditures refers to the basic theory, techniques, and procedures for the appraisal and reappraisal of projects throughout the course of their development. A number of evaluations of a single proposal may be necessary because of:

1. Circumstances that change during the time span from the origin of the project idea to its completion.
2. Alternative solutions of the problem for which the project is designed.
3. Assumptions that vary as to the amount and time pattern of cash flows.

The best available evaluation tools should be used, coupled with an understanding of the risk and danger existing in overreliance on quantitative answers based on many assumptions and estimates. Economic evaluation techniques have received prime attention in literature dealing with capital investment programs. The most advanced methods consider the time value of money in computing an estimated return on investment.

In evaluating capital expenditures, many imponderable factors may affect the decision. These factors include external considerations, such as competition, legal requirements, and social responsibilities, as well as internal factors regarding improved product quality, increased manufacturing flexibility, reduced inventory levels, the capacity for increased product innovations, and emergencies. Furthermore, there is a need to select investments that will keep the firm in balance and be consistent with objectives. The circumstances of each expenditure alternative must be considered in passing judgment on the criteria used. Even then there may be justifiable differences of opinion with respect to governing criteria. The mechanics of various techniques are important, but of still greater importance is their relationship to the overall capital expenditure planning and control process and the need for creative and thoughtful management.

Classification of Capital Expenditures

Capital expenditure projects can be classified as: (1) equipment-replacement expenditures, (2) expansion investments, and (3) improvements of existing products and/or additions of new products. A proposal may involve more than one classification. For example, a firm may consider a proposal to replace an old printing press, whose maintenance cost has become excessive, with a new press that will offer an expanded productive capacity. Also, certain expenditures may be necessary because of tactical or legal requirements, rather than for purely economic reasons: a manufacturer may be forced into the production of a less profitable product because of competitive pressure; recreation facilities may be installed for employee use; or air and water pollution regulations may necessitate an expenditure for a waste disposal unit. Certain projects are musts to the point that use of an evaluation technique is superfluous, e.g., the washout of a section of a railway trestle. Other projects, though indicating an acceptable economic return, may be rejected because of lack of funds, failure to fit into overall objectives, failure to meet other evaluation criteria (such as corner locations for gasoline service stations), or external circumstances (such as current economic conditions or changes in government policies).

Some projects may not be independent of one another and in such cases should be grouped together for evaluation purposes as a compound project. The following quotation illustrates this point:

> Contingent or dependent projects can arise, for instance, when acceptance of one proposal is dependent on acceptance of one or more other proposals. One simple example would be the purchase of an extra-long boom for a crane which would be of little

value unless the crane itself were also purchased; the latter, however, may be justified on its own. When contingent projects are combined with their independent prerequisites, the combination may be called a compound project. Thus, a compound project may be characterized by the algebraic sum of the payoffs and costs of the component projects plus, perhaps, an interaction term.[1]

Equipment-Replacement Expenditures. These include both like-for-like and obsolescence replacements. The basis for decision making is future or prospective cost savings, i.e., comparing future costs of old equipment with future costs of new equipment. In addition to comparisons of operating costs, the analysis of future costs requires the determination of the prospective purchase price less any ultimate resale or salvage value. The most difficult problem is to estimate the probable economic life of the new equipment. This is the core of any capital expenditure decision. For the present equipment, the future decline in disposal value must be estimated. The original cost of the present facility is a sunk and irrecoverable cost, totally irrelevant to the decision-making process. Accumulated depreciation is also independent of the company's real future costs. Book values of existing assets are not relevant for the replacement decision, except for possible income tax consequences. For example, an increase or decrease in income tax liability might result from the recognition of a gain or loss, respectively, from the sale, exchange, or abandonment of an asset in the year of disposition. On the other hand, in the case of an exchange of like-kind assets, the income tax effect results from an adjustment to the tax basis of the new asset and the amount of depreciation available for tax purposes, which in turn affects the amount of income tax liability over the depreciable life of the asset. An increase or decrease in income tax liability has a direct effect on cash flow and is, therefore, relevant to the capital expenditure decision.

Expansion Investments. Expansion investments involve plant enlargement and the invasion of new markets. In these cases, the expected results of doing and not doing the job are compared, with the basis for a decision shifted from cost savings to the expected addition to profits, including the consideration of cash inflow. The added profit is estimated by preparing a projected income statement showing additional revenue and expense over the life of the project. The degree of uncertainty in this type of investment is much greater than in the first category.

Improvements of Existing Products and/or Additions of New Products. The basis for a decision on projects in this category is strategic; that is, the relative competitive market position compels the firm to make investments. Failure to keep abreast of competitors can cause deterioration of the market share. Since no historical basis for making the decision exists and the return on such investments must be based on increasing or maintaining profits in the face of competition, a high degree of sound judgment and business insight is required in making such a decision.

---

[1] H. Martin Weingartner, "Capital Budgeting of Interrelated Projects: Survey and Synthesis," *Management Science*, Vol. XII, No. 7, p. 492.

Cost of Capital

The *cost of capital* represents the expected return that investors demand for a given level of risk. Although this discussion is brief, the cost of capital as related to capital expenditures is a complex concept. It may refer to a specific cost of capital from a particular financing effort to provide funds for a specific product. Such use of the concept connotes the marginal cost of capital and implies linkage of the financing and investment decisions. This view has been challenged as a useful concept for allocating capital because businesses rely on more than one source of funds to finance their activities. The funds available for one or all capital projects are usually considered to be a commingling of more than one source. Therefore, different costs of capital exist, depending upon the mix of the sources of funds used to finance the business. Companies typically obtain funds from (1) bond issues, (2) preferred and common stock issues, (3) use of retained earnings, and (4) loans from banks. If a company obtains funds by some combination of these sources in order to achieve or maintain a particular capital structure, then the cost of capital (money) is the weighted average cost of each money source. This weighted average considers the joint cost of all sources of funds. The relative proportions and the cost of each source of funds used in computing the weighted cost of capital should be those expected over the investment horizon.[2] In practice, the relative proportions used are likely to be those desired by management in the long run, and the costs used are those currently applicable, adjusted for anticipated inflation. The weighted average cost of capital may be computed as follows:

Funds—Source	Proportion of Funds To Be Provided	Aftertax Cost	Weighted Cost
Bonds..	.20	.05	.01
Preferred stock.............................	.20	.10	.02
Common stock and retained earnings......................	.60	.15	.09
	1.00 Weighted average cost of capital.............		.12 = 12%

The cost of capital for each source is described as follows:

1. The cost of bonds is the aftertax rate of interest, i.e., the pretax rate of interest multiplied by one minus the tax rate. If bonds are sold at a premium or a discount, the rate used should be the market yield rate.
2. The cost of preferred stock is the dividend per share divided by the present market price.
3. The cost of common stock and retained earnings is the expected earnings per share, after income tax and after preferred dividends are paid, divided by the present market price.[3]

---

[2] *Statement on Management Accounting, No. 4A,* ''Cost of Capital'' (Montvale, New Jersey: National Association of Accountants, 1984), pp. 3 and 11.

[3] Conflicting opinions exist regarding the treatment of the investors' income tax effect on the cost of equity acquired through the retention of earnings.

Inflationary Considerations in Estimating Cash Flows

Just as a company's cost of capital is affected by inflation's impact, so too are estimates of cash flow. In order for the cash flows to be on an equivalent basis with the acceptance criterion, i.e., the weighted average cost of capital, cash flow estimates must include an allowance for the effect of anticipated inflation. To illustrate this effect, assume that Star Company is considering an investment in a project to produce a new product. A sales volume of 1,000 units of the new product is expected for each of the next five years. The planned sales price is $10 per unit and current period cash costs are expected to be $6 per unit, resulting in a net cash inflow of $4 per unit sold. In addition, assume that management expects the general price level to rise at an annual rate of 10 percent. If management believes that its costs will increase at the same rate as inflation and that the sales price of the new product can be increased at the same rate, the estimated cash flows should be adjusted for the effect of inflation as follows:

Year	(1) Unadjusted Estimate of Cash Inflow	(2) General Price-Level Index	(3) Adjusted Estimate of Cash Inflow	(4) Difference (3) − (1)
1	$ 4,000	1.100	$ 4,400	$ 400
2	4,000	1.210	4,840	840
3	4,000	1.331	5,324	1,324
4	4,000	1.464	5,856	1,856
5	4,000	1.610	6,440	2,440
Total	$20,000		$26,860	$6,860

Unless the cash flows are adjusted for inflation's impact, the cash inflows expected over the life of Star Company's project will be understated by $6,860. Such understatement could result in an erroneous rejection of this project. If the impact of inflation is expected to be different for cash inflows and outflows, separate inflation adjustments must be made. For example, such a difference would occur when either the sales price of output or the purchase price of input is to be under a fixed price contract.[4]

Another effect of inflation is that its increase in discount rates biases the decision-making process in favor of short-term projects because, as rates increase, cash flows in more distant years become less significant. These high rates:

> . . . serve as a destabilizing factor. . . . The high interest rates encourage and even demand that decision makers use high discount rates in their planning. The high discount rates, in turn, tremendously increase the importance of the present—the time horizon becomes biased toward the near future—and the comparative neglect of the long run makes the short run even more unstable.[5]

---

[4]For an elaboration of the effect of inflation in capital budgeting, see Jon W. Bartley, "A NPV Model Modified for Inflation," *Management Accounting*, Vol. LXII, No. 6, pp. 49-52; Debra D. Raiborn and Thomas A. Ratcliffe, "Are You Accounting for Inflation in Your Capital Budgeting Process?," *Management Accounting*, Vol. LXI, No. 3, pp. 19-22; and Allen H. Seed, III, *The Impact of Inflation on Internal Planning and Control* (New York: National Association of Accountants, 1981), pp. 73-78 and 104-105.

[5] C. Torben Thomsen, "Dangers in Discounting," *Management Accounting*, Vol. LXV, No. 7, pp. 37-39.

Income Tax Considerations in Estimating Cash Flows

The effect of income taxes on cash flows is an important consideration in planning and evaluating capital expenditures. The following paragraphs discuss the tax laws regarding depreciation, the investment tax credit, and construction period interest and taxes. Because the tax law changes frequently, the discussion presented in this textbook should be regarded as illustrative only. It is presented to demonstrate the importance of considering the effect of taxes on capital expenditure analysis. Current income tax statutes and regulations should be consulted when planning actual capital expenditures.

Depreciation. Depreciation is not a cash inflow or outflow. However, depreciation allowed for income tax purposes reduces taxable income and, consequently, tax liability, which directly affects cash flow.

The Economic Recovery Tax Act of 1981, with subsequent amendments, represented a substantial change in income tax accounting for capital expenditures. A new system for recovering the cost of capital expenditures, referred to as the Accelerated Cost Recovery System (ACRS), is now used for tangible, depreciable property placed in service after 1980. Although used for federal income tax purposes, some states do not allow the ACRS rates in computing state income taxes. ACRS reduces the impact of inflation by accelerating the recovery of capital expenditures as follows:

1. It eliminates the useful-life concept and replaces it with a shorter recovery period.
2. It allows more cost recovery in the earlier years of the recovery period, i.e., accelerated depreciation rates.

Under the Tax Reform Act of 1986, Modified ACRS (MACRS) increases the number of property classes and lengthens the recovery periods of most kinds of depreciable property.[6] The 1986 Act provides for the recovery of capital expenditures over periods of 3, 5, 7, 10, 15, 20, 27.5, or 31.5 years, depending upon the type of property. Most of the common depreciable business assets, other than buildings, are classified as 5-year or 7-year property. For example, automobiles, trucks, small aircraft, and technological equipment are classified as 5-year property, and railroad locomotives and cars, commercial aircraft, and most manufacturing machinery are classified as 7-year property. Buildings that qualify as residential rental property are depreciated over 27.5 years, and nonresidential buildings over 31.5 years.

The maximum depreciation rate allowable for 3-year, 5-year, 7-year and 10-year property is 200 percent of the declining balance with an automatic switch to straight-line in the first year in which the straight-line deduction determined as of the beginning of the change year exceeds the declining balance deduction for the same year. The maximum depreciation rate allowable is reduced to 150 percent of the declining balance for 15-year and 20-year property and to straight-line for residential rental and nonresidential

---

[6] *Internal Revenue Code*, Section 168. Generally, MACRS rules apply to property placed in service after December 31, 1986.

real property. For most tangible personal property, depreciation is computed as if the property were placed into service at the mid-point of the year (referred to as a half-year convention). Depreciation for real property is based on a mid-month convention (i.e., property placed into service in any month is treated as being placed into service in the middle of the month). For all classes of property, salvage value is treated as zero. An example of the cost recovery rates for 3-year, 5-year, and 7-year property classes follows:

Example of MACRS Recovery Percentages by Property Class
(Half-Year Convention and 200% Declining Balance Method)

Recovery Year	3-Year	5-Year	7-Year
1	.333	.200	.143
2	.444	.320	.245
3	.148	.192	.175
4	.075	.115	.125
5		.115	.089
6		.058	.089
7			.089
8			.045
	1.000	1.000	1.000

Gains on Disposals of Depreciable Property. For federal income tax purposes, gain recognized on the disposal of depreciable property other than buildings is treated as ordinary income to the extent of tax depreciation deducted prior to disposal.[7] Gain, if any, in excess of such depreciation is essentially treated as a capital gain.[8] The Tax Reform Act of 1986 repealed the preferential treatment accorded capital gains by removing the capital gain deduction previously available to individuals and by setting the capital gain rate for corporations equal to the ordinary income rate. However, the law still requires that capital gains be computed and reported separately from ordinary income. This requirement was presumably included in order to permit taxpayers to deduct unused capital loss carryovers. It may also have been included in order to keep in place a mechanism that would make it convenient for Congress to reenact some form of preferential tax treatment for capital gains at a later time.

Investment Tax Credit. The investment tax credit was originally enacted in 1962 for the stated purpose of stimulating the economy and generating additional employment by providing an incentive to business to invest and expand. Congress has repealed, reenacted, increased, and expanded the

[7]*Internal Revenue Code*, Section 1245. *Internal Revenue Code*, Section 1250 generally provides that gain recognized on the disposition of buildings is to be treated as ordinary income to the extent that the depreciation allowed or allowable exceeds the depreciation that would have been allowed under the straight-line method. The remaining gain recognized, if any, is included in the Section 1231 pool. Since MACRS requires that buildings acquired after 1986 must be depreciated under the straight-line method, on such buildings there will be no excess of accelerated over straight-line depreciation to be recaptured as ordinary income under Section 1250.

[8]*Internal Revenue Code*, Section 1231 provides that all gains (i.e., those recognized in excess of the amount treated as ordinary income) and all losses recognized from the dispositions of trade or business properties during the tax year must be pooled. If the total is a net gain, it is added to the capital gain pool. If the total is a net loss, it is treated as an ordinary loss.

investment tax credit to meet varying economic conditions. The investment tax credit was repealed by the Tax Reform Act of 1986. Although the investment tax credit has not been a stable feature of the income tax law, it is an important capital expenditure consideration during periods when it is available because it reduces income tax expense at the end of the project's first year.

When last a part of the law, the investment tax credit was available on the acquisition of most tangible property (other than buildings). The law has sometimes required that the property's depreciable basis be reduced by all or part of the credit claimed. When repealed in 1986, the most recent version of the investment tax credit required that the property's basis be reduced by 50 percent of the amount of the credit claimed. The regular credit rate was 10 percent. If new property was acquired in exchange for a trade-in of an old machine, the qualified cost for purposes of computing the investment tax credit was the tax basis of the old property plus the cash paid. On the other hand, if used property was acquired in a trade-in, the qualified cost was limited to the cash paid for the property.

Construction Period Interest and Taxes. *Statement of Financial Accounting Standards, No. 34,* "Capitalization of Interest Cost," prescribes the capitalization of interest costs incurred in acquiring assets that require a period of time to be made ready for their intended use, provided the periodic income effect, compared with that of expensing interest, is material. The amount capitalized would be recovered through depreciation over the economic life of the new asset. On the other hand, for federal income tax purposes, both construction period interest and taxes must be capitalized.[9] The tax law limits the capitalization of such costs to the acquisition or construction of property that meets any one of the following tests: (1) the property has a class life of 20 years or more, (2) the estimated production period exceeds 2 years, or (3) the estimated production period exceeds one year and the estimated production costs exceed $1,000,000.[10] In addition, the tax law requires the capitalization of not only interest paid or accrued on funds specifically borrowed to construct the property but also a portion of the interest paid or accrued on other liabilities if construction cost exceeds funds borrowed specifically to finance the project.[11]

In evaluating capital expenditure proposals which involve the acquisition or construction of property over a period of time, the initial cash outflow would be increased by both interest and taxes incurred during the construction period. Cash inflows in subsequent periods would be increased by the reduction in income taxes that would result from the amortization of the interest and taxes which had been capitalized during the construction period.

Representative Evaluation Techniques

The following four evaluation techniques are the representative tools in current use: (1) the payback (or payout) period method, (2) the average annual

---

[9]*Internal Revenue Code,* Section 263A(a)(2)(B) and Section 263A(f).
[10]*Internal Revenue Code,* Section 263A(f)(1)(B).
[11]*Internal Revenue Code,* Section 263A(f)(2)(A).

return on investment (or accounting rate of return or financial statement) method, (3) the present value method, and (4) the discounted cash flow (or internal rate of return) method (DCF). None of these methods serves every purpose or every firm. The circumstances and needs of a situation determine the most appropriate techniques to be used. A company may use more than one technique (e.g., payback period and DCF) in evaluating each project; however, the same method or methods should be used uniformly for every project throughout the firm. Confusion could arise if Division A used the discounted cash flow method, while Division B used the average annual return on investment method. Trying to compare different projects which have been evaluated with different techniques would be like trying to compare apples and oranges. To evaluate alternative projects, the same evaluation techniques must be used.

These evaluation techniques, if thoroughly understood by the analysts who use them, should aid management in exercising judgment and making decisions. Certainly the cost of gathering data and applying the evaluation techniques should be justified in terms of the value to management. Moreover, inaccurate raw data used in the calculations or lack of uniform procedures may yield harmful or misleading conclusions.

For purposes of discussing and illustrating the evaluation methods listed, assume that Dartmond Corporation is operating at the limit of the capacity of one of its producing units, and maintenance costs of an existing machine have become excessive. A new machine with greater capacity can be purchased at a cost of $103,000, less a trade-in allowance for the old machine of $8,000, which represents the fair market value of the old machine. Therefore, the initial cash outflow would be $95,000. The old machine has a book value of $5,000 and a tax basis of zero. The net acquisition cost for financial accounting purposes is $100,000 ($95,000 cash price plus $5,000 book value) and for tax purposes is $95,000 ($95,000 cash price plus zero tax basis).[12] The expected economic life of the new unit is eight years. Straight-line depreciation is to be used for financial accounting purposes, with an estimated salvage value of $10,000.[13] For tax purposes, however, the property qualifies as five-year property under ACRS and salvage value is ignored.

---

[12]Both APB Opinion No. 29 and IRC Section 1031 require that no gain be recognized on the exchange of similar or like-kind assets. The book value or tax basis of the new asset is the value or tax basis of the old asset plus boot given (cash paid to the vendor). Note, however, that if the old asset is sold outright rather than traded in, a $8,000 taxable gain would be realized on the sale ($8,000 sales price less zero tax basis) and the net acquisition cost would be the cash price of $103,000. The initial cash outflow would be $95,000 ($103,000 cash price less $8,000 cash proceeds from the sale of the old asset) plus the tax paid on the $8,000 gain recognized. Regardless of whether the old asset is sold or traded in, the book value of the old asset is a sunk cost and irrelevant to the decision. The aftertax gain on the sale of the old asset is irrelevant, since the proceeds received from the sale must be used to purchase the new asset at a greater cash outflow than would be required if the old asset were traded in. However, the tax liability incurred on the sale of the old asset is relevant, because it could be avoided by trading in the old asset instead of selling it outright. Since a trade-in results in a smaller initial cash outflow than a sale, it is assumed for this illustration.

[13]Generally accepted accounting principles require that the cost of a depreciable asset be allocated to expense over the expected useful life of the asset, even though that period is different from the cost recovery period used for tax purposes. See "AcSEC Position on Tax and Depreciation Lives," *The CPA Letter*, AICPA, Vol. 61, No. 21, p. 3. The method of depreciation and the treatment of estimated salvage value for financial accounting purposes must also comply with generally accepted accounting principles, even though such treatment may differ from that required for tax purposes.

The estimated differential aftertax cash inflows yielded by the utilized additional capacity of the new machine for Dartmond Corporation are calculated in the table below. The pretax estimates of cash inflows include consideration of inflation's impact. The aftertax cash flows are computed under the assumption that the investment tax credit is not available. The aftertax cash inflow estimates computed in the table are used to illustrate the capital expenditure evaluation techniques discussed in the following paragraphs. The numbers given in Columns 2 and 3 are uneven, so that the resulting amounts in Column 8 will be easy to use and to follow in subsequent calculations.

DARTMOND CORPORATION—AFTERTAX CASH FLOW
(Assuming No Investment Tax Credit)

(1) Year	(2) Estimated Cash Savings Relating to Present Capacity (Primarily Maintenance)	(3) Estimated Cash Income Relating to Use of Increased Capacity	(4) Total Cash Inflow (2) + (3)	(5) Tax Depreciation*	(6) Taxable Income (Loss) (4) − (5)	(7) Federal and State Income Tax (Reduction) (6) × 40%	(8) Net Aftertax Cash Inflow (4) − (7)
1	$9,100	$26,566	$35,666	$19,000	$16,666	$6,666	$ 29,000
2	7,800	25,267	33,067	30,400	2,667	1,067	32,000
3	6,500	26,340	32,840	18,240	14,600	5,840	27,000
4	5,200	25,850	31,050	10,925	20,125	8,050	23,000
5	3,900	23,817	27,717	10,925	16,792	6,717	21,000
6	2,600	23,727	26,327	5,510	20,817	8,327	18,000
7	1,300	22,033	23,333	0	23,333	9,333	14,000
8	0	20,000	20,000	0	20,000	8,000	12,000
							$176,000

Cash inflow from salvage at end of economic life... 6,000**

Total aftertax cash inflows... $182,000

*Tax depreciation is determined by multiplying the depreciable basis of $95,000 by the MACRS depreciation rates provided on page 742 for the five-year property class.

**The salvage value received at the end of the project would be fully taxable because the tax basis would be zero. Thus, the aftertax cash flow would be $6,000 [$10,000 salvage × (1 − .40)]. Note, however, that no tax would be estimated for salvage if management planned to exchange the asset for a replacement in kind.

This example involves both a replacement and an expansion investment, in which the cash outlay is restricted to the cost of the plant asset unit. Some projects require the commitment of working capital for inventories, receivables, etc., as well as expenditures that may not be capitalized. When such commitments and expenditures exist, they should be included as part of the initial investment and, to the extent that they are recoverable, should be shown as cash inflow in the recovery years.

The Payback Period Method. The payback (or payout) period method is widely used in many firms, if only to serve as an initial screening device or to complement the answers of more sophisticated methods. The technique measures the length of time required by the project to recover the initial outlay.[14] The calculated payback period is compared with the payback period acceptable to management for projects of the kind being evaluated. The computation for the Dartmond Corporation project is:

Year	Net Aftertax Cash Flow	Recovery of Initial Outlay Needed	Recovery of Initial Outlay Balance	Payback Years Required
1	$29,000	$95,000	$66,000	1.0
2	32,000	66,000	34,000	1.0
3	27,000	34,000	7,000	1.0
4	23,000	7,000	0	0.3
Total payback period in years..........................				3.3

Because of the effects of variations in business activity, inflation, and accelerated methods of depreciation used for income tax purposes, it is highly unlikely that estimated cash flows for actual projects would be uniform for each year. However, professional examinations, such as the CPA and CMA examinations, may assume uniform cash flows for simplicity in problems requiring the computation of the payback period. In such cases, the payback period can be computed by dividing the cash outflow in the initial period by the annual cash inflow. For example, if the annual cash inflow from the Dartmond Corporation capital project were $30,000 each year, the payback period would be 3.17 years ($95,000 initial cash investment ÷ $30,000 annual cash inflow).

Advantages of using the payback (or payout) method to evaluate capital expenditures are:

1. It is simple to compute and easy to understand.
2. It may be used to select those investments yielding a quick return of cash, thus placing an emphasis on liquidity.
3. It permits a company to determine the length of time required to recapture its original investment, thus offering a possible indicator of the degree of risk of each investment. Such an indicator is especially useful when the danger of obsolescence is great.
4. It is a widely used method that is certainly an improvement over a hunch, rule of thumb, or intuitive method.

Disadvantages and limitations associated with using the payback (or payout) method of evaluating capital expenditures are:

1. It ignores the time value of money. To illustrate this disadvantage, assume that the "Net Aftertax Cash Inflow" for Dartmond Corporation had been: year 1, $62,000; year 2, $16,000; year 3, $14,000; and year 4, $10,000—with the same 8-year total. The computation would be:

---

[14]The initial outlay used in calculating the payback period should exclude working capital to the extent that the working capital can be recovered through its own liquidation. Investment salvage value at the payback point would further reduce the payback period. Such adjustments result in what is referred to as the "bailout payback."

Year	Net Aftertax Cash Flow	Recovery of Initial Outlay Needed	Recovery of Initial Outlay Balance	Payback Years Required
1	$62,000	$95,000	$33,000	1.0
2	16,000	33,000	17,000	1.0
3	14,000	17,000	3,000	1.0
4	10,000	3,000	0	0.3
Total payback period in years........................				3.3

In both this example and the example on page 745, the payback period is 3.3 years. In this example, however, $33,000 more was received in the first year ($62,000 − $29,000). This situation is more desirable from an investment standpoint because money has a time value; that is, a dollar is worth more the earlier it is received because it can be reinvested.

2. It ignores cash flows which may occur beyond the payback period. In the example on page 745, the payback period is 3.3 years, the economic life is 8 years, and the "Net Aftertax Cash Inflow" is $182,000. Assume that an alternative project indicates a "Net Aftertax Cash Inflow" of $95,000 in the first two years and an economic life of three years, with "Net Aftertax Cash Inflow" of $10,000 in the third year. Although the latter case has a shorter payback period, the original example of a 3.3 year payback and net cash inflow of $182,000 is more desirable when immediate cash problems are not of critical importance.

3. It fails to consider salvage value which may exist after the payback period.

The Average Annual Return on Investment Method. This method is sometimes referred to as the accounting rate of return method or the financial statement method. When this method is used, an investment proposal is evaluated by comparing the estimated average annual rate of return on the investment with a target rate of return. If more than one project exceeds the target rate of return and funds are insufficient to finance all qualified projects, the acceptable projects are ranked and only the most profitable ones selected. The estimated rate of return for the Dartmond Corporation project may be computed as follows:

Net income without deduction for depreciation (net aftertax cash inflow, excluding salvage value)..	$176,000
Less financial accounting depreciation ($100,000 acquisition cost less $10,000 salvage value)*..	90,000
	$ 86,000
Less tax expense on taxable gain from sale of asset at end of economic life ($10,000 salvage value × 40%)...............................	4,000
Net income over economic life of project..	$ 82,000

*Depreciation is assumed to be the only noncash expense and is thus the only adjustment required in converting from cash flow to accrual basis income.

$$\frac{\text{Average annual return}}{\text{on } \textit{original} \text{ investment}} = \frac{\text{Net income}}{\text{Economic life}} \div \text{Original investment}$$

$$= \frac{\$82,000}{8 \text{ years}} \div \$100,000$$

$$= 10.25\%$$

Another approach to estimating a project's rate of return is to divide the average annual net income by the average investment rather than the original investment. The computation for the Dartmond Corporation project is:

Original investment...	$100,000
Investment at end of economic life (salvage value)......................	10,000
	$110,000
Average investment ($110,000 ÷ 2)..	$ 55,000*

*The original book value and the book value at the end of each year can be averaged if the straight-line depreciation method is not used for finanical accounting purposes.

$$\frac{\text{Average annual return}}{\text{on } \textit{average} \text{ investment}} = \frac{\text{Net income}}{\text{Economic life}} \div \text{Average investment}$$

$$= \frac{\$82,000}{8 \text{ years}} \div \$55,000$$

$$= 18.64\%$$

Advantages of using the average annual return on investment method to evaluate capital expenditures are:

1. It facilitates expenditure follow-up due to more readily available data from accounting records.
2. It considers income over the entire life of the project.

Disadvantages and limitations associated with the use of the average annual return on investment method of evaluating capital expenditures are:

1. It ignores the time value of money. Two projects might have the same average return, yet vary considerably in the pattern of cash flow. In such a case, the recognition of the time value of money would point to the desirability of the alternative having greater cash flow in the earlier periods.
2. Inflation's effect is expected to be included in cash flow estimates. But a calculation of net income based on historical cost depreciation and the expression of net income as a return on an investment, which is also stated at historical cost, may be quite misleading.
3. The average return on the original investment technique is inapplicable if any of the investment is made after the beginning of the project.

The Present Value Method. A dollar received a year hence is not the equivalent of a dollar received today, because the use of money has a value. To illustrate, if $500 can be invested at 20 percent, $600 will be received a year later ($500 + 20% of $500). The $600 to be received next year has a present value of $500 if 20 percent can be earned ($600 ÷ 120% = $500). The difference of $100 ($600 − $500) represents the time value of money. In line with this idea, the estimated results of an investment proposal can be stated at its present value, i.e., as a cash equivalent at the present time.[15]

Present value tables have been devised to facilitate the application of present value theory. The "Present Value of $1" table on page 758 presents computations to three decimal places and shows today's value, or the present value, of each dollar to be received or paid in the future for various rates of interest and periods of time.[16] By multiplying the appropriate factor obtained from the table times an expected future cash flow, the present value of the cash flow is easily determined.

The "Present Value of $1 Received or Paid Annually for Each of the Next N Years" table on page 759 shows the present value of a series of $1 periodic receipts or payments. This table is used when the cash flow is estimated to be the same each period. The relationship between this table and the "Present Value of $1" table on page 758 is as follows:

Period	Present Value of $1 at 12%	Present Value of $1 Received or Paid Annually for Each of the Next N Years at 12%
1	.893	.893
2	.797	1.690 (.893 + .797)
3	.712	2.402 (1.690 + .712)
4	.636	3.037 (2.402 + .636)*
5	.567	3.605
6	.507	4.111
7	.452	4.564
8	.404	4.968

*Difference of .001 results from rounding off the results of the formula.

If the flow is uniform, the flow for one period can be multiplied by the cumulative factor to obtain approximately the same answer as by multiplying the individual factors by the flow for each period and totaling the products. For

---

[15]The basic formula for present value is:

$$PV = S\left[\frac{1}{(1 + i)^n}\right] \quad or \quad \left[\frac{S}{(1 + i)^n}\right] \quad or \quad S(1 + i)^{-n}$$

where PV = present value of future sum of money
S = future sum of money
i = earnings rate for each compounding period
n = number of periods

[16]Ordinary tables, such as those included in this chapter, assume that all cash flows occur at the end of each period and that interest is compounded at the end of each period. Either or both of these assumptions can be varied by the use of calculus so that, instead of assuming that the cash flows occur at the end of each period, they can occur continuously, and interest can be compounded continuously. Although the continuous assumptions often are more representative of actual conditions, the tables in this chapter are more frequently used in practice.

example, if a project costing $20,000 is expected to yield a uniform annual aftertax cash flow of $5,000 for seven years, then the present value of the expected cash inflows, discounted at 12 percent, is $5,000 × 4.564, or $22,820, and the net present value is $2,820 ($22,820 − $20,000).[17]

The present value concept can be applied to the Dartmond Corporation problem by discounting at the company's 12 percent estimated cost of capital. For assets requiring a period of time to be made ready for use, the initial cash payment marks the project's origin, at which point the discount factor is 1.000. Subsequent cash payments related to the project's acquisition or construction are shown as outflows to be discounted back to the initial cash outflow date, along with net cash inflows associated with the investment's operating use.

The computation for Dartmond Corporation is as follows:

Year	Net Aftertax Cash (Outflow) Inflow	Present Value of $1 @ 12%	Present Value of Net Cash Flow
0	$(95,000)	1.000	$(95,000)
1	29,000	.893	25,897
2	32,000	.797	25,504
3	27,000	.712	19,224
4	23,000	.636	14,628
5	21,000	.567	11,907
6	18,000	.507	9,126
7	14,000	.452	6,328
8	18,000*	.404	7,272
Net present value....................			$ 24,886

*$12,000 + $6,000 aftertax salvage

The positive net present value of $24,886 indicates that the true rate of return is greater than the cost of capital discount rate. A net present value of zero would indicate a rate of return of exactly 12 percent. If investment funds are not rationed (i.e., the company has sufficient funds available to finance all acceptable projects), all projects with a positive net present value would be accepted. On the other hand, if investment funds are being rationed (the typical case in practice), alternative projects would be ranked according to their net present values.

A project's useful life is one of the uncertainties often associated with capital expenditure evaluations. Equipment obsolescence or shifts in market demands may occur. The conventional payback method determines the time necessary to recover the initial outlay, without regard to present value considerations. However, management may wish to know the minimum life for a project necessary to recover the original investment and earn a desired rate of return on the investment. The *present value payback* calculation focuses on this question and is computed for Dartmond Corporation as follows, using

---

[17]Although unusual in actual capital expenditure evaluation cases, uniform cash flow analysis is included here because it is occasionally required on professional examinations such as the CPA and CMA examinations.

the "present value of net cash flow" figures shown in the previous computation:

Year	Present Value of Net Cash Flow	Recovery of Initial Outlay Needed	Recovery of Initial Outlay Balance	Present Value Payback Years Required
1	$25,897	$95,000	$69,103	1.00
2	25,504	69,103	43,599	1.00
3	19,224	43,599	24,375	1.00
4	14,628	24,375	9,747	1.00
5	11,907	9,747	0	.82
Total present value payback in years.........				4.82

Based on the present value of estimated cash flows, 4.82 years will be required to recover the $95,000 original cash investment and earn a desired 12 percent rate of return on the annual unrecovered balance. Additionally, the present value payback will be shortened by the present value of the project's salvage value.

Advantages of using the present value method of evaluating capital expenditures are:

1. It considers the time value of money.
2. It considers cash flow over the entire life of the project.
3. It allows for different discount rates over the life of the project.

Disadvantages and limitations associated with the use of the present value method of evaluating capital expenditures are:

1. Some argue that this method is too difficult to compute and to understand.
2. Management must determine a discount rate to be used. A well-informed management should already be aware of its cost of capital that should represent the benchmark for discount rate purposes. However, some firms may set as their discount rate something in excess of the cost of capital or use different rates that depend on risk and uncertainty and other characteristics of a particular project. This procedure is conceptually unsound. Cash received in early periods has more value than cash received in later periods only because early cash inflows can be reinvested. If the discount rate is inflated above the reinvestment rate, the value of the cash inflows is misstated. This problem can be overcome by using the reinvestment rate to compute the future value of the cash inflows at the end of the life of the project and then discounting the total terminal value to the start of the project, using a risk adjusted rate (i.e., the cost of capital rate plus an additional component to compensate for risk).[18] Assuming that the cost of capital rate is a reasonable reinvestment rate, the terminal value

[18] See Lester Barenbaum and Thomas Monahan, "Utilizing Terminal Values in Teaching Time Value Analysis," *Journal of Accounting Education*, Vol. 1, No. 2, pp. 79-88.

for the Dartmond Corporation illustration would be computed as follows:

Year	Net Aftertax Cash Inflow	Future Value of $1 at 12%	Terminal Value of Cash Inflows
1	$29,000	$(1.00 + .12)^7 = 2.211$	$ 64,119
2	32,000	$(1.00 + .12)^6 = 1.974$	63,168
3	27,000	$(1.00 + .12)^5 = 1.762$	47,574
4	23,000	$(1.00 + .12)^4 = 1.574$	36,202
5	21,000	$(1.00 + .12)^3 = 1.405$	29,505
6	18,000	$(1.00 + .12)^2 = 1.254$	22,572
7	14,000	$(1.00 + .12) = 1.120$	15,680
8	18,000	1.000	18,000
			$296,820

If a risk premium of 2 percent were added to the 12 percent reinvestment rate, the net present value of the project would be as follows:

Terminal value of aftertax cash inflows....................................	$296,820
Present value of $1 at 14% for 8 periods..............................	.351
Present value of terminal aftertax cash inflows.....................	$104,184
Initial cash outflow..	95,000
Net present value of project..	$ 9,184

More explicit methods of incorporating risk and uncertainty into the capital expenditure analysis are discussed in Chapter 24.

3. If projects being compared involve different dollar amounts of investment, the project with more profitable dollars, as computed by the present value method, may not be the better project if it also requires a larger investment. For example, a net present value of $1,000 on an investment of $100,000 is not as economically wise as a net present value of $900 on an investment of $10,000, provided that the $90,000 difference in investments can be used to realize a net present value of at least $101 in other projects. In this case, a net present value index should be used rather than the net present value dollar figure. This index places all competing projects on a comparable basis for the purpose of ranking them. For Dartmond Corporation, the computation is:

$$\text{Net present value index} = \frac{\text{Net present value}}{\text{Required investment}} = \frac{\$24,886}{\$95,000} = .262$$

This index simplifies finding the optimum solution for competing projects when the total budget for capital outlays is fixed arbitrarily, because it is possible to rank by percentages rather than absolute dollars.

4. It may be misleading when dealing with alternative projects or limited funds under the condition of unequal lives, in that the alternative with the higher net present value may involve longer economic life to the

point that it would be less desirable than an alternative having a shorter life. To illustrate, a firm may be faced with the problem of acquiring equipment for a manufacturing operation. Two alternatives are available: Equipment A, expected to last 18 years, and Equipment B, expected to last 5 years. There are two ways to deal with this problem:

(a) Repeat the investment cycle for Equipment B a sufficient number of times to cover the estimated economic life of Equipment A; in the example, 3⅗ times. An estimate of the salvage value of the fourth equipment investment cycle for Equipment B at the end of the life for Equipment A is needed in order to reflect a common termination date.

(b) The period considered can be the life of the shorter-life alternative, Equipment B, coupled with an estimate of the recoverable value of Equipment A at the end of 5 years. The analysis would then cover only the five-year period, with the recoverable value of Equipment A being treated as a cash inflow at the end of the period. A serious difficulty rests in the need to estimate a value of the longer-life asset at the end of 5 years. Such an intermediate recoverable value may not be an adequate measure of the service value of the equipment at that point in its useful life.

The Discounted Cash Flow (DCF) Method. In the present value method, the discount rate is known or at least predetermined. In the discounted cash flow method, the discount rate is not known but is defined as the rate at which the sum of positive present values equals the sum of negative present values. This discount rate is sometimes referred to as the internal rate of return. Present value theory is used, but the analysis is developed further to determine the discounted rate of return, which is then compared with some standard.

The discounted rate of return for Dartmond Corporation can be determined by trial and error, i.e., by computing net present value at various discount rates to find the rate at which the net present value is zero. This computation is illustrated in the following table:

Year	Net Aftertax Cash (Outflow) Inflow	Present Value of $1 @ 20%	Net Present Value of Cash Flow	Present Value of $1 @ 22%	Net Present Value of Cash Flow
0	$(95,000)	1.000	$(95,000)	1.000	$(95,000)
1	29,000	.833	24,157	.820	23,780
2	32,000	.694	22,208	.672	21,504
3	27,000	.579	15,633	.551	14,877
4	23,000	.482	11,086	.451	10,373
5	21,000	.402	8,442	.370	7,770
6	18,000	.335	6,030	.303	5,454
7	14,000	.279	3,906	.249	3,486
8	18,000	.233	4,194	.204	3,672
			$ 656		$(4,084)

The discounted rate is greater than 20 percent and less than 22 percent. The trial-and-error search should continue until adjacent rates in the table are found—one rate yielding a positive net present value with the other rate yielding a negative net present value, and both as close to zero as possible.

Expanded present value tables permit the determination of a net present value nearer zero. However, an approximation is obtainable by interpolation, as follows:

$$20\% + \left[2\% \times \frac{\$656}{\$656 + \$4,084}\right] = 20\% + [(2\%)(.138)] = .2028 \text{ or } 20.28\%$$

The discounted cash flow method permits management to maximize corporate profits by selecting proposals with the highest rates of return, as long as the rates are higher than the company's cost of capital plus management's allowance for risk and uncertainty and individual project characteristics. In most circumstances, the use of the discounted cash flow instead of the present value method at a given interest rate will not seriously alter the ranking of projects.

Note that the rate of return, using either the discounted cash flow method or the present value method, is computed on the basis of the unrecovered cash outflow from period to period, not on the original cash investment. In the ilustration, the DCF rate of return of 20.28 percent denotes that, over the eight years, the aftertax cash inflow equals the recovery of the original cash investment plus a return of 20.28 percent on the unrecovered cash investment from period to period. The net present value of $24,886 (page 750) indicates that, over the eight years, this additional amount, or a total of $119,886 ($95,000 + $24,886), could have been spent on the machine; and the original cash investment, plus a return of 12 percent on the unrecovered cash investment from period to period, could still have been recovered.

Advantages of using the discounted cash flow rate of return method of evaluating capital expenditures are:

1. It considers the time value of money.
2. It considers cash flow over the entire life of the project.
3. The discounted cash flow rate of return is more easily interpreted than the net present value and the net present value index.
4. Alternative projects which require different initial cash outlays and have unequal lives can be ranked logically in accordance with their respective discounted cash flow rate of return.

Disadvantages and limitations associated with the use of the discounted cash flow rate of return method of evaluating capital expenditures are:

1. Some argue that this method is too difficult to compute and to understand, particularly when cash flows change signs more than once, in which case the project has more than one rate of return.
2. Discounting at the project's internal rate of return implies that cash inflows can be reinvested to earn the rate earned by the investment being evaluated. In contrast, the present value method implies that cash inflows are reinvested at the discount rate being used, which is usually the weighted average cost of capital. The latter assumption

appears more reasonable, particularly when the internal rate of return for the project is high, because the weighted average cost of capital is the company-wide expected earnings rate. Nevertheless, in most circumstances, the use of the discounted cash flow rate of return method instead of the present value method will not seriously alter the ranking of alternative projects.

The Error Cushion. A project whose estimated desirability is near a cutoff point for the type of project being evaluated affords little cushion for errors. For example, if the management of a chain of automotive muffler shops anticipates that a new location should yield a minimum discounted cash flow of 12 percent, there is obviously a greater cushion for errors when the computed rate of return is 20 percent as opposed to 13 percent. Similarly, when one alternative is clearly superior to others for a particular project, there is a better cushion against errors than when two or more of the best alternatives indicate approximately the same expected results.

Reasonably accurate estimates are desirable in evaluating any project. However, a higher degree of sophistication and care, at a higher cost of obtaining the data, may be necessary to add confidence when the evaluation is close to a cutoff point or when two or more project alternatives yield about the same ''best'' answer. Conversely, in many cases, the desirability of a project or the selection from alternatives for a particular project will be so obvious that the costs of making sophisticated data estimates and using evaluation techniques are not justified.

Purchase vs. Leasing. A lease arrangement may be available as an alternative to investment in a capital asset. This possibility can be evaluated by determining the incremental annual cost of leasing versus purchasing. This cost represents purchasing cost savings which, on an aftertax basis, should be sufficient to yield the desired DCF rate of return on the anticipated purchase price.

In evaluating the leasing and purchasing alternatives, the present value method can be used as an alternative to the DCF method in either of two ways:

1. The net present value of the purchase price and the associated aftertax savings is computed, with the resulting net present value used to evaluate the attractiveness of purchasing versus leasing.
2. The net present values of the purchasing alternative and the leasing alternative cash flows are computed separately, each on an aftertax basis. The alternative having the more favorable net present value identifies the preferable choice.

Generally, the capital expenditure or investment decision is first justified, followed by the lease or financing decision. The rationale is that the acquisition must be a sound investment before considering the financing strategy and the operating flexibility, obsolescence, and service/maintenance factors associated with leases versus purchases. With a justified capital expenditure in hand, a lease-purchase decision can be made.[19]

Usually the lease is the more expensive alternative, since a lease involves avoiding various ownership risks for which a price must be paid. In such cases, a relevant question then becomes whether or not the extra cost entailed in leasing is worth paying in order to avoid risks of ownership. Management may prefer leasing if it is thereby able to improve balance sheet position by avoiding a purchase liability. Also, the rate of return on capital employed would be enhanced by reducing the investment in capital assets.[20] However, generally accepted accounting principles prescribe rules that require the capitalization and the recording of an associated liability for leases that are determined to be, in effect, purchases.[21]

▼ CONTROLLING CAPITAL EXPENDITURES

The phase of controlling capital expenditures consists of (1) control and review of a project while it is in process and (2) follow-up or post-completion audit of project results.

Control While in Process

When a project or a series of projects has finally been approved, methods, techniques, and procedures must be set in motion to permit the control and review of all project elements (costs, time, quality, and quantity) until completion. Control responsibility should be clearly designated, recognizing the necessity of assistance from and coordination with many individuals and groups, including those external to the company. Actual results should be compared with approved plans and evaluation results. Variations or trends toward deviations from plans should be reported promptly to responsible authorities in order to facilitate corrective action as quickly as possible. Day-to-day, on-the-scene observation and up-to-date reports should provide good cost control vehicles. Construction engineers have long used such devices as bar charts for planning and controlling the timing of project activities.

PERT/cost (Chapter 16) utilizes the network scheme to show the interrelationships of the multiple activities required to complete the average to

---

[19]William L. Ferrara, *The Lease-Purchase Decision: How Some Companies Make It* (New York: National Association of Accountants; Hamilton, Ontario: The Society of Management Accountants of Canada, 1978), p. 7. For a detailed discussion of the lease-purchase decision model, see William L. Ferrara, James B. Thies, and Mark W. Dirsmith, *The Lease-Purchase Decision* (New York: National Association of Accountants, 1980; Hamilton, Ontario: The Society of Management Accountants of Canada, 1979).

[20]Lawrence A. Gordon, Danny Miller, and Henry Mintzberg, *Normative Models in Managerial Decision-Making* (New York: National Association of Accountants; Hamilton, Ontario: The Society of Industrial Accountants of Canada, 1975), p. 67.

[21]*Statement of Financial Accounting Standards, No. 13,* "Accounting for Leases" (Stamford: Financial Accounting Standards Board, 1976).

large-scale project. Any project—the installation of a single large machine, a complex of machinery and equipment, or the construction of a new factory or office building—will involve many diverse tasks. Some of them can be done simultaneously; others must await the completion of preceding activities. PERT/cost offers a clear and all-inclusive picture of the operation as a whole in contrast to the bars on a chart. The use of this technique is particularly appropriate for those evaluation cases where more than one estimate is needed due to risk and uncertainty and there is a desire to expedite and increase the reliability of difficult estimates.

The cost of administering the control phase should be commensurate with the value derived. Overcontrol is an inefficient use of administrative resources.

Follow-Up of Project Results

Follow-up or post-completion audit means comparing and reporting results as related to the outcome predicted when the investment project was evaluated and approved. Follow-up affords a test of the existing planning and control procedure and therein the possibility of reinforcing successful projects, salvaging or terminating failing projects, and improving upon future investment proposals and decisions.

The same techniques used to evaluate the proposed project should be used for follow-up. For example, if the DCF rate of return projected in support of a project proposal is compared, in the follow-up procedure, with the actual average annual return on investment, the comparison could be quite misleading. Instead, the projected DCF rate should be compared to a DCF rate based on actual data and a reestimation of future data, thus employing the same evaluation technique in the follow-up as in evaluating the project proposal.

Follow-up should aid in determining the optimal point for project abandonment. For example, if the present value of estimated aftertax cash flows for a project's remaining life is less than the aftertax disposal value, it should be abandoned.

Generally, actual work in the area of follow-up lags behind advances made in other capital expenditure phases. Common hindrances to follow-up procedures are management's unwillingness to incur additional administrative costs, difficulty of quantifying the results of certain types of investments, apparent failure of the accounting or cost system to produce needed information, lack of personnel qualified to perform the follow-up tasks, and resentment by those being audited.

Value received as related to the cost of obtaining the follow-up information should determine the extent of the follow-up. For uniformity, efficiency, and independent review, management should designate a centralized group to prescribe procedures and audit the performance of the follow-up activity. The assembled data should be utilized as a control device and be reported to the controlling levels of management. Out-of-line results should then trigger corrective action in harmony with the management by exception principle.

Expected future cash flow

Shows today's value, or the present value of each dollar to be received or paid in the future for various rates of interest and periods of time.

PRESENT VALUE OF $1

Future Years	1%	2%	4%	6%	8%	10%	12%	14%	15%	16%	18%	20%	22%	24%	25%	26%	28%	30%	35%	40%	45%	50%
1	.990	.980	.962	.943	.926	.909	.893	.877	.870	.862	.847	.833	.820	.806	.800	.794	.781	.769	.741	.714	.690	.667
2	.980	.961	.925	.890	.857	.826	.797	.769	.756	.743	.718	.694	.672	.650	.640	.630	.610	.592	.549	.510	.476	.444
3	.971	.942	.889	.840	.794	.751	.712	.675	.658	.641	.609	.579	.551	.524	.512	.500	.477	.455	.406	.364	.328	.296
4	.961	.924	.855	.792	.735	.683	.636	.592	.572	.552	.516	.482	.451	.423	.410	.397	.373	.350	.301	.260	.226	.198
5	.951	.906	.822	.747	.681	.621	.567	.519	.497	.476	.437	.402	.370	.341	.328	.315	.291	.269	.223	.186	.156	.132
6	.942	.888	.790	.705	.630	.564	.507	.456	.432	.410	.370	.335	.303	.275	.262	.250	.227	.207	.165	.133	.108	.088
7	.933	.871	.760	.665	.583	.513	.452	.400	.376	.354	.314	.279	.249	.222	.210	.198	.178	.159	.122	.095	.074	.059
8	.923	.853	.731	.627	.540	.467	.404	.351	.327	.305	.266	.233	.204	.179	.168	.157	.139	.123	.091	.068	.051	.039
9	.914	.837	.703	.592	.500	.424	.361	.308	.284	.263	.225	.194	.167	.144	.134	.125	.108	.094	.067	.048	.035	.026
10	.905	.820	.676	.558	.463	.386	.322	.270	.247	.227	.191	.162	.137	.116	.107	.099	.085	.073	.050	.035	.024	.017
11	.896	.804	.650	.527	.429	.350	.287	.237	.215	.195	.162	.135	.112	.094	.086	.079	.066	.056	.037	.025	.017	.012
12	.887	.788	.625	.497	.397	.319	.257	.208	.187	.168	.137	.112	.092	.076	.069	.062	.052	.043	.027	.018	.012	.008
13	.879	.773	.601	.469	.368	.290	.229	.182	.163	.145	.116	.093	.075	.061	.055	.050	.040	.033	.020	.013	.008	.005
14	.870	.758	.577	.442	.340	.263	.205	.160	.141	.125	.099	.078	.062	.049	.044	.039	.032	.025	.015	.009	.006	.003
15	.861	.743	.555	.417	.315	.239	.183	.140	.123	.108	.084	.065	.051	.040	.035	.031	.025	.020	.011	.006	.004	.002
16	.853	.728	.534	.394	.292	.218	.163	.123	.107	.093	.071	.054	.042	.032	.028	.025	.019	.015	.008	.005	.003	.002
17	.844	.714	.513	.371	.270	.198	.146	.108	.093	.080	.060	.045	.034	.026	.023	.020	.015	.012	.006	.003	.002	.001
18	.836	.700	.494	.350	.250	.180	.130	.095	.081	.069	.051	.038	.028	.021	.018	.016	.012	.009	.005	.002	.001	.001
19	.828	.686	.475	.331	.232	.164	.116	.083	.070	.060	.043	.031	.023	.017	.014	.012	.009	.007	.003	.002	.001	
20	.820	.673	.456	.312	.215	.149	.104	.073	.061	.051	.037	.026	.019	.014	.012	.010	.007	.005	.002	.001	.001	
21	.811	.660	.439	.294	.199	.135	.093	.064	.053	.044	.031	.022	.015	.011	.009	.008	.006	.004	.002	.001		
22	.803	.647	.422	.278	.184	.123	.083	.056	.046	.038	.026	.018	.013	.009	.007	.006	.004	.003	.001	.001		
23	.795	.634	.406	.262	.170	.112	.074	.049	.040	.033	.022	.015	.010	.007	.006	.005	.003	.002	.001			
24	.788	.622	.390	.247	.158	.102	.066	.043	.035	.028	.019	.013	.008	.006	.005	.004	.003	.002	.001			
25	.780	.610	.375	.233	.146	.092	.059	.038	.030	.024	.016	.010	.007	.005	.004	.003	.002	.001	.001			
26	.772	.598	.361	.220	.135	.084	.053	.033	.026	.021	.014	.009	.006	.004	.003	.002	.002	.001				
27	.764	.586	.347	.207	.125	.076	.047	.029	.023	.018	.011	.007	.005	.003	.002	.002	.001	.001				
28	.757	.574	.333	.196	.116	.069	.042	.026	.020	.016	.010	.006	.004	.002	.002	.002	.001	.001				
29	.749	.563	.321	.185	.107	.063	.037	.022	.017	.014	.008	.005	.003	.002	.002	.001	.001	.001				
30	.742	.552	.308	.174	.099	.057	.033	.020	.015	.012	.007	.004	.003	.002	.001	.001	.001					
40	.672	.453	.208	.097	.046	.022	.011	.005	.004	.003	.001	.001										
50	.608	.372	.141	.054	.021	.009	.003	.001	.001	.001												

PRESENT VALUE OF $1 RECEIVED OR PAID ANNUALLY FOR EACH OF THE NEXT N YEARS

Future Years	1%	2%	4%	6%	8%	10%	12%	14%	15%	16%	18%	20%	22%	24%	25%	26%	28%	30%	35%	40%	45%	50%
1	.990	.980	.962	.943	.926	.909	.893	.877	.870	.862	.847	.833	.820	.806	.800	.794	.781	.769	.741	.714	.690	.667
2	1.970	1.942	1.886	1.833	1.783	1.736	1.690	1.647	1.626	1.605	1.566	1.528	1.492	1.457	1.440	1.424	1.392	1.361	1.289	1.224	1.165	1.111
3	2.941	2.884	2.775	2.673	2.577	2.487	2.402	2.322	2.283	2.246	2.174	2.106	2.042	1.981	1.952	1.923	1.868	1.816	1.696	1.589	1.493	1.407
4	3.902	3.808	3.630	3.465	3.312	3.170	3.037	2.914	2.855	2.798	2.690	2.589	2.494	2.404	2.362	2.320	2.241	2.166	1.997	1.849	1.720	1.605
5	4.853	4.713	4.452	4.212	3.993	3.791	3.605	3.433	3.352	3.274	3.127	2.991	2.864	2.745	2.689	2.635	2.532	2.436	2.220	2.035	1.876	1.737
6	5.795	5.601	5.242	4.917	4.623	4.355	4.111	3.889	3.784	3.685	3.498	3.326	3.167	3.020	2.951	2.885	2.759	2.643	2.385	2.168	1.983	1.824
7	6.728	6.472	6.002	5.582	5.206	4.868	4.564	4.288	4.160	4.039	3.812	3.605	3.416	3.242	3.161	3.083	2.937	2.802	2.508	2.263	2.057	1.883
8	7.652	7.325	6.733	6.210	5.747	5.335	4.968	4.639	4.487	4.344	4.078	3.837	3.619	3.421	3.329	3.241	3.076	2.925	2.598	2.331	2.108	1.922
9	8.566	8.163	7.435	6.802	6.247	5.759	5.328	4.946	4.772	4.607	4.303	4.031	3.786	3.566	3.463	3.366	3.184	3.019	2.665	2.379	2.144	1.948
10	9.471	8.983	8.111	7.360	6.710	6.145	5.650	5.216	5.019	4.833	4.494	4.192	3.923	3.682	3.571	3.465	3.269	3.092	2.715	2.414	2.168	1.965
11	10.368	9.787	8.760	7.887	7.139	6.495	5.988	5.453	5.234	5.029	4.656	4.327	4.035	3.776	3.656	3.544	3.335	3.147	2.752	2.438	2.185	1.977
12	11.255	10.575	9.385	8.384	7.536	6.814	6.194	5.660	5.421	5.197	4.793	4.439	4.127	3.851	3.725	3.606	3.387	3.190	2.779	2.456	2.196	1.985
13	12.134	11.348	9.986	8.853	7.904	7.103	6.424	5.842	5.583	5.342	4.910	4.533	4.203	3.912	3.780	3.656	3.427	3.223	2.799	2.468	2.204	1.990
14	13.004	12.106	10.563	9.295	8.244	7.367	6.628	6.002	5.724	5.468	5.008	4.611	4.265	3.962	3.824	3.695	3.459	3.249	2.814	2.477	2.210	1.993
15	13.865	12.849	11.118	9.712	8.559	7.606	6.811	6.142	5.847	5.575	5.092	4.675	4.315	4.001	3.859	3.726	3.483	3.268	2.825	2.484	2.214	1.995
16	14.718	13.578	11.652	10.106	8.851	7.824	6.974	6.265	5.954	5.669	5.162	4.730	4.357	4.033	3.887	3.751	3.503	3.283	2.834	2.489	2.216	1.997
17	15.562	14.292	12.166	10.477	9.122	8.022	7.120	6.373	6.047	5.749	5.222	4.775	4.391	4.059	3.910	3.771	3.518	3.295	2.840	2.492	2.218	1.998
18	16.398	14.992	12.659	10.828	9.372	8.201	7.250	6.467	6.128	5.818	5.273	4.812	4.419	4.080	3.928	3.786	3.529	3.304	2.844	2.494	2.219	1.999
19	17.226	15.678	13.134	11.158	9.604	8.365	7.366	6.550	6.198	5.877	5.316	4.844	4.442	4.097	3.942	3.799	3.539	3.311	2.848	2.496	2.220	1.999
20	18.046	16.351	13.590	11.470	9.818	8.514	7.469	6.623	6.259	5.929	5.353	4.870	4.460	4.110	3.954	3.808	3.546	3.316	2.850	2.497	2.221	1.999
21	18.857	17.011	14.029	11.764	10.017	8.649	7.562	6.687	6.312	5.973	5.384	4.891	4.476	4.121	3.963	3.816	3.551	3.320	2.852	2.498	2.221	2.000
22	19.660	17.658	14.451	12.042	10.201	8.772	7.645	6.743	6.359	6.011	5.410	4.909	4.488	4.130	3.970	3.822	3.556	3.323	2.853	2.498	2.222	2.000
23	20.456	18.292	14.857	12.303	10.371	8.883	7.718	6.792	6.399	6.044	5.432	4.925	4.499	4.137	3.976	3.827	3.559	3.325	2.854	2.499	2.222	2.000
24	21.243	18.914	15.247	12.550	10.529	8.985	7.784	6.835	6.434	6.073	5.451	4.937	4.507	4.143	3.981	3.831	3.562	3.327	2.855	2.499	2.222	2.000
25	22.023	19.523	15.622	12.783	10.675	9.077	7.843	6.873	6.464	6.097	5.467	4.948	4.514	4.147	3.985	3.834	3.564	3.329	2.856	2.499	2.222	2.000
26	22.795	20.121	15.983	13.003	10.810	9.161	7.896	6.906	6.491	6.118	5.480	4.956	4.520	4.151	3.988	3.837	3.566	3.330	2.856	2.500	2.222	2.000
27	23.560	20.707	16.330	13.211	10.935	9.237	7.943	6.935	6.514	6.136	5.492	4.964	4.524	4.154	3.990	3.839	3.567	3.331	2.856	2.500	2.222	2.000
28	24.316	21.281	16.663	13.406	11.051	9.307	7.984	6.961	6.534	6.152	5.502	4.970	4.528	4.157	3.992	3.840	3.568	3.331	2.857	2.500	2.222	2.000
29	25.066	21.844	16.984	13.591	11.158	9.370	8.022	6.983	6.551	6.166	5.510	4.975	4.531	4.159	3.994	3.841	3.569	3.332	2.857	2.500	2.222	2.000
30	25.808	22.396	17.292	13.765	11.258	9.427	8.055	7.003	6.566	6.177	5.517	4.979	4.534	4.160	3.995	3.842	3.569	3.332	2.857	2.500	2.222	2.000
40	32.835	27.355	19.793	15.046	11.925	9.779	8.244	7.105	6.642	6.234	5.548	4.997	4.544	4.166	3.999	3.846	3.571	3.333	2.857	2.500	2.222	2.000
50	39.196	31.424	21.482	15.762	12.234	9.915	8.304	7.133	6.661	6.246	5.554	4.999	4.545	4.167	4.000	3.846	3.571	3.333	2.857	2.500	2.222	2.000

for set amt.

Shows the present value of a series of $1 periodic receipts or payments, used when the cash flow is estimated to be the same each period.

DISCUSSION QUESTIONS

1. Why are effective planning and control of capital expenditures important?

2. Differentiate between the economic and physical life of a project.

3. Describe the procedure for computing the weighted average cost of capital.
   (ICMA adapted)

4. Why would a firm use its weighted average cost of capital as the hurdle rate (minimum rate) for a project investment decision, rather than the specific marginal cost of funds?

5. Discuss the practical difficulties in estimating the firm's weighted average cost of capital.   *(CGAAC adapted)*

6. (a) Is depreciation deducted for tax purposes likely to differ from book (or financial accounting) depreciation? Explain.
   (b) Should book depreciation be considered in estimating the future cash flows from a proposed project? Explain.
   (c) Should tax depreciation be considered in estimating the future cash flows from a proposed project? Explain.

7. Financial accounting data are not entirely suitable for use in evaluating capital expenditures. Explain.   *(AICPA adapted)*

8. Define the payback (or payout) period method.

9. How do the two average annual return on investment methods differ?

10. What is the present value concept and why is it important in capital budgeting?

11. What is the basic difference between the payback method and the present value method?   *(AICPA adapted)*

12. What is the difference between the net present value and the discounted cash flow rate of return calculations?

13. Both the present value method and the discounted cash flow method assume that the earnings produced by a project are reinvested in the company. However, each approach assumes a different rate of return at which earnings are reinvested. Describe the rate of return assumed in each of the two approaches and discuss which of the assumed rates is more realistic.
    (CGAAC adapted)

14. Discuss benefits to be derived from a follow-up of project results.
    (ICMA adapted)

EXERCISES

1. Cost of capital. Wiz Company wishes to compute a weighted average cost of capital for use in evaluating capital expenditure proposals. Earnings, capital structure, and current market prices of the company's securities are:

Earnings

Earnings before interest and income tax	$ 210,000
Interest expense on bonds	30,000
Pretax earnings	$ 180,000
Income tax (assume 45% tax rate)	81,000
Aftertax earnings	$ 99,000
Preferred stock dividends	24,000
Earnings available to common stockholders	$ 75,000
Common stock dividends	30,000
Increase in retained earnings	$ 45,000

Capital structure

Mortgage bonds, 10%, 10 years...	$ 300,000
Preferred stock, 12%, $100 par value..	200,000
Common stock, no par, 50,000 shares outstanding......................	350,000
Retained earnings (equity of common stockholders)....................	150,000
	$1,000,000

Market prices of the company's securities

Preferred stock...	$96
Common stock...	10

Required: Assuming that the current cost and mix of sources of funds are expected to continue over the investment horizon, determine the weighted average cost of capital.

2. Cost of capital. Magnum Tool Company, a manufacturer of diamond drilling, cutting, and grinding tools, has $1,000,000 of its 8% bond issue maturing next month. To meet this debt, an additional $1,000,000 must be raised, and one proposal under consideration is the sale and leaseback of the company's general office building.

The building would be sold to FHR Inc. for $1,000,000 and leased back on a 25-year lease, with annual payments of $110,168, permitting the lessor to recover its investment and earn 10% on the investment. Magnum Tool will pay all maintenance costs, property taxes, and insurance and will reacquire the building at the end of the lease period for a nominal payment.

The current capital structure is:

Capital Component	Amount	Pretax Component Cost
Bonds (including amount to be retired next month)...	$5,000,000	8.0%
Preferred stock (market value)................................	1,000,000	9.0
Common stock and retained earnings (market value)..	4,000,000	12.5

Magnum Tool's income tax rate is 40%.

Required: Compute the weighted average cost of capital before and after the bond retirement and the sale-leaseback transaction.   *(ICMA adapted)*

3. Payback and average annual return on investment methods. Poly Products Inc. is considering the purchase of a $40,000 machine, which will be depreciated on the straight-line basis over an eight-year period with no salvage value for both book and tax purposes. The machine is expected to generate net cash inflow before income tax of $12,000 a year. Assume that the income tax rate is 40%.

Required:

   (1) Determine the payback period.
   (2) What is the average annual return on original investment? *(AICPA adapted)*

4. Investment analysis; uniform cash flow. Apernex Company is evaluating a capital budgeting proposal, requiring an initial investment of $30,000. The project will have a six-year life. The aftertax annual cash inflow due to this investment is $10,000. The desired rate of return is 15%.

Required:

(1) What is the payback period?
(2) Compute the net present value of the project.
(3) What amount would Apernex have had to invest five years ago, at 15% compounded annually, to have $30,000 now?   *(AICPA adapted)*

5. Equipment investment analysis; net present value and present value index. Progression Corporation is considering purchasing a new press, requiring an immediate $100,000 cash outlay. The new press is expected to increase annual net aftertax cash receipts by $40,000 for the next three years, after which it will be sold for $30,000, after taxes. The company desires a minimum return of 16% on invested capital.

Required:

(1) Compute the net present value of the project.
(2) Compute the net present value index.

6. Effect of depreciation methods on cash flow. Kingsgate Corporation is planning to acquire a machine for one of its projects at a cost of $100,000. The machine has an economic life of eight years, but since it is five-year-class property under MACRS, the entire cost will be recovered for tax purposes in six years. The company's cost of capital rate is 14%, and the income tax rate is 40%.

Required: Determine the present value of the income tax benefits which result from the use of the MACRS recovery percentages provided on page 742, as opposed to the straight-line depreciation alternative over the same recovery period.

7. Effect of inflation on investment decision. McLoud Company is evaluating a capital budgeting proposal which will require an initial cash investment of $60,000. The project will have a five-year life. The net aftertax cash inflows from the project, before any adjustment for the effects of inflation, are expected to be as follows:

Year	Unadjusted Estimate of Cash Inflows
1	$20,000
2	18,000
3	16,000
4	10,000
5	10,000

No salvage is expected at the end of the project. Cash inflows are expected to increase at the anticipated inflation rate of 10% each year. The company's cost of capital rate is 15%.

Required:

(1) Compute the estimated cash inflow for each year, adjusted for the anticipated effects of inflation.
(2) Determine the net present value of the cash flows before and after the adjustment for the anticipated effects of inflation.

8. Use of net present value to evaluate asset acquisition. Swift Air Transport Company is considering the acquisition of a new airplane at a cost of $1,000,000. The airplane has an estimated useful life of 15 years, but it qualifies as 7-year property for tax purposes under MACRS. The annual pretax cash inflows from the air freight that will be transported by the new airplane, net of annual operating expenses, is expected to be $120,000 in each of the 15 years the airplane will be used. The company is in a 40% income tax bracket, and its weighted average cost of capital is 15%.

Required: Determine the net present value of the investment in the new airplane. Would you advise management to purchase the airplane? Explain.

9. Equipment replacement analysis. Kipling Company purchased a special machine one year ago at a cost of $10,000. At that time, the machine was estimated to have a useful life of 7 years and a $500 disposal value. A MACRS tax deduction of $2,000 was taken in the year of acquisition. The annual cash operating cost is approximately $20,100.

A new machine that has just come on the market will do the same job but with an annual cash operating cost of only $16,000. This new machine costs $17,000 and has an estimated life of 6 years with no expected salvage value. The old machine could be used as a trade-in at an allowance of $5,000. The tax basis of the old machine is $8,500.

The new machine qualifies as five-year property under MACRS, and the income tax rate is 40%. The company's cost of capital is 12%.

Required: Make a recommendation to management, based on the DCF rate of return. (Use the MACRS depreciation rates provided on page 742.)

10. Net present value and DCF rate of return reinvestment assumption. Aftertax cash flows adjusted for effects of inflation for two mutually exclusive projects (with economic lives of 5 years each) are:

Year	Project A	Project B
0	$(15,000)	$(15,000)
1	5,000	0
2	5,000	0
3	5,000	0
4	5,000	0
5	5,000	35,000

The company's cost of capital is 15%.

Required:

    (1) Compute the discounted cash flow rate of return for each project.
    (2) Determine the net present value for each project.
    (3) Which project should be selected?

PROBLEMS

23-1. Make or buy decision requiring capital expenditure analysis. Lyonal Company manufactures several lines of machine products. One unique part, a valve stem, requires specialized tools that need to be replaced. Management has decided that the only alternative to replacing these tools is to acquire the valve stem from an outside source. A supplier is willing to provide the valve stem at a unit sales price of $20 if at least 70,000 units are ordered annually.

Lyonal's average usage of valve stems over the past three years has been 80,000 units each year. Expectations are that this volume will remain constant over the next five years. Cost records indicate that unit manufacturing costs for the last several years have been as follows:

Direct materials.........................	$ 3.80
Direct labor...............................	3.70
Variable overhead.....................	1.70
Fixed overhead*........................	4.50
Total unit cost........................	$13.70

*Depreciation accounts for two thirds of the fixed overhead. The balance is for other fixed overhead costs of the factory that require cash expenditures.

If the specialized tools are purchased, they will cost $2,500,000 and will have a disposal value of $100,000 after their expected economic life of five years. Straight-line depreciation is used for financial accounting purposes, but the most accelerated method available under MACRS is used for tax purposes. The specialized tools are considered three-year property for MACRS purposes. The company has a 40% marginal tax rate, and Lyonal's weighted average cost of capital is 12%.

The sales representative for the manufacturer of the new tools states: "The new tools will allow direct labor and variable overhead to be reduced by $.80 each per unit ($1.60 total per unit)." Data from another manufacturer using identical tools and experiencing similar operating conditions, except that annual production generally averages 110,000 units, confirm the direct labor and variable overhead savings. However, the manufacturer indicates that it experienced an increase in raw materials cost due to the higher quality of materials that had to be used with the new tools. The manufacturer indicated that its costs have been as follows:

Direct materials.........................	$ 4.50
Direct labor...............................	3.00
Variable overhead.....................	.80
Fixed overhead.........................	5.00
Total unit cost........................	$13.30

Required:

(1) Prepare a present value cash flow analysis covering the economic life of the new specialized tools to determine whether Lyonal Company should replace the old tools or purchase the valve stem from an outside supplier. Use the MACRS depreciation rates provided on page 742.

(2) Identify additional factors that Lyonal Company should consider before a decision is made to replace the tools or purchase the valve stem from an outside supplier.   (ICMA adapted)

23-2. Comparison of investment alternatives. Winsburgh Corporation is considering investing in one of two alternative capital projects. Estimated cash flows relating to the two alternative projects follow:

	Project 1	Project 2
Initial cash investment..	$120,000	$120,000
Estimated economic life of project....................	5 years	5 years
Annual aftertax cash inflows:		
Year 1..	$10,000	$50,000
Year 2..	20,000	45,000
Year 3..	30,000	35,000
Year 4..	60,000	25,000
Year 5..	90,000	20,000

Required:

(1) Compute the net present value for each of the two alternative projects, assuming that the weighted average cost of capital is 12%.

(2) Compute the discounted cash flow rate of return for each of the two alternative projects.

(3) Considering the results of your computations in requirements (1) and (2), what would you recommend? Explain.

23-3. Use of present value to value asset. The City of Grant has been contacted by a downtown bank about purchasing land from the city. The land is adjacent to the bank, and the bank intends to use the property for a parking lot and possibly, at a later date, for expansion. The city is especially interested in working with the bank because of the desirability of maintaining its present downtown location, since the result will enhance the overall health of the downtown business district. Failure to obtain the adjacent property could cause the bank to close its downtown facility. Retention and perhaps expansion of the downtown bank is expected to enhance the city's proceeds from property and sales taxes.

The appraised value of the city's property is $200,000 plus the loss of the continuing use of a water well and storage tank located on the property. The replacement cost of the storage tank is estimated to be $250,000. Loss of the water well means that water must be purchased from the neighboring City of Daniel in addition to what is already being purchased from that city.

The present (19A) cost of producing from the existing well is $32,700 for electricity, $2,500 for labor service, and estimated pump repair and maintenance cost of $20,000 per year for the years 19E through 19H. The annual cost of replacing this lost water supply by additional purchases from the City of Daniel is a fixed demand charge of $46,870 plus a charge of $.2585 per 1,000 for the additional 100,000,000 gallons to be supplied. All costs except for pump repair and maintenance are expected to increase at an annual rate of 8%.

The City of Grant's cost of capital is estimated to be 10%, and it is estimated that the well has a remaining life of 8 years.

Required: Compute an estimated land value that includes the present value of the differential cost of water, and identify other considerations that might affect the final price quoted to the bank.

23-4. Capital expenditure analysis. Vekany Steel Company is considering a process computer for improved production control in its Tin Mill Department. This department receives coils of cold rolled steel from another department of the company. It further reduces the gage of this steel in its own five-stand tandem cold strip mill.The coils of steel, now much thinner in gage, pass through a continuous annealing line, where the strip is heated to 1300 degrees Fahrenheit and allowed to cool slowly in an atmosphere of inert gas. The strip is then cleaned in a pickling line before it moves to the electrolytic tinning line. This last process deposits a thin coating of tin on the continuously moving strip. The coiled tin plate is then shipped to customers in the canning industry.

The Tin Mill Department estimates that the proposed process computer will require an investment of $2,200,000. Resulting aftertax cash savings from reduced costs of labor, materials, utilities, and scrap losses over the useful life of the computer are estimated to be:

Year	Amount
1	$ 300,000
2	350,000
3	400,000
4	450,000
5	500,000
6	550,000
7	600,000
8	650,000
9	700,000
10	750,000
	$5,250,000

Required: With respect to the proposed capital expenditure, compute the following:

(1) The payout period.
(2) The average annual return on original investment, rounded to the nearest $\frac{1}{10}$ of 1%.
(3) The average annual return on average investment, rounded to the nearest $\frac{1}{10}$ of 1%.
(4) The net present value at an assumed 14% cost of capital.
(5) The discounted cash flow rate of return.

23-5. Comparison of equipment alternatives. Two machines are being evaluated for possible acquisition by the Maxfield Corporation. Forecasts relating to the two machines are:

	Machine 1	Machine 2
Purchase price.....................................	$ 500,000	$ 600,000
Estimated economic life.....................	8 years	8 years
Estimated salvage value...................	none	none
Annual aftertax cash benefit:		
Year 1...	$ 125,000	$ 50,000
Year 2...	125,000	75,000
Year 3...	125,000	100,000
Year 4...	125,000	125,000
Year 5...	125,000	150,000
Year 6...	125,000	200,000
Year 7...	125,000	300,000
Year 8...	125,000	400,000
Total cash benefit.........................	$1,000,000	$1,400,000

Required: For each equipment alternative, compute the following:

(1) The payback period.
(2) The average annual return on original investment, rounded to the nearest $\frac{1}{10}$ of 1%.
(3) The average annual return on average investment, rounded to the nearest $\frac{1}{10}$ of 1%.
(4) The net present value and the net present value index, rounded to three decimal places, using an assumed 15% cost of capital.
(5) The discounted cash flow rate of return.

23-6. Feasibility study. Salome Inc. is considering a proposed addition to its Hidden Valley, Colorado ski lift facilities, which will require an investment of $1,000,000 and will have a 6-year useful life with no salvage value. The income tax rate is 40%. The company has sufficient income from other sources to absorb any losses that might be generated from the proposed addition to its facilities in the year in which the loss is incurred. The estimated revenue and expenses over the life of the project, adjusted for the effects of inflation, are:

Estimated Revenues and Expenses
(thousands of dollars)

	Year					
	1	2	3	4	5	6
Revenue..	$450	$800	$800	$800	$700	$500
Cash expenses................................	300	330	408	435	435	342
Net pretax cash inflow.....................	$150	$470	$392	$365	$265	$158
Tax depreciation..............................	200	320	192	115	115	58
Taxable income (loss)......................	$ (50)	$150	$200	$250	$150	$100
Income tax rate................................	40%	40%	40%	40%	40%	40%
Income tax expense.........................	$ (20)	$ 60	$ 80	$100	$ 60	$ 40

Required: With respect to the proposed addition, compute the following:

(1) The payback period.
(2) The average annual return on original investment, rounded to the nearest $\frac{1}{10}$ of 1%.
(3) The average annual return on average investment, rounded to the nearest $\frac{1}{10}$ of 1%.
(4) The net present value and the net present value index, rounded to three decimal places, at an assumed 12% cost of capital.
(5) The present value payback period.
(6) The discounted cash flow rate of return.

23-7. Equipment replacement analysis. Kastlan Corporation is considering the purchase of a replacement machine. The new machine is priced at $64,000. However, the vendor has offered Kastlan a $10,000 trade-in allowance for the old machine. The old machine has a net book value of $4,000 and a tax basis of zero. The new machine will perform essentially the same function as the old machine, except that it will be able to operate at an increased capacity. The following cash flows (which have been adjusted for the anticipated effects of inflation) are predicted over the estimated useful life of the new machine:

Year	Cash Savings Related to Maintenance	Cash Flow from Additional Capacity	Total Increase in Cash Inflow
1	$1,500	$ 6,300	$ 7,800
2	1,200	7,280	8,480
3	900	17,188	18,088
4	600	25,260	25,860
5	300	25,560	25,860
6	0	22,912	22,912
7	0	22,500	22,500

For financial accounting purposes, the new machine is to be depreciated on a straight-line basis over a period of 7 years, with an expected salvage value of $6,000. For tax purposes, however, the machine will be depreciated under MACRS as 5-year-class property. The company's weighted average cost of capital is 12%, and the tax rate is 40%.

Required: Using the MACRS rates provided on page 742, compute each of the following:

(1) Payback period in years.
(2) Average annual return on original investment and average annual return on average investment.
(3) Net present value and the net present value index.
(4) Discounted cash flow rate of return.

23-8. Investment analysis with inflation adjustment. Howison Company is considering the purchase of a giant press costing $100,000. The estimated cash benefits before considering income tax and the effects of inflation follow:

Year	Cash Benefit
1	$25,000
2	25,000
3	25,000
4	25,000
5	25,000
6	20,000
7	20,000
8	15,000
9	15,000
10	10,000

For financial accounting purposes, the press is to be depreciated on a straight-line basis over a period of 10 years, with no expected salvage value. For tax purposes, however, the press will be depreciated under MACRS, using the rates for 7-year property provided on page 742. The company's tax rate is 40%. The annual inflation rate is expected to be 10% for the planning period.

Required: Adjust the cash flows for the expected effects of inflation (round the price-level index used to two decimal places) and compute each of the following:

(1) Payback period in years.
(2) Average annual return on original investment.
(3) Average annual return on average investment.
(4) Net present value and the net present value index at an assumed 16% cost of capital.
(5) Present value payback in years.
(6) Discounted cash flow rate of return.

23-9. Purchase vs. leasing. Wheary Enterprises plans to operate a sightseeing boat along the Charles River in Boston. In negotiating the purchase of a new vessel from Yachts Dynamic Inc., Wheary learned that Yachts Dynamic would lease the boat to them as an alternative to selling it outright. Through such an arrangement, Wheary would not pay the $2,000,000 purchase price but would lease for $320,000 annually. Wheary expects the boat to last for 15 years, when its salvage value would be $200,000. For tax purposes, however, the boat would be 7-year property (i.e., the cost of the boat would be recovered over a period of 8 years, using the MACRS rates for 7-year property provided on page 742).

The annual net cash inflow, excluding any consideration of lease payments and income tax, is expected to be $600,000. The company's income tax rate is 40%, and its cost of capital is 14%.

Required: Make a recommendation to purchase or lease the boat, using the present value method to evaluate each alternative.

23-10. Make, buy, or lease. Egelston Corporation is a manufacturing concern that produces and sells a wide range of products. The company not only mass produces a number of products and equipment components, but is also capable of producing special-purpose manufacturing equipment to customer specifications.

The firm is considering adding a new product, with an estimated six-year market life, to one of its product lines. More equipment will be required to produce the new product. There are three alternative ways to acquire the needed equipment: (1) purchase general-purpose equipment, (2) lease general-purpose equipment, or (3) build special-purpose equipment. A fourth alternative, purchase of the special-purpose equipment, has been ruled out because it would be prohibitively expensive.

The general-purpose equipment can be purchased for $125,000. The equipment has an estimated salvage of $15,000 at the end of its useful life of ten years. After six years, the equipment can be used elsewhere in the plant or be sold for $40,000.

Alternatively, the general-purpose equipment can be acquired by a six-year lease for $40,000 annual rent. The lessor will assume all responsibility for property taxes, insurance, and maintenance.

Special-purpose equipment can be constructed by the Contract Equipment Department of Egelston Corporation. While the department is operating at a level which is normal for the time of year, it is below full capacity. The department could produce the equipment without interfering with its regular revenue-producing activities.

The estimated departmental costs for the construction of the special-purpose equipment are:

Materials and parts...	$ 75,000
Direct labor...	60,000
Variable factory overhead (50% of DL).....................	30,000
Fixed factory overhead (25% of DL)..........................	15,000
Total..	$180,000

Corporation general and administrative costs average 20% of the labor cost.

Engineering and management studies provide the following revenue and cost estimates (excluding lease payments and depreciation) for producing the new product, depending upon the equipment used:

	General-Purpose Equipment		Self-Constructed Equipment
	Leased	Purchased	
Unit selling price...	$5.00	$5.00	$5.00
Unit production costs:			
Materials..	$1.80	$1.80	$1.70
Variable conversion cost.................................	1.65	1.65	1.40
Total unit production cost............................	$3.45	$3.45	$3.10
Unit contribution margin.................................	$1.55	$1.55	$1.90
Estimated unit volume...	40,000	40,000	40,000
Estimated total contribution margin....................	$62,000	$62,000	$76,000

	General-Purpose Equipment		Self-Con-structed Equipment
	Leased	Purchased	
Other costs:			
Supervision...	$16,000	$16,000	$17,000
Property taxes and insurance.........................	—	3,000	5,000
Maintenance..	—	3,000	2,000
Total...	$16,000	$22,000	$24,000

For tax purposes, the company would depreciate both the general-purpose machine and the special-purpose machine over six years, using the MACRS rates for 5-year property provided on page 742. The salvage value of the special-purpose equipment at the end of six years is estimated to be $30,000.

The company uses an aftertax cost of capital of 14%. Its income tax rate is 40%.

Required:

(1) Calculate the net present value for each of the three alternatives that Egelston Corporation has at its disposal.
(2) Explain which, if any, of the three options Egelston Corporation should select.

(ICMA adapted)

CASES

A. Relevant data for investment decision. Clewash Linen Supply Company provides laundered items to various commercial and service establishments in a large city. Clewash is scheduled to acquire some new cleaning equipment in mid-19A, which would enable the company to increase the volume of laundry it handles without any increase in labor costs. In addition, the estimated maintenance costs in terms of pounds of laundry processed would be reduced slightly.

The new equipment was justified not only on the basis of reduced cost but also on the basis of expected increase in demand starting in late 19A. However, since the original forecast was prepared, several potential new customers have either delayed or discontinued their own expansion plans in the market area serviced by Clewash, and the most recent forecast indicates that no great increase in demand can be expected until late 19B or early 19C.

Required: Identify and explain factors which tend to indicate whether the investment should be made as scheduled or delayed.

(ICMA adapted)

B. Decentralization and the management of capital expenditures. Judy Knight founded the Neoglobe Company over thirty years ago. Although she has relied heavily upon advice from other members of management, Knight has made all of the important decisions for the company. Neoglobe has been successful, experiencing steady growth in its early years and very rapid growth in recent years. During this period of rapid growth, Knight has experienced difficulty in keeping up with the many decisions that needed to be made. She feels that she is losing control of the company's progress.

Regular discussions regarding her concern have been held with George Armet, the company executive vice-president. As a result of these discussions, Armet has studied possible alternative organizational structures to the present highly centralized functional organization.

In a carefully prepared proposal, Armet recommended that the company reorganize according to its two product lines, because the technology and marketing methods are quite different. The plastic products require different manufacturing skills and equipment from the brass products. The change could be accomplished easily because the products are manufactured in different plants. The marketing effort is also segregated along product lines within the sales function. The number of executive positions would not change, although the duties of the positions would change. There would no longer be the need for a vice-president for manufacturing or a vice-president for sales. Those positions would be replaced with the vice-president for each of the two product lines. Armet acknowledges that there may be personnel problems at the executive management level, because the current vice-presidents may not be competent to manage within the new structure.

Armet's proposal also contained the recommendation that some of the decision-making power, long held by Knight, be transferred to the new vice-presidents. Armet argued that this would be good for the company. The vice-presidents would be more aware of the problems and solution alternatives of their respective product lines because they are closer to the operations. Fewer decisions would be required of each new vice-president than now are required of Knight. This should reduce the time between problem recognition and implementation of the solution. Armet further argued that distributing the decision-making power would improve the creativity and spirit of company management.

Knight is intrigued by the proposal and the prospect that it would make the company more manageable. However, the proposal did not spell out clearly which decisions should be transferred and which should remain with the president. Knight requested Armet to prepare a supplemental memorandum specifying the decisions to be delegated to the vice-presidents.

The supplemental memorandum presented the recommended decision areas, explaining in each case how the new vice-presidents would be closer to the situation and thereby be able to make prompt, sound decisions. The following list summarizes Armet's recommendations:

(1) Sales
   (a) Price policy
   (b) Promotional strategy
   (c) Credit policy

(2) Operations
   (a) Manufacturing procedures
   (b) Labor negotiations
(3) Development of existing product lines
(4) Capital investment decision—up to amounts not exceeding the division "depreciation flow" plus 25% of its "aftertax income" (excluding ventures into new fields).

The corporate management (Knight and Armet) would be responsible for overall corporate development. Also, they would allocate the remaining available cash flow for dividends, for investment projects above the limits prescribed, and for investment into new ventures.

Required:

(1) Does the company have the characteristics needed for decentralized profit centers? Explain.
(2) Knight believes that the proposal, as presented, will not work. In Knight's judgment, the corporate level management will be unable to control effectively the destiny of the firm because the proposal grants too much investment freedom to the new divisions. Do you agree with Knight that effective control over the future of the firm cannot be maintained at the corporate level if the capital rationing is shared in the manner specified in the proposal? Support your answer with appropriate discussion, including a recommended alternative procedure if you agree with Knight. (ICMA adapted)

C. Capital expenditure administration and project evaluation. The management of McAngus Inc. has never used formal planning techniques in the operation of its business. The president of McAngus has expressed interest in the recommendation of its accountants that the company investigate various techniques it could use to manage the business more effectively.

McAngus, a medium-size manufacturer, has grown steadily. It recently acquired another company located approximately 1,000 miles away. The new company manufactures a line of products which complements the present product line. Both manufacturing plants have significant investments in land, buildings, machinery, and equipment. Each plant is to be operated as a separate division headed by a division manager. Each division manager is to have virtually complete authority for the management of her or his division; i.e., each will be responsible primarily for the profit contribution of her or his division. A complete set of financial statements is to be prepared for each division as well as for the company.

The president and the immediate management team intend to concentrate their efforts on coordinating the activities of the two divisions and investigating and evaluating such things as new markets, new product lines, and new business acquisition possibilities. Because of the cash required for the recent acquisition and the cash needs for desired future expansion, the president is particularly concerned about cash flow and the effective management of cash.

Required: Construct an answer to each of the following requirements to consider known facts about McAngus Inc., as presented in the case. Confine the answer to the accounting techniques and processes involved.

(1) Explain the objectives and describe the process which McAngus can use to plan for and evaluate the long-term commitment of its resources, including cash.

(2) Describe techniques that McAngus can use to help evaluate various alternatives in its long-range plan. Explain the advantages and disadvantages of each.   *(AICPA adapted)*

D. Follow-up of project results. Recap Corporation made a capital investment of $100,000 in new equipment two years ago. The analysis made at that time indicated that the equipment would save $36,400 in operating expenses per year over a five-year period, or a 24% return on

capital before taxes per year based on the discounted cash flow (DCF) rate of return analysis.

The department manager believed that the equipment had lived up to expectations. However, the departmental report showing the overall return on investment (ROI) rate for the first year in which this equipment was used did not reflect as much improvement as had been expected. The department manager asked the accounting section to "break out" the figures related to this investment to find out why it did not contribute more to the department's ROI.

The accounting section was able to identify the equipment and its contribution to the department's operations. The report presented to the department manager at the end of the first year was as follows:

Reduced operating expenses due to new equipment..........................	$ 36,400
Less depreciation (20% of cost).................	20,000
Contribution before taxes..........................	$ 16,400
Investment at beginning of year.................	$100,000
Investment at end of year...........................	80,000
Average investment for the year................	90,000
Return on investment = $16,400 ÷ $90,000 = 18.2%	

The department manager was surprised that the ROI was less than the 24% DCF rate of return, since the new equipment performed as expected.

Required:

(1) Discuss the reasons why the 18.2% return on investment for the new equipment as calculated in the department's report by the accounting section differs from the 24% DCF rate of return calculated at the time the machine was approved for purchase.

(2) Explain how Recap Corporation might restructure the data from the DCF rate of return analysis, so that the expected performance of the new equipment is consistent with the operating reports received by the department manager.   *(ICMA adapted)*

CHAPTER 24

Capital Expenditure Evaluation: Considering Uncertainty

The business world in which companies must operate is one of change and uncertainty. This change may be caused by factors that are often difficult to predict, such as unanticipated technological breakthroughs, changes in the tastes and preferences of consumers, the actions and reactions of competitors, and government regulation or deregulation. Although the capital expenditure evaluation techniques presented in Chapter 23 are theoretically reliable only under conditions of perfect certainty, they are nevertheless widely used in practice in the face of uncertainty. Cash flow estimates are typically based on a management's best guess of the single most likely result for each period. To compensate for the presence of uncertainty, management often relies on intuition and business judgment. Unfortunately, intuition and business judgment are often clouded by personal biases and are typically applied haphazardly among alternatives and over time. As a result, many biased and naive decisions are made. This chapter presents several techniques that specifically consider the effects of uncertainty on proposed capital expenditures.

▼ PROBABILITY ANALYSIS

One way to evaluate the potential effects of uncertainty systematically on proposed capital expenditures is to incorporate probabilistic estimates in the evaluation, i.e., to consider specifically the effect of the distribution of probable outcomes on the expected cash flows and the relative risk of available capital projects. Probabilistic evaluation procedures have been available for many years, but for several reasons they are not widely used in practice. First, many business people are not familiar with the techniques. Second, computational requirements increase when probabilistic estimates are incorporated into capital budgeting analyses. However, with the increased availability and use of computers in business, this deterrent is no longer significant. Third, many managers feel that reliable probability estimates are difficult to obtain because probability distributions relate to future events which are often determined by unfamiliar processes. If the process is unfamiliar, the probability estimates associated with the process must be subjective. In many situations, on the other hand, a wealth of reasonably reliable historical data is available which can be used to make fairly objective estimates about the probabilities associated with future events. Even in those cases in which the probability estimates must be subjective, consideration of the distribution of future outcomes provides a more complete picture of capital investments than a simple estimate of the single most likely outcome.

Probabilistic estimates are most frequently used with the present value method of capital expenditure evaluation. The net present value is computed in the same way as illustrated in Chapter 23, except that the expected value of the net cash flow in each period, rather than the single most likely net cash flow in each period, is discounted to present value.

Expected Value

The *expected value* of an event drawn from a probability distribution is defined as the mean of the distribution and is computed (as in Chapter 21) as follows:

$$E(x) = \Sigma \, [x_i \, P(x_i)]$$

where $E(x)$ = expected value of a random draw from the distribution

x_i = the value of the ith event

$P(x_i)$ = the probability of the occurrence of the ith event

The probability of the occurrence of an individual event is essentially the relative frequency of the occurrence of the event in the distribution, assuming that the events occur randomly; i.e., there is no discernible pattern of the occurrence of these events. For example, if the actual demand for 500 units of a product occurred 5 times out of a sample of 100, the probability that it will occur again (assuming that the future distribution is not expected to change) is 5/100, or .05. If there are no historical data from which to compute the frequency of events, the probability of the occurrence of each event must be subjectively estimated, based on business judgment.

When the effect of the distribution of outcomes of future events is not specifically considered in capital expenditure analysis, decision makers use a single most likely estimate of the outcome in each period. In such cases, decision makers are actually using an estimate of the mode for each event. In contrast, since the expected value of an event drawn from a probability distribution is the mean of the distribution, the most likely event (the mode) will be different from the expected value (the mean) if the probability distribution is not symmetrical. Consequently, if a probability distribution is not symmetrical, the use of expected values rather than estimates of the most likely events will result in a different net present value.

Variance and Standard Deviation

The *variance* of a probability distribution (denoted as σ^2) is a measure of the variability of expected outcomes and is defined here (as in Chapter 21) as:

$$\sigma^2(x) = \Sigma[P(x_i)\ (x_i - E(x))^2]$$

The square root of the variance is referred to as the *standard deviation* (denoted as σ). The standard deviation is generally viewed as a measure of investment risk. For a given level of expected return, the least risky investment is the one with the smallest standard deviation. The relative riskiness of alternative investments which have different levels of expected return can be determined by computing and comparing the coefficient of variation for each alternative. The *coefficient of variation* is a measure of the relative variability of a distribution and is determined by dividing the standard deviation by the expected value (see Chapter 21).

Since capital expenditure problems are multiperiod, the variance and the standard deviation of the expected net present value must be computed differently than for the single period problems discussed in Chapter 21. In a multiperiod problem, the cash flows from different periods must be treated as different random events; i.e., the cash flow possibilities for each period form a separate distribution. As a consequence, the expected net present value for a capital expenditure proposal can be viewed as a random variable drawn from a multivariate distribution. The procedure for computing the variance and the standard deviation for the expected net present value varies, depending upon whether the cash flows in each of the periods are assumed to be independent, perfectly correlated, or partially independent and partially correlated.

If the cash flows in each period are independent (i.e., the magnitudes of the cash flows in subsequent periods are not affected in any way by the magnitude of cash flows that occur in earlier periods), the variance of the expected net present value is computed by adding the discounted variances of the cash flows in each period.[1] For a two-period project, the variance of the net present value under the assumption that periodic cash flows are independent would be:

$$\text{Variance of NPV} = \sigma_o^2 + \frac{\sigma_1^2}{(1 + i)^2} + \frac{\sigma_2^2}{(1 + i)^4}$$

where i is the discount rate (the weighted average cost of capital in this case). The standard deviation would be:

$$\text{Standard deviation of NPV} = \sqrt{\sigma_o^2 + \frac{\sigma_1^2}{(1 + i)^2} + \frac{\sigma_2^2}{(1 + i)^4}}$$

Independent cash flows could occur in practice. For example, independent cash flows could occur when the capital expenditure relates to the production

---

[1]See Frederick S. Hillier, "The Derivation of Probabilistic Information for the Evaluation of Risky Investments," *Management Science*, Vol. 9, No. 3, pp. 443-457.

of an established product or service, and the demand for that product is expected to vary in response to temporary changes in consumer tastes and preferences or the capacity to purchase, which are uncorrelated between periods.

If the cash flows are perfectly correlated (i.e., the magnitude of cash flows in later periods are dependent upon the magnitude of cash flows in early periods), the variance of the expected net present value is the sum of the discounted periodic standard deviations squared.[2] For a two-period project, the variance of the expected net present value would be:

$$\text{Variance of NPV} = \left[\sigma_0 + \frac{\sigma_1}{(1+i)} + \frac{\sigma_2}{(1+i)^2} \right]^2$$

$$= \sigma_0^2 + \frac{\sigma_1^2}{(1+i)^2} + \frac{\sigma_2^2}{(1+i)^4} + \frac{2\sigma_0\sigma_1}{(1+i)} + \frac{2\sigma_0\sigma_2}{(1+i)^2} + \frac{2\sigma_1\sigma_2}{(1+i)^3}$$

The standard deviation would be:

$$\text{Standard deviation of NPV} = \sigma_0 + \frac{\sigma_1}{(1+i)} + \frac{\sigma_2}{(1+i)^2}$$

Notice that the variance of the expected net present value under the assumption that the cash flows are perfectly correlated contains interaction terms. As a result, the variance is larger when the cash flows are dependent than when they are independent.

Perfectly correlated cash flows might occur if the capital expenditure relates to the production of a new product or the entrance into a new market. In such a case, consumer acceptance of the product in one period might be expected to have a direct bearing on the level of sales in the following period.

If the cash flows are neither independent nor perfectly correlated, the cash flows may be treated as though they contain a mixture of independent and dependent periodic cash flows.[3] Mathematically, this procedure is fairly simple. In such a case, the expected periodic cash flows could be divided into two components, the independent cash flows and the perfectly correlated cash flows. Separate periodic variances would then be determined for the independent and the dependent cash flows. Once the periodic variances have been determined, a separate overall variance would be computed for the independent and the dependent cash flows in the manner indicated above. The standard deviation of the expected net present value would then be determined by taking the square root of the sum of the overall variance of the independent cash flows and the overall variance of the dependent cash flows.[4]

The difficult problem in practice is to determine how much of each periodic cash flow is independent and how much is dependent. If the distribution of projected cash flows is based on an historical data set, it may be possible to determine statistically the degree of correlation in the cash flows over time. On

[2]*Ibid.*
[3]*Ibid.*
[4]This computation is illustrated in the following section.

the other hand, if the expected distribution is not based on an historical data set, the degree of correlation would have to be determined subjectively.

▼ NORMALLY DISTRIBUTED CASH FLOWS

The standard normal distribution is a symmetrical continuous probability distribution which has certain mathematical properties that make it attractive. Because it closely approximates a large number of real distributions, it is often applied in practice. Since the normal distribution is symmetrical and has only one mode, the expected value is not only the mean of the probability distribution, but it is also the mode (i.e., the most likely event to occur). As a consequence, the net present value of the expected cash flows would be the same when a normal probability distribution is used in the analysis as it would when the probability distribution of future cash flows is ignored. Nevertheless, if a normal distribution applies, it should be considered in the analysis because it provides a way for management to evaluate risk.

For illustrative purposes, assume that Akira Company is considering a capital investment proposal that will cost $30,000 and have an economic life of five years. Management's best guess is that aftertax net cash inflow will be $9,000 in each year of the five years, and that there will be no salvage value at the end of the life of the project. Although management has no historical data upon which to base its estimate, the aftertax net cash inflows for each year are expected to be normally distributed, which means that management's best guess estimate of the annual cash inflows are also the expected values of the annual cash inflows. In addition, management believes that the standard deviation of the cash inflows will be 1/9 of the expected value, or $1,000 each year. Assuming that Akira's weighted average cost of capital is 12 percent, the expected net present value would be determined as follows:

(1) Year	(2) Expected Value of Aftertax Net Cash (Outflow) Inflow	(3) Present Value of $1 at 12%	(4) Present Value of Expected Aftertax Net Cash Flow (2) × (3)
0	$(30,000)	1.000	$(30,000)
1	9,000	.893	8,037
2	9,000	.797	7,173
3	9,000	.712	6,408
4	9,000	.636	5,724
5	9,000	.567	5,103
Expected net present value............................			$ 2,445

Independent Cash Flows

If the cash flows in each period are independent, the standard deviation of the expected net present value of $2,445 is computed by taking the square root of the sum of the discounted periodic variances. For the proposed Akira Company capital investment, the standard deviation under the independent cash flow assumption would be determined as follows:

(1) Year	(2) Periodic Standard Deviation	(3) Periodic Variance Col. (2)^2	(4) Present Value of $1 at 12%	(5) Present Value of $1 at 12% Squared Col. (4)^2	(6) Present Value of Variance (3) × (5)
0	0	0	1.000	1.000000	0
1	$1,000	$1,000,000	.893	.797449	$ 797,449
2	1,000	1,000,000	.797	.635209	635,209
3	1,000	1,000,000	.712	.506944	506,944
4	1,000	1,000,000	.636	.404496	404,496
5	1,000	1,000,000	.567	.321489	321,489
Variance of net present value...					$2,665,587

$$\text{Standard deviation of net present value} = \sqrt{\text{Variance of net present value}} = \sqrt{\$2,665,587} = \$1,633$$

Perfectly Correlated Cash Flows

If the cash flows in each of the periods are perfectly correlated with one another, the standard deviation of the expected net present value is determined by summing the discounted standard deviations for each period over the life of the project. For the proposed Akira Company capital investment, the standard deviation of the expected net present value under the perfectly correlated cash flow assumption would be determined as follows:

(1) Year	(2) Periodic Standard Deviation	(3) Present Value of $1 at 12%	(4) Present Value of Standard Deviation (2) × (3)
0	0	1.000	0
1	$1,000	.893	$ 893
2	1,000	.797	797
3	1,000	.712	712
4	1,000	.636	636
5	1,000	.567	567
Standard deviation of net present value.......................			$3,605

Notice that the standard deviation of the expected net present value when the cash flows are perfectly correlated ($3,605) is substantially larger than when the cash flows are independent ($1,633). This result is consistent with the intuitive notion that the introduction of established products is less risky than the introduction of new products.

Mixed Cash Flows

If the periodic cash flows are neither independent nor perfectly correlated, the cash flows may be treated as though they contain a mixture of independent and dependent periodic cash flows. The expected periodic cash flows are simply divided into two components, the independent cash flows and the perfectly correlated cash flows. A separate expected value and variance is then computed for the independent and the dependent cash flows in the usual way. The standard deviation of the expected net present value is then determined by taking the square root of the sum of the variance of the independent cash flows and the variance of the dependent cash flows. Assume that of the $9,000 expected annual aftertax net cash inflow for the proposed Akira Company capital investment, $3,000 is determined to be independent with a periodic standard deviation of $500, and $6,000 is determined to be perfectly correlated with a periodic standard deviation of $600. In this situation, the standard deviation of the expected net present value would be determined as follows:

(1) Year	(2) Expected Independent Aftertax Net Cash Inflow	(3) Expected Dependent Aftertax Net Cash Inflow	(4) Total Expected Aftertax Net Cash Inflow (Outflow) (2) + (3)	(5) Present Value of $1 at 12%	(6) Present Value of Expected Aftertax Net Cash Flow (4) × (5)
0			$(30,000)	1.000	$(30,000)
1	$3,000	$6,000	9,000	.893	8,037
2	3,000	6,000	9,000	.797	7,173
3	3,000	6,000	9,000	.712	6,408
4	3,000	6,000	9,000	.636	5,724
5	3,000	6,000	9,000	.567	5,103
Net present value..					$ 2,445

(1) Year	(2) Independent Cash Flow Periodic Standard Deviation	(3) Independent Cash Flow Periodic Variance Col. (2)^2	(4) Present Value of $1 at 12%	(5) Present Value of $1 at 12% Squared Col. (4)^2	(6) Present Value of Variance (3) × (5)
0	0	0	1.000	1.000000	0
1	$500	$250,000	.893	.797449	$199,362
2	500	250,000	.797	.635209	158,802
3	500	250,000	.712	.506944	126,736
4	500	250,000	.636	.404496	101,124
5	500	250,000	.567	.321489	80,372
Variance of net present value for independent cash flows...					$666,396

(1) Year	(2) Dependent Cash Flow Periodic Standard Deviation	(3) Present Value of $1 at 12%	(4) Present Value of Standard Deviation (2) × (3)
0	0	1.000	0
1	$600	.893	$ 536
2	600	.797	478
3	600	.712	427
4	600	.636	382
5	600	.567	340

Standard deviation of net present
value for dependent cash flows....... $2,163

$$\text{Variance of net present value for dependent cash flows} = \left(\text{Standard deviation of net present value for dependent cash flows}\right)^2 = (\$2,163)^2 = \$4,678,569$$

Variance of net PV for dependent cash flows........................	$4,678,569
Variance of net PV for independent cash flows....................	666,396
Variance of total net PV of investment.................................	$5,344,965

$$\text{Standard deviation of total net present value} = \sqrt{\text{Variance of total net present value}} = \sqrt{\$5,344,965} = \$2,312$$

Evaluating Investment Risk

Once the standard deviation of the expected net present value has been determined, it can be used to evaluate the riskiness of the proposed capital investment. The coefficient of variation, computed by dividing the standard deviation by the expected net present value ($1,633 ÷ $2,445 = .668 for the proposed Akira Company project under the assumption of independent cash flows), can be compared to the coefficient of variation for similar projects. Alternatives with the smallest coefficient of variation would be the least risky.

Management may also wish to know the range of the return, measured in terms of net present value, that is likely to occur at some level of probability. One of the properties of the standard normal distribution is that areas of the normal distribution can be related to deviations from the mean expressed in terms of standard deviations. For example, the area under the normal curve from one standard deviation below the mean to one standard deviation above the mean is about 68 percent of the total area under the curve. The area bounded by two standard deviations above and below the mean is about 95 percent, and for three standard deviations, about 99 percent. Since the sum of more than one normally distributed random variable is itself a normally distributed random variable, the net present value of a multiperiod investment for which the cash flows in each period are expected to be normally distributed can be treated as a normally distributed random variable. Thus, for the proposed Akira Company capital investment under the assumption of independent cash flows, there is about a 68 percent probability that the net present value will be between $812 ($2,445 − $1,633) and $4,078 ($2,445 + $1,633), and there is about a 95 percent probability that the net present value will be between −$821 [$2,445 − (2 × $1,633)] and $5,711 [$2,445 + (2 × $1,633)].

Management may also wish to know the probability of achieving a net present value greater than zero. If the expected net present value is positive, the probability of actually achieving a net present value greater than zero is equal to the portion of the area under the normal curve that is above the expected net present value (which is always 50 percent because the expected net present value is the mean, and the distribution is symmetrical) plus the portion of the area under the curve between the expected net present value and a net present value of zero. This area can be measured in standard deviations (by dividing the expected net present value by the standard deviation) and then converted to the percentage of the area under the curve, using a table of Z values for the normal distribution. A partial table of values for selected areas under the normal curve is as follows:

$\frac{\mu - X}{\sigma}$	Area Under Normal Curve Between μ and X	$\frac{\mu - X}{\sigma}$	Area Under Normal Curve Between μ and X	$\frac{\mu - X}{\sigma}$	Area Under Normal Curve Between μ and X
.05	.01994	1.05	.35314	2.05	.47982
.10	.03983	1.10	.36433	2.10	.48214
.15	.05962	1.15	.37493	2.15	.48422
.20	.07926	1.20	.38493	2.20	.48610
.25	.09871	1.25	.39435	2.25	.48778
.30	.11791	1.30	.40320	2.30	.48928
.35	.13683	1.35	.41149	2.35	.49064
.40	.15542	1.40	.41924	2.40	.49180
.45	.17364	1.45	.42647	2.45	.49286
.50	.19146	1.50	.43319	2.50	.49379
.55	.20884	1.55	.43943	2.55	.49461
.60	.22575	1.60	.44520	2.60	.49534
.65	.24215	1.65	.45053	2.65	.49598
.70	.25804	1.70	.45543	2.70	.49653
.75	.27337	1.75	.45994	2.75	.49702
.80	.28814	1.80	.46407	2.80	.49744
.85	.30234	1.85	.46784	2.85	.49781
.90	.31594	1.90	.47128	2.90	.49813
.95	.32894	1.95	.47441	2.95	.49841
1.00	.34134	2.00	.47725	3.00	.49865

Definitions of symbols:
μ = mean of the distribution (which is the expected value of a probability distribution)
X = a value drawn from the distribution
σ = standard deviation of the distribution

For the proposed Akira Company capital investment under the assumption of independent normally distributed cash flows, the area under the curve between the expected net present value of $2,445 and a net present value of zero would be about 1.50 standard deviations [($2,445 − 0) ÷ $1,633], which, according to the table of Z values above, is about 43 percent of the total area under the curve. Consequently, the probability that the proposed investment will yield a positive net present value is 93 percent, i.e., 43 percent (the area below the mean but above zero) plus 50 percent (the area above the mean). On the other hand, if the cash flows are expected to be perfectly correlated, the probability that the proposed investment will yield a positive net present value declines to about 76 percent. The standard deviation of the expected net present value increases from $1,633 to $3,605. The area between the expected net present value of $2,445 and a net present value of zero is about .7 standard deviations [($2,445 − 0) ÷ $3,605], which, according to the table of Z values, is about 26 percent of the area below the mean. The 26 percent of the area below the mean plus 50 percent of the area above the mean is equal to 76 percent.

The reliability of the estimated range for the net present value and the probability of achieving a positive net present value are highly dependent upon the accuracy of the estimates upon which they are based, i.e., the expected values of the annual cash flows and their estimated standard deviations. If these estimates are based on historical data rather than subjective estimates, greater reliance can be placed on the results.

▼ NON-NORMAL PROBABILITY DISTRIBUTIONS

Unfortunately, not all future events that affect cash flows follow the pattern of random variables drawn from a normal distribution. It may be necessary to construct a non-normal probability distribution, using historical data or subjective estimates based on informed business judgment. Although not as convenient to use or as mathematically appealing as normal distributions, such distributions can nevertheless be used to improve decision making. To illustrate the usefulness of a non-normal discrete probability distribution in capital expenditure analysis, assume that Galaxy Air Freight Corporation is considering the purchase of a new airplane to haul freight over a new route. The airplane is expected to cost $30,000 and have an estimated useful life of 5 years with no expected salvage value. Freight demand on the new route is estimated to be between 1,000 and 4,000 tons per year, with the following associated probabilities of occurrence:

Level of Demand	Probability of Occurrence
1,000	.20
2,000	.30
3,000	.40
4,000	.10
	1.00

Since this probability distribution is not symmetrical, the most likely event (demand for 3,000 tons of air freight) is not the mean of the distribution. Consequently, the expected value must be computed. Assuming that the aftertax net cash inflow from hauling a single ton is $5, the expected value of the annual aftertax net cash inflows is determined as follows:

(1) Level of Demand	(2) Aftertax Net Cash Inflow	(3) Probability of Occurrence	(4) Expected Value (2) × (3)
1,000	$ 5,000	.20	$ 1,000
2,000	10,000	.30	3,000
3,000	15,000	.40	6,000
4,000	20,000	.10	2,000
			$12,000

Assuming that Galaxy's weighted average cost of capital is 12 percent, the expected net present value from the proposed capital investment would be determined as follows:

(1) Year	(2) Expected Value of Aftertax Net Inflow (Outflow)	(3) PV of $1 @ 12%	(4) PV of Expected Cash Flow (2) × (3)
0	$(30,000)	1.000	$(30,000)
1	12,000	.893	10,716
2	12,000	.797	9,564
3	12,000	.712	8,544
4	12,000	.636	7,632
5	12,000	.567	6,804
Expected net present value.................			$ 13,260

The variance and standard deviation of the expected annual aftertax net cash inflows would be computed as follows:

(1) Level of Demand	(2) Conditional Value	(3) Expected Value	(4) [(2) − (3)]	(5) [(2) − (3)]²	(6) Probability of Occurrence	(7) Variance (5) × (6)
1,000	$ 5,000	$12,000	$(7,000)	$49,000,000	.20	$ 9,800,000
2,000	10,000	12,000	(2,000)	4,000,000	.30	1,200,000
3,000	15,000	12,000	3,000	9,000,000	.40	3,600,000
4,000	20,000	12,000	8,000	64,000,000	.10	6,400,000
Annual variance........................						$21,000,000

$$\text{Standard deviation} = \sqrt{\text{Variance}} = \sqrt{\$21,000,000} = \$4,583$$

Assuming that the annual cash inflows determined by the demand for air freight on the new route are independent of one another, the standard deviation of the expected net present value is the square root of the sum of the discounted periodic variances and is computed for the proposed Galaxy investment as follows:

(1)	(2)	(3)	(4)	(5)
			PV of $1 @ 12%	Present Value of
	Periodic	PV of $1	Squared	Variance
Year	Variance	@ 12%	(3)²	(2) × (4)
0	0	1.000	1.000000	0
1	$21,000,000	.893	.797449	$16,746,429
2	21,000,000	.797	.635209	13,339,389
3	21,000,000	.712	.506944	10,645,824
4	21,000,000	.636	.404496	8,494,416
5	21,000,000	.567	.321489	6,751,269
Variance of expected net present value.........				$55,977,327

$$\text{Standard deviation of net present value} = \sqrt{\text{Variance of net present value}} = \sqrt{\$55,977,327} = \$7,482$$

$$\text{Coefficient of variation} = \frac{\text{Standard deviation}}{\text{Expected net present value}} = \frac{\$7,482}{\$13,260} = .564$$

Since the probability distribution is not normal, the standard deviation cannot be conveniently used to measure the area under the curve and the probability that the proposed project will yield a positive net present value. Nevertheless, the expected net present value is still the mean of the distribution, which means that, since 50 percent of the probability distribution lies above the mean, there is a better than 50 percent chance that the project will yield a net present value equal to or greater than the expected net present value. Furthermore, the standard deviation and the coefficient of variation provide a measure of the variability of potential outcomes that can be compared with other alternatives to assess relative risk. While not as complete a profile as might be determinable if the probability distribution were normal, more information is available than there would be if the distribution of possible outcomes were ignored.

▼ USE OF PROBABILITIES IN STRATEGY ANALYSIS

In capital expenditure analysis as well as in differential cost analysis (discussed in Chapter 21), probabilities can be used to determine the best strategy under conditions of uncertainty. In the case of capital expenditure analysis, a payoff table can be constructed to evaluate alternative levels of investment. Assume in the Galaxy Air Freight Corporation example that the company has the opportunity to purchase any one of four different sizes of airplanes. For simplicity, assume that the variable cost per air mile per ton is the same for each airplane. As a result, the only cost difference of concern is the size of the initial investment. The four alternatives are as follows:

Airplane	Maximum Freight Capacity on New Air Route (in Tons per Year)	Expected Annual Aftertax Net Cash Inflow	Initial Cost
A	1,000	$ 5,000	$15,000
B	2,000	10,000	20,000
C	3,000	15,000	25,000
D	4,000	20,000	30,000

The first step is to determine the expected value of the annual aftertax net cash inflows. Assuming that the probabilities are .20, .30, .40, and .10 that demand will be 1,000, 2,000, 3,000, and 4,000 tons of freight, respectively, the following payoff table can be constructed:[5]

Possible Actions (Airplane Size To Be Purchased)	Aftertax Net Cash Inflows from Different Levels of Freight Demand				Expected Value of Annual Aftertax Net Cash Inflows
	1,000	2,000	3,000	4,000	
A (1,000 tons)	$5,000	$ 5,000	$ 5,000	$ 5,000	$ 5,000
B (2,000 tons)	5,000	10,000	10,000	10,000	9,000
C (3,000 tons)	5,000	10,000	15,000	15,000	11,500
D (4,000 tons)	5,000	10,000	15,000	20,000	12,000*
Probabilities	.20	.30	.40	.10	

*Σ (probability × conditional value) = [(.20 × $5,000) + (.30 × $10,000) + (.40 × $15,000) + (.10 × $20,000)]

Once the expected value of the annual aftertax net cash inflows has been determined, the expected net present value of each strategy can be determined by discounting the cash inflows for each strategy to present value and subtracting the initial cash outflow, i.e., the cost of the airplane. Assuming that the weighted average cost of capital is 12 percent, the expected net present value of each strategy would be determined as shown at the top of page 786.

The optimal course of action would appear to be to purchase airplane C, which is capable of hauling 3,000 tons of freight, because the expected value of such a strategy is the largest ($16,458 compared to the next best strategy of $13,260 with airplane D). To evaluate the relative riskiness of the four

---

[5]If the periodic aftertax net cash inflows result from the sale of merchandise that could be inventoried, the conditional values computed for each cell in the payoff table should reflect management's decision about whether or not to carry inventory. If the annual expected value of sales demand over the investment horizon exceeds the production capacity of the machine being considered, management may wish to produce at maximum capacity. Although actual production would exceed actual demand in some periods (thereby resulting in an increase in inventory), it would be less than actual demand in other periods (resulting in a decrease in inventory and sales in excess of annual capacity). On the other hand, if the production capacity of the machine being considered exceeds the annual expected value of sales demand, the maximum level of production under uncertainty should not exceed expected demand. Since the annual expected value is the average, inventory increases due to excess production in some periods should be offset by inventory decreases due to excess demand in the other periods. Unless the expected cost of carrying inventory is less than the expected value of the additional sales made possible by carrying inventory, management may elect to adjust production in each year to actual annual demand as actual demand becomes known during the year (in which case the conditional values would be determined in the same way as those determined in the air freight example where inventory is not possible).

(1) Possible Actions (Airplane Size To Be Purchased)	(2) Expected Value of Annual Aftertax Net Cash Inflows	(3) Present Value of 5-Year Annuity of $1 @ 12%	(4) Present Value of Annual Aftertax Net Cash Inflows (2) × (3)	(5) Initial Cash Outflow	(6) Expected Net Present Value (4) − (5)
A (1,000 tons)	$ 5,000	3.605	$18,025	$15,000	$ 3,025
B (2,000 tons)	9,000	3.605	32,445	20,000	12,445
C (3,000 tons)	11,500	3.605	41,458	25,000	16,458
D (4,000 tons)	12,000	3.605	43,260	30,000	13,260

alternative strategies, the coefficient of variation for each alternative could be computed and compared. Assuming that the demand for the air freight in each period is independent of demand in every other period, the variance for each alternative strategy is the sum of the discounted annual variances and, along with the standard deviation and coefficient of variation, is computed for each of the proposed Galaxy capital expenditure alternatives as follows:

1. Risk measures associated with purchase of airplane A (1,000-ton capacity):

(1) Level of Demand	(2) Conditional Value	(3) Expected Value	(4) [(2) − (3)]	(5) [(2) − (3)]²	(6) Probability of Occurrence	(7) Variance (5) × (6)
1,000	$5,000	$5,000	0	0	.20	0
2,000	5,000	5,000	0	0	.30	0
3,000	5,000	5,000	0	0	.40	0
4,000	5,000	5,000	0	0	.10	0
Annual variance with airplane A..						0

Year	(1)	(2) Periodic Variance	(3) PV of $1 @ 12%	(4) PV of $1 @ 12% Squared	(5) Present Value of Variance (2) × (4)
0		0	1.000	1.000000	0
1		0	.893	.797449	0
2		0	.797	.635209	0
3		0	.712	.506944	0
4		0	.636	.404496	0
5		0	.567	.321489	0
Variance of expected net present value...					0

$$\text{Standard deviation of net present value} = \sqrt{\text{Variance of net present value}} = \sqrt{0} = 0$$

$$\text{Coefficient of variation} = \frac{\text{Standard deviation}}{\text{Expected net present value}} = \frac{0}{\$3,025} = 0$$

2. Risk measures associated with purchase of airplane B (2,000-ton capacity):

(1) Level of Demand	(2) Conditional Value	(3) Expected Value	(4) [(2) − (3)]	(5) [(2) − (3)]²	(6) Probability of Occurrence	(7) Variance (5) × (6)
1,000	$ 5,000	$9,000	$(4,000)	$16,000,000	.20	$3,200,000
2,000	10,000	9,000	1,000	1,000,000	.30	300,000
3,000	10,000	9,000	1,000	1,000,000	.40	400,000
4,000	10,000	9,000	1,000	1,000,000	.10	100,000
Annual variance with airplane B..						$4,000,000

(1) Year	(2) Periodic Variance	(3) PV of $1 @ 12%	(4) PV of $1 @ 12% Squared	(5) Present Value of Variance (2) × (4)
0	0	1.000	1.000000	0
1	$4,000,000	.893	.797449	$ 3,189,796
2	4,000,000	.797	.635209	2,540,836
3	4,000,000	.712	.506944	2,027,776
4	4,000,000	.636	.404496	1,617,984
5	4,000,000	.567	.321489	1,285,956
Variance of expected net present value.......				$10,662,348

$$\text{Standard deviation of net present value} = \sqrt{\text{Variance of net present value}} = \sqrt{\$10,662,348} = \$3,265$$

$$\text{Coefficient of variation} = \frac{\text{Standard deviation}}{\text{Expected net present value}} = \frac{\$ 3,265}{\$12,445} = .262$$

3. Risk measures associated with purchase of airplane C (3,000-ton capacity):

(1) Level of Demand	(2) Conditional Value	(3) Expected Value	(4) [(2) − (3)]	(5) [(2) − (3)]²	(6) Probability of Occurrence	(7) Variance (5) × (6)
1,000	$ 5,000	$11,500	$(6,500)	$42,250,000	.20	$ 8,450,000
2,000	10,000	11,500	(1,500)	2,250,000	.30	675,000
3,000	15,000	11,500	3,500	12,250,000	.40	4,900,000
4,000	15,000	11,500	3,500	12,250,000	.10	1,225,000
Annual variance with airplane C..						$15,250,000

(1) Year	(2) Periodic Variance	(3) PV of $1 @ 12%	(4) PV of $1 @ 12% Squared	(5) Present Value of Variance (2) × (4)
0	0	1.000	1.000000	0
1	$15,250,000	.893	.797449	$12,161,097
2	15,250,000	.797	.635209	9,686,937
3	15,250,000	.712	.506944	7,730,896
4	15,250,000	.636	.404496	6,168,564
5	15,250,000	.567	.321489	4,902,707
Variance of expected net present value.........				$40,650,201

$$\text{Standard deviation of} \atop \text{net present value} = \sqrt{\text{Variance of net} \atop \text{present value}} = \sqrt{\$40,650,201} = \$6,376$$

$$\text{Coefficient} \atop \text{of variation} = \frac{\text{Standard deviation}}{\text{Expected net present value}} = \frac{\$ 6,376}{\$16,458} = .387$$

4. Risk measures associated with purchase of airplane D (4,000-ton capacity):

(1) Level of Demand	(2) Conditional Value	(3) Expected Value	(4) [(2) − (3)]	(5) [(2) − (3)]²	(6) Probability of Occurrence	(7) Variance (5) × (6)
1,000	$ 5,000	$12,000	$(7,000)	$49,000,000	.20	$ 9,800,000
2,000	10,000	12,000	(2,000)	4,000,000	.30	1,200,000
3,000	15,000	12,000	3,000	9,000,000	.40	3,600,000
4,000	20,000	12,000	8,000	64,000,000	.10	6,400,000
Annual variance with airplane D..						$21,000,000

(1) Year	(2) Periodic Variance	(3) PV of $1 @ 12%	(4) PV of $1 @ 12% Squared	(5) Present Value of Variance (2) × (4)
0	0	1.000	1.000000	0
1	$21,000,000	.893	.797449	$16,746,429
2	21,000,000	.797	.635209	13,339,389
3	21,000,000	.712	.506944	10,645,824
4	21,000,000	.636	.404496	8,494,416
5	21,000,000	.567	.321489	6,751,269
Variance of expected net present value.........				$55,977,327

$$\text{Standard deviation of} \atop \text{net present value} = \sqrt{\text{Variance of net} \atop \text{present value}} = \sqrt{\$55,977,327} = \$7,482$$

$$\text{Coefficient} \atop \text{of variation} = \frac{\text{Standard deviation}}{\text{Expected net present value}} = \frac{\$ 7,482}{\$13,260} = .564$$

From the computations above, it appears that with respect to the two alternatives with the largest expected values (airplanes C and D), the purchase of airplane C not only results in a larger expected net present value but also a smaller standard deviation and coefficient of variation. The best choice between airplanes C and D is clear: purchase aircraft C because it has the largest expected value and the smallest risk between these two alternatives. On the other hand, the best choice among airplanes A, B, or C is dependent upon management's willingness to assume risk in order to achieve larger profits. Airplane C would be the most profitable but the most risky, whereas airplane A would be the least profitable but the least risky. In this case, management must decide how much risk it is willing to assume in order to increase profit.

Decision Trees

Decision trees may be useful in a capital budgeting context if sequential decisions are required. As explained in Chapter 21, a decision tree is essentially a graphic representation of the decision points, the alternative actions available to the decision maker, the possible outcomes from each alternative decision along with related probabilities, and the expected value of each event. A decision tree is useful in that it gives the decision maker a visual map of the expected result of each alternative action.

Decision trees are applied in a capital budgeting context in essentially the same way as in short-term decision making (see Chapter 21), except that since capital expenditures involve multiperiod events, the expected cash flows should be discounted to present value in order to account for the time value of money. To illustrate the use of a decision tree in a capital budgeting context, assume that Mendez Company is considering building a plant to market a new product. Management believes that consumer response to the new product in the first two years is crucial to the level of sales in subsequent years. Management believes that there is a .7 probability that sales demand will be low in the first year, and a .3 probability that it will be high. If sales demand is low in the first year, there is a .5 probability that subsequent sales demand will be low, and a .5 probability that it will be high. On the other hand, if sales demand in the first year is high, there is a .1 probability that subsequent sales demand will be low, and a .9 probability that it will be high. Sales demand in years after year 2 is expected to remain the same as demand in year 2. Annual aftertax net cash inflow is expected to be $10,000 if demand is low and $50,000 if demand is high.

Mendez has the choice of initially building a small plant at a cost of $50,000 or a large plant at a cost of $150,000. By operating at maximum capacity, the small plant would have the capacity to produce the new product in sufficient quantities to meet the low level of sales demand. At the end of the first or second year, the small plant could be expanded to a size sufficient to meet the high sales demand. The cost of the expansion would be $140,000. If the large plant were built initially, it would have sufficient capacity to satisfy all levels of sales demand and, consequently, subsequent expansion would not be necessary.

Mendez's weighted average cost of capital is 12 percent. If the small plant is built, low demand in the second year makes expansion illogical because future demand will not exceed that of the second year. Conversely, if demand is high in the second year, it would be illogical not to expand the plant because the present value of the expansion benefit ($198,000 present value of large plant cash inflows for 8 years minus $47,570 present value of small plant cash inflows for 8 years = $150,430) exceeds the present value of the expansion cost ($111,580 at the end of year 2). The present values of the payoffs to be derived from each possible combination of events and actions that could occur, given that a small plant is built initially, are as shown on page 790.

Present Value of Payoffs if Small Plant Is Built Initially

(1)		(2)	(3) Present Value of Expansion Cost		(4) Present Value of Cash Inflows		(5) Net Present Value of Payoff
Demand in Year		Initial Cash Outflow	End of Year 1[1]	End of Year 2[2]	Before Expansion[3]	After Expansion[4]	
1	2-10						(4) − (2) − (3)
Low	Low	$50,000	0	0	$56,500	0	$ 6,500
Low	High	50,000	0	$111,580	16,900	$198,000	53,320
Low	Low	50,000	$125,020	0	8,930	47,570	(118,520)
Low	High	50,000	125,020	0	8,930	237,850	71,760
High	Low	50,000	0	0	56,500	0	6,500
High	High	50,000	0	111,580	16,900	198,000	53,320
High	Low	50,000	125,020	0	8,930	47,570	(118,520)
High	High	50,000	125,020	0	8,930	237,850	71,760

(handwritten annotation next to Year 2 column: "in 2 yrs")

(handwritten annotation in left margin: "cost of expansion $140,000")

[1]$140,000 expansion cost × .893 (present value of $1 at 12% for 1 period).

[2]$140,000 expansion cost × .797 (present value of $1 at 12% for 2 periods).

[3]Before expansion, the net aftertax cash inflows would be $10,000 each year, regardless of demand, because the small plant could not produce more than the quantity demanded at the low level of demand. Consequently, the values listed in this column are the present values of $10,000 received in each year for one year (.893 × $10,000 = $8,930), two years (1.690 × $10,000 = $16,900), or ten years (5.650 × $10,000 = $56,500), depending on the period the plant is restricted to the small capacity. The discount rate is 12%.

[4]After expansion, the net aftertax cash inflows would be $10,000 for each year that demand was low and $50,000 for each year that demand was high. If the plant is expanded at the end of year 1 and demand is high in year 2, the post-expansion annual cash inflows are $50,000 in each of the remaining 9 years, in which case the present value of the post-expansion cash inflows discounted at 12% is $237,850 [$50,000 × (5.650 − .893)]. On the other hand, if demand is low in year 2, the post-expansion annual cash inflows are $10,000 in each of the remaining 9 years, in which case the present value of the post-expansion cash inflows discounted at 12% is $47,570 [$10,000 × (5.650 − .893)]. If expansion occurs at the end of year 2 (because demand is high in year 2 and the plant was not expanded at the end of year 1), the post-expansion annual cash inflows are $50,000 in each of the remaining 8 years, in which case the present value of the post-expansion cash inflows discounted at 12% is $198,000 [$50,000 × (5.650 − 1.690)].

Recall that if a large plant is built initially, expansion would not be necessary because the large plant would have sufficient capacity to meet all possible levels of demand. The present values of all possible events given that a large plant is built initially are as follows:

Present Value of Payoffs if Large Plant Is Built Initially

(1)		(2)	(3) Present Value of Cash Inflows		(4) Net Present Value of Payoff
Demand in Year		Initial Cash Outflow	Year 1[1]	Year 2[2]	
1	2-10				(3) − (2)
Low	Low	$150,000	$ 8,930	$ 47,570	$ (93,500)
Low	High	150,000	8,930	237,850	96,780
High	Low	150,000	44,650	47,570	(57,780)
High	High	150,000	44,650	237,850	132,500

[1]The aftertax net cash inflow in the first year is $10,000 if demand is low and $50,000 if demand is high. The present value of $10,000 discounted at 12% for 1 year is $8,930 ($10,000 × .893), and the present value of $50,000 discounted at 12% for 1 year is $44,650 ($50,000 × .893).

[2]The annual aftertax net cash inflows in all years after the first are $10,000 if demand is low in the second year and $50,000 if demand is high in the second year. The present value of $10,000 received in each of the 9 remaining years discounted at 12% is $47,570 [$10,000 × (5.650 − .893)], and the present value of $50,000 received in each of the remaining 9 years is $237,850 [$50,000 × (5.650 − .893)].

In this example, Mendez Company is faced with the decision to build a large plant initially or to build a small plant initially and expand at the end of the first or second year if demand warrants. Based on the data provided, a decision tree can be constructed as follows:

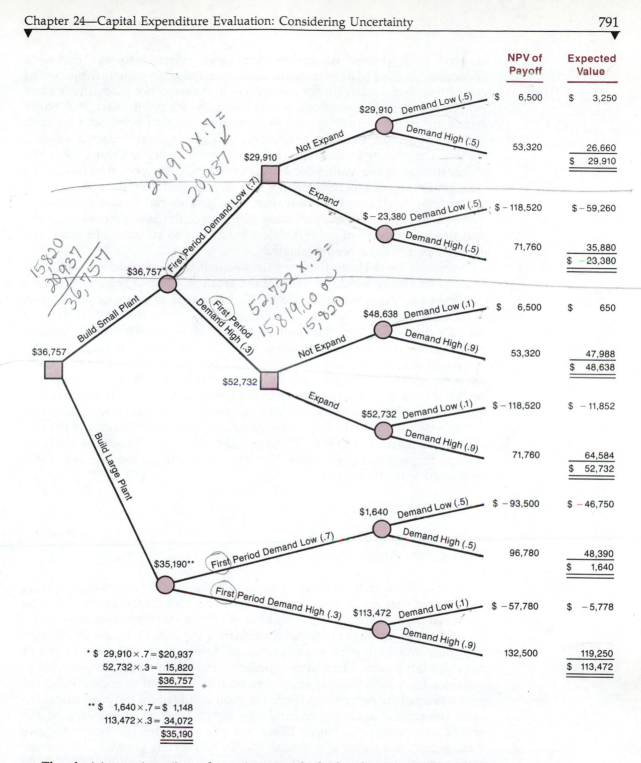

	NPV of Payoff	Expected Value
Demand Low (.5)	$ 6,500	$ 3,250
Demand High (.5)	53,320	26,660
		$ 29,910
Demand Low (.5)	$ −118,520	$ −59,260
Demand High (.5)	71,760	35,880
		$ −23,380
Demand Low (.1)	$ 6,500	$ 650
Demand High (.9)	53,320	47,988
		$ 48,638
Demand Low (.1)	$ −118,520	$ −11,852
Demand High (.9)	71,760	64,584
		$ 52,732
Demand Low (.5)	$ −93,500	$ −46,750
Demand High (.5)	96,780	48,390
		$ 1,640
Demand Low (.1)	$ −57,780	$ −5,778
Demand High (.9)	132,500	119,250
		$ 113,472

* $ 29,910 × .7 = $20,937
   52,732 × .3 = 15,820
               $36,757

** $ 1,640 × .7 = $ 1,148
   113,472 × .3 = 34,072
               $35,190

The decision points (i.e., the points at which the decision maker must choose some action) are denoted with squares, and the chance points (i.e., the points where some event related to the previous decision will occur) are denoted with circles. A process sometimes referred to as "backward deduction" is used to determine the best choice of action. First, the expected value for each of the last chance alternatives in the sequence is determined and written above the circle indicating the related chance point. Next, the chance events are traced to their respective preceding decision point, and for each decision point, the decision alternative with the highest expected value is chosen. The expected value of the best alternative choice is written above the square indicating the related decision point. Then, the expected values for the next preceding chance alternatives are determined (on the basis of the assumption that the best decision alternative for subsequent decisions will be made as determined in the preceding step); then, the best alternative for the next preceding decision point is determined, and so on until all chance and decision points have been evaluated.

Notice in the decision tree on page 791 that the best course of action for Mendez Company would be to build the small plant initially because such a course has an expected value of $36,757, compared to an expected value of $35,190 for the alternative (i.e., building a large plant initially). If the first period's demand is low, the plant should not be expanded until the second period demand is known (the expected value is $29,910 for not expanding compared to $-23,380 for expanding). If the second period's demand is high, the plant should be expanded because demand in all subsequent periods is expected to be high. On the other hand, if the second period's demand is low, the plant should not be expanded because capacity will be sufficient. If the first period's demand is high, the plant should be expanded at the end of the first period (expected value of $52,732 compared with $48,638 if not expanded). By electing this sequence of actions, Mendez will maximize the expected value associated with the project.

Sensitivity Analysis

In a capital budgeting context, *sensitivity analysis* is the process of evaluating the effect of changes in key assumptions or variables on the profitability of a proposed capital expenditure. This kind of analysis is often resorted to when the analyst has no way of reasonably estimating the probability distributions of important variables, such as sales demand, sales price, or the cost of one or more primary inputs. The typical approach would be to make changes in those variables for which there is some uncertainty and then to redetermine the profitability of the proposed project. The profitability of the proposal under the most pessimistic assumptions could be determined and compared to the profitability under the most likely set of conditions in order to give management some idea of potential risk. To balance the analysis and provide management with a full range of possible outcomes, the profitability of the proposed project should also be reevaluated using the most optimistic assumptions. If one variable is of particular concern, it may be desirable to analyze the effect on profitability when only that variable is changed. The impact on profitability that may result from changes in each variable can be analyzed by evaluating the effect of changing only one variable at a time. Microcomputer spreadsheet programs provide an excellent tool for these kinds of analyses because they permit substitution of parameter values and provide rapid recomputation of project profitability with each change.

The effects of parameter changes on project profitability may be communicated to management in graphic or tabular form. To illustrate, assume that a capital project with an initial cost of $600,000 was proposed to produce a new product, X, which is expected to have an annual sales volume of five million gallons. Using the most likely estimates of sales price ($.38 per gallon) and cost for the primary raw material, Z ($.28 per gallon), the expected discounted cash flow (DCF) rate of return is 26 percent. A sensitivity analysis was performed to determine the effect on the DCF rate of return of possible changes in sales prices (ranging from $.34 to $.41 per gallon) and costs for raw material Z (ranging from $.29 to $.27 per gallon). The following graph illustrates the effect of changes in these two variables on the DCF rate of return from the proposed project:

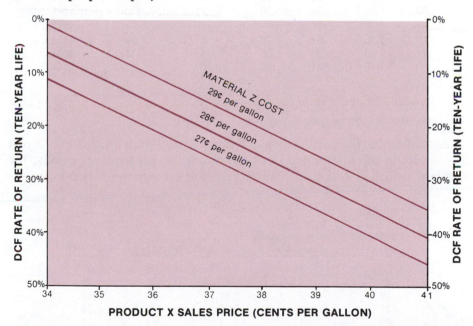

Sensitivity
Analysis
Graph

Sensitivity analysis can be considerably enhanced by incorporating probability estimates into the analysis. This kind of approach is not restricted to the use of any one type of probability distribution; i.e., it is equally applicable to any kind of probability distribution. For illustrative purposes, assume that probability estimates for the sales price of Product X and the cost of Material Z are as follows:

Material Z Cost	Probability of Occurrence	Product X Sales Price	Probability of Occurrence
$.29	20%	$.39	30%
.28	70	.38	30
.27	10	.37	40
	100%		100%

The DCF rate of return for each combination of Product X sales price and Material Z cost can be read from the graph above. Assuming that the variation in the sales price of Product X is independent of the variation in the cost of Material Z, the nine possible outcomes and their associated probabilities are:

(1)	(2)	(3)	(4)	(5)	(6)	(7)
Material Z		Product X		Combined	DCF Rate of Return*	Expected DCF Rate
		Sales		Probability	(Conditional	of Return
Cost	Probability	Price	Probability	(2) × (4)	Value)	(5) × (6)
	.20	$.39	.30	.06	.26	.0156
$.29	.20	.38	.30	.06	.21	.0126
	.20	.37	.40	.08	.16	.0128
	.70	.39	.30	.21	.31	.0651
.28	.70	.38	.30	.21	.26	.0546
	.70	.37	.40	.28	.21	.0588
	.10	.39	.30	.03	.36	.0108
.27	.10	.38	.30	.03	.31	.0093
	.10	.37	.40	.04	.26	.0104
				1.00		

Expected DCF rate of return (expected value)....................................... .2500 = 25%

*These rates were read from the graph on page 793.

Assuming that the combination of Product X sales price and Material Z cost that occurs in the first period does not change in subsequent periods, the standard deviation and coefficient of variation are determined as follows:

(1) DCF Rate of Return (Conditional Value)	(2) Difference from Expected Value (25%)	(3) (2) Squared	(4) Probability	(5) (3) × (4)
26%	1%	1%	.06	.06%
21	−4	16	.06	.96
16	−9	81	.08	6.48
31	6	36	.21	7.56
26	1	1	.21	.21
21	−4	16	.28	4.48
36	11	121	.03	3.63
31	6	36	.03	1.08
26	1	1	.04	.04
Variance..				24.50%

$$\text{Standard deviation} = \sqrt{24.5\%} = 4.9\%$$

$$\text{Coefficient of variation} = \frac{4.9\%}{25\%} = .20$$

If the Product X sales price and the Material Z cost can vary in each period, the standard deviation of the DCF rate of return for the project would be determined in the same manner as illustrated for the Galaxy Air Freight Corporation case discussed previously. If the prices and costs that can occur each period are independent of those that occur in other periods, the standard deviation is determined by taking the square root of the sum of the discounted periodic variances (discounted at the DCF rate of return). If the prices and costs that can occur each period are perfectly correlated with those that occur in other periods, the standard deviation is determined by summing the discounted periodic standard deviations (also discounted at the DCF rate of return).

Not only is the expected DCF rate of return of 25 percent useful to management, but the cumulative probabilities of realizing a rate of return at least equal to each of the various rates are also useful. Beginning with the highest rate for the nine possibilities, the following cumulative probabilities can be determined:

DCF Rate of Return	Cumulative Probability
36%	.03
31	.27 (.03 + .21 + .03)
26	.58 (.27 + .06 + .21 + .04)
21	.92 (.58 + .06 + .28)
16	1.00 (.92 + .08)

Thus, there is a .03 probability that the rate of return will be 36 percent, a .27 probability that the rate will be at least 31 percent, a .58 probability that the rate will be at least 26 percent, etc.

Many economic variables are not independent of one another; e.g., the materials cost may influence the sales price of the finished product. If there is dependence of the variables, computational procedures must be modified by substituting *conditional probabilities*.

The illustration from the previous page can be used to demonstrate variable dependence when the sales price is presumed to be influenced by materials cost. Assume the same probabilities for Material Z cost as before, but assume that the Product X sales price probabilities will be influenced by Material Z cost as follows:

Product X Sales Price	Probability of Sales Price		
	Material Z Cost—$.29	Material Z Cost—$.28	Material Z Cost—$.27
$.39	60%	40%	20%
.38	30	40	30
.37	10	20	50
	100%	100%	100%

The resulting nine possible outcomes for these assumptions and their related probabilities are summarized as follows. Observe that conditional probabilities have been substituted into Column 4.

(1) (2) Material Z		(3) (4) Product X		(5) Combined Probability (2) × (4)	(6) DCF Rate of Return (Conditional Value)	(7) Expected DCF Rate of Return (5) × (6)
Cost	Probability	Sales Price	Conditional Probability			
$.29	.20	$.39	.60	.12	.26	.0312
	.20	.38	.30	.06	.21	.0126
	.20	.37	.10	.02	.16	.0032
.28	.70	.39	.40	.28	.31	.0868
	.70	.38	.40	.28	.26	.0728
	.70	.37	.20	.14	.21	.0294
.27	.10	.39	.20	.02	.36	.0072
	.10	.38	.30	.03	.31	.0093
	.10	.37	.50	.05	.26	.0130
				1.00		

Expected DCF rate of return (expected value)... .2655 = 26.55%

Again, assuming that the combination of Material Z cost and Product X sales price that occurs in the first period does not change in subsequent periods, the standard deviation and the coefficient of variation are determined as follows:

(1) DCF Rate of Return (Conditional Value)	(2) Difference from Expected Value (27%)*	(3) (2) Squared	(4) Probability	(5) (3) × (4)
26%	− 1%	1%	.12	.12%
21	− 6	36	.06	2.16
16	−11	121	.02	2.42
31	4	16	.28	4.48
26	− 1	1	.28	.28
21	− 6	36	.14	5.04
36	9	81	.02	1.62
31	4	16	.03	.48
26	− 1	1	.05	.05
				16.65%

*26.55% rounded = 27%

$$\text{Standard deviation} = \sqrt{16.65\%} = 4.1\%$$

$$\text{Coefficient of variation} = \frac{4.1\%}{26.55\%} = .15$$

Monte Carlo Simulations

Computer simulations that contain stochastic variables are often referred to as *Monte Carlo simulations*. As discussed in Chapter 21, Monte Carlo simulations are especially useful in evaluating problems that contain numerous stochastic variables because such problems are difficult, and in some cases impossible, to evaluate analytically. The economic analysis of many capital expenditure proposals is complicated by the multiperiod nature of long-term investments. When stochastic processes are imposed on more than one variable, complexity increases, and when these stochastic processes are ill-behaved because the distributions are irregular or because different variables have different distributions, an analytical solution becomes virtually impossible. However, as long as the underlying cost and revenue generating processes can be modeled with one or more mathematical equations, even multiperiod capital expenditure proposals can be evaluated relatively efficiently using a Monte Carlo simulation.

In capital budgeting, a Monte Carlo simulation utilizes statistical sampling techniques in order to obtain a probabilistic approximation of the profitability of a capital expenditure proposal. The probability distributions of the stochastic variables in the decision problem are simulated in the computer model using a random number generator. The form of the stochastic processes simulated can be based on historical data or on estimates. The simulation is run numerous times in order to model the output of the system. Based on the frequency distribution of the simulated results, the analyst can determine the expected value and the variance (and/or standard deviation) for the capital expenditure proposal, which provide a basis for evaluation and comparison with alternatives.

DISCUSSION QUESTIONS

1. Why should analysts incorporate probability analysis into capital expenditure evaluation?

2. The best estimate of future cash flows will differ from the expected value of future cash flows in some cases but not in others. Explain.

3. Even if the cash flows are normally distributed, it is desirable to incorporate probability analysis into capital expenditure evaluation. Why?

4. What are the variance and the standard deviation of a probability distribution? Why would these measures be of interest to decision makers?

5. In what way does the computation of the variance of multiperiod cash flows differ from the variance of a single period cash flow?

6. In a capital budgeting context, what is meant by independent periodic cash flows and under what conditions might they be expected to occur?

7. In a capital budgeting context, what is meant by perfectly correlated periodic cash flows and under what conditions might they be expected to occur?

8. How might the variance of the net present value of a capital expenditure proposal be computed if the periodic cash flows are neither independent nor perfectly correlated?

9. Under what conditions would a decision tree be useful in capital expenditure analysis?

10. In what way would the use of decision trees in capital expenditure evaluation differ

from the use of decision trees in short-term decision making?

11. How might an analyst evaluate the potential range of the net present value to be derived from an investment when the probability distribution associated with the most likely cash flows is not known?

12. What is a Monte Carlo simulation and when might it be useful in capital expenditure evaluation?

EXERCISES

1. Expected net present value of investment with normally distributed cash flows. Allset Enterprises is considering a capital expenditure proposal that will cost $20,000 and yield an expected aftertax cash inflow of $5,000 each year for 6 years. There is no expected salvage value at the end of the life of the project. The aftertax net cash inflows for each year are expected to be normally distributed with a standard deviation of $800. Allset's weighted average cost of capital is 10%.

Required: Compute the expected net present value of the capital expenditure proposal.

2. Standard deviation of expected net present value when periodic cash flows are normally distributed and independent. Purvis Company is considering a capital proposal that has an expected net present value of $3,000. The periodic cash inflows are normally distributed with a standard deviation of $500 each period. The initial cash outflow has a zero standard deviation. The company's weighted average cost of capital is 12%, and the capital project has an expected life of 8 years. The periodic cash inflows are expected to be independent of one another.

Required: Compute the standard deviation of the expected net present value for the Purvis Company investment.

3. Standard deviation of expected net present value when periodic cash flows are normally distributed and dependent. Ramos Company is considering a capital expenditure for which the periodic cash inflows are expected to be normally distributed and perfectly correlated. The expected net present value of the proposed project is $5,000, and the standard deviation of the cash inflows is $1,000 in each period. The initial cash outflow has a zero standard deviation. The company's weighted average cost of capital is 10%, and the capital project is expected to have a life of 5 years.

Required: Compute the standard deviation of the expected net present value for the Ramos Company investment.

4. Standard deviation of expected net present value when periodic cash flows are neither independent nor perfectly correlated. Vincent Corporation is considering an investment in new machinery with a seven-year estimated useful life and an estimated net present value of $12,000. The cash inflows are expected to be normally distributed; however, 60% of each period's cash inflow is expected to be independent, and the remaining 40% is expected to be perfectly correlated. Cash inflows are expected to be $10,000 each period. The independent cash inflows have a standard deviation of $1,000, and the dependent cash inflows have a standard deviation of $1,500. The initial cash outflow has a standard deviation of zero. The corporation's weighted average cost of capital is 12%.

Required: Compute the standard deviation of the expected net present value for Vincent Corporation.

5. Evaluating capital project risk. Oskervale Company is considering investing in a new plant that will produce a product for which there is an established market. Demand for the product has historically followed a random normal distribution and has been independent from one period to the next. Management has determined that the expected net present value of the investment is $30,000, and the standard deviation of the expected net present value is $25,000.

Required:

(1) Determine the 95% confidence interval for the net present value, i.e., the range within which the net present value of the proposed investment will fall about 95% of the time.
(2) Using the table of selected areas under the normal curve, determine the probability that the net present value of the proposed investment will exceed zero.

6. Expected net present value of capital project with non-normally distributed cash flows. Indeto Company is considering a capital expenditure proposal with the following possible periodic aftertax net cash inflows:

Aftertax Net Cash Inflows	Probability
$10,000	.10
15,000	.25
20,000	.50
25,000	.15

The initial cash outflow will be $50,000, and the project will have a four-year life with no expected salvage value. The company's weighted average cost of capital is 10%.

Required: Determine the expected net present value for Indeto Company's capital expenditure proposal.

7. Expected net present value with more than one non-normally distributed random variable. MacFadden Corporation is considering purchasing a new piece of machinery at a cost of $9,000. The estimated useful life and the estimated annual aftertax cost savings are not known with certainty but are believed to have the following probabilities of occurring:

Years of Estimated Useful Life	Probability of Occurrence	Estimated Annual Aftertax Cost Savings	Probability of Occurrence
4	.20	$2,000	.10
5	.50	3,000	.50
6	.30	4,000	.40

The estimated useful life of the machine is unrelated to the estimated annual aftertax cost savings.

Required: Determine the expected net present value of the machine using a 10% discount rate.

8. Standard deviation of expected net present value when cash flows are independent but not normally distributed. Management of Seamaid Corporation is considering a capital investment that will cost $100,000 and yield an expected net present value of $39,436. The expected net present value of the project was determined as follows:

Annual Aftertax Net Cash Inflows	Probability	Expected Value
$30,000	.20	$ 6,000
40,000	.30	12,000
50,000	.40	20,000
60,000	.10	6,000
		$44,000

Years	Expected Value of Aftertax Net Inflow (Outflow)	PV of $1 @ 10%	PV of Expected Cash Flow
0	$(100,000)	1.000	$(100,000)
1	44,000	.909	39,996
2	44,000	.826	36,344
3	44,000	.751	33,044
4	44,000	.683	30,052
Expected net present value...............			$ 39,436

Required: Assuming that the cash inflows in each year are independent of the cash inflows in other years, compute the variance and the standard deviation of the expected net present value.

9. Standard deviation of expected net present value when cash flows are dependent but not normally distributed. The management of J. Valrath Company is considering a capital investment that will cost $70,000 and yield an expected net present value of $39,436. The expected net present value of the project was determined as follows:

Annual Aftertax Net Cash Inflows	Probability	Expected Value
$20,000	.25	$ 5,000
25,000	.30	7,500
30,000	.35	10,500
35,000	.10	3,500
		$26,500

Years	Expected Value of Aftertax Net Inflow (Outflow)	PV of $1 @ 12%	PV of Expected Cash Flow
0	$(70,000)	1.000	$(70,000)
1	26,500	.893	23,665
2	26,500	.797	21,120
3	26,500	.712	18,868
4	26,500	.636	16,854
5	26,500	.567	15,026
Expected net present value...............			$ 25,533

Required: Assuming that the periodic cash inflows are perfectly correlated, compute the standard deviation of the expected net present value.

10. Use of payoff table in capital expenditure analysis. Dealdorf Corporation is considering constructing a new hotel in a city where it does not currently have a hotel. Data relevant to the decision follow:

Annual Demand	Probability of Demand	Annual Aftertax Net Cash Inflows	Cost of Building with Capacity To Meet Demand
30,000	.40	$300,000	$1,100,000
40,000	.30	400,000	1,500,000
50,000	.20	500,000	1,800,000
60,000	.10	600,000	2,000,000

The present value of an annuity of $1 discounted at the company's weighted average cost of capital (12%) over the investment horizon (20 years) is $7.469.

Required:

(1) Construct a payoff table to determine the expected value of the annual aftertax net cash inflows for each size of hotel.
(2) Determine the expected net present value of each alternative hotel size and indicate which size Dealdorf should build.

PROBLEMS

24-1. Capital expenditure proposal with normally distributed, independent periodic cash flows. Nevron Corporation would like to expand the production of one of its product lines. To provide sufficient capacity, it will be necessary to purchase a new machine at a cost of $200,000. The new machine will have an estimated useful life of 6 years, with no expected salvage value. The historical demand for the product is normally distributed. Management believes that future demand will also be normally distributed and independent from one period to another. The expected value of the annual demand for the product produced by the new machine is 5,000 units with a standard deviation of 900 units. The aftertax net cash inflow from the sale of each unit is $10. Nevron's weighted average cost of capital is 12%.

Required:

(1) Determine the expected net present value of the machine.
(2) Determine the variance and the standard deviation of the expected net present value of the machine.
(3) Compute the coefficient of variation for the capital expenditure proposal.
(4) Determine the probability that the net present value from this machine will be greater than zero.

24-2. Capital expenditure proposal with normally distributed, dependent periodic cash flows. Haverland Manufacturing Company is considering purchasing a machine that will cost $50,000. The machine is expected to have a useful life of 4 years, with no expected salvage value. The aftertax net cash inflows for each year are expected to be $20,000. The periodic cash inflows are believed to be normally distributed with a standard deviation of $2,000. Since the machine will be used to produce a new product, the periodic cash flows are expected to be perfectly correlated. Haverland's weighted average cost of capital is 15%.

Required: With respect to the capital expenditure proposal, compute the following:

(1) The expected net present value of the capital expenditure proposal
(2) The standard deviation of the expected net present value
(3) The coefficient of variation

24-3. Capital expenditure proposal with normally distributed cash flows that are neither independent nor perfectly correlated. Lasko Company is considering a capital expenditure proposal that will cost $300,000 but is expected to yield an aftertax net cash inflow of $100,000 a year for five years. The cash flows are expected to be normally distributed; however, the cash flows from year to year are not likely to be completely independent of one another. Management believes that for all practical purposes 70% of each year's cash inflows should be treated as independent and 30% as perfectly correlated. The best estimate of the periodic standard deviation of the independent portion of the cash inflows is $10,000, and the periodic standard deviation of the dependent portion is believed to be $5,000. The company's weighted average cost of capital is 10%.

Required:

(1) Compute the expected net present value of the Lasko Company proposal.
(2) Compute the variance and the standard deviation of the expected net present value.
(3) Compute the coefficient of variation for the capital expenditure proposal.

24-4. Capital expenditure proposal with non-normally distributed cash flows. Thuley Company is considering renting a new machine at a total cost of $50,000 for a 5-year period, to be paid in $10,000 installments at the beginning of each year. Demand for the product to be produced by the machine and the associated probabilities of occurrence are as follows:

Unit Demand	Probability
4,000	.20
5,000	.40
6,000	.30
7,000	.10

Demand for the product is believed to be random and independent from one period to another. The contribution margin from the sale of each unit of product is $5. The company's weighted average cost of capital is 12%, and the company is in the 40% income tax bracket.

Required:

(1) Compute the expected net present value for the capital expenditure proposal.
(2) Compute the variance and the standard deviation of the net present value.

24-5. Use of payoff table in capital expenditure evaluation. The City of Pascal is considering the purchase of a new electric generator. Four alternative sizes are being considered, each of which has a useful life of 10 years and no expected salvage value. The alternative sizes denoted by their respective capacities, the probabilities of demand at each of the rated capacity levels, the cost of the alternative generators, and the annual cash inflow expected at maximum capacity are as follows:

Annual Capacity in Millions of KWH	Probability of Demand	Cost of Generator	Annual Cash Inflow at Maximum Capacity
50	.20	$2,000,000	$500,000
60	.40	2,300,000	600,000
70	.30	2,550,000	700,000
80	.10	2,700,000	800,000

If demand exceeds generator capacity, additional electric power can be purchased from a nearby electric co-op for an amount exactly equal to Pascal's price to the consumer. Any profit made by Pascal in generating its own electricity will be transferred to the city's general operating fund, thereby reducing the need for city tax increases. Pascal's excess production capacity cannot be sold. Demand is expected to be independent from period to period. Pascal's cost of capital is 10%.

Required:

(1) Construct a payoff table to determine the expected value of the periodic net cash inflows for each size of generator. Taxes are not a factor in this problem because municipalities are not taxed by the state or federal governments.

(2) Determine the expected net present value of each alternative generator size, and indicate which size Pascal should purchase.

(3) Compute the variance and the standard deviation of the expected net present value for the most profitable alternative and the second most profitable alternative. Which size generator should Pascal purchase? Explain.

24-6. Use of decision tree in capital expenditure analysis. Fargo Express Company is considering building a new warehouse in a newly opened territory. Management believes that customer response to their service in the first two years is critical to the demand for services in subsequent years. There is a .8 probability that demand will be low in the first year and a .2 probability that it will be high. If demand is low in the first year, there is a .6 probability that subsequent demand will be low and a .4 probability that it will be high. On the other hand, if demand in the first year is high, there is a .3 probability that demand in subsequent years will be low and a .7 probability that it will be high. Demand in all years subsequent to the second year is expected to be the same as in the second year.

Fargo has the choice of initially building a small warehouse at a cost of $200,000 or a large warehouse at a cost of $500,000. The small warehouse would be large enough to meet the low level of demand (which would result in an annual aftertax net cash inflow of $50,000); however, there would be no excess capacity. The large warehouse would be large enough to meet the high level of demand (which would result in an annual aftertax net cash inflow of $150,000). If Fargo chooses to build the small warehouse, capacity could be expanded at the end of the first or second year to the same capacity as the large warehouse for an additional cost of $400,000. If the large warehouse is built initially, it would not have to be expanded. Either investment will have an estimated useful life of 10 years and no expected salvage value.

Required:

(1) Assuming that Fargo's weighted average cost of capital is 12%, compute the payoffs to be derived from each possible combination of events and actions.

(2) Construct a decision tree for Fargo's investment decision, and indicate whether Fargo should initially build a large warehouse or a small one. Support your recommendation by computing the expected net present value for each alternative.

24-7. Use of decision tree in capital expenditure analysis. Whole Grain Bread Company is considering building a bakery in a nearby state which has not previously been served by Whole Grain Bread Company. Management believes that customer response to their product in the first two years is critical to the demand for the product in subsequent years. There is a .6 probability that demand will be low in the first year and a .4 probability that it will be high. If demand is low in the first year, there is a .5 probability that subsequent demand will be low and a .5 probability that it will be high. On the other hand, if demand in the first year is high, there is a .1 probability that demand in subsequent years will be low and a .9 probability that it will be high. Demand in all years subsequent to the second year is expected to be the same as in the second year.

Whole Grain has the choice of initially building a small bakery at a cost of $400,000 or a large bakery at a cost of $800,000. The small bakery would be large enough to meet the low level of demand (which would result in an annual aftertax net cash inflow of $100,000); however, there would be no excess capacity. The large bakery would be large enough to meet the high level of demand (which would result in an annual aftertax net cash inflow of $300,000). If Whole Grain chooses to build the small bakery, capacity could be expanded at the end of the first or second year to the same capacity as the large bakery for an additional cost of $600,000. If the large bakery is built initially, it would not have to be expanded. The useful life of either size bakery is 8 years, with no expected salvage value.

Required:

(1) Assuming that Whole Grain's weighted average cost of capital is 14%, compute the payoffs to be derived from each possible combination of events and actions.
(2) Construct a decision tree for Whole Grain's investment decision, and indicate whether the company should initially build a large bakery or a small one. Support your recommendation by computing the expected net present value for each alternative.

24-8. Product analysis using discounted cash flow method; sensitivity analysis. Virginia Company is considering a capital investment in a product that represents an improvement on existing products and is in a market not presently served by the company.

Management's *best guess* is that the company can expect annual sales of 1,000,000 units at a price of $5. Cost of goods sold are estimated to be $2.50 variable cost per unit plus a $500,000 annual fixed cost (including depreciation) for manufacturing and an additional $100,000 annually for general and administrative expenses. Variable marketing costs are 2% of sales.

The investment in the plant is expected to be $3.5 million, with an economic and physical life of 10 years and no salvage value. Depreciation will be computed by the straight-line method. Working capital, which will be recovered at the end of 10 years, is to be 10% of sales and 10% of cost of goods sold. The income tax rate is 50%.

Required:

(1) Compute the discounted cash flow rate of return.
(2) Assuming a range of the $5 sales price from a drop of 30% to an increase of 30%, at 10% intervals, determine the sensitivity of the discounted cash flow rate of return at the 1,000,000-unit annual sales level.
(3) Assuming a range of 1,000,000 units of annual sales from a decline of 30% to an increase of 20% (plant capacity), at 10% intervals, determine the sensitivity of the discounted cash flow rate of return at the $5 unit sales price.

24-9. Equipment feasibility study with allowance for risk and uncertainty. The plant manager of Ostende Corporation is confronted with a need to purchase a machine. Machine A will cost $5,000, Machine B's initial cost will be $10,000, and each machine has an estimated life of 3 years. However, an analysis of the operating costs associated with each of the machines reveals that the cost per unit with Machine A is $1 and with Machine B is $.50, excluding depreciation. The product's sales price is $4.

Estimates of the probability of the number of units required for each of the next 3 years, based in part upon analysis of the past and in part on the manager's best appraisal of the future, are as follows:

Annual Requirements	Probability of Occurrence
2,000	.20
3,000	.60
5,000	.20

Required:

(1) Compute the net present value for each of the three activity levels for Machines A and B, using a discount rate of 6%.
(2) Determine the expected net present value for each machine. (Ignore income tax considerations.)
(3) Assuming that the quantity of units determined in the first period will not change in subsequent periods, compute the standard deviation and coefficient of variation for each machine, rounding data used to the nearest dollar.

24-10. New product analysis considering risk and uncertainty; net present value. Grant Enterprises designs and manufactures toys. Past experience indicates that the product life cycle of a toy is 5 years. Promotional advertising produces large sales in the early years, but there is a substantial sales decline in the final year of a toy's life.

A new toy has been developed, and the following sales projections were made by carefully evaluating its consumer demand:

Consumer Demand for New Toy	Probability of Occurrence	Estimated Sales in Thousands of Dollars				
		Year 1	Year 2	Year 3	Year 4	Year 5
Most probable	60%	$1,000	$1,500	$2,000	$1,200	$ 600
Pessimistic	30%	300	400	500	300	200
Optimistic	10%	1,500	2,000	3,000	2,500	1,000

Variable costs are estimated at 30% of the sales price. Special machinery must be purchased at a cost of $1,100,000 and will be installed in an unused portion of the factory, which Grant has unsuccessfully been trying to rent for several years at $50,000 per year, with no prospects for future utilization. Fixed costs (excluding depreciation) of a cash-flow nature are estimated at $60,000 per year on the new toy. The new machinery is to be depreciated by the straight-line method for financial accounting purposes, with an estimated salvage value of $500,000, and will be sold at the end of the fifth year. Advertising and promotional expenses will total $200,000 in the first year, $300,000 in the second year, and $100,000 in the third, fourth, and fifth years.

The machinery is 7-year-class property under MACRS and will be depreciated by the most accelerated method available for income tax purposes. The income tax rate is 40%.

Required:

(1) Prepare a schedule of the new toy's probable sales for each year.
(2) Prepare a schedule of the aftertax cash inflows from the new toy's sales for each of the five years involved and from the disposition of the machinery at the and of the fifth year.
(3) Prepare a schedule of the net present value of the net cash flows, assuming a minimum desired rate of return of 12%.   *(AICPA adapted)*

CHAPTER 25
Marketing Cost and Profitability Analysis

This chapter presents techniques and procedures that are useful in analyzing and controlling marketing costs and in analyzing market profitability. *Marketing* is the matching of a company's products with markets for the satisfaction of customers at a reasonable profit for the firm. Marketing managers must decide the (1) product selection, design, color, size, and packaging, (2) prices to be charged, (3) advertising and promotion needed, and (4) physical distribution to be followed. These numerous decisions require organization, planning, and control. Marketing is usually organized by product or brand lines or by territories or districts. The planning and control phases should be based on a well-structured marketing cost and profitability analysis system.

The preparation of budgets and the need for budgeting in planning and controlling the marketing effort of a firm are discussed in Chapter 15. At the end of each month, budget reports that indicate the success or failure of the budgetary boundaries are issued. However, the problems associated with marketing costs do not end with these budgetary procedures. Cost control at the departmental level is the important feature of any cost improvement program. Yet, in marketing, the emphasis ordinarily rests on selling rather than on costs. To limit marketing costs unreasonably might lead to a curtailment of sales activities, which in turn could mean the gradual deterioration or elimination of certain types of sales. Conversely, indiscriminate and wasteful spending should not be sanctioned.

▼ SCOPE OF MARKETING COSTS

Control and analysis of marketing costs complement each other and involve the assignment of marketing expenses to various costing groups such as territories, customers, and products. However, assigned costs must be controlled through analysis within the jurisdictional function as well, in order to hold each marketing activity to the budgeted level.

This phase of cost accounting also calls for the determination of marketing costs for managerial decisions, thereby making it an integral part of business planning and policy formulation. Management requires meaningful marketing cost information in order to determine and analyze the profitability of (1) a territory or territories; (2) certain classes of customers, such as wholesalers, retailers, institutions, and governmental units; (3) products, product lines, or brands; and (4) promotional efforts by salespersons, telephone, mail, television, or radio.

The scope of today's marketing activities includes not only the fulfilling of existing demands, but also the creation and discovery of new demands for a company's products and services. Industry must concentrate on satisfying customers rather than on merely producing products. This outlook requires the best available working tools for management's use. In many organizations, the marketing activity has always received management's attention, and in some cases even more attention than that rendered to other business operations. In today's economy, the strategic importance and magnitude of marketing activity merit still greater attention to marketing costs.

▼ COMPARISON OF MARKETING AND MANUFACTURING COSTS

The control and analysis of marketing costs present certain complexities. First of all, logistic systems are many and varied. Manufacturers of certain products use basically the same materials and machinery. However, these companies may use vastly different channels of distribution, ranging from a simple, direct distribution to a complex marketing system, with promotional efforts directed to narrow or broad customer groups. Therefore, a meaningful comparison of the marketing costs of one company with another is almost impossible.

Not only do distribution methods vary, but they are also extremely flexible. A company may find that a change in market conditions necessitates a change in its channels of distribution. Distribution standards must be revised with every change in the method of distribution, so tactics may change several times before the best method is found. Such sweeping changes are uncommon in production, however. Once a factory is set up, management is not likely to change its manufacturing techniques until machinery is replaced or new products are introduced. Therefore, standards set for a particular machine do not require much revision.

The psychological factors present in selling a product are perhaps the main reasons for differences between manufacturing and marketing costing. Management can control the cost of labor, hours of operation, and number of machines operated; but management cannot control what the customer will do. Various salespersons may have different effects on a customer, who may respond differently to varying appeals. Customer resistance is the enigma in marketing cost analysis. The customer is a controlling rather than a controllable factor, whose wishes and peculiarities govern the method of doing business.

The attitudes of marketing and manufacturing management also differ. Although factory managers are eager to measure their accomplishments in terms of reduced cost per unit, most sales managers consider sales the yardstick for measuring their efficiency, although increased sales do not always mean greater profits.

Cause and effect, generally obvious in the factory, are not so readily discernible in the marketing processes. For example, many promotional costs are incurred for future results, creating a time lag between cause and effect. Conversely, the effects of manufacturing changes are usually quickly observable, and matching between effort and result can usually be achieved. Furthermore, manufacturing results are more readily quantified than are marketing results. For marketing, it is often not easy to identify quantities or units of activity with the cost incurred and results achieved.

Generally accepted accounting practice does not charge Cost of Goods Sold and ending inventories with marketing and administrative expenses. These and other nonmanufacturing expenses usually fall into the category of period costs, which are charged off in total at the end of the accounting period. Thus, marketing costs are generally charged against the operations of the accounting period in which they are incurred, while production costs are held in inventory until the units are sold. This practice is followed because too much uncertainty exists as to the probable results in future periods arising from marketing expenditures. Of course, depreciable marketing assets (such as delivery trucks) should be expensed over their useful lives, not when acquired.

In the field of marketing, it is more common to speak of marketing cost analysis rather than of marketing cost accounting. A tie-in of marketing costing with the general accounts, although desirable, is often not necessary.

▼ MARKETING COST CONTROL

The control and analysis of marketing costs should follow methods that are similar to those used for manufacturing costs. The first step in the control of marketing costs is the classification of natural expenses according to functions or activities. It is essential that each function and its associated expenses be made the responsibility of an individual department head.

Marketing functions are of many types, depending on the nature of the business and its organization, size, and method of operation. Each function should be a homogeneous unit, whose activity can be related to specific items of cost. A function might follow a particular pattern of natural expenses, but most functions will have similar expenses, such as salaries, insurance, property taxes, heat, light, power, and supplies.

Functional classifications of marketing costs might be structured in the following manner:

1. Selling
2. Advertising
3. Warehousing
4. Packing and shipping
5. Credit and collection
6. General accounting (for marketing)

These functional classifications can be grouped into two broad categories: order-getting costs and order-filling costs. Order-getting costs are the costs of activities carried on to bring in the sales orders and include selling and advertising. Order-filling costs are the costs of warehousing, packing and shipping, credit and collection, and general accounting.

A broad category of marketing administration costs may also be identified. This category includes the costs of marketing planning and organization, market research and forecasting, product design and development, and product-line planning.

Direct and Indirect Expenses

Direct expenses are those expenses that can be traced directly to a function or department, such as the salary of a department manager or the depreciation of a delivery truck. Expenses which can be traced to a territory, customer, product, or definite type of sales outlet may also be considered direct expenses. Conversely, indirect expenses are incurred for more than one function or other classification and hence must be allocated. A direct expense may also be allocated when direct identification requires excessive clerical expense.

Marketing expenses may be considered direct, indirect, or a combination of both. For example, marketing expenses may be directly identifiable with functional classifications while being only indirectly identifiable with regard to other classifications, such as territories or products.

Functionally classified marketing costs which are indirect with respect to other classifications may be allocated to such classifications as territories and products by (1) using a percentage based on actual sales, manufacturing cost, or some other appropriate basis, or (2) creating a standard unit cost for each activity—similar to factory costs. However, the assignment of functional marketing expenses as percentages of actual sales or manufacturing costs, or on some other basis, is of dubious analytical value. The procedure has been used in the past for want of more satisfactory methods. The determination of a functional standard unit costing rate is a more dependable solution. The charging of marketing expense activities on the basis of a costing rate is a logical extension of widely adopted factory standard costing procedures. Furthermore, the availability of such a rate permits quick and decisive analysis. Actual expenses would be collected in the customary manner and charged to their departmental and natural expense classifications in a subsidiary ledger controlled by a marketing expenses control account in the general ledger.

Selection of Bases for the Allocation of Functional Costs. The marketing cost allocation process poses two basic questions: (1) what bases should be used for the allocation and (2) how far should the allocations be carried out? As a solution to the first, the bases used should be fair and equitable. Ideally, the base selected should be the one most closely related to the incurrence of the costs being allocated. The second question occurs because of doubts raised as to the advantages of full allocation of all indirect expenses. Certain expenses should be omitted from the allocation procedure when they are not measurable in relation to the function or activity. This is especially true when the costs are being allocated for analytical purposes. On the other hand, full marketing cost allocation may be desirable in cost-plus pricing of contracts. With respect to government contracts, CAS 418 calls for the allocation of indirect costs to be based on one of the following, listed in order of preference: (1) a resource consumption measure, (2) an output measure, or (3) a surrogate that is representative of resources consumed.[1]

Factory overhead rates should have a base which most closely expresses the effort connected with the work of the department, such as labor hours, machine hours, or labor cost. A similar procedure for allocating marketing expenses is to divide the total cost of each marketing function by the units of functional service (the base) to obtain the cost per unit. Either an actual rate or a predetermined standard rate may be used, but the latter is preferable.

The selection of bases or units of measurement requires careful analysis, because the degree to which the final rates represent acceptable costs is greatly dependent upon the adequacy of the bases selected. Each function must be examined with respect to that factor which most influences the volume of its work. Some examples of allocation bases for different marketing functions are as follows:

Function	Cost Allocation Bases
Selling	Gross sales dollar value of products sold or number of salespersons' calls on customers (based on salespersons' time reports)
Advertising	Quantity of product units sold, relative media circulation, or cost of space directly assignable
Warehousing	Size, weight, or number of products shipped or handled
Packing and shipping	Number of shipping units, weight, or size of units
Credit and collection	Number of customers' orders, transactions, or invoice lines
General accounting	Number of customers' orders, transactions, or invoice lines

Determination of Functional Unit Cost. The unit cost of an activity is calculated by dividing the total cost of the function by the measurement unit or base selected. A vast amount of information must be collected in order to establish a functional unit costing rate. The tedious assembly of such underlying information is often the reason for the lack of a marketing cost system. When the system is based on standards, the initial work might be more elaborate. However, once the procedure is established, its actual operation should not only be less expensive, but the value derived should far outweigh any previous expenses incurred in establishing the system.

Fixed and Variable Expenses

Recognition of the fixed-variable cost classification is valuable in controlling marketing costs and in making decisions dealing with the possible opening or closing of a territory, new methods of packaging goods, servicing different

---

[1] *Standards, Rules and Regulations, Part 418,* "Allocation of Direct and Indirect Costs" (Washington, D.C.: Cost Accounting Standards Board, 1980).

types of outlets, or adding or dropping a product line. Fixed marketing expenses include salaries of executive and administrative sales staffs; salaries of warehousing, advertising, shipping, billing, and collection departments; and rent and depreciation of associated permanent facilities. These fixed costs have also been called *capacity costs*.

Variable marketing costs include the expenses of handling, warehousing, and shipping that tend to vary with sales volume. They have been referred to as *volume costs* or as expenses connected with the filling of an order. Another type of variable marketing cost originates in connection with promotional expenses such as salespersons' salaries, travel, and entertainment and some advertising expenses. Management must examine these costs carefully in the planning stage, since sales volume may have little influence upon their behavior. These expenses are variable because of management decisions. In fact, once agreed to by management, these expenses may be fixed, at least for the budget period under consideration.

Flexible Budget and Standards for Marketing Functions

Sales estimates are basically the most important figures in any budget. The accuracy and usefulness of most other estimates depend on them. Methods used in determining sales budget estimates are discussed in Chapter 15. Total sales are ordinarily broken down into the various kinds of products to be sold, into monthly or weekly sales and into sales by salespersons, territories, classes of customers, and methods of distribution. In each division, quotas may be useful for determining the desirability of cultivating various outlets and for judging the efficiency of sales methods and policies.

Budgets are prepared to anticipate the amount of functional expenses for the coming period and to provide a basis for comparing and evaluating the actual expenses. Because of the influence of volume and capacity, a comparison of actual costs with predetermined fixed budget figures does not always give a fair evaluation of the activities of a function. Therefore, the use of flexible budgets for the control of marketing costs should be considered.

The flexible budget for a distributive function such as billing might take the following form:

FLEXIBLE BUDGET FOR BILLING DEPARTMENT

Expenses	Functional Unit—Invoice Line			
	50,000	55,000	60,000	65,000
Clerical salaries	$ 4,000	$ 4,000	$ 4,000	$ 4,000
Supervision	3,000	3,000	3,000	3,000
Depreciation—building	750	750	750	750
Depreciation—equipment	1,250	1,250	1,250	1,250
Supplies	2,500	2,750	3,000	3,250
Total	$11,500	$11,750	$12,000	$12,250

A standard functional unit cost is then established for each activity or function on the basis of normal capacity. These standard unit costs will furnish bases for comparisons with actual costs, and spending and idle capacity variances can be isolated. Using the Billing Department as an example and assuming that 60,000 invoice lines represent normal capacity, the following standard billing rate per invoice line would be computed:

$$\frac{\$12,000}{60,000 \text{ invoice lines}} = \$.20 \text{ per invoice line}$$

Assuming $9,000 fixed expense and $3,000 variable expense, the variable portion of the rate is:

$$\frac{\$3,000}{60,000 \text{ invoice lines}} = \$.05 \text{ per invoice line}$$

The cost variances for billing expenses can be computed in a manner similar to that discussed in connection with factory overhead (Chapter 12) and consistent with the basic idea of flexible budgeting. If actual sales required 63,000 invoice lines for a month at a total of $12,500, the variances for the Billing Department would be determined as follows:

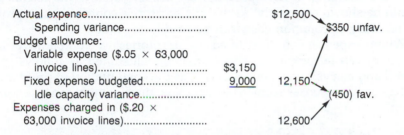

The increased volume leads to a favorable idle capacity variance due to overabsorption of fixed expenses. On the other hand, the supervisor overspent the $12,150 budget allowance by $350.

Accountants usually do not favor carrying this type of variance analysis through ledger accounts. The analysis is usually statistical and is presented to management in report form. However, the following journal entries similar to those for factory overhead could be made:

Billing Expense Charged In	12,600	
Applied Billing Expense		12,600
Actual Billing Expense	12,500	
Sundry Credits		12,500
Applied Billing Expense	12,600	
Billing Expense—Spending Variance	350	
Billing Expense—Idle Capacity Variance		450
Actual Billing Expense		12,500

▼ MARKETING PROFITABILITY ANALYSIS

The functional unit costs are used to analyze costs and determine the profitability of territories, customers, products, and salespersons. In most cases, a continuous reshuffling or rearranging of expense items is needed to find the required costs and profits. The possibility of improving marketing cost and profitability analysis has been enhanced by the availability of electronic data processing equipment capable of processing the great amount of quantitative detail so characteristic of these analyses.

Analysis by Territories

Perhaps the simplest analysis of marketing profitability is by territories. When marketing activities are organized on a territorial basis, each identifiable geographical unit can be charged directly with the expenses incurred within its area, thereby minimizing the proration of expenses. Expenses that can be traced directly to a territory are: salespersons' salaries, commissions, and traveling expenses; transportation cost within the delivery area; packing and shipping costs; and advertising specifically identified with the territory. Nontraceable expenses that must be allocated to the territory are: general management, general office, general sales manager, credit and collection, and general accounting. If nontraceable costs are allocated to the territory, they should be shown separately, so that the territory's contribution to profit and the recovery of common costs can be readily identified.

When expenses are identified by territories, a comparative income statement can be prepared. This statement, illustrated as follows, permits control and analysis of expenses as well as the computation of profit margins. When sales or expenses seem to be out of line, management can take corrective action.

INCOME STATEMENT BY TERRITORIES

	Territory		
	No. 1	No. 2	No. 3
Net sales	$210,000	$80,000	$175,000
Cost of goods sold	160,000	60,000	140,000
Gross profit	$ 50,000	$20,000	$ 35,000
Traceable marketing expenses:			
Selling	$ 15,000	$ 8,600	$ 23,900
Warehousing	3,600	1,400	3,100
Packing and shipping	1,500	400	1,900
Advertising	2,000	1,000	500
Credit and collection	800	250	1,200
Total traceable marketing expenses	$ 22,900	$11,650	$ 30,600
Contribution to profit and common costs	$ 27,100	$ 8,350	$ 4,400
Allocated indirect costs:			
Institutional advertising	$ 1,400	$ 1,400	$ 1,400
General administration	5,000	5,000	5,000
Total allocated indirect costs	$ 6,400	$ 6,400	$ 6,400
Operating income (loss) per territory	$ 20,700	$ 1,950	$ (2,000)

Analysis by Customers

Although most marketing costs can be assigned directly to territories, relatively few of these costs can be traced directly to customers. Perhaps sales commissions, transportation expenses, and sales discounts can be considered direct, but all other expenses are allocated on the basis of functional unit costing rates.

The large number of customers makes the allocation and analysis of marketing costs by customers rather cumbersome if not impossible. For this reason, customers are grouped according to certain characteristics to make the analysis meaningful. The grouping may be by (1) territories, (2) amount of average order, (3) customer-volume groups, or (4) kinds of customers.

Analysis of Customers by Territories. This type of analysis reflects territorial cost differences due to the customer's proximity to warehouses, volume of purchases, service requirements, and the kinds of merchandise bought. These factors can make some sales profitable or unprofitable. The analysis proceeds in the same manner outlined for territories, except that the costs would be broken down by customers or kinds of customers within each territory.

Analysis of Customers by Amount of Average Order. The amount of a customer's order is closely related to profitability. An analysis might indicate that a considerable portion of orders comes from customers who cost the company more in selling to them than the orders are worth in terms of gross profit. Companies have therefore resorted to setting minimum dollar values or minimum quantities for orders as well as price differentials, thereby reducing the number of transactions and increasing profits. Although selective selling has found much favor among many executives, it requires changes in habits and routines.

To present management with a quick view of the situation regarding the amount of the average order in relation to the number of customers, time spent, and total dollar sales, the following chart might be helpful:

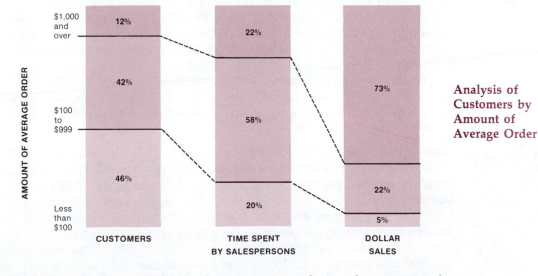

Analysis of Customers by Amount of Average Order

Analysis by Customer-Volume Groups. An analysis of customers by customer-volume groups is similar to that of the amount-of-average-order analysis. Instead of classifying customers by an order's dollar value, however, the customer-volume group analysis is based on quantity or volume. This type of analysis yields information concerning (1) the profitability of various customer-volume groups and (2) the establishment of minimum orders and price differentials.

The following analysis indicates that only sales to customers who buy more than 150 units during a week result in a positive contribution margin:

ANALYSIS BY CUSTOMER-VOLUME GROUPS

Customer-Volume Group (Number of Units Purchased During Week)	Customers (% of Total)	Volume (% of Total)	Gross Contribution Margin per 100 Units	Variable Commercial Expenses per 100 Units	Contribution Margin per 100 Units
Customers unsuccessfully solicited.....................	17.1%	....	....	....	....
1-25...	7.6	0.2%	$1.66	$4.01	$(2.35)
26-50.....................................	8.3	0.7	1.38	2.55	(1.17)
51-100...................................	12.0	1.9	1.25	1.78	(.53)
101-150.................................	9.3	2.4	1.26	1.32	(.06)
151-200.................................	7.8	2.9	1.14	1.13	.01
201-250.................................	6.4	3.0	1.12	.95	.17
251-500.................................	17.1	13.2	1.06	.75	.31
501-1,000..............................	12.7	18.6	1.02	.49	.53
1,001-10,000.........................	1.7	57.1	.81	.24	.57
Total.................................	100.0%	100.0%			

The variable cost of goods sold is subtracted from sales to compute the gross contribution margin, from which the variable commercial (marketing and administrative) expenses are subtracted to compute the contribution margin. Although the customers buying more than 150 units weekly represent only about 46 percent of the customers, they purchase approximately 95 percent of the units sold and thus provide the profits.

In spite of the higher gross contribution margin received from orders by customers who buy less than 150 units, it is not sufficient to cover variable commercial expenses. As a result, the sales to this group provide nothing for fixed expenses and profit.

Analysis by Kinds of Customers. This type of analysis makes a distinction between manufacturers, wholesalers, retailers, government (local, state, and federal), schools, colleges and universities, and hospitals. Prices might be uniform within each customer group but might vary between groups. Different salespersons are often employed for each category; hence their salaries and related expenses can be assigned directly to the group. Delivery to such groups might be different, with one delivery contracted with outside truckers and another made by the firm's own trucks. For analytical purposes, revenue and costs should be related to each kind of customer.

Analysis by Products

The effect of the sales of each product or product line is of considerable importance in planning and controlling the marketing effort. The existence of a high sales volume and a companywide profit does not necessarily mean that all is well. Profitable and unprofitable products must be identified in order to plan and control costs and profits effectively.

Just as customers are grouped for purposes of analysis, products sold can be grouped according to product lines or brands possessing common characteristics. With the aid of functional costing rates, a product-line (or brand-line) income statement can be prepared for the evaluation of profitable and unprofitable product lines. The statement below relates the actual contribution of each product line to total profits and to the recovery of common costs for the year.

PRODUCT-LINE INCOME STATEMENT
(CONTRIBUTION MARGIN APPROACH)

		Product Line		
	Total	1	2	3
Net sales......................................	$3,100,000	$1,540,000	$1,070,000	$490,000
Less variable cost of goods sold......................................	1,927,000	925,000	590,000	412,000
Gross contribution margin...................	$1,173,000	$ 615,000	$ 480,000	$ 78,000
Less variable marketing expenses:				
Selling......................................	$ 243,300	$ 112,300	$ 89,000	$ 42,000
Warehousing................................	87,100	48,000	27,500	11,600
Packing and Shipping.......................	66,000	39,000	17,800	9,200
Advertising................................	38,000	20,000	12,000	6,000
Credit and collection.....................	19,700	12,300	4,200	3,200
General accounting........................	52,200	23,000	16,800	12,400
Total variable marketing expense*......................................	$ 506,300	$ 254,600	$ 167,300	$ 84,400
Margin available for fixed expenses and operating income (contribution margin)........................	$ 666,700	$ 360,400	$ 312,700	$ (6,400)
Less fixed expenses (manufacturing and nonmanufacturing) directly related to individual product lines......................................	120,000	40,000	60,000	20,000
Margin available for common fixed expenses and operating income......................................	$ 546,700	$ 320,400	$ 252,700	$(26,400)
Less common fixed expenses (manufacturing and non-manufacturing)...........................	230,000	Not allocated		
Operating income...........................	$ 316,700			

*In this illustration, all administrative expenses are fixed.

It is also useful to compare actual gross profit with planned or prior period gross profit and to analyze the sources of the observed difference. The difference may be the result of one or a combination of the following:

1. Changes in sales prices of products.
2. Changes in volume sold.
   a. Changes in the number of physical units sold.
   b. Changes in the types of products sold, often called the *product mix* or *sales mix*.
3. Changes in cost elements, i.e., materials, labor, and overhead costs.

The determination of the various causes for an increase or decrease in gross profit is similar to the computation of standard cost variances, although gross profit analysis is often possible without the use of standard costs or budgets. In such a case, prices and costs of the previous period, or any period selected as the basis for the comparison, serve as the basis for the computation of the variances. When standard costs and budgetary methods are employed, however, a greater degree of accuracy and more effective results are achieved.

As the basis for illustrating the analysis of gross profit using budgets, the following gross profit sections of Spanton Company's operating statements are presented:

	Budgeted	Actual	Difference
Sales (net)...............................	$120,000	$140,000	+$20,000
Cost of goods sold....................	100,000	110,000	+ 10,000
Gross profit................................	$ 20,000	$ 30,000	+$10,000 net increase

In comparison with the budget, actual sales increased $20,000 and costs increased $10,000, resulting in an increase in gross profit of $10,000.

Additional data taken from various records indicate that the sales and the cost of goods sold figures can be broken down as follows:

Product	Quantity	Budgeted Sales Unit Price	Budgeted Sales Amount	Budgeted Cost of Goods Sold Unit Cost	Budgeted Cost of Goods Sold Amount
X......................	8,000 units	$5.00	$ 40,000	$4.000	$ 32,000
Y......................	7,000	4.00	28,000	3.500	24,500
Z......................	20,000	2.60	52,000	2.175	43,500
		Total sales	$120,000	Total cost	$100,000

Product	Quantity	Actual Sales Unit Price	Actual Sales Amount	Actual Cost of Goods Sold Unit Cost	Actual Cost of Goods Sold Amount
X......................	10,000 units	$6.60	$ 66,000	$4.00	$ 40,000
Y......................	4,000	3.50	14,000	3.50	14,000
Z......................	20,000	3.00	60,000	2.80	56,000
		Total sales	$140,000	Total cost	$110,000

In analyzing the gross profit data of Spanton Company, the budgeted sales and costs are used as the basis (or standard) for all comparisons. A sales price variance and a sales volume variance are computed first, followed by the computation of a cost price variance and a cost volume variance. The sales volume variance and the cost volume variance are analyzed further as a third step, which results in the computation of a sales mix variance and a final sales volume variance.

The sales price and sales volume variances of Spanton Company are computed as follows:

Actual sales..		$140,000
Actual sales at budgeted prices:		
X: 10,000 units @ $5.00..	$50,000	
Y: 4,000 @ 4.00..	16,000	
Z: 20,000 @ 2.60..	52,000	118,000
Sales price variance...		$ 22,000 fav.
Actual sales at budgeted prices................................		$118,000
Total budgeted sales (used as standard).....................		120,000
Sales volume variance...		$ 2,000 unfav.

The cost price and cost volume variances are computed as follows:

Actual cost of goods sold......................................		$110,000
Actual sales at budgeted costs:		
X: 10,000 units @ $4.000..	$40,000	
Y: 4,000 @ 3.500..	14,000	
Z: 20,000 @ 2.175..	43,500	97,500
Cost price variance..		$ 12,500 unfav.
Actual sales at budgeted costs................................		$ 97,500
Budgeted cost of goods sold (used as standard)............		100,000
Cost volume variance..		$ 2,500 fav.

The results of the preceding computations explain the reason for the $10,000 increase in gross profit:

Sales price variance...		$22,000 fav.
Volume variances (net) consisting of:		
Cost volume variance...	$2,500 fav.	
Less sales volume variance...................................	2,000 unfav.	
Net volume variance..		500 fav.
		$22,500
Less cost price variance..		12,500 unfav.
Net increase in gross profit.....................................		$10,000

The net $500 favorable volume variance is a composite of the sales volume and cost volume variances. It should be further analyzed to determine the more significant sales mix and final sales volume variances. To accomplish this analysis, one additional figure must be determined—the budgeted average gross profit per unit. The computation is:

$$\frac{\text{Total budgeted gross profit}}{\text{Total budgeted number of units sold}} = \frac{\$20,000}{35,000} = \$.5714 \text{ per unit}$$

The $.5714 average budgeted gross profit per unit sold is multiplied by the actual total number of units sold (34,000 units). The resulting $19,428 is the total gross profit that would have been achieved if all units had been sold at the budgeted average gross profit per unit.

The sales mix and the final sales volume variances can now be calculated:

Actual sales at budgeted prices..	$118,000
Actual sales at budgeted costs..	97,500
Difference..	$ 20,500
Actual sales at budgeted average gross profit..........................	19,428
Sales mix variance...	$ 1,072 fav.

Actual sales at budgeted average gross profit..........................		$ 19,428
Total budgeted sales (used as standard)................................	$120,000	
Budgeted cost of goods sold (used as standard)....................	100,000	
Difference..		20,000
Final sales volume variance...		$ 572 unfav.

Check: Sales mix variance...	$ 1,072 fav.
Final sales volume variance...	572 unfav.
Net volume variance..	$ 500 fav.

The sales mix variance can be viewed in the following manner:

	(1) Actual Sales in Units	Budgeted Sales Units	Budgeted Sales %	(2) Actual Sales (In Budgeted Proportions)	(3) (1) − (2)	(4) Budgeted Unit Gross Profit	Sales Mix Variance (3) × (4)
Product							
X......................	10,000	8,000	22.86	7,772*	2,228	$1.000**	$2,228 fav.
Y......................	4,000	7,000	20.00	6,800	(2,800)	.500	(1,400) unfav.
Z......................	20,000	20,000	57.14	19,428	572	.425	243 fav.
Total..................	34,000	35,000	100.00	34,000	-0-		

Rounding difference...	1
Net sales mix variance..	$1,072 fav.

*34,000 × 22.86% = 7,772
**$5 sales price − $4 cost of goods sold = $1

With such an analysis, the influence of individual products on the total sales mix variance is specifically measured. The interactive effect of shifts in the mix is also revealed. This detailed information enables management to assess the effects of past as well as future sales mix variations.

The final sales volume variance is the difference in the number of units budgeted and sold, multiplied by the budgeted average gross profit per unit:

Actual sales in units....................................	34,000
Budgeted sales in units...............................	35,000
Unit sales difference..............................	1,000
Average budgeted gross profit per unit.....	× $.5714
	$571.40
Rounding difference................................	.60
Final sales volume variance......................	$572.00 unfav.

Combining two or more products or product types having different cost or sales prices into a single product category should be avoided. Such aggregation will result in the price variances including a portion of what is actually the mix variance as the mix within such a combination changes.[2]

The variances identified in the preceding computations are summarized as follows:

	Gains	Losses
Gain due to increased sales price	$22,000	
Loss due to increased cost		$12,500
Gain due to shift in sales mix	1,072	
Loss due to decrease in units sold		572
Total	$23,072	$13,072
	13,072	
Net increase in gross profit	$10,000	

The gross profit analysis based on budgets and standard costs depicts the weak spots in the period's performance. Management is now able to outline the remedies that should correct the situation. As the planned gross profit is the responsibility of the marketing as well as the manufacturing functions, the gross profit analysis brings together these two major functional areas of the firm and points to the need for further study by both of them. The marketing function must explain the changes in sales prices, the shift in the sales mix, and the decrease in units sold, while the production function must account for the increase in cost. To be of real value, the cost price variance should be further analyzed to determine variances for materials, labor, and factory overhead.

Analysis by Salespersons

The selling function includes costs such as salaries, travel, and other expenses connected with the work of sales representatives. In many instances, salespersons' expenses form a substantial part of the total expense incurred in selling. The control and analysis of these expenses should, therefore, receive management's closest attention. To achieve this control, performance standards and standard costs should be established. These standards are used not only for the control of costs but also for determining the profitability of sales made by salespersons.

Cost Control. The allocation table on page 811 indicates that selling expenses may be allocated on the basis of the number of calls made. A call or visit by a salesperson is usually made for two reasons: to sell and to promote the merchandise or products. The problem is to determine the cost of doing each of these types of work and to compare the actual cost with the standard cost allowed for a call.

A salesperson's call often involves several kinds of work: not only calling on the customer, but also helping the merchant with the display in the store. This practice is common in cosmetic, pharmaceutical, and fast-food businesses. Because the salesperson's time is consumed by such activities, a standard time

---

[2] Robert E. Malcolm, "The Effect of Product Aggregation in Determining Sales Variances," *The Accounting Review*, Vol. LIII, No. 1, pp. 162-169. Problem 25-8 is adapted from this article.

allowed per call is often very difficult to establish. To obtain the necessary statistics for establishing such standards and to make comparisons, the sales representative might be asked to prepare a report providing information regarding the type of calls made as well as the quantity, type, and dollar values of products sold. This information is the basis for much of the analysis discussed previously.

Profitability Analysis. It is also possible to analyze sales in relation to profitability. Sales volume alone does not tell the complete story. High volume does not always insure high profit, and the sales mix plays an important part in the final profit. Although a sales representative might wish to follow the line of least resistance, management must strive to sell the merchandise of all product groups, particularly those with the highest profit margins. Since sales territories are often planned for sales according to product groups, it is necessary that anticipated sales be followed up by analyzing the salespersons' efforts. The following table indicates how such an analysis can be made:

SALES, COSTS, AND PROFITS BY INDIVIDUAL SALESPERSONS
FOR APRIL, 19—

(1)	(2)	(3)	(4) Salary and Commis- sion	(5)	(6)	(7) Total Cost (4) + (5) + (6)	(8)	(9)	(10) Profit, % of Sales	(11) Ship- ments, % of	(12)
Sales- person	Ship- ments	% of Quota		Travel Expense	Cost of Handling		Gross Profit	Profit (8) − (7)	(9) ÷ (2)	Total*	Potential, % of Total*
A	$26,000	80%	$2,000	$3,000	$2,340	$ 7,340	$ 7,540	$ 200	.8%	6.7%	9.0%
B	26,000	122	1,900	1,800	2,340	6,040	7,800	1,760	6.8	6.7	5.5
C	39,000	100	2,800	2,100	3,500	8,400	11,700	3,300	8.5	10.1	10.5
D	22,000	108	1,800	2,000	1,980	5,780	7,050	1,270	5.8	5.8	5.5
E	21,000	110	1,700	1,700	1,890	5,290	6,720	1,430	6.8	5.4	5.0
F	54,000	125	3,500	3,100	5,700	12,300	14,600	2,300	4.3	14.0	10.0
G	21,000	98	1,600	1,200	1,700	4,500	6,720	2,220	10.6	5.5	5.5
H	46,000	101	3,400	1,000	4,100	8,500	13,800	5,300	11.5	12.0	12.0

*For 8 salespersons out of a total of 15 salespersons.

▼ THE CONTRIBUTION MARGIN APPROACH

Generally, the income statement shows a profit figure after all marketing and administrative expenses have been deducted. The total cost and profit approach assigns all the expenses, direct or indirect, fixed or variable, to each segment analyzed. This procedure is commonly used, since management is familiar with it and believes that no profit is realized until all manufacturing and nonmanufacturing expenses have been recovered.

Marketing cost analysis attempts to allocate marketing expenses to territories, customers, products, or salespersons. However, because these marketing costs contain direct, indirect, fixed, and variable amounts, allocations are extremely difficult and the end results may be misleading. It has been suggested that only the variable manufacturing cost be subtracted from each segment's sales, thus arriving at a figure described as "gross contribution margin." (The conventional income statement deducts all manufacturing costs in arriving at a figure described as "gross profit.") Furthermore, only the variable nonmanufacturing expense would be subtracted from the gross contribution margin of a territory, customer class, product, or salesperson, resulting in the contribution margin for each segment. Fixed expenses would be shown separately and not allocated unless specifically attributable to a segment. When a territory, customer class, or product group contributes nothing to the recovery of fixed expenses, the situation should be examined and remedial steps taken. The product-line income statement on page 817 illustrates this approach. Moreover, nontraceable variable costs, such as variable joint product costs, should be viewed as they relate to the contribution made by the group of products or territories rather than based on arbitrary allocations, e.g., to individual products or territories (pages 137-138). The arbitrary nature of such joint cost allocations is also a fundamental reason for criticism of requirements to report segment or product-line revenue, costs, and profits in published financial statements.

Although sales volume is the ultimate goal of most sales managers, the trend has been toward a greater recognition of contribution margin as the basis for judging the success and profitability of marketing activities. The increased use of standard production costs has aided the analysis of gross profit, as discussed on page 818. Even though a manufacturer might know the production costs, the question remains: "How much can the company afford for marketing costs?" The problem of determining allowable marketing expenses is intensified because once a sales program gets under way, the majority of expenses become fixed costs, at least in the short run.

In summary, proponents of the contribution margin approach point out that only specific and direct costs, whether variable or fixed, should be assigned to territories, customers, product groups, or salespersons, with a clear distinction as to their fixed and variable characteristics. Moreover, for the purpose of identifying costs with responsible managers, it is desirable to identify each reported cost with its controllability by the manager in charge of the reported activity.

The contribution margin approach has influenced the thinking of the volume-minded sales manager or salesperson who must recognize that profit is more beneficial than volume. The contribution margin is a better indicator than sales as to the amount available for recovery of fixed manufacturing cost, fixed marketing and administrative expenses, and a profit.

▼ EFFECT OF THE ROBINSON-PATMAN ACT ON MARKETING COST ANALYSIS

The Robinson-Patman Act of June, 1936, amended Section 2 of the Clayton Act, which was enacted to prevent large buyers from securing excessive advantages over their smaller competitors by virtue of their size and purchasing power. Since the Clayton Act prohibited discrimination only where it had a serious effect on competition in general, and since it contained no other provisions for the control of price discrimination, the act was amended in order to insure competitive equality of the individual enterprise. The following clause of the Robinson-Patman Act is of special interest in connection with marketing costs:

> *To make it unlawful for any person engaged in commerce to discriminate in price or terms of sale between purchasers of commodities of like grades and quality; to prohibit the payment of brokerage or commissions under certain conditions; to suppress pseudo-advertising allowances; to provide a presumptive measure of damages in certain cases; and to protect the independent merchant, the public whom he serves, and the manufacturer who sells him his goods from exploitation by unfair competitors.*

The Robinson-Patman Act intends to preclude price discrimination that decreases competition. The seller has three acceptable defenses for price cuts:

1. They resulted from changing conditions in the market place (discontinued products, distress sales, perishable goods, etc.),
2. They temporarily changed in a good-faith attempt to meet an equally low and lawful price of a competitor, or
3. They reflect lower costs that resulted from different methods or quantities of sale or delivery.

The amendment does not imply that price discriminations in the sense of price differentials are entirely prohibited or that a seller is compelled or required to grant any price differential whatever. A vendor may sell to all customers at the same price regardless of differences in the cost of serving them. At the core of the amendment are the provisions that deal with charging different prices to different customers. To meet the third of the defenses for price cuts, differentials granted must not exceed differences in the cost of serving different customers. The cost of serving includes the cost of manufacturing, selling, and delivering, which may differ according to methods of selling and quantities sold. The burden of proof is on both the buyer and the seller and requires a definite justification for the discounts granted and received. It is necessary to prove that no discrimination took place with respect to (1) price differences, (2) discounts, (3) delivery service, (4) allowances for service, (5) advertising appropriations, (6) brokerage or commissions, or (7) consignment policies.

These possibilities for discrimination fall chiefly into the field of marketing costs. Many interesting problems have arisen because of the nature of these costs and the numerous variations and combinations in the manner of sale and delivery. As indicated, it is difficult to apply many marketing costs to particular products. Therefore, it is important for concerns performing distribution functions to accumulate cost statistics regarding their marketing costs, because the act makes allowances for differences in costs. The act increases the interest in marketing cost analysis and its part in the determination of prices. The following cost justification study illustrates this point:

COST JUSTIFICATION STUDY

A producer of a heavy bulk chemical, which sells FOB point of manufacture at $25 a ton in minimum quantities of a full rail carload (approximately 40 tons), is offered a contract for 500 to 1,000 carloads a year if it will reduce its FOB shipping point price by 6 percent. The producer does not want to reduce the selling price to other customers, to whom annual shipments range from 10 to 200 carloads. The only source of cost differences is sales solicitation and service expense.

The sales manager estimates (since exact records are not available) that salespersons typically pursue the following call schedule:

Customer Size (in Carloads)	Annual Number of Sales Calls
10-40	12
41-80	24
81-150	36
151 and up	50

The sales manager further estimates that each sales call costs approximately $50-$70 regardless of customer size. After questioning, the manager agrees that study would probably show that calls on large customers (more than 100 carloads) are longer in duration than calls on smaller customers. For study and testing purposes, it was assumed that a call on a small customer costs $60 and a call on a large customer costs $90. The following cost-sales relationship can now be developed:

DIFFERENTIAL COST
LARGE VS. SMALL CUSTOMERS

	\$25,000	\$50,000	\$100,000	\$200,000	\$500,000
	25	50	100	200	500
Sales value	$25,000	$50,000	$100,000	$200,000	$500,000
Number of sales calls	12	24	36	50	50
Assumed cost per call	$ 60	$ 60	$ 90	$ 90	$ 90
Assumed cost of call per customer	720	1,440	3,240	4,500	4,500
Assumed cost of call as a percent of sales	2.9%	2.9%	3.2%	2.25%	0.9%

Annual Carloads per Customer

Since the assumed differential costs are less than the 6 percent proposed discount, it appears obvious that a discount of that magnitude is not susceptible to cost justification. Indeed, it is possible that even a one percent discount to a 500-carload customer might be hard to justify since it is probable that more exact costing would narrow the spread in the percentages among the various classes.

Adapted from "Cost Justification of Price Differences" by Herbert G. Whiting, *Management Services*, Vol. 3, No. 4, pp. 31-32. Copyright 1966 by the American Institute of Certified Public Accountants.

A competitor who believes that discrimination exists must file a complaint substantiated by evidence acquired from published price lists or from other persuasive evidence of this kind. The complaint is valid if all of the following violations have been committed:

1. Price discrimination.
2. Discrimination between competitors.
3. Discrimination on products of like grades and quality.
4. Discrimination in interstate commerce.
5. Injurious effect on competition.

The most effective method for a firm to answer any such complaint is to have a functional unit cost system for marketing costs. In fact, no firm should be placed in a situation of having to make a cost study after being cited. Experience has proven that such belated cost justification studies seldom are successful. Therefore, the firm should (1) establish records that show that price differentials are extended only to the extent justified by maximum allowable cost savings and (2) maintain the cost data currently through spot checks conducted periodically to insure that the price differentials are in conformance with current cost conditions.

In justifying price differentials, marginal costing cannot be utilized; i.e., a plant operating at 80 percent capacity and wishing to add an order to increase its capacity to 90 percent cannot restrict its cost considerations to that incremental element of variable cost due to the volume change. The reduced cost per unit resulting from the greater volume must be spread over all units. Thus, the government, in consistently rejecting the marginal approach, endorses instead a method which is often called fully distributed cost analysis and only these fully distributed or average total costs are acceptable for a cost justification defense under the Robinson-Patman Act. The government has held that only identifiable savings, whether manufacturing or marketing, resulting from specific methods or quantities connected with given orders can be properly passed in their entirety to specific customers. For example, if the price difference is related to special manufacturing runs, then cost factors that can be considered include the differences between customer runs, which can cause a difference in unit costs. Typical of such costs are setup costs, skill and number of direct laborers, tool-wear costs, machine downtime, scrap rates, order scheduling, and inspection.

In general, the Robinson-Patman Act seems to work toward greater equity beween prices, since pricing schedules appear to be more carefully attuned to differences in costs than they were before the enactment of this particular type of control. The accountant must be prepared to study the subject actively and continuously to help management avoid unintentional price discriminations that might be in violation of the law. The marketing manager must also follow the effect of any pricing policy to determine whether it is profitable and produces the kind of business necessary for the wholesome operation of the enterprise.

▼ ILLUSTRATIVE PROBLEM IN MARKETING COST AND PROFITABILITY ANALYSIS

Ambler Company manufactures and sells a variety of small power tools, dies, drills, files, milling cutters, saws, and other miscellaneous hardware. The company's catalog lists the merchandise under sixteen major classifications.

Customers fall into five categories: retail hardware stores, manufacturers, public school systems, municipalities, and public utilities. Territories include New Jersey and Pennsylvania. The company's president believes that in certain areas the cost of marketing the products is too high, that certain customers' orders do not contribute enough to cover fixed costs and earn a profit, and that certain products are being sold to customers and in territories on an unprofitable basis. Therefore, the president has instructed the controller to review the firm's marketing costs and to study the steps, methods, and procedures necessary to provide more accurate information about the profitability of territories, products, and customers.

The controller has designed and operated a standard marketing cost system which gives management the desired information for the control and analysis of marketing and administrative expenses. The preparation and assembling of statistical and cost data were carried out in the following sequence:

1. Total marketing expenses were estimated (or budgeted).
2. Six marketing functions (selling, warehousing, packing and shipping, advertising, credit and collection, general accounting) were established.
3. Direct costs were assigned directly to functions; indirect expenses were allocated to functions via a measurement unit, such as kilowatt-hour, footage, or number of employees.
4. Fixed and variable expenses were determined for each function.
5. Functional unit measurement bases were selected for the purpose of assigning costs to the segments to be analyzed, i.e., territory or product.
6. Functional unit measurements or bases applicable to a territory or a product were determined.
7. Unit standard manufacturing costs and standard product sales prices were established.
8. Data regarding the types and number of units sold in the territories were prepared.
9. Income statements by (a) territories and (b) product lines in one territory were prepared for management.

Exhibit 1 on page 828 summarizes the results of the study prepared by the controller. Column 1 shows the total budgeted expense per function. Each total is supported by a budget showing the amount for each individual expense of the function. Columns 2 and 3 place total expenses in a variable and fixed expense classification. Column 4 indicates the functional unit measurement selected as being reliably applicable to that function. Column 5 lists the quantity or value of the measurement unit used to determine the functional unit costing rate. Columns 6, 7, and 8 indicate the variable, fixed, and total functional unit costing rates.

Exhibits 2 and 3 list the details necessary for the preparation of Exhibits 1, 4, and 5. To simplify the illustration, nonmanufacturing costs other than marketing costs have been excluded.

The product-line income statement for the territory of Pennsylvania (Exhibit 5) indicates that the volume and/or price of Product 1 is not sufficient to

Exhibit 1

DETERMINATION OF FUNCTIONAL UNIT COSTING RATES

Function	Budgeted Expenses			Functional Unit Measurement Base (4)	Quantity (5)	Functional Unit Costing Rates		
	Total (1)	Variable (2)	Fixed (3)			Variable (6)	Fixed (7)	Total (8)
Selling	$ 95,500	$ 38,200	$ 57,300	Gross sales dollar value of product sold	$1,910,000	2%	3%	5%
Warehousing	75,000	45,000	30,000	Weight of units shipped	375,000	$ .12	$ .08	$ .20
Packing and shipping	63,000	37,500	25,500	Quantity of product units sold	150,000	.25	.17	.42
Advertising	54,000		54,000	Quantity of product units sold	150,000		.36	.36
Credit and collection	28,800	18,720	10,080	Number of customers' orders	7,200	2.60	1.40	4.00
General accounting	49,200	21,300	27,900	Number of times product items appear on customers' invoices	15,000	1.42	1.86	3.28
Total functional distribution expense	$365,500	$160,720	$204,780					

Exhibit 2

DATA CONCERNING PRICE, COST, QUANTITY, WEIGHT, AND TRANSACTIONS OF PRODUCTS

Product Class	Product 1	Product 2	Product 3
Standard product sales price	$10.00	$15.00	$18.00
Unit standard manufacturing cost	8.00	11.00	12.00
Quantity of product units sold	80,000	50,000	20,000
Weight of units shipped (kilograms)	2.25 kg	2.5 kg	3.5 kg
Number of times product items appear on customers' invoices	6,400	5,700	2,900
Number of customers' orders	2,400	3,000	1,800

Exhibit 3

DATA CONCERNING TRANSACTIONS IN TERRITORIES

Territory	Quantity of Product Solds			Number of Times Product Items Appear on Customers' Invoices			Number of Customers' Orders		
	Product 1	Product 2	Product 3	Product 1	Product 2	Product 3	Product 1	Product 2	Product 3
Pennsylvania	55,000	30,000	16,000	4,000	2,900	1,000	1,000	1,900	900
New Jersey	25,000	20,000	4,000	2,400	2,800	1,900	1,400	1,100	900

result in a profit. In Exhibit 6, this analysis is carried further with the aid of a fixed-variable analysis of manufacturing costs and marketing expenses to determine the contribution made by the product line to the total fixed cost and profit. This exhibit assumes the nonexistence of unallocated cost, fixed or variable. The product-line income statement on page 817 illustrates a presentation with unallocated costs.

Next, the steps required to bring about an improvement in the profitability of this product line should be determined. Functional marketing cost analysis permits this type of analysis, which should eventually lead to a selective selling program supported by product break-even analyses and by cost-volume-profit and differential cost analyses (Chapters 20 and 21).

Exhibit 4
INCOME STATEMENT FOR ALL PRODUCT CLASSES IN THE TWO TERRITORIES

	Total	Territory	
		Pennsylvania	New Jersey
Gross sales..	$1,910,000	$1,288,000	$622,000
Less cost of goods sold....................	1,430,000	962,000	468,000
Gross profit..	$ 480,000	$ 326,000	$154,000
Less marketing expenses:			
Selling...	$ 95,500	$ 64,400	$ 31,100
Warehousing...................................	75,000	50,950	24,050
Packing and shipping.....................	63,000	42,420	20,580
Advertising......................................	54,000	36,360	17,640
Credit and collection......................	28,800	15,200	13,600
General accounting.........................	49,200	25,912	23,288
Total..	$ 365,500	$ 235,242	$130,258
Operating income.................................	$ 114,500	$ 90,758	$ 23,742

Exhibit 5
INCOME STATEMENT BY PRODUCT CLASSES IN THE PENNSYLVANIA TERRITORY

	Total	Product Class		
		Product 1	Product 2	Product 3
Gross sales..	$1,288,000	$550,000	$450,000	$288,000
Less cost of goods sold....................	962,000	440,000	330,000	192,000
Gross profit..	$ 326,000	$110,000	$120,000	$ 96,000
Less marketing expenses:				
Selling...	$ 64,600	$ 27,500	$ 22,500	$ 14,400
Warehousing...................................	50,950	24,750	15,000	11,200
Packing and shipping.....................	42,420	23,100	12,600	6,720
Advertising......................................	36,360	19,800	10,800	5,760
Credit and collection......................	15,200	4,000	7,600	3,600
General accounting.........................	25,912	13,120	9,512	3,280
Total..	$ 235,242	$112,270	$ 78,012	$ 44,960
Operating income (loss)........................	$ 90,758	$(2,270)	$ 41,988	$ 51,040

Exhibit 6

INCOME STATEMENT OF PRODUCT CLASS WITH FIXED-VARIABLE ANALYSIS OF MANUFACTURING AND MARKETING COSTS IN THE PENNSYLVANIA TERRITORY

		Product 1
Gross sales		$550,000
Less cost of goods sold (variable unit cost = 60% of $8)		264,000
Gross contribution margin		$286,000
Less variable marketing expenses:		
Selling	$ 11,000	
Warehousing	14,850	
Packing and shipping	13,750	
Credit and collection	2,600	
General accounting	5,680	47,880
Contribution margin		$238,120
Less fixed costs and expenses:		
Manufacturing cost—fixed	$176,000	
Marketing expenses—fixed:		
Selling	$ 16,500	
Warehousing	9,900	
Packing and shipping	9,350	
Advertising	19,800	
Credit and collection	1,400	
General accounting	7,440	240,390
Operating loss—Product Class 1—Pennsylvania		$ (2,270)

DISCUSSION QUESTIONS

1. What general principles should be observed in planning a system of control for marketing expenses?

2. How should marketing expenses be classified in order to find the cost of selling jobs or products?

3. A method still commonly used today in analyzing marketing expenses is to relate them to either the total factory cost or the total sales value. This method is merely a relationship and not a scientific basis. Discuss.

4. Outline a procedure for determining the marketing costs for a concern manufacturing two products. This organization uses national advertising and assigns salespersons to definite territories for contact with established dealers and also to secure additional retail outlets.

5. What are the objectives of profit analysis by sales territories?

6. What causes changes in the gross profit?

7. By what methods can a change in the gross profit figure be analyzed?

8. Whose task is it to see that the planned gross profit is met?

9. What difficulties may arise if an attempt is made to set standards for marketing expenses?

10. Explain briefly the difference between the profit approach and the contribution margin approach in marketing cost analysis.

11. Why did the Robinson-Patman Act lead to the establishment of marketing cost procedures in business?

EXERCISES

1. Controlling functional activity by using a flexible budget and standards. The flexible budget for the Warehousing Department of Abernathy Supply Company is as follows:

Expense	Functional Unit—Number of Transactions			
	1,000	2,000*	3,000	4,000
Supervision..........................	$2,000	$2,000	$2,000	$2,000
Other labor..........................	1,000	1,100	1,200	1,300
Depreciation........................	750	750	750	750
Supplies..............................	250	300	350	400
Insurance............................	250	250	250	250
Rent....................................	200	200	200	200
Total expense.....................	$4,450	$4,600	$4,750	$4,900

*Normal capacity

During April, the Warehousing Department handled 1,800 transactions. The actual expense was $4,510.

Required: Compute the spending and idle capacity variances for the Warehousing Department.

2. Marketing cost control using flexible budget and standards. The monthly flexible budget for the General Accounting Department is as follows:

Expense	Functional Unit—Number of Transactions			
	10,000	15,000	20,000	25,000
Supervision..............................	$ 3,000	$ 3,000	$ 3,000	$ 3,000
Clerical salaries......................	11,500	11,500	11,500	11,500
Utilities...................................	500	500	500	500
Depreciation—building.............	750	750	750	750
Depreciation—equipment.........	1,250	1,250	1,250	1,250
Supplies..................................	2,500	3,000	3,500	4,000
Total.......................................	$19,500	$20,000	$20,500	$21,000
Cost per transaction...............	$1.9500	$1.3333	$1.0250	$ .8400

During June, the General Accounting Department handled 23,500 transactions; actual costs were $20,930. Normal capacity calls for the handling of 20,000 transactions.

Required: Compute the budget allowance for 23,500 transactions, the spending variance, and the idle capacity variance.

3. Marketing cost analysis by territories. Klumb Auto Supply Company of Waco, Texas, markets automotive supplies in Waco and Dallas. Marketing expenses for the past year were:

Sales salaries...	$ 86,000
Salespersons' expenses............................	16,200
Advertising...	24,000
Delivery expense..	25,200
Credit investigation expense.....................	6,800
Collection expense....................................	11,400
Total...	$169,600

Additional information:

(a) The company has five salespersons, three in Dallas and two in Waco, and each is paid the same salary.

(b) The salespersons receive equal allowances for expenses, except that the Dallas salespersons each receive $400 per year extra for turnpike toll fees.

(c) All advertising is placed according to the number of subscribers to the Waco and Dallas daily newspapers, 150,000 and 750,000 respectively.

(d) Delivery is made by an outside agency which charges a flat annual fee. The agency made 4,800 deliveries (3,000 in Dallas, 1,800 in Waco) from a centrally located warehouse.

(e) 680 new customers were obtained (400 from Dallas, 280 from Waco).

(f) 6,000 customers' remittances were received (4,500 from Dallas, 1,500 from Waco).

Required: Prepare a marketing cost analysis for the two territories.

4. Marketing cost analysis by territories. Riney Company is a wholesaler of novelty items sold through campus bookstores in Alabama, Georgia, and Florida. Marketing expenses for the past month were:

Sales salaries	$25,200
Sales commissions	2,550
Travel	3,400
Advertising	6,060
Warehousing	4,747
Delivery	3,170
Collection	3,744

The company has developed the following survey data:

(a) Nine salespersons are employed (four in Alabama, three in Georgia, and two in Florida) at the same base salary.

(b) The following commission schedule has been established:

Sales	Commission (% of Sales)
First $20,000	0%
Second $20,000	2
Sales over $40,000	5

Sales were:

State	Salesperson #1	#2	#3	#4
Alabama	$35,000	$30,000	$41,000	$26,000
Georgia	31,000	29,000	36,000	
Florida	42,000	33,000		

(c) The salespersons receive $.20 per mile for travel. Salespersons in Alabama traveled 8,000 miles; Georgia, 5,000 miles; Florida, 4,000 miles.

(d) Advertising allowances of 2% of sales are granted to purchasers.
(e) Warehousing expenses are distributed on the basis of the number of products handled, with the average cost of units shipped being $3.
(f) Delivery expenses are allocated on the basis of weight. Shipments of merchandise to Alabama weighed 50,000 pounds; to Georgia, 30,000 pounds; and to Florida, 20,000 pounds.
(g) A total of 120 remittances were received from customers, of which 70 were from Alabama, 30 from Georgia, and 20 from Florida.

Required: Prepare a marketing cost analysis by territories.

5. Marketing expense analysis by territories. Red River Hardware Company sells hardware items in New Mexico, Colorado, and Wyoming. Marketing expenses for the past quarter were as follows:

Sales salaries	$58,100	Advertising expense	$14,920
Sales commissions	8,460	Warehousing expense	2,940
Travel expense	2,240	Collection expense	900

The company wishes to know the cost of distributing its products in each of the three states. A survey reveals the following information:

(a) Ten salespersons are employed (five in Colorado, three in New Mexico, and two in Wyoming). All are paid at the same base salary.
(b) Sales were as follows:

Salesperson	Colorado	New Mexico	Wyoming
#1	$54,000	$11,000	$48,000
#2	32,000	23,000	51,000
#3	6,000	50,000	
#4	49,000		
#5	49,000		

(c) The following commission schedule has been established:

Sales for each Salesperson	Commission (% of Sales)
For portion under $10,000	0%
For portion $10,000 − $50,000	3
For portion over $50,000	6

(d) Travel expense is allocated 4:3:1 among Colorado, New Mexico, and Wyoming, respectively.
(e) Advertising expense is allocated on the basis of sales.
(f) Warehousing expense is allocated by assigning Colorado and Wyoming $200 and $100, respectively, with the balance distributed in the same ratio as travel expense.
(g) A total of 15,000 remittances were received from customers, of which 3,000 were from Wyoming and 4,500 from New Mexico.

Required: Prepare a marketing expense analysis by territories, detailing each expense category.

6. Income statement by customer classes. Central Manufacturing Company assembles a washing machine that is sold to three classes of customers. The data with respect to these customers are as follows:

Customer Class	Sales	Gross Profit	Number of Sales Calls	Number of Orders	Number of Invoice Lines
Department stores............	$180,000	$ 26,000	240	120	2,100
Retail appliance stores.....	240,000	80,000	360	580	4,600
Wholesalers......................	300,000	71,000	400	300	3,300
Total.........................	$720,000	$177,000	1,000	1,000	10,000

Actual marketing costs for the year are:

Function	Costs	Measure of Activity
Selling...	$65,000	Salespersons' calls
Packing and shipping.....................	12,000	Customers' orders
Advertising......................................	20,000	Dollar sales
Credit and collection.......................	15,000	Invoice lines
General accounting..........................	18,000	Customers' orders

Required: Prepare an income statement by customer classes, with functional distribution of marketing expenses. (When allocating the advertising expense, round to the nearest $100.)

7. Gross profit analysis. K. M. Harrison Company presents the following data for two retail inventory items:

	Budget			Actual		
	Units	Per Unit	Amount	Units	Per Unit	Amount
Sales:						
X..................................	11,000	$2.50	$27,500	13,000	$2.55	$33,150
Y..................................	5,000	2.00	10,000	8,000	1.95	15,600
			$37,500			$48,750
Cost of goods sold:						
X..................................	11,000	$2.00	$22,000	13,000	$2.02	$26,260
Y..................................	5,000	1.40	7,000	8,000	1.45	11,600
			$29,000			$37,860
Gross profit......................	16,000	$.53125	$ 8,500	21,000	$.51857	$10,890

Required: Compute the price and volume variances for sales and cost, and the sales mix and final sales volume variances.

8. Gross profit analysis. A cost analyst has prepared a monthly gross profit analysis for Alboc Company, comparing actual to budget for two products, Alco and Bacco. June budget and actual data follow:

| | Sales | | | Cost of Goods Sold | | Gross Profit | |
	Units	Unit Price	Amount	Unit Cost	Amount	Per Unit	Amount
Budget:							
Alco.....................................	8,000	$20.00	$160,000	$16.00	$128,000	$4.00	$32,000
Bacco..................................	4,200	14.00	58,800	12.00	50,400	2.00	8,400
Total budget....................	12,200	17.9344*	$218,800	14.6229*	$178,400	3.3115*	$40,400
Actual:							
Alco.....................................	7,500	21.00	$157,500	16.50	$123,750	4.50	$33,750
Bacco..................................	4,500	13.50	60,750	11.50	51,750	2.00	9,000
Total actual......................	12,000	18.1875*	$218,250	14.625*	$175,500	3.5625*	$42,750

*Weighted average

Required: Compute the price and volume variances for sales and cost, and the sales mix and final sales volume variances.

9. Gross profit analysis. Spiffy Sporting Goods Shop presents the following data for two types of racquetball gloves, leather and fabric, for 19A and 19B:

| | 19A | | | 19B | | |
	Units	Per Unit	Amount	Units	Per Unit	Amount
Sales:						
Leather racquetball gloves.....	8,000	$8.00	$64,000	12,000	$10.00	$120,000
Fabric racquetball gloves.......	8,000	4.00	32,000	20,000	6.00	120,000
			$96,000			$240,000
Cost of goods sold:						
Leather racquetball gloves.....	8,000	$6.00	$48,000	12,000	$ 9.00	$108,000
Fabric racquetball gloves.......	8,000	3.00	24,000	20,000	5.00	$100,000
			$72,000			$208,000
Gross profit.................................	16,000	$1.50	$24,000	32,000	$ 1.00	$ 32,000

Required: Compute the price and volume variances for sales and cost, and the sales mix and final sales volume variances.

10. Gross profit analysis. Kleinfuss Shoe Company manufactures a wide line of ladies' footwear. Sales volume had been increasing rapidly for seven years. However, after a change in executive management, the new president believed that sales volume should increase at an even faster rate. The plan was to increase volume, with the price level remaining the same or declining. After lengthy discussions with the plant manager and the sales manager, a mutually agreeable plan was formulated, whereby the volume was expected to increase with a decrease in the sales price. At the time of this proposal, both the plant manager and the sales manager believed that the existing level of gross profit could be maintained.

In 19A, the last year before adoption of the new plan, the following company data had been recorded with respect to two lines of ladies' footwear—Loafers and Sandals.

	Loafers	Sandals
Shoes sold	10,000	5,000
Revenue	$200,000	$150,000
Gross profit	70,000	60,000

The proposed plan did have the desired effect on 19B gross profit. The president was quite enthusiastic over the success of the plan, but wanted to know if the increased gross profit was attributable to increased sales or reduced costs.

Data for 19B:

	Loafers	Sandals
Shoes sold	12,000	6,000
Revenue	$208,000	$144,000
Cost of goods sold	124,000	86,000
Gross profit	$ 84,000	$ 58,000

Required: Prepare an analysis to indicate the underlying reasons for the change in gross profit.

11. Salesperson's performance reports. A corporate budget director designed a control scheme in order to compare and evaluate the efforts of the company's three salespersons and the results attained. Specifically, each salesperson is to make five calls per day; the budget provides for $40 per day per salesperson for travel and entertainment expenses; each salesperson was assigned a sales quota of $400 a day. The Budget Department collects the data on actual performance from the daily sales reports and the weekly expense vouchers and then prepares a monthly report. This report includes variances from standard and performance indexes. For the performance index, standard performance equals 100.

The records for November, with 20 working days, show:

Salesperson	Sales Calls	Travel Expenses	Sales
Palmer, K.	70	$1,000	$14,000
Thompson, J.	100	800	8,400
Miller, O.	120	720	6,000

Required: Prepare a monthly report comparing the standard and actual performances of the salespersons, including the performance indexes for (1) sales calls, (2) travel expenses, (3) sales, and (4) sales revenue per call.

12. Product-line income statement—contribution margin approach. Pralina Products Company has three major product lines—cereals, breakfast bars, and dog food. The following income statement for the year ended April 30 was prepared by product line, using full cost allocation:

Pralina Products Company
Income Statement
For the Year Ended April 30, 19—
(000s omitted)

	Cereals	Breakfast Bars	Dog Food	Total
Sales (in pounds)...	2,000	500	500	3,000
Revenue from sales..	$1,000	$400	$200	$1,600
Cost of goods sold:				
Materials..	$ 330	$160	$100	$ 590
Direct labor..	90	40	20	150
Factory overhead...	108	48	24	180
Total cost of goods sold....................................	$ 528	$248	$144	$ 920
Gross profit...	$ 472	$152	$ 56	$ 680
Commercial expenses:				
Marketing expenses:				
Advertising...	$ 50	$ 30	$ 20	$ 100
Commissions..	50	40	20	110
Sales salaries and related benefits.................	30	20	10	60
Total marketing expense.................................	$ 130	$ 90	$ 50	$ 270
General and administrative expenses:				
Licenses..	$ 50	$ 20	$ 15	$ 85
Salaries and related benefits..........................	60	25	15	100
Total general and administrative expenses......	$ 110	$ 45	$ 30	$ 185
Total commercial expense....................................	$ 240	$135	$ 80	$ 455
Operating income...	$ 232	$ 17	$(24)	$ 225

Explanatory data:

(a) Cost of goods sold. The company's inventories of materials and finished products do not vary significantly from year to year. Factory overhead was applied to products at 120% of direct labor dollars. The factory overhead costs for the year were as follows:

Variable indirect labor and supplies....................................	$ 15,000
Variable employee benefits on factory labor.....................	30,000
Supervisory salaries and related benefits..........................	35,000
Plant occupancy cost..	100,000
	$180,000

There was no over- or underapplied factory overhead at year end.

(b) Advertising. The company has been unable to determine any direct causal relationship between the level of sales volume and the level of advertising expenditures. However, because management believes advertising is necessary, an annual advertising program has been implemented for each product line, independent of the others.

(c) Commissions. Sales commissions are paid to the sales force at the rate of 5% on the cereals and 10% on the breakfast bars and dog food.

(d) Licenses. Various licenses are required for each product line, renewed annually for each product line at a fixed amount.

(e) Salaries and related benefits. Sales and general and administrative personnel devote time and effort to all product lines. Their salaries and wages are allocated on the basis of management's estimates of time spent on each product line.

(f) Fixed factory overhead and the salaries and related benefits for sales and general and administrative personnel are not traceable to individual product lines on any objective basis.

Required: Prepare a product-line income statement, using the contribution margin approach.   (ICMA adapted)

PROBLEMS

25-1. Standard cost variance analysis; revision of sales prices. Delgado Corporation's actual and standard (for budgeted hours) marketing costs for January are:

	Budget at Standard Cost	Actual
Sales..	$750,000	$750,000
Direct marketing costs:		
Selling......................................	$ 12,000	$ 15,000
Shipping salaries......................	21,000	28,350
Indirect marketing costs:		
Order filling..............................	17,250	21,500
Other costs..............................	2,100	2,500
Total cost...................................	$ 52,350	$ 67,350

Additional data:

(a) The company sells one product at $10 per unit.
(b) The other indirect marketing costs and shipping salaries are allocated on the basis of shipping hours. January shipping hours are:

Budgeted hours...	3,500
Standard hours (at January operating level).....................	4,400
Actual hours...	4,500

(c) Order-filling costs are allocated on the basis of sales and are comprised of freight, packing, and warehousing costs. An analysis of the amount of these standard costs by unit order size follows:

Unit-Volume Classification	Order-Filling Standard Costs Classified by Unit Order Size			
	1-15	16-50	Over 50	Total
Freight............................	$ 1,200	$ 1,440	$ 2,250	$ 4,890
Packing............................	2,400	3,240	4,500	10,140
Warehousing....................	600	720	900	2,220
Total.............................	$ 4,200	$ 5,400	$ 7,650	$17,250
Units sold.........................	12,000	18,000	45,000	75,000

Management realizes that the marketing cost per unit decreases with an increase in the size of the order and, hence, wants to revise its unit sales prices upward or downward on the basis of the quantity ordered in proportion to the allocated freight, packing, and warehousing standard costs. Management assumes that the revised unit prices will require no changes in standards for sales volume, the number of units sold in each order-size classification, and the profit per unit sold.

Required:

(1) Compute and analyze variances from standard cost for (a) other indirect marketing costs and (b) shipping salaries. The analysis should compare actual and standard costs at the January standard operating level.

(2) Prepare a schedule computing the standard cost per unit for each order-filing cost in each unit-volume classification. Use the same format as in item (c).

(3) Prepare a schedule computing the revised unit sales prices for each unit-volume classification. *(AICPA adapted)*

25-2. Marketing cost analysis by territories. Starnes Company sells toiletries to retail stores throughout the United States. For planning and control purposes, the company is organized into twelve geographic regions, with two to six territories within each region. One salesperson is assigned to each territory and has exclusive rights to all sales made in that territory. Merchandise is shipped from the manufacturing plant to the twelve regional warehouses, from which the sales in each territory are shipped. National headquarters allocates a specific amount at the beginning of the year for regional advertising.

The net sales for Starnes Company for the six months ended September 30 total $10 million. Costs incurred by national headquarters are:

National administration.....................	$250,000
National advertising.........................	125,000
National warehousing......................	175,000
	$550,000

The results of operations for the South Atlantic Region for the six months ended September 30 are:

Starnes Company
Statement of Operations for South Atlantic Region
For the Six Months Ended September 30, 19—

Sales..		$900,000
Costs and expenses:		
Advertising fees..	$ 54,700	
Uncollectible accounts expense....................	3,600	
Cost of goods sold..	460,000	
Freight out..	22,600	
Insurance..	10,000	
Salaries and employee benefits....................	81,600	
Sales commissions..	36,000	
Supplies..	12,000	
Travel and entertainment..............................	14,100	
Wages and employee benefits......................	36,000	
Warehouse depreciation................................	8,000	
Warehouse operating cost.............................	15,000	
Total cost and expense.............................		753,600
Territory contribution...		$146,400

The South Atlantic Region consists of two territories—Green and Purple. The salaries and employee benefits consist of the following items:

Regional vice-president..	$24,000
Regional marketing manager...	15,000
Regional warehouse manager..	13,400
Salespersons (one for each territory, with both receiving the same salary base)........	15,600
Employee benefits (20%)..	13,600
	$81,600

The salespersons receive a base salary plus a 4% commission on all items sold in their territory. Uncollectible accounts expense has averaged .4% of sales in the past. Travel and entertainment costs are incurred by the salespersons in calling upon their customers and are based on a fixed authorized amount. Freight out is a function of the quantity of goods shipped and the distance shipped. Thirty percent of the insurance is expended for protection of the inventory while it is in the regional warehouse, and the remainder is incurred for the protection of the warehouse. Supplies are used in the warehouse for packing the merchandise to be shipped. Wages (a variable cost) relate to the hourly employees who fill orders in the warehouse. The warehouse operating cost account contains such costs as heat, light, and maintenance.

The following cost analyses and statistics by territory for the current period are representative of past experience and of expected future operations:

	Green	Purple	Total
Sales..	$300,000	$600,000	$900,000
Cost of goods sold*................................	184,000	276,000	460,000
Advertising fees......................................	21,800	32,900	54,700
Travel and entertainment.........................	6,300	7,800	14,100
Freight out..	9,000	13,600	22,600
Units sold...	150,000	350,000	500,000
Pounds shipped**...................................	210,000	390,000	600,000
Sales travel (miles).................................	21,600	38,400	60,000

*Use to allocate inventory insurance to territories.
**Use to allocate supplies and wages and employee benefits to territories.

The executive management of Starnes Company wants the regional vice-presidents to present their operating data in a more meaningful manner. Therefore, management has requested that the regions separate their operating costs into the fixed and variable components of order-getting, order-filling, and administrative. The data are to be presented in the following format:

	Territory Cost		Regional	Total
	Green	Purple	Cost	Cost
Order-getting.......................				
Order-filling.........................				
Administrative.....................				

Required:

(1) Prepare a statement which presents the cost for the region by territory, with the costs separated into variable and fixed categories and using management's suggested format.

(2) Identify the data presented that are relevant to a decision (either for or against) to split the Purple Territory into two separate territories (Red and Blue), and specify other data needed to aid management in its decision.

(3) Explain the use of standards and flexible budgets for planning and controlling marketing costs, assuming that Starnes Company keeps its records in accordance with the classification required in (1). *(ICMA adapted)*

25-3. Income statements by products and amount-of-order classes. The feasibility of allocating marketing and administrative expenses to products or amount-of-order classes for managerial purposes has been considered by Brentwood Company. It is apparent that some costs can be assigned equitably to these classifications, while others cannot. The company's cost analyst proposed the following bases for apportionment:

Expense	Type of Analysis	
	By Products	By Amount of Order
Sales salaries...	Not allocated	Sales dollars times number of customers in class
Sales travel...	Not allocated	Number of customers in class
Sales office...	Not allocated	Number of customers in class
Sales commissions......................................	Direct	Direct
Credit management......................................	Volume of sales in dollars	Number of customers in class
Packing and shipping...................................	Weight times number of units	Weight times number of units
Warehousing..	Weight times number of units	Weight times number of units
Advertising..	Not allocated	Not allocated
Bookkeeping and billing...............................	Volume of sales in dollars	Number of orders
General marketing and administrative..............	Not allocated	Not allocated

From books, records, and other sources, the following data have been compiled:

Amount of Order	Number of Customers	Number of Orders	Cost of Goods Sold	Total Sales	Product Sales		
					X	Y	Z
Under $25	1,000	6,000	$ 59,000	$ 100,000	$ 35,000	$ 40,000	$ 25,000
$26-$100	250	4,000	177,000	300,000	105,000	120,000	75,000
$101-$200	100	4,000	354,000	600,000	210,000	240,000	150,000
Over $200	50	1,000	236,000	400,000	140,000	160,000	100,000
Total	1,400	15,000	$826,000	$1,400,000	$490,000	$560,000	$350,000

Other data:

Product	Weight	Cost of Goods Sold	Units Sold
X......................	1 kg	$252,000	98,000
Y......................	3 kg	294,000	70,000
Z......................	2 kg	280,000	175,000

Marketing and administrative expenses for the year:

Sales salaries..	$ 38,250
Sales travel..	28,000
Sales office (variable)...	15,400
Sales commissions (5%)..	70,000
Credit management...	14,000
Packing and shipping..	32,900
Warehousing..	16,450
Advertising..	150,000
Bookkeeping and billing..	42,000
General marketing and administrative....................................	90,000
Total...	$497,000

Required:

(1) Prepare a product income statement showing the allocation of marketing and administrative expenses to each product.

(2) Prepare an income statement showing the allocation of marketing and administrative expenses to each order class.

(For both requirements, round off all base computations to five decimal places and all allocated amounts to the nearest dollar.)

25-4. Cost allocations to individual stores; sales expansion decision. McNamara Foods Inc., a grocery chain consisting of three stores, operates in a state that permits each of its municipalities to levy an income tax on corporations operating within their respective city limits. This legislation establishes a uniform tax rate that may be levied by the municipality. Regulations also provide that the tax is to be computed on income derived within the taxing municipality after a reasonable and consistent allocation of general overhead expenses, which include warehouse, central office, advertising, and delivery expenses. General overhead expenses have not been allocated previously to McNamara's stores.

Each municipality in which McNamara operates a store has levied the corporate income tax as provided by state legislation, and management is considering two plans for allocating general overhead expenses to each store.

General overhead expenses for the year were as follows:

Delivery and warehousing expenses:		
Delivery expense..	$40,000	
Warehouse operations...	30,000	
Warehouse depreciation.......................................	20,000	$ 90,000
Central office expenses:		
Advertising...	18,000	
Central office salaries..	37,000	
Other central office expense..............................	28,000	83,000
Total general overhead expense.....................		$173,000

Additional information:

(a) One fifth of the warehouse space is used to house the central office, and depreciation of this space is included in the other central office expense. Warehouse operating expenses vary with the quantity of merchandise sold.

(b) All advertising is prepared by the central office and is distributed in the areas in which stores are located.

(c) As each store was opened, the fixed portion of central office salaries increased by $7,000, while other central office expense increased by $2,500. Basic fixed central office salaries were $10,000 and the basic fixed other central office expense was $12,000. The remainder of central office salaries and the remainder of other central office expense vary with sales.

(d) The delivery expense varies with the distance and the number of deliveries. The distances from the warehouse to each store and the number of deliveries made during the year were:

Store	Miles	Number of Deliveries
Ashville.....................	120	140
Burns........................	200	64
Clinton.....................	100	104

The year's operating results, before deducting general overhead expense and the tax for each store, were:

| | Store | | | |
	Ashville	Burns	Clinton	Total
Net sales..	$416,000	$353,600	$270,400	$1,040,000
Less cost of goods sold	215,700	183,300	140,200	539,200
Gross profit.....................................	$200,300	$170,300	$130,200	$ 500,800
Less other local operating expenses:				
Fixed..	$ 60,800	$ 48,750	$ 50,200	$ 159,750
Variable...	54,700	64,220	27,448	146,368
Total..	$115,500	$112,970	$ 77,648	$ 306,118
Operating income before general overhead and income tax...............	$ 84,800	$ 57,330	$ 52,552	$ 194,682

Required:

(1) Under each of the following allocation plans, compute the operating income for each store that woud be subject to the municipal tax levy on corporation income:

Plan 1: Allocate all general overhead expenses on the basis of sales volume.

Plan 2: First, allocate central office salaries and the other central office expense equally to warehouse operations and to each store.

Second, allocate the resulting warehouse operations expense, warehouse depreciation, and advertising to each store on the basis of sales volume.

Third, allocate delivery expense to each store on the basis of delivery miles multiplied by number of deliveries.

(2) Formulate a management decision to determine which store should be selected for expansion in order to maximize corporate profits. This expansion will increase McNamara's sales by $60,000 and its local fixed operating expense by $7,500, and it will require ten additional deliveries from the warehouse.

(AICPA adapted)

25-5. Final sales volume and sales mix variances using contribution margin. Orion Carpet Co. makes three grades of indoor-outdoor carpets. The sales volume for the annual budget is determined by estimating the total market volume for indoor-outdoor carpet and then applying the company's prior year's market share, adjusted for planned changes due to company programs for the coming year. The volume is apportioned between the three grades, based upon the prior year's product mix, again adjusted for planned changes due to company programs for the coming year.

The company's budgeted income statement and the results of operations for the current year are as follows:

Income Statement (Budgeted)
(in thousands of dollars)

	Grade 1	Grade 2	Grade 3	Total
Sales in units.......................................	1,000 rolls	1,000 rolls	2,000 rolls	4,000 rolls
Sales in dollars....................................	$1,000	$2,000	$3,000	$6,000
Variable expense..................................	700	1,600	2,300	4,600
Contribution margin.............................	$ 300	$ 400	$ 700	$1,400
Traceable fixed expense.....................	200	200	300	700
Traceable margin.................................	$ 100	$ 200	$ 400	$ 700
Marketing and administrative expenses..				250
Operating income.................................				$ 450

Income Statement (Actual)
(in thousands of dollars)

	Grade 1	Grade 2	Grade 3	Total
Sales in units....................................	800 rolls	1,000 rolls	2,100 rolls	3,900 rolls
Sales in dollars.................................	$810	$2,000	$3,000	$5,810
Variable expense..............................	560	1,610	2,320	4,490
Contribution margin...........................	250	$ 390	$ 680	$1,320
Traceable fixed expense....................	210	220	315	745
Traceable margin...............................	$ 40	$ 170	$ 365	$ 575
Marketing and administrative expenses...				275
Operating income..				$ 300

Industry volume was estimated at 40,000 rolls. Actual industry volume for the year was 38,000 rolls.

Required:

(1) Compute the final sales volume variance, using budgeted contribution margins.
(2) Explain the effect of the present condition of the carpet industry on the final sales volume variance.
(3) Compute the dollar impact on profits (using budgeted contribution margins) of the shift in product mix from the budgeted mix.   *(ICMA adapted)*

25-6. Gross profit analysis. Tribal Products Inc. was organized ten years ago by James Littlebear for the purpose of making and selling souvenirs to tourists in Southwestern Arizona. After much experimentation, the product line has been limited to five products: moccasins, strings of beads, rawhide vests, leather belts, and feathered headdresses. All transactions take place in two small buildings located on tribal land.

In 19B, despite an increase in the total number of units sold, the gross profit of the firm dropped. As a result, Littlebear tentatively blamed the drop in profit on a change in the sales mix.

The accountant has been given the task of analyzing the gross profit of the past two years, shown as follows, in an attempt to pin down the cause of the loss in profits.

				19A		
Product	Quantity	Unit Cost	Total Cost	Unit Price	Total Sales	Gross Profit
Moccasins.........................	1,000	$2.50	$ 2,500	$5.00	$ 5,000	$ 2,500
Beads..............................	6,000	.20	1,200	.50	3,000	1,800
Vests...............................	1,500	1.75	2,625	3.50	5,250	2,625
Belts................................	4,000	.45	1,800	1.00	4,000	2,200
Headdresses....................	500	4.00	2,000	7.50	3,750	1,750
Total.............................	13,000		$10,125		$21,000	$10,875

				19B		
Product	Quantity	Unit Cost	Total Cost	Unit Price	Total Sales	Gross Profit
Moccasins.........................	1,100	$2.60	$2,860	$5.00	$ 5,500	$ 2,640
Beads..............................	6,800	.20	1,360	.50	3,400	2,040
Vests...............................	1,200	1.80	2,160	3.50	4,200	2,040
Belts................................	4,200	.50	2,100	1.00	4,200	2,100
Headdresses....................	350	3.80	1,330	7.50	2,625	1,295
Total.............................	13,650		$9,810		$19,925	$10,115

Required: Prepare an analysis of the gross profit decline from 19A to 19B (Round off the 19A average gross profit per unit to four decimal places.)

25-7. Gross profit analysis. H. Pacer is the general manager for Ace Chemicals Division. The following is the division's gross profit data for November, in thousands of dollars:

	Actual	Budget
Sales..	$14,005	$12,600
Cost of goods sold.....................	11,323	9,850
Gross profit.................................	$ 2,682	$ 2,750

Pacer knew before receiving the statement that sales were above budget for the month and that the effect of recent price increases on most products would be realized this month. Upset upon finding that income results were below budget while sales were more than 10% above budget, Pacer asked the Accounting Department for an explanation. The Accounting Department looked at the detailed budget and found the following data:

Product	Sales in Pounds (000s omitted)	Sales Price per Pound	Cost of Goods Sold per Pound	Gross Profit (000s omitted)
1......................	2,000	$ .60	$ .60	—
2......................	5,000	.80	.65	$ 750
3......................	7,000	.20	.12	560
4......................	4,000	1.50	1.14	1,440
	18,000			$2,750

$2,750 ÷ 18,000 = $.1528 budgeted gross profit per pound

The following gross profit data pertain to November results:

Product	Sales in Pounds (000s omitted)	Sales Price per Pound	Sales in Dollars (000s omitted)	Cost of Goods Sold (000s omitted)	Gross Profit (000s omitted)
1..........	2,845	$ .735	$ 2,091	$ 1,692	$ 399
2..........	3,280	1.023	3,355	3,240	115
3..........	7,340	.195	1,431	991	440
4..........	4,320	1.650	7,128	5,400	1,728
	17,785		$14,005	$11,323	$2,682

Required: Compute the price and volume variances for sales and cost, and the sales mix and final sales volume variances.

(Based on a problem in *Management Accounting Campus Report*)

25-8. Gross profit analysis and the effect of product aggregation. Hampton Appliance Company markets irons for home use, classified as nonsteam and steam. For 19A, budgeted and actual sales, cost, and gross profit follow:

19A Budget:

Item	Units	Sales Per Unit	Sales Total	Cost Per Unit	Cost Total	Gross Profit Per Unit	Gross Profit Total
Nonsteam..........	4,000	$22.500	$ 90,000	$20.000	$ 80,000	$2.50	$10,000
Steam................	8,000	31.875	255,000	28.625	229,000	3.25	26,000
	12,000	28.75*	$345,000	25.75*	$309,000	3.00*	$36,000

*Weighted average

19A Actual:

Item	Units	Sales Per Unit	Sales Total	Cost Per Unit	Cost Total	Gross Profit Per Unit	Gross Profit Total
Nonsteam..........	4,000	$21.75	$ 87,000	$19.40	$ 77,600	$2.35	$ 9,400
Steam...............	10,000	32.50	325,000	29.10	291,000	3.40	34,000
	14,000	29.43*	$412,000	26.33*	$368,600	3.10*	$43,400

*Rounded weighted average

Each iron is of two types—noncoated and coated. The above data, further segmented into four categories, rather than two, follow:

19A Budget:

Item	Units	Sales Per Unit	Sales Total	Cost Per Unit	Cost Total	Gross Profit Per Unit	Gross Profit Total
Nonsteam-Noncoated..........	2,000	$20.00	$ 40,000	$18.00	$ 36,000	$2.00	$ 4,000
Nonsteam-Coated...............	2,000	25.00	50,000	22.00	44,000	3.00	6,000
Steam-Noncoated...............	5,000	30.00	150,000	27.20	136,000	2.80	14,000
Steam-Coated.....................	3,000	35.00	105,000	31.00	93,000	4.00	12,000
	12,000	28.75*	$345,000	25.75*	$309,000	3.00*	$36,000

*Weighted average

19A Actual:

Item	Units	Sales Per Unit	Sales Total	Cost Per Unit	Cost Total	Gross Profit Per Unit	Gross Profit Total
Nonsteam-Noncoated..........	2,600	$20.00	$ 52,000	$18.00	$ 46,800	$2.00	$ 5,200
Nonsteam-Coated...............	1,400	25.00	35,000	22.00	30,800	3.00	4,200
Steam-Noncoated...............	5,000	30.00	150,000	27.20	136,000	2.80	14,000
Steam-Coated.....................	5,000	35.00	175,000	31.00	155,000	4.00	20,000
	14,000	29.43*	$412,000	26.33*	$368,600	3.10*	$43,400

*Rounded weighted average

Required:

(1) Prepare a gross profit analysis of irons segmented into two categories: nonsteam and steam.
(2) Prepare a gross profit analysis of irons segmented into four categories: nonsteam—noncoated and coated, and steam—noncoated and coated.
(3) Explain the differences in the answers to (1) and (2).

(Based on an article in The Accounting Review)

CASES

A. Use of standard rates and selection of cost allocation bases. Cintron Company is a regional office supply chain with 26 independent stores. Each store has been responsible for its own credit and collections. The assistant manager in each store has been assigned the responsibility for credit activities, including the collection of delinquent accounts, because the stores do not need a full-time employee assigned to credit activities. The company has experienced a sharp rise in uncollectibles the last two years. Therefore, corporate management has decided to establish a Collections Department in the home office to be responsible for the collection function company-wide. The home office will hire the necessary full-time personnel. The size of this department will be based upon the historical credit activity of all of the stores.

The new centralized Collections Department was discussed at a recent management meeting. A method to assign the costs of the new department to the stores has been difficult to determine because this type of home office service is somewhat unique. Alternative methods are being reviewed by executive management. The controller favors using a standard rate for charging the costs to the stores. The standard rate would be based on budgeted costs. The vice-president of sales has a strong preference for an actual cost charging system.

In addition, the basis for the collection charges to the stores was discussed. The controller identified the following measures of services (allocation bases) which could be used:

(a) Total dollar sales.
(b) Average number of past-due accounts.
(c) Number of uncollectible accounts written off.
(d) One twenty-sixth of the cost to each of the stores.

The executive vice-president stated that he would like the Accounting Department to prepare a detailed analysis of the two charging methods and the four allocation bases.

Required:

(1) Evaluate the two methods identified— standard rate versus actual cost—in terms of:
  (a) Practicality and ease of use.
  (b) Cost control.
(2) For each allocation base, discuss whether or not it is appropriate to use in this situation, and identify possible behavioral problems. (ICMA adapted)

B. Marketing profitability analysis by products and by salespersons. Caprice Company manufactures and sells two products, a small portable office file cabinet that it has made for over 15 years and a home-travel file introduced in 19A. The files are made in Caprice's only manufacturing plant. Budgeted variable production costs per unit of product are as follows:

	Office File	Home-Travel File
Sheet metal	$ 3.50	—
Plastic	—	$3.75
Direct labor (@ $8 per DLH)	4.00	2.00
Variable factory overhead (@ $9 per DLH)	4.50	2.25
	$12.00	$8.00

Variable factory overhead costs vary with direct labor hours. The annual fixed factory overhead costs are budgeted at $120,000. A total of 50% of these costs are directly traceable to the Office File Department, and 22% are traceable to the Home-Travel File Department. The remaining 28% of the costs are not traceable to either department.

Caprice employs two full-time salespersons, Pam Price and Robert Flint. Each salesperson receives an annual salary of $14,000 plus a sales commission of 10% of his or her total gross sales. Travel and entertainment expense is budgeted at $22,000 annually for each salesperson. Price is expected to sell 60% of the budgeted unit sales for each file and Flint the remaining 40%. Caprice's remaining marketing and administrative expenses include fixed administrative costs of $40,000 that cannot be traced to either file, plus the following traceable marketing expenses:

	Office File	Home-Travel File
Packaging expenses per unit	$ 2.00	$ 1.50
Promotion	30,000	40,000

Data regarding Caprice's budgeted and actual sales for the fiscal year ended May 31, 19D, are presented in the following schedule. There were no changes in the beginning and ending balances of either finished goods or work in process inventories.

	Office File	Home-Travel File
Budgeted sales volume in units	15,000	15,000
Budgeted and actual unit sales price	$29.50	$19.50
Actual unit sales:		
Pam Price	10,000	9,500
Robert Flint	5,000	10,500
Total units	15,000	20,000

Data regarding Caprice's operating expenses for the year ended May 31, 19D, are as follows:

(a) There were no increases or decreases in raw materials inventory for either sheet metal or plastic, and there were no usage variances. However, sheet metal prices were 6% above budget and plastic prices were 4% below budget.

(b) The actual direct labor hours worked and costs incurred were as follows:

	Hours	Amount
Office file	7,500	$ 57,000
Home-travel file	6,000	45,600
	13,500	$102,600

(c) Fixed factory overhead costs attributable to the Office File Department were $8,000 above the budget. All other fixed factory overhead costs were incurred at the same amounts as budgeted, and variable factory overhead costs were incurred at the budgeted hourly rates, except for a $9,000 unfavorable variance in the Home-Travel File Department.

(d) All marketing and administrative expenses were incurred at budgeted rates or amounts, except the following items:

Nontraceable administrative expenses..		$ 34,000
Promotion:		
Office files	$32,000	
Home-travel files	58,000	90,000
Travel and entertainment:		
Pam Price	$24,000	
Robert Flint	28,000	52,000
		$176,000

Required:

(1) Prepare a segmented income statement of Caprice Company's actual opera-tions for the fiscal year ended May 31, 19D. The report should be prepared in a contribution margin format by product and should reflect total operating income (loss) for the company.

(2) Identify and discuss any additional analyses that could be made from the data presented that would be of value to Caprice Company.

(3) Prepare a performance report for the year ended May 31, 19D, that would be useful in evaluating the performance of Robert Flint. Include variable manufacturing costs at budgeted rates and compute Flint's contribution margin as well as his contribution net of traceable fixed costs. The only fixed costs traceable to individual salespersons are travel and entertainment and salary.

(4) Discuss the effects of Robert Flint's sales mix on Caprice Company's:
   (a) Manufacturing operations.
   (b) Profits.   (ICMA adapted)

C. Sales force motivation and performance. XYZ Recreational Products Company, in an attempt to increase its sales and profits, has decided to change from a straight salary system to a commission-plus-bonus arrangement for compensating its salespersons. XYZ Company manufactures and sells a line of fiberglass canoes and water skis. The company's sales are highly seasonal, with more than 75% of its business occurring between May and September.

The compensation plan under consideration calls for the salespersons to receive monthly a 10% commission on all sales that exceed the monthly sales quotas. If sales do not exceed the monthly quota, the salespersons will receive a 5% commission on the amount sold. The commission would be earned in two installments, one half in the month the order is shipped and one half in the month the customer pays for the product. Sales personnel can earn an additional 2% bonus on all their sales for the year if the quota is attained each month for a 12-month period.

At the beginning of each year, the yearly sales quota for each salesperson is determined by joint agreement between the salesperson and his or her supervisor. The monthly sales quota for each territory is then determined by dividing the annual sales quota by 12.

Required:

(1) List aspects of the new compensation plan that are likely to have a positive effect on employee motivation and performance.
(2) List aspects of the new compensation plan that are likely to have a negative effect on employee motivation and performance. (CIA adapted)

D. Compensation program for salespersons. Betterview Corporation manufactures a full line of windows and doors, including casement windows, bow windows, and patio doors. The bow windows and patio doors have a significantly higher profit margin per unit than casement windows, as shown in the following schedule:

	Casement Windows	Bow Windows	Patio Doors
Sales price	$130	$250	$260
Manufacturing costs:			
Direct materials	$ 25	$ 40	$ 50
Direct labor	20	35	30
Variable overhead	16	28	24
Fixed overhead	24	42	36
Total manufacturing cost	$ 85	$145	$140
Gross profit	$ 45	$105	$120

The company sells almost entirely to general contractors of residential housing. Most of these contractors complete and sell 15 to 50 houses per year. Each contractor builds tract houses that are similar, with some variations in exteriors and rooflines.

When contractors contact Betterview, they are likely to seek bids for all the windows in the houses they plan to build in the next year. At this point, the Betterview salespersons have an opportunity to infuence the window configuration of these houses by suggesting patio doors or bow windows as variations for one or more casement windows for each of the several exteriors and rooflines built by the contractor.

The bow windows and patio doors are approximately twice as wide as the casement windows. A bow window or a patio door usually is substituted for two casement windows. Casement windows are usually ordered in pairs and placed side-by-side in those houses which could be modified to accept bow windows and patio doors.

Joseph Hite, president of Betterview Corporation, is perplexed with the company's profit performance. In a conversation with his sales manager, he declared, "Our total dollar sales volume is growing, but our net income has not increased as it should. Our unit sales of casement windows have increased proportionately more than the sale of bow windows or patio doors. Why aren't our sales representatives pushing our more profitable products?" The sales manager responded with a sense of frustration, "I don't know what else can be done. They have been told which type of windows we want sold, due to the greater profit margin. Furthermore, they have the best compensation plan in the industry, with a $1,000 base monthly salary and commissions of 5% on sales dollars."

Required:

(1) Identify the needs of the salespersons that are being met by the current compensation program.
(2) Explain why Betterview's present compensation program for its salespersons does not support the president's objectives to sell the more profitable units.
(3) Specify alternative compensation programs which may be more appropriate for motivating the salespersons to sell the more profitable units.
(ICMA adapted)

E. Sales compensation plans. Pre-Fab Housing Corporation, a relatively large company in the manufactured housing industry, is known for its aggressive sales promotion campaigns. Pre-Fab's innovative advertising and sales strategies have resulted in generally satisfactory performance in the last few years.

One of Pre-Fab's objectives is to increase sales revenue by at least 10% annually. This objective has been attained. Return on investment is considered good and has increased annually until last year, when net income decreased for the first time in nine years. The latest economic recession could be the cause of the change, but other factors such as sales growth discount this reason.

A significant portion of Pre-Fab's administrative expenses are fixed, but the majority of the manufacturing expenses are variable in nature. The increases in sales prices have been consistent with the 12% increase in manufacturing expenses. Pre-Fab has consistently been able to maintain a companywide manufacturing contribution margin of approximately 40%. However, the manufacturing contribution margin on individual product lines varies from 25 to 55%.

Sales commission expenses increased 30% over the past year. The prefabricated housing industry has always been sales-oriented, and Pre-Fab's management has believed in generously rewarding the efforts of its sales personnel. The sales force compensation plan consists of three segments:

(a) A guaranteed annual salary, which is increased annually at about a 6% rate. The salary is below industry average.
(b) A sales commission of 9% of total sales dollars. This is higher than the industry average.
(c) A year-end bonus of 5% of total sales dollars to each salesperson when their total sales dollars exceed the prior year by at least 12%.

The current compensation plan has resulted in an average annual income of $42,500 per sales employee, compared with an industry annual average of $30,000. However, the compensation plan has been effective in generating increased sales. Further, the Sales Department employees are satisfied with the plan. Management, however, is concerned about the financial implications of the current plan. Management believes that the plan has caused higher selling expenses and a lower net income relative to the sales revenue increase.

At a recent staff meeting, the controller suggested that the sales compensation plan be modified so that sales employees could earn an annual average income of $37,500. The controller believes that such a plan would still be attractive to its sales personnel and, at the same time, allow the company to earn a more satisfactory profit.

The vice-president for sales voiced strong objection to altering the current compensation plan because employee morale and incentive would drop significantly if there were any change. Nevertheless, most of the staff believes that the area of sales compensation merits a review. The president stated that all phases of a company operation can benefit from a periodic review, no matter how successful they have been in the past.

Several compensation plans known to be used by other companies in the manufactured housing industry are:

(a) Straight commission as a percentage of sales.
(b) Straight salary.
(c) Salary plus compensation based on sales to new customers.
(d) Salary plus compensation based on manufacturing contribution margin.

Required:

(1) Discuss the advantages and disadvantages of Pre-Fab's current sales compensation plan with respect to:
   (a) The financial aspects of the company.
   (b) The behavioral aspects of the sales personnel.
(2) For each of the listed alternative compensation plans, discuss whether or not the plan would be an improvement over the current plan in terms of the financial performance of the company and the behavioral implications for the sales personnel. (ICMA adapted)

F. Gross profit variances. Handy Home Products Company distributes two home-use power tools to hardware stores, a heavy duty ½" hand drill and a table saw. The tools are purchased from a manufacturer that attaches the Handy Home Products label on the tools. The wholesale selling prices to the hardware stores are $60 each for the drill and $120 each for the table saw.

The budget for the current year and the actual results are presented as follows. The budget was adopted late in the preceding year and was based on Handy Home Products' estimated share of the market for the two tools.

Handy Home Products Company
Income Statement
For the Year Ended December 31, 19—
(000s omitted)

	Hand Drill		Table Saw		Total		
	Budget	Actual	Budget	Actual	Budget	Actual	Variance
Sales in units................................	120	86	80	74	200	160	40
Revenue...	$7,200	$5,074	$9,600	$8,510	$16,800	$13,584	$3,216 unfav.
Cost of goods sold......................	6,000	4,300	6,400	6,068	12,400	10,368	2,032 fav.
Gross profit..................................	$1,200	$ 774	$3,200	$2,442	$ 4,400	$ 3,216	$1,184 unfav.
Unallocated costs:							
Selling.......................................					$ 1,000	$ 1,000	$ 0
Advertising................................					1,000	1,060	60 unfav.
Administration...........................					400	406	6 unfav.
Income taxes (45%).................					900	338	562 fav.
Total..					$ 3,300	$ 2,804	$ 496 fav.
Net income....................................					$ 1,100	$ 412	$ 688 unfav.

During the first quarter of the current year, Handy Home Products' industry projections indicated that the total market for these tools would actually be 10 percent below original management estimates. In an attempt to prevent unit sales from declining as much as industry projections, management developed and implemented a marketing program. Included in the program were dealer discounts and increased direct advertising. The table saw line was emphasized in this program.

Required:

(1) Analyze the unfavorable gross profit variance of $1,184,000 in terms of sales price variance, cost price variance, sales mix variance, and final sales volume variance.

(2) Discuss the apparent effect of the special marketing program (i.e., dealer discounts and additional advertising) on actual operating results. Provide supporting numerical data where appropriate.   *(ICMA adapted)*

CHAPTER 26

Profit Performance Measurements; Intracompany Transfer Pricing; Product Pricing Methods

The establishment of a profit goal based on marketing and manufacturing plans expressed as budgets and standards, the delegation of authority and the assignment of responsibility to middle and lower management levels, and finally the creation of decentralized, autonomous divisions of a company lead to the need for measuring the operating and profit performance of top as well as subordinate executives. This chapter discusses the return-on-capital-employed concept, a measure used by management in appraising company-wide as well as divisional operating performance, and intracompany transfer pricing, which plays a significant role in measuring divisional results. The chapter also deals with different methods by which management can establish the product prices needed to cover costs and return a profit.

▼ THE RATE OF RETURN ON CAPITAL EMPLOYED

The term "return on capital employed" used here refers to an internal measure of operating management. The term "return on investment" is sometimes used to refer to this notion, but such usage may be confusing because the term also refers to the average annual return on investment method (discussed in Chapter 23), which is a capital expenditure evaluation technique, and to a return or yield on equity capital, which is primarily an investor's guide. The return on equity capital also has some value as an internal measure, but for financial, not operating, management.

The rate of return on capital employed may be expressed as the product of two factors: the percentage of profit to sales and the capital-employed turnover rate. In equation form, the rate of return is developed as follows:

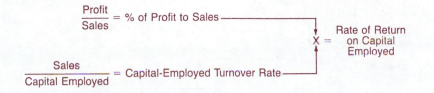

Notice that sales cancels out in the two fractions to yield the rate of return on capital employed measure. Although the final measure can be computed directly by dividing profit by capital employed, an evaluation of the full formula that includes profit on sales and turnover of capital employed gives management a better comprehension of the elements leading to the final result. The profit percentage reflects a cost-price relationship affected by the level and mix of sales, the price of products sold, and the success or lack of success in maintaining satisfactory control of costs. The turnover rate reflects the rapidity with which committed assets are employed in the operations.

Because the rate of return on capital employed is the product of two factors, numerous combinations can lead to the same result, illustrated as follows for a 20 percent rate of return:

Percentage of Profit to Sales	Capital-Employed Turnover Rate	Rate of Return on Capital Employed
10%	2.000	20%
8	2.500	20
6	3.333	20
4	5.000	20
2	10.000	20

There is no single rate of return on capital employed that is satisfactory for all companies. Manufacturing companies in various industries will have different rates, as will utilities, banking institutions, merchandising firms, and service companies. Management can establish an objective rate by using judgment and experience supported by comparisons with other companies. Every industry has companies with high, medium, and low rates of return. Structure and size of the firm influence the rate considerably. A company with diversified divisions might have only a fair return rate when all of them are pooled in the analysis. In such cases, it seems advisable to establish separate objectives for each division as well as for the total company. Methods for divisional analyses are discussed in a later section of this chapter.

The Formula's Underlying Data

None of the factors or elements that produce the final rate can be disregarded, minimized, or overemphasized without impairing the quality of managerial decisions. Complete details of the relationships of the capital-employed ratio to the underlying ratios—percentage of profit to sales and capital-employed turnover rate—are portrayed in the following chart:

Relationship of
Factors Influencing
Rate of Return on
Capital Employed

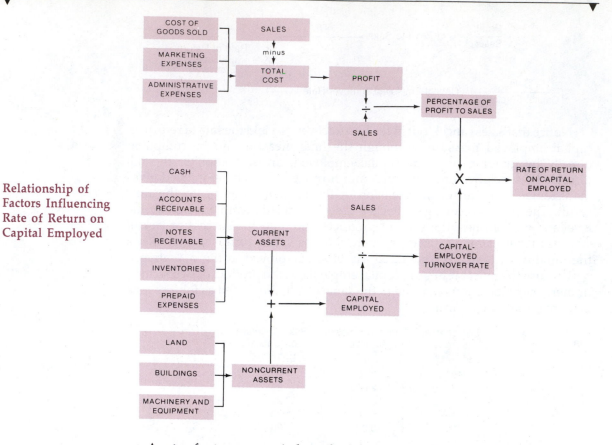

A rate of return on capital employed is computed by using figures from the balance sheet and income statement. Probability estimates can also be incorporated as a part of the computation.[1] The sales figure commonly used is net sales—gross sales less sales returns, allowances, and discounts. No general agreement exists with respect to the profit and capital-employed figures used in computing the rate. Consistency and uniformity are primary requisites, however, since the return on capital employed generally deals with a complexity of operations and/or a great diversity of divisions. Under such circumstances, it seems wise to avoid additional complexity and to seek clarity in the presentation of operating results without sacrifice of substance.

The income statement generally reports several profits, such as (1) operating income, which includes cost of goods sold and marketing and administrative expenses but excludes nonoperating income and expenses; (2) income before income tax, which would include the nonoperating income and expense items, and (3) the net income, which is the amount that is transferred to retained earnings. Using operating income means that only transactions of an operating nature should be considered. This profit figure is preferred for divisional analyses, since nonoperating items are usually the responsibility of

[1] William L. Ferrara, "Probabilistic Approaches to Return on Investment and Residual Income," *The Accounting Review*, Vol. LII, No. 3, pp. 597-604.

the entire company. The use of income before or after income tax is significant when judging the enterprise as a whole. Net income is more defensible because tax money is not available to management, and managerial efficiency should be judged only by the ultimate result. If capital employed is restated to give recogition to inflation accounting, as discussed later in this chapter, then comparability calls for a similar restatement of the effect of inflation accounting on profit.

Capital employed refers to total assets or the sum of current assets and noncurrent assets. In describing capital employed, the word "investment" is intentionally avoided because it is used in connection with capital investment (noncurrent assets) and owner's investment (net worth or equity capital), and its meaning would be confusing.

Many accountants suggest that the amount of capital employed should be averaged over the fiscal period, if possible. Such a procedure tends to equalize unusually high or low year-end asset values or seasonal influences, particularly in divisional comparisons. Also, the sources of funds are not considered in determining the amount of capital employed. Therefore, current and long-term liabilities, which provided the money used in the purchase of assets, are not deducted from the assets. However, some accountants believe that current liabilities should be deducted from current assets to obtain a working capital figure to be used in place of the current assets figure.

Current Assets. The three most significant items classified as current assets are cash, receivables, and inventories. Problems of valuation are connected with each of these assets.

Cash. Ordinarily, the cash shown on the balance sheet is the amount required for total business operations. Cash funds set aside for pensions, taxes, or future expansion or development programs should be excluded. However, some companies believe that if such items are treated uniformly in relation to total cash or assets, no change of the cash balance sheet figure is warranted. On the other hand, certain managers do not accept the stated cash figure but consider a predetermined percentage based on the cost of goods sold or the annual operating expenses.

Receivables. Values used for receivables should be either the gross amount or the net amount after deducting the allowance for doubtful accounts. The procedure should be uniform for all receivables allowances.

Inventories. Different inventory costing methods, such as fifo, average, or lifo, give rise to some balance sheet and income statement differences. When return ratios of companies in the same industry are compared, an allowance for such differences should be made. Again, if an allowance account is used for lower of cost or market adjustments, the question arises as to whether the inventory figure used should be net of the allowance. Here, too, uniformity plays a significant role.

Some companies' inventories are costed on a standard cost or direct costing basis. Use of these two bases will, as in the case of lifo, generally depress inventory values on a company's balance sheet. For internal comparison, however, the use of either method on a uniform basis should not influence results. The same reasoning applies to other deviations from normal procedures.

Noncurrent Assets. In dealing with noncurrent assets, three possible valuation methods have been favored: (1) original cost (original book value), (2) depreciated cost (original cost less the depreciation allowance, i.e., net book value), and (3) inflation accounting.

Original Cost. Those accountants favoring the original cost basis argue that:

1. Assets of manufacturing companies, unlike those of mining companies, are on a continuing rather than on a depleted and abandoned basis.
2. Gross assets of one plant can be compared better with those of another plant, where depreciation practices or the age of the assets may be different.
3. Accumulated depreciation should not be deducted from the gross asset value of property, since it represents retention of the funds required to keep the stockholders' original investment intact. Actually, noncurrent assets are used to produce a profit during their entire life. Therefore, full cost is considered an investment until the assets are retired from use.

Depreciated Cost. Those accountants who favor the use of the depreciated cost for noncurrent assets state that:

1. While noncurrent assets are conventionally understated at the present time, the wrong method of increasing the original cost cannot be relied on to furnish the correct results. The attempt can only add to the existing confusion in accounting thinking.
2. An investment is something separate and distinct from the media through which it is made. The purchase price of a machine should be regarded as the prepaid cost for the number of years of production expected. Each year this number will decline. The function of depreciation accounting is to maintain the aggregate capital by currently providing substitute assets to replace the aggregate asset consumption (depreciation) of the year.

The several acceptable depreciation methods, such as straight-line or the various accelerated methods, result in the balance sheet and income statement differences. When return ratios of companies in the same industry are compared, such differences should be considered.

Inflation Accounting. Those accountants who maintain that noncurrent assets should be included at current cost or at historical cost adjusted to constant dollars argue that such values are more realistic. They believe that a company receiving a certain and apparently satisfactory return based on book values should recognize the situation as being out-of-step with actual conditions. They further assert that some equalization of facility values of different divisions or companies should be provided, especially between those with old plants that were built at relatively low cost and those with new plants that were built at high cost. This method, of course, poses the serious problem of finding proper values.

Closely allied to any discussion of appropriate noncurrent asset values in an inflation accounting context are considerations as to the effect on profits, sales, and capital employed. Sales, costs currently incurred, and current assets might be measured in current dollar values, while the noncurrent assets and their expired cost might lag years behind. When the noncurrent asset effects are translated into current costs or constant dollars, the rate of return on capital employed is more realistic.

Divisional Rates of Return

The determination of divisional (segment) return on capital is a matter of relating performance to assets placed at the disposal of divisional management.[2] This involves certain allocation difficulties. Some analysts believe that only a segment's sales, costs, and capital employed should be included in calculating a divisional rate of return, because only these figures are under the control of the divisional manager. Others argue that if certain expenses or capital employed are not allocated, the segments will show a higher return in the aggregate than that of the company. Such a result might create a psychological dilemma which would make it difficult to obtain additional effort from the unit supervisory staff that shows a higher or better return than the company average. Consequently, the calculation of a rate of return based on sales, costs, and capital employed specific to the segment is often followed by a rate of return calculation that includes a full allocation of total company sales, costs, and capital employed, so that both rates of return are clearly presented.

Sales figures usually can be identified directly with specific divisions. The allocation of costs, however, involves the same rationale as the allocation of overhead; i.e., direct departmental expenses are charged to the departments, followed by allocations of general and service department expenses.

The allocation of capital employed that is not directly identified with segments might be achieved as follows:

Cash might be allocated to segments on the basis of (1) gross sales billed, (2) cost of goods sold, (3) a ratio to total product cost, (4) a standard percentage of sales or cost of goods sold, or (5) manufacturing cost less any noncash items.

Accounts Receivable might be allocated to segments or products based on gross sales billed, or allocated on the basis of gross sales for the average number of days reflected in the receivables.

Materials might be allocated on the basis of (1) materials consumed, (2) annual consumption figures, or (3) a ratio to actual or normal usage or standard direct materials cost.

Finished Goods would be directly assigned.

Noncurrent Assets might be allocated on the basis of use of facilities at either normal, standard, or actual volume.

---

[2] Although this discussion refers to divisions as segments, the rate of return on capital employed may be computed for other segments, such as products, following the procedures described for divisions.

Divisional return-on-capital-employed measures have been criticized as a motivational tool because a division may seek to maximize relative profits rather than absolute profits. Assume that a division which is presently earning 30 percent on capital employed is considering a project whose return would be only 25 percent. The divisional management might decline the project because the return on total divisional capital would decrease. Yet, if the acceptance of the project would make the best use of these divisional resources from a total company point of view, then even with a lower rate of return for the segment or for the total company, the project should be accepted.

This suboptimum behavior might be overcome by calculating a *residual income figure*—a division's income less an amount representing the company's cost of capital employed by the division. This additional calculation would emphasize marginal profit dollars above the cost of capital, rather than the rate of return on capital employed.

Residual income is a counterpart to the return-on-capital-employed computation and is a dollar measure of profitability. The concept is analogous to the net present value obtained when discounting cash flows (Chapter 23). A positive residual income indicates earnings in excess of the desired return, while a negative residual income indicates earnings less than the desired return.[3]

Using the Rate of Return on Capital Employed

The return on capital employed is a measure of profitability for the total company as well as for divisions and individual plants and products. While a company's total analysis and comparison with the industry's ratios are significant for executive management, the real purpose of the return-on-capital-employed ratio is for internal profit measurement and control, with trends more meaningful than single ratios. It is not a guide for shareholders or investors who measure profitability or earning power by relating profit to equity capital.

Executive management of many companies has shown a growing acceptance of the rate-of-return-on-capital-employed concept as a tool in planning, in establishing sales prices, and in measuring operational profitability. Return-on-capital-employed information is useful to executives, plant managers, plant engineers, and salespersons. It provides executives with a brief yet comprehensive picture of overall operations, of operations in each division, and of operations for plants and products. The plant manager receives a statement which measures the plant's operating results in a single figure. The product engineer's responsibility is to create products which can be manufactured at minimum cost and sold in profitable quantities without abnormal increases in asset investment. The sales staff realizes that price changes, justified as they may seem, are effective only if they contain a profit increment which yields an adequate return.

---

[3] *Ibid.*, p. 599.

The return on capital employed not only acts as a measurement of the cooperative efforts of a company's segments but also shows the extent to which profitable coordination exists. A company's interlocking efforts are most effectively demonstrated by this rate. An appreciation of this concept by all employees will build an organization interested in achieving fair profits and an adequate rate of return.

Budgeting is the principal planning and control technique employed by most companies. Among the multiple phases of budgeting, sales estimating is still considered the most difficult profit-planning task. Assuming that an acceptable sales budget has been established and that production, manufacturing, and commercial expense budgets have been prepared, return-on-capital-employed ratios are useful in evaluating the entire planning procedure.

Management's objectives with respect to the long-range return, as well as the immediate returns for each division, plant, or product, influence and guide budget-building procedures. As sales, costs, and assets employed are placed in the perspective of the rate of return on capital employed as envisioned by management, there is a marked change in the attitude of the people responsible for assembling the figures. Segment budgets are compared with predetermined goals. If too low, examination and revision can perhaps achieve the desired result. If an unusually excellent return is calculated, the reasons for it can be investigated. Management can either accept the situation as is or decide on a temporary modification of its planning goal. At any rate, the return on capital employed offers a satisfactory foundation for the construction of both annual and long-range planning budgets. When considering long-range plans regarding addition of new products, dropping of old products, expansion of production facilities, or investing additional capital in research and development, application of the return on capital employed on any future projects has a sobering effect if these projects have been conceived haphazardly or overoptimistically.

A successful technique in planning for profit improvement is to (1) define quantitatively (for sales, profits, and capital employed) the gap which exists between performance at present and that represented by long-term objectives, (2) fix the problems precisely by examining the details of each factor, (3) formulate a specific scheduled program of action for each factor, and (4) translate the planned results of each program in terms of its effect upon income and asset accounts. The application of this technique is shown in the table on page 860:

Advantages of the Use of the Return on Capital Employed. In general, the advantages of the use of the rate of return on capital employed are its tendency to:

1. Focus management's attention upon earning the best profit possible on the capital (total assets) available.
2. Serve as a yardstick in measuring management's efficiency and effectiveness for the company as a whole and its divisions.
3. Tie together the many phases of financial planning, sales objectives, cost control, and the profit goal.

EFFECT OF PLANNED PROGRAMS FOR PROFIT IMPROVEMENT

	Present		Change by Volume	Change by Cost Reduction	Asset Curtailment	Future	
Assets:							
Inventory	$ 500,000				−$100,000	$ 400,000	
Other current assets	200,000		+$ 20,000			220,000	
Noncurrent assets	300,000			+$80,000		380,000	
Total assets	$1,000,000		+$ 20,000	+$80,000	−$100,000	$1,000,000	
Profit:							
Sales billed	$1,000,000	100.0%	+$200,000			$1,200,000	100.0%
Manufacturing cost	$ 770,000	77.0%	+$140,000	−$88,000		$ 822,000	68.5%
Marketing and administrative							
expenses	130,000	13.0	+ 10,000	− 2,000		138,000	11.5
Total cost and expense	$ 900,000	90.0%	$150,000			$ 960,000	80.0%
Operating profit	$ 100,000	10.0%	+$ 50,000	+$90,000		$ 240,000	20.0%
Return on capital employed:							
% of profit to sales		10.0%					20.0%
Capital-employed							
turnover rate (times)		1.0					1.2
Return on capital employed (%)		10.0%					24.0%

4. Afford comparison of managerial results, both internally and externally.

5. Develop a keener sense of responsibility and team effort in divisional managers by enabling them to measure and evaluate their own activities in the light of the results achieved by other managers.

6. Aid in detecting weakness with respect to the use or nonuse of individual assets, particularly in connection with inventories.

Limitations of the Use of the Return on Capital Employed. The use of the return-on-capital-employed ratio may be subject to some of the following limitations:

1. It may not be reasonable to expect the same return on capital employed from each division if the divisions sell their respective products in markets that differ widely with respect to product development, competition, and consumer demand. Lack of agreement on the optimum rate of return might discourage managers who believe the rate is set at an unfair level.

2. Proper allocation requires certain data regarding sales, costs, and assets. The accounting and cost system might not give such needed details.

3. Valuations of assets of different vintages in different divisions might give rise to comparison difficulties and misunderstandings.

4. For the sake of making the current period rate of return on capital employed "look good," managers may be influenced to make decisions

that are not the best for the long-run interests of the firm. This problem is especially likely if managers are presumed to be in positions for only a short time before being reassigned, thus personally avoiding responsibility for long-run consequences.

5. A single measure of performance, such as return on capital employed, may result in a fixation on improving the components of the one measure to the neglect of needed attention to other desirable activities. Product research and development, managerial development, progressive personnel policies, good employee morale, and good customer and public relations are just as important in earning a greater profit and assuring continuous growth.

Multiple Performance Measurements. Many well-managed companies use multiple performance measurements in order to overcome limitations of a single measure. Multiple performance measures provide central management with a more comprehensive picture of divisional performance by considering a wider range of management responsibilities. The implementation of an evaluation and reward structure that includes multiple performance measures provides an incentive to divisional managers to engage in desirable activities, such as research and development, employee development, and improvement of market position, as well as to seek profitability. In turn, such measures will mitigate the problem of trying to evaluate divisional performance on the basis of a single profit measure that may be computed on different bases in each division, and they will provide managers with long-run as well as short-run incentives.

A multiple performance measurement system may be difficult to implement and administer. Since measurement criteria are not all equally quantifiable, it may be difficult to compare the overall performance of one division with another. It may be difficult for central management to apply the multiple, nonquantifiable criteria on a consistent basis between periods and among divisions. Uncertainty about the weight being placed on the various measures may result in confusion for divisional managers, which in turn may result in diffusion of effort and instability in divisional performance. One company that uses multiple measurements for rating divisional performance describes its method as a quantification of progress against agreed-upon standards. Each year, common standards are adopted by agreement of divisional managers and corporate management. Points are assigned to standards, reflecting those areas which require special attention in each division, as determined by management. Performance is measured as follows:

1. Profits for the current year are compared with the profits for the preceding year in absolute dollars, margins, and return on capital employed.
2. Profits are compared with the budget.
3. Cash and capital management measures are employed. Here, the emphasis is on effective management of inventory and receivables.

The claimed advantages of this method are that:

1. Performances of division managers are measured more fairly than would result from using solely a return-on-capital-employed figure.
2. Management can readily see those divisions which are performing well and those which are not.
3. Lost points serve as "red flags" by directing management to areas requiring attention and to the reasons and the corrective actions taken or needed.
4. The system has flexibility as to timely, needed shifting of management emphasis.

In this company, management concludes that it is not enough to tabulate performance statistics. The results must be effectively communicated, corrective action taken, and good performance rewarded. The system must also have the interest and support of division and corporate management.[4] On a more gobal basis, performance measurements and related compensation plans should (1) reward performance over extended time periods; (2) tie incentive plans to achieving strategic (not financial) goals, such as target market share, productivity levels, product quality and product development measures, and personnel development measures; and (3) evaluate operating profits before gains from financial transactions, before deductions for approved expenditures on research and development, quality improvements, and preventive maintenance, and before deductions for the incremental amount of accelerated depreciation.[5]

Graphs as Operating Guides. Sound planning and successful operation must point toward the optimum combination of profits, sales, and capital employed. As stated earlier, the combination will necessarily vary, depending upon the characteristics of the operation. An industry with products tailor-made to customers' specifications will not have the same profit margins and turnover ratios as industries that mass produce highly competitive consumer goods.

In multiproduct companies, the three basic factors cannot be uniform, due to different types of operations. However, a special type of graph can be of assistance in judging the performance of segments or products in their relationship to a desired overall return on capital employed. Such a graph has the advantage of flexibility in appraising profit performance and offers an approach by which performance can be analyzed for improvement.

The following graph shows possible combinations of percentage of profit to sales and capital-employed turnover rate which yield a 20 percent return. When individual divisions or products are plotted on the graph, the segment's data might appear to the left or right of the basic curve. If on the left, the unit has a capital-employed-return performance below that expected for the company as a whole. A segment whose ratios appear to the right of the basic curve has a return in excess of that expected for the entire company. The same interpretation applies when the company's total return is plotted.

[4] Frank J. Tanzola, "Performance Rating for Divisional Control," *Financial Executive*, Vol. XLIII, No. 3, pp. 20-24.
[5] Alfred Rappaport, "Executive Incentives vs. Corporate Growth," *Harvard Business Review*, Vol. 56, No. 4, pp. 85-86.

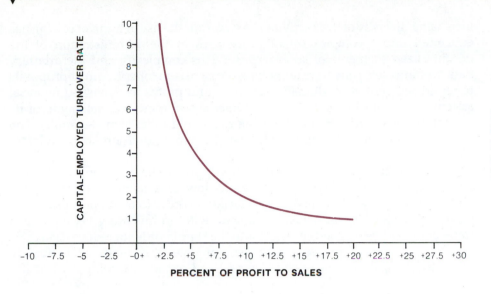

Relationship Between Percent of Profit to Sales and Capital-Employed Turnover Rate

▼ INTRACOMPANY TRANSFER PRICING

The effectiveness of the return on capital employed as a device for measuring the performance of divisional segments of a company depends considerably on the accuracy of allocating the costs and assets associated with the segment. In a decentralized multiplant or multiproduct organization, the unit managers are expected to run portions of the enterprise as a semiautonomous business. Thus, a shift to the return-on-capital-employed concept for measuring operational performance requires some rather fundamental policy changes.

As long as a segment is not entirely independent and separable, goods and services are generally transferred from one unit to another, a situation common to integrated corporations. The finished or semifinished product of one or more divisions or subsidiaries frequently becomes the raw material of one or more other divisions. In addition, some service functions are centralized and might conceivably deal with a number of profit centers. When transfers of goods or services are made, a portion of the revenue of one segment becomes a portion of cost of another, and the price at which transfers are made influences the earnings reported by each profit center. The value of these earnings as a measure of performance depends not only upon the manager's executive abilities but also upon the transfer prices used. The transfer pricing system used can distort any reported profit and make profit a poor guide for evaluating divisional performance. In the end, the cost or price used for the transfer will be used in the calculation of the return on capital employed, due to the very nature of the formula.

Years ago, transfer pricing played only a minor role in cost control. Today, many businesses have become large due to merger, acquisition, or internal growth and have turned to decentralization as a way of managing the increasing diversity of their activities. As a result, the use of transfer pricing has expanded into a complex set of procedures in the administration of the decentralized segments of an enterprise. This complexity and the arbitrary nature of intracompany transfer pricing is one reason for criticism of proposals to report segment or product-line revenues and profits in published financial statements. A steel company may operate a coal mine and sell some of its output on the open market but use the remainder in its own steel mills. The coal's transfer price can control whether the mining division shows a large, small, or zero profit.

External factors may influence the transfer price determination. A company with an overseas plant, where tax rates are low, may keep the transfer price high for materials sent to the domestic facility in order to retain profits abroad. Or a company with warehouses in a state with an inventory tax may keep transfer prices low on goods brought into the state in order to reduce its tax bill.

The existence of multiple management objectives makes it extremely difficult for a company to establish logical and sound intracompany transfer prices. A pricing method can be chosen only after the primary purposes for the use of the information from transfers have been identified. Therefore, a transfer pricing system must satisfy these three fundamental criteria: (a) allow central management to judge as accurately as possible the performance of the divisional profit center in terms of its separate contribution to the total corporate profit, (2) motivate the divisional manager to pursue the division's own profit goal in a manner conducive to the success of the company as a whole, and (3) stimulate the manager's efficiency without losing the division's autonomy as a profit center.[6] The system should also be easy to apply, meet legal and external reporting requirements, and permit each unit of a company to earn a profit commensurate with the functions it performs. As a practical matter, these criteria may be difficult to satisfy, because behavioral considerations are of paramount importance. Accordingly, a transfer price should be a just price to both the selling and buying parties. An advantage gained by one will be a disadvantage to the other and, in the end, may be detrimental to the corporate profit goal.

A profit center manager's interest must remain congruent with the firm's interest. For example, assume that Division X offers its Product A to Division Y at a transfer price of $14, which includes a $2 profit, a $9 variable cost, and a $3 fixed cost that presumably will remain unchanged in total as activity fluctuates. The same product is also available from an outside supplier at $11. Division Y, acting to minimize its costs, will prefer to purchase Product A at the lower external price of $11. However, assuming that, from the total firm point of view, no more profitable use could be made of the Division X facilities used in supplying Product A to Division Y, such a decision would not be congruent with the best interests of the total firm. This incongruence results because the $11 external price is greater than the $9 variable cost which, in this example, is the differential cost, i.e., the incremental cost incurred to produce additional

---

[6] Joshua Ronen and George McKinney III, "Transfer Pricing for Divisional Autonomy," *Journal of Accounting Research*, Vol. 8, No. 1, pp. 99-112.

units. Additionally, it should be observed that, in the long run, full cost must be recovered and a reasonable profit achieved on the facilities that are to be employed.

Five basic methods of pricing intracompany transfers are available: (1) transfer pricing based on cost, (2) market-based transfer pricing, (3) cost-plus transfer pricing, (4) negotiated transfer pricing, and (5) arbitrary transfer pricing. No one method of transfer pricing can effectively satisfy all of the requirements in all circumstances, so the best transfer price can be defined only as it is best for a particular purpose in a particular circumstance. Regardless of what transfer price is used, the differential cost of goods transferred from division to division should be determined and used for decision-making purposes.[7]

Transfer Pricing Based on Cost

In a totally centralized firm, executive management basically makes all decisions with respect to the operations of the divisions. This responsibility makes cost control the basis for measuring a manager's performance. A cost-based transfer price is usually sufficient in this situation. A company without any integrated operations might have so little volume of intracompany transfers that it would be too time consuming and costly to price the transfer at other than cost.

The cost figure may be the actual or standard cost or based on direct or absorption costing. The company's cost system should permit the computation of a product's unit cost, even at various stages of production. When service departments are involved in a company's operations, a service charging rate similar to the one described on page 394 should be established in advance of the work performed, so that servicing and benefiting departments or plants know in advance the costs connected with services.

The cost method's primary advantage is simplicity, in that it avoids the elimination of intracompany profits from inventories in consolidated financial statements and income tax returns. Also, the transferred cost can readily be used to measure production efficiency by comparing actual with budgeted costs. Finally, the method allows simple and adequate end-product costing for profit analysis by product lines.

Considering the disadvantages, a transfer price based on cost is not suited to decentralized companies that need to measure the profitability of autonomous units. Also, producing segments may not be sufficiently conscientious in controlling costs that are to be transferred, although the use of standard costs for transfer pricing may alleviate this problem. A transfer price based on cost lacks not only utility for divisional planning, motivating, and evaluating, but also the objectivity required of a good performance standard.

---

[7] For further study, the nature and scope of several major transfer pricing models categorized as to (1) the economic theory of the firm, (2) mathematical programming approaches, and (3) other analytical approaches, are covered in "Transfer Pricing—A Synthesis," by A. Rashad Abdel-khalik and Edward J. Lusk, *The Accounting Review*, Vol. XLIX, No. 1, pp. 8-23.

In an analysis of a study of interdivisional transfer pricing, made by the National Industrial Conference Board, Sharav observes that in most cases of vertical transfers (meaning transfers between divisions at different stages of the manufacturing and marketing processes), transfers are priced at cost if the transferring division is viewed as a cost center (where the manager is responsible for cost only). However, if the transferor is a profit center (where the manager is responsible for cost and revenue), the transfer price may include a profit factor, thus approximating outside market prices. In horizontal transfers (meaning that transferer and transferee are situated at the same stage of the production and marketing processes), the transfers are usually executed at cost, which may include freight and handling charges. In many cases, companies using cost-based transfer prices choose actual costs which are derived from divisional operating statements and underlying cost records. Standard or budgeted costs are employed when available. Variable costs are used by only a few companies. A modified version of cost is the so-called cost-plus transfer price. It is comprised of cost plus a markup that is meant to provide a return on investment in divisional assets. Much less frequently used, this transfer price may be applied in lieu of the market price.[8]

Another cost-based transfer price that has been advocated is standard variable cost plus the per unit contribution margin given up on the outside sale by the company when a segment sells internally. For profit centers, the result generally approximates market price, while for cost centers, the transfer price is standard variable cost plus the possibility of an assigned portion of fixed cost.[9]

Market-Based Transfer Pricing

The market-based transfer price is usually identical with the one charged to outside customers, although some companies apply a discount to the market price to reflect the economies of intracompany trading. This method is the best profitability and performance measurement because it is objective. It reflects product profitability and division management performance, with divisions operating on a competitive basis. It also aids in planning and is generally required by foreign tariff laws and income tax regulations.

The most serious drawback to this method is the requirement for a well-developed outside competitive market. Unfortunately, a market price is not always determinable for intermediate or unique products. Also, the market-based price adds an element of profit or loss with each transfer of product. Consequently, the determination of the actual cost of the final product may be difficult, and intracompany profit must be eliminated from inventories in financial statements and consolidated income tax returns.

Statement of Financial Accounting Standards No. 14, "Financial Reporting for Segments of a Business Enterprise," does not specify the transfer pricing

---

[8] Itzhak Sharav, "Transfer Pricing—Diversity of Goals and Practices," *The Journal of Accountancy*, Vol. 137, No. 4, p. 59.
[9] Ralph L. Benke, Jr. and James Don Edwards, *Transfer Pricing: Techniques and Issues* (New York: National Association of Accountants, 1980).

method to be used in segment reporting, but it does require disclosure of the method used. A review of 250 annual reports for a recent year indicated that of the surveyed companies which were required to make such a disclosure, 75 percent used a market-based transfer price.[10] The SEC, however, requires disclosure of:

1. *When and where intersegment transfers are made at prices substantially higher or lower than the prevailing market price or the price charged to unaffiliated parties for similar products or services, and*
2. *The estimated or approximate amounts (or the percentage of increase or decrease in the amounts) of the revenue and operating profit or loss that the particular segments would have had if the intersegment transfers had been made at the prevailing market price.[11]*

Cost-Plus Transfer Pricing

A cost-plus transfer price, i.e., the cost to manufacture plus a normal profit markup, is often used when a market price is not available. In a sense, it is a surrogate for a market price. Although a cost-plus price has the virtue of being easy to compute, it is an imperfect price that can lead to distortions in the relative profitability of the selling and buying divisions. A cost-plus transfer price provides no incentive to the selling division to be efficient. To the contrary, since the profit markup is often a percentage of cost, there is an incentive to inflate cost through arbitrary allocation of common costs and production inefficiency. In addition, cost-plus transfer pricing also has the disadvantage of inflating inventories with intracompany profits that must be eliminated from the financial statements and consolidated income tax returns.

Negotiated Transfer Pricing

Setting the transfer price by negotiation between buying and selling divisions allows unit managers the greatest degree of authority and control over the profit of their units. The managers should consider costs and market conditions and neither negotiating party should have an unfair bargaining position.

A serious problem encountered with this method is that negotiation can not only become time-consuming but can also require frequent reexamination and revision of prices. Negotiated transfer prices often divert the efforts of divisional managers away from activities that are in the best interests of the company to those that benefit the division, and negotiation diverts the efforts of divisional managers away from productive activities. The divisional profit measures may be more of a reflection of the divisional manager's negotiating ability than the division's productive efficiency. As a result, evaluations of the relative operating performance of divisions may be distorted when negotiated

---

[10] Robert Mednick, "Companies Slice and Serve Up Their Financial Results Under FASB 14," *Financial Executive,* Vol. XLVII, No. 3, p. 54.
[11] *Ibid.,* p. 55.

transfer prices are used. In addition, since the transfer price includes a profit markup, intracompany profits must be eliminated from inventories for financial statements and consolidated income tax returns.

Arbitrary Transfer Pricing

An arbitrary transfer price is simply a price set by central management. The price is generally chosen to achieve tax minimization or some other firmwide objective. Neither the buying division nor the selling division controls the transfer price. The advantage of this method is that a price can be set that will achieve the objectives deemed most important by central management. Since central management is responsible for the overall performance of the company, transfer prices set by central management should result in divisional actions that enhance firmwide performance. The method's disadvantages, however, far outweigh any advantage. It can defeat the most important purpose of decentralizing profit responsibility, i.e., making divisional personnel profit-conscious, and it severely hampers the profit incentive of division managers. Again, since arbitrary transfer prices include some markup for profit, intracompany profits must be eliminated from inventories for financial statement and consolidated income tax reporting.

Dual Transfer Pricing

The consuming (buying) and producing (selling) divisions may differ in the purpose a transfer price is to serve. For example, a consuming division may rely on a transfer price in make-or-buy decisions or in determining a final product's sales price based on an awareness of total differential cost. A producing division may use a transfer price to measure its divisional performance and, accordingly, would argue against any price that would not provide a divisional profit. In such circumstances, a company may find it useful to adopt a dual transfer pricing approach in which the:

1. Producing division uses a market-based, cost-plus, negotiated, or arbitrary transfer price in computing its revenue from intracompany sales.
2. Variable costs of the producing division are transferred to the purchasing division, together with an equitable portion of the fixed cost.
3. Total of the divisional profits will be greater than for the company as a whole, and the profit assigned to the producing division would be eliminated in preparing companywide financial statements and for income tax purposes.

Under this system, a producing division would have a profit inducement to expand sales and production, both externally and internally. Yet, the consuming divisions would not be misled. Their costs would be the firm's actual costs and would not include an artificial profit. Variable costs, as well as fixed costs, should be associated with the purchase to ensure that the consuming division is aware of the total cost implications. Of course, the benefits from a dual transfer pricing approach can be achieved only if the underlying cost data are accurate and reliable.

Although the dual transfer pricing method appears to overcome many of the problems inherent in the other transfer pricing methods, it is not commonly used in practice. This lack of use may be due in part to recordkeeping complexity created by the method and in part to the difficulty inherent in evaluating the relative performance of the selling and buying divisions when their profits have been determined on different bases.

▼ PRODUCT PRICING METHODS

Product pricing is a complex subject and is neither a one-person nor a one-activity job. Theorists and practitioners differ on various pricing theories. In practice, the solution to a pricing problem becomes a research job that requires the cooperation and coordination of the economist, statistician, market specialist, industrial engineer, and accountant. Since the determination of a sales price requires consideration of many factors, some of which defy measurement or control, prudent and practical judgment is necessary. Accountants can provide executive management and marketing managers with mileposts to be used as guides when traveling the relatively uncharted road toward successful pricing.

Costs are generally considered to be the starting point in a pricing situation, even though a rigid relationship may not be expected to exist. Prices and pricing policy vary in relation to costs and market conditions as well as to the selection of a long- or short-range view. The long-run approach allows changes in products, manufacturing methods, plant capacity, and marketing and distribution methods. It aims to obtain prices which will return all costs and provide an adequate return on the capital invested. A normal or average product cost is the basis used for long-range pricing. A short-range pricing policy looks toward the recovery of at least part of the total cost in order to meet changing needs resulting from fluctuating sales volume, sales mix, and prices. In such cases, the differential cost of a product may serve as a guide for the determination of prices. Variable costs are the principal source of cost differentials which must be computed in such pricing problems (Chapters 19 and 21). In any case, the figures used should be current, which may require adjusting historical costs to reflect inflation accounting.

The relationship between costs and prices is one of the most difficult for a manager to determine. Price setting is that field of business in which management truly becomes an art. A sales price, generally thought of as the rate of exchange between two commodities, is determined in many industries in a manner that gives individual companies some degree of control over the price. Even companies that experience a great deal of competition have some measure of control, since products, quality, and/or the services rendered may differ. Although a firm may exercise some control over sales prices, the costs incurred in order to do business are usually more within its control.

Prices may be influenced not only by competition but also by what customers are willing to pay and by governmental regulations and controls. The Robinson-Patman Act must be complied with to avoid alleged price discrimination. Even if a company has little or no control over a sales price, it faces the question of whether it can operate profitably at the price that can be charged. Costs must be known and used as building blocks for determining the minimum price required to justify entering or continuing in a given market.

The accountant's assistance to management in the highly important field of pricing products requires knowledge and recognition of inventory costing methods as well as all cost items as they flow through the cost accounting cycle. The development of an appreciation for and an understanding of economic, social, and legal considerations is also required. The accountant must be not only an economist but also an investment analyst and must be able to see problems through management's eyes. By doing so, the accountant becomes a vital part of management, with cost accounting as a necessary tool.

Even though price-setting procedures are difficult, several cost-oriented methods are available that will assist in their computation and determination. These methods include (1) profit maximization—relating total revenue to total cost, (2) pricing based on a return on capital employed, (3) conversion cost pricing, (4) the contribution margin and the differential cost approach to pricing, and (5) standard costs for pricing.

Profit Maximization

A key objective of most business enterprises is to obtain a price that contributes the largest amount of profit. Economic theorists describe this as *profit maximization*. The profit return on each unit sold is not so important as the total profit realized from all units sold. The price that yields the largest total profit is the price to be charged to a consumer.

The following schedule shows the variable cost at $7 per unit, with fixed cost at $300,000 for all ranges of output. The most profitable sales price is $14 per unit, with a contribution margin of $560,000 and a profit of $260,000, after deducting the fixed cost.

Sales Price per Unit	Number of Units To Be Sold	Total Sales Volume	Variable Cost ($7 per Unit)	Fixed Cost	Profit (Loss)
$20	20,000	$ 400,000	$140,000	$300,000	$ (40,000)
18	40,000	720,000	280,000	300,000	140,000
16	60,000	960,000	420,000	300,000	240,000
14	80,000	1,120,000	560,000	300,000	260,000
12	100,000	1,200,000	700,000	300,000	200,000
10	120,000	1,200,000	840,000	300,000	60,000
8	140,000	1,120,000	980,000	300,000	(160,000)

In other situations, the unit variable cost and the total fixed cost may vary according to the total number of units to be sold, thus influencing the most profitable sales price.

Profit maximization is not to be looked upon as the immediate return expected, but rather as a goal to be realized over several months or years. However, during these months and years, sales policies, competition, customer practices, cost changes, and other economic influences might radically alter all previous assumptions. Profit maximization is not necessarily the single objective or even the dominant objective of firms. A recent study found that firms pursue multiple objectives in setting their prices. These include major objectives—profits, return on investment, market share, and total sales—and lesser objectives—price-earnings ratio, liquidity, employee job security, and industrial relations. While each firm surveyed gave weight to many of these objectives, certain patterns of dominance were found:

> . . . for firms selling standard products, market share was the dominant pricing policy objective. In contrast, firms handling custom-made products were more concerned with return on investment and [employee] job security. . . . Where firms seemed to be competing on the basis of price and service, sales maximization was the principal pricing objective. Where product innovation was the major source of competition, profits seemed to dominate. . . .[12]

Pricing Based on a Return on Capital Employed

Some companies attempt to develop prices that will yield a predetermined or desired rate of return on capital employed. To illustrate, assume that a single-product company's total cost is $210,000, total capital employed is $200,000, the sales volume is 50,000 units, and the desired rate of return on capital employed is 20 percent. The formula used and the determination of the product's sales price would be:

$$\text{Price} = \frac{\text{Total cost} + (\text{Desired rate of return} \times \text{Total capital employed})}{\text{Sales volume in units}}$$

$$\text{Price} = \frac{\$210,000 + (20\% \times \$200,000)}{50,000 \text{ units}} = \frac{\$250,000}{50,000 \text{ units}} = \$5$$

Proof: Sales (50,000 units × $5)............ $250,000
Less total cost................................ 210,000
Profit (20% × $200,000).............. $ 40,000

Pricing procedures using capital employed as part of the pricing formula may be complex, however. The illustrations assume no change in capital employed. Actually, as prices and costs change, capital employed may be expected to change. With an increase in capital employed, more cash will be required to serve the business. With higher prices, accounts receivable will be higher, and inventory costs will increase in proportion to increases in factory costs. Decreases would have the reverse effect.

---

[12]Lawrence A. Gordon, Robert Cooper, Haim Falk, and Danny Miller, *The Pricing Decision* (New York: National Association of Accountants, 1981; and Hamilton, Ontario: The Society of Management Accountants of Canada, 1980), pp. 9, 15-17.

If it is assumed that a firm is in business to maximize its value to the shareholders, then its pricing policy should be based largely on a target rate of return on capital employed. To be effective in its control and analysis, management's pricing decisions should be made after this rate, the standard cost, and the estimated plant capacity have been considered.

Conversion Cost Pricing

Conversion cost pricing attempts to direct management's attention to the amount of labor and factory overhead that products require. To illustrate, assume that a company manufactures two products, each selling for $10. The manufacturing cost for each is $9, resulting in a gross profit of $1 per unit, indicating that from a profit point of view it does not matter which product is promoted. However, a breakdown of the costs reveals the following:

Item of Cost	Product A	Product B
Direct materials.....................................	$ 6	$ 3
Direct labor..	2	4
Factory overhead..................................	1	2
Total manufacturing cost......................	$ 9	$ 9
Sales price..	10	10
Gross profit..	$ 1	$ 1

The cost breakdown indicates that Product A requires only half the labor and factory overhead that is required for Product B. If it were possible to shift all efforts to A, a greater number of units could be produced and sold with the same gross profit per unit. Marketing costs of A versus B must also be considered. Of course, any volume increase might disturb market equilibrium and even cause a decrease in the price because of increased supply. These difficulties are discussed in Chapter 20.

Contribution Margin Approach to Pricing

In direct costing, the contribution margin figure indicates a product's contribution to the recovery of fixed costs and to profit. The fixed and variable cost classifications permit an evaluation of each product by a comparison of specific contribution margins. While this contribution margin approach might be used for a firm's entire business, it is of even greater value in the analysis of its divisions, plants, products, product lines, customers, and territories. Care must be taken, however, not to confuse contribution with profit, since profit is realized only after all fixed costs are covered.

The differential cost of an order is the variable cost necessary to produce the additional units, plus additional fixed costs (if any) at the new production level.

If the cost of additional units is accepted as a basis for pricing them, any price over and above total differential cost would be acceptable. This procedure is, of course, applicable only to the additional units.

To base sales prices on differential cost requires careful scrutiny of all related factors. For example, long-term sales promotion should not be used for a product priced on the basis of differential costs when total cost recovery and a reasonable profit will not result.

Standard Costs for Pricing

If cost estimates used for pricing purposes are prepared on the basis of the standard costs for materials, labor, and factory overhead, the tasks of preparing the estimate and using the data to set the price will be considerably easier. The use of standard costs for pricing purposes makes cost figures more quickly available and reduces clerical detail. Since a standard cost represents the cost that should be attained in an efficiently operated plant at normal capacity, it is essential, once the sales price has been established, that the cost department furnish up-to-the-minute information to all parties to make certain that the cost stays within the rate set by the estimate. Any significant deviation between actual and standard costs should come to light for quick action through the accounting system.

The National Association of Accountants has stated that companies can be divided into four groups with respect to the type of cost figures which they supply to pricing executives. These groups are composed of:

1. Companies which supply executives with standard costs without the application of any adjustments to the standards.
2. Companies in which the standard costs are adjusted by the ratio of actual costs to standard costs as shown by the variance accounts.
3. Companies which use current market prices for materials, and in a few cases for labor, with standard costs for other elements of product cost.
4. Companies which adjust standard costs to reflect the actual costs anticipated during the period for which the prices are to be in effect, including inflation's impact on costs.[13]

When standard costs are used for bid prices, they might be based on estimates previously submitted. However, while some materials parts or labor operations might be identical with those used for another product, executives need the most up-to-date information on all cost components in order to set a profitable price. Companies that must present bids adjust the costs developed from the detailed standards to approximate actual costs expected.

---

[13] Research Series, No. 14, "Standard Manufacturing Costs for Pricing and Budgeting," *NAA Bulletin*, Vol. XXX, No. 3, pp. 165-166.

DISCUSSION QUESTIONS

1. How is the return on capital employed computed?

2. What management activities are measured by each of the factors involved in determining the rate of return on capital employed?

3. What items are generally included in the term "capital employed"?

4. State two major objectives that management may have in mind when setting up a system for measuring the return on divisional capital employed.

5. Identify the basic methods used in pricing intracompany transfers.

6. A cost-plus transfer price is often used as a surrogate for a market-based transfer price. Explain the primary disadvantage of using a cost-plus transfer price relative to using a market-based transfer price.

7. From an organizational point of view, two approaches to transfer pricing are (a) to let the managers of profit centers bargain with one another and arrive at their own transfer prices (negotiated transfer pricing) and (b) to have the firm's executive management set transfer prices for transactions between the profit centers (arbitrary transfer pricing). State the fundamental advantage and disadvantage of each approach.

(CGAAC adapted)

8. Explain the dual transfer pricing approach in intracompany transfer pricing.

9. Discuss the statement, "Price setting is truly an art."

10. What accounting-based methods are available that might assist and permit the computation and determination of a sales price?

11. Discuss the profit-maximization method of pricing.

12. Why are standard costs helpful in setting prices?

EXERCISES

1. Rate of return on capital employed. During the past year, Kaw Waterworks Company had a net income of $160,000. Net sales were $800,000 and total capital employed was $1,600,000.

Required: Compute (1) the capital-employed turnover rate, (2) the percentage of profit to sales, and (3) the rate of return on capital employed.

2. Rate of return on capital employed; minimum price. Mastertech Corporation manufactures a highly specialized alloy used in missile skins. Rising materials costs led the company to adopt the lifo method for inventory costing. In 19A, the company produced 702 000 kilograms of alloy. New government contracts and other new business should increase volume by about 30%. In spite of increased costs, management felt that it could reduce the sales price from $12.30 per kilogram in 19A to $11.40 in 19B and still maintain the same rate of return on capital employed. However, prices of basic raw materials climbed higher than expected and the desired return and profit did not materialize. The following data are available (000s omitted):

	19A	19B
Sales...	$8,450	$8,835
Cost of goods sold and commercial expenses....................	7,549	7,939
Profit..	901	896
Cash...	1,200	500
Accounts receivable...	1,000	1,000
Inventories...	1,750	2,300
Noncurrent assets...	6,650	7,400

Required: Compute (1) the actual rate of return on capital employed for the past two years, and (2) the minimum price that the company should have charged.

3. Rate of return on capital employed for regions. Hutton Sales Company has three regions: Eastern, Central, and Western. The cost of assets employed is determined by averaging the December 31, 19A balance of $1,446,000 and the December 31, 19B balance of $1,632,000. The assets are distributed among the Eastern, Central, and Western regions in a ratio of 3:1:2, respectively. The 19B condensed income statement is as follows:

Hutton Sales Company
Income Statement
For the Year Ended December 31, 19B

	Eastern	Central	Western	Total
Sales...............................	$3,078,000	$513,000	$2,308,500	$5,899,500
Cost of goods sold..........................	2,016,000	383,000	1,818,500	4,217,500
Gross profit.......................................	$1,062,000	$130,000	$ 490,000	$1,682,000
Commercial expenses.....................	908,100	88,960	443,830	1,440,890
Operating income...........................	$ 153,900	$ 41,040	$ 46,170	$ 241,110

Required: For each region and in total, compute:

(1) The capital-employed turnover rate. (Compute answers to one decimal place.)
(2) The percentage of profit to sales. (Compute answers to $\frac{1}{10}$ of 1%.)
(3) The rate of return on capital employed. (Compute answers to $\frac{1}{10}$ of 1%.)

4. Rate of return on capital employed for product lines. Hayashi Company has three product lines: Recreational, Household, and Hand Tools. The December 31, 19A balance sheet shows total assets of $4,117,000, and the year-end 19B balance sheet totals $5,117,000, with the average of the two balances used to compute the rate of return on capital employed. Asset utilization is allocated one third to Recreational, one sixth to Household, and one half to Hand Tools. The 19B condensed income statement is as follows:

HAYASHI COMPANY
Income Statement
For the Year Ended December 31, 19B

	Recreational	Household	Hand Tools	Total
Sales................................	$3,078,000	$513,000	$2,308,500	$5,899,500
Cost of goods sold..........................	2,016,000	383,000	1,818,500	4,217,500
Gross profit.......................................	$1,062,000	$130,000	$ 490,000	$1,682,000
Operating and other expenses.......	815,760	68,440	420,745	1,304,945
Profit...	$ 246,240	$ 61,560	$ 69,255	$ 377,055

Required: For each product line and in total, compute:

    (1) The capital-employed turnover rate, computed to one decimal place.
    (2) The percentage of profit to sales, computed to $\frac{1}{10}$ of one percent.
    (3) The rate of return on capital employed, computed to $\frac{1}{10}$ of one percent.

5. Transfer pricing. Wallach Iron Mill produces high-grade pig iron in its single blast furnace in Bedford, Pennsylvania. Coal from nearby mines is converted into coke in company-owned ovens, and 80% of the coke produced is used in the blast furnace. The management of the mill is experimenting with divisional profit reporting and control and has established the blast furnace as well as the coke-producing activity as profit centers. Coke used by the blast furnace is charged to that profit center at $6 per ton, which approximates the current market price less costs of marketing (including substantial freight costs). The remaining 20% of the coke produced at a normal annual volume output of 80,000 tons is sold to other mills in the area at $7.50 per ton.

    The cost of coal and other variable costs of coke production amount to $4.50 per ton. Fixed costs of the coke division amount to $40,000 a year.

    The blast furnace manager, with authority to purchase outside, has found a reliable, independent coke producer who has offered to sell coke at a delivered price of $5 per ton on a long-term contract. The manager of Wallach Iron Mill's coke division claims it cannot match that price and maintain profitable operations.

    The manager of the coke division indicates that with an additional expenditure of $60,000 annually for fixed productive and delivery equipment, the division's entire annual normal output could be sold to outside firms at $6 per ton, FOB the Wallach Iron Mill plant. Other marketing expenses will be $.50 per ton. The increased fixed costs would reduce variable production costs by $1.50 per ton.

Required:

    (1) Prepare calculations to guide the coke division manager in deciding whether to accept the offer, assuming that Wallach Iron Mill cannot increase its sales of coke to outsiders above the 20% of normal production.
    (2) Prepare calculations to aid executive management in deciding whether to make the additional investment and sell the entire coke division's output to outsiders.

6. Product pricing. Mercado Company is considering changing its sales price of Salien, which is presently $15. Increases and decreases of both 10% and 25%, as well as increases in advertising and promotion expenditures, are being considered, with the following estimated results for 19A and 19B:

	Estimated Unit Sales		Estimated Advertising and Promotion Expenditures	
Price	19A	19B	19A	19B
−25%	190,000	200,000	$200,000	$210,000
−10%	180,000	190,000	250,000	250,000
No change	160,000	170,000	300,000	300,000
+10%	140,000	150,000	400,000	450,000
+25%	130,000	140,000	450,000	550,000

The company has the necessary flexibility in its production capacity to meet these volume levels. The variable manufacturing cost per unit of Salien is estimated to be $7.25 in 19A and $7.80 in 19B.

Required: Determine the recommended sales price.   *(ICMA adapted)*

7. Contribution margin approach to pricing. The Gelotech Company is a large manufacturer of refrigeration units. The firm's product line includes refrigerators for homes, industry, and ships. The firm is composed of three divisions. The Motor Division is responsible for manufacturing the motors for all of the various refrigeration units. In the Shell Division, the refrigerator shells are produced and the motors transferred from the Motor Division are installed. The Marketing Division is responsible for the sale and distribution of the final product.

While a market exists outside the firm for both the motors and shells, the transfer price between divisions is set by executive management. This is done to avoid unnecessary friction, which management feels might impair efficiency and prove wasteful.

Recently the company was asked to submit a bid for 100 refrigeration units for a local shipbuilding firm. The following unit cost estimate has been prepared:

	Motor	Shell	Marketing
Manufacturing materials..	$195	$ 180	—
Receiving and handling (60% fixed)....................	10	25	$ 20
Motor...	—	600	—
Refrigeration units..	—	—	1,240
Shipping materials..	—	—	30
Direct labor..	190	220	35
Factory overhead:			
Fixed...	55	45	15
Variable...	100	80	10
General administrative cost.................................	28	57	67
Transfer price..	600	1,240	—

Prior to submitting its bid, Gelotech has learned that its principal competitor has submitted a bid of $1,200 per unit.

Required: Prepare an analysis as to whether or not Gelotech can match the competitor's bid.

PROBLEMS

26-1. Rate of return on capital employed. Westworth Corporation's management is concerned over its current financial position and return on capital employed. In a request for assistance in analyzing these financial conditions, the controller provides the following statements:

Westworth Corporation
Statement of Working Capital Deficit
December 31, 19A

Current liabilities..		$198,625
Less current assets:		
Cash..	$ 5,973	
Accounts receivable (net).....................	70,952	
Inventory...	90,200	167,125
Working capital deficit.............................		$ 31,500

Westworth Corporation
Income Statement
For the Year Ended December 31, 19A

Sales (90,500 units)...	$751,150
Cost of goods sold...	451,000
Gross profit...	$300,150
Marketing and general expenses, including $22,980 depreciation....................	149,920
Income before income tax..	$150,230
Less income tax (50%)...	75,115
Net income..	$ 75,115

Noncurrent assets consist of land, a building, and equipment, with a net book value of $350,000 on December 31, 19A.

Sales of 100,000 units are forecast for 19B. Within this relevant range of activity, costs are estimated as follows (excluding income tax):

	Fixed Cost	Variable Cost per Unit
Cost of goods sold...		$4.90
Marketing and general expenses, including $15,450 depreciation....................	$125,750	1.10
Total...	$125,750	$6.00

The income tax rate is expected to be 50%. Past experience indicates that current assets vary in direct proportion to sales dollars. Management feels that in 19B the market will support a sales price of $8.40 at a sales volume of 100,000 units.

Required:

(1) Compute the 19A return-on-capital-employed ratio (after income tax), to $\frac{1}{10}$ of one percent.
(2) Compute the 19B rate of return (after income tax) on net book value of total assets, to $\frac{1}{10}$ of one percent. *(AICPA adapted)*

26-2. Profit and rate of return on capital employed using various proposals. Lauren Toy Company manufactures two specialty children's toys marketed under the trade names of Springy and Leapy. During the year, the following costs, revenue, and capital employed by the company in the production of these two items were:

	Springy	Leapy
Sales price per unit...	$ 1.50	$ 1.95
Sales in units..	280,000	150,000
Materials cost per unit......................................	$ .20	$ .30
Labor cost per unit...	.50	.75
Variable factory overhead per unit.....................	.15	.20
Variable marketing cost per unit.........................	.05	.10
Fixed factory overhead.....................................	100,000	30,000
Fixed marketing cost...	30,000	15,000
Variable capital employed.................................	10% of sales	20% of sales
Fixed capital employed......................................	$148,000	$ 91,500

Fixed administrative and other nonallocable fixed costs amounted to $28,000, and nonallocable capital employed was $25,000.

Management, dissatisfied with the return on total capital employed, is considering a number of alternatives to improve this return.

The market for Springy appears to be underdeveloped, and the consensus is that sales can be increased to 325,000 units at the same price with an increase of $9,500 in the fixed advertising cost. An increase in the production of Springy will require use of some equipment previously utilized in the production of Leapy and a transfer of $10,000 of fixed capital and $5,000 of fixed factory overhead to the production of Springy.

For Leapy, it would mean limiting its production to 100,000 units, which could be marketed with the current sales effort at (a) an increase in price of $.15 per unit; (b) without a price increase and with a reduction in current fixed advertising cost of $9,000; or (c) with a $.05 per unit increase in price and a $7,500 reduction in the current fixed advertising cost.

Required:

(1) Compute the income before income tax and the return on capital employed for each product and in total for the year, to $\frac{1}{10}$ of one percent.
(2) Compute the income before income tax and the return on capital employed for each product and in total under each alternative, to $\frac{1}{10}$ of one percent.

26-3. Public utility rate based on capital employed. Mauford Water Company is a public utility providing water service to 3,000 customers. As a privately owned public utility, its rates are subject to government regulation. Its rate structure is designed to provide a reasonable rate of return, calculated by expressing net income as a percentage of the company's rate base. The rate base, in turn, is the depreciated cost of the utility plant, averaged between the beginning and end of the year. Operating results for the year were as follows:

Water revenue...		$90,000
Expenses:		
Fixed..	$38,668	
Variable...	12,852	
Depreciation on utility plant.....................	17,000	68,520
Income before income tax...........................		$21,480
Income tax...		4,510
Net income...		$16,970

Mauford's directors feel that the present net income is inadequate and are considering applying for higher rates. At present, each customer is charged a flat rate of $30 per annum.

An analysis of metered water consumption data indicates the following ranges of average monthly usage:

Range	Consumption	Number of Customers
A	0-100 cu. ft. (average: 50 cu. ft.)	900
B	101-500 cu. ft. (average: 300 cu. ft.)	1,800
C	over 500 cu. ft. (average: 700 cu. ft.)	300
		3,000

Other data:

Utility plant in service, January 1......................................	$800,000
Less accumulated depreciation..	200,000
Depreciated cost of utility plant, January 1.....................	$600,000
Utility plant addition during the year................................	$ 81,000

The income tax rate on earnings up to $80,000 is unchanged.

Required:
(1) Calculate the rate base and rate of return for the year, to $\frac{1}{10}$ of one percent.
(2) Based on the information:
(a) Compute the flat rate annual customer charge necessary to provide a 10% rate of return.
(b) For each of the three consumption ranges, compute the charge per cubic foot of water necessary to provide a 10% rate of return, with the charge for consumption within Range B being double that within Range C, and two thirds of that within Range A; i.e., a customer consuming 150 cu. ft. of water would be billed at the Range A rate for the first 100 cu. ft. and at the lower Range B rate for the additional 50 cu. ft. (Compute answers to nearest $\frac{1}{10}$ of a cent.) *(CGAAC adapted)*

26-4. Product pricing and transfer pricing. National Industries is a diversified corporation with separate and distinct operating divisions. Each division's performance is evaluated on the basis of total dollar profits and return on division investment.

The WindAir Division manufactures and sells air conditioner units. The coming year's budgeted income statement, based on a sales volume of 15,000 units, is as follows:

WindAir Division
Budgeted Income Statement
For 19A

	Per Unit	Total
Sales revenue...	$400	$6,000,000
Manufacturing costs:		
Compressor...	$ 70	$1,050,000
Other raw materials.................................	37	555,000
Direct labor..	30	450,000
Variable factory overhead........................	45	675,000
Fixed factory overhead.............................	32	480,000
Total manufacturing cost.....................	$214	$3,210,000
Gross profit...	$186	$2,790,000
Commercial expenses:		
Variable marketing....................................	$ 18	$ 270,000
Fixed marketing.......................................	19	285,000
Fixed administrative.................................	38	570,000
Total commercial expense...................	$ 75	$1,125,000
Income before income tax...........................	$111	$1,665,000

WindAir's division manager believes sales can be increased if the unit sales price is reduced. A market research study conducted by an independent firm at the request of the manager indicates that a 5% reduction in the sales price ($20) would increase sales volume 16%, or 2,400 units. WindAir has sufficient production capacity to manage this increased volume with no increase in fixed cost.

At the present time, WindAir uses a compressor in its units, which it purchases from an outside supplier at a cost of $70 each. The division manager of WindAir has approached the manager of the Compressor Division regarding the sale of compressor units to WindAir. The Compressor Division currently manufactures and sells a unit exclusively to outside firms which is similar to the unit used by WindAir. Specifications for the WindAir compressor are slightly different, which would reduce the Compressor Division's raw materials cost by $1.50 per unit. In addition, the Compressor Division would not incur any variable marketing cost for the units sold to WindAir. The manager of WindAir wants all of the compressors it uses to come from one supplier and has offered to pay the Compressor Division $50 for each unit.

The Compressor Division has the capacity to produce 75,000 units. The coming year's budgeted income statement for the Compressor Division, shown as follows, is based on a sales volume of 64,000 units, without considering WindAir's proposal:

Compressor Division
Budgeted Income Statement
For 19A

	Per Unit	Total
Sales revenue..	$100	$6,400,000
Manufacturing costs:		
Raw materials...	$ 12	$ 768,000
Direct labor..	8	512,000
Variable factory overhead..........................	10	640,000
Fixed factory overhead...............................	11	704,000
Total manufacturing cost........................	$ 41	$2,624,000
Gross profit..	$ 59	$3,776,000
Commercial expenses:		
Variable marketing......................................	$ 6	$ 384,000
Fixed marketing...	4	256,000
Fixed administrative....................................	7	448,000
Total commercial expense.....................	$ 17	$1,088,000
Income before income tax.............................	$ 42	$2,688,000

Required:

(1) Compute the estimated result if the WindAir Division reduces its sales price by 5%, even if it cannot acquire the compressors internally at $50 each.

(2) Compute the estimated effect on the Compressor Division, from its own viewpoint, if the 17,400 units are supplied to WindAir at $50 each.

(3) Determine whether it would be in the best interests of National Industries for the Compressor Division to supply the 17,400 units at $50 each.

(ICMA adapted)

26-5. Transfer pricing. Martin Corporation, a diversified company, recently implemented a decentralization policy under which divisional managers are expected to make their own operating decisions, including whether to do business with other divisions. The performances and year-end bonuses of divisional managers are measured by the return on capital employed of their divisions. Because most divisions have operated at full capacity, it is company policy that all transfers between divisions are to be priced at 120% of standard manufacturing cost (to allow for a "normal" divisional profit margin). This transfer price is not negotiable.

The president of the company is currently faced with a dispute between the general managers of two divisions: the Consumer Products Division and the Engineering Division. The Consumer Products Division makes and sells several household articles, including a home appliance that has, until recently, been one of the company's steadiest sellers. Recently, this division has had marketing difficulties and has reduced its production of the appliance to 56,000 a year from its usual production at capacity. The unused capacity cannot be utilized for other products. The Engineering Division makes a wide variety of items, incuding a specialized part (Part TX) that is sold to the Consumer Products Division and to a few small outside companies. The latter buy a steady 12% of the Engineering Division's annual production capacity for the part.

The Consumer Products Division uses four of these parts in each home appliance unit and maintains no significant inventory of unused parts but acquires them from the Engineering Division as needed to meet its production requirements. The parts are not available from any other source.

Because the Consumer Products Division has recently reduced its requirement for Part TX, the Engineering Division has been seeking new customers and has received an offer to buy 100,000 units of the part annually, at a price of $5 each, which is less than the $5.40 each paid by the small outside companies but more than the transfer price paid by the Consumer Products Division. The company making the offer is in a market unrelated to that of either the Consumer Products Division or the small outside companies.

Following are data with respect to Part TX and the home appliance involved in the dispute between the two managers:

	Part TX (Engineering Division)	Home Appliance (Consumer Products Division)
Annual production capacity..	300,000 units	66,000 units
Unit sales price to outside customers.............................	$5.40	$80.00
Standard manufacturing cost per unit (based on production at full capacity):		
Division's own costs:		
Variable..	$2.00	$37.00
Fixed..	1.75	13.00
Transfers from the Engineering Division..................	—	18.00
Standard manufacturing cost per unit.......................	$3.75	$68.00

The manager of the Consumer Products Division has requested that the president instruct the manager of the Engineering Division to refuse the offer received, since (1) no other source for Part TX can be found, (2) the marketing problems with the home appliance are expected to be temporary, and (3) the Engineering Division cannot expand its production capacity for Part TX.

Required:

(1) Determine the action that the manager of the Engineering Division should take as a result of the offer, in order to maximize the results of that division. Include calculations of the offer's effect on the Engineering Division.
(2) Determine the overall effect on the company, under existing circumstances, if the Engineering Division's manager accepts the offer.
(3) Identify the factors that the president should consider in deciding whether to intervene in the dispute.
(4) Revise the transfer pricing policy to assist the divisional managers in making optimal decisions for the company.   (CICA adapted)

26-6. Product pricing. Brazos Corporation produces an electronic component. Product demand is highly elastic, within a specified range. At present, 100,000 units are sold at $10 each, and the additional demand expected with price reductions is:

Unit Price	Units of Estimated Demand
$9.75	120,000
9.50	150,000
9.25	190,000
9.00	240,000
8.75	300,000

Present capacity is 125,000 units. Further estimates are that the first capacity increase will require a $500,000 capital expenditure and, including depreciation, will increase annual fixed costs by $100,000 from the present $250,000 level. Each subsequent addition of 75,000 units will require further capital investment of $450,000 and will increase annual fixed costs by $75,000. Commercial expenses included in the present $250,000 figure will not change at the higher volumes. Other unit costs are estimated as follows:

	Less Than 150,000	150,000 to 200,000*	More Than 200,000*
Direct materials....................	$4.00	$3.80	· $3.60
Direct labor...........................	1.00	1.00	1.10
Variable factory overhead and commercial expenses	1.00	1.00	1.00

*Average costs for total production.

The board of directors will not approve additional capital expenditures unless a minimum pretax return of 20% is anticipated.

Required: Prepare a profitability statement at the various operating volumes, including the required 20% return on additional investment.

26-7. Contribution margin approach to pricing. J. Schifflein manufactures custom-made pleasure boats ranging in price from $10,000 to $250,000. For the past thirty years, Schifflein has determined each boat's sales price by estimating the costs of materials, labor, and a prorated portion of overhead and by adding 20% to these estimated costs. For example, a recent price quotation was determined as follows:

Direct materials.....................	$ 5,000
Direct labor...........................	8,000
Overhead..............................	2,000
	$15,000
Plus 20%..............................	3,000
Sales price...........................	$18,000

The overhead figure was determined by estimating the total overhead cost for the year and allocating it at 25% of direct labor.

If a customer rejects the price and business is slack, Schifflein is often willing to reduce the markup to as little as 5% over estimated costs. Thus, average markup for the year is estimated at 15%.

Schifflein has just completed a pricing course and believes that the company could use some of the modern techniques taught in the course. The course emphasized the contribution margin approach to pricing, and Schifflein feels that such an approach would be helpful in determining the sales prices of custom-made pleasure boats.

Total overhead (including marketing and administrative expenses for the year) has been estimated at $150,000, of which $90,000 is fixed and the remainder is variable in direct proportion to direct labor.

Required:

(1) (a) Compute the difference in profit for the year if a customer's offer of $15,000 instead of the $18,000 quotation shown above is accepted.
    (b) Determine the minimum sales price Schifflein could have quoted without reducing or increasing profit.

(Continued)

(2) State the advantages that the contribution margin approach to pricing has over the approach used by Schifflein.
(3) Identify the pitfalls, if any, to contribution margin pricing.   (ICMA adapted)

CASES

A. Divisional rates of return. Notewon Corporation is a highly diversified company which grants its divisional executives a significant amount of operating authority. Each division is responsible for its own sales, pricing, production, costs of operations, and management of accounts receivable, inventories, accounts payable, and use of existing facilities. Cash is managed by corporate headquarters. All cash in excess of normal operating needs of the divisions is transferred periodically to corporate headquarters for redistribution or investment.

Divisional executives are responsible for presenting investment project requests to corporate management, which has authority for decisions to commit funds.

Corporate management evaluates the performance of division executives by the return-on-capital-employed (RCE) measure, with an asset base composed of fixed assets employed plus working capital exclusive of cash.

RCE is the most important appraisal factor for divisional executives in salary adjustments. Additionally, RCE affects the annual bonus, with increases in RCE being especially important. The company adopted the RCE performance measure and related compensation procedures about ten years ago to increase divisional management awareness of the importance of the asset-profit relationship and to provide additional incentive to divisional executives in seeking investment opportunities.

Although the RCE has continued to grow in each division, the corporate RCE has declined in recent years, and during the past three years the corporation has accumulated a sizeable amount of cash and short-term marketable securities.

Required:

(1) Specify actions division managers might have taken to cause RCE to grow in each division but decline for the corporation.
(2) Explain how Notewon's emphasis on the use of RCE might have resulted in the recent decline in the corporation's return on capital employed and the increase in cash and short-term marketable securities.
(3) Suggest changes in the compensation policy to avoid this problem.
   (ICMA adapted)

B. Rate of return on capital employed as measure of division performance. Torres Corporation is a large, divisionalized manufacturing company. Each division is viewed as an investment center and has virtually complete autonomy for product development, marketing, and production.

Performance of division managers is evaluated periodically by senior corporate management. Divisional rate of return on capital employed is the sole criterion used in performance evaluation under current corporate policy. Corporate management believes that rate of return on capital employed is an adequate measure because it incorporates quantitative information from the divisional income statement and balance sheet in the analysis.

Some division managers complain that a single criterion for performance evaluation is insufficient and ineffective. These managers have compiled a list of criteria which they believe should be used in evaluating division managers' performance. The criteria include profitability, market position, productivity, product leadership, personnel development, employee attitudes, public responsibility, and balance between short-range and long-range goals.

Required:

(1) Discuss the shortcomings or possible inconsistencies of using rate of return on capital employed as the sole criterion to evaluate divisional management performance.

(2) Discuss the advantages of using multiple performance measures versus a single performance measure in evaluating divisional management performance.

(3) Describe the problems or disadvantages which can be associated with the

implementation of a system of multiple performance measures as suggested to Torres Corporation by its division managers. *(ICMA adapted)*

C. Using the rate of return on capital employed to evaluate divisions. A distributor of sporting goods to educational institutions relies upon sales personnel to market its goods directly. The company is organized by geographical regions: Northeast, Southeast, Northwest, and Southwest. Each year, bonuses are awarded to the personnel in the region with the highest rate of return on capital employed, provided that the rate of return exceeds the established minimum rate. The current minimum acceptable rate of return on capital employed has been established at 10%. The current year's actual regional results are shown in the table below.

Region (in 000s)					
	Northeast	Southeast	Northwest	Southwest	Total
Estimated market..........................	$ 200,000	$ 75,000	$ 50,000	$ 100,000	$ 425,000
Regional sales.............................	$ 90,000	$ 40,000	$ 5,000	$ 25,000	$ 160,000
Variable costs..............................	$ 50,625	$ 22,500	$ 2,813	$ 14,062	$ 90,000
Discretionary costs[1].....................	9,750	3,500	250	6,500	20,000
Committed costs[2]........................	22,500	10,000	1,250	6,250	40,000
Total costs.................................	$ 82,875	$ 36,000	$ 4,313	$ 26,812	$ 150,000
Profit.......................................	$ 7,125	$ 4,000	$ 687	$ (1,812)	$ 10,000
Assets employed.........................	$ 80,000	$ 35,000	$ 6,500	$ 16,000	$ 137,500
Liabilities...................................	$ 20,000	$ 15,000	$ 2,300	6,000	$ 43,300
Net investment............................	$ 60,000	$ 20,000	$ 4,200	$ 10,000	$ 94,200

[1] Escapable or avoidable costs.
[2] Costs that will be incurred during the period in which the decision is made, regardless of the action chosen. Committed costs are assigned by central management on the basis of actual regional sales.

The president of the company would like to determine which region has the best performance, so that bonuses may be awarded. The following information is available:

1. The Northwest region leases its main warehousing facility on a twenty-year operating lease. The purchase price of the building would be $3,750,000.

2. The regions were established several years apart in the following order: Northeast, Southeast, Southwest, and Northwest.

3. Inventories are kept on a lifo basis in all regions.

Required:

(1) On the basis of the information available, which region, if any, deserves to be awarded the bonuses? Show and label all supporting calculations.

(2) What factors make the rate of return on capital employed criterion inappropriate for this analysis? What factors would make it appropriate?

(3) Does the use of a minimum rate of return seem appropriate in this case? What other measures should be used in the evaluation of the regions?

(CIA adapted)

D. Transfer pricing. MBR Inc. consists of three divisions which formerly were three independent manufacturing companies. Bader Corporation and Roach Company merged in 19A and the merged corporation acquired Michael Company in 19B. The name of the corporation was subsequently changed to MBR Inc., and each company became a separate division, retaining the name of the original company.

The three divisions have operated as independent entities, each having its own sales force and production facilities. Each division manager is responsible for sales, cost of operations, acquisition and financing of divisional assets, and working capital management. The corporate management of MBR evaluates the performance of the divisions and division managers on the basis of rate of return on capital employed.

Michael Division has just been awarded a contract for a product which uses a component manufactured by the Roach Division as well as by outside suppliers. Michael used a cost figure of $3.80 for the component manufactured by Roach in preparing its bid for the new product, a figure supplied by Roach in response to Michael's request for the average variable cost of the component. It represents the standard variable manufacturing cost and variable marketing expense.

Roach has an active sales force that is continually soliciting new prospects, and its sales price for the component Michael needs is $6.50. Sales of this component are expected to increase; however, the Roach management has indicated that it could supply Michael with the required quantities at the regular sales price less variable marketing expense. Michael's management has responded by offering to pay standard variable manufacturing cost plus 20%.

The two divisions have been unable to agree on a transfer price. Corporate management has never established a transfer price policy because interdivisional transactions have never occurred. As a compromise, the corporate vice-president of finance has suggested a price equal to the standard full manufacturing cost (i.e., no marketing expense) plus a 15% markup. This price has also been rejected by the two division managers, because each considered it grossly unfair.

The unit cost structure for the Roach component and the three suggested prices are as follows:

Regular sales price..	$6.50
Standard variable manufacturing cost..................	$3.20
Standard fixed manufacturing cost.......................	1.20
Variable marketing expense...................................	.60
	$5.00
Regular sales price less variable marketing expense ($6.50 − $.60)..................	$5.90
Variable manufacturing cost plus 20% ($3.20 × 1.20)............................	$3.84
Standard full manufacturing cost plus 15% ($4.40 × 1.15)....................................	$5.06

Required:

(1) State the effect of the three proposed prices on the Roach Division's attitude toward intracompany business.
(2) Evaluate the negotiation method for setting the transfer price.
(3) Specify the extent of desired MBR corporate management involvement in setting the transfer price.

(ICMA adapted)

E. Transfer pricing. Defco Division of Gunnco Corporation requests of Omar Division, operating at capacity, a supply of Electrical Fitting #1726 that is not available from any other source. Omar Division sells this part to its regular customers for $7.50 each. Defco, operating at 50% capacity, is willing to pay $5 each for this fitting. Defco will put the fitting into a brake unit which it manufactures on essentially a cost basis for a commercial jet plane manufacturer.

Omar Division produces Electrical Fitting #1726 at a variable cost of $4.25. The cost (and sales price) of the brake unit as it is being built by the Defco Division is:

Purchased parts (outside vendors).....................	$22.50
Omar Electrical Fitting #1726............................	5.00
Other variable costs...	14.00
Fixed factory overhead and administrative expenses..	8.00
Total...	$49.50

Defco believes that the price concession is necessary to obtain the job.

Gunnco uses return on investment and dollar profits in measuring division and division manager performance.

Required:

(1) Recommend whether or not the Omar Division should supply Electrical Fitting #1726 to the Defco Division. (Ignore income tax.)

(2) Discuss whether or not it would be to the short-run economic advantage of the Gunnco Corporation for the Omar Division to supply the Defco Division with Electrical Fitting #1726 at $5 each. (Ignore income tax.)

(3) Discuss the organizational and managerial behavior difficulties inherent in this situation and recommend to Gunnco's president how the problem should be handled.   (ICMA adapted)

F. Transfer pricing. Lorax Electric Company manufactures a large variety of systems and individual components for the electronics industry. The firm is organized into several divisions, with division managers given the authority to make virtually all operating decisions. Management control over divisional operations is maintained by a system of divisional profit and return on investment measures which are reviewed regularly by executive management. The executive management of Lorax has been quite pleased with the effectiveness of the system they have been using, and believes that it is responsible for the company's improved profitability over the last few years.

The Devices Division manufactures solid-state devices and is operating at capacity. The Systems Division has asked the Devices Division to supply a large quantity of integrated circuit IC378. The Devices Division currently is selling this component to its regular customers at $40 per hundred.

The Systems Division, which is operating at about 60% of capacity, wants this particular component for a digital clock system. It has an opportunity to supply large quantities of these digital clock systems to Centonic Electric, a major producer of clock radios and other popular electronic home entertainment equipment. This opportunity is the first that any of

the Lorax divisions have had to do business with Centonic Electric. Centonic Electric has offered to pay $7.50 per clock system.

The Systems Division prepared an analysis of the probable costs to produce the clock systems. The amount that could be paid to the Devices Division for the integrated circuits, five of which are required for each clock system, was determined by working backward from the selling price. The cost estimates employed by the division reflected the highest per unit cost the Systems Division could incur for each cost component and still leave a sufficient margin so that the division's income statement could show reasonable improvement. The cost estimates are summarized below.

Proposed selling price.........................		$7.50
Costs excluding required integrated circuits IC378:		
Components purchased from outside suppliers..............................	$2.75	
Circuit-board etching—labor and variable factory overhead........................	.40	
Assembly, testing, packaging—labor and variable factory overhead.........	1.35	
Fixed factory overhead allocations..	1.50	
Profit margin......................................	.50	6.50
Amount which can be paid for integrated circuits IC378 (5 @ $20 per hundred)...		$1.00

As a result of this analysis, the Systems Division offered the Devices Division a price of $20 per hundred for the integrated circuit. This bid was refused because the manager of the Devices Division felt that the Systems Division should at least meet the price of $40 per hundred which regular customers pay. When the Systems Division found that it could not obtain a comparable integrated circuit from outside vendors, the situation was brought to an arbitration committee which had been set up to review such problems.

The arbitration committee prepared an analysis which showed that $.15 would cover the variable costs of producing the integrated circuit; $.28 would cover the full cost, including fixed factory overhead; and $.35 would provide a gross margin equal to the average gross margin on all of the products sold by the Devices Division. The manager of the Systems Division reacted by stating, "They could sell us that integrated circuit for $.20 and still earn a positive contribution toward profit. In fact, they should be required to sell at their variable cost—$.15—and not be allowed to take advantage of us."

The manager of Devices countered by arguing that, "It doesn't make sense to sell to the Systems Division at $20 per hundred when we can get $40 per hundred outside on all we can produce. In fact, Systems could pay us up to almost $60 per hundred, and they would still have a positive contribution to profit."

The committee recommended that the price be set at $.35 per unit ($35 per hundred) so that Devices could earn a "fair" gross margin. When this price was rejected by both division managers, the problem was brought to the attention of the vice-president of operations.

Required:

(1) What is the immediate economic effect on Lorax Electric Company as a whole if the Devices Division is required to supply IC378 to the Systems Division at $.35 per unit—the price recommended by the arbitration committee? Explain.

(2) Discuss the advisability of intervention by executive management as a solution to transfer pricing disputes between division managers, such as the one experienced by Lorax Electric Company.

(3) Suppose that Lorax adopted a policy requiring that the price to be paid in all internal transfers be equal to the variable costs per unit of the selling division for that product and that the supplying division must sell if the buying division decides to buy the item. Discuss the consequences of adopting such a policy as a way of avoiding the need for the arbitration committee or for intervention by the vice-president.

(ICMA *adapted*)

G. Performance measurement and transfer pricing. Frederick Industries manufactures carpets, furniture, and foam in three separate divisions. Frederick's operating income statement for the current year is shown below.

Frederick Industries
Income Statement
For the Year Ended December 31, 19—
(000s omitted)

	Carpet	Furniture	Foam	Total
Sales revenue	$3,000	$3,000	$4,000	$10,000
Cost of goods sold	2,000	1,300	3,000	6,300
Gross profit	$1,000	$1,700	$1,000	$ 3,700
Commercial expenses:				
Administrative	$ 300	$ 500	$ 400	$ 1,200
Marketing	600	600	500	1,700
Total	$ 900	$1,100	$ 900	$ 2,900
Income from operations	$ 100	$ 600	$ 100	$ 800

Additional information regarding Frederick's operations follows:
1. Included in Foam's sales revenue is $500,000 that represents transfers made to the Furniture Division at manufacturing cost.

2. The cost of goods sold is comprised of the costs shown in the table below.
3. Marketing expenses are all incurred at the division level and are 80% variable for all divisions.

	Carpet	Furniture	Foam
Direct materials	$ 500,000	$1,000,000	$1,000,000
Direct labor	500,000	200,000	1,000,000
Variable factory overhead	750,000	50,000	1,000,000
Fixed factory overhead	250,000	50,000	0
Total cost of goods sold	$2,000,000	$1,300,000	$3,000,000

4. Administrative expenses are listed in the table below.

	Carpet	Furniture	Foam
Administrative expenses:			
Division expenses:			
Variable	$ 85,000	$140,000	$ 40,000
Fixed	85,000	210,000	120,000
Fixed home office expenses:			
Directly traceable to division	100,000	120,000	200,000
Allocated common costs	30,000	30,000	40,000
Total	$300,000	$500,000	$400,000

J. Williams, manager of the Foam Division, is not pleased with Frederick's presentation of operating performance. Williams claimed, "The Foam Division makes a greater contribution to the company's profits than what is shown. I sell foam to the Furniture Division at cost and it gets our share of the profit. I can sell that foam on the outside at my regular markup, but I sell to Furniture for the well-being of the company. I think my division should get credit for those internal sales at market. I think we should also revise our operating statements for internal purposes. Why don't we consider preparing these internal statements in a contribution margin reporting format showing internal transfers at market?"

Required:

(1) (a) Explain why Williams is correct.
    (b) Identify and describe three approaches used for setting transfer prices other than the manufacturing cost used by Frederick Industries and the market price as recommended by Williams.
(2) Using the contribution margin approach and market-based transfer prices, prepare a revised operating income statement, by division, for Frederick Industries for the current year.
(3) Discuss the advantages of the contribution margin approach for internal reporting purposes. (ICMA adapted)

H. Product pricing. Kolesar Company manufactures office equipment for sale to retail stores. The vice-president of marketing has proposed that Kolesar introduce two new products to its line—an electric stapler and an electric pencil sharpener.

Kolesar's Profit Planning Department has been requested to develop preliminary selling prices for the two new products for review. The Profit Planning Department is to follow the company's standard policy for developing potential selling prices, using as much data as available for each product. Data accumulated by the Profit Planning Department are shown in the table below.

	Electric Stapler	Electric Pencil Sharpener
Estimated annual demand in units	12,000	10,000
Estimated unit manufacturing costs	$10	$12
Estimated unit selling and administrative expenses	$4	Not available
Assets employed in manufacturing	$180,000	Not available

Kolesar plans to employ an average of $2,400,000 of assets to support its operations in the current year. The condensed pro forma operating income statement represents Kolesar's planned goals with respect to cost relationships and return on capital employed for the entire company for all of its products.

Kolesar Company
Pro Forma Operating Income Statement
For the Year Ending May 31, 19—
($000s omitted)

Sales revenue	$4,800
Cost of goods sold	2,880
Gross profit	$1,920
Marketing and administrative expenses	1,440
Operating income	$ 480

Required:

(1) Calculate a potential selling price for:
   (a) The electric stapler, using return-on-capital-employed pricing.
   (b) The electric pencil sharpener, using gross-profit-margin pricing.

(2) Could a selling price for the electric pencil sharpener be calculated using return-on-capital-employed pricing? Explain your answer.

(3) Which of the two pricing methods (return on capital employed or gross profit margin) is more appropriate for decision analysis? Explain your answer.

(4) The vice-president of marketing has received from the Profit Planning Department the potential selling prices for the two new products (as calculated in the first requirement). Discuss the additional steps that the vice-president is likely to take in order to set an actual selling price for each of the two products.   *(ICMA adapted)*

INDEX

A

ABC plan, 217
Abnormal loss of units, 83
Absorption costing, 333, 588
Accounting, responsibility, 392
Accountability, *def.*, 5
Accounting period, costs in relation to, 26
Accounts, chart of, 19, *illus.*, 20
Accumulation procedures, cost, 68
Activity, 476
Activity level selection for factory overhead rate, 329
Actual cost system, *def.*, 44
Actual factory overhead, 335
Actual factory overhead, departmentalized, 370
Actuary, 277
Additional orders, accepting, 644
Addition of materials in process costing, 84
Additions of new products, 738
Administrative budget, flexible, 485
Administrative expenses, *def.*, 22
  budget, 443
Alternatives, choosing among, 11
American Accounting Association (AAA), 12
American Institute of Certified Public Accountants (AICPA), 12
Analysis,
  break-even, 609
  correlation, 303
  cost behavior, 294
  cost-volume-profit, 609
  variance, 322
Analysis budgets, 651; *illus.*, 652
A posteriori method, 425
Applied acquisition costs, 158
Applied factory overhead, *def.*, 46, 52
  mechanics of, 336
Apprenticeship programs, 272
A priori method, 425
Arbitrary transfer pricing, 868
Artificial variable, *def.*, 709
Authority, *def.*, 5

Authority for Expenditures (AFE), 736
Average annual return on investment method, 747
Average costing, 95, 166
  combined cost of production report, 100
  cost of production report, *illus.*, 97, 99, 101, 102
  vs. fifo costing, 110
Average order, analysis of customers by amount of, 815
Average unit cost method, 134
Autocorrelation, 308

B

Balance sheet, 34; *illus.*, 29, 34
  budgeted, 470
Barometric methods, 212
Base, for overhead rates, 325
Base rate, 235
Basic standard, 511
Behavioral variables, approach, 273
Benefits, fringe, 235
Bill of materials, def., 162
Bin cords, 160
Billing rate, 394
  for EDP services, 395
Blending department, 73, 96, 103
  cost of production report for, *illus.*, 74, 81
    average costing, *illus.*, 97, 102
    fifo costing, *illus.*, 104, 109
  Blend variance, 527
Bonus payments, 270
Bonus plan,
  group, 243
  100%, 242
Break-even analysis, 609
  for decision making, 615
  uses of, 630
Break-even chart, *illus.*, 613, 614, 615, 617
  constructing a, 613

Break-even point, 609
Budget, *def.*, 9, 591
  administrative expenses, 443
  capital expenditures, 461
  cash, 465
  development and implementation of, 429
  direct labor, 438
  direct materials, 437
  factory overhead, 439
  fixed, 480
  flexible, 480
  manufacturing, 436
  marketing expenses, 443
  periodic, 430
  probabilistic, 480
  production, 435
  research and development, 462
  sales, 432
Budget committee, 429
Budgeted balance sheet, 470
Budgeted cost of goods manufactured and sold statement, 442
Budgeted income statement, 444
Budgeting, 9, 424
  capital expenditures, 735
  computerized, 471
  principles of, 428
  zero-base, 475
By-products, def., 124
  nature of, 125
By-product costing, 124, 126
  difficulties in, 126
  tax laws and, 136
  market value method, 129
  recognition of gross revenue, 127
  recognition of net revenue, 128
  replacement cost method, 129

C

Capacity,
  excess, 332
  expected actual, 330
  idle, 332